National Intelligencer Newspaper Abstracts 1846

Joan M. Dixon

HERITAGE BOOKS
2006

HERITAGE BOOKS
AN IMPRINT OF HERITAGE BOOKS, INC.

Books, CDs, and more – Worldwide

For our listing of thousands of titles see our website
at
www.HeritageBooks.com

Published 2006 by
HERITAGE BOOKS, INC.
Publishing Division
65 East Main Street
Westminster, Maryland 21157-5026

COPYRIGHT © 2006 JOAN M. DIXON

Other Heritage Books by the Author:

National Intelligencer Newspaper Abstracts, Special Edition: The Civil War Years, 1861-1863
National Intelligencer Newspaper Abstracts, 1845
National Intelligencer Newspaper Abstracts, 1844
National Intelligencer Newspaper Abstracts, 1843
National Intelligencer Newspaper Abstracts, 1842
National Intelligencer Newspaper Abstracts, 1841
National Intelligencer Newspaper Abstracts, 1840
National Intelligencer Newspaper Abstracts, 1838-1839
National Intelligencer Newspaper Abstracts, 1836-1837
National Intelligencer Newspaper Abstracts, 1834-1835
National Intelligencer Newspaper Abstracts, 1832-1833
National Intelligencer Newspaper Abstracts, 1830-1831
National Intelligencer Newspaper Abstracts, 1827-1829
National Intelligencer Newspaper Abstracts, 1824-1826
National Intelligencer Newspaper Abstracts, 1821-1823
National Intelligencer Newspaper Abstracts, 1818-1820
National Intelligencer Newspaper Abstracts, 1814-1817
National Intelligencer Newspaper Abstracts, 1811-1813
National Intelligencer Newspaper Abstracts, 1806-1810
National Intelligencer Newspaper Abstracts, 1800-1805

All rights reserved. No part of this book may be reproduced or transmitted in any form or by any means, electronic or mechanical, including photocopying, recording or by any information storage and retrieval system without written permission from the author, except for the inclusion of brief quotations in a review.

International Standard Book Number: **0-7884-4072-1**

NATIONAL INTELLIGENCER NEWSPAPER WASHINGTON, D C 1846

TABLE OF CONTENTS

Daily National Intelligencer
Washington, D C, 1846 ---1

Alexandria volunteers ---263
American Colonization Society ---87-88
Army appointments and promotions ----71-74; 233; 287; 364-365; 382-288 548-551
Army-Mexico-killed and wounded ---456-457
Army-Mexico-killed and wounded-8th regt ---358-359
Army Surgeons ---309-310
Balt and Wash volunteers ---249; 268
Chew, Thomas J, Navy ---329
Church Directory-Wash ---16
Commencements:
    Columbian College, D C ---453
    Gtwn College, D C ---336-337
    Gtwn College, D C-Med Dept ---119
    St Mary's, Chas Co, Md ---378
    Visitation, Gtwn, D C ---202; 347-349
Disaster-brig Somers sunk ---578-579
Disaster of steamship Atlantic ---532-534; 538; 540
Disaster on the steamer Enterprise ---422
Disaster-fire in the Theatre Royal, from the Quebec Mercury ---267-268
Disaster-fire at Fayetteville, N C ---327
Dayton, Gen Elias B ---111
Female smokers ---310
Fulton, Robt ---473
German Catholic Church cornerstone ---140
Ky volunteers ---247; 260
Killed and wounded-1st Ohio regt ---497-498
Lands for sale Hardy Co, Va ---193; 253
Licenses for taverns or ordinaries ---79-486; 553-557

Methodist Episcopal Conference----------148
Methodist Protestant Conference----------132
Mounted riflemen-Army----------255-256
Murder of Mr F Adolphus Muir----------319
Ofcrs of the Army----------158
Ofcrs of the Boxer-36; Columbus-374; Cumberland-36; 458
Independence-379; Jamestown-360; Plymouth-451; Preble-441;
Vixen-581; Warren-80; Yorktown-246
Ofcrs who fell at Monterey----------474; 504-512; 524-525
New buildings in Wash, D C----------188; 437
Page, Capt John-Army----------320
Passed Midshipmen----------307
Revolutionary patriots----------143
Sale of lots in Gtwn, D C, for taxes----------232
Texas volunteers----------264
Thomas J Chew, Navy----------329
Wash City property sold for taxes----------426-429
Wash City Riflemen----------219
Will of Thomas Pentecost----------327
Williamsburg, Va 1770----------400-403
Woodlawn for sale----------203

Index----------511

Dedicated to the memory of
Andrew J S Dixon, Sr: b. Mar 1867-Gtwn, D C;
d. 1935-Gtwn, D C
m. Mar 19, 1889
Estelle Campbell: b. Nov, 1867, Balt, Md;
d. Apr 1950-Silver Spring, Md
[Grandparents of Roland C Dixon, my husband.]

PREFACE

Daily National Intelligencer Newspaper Abstracts
1846
Joan M Dixon

The National Intelligencer & Washington Advertiser is hereafter the Daily National Intelligencer. It was the first newspaper printed in Washington, D C; Samuel H Smith, the originator. The same was transferred to Jos Gales, jr on Aug 31, 1810; on Nov 1, 1812, the paper was under the firm of Jos Gales, sr, & Wm W Seaton. The Library of Congress has microfilm of the paper from the first issue of Oct 31, 1800 thru Jan 8, 1870, the final paper. The Evening Star Newspaper of Jan 10, 1870 reports: The Intelligencer is discontinued: the proprietor, Mr Delmar, says that having lost several thousand dollars, & being in poor health, he has resolved to discontinue its publication.

Included in the extractions are advertisements; appointments by the President; Hse o/Rep petitions; passed Acts; legal notices; marriages; deaths; mscl notices; social events; tax lists; military promotions; court cases; deaths by accident; prisoners; & maritime information-crews. Items or events which might be a clue as to the location, age or relationship of an individual are copied.

No attempt has been made to correct the spelling. Due to the length of some articles, it was necessary to present only the highlights of same. Chancery and Equity records are copied as written.

The index contains all surnames and *tracts of lands/places*. **Maritime vessels** are found under barge, boat, brig, frig, schn'r, ship, sloop, steamboat, tugboat, yacht or vessel.

ABBREVIATIONS:
AA CO	ANNE ARUNDEL COUNTY
CO	COMPANY/COUNTY
CMDER	COMMANDER
CMDOR	COMMODOR
D C	DISTRICT OF COLUMBIA
DWLG	DWELLING
ELIZ	ELIZABETH
ELIZA	ELIZA
MICHL	MICHAEL
MONTG CO	MONTGOMERY COUNTY
NATHL	NATHANIEL
PG CO	PRINCE GEORGES CO
WASH	WASHINGTON
WASH, D C	WASHINGTON, DISTRICT OF COLUMBIA

BOOKS IN THE NATIONAL INTELLIGENCER NEWSPAPER SERIES-:
1800-1805/1806-1810/1811-1813/1814-1817/1818-1820/1821-1823/1824-1826/1827-1829/1830-1831/1832-1833/1834-1835/1836-1837/1838-1839/1840/1841/1842/1843/1844/1845/1846/SPECIAL: CIVIL WAR 2 VOLS, 1861-1865

DAILY NATIONAL INTELLIGENCER NEWSPAPER
WASHINGTON, D C
1846

THU JAN 1, 1846
Washington Seminary: N Y ave, near the Navy Dept. The subscriber, a native of Va & graduate of Columbian College, D C, having taken the above well-known school, solicits the patronage extended to its former proprietors. Refer to: President & Faculty of Columbian College, Rev G W Samson, B F Pleasants, Dr S C Smoot. –Jos B Pleasants, A B

Fatal accident in Rochester, N Y, on Christmas, which resulted in the death of Mrs C A McBane. With her husband & child, they occupied rooms at Bradley's Hotel, Main st. In the morning she went to the fireplace to reach an article from the shelf & her clothes caught fire. She was shockingly burnt & lived in a state of great suffering till evening. -Democrat

Senate: 1-Ptn of Edw D Tippett, asking the payment of an amount due him for military services. 2-Ptn of Caroline E Sanders, wid/o a dec'd ofcr in the Florida war, asking a pension. 3-Ptn of Fred'k Vincent, adm of Jas Le Cage, surviving partner of Le Cage & Mallet, for amount of balance standing to their credit on the books of the Treasury. 4-Ptn of Jos Radcliffe, asking compensation for timber destroyed at the Wash Navy Yard in the war of 1814. 5-Bill for the relief of Wm Elliott, jr, of Fulton Co, Ill, was ordered to be engrossed.

Died: yesterday, in Gtwn, Eleanor Thomas, in her 64th year, after a long protracted illness. Her funeral is this afternoon at 3 o'clock, from the residence of her son Jenkin Thomas, High st, Gtwn.

Died: on Dec 30, in Gtwn, Wm Henry Palmer, in his 36th year. His funeral is today at 2 o'clock, from his late residence on Bridge st.

Criminal Court-Wash. In the case of Thos Cook, tried for the murder of Thos Naylor, by beating him with a heavy bludgeon in a drunken affray, was found guilty of manslaughter. He implored the mercy of the Court. Judge Crawford sentenced him to 7 years in the penitentiary.

W H Gunnell informs his customers that their accounts are ready. My nephew, J G Hayden, will be associated with me from & after Jan 1, 1846, in the Lumber business, Canal & 6th sts. –W H Gunnell & Co

House of Reps: 1-Cmte of Claims: bill for the relief of Jos Kimball: committed. 2-Cmte of Claims: unfavorable report in the case of Wm Brook & other citizens of Ill, for compensation for property destroyed by the Sac & Fox Indians in 1832: ordered to be printed. 3-Cmte of Claims: adverse report on the ptn of Mary W Harrison, excx of Benj Harrison: laid on the table. 4-Cmte of Claims: adverse report on the ptn of Lyman King: laid on the table. 5-Cmte of Claims: bill for the relief of Chas Benns: committed. 6-Cmte on the Public Lands: bill for the relief of Semington Buffenbarger: committed. 7-Cmte on the Public Lands: adverse report on the case of *Mary Ann Bruner: moved that it be laid on the table. 8-Cmte on Revolutionary Claims: bill for the relief of the heirs of Col Wm Grayson: committed. 9-Cmte on Revolutionary Claims: bill for the relief of the heirs of Capt Presley Thornton: committed. 10-Cmte on Revolutionary Claims: the heirs of Wm Pratt have leave to withdraw their papers: agreed to. 11-Cmte on Military Affairs: adverse report in the case of Lucien B Webster: laid on the table. Same cmte: adverse report in the case of Pierre Gideon: laid on the table. 12-Cmte on Revolutionary Pensions: bill for the relief of the heirs of John Carr & a bill for the relief of Thompson Hutchinson: committed. Also made an adverse report in the cases of John Spalding & others, & of Wm Randall: laid on the table. 13-Cmte on Invalid Pensions: adverse reports on cases of John Napper Tandy & Jas Bumbaugh: laid on the table. 14-Cmte on Invalid Pensions: bill for the relief of Jas Davidson: committed. 15-Cmte on Patents: adverse report on the case of Sherburne C Blodget: laid on the table. 16-Cmte of Claims: bill to provide for the payment of the passage of Gen Lafayette from France in 1824: committed. 17-Cmte of Claims: bill for the relief of G D Spencer: committed. [Jan 3rd newspaper: the Cmte on Public Lands instructed to report a bill in the claim of Mary Ann Bruner. –E W McGaughey]

List of letters remaining in the Post Ofc, Wash, Jan 1, 1846.

Almond, Thos M	Bleight, Dr S R	Browne, Peter A
Anderson, Mrs H	Brown, John	Bettinger, T A
Ashby, Jas	Beard, Aquilla J	Bainbridge, M
Ashby, Philip S	Beall, L B A C	Beaseley, Jos
Artman, Jacob	Brown, Mrs M C	Bishop, Absolem
Ayres, Saml	Brent, Wm L	Baker, Lewis
Anderson, Lucy B	Brooke, John C-2	Berchil, A
Anderson, John	Brown, Thos	Burgwin, Miss M
Adams, Mrs M A	Briggs, Mrs A C J	Broadhead, John C
Aldrick, P Emery-3	Byrne, C R	Brainard, H-2
Anderson, Walker	Ball, Mrs Fanny	Burgess, Saml
Brooks, Edw J	Boyd, Saml C	Bryan, Benj
Crooks, Correll	Barnes, Mrs M	Bentley, Dr M A-2
Brent, Dr A Lee	Birch, Mr	Bowen, Henry M
Baird, Matthias	Bibb, T P Attieus	Beaumont, Francis
Brown, Wm J	Beams, Miss Susan	Bowman, Jas
Beck, Jas L	Bull, Jas H	Baldwin, H
Beck, Octavia	Brown, Wilson	Barnard, Edw

Bruning, John H	Cooper, Miss Harriet	Davis, Mrs Malinda
Brayton, R	Canfield, G R	David, Richd [col'd]
Brannan, Saml	Chambers, Thos	Edds, Major
Boyden, Henry	Courter, Jas	Everett, Alex H
Butler, Mrs Ann	Coffin, Isaac N	Ergood, Jessee
Bowman, Mrs H	Corbin, P'd M'd T G	Emory, Fred'k
Brady, N	Digges, Geo A	Entwistle, Saml
Briscoe, Palm	Diggs, Thos	Evans, Edwin P
Biddle, Edw	Doods, Jos	Emmons, Mrs M E
Braiden, Miss E-2	Dodge, Francis	Ellis, Chesselden-2
Basil, Washington	Dunn, Jas R	Elliott, Dr A B
Blanchard, John	Dean, Rev Wm	Edelin, Capt Jas-3
Bickley, L W-5	Denham, Elkanah	Edelin, Miss E S-2
Butler, Mrs F L-5	Dixon, Augustus	Edmonds, Mrs Mary
Butler, Miss Julia H	Dickson, Mrs Sarah	Fleet, Jas H
Barry, Mrs Eliza	Dinnies, Alfred C	Flagg, Mrs
Burnett, J H	Dodson, Mrs Airy	Fowler, Mary I
Browne, Dr Orris A	Dougherty, John	Faber, Dr J C-2
Beall, Miss Mary A	Dana, Jas D	Fleming, Mrs G
Bayard, Richd H-2	Draper, Lyman C	Fuller, Mr J H
Clagett, Hezekiah	Dedman, Robt B	Fugett, Miss S B-2
Cox, M A	Danforth, Mrs Jane	Fitzgerald, P'd M'n
Cook, John	Dwinell, Thos A	Fulmer, Henry G
Carr, Horatio N	De Witt, John	Fulton, John S-2
Crump, Dr Geo W	Donnelly, P-2	Fardy, John
Coumbe, John T	Dement, Geo C	Fahy, John
Crown, Jas E	Douglass, Mrs L A	Feinour, Dr T
Combs, Gen Leslie	Dunham, Francis S	French, Mrs Philippa
Clarke, Oswald B	Davis, Mrs Jane	Grawford, Ed
Cormick, Wm	Davis, Amos	Green, John
Cooper, Maj S	Davis, John	Greene, C K-4
Carver, Miss M A	Davis, Geo T M-3	Greene, Caleb
Cockrill, Miss A M	Davis, Wm	Griggs, Mrs Mary
Curtis, Henry	Davis, Geo S	Gould, C D
Cutler, Willard	Darnell, Gen N H-3	Gates, Wm
Corbitt, Abraham	Duvall, Gen John P	Gwinn, Dr Wm-4
Campbell, Mrs R	Duvall, A J	Gibson, Mid
Custis, Mrs S C	Diggs, Miss Mary A	Galer, I O
Crandal, Mrs H	Dickinson, Rev R H	Garland, H A-2
Crawford, A C	Dulany, Washington	Godwin, Parke
Coury, Miss Mary	Dunbar, Miss Eliza J	Gammon, A L-2
Calvert, Chas B	Duley, Mrs Eliz	Gwinn, Capt John
Callaghan, Edw	Delaney, sur'n, M G-2	Gibons, John W
Costin, Wm Custis	DeBemo, Rev John	Gallagher, Col David
Cavillion, Robt	Delaney, Lt D French	Griggsby, Eliz

Griffith, Jas	Hill, Geo	Latson, John W
Gillespie, Lt A H	Hughes, Robt	Lighthall, Wm
Graham, Maj J D-3	Hines, Jas	Lebrun, Napoleon
Hunter, Jas	Hall, Danl D	LeTruit, Barbara V
Hutton, Geo	Hall, Mrs Mary	Lewis, Robt T
Henderson, Jas	Hunt, H-2	Lewis, Mary A
Higgins, Miss C	Hunt, Seth B	Lofftus, Ralph W-2
Hammond, A A	Hall, Col Jos	Meek, A B-3
Herdelbrinck, Mr	Irons, Wm	Mountz, Geo W
Harvey, Thos H	Iardella, Lawrence	Mount, Mrs M A
Hammock, Miss L	Irwin, Maj Wm	Marks, Isaac D
Heckrott, A G	Jones, Jas H	Miles, Col John-2
Hamilton, Mrs E	James, Banning W	May, John
Hamilton, A	Jones, Mrs Lucretia	Mead, John
Hammond, A A	Jones, John B-2	Munn, St Saml E-4
Hogans, Miss E	Jones, Mrs Maria H	Moore, Eli
Hopkins, Jas A	Johnson, Matthew	Marvin, R P
Herrick, Benj	Jackson, Saml	Markwood, Wesley
Hutchison, Jas	Johnson, Jas H	Murphy, Henry
Hopkins, John	Jamaison, Miss J	Morrow, Francis
Hubbard, Wm H-2	Johnson, Henry	McGee, Jos H
Henderson, Jos	Judik, Jos	Magee, Miss Mary
Humphreys, J C	Johnson, Orange	McCabe, M
Hazeltine, Robt-2	Johnson, Wm	McLean, J of N Y
Hoover, Chas	Jackson, Alphonso-2	Nes, Henry
Hoffman, M	Keitt, L M	Newland, Saml
Hancock, L R	Kane, Thos L	Nalle, Thos B, U S N
Hutchison, H	Kerr, John L	Noble, Wm T
Haistor, Peter W	Knott, Wm	Nicholas, Malcolm-2
Hurdle, Geo N	Knowles, Mrs E	Nicholson, Com J B-2
Hardin, John J	Kern, Fred'k S	Nelson, John
Hawkins, Chas	Kiger, Alfred	Neiser, J P Michl
Holdridge, Harrison	Kelly, Miss Ann	Owen, Robt
Hernandez, Gen	Kellogg, Augustus	Points, Jas
Hanson, Mid J J-2	Kugur, Capt John	Price, Jas
Hickman, Hon Beau	Kennedy, Chas	Paige, David S
Hall, Mrs Polly	Killum, John H	Poole, Mrs Mary M
Hill, Richd	Kidwell, John L	Pratt, Z
Hill, Francis H	Lee, Mgt	Pierce, Richd
Hunt, John C	Lloyd, Wm-2	Porter, Wm H
Hill, John C	Lamb, David S	Perrie, Mrs S H
Heser, Jas	Leighton, Miss J	Porter, Rev Robt
Hooe, Jesse	Latimer, Mid C-2	Parrott, Henry
Hoff, Fred'k J	Leman, Jas	Preston, E D C
Hall, Edw	Lacy, Miss F M	Penrose, Lt J W

Purdy, Leonard
Powell, Alex
Powders, Miss Kitty
Patterson, Wm
Penney, Miss H
Poindexter, T B
Quarls, Mrs Milly
Quantrill, Maj T
Raub, Maj Saml
Rice, Richd D
Ricks, Jas Thos
Rhodes, Eliz
Rhodes, Mrs Lucy
Robertson, John
Roby, Miss Azubah
Raggio, Jos
Rupell, F S K-4
Reiley, Mrs Frances
Radcliffe, Miss C
Robinson, H H
Reider, John Thos
Rucker, Miss J-2
Reeder, Richd
Robinson, Wm
Roberts, Lt B F
Ragan, Jackson
Richardson, O D-3
Robinson, John W
Rockwell, C W
Ramsay, Mrs A E
Rodgers, Dr Jos
Soule, Geo W-2
Staines, Julia
Scott, Mrs Maria
Smith, Miss Jane O
Smith, Thos R
Smith, f O J
Streets, G
Smith, Miss Clara
Smith, Miss C
Shade, Jas G
Sehwier, Heur
Smith, Wm H
Stone, Col Alfred J
Smith, Wm O

Smith, Geo Clinton
Stone, Mid E E
Simms, Miss F-2
Shields, Edw M
Stepper, Andrew-2
Slidell, Geo
Stephens, R H
Saltmarsh, D A-2
Simpson, Wm E
Salisbury, John L
Simmons, Miss C
Summers, J F
Scheffer, John
Snodgrass, Wm
Searight, Capt J D
Soper, Miss Sarah E
Shankland, Thos
Stewart, W W
Snowden, Mrs C
Sergeant, H J
Sollers, Jane C
Shaler, Chas
Soper, Miss C
Stewart, Wm
Simmons, B F
Sabine, H W
Stone, M M
Selby, Hoyt
Stubbs, Wm E-2
Sinclair, Rev Jos
Smallwood, Mrs M J
Thrift, Wm
Todd, Wm H
Titus, Benj N
Turner, Wm R
Tascho, Thos
Thompson, Mr C
Thompson, E H-2
Thompson, Mrs M
Tilghman, Henry
Talbot, Geo
Trescott, W H
Tolson, John F
Thomas, Ross
Trabue, Mr

Thomas, Mrs R
Thruston, Miss C
Tiffany, O C
Thompson, Chas
Thompson, Mrs C
Torplen, Miss B
Thornton, Miss J W A
Townley, Jona D
Tracy, Mrs P M
Territt, Lt Geo
Vanforsen, Miss E
Van Tyne, J S-2
Vincins, E
Vinton, Miss M S
Vernooye, Chas
Van Tyne, Dr J P
White, Wm W
Wells, Mrs Ann-2
Wood, Mrs A C-2
Woods, Sarah
Wright, Geo
Wright, Jas
White, Albert J
Wolfe, Danl
Webb, Horatio
Wood, Miss Mary
Ward, Nahum
Ward, Henry S
Waddell, Mid
Willett, Mrs E
Winne, Thos
Waters, Miss Sarah
Williams, W L-2
Whigeron, J
Walker, Jos W
Wilson, Henry
Woolman, S B-2
Whitmore, Albert
Westbrook, Miss E
Wheeler, John H
Walker, Nat
Winslow, Phebe P
Weaver, Capt Wm
Wilson, Jos, U S N-2
Wilson, Jos

Widbeck, Danl P
Warder, Miss M C
Williams, J W-2
Williams, J C
Williams, F H
Waller, Capt Robt
Waldron, Mrs M

Watson, Sumner F
Waters, David S-3
Wiggins, Benj-3
Whittlesey, T T-2
Whittlesey, Chas-2
Wright, Capt J D C
Williams, Saml S

Williams, Zachariah
Walker, sen, John
Yates, Giles F-5
Young, Wm
Young, Mrs Susan B

FRI JAN 2, 1846
The demise of the Most Rev Jos Sequire, Archbishop of Manilla, is mentioned in the Singapore papers.
Census of the island of Singapore taken Jul last: 57,421, of these 336 Europeans.

M Barrot, father of M Odilon Barrot, member of the Convention of the Legislative Assemblies up to 1815, died lately in Paris in his 93rd year.

House of Reps: [Presented during the present week.] 1-Ptn of Elisha Deming, of Chester, Mass, for an increase of his invalid pension. 2-Claims of Chas Roby, of Ohio, for claims on the Ottawa Indians. 3-Ptn of John Skirving, praying remuneration for drawing plans for & superintendence of the alteration at the old Jail, converting the same into a lunatic asylum. 4-Ptn of Mgt & Agnes Brigham, heirs at law of Thos Armor, praying the reimbursement of advances made, & payment for services rendered by him during the Revolutionary war. 5-Ptn of Amelia Brereton, for an adjustment of her late husband's accounts. 6-Ptn of the Vestry of <u>Washington Parish</u>, for liberty to purchase land for the extension of their burial ground. 7-Ptn of G P A Healy, that Congress would purchase Stuart's portraits of the Presidents. 8-Ptn of Henry Whiting, of Mass, for pension, was taken from the files & referred. 9-Ptn of Eli Merrill, of Belleville, N J, for relief in the matter of a land pension. 9-Ptn of Geo V Mitchell, late postmaster in Belleville, Mifflin Co, Pa, for relief. 10-Ptn of Elijah Buchanan, Lansing, N Y, for an invalid pension. 11-Ptn of Mrs Sarah Hammond, wid/o John Hammond, dec'd, praying that a law may pass allowing to her a pension commensurate with the services of her husband in the Revolutionary war. 12-Ptn of Lt Jas F Miller, for certain back pay. 13-Ptn of Nathl Bird, for a Revolutionary pension. 14-Ptn of Geo M Fowl, for remuneration for services as deputy collector & inspector at Barcelona harbor. 15-Ptn of Hiram Humphreys, praying remuneration for losses sustained by him in building a bridge for the U S. 16-Ptn of Benj J Porter, for the allowance of 7 years' half-pay for services rendered during the Revolutionary war as a Surgeon's mate. 17-Ptn of John Ambrozine, praying for permission to surrender a patent for 160 acres of land granted him for services rendered during the last war, [said land proving of no value,] & for compensation. 18-Claim of Paul Vandervoort, for transportation during the Revolutionary war. 19-Ptn of Roswell Hale, praying Congress for increase of pension. 20-Ptn of Eliz Fays, praying the payment of certain moneys due her grandfather, Robt Smith, for Revolutionary services.

New Orleans Picayune of Dec 24. Steamboat disaster on Dec 18: the steamboat **Belle Zane**, Capt Brazier, on her way from Zanesville, Ohio, to New Orleans, struck a snag & immediately turned bottom up. Upwards of 50 perished. Known lost: Mr Bowen, lady, & child, of Zanesville. Some who came down to this city: John P Nesle, of Albany, N Y, Jas Sheridan, John Mick, Robt H Foster, J Gibson, & Henry Platte. The feet of some were badly frost-bitten. [Jan 9th newspaper: Rev Dr Maclay, Rep in Congress, is one of those who escaped with his life from the wreck of the steamer **Belle Zane**. –N Y Eve Post.]

U S Gas: Obit of a Reverend Revolutionary Patriarch: Died, Aug last, at his residence in Hartland, Vt, Rev Danl Breck, whose age lacked only 3 years of 100 years. He was born in Boston, Aug 18, 1748: was religiously educated at Princeton, & graduated there in 1774; he entered the army as Chaplain & accompanied Col Porter's Regt into Canada. He was father of Hon Danl Breck, a Judge of the Supreme Court of Ky, & Dr Breck, of Alabama, & uncle of Saml Breck, of Phil, & Geo Breck, of Bristol, Pa.

E W Bull, a well-known druggist of Hartford, Conn, in a fit of insanity, jumped from a window & killed himself last Saturday.

Oliver Smith, who died recently at Hatfield, Mass, left half a million of property. Much of this is disposed of for charitable purposes, & a large amount for benevolent & philanthropic objects.

The co-partnership heretofore existing under the firm of R W Dyer & Co, has been dissolved. The subscriber will continue to carry on the business as heretofore.
-R W Dyer, Auctioneer & Commision Merchant

SAT JAN 3, 1846
House of Reps: 1-Cmte of Claims: adverse reports on the cases of Ebenezer Atwell & of Henry Bogardus & others. Same cmte: bill for the relief of John Anderson, of Missouri: committed. 2-Cmte of Claims: bill for the relief of Chas M Gibson, & a bill for the relief of the sureties of Elijah J Weed, late Quartermaster of Marines: bills were committed. 3-Cmte of Claims: bill for the relief of Lyon & Howard: committed. 4-Cmte on Public Lands: adverse report in the case of Jesse Johnson: ordered to be printed.

RCC Church. The bldg cmte of the German Roman Catholic Church of Wash tender their thanks to Mr M Duffy, of Gtwn, for the plan of the edifice they are about to erect on 5th st, & will, in accordance of said plan, receive proposals until Jan 14 for the carpenter's work & the brick & stone work. The plan of said bldg can bee seen daily, except Sunday, by calling on Rev Mr Oliy, between 10 & 12 m, at the residence of Mr Fundler, 10th st, Northern Liberties, Wash.
–Sauter, Roth, Fundler, Hoskum, & Filler

Will be opened this day, at Mrs S A Parker's, a new style Evening Dresses: Pa ave, between 9th & 10th sts.

Public sale of valuable books: on Jan 6, at the Bookstore of the late Thos R Hampton, Pa ave & 13th st, [Traver's corner,] a lot of Books & Stationery, seized & taken to satisfy rent in arrears due John McDuell. Terms cash. –John Waters, Bailiff

New Boarding House, at Bladensburg, Md. Subscriber has taken the commodious house known as Ross' Tavern. His stable is warm & dry, & an attentive good man has it in charge. –Henry L Carlton

Orphans Court of Wash Co, D C. In the case of Francis A Dickens, adm of Jos Haylate, a Surgeon in the Virginia State Navy of the Revolution, dec'd. The adm & Court have appointed Feb 10 next for settlement of said estate.
–Ed N Roach, reg/o wills

Rev H H Shropshere, of the Helena [Louisiana] Circuit, has been expelled from the Ministry by the Methodist Episcopal Conference, in session at New Orleans, for attempting to seduce a young lady on whom he was pratising some mesmeric experiments in Jul last. Bishop Soule, Pres of the Conference, strongly reprehended the practice of mesmerism. –N Y Tribune

Drowned: a little boy, s/o Mr Keller, who resides on the Belair road from Balt, near Herring run, while skating on the run on Sun, broke through, & notwithstanding the effects of a younger brother to save him, was drowned.

House of Reps: 1-Ptn of Chas W Bingley, for an act of Congress authorizing the Collector of Charleston, S C, to grant an enrolment of register for his vessel. 2-Ptn of Oris Crosby, for a pension. 3-Ptn of A Butterfield & others for a harbor at Eighteen Mile Creek, N Y. 4-Ptn of Jeremiah Murphy, for a pension. 5-Ptn of Geo Wade, for a pension. 6-Ptn of Chauncey Whetmore, adm of Elisha Hubbard, for arrears of pension due said Hubbard. 7-Ptn of the legal reps of Hugh Hughes, for the payment of certain loan ofc certificates. 8-Ptn of Sophia Albrecht, of Pa, wid/o a Revolutionary soldier, praying for relief.

Temperance: Mr Geo Collett, a reformed tavernkeeper of Balt, & Messrs West & Dewee of N Y, will address the friends of temperance, & all others who will attend, at the 9th st Church, Rev Mr Smith's, on Jan 4, at 3 o'clock.

Mrd: On Jan 1, by Rev Mr Stringfellow, Mr Wm Lightfoot, of Alexandria, D C, to Miss Mary Ann Stewart, of Wash City.

Died: on Dec 31, 1845, after a distressing & protracted illness, [dropsy of the heart,] Wm P Zantzinger, a native of Lancaster, Pa, late a Purser in the U S Navy. His funeral will take place today at 12 m.

MON JAN 5, 1846

Senate: 1-Ptn of Sarah Little, asking a pension in consideration of the services of her late husband. 2-Ptn of David L White, of Florida, asking arrears of pension & reimbursement of certain expenditures made for the public service. 3-Ptn of Geo W Jones, for himself, & as atty for the other heirs of John Rice Jones, dec'd, asking confirmation of a title to 2 tracts of land. 4-Ptn of Jas Bogardus, asking an extension of his patent for the improvement of grist milles. 5-Bill for the relief of Wm Elliot, jr, of Fulton, Ill, was passed.

Company D of the U S dragoons, commanded by Lt Johnson & 2nd Lt Gardner, & Company G, commanded by Capt Steen with Lt Buford, were at Evansville, Ark, [the scene of the Indian disturbances,] on Dec 13th.

The home farm belonging to the estate of the late John Nixon, containing 619 acres, was sold at $48.80 per acre. Purchaser, Dr Thos Clagett. On the same day, belonging to the same estate, 270 acres, unimproved, at $38.15 per acre. Purchaser, Mr Nichols. -Washingtonian

N Y Express of Sat: we notice with sincere regret the death of Eli Hart, age 65. He acquired an ample fortune, & retired from active pursuits a year or two since, when his health became impaired. He was a man of great business capabilities. He was a kind husband, father, & friend, & an upright citizen.

Appointments by the Pres, by & with the advice & consent of the Senate.
Levi Woodbury, of N H, Assoc Justice of the U S Supreme Court, in place of Jos Story, dec'd.
Jas Shields, of Ill, Com'r of the Genr'l Land Ofc, in place of Thos H Blake, removed.
Wm Medill, of Ohio, Com'r of Indian Affairs, in place of Thos H Crawford, resigned.
Collectors:
Jas K Hatton, for the port of Wash, N C, vice Thos H Blount, resigned.
Rizop Rawls, for the port of Edenton, N C, vice Thos J Charleton, whose commission expired.
Henry Hicks, for the port of Wilmington, Dela, vice Arnold Naudain, whose commission expired.
Wm J Grayson, for the port of Charleston, S C.
Rufus O Pray, for the port of Shieldsborough, Miss, vice Wm H Arnold, whose commission expired.
Nathl W Walker, for the port of St Marks, Fla, vice Wm H Ware, whose commission expired.
Thos L Shaw, for the port of Gtwn, S C.

Surveyor & Inspectors:
Chas N Lawson, for the port of Carter's Creek, Va, vice Robt Edmonds, whose commission expired.
Robt B Merchants, for the port of Dumfries, Va, vice Geo H Cockrell, whose commission expired.
Michl Edwards, jr, for the port of Wheeling, Va, vice Saml Atkinson, whose commission expired.
Thos H Jerrey, for the port of Charleston, S C, reappointed from Jan 12, 1846.
Naval Ofcr:
Alcee Labranche, Naval Ofcr for the district of New Orleans, La, vice Martin Duralde, whose commission expired. –Union

Mrd: on Dec 31, by Rev W A Turner, Mr Jas Martin, of PG Co, Md, to Miss Joanna C S Everett, of Rockville, Montg Co, Md.

Mrd: on Dec 20, in Phil, by Rev Wm W Spear, Mr Alex'r Hull, of Wash City, to Miss Georgiana H, y/d/o Col John H Sherburne, of Phil.

Died: on Jan 4, of croup, Beverly Osmond, s/o Geo W & Joanna Thompson, in his 5th year. His funeral is this afternoon at half-past 2 o'clock, from the residence of his father, near the Navy Yard.

Died: on Sunday, in Wash City, Jas Rozzell, s/o Archibald B & Mary Ann Quantrill, aged 4 years. His funeral will take place from his father's residence on tomorrow at 2 o'clock, corner of 18th & K sts. Friends of the family & the members of St Paul's Lutheran Church are respectfully invited to attend.

Trustee's sale: by deed of trust from Geo Hill, jr, to me, dated Dec 4, 1841, recorded in Liber W B, #90, folios 405 thru 407, of the Land Records of Wash Co, D C: sale on Jan 6: a negro woman named Louisa, aged about 35 years, to serve until Dec 4, 1851, & then to be free; & her female child Rosannah, now aged about 13 years, a slave for life. –Henry Haw, Trustee -E S Wright, auctioneer

Criminal Court-Wash: 1-John Angell guilty of an assault & battery upon Richd Plummer, a colored man, with intent to kill Plummer, on Jun 23. Not yet sentenced. 2-The case of Richd Bland Randolph, an old sailor belonging to the U S Navy, & who has been confined in jail since May 5 last, was before the Court on Fri. The prisoner was brought before the Court under a writ of habeas corpus, on his own application. [He was committed to jail by Justice Goddard as a dangerous lunatic, at the instance of the Mayor, who received a communication on the subject of the prisoner's escape from confinement in Norfolk, Va, & of his being a dangerous person to go at large. No notice of the matter was taken, & he has been in prison every since May, upwards of 8 months. He has committed sundry acts of violence as a prisoner.]

House of Reps: 1-Ptn of Benj G Perkins, praying for a pension, as an invalid, in consideration of disabilities incurred during his service in the U S Army. 2-Ptn of Jose Carscillo, praying confirmation for a claim to a tract of land therein described. 3-Ptn of Jas H Caldwell, praying for compensation for work done on the Marine Hospital at New Orleans not included in the contract, but ordered & approved by the agents of the Gov't. 4-Ptn of W B Snowhook & others, for a mail route from Chicago, via Mulford, Stebbins, Gross Point, Ellisville, & Littlefort, to Southport, Wisconsin.

30th Annual meeting of the Columbia Typographical Society, was held on Jan 3. Ofcrs elected for the ensuing year: Chas F Lowrey, Pres; Jas D Chedal, V P; Michl Caton, Treas; P H Brooks, Cor Sec; Thos Rice, Rec Sec. Deep regret of the death of Alex'r Graham, the oldest member & 1st Pres of the Society, who died lately at his residence, in Easton, Md. Condolences to the family of the dec'd.

Sale of valuable property: by decree made by the Orphans Court of Wash Co, D C, in the matter of the ptn of John H Hendley, guardian of Geo, Cecilia V, & Sophia J Hendley, the undersigned will sell, on Feb 12, the following pieces or parcels of ground, in Wash City, with improvements: all that part of lot 16 in square 431; also, the eastern equal half of lot 12 in square 431: property is at 7th & E sts, & is at present occupied by Mr De Saule as a refectory. Title believed to be unquestionable. Apply to the undersigned, or to Walter Lenox, atty at law. –John H Hendley, Guardian -A Green, Auctioneer

TUE JAN 6, 1846
Missing men found. The barque **Quebec**, which arrived at St John [N] on 27th ult, from Plymouth, England, reports having picked up at sea, on Nov 11, a boat & crew lost from the whale ship **Minerva Smyth**, of & from New Bedofrd, consisting of Wm Marble, mate, J E Farmer, A C Farnsworth, Wm Hews, Jas Ward, & Alex'r Curry, while alongside a whale on the 7th. They are now under the care of the U S Consul at St John, N V. [The M S touched at Fayal Nov 15, & reported that she had lost a boat containing 1st ofcr & 5 men, taken down by a sperm whale.]

The Rockaway House at Lynn, Mass, kept by Mr John Tilton, was destroyed by fire on Thu last, with most of the furniture. Insured for $6,500.

Died: on Jan 2, in PG Co, Md, Aquila D Hyatt, aged 73 years. He had been by profession a practical printer, & was for many years, beginning more than 40 years ago, a steady & faithful workman in the ofc of the Nat'l Intelligencer.

Died: on yesterday, in Wash City, Mr A F Agate, late of N Y, in his 28th year. His funeral will take place from his late residence, Mrs Kenneday's, Indiana ave, near 4½ st, at 1 o'clock, today.

Died: on Sunday last, at his residence, near the Navy Yard, Wash, with Christian composure, Salvadore M Catalano, Sailingmaster U S Navy, aged 70 years, a native of Palermo, in Sicily, but for the last 41 years a resident of Wash City. His admissioin into the American Navy was the reward of services as a volunteer to pilot the gallant Decatur into the harbor of Tripoli, when he set fire to the American frig **Philadelphia**, then in possession of the Corsairs. The dec'd at the time, 1804, was a pilot on board the ship **Enterprise**, then under the command of Lt [afterwards Cmdor] Decatur. Lt Decatur, being aware that his pilot understood the language of the Corsairs, first proposed to him, & afterwards to Cmdor Preble, then commanding the squadron, the daring project of entering the harbor of Tripoli by night & destroying the frig **Philadelphia**. The dec'd immediately volunteered his services, & the project being approved by Cmdor Preble, the gallant Decatur, with the dec'd, [one midshipman & 20 men being concealed in the bottom of a xebec,] sailed for the **Philadelphia**. On approaching the frig the xebec was hailed, when the dec'd answered that he had lost his cable & anchor, & requested permission to make fast to the frig until morning. Having obtained leave to make fast to her stern, Decatur & his brave companions boarded the **Philadelphia** & swept her decks. Out of 50 Corsairs not one escaped. The frig was then set on fire, & the heroic band set sail for the American squadron with only 1 seaman wounded. As a reward for this brave & heroic service, the dec'd, upon the recommendation of Cmdor Decatur, was admitted into the American Navy. His funeral will take place today at 2 o'clock, from his late residence.

WED JAN 7, 1846
Foreign Item: the will of the late Earl Gray was proved in the Consistory Court of Durham on the 18th ult, by the present Earl, the sole executor. The personal effects in the diocese of Durham were sworn under L30,000.

Criminal Court-Wash. 1-John Carroll was found guilty of manslaughter in the murder of Benj Adams, a free negro, during an affray in Sep last. 2-John Seitz & Geo Seitz were convicted of an assault & battery. 3-Thos Gardiner was found guilty of a burglary in the house of Eliz & Eliza Mattingley, & recommended by the jury to the mercy of the Court. [Jan 9th newspaper: John Carroll sentenced to 6 years in the penitentiary. Thos Gardiner sentenced to 3 years in the penitentiary.]

Wash Corp: 1-Relief of Pringle Slight was taken up & passed. 2-Cmte of Claims: bill for the relief of Jacob Martin: passed. 3-Ptn of Michl Downey, praying remission of a fine: referred to the Cmte of Claims. 4-Ptn of K H Lambell, praying payment of an account due him for repairing scows: referred to the Cmte on Police. 5-Select cmte will ascertan & report the amount of damages claimed by A B McClean or his assigness: in relation to the difficulties which have arisin in the transfer to the Corporation of the fish wharf on the Potomac, at the end of 6th st west.

Mr Chas L Voltz, an aged & much respected citizen of Pittsburg, was killed on Fri by the falling of a wall of a burnt bldg whilst he was passing along the street.

Senate: 1-Ptn of Francis Summeraner, praying a pension for disabilities contracted in the military service of the U S. 2-Ptn of Preston Stanitt & others, claimants under the Cherokee treaty of 1835, praying the appointment of a Board of Com'rs. 3-Ptn of Jane Heyl, the wid/o Christopher Heyl, a dec'd Revolutionary ofcr, asking a pension. 4-Memorial of Lt John L Worden, for compensation for extra services while doing duty in a higher grade. 5-Cmte of Claims: to inquire into erecting light-houses at the following points on the east of Missouri: one at St Joseph's island, one at Merrills' shell-bank, one at Mississippi city, opposite John J McCorgle's dwlg-house, & one at or near Belexia. 6-Cmte of Claims: bill for the relief of Nathl Goddard & others. 7-Cmte of Public Lands: bill for the relief of David M Williamson, of Oak Co, Ark, without amendment.

Mr Lyman D Scott, an intemperate man, burnt his house & himself in it at Monkton, Vt, on Sat before last. He was about 45 years old, & has left a wife & 2 children.

Look Here! With a view of moving to the West, the subscriber will sell on accommodating terms his stock of Groceries for a family grocery. The stand is in the best part of the city for a business of that kind. –T C Duckworth, corner of E & 7th sts, opposite the Post Ofc Dept.

Susan Bump, about 12 years old, was accidentally killed at Bridgewater, Mass, last week by her brother, who discharged a gun at her not knowing that it was loaded.

Geo W C Hujill, jr, was killed at Clarksburg, V, on Christmas day. He was shooting at a mark, & put his mouth to the muzzle to ascertain whether it was loaded, at the same time placing his foot on the hammer to press it back. His foot slipped, & the ball entered his mouth, & he fell dead on the spot.

Mrd: on Nov 30, at the Wilcox Settlement, Clayton Co, Iowa Territory, by Rev J L Elliott, Chaplain U S Army, Mr Geo Vandon to Miss Amelia Messinger, both of Clayton Co, I T.

Mrd: on Jan 6, by Rev Henry Tarrington, Mr John G Lare, formerly of Fred'k city, Md, to Miss Martha M Ross, of Wash City.

Died: on Jan 5, at the residence of his dght, corner of 3rd & G sts, Mr Lewis Knott, in his 89th year, after a long & painful illness. His funeral is this day at 3 o'clock.

Died: on Dec 24, of consumption, at the residence of Chas King, [Gtwn, D C,] Dr Nathl M King, in his 28th year. He was graduated at the Jefferson Medical College, Phil, but was prevented by the early approach of his disease from ever practicing the duties of his profession. During his stay of 9 months among us, he daily prepared for death with Christian calmness. His relatives & numerous friends will regret his loss.

Mrd: on Dec 17, by Rev A B Brown, Richd S McCulloh, late Prof of Math & Nat'l Philiosophy in Jefferson College, to Miss Mary Stewart, d/o Dr John D Vowell, of Canonsburg, Pa, & formerly of Alexandria.

Orphans Court of Wash Co, D C. Letters of administration on the personal estate of John H Offley, late of said county, dec'd. –Catharine Offley, admx

Trustee's sale on Jan 25, at public auction, 40 shares of the capital stock of the Wash & Fredericksburg Steamboat Co. –Jos H Bradley, trustee

THU JAN 8, 1846
Notice: by an order for distress, I shall sell, for cash, on Jan 15, in Wash City, one hackney carriage, seized & taken for stable rent due in arrears by Benj Lanham to Dorcas Galvin, & will be sold to satisfy the same. -R R Burr, Bailiff -A Green, auct

Senate: 1-Memorial of Col J B Walbach, for compensation for extra services in the army. 2-Ptn of Blair & Rives, praying compensation for printing the Compendium of the 6th Census. 3-Ptn of John Wilson, one of the heirs of Gilbert Denel, praying indemnity for a depreciation in the currency in which he was paid for his services in the Revolutionary war. 4-Cmte on Military Affairs: bill for the relief of Mary McRea, reported the same without amendment. 5-Cmte on the Judiciary: reported without amendment, the bill to authorize the Sec of the Treas to compromise with M M Quackenboss & his co-obligors as sureties to the U S. 6-Bill for the relief of Jas Bogardus was passed.

Wm Harper, convicted at N Y of the murder of John G Kemff, has been sentenced to be hanged on the 24th of next month.

Rev Dr Blue, of the Methodist Episcopal Church, was killed near Ontario Indiana, on Dec 19, by his horse taking fright.

People's Advocate [York, Pa,] states that a duel fought a few days ago in Hopewell, York Co, between Mr Jesse Gilbert, of Hartford Co, & Mr Wm B Blair, of Ohio, arose in an argument about the Oregon question. They fought with rifles at 60 paces. After the first fire, neither of the parties being wounded, the difficulty was adjusted by the seconds.

Household & kitchen furniture at auction on Jan 14, at the residence of the late Saml Harrison Smith, aon 15th st, near the banking-house of Messrs Corcoran & Riggs. -R W Dyer, auct

Stray cow came to my farm. Owner is to come forward, prove property, pay charges, & take her away. -Jacob Harshman, between the Navy Yard Bridge & Good Hope Tavern.

Appointments by the Pres, by & with the advice & consent of the Senate.
Chas A Bradford, of Mississippi, to be Surveyor Genr'l of the public lands for the district south of Tenn, in place of Alex'r Downing, removed.
Geo W Jones, of Wisconsin, to be Surveyor Genr'l of the public lands for the Territories of Wisconsin & Iowa, in place of Jas Wilson, removed.
Wm Pelham, of Arkansas, to be Surveyor General for the State of Arkansas, his former commission having expired.
Lucius Lyon, of Michigan, to be Surveyor Genr'l of Ohio, Indiana, & Michigan, in place of Wm Johnston, resigned.
Robt Butler, of Florida, to be Surveyor Genr'l of the public lands in the Territory of Florida, in place of Valentine Y Conway, resigned.
Fred'k R Conway, of Missouri, to be Surveyor Genr'l of the public lands in Illinois & Missouri, in place of Silas Reed, removed.
Loren Spencer, of Missouri, to be Recorder of land titles in Missouri, in place of Fred'k R Conway, appointed Surveyor Genr'l for Illinois & Missouri. –Union

Mrd: on Thu last, in Balt, by Rev Dr Wyatt, Thos Hollingsworth Morris to Mary, d/o the Hon Reverdy Johnson, all of Wash City.

FRI JAN 9, 1846
Senate: 1-Ptn from Mary Williams, praying compensation for property destroyed by the Seminole Indians in consequence of its military occupation by the U S troops. 2-Ptn from Sally Bass, d/o a Revolutionary surgeon, dec'd, for commutation pay. 3-Ptn from the reps of the late Wm A Slacum, for compensation for his services in obtaining information in relation to the settlements in the Oregon territory. 4-Ptn from Jonathan Thompson, praying the reimbursement of certain moneys illegally charged against him in the settlement of his accounts as Collector of the Port of N Y. 5-Ptn from Hugh Munn McLean, for payment of 3 certificates standing in his name for money lent by his father to the U S during the Revolution.

The Hon Chas Carroll is still detained from his seat in Congress by his own illness, & the illness of 2 members of his family, who have been attacked with scarlet fever. –Rochester Democrat

A young man, Arthur B Salmon, an agent of the New Orleans Commercial Times newspaper, drowned himself in the Ohio river, near New Albany, Indiana, last week.

Criminal Court-Wash: 1-John Angel found guilty of simple assault on Thos O Thorn: sentenced to 2 weeks' in the county jail. John Angel convicted of an assault with intent to kill Richd Plummer: sentenced to 2 years in the penitentiary. 2-Jas Bland Randolph, having been presented by the Grand Jury to be of unsound mind, to be removed to a lunatic asylum.

Died: on Dec 28, in Wilmington, Lt Wm Henry Wright, of the U S Crops of Engineers, aged 31.

Church Directory: Wash.
Baptist: Rev O B Brown, 10th st, between E & F sts.
Baptist: Rev Mr Samson, E st, between 6th & 7th sts.
Baptist: Rev Mr Hendrickson, 4th & Va ave.
Baptist, Shiloh: Elder Robt C Leachman, Va ave, near 4½ st.
Catholic, St Patrick's: Very Rev Mr Mathews, assistant Rev Jas B Donelan, F st, between 9th & 10th sts.
Catholic, St Mathew's: Rev J P Donelan, H & 15th sts.
Catholic, St Peter's: Rev Mr Van Horseigh, 2nd st, between C & D sts, Capitol Hill.
Episcopal, Christ's Church: Rev Mr Bean, G st, between 6th & 7th sts.
Episcopal, St John's: Rev Mr Pyne, corner of 16th & H sts.
Episcopal, Trinity: Rev Mr Stringfellow, 5th st, between La ave & E sts.
Episcopal, Epiphany: Rev Mr French, G st, between 13th & 14th sts.
Episcopal, Ascension: Rev Mr Gillis, H st, between 9th & 10th sts.
Friends: I st, between 18th & 19th sts.
German Evangelical: Rev A Biewand, 21st & G sts.
Lutheran, English: Rev Dr Muller, 11th & H sts.
Methodist, Ebenezer: Rev Messrs Ege & Hanson, 4th st, between F & G sts, Navy Yard.
Methodist, Foundry: Rev Messrs Tarring & T A Morgan, 14th & G sts.
Methodist, Wesley Chapel: Rev Norval Wilson, F & 5th sts.
Methodist, McKendree Chapel: Rev Mr Eggleston, Mass ave, between 9th & 10th sts.
Methodist, Ryland Chapel: Rev F S Evans, Md ave & 10th sts.
Methodist Protestant: Rev J J Murray, Va ave, between 5th & 6th sts, Navy Yard.
Methodist Protestant: Rev Mr Matchett, 9th st, between E & F sts.
Presbyterian: Rev Dr Laurie, F st, between 14th & 15th sts.
Presbyterian: Rev Mr Sprole, 4½ st, between C & D sts.
Presbyterian: Rev Mr Knox, H st & N Y ave.
Presbyterian [Old School:] Rev Mr Eells, meet in the Protestant Methodist Church, 9th st.
Presbyterian: Rev J C Smith, 9th st, between G & H sts.
Presbyterian, [nearly finished:] Rev S Tuston, 8th st, between H & I sts.
Unitarian: Rev J Angier, D & 6th sts.

Mrd: on Jan 7, in Wash City, by Rev Dr Jas Laurie, John Cornog to Sarah D, d/o the late Robt V Sharples, of Chester Co, Pa.

For rent: the old & well known store & dwlg, corner of M st & 9th st, near the Navy Yard gate. Mr Wm Morgan, the present occupant will show the same, or Wm D Acken.

$25 reward for runaway, my negro man Bob, about 45 years old. He has a wife & child renowned by Mr Jas Payne, in Westmoreland Co, Va. –Cornelius Barber, farm in St Mary's Co, Md.

House of Reps: 1-Cmte of Claims: bill for the relief of John G Pierre: committed. 2-Cmte on Commerce: bill for the relief of Asa Armington & others: committed. 3-Ptn of Geo M Fowle, deputy collector & inspector at Barcelona: laid on the table. 4-Cmte of Claims: bill for the relief of Wm Culver: committed. 5-Cmte of Claims: adverse report on the ptn of Chas Foreman: laid on the table. 6-Cmte on Public Lands: bill for the relief of Mary Ann Bruner: committed. 7-Cmte on Invalid Pension: adverse reports in the cases of Andrew Ferguson, Elisha Foster, & Alex S Jackson: all laid on the table. 8-Cmte on Revolutionary Pensions: against the ptn of Saml S Smith: laid on the table. 9-Cmte on Invalid Pension: bill for the relief of Aaron Rollins; bill for relief of Jas Mains; bill for the relief of Jas Wyman; bill for the relief of Arthur R Frogge: committed. Same cmte: adverse reports on the cases of John Stone, Juliana Birchmore, & Isaac Barker: laid on the table. Same cmte: bill for the relief of John Ficklin; bill for the relief of Jos Watson: committed. Same cmte: adverse report on the ptn of Elijah Blodget; of Lucy O'Bryon; of Jesse Ellis; Theophilus Somerly; & of Thos H Brown: laid on the table. 10-Bill granting a pension to Jos M Rhea, of Tenn, to commence Jan 1, 1846: passed in the affirmative. 11-Bill for the relief of Saml D Walker: committed.

SAT JAN 10, 1846
By virtue of 6 writs of fieri facias, issued by T C Donn, a Justice of the Peace for Wash Co, D C, I shall expose to public sale, for cash, at the Canal Bridge, on 7th st, on Jan 10, the following, to wit: the long boat **Elizabeth**, an anchor & chain, seized & taken as the property of Jas M Donald, & Chas West, superseder, & will be sold to satisfy 6 judgments in favor of Chas Rosenthal. –John Magar, Constable

House of Reps: 1-Cmte of Claims: unfavorable report on the ptn of Chas Freeman; adverse report on the case of Elbert H Hungerford: both laid on the table. 2-Bill for the relief of the legal reps of John Lawson, dec'd: introduced. 3-Cmte on the Judiciary: bill for the relief of Wm Sanders & Wm R Porter: committed. 4-Cmte on Revolutionary Claims: bill for the relief of the heirs of Larkin Smith: committed. 5-Cmte on Naval Affairs: bill for the relief of John E Holland: committed. 6-Cmte on Invalid Pensions: adverse report on the ptn of John Martin: laid on the table. 7-Bill for the relief of Jas Bogardus: referred to the Cmte on Patents. 8-Bill for the relief of Jeremiah Moore: referred to the Cmte of Claims.

Pippin Apples, Md Bacon Hams [old] & 3 hogsheads Sugar-house Sirup: in Store, & for sale by D L Jackson & Brother.

Wanted, a first-rate woman servant, for a small private family on 3rd st. She must be a good cook, & handy. Wanted, a Cook & Chamber Servant, for a small family on 3rd st. Inquire of Mr Mankin, Patriotic Bank. One from the country would be preferred.

The Red River Republican, published at Alexandria, in Louisiana, announces the death, near that place, of Gen Walter H Overton, in his 57th year. During the memorable defence of New Orleans, Gen Overton was entrusted with the command of **Fort St Philip**, below the city, which fort he defended against the bombardment of the enemy with signal bravery; & he was one of the Reps of Louisiana in Congress. [No date-news item.]

Benj Tevis, of Phil, died on Wed, after a very short but severe illness of an inflammation of the breast.

The Whig Genr'l Cmte of N Y C organized on Wed, at the Broadway House, by electing: J Phillips Phoenix, as Chairman; Abraham R Lawrence, Assist Chairman; Jas H Pinkney & Chas Chamberlain, as Secretaries.

Geo Pepper died on Tue, at his residence in Phil. He was among the most respectable & wealthy of our citizens, perhaps the wealthiest. He lived an irreproachable life, & sustained a lofty integrity. –U S Gaz

Cabinet-maker & Undertaker: old stand on 7th st, north of the Patent Ofc. –Peter Callan

Trustee's sale of valuable city property: decree of the Circuit Court of Wash Co, D C, in the case of Frances Clarke against John F Clark & others: sale on Feb 2, upon the premises, the western most dwlg-house on F st, with ground belonging to the same, & as now occupied, the 2nd & upper stories of said house extending over the alley, being part of lot 5 in square 224, with the privilege of the alley; also lot 27 in square 252, in Wash City; both parcels constituting lot 5 in the division of the real estate of Francis Clark, dec'd, as by the report of the com'rs, on record, may appear. –W Redin, Trustee The adjoining lot #26, square 252, will also be offered for sale at the same time. –W Redin -B Homans, auctioneer [Note: the spelling of Clark/Clarke-copied as written.]

Valuable bldg lots for sale: decree made by the Orphans Court of Wash Co, D C, on Oct 10, 1845: sale on Feb 3 next, on the premises, lots 9 & 10 in square 220, fronting on H st, near St Matthew's Church: each lot is 24 feet 8 inches front, by 150 feet deep, with an alley 30 feet wide in the rear. Please call at my ofc, in the west wing of the City Hall. –John A Linton, Atty -R W Dyer, auct

Orphans Court of Wash Co, D C. Letters of administration on the personal estate of Chas Ungher, late of said county, dec'd. –Jacob Smull, adm

Household & kitchen furniture at auction on Jan 12, at the house of Mr W Smith, 7th & I sts. –Wm Marshall, auctioneer

Appointments by the Pres, by & with the advice & consent of the Senate.
Edmund Burke, of N H, to be Com'r of Patents, in place of Henry L Ellsworth, resigned.
Gansevoort Melville, of N Y, to be Sec of Legation of the U S near her Britannic Majesty, in place of Francis R Rives, resigned.
Wm H Stiles, of Ga, to be Charge d'Affiares to the Court of his Majesty the Emperor of Austria, in place of Danl Jenifer, Envoy Extra & Minister Pleni to that Court.
Benj A Bidlack, of Pa, to be Charge d'Affaires to the Republic of Granada, in place of Wm M Blackford, recalled.
Anthony Ten Eyck, of Michigan, to be Com'r to the Sandwich Islands, in place of Geo W Brown, at his own request recalled.

Custom-House Ofcrs:
Michl McBlair to be Appraiser of merchandise for the port of Balt, Md, vice John Lester, removed.
J Travis Rosser, to be Collector of customs for the district of Petersburg, Va, vice Hugh Nelson, removed.
Hiram G Reynolds, to be Collector of the customs for the district of Texas, & Inspector of the Revenue for the port of Galveston, in the State of Texas.

Justices of the Peace-8:
Benj K Morsell, of Wash
Nicholas B Vanzandt, of Wash
Nathl Brady, of Wash
David Saunders, of Wash
Benj B French, of Wash
Robt H Clements, of Wash
Robt White, of Gtwn
Jas Callaghan, of Wash, in place of Thos R Hampton, dec'd

Postmasters:
Jas M Buchanan, Balt, Md, in place of Thos Finley, removed.
Paul Dean Carrique, Hudson, N Y, in place of Justus McKinstry, removed.
Robt H Morris, N Y, N Y, in place of John L Graham, removed.
Geo F Lehman, of Phil, Pa, in place of Jas Hoy, jr, removed.
Henry C Conklin, Brooklyn, N Y, in place of Geo Hall, removed.
Geo Sanderson, Carlisle, Pa, in place of Wm M Porter, removed.
Stephen Isley, Newburyport, Mass, in place of Benj W Hale, whose commission has expired.

N Y Tribune: N Y, Dec 30, 1845. I take pleasure in acknowledging, on behalf of Mrs Fanny M Preston, wid/o the late John H Preston, dec'd, the payment of $5,000, being the amount of a policy of insurance effected by her late husband upon his life at your ofc, for the benefit of his wife, on Sep 25 last. By means of this policy the wife & children of the dec'd are guarantied a comfortable support. –Richd B Kimball, 53 Wall st. Robt L Patterson, Pres of the Mutual Benefit Life Ins Co.

Household & kitchen furniture at auction on Jan 12, at the house of Mr W Smith, 7th & I sts. –Wm Marshall, auctioneer

MON JAN 12, 1846
House of Reps: 1-Cmte of Claims: adverse report on the case of Patrick Smith: laid on the table. 2-In the case of Jas Bumbaugh, which the Cmte on Invalid Pensions had reported adversely, same to be recommitted to the same cmte due to additional testimony.

Applicants for repairing & gravelling Pa ave-Wash: [W Noland, Comr of Public Bldgs]

Geo Scott	Philip Ennis
Peter Little	Mich Dooley
R R Farr	Nicholas Feriton
Wm Bush	John Ready
C & R Coltman	Roach & Rogers
P Crowley	Peter Gorman

Applicants for paving in front of the Treasury bldg-Wash:

Robt Isherwood	John Holoham
Thos Berry	Patrick Hartnett
Thos Hunter	Richd Joyce
Gault & Emory	Eugene Daly
Jas A Tait	Henry Ellis
Jeremiah M Smith	J Hopkins
McMoreland & Rutherford	Jas T Brown
M Gault	

Applicants for contract painting the President's Mansion-Wash:

John Purdy: $4,466.	Wm A Godey: $3,600.
Thos Stanly: $4,000.	Moore & Kellum: $3,495.
Henry Diffenbach: $4,000.	Benj F Bunker: $2,996.
John M Seely, $4,383.	Benj J Williams: $2,956.69
Levi Hurdle, Thos F Hurdle, & Albion Hurdle: $2,700.	

Applicants for repairing & gravelling Pa ave, from 17th st to Rock creek:

Fletcher & Hagerty	R R Farr
Wm R Burton	P Crowley
Lewis L Coryell	Saml O'Riley
M Dooley	P Gormly
Kidwell & Ennis	J H King
C & R Coltman	Coburn & Dove
Prather & Wilson	Roach & Rogers
Peter Gorman	

Applicants for furnishing & setting curbstone in front of the new Treasury bldg:

Jas A Tait	Richd Joyce
Gault & Emory	Robt Isherwood
Wilkins, Cassidy & Co	Eugene Dayly-withdrawn
John Holohan	

On Dec 24, as Mr Edw Doyle, of Charleston, was on his way from Charleston to Columbia, to see his wife, resident in Camden, in endeavoring to pass from one car to another, accidentally fell, when the whole train passed over him, crushing both his legs. He expired the next morning. –Charleston Courier

The Hon Elias Glenn died yesterday, at his seat neat this city, at a ripe old age. He was formerly the Judge of the U S District Court of Md, which ofc he resigned some years since on account of ill health. He was among the oldest residents of Balt, & was universally respected for his high public character & excellence as a private citizen. –Balt Patriot

Wilmington, Dela, Jan 9. Yesterday an accident occurred at the paper mill of Jos Scott & Co, when the revolving boiler was blown from the back part of the mill into 2nd st, & struck the lower part of Mr Jos Beggs' dwlg, breaking his door & steps into atoms. The engineer, Patrick McCoy was killed instantly; John Stewart, fireman, was very badly scalded; John Bennett was much injured. -Journal

Mrd: on Jan 8, by Rev J P Donelan, Mr Jas Herrity to Miss Julia Coninx, all of Wash City.

Four of Dupont's workmen were drowned on Wed last, whilst crossing Riddle's dam, on their way home from their daily work. They were: Chas Armstrong, Andrew McCann, Owen, McCarran, & David McCallen. –Del Jour

It is stated in the Colonization Journal that Judge Leigh, the exc of John Randolph, has purchased a large tract of land in Mercer Co, Ohio, on which to locate the slaves [some 300] manumitted by Mr Randolph at the time of his death.

Mr Benj Lamborne, a respectable citizen of London Grove, Chester Co, Pa, committed suicide on Sat last. He inflicted severe wounds upon his person & then threw himself in a stream & was drowned.

Criminal Court-Wash: 1-Ignatius Grimes, [free negro,] was found guilty with grand larceny in stealing $26 from Darnel Chew, [free mulatto.] He was sentenced to 18 months in the penitentiary. 2-Geo W Talburt was acquitted of assault & battery on Zachariah Berry.

Wash City Ordnance: Act of the relief of Pringle Sleight: payment of the claim, for making a platform & fixtures at the east front of the Capitol, by request of the Cmte of Arrangements, on the occasion of the funeral solemnities in honor of the memory of the late ex-Pres Jackson, the sum of $25.75 is hereby appropriated, & payable to Pringle Sleight out of the general fund.

The copartnership heretofore existing between the undersigned was dissolved by mutual consent on Jan 1. –J W Henderson, Fred Iddins [The business will hereafter be conducted by J W Henderson.]

TUE JAN 13, 1846
Senate: 1-Memorial of Joshua Dodge, for further compensation for services as a special agent of the U S to negotiate with certain European Gov'ts for a modification of the duties on tobacco. 2-Ptn of Jos Wilson, a purser in the navy, praying to be released from responsibility for public money deposited in a suspended bank. 3-Ptn from the wid/o the late Alex'r Hamilton, praying the patronage of Congress in the publication of the papers of her late husband. 4-Ptn of the excs of Jos Wood, dec'd, praying the renewal of a patent. 5-Ptn of Angier M Perkins, praying an extension of his patent for heating bldgs. 6-Ptn of Eliz A Sevier, wid/o Alex'r G Sevier, late an ofcr in the U S marine corps, for arrears of pension. 7-Ptn of Wm Pumphrey, praying the confirmation of his title to a tract of land in Louisiana. 8-Ptn of the heirs of the late C C B Thompson, praying compensation for diplomatic services near the Gov'ts of Chili & Peru, while in command of the U S squadron. 9-Ptn of Andrew Moore, for a pension for wounds received in the last war. 10-Memorial of the legal reps of Moses Shepperd, dec'd, for compensation for work done by him on the Cumberland Road. 11-Cmte on Indian Affairs: bill for the relief of Elijah White. Same cmte: bill for relief of the legal reps of Geo Duvall, a Cherokee Indian. 12-Bill for relief of David Williamson, of Pope Co, Ark: passed.

The Charleston papers announce the death of the venerable Dr Le Seigneur, at the advanced age of 84, after a residence of more than half a century in that city. He was a native of Caen, France, whence he emigrated to St Domingo, from which place he was forced to fly during the revolutionary troubles in that country.

Allison Floyd was arrested on Sat, at Balt, upon suspicion of being connected with hotel robberies which have lately taken place.

Mrd: on New Year's Day, at York Springs, Adams Co, Pa, by Rev D Hartman, John B McCreary, of that place, to Miss Rachel Funk, d/o Geo Deardorff, of Latimore Place, Adams Co.

Mrd: on Jan 8, by Rev Mr Ege, Mr Wm Beron to Miss Eliz Ann Bright, all of Wash City.

Died: on Dec 27 last, at the Monastery of the Visitation, D C, Mauguerite Rutherford Hite, d/o the late Mr Geo Hite, of Charleston, Jefferson Co, Va.

Steamboat explosion on Jan 3, killing Mr Chas Whon, 2nd engineer, & dangerously scalding Mr Kew, first engineer. –N O Bulletin

WED JAN 14, 1846
Arrest of Mary F Clark, alias Mary F Ellis, who is suspected of being the accomplice of Albion Floyd in the late robbery at the U S Hotel, was on Mon last arrested in this city.

Criminal Court-Wash-Mon: the trial of John Wesley Scott, alias Wesley Acott, convicted of grand larceny, [stole of certificate for $126.73, belonging to Wm Laird, of Balt,] also of forgery, was found guilty of both & sentenced to 2 years in the penitentiary for each offence.

The Small-Pox has extended itself into some of our principal streets: a family in C st, & another family in 5th st, both are in the same distressing situation. Vaccination is an antidote to the small-pox. [Jan 17th newspaper: from the Health Physician-the cases on C st turn out to be no cases of small-pox at all.]

Wash Corp: 1-Ptn of Geo Stewart: referred to the Cmte of Claims. 2-Ptn of H B Sawyer & others, for a flag footway at 22nd & Pa ave: referred to the Cmte on Improvements.

Keene [N H] Sentinel of Wed last: last week, on the border of Langdon, near Drewsville, Mr Derrick Hartwell, of Langdon, went into the woods with a 2 horse team, & was returning, seated on the top of his load, when he was thrown forward, & fell under the sled. The reins were wound around him so that the horse could not proceed. He remained like this during the bitter cold night, & died the following Monday.

Arkansas Intelligencer, published at Van Buren, of Dec 26, notices the death by drowning of Fred'k Gibboner & Mattois Myer. They had been employed at *Fort Smith*, & were descending the Arkansas river in a skiff, & about 25 miles below Van Buren, & were drowned.

Senate: 1-Ptn of Deliverance Slaston, an old soldier, for an increase of his Revolutionary pension. 2-Ptn of Jas Updike, a Revolutionary ofcr, praying a pension. 3-Ptn of Simon Hubbard, on behalf of Cooper Pollygreen, a Revolutionary musician, praying a pension. 4-Memorial of Cadwallader Wallace, praying relief for certain lands located by him in the Virginia military reservation, Ohio, between Ludlow's & Roberts' lines. 5-Ptn of W B R Gale, praying compensation for services as bearer of dispatches from the American Consulate at Tunis to the U S. 6-Cmte on Naval Affairs: adverse report on the ptn of David D Porter, in behalf of his mother, Mrs Evelina Porter, wid/o the late Cmdor Porter. 7-Cmte of Claims: bill for the relief of the legal reps of Pierre Menard & others, sureties of Felix N Vrain, late Indian agent, with amendments. 8-Cmte of Claims: bill for the relief of the heirs of Wm D Cheever, with an amendment. 9-Bill for the relief of Nathl Goddart: passed over informally. 10-Bill for the relief of Mary MacRea, wid/o Lt Col Wm MacRea, late Colonel of Artl in the service of the U S, was taken up in Cmte of the Whole: it was postponed. Note of the Nat'l Intelligencer: The subjoined report on the subject, so interesting, that we think we cannot do better than place it before our readers. In Senate of the U S, Jan 7, 1846. The petitioner sets out the long, faithful, & meritorious services of her dec'd husband, & his death while in the service, & her own destitute condition, & prays remuneration or relief from Congress for these extraordinary services. His service extended over 41 years, embracing the Indian wars of the N W & the late war with Great Britain, including arduous services on the frontiers during peace: he commenced service in 1791 as a Lt, & served in the campaign under Maj Gen St Clair in the then Northwestern territory, now State of Ohio, & was in the engagement of Nov 4, of that year, & commanded a company of 57 men, 46 of whom were killed or wounded, himself among the latter. He was next under the order of Maj Gen Anthony Wayne, in the same territory, with whom he served in 1792 until 1796-97, & fought under his order in the action of Aug 20, 1794, as a brig major, being that year a captain in the 3rd sub-legion of the U S. In May, 1796, on the death of Maj Gen Wayne, he was appointed to perform that duty, which he continued until the army arrived at Detroit, & took possession of the posts on the lakes which were surrendered to the U S under Mr Jay's treaty in the fall of 1796. A new organization of the army having taken place in the winter of 1796-97, being then a junior captain, his company was reduced; in the spring following he was appointed a captain of the artillery. On Jul 31, 1800-promoted to a majority in the 2nd regt of artl & engineers; & after commanding some time at **Fort Mifflin**, Dela, & posts in R I & Conn; in the spring of 1802 he proceeded to Tenn, & took command of the troops on the frontier of Tenn; in summer of 1807, he was ordered to **Fort Adams**, on the **Mississippi**, & thence to New Orleans, to take command of the troops in that city. He remained there until 1815. On Dec 23, 1814, when Gen Jackson moved with his disposable forces to meet the enemy, he accompanied him. Col MacRae continued to serve for 11 years after the reorganization of the army in 1821, his health becoming greatly impaired by his long exposure on the frontiers, & in the South. He was twice struck with paralysis, & was attacked with cholera on Nov 3, 1832, on board a steamboat on the Ohio river, & died in a few hours, & his dead body was buried on the banks of the river, on the Illinois side, with all the precipitation which the alarm of his death inspired. At his death he left a widow & 2 dghts; the 2 latter have since died. The widow alone now survives, & is now in great want-having expended, since the death of her husband, in her necessary support, the little property she possessed, & being now dependent on the benevolence of friends. If Col MacRea had been killed in the line of his duty, his widow would have been entitled to 5 years' half-pay; whether the ofcr was killed in service, or wore out his life & died in the service, the loss is the same to the family.

Trustee's sale of valuable warehouse: sale on Jan 27, on the premises, the piece of ground, with improvements, fronting 32 feet on La ave, back to the line of lot 76: with a 3 story brick warehouse, with a slate roof, now occupied by Wm Noyes & Co above, & Gould & Co below. The property is free from all incumbrance: title indisputable. –G R Gaither, Edm Pittman, Trustees

Died: on Dec 15, at Deep Creek, Eastern Shore, Va, Mrs Margaret T, w/o Tully W Parker, after a short illness, leaving a husband & 3 children to mourn her untimely death.

House of Reps:: 1-Cmte on Revolutionary Pensions: adverse report on the case of Bartholomew Braddock: laid on the table. Same cmte: bill for the relief of Jas Hillman: committed. 2-Cmte on Invalid Pensions: adverse reports on the cases of Saml Cochran & Dennis Dygert: laid on the table. Same cmte: adverse reports on the cases of John L Allen, Elias Carpenter, Hector St John Beetley, Nathan Ashby, Aaron Tucker, Andrew & John Moddrell, Eli West, John Biddle, & Elijah Buchanan: laid on the table. Same cmte: bill for the relief of the heirs of Wm Evans, dec'd: committed. 3-Bill for the relief of Thos Copeland, on account of services rendered at the U S arsenal near Pittsburg: introduced. 4-Memorial of Dowry Williams, of Cass Co, Ga, who seek indemnity for damages sustained by him in being dispossessed of his improvements contrary to the stipulations of the 10th article of the Cherokee treaty of 1835: referred to the Cmte on Indians Affairs.

Gtwn Assemblies will be held at the Ball Rooms, Union Hotel, on Jan 20th next, & continue throughout the Winter at intervals of 2 weeks. Managers:

E M Linthicum	Manadier Mason	Peter Wilson
Col L Humphrey	E S Wright	L M Morton
Wm S Nicholls	R Ould	Robt Dick
O M Linthicum	Dr W Plater	Jno E Addison
Hugh Caperton	Clem Smith	J F Pickrell
Dr Wm Sothoron	J M Ramsey	

For rent: a house & store, in Gtwn, for the last 20 years occupied as a China, Glass, & Earthenware establishment. Old age & increasing infirmities is the reason of the present occupant wishing to decline business. For further particulars inquire of John Claxton, on the premises.

For sale: valuable farm in Fairfax Co, Va: land bounds on the Columbia turnpike, leading from Wash City by a free bridge to Loudoun Co: contains about 500 acres, with comfortable improvements. Also, a house & lot in Duke st, Alexandria. For particulars apply to the subscriber on Louisiana ave, between 6th & 7th sts, or to Genr'l Hunter, Marshal, Washington. –Julia Terret

THU JAN 15, 1846
Letters remaining in the Post Ofc, Wash, Jan 15, 1848.

Atocho, A T	Alexander, Mrs M B	Bruce, Miss S
Archer, Wm B-2	Anderson, Chas C	Bill, Tracy L-2
Andrews, B F	Antomarchi, J M	Brooks, Col Ed
Allen, John W	Bush, Jas W	Brown, Miss Mary
Allen, Gen Jas	Banks, T G	Beall, John H
Adams, John G	Brent, Mrs Eliza	Brown, Dr O A

Burke, Mrs Teresa
Beirne, Oliver
Boswell, Jas
Baldwin, Harvey
Brokenborough, C
Ballman, John H
Baker, Stephen M
Berry, Mrs B L
Baker, Mrs Eliza
Banghart, J
Belsher, J Henshaw
Boteler, John D-2
Baldwin, Geo R
Burdell, Wm
Buckey, Danl
Bronough, Mrs
Bulley, T, or B Dant
Branson, Benj
Breadford, Purser
Broadhead, John C
Barnum, Capt E K
Brady, Nathl
Cole, Mrs F A
Cross, Miss Eliza
Cooke, Eliuths
Crump, Dr G W-2
Clark, Miss M A-2
Cutler, Abraham-2
Colton, Rev Calvin-2
Cuyler, Theodore
Coston, John F
Coffee, Geo W
Collings, Saml P
Coleman, Nathan
Clements, Miss C
Corbin, T G, U S N
Comstock, Dr W W
Canfield, Capt Aug
Crutchett, Jas-2
Cochrane, J T
Cabell, Jos C
Courtney, Miss Ann
Chenowith, S W
Claxton, Richd W
Carey, Shepherd

Calloway, Dr J W
Carusi, Lewis
Cushing, Caleb-2
Coffin, Isaac N
Dorn, Philip
Dwight, Tim C
Dulay, Robt
Dailey, Oliver A
Dwey, Rev L D
Downing, Robt
Dumas, P C
Donley, Danl
Dunbar, Miss E J
Darnell, Gen N H
Dixon, Wm
Darrah, Jas
Duncan, Wm
DeKoven, Mid W
Degraff, John T
DeLand, Dr M G, U S N
Dickinson, T-4
Drummond, Mrs H A
Duvall, Mrs Harriet
Davis, Geo T M-3
Duvall, Gen John P
Donelson, A J-3
Elting, Henry J
Ellsworth, C L
Elting, A
Ewing, E H-3
Ellis, V
Elliott, Mrs Mary
Fry, Wm A
France, Jas-2
Forbes, Col G V H
Fitch, Horatio
Failes, Wm H
Fuller, J H
Ferguson, F
Feagans, Benj
Feady, Matthew
Falknew, Thos
Forney, John W-2
Fenwick, Phil

Greene, Rich W
Glenn, Jos B
Grose, David
Grant, Jas
Greene, C K-5
Gulick, John-4
Gratiot, Chas H-2
Gorman, Peter
Gibert, A
Griffith, Miss M J
Grammer, Fred'k
Gibson, Richd
Gleason, Thos M
Galley, Isaac
Griffith, Jas
Garner, Miss Car
Greene, Thorp, & Davis
Griner, Anthony W
Guerber, Auguste
Hunt, Mrs Sarah A
Hess, Wm R
Hill, Miss Ann
Hays, John
Hoit, Stephen
Hall, Wm
Hart, Rufus E
Hall, Jas
Hall, Edw
Hallett, Benj F
Hebard, Andrew
Heaton, D F-3
Hamilton, R C
Hollaga, sr, Thos
Harris, Geo F
Hubley, Ed B-2
Henrie, Dr Drake
Henley, Thos Jef
Hodskin, Mrs P
Handy, John W
Hickman, J C
Hurseley, J G
Humphrey, L S
Humphrey, H B-2
Hipkins, John

Harvey, Thos H	Lawrence, Henry	McDonald, Jas
Herrick, John B	Lawrence, Jno W	McReynolds, John
Harris, J G	Larner, Thos D	McIntosh, Jas T
Holland, Geo	Leonard, Byram	McIntosh, Mrs
Hornblower, J H	Leighton, Miss J	McDuffee, Thos
Hamilton, W B	Lamme, David S-5	McFarlan, Miss E
Helfrichoder, J	Lowry, M B	McKenny, J
Hickox, Col S B	Means, Jos-2	McArthur, Lt W P
Holland, Mrs Eliz	Moore, Joshua J	McLemore, Jno C
Hoomer, Miss M W	Mules, Thos	North, Dr Mile L
Hamlin, L F	Moore, Geo F	Neff, Mr
Harrett, Miss Mary	Moore, Robt	Nevit, Mrs Lucy A
Hayward, Chas	Moore, Henry W	Nicholson, A O P
Hopkins, Alfred	Moore, Miss M E	O'Neill, Mich
Hooper, Chas	Mann, Hamilton	Orme, W C
Hardin, Mr	Marshall, Jas D	O'Neill, G P
Hunt, Mrs Belinda D	Mattingly, T J	O'Brien, Dr P W
Hanover, Rep of the Kingdom	Matthews, C F-2	Offley, J H-2
	Mixner, L B	Prime, Rufus-2
Irwin, Jared	Morgan, Geo W	Pool, Wm C
Isherwood, Robt	Murphy, H C	Pease. L T
Irvine, Washington	Meyer, Frank	Page, Thos
Irwin, Wm	Milstead, Robt A	Peak, Wm
Jones, Mrs Mary	Morse, Mrs Rosena	Phelps, Francis P
Jordon, Jas W	Murphy, Ellen	Porter, Benj F
Jefferson, Maj P-3	Martin, John	Pleasants, J B
Jackson, Miss Mary	Manning, Dr W A-2	Philips, Mrs C A
Johnston, Edw	Martin, Mrs M A	Powell, John A
Jewett, Jos	Morrison, Coke	Pringle, Wm
Jenkins, Miss M E	Martin, J	Porter, Wm T
Krebs, H H	Mahon, John D	Potter, jr, Gilbert
Keith, Chas R	Maron, David	Petticord, Mrs C
Kolb, Henry	Matthews, Henry C	Patton, Geo
Kemble, S	Morrison, Cornelius	Partee, A Y-2
Kanally, J	Morgan, Col Gid	Parmenter, Wm
Long, Edw	Moran, Patrick	Porter, Rev Robt
Latson, John W-2	Morrison, Enoch B	Prentiss, Saml S
Lukins, Miss W	Mitchell, W H	Quimby, Thos B
Lomax, Wm	McGraw, Jas	Quinter, Jos R
Livingston, Edw	McMakim, John	Reed, John-2
Latreal, Mrs	McNeil, Gen W H	Reeves, J, of Uhgatt
Lovelace, Miss M D	McClure, Chas	Roberts, E
Loomiss, E G	McKeim, Jno W	Ryon, Jas S
Learcock, G F D	McCrery, Dr J	Rowand, Chas L
Littleton, Jas	McKeever, Miss B	Rantoul, jr, Robt

Russell, Jeremiah-2
Retter, Ann G
Rigdon, Miss Ann
Randolph, Francis
Ryan, Michl
Ritter, Dr
Reily, Jas A
Russell, Jos
Rawlett, Edw
Randolph, Mr
Simms, Mrs E C
Skaggs, S B
Smith, T C H
Smith, Miss Hannah
Shields, Edw
Stras, Miss E C
Smith, Algernon C
Smith, David
Stone, Col Alfred J
Smith, Benj P-3
Shellenberger, E T
Savage, Col John
Schuyler, G L
Stewart, Wm H
Simmes, Thos E
Slocum, Geo W
Sidney, J C
Skinner, Miss M
Sinclair, Jos-2
Smith, A, of Maine-2
Seymour, N'y or Jno
Sanders, Jas A
Speicer, Wm
Saunders, Mrs A
Scofield, Miss H
Sanford, Jas
Skillman, S
Stewart, Capt W-2
Trieste, Wm
Thrift, John T

Thorne, Miss M J
Tuner, Orsamus
Taylor, Miss Eliza
Tompkins, M
Tyson, J W
Truston, Jas L
Tappan, Benj-2
Thompson, E H-2
Thompson, J E
Titcomb, Moses
Thurber, jr, Wm
Thillon, Jos
Titus, Jonas H-5
Tatum, Amy Y
Taylor, Col of Texas
Thompson, Mrs C A
Tallman, Henry
Taylor, Philip R
Thornton, Jas B-2
Thompson, R A
Timberlake, Dixon
Usher, Mrs Eliz
Vanderpool, J V
Vermillion, Miss M
Varney, Ivory
Van Sissen, Hendrick
Vinton, Miss M
Webb, S H
Wood, Mrs Abby C
Wells, Gideon
Welles, R S
Wright, Real
West, B R
West, John W-2
Wood, Francis J
Whales, Wm
Wright, Jas
Werle, Wm
White, Miss Jane E
White, Thos D H

Watts, Philip
Watts, Philip
Watts, Mrs M-2
Wilson, R R
Wilson, John
Williams, Ruel
Williams, Danl
Williams, Miss C
Wolfinger, Henry
Watson, Miss M A
Whittlesey, Chas
Wallace, John T
Wadsworth, Jas S
Woodworth, S E
Williams, W L
Walker, S P
Whiten, Simeon-2
Wescott, John S-3
Washburn, Rev C
Whitney, S W-2
White, Dr E, of Oregon-8
Walker, Mrs M B
Wilson, Mrs A R
Watson, Reason
Wilkins, Wm
Williams, Miss M V-2
Webster, Sandy
Wilson, Francis S
Woolman, S B
Watson, Miss M R
Waters, Wm B
Warren, John P
Williams, Mrs Sarah
Wickliffe, Chas A
Young, Mrs Ann E
Young, Notley
Yates, Giles F
Yager, Hiram
Young, J, of Canada-2

The inland postage on all letters intended to go by ship must be paid, otherwise they remain in this ofc. -C K Gardner, P M

House to let: on 14th st, between F & G sts, lately occupied by N Callan. Rent $150 per annum. Inquire of Mrs Billing, on E st, between 9th & 10th sts.

Senate: 1-Ptn of Jemima Wood, wid/o a dec'd Revolutionary soldier, praying a pension. 2-Ptn of Philip Pearce, praying the right of pre-emption to a tract of land. 3-Ptn of Edw Bolon, praying compensation for his trouble & expense in keeping in confinement persons charged with the violation of the laws of the U S. 4-Ptn of Janna Juicey, asking for a pension. 5-Bill for the relief of Nathl Goddard & others was postponed.

The Martinsburg [Va] Gaz says that Washington Cross, of Morgan Co, a s/o the late Gassaway Cross, was curshed to death a few days ago in the machinery of his mill, on Capon river.

House of Reps:: 1-Bill for the relief of Chas M McKenzie: referred to the Cmte on Public Lands.

Mrd: on Jan 12, by Rev Jas B Donelan, Benj A Miller, of Shepherdstown, Va, to Caroline E, eldest d/o the late Phillip Eberle, of Phil.

On Jan 13 Rev Ninian Bannatine was installed co-pastor of F st church. He had previously been ordained to the Holy Ministry by the Presbytery of Balt. Rev Dr Laurie, is senior pastor.

Orphans Court of Wash Co, D C. Letters of administration on the personal estate of Alfred T Agate, late of said county, dec'd. --Stans Murray, adm

Valuable improved property on Pa ave for sale at public auction, on Feb 25 next: part of lots 17 & 18 in square B, with a 3 story brick dwlg & store: dwlg is occupied by Mrs Preuss as a boarding house. Lots 26 & 27 in square B, with a large 3 story brick dwlg & large back bldg & store: dwlg is occupied by Mrs Hamilton as a boarding house. It is the square immediately in front of Coleman's Hotel. -R W Dyer, auct

FRI JAN 16, 1846
House of Reps: 1-Ptn of Chauncey Wetmore, adm of Elisha Hubbard, late of Middletown, Conn, praying for arrears of pension. 2-Ptn of Seth Overton, of Portland, Conn, asking for remuneration of services rendered in the Revolutionary war. 3-Ptn of Gardiner Herring, praying for a pension. 4-Ptn & papers of John Owen, of China, Maine; of Solomon Russell; of Isaac Davenport: all presented. 5-Ptn of Esther Russell, praying for an increase of pension. 6-Ptn of Levi Colemus, praying that a pension may be allowed him from 1814 to 1844, when he was placed on the pension roll. 7-Memorial of the heirs of Robt Fulton praying the attention of Congress to their claim against the U S Gov't, in consideration of the use of his invention of the application of steam-power to vessels. 8-Ptn of Isaac Davis, of Nelson Co, Ky, asking compensation for services rendered by his father, Cornelius Davis, during the Revolutionary war, & for property lost in the early settlement of Ky. 9-Ptn & papers of Catharine Fulton, of Wash Co, Pa, praying a pension for the

services of her dec'd husband during the Revolutionary war. 10-Ptn of Ralph French, of Hardin Co, Ky, praying a pension for Revolutionary services. 11-Ptn of Mrs Catharine Adair, wid/o the late Gen John Adair, asking a pension from the time the first act allowing pensions to widows of Revolutionary ofcrs expired up to the time when the act was revived, a period of 2 years. 12-Memorial & papers of Christopher Millers' heirs, of Hardin Co, Ky, praying for compensation for services rendered by said Miller in the Northwestern army. 13-Ptn of Geo Lee, of Norwich, Conn, to have refunded to him the proceeds of the wreck of the brig **Plato** paid into the U S Treasury. Also, for money expended for the shipwrecked seamen on board the brig. 14-Ptn of Jacob Stonecipher, for compensation for a horse lost whilst engaged in the service of the U S during the late war with Great Britian. 15-Ptn of Ignatius Peirce, for bounty on fishing schnr **Fortune**. 16-Ptn of Seneca Thomas, of Worcester, Mass, praying for arrears of pension for a wound received in the late war with Great Britain. 17-Memorial of Passed Midshipman John L Warden, of the U S Navy, for compensation for performing duties belonging to those of a higher grade, from Dec 1, 1840 to May 30, 1842, inclusive, on board the U S ship **Relief**, under the command of [now] Cmder John S Nichols. 18-Ptn of Jas Journey, of Missouri, asking Congress to confirm to him a tract of land in Missouri, favorable reported on & placed in the first class by report of Com'rs appointed under the act of Jul 9, 1832. 19-Ptn of Reuben Taylor, for relief. 20-Ptn of Nathl Cole, jr, of Palmyra, Maine, for a pension on account of injuries sustained in the last war with Great Britain. 21-Ptn of Luke Hilton, of Canada line, State of Maine, for injuries sustained while in the service & employ of the Gov't in hauling & distributing the monuments on the boundary line in Mar, 1845. 22-Papers presented relating to the claim of the wid/o Seth Babb, sen, dec'd, for arrears of pension. 23-Ptn of John Strobecher & others, praying to be indemnified for losses by insurance on the schnr **Enterprise**, driven by stress of weather into Bermuda, & forcibly detained by the authorities of the Island. 24-Ptn of J Wilson for relief. 25-Ptn of Nancy G Van Renssealer & of Jonas D Platt, for pensions. 26-Ptn of Wm Briscoe & Eliza, his wife, heirs of Peter B Bruen, of Mississippi, for arrears of pension. 27-Ptn of Thos Gregg, of Pa, praying Congress to authorize an experiment to test the value of a model invented by him of ball-proof vessels for the naval service. 28-Ptn of Jacob Gideon, of Wash, D C, praying compensation in damages for a violation of his contract with the Navy Dept. 29-Papers of Mrs Ann Dodd, wid/o John Dodd, on file in the Pension Ofc, referred to the Cmte on Revolutionary Pensions. 30-Ptn of Ann Bissel, wid/o Saml Bissel, praying a pension. 31-Ptn of Mathew Thompson, for a pension. 32-Ptn of the heirs of Jas Williams, for a pension. 33-Ptn of the heirs of Lott Hall, dec'd, for remuneration for revolutionary services & prize money, & that the papers relating to this case be taken from the files of the House, & referred to the Cmte on Revolutionary Claims. 34-Ptn & documents of Andrew C Armstrong, praying a readjustment of his accounts as navy agent. 35-Ptn & documents of Jos H Brigham, praying to be confirmed in the occupation of a tract of land. 36-Ptn of Danl Spencer, accompanied with additional testimony. 37-Ptn of the heirs of Gen Arthur St Clair, for payment of moneys advanced by him for the use of the Gov't in the Revolutionary war. 38-Ptn of Mott Wilkinson, for a pension. 39-Memorial of the heirs of Capt John Oldham, for half-pay. 40-Ptn of Jas Conway. 41-Ptn of Polly Muhl, of Vincennes, for a pension. 42-Ptn & documents of the heirs of Reynal Hilliary, for remuneration in lieu of bounty land of which they allege they were defrauded: presented. 43-Ptn of the administrators of Col John Anderson, for compensation for property destroyed by the British & Indians during the last war. 44-Ptn of Moses Davis, for a pension for injuries received while in the service of the U S during the late war with Great Britain. 45-Ptn of Jos Thomure, of Missouri, legal rep of Nicholas Janis, praying the confirmation of a tract of land granted to said Janis by Don Henry Peyroux, civil & military commandant of the port of St Genevieve, on Apr 9, 1800. 46-Cmte on Revolutionary Claims: reported a bill for the relief of the reps of Lt Jonathan Dye: committed. 47-Cmte of Claims: adverse report on the case of Derrin Farrer: laid on the table. 48-Cmte of Claims: adverse report in the case of Robt Brady: laid on the table. Also, reported on the case of W Frost: which was agreed to. 49-Cmte on Indian Affairs: made an adverse report on the cases of Chas Roby & Willis Stephens: laid on the table. 50-Cmte on Invalid Pension; adverse reports on the cases of Benj Hunt & John Farnham. 51-Cmte on Revolutionary claims: reported a bill for the relief of Nathl Bird: committed. 52-Cmte of Claims: was discharged from the case of Wm J Bradford: it was laid on the table. 53-Cmte of Claims: discharged from the case of A Hathway, & it was committed to the Cmte of the Whole House. 54-Bill from the Senate for the relief of David F Williamson, of Pope Co, Ark, was committed to the Cmte on Public Lands. 55-Cmte of Claims: adverse report on the case of Robt Sewall: laid on the table. 56-Resolved: that the Cmte on Revolutionary Pensions inquire into the propriety & expediency of placing Benj Kerlin, of Ky, on the pension roll.

Herr Alexander, the great magician who has attracted so much notice in Phil & Balt, proposes to visit Wash City this week. He has been engaged at Carusi's Saloon.

Wash City Orphan Asylum meeting on Jan 13: Rev L J Gilliss called to the chair; Rev J W French appointed sec. Motion by Rev Smith Pyne: notice of the death of Rev Wm Hawley, Rector of St John's Church, in Wash City, which occurred since the last annual assemblage. Ladies elected for the ensuing year:

Mrs Hawley, First Directress	Mrs Laurie, 2nd Directress	Miss Smith, Treas Miss Van Ness, Sec
Managers:		
Mrs Brown	Mrs Richd Smith	Mrs R S Coxe
Mrs Lear	Mrs McLaughlin	Mrs Tucker
Mrs Dr Washington	Mrs Gilliss	Mrs Stone
Mrs Luce	Mrs Henderson	Miss Bingham

The Salem Register tells of a gentleman of Boston, who, 20 years ago was an endorser upon a note of a failing firm, which afterwards settled & received a discharge from all its creditors by paying 76%. Last week, the endorser, Mr John Williams, of Boston, paid up the amount due, with interest, which was $1,450.

Obit-died-Dr McCaw, of Richmond. Notice was in the Richmond papers. He was there at the burning of the Richmond Theatre in the winter of 1811, leaped from the side box of the stage, in the hope of securing the escape of his party behind it. He saved many lives, including that of his wife, but was much injured himself. His own son dragged him out of danger from the falling wall. Months of severe pain followed. [No other information.]

Major Reybold, of Dela, & his four sons, sent the following quantity of peaches to market last season: Maj Philip Reybold, from Md & Delaware orchards, 44,000 baskets; John Reybold, 17,760; Philip Reybold, 9,000; Wm Reybold, 10, 095; Barney Reybold, 10,000. Average them only at a $1 a basket. –N Y Sun

Biographical sketch of Clemens Weinzel Lothar, Prince of Metternich. He was born at Coblentz, on the Rhine, on May 15, 1773: descended from an ancient Rhenish family. Studied at Strasbourg & Mains, Mayence, on the Rhine: in 1795 he married the Countess Eleonore von Kaunitz. In 1801 was appointed Minister to Dresden; in 1806 was ambassador to France until 1809, when having been refused passports at Paris, Bonaparte's army then marching to Austria, he succeeded in reaching the encampment of the Emperor Francis at Komoen, a short time before the battle of Wagram. In 1810 he accompanied Maria Louisa, Archduchess of Austria, as Empress of France to Paris. Owing to Metternich's indefatigable efforts at Dresden, in 1812, the threatened outbreak in the North was prevented, by which Napoleon's plans were completely frustrated. Emperor bestowed on him the title of Austrian Prince for himself & his descendants. Prince Metternich is Knight of the Golden Fleece & of all the first class of orders in Europe, except the English Garter. His wife died in 1819; 10 years after he lost his second, the Countess Beilstein; & in 1831 he married, for the 3rd time, Countess Melanie Zichy Ferraris, his present wife, one of the most beautiful & charming of the Hungarian nobility. Two dghts by his first, one of whom is married to an Hungarian nobleman, one son by his second, & one dght & son by his present Princess, grace his family circle. [Pronounced Metternik.]

Geo Pepper, the wealthiest citizen of Phil, after the demise of the late Jacob Ridgway, whose death has been lately mentioned, has left a fortune of upwards of two million dollars, invested almost wholly in real estate & bond & mortgages. This large estate will be divided among some 8 or 10 children.

Pittsburg Gaz of Mon announces the death of Chas McClure, formerly a Rep in Congress from the Cumberland district, & late Sec of State of Pa. He was out late on Thur night last, & in passing to his room in his boarding house in the dark he fell down a back stairs, not used in the winter season, & it is supposed broke his neck by the fall. He leaves a family in Carlisle to mourn his untimely death.

On Tue last a young fellow at Burlingham was handling a gun in Mr Abbott's barroom, when it accidentally discharged, & the contents entered the arm & side of Miss Harriet Abbott, age 17, the y/d/o the landlord, who lingered until Thu morning, when death put an end to her sufferings. –Sullivan Whig

Senate: 1-Ptn of Benj Ballard, praying confirmation of a claim to a tract of land. 2-Addition documents in relation to the claim of Peter Ingles, a soldier in the last war with Great Britain: presented. 3-Cmte on Military affairs: bill for relief of widow of the late Zebulon M Pike. 4-Cmte on Pensions: adverse report on ptn of Jas Morgan.

Farm at auction: the subscriber having engaged in a business in Washington which will require his constant personal attention, will sell at public auction on Feb 2, the Farm on which he resides, containing 125 acres, on Rock creek: with a comfortable 2 story frame dwlg house. Also, for sale, the crops, stock, & farming utensils on the same. –L J Middleton -R W Dyer, auct

By virtue of a writ of fieri facias, at the suit of Robt W Hinton, use of Geo Collard, & against Wm B Cook, I have seized & taken in execution all the right, title, & interest of said Wm B Cook, to wit: a stove, 6 chairs, 2 table, 1 looking-glass, a teakettle, dripping pan, a small waiter, 2 mugs, & 1 pitcher: to be offered for sale on Jan 22. –John S Hutchins, Constable

By virtue of a writ of fieri facias in the suit of Richd G Briscoe & Jos S Clarke, trading under the firm of Briscoe & Clarke, against the goods & chattels, lands & tenements, rights & credits of Wm Young, I have seized & taken in execution all the right, title, & interest of the said Wm Young in a clock & a large looking-glass: sale, for cash, on Jan 22. –H R Maryman, Constable

By virtue of a writ of fieri facias at the suit of Richd C Washington, against the against the goods & chattels, lands & tenements, rights & credits of Wm Young, I have seized & taken in execution all the right, title, & interest of the said Wm Young in 4 mahogany tables, 2 ottomans, 2 table covers, 2 pair of andirons, shovel & tongs, 6 chairs, 2 fenders, 1 bellows, 2 waiters, 1 hearth rug, 1 sofa: to be sold for cash on Jan 22. -John H Locke, Constable

By virtue of a writ of fieri facias, at the suit of Joshua Pierce, use of John F Callan, against the goods & chattels, lands & tenements, rights & credits of Jonas W Nye: I have seized & taken in execution: one wardrobe, a desk, a lot of books, 1 stove, 16 chairs, knives, forks & spoons, 3 tables, 2 buckets, 1 fender, a pair of andirons, & 2 candlesticks: for sale on Jan 22, for cash. –H R Maryman, Constable

By virtue of a writ of fieri facias, at the suit of Thos A Doniphan, against the goods & chattels, lands & tenements, rights & credits of Wm Young: I have seized & taken in execution: a mahogany sideboard & one looking-glass: sale on Jan 22: for cash. –H R Maryman, Constable

By virtue of a writ of fieri facias, at the suit of Thos Faithful, Chas Faithful, & Wm Faithful, against the goods & chattels, lands & tenements, rights & credits of Wm B Cooke: I have seized & taken in execution: a bureau, 2 stands, a lot of books, 2 pictures, a silver watch, & 6 silver spoons: sale on Jan 22, for cash.
-H R Maryman, Constable

By virtue of a writ of fieri facias, at the suit of Susan Joyce, against the goods & chattels, lands & tenements, rights & credits of Jonas W Nye: I have seized & taken in execution: one wardrobe, a washstand, a desk, a stove, & 16 chairs: to be sold on Jan 22, for cash. –H R Maryman, Constable

Mrd: on Jan 14, by Rev Smith Pyne, Jas Blair, of the U S Navy, to Miss Mary L E, d/o Gen Thos Jesup.

Died: on Jan 14, aged about 66 years, Fred'k Augustus Wagler, professor of music, a native of Brunswick, in Germany, but for the last 40 years a resident of Wash City. His funeral is this day, at 10 o'clock, from his late residence, north side of Pa ave, between 17th & 18th sts.

For rent: I will rent my house, situated on the corner of 7th & I sts, for either a store or tavern, inasmuch as it is so constructed as to suit in every respect either business. Can be had immediately. –Jas H Shreve

SAT JAN 17, 1846
House of Reps: 1-Cmte of Claims: report a bill for the relief of Alborne Allen: committed. 2-Cmte of Claims: made an adverse report on the ptn of Mary Bowen: laid on the table. 3-Cmte on the District of Columbia: reported a bill for the relief of J W Nye, assignee of Peter Bargy & Hugh Stewart: committed. 4-Cmte on Foreign Affairs: reported a bill directing the mode of settlement of the accounts of Cmdor Thos Ap Catesby Jones: committed. 5-Cmte on the Military: reported it is inexpedient to act upon the ptn of John R Pollard, & asked that the cmte be discharged from its consideration. Agreed to. 6-Cmte of Claims: adverse report on the case of Wm Ausment: laid on the table. 7-Cmte on Revolutionary Pensions: adverse report on the ptn of Catharine Keller: laid on the table. Same cmte: bill for the relief of Saml Jourdan: committed. 8-Cmte on Revolutionary Pension: ptn of Mrs Judith Keith, wid/o Capt Thos Keith, made a report that in the opinion of the cmte the claims of the petitioner is reasonable, & ought to be allowed, & that the present laws are sufficient to afford the relief without further legislation in her case, & the cmte advise that the papers be sent by the Clerk of the House of Reps to the Sec of War, to the end that he may review the case, & grant relief to the petitioner. Done accordingly. 9-Cmte on Naval Affairs: bill for the relief of Philip B Holmes & Wm Pedrick: committed. 10-A bill to abolish public execution in capital cases. Bills were read & committed to the Cmte of the Whole on the state of the Union.

Orphans Court of Wash Co, D C. Letters of administration on the personal estate of Wm P Zantzinger, late of said county, dec'd. –Louisa F Zantzinger, Wm C Zantzinger, adms

MON JAN 19, 1846
Mr Hines, who keeps a grocery store on Pa ave, does not have a case of small pox in his family. Such a report is altogether without foundation.
–Harvey Lindsey, Pres/G C Gardner, Sec: Board of Health

Criminal Court-Wash: 1-Jury returned a verdict of guilty of murder in the first degree against Chas Williams, free negro, for the murder of his wife Delilah Williams, near Gtwn, on Jun 25, 1842. He has been confined in the jail of Wash Co for the long period of 3½ years, awaiting the action of the law. His wife Delilah, a woman of good character, was found dead, with her skull fractured, on the ledge of a stone quarry, a few miles from Gtwn. A man named Lightfoot, to whom the prisoner made a confession that he had murdered his wife, was mainly relied upon to prove the heinous offence charged in the indictment. [Mar 23rd newspaper: Chas Williams was brought into the Court & tried the 3rd time for his heinous offence. The prisoner was quite feeble & emaciated, almost unable to walk, even with help. The Court ruled that the plea enterd by the prisoner was sustained by the record, & ordered his discharge.]

Saml W Tucker, Coleman's Hotel, 6th st, is now selling splendid French Embroidered Vestings [genuine needlework,] lower than they can be brought in N Y.

House of Reps: 1-Ptn & papers of Jno Kleine, a soldier of the late war, asking for relief. 2-Application of the widow Johnson, wid/o Homer Johnson, late of Indiana, asking compensation for certain extra services rendered by her late husband as superintendent on the Cumberland Road. 3-Ptn of Danl B Perkins, praying for an allowance in consideration of injuries received in preserving the property of the U S at the armory at Springfield, Mass, from destruction by fire. 4-Mr Relfe withdrew from the files of the last Congress the ptn & papers of Joshua Shaw, praying compensation for the use of percussion lock, cap, & primer, invented by him, & used by the U S in violation of his letters patent. 5-Ptn of John Ingraham for an increase of his pension: referred. 6-Ptn of Lemuel Cushman, of Stafford, Conn: referre. 7-Ptn & papers of Niel Shannon, praying a pension. 8-Papers relating to the claim of John Robinson, of Carroll Co, Ga, administrator of Geo M Lavender, dec'd: referred. 9-Papers relating to the claim of Johnson Frost, of Troup Co, Ga: referred. 10-Ptn of Isaac Gray, of Campbell Co, Ga, heir at law of Jas Heath, praying remuneration for property carried away by the Cherokee Indians during the years 1791 & 1782: referred. 11-Memorial of Conrad House, of Wood Co, Ohio, heretofore referred Jan 16, 1837: referred. 12-Memorial of D & J Wilkinson, heirs of John Wilkinson, dec'd, of Wood Co, Ohio, heretofore referred Jan 16, 1837: referred

Notice: I have withdrawn from the Agency of the Balt Life Inso Co. –Jas H Causten

The barn of Augustus Hiester, near Harrisburg, was destroyed by fire on Sat last, together with all its contents. Loss $4,000; insured for $3,000.

The frig **Cumberland** & the brig **Boxer** are now in the stream of Boston harbor & ready for sea. They are both bound to the coast of Africa, from whence the fomer will proceed to the Mediterranean. Ofcrs of the U S frig **Cumberland**:

Geo C Read, Cmdor   Bladen Dulany, Capt
Lts:
J Bisham   J H Sherburn   S F Hazard
Edw Middleton   J A Winslow   Thos S Brasher
A D Howell, Passed Midshipman, Acting Master
Passed Midshipmen:
M C Perry   R Fairfax   Henry Ashton
Jos H Day   A J Dallas
E Ross Calhoun   Beverly Randolph
Fitch W Taylor, Chaplain
Nathl Wilson, Purser
Waters Smith, Fleet Surgeon
R T Maxwell, & W S Bishop, Assist Surgeons
Midshipmen:
Jos Seawell   J L Johnston   Robt Stuart
Walter Queen   Marshall J Smith
A T West   Edw E Stone
G B Hodge, Acting Midshipman
Chas Johnston, Boatswain
Elijah Haskell, Gunner
Amos Chick, Carpenter
T A Boyce, Sailmaster

Ofcrs attached to the brig **Boxer**:
W L Howard, Cmder
Lts: Thos T Hunter & C L Vanalston
Passed Midshipmen: John Stuart, Mayo C Watkins, & Julian Myers
W B Hartwell, Purser
Jos Beal, Passed Assist Surgeon
John McCullum, Midshipman

The Hon Wm Taylor, a Rep in Congress from the State of Va, died suddenly at his lodgings in Wash City on Sat last. The Cmte will attend funeral is 11½ a m on Mon, at the residence of the Hon Thos H Benton: the corpse will be removed in charge of the Cmte of Arrangements to the Hall of the House. At 12½ the funeral service will be performed, & immediately thereafter the procession will move to the ***Congressional Burial Ground***. His afflicted family was in the procession.

An act divorcing Mrs S C P Thomas from her husband, Francis Thomas, & changing her name to S C P McDowell, passed the Senate of Virginia on Wed, & has become a law.

Disaster at the coal mines, in Carbondale, Pa, on Jan 12, by which some 50 or 60 persons were literally buried alive, of whom it is supposed that 15 have lost their lives. John Hosie, one of the overseers, was rescued on the 3rd day after the occurrence. His escape was remarkable.

Mrd: on Jan 15, by Rev John P Donelan, Mr Andrew Sessford to Miss Josephine Kelly, of Balt, Md.

Mrd: Jan 15, by Rev H H Bean, Mr Rufus P Littlefield, of Balt, to Miss Eugenia McDonald, of Wash City.

Saml T McAllister, of Natchez, died at his residence on Jan 3. He was a prominent merchant & a benevolent man, whose loss will long be felt in our sister city. –New Orleans Times

On Jan 2 the house of Mr Geo Miller, in Encore, below Detroit, Mich, was consumed by fire, including 2 promising children of from 4 to 6 years. Mr Miller was a widower, & absent from home at the time.

Valuable real estate in Wash City & Wash County for sale: North half of square 472; lots in square 501, on M & 4½ sts; south half of square 544; north half of square 594; west half of 595; west half of square 595; half of lot 11 in square 653; lots 25 & 26 in square 555; lots 20 thru 26 in square 616; & lot 23 in square 673. I will sell the whole or any part of the tract of land owned by me in Wash Co, D C, containing 62 acres, on the new Bladensburg road, adjoining Brentwood & the lands of Messrs Gales, Derringer, & others. I would also dispose of on liberal terms the landed estate on which I reside in Montgomery Co, Md, 8 miles from the city, on Rock creek. For information apply to H H Dent, 4½ st, near City Hall, Wash, with whom I have left the plots, or to the subscriber. –R Y Brent

The partnership between Theopilus Fisk & Jesse E Dow is this day dissolved by mutual consent. The U S Journal, Democratic Expositor, & Congressional Journal, will be continued, heretofore, by the undersigned, assisted by an able Democratic Editor, who is daily expected to take his post. –Jesse E Dow

TUE JAN 20, 1846
N Y: Died: Jan 16, Henry Inman, in his 45th year, a distinguished painter. He died of a disease of the heart.

Jas Hoban, the U S Atty for this District, died last night at his residence in this city. [Jan 21st newspaper: the funeral of the late Jas Hoban will be at St Patrick's Church, this day, at 11 a m. Pall-bearers, viz:
Hon T Hartley Crawford
Gen Alex'r Hunter
Mr Thos Carbery
John Marbury
Wm Brent
Mr Gregory Ennis
[Jan 28th newspaper: Meeting of the Union Literary Society, on Jan 24, to pay a tribute of respect to Jas Hoban, a devoted husband & an affectionate parent.]

Senate: 1-Word received of the death of the Hon Wm Taylor, one of the Reps in Congress from Va, who died suddenly, at his residence/lodgings in Wash City, on Sat last, cut off in the vigor of his age & usefulness. He breathed his last in the midst of home associations, surrounded by his family & by dear cherished friends, at no great distance from the spot where the light of heaven first met his eyes, having been born in the city of Alexandria, in this District. As a lawyer he stood well at the bar.

The subscriber has a large body of land lying contiguous to Wash City & Gtwn. He wishes to dispose of the greater portion. Much of the land is in its primitive state. There are several valuable mill-seats, having an abundant supply of water, with falls of any height, up to 80 feet. –Abner C Peirce

Mrd: on Jan 18, in Wash City, by Rev Geo W Samson, Mr Robt Martin to Miss Mary E Davis, both of Wash City.

Mrd: on Jan 15, by Rev Ulysses Ward, Mr Geo W Ward, of Wash, to Miss Frances A Jackson, of Fairfax Co, Va.

Died: on Jan 19, the Rev Wm Ryland, chaplain of the Navy, in his 76th year. His funeral will take place on Jan 21, at 1 o'clock, from his late residence on 8th st opposite the Barracks. [Jan 21st newspaper: Rev Ryland was for many years a laborious & zealous Minister of the Methodist Episcopal Church: his services rendered us the erection of the Wesley Chapel. Rev N Wilson will preach a sermon at the funeral.]

WED JAN 21, 1846
Mr Philip Otterback yesterday exposed for sale in our Centre Market a parcel of the finest mutton ever exhibited in this city. It was fed by that eminent grazier, Jacklin Smith, of Clarke Co, Va.

Died: on Sunday last, at N Y, Mrs Joanna Bayard Neilson, d/o the late John G Warren.

Wash Corp: 1-Cmte of Claims: bill for the relief of Robt Farnham: passed. 2-Bill for the relief of John Fletcher, assignee of A C Kidwell: referred to the Cmte of Claims & passed. 3-Ptn of Jos C Harris, praying remission of a fine: referred to the Cmte of Claims. 4-Cmte of Claims: bill for the relief of Eliz G Dulany: read twice.

Samaritan Association held at Franklin Engine House, on Jan 14:

W W Seaton, Pres	John Devlin, 2nd V P	Edw Stubbs, Treas
John E Norris, 1st V P	Wm Flinn, Sec	W C Reddall, Register

Gentlemen appointed a Board of Managers for the ensuing year:

Dr Richmond Johnson	J C McGuire	P Brady
Capt W Easby	P Ennis	J H Houston
F Markoe, jr	L Parmele	J C Fitzpatrick
Gregory Ennis	Dr Speer	Robt Coltman
Giles Dyer	W Ridgly	W Miller
Wm Dietz	P Gallant	S Byington
S L Gouverneur	L Washington, jr	J H Ellis
Jas Harvey	Jas Adams	W Rhodes
W P Faherty	B B French	T Thornly

House of Reps: 1-Cmte of Claims: adverse reports on ptns of Ichabod Peck, wid/o Saml Scott, & heirs of Thos Underhill: which were laid on the table. 2-Cmte of Claims: adverse report on ptn of John B Fitch & others, heirs of John Fitch: laid on the table. Same cmte: adverse report on ptn of Thos F Harkness: laid on the table. 3-Cmte of Claims: report on ptn of Nathan Smith & Chas K Smith, with a bill for their relief: committed to a Cmte of the Whole House. 4-Cmte on Revolutionary Claims: adverse report on ptns of Saml Frothingham & Chauncey Wetmore, adms of Eliz Hubbard, dec'd: laid on the table. 5-Cmte of Claims: ptn of Adam McCulloch, with a bill for his relief: committed to a Cmte of the Whole House. Same cmte: bill for relief of Jeremiah Moors, reported same without amendment. 6-Ptn of J H Dickey & 94 others, against slavery in D C. 7-Ptn of J G Laughlin & 74 others, against admission of Texas. 8-Ptn of Jas McCutcheon, praying compensation for losses sustained during the year 1812 by Genr'l Hopkins' army. 9-Ptn of Saml Gregory, of Michigan, a Revolutionary soldier, for a pension. 10-Ptn of Seth M Leavenworth, with a joint resolution for his relief: committed to a Cmte of the Whole House. 11-Bill for relief of Emanuel Berri & John W Reese: referred to the Cmte of Claims. 12-Memorial of Jas Meade, for remuneration for property lost & destroyed by the enemy in the last war. 13-Ptn of Wm Bailey Lang, of Boston. Also, ptn of Joshua Lawrence & others, of Mass, for relief. 14-Bill for relief of Thos Copeland, for services rendered at the U S arsenal near Pittsburg: referred to Cmte of Claims.

Dec 27, the house of Mr Antoine Baly, 3 miles below Thibodaux, La, was destroyed by fire, & 2 of his little dghts died. Another's life is much despaired of. Mr Baly was severely burnt in attempting to save his family, who were all asleep at the time the fire broke out.

Correspondent of the Norfolk Herald writes as follows from Plymouth, N C, under date of Jan 14. Shipwreck on Jan 6, the schnr **Comet**, of this place, was wrecked on the North Point of Breakers, near Ocracoke, & all on board perished. Besides the crew, there were 2 young men, the sons of Mr Stephen Long, of Williamston, promising youths, in the very morning of manhood, the pride & hope of their heart-stricken parent. Awful calamity which effects of the news of the death of her commander, Capt Thos S Chase, our townsman, has brought on his poor disconsolate widow & 2 helpless babes. Last night she arose from her bed, & though severely cold, plunged into the river with both her children. The body of Mrs Chase has been recovered, but as yet neither of the poor innocents.

Died: on Tue last, after a lingering illness, in her 34th year, Mrs Martha Edes, consort of Wm H Edes, of Gtwn, & d/o Jos Radcliffe. Her funeral is from her late residence, in Gay st, near High, on Thu, at 3 p m.

Law Notice: the partnership existing between Donoho & Warner was dissolved on Jan 17, by mutual consent. The unfinished business of the late firm will be attended to at the Ofc of the undersigned, on 9th st, near D st. –T S Donoho, Atty at Law

Appointments by the Pres, by & with the advice & consent of the Senate:
John W Brockenbrough, of Va, to be Judge of the district court of the U S for the western district of Va, in place of Isaac S Pennybacker, resigned.
Geo H Lee, to be U S Atty for the western district of Va, in place of Moses C Good, removed.
Wm S Parrott, of Wash, to be Sec of the U S Legation to the Mexican Republic.
Edw Warrens, of Missouri, to be Consul for the port of Trieste, in place of A D Mann, resigned.
Hiram G Runnells, to be Collector of the Customs for the district of Texas, & Inspector of the Revenue for the port of Galveston, in the State of Texas.
Postmasters:
Chambers McKibbin, of Pittsburg, Pa, in place of Robt M Riddle, whose commission expired.
Pearson Mundy, of Watertown, N Y, in place of John F Hutchinson, resigned.
Land Ofcrs:
Thos J Winship, Register of the Land Ofc for the district of lands subject to sale at Chillicothe, Ohio, vice Thos Scott, removed.
John Hough, to be Receiver of Public Moneys for the district of lands subject to sale at Chillicothe, Ohio, vice Wm Y Strong, removed.
Robt McKelly, to be Register of the Land Ofc for the district of lands subject to sale at Upper Sandusky, Ohio, vice Abner Root, removed.
Christian Huber, to be Receiver of Public Moneys for the district of lands subject to sale at Upper Sandusky, Ohio, vice Moses H Kirby, removed.
John F Real, to be Register of the Land Ofc for the district of lands subject to sale at Jeffersonville, Indiana, vice Jas Scott, whose commission expired.

Philip E Engle, to be Receiver of Public Moneys for the district of lands subject to sale at Crawfordsville, Indiana, vice John Beard, whose commission expired.
Hugh P Caperton, to be Register of the Land Ofc for the district of lands subject to sale at Lebanon, Alabama, vice Jacob T Bradford, removed.
John G Winston, to be Receiver of Public Moneys for the district of lands subject to sale at Lebanon, Alabama, vice Levi W Lawler, whose commission expired.
Geo H Walker, to be Register of the Land Ofc for the district of lands subject to sale at Milwaukie, in the Territory of Wisconsin, vice Paraclete Patter, whose commission expired.
Paschal Bequette, to be Receiver of Public Moneys for the district of lands subject to sale at Mineral Point, in the Territory of Wisconsin, vice Robt W Lansing, removed.
Bernhart Herin, to be Register of the Land Ofc for the district of lands subject to sale at Fairfield, in the Territory of Iowa, vice Arthur Bridgman, removed.
Ver Planck Van Antwerp, to be Receiver of Public Moneys for the district of lands subject to sale at Fairfield, in the territory of Iowa, vice Saml J Bayard, removed.
Warner Lewis, to be Register of the Land Ofc for the district of lands subject to sale at Dubuque, in the Territory of Iowa, vice Wm H H Scott, removed.
Stephen Langworthy, to be Receiver of Public Moneys for the district of lands subject to sale at Dubuque, in the Territory of Iowa, vice Thos McKnight, removed.
Robt K McLaughlin, re-appointed Register of the Land Ofc for the district of lands subject to sale at Vandalia, Illinois, his last commission having expired.
Danl Gregory, to be Receiver of Public Moneys for the district of lands subject to sale at Vandalia, in Illinois, in place of Henry Smith, to take effect on Jan 31, 1846, when the commission of said Henry Smith will expire.
<u>Land Ofcrs:</u>
John A Langlois, to be Receiver of Public Moneys for the district of lands subject to sale at Kaskaskia, Illinois, vice Richd B Servant, removed.
Braxton Parish, to be Receiver of Public Moneys for the district of lands subject to sale at Shawneetown, Illinois, vice Stephen R Rowan, removed.
Harman Alexander, to be Register of the Land Ofc for the district of lands subject to sale at Palestine, Illinois, vice Jas M McLean, removed.
Wm E Russell, to be Register of the Land Ofc for the district of lands subject to sale at Danville, Illinois, vice John W Vance, whose commission expired.
John Dement, to be Receiver of Public Moneys for the district of lands subject to sale at Dixon, Illinois, vice Jas Swan, removed.
Thos Dyer, to be Receiver of Public Moneys for the district of lands subject to sale at Chicago, Illinois, vice Geo L Ward, removed.
Jonathan Kearsley, to be Receiver of Public Moneys for the district of lands subject to sale at Detroit, in Michigan, vice Sylvester W Higgins, resigned.
Benj Sherman, to be Register of the Land Ofc for the district of lands subject to sale at Ionia, Michigan, vice Ira Porter, whose commission expired.
Fred'k Hall, to be Receiver of Public Moneys for the district of lands subject to sale at Ionio, Michigan, vice Thos Fitzgerald, resigned.
Thos Watson, to be Register of the Land Ofc for the district of lands subject to sale at St Louis, Missouri, vice Wm S Allen, removed.

Wm McNair, to be Register of the Land Ofc for the district of lands subject to sale at Fayette, Missouri, vice John B Clark, resigned.

Alfred W Morrison, to be Receiver of Public Moneys for the district of lands subject to sale at Fayette, Missouri, vice J W S Mitchell, resigned.

Franklin Cannon, to be Register of the Land Ofc for the district of lands subject to sale at Jackson, Missouri, vice Greer W Davis, removed.

Aaron Snyder, to be Receiver of Public Moneys for the district of lands subject to sale at Jackson, Missouri, vice Ralph Guild, whose commission expired.

Benj Davies, to be Register of the Land Ofc for the district of lands subject to sale at Palmyra, Missouri, vice Cyril C Cady, removed.

Jas H McBride, to be Register of the Land Ofc for the district of lands subject to sale at Springfield, Missouri, vice Joel H Hayden, removed.

Nicholas R Smith, to be Receiver of Public Moneys for the district of lands subject to sale at Springfield, Missouri, vice Geo R Smith, removed.

Wm Monroe, to be Register of the Land Ofc for the district of lands subject to sale at Clinton, Missouri, vice Abraham B Morton, removed.

Benj P Jett, to be Register of the Land Ofc for the district of lands subject to sale at Washington, Arkansas, vice Saml C Wheat, removed.

John Bruton, to be Register of the Land Ofc for the district of lands subject to sale at Johnson Court-house, Arkansas, vice Jas Woodson Bates, removed.

David C Glenn, to be Receiver of Public Moneys for the district of lands subject to sale at Jackson, Mississippi, vice Isaac McFaran, resigned.

Wm S Taylor, to be Receiver of Public Moneys for the district of lands subject to sale at Pontotoc, Mississippi, vice John F Wray, removed.

Armistead D Cary, to be Receiver of Public Moneys for the district of lands subject to sale at Sparta, Alabama.

Saml Curse, to be Receiver of Public Moneys for the district of lands subject to sale at Huntsville, Alabama.

Information wanted concerning Robt & Martha McFee, who are supposed to reside either in the U S or Canada. This information is desired by their brother, now residing in this country. Any person knowing them will bestow a favor upon him by informing them of this notice. For his present residence inquire of Wm Lamb, Parkman, Geauga Co, Ohio.

Private sale: the subscriber, being desirous of removing from the city, wishes to dispose of several articles of too great bulk to take with him, such as follows: a large plated French Dinner Service, equal to silver for wear. Also, Dessert China, Bronze Lustre, & a large French Pier Glass, with some very valuable Prints, Oil Paintings, & Books. He would likewise sell some city property: two 3 story brick houses, in good order, in the First Ward. Inquire at his residence, on 24th st, 1st 3 story brick house north of Pa ave. –J Boulanger

Rev Father Alig, of the Congregation of the Redemptionist, is authorized to collect subscriptions in my diocese for the bldg of a German Church in Wash, D C. Given at Balt, Jan 2, 1846. –Saml, Archbishop of Balt. [Rev Father Alig intends to collect this week in Gtwn, with Mr Miller of the same place, Trustee of the said Church.]

Senate: 1-Ptn from Asa Andrews, asking balance of pay due him in a suit brought against him by the U S for an alleged deficiency. 2-Ptn from Welcome Parmeter, asking a pension. 3-Ptn from the legal reps of Richd Buller, dec'd, asking payment of certain sums of money due them. 4-Ptn from John Strobecker & others, asking indemnities for losses in consequence of the improper interference of the British authorities in the island of Bermuda. 5-Ptn from Saml Martin, exhibiting a plan of Lake defence. Also, from the same, proposing a plan for regulating the currency of the U S. 6-Ptn from John B Baldwin, asking indemnity for losses sustained by the burning of his vessel by order of the U S ofcr commanding on the coast of Florida. 7-Ptn from Sophia Fleming & others, asking that a board of com'rs may be appointed to settle claims for losses sustained in consequence of the Indian wars in Florida. 8-Ptn from Peter Capella, adm of Andrew Capella, asking indemnity for losses sustained through occupation by the U S troops in Florida. 9-Ptn from J Bigelow, administrator on the state of Francois Cazeau. 10-Ptn from Balie Peyton, asking the U S to purchase the tract of land belonging to him at the S W Pass of the Mississippi, now occupied by the U S. 11-Cmte of Claims: bill for the relief of the legal reps of John J Bulow, jr, dec'd, with a report: ordered to be printed. 12-Cmte on Naval Affairs: bill for the relief of Nathl Philips, with a report: ordered to be printed. 13-Cmte of Claims: bill for the relief of J Thorckmorton, with a report: ordered to be printed. 14-Cmte on Naval Affairs: to inquire into Dr Wm P McConnell's submerged propeller & other improvements, & report on their utility & practicability to propel war steamers.

To Capitalists: for sale-large 3 story brick house, with a back bldg & yard attached, on Pa ave, between 10th & 11th sts, Wash, & now in the occupancy of Mr Nathl Carusi, & will be sold a very great bargain. Also, the 2 story brick house, south side of G st, opposite the Foundry Meeting-house, now tenanted by Mrs Wilson, will be sold very low. Apply to Mr John J Joyce, Grocer, N W corner of F & 13th sts.

THU JAN 22, 1846
Senate: 1-Cmte of Claims: adverse report on the ptn of Jos Ratcliffe; also, adverse report on the ptn of Amos Holton, late a Paymaster in the Army. 2-Cmte on the Post Ofc & Post Roads: a joint resolution for the relief of Orlando Saltmarsh & Wm Fuller, with a report.

Appointments by the Pres, confirmed by the Senate. 1-John Slidell, of Louisiana, to be Envoy Extra & Minister Pleni to the Mexican Republic. 2-Sylvester Churchill, late Inspector Genr'l to be Inspector Genr'l in the Army, with the rank of Colonel, to take rank from Jun 25, 1841, the date of his former commission.

Mr Bryant, late senior editor of the Louisville Morning courier, announced his retirement from that paper.

Last Week: Titian's Venus exhibition of this beautiful painting positively closes this week, & goes immediately to Balt, on its way to N Y. This picture was formerly in the possession of Sir Thos Lawrence; passing at his death into the Pall Mall Gallery, London, it was visited by more than 100,000 persons. The picture is supposed to have been painted by Titian, after his own masterpiece in the Florentine Gallery; it is nearly 300 years old, & sold in London for L2,000 sterling. Plumbe's Daguerreotype of the picture for sale at the room. Ladies Day on Sat, from 11 a m till 2 p m, exclusively for ladies. Open from 9 a m till 9 P M: admission $25.

Richmond Daily Whig, Jan 20. The undersigned, proprietors of the Whig, announce that Richd H Toler, will take charge of the editorial dept of the Whig about the middle of March next. --Thos M Bondurant, Robt H Gallaher, Wyatt M Elliott. The firm will be known as Gallaher, Elliott & Co.

FRI JAN 23, 1846
New School Com'rs: Andrew Coyle & John F Callan, lately elected Trustees of the 2nd School District, in place of Peter Force & John Marron, who had previously tendered their resignations.

The funeral services of the late lamented Jas Hoban took place last Wed morning. The remains of the distinguished advocate were followed from his late residence on La ave to St Patrick's Church by a numerous body of friends of the dec'd, members of the Bar, & other citizens. The ceremonies were performed by the Very Rev Wm Matthews & the Rev John P Donelan.

House of Reps: 1-Ptn of S B Hays, asking for compensation from the Post Ofc Dept for services rendered. 2-Memorial of Theodore Foster & other citizens of Michigan for a post road from Ann Arbor to Flint, Michigan. 3-Ptn & accompanying documents of Michl Weidnen, asking for a pension for his services as a soldier in the war of the Revolution. 4-Ptn of Zadoc Motlow & others, heirs of John Motlow, dec'd, heretofore referred, Jan 20, 1830. 5-Ptn of Saml Reed,of Pike Co, Ohio, praying compensation for the loss by him of certain lands in Ohio, sold by the U S & mediately purchased by him; the title to which, derived from the U S, has failed. 6-Ptn of Susan Brum, widow of Philip Brum, sailingmaster of the ship **Saratoga**, in the battle of Lake Champlain, asking for a pension. 7-Ptn of Danl Witt, of Jefferson Co, Tenn, praying Congress to grant him a pension for disabilities incurred as a soldier in the late war with Great Britain. Ptn of Jas P H Porter, of Sevier Co, Tenn, with a similar prayer. 8-Ptn of Luke Stansberry, of Blount Co, Tenn, praying Congress for an increase of pension as a Revolutionary soldier. 9-Ptn of Jane Rankin, wid/o Richd Rankin, dec'd, a Revolutionary soldier, asking Congress to grant her a pension. 10-Ptn of Mr Santangelo in regard to the Mexican indemnity. 11-Ptn of Geo E Graves, for payment of certain losses sustained by him as mail contractor.

Orphans Court of Wash Co, D C. Letters testamentary on the personal estate of Henry Orr, late of said county, dec'd. –Sarah L Orr, excx

European paper: during the 3 centuries which have elapsed since 1545, when Jacques Bourdon was Minister of War, 110 Ministers have filled the same ofc, including Marshal Soult, making upon the average a service of rather less than 3 years for each Minister.

Senate: 1-Ptn from Godfrey Pattison & others, asking the reimbursement of certain duties illegally exacted from them. 2-Ptn from Mira Clarke Gaines, asking to be allowed to locate a grant made to the Marquis de Maison Rouge in the year 1797, on any unappropriated public lands. 3-Ptn from Benj Watson, for a pension. 4-Ptn from N D McDowell, asking relief for losses sustained during the late war. 5-Ptn from Calvin Read, by his attys, asking payment for pine tress sold to the U S for the erection of a fort in Florida. Also, from Geo W Walton, by his attys, asking payment for the same thing. 6-Ptn from Saml H Morse, asking to be allowed certain items in his accounts when acting as Collector of Passamaquoddy. 7-Ptn from G D Duvall, asking remuneration for losses sustained during the late war with England. 8-Additional documents in the case of Wm Pennoyer. 9-Ptn from the heirs of Abner L Duncan, asking pay for a vessel sold for an alleged violation of the neutrality laws. 10-Ptn from Philip Pollard & others, praying to be confirmed in their titles to certain reserved lands purchased from the Pottawatamie Indians. 11-Ptn from the heirs of Capt Richd McCarty, asking payment for certain advances made by him during the Revolutionary war. 12-Ptn from Thos F Gordon, asking aid for the completion of his design of the arrangement & publication of the indices of the public records. 13-Documents relating to the claim of E Ware: presented. 14-Ptn from the legal reps of John Campbell, asking the settlement of his accounts as Quartermaster during the Revolutionary war, with interest on such sums as may be found due him. 15-Cmte on Pensions: adverse report in the case of Calra F Coble. 16-Adverse reports made from cmtes, named in prior proceedings, were taken up & concurred in, with the exception of the case of Mrs Evelina Porter, which was passed over informally.

Hon Judah Dana, formerly a U S Senator from Maine, & a lawyer of good attainments & high character, died on Dec 27, at Fryeburg, Maine, aged 73. He was a native of Vermont.

Mrd: on Jan 15, at Tudor Hall, St Mary's Co, Md, by Rev Mr Gallagher, Mr Douglass Clopper, of Montg Co, Md, to Miss Mary Sophia, d/o the late Philip Key, of St Mary's.

Died: on Jan 21, after an illness of 24 hours, of typoid fever, Eliz Powell Massey, aged 60 years, formerly of King Geo Co, Va, but for the last 32 years a resident of Wash City. Her funeral is this day at 2 o'clock, from her residence on 22nd st, near N Y ave.

Died: on Dec 24, Henry Orr, in his 55th year, long a respectable inhabitant of the 1st Ward.

Died: on Jan 19, Mary Eliz, y/d/o Jas & Catharine Chezum, aged 1 year & 28 days.

Teacher wanted, to take charge of the primary school on Calvert's Manor, near Piscataway, PG Co, Md. For further particulars, apply to Wm Bryan, [of Richard,] near Piscataway.

New Fancy Goods: between 9th & 10th sts, on Pa ave. –H N Roby

SAT JAN 24, 1846
Notice: by virtue of a writ of distrain by Dr Wm Jones, I have this day seized & taken all the improvements on the premises occupied by Jos Martine & others, being on 10th st, between D & E sts, in square 348, consisting of 2 shops; all of which I will proceed to sell for cash, on Feb 1. –Richd I A Culverwell, Bailiff

For hire, for the balance of the year, an intelligent negro man. He is a first rate carriage-driver, & a careful hand with horses. He is sober & trustworthy. –J B Holmead, between 3rd & 4th sts, Pa ave.

Orphans Court of Wash Co, D C. Letters of administration on the personal estate of Fred'k A Wagler, late of said county, dec'd. –Geo F Todsen, adm

Mrd: Jan 22, in Wash City, by Rev Geo W Samson, Mr Edw L Waller to Miss Eliz Killmon, both of Wash.

Mrd: on Jan 20, at Phil, by Rev H J Morton, Lt Jas S Biddle, U S Navy, to Meta Craig Biddle, eldest d/o the late Nicholas Biddle.

MON JAN 26, 1846
Criminal Court-Wash: Wm B Whiting acquitted. The Court directed that shoes charged to have been stolen by the accused to be given up to him.

Coroner's Inquest on the body of Jas Heatley, on Sat, living in an alley near the soap-factory of Messrs Bates & Brother, on G st, between 6th & 7th sts. Verdict: the dec'd came to his death from exposure.

Samaritan Society, held at Wash City, the following ladies were appointed to compose the Visiting Cmtes in the several Wards. The duty of the Visiting Cmte is to ascertain the number, residence, name & condition of the indigent in their respective districts, report the same to the monthly meetings of the Managers, & distribute relief in such articles & funds as may be place in their hands by the Managers; also to solicit funds for the Society.

Mrs Redfern	Mrs Walter Clarke	Mrs Simon Brown
Mrs Easby	Miss Mary Masi	Miss Julia Franzonia
Miss Rebecca Lowry	Rev Mr Eggleston	Mrs Edw Stelle
Miss Catharine Smith	Mrs Thos Anderson	Mrs Robt Beall
Mrs Davidson	Miss Ann Scott	Mrs E Brooks
Mrs Major Scott	Mrs Capt Williams	Mrs Watterston
Mrs Chislom	Mrs John Harkness	Mrs Fitzpatrick
Mrs Parker	Mrs John E Norris	Mrs J W Jones
The Misses Reddall	Miss Anna E Hyde	Mrs Blagden
Miss Belt	Miss Ann Eliz Caden	Mrs Richd Berry
Mrs Belt	Mrs Griffen	Mrs Geo Mattingly
Mrs Trenholm	Mrs Allen	Mrs Byington
Miss Manning	Mrs Mary Ann Sturgeon	Mrs Genr'l Henderson
Mrs Deitz	Mrs John Thaw	Mrs Fulmore
Mrs Ferguson	Mrs Tastet	Mrs Lawrence
Miss Parris	Mrs John Hoover	Mrs Martin King
Miss Sarah Waggaman	Mrs Maria Dyer	Mrs Wm Howard
	Mrs Wannell	Rev Mr Bean
Miss Sarah Devlin	Mrs Best	Mrs Dr Young
Miss Mary Devlin	Mrs Mary Sullivan	

Last Monday night a female servant belonging to Genr'l Jesup was dreadfully burnt, so as to cause her death a few days afterwards. Some of the Genrl's family were out visiting, & orders were left with the girl to sit up for them. She made a large fire, lay down by the side of it & fell asleep. Her clothes caught fire. The hands of another servant were so severely burnt, in her attempt to save the dec'd, that the amputation of one of them is deemed necessary.

House of Reps: 1-Memorial of Chas Reeder, a member of the Board of Examiners to make experimental trials in relation to the explosion of steam-boilers, praying Congress to make provision for the liquidation of his claim against the Gov't for services rendered while a member of said board. 2-Memorial of John S Tyson, adm of Jonathan W Sherburne, praying compensation for services rendered by said Sherburne in constructing a buoy at the entrance of Port Royal. 3-Ptn of Guy Carpenter, praying Congress to appropriate lands for draining Cotton Wood swamp, Lenaire Co, Michigan. Also, the claim of Guy Carpenter for expenses, incurred on account of sickness during his service in the Black Hawk war as a volunteer. 4-Ptn of John Murphy, for a pension. 5-Ptn of Mary Stanton, of Kane Co, Ill, for a pension. 6-Ptn of Thos Scott, of Ohio, was taken from the files & referred to the Cmte of Claims.

Col Jas K Morse, of Hernando, Miss, was brutally murdered on Jan 7, by a man named Jas Dyson, who shot him dead, as he was riding along the road. Col Morse was a gentleman, & a successful practitioner at the bar.

Fire at Balt on Sat in the upper part of the house occupied by Mr H Colburn as a bookstore, near Charles st, which, with the adjoining jeweller's store of Mr Geo W Webb, was entirely destroyed. The Antiquarian Bookstore adjoining J W Bond & Co, to the east of Colburn's, was also destroyed, but the greater part of their books were saved. The store of P B Sadtler & Sons was seriously injured.

Leon Shackleford, 11 years old, s/o Wm H Shackleford, of Branch village, Smithfield, was shot dead a few days ago by a boy named Beacon, who came into the yard, loaded a guy with a ball, & fired at an outhouse, in which young Shackleford was standing. He was found dead in about half an hour after the report of the gun was heard. –Providence Journal

Died: on Sat last, in Wash City, after a short illness, Mrs Mary Amidon, w/o Mr Hollis Amidon. Her funeral is this morning, at 11 o'clock, from her late residence, on La ave, between 9th & 10th sts.

Died: on Jan 22, at his residence, on Capitol Hill, Mr Wm French, formerly a Clerk in the Land Ofc, in his 63rd year.

Died: on Jan 24, at her residence, near the Navy Yard, Wash, Mrs Mary Kealey, aged 62 years, a native of Ireland, but for 38 years a resident of Wash City. Mrs Kealey was a member of the Roman Catholic Church, & a faithful & devout adherent to its sacred doctrines. Her life was spent in amiable associations, exemplary piety, & devoted attachment to her affectionate children, who, during her long & severe illness, manifested their love for the kindest of parents. Her funeral is on Jan 26, at 2 o'clock.

Died: on Jan 18, at Newbern, S C, Mrs Margaret S Scott, relict of Dr Andrew Scott, in her 60th year.

TUE JAN 27, 1846
L S Beck & Son are ready to supply all wants in the House Furnishing Goods, new & old: Pa ave, south side, between 9th & 10th sts.

Senate: 1-Ptn from the administrator of Wm Starke Jett, asking payment of certain outstanding loan certificates which had been lost or destroyed. 2-Ptn from Jas L Sawyer, asking payment for services performed in the custom-house at N Y. 3-Ptn from Henry Northup, asking compensation for a horse lost in the service of the U S. 4-Ptn from Jas H Causten, asking payment for certificates issued by the U S to claimants under the Mexican Convention. 5-Cmte on the Judiciary: asked to be discharged from the further consideration of the ptn of John A Ragon. 6-Cmte on the Post Ofc & Post Roads: bill for the relief of Francis A Harrison.

Furnished rooms: a parlor & 2 chambers on the same floor, genteely furnished, can be had on early application to Mrs M Johnson, on E, between 10th & 11th sts.

Sale of jewelry at the Jewelry Store of C W Heydon, Pa ae, between 4½ & 6th sts, Wash.

For rent: desirable 2½ story brick dwlg on 8th st, between G & H sts, occupied at present by Mrs Queen. Possession given Feb 1st. Inquire on the premises, or of the subscriber on 11th st, between G & H sts.
-Margaret Stewart

Sale of fancy articles: store is on Pa ave, one door from the corner of 11th st.
–Alice Pilling

Govn'r Wright, of N Y, declined to exercise the executive clemency in the case of Eliz Van Valkenburgh, convicted of the murder of her husband, & sentenced to be executed in Fulton Co on Sat last.

Accident at Elizabethtown, N J, Tue, by which a single man, Jacob Vanderpoel, residing at Galloping Hills, drove his horse across the railroad track as the Phil train was passing. The pilot, or cow catcher, caught the wagon & turned it over, & carried it to Grand st. Vanderpoel lived but a few minutes.

Mrd: on Jan 14, at Millville, Jefferson Co, Va, by Rev R H Wilmer, Geo Read Riddle, of Wilmington, Dela, to Margaret S Opie, of the former place.

The little son, some 10 or 12 years of age, of the late Michl Hoke, of Lincolton, was shot on Sat last, & died instantly. Another young boy, Fulenwider, accidentally discharged a gun at Hoke. Mrs Hoke has been in a very critical state of health since the death of her husband. –Rutherfordton Republican

Died: on Jan 25, at the residence of his son, in Fairfax Co, Va, the Hon Chas Cutts, in his 77th year. Mr Cutts was a U S Senator at the most critical period of history of this country, &, after ceasing to be a Senator, filled the ofc of Sec of the Senate of the U S for about 14 years. He was one of the most benevolent of human beings.

Died: on Jan 25, Mrs Mary E Phelps, in her 41st year. Her funeral is today at 2 o'clock from her late residence on 20th st.

Died: on Jan 11, in Albany, N Y, in his 74th year, Wm Gould. As the head of the extensive publishing & book selling house of W & A Gould, he was well known through the State, & as widely esteemed for the uprightness of his character.

Died: on Jan 11, at his residence near Albany, Thos Russell, long known as a merchant of probity & wealth in the city of Albany, but for many years retired from active pursuits. He was one of the house of Thomas & Jos Russell, the other member of which Jas Russell, Pres of the Canal Bank, died several years since.

Died: on Jan 21, at his residence, West River, Md, Mr Geo T Ditty, leaving a wife, 3 children, & a large circle of acquaintances to regret his demise.

Died: on Jan 4, at Quincy, Illinois, after a protracted illness, Capt Jos A Phillips, formerly of the 8th Regt U S Infty, aged 40 years.

The funeral of Gen Elias B Dayton was attended, a few days ago, by a large circle of friends, from the residence of his nephew, J J Chetwood, in Elizabethtown, N J. Gen Dayton was a native, & for the greater part of his life a resident of that old borough. He received an appointment in the N Y Custom-house some years ago, & according removed to the city, where, though he had nearly attained the aged of 84 years, he continued to discharge its duties daily with remarkable vigor until within a few days of his death. Gen Dayton was a brother of the late Gen Jonathan Dayton, who bore a conspicuous part in the early councils of the nation, & we believe, the only Speaker of the House of Reps taken from N J. He leaves a number of children, among whom is the Hon Aaron O Dayton, 4th Auditor in the Treas Dept.
–Newark Daily Advertiser

$5 reward for strayed or stolen bright yellow setter Dog. –Chas W Stewart, residence on Capitol Hill.

WED JAN 28, 1846
Senate: 1-Ptn from Benj E Green, asking to be allowed the usual pay & allowances of a Charge d'Affaires for services in Mexico. 2-Ptn from Jas B Davenport, asking confirmation of his title. 3-Ptn from Lewis Evans, asking compensation for losses sustained by him. 4-Ptn from Maj Chas Larrabee, late a Major in the U S Army, for arrears of pension. 5-Cmte on the Judiciary: bill for the relief of Henry Gardiner & others, directors of the association known as the New England Mississippi Land Co, accompanied by a report; which was ordered to be printed. 6-Bill for the relief of Benj Harris, of La Salle Co, Ill, to be introduced. 7-Bill for the relief of Chas B Page, of the Patent Ofc, was considered in Cmte of the Whole, & ordered to be engrossed for a 3rd reading.

Fred'k Koones offers himself as an agent for the sale of real & personal estate.

Philip Barton Key has been appointed by the Pres of the U S to be Atty of the U S for the District of Columbia, & the appointment was yesterday confirmed by the Senate.

The extensive cotton manufactory of Mr Geo C Ballou, at Woodsocket, R I, was totally consumed by fire on Thu. The mill of Mr Edw Harris was much damaged, while the dye-house of Mr John U Ruegger was almost wholly destroyed. Aggregate loss $30,000.

The extensive milling establishment of Messrs Thos Dugdale & Son, at Burlington, N J, was destroyed by fire on Sunday: loss estimated at $40,000; insurance $10,000.

House of Reps: 1-Cmte on Naval Affairs: bill for the relief of the heirs of Robt Fulton: committed. 2-Cmte of Claims: report against the ptn of John Otis: laid on the table. 3-Cmte on Naval Affairs: bill for the relief of Francis Martin. 4-Cmte on Naval Affairs: referred the ptn of Jas F Miller. 5-Cmte of Claims: bill for the relief of the heirs of Dr John Gray, dec'd; a bill for the relief of Matilda Drury: both bills committed. Same cmte: adverse to the ptn of Wm A Duer: laid on the table. 6-Adverse report on the ptn of Walter Titus, for a return of duties paid in consequence of the increased rate between the time the goods were ordered & their arrival: laid on the table. 7-Cmte on Military Affairs: bill for the relief of John Stockton, late a Lt in the army: committed. 8-Cmte on Naval Affairs: bill for the relief of Capt John Ericson: committed. 9-Sec of the Navy & the Sec of the Treasury to appoint 5 scientific persons to examine the invention of Jas Montgomery, called the 'Safety Guard, to prevent the explosion & burning of steam-boilers, & to save fuel in their use;" & if expedient to use the said invention, to pay said Montgomery such sum as it shall be adjudged to be worth to the Gov't: read & committed. 10-Cmte on the Judiciary: against the ptn of Wm Lamphier & Jos Harris: concurred in. 11-Cmte on the Judiciary: adverse on the ptn of Harry Richardson, of Vt: laid on the table. 12-Cmte on Revolutionary Claims: against the claim of Isaac Davis: laid on the table. Also, a bill for the relief of the heirs of Lt Thos Wishart: committed. 12-Cmte on Revolutionary Claims: against the claims of Henrietta Barnes, one of the heirs of Lathrop Allen, & the heirs of Gustavus B Horner: laid on the table. Also, against the ptn of the heirs of Compte de Grass, & the heirs of Christopher Miller: laid on the table. 13-Ptn of John Gilleylew, of Mississippi, heretofore referred Jan 18, 1845. 14-Ptn of John R Chapman, of Alabama, praying that Congress would grant him the balance of the appropriation voted by the last Congress for the improvement of the Choctawhatchie river. 15-Ptn of Israel Griffin, for a pension. 16-Ptn of Giles London, for a pension. 17-Ptn of Jonathan Shaiffer, one of the heirs of Christian Orndorff. 18-Ptn of Wolcott M Morse. 19-Ptn of John Turner, of Wayne Co, Ky, praying a pension for injuries received while in the service of the U S during the late war with Great Britain. 20-Ptn of Mrs Catharine Gale, wid/o the late Col Anthony Gale, praying a pension. 21-Ptn of Col Geo Boyd, late Indian agent, to have certain allowances made him in a settlement of his accounts. 22-Memorial of Dr Edw Earle, of Phil, asking that his process for preserving canvass & cordage may be adopted for the service of the U S Navy. 23-Ptn of the heirs of John Mountjoy, praying for the allowance of the commutation of 5 years' full pay, with the interest, for the services of the said Mountjoy during the Revolutionary war. 24-Ptn of M H Debow, exc of Dr Thos Cooper, to be refunded moneys paid under the act of 1798, called the alien & sedition act. 25-Ptn & papers of Geo Cochran, asking for a settlement of his claims against the U S, by reason of the non-fulfillment of a contract with the Commissary Dept in 1815.

Mrd: on Christmas eve, by Rev R S Killin, Mr Saml N Smallwood, of Portsmouth, Va, to Miss Eliza M Curtis, of Richmond, Va.

Died: on Jan 27, Mr Thos Riley, a native of Accomac Co, Va, but for the last 20 years a resident of Wash City. His funeral is on Thu next, at 2 o'clock.

Died: on Jan 24, at the residence of his grandfather, Robt B Boyd, of the croup. John, only s/o John & Amanda Greaves, aged 3 years & 6 months.

City Councils of Balt city have elected Dr John J Graves to the ofc of City Register for ensuing 2 years, in place of Jesse Hunt, whose term of service had expired.

There were 18 deaths by small-pox in Phil last week. There were 10 deaths in the city of Balt last week by the same disease.

THU JAN 29, 1846

Exercising chairs just received, a new lot of Halsted's Anti-Dyspeptic or Exercising Chairs. Apply at the book & publishing store of Wm M Morrison, Pa ave, 2nd door west of 4½ st.

Orphans Court of Wash Co, D C. Letters of administration on the personal estate of Fred'k A Wagler, late of Wash Co, dec'd. –Saml Redfern, adm

Mrd: on Jan 27, in Wash City, by Rev Dr Jones, of Balt, Lt Simon F Blunt, of the U S Navy, to Miss Ellen L Key, d/o the late Francis S Key.

Mrd: on Jan 20, in Rockingham Co, N C, by Rev Mr Mebane, Nathl W Williams, of Smith Co, Tenn, to Mary E, d/o the late Robt Galloway.

Died: on Jan 27, in Wash City, Mrs Ann Kedglie, a native of Scotland, aged about 78 years, an old & highly estimable resident of this place. Her funeral is at 3 o'clock on Fri, from her late residence near the West Market.

FRI JAN 30, 1846

City Ordinance-Wash: An Act to authorize the arbitration of a certain claim of A B McLean, or his assigns. In the arbitrament to ascertain the present fair valuation of the sheds, vats, & fixtures pertaining to the Fish Wharf & Dock, at the lower end of 6th st west, on the Potomac river, authorized by the act of Mar 8, 1841, to inquire into & assess what reasonable compensation, if any, shall be allowed to A B McLean, or his assigns, by reason of the damage or loss, if any, which he the said A B McLean, or his assigns, may have sustained by reason of the partial loss of the privilege granted by the said act, in the landing of fish brought to this city, during the regular fishing seasons, during 1842 thru 1845, at his wharf at the foot of 6th st aforesaid. –Saml Bacon, Pres of the Board of Common Council -Jas Adams, Pres of the Board of Aldermen -W W Seaton, Mayor. Approved, Jan 22, 1846.

Rev Matthew Hale Smith has accepted a call to the pastoral charge of the Second Presbyterian Church, on N Y ave, formerly under the care of the Rev Mr Knox.

Senate: 1-Ptn from Chas Stearns, asking reimbursement of expenses of a criminal prosecution instituted against him, upon information of an ofcr of the U S, on which he was acquitted. 2-Cmte on Pensions: adverse reports on the ptns of Wm Nicholls; & of Lydia Ruth. 3-Ptn from Eli Hobb, asking compensation for property taken by the U S troops at Lower Sandusky. 4-Ptn from Orlando S Reese, asking indemnification for losses during the Seminole war. 5-Ptn from the heirs of *John Smith T, asking to be allowed to enter certain lands at the minimum price. [*Copied as written.]

Dr French, of Adams Co, Pa, was thrown from his sleigh on Thu last, & died of his injuries on Fri last.

Matthew C Patterson, District Atty for the city & county of N Y, died on Mon night.

John Bannon, an industrious mechanic, a stone-cutter, was deliberately shot at Albany on Sat, whilst coming out of a neighbor's house, being mistaken for the other person. [Jan 31st newspaper: John Bannon was shot in the streets of Albany on Sat last, by Chas Gouche, who mistook him for another person. He died on Sunday morning.]

New expedition has recently sailed from Liverpool for the interior of Western Africa, under the control of Mr G W Daniell, a surgeon of some experience, in order to explore further the discoveries of Mr McGregor Laird & others, from which it is expected that commercial & political information will be obtained.

Wash Corp: 1-Ptn of Wm King, praying remission of a fine: referred to the Cmte of Claims. 2-Ptn of Thos R Mackey, praying a remission of a fine: referred to the Cmte of Claims. 3-Cmte of Claims: reported a bill for the relief of Geo Stewart: passed.

The Northampton Courier notices the death, at the almshouse, in that town, of Capt Wm Smith, aged 73 years. He had for the last 14 years been an inmate of the poor house. He was born in Md, & was one of the original claimants for indemnification for French Spoliations, having been captured thrice, on 3 different vessels, by French privateers, his property confiscated, & himself made prisoner. He has had his claim, among others, for $10,000, which, with interest, would now have amounted to over $40,000.

Mr John Hough, of Cincinnati, was mulcted in the sum of $1,700 for seducing Miss Roberts, & $2,750 for a breach of the marriage promise made to Miss Sarah Watson.

Miss Maria Lytle, d/o Thos Lytle, of Balt Co, was thrown from her horse on Sat last, & so seriously injured by the horse treading upon her arm, that amputation was found to be necessary. The arm was taken off by a physician living in the neighborhood. Miss Lytle expected to be married in the course of the next 2 weeks. –Balt Clipper

Jos Fiddler Reddy, teller of the Bank of the British North America, at Montreal, absconded recently with about L5,000, the property of the institution. It is supposed that he fled to N Y. [Jan 31st newspaper: Reddy was arrested in N Y C, & delivered over to the Canadian ofcrs. Augustus Harnfeldt, a gambler, who was an accomplice of Ready, share the same fate.]

Died: on Jan 27, Mr Thos Robinson Riley, a native of Occomac Co, Va, but for the last 20 years a resident of Wash City.

Died: on Jan 27, Edwin Richard, infant s/o Danl & Emeline Bidleman.

Died: on Jan 14, at St Augustine, Fla, Col Geo W Cole, Receiver of the Land Ofc in that district, in his 56th year.

Died: on Jan 29, of catarrh fever, Andrew, infant s/o Thos & Mary Young, aged 6 months. His funeral is tomorrow at 2½ o'clock, from the residence of his father, on Missouri ave.

SAT JAN 31, 1846
The N Y Express has papers from *Van Dieman's Land* as late as Sep 23. The Melbourne Herald, of the 13th, gives the particulars of one of the most horrible shipwrecks on record, by which 414 lives were lost. The ship **Cataraqui**, Capt C W Finlay, [emigrant ship of 800 tons,] sailed from Liverpool on Apr 20, with 369 emigrants, & a crew, including 2 doctors, of 46 souls. The emigrants were principally from Bedfordshire, Staffordshire, Yorkshire, & Nottinghamshire. About 120 passengers were married, with families, & in all 73 children. On Aug 4, the ship went ashore in a violent gale, on a reef, on the west coast of King's Island, at the entrance of Bass' Straits. The ship filled in a few hours at night. Before morning but 30 of the company were alive, the rest having been swept into eternity by the waves. Out of the whole crew only 9 were saved.

New Orleans: Mr Kane, a young lawyer, was shot in a duel on Jan 21 by his antagonist Mr Hyman, a merchant of this city. The weapons were pistols at 10 paces. The difficulty arose about a question of right to a certain place in a cotillion.

Mr John Hough, of Cincinnati, was mulcted in the sum of $1,700 for seducing Miss Roberts, & $2,750 for a breach of the marriage promise made to Miss Sarah Watson.

Loudoun Land for sale: by virtue of a decree of the Circuit Superior Court of Law & Chancery for Loudoun Co: sale of the very valuable estate of the late Wilson C Selden known as *Exeter*, containing about 824 acres, lying contiguous to the town of Leesburg, Loudoun Co, Va: improvements are a large dwlg house, with the necessary out-bldgs. Mr Wm Ball, one of the tenenats, will show the estate to any one desiring to buy. –John A Washington, Burr W Harrison, com'rs

Appointed by the Columbia Typographical Society to collect & secure the property of the same: John Thorn, Geo Amridge, & W A Kennedy.

House of Reps: 1-Cmte on Revolutionary Pensions: bill for the relief of Isabella Baldridge, wid/o John Baldridge: read & committed. Same cmte, reported a bill for the relief of Silas Waterman; also, a bill for the relief of Sampgon Brown: committed. Same cmte: unfavorable report in the case of Nathl Shiflett: laid on the table. 2-Cmte on Invalid Pensions: adverse reports on the cases of Saml Bump, John Owen, Richd Buchanan, & Jos Johnson: laid on the table. 3-Same cmte: adverse reports on the cases of Pliny Pierce, Jos Bell, Stacy Lamphere, & Jos Craigmiles: laid on the table. Same cmte: bill for the relief of John Porter: committed. 4-Cmte on Invalid Pensions: bill to authorize the Pension Agent at Cincinnati to pay to John Wing the arrears of pension due to Dorothy Ferrell: committed. Same cmte: bill for the relief of Orris Crosby; also, a bill for the relief of Elijah C Babbatt: both committed. 5-Cmte on Invalid Pensions: adverse report on the cases of Jos Pulsifer & Enoch Dobbyns: laid on the table. Same cmte: bill for the relief of Isaiah Parker: committed. 6-Cmte on Patents: bill for the relief of Elisha H Holmes: committed. 7-Cmte of Claims: bill for the relief of Saml D Enochs: committed. Also, made an adverse report on the ptn of Teakle Savage, administrator of Bolitha Laws: laid on the table. 8-Cmte of Claims: bill for the relief of Gregory Thomas & another: committed. Same cmte: adverse reports on the cases of David B Ogden & Ira Carpenter: laid on the table. 9-Cmte on Commerce: adverse report on the case of Chas W Bingley: laid on the table. Also, bill for the relief of Philip & Eliphalet Greely. Also, a bill for the relief of N L Dana & Co. 10-Cmte on Commerce: bill for the relief of Emanuel Berri: committed. 11-Cmte on Public Lands: bill for the relief of John G McCloud & a bill to confirm the entry of land made by the administrator of Jas Anderson, dec'd, of Iowa: bills were committed. Same cmte: adverse report on the case of Richd Church & others, of Gallatin Co, Il: laid on the table. 12-Cmte on the Post Ofc & Post Roads: reported a joint resolution to settle the claim of Alex'r M Cumming: read & committed. 13-Cmte on Revolutionary Claims: bill for the relief of Jos Warren Newcomb & a bill for the erection of a monument to the memory of Gen Jos Warren: read & committed. 14-Cmte on Revolutionary Claims: adverse report on the case of the legal reps of Adney Hay: laid on the table. Same cmte: bill for the relief of the legal reps of Simon Spalding, dec'd: committed. 15-Cmte on Private Land Claims: referred the bill to amend the act of Feb 24, 1843, for the relief of Geo Mayfield, reported the same back to the House without amendment: bill was then committed. 16-Cmte on Naval Affairs: was discharged from the ptns of Danl Sampson & Holt Ingraham: they were laid on the table.

Orphans Court of Wash Co, D C. In the case of John F Callan, adm of Thos Magnier, dec'd, the administrator & Court have appointed Feb 20 next, for settlement of the estate of Thos Magnier. -Ed N Roach, reg/o wills

The U S sloop-of-war **Boston** arrived in Hampton Roads on Sat last, & then departed for N Y, under orders from the Dept at Washington. The Norfolk Beacon says: part of her crew were frostbitten. Cmdor Turner, Lt Peter Turner, flag Lt Mr Habersham, Cmdor's Sec, & Purser White, [relieved,] & Lt Goden & Purser Barry, of the Boston, came up yesterday morning; & the 2 last named ofcrs left for the ship in Hampton Roads, in the U S steamer **Engineer**.

$100 reward for runaway negro man Richd Neale, 25 years of age, who ran away from the residence of Noble S Braden, 5 miles west of Leesburg, Loudoun Co, Va. –Thos Rogers, Deputy of A Gibson, late Sheriff of Loudoun, Va, & administrator of Geo M Chichester.

List of letters remaining in the Post Ofc, Wash, Feb 1, 1846.

Adams, Henry	Brown, J P	Butler, Abraham B
Adams, Mrs M A	Brick, Saml R-3	Benedict, Prof
Adam, Rev Wm	Bird, Wm P	Barton, Henry
Allen, Gen Jas-2	Burt, Mrs Martha	Brower, Jas
Alston, Jas T	Bayne, Miss Mgt	Beaman, D E
Anderson, Saml J	Beard, Lewis	Blatchford, R M
Adams, L C	Beck, Lemuel J	Bradford, Miss Mary
Allen, Miss S E	Bond, Wm S	Barker, John
Aldrick, P Emory	Bean, Benj	Bradford, Freeman
Adams, Mary H	Beam, M M	Bartlin, A S H-2
Applegate, John	Bellows, Geo-2	Bacon, D Francis
Alexander, Mrs E	Baker, John J	Bishop, J A
Arundell, R J	Butler, Henry	Baltzell, Miss A M-2
Ball, Luellan	Bayard, J A	Bowen, Chas
Beirne, Oliver	Blanchard, John	Barker, Dr M
Bull, Mrs Wm G	Butler, Andrew W	Bellville, Rev Jacob
Brooks, Hananiah	Bulger, John	Coxe, Benj
Brooke, C W	Brokenboro, Carter	Chase, Miss E-2
Besch, John	Brannan, Robt	Comb, Mrs Ann
Breese, Capt S L	Burbank, Abner-3	Clark, Darius-2
Boun, Philip	Bogart, John A	Clark, Mr
Brown, Wm-2	Broadhead, D M	Cook, C H-2
Brown, L D-3	Braxton, Richd	Chase, Britain
Boyle, Mrs Ellen	Bryan, John F-2	Coutts, Miss Mary
Bitts, Royston	Bontz, Miss E M K-2	Cook, John
Brown, Miss Eliz	Bayly, J	Coles, Oscar
Botner, M	Butler, Mrs Ann	Clark, Wm R

Clarke, J C R-5	Curtis, Edw	Edgerton, sr, A P
Crump, Geo W-2	Chipman, Mrs Ruth	Elmondorf, Dorothea
Cox, Walter S	Dunn, Mrs Ann-2	Elliott, C E
Cook, Miss M E	Day, Hoven H-2	Edelin, Francis S
Colt, Saml	Dennett, Sarah	Eckhart, Thos
Carver, Miss Maria	Dockerty, John	Erwin, John-7
Campbell, Hy R	Donaldson, T H	Edelin, Capt Jas-2
Chapman, Mrs S P	Dowson, Wm	Elwell, Francis
Carusi, Lewis-3	Dewey, Rev L D-2	Fox, Gracy Ann
Conlin, Peter	Donnelly, Patrick	Forbes, Saml C
Colley, Jas W	Danforth, W R	France, W
Cisson, Mrs Ann	Darnell, Gen W H	Ford, Miss Lucinda
Coleman, Nathan F	Dunlap, Gen H W	Fales, Wm
Cockerill, Miss A E	Dulany, W H	Fowle, Wm B
Carnan, John R H	Daniel, B R	Fisher, Mr
Chamberlain, C F	Downing, Aug C	Favor, Col Jos
Campbell, Mrs S B	Dandridge, Miss	Flewellen, Miss A J
Curtis, Mrs Eliza	Dixon, Alex'r	Flyblock, Jack
Carnell, Mrs, of Balt	Dixon, Augustus	Fenwick, Benj J
Curtis, Henry	Duncan, Thos-2	Freidenberger, A
Corwin, John F	Davidson, Geo	Fenton, Maj D G
Cuyler, Theodore	Dorsey, A	Fannon, Col A B
Cooper, Saml-2	Dickover, Mrs L M	Farrish, Robt O
Comier, Edw	Dockray, Jas P	Fuller, John
Carroll, Anne	Dinnies, Alfred	Grey, Wm
Collins, John F	Dailey, Oliver	Griggs, A
Colton, Levi-2	Dickson, Jas N	Green Geo
Cooper, Lloyd N	Davies, Maj Chas	Graves, Miss Marg
Carter, Mrs Matilda	Donely, Isaac	Green, Dr Solomon
Churchill, Peleg	Deleny, Miss R	Grice, Saml B
Crepon, Geo W	De Neale, Mrs Jane	Guthrie, G W
Croghan, Col Geo-2	English, Jno A-2	Grimes, Susan M
Cadden, Jas-2	Eaton, L M-2	Gibson, Jas M
Campbell, Cornel's-2	Evans, Miss F | Ed	Gibson, Jas K-3
Camara, Joze D de	Ewing, R M	Gillott, Geo
Chapman, Alex	Emory, Fred'k	Gibbons, John W
Craypo, L A	Edwing, Edwin H-5	Gatton, Mrs Mary
Canfield, Danl B	Esher, Jacob	Gatsell, O
Comelly, Michl	Engelbrecht, T F	Giddings, Saml S
Carryl, Nathan T	Emmons, Jno B	Glendy, Lt W M-2
Cadwell, Miss E	Emerson, Ethan A	Goodrich, Chas B
Chaney, Richd	Eaton, Danl C	Garonski, L R
Caldwell, Mrs Eliza	Equal Div'n, R S of	Graham, Carson
Chilton, S	Elzey, Mrs Mary H	Griffin, Mary
Carlyle, C M	Evans, Edw G	Grammer, F A

Gordon, Enoch	Harvey, Wm E	Ketchum, Mrs M H
Gipson, John H	Harvie, Lewis E	Kerney, Mrs-2
Goodwin, F C	Huger, Danl E	Kelsey, Wm
Gordon, Chas	Hammond, c G	Kellogg, Miss J A
Gillespie, Lt A H	Handy, Col Levin-2	Ketchum, Israel
Gratiot, C H-3	Heckrote, A G	Lunt, Miss Ann-2
Graham, Wm S	Herbert, Henry	Long, Robt C
Hunt, Lt E B	Howard Div'n, R S of	Lewis, Harrison J
Hall, Edw	Haskell, Danl B	Lannum, Miss C
Hall, Jas D	Horncastle, Prof	Lowry, Geo W
Hooe, Jessee	Harris, Wm	Lindsley, Mrs E C
Hoge, John Blair	Hunter, Miss M E	Ludlow, Augustus
Hook, Wm T	Hager, J H	Lanier, Lt Edmund
Howe, Wm	Harise, W	Lambert, Capt J H
Hunt, J C	Hinton, Gen O	Lanier, J F
Hays, S	Horrel, Thos	Lanier, Mr, of Ind
Hall, Henry	Harrison, Rev Hy	Lewis, Lewis
Hall, Jas	Hussey, J G	Lightall, Ahasuerus
Humes, Mrs Judy	Hollins, Francis	Livingston, J C
Hum, W Thruston	Hepburn, Peter	Lindenberger, Mrs R
Hill, Dr H H	Harrison, Columbus	Lendrum, Maj T W
Hughes, Mrs S S	Hammond, Lt R P	Lawrence, Mr
Hardin, Gen J J-2	Ireland, Eliza	Lanton, Mr
Howard, Jas M	Ingle, J	Larner, A J
Haller, Jacob	Ishy, J H	Lamnie, D S-4
Heben, A E, U S N	Ingram, Mrs	Mills, Lewis
Harding, Capt E	Jones, Washington	Moore, Pres W-2
Hooper, Chas	Jones, Gen E	Moore, Mrs Mary
Harris, Geo F	Jamaison, Miss J	Mead, Simeon
Hoffman, Josiah	Jorden, Isam	Moore, H W
Hildreth, F A-2	Johnson, Chas F	Maus, Isaac R
Howard, Miss I J	Jackson, L E	Morse, John G
Hurlbert, Dr O	Johnson, Miss S	Martin, Fayette, W
Herbert, Geo	Jackson, Eliza	Mason, Jas M
Hassard, Thos	Johnson, Jacob	Mason, M B
Holley, Mrs E H	Jordan, Thos W	Morsell, Saml T
Hopkins, Mrs A M	Jervis, John H	Morgan, Rudolph S
Hollins, Francis	Jamaison, Elias	Martin, Miss E P
Hubley, Edw B	Jennings, Augustus	Mathews, C S
Hetzel, Lt Calvin	Kurtz, Danl	Murphy, Henry
Hopkins, Col W-3	Knott, Wm E	Moses, J T
Humphrey, L S	King, D C	Massoletti, J R
Howard, Miss M A	Key, Tayloe	Major, Danl-2
Hamlin, J E	Knight, Cavendish	Miler, Christian
Hompkins, Wm	Krebs, Chas W	Mitchell, Wm L

Martin, Henry C	Pool, Miss Mary	Reaney, Caleb E
Murray, Henry T	Powel, Capt J A-2	Ramsay, Miss M A-3
Myer, C F	Pierce, A C	Ramsay, Jas
Marcy, Laban	Pool, Elder W C	Roberson, Eliz
Mason, W T T	Phelps, Dr	Rodgers, Wm T
Morgan, John B	Pratt, Jos	Rayan, Michl
Maruder, Capt G A	Phelps, Dr Francis	Russell, Jeremiah
Martin, John P	Pearks, Miss A E	Robinson, Mr
Moulton, Dr Ed	Phelps, A Lincoln	Roberts, E
Marion Div's, R S of	Price, Col J W	Roswell, Rosson J
Mitchell, Wm S	Peddicord, Mrs A E	Robbins, S E-2
Mitchell, John	Peters, R, of Phil'a	Rogers, J C
Marshall, Gen A	Phillips, Miss J	Smith, E J
Martin, Mrs I J	Poensel, Geo	Scott, Miss Alexena
Marshall, Jas	Porter, Sidney D	Stone, Hiram
Mulloy, John J	Perison, Wm	Smith, Miss Lixxy
Murphy, Jeremiah	Pouiston, R J	Smoot, Dr Henry
Maddox, Mrs Sarah	Patrick, John	Spires, A W
McLean, Mrs M	Philips, Jas B-2	Swartz, Dr
McGrath, Rebecca	Pendleton, T J	Smith, T C H
McEndree, Mrs M-2	Prentiss, Lt G A	Shunk, Edmund
McIntyre, Arch	Pilling, Jos	Smith, John G
McFarland, John	Quimby, Thos R-2	Smith, Delazon
Maguire, H	Quinlein, Chas	Simms, Miss J E
McDuffie, J T	Reed, Jas H	Sprigg, Osborn
McKenny, Jno F	Reid, jr, S C-2	Scott, Mrs Ruth
McCullough, Geo	Read, Wm	Swett, Benj
McNamara, John	Rose, Dr Wm R	Shore, Jonathan
McHenry, H	Ruff, C F	Smith, Mrs Eleanor
McKenny, Saml	Rhodes, Mr	Smith, Maj A J
Makintosh, Capt J M	Ritchie, Wm H	Scovell, Col H W
McDonnell, Patrick	Richards, Alfred	Simmons, Mrs E D
McLemore, Jno C	Robertson, Miss E	Sayers, Jas-3
McClelland, Capt J-2	Robertson, N R	Seymour, Wm B
McGray, Miss Susan	Rickards, Benj	Sillcox, Josiah
Nice, Decatur	Robert, Sanderson	Spencer, Col J-3
Nally, J H	Roberts, Geo	Sothoron, John R
Noel, Miss	Reiley, John	Sanford, Capt J C
Newton, Wilboughly	Roers, Henry	Salter, Benj
O'Neill, G P	Rogers, Prof H D	Sloman, John
Oliver, Geo	Renolds, Saml	Simpson, Marcellus
Osborn, Danl	Rodgers, Robt S	Sweeney, Mrs Jas
O'Brien, Timothy	Russel, F S	Skidmore, Mrs M
Price, Capt John	Ritter, Mrs Cath	Seymour, John S
Price, John C	Reynolds, Mr	Scribner, Rev J M

Seymour, Wm B	Titus, J H	Wagoner, Anthony
Sweeney, Thos	Thurber, jr, Wm	Washington, L W
Stewart, Mrs Com	Thomas, Gen Isaac	Williams, Wm
Smallwood, Mrs A	Tappan, Benj-5	Williams, Miss M
Sewall, Robt D	Van Zandt, Jos A	Wilson, Wm
Staples, Henry	Verdon, Morden	Weaver, Mrs J G
Staples, Seth P-2	Vanderpoel, J V	Wilson, Fred'k
Sinclair, John-2	Van Dusen, Mathew	Whistler, Geo W
Sansbury, Jas	Vaden, Dr J R	Walker, Dr A M
Towns, John	Weil, Wm	Whitter, Wm
Trochart, Henry	Welch, Wm-2	Williams, Wm
Thomas, Philip W	Wright, Jas M	Waters, David S
Taliaferro, John	White, O H	Warren, Wm E
Totten, Lt Jas	White, Jas	Wheeler, Thos B
Turner, H S	Walch, J	Wilkinson, Maj J
Tatham, G N	Ward, W Cont'r	Washington, Simeon
Taylor, Capt T M-2	Ward, Catharine	Wetmore, C W
Tenny, Miss Helen	West, B R	Williamson, J C
Townsend, Gen	Welch, Mrs Sarah	Wilheim, H
Taylor, John B	Wall, Geo W	Watmough, E C
Taylor, Henry	Ward, C L	Whitney, Danl-2
Trunnell, Thos	Wood, Saml	Williams, Wm A
Thompson, Jno R	Wood, Lt Thos J	Williams, F A
Thompson, Judge	Whitney, Mss M P	Walley, Miss Mary
Thomas, A M-2	Williams, Jas	Yates, Giles F-3
Tenny, Mrs A R	Washington, N	Yell, Mrs Lucy
Timothy Div, R S of	Williams, Ruel	Young, J, of Mordecai
Thompson, Col G W	Williams, G Mott	Zabriskie, Col Jas C
Templeton, Mr	Winne, Thos	

The inland postage on all letters intended to go by ship must be paid, otherwise they remain in this ofc. -C K Gardner, P M

Fairfax Institute, Fairfax Co, Va, near Alexandria, D C. The second term of the 8th annual session will commence with Feb, & continue to the 2nd week in Jul. Apply to the subscriber, Theological Seminary post ofc, Fairfax Co, Va.
--Geo A Smith, Principal

Mrd: Dec 30, at Phil, by Rev Dr Boardman, Alex'r R McHenry to Roxalene, d/o Jas Orne, all of that city.

Mrd: on Jan 27, by Rev Mr Kepler, Benj O Mullikin to Mary E, d/o the Hon Wm T Wootton, all of PG Co, Md.

MON FEB 2, 1846
City Ordinance-Wash: 1-Act for the relief of Robt Farnham: fine improsed for an alleged violation of the law in relation to licenses for the sale of stationery be & the same is remitted, provided he pay the cost or prosecution, & the amount of the fine shall be refunded. 2-Act for the relief of A C Kidwell: the sum of $81.32 be appropriated for the purpose of paying Kidwell for taking up & relaying the stone gutter & curbing on square 168. 3-Act for the relief of Henry Hoffman & others: sum of $129.75 be appropriated as follows: $69.75 to Henry Hoffman; $51.50 to Jas Lee; $6 to Wm Donohon; $2.50 to Basil Lee, the same being in full payment to them for work done in filling up in Centre Market space.

1-Ptn of Eli Pember, a Lorain Co, Ohio, a Canadian volunteer, for relief. 2-Ptn of John Stanert, of Phil, an invalid pensioner, praying that his pension shall commence from the time he received his wounds. 3-Memorial & documents of Lucretia Haymaker & other heirs of John Bowen, for leave to locate a Virginia military land warrant. 4-Ptn of R G Ward & F Mauzy, of Va, for relief. 5-Ptn of Lucy P Brent & Eliza B Horner, of Va. 6-Ptn of Mrs Nancy Hazzard, of Cumberland Co, Ky, asking for a pension. 7-Ptn of Moses Wright, of Wayne Co, Ky, asking a pension for certain services rendered & disabilities incurred whilst in the service of the U S during the late war with Great Britain. 8-Ptn of Joshua Dodge, praying compensation for extra services as a special tobacco agent. 9-Ptn of Capt Jas Whaley, of Fayette Co, Pa, for an increase of pension. 10-Ptn & documents of Thos Thompson, a soldier of the late war, praying to be placed on the pension list. 11-Application on behalf of Jos Taylor. 12-Ptn of March Farrington for an increase of pension. 13-Ptn & documents of John S Vandyke, of Phil, praying that certain prize moneys due to his dec'd brother, Henry Vandyke, may be paid. 14-Memorial of Edmund H Taylor, of Frankfort, Ky, praying an allowance of the commutation of 5 years full pay, with interest thereon, in lieu of half pay for life promised by the resolved of Oct, 1780, & Mar 22, 1783, in consideration of the services of Col Francis Taylor, in the Continental Line of Va, in the war of the Revolution. 15-Ptn of Adam Swart, for pay for Revolutionary services. 16-Ptn of Silas Chatfield, for a pension. 17-Ptn of Benj Hansford & other citizens of Pulaski Co, Ky, praying a pension for said Hansford on account of services rendered as a spy during the year 1787, in the war of the U S against the Indians.

Homicide: Memphis Enquirer of the 22nd ult: Dr Jenifer was shot & killed by Dr Grant, in Helena, Arkansas, on Tue last, in a street rencontre. The dec'd was a son of the Hon Danl Jenifer, of Md. Dr Grant has recently settled in Helena, having removed there from the neighborhood of Vicksburg.

Mary L Marble recovered a verdict of $1,500 in the Court of Common Pleas of Worcester Co, Mass, last week, against Origen Halbach, for slanderous words uttered against the fair fame of the plntf by the wife of the dfndnt.

Died: on Sat last, Mrs Charlotte E Mason, wid/o the late Gen Armistead T Mason, of Va. Her funeral is this day, at 12 o'clock, from the residence of her son, Mr S T Mason, at the U S Arsenal.

Died: on Sat last, near the Navy Yard, after a lingering illness, Mr Thos J Bright, aged 21 years & 3 months. He promised to become a source of comfort & support to his widowed mother in her old age, but Providence ordered otherwise, & removed him from this scene. His funeral obsequies will take place at St Peter's Church, Capitol Hill, Tue, at 10 o'clock.

Fulton Co, [N Y] Democrat: Execution of Mrs Valkenburgh on Jan 24: she acknowledged having poisoned 2 husbands. She gave her first husband a dose of arsenic, which, although he did not die immediately, was untimately the cause of his death.

TUE FEB 3, 1846
Just published: Oregon, Our Right & Title, by Windham Robertson, jr, of Virginia. Price .50. For sale by Wm Q Force, corner of Pa ave & 10th st.

Old Capitol: wanted immediately a first-rate Cook. One of sober habits & honest. --H V Hill

Orphans Court of Wash Co, D C. Letters of adminstration on the personal estate of Jas Hoban, late of said county, dec'd. --John F Callan, adm

Senate: 1-Ptn from the exc of Thos Cooper, asking the reimbursement of the fine imposed under the alien & sedition laws. 2-Ptn from Peter Von Schmidt, asking for compensation for a model of a pneumatic dry-dock, constructed under direction of the Sec of State for the use of the China mission. 3-Ptn from John Jones, asking compensation for work performed at the Pea Patch Island under contract with the U S. 4-Ptn from Jas Hamilton & P Schuyler, asking the Gov't to purchase their right to an improvement in certain machinery. 5-Ptn from Saml Simpson, asking a pension. 6-Ptn from Geo Wingard, for a pension. 7-Ptn from Meledge Galphin, of S C, asking the recognition of certain claims by the Gov't. 8-Cmte on Indian Affiars: bill to authorize the settlement of the accounts of John Crowell. 9-Cmte of Claims: adverse report on the ptn of Wm Morrow. Same cmte: adverse report on the claim of Ed D Tippett. 10-Cmte of Claims: adverse report on the memorial of Ed Bolan. Also, asking to be discharged from the further consideration of the ptn of Caleb Greene, & that it be referred to the Cmte on the Judiciary. 11-Cmte of Claims: bill in addition to an act for the relief of Walter Loomis & Abel Gay. Same cmte: asking to be discharged from the further considerationof the claim of Chas F Sibbald, & that it be referred to the Cmte on the Judiciary. 12-Cmte on Indian Affairs: bill for the relief of Elijah White. 13-Cmte on Patents: bill to further extend the patent of Jethro Wood. Same cmte: bill for the relief of Ross Winans.

New provision store: now selling at Stalls #s 18 & 20, in the Centre market, & the Capitol Hill market, a fine lot of well-fattened Beef. Also opened, a provision store in the new bldg on the corner of 8th & D sts. -John Hoover

House of Reps: 1-The widow of Robt Gray rose to present a paper: her ptn sets forth that she is the widow of Capt Robt Gray, well known as the navigator who discovered, first entered, & gave its present name to the Columbia river. That your petitioner was left a widow nearly 40 years ago, with 4 young dghts, & without adequate means for their education & support. In her advanced age is still in circumstances requiring the strictest economy: her dghts are yet living, & 3 of them remain unmarried. Her late husband was in the naval service of his country during a part of the war of the Revolution, but she is unable under the existing laws to entitle herself to be placed upon the list of U S pensioners, the act granting half-pay & pensions to certain widows & for other purposes, providing only for widows whose marriage took place before Jan 1, 1794, & her marriage having taken place in Feb, 1794. Neither her late husband during his lifetime, nor his family since his decease, have received the slightest pecuniary benefit from the great discovery herein referred to; & your petitioner now, for the first time, appeals to the justice of her country with confidence. Boston, Jan 17, 1846 -Martha Gray [Memorial to be referred to the Cmte on Revolutionary Pensions, & printed.]

Fatal duel fought yesterday, near Bladensburg, between Dr Danl Johnson & Thos F Jones, of Perquimons Co, N C, which terminated at the first fire in the instant death of Dr Johnson. It is said the surviving combatant, & his second, were arrested upon the spot by the civil authorities of the county, P G Co, Md. [Feb 7th newspaper: a Judge of the Superior Court of Md re-examined the case, & decided that, as killing in a duel was not a capital offence, according to the laws of Md, & the parties under arrest were entitled to be admitted to bail; which was tendered & accepted, & they were discharged. Last night, the 2nd, the parties returned to Elizabeth City, N C, where they reside, & the corpse of Dr Johnson was at that time taken to his friends.]

I will sell *Indiantown*, the Farm on which I reside, containing 884 acres; also, a piece of land detached from the said Farm, containing 57 acs. *Indiantown* has a west front on Nanjemoy creek; on the north it is bound by Avon river, on the south by King's creek, requiring less fencing than any farm of its size in Md. On the farm is a comfortable frame dwlg, & all necessary out-bldgs. It will be offered on Feb 24 at private sale. -John D Freeman

For sale, a fine estate in the valley of Va, on a credit of 10 years. The estate on which I reside, lying 1 miles from the Shenandoah river: contains upwards of 1,100 acres; the dwlg house is of brick, 2 stories high, well finished, covered with slate, contains 8 rooms, &, with the adjacent ofcs, cost about $12,000. The whole tract may be had at $38 per acre, or 500 acres with the dwlg house at $45 per acre. The *Wolf Marsh* tract, about 350 acres, at $37, & the *Stone Bridge* tract, near 300 acres, at $36. -J M Hite, White Post Ofc, Clarke Co, Va

Loudoun Farm for sale: adjoining the town of Leesburg, containing 225 acres; was formerly part of *Exeter*; about 33 miles from Washington. Mr Wm Ball, at *Exeter*, will show the property. –John A Washington, Mount Vernon

Mrd: on Jan 28, at N Y, Wm C Ellison, of Phil, to Annie Alexander Dibble, d/o the late John Hull, of N Y.

Died: on Jan 30, suddenly, at Megeville, the seat of her son, Wm Temple Washington, of Jefferson Co, Va, Mrs Lucy P Todd, only surviving sister of Mrs Madison. This amiable & excellent lady had in early life married Geo S Washington, nephew & one of the heirs of Genr'l Washington. After the death of Mr Washington she became united in marriage with the Hon Thos Todd, of Ky, one of the Judges of the Supreme Court of the U S, whom she survived for many years, to guide & protect the fatherless children, whose love & tears follow her to the grave.

Died: on Feb 2, in Wash City, Nicholas Ignatius Ennis, s/o Philip & Jane Ennis, in his 15th year. His funeral is this afternoon, at half past 3 o'clock, from the residence of his parents on 6th st.

WED FEB 4, 1846
Wash Corp: 1-Bill for the relief of M P Mohun: passed. 2-Cmte of Claims: bill for the relief of Joshua L Henshaw: passed. Same cmte: bill for the relief of Thos Welsh. 3-Ptn from Edw D Tippett: referred to the members from the First Ward. 4-Ptn from Richd T Smallwood: referred to the Cmte of Claims. 5-Ptn of Geo P Kensett, praying that certain certificates of deposite may be transferred to Thos Pursell: referred to the Cmte of Claims. 6-Ptn of Chas McDonald, praying a remission of a fine: referred to the Cmte of Claims.

Senate: 1-Ptn from Joshua Appleby, keeper of a light-house at Sand Key, Florida, asking to be remunerated for property lost by the destruction of said light-house in 1842. 2-Ptn from Mary B Hook, wid/o Col Jas H Hook, asking remuneration for his services in the bureau for emigrating Indians in the years 1845 & 1846. 3-Ptn from Robt & Wm Armstrong, for compensation as spies under Gen Wayne in 1793. 4-Cmte on Pensions: bill granting a pension to Jos Morrison. Same cmte: asked to be discharged from the further consideration of the ptn of Jas Low: referred to the Cmte on Naval Affairs. 5-Cmte on Indian Affairs: adverse report on the claim of A R S Hunter: ordered to be printed. 6-Cmte on Naval Affairs: bill for the relief of Henry Etting, a purser in the U S Navy. Same cmte: asked to be discharged from the further consideration of the ptn of Jonathan Thompson & others, of N Y C: to be referred to the Cmte on Commerce. 7-Cmte of Claims: asking to be discharged from the further consideration of the memorial of Fed'k Vincent, administrator of Jas La Caze: to be referred to the Cmte on Revolutionary Claims.

Inquests were held in Wash City last Sunday by Coroner Woodward over a white man, Owen Gorman, & a colored woman, Ellen Day, whose deaths were caused by intemperance. Gorman belonged to the almshouse.

St Charles Hotel: dissolution of copartnership under the firm of Brown & Roff, by mutual consent. -Burlin Brown, Wm Roff, Jan 31, 1846. Mr Brown has purchased the interest of Mr Roff in the establishment, & the business will hereafter be conducted by himself personally.

House of Reps: 1-Ptn of S Nickerson & Solathiel C Nickerson, owners of the schnr **Martha**, of Belfast, Maine, that the sum to which said schnr is entitled as bounty or drawback for having been employed at sea in the cod fisheries during the fishing season of 1837, may be allowed & paid to them. 2-Affidavits in support of the ptn of Amanda King, excx of Geo W Fox, dec'd, for compensation for property destroyed by the enemy in the late war with Great Britain. 3-Ptn of Solomon Price, adm of Richd, dec'd, praying for a law authorizing the payment to him by the Post Ofc Dept of a balance which was due to the said dec'd at the time of his death. 4-Ptn of Moses Noble, praying for the allowance of the bounty to the fishing schnr **Ruth**, lost at sea while pursuing her fishing voyage. 5-Ptn of Wm Shapley, praying Congress to allow him the sum of $40, with interest, to which he is entitled by virtue of a resolution of Congress of Sep 26, 1778. 6-Ptns of P Young, mate of the schnr **Brewster**, & of Capt Lamaris, of schnr **Rainbow**, for an appropriation for harbor at Cattaraugus harbor, N Y. 7-Ptn of Geo Alford, of Monroe, Mich, praying to be restored to the roll of the Revolutionary pensioners. 8-Ptn of D Pugh,adm for the benefit of the children of Mrs H Watkins, claiming arrears of pension under the act of Jul 7, 1838. 9-Ptn of John Rareshide & others, praying compensation for their services as volunteers from the State of Louisiana to Texas in 1845.

By virtue of a writ of distrain by Thos Sewel, against the goods & chattels of Patrick Crowley, I have taken the following: a butcher's cart, one wagon, & 2 horses, which I will expose at public sale, at the Centre Market-house, on Feb 7, for cash.
–Jas H Boss, Bailiff

The bill which passed the House a few days since, divorcing Eliz Booth, of Delaware, from Wm Chase Barnet, of Md, passed the Senate yesterday. She is restored by the law to all her former rights & privileges. The reason assigned for the divorce is, that the marriage ceremony was performed in a language unknown to the young lady, & therefore declared a fraud; &, as such, null & void.
–Annapolis [Md] Herald

Capt McGrath, of the 6th ward police, arrested yesterday at Newark, Robt Henry Beaudont, charged with having in Montreal committed forgery. –N Y Com Adv

New Flour Store: subscriber has taken the warehouse on the north side of Water st, opposite Messrs Read & Son, & intends on keeping a supply of all the various grades of flour. –Lewis Brooks, Water st, Gtwn

By a private letter from Covington, La, we learn that on Friday C Y Kimball, the proprietor of the hotel at that place, shot at Mr Jesse Kirkland, the successful candidate for clerk of the district court, through the window, as he was sitting in his house. Kimball returned to Kirkland's house, inquired if he was dead, & on finding out he was not, said he was determined to kill him. On this, when he returned, Kirkland met him again, he raised his gun, & shot him dead. Mr Kirkland immediately gave himself up.

On Thu in Attakapas, La, the day appointed by Govn'r Mouton for public thanksgiving & prayer, a cannon was to be fired as part of the ceremony. On the 3rd discharge, the gun went off as Mr C Benson was ramming the cartridge down; his hand was most horribly mangled & amputation was necessary. -Gaz

Died: yesterday, after a lingering illness, Mrs Catherine Covell, in her 33rd year, w/o Gen M L Covell, of Bloomington, Ill. Her funeral will take place at her late residence, Mrs M Hill's, 4½ st, south of Pa ave, this afternoon, at 3 o'clock.

Died: on Nov 29 last, in Wash City, aged 41 years, Anthony Reintzel, [s/o the late Danl Reintzel, well known as one of the most respected citizens of Gtwn,] after a sudden & brief illness. Among those who mourn is one peculiarly bereaved-one whose tenderest affections gathered around him as the last pillar of the early home, & to whom human sympathy can avail little when he who was so much her pride & joy.

Died: on Jul 3 last, at Houston, Texas, Mr Saml A Childs, for many years a resident of Wash City. [Per letter dated Houston, Texas, Dec 22, 1845.]

THU FEB 5, 1846
Senate: 1-Ptn from Thos Wilson, asking payment of the award made in his favor by the convention for settling claims on Mexico. 2-Ptn from John Bronson, asking compensation for property destroyed during the last war. 3-Ptn from Simeon Rousseau, asking a right of pre-emption to a certain tract of land in Michigan. 4-Cmte on Pensions: to inquire into placing Lt Thos Hall on the pension list. 5-Bill for the relief of Nathl Goddard & others was considered in Cmte of the Whole, & reported without amendment. [This bill is for reimbursing the parties the value of a ship & cargo confiscated during the last war.]

For sale, a valuable lot of ground, corner of 6th & Pa ave. Apply to J Hellen, at his ofc, on 5th st.

A young d/o Mr Titus Dort, of Dearborn, Mich, was killed by the accidental discharge of a pistol in the hands of her father. The grief & horror of the parent need not be told. –Detroit Daily Adv

I am authorized to sell the following valuable lands, lying on the Missouri river, in Ray Co, about 6 miles from Lexington, Missouri. A tract of about 1,297 acres, with 2 commodious warehouses; also, 2 log dwlg-houses, with out-houses. Also, a farm containing about 320 acres, with a comfortable dwlg-house & out-houses. For further particulars, address, post paid, E A Lewis, Atty at Law, Richmond, Missouri.

I certify that Geo Bean brought before me as a stray, a bay horse. –Jas Marshall, J P, Wash Co, D C. [Owner is to come forward, prove property, pay charges, & take him away. –Geo Bean, living on 11th st east, near the Navy Yard Bridge.]

Evening dresses just received at the Philadelphia Fancy Store, Pa ave, below 3rd st. –P Crerar

$10 reward: stolen from the farm of the subscriber, a large sorrel horse. Reward will be paid for the return of the horse. –Saml Sprigg, Northampton, PG Co, Md

For sale: 2 valuable plantations in the neighborhood of Upper Marlborough, PG Co, Md. One contains between 350 & 400 acres, the other between 250 & 300 acs. Inquire of the editor of the Marlborough Gaz, or N Callan, Genr'l Agent, Washington.

Mrd: Jan 29, by Rev Mr Van Horseigh, Mr Patrick Hefferman to Miss Louisa Greenwell, all of Wash City.

Died: yesterday, Mr Jas Baker, in his 51st year, a native of county Kilkenny, Ireland. His funeral is this afternoon, at 3 o'clock, from the corner of 9th & E sts.

Died: on Jan 28, at her residence, in Montg Co, Md, after a long & painful illness, Mrs Mary Gattrell, in her 70th year, leaving a large circle of relatives & acquaintances to mourn her loss.

Died: on Sunday, at Md Square, in his 91st year, Dr Jas Steuart, one of the oldest citizens of Balt, perhaps as generally known & as universally respected as a member of that community.

Dissolution of copartnership under the firm of Jacob Tabler & Jas A Clark: dissolved on Feb 4, by mutual consent. Jacob Tabler will settle all claims against the firm. –Jacob Tabler, Jas A Clark

Groceries & store fixtures at auction: on Feb 5, at the Grocery Store of Mr T Pierce, on N Y ave, between 7th & 8th sts. –A Green, auctioneer

FRI FEB 6, 1846

The new Presbyterian Church, on 8th st, under the pastoral care of the Rev Septimus Tuston, Chaplain of the U S Senate, is rapidly progressing its completion. A valuable lot having been given in May last by Gen Van Ness, as a site for the edifice, & the corner stone was laid on Jun 2.

Senate: 1-Ptn from Abraham W Smith & others, asking the recognition of Liberia as an independent Gov't. 2-Ptn from the legal reps of John Brook, asking commutation pay. 3-Ptn from Gen Wentling, an ofcr in the Revolution, asking a pension. 4-Ptn from J W Vaye, asking remuneration for losses. 5-Ptn from Oliver C Harris, for an extension of a patent. 6-Ptn from Calvin J Keith, asking Gov't to pay the awards made under the convention with Mexico. 7-Cmte on Public Lands: bill for the relief of Benj Harris, of La Salle Co, Ill.

House of Reps: 1-Ptn of Thos B Scott, in reference to a land claim. 2-Ptn of Mrs Rebecca White, of Lancaster, N H, for an increase of pension for Revolutionary services performed by her husband, Nathl White. 3-Ptn of Jas B Davenport, for the confirmation of a tract of land in the southwestern district of Louisiana. 4-Ptn of Chas Cappell, prayint the confirmation of a certain tract of land he held under a Spanish title. 5-Ptn of Moses Fowler, of Mason Co, Ky, praying Congress to allow him a pension for his services in the Indian wars. 6-Ptn of the heirs of Capt Nehemiah Stokely, for commutation pay. 7-Memorial of Calvin Keith, Anne B Coy, & Cora Ann Slocumb, praying for the adjustment & payment of the awards made in their favor under the convention with Mexico. 8-Ptn & other documents of Jos Carter, of Morgan Co, Ky, praying for a pension for services rendered during the Revolutionary war. 9-Ptn of Tycey Nelson, of Jefferson Co, Tenn, praying Congress to grant him a pension for hardships endured & disabilities incurred as a soldier in the late war with Great Britian. 10-Ptn of John Semple, of Michigan, for compensation for services in the last war.

<u>Appointments by the Pres. by & with the advice & consent of the Senate.</u>
Auguste Davezac, of N Y, to be Charge d'Affaires at the Court of his Majesty the King of the Netherlands, in place of Christopher Hughes, recalled.
Henry W Ellsworth, of Indiana, to be Charge d'Affaires at the Court of Sweden, in place of Geo W Lay, recalled.
Jas Dunlop, of the District of Columbia, to be Assist Judge of the Circuit Court of the U S for D C, in place of Buckner Thruston, dec'd.
Henry Dodge, to be Govn'r of Wisconsin, in place of Nathl P Tallmadge, removed.
Jas Clarke, of Iowa, to be Govn'r of Iowa, in place of John Chambers, removed.
Jesse Williams, of Iowa, to be Sec of Iowa, in place of Saml J Burr, removed.
Stinson H Anderson, to be U S Marshal for the district of Illinoie, in place of Thos M Hope, removed.

Consuls:
Wm H Robertson, of Louisiana, for the port of Bremen, vice A D Mann, recalled.
Wm A Sparks, of S C, for the port of Venice, vice Albert Dabadie, recalled.
Simeon M Johnson, of Michigan, for the port of Matanzas, in place of Thos M Rodney, recalled.

Navy Ofcrs:
Cornelius Vanalstine, to be a Lt in the Navy, from Apr 11, 1845, at which time he was promoted to fill a vacancy.
George W Doty, to be a Lt in the Navy, from May 13, 1845, in place of Lt Wm A Jones, resigned.
Washington Sherman, to be an Assist Surgeon in the Navy from Apr 25, 1845, in place of Assist Surgeon Wm Pitt Canning, dec'd.
Felix Grundy Mason, to be a 2nd Lt in the Marine Corps from Nov 14, 1845, in place of Lt Robt D Taylor, dec'd.
David Harlan, now a passed Assist Surgeon, to be a Surgeon in the Navy, from Dec 6, 1845, in place of Surgeon John Haslett, resigned.

District Attys:
Philip Barton Key, for the District of Columbia, in place of Jas Hoban, dec'd.
Solomon W Downes, for the district of Louisiana, in place of Balie Peyton, removed.
Thos M Pettit, for the eastern district of Pa, in place of Henry M Watts, removed.
Thos T Gantt, for the district of Missouri, in place of Wm M McPherson, removed.
Chas Linsley, for the district of Vermont, in place of Chas Davis, whose commission had expired.
John L Dawson, for the western district of Pa, in place of Wm O'Hara Robinson, removed.
Franklin Pierce, for the district of N H, in place of Joel Eastman, removed.
Robt Rantoul, jr, for the district of Massachusetts, in place of Franklin Dexter, removed.
Thos W Bartley, for the district of Ohio, in place of Chas Anthony, removed.
Wm F Allen, for the northern district of N Y, in place of Joshua A Spencer, removed.
Wm L Marshall, for the district of Md, in place of Z Collins Lee, removed.
Augustine Haines, for the distict of Maine, in place of Gorham Parks, resigned.

Ofcrs of the Customs:
Dillon Jordan, Collector of the district, & inspector of the revenue for the port of Pensacola, Fla, vice Robt Mitchell, removed.
Chas W Rand, Collector of the district, & inspector of the revenue for the port of Nantucket, Mass, vice Wm R Easton, whose commission has expired.
Isaac H Wright, to be Navy Agent for the port of Boston, Maass, in place of J Vincent Brown, removed.
Saml Cushman, to be Navy Agent for the port of Portsmouth, N H, in place of Timothy Upham, resigned.
Jos White, to be Navy Agent for the port of Balt, Md, in place of Saml McClellan, removed.

Walker Anderson, to be Navy Agent for the port of Pensacola, Fla, in place of Jackson Morton, whose commission has expired.

Land Ofcrs:

Danl B Richardson, to be Register of the Land Ofc for the district of lands subject to sale at Ouachita, Louisiana, vice Henry O McEnery, removed.

Hardy Holmes, re-appointed Receiver of Public Moneys for the district of lands subject to sale at Ouachita, Louisiana, his former commission having expired.

Alex'r J Irvin, to be Receiver of Public Moneys for the district of lands subject to sale at Green Bay, in the Territory of Wisconsin, vice Stoddard Judd, whose commission expired.

Postmasters:

Henry Campbell, at Rochester, N Y, in place of S J Andrews, removed.
John K Wright, Reading, Pa, in place of Chas Troxell, whose commission expired.
John McClintock, Chambersburg, Pa, in place of David D Durborrow, removed.
Hart L Stewart, Chicago, Ill, in place of Wm Stuart, removed.
John M Wimer, St Louis, Missouri, in place of Saml B Churchill, removed.
Geo M Horton, Geneva, N Y, in place of Jas Rees, whose commission expired.
Jos M Doty, Ogdensburg, N Y, in place of P B Fairchild, whose commission expired.
Thos B Hahn, Canandaigua, N Y, in place of J M Wheeler, whose commission expired.
David P Brewster, Oswego, N Y, in place of Jas Cochran, removed.
Amos S Rathbun, Auburn, N Y, in place of Wm C Beardsley, removed.
Wm W Teal, Syracuse, N Y, in place of Henry Raynor. removed
John L Slaymaker, Galena, Ill, in place of Robt W Carson, removed.
Jos W McCorkle, Dayton, Ohio, in place of Thos Blair, removed.
Benj F Rawls, Columbia, S C, in place of A H Gladden, whose commission expired.
Wm G Smith, Macon, Ga, in place of K Tyner, whose commission expired.
Geo Crawford, Cincinnati, Ohio, in place of W H H Taylor, whose commission expired.
Jacob Medary, Columbus, Ohio, in place of John G Miller, whose commission expired.
Truman C Everts, Toledo, Ohio, in place of Andrew Palmer, resigned.
Benj F Johnson, Frankfort, Ky, in place of Wm Hardin, resigned.
John Forsyth, Columbus, Ga, in place of G W E Bedell, whose commission expired.
Thos J Read, Louisville, Ky, in place of L H Mosby, removed.
Whitacre O'Neal, Steubenville, Ohio, in place of Wm Collins, whose commission expired. –Union

The Western Star published at Elkhorn, Wisc Terr, publishes a letter dated Jan 2, announcing the suicide of Thos K La Barron, who shot himself through the heart. He left a number of letters in his trunk referring to his suicidal purpose.

For rent: 3 story brick house on Pa ave. Property will be rented for a moderate price, which will be made known by Geo Watterston, on Capitol Hill. –C B Hamilton

On Apr 1, Mr Edwin Pinkney married Mary Ann Gale, in front of the altar railings of St Mary's Church, Islington. He met her 2 years ago, when age 28 years. His brother, Henry, was in attendance.

Orphans Court of Wash Co, D C. Letters of administration on the personal estate of Thos R Riley, late of said county, dec'd. --Wm R Riley, adm

SAT FEB 7, 1846
Appointments by the President, with the advice & consent of the Senate: 1-Elias Rector, to be U S Marshal for the district of Arkansas, in place of Henry M Rector, removed. 2-John M Fontane, to be Receiver of Public Moneys for the district of lands subject to sale at St Augustine, Fla, in place of Geo W Cole, dec'd. 3-John S Bagg, to be postmaster at Detroit, Mich, in place of Thos Rowland, removed.

Promotions & appointments in the Army. Promotions:
1st Lt Wm Eustis, to be Captain, Mar 17, 1845, vice Terrett, dec'd.
2nd Lt Andrew J Smith, to be 1st Lt Mar 4, 1845, vice Schaumburg, whose appointment ceased on that day.
2nd Lt Jas H Carleton, to be 1st Lt Mar 17, 1845, vice Eustis, promoted.
2nd Lt Richd S Ewell, to be 1st Lt Sep 18, 1845, vice McCrate, dec'd.
Brevet 2nd Lt Thos C Hammond, to be 2nd Lt Mar 4, 1845, vice Smith, promoted.
Brevet 2nd Lt Rufus Ingalls, of the 2nd Regt of Dragoons, to be 2nd Lt Mar 17, 1845, vice Carleton, promoted.
Brevet 2nd Lt Cave J Couts, of the 2nd Regt of Dragoons, to be 2nd Lt Mar 31, 1845, vice Rust, resigned.
Brevet 2nd Lt Jos H Whittlesey, of the 2nd Regt of Dragoons, to be 2nd Lt Sep 18, 1845, vice Ewell, promoted.
2nd Regt of Dragoons:
Brevet 2nd Lt Alfred Pleasanton, of the 1st Regt of Dragoons, to be 2nd Lt Nov 3, 1845, to fill a vacancy occasioned by the dismissal of 1st Lt Ranson.
3rd Regt of Artl:
Lt Col Wm Gates, to be Colonel Oct 13, 1845, vice Armistead, dec'd.
Maj Francis S Belton, of the 4th Regt of Artl, to be Lt Col Oct 13, 1845, vice Gates, promoted.
Brevet 2nd Lt Lucien Loeser, of the 2nd Regt of Artl, to be 2nd Lt May 31, 1845, vice A P Stewart, resigned.
4th Regt of Artl:
Brevet Maj John L Gardiner, Captain of the 4th Regt of Artl, to be Major Oct 13, 1845, vice Belton, promoted.
1st Lt Raphael C Smead, to be Captain Oct 13, 1845, vice Gardiner, promoted.
2nd Lt Francis N Clarke, to be 1st Lt Oct 13, 1845, vice Smead, promoted.
2nd Lt Geo W Getty, to be 1st Lt Oct 31, 1845, vice Soley, dec'd.
Brevet 2nd Lt Danl H Hill, of the 3rd Regt of Artl, to be 2nd Lt Oct 31, 1845, vice Getty, promoted.

3rd Regt of Infty:
1st Lt Jos L Coburn, to be Captain Nov 3, 1845, vice Cotton, resigned.
2nd Lt Oliver L Shepherd, to be 1st Lt Nov 3, 1845, vice Coburn, promoted.
Brevet 2nd Lt Robt Hazlitt, of the 4th Regt of Infty, to be 2nd Lt Nov 3, 1845, vice Shepherd, promoted.

4th Regt of Infty:
Lt Col Wm Whistler, of the 7th Regt of Infty, to be Colonel Jul 15, 1845, vice Vose, dec'd.
Brevet 2nd Lt Christopher C Augur, of the 2nd Regt of Infty, to be 2nd Lt Sep 12, 1845, vice Higgins, dec'd.
Brevet 2nd Lt Ulysses S Grant*, to be 2nd Lt Sep 30, 1845.

5th Regt of Infty:
1st Lt Wm Chapman, to be Captain Jun 8, 1845, vice Johnston, dec'd.
2nd Lt John A Whiteall, to be 1st Lt Jun 8, 1845, vice Chapman, promoted.
2nd Lt Geo Deas, to be 1st Lt Nov 17, 1845, vice Reid, dec'd.
Brevet 2nd Lt Mortimer Rosecrants, to be 2nd Lt Jun 8, 1845, vice Whiteall, promoted.
Brevet 2nd Lt Lafayette B Wood, of the 8th Regt of Infty, to be 2nd Lt Nov 17, 1845, vice Deas, promoted.

6th Regt of Infty:
Capt Benj L E Bonneville, of the 7th Regt of Infty, to be Major Jul 15, 1845, vice Hoffman, promoted.
1st Lt Wm H T Walker, to be Captain Nov 7, 1845, vice Searight, resigned.
2nd Lt Edw H Fitzgerald, to be 1st Lt Nov 7, 1845, vice Walker, promoted.
Brevet 2nd Lt Edwin Howe, of the 5th Regt of Infty, to be 2nd Lt Nov 7, 1845, vice Fitzgerald, promoted.

7th Regt of Infty:
Maj Wm Hoffman, of the 6th Regt of Infty, to be Lt Col Jul 15, 1845, vice Whistler, promoted.
1st Lt Danl P Whiting, to be Captain Apr 18, 1845, vice Davis, dismissed.
1st Lt Roger S Dix, to be Captain Jul 15, 1845, vice Bonneville, promoted.
1st Lt Richd C Gathir, to be Captain Sep 30, 1845, vice Dix, appointed paymaster.
2nd Lt Henry Little, to be 1st Lt Apr 18, 1845, vice Whiting, promoted.
2nd Lt Has R Scott, to be 1st Lt Jul 15, 1845, vice Dix, promoted.
2nd Lt Chas H Humber, to be 1st Lt Sep 30, 1845, vice Gathir, promoted.
Brevet 2nd Lt John M Jones, of the 5th Regt of Infty, to be 2nd Lt Apr 18, 1845, vice Little, promoted.
Brevet 2nd Lt Franklin Gardner**, to be 2nd Lt Sep 12, 1845.
Brevet 2nd Lt Jos H Potter, of the 1st Regt of Infty, to be 2nd Lt Oct 21, 1845, vice Quimby, resigned.

8th Regt of Infty:
2nd Lt Calvin Hetzel, to be 1st Lt May 30, 1845, vice Johnson, cashiered.
Brevet 2nd Lt Jacob J Bohee, of the 1st Regt of Infty, to be 2nd Lt Jun 1, 1845, vice Hanson, resigned.

Brevet 2nd Lt Theodore L Chadbourne, of the 2nd Regt of Infty, to be 2nd Lt Sep 10, 1845, vice Darne, resigned.
Brevet 2nd Lt Edmund B Holloway, of the 4th Regt of Infty, to be 2nd Lt Sep 26, 1845, vice Handy, dec'd.

Appointments: Quartermaster's Dept:
1st Lt Morris S Miller, of the 3rd Regt of Artl, to be Assist Quartermaster, with the rank of Capt, Sep 13, 1845.

Pay Dept:
Benj F Larned, Paymaster, re-appointed, to take effect Nov 24, 1845, when his former commission expired.
Thos J Leslie, Paymaster, re-appointed, to take effect Nov 27, 1845, when his former commission expired.
St Clair Denny, Paymaster, re-appointed, to take effect Oct 15, 1845, when his former commission expired.
Roger S Dix, late Capt of the 7th Regt of Infty, to be Paymaster, Sep 30, 1845, vice Davies, resigned.

Corps of Engineers:
Cadet Wm H C Whiting, to be 2nd Lt Jul 1, 1845

Ordnance Dept:
Stephen T Mason, of Va, to be Military Storekeeper Jul 1, 1845.

Graduates of the Military academy attached to the Army as Brevet 2nd Lts, in conformity with the 4th section of the act of Apr 29, 1812, to take rank, respectively, from Jul 1, 1845.

Brevet 2nd Lts attached to the Corps of Engineers:
Cadet Edw B Hunt, of N Y
Cadet Louis Hebert, of Louisiana

Brevet 2nd Lts attached to the Corps of Topographical Engineers:
Cadet Wm F Smith, of Vt
Cadet Thos J Wood, of Ky

Brevet 2nd Lts attached to the Ordnance Dept:
Cadet Thos G Rhett, of S C
Cadet Chas P Stone, of Mass

Brevet 2nd Lts attached to the Dragoon Arm
Cadet Bezaleel W Armstrong, of Ohio
Cadet Wm T Allen, of Va
Cadet John W Davidson, of Va
Cadet Jas M Hawes, of Ky
Cadet Newton C Givens, of Ky
Cadet Richd C W Radford, of Va
Cadet Delos B Sacket, of N Y
Cadet Jos McIlvain, of Indiana

Brevet 2nd Lts attached to the Artl Arm
Cadet Fitz John Porter, of N H
Cadet Josiah H Carlisle, of Maine
Cadet Geo Edwards, of England
Cadet Henry Coppee, of Ga
Cadet Francis Collins, of N Y
Cadet Jos F Farry, of Pa
Cadet Louis D Welch, of Conn
Cadet Geo P Andrews, of Conn
Cadet Thos B J Weld, of Maine
Brevet 2nd Lts attached to the Infty Arm
Cadet John P Hache, of N Y
Cadet John A Richey, of Ohio
Cadet Patrick A Farelly, of Pa
Cdet Abram B Lincoln, of N Y
Cadet Jas G S Snelling, of Iowa
Cadet Edmund K Smith, of Florida
Cadet Thos J Montgomery, of Maine.
Cadet Jas N Ward, of Ky
Cadet Barnard E Bee, of S C
Cadet Wm Rhea, of Va
Cadet Gordon Granger, of N Y
Cadet Henry B Clitz, of N Y
Cadet Wm H Wood, of Mass
Cadet David A Russell, of N Y
Cadet Thos G Pitcher, of Indiana.
Cadet Wm L Crittenden, of Ky
*Lt Grant was promoted in the 7th Regt of Infty, vice Humber, promoted & exchanged into his present Regt-the 4th, with Lt F Gardner.
**Lt Gardner was promoted in the 4th Regt of Infty, vice Berry, dec'd, & exchanged into his present Regt-the 7th, with Lt Ulysses S Grant.

Sale of papermill, land, & negroes, on Apr 13 next: under a deed of trust to me, executed by David Clewell, of Stokes Co: sale on the premises near Salem, 239 acres of land, more or less, in 3 adjoining tracts, lying in Stokes Co, on both sides of Peter's creek, [a branch of Middleford of Muddy creek,] including the papermill & outhouses, & bldgs; & the machinery. Also, 3 negro men, all more or less acquainted with making paper. –F C Meinung, Trustee, Salem, N C, Feb 2, 1845

Runaway committed to the jail of Wash Co, on Jan 22 last, a dark mulatto boy, who calls himself Saml Dixon, about 20 years of age. He says he belongs to Wm Turner, of Jefferson Co, Va, & that his master is now at Richmond, in the House of Delegates. The owner is to come forward & prove his property, otherwise he will be released according to law. –Thos Martin, Sheriff

Mrs Clavadetscher, formerly Mrs Bihler, informs those who are interested in the Raffle for Shawls, that they will be raffled off this afternoon, at 4 o'clock.

Writing Academy, evening classes, at his academy on Pa ave, between 12th & 13th sts. –W B Malcolm

Notice: The heirs of Geo Read & Geo Read, jr, late of Newcastle Co, Dela, dec'd, will take notice, that whereas, upon application made in the Orphans' Court of Crawford Co, Pa, on Nov 12, 1845, an inquest of partition was awarded by the said Court of a tract of land, being donation land #118, in Crawford Co, containing 500 acres with allowance, of which the said Geo Read was, in his lifetime & at his death, seised in fee simple, in pursuance of which order & award an inquest of partition of said land will be held on Apr 1, 1846. –S B Long, Sheriff

The King of Bavaria has issued a decree ordering that in future all persons killed in duels, or who have committed suicide, shall be interred without religious ceremonies of any kind.

Corporation Stock, Franklin Ins Stock, Bank of Metropolis, & Bank of Washington Stocks wanted. Apply to Andrew Carothers, 11th & F sts.

Piano fortes, guitars, violins, oil paintings, household furniture, for sale, on Feb 11, at the residence of the late F A Wagler, on H st, between 17th & 18th sts, by order of the Orphans Court of Wash Co, D C. –R W Dyer, auct

Circuit Court of Wash Co, D C: Augusta Davis has applied to be discharged from imprisonment under the act for the relief of insolvent debtors, on Feb 16, at the Court Room, when & where her creditors are requested to meet. –W Brent, clk

Columbia Typographical Society: meeting this evening at half-past 7 o'clock. –Thos Rich, Rec Sec

Post ofc Dept: The ofc in Bedford Co is here known as Dickinson's store; the one in Russell Co is called Dickensonville; the one in Franklin Co is Dickinson. In Powhatan & Tazewell Co there is no post ofc or postmaster named Dickinson's, or anything like it. –W J Brown, 2nd Assist Postmaster Genr'l

Died: yesterday, in Wash City, Wm Henry, of the Land Ofc, formerly of Ky, in his 73rd year. His funeral is tomorrow at 3 p m, from his late residence on H st, near 9th.

Died: on Feb 4, Emma, d/o Capt Alfred Mordecai, U S Army, aged 15 months.

MON FEB 9, 1846

The new Baptist Church on E st, between 6th & 7th sts, is now under the pastoral care of Rev Mr Samson, is now under the direction of Mr Mann, the skilful superintendent, progressing towards it completion.

Monument to the Memory of Jas Hoban; meeting held last Wed at the house of Mr John Foy, on D st: appointed Peter Brady, chairman, & J F Ennis, sec. The Cmte of arrangements appointed: Messrs Henry May, John F Callan, Gregory Ennis, John W Maury, & J Sullivan.

Mrs H T Weightman has 3 comfortable rooms unoccupied, which she is desirous of renting. She will furnish breakfast, if required. The house is on E, between 9th & 10th sts.

Capt John H Aulick, the esteemed Commandant of the Wash Navy Yard, has been appointed to the command of the U S frig **Potomac**, now preparing for sea: & Cmdor Wm B Shubrick, Chief of the Bureau of Provisions & Clothing, is to succeed him in the command of said yard.

The Democrat of Carbondale says that on Jan 30, the bodies of Patrick Walker & Mark Brennan, were discovered near the main road. Walker had his legs broken, probably by the flying car boxes. Brennan had been thrown by the wind upon the top of a loaded car, & was there caught by the falling roof, crushing him.

Juanito Capella, aged 16, while romping over a lawn with friends, at Shell Bank, near St Augustine, Fla, on Jan 22, fell dead instantly.

Mr Jos Price & his dght, Miss Price, at Toronto, Canada, a few day since, near that city, were riding in a carriage when the horses set off at full speed. Miss Price sprang out & was badly injured; Mr Price, leaped out immediately, & was so injured that he died soon after.

House of Reps: 1-Ptn of Robt Ellis, of Campbell Co, Tenn, praying a pension for disability incurred as a soldier in the war of the Revolution. 2-Ptn of Jacob Slade, for a pension. 3-Memorial of Wm Y Hansell, Wm H Underwood, & the reps of Saml Rockwell, praying that an allowance be made to them for professional services rendered to the Cherokee nation as solicitors, counselors, attys, & advocates, prior to their removal west of the Mississippi river. 4-Ptn of Mary Stanton, for a pension. 5-Ptn of Julius Eldred & sons, praying remuneration for services & the reimbursement of expenses in removing the copper rock from Lake Superior to Washington. 6-Ptn of Felicite McKocky for a new warrant for land, in lieu of lost land warrant $1,628 for 300 acres of land. 7-Ptn of Mrs Eliz Randolph, of Mercer Co, Ky, asking a pension for the Revolutionary services of her dec'd husband. 8-Ptn & papers of J Speakman, asking for indemnity for loss sustained by him in a contract with the War Dept.

On Jan 18, at Middlesex, Pa, Mr Saml Graham, one of the proprietors of the Middlesex furnace, was injured & his horse killed, when the horse leaped from a bridge, & fell 53 feet to the ice below. Mr Graham survived until the evening of the ensuing day.

Died: on Jan 28 last, at Culpeper Court-house, Va, John Shackelford, atty at law, in his 74th year. He will be cherished as a warm-hearted friend, kind neighbor, & an honest man.

Died: on Feb 4, at Guilford, Conn, Gregory E Lay, in his 20th year.

Obit-died: in Washington, aged 72 years, 1 month & 16 days, Wm Henry, who was born in Lancaster, Pa, late a clerk in the Genr'l Land Ofc. Wm Henry was born Dec 21, 1773, submitted on the morning of Feb 6, 1846, to the supreme fiat. His wife, children, & grand-childrenmourn his loss.

Franklin Fire Co: ofcrs elected for the ensuing year:
Wm Durr, Pres   John Ward, 2nd Assist
Jos Sessford, V P   John Minnix, 3rd Assist
Wm Cammack, Sec   John Sessford, Capt of Hose
Louis Lepreux, Assist Sec   Jos Williams, 1st Director
Thos J Fisher, Treas   Louis Lepreux, 2nd Director
John Mitchell, Capt of Engine   Ferdinand Butler, 3rd Director
Edw Edmonston, Chief Engineer
Cmte on Honoray Members: Thos J Fisher, Jos Sessford, & Robt Doyle.

Mrs Crossfield, 10th st, west of Pa ave, has 2 rooms for rent, with or without board.

Valuable farm hand at auction, on Feb 7, by order of the Circuit Court of Wash Co, D C, a negro man about 35 years old. Terms cash. –John H Bayne, Com of Geo Semmes. -R W Dyer, auct

The subscribers [as successors of O Fish & Co,] have formed a copartnership under the firm of M H Stevens & Emmons. –M Henry Stevens, John A Emmons

TUE FEB 10, 1846
Senate: 1-Ptn from Joel M Smith, asking compensation for services as pension agent at Nashville. 2-Ptn from Wm B Slaughter, late Sec of Wisconsin Territory, asking indemnity for loss sustained on account of money deposited in a bank that had failed. 3-Ptn from Elijah Buchanan, asking for a pension. 4-Ptn from Hector St John Berkeley, for a pension. 4-Ptn from Harriet Ward, for a pension. 5-Ptn from Louis de la Housage, asking confirmation to certain lands in the State of Louisiana. 6-Ptn from Nahun Ward, Treasurer of the Ohio Co, asking the payment of certain outstanding loan certificates. 7-Ptn from the excs of Benj Chaires, Gad Humphreys,

& Pedro Miranda, asking to be allowed to locate a tract of land held under a Spanish title, agreeably to the bounds thereof. 8-Cmte on Indian Affairs: adverse report on the ptn of John a Ragan: ordered to be printed. Same cmte: adverse report on the ptn of Louis Evans: ordered to be printed. 9-Cmte on Indian Affairs: asking to be discharged from the further consideration of the memorial of Wm Gentry & others. 10-Adverse reports made in the case of Wm Morrow & A R S Hunter were taken up & concurred in. 11-In the case of Jos Ratcliffe: asking to be discharged from its further consideration, was taken up & concurred in. 12-Bill for the relief of Nathl Goddart & others was passed over for the present. 13-Bill for the relief of Mary McRea, wid/o Col Wm McRae, late of the U S army, was taken up: bill passed over for the present.

Lost, a gold seal & ring. Finder please return to Rev R R Gurley, C st. Any reasonable reward will be given.

Prime new bacon just received, cured in the best manner for family use. --Presley Simpson, Pa ave, 2nd door east of 11th st, Wash.

WED FEB 11, 1846
House of Reps: 1-Cmte of Claims: adverse reports on the ptns of Wm Wilson, Henry Disbrow, & G T Beyer: laid on the table. Same cmte: bill for the relief of Langtry & Jenkins: committed. Same cmte: bill for the relief of John R Williams, & a bill for the relief of Andrew A Jones: committed. Same cmte: adverse report on the ptn of Geo J Knight: laid on the table. Same cmte: adverse reports on the cases of Hugh Hughes & John White: laid on the table. Same cmte: bill for the relief of Jacob L Vance, & a bill for the relief of the legal reps of Wm Bunce, dec'd: committed. 2-Mr Rockwell, of Conn, on behalf of Mr Pollock, from the Cmte of Claims: bill for the relief of the exc of John Norris, dec'd: committed. 3-Cmte of Claims: bill for the relief of Farrow & Harris: committed. Same cmte: adverse report on the case of Jas Hampson: laid on the table. 4-Cmte on Commerce: bill for the relief of Robt T Norris: committed. 5-Cmte on Public Lands: bill for the relief of the legal reps of John Smith, T, & to grant pre-emption rights to said heirs: committed. 6-Cmte on Public Lands: bill for the relief of Chas M McKenzie: committed. Same cmte: bill from the Senate for the relief of David T Williamson, of Pope Co, Arkansas, reported the same without amendment: committed. 7-Cmte on the Post Ofc & Post Roads: joint resolution for the relief of S B Hayes: committed. 8-Cmte on the Judiciary: bill for the relief of the heirs of Danl D Thompkins: committed. Also, reported a bill for the relief of Abraham Horback: committed. 9-Cmte on the Judiciary: adverse to the case of Wm Wilcox & Jos Wilcox, sureties of Martin Wilcox: laid on the table. 10-Cmte on Revolutionary Claims: to discharge the cmte from the case of Eliz Sailor, & to lay it on the table: agreed to. 11-Cmte on Revolutionary Claims: adverse to the case of Eliz Tays, of N C: laid on the table. Same cmte: to be discharged from the consideration of the case of Mgt & Agnes Bigham, heirs-at-law of Thos Armor: laid on the table. Same cmte: bill for the relief of the heirs of Marshal De Rochambeau: committed. Same cmte: adverse report on the cases of

Henry A Livingston, & the heirs of Lt Seth Chapin: laid on the table. 12-Cmte on Private Land Claims: adverse report on the cases of John McLaughlin & Marcus Spalding: laid on the table. 13-Cmte on Indian Affairs: bill for the relief of the heirs & legal reps of Cyrus Turner, dec'd: committed. Also, made a report on the case of P Prescott, interpreter at St Peters, in Iowa: laid on the table. 14-Cmte on Military Affairs: bill for the relief of Gad Humphreys & Geo Center: committed. 15-Cmte on Naval Affairs: bill for the relief of the heirs of John Paul Jones, & a bill for the relief of Saml D Anderson: both committed. Also, made an adverse report on the case of John P Anderson: laid on the table. Same cmte: bill for the relief of H D Johnson: committed. 16-Cmte on Invalid Pensions: adverse report on the case of Chas Cortwite: laid on the table. Same cmte: bill to increase the pension of Roswell Hale: committed. Same cmte: adverse report on the cases of Seneca Thomas, Elisha Deming, Thos Dresser, & Danl Ladd: laid on the table. 17-Cmte on Patents: bill for the relief of Joshua Shaw: committed. 18-Cmte on Revolutionary Pensions: bill for the relief of Peter Rife, & a bill for the relief of Martha Clarke: committed. Same cmte: adverse report on the case of Mary E Thompson: laid on the table. Same cmte: bill for the relief of Geo Roush: committed. Same cmte: adverse report on the case of Lucy Johnson: laid on the table. Same cmte: bill for the relief of Patrick Kelly, sr, & a bill for the relief of Fred'k Hopkins: committed. Also, adverse reports on the cases of Thos P Franklin, Nathl Bird, Lawrence Van Dyck, Mary Child, Seth Overton, Mary Buck: laid on the table. 19-Cmte on the Public Lands: discharged from the cases of John Newton, John Gilleylieu, the heirs of Wm Arnold, & the heirs of John Bowen: laid on the table. 20-Cmte on Foreign Affairs: Bill directing the mode of settling the claim of Cmdor Chas Ridgely: committed. 21-Memorial of Jos Gideon, praying to be allowed the pay of an acting purser in the navy. 22-Ptn of Jas H Coaly, praying the allowance of the pay of a carpenter in the navy. 23-Memorial of Henry Bernard, praying that a balance standing on the books of the Navy Dept as due him may be paid. 24-Ptn of Jos Dusean, of Monroe Co, Mich, for a pension. 25-Ptn of John Trimble, of Pa, for an increase of pension. 26-Ptn & papers in relation to the claim of the heirs of Capt John Oldham.

Mrs Ellen Jones has commenced a School for Young Ladies on F st, between 19th & 20th sts.

For rent: a large 2 story frame house on 11th st, containing 8 large rooms.
--J H Wheat

Orphans Court of Wash Co, D C. Letters of administration on the personal estate of Wm Hawley, late of said county, dec'd. --Wilhelmina D Hawley, admx

Orphans Court of Wash Co, D C. Letters of administration on the personal estate of Wm Ryland, late of said county, dec'd. --Enoch Tucker, Thos Pursell, excs

For rent: 2 story frame house on L st, between 13th & 14th sts. Apply to the present occupant, who will show the hosue, or to Luke Richardson, M st, near 14th.

The Poorhouse in Uxbridge, Mass, was destroyed by fire on Tue, with all its contents. Three aged persons, Leonard Taft, Mr Balster, & a female whose name is not given, were burnt to death.

Mrd: on Feb 8, by Rev Mr Muller, Mr Wm T Newton to Miss Eliza Ann Jackson, all of Balt.

Mr Francis D Newcomb, late U S Surveyor for the State of Louisiana, has been indicted in the U S Circuit Court at New Orleans for forgery. A large amount of public funds is said to be involved.

Died: on Feb 3, at *Oakwood*, the residence of his father, Judge Scott, in his 18th year, Chas Francis Scott, a youth of great promise, the idol of his bereaved parents.

The U S ship **Warren** was at Panama on Jan 3. Ofcrs & crew all well. She brought as passengers from Mazatlan, Lt J M Watson, bearer of dispatches, Passed Midshipman J Wilkinson, & Sailmaker Bennett on sick-ticket. She left an anchor in the roads of Mazarlan the frig **Savannah**, bearing the broad pennant of J D Sloat, & the sloop **Levant**, Hugh N Page, Cmder. The ship **Portsmouth**, Cmder Montgomery, was shortly expected from Guaymas. List of the Ofcrs of the **Warren**: Jos B Hull, Cmder

Lts-4:
Wm Radford, 1st	Wm B Renshaw, 3rd
Wm L Maury, 2nd	John Rutledge, acting 4th
Wm H Montgomery, Acting Master	Wm Grier, Assist Surgeon
Wm J Powell, Surgeon	Thos R Ware, Purser

Midshipmen:
Fred'k Kellogg	P H Haywood
John Geo Whitaker	N W Johnson
Thos J McRoberts	A M De Bree
Cmder's clerk, E L Stetson	Purser's clerk, Edw Jones

Forward Ofcrs
John Owens, gunner	John Joines, sailmaker
Jas Barret, sailing boatswain	Wm Knight, carpenter

John B Gough's Life, for sale by L S Beck & Son: at the house furnishing store, south side of Pa ave, between 9th & 10th sts. Boarding: Mrs R A Beck can accommodate 5 or 6 gentlemen with board: location is pleasant: Pa ave, over L S Beck & Son's house-furnishing store.

For sale: valuable farm, 65 acres, fronting on the road leading from the toll-gate to the Anacostia bridge. Call on the subscriber residing thereon. –John A Bartruff

Dr Alexander was appointed a few years ago the Bishop of Jerusalem. Being a Jew himself, it was supposed that his elevation to this new bishopric would exert a happy influence in hastening the introduction of Israelites generally into the true fold. Papers received by the last steamer informs us, that the Bishop died on his way from Jerusalem to Egypt, via Gaza, Nov 21. He was arrested by apoplexy.

Senate: 1-Ptn from Phoebe Pack, asking a pension. 2-Ptn from Saml Grice, asking compensation for losses sustained by having his vessel impressed into the service of the U S. 3-Ptn from the legal reps of Wm Shippen, asking payment of a certificate issued under the Continental Congress. 4-Cmte on the Post Ofc & Post Roads: bill for the relief of Nathl Kuykendall, with a report, was ordered to be printed. 5-Cmte of Claims: adverse report on the ptn of Isaac Lilley. 6-Cmte of Claims: the case of Jos Ratcliffe was ordered to lie on the table for the present. 7-The bill for the relief of Pierre Menard & others, sureties of Felix St Vrain, was passed.

Coroner's Inquest: on Monday at the house of Chas Finnegan, on C st, over the body of a well know hack-driver, Henry Bershandt, commonly called Dutch Henry, who died very suddenly the day previously while calling at the house of the said Finnegan. Verdict: his death had probably been caused by a fixed habit of intemperance.

Beautiful residence for sale: the subscriber, being desirous of returning to Barbadoes in March, offers for sale his residence, called **The Retreat**, in Wash Co, D C. The improvements consist of a spacious brick mansion, with every outbldg, for the accommodation of a large family or boarding school. It is on the Rockville turnpike road: will be sold with 34 or 64 acres of land. The title is indisputable. Possession can be given on Mar 1, or earlier if desired. Apply on the premises to Richd P Pile.

Sale of valuable property: by virtue of a decree made by the Orphans Court of Wash Co, D C, in the matter of the ptn of Leonard Storm, guardian of the minor children of John & Sarah Boose, dec'd, the undersigned will sell, on Mar 6, 12½ acres, more or less, of land, lying on Piney Branch & north of the farm of Wm Holmead, being the late residence of said John Boose. Title undisputed. For further particulars, apply to the undersigned, or to A H Lawrence, Atty at Law. –Leonard Storm, Guardian

THU FEB 12, 1846
House of Reps: 1-Ptn of Jos Mace, a Revolutionary soldier, asking for additional pension. 2-Ptn of Nicholas Siscoe, asking for a pension. 3-Ptn of John Pickett & others, of Mass, for remuneration & indemnity. 4-Ptn of Sarah Felton, of Wendell, Mass, wid/o Stephen Felton, a private in the Revolutionary war, praying for a pension. 5-Ptn of Relief Gibson, of Mass, wid/o Thos Gibson, a private, & also a non-commissioned ofcr in the Revolutionary war, praying for a pension. 6-Ptn of John Mason, of Va, asking pay for certain cannon manufactured by him for the naval service. 7-Ptn of Zachariah Walker, for compensation for services rendered in saving the records in the Capitol at the time of its conflagration in 1814. 8-Ptn of

Ephraim Shaler, late a Capt of the U S army, for a pension. 9-Ptn of Thos Reed, of New Orleans, praying for a pension. 10-Ptn of Griffin Kelley, of Clark Co, Ky, praying for a pension for injuries received in the service of the U S in the defence of the Northwestern frontier from the attacks of the Indians.

Senate: 1-Cmte on pensions: an adverse reports on the ptns of Caroline E Saunders; on the ptns of Hannah Branch & Jane Heyl: ordered to be printed. 2-Cmte on Private Land Claims: bill for the relief of Benj Ballard.

FRI FEB 13, 1846
House of Reps: 1-Bill from the Senate for the relief of the legal reps of Pierre Menard, Josiah F Betts, Jacob Feaman, & Edmund Roberts, of Illinois, sureties of Felix St Vrain, late Indian agent, dec'd, was read & referred to the Cmte of Claims. 2-Cmte on Foreign Affairs: adverse report on the ptn of A H Everett: laid on the table. 3-Cmte on Revolutionary Pensions: adverse report on the ptn of Thos Harvey: laid on the table. 4-Cmte of Claims: bill for the relief of Josiah Haskell: committed. Same cmte, bill for the relief of Danl Steenrod: committed.

The business of the subscriber conducted by Gibson & Mitchell, agents, at 8th & Market Space, was discontinued on Jan 19. Books have been left with Henry Carter. The stock of goods will be supplied at the lowest N Y & Phil auction prices.
–W G W White

On Jan 27, the dwlg of the Hon Marshall M Strong, of Racine, w T, was consumed by fire, & Mrs Strong, together with her son about 4 years, & dght 2 years of age, perished in the flames. Mr Strong was absent at Madison.

Mrd: on Feb 10, at Winter Hill, Fairfax Co, Va, by Rev Robt T Nixon, Mr Thos Murgatroyd to Miss Sarah Ann Virginia, d/o Col John Crump, of Fairfax Co, Va.

Mrd: on Feb 10, by Rev N Wilson, Thos H Havenner to Mary Cornelia, d/o the Rev Norval Wilson, all of Wash City.

Died: on Feb 4, in N Y, Mrs Emma, w/o the Hon Ely Moore, & d/o the late Gilbert Coutant. She leaves a young family of helpless & weeping children, & a heart-broken bereaved husband. -Herald

Fruit trees from the celebrated nursery of John Perkins, of N J. Please hand orders to the subscriber. -Enoch Tucker

Notice: By writ of fieri facias, at the suit of Jeremiah Murphy, I have levied on all the right & title of Jos Marteni to the improvements in the premises now in the occupancy of said Marteni & others, on 10th st, in square 348, to satisfy the said Murphy in plea of debt. I will proced to sell the same for cash, on Feb 18.
–Richd I A Culverwell, Constable

Senate: 1-Ptn from Ann Kelly, asking a pension. 2-Ptn from Hezekiah Wingate, asking a pension. 3-Cmte on Pensions: adverse report in the case of Mary Jane West. 4-Bill to authorize the Sec of the Treas to make an arrangement or compromise with Mangle M Quackenboss & his co-obligors, or any of them, for claims on bonds given by them as sureties to the U S: read & passed. 5-Bill for the relief of the legal reps of Wm D Cheever, dec'd: ordered to be engrossed & read a 3rd time. 6-Bill for the relief of the legal reps of Geo B Duvall, a Cherokee Indian, was considered in Cmte of the whole, & ordered to be engrossed & read a 3rd time.

The late Chas Cutts: was born in Portsmouth, N H, of an ancient & honorable family: maternal grandfather was the venerated Pres Holyoke, of Cambridge College, Mass; he himself was a distinguished graduate of that university; for many years represented his native town in the State Legislature; was Speaker of that body, a member of the U S Senate, & Sec of the Senate. His last illness was short. His afflicted widow & children find consolation in the belief that he left not an enemy or an ill-wisher behind him. [The N H & Maine papers will please copy.]

Death of Dr J C Jenifer, from the St Helena [Arkansas] Star. On Jan 20, there was a rencontre in this place between Dr John C Jenifer & Henry M Grant, in which Jenifer was shot in the abdomen, causing death in a few minutes. Society has been deprived of one of its most useful members, the medical profession of one of its brightest ornaments. Dr Jenifer had resided in this place & vicinity since 1836. The cause was a professional misunderstanding between Jenifer & Grant. Dr Grant gave himself up to the civil authorities immediately after the occurrence. To his friends in Md, Dr Jenifer he died remote from them & the scenes of his childhood. His body was attended to the grave by the largest attendance of mourning friends that we have witnessed since our sojourn in Arkansas.

The undersigned have formed a copartnership, under the name of C Eckloff & Sons, & will continue in the Merchant Tailors & Fashionable Clothing Store, on Pa ave, south side, between 12th & 13th sts. –C Eckloff, Jo W Eckloff, Fred Eckloff. [It being necessary to close my late business, I urgently request all who are indebted to me to make an early settlement & solicit a continuation of their custom by my friends at the above store. –C Eckloff]

Fatal accident yesterday by an explosion in the laboratory at the Navy Yard: Mr Jas Dailey, from Phil, was killed. He was a man of excellent character. A s/o Capt Mitchell, of the steamboat **Oceola**, had an arm broken.

Perserverance Fire Co: following were elected ofcrs on Feb 5:
C Buckingham, Pres   Valentine Harbaugh, Sec
Geo S Gideon, V P   Silas M Hill, Treas

Wash Corp: 1-Ptn from Kinlaugh Deneale: referred to the Cmte of Claims. 2-Bill for the relief of M P Mohun: referred to the Cmte on Improvements. 3-Bills for the relief of Geo Stewart & the relief of Thos Welch: referred to the Cmte of Claims.

SAT FEB 14, 1846
Senate: 1-Cmte of Commerce: Bill for the relief of Jos Holmes & others, owners of schnr **Industry**. Same cmte: bill for the relief of Joshua Knowles, jr, & others, owners of schnr **Garnet**. Same cmte: bill for the relief of Levi Eldridge & others, owners of the schnr **Union**. Same cmte: bill for the relief of Andrew Blake & others, owners of the schnr **Two Brothers**. 2-Cmte on Private Lands: bill for the relief of Ann Hackett & others, heirs of Thos Kelly: committed. Same cmte: adverse report on the case of Garland R Lincecum: laid on the table. 3-Bill for the relief of Jos Kimball & the bill for the relief of Symington Buffenbarger: were read: to be reported to the House. 4-Bill for the relief of the heirs of Col Wm Grayson was read. 5-Bill for the relief of the heirs of Capt Presley Thornton: bill was rejected in cmte. 6-Bill for the relif of Eliz Jones & other children, if any, of John Carr: reported to the House with a recommendation that it do not pass.

Mrs E O Robinson, 1st & B sts, Capitol Hill, has 3 chambers & 1 parlor, which she is desirous of filling. They can be had with or without board.

Household & kitchen furniture at auction on Feb 18, at the residence of Mr Wm Browne, on G st, between 17th & 18th sts. -R W Dyer, auct

The Moosup Mill, in Sterling, Conn, owned by Henry Valentine, of N Y, was totally destroyed by fire on Feb 7. Loss about $25,000.

Mrd: on Feb 12, by Rev John P Donelan, Mr Richd White to Miss Sarah A Fletcher, both of Wash.

Died: on Feb 13, Mrs Eliz Lenman, in her 49th year. Her funeral is this day at 4½ o'clock, from her late residence on 11th st.

MON FEB 16, 1846
On Sat last, as a respectable colored man named Isaac Taylor, was going to his work, he fell down on Md ave & died almost immediately. He was a person of sober & industrious habits, & died of a fit of epilepsy.

A great number of person assembled last Fri night at Brown's Hotel, to witness the lightning up of that old & popular establishment with gas. The patentee of this apparatus is Mr Benj Franklin Coston, of the navy. The light in front of the hotel was observable for at least a mile. In the ladies' parlor, the splendid glass chandelier has 4 burners of gas light, which makes the room alike brilliant & beautiful.

Dr Boussac, of the Parish of Plaquemines, La, was killed on Feb 4, when his horse took fright, ran away, & broke the carriage to pieces. The doctor was thrown to the ground, his skull fractured, & he died instantly.

A petition was recently presented in the Ohio Legialature from John Noel, of Jackson Co, praying that Geo Rodebaugh be divorced from his wife, & that she be given to petitioner, in pursuance of a previous contract of marriage.

House of Reps: 1-Bill introduced to pay Capt John B Crozier's company of Tennessee mounted volunteers: referred to the Cmte of Claims. 2-Bill for the relief of the heirs of Col Wm Grayson was again passed over informally. 3-Bill for the relief of Thompson Hutchinson: rejected. 4-Bill granting a pension to Jas Davidson, of Fentress Co, Tenn: sent to the Senate. 5-Bill for the payment of the passage of Gen Lafayette to the U S: postponed. 6-Bill for the relief of Geo D Spencer: sent to the Senate. 7-Bill for the relief of John Anderson, of Missouri: laid aside. 8-Bill for the relief of Chas M Gibson: laid aside. 9-Bill granting a pension to Jas Mains, & the bill granting a pension to Jas Wyman: passed over informally. 10-Bill for the relief of the sureties of Elijah J Weed, late Quartermaster of the Marine Corps: passed over informally. 11-Bill granting a pension to Wm McCauley was ordered to be reported to the House. 12-Bill granting a pension to John Ficklin: read. 13-Ptn of Mrs Cecilia Higgins & documents: referred. 14-Additional evidence in the matter of Simeon Caswell, praying for an invalid pension. 15-Ptn of Gustavus Denevue, of the Territory of Wisconsin, asking repayment of certain moneys paid for lands covered by water. 16-Ptn of Geo Alexander & A Cornwall, of Missouri, praying to be allowed a pre-emption to a tract of land in said State upon which they have a mill erected. 17-The ptn of Sally Hart, for the allowance of a pension for services of her husband, Fred'k A Hart, in the war of the Revolution. 18-Ptn of Capt Staring, for the completion of Cattaraugus harbor. 19-Ptn of Hugh Riddle, of the State of N Y, for an invalid pension. 20-Ptn of Wm Causey, of Guilford Co, N C, a soldier of the last war, wounded in defence of his country, asking to be placed on the invalid pension roll.

Died: on Feb 15, Major Saml Raub, jr, formerly of Pa, but for several years a resident of Wash City, in his 54th year. His funeral is on Tue at 2 o'clock, from his late residence on 13th st, near Md ave.

Died: yesterday, in Gtwn, Mrs Mary K, consort of Jos Mountz, & d/o the late Rezin B Offutt, aged 35 years. Her funeral is from her late residence on Green st, tomorrow, at 9 a m.

Died: on Feb 2, at Cambridge, Md, Capt Edw Trippe, aged 75 yers, long known as cmder of the first line of steamboats established between Balt & Phil, & who after the close of the last war, superintended, & after commanded, the first steamboat upon the waters of Chesapeake Bay.

Died: at St Augustine, Fla, Col Geo W Cole, Receiver in that district, in his 58th year, a native of Chesterfield Co, Va. [The date is not readable. This is a current death notice.]

Orphans Court of Wash Co, D C. Ordered, on application that letters of administration on the personal estates of Philip Brady, Chas Cook, Oliver Dunin, & Sutherland Bell, late of the U S Army, dec'd, be granted to Thos S Bryant, unless cause to the contrary be shown on or before Mar 6 next. –Ed N Roach, Reg/o wills

Obit-died: on Jan 31, on board the U S frig **Cumberland**, in his 23rd year, Passed Midshipman Henry Ashton, s/o the late Col Henry Ashton, of Wash City. But a few weeks since he left his city in apparently full health; his orders to sea came at a most inopportune & unfortunate moment, at a moment when he was about to experience the consummation of the dearest hopes a young & ardent heart can entertain, the union in marriage with her whom he had chosen as his companion through the uncertain sea of life. In obedience to his orders, he joined the **Cumberland**, then lying at Boston. On the very day that would have witnessed his bridal, he was borne, with military honors, to the tomb.

TUE FEB 17, 1846
Senate: 1-Ptn from E Whitten, for loss property while in the naval service of the U S. 2-Ptn from Wm Davis, asking indemnification for property lost during the war. 3-Ptn from John S Gilbert, asking to be allowed to construct a dry-dock for the U S, agreeably to the patent of said Gilbert. 4-Ptn from Eli Hinds, for a pension. 5-Cmte on the Judiciary: asked to be discharged from the futher consideration of the ptn of the legal reps of Eliza W Ripley, & that it be referred to the Cmte of Claims. Same cmte: asking to be discharged from the further consideration of the ptn of Asa Andrews, & that it be referred to the Cmte of Claims. 6-Cmte on Military Affairs: adverse report on the ptn of Danl Raub. 7-Bill for the relief of True Putney & Hugh Riddle. 8-Bill for the relief of Jos Kemball; relief of Symington Buffenbarger; relief of Jas Davidson, of Fentress Co, Tenn; relief of Geo D Spencer; relief of the legal reps of Wm D Cheever, dec'd; & relief of the legal reps of Geo B Duvall, a Cherokee Indian: all appropriately referred. 9-Relief of Elijah White was taken up in Cmte of the Whole. Elijah White represents that he was appointed sub-agent for the Indians west of the Rocky Mountains in 1842; in pursuance of instructions from the War Dept, he proceeded in the spring of 1842 to the western frontier of Missouri, where he succeeded in getting together a band of Oregon emigrants, whom he conducted on their journey to the Willamette valley. In 1845 he returned to the U S at the request of the Oregon Legislature, as a sort of bearer of dispatches. On his way to the U S he was attacked & robbed by the Pawnee Indians, & he claims to be reimbursed by the U S the amount of the value of the property of which he was thus despoiled. He engaged 3 men to accompany him, & they too were robbed. Even if this were sufficient, the objection is fatal thay they were not lawfully within the Indian country according to the act of 1834. Bill was laid on the table.

House of Reps: 1-Cmte of the Whole House be for the present discharged from the consideration of the bill 107, for the benefit of Jas Dixon: the same be recommitted to the Cmte for the District of Columbia. 2-Bill for the relief of John Chasseand, Consul for Syria & Palestine: referred to the Cmte on Commerce. 3-Relief of the reps of Jno Habersham, dec'd: referred to the Cmte of Claims. 4-Bill for the relief of Jas Green; bill for the relief of Israel McBee, a Revolutionary soldier; & bill for the relief of Jas Jones: all bills to be introduced. 5-Ptn of Thos Thody was referred to the Cmte on the Judiciary. 6-The Sec of War is to furnish this House with certified copies of the papers on file in the Pension Ofc in support of the ptn of Freelove Waid, wid/o Increase Waid.

Orphans Court of Wash Co, D C. Letters of administration on the personal estate of Thos R Hampton, late of said county, dec'd. –Robt Ricketts, adm

The Indianapolis Democrat states that the public in the vicinity of the residence of the Rev Nelson R Ellis, of Wash township, Marion Co, have been much shocked by finding his lifeless body in his own barn, on Jan 29, with a bullet hole through it. His gun was laid across the wind mill, with a string fastened to the trigger, & the string passed around the guard or breach of the gun, so as to have easily caused it to fire.

Died: on Sunday, Miss Mary C Hamilton, in her 60th year. Her funeral is tomorrow at 3 o'clock, from the residence of Stanislaus Murray, on 5th st.

Barton Hall for sale: by virtue of a decree of St Mary's Court, sitting as a Court of Equity, passed Dec 3, 1845, the subscribers, as trustees, will expose to public sale on Mar 10, 1846, at the Court-house in Leonardtown, the tract of land known by the name of *Barton Hall*-331 acres more or less. This land is situated on the west side of St Clement's Bay, in St Mary's Co, Md. –B G Harris, John H Key, Trustees

Orphans Court of Wash Co, D C. In the case of Danl Whitney, adm of Peter Sherman, of Wisconsin Territory, the adminstrator & Court have appointed Mar 6 next, for final settlement of his administration. –Ed N Roach, reg/o wills

For rent, dwlg house on Capitol Hill lately occupied by Mr Serruys, the Belgian Minister. Apply to D Vass.

WED FEB 18, 1846
American Colonization Society: 29th annual meeting: held in Washington on Jan 20.
Following ofcrs elected: Pres: Hon Henry Clay
Vice Presidents:

John C Herbert, of Md	Theodore Frelinghuysen, of N Y
Gen John H Cocke, of Va	Louis McLane, of Balt
Danl Webster, of Mass	Moses Allen, of N Y
Chas F Mercer, of Florida	Gen W Jones, of Wash
Rev Jeremiah Day, D D, of Conn	Jos Gales, of Wash

Rt Rev Wm Meade, D D, Bishop o/Va
John McDonogh, of Louisiana
Geo Wash Lafayette, of France
Rev Jas O Andrew, Bishop o/M E Church
Wm Maxwell, of Va
Elisha Whittlesey, of Ohio
Walter Lowrie, of N Y
Jacob Burnet, of Ohio
Joshua Darling, of N H
Dr Stephen Duncan, of Miss
Wm C Rives, of Va
Rev J Laurie, D D, of Wash
Rev Wm Winans, of Miss
Jas Boorman, of N Y C
Henry A Foster, of N Y
Dr John Ker, of Miss
Robt Campbell, of Ga
Peter D Vroom, of N J
Jas Garland, of Va
Rev T Morris, Bishop o/M E Church, Ohio
Rt Hon Lord Bexley, of London
Wm Short, of Phil
Williard Hall, of Delaware
Rt Rev Bishop Otey, of Tenn
Gerald Ralston, of London
Rev Courtland Van Rensselaer, of N J
Dr Hodgkin, of London
Rev E Burgess, D D, of Mass
Thos R Hazard, of Providence, R I
Dr Thos Massie, o/Tye River Mills, Va
Gen Alex'r Brown, of Va
Maj Gen Winfield Scott, Wash
Rev Thos E Bond, D D, N Y
Rev A Alexander, D D, N J
Saml Wilkeson, of N Y
L Q C Elmer, of N J
Jas Railey, of Miss
Rev Geo W Bethune, D D, of Phil
Rev C C Cuyler, D D, of Phil
Elliot Cresson, of Phil
Anson G Phelps, N Y
Rev Leonard Woods, D D, Andover, Mass
Jonathan Hyde, Bath Maine
Rev J P Durbin, D D, Carlisle, Pa
Rev Beverly Waugh, Bishop o/M E Church-Balt
Rev Dr W B Johnson, of S C
Moses Shepherd, of Balt
John Gray, of Fredericksburg, Va
Bishop McIlvain, of Ohio
Rev Dr Edgar, of Nashville, Tenn
Rev P Lindsley, D D, of Tenn
Hon J R Underwood, of Ky
Hon J W Huntington, of Conn
Hon P White, of Putney, Vt
Hon C Marsh, of Woodstock, Vt

Wash Corp: 1-Ptn from Henry Gray: referred to the Cmte of Claims. 2-Ptn from Chas Borremans: referred to the Cmte of Claims. 3-Ptn from Robt Beale: referred to the Cmte of Claims. 4-Cmte on Improvements: referred the ptn of H B Sawyer, for an appropriation for a flag footway in the First Ward. 5-Bill for the relief of Joshua L Henshaw: referred to the Cmte on Public Schools. 6-Cmte of Claims: asked to be discharged from the further consideration of the ptn of Thos R Mackey.

Notice: the undersigned Com'rs appointed by Worcester Co Court-Md, to value & divide the real estate of Eliz Cottman, late of Somerset Co, [the said real estate being in Worcester Co,] according to the provisions of the act of Assembly, do hereby give notice to all concerned that we shall meet at Col Wm S B Cottman's on Apr 22 next, to proceed in the business for which we are appointed. –Cord Hazzard, John E Hayward, Peter Dickerson, Moses C Smith, Saml D Harper, Com'rs

House of Reps: 1-Cmte of Claims: adverse reports on the cases of Pacificus Ord; on the case of Geo E Graves, Jos T Atchison, of the administrators of Col John Anderson, & of Jas B Watson, assignee of P G Hambaugh: all laid on the table. 2-Cmte of Claims: adverse report on the case of Jos Sawyer; on the cases of Benj Sayre, Thos Jarrett, & R A Clements: all laid on the table. 3-Cmte of Claims: discharged from the consideration of the memorial of B S Roberts: laid on the table. 4-Cmte on the Judiciary: adverse report on the case of Jos De La Francis: laid on the table. Same cmte: discharged from the case of Benj Balch & associates, for the incorporation of a Nat'l Life Insurance Co: laid on the table. 5-Cmte on Revolutionary Claims: discharged from the case of Elijah W Brown: laid on the table. Same cmte: reported adversely in the case of Susan Campbell: laid on the table. 6-Cmte on Private Land Claims: bill for the relief of Eli Merrill: committed. 7-Cmte on Indian Affairs: adverse reports on the cases of Wm Mathias: laid on the table. 8-Cmte on Revolutionary Pensions: discharged from the consideration of the cases of Benj J Porter, Lucy Forbes, Mary B Perry, & other heirs of John Donnell & John Hoge: laid on the table. Same cmte: reported a bill for the relief of Wm Bean: committed. Same cmte: bill for the relief of Ebenezer Contant: committed. 9-Cmte on Invalid Pensions: made adverse reports on the cases of Joshua Pittman, Littleton Crabtree, & John Ashton: laid on the table. 10-Cmte on Revolutionary Pensions: adverse report on the case of Wm Anglea: laid on the table. 11-Cmte on Invalid Pensions: was discharged from the cases of F B DeBellevue, Edith, wid/o Jno Alexander, & Patrick Goss: laid on the table. Same cmte: reported verbally against the case of Darius Hawkins: laid on the table. Same cmte: adverse reports on the cases of John Dixon, Saml Coney, Richd Robins, & of citizens of Alabama asking the allowance of a back pension to N A Penland: laid on the table. 12-Bill for the relief of Geo Jackson & others. 13-A select cmte reported a bill for the relief of Alvan C Goel, with a detailed report: committed. 14-Cmte on the Judiciary: adverse report on the case of Benj Crawford: laid on the table.

N Y Sun on Mon: Express from Squam Inlet-ship **John Milton**, Capt Starkey, N Y & New Orleans packet, driven ashore on Sun morning about 8 o'clock. The Capt & his wife, their child & servant, & 37 persons, passengers or sailors, perished in attempting to save themselves. Cargo all lost. The snow storm of Sat & Sun was the most severe ever known in that vicinity. [Feb 24th newspaper: wreck of the ship **John Minturn**, which left New Orleans on Jan 24, & went ashore on Sun, in the very height of the storm. The captain, his wife, son, dght, & servant were among the sufferers. Among the passengers who perished, was Mrs Stark, with her son, about 12 or 14 years of age, her dght, a female servant, & Mrs Forbes, the w/o Mr Forbes, one of the cabin passengers. On board the vessel were Capt Babcock & mate of the schnr **Van Buren**, which was wrecked at Galveston bar, both of whom drowned.]

Senate: 1-Ptn from Mary D Wade, for a pension. 2-Ptn from Isaac Barnes, asking a pre-emption tight to a portion of public lands in Oregon. 3-Papers in the case of Mira Alexander were taken from the files, & referred to the Cmte on Military Affairs. 4-Documents in relation to the claim of Jas Foster were submitted.

5-Documents in relation to the claim of the wid/o Jas Ware were submitted. 6-Peter Frost had leave to withdraw his petition & papers. 7-Cmte of Claims: asking to be discharged from the ptn of Mary B Hook, wid/o Col Jas Hook, & that it be referred to the Cmte on Military Affairs. 8-Cmte on Naval Affairs: bill for the relief of Ebenezer Ballard, with a report, was ordered to be printed. Same cmte: bill for the relief of Jas Lowe, with a report, was ordered to be printed. 9-Cmte on the Judiciary: bill for the relief of Jos Chaires, exc of Benj Chaires, dec'd. 10-Cmte on Public Lands: bill for the relief of Geo Gordon, with a report, & ordered to be printed. 11-Cmte on Pensions: discharged from the further consideration of the ptn of Carey H Seely: referred to the Cmte on Naval Affairs.

THU FEB 19, 1846
Senate: 1-Ptn from Thompson Hutchinson, asking arrears of pension. 2-Ptn from the heirs of John Carr, asking for arrears of pension. 3-Ptn from F A Thornton & others, for commutation pay due their father. 4-Ptn from Oliver K Freeman, praying the passage of a joint resolution for furnishing the clerk of the county court of Macon Co, Ala, with copies of all the public documents which have been published in relation to the lands ceded to the U S by the Creek Indians. 5-Ptn from Maria Ostrander, wid/o a dec'd Revolutionary soldier, praying to be allowed arrears of pension. 6-Adverse reports made in the cases of Louis Evans, Henry Northup, Caroline E Saunders, Jas Hyde, & Hannah Branch. 7-Adverse report in the case of Isaac Lilly came up: it was recommitted to the Cmte of Claims. 8-Mr Jonathan Thompson, of N Y, had leave to withdraw his papers.

House of Reps: 1-Cmte of Claims: bill for the relief of the legal reps of Pierre Menard, Josiah T Betts, Jacob Sherman, & Edmund Roberts, of the State of Illinois, sureties of Felix St Vrain, late Indian agent, reported the same with an amendment: bill was then committed. 2-Papers of Jos Nock, now on file, were referred to the Cmte of Claims. 3-Cmte on the Judiciary: adverse report on the memorial of Sarah B H Stith: laid on the table. 4-Cmte on Revolutionary Claims was discharged from the memorial of Eleazey Blake: laid on the table. 5-Cmte on Foreign Affairs: made an adverse report on the ptn of H Gold Rogers: laid on the table. 6-Cmte on Revolutionary Pensions: bill for the relief of Lewis Mattison: committed. 7-Cmte on Invalid Pensions: adverse report on the case of Amelia Baldwin, wid/o Alfred Baldwin: laid on the table. Same cme: bill for the relief of John Patten: committed. Also, made adverse reports on the cases of Benj Kerlin, John L Watson, Susannah Langreen, & Jas Campbell: laid on the table.

The slander suit, Mary N Ladd vs Marietta Ingham, tried last week at the Orleans [N Y] Circuit, resulted in a verdict for the plntf of $3,000. This suit grew out of the celebrated watch case, which occurred at the Le Roy Female Seminary, some 3 or 4 years since. The plntf, who was a pupil, was charged by the dfndnt, the teacher, with having stolen a gold watch. The dfndnt was indicted in Genesee Co for false imprisonment in reference to the same matter, & suffered a slight fine.

Fatal railroad accident on Fri, this side of Lynn Hotel depot, by the train of cars which left Boston, by which the engine was thrown off the track, & the baggage-master & brakeman, Mr Joshua Gardiner, was instantly killed. Mr Gardiner was standing on the platform car.

Mrd: on Feb 12, by Rev Mr French, Saml Bush Bleight, M D, of Phil, to Georgianna Alexander, y/d/o the last Geo Chapman, of Prince Wm Co, Va.

Mrd: on Feb 5, at the residence of Maj K B Gibbs, of *Fort George* Island, Florida, by Rev I F Young, Gen Duncan L Clinch to Sophia H Couper, d/o Geo Gibbs.

Mrd: on Feb 12, at *Spring Hill*, West River, Md, by Rev John Miller, Richd W Templeman to Annie Caroline, only d/o Rev D H Battee, of that place.

Died: on Feb 16, Mrs Eleline G Waring, w/o Mr John P Waring, about a day after the death of her infant child of 2 months old. Her recent return to reside among those who knew her longest & best, was hailed with much satisfaction; but an all wise Providence disappointed our expectations by removing her to a better world. –C

Circuit Court of Wash Co, D C-in Chancery. Wm S McPherson vs John McPherson, et al. Notice is given that I shall attend at my ofc, in Gtwn, on Feb 28, to hear parties & receive proofs, & shall proceed to state for the Court a distribution of the nett fund in the Trustees hands among the heirs at law of Sarah McPherson, dec'd, & their reps or assignees. –Clement Cox, auditor

Circuit Superior Court of Law & Chancery for Fauquier Co, Va: the Bank of the U S vs John B Steenbergen. The parties, cmplnts & dfndnts, in the said cause, are notificed that on Mar 24 next, at the ofc of Jas B Latimer, a Com'r for the State of Va, residing in the city of Balt, in Fayette st, shall proceed to take the depositions of sundry witnesses, to be offered in evidence on my behalf, as a petitioning creditor of said John B Steenbergen's said cause. –Marcus Denison -John M Herndon, Atty

Orphans Court of Wash Co, D C. Letters testamentary on the personal estate of Ann Kedglie, late of said county, dec'd. –Saml Stott, David Munro, excs

FRI FEB 20, 1846
Providence Journal: announces the death of Wm G Goddard, late Prof of Belles Lettres in Brown Univ, who died very suddenly on Feb 16, at aged 52 years. While seated at the dinner table with his family, he was surprised with sensations of intense suffocation in the throat, proceeding, as is supposed, from a paralysis of the muscles of deglutition, & in a few moments his life was at an end.

House of Reps: 1-The Speaker laid before the House a letter from the Sec of the Navy, transmitting the report of the Naval Court of Inquiry appointed to investigate the legality of the expenditures of the squadron in Florida during the late Seminole Indian war, under the command of Lt John T McLaughlin: referred to the Cmte on Expenditures in the Navy Dept. 2-Com'r of Pensions to transmit to the Clerk of this House the papers on file in his ofc connected with the application of Wm Paton, of Ky, a soldier of the Revolutionary war, for a pension. 3-Cmte on Revolutionary Pensions: reported a bill for the relief of John Hawkins: committed. 4-Ptn of Cadwallader Ringgold, Lt in the U S Navy. 5-Ptn of Jos Bryan, a purser in the U S Navy. 6-Ptn of Benj Crawford, on the subject of preventing explosions of steam boilers. 7-Memorial of Dr John Baldwin in relation to certain certificates issued by the U S Treas as evidence of the award made in his favor by the mixed commission between the U S & Mexico, authorized by the convention of Apr 11, 1839. 8-Ptn of Lydia Bridgman & others, widow of Revolutionary soldiers, praying for pensions under the act of 1838. 9-Ptn of Catharine Stover, praying for a pension.
10-Memorial of Saml P Todd, asking an allowance for commissions on certain bills of exchange. 11-Ptn of the heirs of Capt Richd Lucas, praying for commutation pay. 12-Ptn of Linchfield Sharp, for a pension. 13-Ptn of Wm Stubblefield, praying for a pension.

Senate: 1-Ptn from Solomon Drew, of Wash City, asking compensation for services as provost marshal of the legionary court. 2-Ptn from Edw Earle, asking Gov't to purchase his patent for preventing canvas & cordage from mildew & dry-rot. 3-Ptn from J W Taylor & others, asking the adjustment of certain private land claims. 4-Ptn from Cornelius P Van Ness, late collector of the port of N Y, asking repayment of certain moneys improperly paid by him into the Treas of the U S. 5-Ptn from Capt Holmes & mate of the schnr **Victory**, asking that a light-house may be fixed at Cattaraugus harbor. 6-Ptn from C W Young, asking a grant of land in the Oregon territory. 7-Saltmarsh & Fuller had leave to withdraw their papers from the files of the Senate. 8-Cmte on Patents: adverse report on the claim of David Little. 9-Cmte on the Public Lands: asking to be discharged from the further consideration of the ptn of John A Rogers, & that it be referred to the Cmte of Claims. 10-Cmte of Claims: bill for the relief of Amos Kendall.

New Third Ward Market-house meeting held at Mr John McLeod's Academy on Feb 17: Col Wm Doughty called to the chair, & J A M Duncanson appointed sec. On motion of Mr Hugh B Sweeney, a cmte of 6 were appointed in regard to the erection of a market-house in the northern portion of the Third Ward:

Wm Doughty	Hugh B Sweeney
John Y Bryant	Isaac Clark
David Saunders	Jos Downing
Harvey Cruttenden	Simeon Matlock
John C Harkness	John T Walker
N P Van Zant	Geo Crandall
H G O'Neal	Henry Davis

Circuit Court of Wash Co, D C-Chancery sale: in the cause of Jas Dundas et al, vs the reps or Jos Forrest, dec'd: on Mar 5, all the valuable real estate of which Jos Forrest was seised at the time of his death, situated in Wash City: part of lot 14 in square 490, fronting on La ave, adjoining Copp's Bowling Saloon; with improvements, including a tavern, in the occupancy of Mr Douglass, enjoying a good run of business. Also, lots 13 & 14 in square 80, with a 2 story frame bldg, now occupied by Wm Anderson & Mr Hill. Also, lot 5 in square 120, part of which is under ground rent of $21 per annum. –J Forrest, Clement Cox, trustees
-R W Dyer, auct

Orphans Court of Wash Co, D C. In the case of Eleanor Dewees, admx de bonis non of Eleanor De Krafft, dec'd, the admx & Court have appointed Mar 10, for final settlement of the said dec'd's estate, & distribution of the assets in her hands.
–Ed N Roach, Reg/o wills.

Orphans Court of Wash Co, D C. In the case of Eleanor Dewees, excx of Wm Dewees, dec'd, the excx & Court have appointed Mar 10 next for final settlement of the said dec'd's estate, & distribution of the assets in her hands.
–Ed N Roach, Reg/o wills

SAT FEB 21, 1846
Imaum for sale: at public auction, on Mar 13, the splendid Arabian horse: sent by the Imaum of Museat, in one of his own ships, as a present to the President in 1840. He is of the purest blood of the desert, as was certified by the Admiral who commanded the ship which brought him over. -R W Dyer, auct

Teacher wanted at Newark Academy, at Newark, Dela: it is desirable that the teacher should be a married man, that he may board & lodge all the pupils from abroad. During the last year between 60 & 70 pupils have attended the institution, of whom some 50 were boarders. Apply to E W Gilbert, Pres of Delaware College, or to Jas L Miles, at Newark, Dela.

We the subscribers, having purchased the entire right to Saml Casey's substitute lamp oil or gas-light in the following named States: N C, S C, Ga, Ala, La, Miss, Ark, Fla, & Texas, & do hereby forewarn all persons from purchasing the same from any person except us. –Thos N Davis, Edwin Walker [Feb 27th newspaper: I am the only & sole agent for the said Saml Casey's composition or substitute for lamp oil or gas light. –H R Smeltzer]

Died: on Feb 20, Marion Virginia, y/d/o Chas W Boteler, sen, aged 8 years. Her funeral will take place from the residence of her father, on D st, on Feb 22, at half past 2 o'clock.

Died: yesterday, at the residence of Capt Forrest, Mrs Eleanor Carrol Simms, relict of the late John D Simms. Her funeral is on Mon next, at 1 p m.

Died: on Feb 17, at the residence of Geo G Coe, near Piscataway, Md, Henry Culver, in his 21st year.

MON FEB 23, 1846
House of Reps: 1-Ptn of Saml T Winlow, for a pension. 2-Ptn of Dunning R McNair, asking to be relieved from certain fines imposed on him as a mail contractor by the Postmaster Genr'l, & praying that the sum of $2,427 allowed by law to him should be paid him. 3-Memorial of Nicholas Murray & others, heirs of Jas Murray, asking to be paid arrears due to Jas Murray for Revolutionary services. 4-Papers of Jos Coe, in relation to an invalid pension. 5-Ptn & papers of Stephen Johnston, of Miami Co, Ohio, asking that a certificate therein named may be taken in payment for certain lands agreeable to the decision of Mr Whitcomb, late Com'r of the Genr'l Land Ofc. 6-Memorial of Catharine Henrietta F Johnson, wid/o Capt Hezekiah Johnson, late of the U S Army, setting forth the long & arduous services of her late husband, which resulted in his premature death; & asking for a pension as the wid/o said Capt Hezekiah Johnson. 7-Cmte of Claims: adverse reports on the cases of Zachariah Lawrence; & of Conrad House & D & J Wilkinson: laid on the table. Same cmte: bill for the relief of Jacob L Vance: committed. 8-Cmte on Public Lands: bill for the relief of the heirs of John Whitsett: committed. 9-Cmte on the Judiciary: bill from the Senate on the case of Mangle M Quackenboss & his co-obligors: laid on the table. Also, made an adverse-verbal, report on the case of Mason Vannoy, Wm Harris, & Wm H Moore: laid on the table. 10-Cmte on the Judiciary: adverse report on the case of Jacob Thody: laid on the table. 11-Cmte on Revolutionary Claims: bill for the relief of the legal reps of Tarlton Woodson, dec'd: committed. 12-Bill for the relief of Geo Jackson: referred to the Cmte on Indians. 13-Cmte on the Post Ofc & Post Roads: reported a joint resolution for the relief of Wm B Stokes, surviving partner of John C Stockton & Co: committed. 14-Cmte of Claims: adverse report on the case of Jas K Blount: laid on the table. 15-Cmte on Private Land Claims: bill for the relief of Solomon Russell: committed. 16-Cmte on Indian Affairs: bill for the relief of Wm J Price: committed. Same cmte: bill for the relief of J & L Ward, of Wisconsin: committed. 17-Bill granting a pension to Wm McCauley, reported from the Cmte of the Whole, came up in order, & was sent to the Senate for concurrence. 18-Bill granting a pension to John Ficklin was sent to the Senate for concurrence. 19-Bill introduced for the relief of Israel McBee, of Tenn, which was referred to the Cmte on Revolutionary Claims. Same for the bill for the relief of Jas Green. 20-Cmte on Patents: bill from the Senate for the relief of Chas G Page, asked that the bill be put on its passage. [The 2nd, 7th, & 15th sections of the act of Jul 4, 1836, prohibits the granting of patents to any person appointed or employed in the Patent Ofc.]-laid on the table. 21-Bill to pay Chas M Gibson for a wagon & horse lost in the public service in the late Indian war in Florida: laid on the table. 22-Bill granting a pension to John Ficklin: sent to the Senate for concurrence. 23-Bill for the relief of Chas Benns: passed over informally. 24-Bill granting

commutation of half-pay to the heirs of Col Wm Grayson, dec'd: cmte rose without coming to any decision.

The Mobile Advertiser records the death by lightning of Miss E A C Goodman, an amiable young lady of 18 years, which happened on Feb 13.

Mrd: on Feb 19, by Rev Jas B Donelan, Mr Jos Williamson to Miss Ann Toomy, all of Wash City.

Died: at her residence in Wash City, Mrs Eliza Forrest, in her 46th year, leaving a husband & 9 children to mourn their loss. [No date-recent notice.]

Died: on Jan 7, in Paris, France, after a protracted illness, Mrs Eliz C, w/o Mr Henry J Brent, of Wash, U S A, & d/o Danl Carroll, of Duddington, of the same place.

The Verandah, a new Hotel on the European Plan, Pa ave, between 4½ st & Jackson Hall. –John Cotter, late of N Y. -Rich R Thompson, late of Coleman's Nat'l Hotel

TUE FEB 24, 1846
Philemon Chew, of PG Co, Md, has been elected Treasurer of the Chesapeake & Ohio Canal, vice Robt Barnard, resigned.

I certify that Saml Perkins, of Wash Co, D C, brought before me as a stray trespassing on his enclosures, a bay horse Colt. –Jas Crandell, Justice of the Peace [The owner is to prove property, pay charges, & take him away. –Saml Perkins, living near the *Congressional Burial Ground.*]

Pensacola, Feb 14. On Sat last, as a party of 3 men were hunting about 10 miles from East Bay, they were fired upon by Indians. One of the party, Mr Pitts, was instantly killed, & his brother severely wounded; the other, Mr Silcox, with the wounded man, succeeded in escaping. Col Crane, commanding the forticifactions in the harbor dispatched a detachment of men under the command of Lt Donalson, to cut off this body of roving Indians. We have not yet heard of the return of the troops. -Gazette

Mrd: on Feb 10, in Hinds Co, Miss, by Rev L Wylie, Col David Gordon, of Hinds Co, Miss, to Mrs Susan E Fisher, formerly of Fauquier Co, Va, but more recently of Tallahassee, Middle Florida.

Died: on Feb 15, at Phil, Lt John Cassin Henry, of the U S Navy, aged 28 years. [Feb 26th newspaper: obit-entered the navy in 1833; was examined in 1839; awarded the highest honors of his class, placing him at its head.]

Died: on Feb 11, at his residence, near Nottingham, PG Co, Md, Mr Elisha Skinner, in his 74th year.

Died: on Jan 9, Capt John Baden, aged 89.

Culpeper [Va] County Court, Feb 16, 1846: on the motion of Philip Lightfoot, the following minute was made. The Court has been informed that the death of John Shackelford, late Atty for the Commonwealth, has occurred since the last term. For more than 50 years he was a prominent member of this bar, & for 35 years the counselor of the court as Atty for the Commonwealth. A copy of this entry is to be communicated to the his widow by the Clerk in respectful condolence for her loss. –G Mauzy, Clerk

The Kilmiste Family, from Euwope, will perform at Carusi's Saloon this evening. Also, Wattie Ferguson, whose skill upon the War-pipes of the ancient Gael has been rewarded in presence of her Majesty Queen Victoria, will perform. Mr Ferguson will appear in the dress worn by him on that occasion.

House & Garden for rent: the house is on I st, between 5th & 6th sts, with a large garden & barn attached. The garden comprises about $2/3^{rd}$s of square 485. Apply to Saml Wroe, H & 5th sts.

Washington's Birthday was celebrated yesterday in Wash City with a good deal of spirit by our volunteer companies. Sgt Hiram Richey won the silver medal for the best shot. An oration was delivered by Thos J Semmes. Mr Columbus Drew read Washington's Farewell Address.

Benj Young, a young man, was stabbed in Walker's Refectory by a person named Robinson. He was arrested by John Waters, constable. Prof May considers Young to be dangerously wounded. [Feb 25th newspaper: Isaac Robinson was arrested for stabbing Benj Young. Wm Hines, who appeared to be acting in concert with him, was also arrested. They were tried last term for assaulting, with intent to kill, Wm Cox, a member of the Auxiliary Guard, on Sep 12th last. They were convicted & fined $5 each.] [Mar 20th newspaper: Robinson & Hines were both found guilty. Robinson was sentenced to the penitentiary for 3 years. Hines was sentenced to be imprisoned for 6 months in the county jail.]

The undersigned, having closed his business in this place, & about to leave the city, expresses his gratitude for the kindness & generosity manifested towards him during his residence here. –Thompson Tyler
+
The Copartnership between the subscribers, keepers of the U S Hotel in Wash City, has been this day dissolved by mutual consent. –Thompson Tyler, Jas H Birch [Jas H Birch has become the sole proprietor.]

Orphans Court of Wash Co, D C. Letters of administration on the personal estate of Beman Kelley, late of said county, dec'd. –Patrick Moran, adm

Loudoun Farm for sale: in Loudoun Co, Va: adjoins the lands of Gen Geo Rust & Messrs Hoffman & Ball, & consists of 350 acres; improvements consist of a comfortable dwlg house, built of stone, with all necessary outbldgs. Call on the subscriber, at Col Osborne's Hotel, Leesburg. –Chas Gassaway

Notice: on Mar 6 next, will be offered for sale at public auction all the Fish Stalls in the Eastern Branch Market-house, for a term ending on Mar 1, 1847. And, on Mar 7, in the same manner, all the Fish Stalls in the Centre Market-house. Terms cash, to be settled after sale. –W W Seaton, Mayor

Valuable brick house & lot for sale: situated on 5th st, near E, next to the residence of Wm Morrow, being lot 12 in square 489. Apply to A Green, Auctioneer & Commission Merchant, Concert Hall.

WED FEB 25, 1846
U S Navy Yard: Feb 21, 1846. Letter to Capt John H Aulick, U S Navy, on his leaving the yard, the workmen beg leave to express their sentiments of esteem.
John Davis, [of Abel] Master Plumber   John H Smoot, Master Joiner
Jas Tucker, Master Blacksmith   Jas McCathran, Master Carpenter
Wm M Ellis, Engineer & Machinist   John H Peake, Master Painter
Amon Woodward, Mstr Blockmaker   Jos M Padgett, Overseer of Laborers

Senate: 1-Ptn from A Whitney, asking a grant of land for the construction of a railroad from Lake Michigan to the Pacific Ocean. 2-Ptn from the heirs of Edw Armstrong, asking to be allowed arrearages of pension. 3-Cmte on Public Lands: bill for the relief of Henry Newman. Same cmte: adverse report on the ptn of Wm Pearce. 3-Bill for the relief of Semmington Buffenbarger, without amendment. 4-Cmte of Claims: bill for the relief of Peter Von Schmidt. Same cmte: adverse reports on the memorials of Jas L Sawyer & Saml Grice. Same cmte: bill for the relief of Jos Kemball, without amendment. Also, same cmte: adverse report on the ptn of Richd & Wm Armstrong: ordered to be printed. 5-Cmte on the Judiciary: adverse reports on the ptn of Edw S Osgood & on that of Caleb Green. 6-Cmte on Pensions: adverse reports on the ptns of Danl M Baker, Eliz Sailor, w/o Jacob Sailor, & Jacob Perkins: all ordered to be printed. 7-Sec of War to send to the Senate the papers in the case of John C Whittell, in which he claims 2 tracts of land under the Choctaw treaty of Dancing Rabbit Creek. 8-House bills for the relief of Wm McCauley, & for the relief of John Ficklin, were referred to the Cmte on Pensions. 9-Adverse reports on the ptn of Wm B Baker; & of Nathan Ward.

House of Reps: 1-Cmte of Claims: case of Peter Schaeffer recommitted. 2-Com'r of Pensions to transmit to the House copies of the file in his ofc connected with the application of the heirs of Eliz Conklin, of N Y, for a pension.

Died: on Feb 23, Mrs Jane, w/o Thos J Mudd, after a short illness, in her 66th year. Her funeral is this afternoon at 4 o'clock, from her late residence on 10th st.

Died: yesterday, Mrs Virginia S Essex, consort of Mr Jas F Essex, aged 23 years. Her funeral is tomorrow at 2 o'clock, from her late residence on High st, Gtwn.

Died: on Feb 24, Mrs E C Peale, consort of T R Peale, late of Phil.

THU FEB 26, 1846
Senate: 1-Ptn from the executor of Nathan Lamme, praying to be allowed commutation pay. 2-Ptn from Bancroft Woodcock, asking an extension of a patent for an improved plough. 3-Ptn from John Baldwin, asking payment of the award made in his favor under the convention for the settlement of Mexican indemnities. 4-Cmte on Finance: bill for the relief of Richd Kidd & Benj Kidd. 5-Cmte on Pensions: bill for the relief of Francis Sommeraner, with a report: ordered to be printed. 6-Adverse reports on the ptns of Wm Pennoyer, John England, & Saml Simpson: ordered to be printed. 7-Cmte on Pensions: ptns of Mary Jane West, David Ross, Eliz Sailor, & Hector Perkins: concurred in. 8-Adverse report in the case of David Little, from the Cmte on Patents, & of Edw S Osgood, from the Cmte on the Judiciary, were also concurred in. 9-Cmte of Claims: ptn of Caleb Green: passed over informally.

Citizens desiring the services of the Sweep of the Second Ward will send a note to his residence on 11th st, between L & M sts, or to the grocery store of Geo W Stewart, or Mr Reed's, F & 13th sts. –Geo Y Bowen

Orphans Court of Wash Co, D C. Letters testamentary on the personal estate of Mary C Hamilton, late of said county, dec'd. –Stans J Murray, exc

Mrd: on Feb 17, at Friendly Hall, Chas Co, Md, by Rev Mr Cruse, Mr Benj H Clements, of Wash City, to Miss Mary L C Norriss, of Chas Co, Md.

House of Reps: 1-Cmte on Naval Affairs: asked to be discharged from the consideration of the case of Benj Crawford: laid on the table. 2-Cmte on Naval Affairs: to be discharged from the consideration of the ptns of Polly Clough, & of Eliza Stevens, wid/o Cmdor Thos Holdup Stevens: laid on the table. 3-Cmte on Revolutionary Pensions: asked to be discharged from the consideration of the case of Christian Wise: laid on the table. Same cmte: adverse reports on the cases of Judith Worthen, Luke Stansbury, Ralph Young, Barbos Haley, & Rebecca White: laid on the table. 4-Cmte on Invalid Pensions: bill for the relief of Maj J P H Porter, of Tenn; & a bill for the relief of Zachariah Simmons, of Tenn: both committed. Same cmte: adverse reports on the cases of Savil Mores, Henry Sliver, Benj Holland, Thos Reed, Geo Dimsdale, Wm Turney, Wm King,Thos Rowland, Leonard Wardwell, John Brady, Jas Bumbough, Jas Parker, & Jas L Loyd: laid on the table. Same cmte: bill for the relief of Jas Gee: committed. Same cmte: bill for the relief of Lewis

Hastings; for the relief of Wm Pooler; bill granting arrears of pension to Anthony Walton Bayard; bill granting a pension to Gideon A Perry: committed. 5-Cmte of Claims: adverse reports on the cases of Jas Wood, John Felt, Henry Adams, & Catharine Adams, reps of Francis Zock & Geo Parsons: laid on the table. Same cmte: adverse report on the case of Jas McCuchen: laid on the table. Same cmte: adverse reports on the cases of Danl Spencer, Luke Hilton, Jonathan Scott, Hiram Humphreys, Chas Sampson, Henrietta M Hall, & on the reps of Richd & Jonathan Hall: laid on the table. 6-Cmte on Revolutionary Claims: asked to be discharged from the consideration of the case of Lemuel Cushman, heir of Hannah Cushman: to lie on the table. Same cmte: bill for the relief of the heirs of Sgt Maj John Champe: committed. 7-Cmte on Military Affairs: adverse report on the case of Saml M Hughes: laid on the table. Same cmte: reported a joint resolution relating to Wm S Kerchum's hand-grenade: committed. Same cmte: asked to be discharged from the consideration of the memorial of H Shubart, of Berks Co, Pa, proposing a national defence: laid on the table. 8-Com'r on Pensions to send the papers on file to the clerk of this House in relation to the application of Adam Swart, of Rochester, N Y, for a pension.

FRI FEB 27, 1846
House of Reps: 1-Ptn of Saml Billings, of Portsmouth, N H, for the allowance & payment of a fishing bounty on the schnr **Lurana**. 2-Ptn of John Loyd, for compensation for services in the last war with Great Britain. Also, the ptn of Ira Race & others, in favor of the same. 3-Ptn of Eliz Taylor, wid/o the late Maj Wm Taylor, a Revolutionary pensioner, for arrears of pension due her late husband. 4-Ptn of Judith Eggleston, of Amelia Co, Va, asking that the provision made for widows of ofcrs & soldiers of the war of the Revolution may be extended to her. 5-Ptn of Francis Yost & of John R Rogers, for a change of entries of land entered by mistake. 6-Memorial of Catharine Hodges, wid/o Benj Hodges, asking payment for a deported slave under the treaty of Ghent.

Senate: 1-Ptn from the heirs of Saml Beach, from the adm of Benj Durkee, from the legal reps of Christopher Delezenne, from Catharine Van Valkenburg, exc of B Van Valkenburg; & from the exc of Henry Tatum. 2-Cmte on Patents: bill for the relief of Calvin Emmons. 3-Cmte of Claims: bill for the relief of Jas H Causten, assignee of Col John B Hogan. 4-Cmte on Revolutionary Claims: adverse reports on the ptn of Simon Summers, Wm Shippen, & Wm Starke Jett. 5-Ptn from J Dutton, asking payment of a continental bill.

Margaret Callayham, convicted at Rochester, N Y, of arson in the 2nd degree, has been sentenced to 10 years & 6 months in the Sing Sing Penitentiary.

Accident on Wed near Schoharie court-house, N Y: Wm Getter, accidentally shot & killed his son Peter Getter, when they went out to try the barrel of a new rifle, which the young man had made.

Mrd: on Feb 23, at St Peter's Church, by Rev J Van Horseigh, Mr John Riley to Miss Catharine Carroll, all of Wash.

Died: on Feb 24, Mr Lazare Hervand, a native of Switzerland, but for the last 30 years resident of Wash. His funeral is on Feb 28 at 11 o'clock, from his late residence at Woodley, near Gtwn.

Died: on Feb 11, at her residence, on the Bayou Grosse Tete, parish of Iberville, La, Mrs Maria Brent, wid/o the late Dr John Carroll Brent, formerly of Wash City.

For rent: brick dwlg-house on 10th st. Inquire of Mr Robt W Dyer, or John F M Lowe, Alexandria, D C.

Stray cow came to my farm in Montg Co, Md, early last fall. Owner is to come forward, prove property, pay charges, & take her away. –Thos M Wilson

SAT FEB 28, 1846
Obit-died: on Feb 18, in Quincy, Mass, Mrs Lucy Greenleaf, w/o Mr John Greenleaf, aged 78. She was a d/o the late Hon Richd Cranch, of Braintree, Mass, & a sister of Judge Cranch, of Wash City. Her memory of a mother is hallowed by the dearest remembrances; she lived a pattern of admirable affection with her husband more than 50 years, who survives, but on the brick of eternity, patiently awaiting a release from his dying body, & eager to join his consort in the skies. –D

Albert Todd, Chas H Haven: Todd & Haven, Attys & Counsellors at Law, St Louis, Missouri. [Ad]

House of Reps: 1-Ptn of Moses Harris, Mason Vanroy, & others, recommitted to the Cmte on the Judiciary. 2-Bills on the calendar passed: relief of Chas Benris; Jas Mains; Jas Wyman; Jos Watson; Arthur R Frogge; Jos M Rhea; Saml D Walker; Smith, Thurgar & Co; John G Pierre; John E Holland; Danl Ingalls; heirs of Wm Evans; Wm Eliot, jr, of Illinois; relief of Adam McCulloch. 3-Bill for the relief of the heirs of Wm Evans: reconsidered & passed with no quorum.

Appointment by the Pres: Romulus M Saunders, of N C, to be Envoy Extra & Minister Pleni of the U S at the Court of her Catholic Majesty, in the place of Washington Irving, at his own request recalled.

Orphans Court of Wash Co, D C. Letters of administration on the personal estate of Bernard Kelley, late of said county, dec'd. –Patrick Moran, adm

Orphans Court of Wash Co, D C. Letters of administration on the personal estate of John Douglas, late of said county, dec'd. –Wm G Gorsuch, adm

Orphans Court of Wash Co, D C. Letters of administration on the personal estate of Jas Douglas, late of said county, dec'd. –Wm G Gorsuch, adm

Richmond Compiler of yesterday: fatal rencontre near our city on Wed, on the Manchester side of the river, between Mr John Hampden Pleasants & Mr Thos Ritchie, jr. Mr Pleasants received 5 wounds, in his arm, shoulder, upper part of the left breast, left hand, & upper & inner part of the thigh–of which the last 2 are the most serious. Mr Ritchie was not seriously hurt. [Mr Pleasants has since died.] [Apr 7th newspaper: the trial of Mr Thos Ritchie, jr, on an indictment for the murder of John H Pleasants was concluded at Chesterfield Court-house, Va, on Sat last, & resulted in a verdict of not guilty.] [Jul 2nd newspaper: Ritchie found guilty of a simple assault.] [Jul 13th newspaper: Dr Ritchie found guilty and sentenced to pay a fine of $30.]
+
Died: yesterday, at Richmond, Va, John Hampden Pleasants, the founder & long the distinguished editor of the Richmond Whig. To a future notice must be left the justice due to the personal worth & professional eminence of this lamented gentleman. [Mar 2nd newspaper: Mr Pleasants died on Feb 27, after great suffering. He was the eldest s/o the late Govn'r Jas Pleasants, & has left an aged mother, 2 children, & many other relatives, for no man was ever more tenderly beloved by his family, & no one ever had more devoted friends.] [Mar 3rd newspaper: he established the Richmond Whig in the spring of 1824; he would have been 49 years of age some time in March; he left an aged mother, 2 children, several sisters, & 2 brothers.]

Died: on Tue, at Alexandria, Harriet Easton Neale, w/o Christopher Neale, after a painful & lingering illness, which she bore with firmness & Christian submission.

Died: on Feb 27, Mrs Dorcas Hull, in her 65th year, after a long & protracted illness, which she bore with Christian resignation. She was a resident of Fredericktown, Md, for 50 years, but for the last 4 years a resident of this place. Her funeral will take place tomorrow, at 2 o'clock, from the residence of her son-in-law, Mr John F King, on 5th, between I & K sts.

Died: on Feb 18, at Bryorfield, Andrew Bartle, in his 69th year. He was a native of Pa, & has been a resident of Eliz City Co, Va, for nearly 27 years.

Died: on Feb 24, Mr Lazare Kervand, a native of Switzerland, & for the last 30 years a resident of Wash City. His funeral is on Feb 28, at 11 o'clock, from his late residence at Woodley, near Gtwn.

For sale: neat 2 story brick house & lot, on E st, next the residence of John F Callan. –Wm Graham

MON MAR 2, 1846

House of Reps: 1-Bill for the relief of the legal reps of Wm D Cheever, dec'd: committed. 2-Ptn of Nancy Martin for the 5 years' pension due to her mother at her death. 3-Ptn of Jacob Boston, of Luzerne Co, Pa, praying for a pension in consideration of his services as a marine in the U S Navy at the siege of Tripoli in 1804. 4-Ptn of Jas Titus, of Crawford Co, Pa, praying legislation relative to an invention for exploding powder under water, called the diving peace machine. 5-Ptn of Geo Hix, of Monroe Co, Tenn, praying Congress to grant him compensation for depredations committed by Lt Fowler, while in the service of the U S, in the Cherokee nation, in the year 1831. 6-Cmte of Claims: adverse reports on the cases of John P Converse, Wm H Topping, & Jos Nock: laid on the table. 7-Cmte on Commerce: bill for the relief of Chas W Bingley, of Charleston, S C: passed & sent to the Senate for concurrence. 8-Cmte for D C: bill for the relief of Jas Dixon: committed. 9-Cmte on the Judiciary: adverse report on the case of Maria L Nourse: laid on the table. 10-Cmte on the Post Ofc & Post Roads: reported a joint resolution for the relief of John B Denton & Curtis Humphreys: committed. Same cmte: adverse reports on the cases of Nathl Patton's heirs & legal reps & of Jas A McHatton & Ed Herndon: laid on the table. 11-Cmte on Revolutionary Claims: bill for the relief of the heirs of Thos Knowlton: committed. Same cmte: bill for the relief of the grandchildren of Maj Gen Baron de Kalb: committed. 12-Cmte on Private Land Claims: bill for the relief of Wm Moss, of Missouri: committed. Same cmte: asked to be discharged from the case of Henry Asbury, & that leave be given to withdraw the papers: agreed to. 13-Cmte on Indian Affairs: bill for the relief of Doctor Clark Lillybridge: committed. 14-Cmte on Naval Affairs: bill for the relief of W P S Sanger & Geo T De la Roche: committed. 15-Cmte on Patents: bill for the relief of Henry M Shreve, & to authorize the purchase of his patent: committed. 16-Bill for the relief or Pierre Menard, Antoine Peltier, & Jos Placy: referred to the Cmte on Revolutionary Claims. 17-Bill granting commutation of half-pay to the legal reps of Col Wm Grayson, of the Revolutionary army, was passed in the affirmative, 73 to 69.

Died: on Feb 28, Edw Barnard, in his 59th year. He was a native of Massachusetts, & for many years a clerk in the Genr'l Land Ofc. His funeral is this evening, at 2 o'clock, from his late residence, on N Y ave, between 7th & 8th sts.

List of letters remaining in the Post Ofc, Wash, Mar 1, 1846.

Adams, John Geo	Brown, Miss M A	Brooke, C Wallace
Anderson, Esther	Boyd, Jas K	Bates, John A, U S N
Abert, Silvanus T	Bates, Elizur-3	Bean, Miss Marg A
Alnutt, Miss C B	Burch, Jos A	Brass, John
Adams, John	Beach, Albert H-2	Beall, Ann J
Allerson, Henry	Brown, Wm C	Banks, Thos
Aspinwall, Geo W	Brown, John	Boyd, Thos J
Adams, J B	Brown, Dr Chas D	Burke & Elliott
Boyd, Cooper S	Bess, Mr	Bright, Michl G-3

Byrne, Miss Cath	Clark, Mrs Sarah	Cooke, Capt P St
Birch, Wm	Crane, Wm R	Geo-4
Blanchard, F	Choate, Rufus	Diggs, Jas
Bohrer, J S, U S N	Colt, Col Saml	Dade, John or
Boarman, Miss Eliz	Crump, G W	Langhorn
Butler, Richd	Crescraft, E G	Dunn, Mrs A
Bowrum, Chas H	Clinton, Chas	Dann, Geo
Bryan, Maj N A	Crittenden, A F	Dow, Henry
Brackenridge, H M	Codman, Rev Dr-3	Dwight, T C
Bergman, E H	Crosby, Elias	DeGeisse, Lt Paul
Butler, Hon B F	Clements, Mrs	D'Anville, Madam V
Baker, John J	Carter, Francis	Dixon, Edw
Burbank, M Abner	Colgate, Saml	Dixon, L A
Butler, Richd	Carter, Hart	Dyer, Mrs Eliz
Barton, Henry	Carroll, Nicholas	Dinnies, Alfred
Buckham, John	Cullum, J	Decker, Jas
Barry, John A	Clements, Richd	Dornay, Mrs
Bidwell, H	Calhoun, Wm B	Davidson, Mrs M T
Blatchley, J S	Covert, Cornelius	Davis, Bealis
Bayley, Henry	Chalmers, Dr J G	Duvall, Edm B
Biddle, Mrs Jas S	Conroy, T of N Y	Downey, Thos A
Birch, Miss Amanda	Carter, Valentine	Devenish, Miss H
Buckler, Miss H P	Cummings, Sam T	Derby, L
Burnell, Barker	Crown, Miss Ann	Dickinson, Town'd-2
Barlow, Dr B W	Clements, Gen J B	De Witt, jr, Peter-2
Bryan, Purser Jos	Chilton, Saml	David, Jas Y
Brannan, R	Colton, C L	Dunning, Jas
Butler, Keyron	Chatman, Basil	Deacon, Mrs E P
Bayma, A W	Cattin, Abijah	Eichner, Jacob
Bayly, W P	Cassidy, H	Enwisle, Saml
Beldon, C, U S N	Carter, John P	Edwards, Alfred P
Besaneon, Gen L A	Clayton, Jas F-2	Elzy, Miss Maria H
Berry, Messrs W & Z	Clements, Miss S A	Evans, Mrs Mary
Berry, Zach	Claxton, Col Richd	Ehringhaus, J C B
Bayard, A W	Collier, John	Evans, Evan
Brown, Mrs S A	Carter, Chas H	Elliott, Henry
Burner, Wm R	Campbell, A	Evans, Miss Frances
Bartell, Harvey, Geo	Colman, Jas	Evans, Mrs Mary
Norman, or Alfred	Caulison, Miss Susan	Edwards, Miss Chr
Cook, Dr H B	Casper, Jno Antonia	Echardt, Thos
Cox, Mrs E M-2	Caperton, Overton H	Farr, John
Crane of Crane &	Cummins, Mr Att'y	Fry, Jas T
Swan	Cooper, Mrs Matilda	Foy, John
Coale, Col Jas M	Callan, Mrs Christina V	Ford, Mary
Cearnes, Miss M A	N	Forbes, John G-2

Ford, Jas
Forbes, G H
Flocke, Henry
Fowler, Miss M E
Fillies, Thos
Fuller, John
Foster, Wm
Flemming, Miss G
Fisher, Chas
Fording, Miss Eliz
Favor, Jos
Forney, John W
Fenwick, Marion A
Fitzhugh, jr, W H
Fenton, D G-2
Gray Eyes, John
Gray, Rev S T-2
Galt, Capt P H
Grice, Saml
Gist, Judge
Graeve, Ludwig
George, John C
Green, J W
Gross, M
Gough, John B
Grey, Jas P
Garrison, Amos J
Gorman, Peter
Garnett, r H
Greenwell, C J
Gideon, Jos
Gedney, Capt T R
Grignon, C A-2
Graham, Mrs M
Goodyer, Mrs S
Gibons, John B
Glover, Mr, late o/NY
Goble, Dr J G
Gibson, Jas K
Gregory, John
Gordon, R C
Gardiner, Alex-2
Grant, Miss J
Greene, Mr, Boston
Guytan, Mrs Ophelia

Heaight, Silas
Helm, Chas J
Hoyt, J C
Hanks, Miss Sylvia
Hoyt, Levi
Hume, Geo
Hill, Dr M J-2
Hale, Andrew L
Hurst, John T
Hays, Gen S-2
Halt, Danl E
Hough, Col Jas
Hirst, Wm L
Hall, Jas D
Hall, Hamilton
Hume, Chas
Hall, Miss Clara
Hunt, Hiram
Hall, Raymond B
Hart, Mr
Hord, Robt
Hager, E W
Hunter, Chas S
Hammond, Edw
Hipkins, Mrs
Hamilton, R C-2
Homer, Chas
Harris, Thos W
Howard, Volney E
Harris, A
Hawkins, Chas G
Hickman, Mrs J
Hewett, Danl
Holden, Richd-2
Houston, Gen S
Howard, Jos
Holbourn, A
Howard, Francis
Hocke, Henriech
Haven, Franklin
Harris, Col J G
Horwell, Thos J
Harvie, Lewis E
Hilcox, Jos
Heckerman, J W

Hopkins, Lewis
Hutchins, Miss M
Hansell, Maj W Y
Harney, Bt Col W S
Hagerty, Lt F S-2
Henderson, J, of Mi
Harris, Hurbert
Hutchins, Mrs S G
Higinbotham, John
Hillstock, Mrs M
Hooper, Chas C
Indeman, Jas
Isherwood, B F-2
Jones, Thos
Jones, Capt Fountain
Jones, Owen
Johnson, Alford
Janney, John W
Jackson, Henry
Johnson, Thos
Jacobs, Benj F
Jackson, Wm
Johnston, Miss H A
Jackson, Jas W
Johnson, Richd H-3
Johnson, Litty
Jamaison, R
Johnson, Mrs E
Jonston, Miss M M
Johnson, Mrs Tenor
Jackson, Fred'k
Kooms, C
Kerr, Geo
King, Isaac
King, Miss M A A
King, Chas
Kellogg, John P
Kearney, Lt P
Kendrick, Miss M
Kezer, Mrs E T
Kerney, Mrs A-2
Kelly, Michl
Leake, Mrs Rebecca
Lee, Hugh H
Lunt, Miss E

Laird, John	Mason, M	Phelps, Lt J W-2
Laird, Jas D	Mattingley, Jos	Pease, L T
Lord, Lt Francis B	Marshall, Mrs T	Prall, David M-3
Lyne, Miss L H	Mitchell, Wm	Perry, Thos H
Lee, Miss A	Manning, Dr W A	Perry, Chas M
Lewis, Winslow	Moorehead, J K	Paschal, Geo W
Lippincott, T K	Morgan, Rudolph S	Phelan, Patrick
Lupton, W H	Maynard, E A-3	Prestman, Benj C
Loomis, A J	Miller, Benj A	Perry, Miss Ann E
Lyon, L	Mason, Lewis E	Pennington, Josias
Leekie, Mrs M	Manning, Cpat T J	Philips, Geo S
Lyon, Miss E B	Morrison, David-2	Pickett, John
Lewis, Chauncy	Morsell, B R	Parmenter, Wm
Lunen, Nicholas	Maclane, W	Philips, Jas
Lomax, Madame	Mahon, Miss Sally	Pettit, John
Leseur, Dr Francis	McCook, Danl-2	Power, Wm
Luffobrough, Dr	McReam, Jas	Power, Michl
Lansdale, H A	McCallion, Geo	Pringle, W G
Latruit, Miss B V	McFarlane, John	Pendergrast, Com't
Lippincott, I K	McNamara, John	Pickins, Mrs Matilda
Leavens, jr, Jessee	McGraw, Jas	Porter, Col Andrew
Latruit, Mrs E	McClaughey, Jas	Perry, Mrs Sophia
Lagrand, John C	Mackabee, John B	Polkenhorn, Miss C
Lally, F T	McCollins, Jas	Polkenhorn, Miss J
Leiper, Col Wm	McDougal, John	Reeves, Randolph
Mines, J L B	McCausleind, John	Roste, Danl
Morse, Edw	McLemore, Col J C	Rust, Genr'l
May, Geo R	McBridge, Arch A	Rust, Robt B
Moore, Wm	McNeill, Maj W G	Ray, Thos
Moore, J A	McDowell, Miss R A	Rea, Archelaus
May, May J M	McClelland, Miss M	Ritchie, Harrison
Mace, Mrs Lydia	Niles, John S	Rardaf, Francis
Miller, Mrs C E	Norris, John	Ratcliff, Jas A
Mitchell, N O-2	Northe, Jas	Russell, F S K
Matthews, Susan S	Newbury, Oliver-2	Robinson, T R
Milsteads, Isaac	Noble, Wm T	Ripley, Lt R S
Magum, Wm	Newton, Eliz	Robinson, Orville
Morris, Mrs M-2	Norton, Mr, Boston	Ripley, Geo B
Martin, Mrs Ca'ne	Ochis, Wilhelmn	Richardson, I F-2
Mattock, Col Go C	O'Neill, G P	Ramsay, Mrs Anna
Monroe, Jas M	Pierce, Wm B-6	Ramsford, Geo
Moulden, Mrs M J	Page, Benj	Reiley, Chas
Manly, Miss Cara	Payne, D A	Robertson, Miss E
Martin, Fayette W	Pool, Edler W C	Richard, Benj
Murray, Nicholas	Potts, Richd	Rodgers, John F

Robertson, jr, W W	Stewart, W W	Thornton, Francis A,
Rogers, Col John A	Stewart, John	U S N
Rynders, Capt I-2	Symington, Maj J	Thompson, Mrs
Russell, Lt W W-3	Sutton, Wm M	Josephine A
Rolando, P'd Mid H-2	Skinner, Mrs R	Turner, Orsemas-5
Robinson, Col T D	Sprague, Wm	Tappan, Lewis W-4
Ruggles, Mrs Oliver	Stevens, E A	Taylor, Knowles-2
Reiley, Mrs Frances	Smallwood, D A	Turner, Robt B
Russell, Francis S-2	Sherlock, Miss V	Von Ritter, Fred
Shaw, Elwood C	Street, Jesse	Vesey, Wm H
Scott, Chas G-2	Shoemaker, Abner	Van Buren, L B
Smith, Miss Sarah J	Satterwhite, Geo	Van Ness, Geo H
Sprigg, Osborn	Stewart, Robt	Vanzandt, Jos
Smith, Wm	Smith, Miss Hannah	Ward, John L
Smith, Wm O	Scott, Miss Eliz	White, Moses F-2
Smith, Thos H	Tate, Dr Jas H	Walsh, Thos S
Smith, Jackson	Todd, Wm H-2	Woods, John-2
Slack, Lt W B	Thrift, Jas W	Woodward, Mrs M
Smith, John C	Todd, J P	Wood, Ransom E
Spice, Wm	Tilghman, Gen T	Wofford, John
Smith, Miss E J	Tyler, jr, John	Woodford, Morris
Smith, Geo Clinton	Tennant, Wm	Wallace, Geo
Staines, Julia	Taylor, Col S G	Wilson, Wm
Stone, Mrs C-3	Tucker, J R	Washington, R R
Starke, E E	Thompson, Miss M	Williams, Wm
Stearners, Onslow	Trontfeller, Jason	Whittley, G B
Searle, Maj F	Taylor, Wm-2	Woodford, Asa M
Sprague, L H	Townley, Eugene	Wall, Thos Welsh,
Shonenburg, Lewis	Taylor, Wm P	Ward, N W
Seymour, Wm H	Thompson, Jas H	Wailes, Geo B N
Shurtcliff, Jonas	Tucker, Henry	Webb, Miss E G
Stevens, John G	Thompson, Ro A	Wells, Gideon
Sommers, S La F	Tschiffely, A G	Williams, G Mott-2
Scribner, Jas	Thompson, Benj	Whitney, Chas H
Stoddard, Gen M	Taylor, Gen D	Webster, Edw
Searight, Capt Jos	Toler, H A	Wilson, Jas
Shepherd, Col T	Travers, John	Wargatt, Cornelius
Spelman, John R	Tompkins, Ray	Wilson, Wm
Spencer, Col John	Thomas, Philip W	Wilson, Edmond-2
Shaffer, Fred'k I	Titus, Henry	Watson, Thos S
Stevens, Jas	Timberlake, D	Wall, Geo W
Summers, John F	Tupper & Smith	Wade, W G
Seymour, Wm B	Trimble, J R	Wood, Miss Eliz
Seoncia, Master	Thomas, Wm H, o/Mi	White, Geo H
Stantan, Stephen K-3	Turner, Com Danl	Wilson, Rev Dr H D

White, Miss Mary A	Washington, Col H	Young, Wm
Walback, Lt J J B	Young, Willis	Young, Wilfred
Wilson, Nathl H	Young, Jas C	Yeatman, S M
Watson, Thos H	Young, Notley	Younger, Mrs Sarah
Willis, R	Yates, Giles F-3	Zachman, Chas-2
Willard, Wm H	Young, Jas	
Williams, Jas-3	Young, Miss Eliz	

To the owners of one piper & two half pipes Gin, marked [T] Washington city. The inland postage on all letters intended to go by ship maust be paid, otherwise they remain in this ofc. -C K Gardner, P M

Mar 2: Philip Barton Key, the new District Atty, will make his debut this morning.

Mr Jos Burke, formerly known as Master Burke, one of the most celebrated violinists of the day, will commence a series of concerts at Carusi's Saloon. Leopold De Meyer, the lion pianist, will pay us a flying visit shorly.

TUE MAR 3, 1846

Senate: 1-Ptn from Saml Veasie & others, asking that a marine hospital may be erected in the State of Maine. 2-Ptn from Prof Espy, asking to be allowed to ventilate the Senate Chamber of the U S. 3-Ptn from S Hall, asking an increase of pension. 4-Ptn from Theodore Frelinghuysen, asking that certain scientific works may be imported free of duty. 5-Cmte on the Post Ofc & Post Roads: bill for the relief of Thos Rhodes. 6-Cmte of Claims: bill for the relief of Mary Williams. 6-Cmte on Indian Affairs: bill for the relief of Jas Irving, of Arkansas, & others. Same cmte: adverse report on the 2 ptns of Wm H Thomas. 7-Cmte on the Judiciary: adverse reports in the cases of Saml Grisse, Jas L Sawyer, & Robt & Wm Armstrong. Also, adverse report in the case of Caleb Green: laid aside.

Valuable property at auction: one of the Stores [the western] occupied by Messrs Geo & Thos Parker, opposite the Centre Market: sale on Mar 5. The store is now under lease to the Messrs Parker until Jul 1, 1849, at $650 per annum, clear of repairs. –Wm Marshall, auctioneer

Notice: application has been made to the Bank of the Metropolis for renewal of a certificate for 8 shares of the stock of said Bank, #115, issued in favor of the heirs of the late John Douglass. –Wm G Gorsuch, adm

For rent: commodious brick dwlg house on Pa ave, next door to Rev Dr Laurie. The key is left with Saml W Handy, a few doors below. –John L Smith, near Steamboat wharf, or at Mr Smith's boarding house, on La ave, near 7th st.

For sale: a small farm of about 300 acs. –Chas A Pye, near Port Tobacco, Md.

Circuit Superior Court of Law & Chancery for Tyler Co, Va. Jos A Clay, cmplnt, vs Chas Woodward, exc of Gavin Hamilton, ___ Starr, husband of Mary Starr, late Mary Hamilton, late of Wilmington, Delaware, Moses Bell, of Marshall Co, & Jacob Keek, & the heirs of Gavin Hamilton, the son of John, dfndnts. Be it known that Jos A Clay, of Phil City, Pa, had filed his bill, the material allegations of which are as follows: That, in 1788, 2 tracts of land were granted by the Commonwealth of Va to Abraham Nelson, one for 6,800 acres & the other for 2,000 acres of land, which said lands are in Tyler Co; that the said Abraham Nelson, on Mar 21, 1789, by his atty in fact, Amassa Nelson, sold & conveyed the said lands to Gavin Hamilton, the elder, Gavin Hamilton, the younger, & Gavin Hamilton, the son of John. That, on Feb 20, 1786, 2 grants were issued by the said Commonwealth to Danl Vardin, jr, for 4,000 acres each, which said lands are in Marshall Co; that the said Vardin, on Feb 16, 1789, sold & conveyed the said lands to the aforesaid Hamiltons; that, on Feb 20, 1786, another grant was issued by said Commonwealth to the said Danl Vardin, jr, for a tract of 5,000 acres of land, in Ritchie Co; that the said Vardin on ___ day of___ sold & conveyed the said tract of land to the said Hamiltons; that Gavin Hamilton, the elder, died intestate, leaving as his only child & heir the said Gavin Hamilton, the younger, to whom his interest in the lands aforesaid descended; that the said Gavin Hamilton, the younger, died without issue, having by his last will & testament constituted & appointed Chas Woodward, of Phil, Pa, his exc, with power to sell his lands for certain purposes mentioned in the said will; that the said Gavin Hamilton, the son of John, died intestate, leaving an only child, by the name of Mary, who married a gentleman of Wilmington, Delaware, by the name of Starr; that the said Mrs Starr died intestate, leaving a dght, an only child, who died under the age of 21, without issue, & that the kindred of the said Gavin Hamilton, the son of John, to whom his interest in the said lands descended by the laws of the Commonwealth of Va, subject to the tenancy by the curtesy, in the husband of said Mrs Starr, are unknown & supposed to reside in Scotland. The bill further alleges that the said Jos A Clay has been appointed the trustee of the estate of said Gavin Hamilton, the younger, & that, as such trustee, he claims 2 undivided thirds of the aforesaid lands. The said bill alleges that the said Chas Woodward, of Phil was exc of Gavin Hamilton, the younger, but that he, by mistake, supposed himself the exc of Gavin Hamilton, the elder, & as such made certain irregular sales & conveyances of portions of the aforesaid tracts of land to Jacob Keek & Moses Bell, & asks that the same be corrected, & that the several tracts of land may be divided & apportioned among the owners thereof, so as to protect the said Keek & Bell, & 1/3rd thereof assigned to the unknown heirs of the said Gavin Hamilton, the son of John, & 2/3rds thereof to the said Clay. Now, in pursuance with the act of the Genr'l Assembly of Va in such cases made & provided, it is ordered that all persons interested in the lands aforesaid, as heirs of Gavin Hamilton, the son of John, formerly of Phil City, Pa, & all others interested in the said lands, are warned & notified to appear & make themselves parties dfndnt to the suit aforesaid, & to file their answers to the said bill, asserting their rights or claims to the said lands; & that this order be published for 6 successive weeks in the Nat'l Intelligencer, published in Wash City.
-D Hickman, clerk

Valuable land on the Potomac for sale: a tract of 250 acres, in Loudoun Co, Va. Address, L Cary Selden, Mount Ida, near Alexandria, D C.

WED MAR 4, 1846
Wash Corp: 1-Ptn of L M Dippel, praying remission of a fine: referred to the Cmte of Claims. 2-Ptn of Wm Doughty & others, as a cmte, praying the establishment of a Market at the intersection of N Y & Mass aves, & between 9th & 10th sts west: laid on the table. 3-Ptn of John Lee, praying remission of a fine: referred to the Cmte of Claims. 4-Bill for the relief of Joshua L Henshaw: passed. 5-Cmte on Canals: recommitted the bill for the relief of Wm Easby & K H Lambell: passed. 6-Bill for the relief of Kinslaugh DeNeale: referred to the Cmte of Claims. 7-Resolved: that the markets shall be held on Tues, Thu, & Sats, at such hour as the Mayor may designate. 8-Mayor nominates Jas A Tait, as Com'r of the Western Section of the Wash Canal, in place of John A Bender, which was confirmed. 9-Cmte of Claims: bill for the relief of John Fletcher, assignee of A C Kidwell: passed. Same cmte: bill for the relief of Henry Gray: passed. Same cmte: bill for the relief of Richd T Smallwood: passed. 10-Ptn of H G Corcoran: referred to the Cmte of Claims. 11-Bill authorizing Patsy R Walker to erect a wharf opposite the west corner of square 355, on the Potomac river: ordered to lie on the table.

Criminal Court-Wash: Grand Jurors sworn on Mon.

John W Maury, Foreman	Geo Watterston	Wm I Stone
Roger C Weightman	Thos P Jones	Wm A Bradley
Abner C Pierce	G W Riggs	John Cox
Thos Corcoran	Saml Bacon	W D C Murdoch
Lewis Carbery	John F Callan	Philip T Berry
John Boyle	Henry McPherson	John T Sullivan
Eleazer Lindsley	Hamilton Lufborough	Geo W Phillips
	John C Rives	Jabez Travers

Petit Jury:

Geo Crandell	S Duvall	D A Gardiner
J C Harkness	S Matlock	B W Reed
G A W Randall	D Homans	J H Lusby
J G Robinson	W Bond	F A Tucker
L H Haslup	T Parker	D Campbell
A H Boucher	O Connolly	J H Daniel
Z Walker	R H Harrington	W A Williams
J L Brightwell	W H Simms	B Bohrer
L Beeler	Jas Maguire	T Bangs
J H Kidwell	T Baker	G Lamb
Elexius Simms	D Koones	
J S King	B Burns	

Several trials which took place in this Court: 1-U S vs Dick Plummer, free negro, found guilty for an assault: fined $3 & discharged. 2-U S vs Mgt Coyle, alias Mary Ann Lackey: found guilty of keeping a disorderly house. 3-U S vs John Wade, found not guilty of riot & assault upon Conrad Heiss. 4-U S vs Wm Dippel, found guilty for keeping a disorderly house: recommended by the jury to the mercy of the Court. 5-In the case of the U S vs Isaac Robinson & Wm Hines, charged with suspicion of stabbing Benj Young, jr, we learn that the Justices have decided to take bail in $500 for the appearance of Hines at the Criminal Court now in session. Dr May does not consider Mr Young out of danger, & has objected to the taking of his deposition while in his present critical condition. Robinson remains in jail for the action of the Grand Jury in his case.

Another Jersey Blue gone. Jeremiah Howell died at Parsippany, Morris Co, on Feb 18, aged 98 years & 5 months. He was at the battle of Monmouth, & participated in other scenes of strife & glory in our golden age. And still another: Abijah Harrison, a venerable citizen of Orange, &, we presume, the oldest man in the county, died this moring at the advanced age of 96 years. –Newark Advertiser [No date-recent news.]

Dr Bradley, convicted of robbing the mails, & imprisoned for the offence in 1841, died in his cell at Pittsburg on Fri week. Previous to his death he confessed his guilt.

Senate: 1-Ptn from Nahum Haskell, of Vt, asking reimbursement for a forfeiture paid by him as surety for an absconding criminal who was afterwards retaken & tried. 2-Ptn from Wm B Foster, late Quartermaster in the U S Army, asking compensation for losses sustained by negotiating a loan for the purchase of supplies for U S troops. 3-Ptn from Thos Brownett, asking a continuation of his pension; also, from Ray Tompkins & other heirs of Danl Tompkins, asking payment of interest on the sum due him for service in the late war with Great Britain. 4-Ptn for the relief of John C Whitsett. 5-Cmte on Naval Affairs: adverse report on the ptn of S H Thompson. 6-Ptn of Asa Andrews, which was referred to the Cmte on the Judiciary, was referred to the Cmte of Claims. 7-Adverse reports in the cases of Wm Pennoyer, Saml Simpson, & Wm Shippen: taken up & concurred in. 8-The case of Caleb Green was recommitted to the Cmte on the Judiciary.

House of Reps: 1-Ptn of Asa Hall, of Will Co, for payment of back pension from Apr 26, 1814, to Jul 22, 1830. 2-Papers of the heirs of Israel Cryder: presented.

Mrd: on Feb 26, by Rev J J Murray, Rev John B Ferguson to Mrs Frances Fugitt, all of Wash City.

Died: on Mar 2, Mrs Margaret Merrit, in her 65th year. Her funeral is this afternoon, at 2 o'clock, from her late residence on 8th st.

The Late Gen Elias B Dayton. Elizabethrown, N J, furnished 29 commissioned ofcrs to the regular line of the army during the Revolutionary War. Gen Dayton, whose death occurred in N Y C, a short time since, at age 83 years, was nearly the last of those who, from that little town, participated actively in the glorious struggle for liberty. His father, Gen Elias Dayton, served through the whole war, part of the time as colonel of a regt, & afterwards as Brig Gen & commander of the Jersey brig; was in nearly all the principal engagements, & had 3 horses shot under him: his brother, the late Gen Jonathan Dayton, was a captain in the Continental line, & his brother-in-law, Col Matthias Ogden, commanded one of the Jersey regts. The necessity of some protection for his mother & her infant children, prevented his enrolling himself in the regular army; but the same zeal in the great cause led him to volunteer upon several dangerous expeditions against the enemy. He was one of a party of 30 or 40 who, under the command of Capt [afterwards Gen] Wm Crane, the father of the present Cmdor Crane, captured 2 British gun-boats at Staten Island. Mr Dayton, Luther Baldwin, of Newark, & a dozen other men, crossed Newark bay at night & succeeded in taking 5 or 6 prisoners. His whole life was marked by an ardent love of country. –N Y Courier & Enquirer [Mar 28th newspaper: Cmdor Crane was born at Elizabethtown, N J, Feb 1, 1776, & was the s/o Gen Wm Crane, who served with distinction as Colonel in the Revolutionary army before Quebec, where he received a wound of which he ultimately died. Cmdor Crane entered the Navy on May 23, 1799, & first served as Midshipman on board the frig **United States** in the following June. He served on board the ship **Chesapeake**, & as Master in the ship **Genr'l Greene**, & joined the brig **Vixen** in 1803 at Lt, & was present at all the attacks on Tripoli. He leaves a wife, a lady of Norfolk, Va, of rare personal merit, & 2 brothers, the gallant Col Crane of the U S Artl, & Judge Crane of Ohio. The Cmdor was the 2nd son, & was 62 years of age Feb 1 last. He was tall & of large & massive frame, of commanding & imposing presence.]

Orphans Court of Wash Co, D C. In the case of the administrator of Patrick A Orme, dec'd, the administrator & Court have appointed Mar 20th next for settlement of said estate, & distribution of the assets in the hands of the administrator.
–Ed N Roach, Reg/o wills

Orphans Court of Wash Co, D C. In the case of the administrator, with the will annexed, of John Emmerick, dec'd, the administrator & Court have appointed Mar 20th next for the settlement of said estate, & distribution of the assets in the hands of the administrator. –Ed N Roach, Reg/o wills

TUE MAR 5, 1846
Retrocession in the District of Columbia: recent movements in Alexandria, the Legislature of Va, & the House of Reps, have added increased interest in the subject-matter of this discussion. Mr Hunter, from the Cmte on D C, reported a bill to retrocede the county of Alexandria, in D C, to the State of Va. Read & committed.
–Justice

Senate: 1-Ptn from the heirs of Gustavus B Horner, asking bounty land & commutation pay for services as surgeon's mate during the Revolutionary war. 2-Ptn from Thos P Shepherd, asking that the apparatus employed making oil of vitriol may be imported dury free. 3-Ptn from Thos & Eliz Armstrong, legal reps of Josiah Fletcher, asking indemnity for property destroyed by hostile Indians. 4-Ptn from J M Wendall & others, asking payment of their claims under the 5th article of the treaty with the Saginaw Indians. 5-Ptn from Jacob Dyckman, asking the adoption of his system of military instruction for the use of the militia. 6-Ptn from Wm Bell & Mgt P Cameron, asking payment of balances for advances made by their ancestors during the Revolution. 7-Cmte on Pensions: bill for the relief of Wm Macauly, without amendment. House bill for the relief of John Ficklin, without amendment. House bill for the relief of Arthur R Frogge, of Tenn, without amendment. House bill for the relief of Jas Davidson, of Tenn, without amendment. Same cmte: asking to be discharged from the further consideration of the ptns of Eliz Sevier & Harriet Ward, & that they be referred to the Cmte on Naval Affairs. 8-Cmte on Revolutionary Claims: adverse reports on the memorial of John Fulford, on the ptn of the legal reps of Maj John Brooks, on the ptn of Sally Bass-a written report in each case: ordered to be printed. 9-Cmte on the Judiciary: bill for the relief of Peter Capella, adm of Andrew Capella, dec'd. 10-Cmte on Pensions: bill to allow arrearages of pension to Hugh W Dobbin, with a report: ordered to be printed.

The elegant mansion of Stephen Weld, at Jamaica Plain, near Boston, has been burnt down. The house was valued at $10,000, insurance $6,000.

The Hon Thos Stockton, Govn'r of the State of Delaware, died very suddenlty at Newcastle on Mon last. Whilst in one of the public ofcs, without any premonition of his approaching end, his head fell suddenly upon his breast, & he died without a struggle or a groan. A rupture of the large blood vessels in the vicinity of the heart is supposed by the physicians to have been the cause of his death. We tender to the family of Govn'r Stockton an expression of our heartfelt sympathy in the loss they have sustained.

Mrd: on Mar 3, at Martinsburg, Berkeley Co, Va, by Rev John O'Brien, Mr Robt P Bryarly to Miss Sally Abell, d/o Capt Chas Boarman, of the U S Navy.

FRI MAR 6, 1846
Died: on Mon last, at **Mount Ida**, near Alexandria, Mrs Mary B Selden, wid/o Dr Wilson Cary Selden, of Loudoun Co, Va.

Addison Ferguson was drowned last Tue whilst engaged in shooting ducks on the Potomac, near the Arsenal. He has left a wife & 7 children. [Mar 9th newspaper: The body of Addison Ferguson, who was drowned in the Potomac, near the Arsenal, was found on Thu.]

The dwlg-house of Mr Lewis Bailey, of Fairfax Co, Va, about 4 miles from Alexandria, was burnt down on Mon night. The family barely escaped with their lives. All the furniture was consumed.

Criminal Court-Wash: 1-Charged with a riot at Hazeltown, Capitol Hill, on Feb 28, 1845-being a party from *English Hill* against another on Capitol Hill. John Webster, Jos Sanford, John Beech, & Mary Sandford were discharged by the Court on payment of costs. 2-John H Locke, Lucien Roane, Jas Stewart, Wm Webster, Lyon Sanford, & Jas Brown with tried & found not guilty. 3-Alfred Henning, was found not guilty. 4-John Wade was convicted of an assault upon Moses Gilbert. 5-Rezin Turvey was found guilty for an assault with intent to kill Geo Doyle in 1838. 6-Francis Nolan was found guilty for a riot on Dec 25, 1845. 7-Francis Nolan was indicted for an assault upon B Queen at the same time. No verdict returned as yet. 8-John Gross, indicted for a riot at Gtwn on Dec 25, 1845, was found guilty.

On Sat last Wm Richardson, s/o Wm S Richardson, living near the Hill Top, in Chas Co, Md, was killed by the fall of a tree. It appears that he had cut into the tree sufficiently to cause it to fall; it suddenly fell, striking him upon the head & felling him to the earth; he got up & walked a quarter of a mile to the house, but in a short time after arriving there expired. He was about 22 years of age.
–Port Tobacco Times

Letter dated Feb 11, 1846, to Gen John Mason, Clermont, Fairfax Co, Va from Francis L Smith, Chas T Stuart, & Robt Brockett: subject-recession of Alexandria. The inhabitants of the town & county of Alexandria are, as we conceive, subject to all the evils, without any of the benefits, of being citizens of this District; & are denied many valuable privileges enjoyed by citizens of the States. Reply by Gen John Mason: Mar 2, 1846: I must conclude that there is nothing in the Constitution to bar the action of Congress in retroceding, in compliance with the invitation of Virginia, that portion of the district originally belonging to her. The good town of Alexandria, of which I was a neighbor in my boyhood, & which I then knew by its appropriate name of *Belle Haven*, would have been better fostered by its natural mother, the *Old Dominion*, than by the care of the U S Congress. -J Mason

Senate: 1-Ptn from Isaac Stout, heir of Jas Sampson, asking confirmation of a land title held in virtue of a Spanish grant. 2-Ptn from Henry & G K Cheatham, asking compensation for the removal of the raft on Red River. 3-Ptn from Frances Moore, asking repayment of advances made by her ancestor during the Revolutionary war. 4-Ptn from Geo W Billing, asking that the Sec of the Navy be authorized to contract for a supply of water-rotted hemp, for the use of the Navy, with said Billing.

Died: on Mar 1, in Wash City, Jas E, s/o Patrick & Margaret Dowling, aged 3 years & 6 months.

Died: on Mar 2, at Alexandria, Timothy Mountford, about 70 years of age. He has for a number of years been well known as the manager of the Alexandria Museum, to which institution he devoted much of his time & his efforts. He was a patriotic citizen, always ready, as far as his means would permit, to advance the interests of the town. --Alexandria Gaz

Household furniture, wagon, vinegar, at auction: on Mar 10, at the late residence of Bernard Kelly, dec'd, on K st, near the lower bridge leading to Gtwn. Terms cash. --A Green, auctioneer

For sale: a likely colored boy, aged about 15 years, a good house servant. --H R Maryman

Appointments by the Pres, by & with the advice & consent of the Senate.
Jas L Edwards, Com'r of Pensions, to take effect from after Mar 3 next, when his present commission will expire.
Consuls:
Wm Crosby, of Ohio, for the port of Talcahuano, Chili, in place of Paul H Delano, recalled.
Chas Sherwood, of N Y, for the port of Messina, Sicily, in place of John L Payson, recalled.
Henry G Hubbard, of N Y, for the port of St Johns, Puerto Rico, in place of O S Morse, recalled.
Thos N Carr, of N Y, for the Empire of Morocco, in place of John F Mallowny, recalled.
Nicholas B Boyle, of Wash, for Port Mahon, in the Island of Minorca, in place of Obadiah Rich, resigned.
John F Bacon, of N Y, for the port of Nassau, in the island of New Providence, in place of Timothy Darling, recalled.
John W Holding, of Md, for the port of San Jago de Cuba, in place of Jas J Wright, dec'd.
Ramon L Sanchez, of Florida, for the port of Carthagena, in New Grenada, in place of Saml H Kneass, resigned.
Jos Cowdin, of N Y, for the port of Glasgow, Scotland, in place of Thos McGuire, recalled.
Nicholas Browne, of N Y, of the city of Rome, in place of Geo W Greene, recalled
Joel Turrill, of N Y, for the Sandwich Islands, in place of Alex'r Abel, recalled.
Geo P Manouvrier, of Louisiana, for the port of Pernambuco, in place of G T Snow, recalled.
Thos McGuire, of Ohio, for the port of Rio Grande, Brazil, in place of John C Pedrick, resigned.
Francis V Clark, of Pa, for the port of San Juan de Nicarague, in the Republic of Guatemala.

Navy Ofcrs:
Henry L Chipman, Lt in the navy from Apr 13, 1845, at which time he was promoted to fill a vacancy created by the dismission of Lt Wm D Hurst.
Henry O Mayo & John Rudenstein, Assist Surgeons in the navy, to fill the vacancies occasioned by the promotion of David Harlan & the resignation of Assist Surgeon Joshua Huntington.

Postmasters:
Stanley G Trott, New London, Conn, in place of Jas H Turner, whose commission expired.
Philo F Barnum, Bridgeport, Conn, in place of Isaac Sherman, jr, removed.
Nehemiah Moses, Portsmouth, N H, in place of Saml Gookin, removed.
Henry F Baker, Winchester, Va, in place of John Wall, whose commission expired.
Jacob Fetchtig, Cumberland, Md, in place of Wm Lynn, removed.
Robt Cochran, Erie, Pa, in place of Andrew Scott, removed.
Jonas J Bell, Tuscumbia, Ala
Wm White, Raleigh, N C, in place of Thos G Scott, resigned.
Elihu Stout, Vincennes, Indiana, in place of Jas W Greenhow, removed.
Livingston Dunlap, Indianapolis, Indiana, in place of Saml Henderson, removed.
Jos S May, Apalochicola, Florida, in place of Geo F Baltzell, resigned.
Jeremiah Cherry, Columbia, Tenn, in place of Hillary Langtry, resigned.
Wm S Hill, Greensborough, N C, in place of I J M Lindsay, removed.

Land Ofcrs:
Amzi L Wheeler, Receiver of Public Moneys for the district of land subject to sale at Winamac, in Indiana, in place of Jeremiah Grover, whose commission expired.
Nathl Bolton, Register of the land ofc for the district of land subject to sale at Indianapolis, Indiana, from & after Mar 1, 1846, in place of David V Cully, whose term of office will expire then.

Ofcrs of the Customs:
Cornelius W Lawrence, Collector of the customs for the district of N Y, vice Cornelius P Van Ness, resigned.
Saml Jones Willis, Appraiser of Merchandise for the port of N Y, vice Amos Palmer, removed
Chas Parker, Surveyor & Inspector of the Revenue for the port of Snow Hill, Md, vice Geo Hudson, removed.
Saml S Spencer, Collector of Customs for the distict, & Inspector of the Revenue for the port of Apalachicola, Florida, vice Hiram Nourse, resigned.
Ezra Chesebro, Collector for the district, & Inspector for the port of Stonington, Conn, vice Giles R Hallam, removed.
Smith Inglehart, Collector for the district of Cuyahoga, & Inspector for the port of Cleveland, Ohio, vice Wm Milford, removed.
Reuben H Boughton, Collector for the district of Niagara, & Inspector for the port of Lewiston, N Y, vice Amos S Tryon, removed.
Phineas W Leland, Collector for the district, & Inspector for the port of Fall River, Mass, vice Chas H Holmes, removed.

John Duncan, Appraiser of Merchandise for the port of New Orleans, La, vice Robt M Wellman, removed.
Chas G Hammond, Collector for the district, & Inspector for the port of Detroit, Michigan, vice Edw Brooks, resigned.
Saml C White, Surveyor & Inspector of the Revenue for the port of Accomack Court-house, Va, vice Wm Wallston, removed.
Jos P Junkins, Collector & Inspector for the port of York, Maine, vice Jeremiah Brooks, removed
Rowland H Bridgham, Collector for the district of Penobscot, & Inspector for the port of Castine, Maine, vice Chas J Abbott, removed.
Wm Brown, Collector & Inspector for the port of Machias, Maine, vice Wm B Smith, removed.
Henry Welch, Naval Ofcr for the district of Phil, Pa, vice Joel B Sutherland, removed.
John McNeil, Surveyor for the district of Boston & Charlestown, & Inspector for the port of Boston, vice Jos Grafton, removed.
Wm B Bullock, Collector for the district of Savannah, Georgia, vice Edw Hardin, removed.
Edw Green, Collector for the district of Alexandria, in D C, vice Geo Brent, dec'd.
Jas R Thompson, Surveyor & Inspector for the port of Town Creek, Md, vice Lewis Stone, dec'd.
Peter Dixey, Collector, Marblehead, Mass, vice Jas Gregory, removed.
Jos T Pease, Collector & Inspector for the port of Edgartown, Mass, vice Leavitt Thaxter, removed.
Jas T Miller, Naval Ofcr in the district of Wilmington, N C, vice Jas Owen, removed.
Denis Prieur, Collector of New Orleans, La, vice Thos Barrett, removed.
Jas E Saunders, Collector & Inspector for Mobile, Ala, vice Collier H Minge, removed.
Robt White, Collector & Inspector for the port of Gtwn, in D C, vice Henry Addison, whose commission expired.
Wm Nichols, Collector for Newburyport, Mass, vice Henry W Kinsman, whose commission expired.
Enoch Fowler, Naval Ofcr for Newburyport, Mass, vice Thos M Clark, whose commission expired.
Geo Center, Collector & Inspector for the port of St Augustine, Florida, vice Augustus W Walker, resigned.
Attys:
Robt C Nicholas, for Eastern District of Va.
Wm S Burges, for the district of Rhode Island, vice Richd W Green, removed.
John Norvell, for the district of Michigan, vice Geo C Bates, resigned.
Edw Johnston, Atty for Iowa, vice John G Deshler, removed.
Marshals:
Austin E Wing, for the district of Michigan, in place of L S Humphrey, resigned.
Eli Moore, for the Southern district of N Y, vice Silas M Stillwell, removed.

Thos Fletcher, for the Southern District of Mississippi, vice Anderson Miller, removed.
Danl A Robertson, for the district of Ohio, vice John McElvain, removed.
Wm F Wagner, for the district of Louisiana, vice Algernon S Robertson, removed
Gideon S Bailey, for the district of Iowa, vice Isaac Leffler, removed.
Cyrus Barton, for the district of N H, vice Israel W Kelley, whose commission has expired.
Arthur R Crozier, for the Eastern district of Tenn, vice Richd M Woods, dec'd.
Abel C Pepper, for the district of Indiana, vice Robt Hanna, whose commission had expired.
Jas G Lyon, for the Southern district of Alabama, vice Wm Armistead, removed.
Alex'r Porter, for the district of Delaware, vice John McClung, resigned.
+
John Catlin, Sec of the Territory of Wisconsin, vice Geo R C Floyd, removed.
Wm A Richmond, of Michigan, to be Indian Agent for the agency of Michilimackinac, vice Robt Stuart, removed.

House of Reps: 1-Cmte on the Post Ofc & Post Roads: adverse report on the case of Farley D Thompson & others, sureties of Killian White, late postmaster at Lagrange, in Alabama. 2-Cmte of Claims: adverse reports on the cases of John Chaffee & Guy Carpenter; also on the case of Matthew Scoby; also on the cases of Jas Mitchell, Wm Marshall, & Jas Mead; also, adverse reports on the cases of Caleb Bell, adm of Matthew Bell, & of Jeremiah Carpenter: laid on the table. Same cmte: bill for the relief of Amelia Brereton: committed. Same cmte: adverse report on the case of the reps of Jas Rumsey: laid on the table. 3-Cmte on Commerce: adverse report on the case of Josiah Sturgis: laid on the table. 4-Cmte on Revolutionary Claims: adverse report on the case of the heirs at law of Wm Cherry: laid on the table. Same cmte: bill for the relief of the administrator of Col Francis Taylor, dec'd: committed. Same cmte: bill for the legal reps of Lt Francis Ware: committed. Also, made an adverse report on the case of the heirs of Lt Henry Dygert: laid on the table. 5-Cmte on Indian Affairs: bill from the Senate for the relief of the legal reps of Geo Duval, a Cherokee Indian, reported the same without amendment: committed. 6-Cmte on Military Affairs: adverse report on the case of John Dorsey: laid on the table. 7-Cmte on Revolutionary Pensions: adverse reports on the cases of Sarah Miles, Christopher Moon, & Danl Flick. Same cmte: adverse reports on the cases of Pearson Freeman, John Taylor [of Jefferson Co, Va,] & Ebenezer Stone: laid on the table. 8-The ptn & papers of Henry A Livingston were recommitted to the Cmte on Revolutionary Claims, with additional & important papers now presented. Same cmte: Bill for the relief of Mgt Gwinnup: committed. 9-Ptn of Rebecca Boyd, of Northumberland Co, Pa, praying for a pension. 10-Report of Dr Richd Fraser, touching the necessity of having a physician on board emigrant vessels. 11-Ptn of Antoine Dupre, praying to be confirmed in a certain tract of land. 12-Ptn of Thos Blanchard, of Boston, for the renewal of his patent. 13-Ptn of Mgt Cowan & others, of Massachusetts, for a renewal of their pensions.

For rent: with board, a large double room. Apply to Mrs Clitz, between 3rd & 4½ sts, Pa ave.

SAT MAR 7, 1846
House of Reps: 1-No objection was made to the following bills: relief of Saml Jordan; relief of Wiley B Parnell; relief of Isabella Baldridge, wid/o Capt John Baldridge; & relief of Saml Brown. 2-Ptn of J A E Degrand, of Paris, France, for the reimbursement of 2/3rds of the amount paid by him to the Patent Ofc, he having abandoned all claim to a patent. 3-Ptn of Elijah Rose, of Penfield, N Y, asking pay for unrequited services in the last war. 4-Ptn of Richd Melvin, Jas Perham, Martha Jeffers, & Nancy C Hardy, children & legal reps of Mary Patten, late of Chester, N H, for the amount of pension due the said Mary Patten at the time of her decease. 5-Ptn of Peter Myers, of Greene Co, Pa, a soldier of the late war. 6-Memorial of Theodore Frelinghuysen, John Delafield, W C Redfield, & others, for repealing the law imposing duties on scientific works. 7-Claim of the heirs of Capt Andrew Englis, for forage, furnished the army in the Revolutionay war by the said Englis.

Dr E Hall offers his professional services as Practitioner of Medicine & Surgery to the inhabitants of Wash & its vicinity. Ofc north side of Pa ave, a few doors below Coleman's Hotel.

Money found: owner can have proving property & paying for this ad. Apply to John Foy, Republican House, D st.

The death of Govn'r Stockton invests Dr Jos Maull, Pres of the Senate, in ofc, with the gubernatorial powers.

Consulting a Doctor by Telegraph. Early yesterday, a gentleman stepped into the telegraph ofc at Buffalo & desired to have Dr Stevens, who resides & practices in the village, called into the ofc here, as he wished to have a conversation with him. Mr Boughton immediately called the Doctor. The gentleman at Buffalo said his wife was ill, & desired that Dr Stevens should prescribe for her. After a full account of her condition & symptoms, he made the proper prescriptions.
–Lockport Daily Courier

Gov Smith, of Va, has respited Hunter Hill, the murderer of Maj Smith, until Feb 7, 1847; & it is said that the Govn'r has avowed his determination to prevent the execution of the criminal during his term of ofc.

A lovely child of 7 years, a d/o of Dr Gunn, of Louisville, Ky, was crushed to death at New Orleans, on Feb 22, by a hogshead of sugar carelessly rolled from a dray.

Norfolk Beacon: Mrs Mason, [w/o of Bennett Mason, of Fox Hill, Eliz City Co,] 3 children, & Miss Sarah Melson, were all drowned at their residence during the late gale, the tide being so high as to effectuallay interdict their egress.

A new Diamond Mine was discovered in Brazil. It was discovered in oct, 1844, by a negro shepherd.

A letter to a gentleman in N Y C, dated Copper Harbor, Lake Superior, Jan 6, 1846, says: within the last 2 weeks a discovery has been made by the Pittsburg Co, at Eagle river, that beggars description. Mr Kendrick, who passed her a few days ago, was directly from the vein. He described as excelling any thing ever discovered in the civilized world: copper, mixed with silver, weighing from 3 to 4,000 pounds.

Mrd: on Mar 5, by Rev Mr French, Mr Junius Slemaker, of Anne Arundel Co, Md, to Miss Ellen, d/o Wm Gordon, of Wash City.

Died: yesterday, Mr Henry Teachum, a native of Germany, but for the last 50 years a resident of Wash City, in his 75th year. His funeral is Sun, at 2 ½ o'clock, from his late residence near Blagden's wharf.

Died: on Mar 1, at the residence of her father, Rev J E Weems, Summerfield, Prince Wm Co, Va, of pulmonary consumption, in her 24th year, Mrs Frances Ann, consort of Lt Robt Tansill, of the U S Marine Corps.

St Patrick's Day celebration on Mar 17, by a dinner at the hall of the Wash City Benevolent Society on G st, between 6th & 7th sts. Cmte: Philip Ennis, Wm Dowling, Jeremiah Calnan, & Jeremiah Sullivan.

Dr Filander Gould offers his professional services to the citizens of Wash. Ofc between 6th & 7th sts.

MON MAR 9, 1846
Commencement of the Medical Dept of the Columbian College was held last Thu in the Baptist Church, E st: degree of Doctor of Medicine was conferred on:

R M Worthington, of N C	John C Morfit, Wash
A McWilliams, Wash	Francis M Gunnell, Wash
John V Hackerman, Pa	Jas R Gregory, N Y
Alfred Ball, Ohio	G E Bomford, Wash
Wm Beall, Md	Aaron W Miller, Wash
Wm L Frazer, Alexandria	Cyrus Colby, Alabama

Criminal Court-Wash: 1-Geo Kendall, free negro, guilty of grand larceny: sentenced to 1 year in the penitentiary. 2-Thos Johnson alias Thos Williams, free negro, an old offender, was convicted of stealing shoes the property of Wm Noyes & Son: sentenced to 2 years in the penitentiary. 3-John Gross found not guilty for a riot at Gtwn on Dec 25. 4-Thos Taylor found not guilty for stealing a wheel-barrow, the property of the Corp of Wash. 5-Wm M Stewart found not guilty with an assault & battery upon Thos Nairy. 6-U S vs *Lydia Thompson, charged with keeping a house

of ill-fame & a disorderly house on Capitol Hill. There was a good deal of amusement, arising from the fact that Mr Zachariah Hazell undertook, at his own request, & with the leave of the bench & the bar, to act as counsel for the dfndnt. In the end, Mr Hazell, was not a successful advocate, for the jury found the dfndnt guilty on the 2nd count, & sentenced to pay a fine of $10, the Court adding that, but for her advanced age, she would have been sentenced to imprisonment.
[*Mar 3 newspaper: correction-the charge of keeping a house of ill fame was abandoned in the case of Lydia Thompson. She was found guilty of a disorderly house.]

Yesterday, the chimney on the house of Mr G Brooks, at 15th & Pa ave, caught fire. It was extinguished before damaging the bldg.

Vicksburg, [Miss] Feb 23. A party of Choctaws [about 300] are encamped near the plantation of Col Hebron, 9 miles from this city, where they were met by Gen Armstrong, preparatory to the delivery of their scrip & land patents. These Indians are under the charge of Col H N Barstown, Contractor for the Emigration, & Col Geo W Clarke, U S Agent. -Intelligencer

Turkish Feast. The marriage of the d/o Mehemet Ali was celebrated in Cairo in Dec. The festivities lasted 6 days.

Hon Dudley Chase died at his residence in Randolph, Vt, on Feb 23, aged 74 years. He was Speaker of the House of Reps from 1808 to 1812, when he was elected Senator in Congress for 6 years. In 1817 he was made Chief Justice of the Supreme Court: held ofc for 4 years, & resigned in 1821. At the 1824 session he was again elected to the U S Senate, &, having served out his time, he declined a re-election, & retired from public life in 1830.

Col Henry Purkitt died in Boston on Wed at the venerable age of 91. He was a soldier of the Revolution, & saw the memorable destruction of the tea in Boston harbor.

Doyleston Intelligencer: states that the country seat of the late Nicholas Biddle, of Andalusia, in that county, is to be sold at public auction on Mar 10.

Wash City Ordinances: 1-Act for the relief of John Fletcher, assignee of A C Kidwell: payment of the balance of the claim for regulating the gutter on square 287, & paving the same adjoining curb, the sum of $33.44, to be paid. 2-Act for the relief of Joshua L Henshaw: to refund to him the sum of $25, paid by him as rent of the lot in the rear of the school-house of the first district. 3-Act for the relief of M P Mohun: to pay him $16.39, being for work done in the repairing of the pavement on 12th st.

Died: Feb 20, at Vicksburg, Mr Richd Johnson, aged 65 years, formerly a resident of Balt & of Wash City.

By virtue of an order of distrain for house rent due to Jas Fitzgerald by Mrs Ford: I will offer at public sale, on Mar 14, in front of the Centre Market-house, to wit: 1 bureau, 3 tables, 1 stove, 7 chairs, a lot of carpeting, 7 pictures, 1 mantel clock, 1 bed, 1 bedstead & bedding, 6 glass jars, 2 jugs, 3 jars, 1 demijohn, & a lot of crockery ware. –H R Maryman, Bailiff

Died: on Mar 7, Gen John P Van Ness, in his 77th year. His funeral will take place at his late residence, on Tue at 4 o'clock. He was one of the oldest & most respected inhabitants of this city. He was a native of N Y, & elected to Congress from that State during the first term of Mr Jefferson's administration; & he shortly afterwards married the only child of the late David Burns, one of the original proprietors of the land on which Wash City was built. Having accepted from Mr Jefferson a commission of major of the militia in this District, it was deemed that by so doing he had forfeited his right to his seat in the House of Reps. He then fixed his permanent residence in Wash City. The Bank of the Metropolis was established in 1814, & he became its President, which ofc he held at the time of his death. He filled the ofc of Mayor. His loss will be sensibly felt by a large circle of acquaintances. The property which he received with his wife enabled him to extend an elegant hospitality to acquaintances & to strangers visiting the city, & to patronise all the purblic improvement & charitable & religious institutions in this city, without respect to sect or denomination. –S

Died: on Mar 1, suddenly, of an enlargement & ossification of the heart, at Rochester, journeying towards Washington, Henry C Mayer, of Chatauque Co, N Y, aged 24 years, leaving a disconsolate widow & 2 children. He was a native of Md, a learned member of the Balt Bar, an accomplished scholar; a sincere friend & Christian, & affectionate husband & father. He was the s/o Chas F Mayer, of Balt, & son-in-law of Jas W McCulloh, of Wash. He leaves his widow, 2 children, & his parents.

TUE MAR 10, 1846
Senate: 1- Ptn from Saml R Read, for a pension. 2-Ptn from Geo G Glazier & others, asking a reorganization of the navy. 3-Ptn from Mgt C Brown, widow of Thos Murray, asking compensation for services of her dec'd husband, as clerk of the Cherokee Indians while negotiating a treaty with the U S. 4-Ptn from the reps of John Anderson, asking indemnity for property destroyed by the British & Indians during the late war. 5-Ptn from Alex'r D Peck, of Louisiana, asking leave to have his title confirmed to a certain tract of land. 6-Cmte of Claims: bill for the relief of John Jones, surviving partner of John & Chas Souder. 7-Cmte on the Judiciary: bill for the relief of Richd S Coxe, with a report Same cmte: bill for the relief of Harriet L Catching. Same cmte: asking to be discharged from the further consideration of the ptn of Ray Tompkins & others, heirs of D D Tompkins, & that it be referred to

the Cmte of Claims; & from the ptn of Franklin Whitney, that it be referred to the Cmte on Patents. 7-Cmte of Claims: bill for the relief of Asa Andrews, with a report. 8-Cmte on Pensions: bill for the relief of Geo Wentling; written reports on the ptn of Carey H Seeley, & on the ptn of Mary D Wade. Same cmte: bill for the relief of Thos Brownell.

Take notice: I have just received, from Middletown Valley, Md, a lot of choice Roll Butter, which I shall offer to the lovers of this article this morning, on the stall next to Mr Chas Miller, butcher, old Centre Market-house, at a price to suit the times. --Richd Cruit

The Martinsburg [Va] Gaz has entered upon its 47th volume, & will hereafter be published by Messrs J E Stuart & H K Gregg. Mr S will continue to be its editor.

To Teachers: a Classical School, in situation one of the most desirable in the city, & worth from $500 to $800 or $1,000 per annum, is offered on the most reasonable terms. Address [post paid] John H H, Wash.

For rent: large house on C st, next door to the Exchange Hotel. Apply to the present occupant, Miss Gurley.

WED MAR 11, 1846
Fine South Branch Beef raised by Mr Cunningham. Mr Saml Little killed this beef & brought it to our principal market, Centre Market, & is deserving of great credit for this extraordinary display.

<u>Ladies of the Benevolent Society managers:</u>

Mrs M St C Clarke	Mrs Dr Bradley	Mrs Purdy
Mrs Latimer	Mrs Morton	Mrs Tucker
Mrs Easby	Mrs Fowler	Mrs Cox
Miss Crawford	Mrs Rice	Mrs S Brown
Miss Stott	Mrs W A Bradley	Mrs Stelle
Mrs Macomb	Mrs Col Munroe	Mrs Davis
Mrs Lyons	Mrs Anderson	Mrs Mills
Miss Moore	Mrs Hall	Mrs Milburn
Mrs Laurie	Mrs O B Brown	Mrs S King
Mrs Drake	Mrs Powell	

Senate: 1-Ptn from Benj Crawford, asking compensation for injuries received, while trading with the Creek Indians, by a U S ofcr. 2-Ptn from Jas Baker & others, asking indemnity for loss of certain Treasury notes. 3-Ptn from John Hurlburt, asking pay for certain services performed. 4-Cmte on the Judiciary: asking to be discharged from the further consideration of the ptn of Pearson Coggswell, late U S Marshal of N H, & that it be referred to the Cmte of Claims. 5-Cmte on Naval Affairs: bill for the relief of Jos Wilson, with a report.

For sale: 2 story brick dwlg-house on the west side of N J ave, below the residence of Thos Blagden. Also, a 2 story brick dwlg on the north side of N st south, next to 3rd st. –Richd Barry, opposite the property first named.

House of Reps: 1-Ptn of Alex'r D Peek, praying for confirmation of a tract of land in the parish of Morehouse. 2-Ptn of Isaac Guess, of Atala Co, Miss, praying to be confirmed in the entry of certain lands therein described. 3-Ptn of Henry Thompson, of Cynthiana, Ky, praying for a pension. 4-Ptn & papers of Andrew Flanagan, a Lt in the late war.

Dwlgs for rent on the heights of Gtwn. One large brick tenement, with near 2 acres of ground, now occupied by Lt Bissell, on Congress st; possession given on May 1 next. The other is a neat cottage, with 5 rooms & a kitchen, with a small garden, adjoining the residence of the subscriber; immediate possession of this can be had. –John Harry, Gtwn

Wash Corp: 1-Ptn from Wm Marshall & John Moore: referred to the Cmte on Improvements. 2-Ptn of Wm R Dempster, praying a remission of a fine: referred to the Cmte of Claims. 3-Ptn of C Doverwater, praying the renewal of a license: referred to the Cmte on Police. 4-Cmte of Claims: bill for the relief of Geo Stewart: passed. Same cmte, to which was referred the bill for the relief of Kenslaugh DeNeale: laid on the table.

Boston papers: Mr J Hoffman Collamore, who failed in Boston last year, owing $50,000, paid .30 on the dollar & received from his creditors a full & legal discharge. Soon afterwards property came into his possession by the death of a near relative, a portion of which he immediately placed in the hands of a trustee to make good his old liabilities.

Old manuscripts found several weeks since, whilst some workmen were taking down an old stone bldg on the dock of Rondout, in this town, a box was discovered hiddin some way between the floor & ceiling, & in it a large quantity of continental money, [several millions of dollars,] together with old papers relating to Revolutionary affairs. We saw the letter signed by Pierre Van Cortlandt, Pres of the Senate, & Evert Bancker, Speaker of the assembly, dated at Kingston, Jun 30, 1780, & directed to some persons at Rochester, Ulster Co, calling on them to aid the case of Independence by furnishing clothing for the soldiers. Some papers were scattered about the village-we are sorry for this. –Kingston [N Y] Jour

On Sunday, our old & estimable fellow-citizen, Thos Kell, died, after an illness of 3 or 4 weeks. Judge Kell was well known throught this State, in which, for a series of years, he was a very prominent citizen. -Baltimore American

J F Ready, who was concerned in the late bank robbery at Montreal, after being allowed to turn States' evidence against his accomplice, was admitted to bail. He absconded & went to one of the Southern States.

Mrd: on Mar 2, in St Paul's Church, Louisville, by Rev John B Gallagher, the Rev Wm A Smallwood, of Zanesville, Ohio, to Mrs Mary L Douglas, of N Y C.

Died: on Mar 8, after a painful illness of 3 months, which she bore with Christian fortitude, Mrs Sarah Hooper.

Died: on Mar 7, at the residence of his father, Sligo, Montgomery Co, Md, of pulmonary consumption, Wm S Prout, in his 17th year.

Furnished room for rent: F Lombardi, 11 st, east side, 2nd house north of Pa ave.

THU MAR 12, 1846

The Patapsco Female Institute, near Balt, [Ellicott's Mills Post Ofc,] Mrs Lincoln Phelps, Principal: will be in session for the summer after May 6.

For rent: commodious 3 story brick house, in the immediate vicinity of Capitol square. –Geo Watterston

Union Hotel, Winchester, Va: large & commodious house, recently erected by Mr Isaac Paul on Market st, [Cameron,] convenient to the Railroad, is now open to the public. The Daily Line of Stages to the South [via Staunton] run to & from this house. –A S Rhodes, late proprietor Cloverdale Hotel, Winchester, Va.

Desirable farm for sale: subscriber, having determined to remove to Loudoun Co, Va, is desirous of dispose of his farm, *Aspin Grove*, at private sale. It is in Alexandria Co, D C, 5 miles distant from Gtwn; contains 187½ acres; improvements are a comfortable frame house, 2 rooms above & 2 rooms below stairs, with a portico extending the length of the house. And kitchen & meat-house new, with some few outbldgs. Information can be obtained from either Col Wm E Minor, residing in the neighborhood, John E Addison, Gtwn, or from the subscriber at Leesburg, Va. –John West Minor

Senate: 1-Cmte on Naval Affairs: bill for the relief of John E Holland, without amendment. 2-Cmte on Pensions: House bills for the relief of Danl Ingalls; relief of Jos Watson; relief of Jas Wyman; relief of Jas Maine.

C C Langdon, the proprietor of the Mobile Daily Advertiser, is desirous of disposing of an interest in said establishment to some gentleman competent to take charge of the commercial dept of the paper.

For rent: comfortable 2 story brick dwlg near the corner of I & 7th sts, & next adjoining the residence of A Rothwell. To a good tenant the rent will be at the reduced rate of $200 per annum. Inquire of Mr R W Dyer, auctioneer, or of the subscriber, on 8th, between E & F sts. –Jane Maria Dyer

Died: on Wed, of consumption, Jas Staughton Gibson, s/o the late Jos Gibson, in his 21st year. His funeral is from his mother's residence, on 9th st, between I & N Y ave, this evening, at 4½ o'clock.

Died: on Feb 27, in Wash City, Mr Jas H Tuston, in his 42nd year.

FRI MAR 13, 1846
Senate: 1-Ptn from the Female Anti-Slavery Society of Phil, asking such change of the Constitution as will abolish slavery in the U S, & release the citizens of Pa from all participation in the support of American Slavery. Signed Hannah L Stickney, President, & Sarah A McKim, Sec. 2-Ptn from Gen Guier, guardian of the children of Jno S Ardis, for arrears of pension. 3-Ptn from Jas Bell & Allen G Johnson, asking to be allowed to enter a section of land on condition that they drain the inundated lands adjacent thereto.

Criminal Court-Wash: trial of the U S vs Julia Cross: witnesses for the defence: Mr Jas C Davidson, Mrs Davidson, Mr C Hunt, Mr David Hines, Misses Eliz & Virginia Cross, Mr Abraham Hines, Mr Theodore Kane, Mr Robt Ricketts, Mr Jas Barker, Saml Drury, & Mr Wagner. Mr Jos H Bradley spoke to the jury on behalf of Mrs Cross. Gen Jones followed Mr Bradley the next day. [Mar 16th newspaper: Mrs Cross was indicted for an attempt to poison the family of Mr Aquila Ricketts: jury found the accused not guilty.]

House of Reps: 1-Ptn of the heirs of Saml Ransom, who was killed at the battle of Wyoming, in 1778, praying compensation for the services of the said decendent as an ofcr in the Pa Continental Line. 2-Ptn of Thos Withrow for indemnity for losses as mail contractor. 3-Ptn of Wm C Crain & 9 others, members of the Legislature of N Y, in favor of the claim of Moses Van Campen, an ofcr of the Revolutionary war, for interest on his commission pay. 4-Ptn of John Morrison, an invalid pensioner, for back pay. 5-Ptn of Jones & Boker, & others, of Wash City, praying for an appropriation for the payment of certain Treasury notes lost by robbery of the U S mail. 6-Cmte of Claims: adverse reports on the cases of John Martin, Wm B Molt, & the heirs of Christopher Miller, dec'd: laid on the table. Same cmte: adverse reports on the cases of S F Chapman & Wm Jenkins: laid on the table. Same cmte: adverse reports on the cases of Saml D Sizer & of Harvey & Margaret Holgate: laid on the table.

Appointments by the Pres: 1-Alex'r Hunter, to be U S Marshal for the District of Columbia. 2-Jas McKissick, of Arkansas, to be Indian Agent for the Cherokee Agency, in place of P M Butler, whose commission had expired.

Died: on Mar 12, at the residence of her sister, Mrs Rachael Wheat, near Coombe's wharf, Mrs Amelia Radcliff, aged 74 years. Her funeral is today at 10 o'clock.

Died: on Thu, Jonathan Elliot, in his 62nd year, & for more than 30 years a resident of Wash City. His funeral is today at 4 o'clock, from his late residence on Capitol Hill, [formerly Jas Greenleaf's,] corner of 2nd st east & C st north. Mr Elliot was born near Carlisle, England, in 1784, & came to N Y about 1802, where he commenced the business of book printing. In 1810 he left N Y to take part in the revolutionary movement in Caraccas, to establish the independence of New Grenada, & was in several engagements under Bolivar, in one of which he was severely wounded. He was taken prisoner when Gen Miranda surrendered in 1812, & suffered many hardships. He was finally liberated, & returned to the U S in 1813; he then served in the American army in the last war. In 1814 he became a permanent resident of Wash City, &, during 13 years, edited the Wash Gaz with much ability. Mr Elliot is known as the author of "The American Diplomatic Code," "Debates on the Adoption of the Constitution," " The Comparative Tarriffs," "Funding System of the U S, &, "Statistics of the U S." In private life he was frank, generous, & warm-hearted, an affectionate father, & a kind husband.

Thos B Griffin has for the present removed his Boot & Shoe establishment on the opposite side of the street, next door to Mr Kinchey's Confectionary, & opposite to Mr Dyer's Auction Store, south side of Pa ave, between 10th & 11th sts.

Navy Dept: letter to the Hon John W Davis, Speaker of the House of Reps: from Geo Bancroft. Subject-Expenditures made by Lt John T McLaughlin, at the Florida expedition or squadron, from Oct 1, 1838, to Aug 3, 1842. Lt McLaughlin was paid for his services as captain commanding: $13,714.98. The Court is of the opinion that he did not waste, or permit any person under his command to waste any ammunition, provisions, or other public stores. 2-Letter from M C Perry, Pres of the Court: Phil Barton Key, Judge Advocate: Oct 29, 1845. [After the 10th head of inquiry is answered,] is the following: From the files of the Navy Dept it appears that the schnr **Wave**, under command of Lt John T McLaughlin, was, by an order from the Navy Dept dated Jun 12, 1838, placed under the orders of Cmdor Dallas, then in command of the West India station. On Jun 18, 1839, Lt McLaughlin was transferred from the West India squadron, & to report to Cmder Mayo, to whom had been assigned the command of the Florida expedition, & who continued in said command until Dec 2, 1839. The period for which Lt McLaughlin was allowed pay as a captain in command commenced on Oct 1, 1838; it appears that 14 months of the time he received pay as captain in command, he was under orders of ofcrs senior to himself. On Jun 8, 1840, Mr Sec Paulding wrote to Lt McLaughlin, informing him the Navy dept did not recognize him as cmder of a squadron, nor does the court consider his command at any time during the period of his service in Florida, entitle him to the pay of captain in command. The precedents referred to by Lt McLaughlin are not, in the opinion of the court, analogous to the case under consideration. –M C Perry

Anniversary of Ireland's Patron Saint will be celebrated by a public dinner at 4 o'clock, at Carusi's Saloon, on Mar 17. Cmte of Arrangements:

Philip Ennis
W Dowling
Jeremiah Sullivan
Jeremiah Calnan
Gregory Ennis
Edw Stubbs
John McDermott
Dr Carson, Alexandria
Jas Roach, Alexandria
Tim'y O'Neil, Gtwn
Tim'y Donoghue, Gtwn

-P Brady, Chairman: Geo D Dowling, Sec

SAT MAR 14, 1846

Cape of Good Hope newspapers to Dec 14 contain an account of the murder of the Rev Mr Scholtz, of the Berlin Society mission. He was assailed while on his way to Kaffirland to join the mission. 3 or 4 Kaffirs stabbed & killed Rev Scholtz & another man on the Fish river, near Port Peddie, in the encampment.

Mrd: on Feb 19, by Rev French S Evans, Wm Worrell, of Montg Co, Md, to Miss Ermenia C Franzoni, of Wash City.

Orphans Court of Wash Co, D C. In the case of Jas C Zabriskie, administrator of Borden M Voorhees, late of Wash Co, dec'd, the administrator & the Court have appointed Apr 7 next for the settlement of said estate, as far as the assets in the hands of the administrator. –Ed N Roach, Reg/o wills

MON MAR 16, 1846

Mrs Widdicombe has several furnished rooms for rent: on F st, near the Treas bldg, next door to Mr Pairo's exchange ofc.

New Spring Goods: Jas B Clarke, Pa ave, 7 doors west of Brown's Hotel.

Newburyport Herald announces the death, in that town, on Mon last, of Ephraim W Allen, aged 66 years, who was the conductor of the Herald for 30 years, interrupted only by 1 or 2 intervals of absence.

Salem Register has received intelligence of the death of Rev John Brazer, a distinguished Unitarian clergyman, & pastor of the North Church in Salem. He left Salem about 2 months ago for the South with impaired health, & died of dropsy on the chest & organic disease of the heart, on Feb 26 last, at the residence of his friend, Dr B Huger, in S C. He was 57 years of age.

John U Waring was shot in Versailles, Woodford Co, on Sat, from the window of an upper room in one of the hotels. The wound was supposed to be mortal. Through the whole of his most unhappy life, Waring was a man of violence & blood. He must have been nearly 70 years of age. –Louisville Jour

Dr Pardon Brownell, eminent physician of East Hartford, Conn, died from the bursting of a blood vessel in the head on Mar 10. He stepped into a democratic meeting; was called on to make some remarks; said a few words & said he had to stop because he was dizzy. He died in an hour & 20 minutes. He was 56 years of age, & a brother of Bishop Brownell. –Connecticut paper

Died: on Sat, suddenly, at **White Cottage**, Mrs Anna Gilman, w/o Ephraim Gilman, of the Genr'l Land Ofc, in her 59th year, for more than 30 of which a devoted disciple of her Redeemer. Her funeral will take place from her late residence today at 2 o'clock.

The undersigned informs he has sold his stock in trade, consisting of Boots & Shoes, to Mr John A Ruff. All persons having claims against him will hand them in & they will be paid. –Edw Lacy [John A Ruff, is at the old stand, a few doors east of Coleman's Hotel, & next door to Mr Frank Taylor's Bookstore.]

House of Reps: 1-Cmte on Private Land Claims: adverse report on the claim of Pierre Choteau & others, proprietors of the Dubuque land claim: laid on the table. 2-Cmte on Revolutionary Pension: bills for the relief of Leah Gray; relief of Mary Campbell: both committed. Same cmte: adverse reports on the cases of Edw Smith, Abner Watson, & John Murphy: laid on the table. 3-Cmte on Invalid Pensions: bill for the relief of Wm Gump: bill for the relief of Lewis Lang: bills were committed. 4-Ptn of Sally Ketchum, wid/o Jos Ketchum, for a pension. 5-Memorial of Geo Coombs, exc of Cornelius Manning, asking payment for an exported slave. 6-Additional evidence in support of the claim of Peter Shaffer. 7-Papers in the case of Elisha Tracey, of Norwich, Conn, asking Congress for additional pay. 8-Ptn of the heirs of Capt John Slaughter, of the N C Continental line, for commutation. 9-Memorial of Mrs Mary Bentley, wid/o Col Wm Bentley, asking to be allowed the same remuneration for the services of her husband in the war of the revolution which has been allowed to the widows of other ofcrs who were married prior to 1794.

TUE MAR 17, 1846
Household & kitchen furniture at auction on Mar 20, at the residence of the late Edw Ingle, B st north & 3rd st. –A Green, auctioneer

Anthracite & Cumberland Coal for sale, delivered punctually to order, it can be had at the corner of 13½ st & Md ave, near the Long Bridge. –John Pettibone

Meeting of the citizens of the First Ward this evening at 7½ o'clock: Foget not the Poor-provide means for the relief of the destitue poor. –Geo J Abbott, sec

Meeting of the citizens of the Northern portion of the 2nd, 3rd, & 4th Wards at the Academy of Mr John McLeod this evening, at half past 7 o'clock.
–J A M Duncanston, sec

Theatre-Odeon Hall, 4½ st & Pa ave. The Misses Kilmiste appearing in a variety of pieces, original songs, & brilliant dances; Mr Ferguson playing upon the war pipes of Scotland & the union pipes of Ireland. Performance at 8 o'clock. Tickets 50 cents.

WED MAR 18, 1846
Macon [Geo] Messenger of Mar 5: announces the death of our fellow-citizen Dr Ambrose Baber, who died on Sun last, very suddenly, while in the room of one of his patients in East Macon. He was a native of Rockingham Co, Va, & was among the earliest settlers of our city, having resided here since the spring of 1824, [except for a short time.] In the war with England in 1812 he served for some time as a volunteer soldier, & in the Creek & Seminole wars, a few years after, he was a surgeon in the army under Gen Jackson. In 1826, 1831, 1835, & 1838, he served in the U S Senate. In 1841 he was appointed Minister to Sardinia by Gen Harrison, where he remained about 3 years. On his return he resumed his profession. Dr Baber had prescribed for a consumptive patient a remedy often given, of which prussic acid is a material component, & known among the medical faculty as cyanuret of potass. The medicine was in a much stronger from than it should be administred. The error probably occurred by a reference to Elis' Formula, a work in which it exists on page 83, 7th edition, where an ounce of the medicated article prescribed in place of a drachm. The patient believing the medicine too strong, did not take it. Dr Baber had been in the practice of taking or administering the medicine, &, not being aware of the error, had a large dose of it, which terminated his life in a few minutes. No blame can be attached to the druggist. The health of Dr Baber at the time was very feeble, & perhaps hastened the operation of the fatal dose.

Wash Corp: 1-Cmte of Claims: asked to be discharged from the further consideration of the ptn of Chas Borremans: agreed to. 2-Ptn from Lewis Carusi & R R Golden: referred to the Cmte of Claims.

Senate: 1-Ptn from Wm P Fail, asking to be allowed to change a location of a grant of land. 2-Ptn from the heirs of Willis Wilson, for commutation pay. 3-Ptn from Chas Callaghan, asking that the awards made under the convention with Mexico may be paid. 4-Documents relating to the claim of Agnes Williams, for an increase of pension: referred. 5-Ptn from the widow of John T King, asking a pension for services performed by her husband. 6-Cmte on the Judiciary: bill for the relief of certain bail of Thaddesu C Haskell, of the State of Vt. 7-Cmte on Revolutionary Claims: asking to be discharged from the further consideration of the ptn of the heirs of Gustavus B Horner, on the ground of irregularity, the ptn having been reported against at a previous session. Same cmte: adverse report on the claim of the heirs of Lord Sterling. 8-Cmte on Indian Affairs: report on the memorial of Preston Sterritt & others: which was ordered to be printed.

Notice: by writ of fieri facias, I shall expose to public sale, for cash, on Mar 24. one hackney carriage, seized & taken as the property of Jos Sill, & will be sold to satisfy a judgment in favor of Geo W Walker. -R T Mills, Constable

House of Reps: 1-Ptn of Archibald Bull & Lemuel S Finch, for services rendered & money advanced to detect a forgery on the pension fund. 2-Memorial of John Cook, asking pay for services of his father, Capt Geo Cook, in the war of the Revolution. 3-Ptn of Betsey Baine, of Cornville, Maine, for money or land due her for services of her former husband, Job Kenniston. 4-Ptn of Pethuel Foster, an invalid Pensioner, for back pay.

A Card: Mrs M Lare, formerly Miss M Ross: Plain & Fancy Dress & Habitmaker, informs she has removed from her old stand, next door to Woodward & King's, & taken a house on 10th st, west side, near Pa ave, to execute all orders in her line with her usual promptness. –M Lare

Died: on Fri last, at Balt, Henrietta, w/o Mr Wm Samuels, of Wash City. Her sufferings were intense, but her last moments were peaceful, & she expired with a firm reliance in the promise of her Redeemer. Her funeral is this day at 11 o'clock, from the house of Mr Jas Handley on 7th st, between G & H sts.

Died: on Mar 12, at the house of her son, Hiram Richey, Mrs Jane Richey, aged 63 years, after a long & painful illness, being for nearly 5 years confined to her bed, which she endured with perfect resignation to the holy will of the Lord. She was a native of Ireland, born in the county of Tyrone, came to this country when a child, with her parents, & for the last 25 years had lived in this District.

THU MAR 19, 1846
One Cent Reward: ran away from the subscriber, on Mar 16, Robt Clements, an indented apprentice to the Confectionary & Bakery Business. I forewarn all persons from employing or harboring said apprentice, as I am determined to enforce the rigor of the law on all persons so doing. I will give the above reward, but no thanks. –Geo Krafft

Senate: 1-Ptn from Henry R Schoolcraft, asking to be allowed a credit on certain disbursements made by him, & compensation for extra services. 2-Ptn from the reps of Jean Baptiste les Compte de Lomagne, asking commutation pay. 3-Cmte on the Judiciary: bill to refund a fine imposed on Thos Cooper under the sedition law. 4-Cmte on Naval Affairs: adverse report on the ptn of Eliza Sevier.

Sandwich Islands. When Capt Cook first discovered these islands, in 1778, he found a people immersed in the grossest barbarism, the subjects of the most degrading superstition & idolatry, & offering human victims to appease the wrath or to win the favor of their imaginery deities.

$3,000 wanted, to be secured by mortgage on improved & unincumbered real estate. Inquire of Fred Koones, Genr'l Agent, ofc #6, Pollard Row.

Horrible Butchery. We learn by Mr Fink, conductor from Auburn, that the house of Mr Van Ness, a farmer & supervisor of the town of Fleming, on Owasco lake, 4 miles from Auburn, was entered Fri, by some one disguised as a negro, & Mr Van Ness, his wife & child were stabbed by the villain, & are dead. His mother-in-law and hired man were also stabbed, but are still living. The above is from the Albany Citizen of Sat. The supposed murderer has been taken at Fulton, Oswego Co, & is in the custody of the Sheriff. [Mar 20th newspaper: the murderer is a negro, Wm Freeman, about 23 years old. He has been for 5 years in the State prison for stealing a horse, of which he was convicted through Mr Van Ness. Four of the persons stabbed have already died, & it is probable that a 5th victim will be added: Cayuga Co, N Y.]

Died: yesterday, suddenly, in Wash City, Cmdor Wm M Crane, of the Navy, & Chief of the Bureau of Ordnance & Hydropgraphy. [Mar 20th newspaper: the funeral of Cmdor Crane is this day, Fri, at 11 o'clock, from the residence of Cmdor Warrington.]

Died: on Feb 27, at Havana, Mrs Juliana Jenkins, in her 36th year, w/o Edw Jenkins, & d/o Basil S Elder, all of Balt.

Died: on Mon last, at his residence, in Nottingham District, after an illness of but 2 days, Francis E Mudd, Pres of the Levy Court of PG Co, Md. Few men have descended to the grave more universally respected & esteemed than Mr Mudd. By his honest & upright walk in life, he had endeared to him the neighborhood in which he lived.

FRI MAR 20, 1846
A beautiful monument, to be place over the remains of Capt E R Shubrick, who died about 2 years ago on board the U S frig **Columbia**, at Rio Janeiro, has been finished in Boston. It was made by order of the ofcrs & crew of the **Columbia**, to whom Capt Shurbrick endeared himself by his many excellent qualities. Capt Shubrick was buried in Charleston, & thither the monument is to be taken.

The great pianist, Leopold De Meyer, is now on a professional visit to this metropolis.

Criminal Court-Wash: 1-Geo Drudge, not guilty for assault & battery upon Hon Mr Sprigg, of Ky, by biting off his ear several years ago, in a refectory on Pa ave.

The 4 companies of volunteers called out at New Orleans, by Gen Gaines, for Texas, without any orders from the War Dept, & without any occasion for their services, were paid $51,600 for 3 months' service.

Methodist Protestant Conference adjourned on Wed. Annual appointments for 1846:
Pres-Eli Hinkle
Conference Missionary-Fred'k Stier
Kensington station, Phil-John G Wilson
First Methodist Protestant Church, Phil-unsupplied by Conference
Brickmaker's station, Phil-J R Nichols, Thos J Desberry, J Mallison, sup assistant
Wilmington station, Delaware-S B Southerland
Newport circuit-Wm D Hamilton
Cecil circuit-Jas M Eldendice
Smyrna mission-Thos M Bryan
Kent circuit-W Roby, Wm Dale
Queen Anne's circuit-T M Wilson [one to be supplied]
Caroline circuit-Geo Heritage
Lewis mission-D A Shermer
Sussex circuit-Wm T Wright
Dorchester circuit-Theodore D Valiant
Cambridge circuit-D W Bates, T A Moore
Union circuit-L W Bates, H Day
Newtown circuit-Danl F Ewell, J D Brooks
Snow Hill circuit-John Roberts
Accomac circuit-Wm Fisher, [one to be supplied.]
Deer Creek circuit-D Evans Reese, [one to be supplied.]
Newmarket circuit-G D Hamilton, F Swentzell
Carlisle circuit-John Elderdice
Concord circuit-Henry Rowan
Juniata circuit-David Wilson, [one to be supplied]
Cumberland station-H P Jordan
Alleghany circuit-R Adkinson
Pipe Creek circuit-W Collier, J K Nichols
Fred'k circuit-L P Wilson
Howard circuit-T L McLean, J C Davies
Baltimore circuit-J Webster, J McClelland
East Baltimore station-J J Murray
Central Baltimore station-to be supplied.
West Baltimore station-L R Reese, D T Waters, super assist
Liberty street mission-unsupplied by Conference
Anne Arundel circuit-R S Norris, J M Henckle
First Methodist Protestant Church, Wash-Wm T Eva
9th st Methodist Protestant Church, Wash-S K Cox
Gtwn station-Jas Varden
Alexandria station-Dr J S Reese
Potomac circuit-Wm T Dunn
Prince Wm circuit-A Eversole
Franklin mission-to be supplied.
Hummelstown mission-to be supplied.

A correspondent of the Tallahassee Sentinel, writing from Tampa Bay, mentions the recent discovery of an old *Spanish fort*, about 40 miles from that place. It is some 80 feet high, for an area of about 60 feet long & 50 broad, among which were fragments of cannon, swords & muskets, so far eaten by time to be scarcely recognized. Half of a wall of the fort was still standing. An old musket barrel dated 1539 was found amid the rubbish.

The Wheeling Times announces the arrival there of the new schnr **Cyrus Chamberlain**, 13 tons, built at Freedom, Pa, & bound for New Haven, Conn: Cyrus Chamberlain owner, builder, & master. She is intended for the coasting trade, & is as pretty a vessel as sails.

The Gloucester Machine Company, having commenced operations at their New Works at Gloucester, N J, are prepared to make contracts for every description of Cotton Machinery; also, Slide & Screw Engine Lathes, & all other Machine Shop Tools. Reference to Siter, Price & Co, Phil. Address J Cooke Siter, Treas, Gloucester, N J.

Senate: 1-Ptn of Abraham P Housman, asking indemnity for property destroyed by Seminole Indians. 2-Ptn from Edw Hardy, asking reimbursement of duties unlawfully extracted by the Collector of N Y. 3-Citizens of Cayuga Co, remonstrating against the renewal of Jethro Wood's patent for a plough. 4-Ptn from Geo Trull, praying reimbursement of duties illegally exacted by the Collector of N Y. 5-Ptn from the legal reps of Cornelius Oakley, for a pension for his services. 6-Cmte on Patents: bill for the relief of Oliver C Harris.

Appointments by the Pres, by & with the advice & consent of the Senate.
Andrew J Donelson, of Tenn, to be Envoy Extra & Minister Pleni of the U S, at the court of his Majesty the King of Prussia, in place of Henry Wheaton, recalled.
Ofcrs of the Customs:
Henry W Rogers, to be Collector for the district of Buffalo Creek, & Inspector of the Revenue for the port of Buffalo, in N Y, vice Jedediah H Lathrop, removed.
Otis N Cole, to be Collector of the Customs for the district, & Inspector of the Revenue for the port of Sackett's Harbor, in N Y, vice John O Dickey, removed.
Michl Hoffman, to be Naval Ofcr for the district of N Y, in N Y, vice Jeremiah Towle, removed.
Geo W Pomeroy, to be Appraiser of Merchandise for the port of N Y, in N Y, vice Mathias B Edgar, removed.
Stephen R Mallory, to be Collector of the Customs for the district, & Inspector of the Revenue for the port of Key West, in Florida, vice Adam Gordon, removed.
Isaac II Wright, to be Navy Agent for the port of Boston, in Mass, in place of J Vincent Browne, removed.

Land Ofcrs:
Jas C Sloo, to be Register of the Land Ofc for the district of lands subject to sale at Shawneetown, Ill, from Mar 25, 1846, when his present commission will expire.
Wyatt J Draugn, to be Receiver of Public Moneys for the district of lands subject to sale at Augusta, Miss, from Apr 21, 1846, when his present commission will expire.
Jas H Weakly, to be Surveyor Genr'l of the Public Lands in the State of Alabama, from Apr 1, 1846, when his present commission will expire.

Postmasters:
Nathan L Woodbury, Portland, Maine, in place of S R Lyman, removed.
Harvey Chapin, Springfield, Mass, in place of Galen Ames, removed.
Edw W Green, New Bedford, Mass, in place of Simeon Bailey, removed.
Geo F Worth, Nantucket, Mass, in place of S H Jenks, whose commission expired.
Thos Shepherd, Northampton, Mass, in place of Amos H Bullen, removed.
Richd H Stanton, Maysville, Ky, in place of Jas W Coburn, whose commission expired.

Justices of the Peace:
Wm Minor for Alexandria Co, D C, in place of John W Minor, who has removed from said District.
Jas Carson, for Alexandria Co, D C, in place of Tench Ringgold, dec'd.
John M Thayer & John M Williams, for Wash Co, D C.
Wm F Purcell, & Jas M Fearson, for Wash Co, D C.

Charleston papers announce the death on Mar 12 of Capt Thos Hervey, in his 68th year, who held the ofc of Surveyor of the port of Charleston for the last 32 years.

Mrd: on Mar 19, by Rev Mr French, Rector of the Church of the Epiphany, in Wash City, Lewis R Hammersly, formerly of York, Pa, to Catherine E, d/o the late Cmdor Thos Holdup Stevens, U S Navy, both of Wash.

Mrd: on Feb 25, in Gallatin Co, Ill, Mr Chas H Lanphier, of Springfield, Ill, to Miss Mgt T Crenshaw, of the above county.

House of Reps: 1-Ptn of Archibald Bull & Lemuel S Finch, for services rendered & money advanced to detect a forgery on the pension fund. 2-Memorial of Phebe Breasha for arrearages of pension due her late husband, John Lang, dec'd, for wounds received on board of the U S ship **Wasp**, in her engagement with His Britannic Majesty's ship **Frolic**, Oct 18, 1812. 3-Ptn of Isaac Cobb, praying for a pension. 4-Ptn of Gilman B Shaw, of the State of Maine, for arrearages of pension. 5-Application of Hannah Jane Wick, for an increase of pension on account of the services of her husband. 6-Ptn of Wm Armstrong, of Cuyahoga Falls, Ohio, for a pension. 7-Ptn of Eliza Bostwick, of Edinburgh, Ohio, asking compensation for Revolutionary services. 8-Ptn of Benj J Cahoone, Purser in the U S Navy, for relief.

Died: on Mar 18, in Wash City, Walter Luke, infant s/o the Hon Walter T Colquitt, Senator from the State of Georgia. Though the parents have lost a child, Heaven has received another Cherub.

Orphans Court of Wash Co, D C. In the case of John P Pepper, adm of Wm Hicks, dec'd, the administrator & Court have appointed Apr 7 next, for the final settlement of the said estate, with the assets in the administrator's hands, so far as have been collected & turned into money. –Ed N Roach, Reg o/wills

For rent or exchange: 3 story brick house on First st, Gtwn, in Smith's Row. Mr Pettit, who is to be found in his carpenter's shop, a few doors west of the house, has the key, & will show the premises. For further particulars apply to M Adler, Agent.

For rent: new brick house on 16th st west, opposite Cmdor Morris'. Also, a 2 story house on G st, opposite the War Ofc, lately occupied by Mr Wm Browne.
–Jas Carrico

For rent: 2 story brick dwlg-house, nearly new, on Mass ave, between 11th & 12th sts. Inquire of Richd Elliott, on N Y ave, between 12th & 13th sts, or of J Goodrich, at the City Post Ofc.

SAT MAR 21, 1846
House of Reps: 1-Letter from the Sec of War, containing the report of Capt J Allen, of the 1st Regt of Dragoons, of his expedition during the past summer to the heads of the Des Moines, Blue Earth, & other rivers in the northwest. Letter was referred to the Cmte on Military Affairs. [Note: Letter is not in the paper.]

Zachariah Hazel has taken the Fish Wharf on the Eastern Branch, near the Navy Yard, at which the highest price will be given for all kinds of fish that may be brought to the wharf. –Z H

Madame Clermon has removed to the n w corner of 10th st, one door from Pa ave, round the corner from Mr Dyer's auction store, where she has for sale a fresh supply of the best linen drilling corsets.

Paper-hanging & Upholstering Store, on Pa ave, between 9th & 10th sts. Latest styles will be sold at the old stand of Muller & Moore. –D Moore

Died: yesterday, after an illness of only a few days, Ezra Holden, one of the editors of the Phil Sat Courier, aged about 40 years.

Died: on Feb 20, in PG Co, Md, at the residence of Richd Young, Mr Jas M Timms, of Wash, in his 34th year. His funeral is this evening at 4 o'clock, from the residence of his mother, on A st south, Capitol Hill.

Orphans Court of Wash Co, D C. Letters of administration on the personal estate of Lezan Kervand, late of said county, dec'd. –Anne Eliz Kervand, admx

MON MAR 23, 1846

Criminal Court-Wash. 1-Bayes, an old offender, was found guilty for stealing sundry article, the property of Mr Ball, the jailer: & sentenced to 6 months in the county jail.

Orphans Court of Wash Co, D C. In the case of Jas M Cutts & Richd D Cutts, adms of Richd Cutts, dec'd, the administrators & Court have appointed Apr 13 next, for the final settlement of said estate, with the assets in the hands of the administrators. –Ed N Roach, Reg/o wills

The Frankfort [Ky] Commonwealth says that John U Waring, who was shot at Versailles a few days ago, died about 24 hours after the shot. He was a violent man, & a post-mortem examination disclosed a fact long suspected, that he wore a strong coat of mail, made of steel.

Laying the Corner-stone of the new Roman Catholic Church, 5th st, between G & H sts, will take place on Mar 25, the feast of the Annunciation, at 11 o'clock. Holy Mass for the Germans will be in the Chapel on 8th st by Rev M Arlig on that morning, at 8 o'clock, after which the German Society for bldg the Church will go in procession, with their Pastor, to St Matthews' Church, & proceed to the site of the new Church: named Church of <u>Saint Mary Mater Dei</u>. The corner-stone will be laid by the Most Rev Archbishop Eccleston in pontificals, at the conclusion of which sermons will be delivered in German & in English, & a collection will be taken up to aid in erecting the bldg.

Notice: Application is intended to be made to the Treas of the U S for the payment of a lost certificate issued by the Register of the U S, on Aug 26, 1782, for $16.94, to Clemens Green, who was a soldier in Col Armand's Legion, in the war of the Revolution.

Mrd: on Mar 19, by Rev John P Donelan, Mr Geo A Fisher to Miss Eve Hesler, both of Wash City.

Mrd: on Mar 11, in Utica, N Y, by Rev Geo Leeds, J Sidney Henshaw, U S Navy, of Phil, to Jane, d/o the late John H Handy, of Utica.

Mrd: on Mar 2, in N Y, by Rev A Bloomer Hart, Mr Chas A Dana, of Brook Farm, Mass, to Miss Eunice, d/o the late John Macdaniel, of Wash.

Household & kitchen furniture at auction on Mar 25, at the residence of Mrs Brook, on 12th between G & H sts. –A Green, auctioneer

TUE MAR 24, 1846
Senate: 1-Ptn from Danl Simmons & others, asking indemnity for property destroyed by Seminole Indians. 2-Ptn from the heirs of Jonathan Johnson, asking to be allowed commutation pay. 3-Ptn from Martha More, for a pension. 4-Ptn from Michl Boden, for a pension. 5-Additional documents in relation to the claim of Hugh Wallace Wormley. 6-Cmte on the Public Lands: bill to compromise the claim of the heirs of John Smith T to certain lands under a Spanish grant. 7-Cmte on Pensions: bill for the relief of Geo Wingerd. 8-Cmte on Private Land Claims: bill for the relief of Robt Barclay, of Missouri. 9-Cmte on Revolutionary Claims: adverse report in the case of Simeon Hubbard, W S Jett, & Beebee Wadhams; which was order to be printed. 10-Cmte on Privatr Land Claims: bill for the relief of Wm Marrin. Adverse report on the ptn of the heirs of Erastus Brown.

Valuable lands for sale in Prince Wm & Fairfax Co, Va. By virtue of a decree of the Circuit Superior Court of Law & Chancery for Fairfax Co, pronounced at its Nov Term, 1845, in 2 suits therein depending, in the name of John H Bernard, exc of Eliz Hipkins, against Jas H Hooe's administrator & others, & Aris Buckner & wife against the same dfndnts, the undersigned will sell at Centreville, in Fairfax Co, on May 25, 1846, the following desirable tracts of land, belonging to the estate of Jas H Hooe, dec'd: 1-In Prince Wm Co: Tract on Little Bull Run, called *Poplar Fields*, containing about 600 acres, now rented by C C Magruder. One tract in the immediate neighborhood of Bethlehem Meeting-house, containing about 127 acres, now occupied by Hanson Pinn. One other tract in the same neighborhood, containing about 240 acres, now occupied by Walter Woodyard. Another called *Bradley tract*, containing about 1,376 acres, now occupied by Wm Duvall. One tract, adjoining *Bradley*, containing 10 acres; & one other tract containing about 80 acres, adjoining Hazle Plain, the former residence of Bernard Hooe, sr, dec'd, now occupied by Jas Robinson. 2-In Fairfax Co: one tract of land on Cub run, containing about 650 acres, now occupied by Mr Legg. One other tract called *Wood Lawn*, containing about 350 acres, now occupied by Garret Freeman & Henry Hanison. One other tract containing about 477 acres, now occupied by Jas Fewell; & one other tract containing about 53 acres, also occupied by Jas Fewell. Mr Thos B Gaines, living near Haymarket, in Prince Wm Co, will show the lands in that county.
–F L Smith, Alexandria, T R Love, Fairfax C H, Com'rs

SAM WINTER-If Saml Winter, who, it is believed, left England about the year 1780, & went to reside in Alexandria city, in Va, in the U S A, & carried on there the trade or business of a shipwright, or his children or lawful descendants, will apply to Messrs Brooke & Mertons, solicitors, Margate, they may hear of something to their advantage. –London Times, Feb 9, 1846.

Orphans Court of Wash Co, D C. Letters of administration on the personal estate of Henry Ashton, late of the U S Navy, dec'd. –Caroline H Watkins, Geo S Watkins, admx

Orphans Court of Wash Co, D C. Letters of administration on the personal estate of Eleanor C Simms, late of said county, dec'd. –F Forrest, exc

The Evansville Journal states that Messrs Geo Schlamp, John Schnell, & Fred Sauter, were drowned on Tue week within a mile or 2 of Mount Vernon. They, with 2 others, were in a 2 horse wagon, & attempted to cross a creek, which they thought fordable.

On Mar 15 the bldg occupied as the Buffalo Woollen Manufactory, by R B Heacock, was totally destroyed by fire. There were about 10,000 yards of cloth destroyed. The total loss is estimated at $20,000.

Foreign Obituary. In Dec, in the battle with the Sikhs, Sir Robt Sale, Sir John McCaskill. In Feb, Sir Jas R Carnac, formerly Govn'r of Bombay. In Ireland, Rear Admiral Saml C Romley, aged 71. On the 3rd ult, the Dowager Dutchess of Anhalt Dessau, aged 70. On the 13th ult, John Loder, the eminent violinist, aged 58. On the 12th ult, Sir Geo W L Knight, late physician to the embassy of Russia, committed suicide by taking prussic acid while laboring under insanity. On the 14th ult, in Dublin, much regretted, Miss Moore, the only surviving sister of Thos Moore, the poet. At Fintray House, Aberdeenshire, Sir John Forbes, aged 61. –London paper

Mrd: on Mar 23, at the U S Hotel, by the Rev W T Sprole, Burgis D Bartlett to Miss Armenia Timms, all of Virginia.

Rooms to let: 4 large rooms on Pa ave, near 9th st. –J Visser, at his Fancy Store, near 9th st.

WED MAR 25, 1846
On Sun a colored man named Clark was caught by 2 of the Auxiliary Guard in the Billiard Saloon belonging to Messrs Provest & Wallingsford, which he had broken into with a felonious intent. He was armed with a loaded pistol, which he fired. The pistol missed fire or officer Colclasier would have been killed on the spot. The prisoner has been full committed for trial by Justices Morsell & Goddard.

Senate: 1-Ptn from John B Clarke, of N Y, asking remuneration for duties illegally exacted by the collector of that port. 2-Ptn from Francis Le Beau, Jean Bevin, & Alexis Perche, remonstrating against the confirmation of certain private land claims in Louisiana.

Mr Loring Larkins, formerly captain of the schnr **Merchant**, was tried at Charleston last week on a charge of being about to engage in the slave trade, & convicted. The punishment is a fine of not more than $7,000, & imprisonment for not more than 5 years. [Apr 2nd newspaper: Mr Lorin Larkins to pay a fine of $1,000 & remain in jail 3 years, being the least punishment allowed under the law.]

Painting by Mr J H Beard, of Cincinnati, "The North Carolina Emigrants," is on display in the Rotundo of the Capitol. It is a large picture representing a party of humble & hardy emigrants on their way from N C to Ohio.

Murderous affray at Nashville, Tenn, on Sun week, in the street, between E Z C Judson & Robt Porterfield, in which the latter was shot dead. About 12 or 15 balls were fired at Judson by the brother of the dec'd & his friends, none of which struck him. The sheriff conveyed him to prison, but the people took the law into their own hands. A mob broke into the jail, dragging Judson, the prisoner, & hung him over an awning post. He was only saved from death by the breaking of the rope, when he was again conveyed to jail.

Mrd: on Mar 23, at the residence of Mr J P Heiss, by the Rev A A Muller, D D, Pastor of St Paul's Lutheran Church, Marinus Stacker, of Tenn, to Maria, 2nd d/o B Richmond, of Nashville.

Pathological Society meeting this day at the City Hospital, at 1 o'clock.
–F Howard, sec

To builders: proposals will be rec'd until Apr 15 for the erection of a portico & belfry in front of the First Presbyterian Church. Information to Mr Robt Brown, Capitol Hill, or Mr Harvey Cruttenden, bldg cmte.

Groceries at auction on Mar 30, at the store of Wm McLean, corner of B st south & N J ave, his entire stock of Groceries. Also, his scales, weights, & drawers.
–A Green, auctioneer

$10 reward for lost bright leather Trunk, with the marks J B. Lost in going between the Railroad Depot to the lower end of N J ave. Information to Capt Goddard, of the Auxiliary Guard, or to T F Hickey, N J ave, near Mr Blagden's.

House of Reps: 1-Ptn of Reuben B Heacock, & A M & S H Grosman, for compensation for property destroyed by the army at Buffalo in 1813. 2-Ptn of S Calvert Ford, asking that his account may be settled, & the amount paid out by him for the benefit of the troops while at Carlisle may be refunded. 3-Ptn of Wm Hilton, of Solon, Somerset Co, Maine, for increase of pension. 4-Remonstrance of Francis Deming & a great number of others, masters of vessels & others interested in the commerce of Alexandria, D C, against the repeal of the pilot law of Mar 2, 1837. 5-Ptn of B F H Witherell & others, for appropriation in lands for the construction of a military road from Saginaw to the Straits of Mackinaw, in the State of Michigan. 6-Ptn of M E Davis, praying for a confirmation of a tract of land. 7-Ptn of Jacob Lehman, a soldier in the war of 1812, for arrears of pension. 8-Ptn of Nicholas James, a soldier of the Revolutionary war, for a pension. 9-Ptn of Isaac Fowler & 28 others citizens of Ohio, for a naval depot at Huron. 10-Ptn of Jas Otis & 22 others, citizens of Ohio, for a naval depot at Sandusky.

The subscriber will undertake to do Stone-mason's & Bricklayer's Work in all its branches, fix Boilers & all firework flues which require brick & mortar, & will be thankful to the citizens of Washington for employment. Reference: the work done in his line of business for the last 30 years in Wash City. -Jacob A Bender

Valuable bldg lots for sale: lots 9, 10, & 11, in square 220, fronting on H st, near St Matthew's Church. Please call at my ofc, in the west wing of the City Hall, John A Linton, Atty.

Public sale of that beautiful piece of property on C st, between 3rd & 4½ st, lately occupied by Robt N Johnson. I believe the title to be perfectly good.
–Jos H Bradley

Valuable property on Pa ave for sale at public auction: on Apr 29: parts of lots 17 & 18, in square B, with a 3 story brick dwlg: occupied by Mrs Preuss as a boarding-house. Lots 26 & 27, in square B, with a 3 story brick dwlg & a back bldg & store: dwlg occupied by Mrs Hamilton as a boarding house. -R W Dyer, auct

For rent, my 3 story brick house on Bridge st, Gtwn, nearly opposite the Farmers' & Mechanics' Bank, & opposite the Post Ofc. Also, a snug brick house on Gay st, next door to Mr Jos Reynolds, in good order; rent very law. Apply to W S Nicholls.

THU MAR 26, 1846
The corner-stone of the new German Catholic Church intended for the use of German Catholics under the pastoral care of the Rev M Arlig, of Wash City, was laid yesterday by the Most Rev Archbishop Eccleston, in the presence of an immense body of people. A large procession, accompanied by the German Band, moved along Pa ave, from St Mathew's Church, passing into 4½ st, & thence to the site of the Church of <u>St Mary Mater Dei</u>, which is situated on 5th st, between G & H sts. Procession: The German Band; German Beneficial Society; the German Male & Female Sodality; the Wash Benevolent Society; the Rev Messrs Flannegan & Ray, of Gtwn, the Rev Messrs Donelan, of Wash, & clergy of Balt. A numerous body of Germans & citizens, walked two by two. Rev J P Donelan delivered a sermon in English, & Rev Mr Haslinger, of Balt, delivered a sermon in German.

Mr Saml F Wright, formerly of PG Co, Md, was killed at Maysville, Ky, last week by the falling of a heavy iron shaft in a cotton factory.

Mrd: on Mar 24, by Rev F S Evans, Mr Wm Glover to Miss Henrietta E Clarke.

Mrd: on Mar 24, by Rev F S Evans, Mr Richd Gray to Miss Mary Dover.

Mrd: on Mar 24, at St John's Church, by Rev Mr Pyne, Mr Geo B Ironside, of N Y, to Mary E, d/o Capt W H Swift, of the U S Army.

Senate: 1-Ptn from Jas Buchanan, late British Consul, at N Y, asking reimbursement of moneys expended in case of a vessel brought into that port under charge of a British ofcr. 2-Ptn from E Ley & others, citizens of Florida, remonstrating against the passage of a bill for the relief of Jos Chaires. 3-Ptn from Haym M Salonron, asking reimbursement for moneys expended by his father during the Revolutionary war. 4-Ptn from citizens of Florida, remonstrating against the confirmation of the claim of Aredondo's heirs. 5-Cmte on Revolutionary Claims: adverse report on the ptn of the heirs of Willis Wilson. 6-Cmte on the Judiciary: bill for the relief of John P Skinner & the legal reps of Isaac P Green. Same cmte: adverse report on the ptn of Chas Stearns.

Appointments by the Pres, by & with the advice & consent of the Senate:
Ephraim D Dickson, to be Register of the land ofc for the district of lands subject to sale at Fayetteville, Ark, vice Jas H Stirman, removed.
Thos Mussey, Collector of Customs for the district of New London, Conn, vice Chas F Lester, dec'd.
Chas S A Davis, Surveyor of the District & Inspector of Revenue for the port of New Haven, Conn, vice Chas A Judson, removed.
Wm A Pritchard, Collector of Customs for the district of Camden, & Inspector of Revenue for the district of Eliz City, N C, vice Geo W Charles, removed.
Christopher R Dickson, to be Postmaster at Jackson, Miss, vice Howell Hobbs, removed.
Alex'r B Meek, U S Atty for the souther district of Alabama, vice Geo J S Walker, whose commission has expired.

Promotions & appointment in the U S Army.
Promotions:
2nd Lt Jeremy F Gilmer, to be 1st Lt, Dec 29, 1845, vice W H Wright, dec'd.
Brevet 2nd Lt Edw B Hunt, to be 2nd Lt, Dec 29, 1845, vice Gilmer, promoted.
2nd Regt of Dragoons:
2nd Lt Reuben P Campbell, to be 1st Lt, Nov 3, 1845, vice Ransom, dismissed.
3rd Regt of Artl:
2nd Lt Geo W Ayers, to be 1st Lt, Dec 20, 1845, vice Rankin, dec'd.
Brevet 2nd Lt Isaac F Quinby, to be 2nd Regt of Artl, to be 2nd Lt, Dec 20, 1845, vice Ayers, promoted.
7th Regt of Infty: Maj Greenleaf Dearborn, of the 1st Regt of Infty, to be Lt Col, Nov 26, 1845, vice Hoffman, dec'd.
8th Regt of Infty:
2nd Lt Robt P Maclay, to be 1st Lt, Dec 31, 1845, vice Browne, resigned.
2nd Lt John G Burbank, to be 1st Lt, Dec 31, 1845, vice Hetzel, resigned.
Brevet 2nd Lt Alfred Crozet, of the 7th Regt of Infty, to be 2nd Lt, Dec 31, 1845, vice Burbank, promoted.
Appointments: Medical Dept:
Wm Roberts, of Ga, to be Assist Surgeon, Dec 31, 1845, vice Van Buren, resigned.
Grayson M Prevost, of Pa, to be Assist Surgeon, Dec 31, 1845, vice Buist, resigned.

By virtue of a writ of distrain, to me directed, against the goods & chattels of Edw Barnard, dec'd, to satisfy Harvey Cruttenden, for rent due & in arrears, I have the following articles, viz: [furniture, carpet, window curtains; China dinner set; andirons; looking glass; bottles; waiters; iron-ware, & sundry articles.]
Sale at the house on N Y ave, between 8th & 9th sts. –Rich I A Culverwell, Bailiff; B Homans, auctioneer

Phil, Jan 4, 1845. I certify that I became deaf at age 12, & have been deaf for the past 18 years, when I heard about & used Scarpa's Compound Acoustic Oil. Like magic, it quite cured me. My residence is on Concord st, 1st door above 2nd st. –Mrs Rebecca Baxter   Only agent for Wash: F W Fuller, Pa ave & 12th st.

To the lovers of good mutton! I purchased of Maj Geo D Washington Peters, of Montgomery Co, Md, a very fine lot of Southdown Mutton, & will offer it for sale on Sat & Tue, at my stalls, in New Centre Market. –Chas Homiller

FRI MAR 27, 1846
Senate: 1-Cmte of Claims: a bill for the relief of Saml A Morse: which was read & ordered to a 2nd reading. 2-Mr Thos F Rusk, Senator elect from the State of Texas, who, after being duly qualified, took his seat.

House of Reps: 1-Ptn of Isaac Beall, praying compensation & pay for services of his father, Thos Beall, of Saml, a Revolutionary ofcr. 2-Ptn of Gabriel Friend, praying to be released from the payment of a note given for arrears due the Post Ofc Dept as Postmaster at Friendsville, Md. 3-Ptn of Jas Taylor, a Revolutionary soldier, asking a pension. 4-Ptn of Edw Raymers, for a pension. 5-Ptns of Mrs Catharine E Moreland, of Alabama, praying payment for loses sustained in the Indian hostilities of the Creek country. 6-Memorial of John N Ford & John Scrivener, for additional compensation, for extra services as messengers in the Genr'l Land Ofc. 7-Ptn from John E Jones & others, in relation to the tenure of ofc of steamboat inspectors. 8-Ptn of Geo Ramey, of Missouri, asking Congress to confirm to him a certain entry made under the authority of the Com'r of the Genr'l Land Ofc, but which was afterwards revoked. 9-Memorial of C Rogers & 34 other citizens of Freeport, & Asa Clapp & 96 other citizens of Portland, Maine, remonstrating against the withdrawal of bounties on pickled fish exported to other countries.

New expeditions to start for California: one from *Fort Smith* on the Arkansas, of about 1,000 souls, under the charge of Mr Leavitt, & another under the command of Maj Russell, of Missouri, embracing many emigrants from Ky, & another under the guidance of Mr Grayson, who leaves Independence, Missouri, on Apr 15, for the valley of Sacramento, in N C.

Died: on Mar 14, at his residence, in Jefferson Co, Missouri, Capt Geo W Waters, late of the 6th Regt of Infty, U S Army.

They are passing away: decease of Revolutionary patriots & other aged persons, selected from exchange papers within a week last past:
In Durham, Conn, Mar 14, Jas Parmele, aged 82 years, a Revolutionary pensioner.
In Stamford, Conn, Mar 16, Capt Jos Sellick, aged 88 years, a Revolutionary ofcr.
In Harpswell, Maine, Mar 4, Mr Wm Coombs, aged 92, a Revolutionary pensioner.
In Waterford, Vt, Deacon Moses Hartly, aged 85, a Revolutionary soldier.
In Pefferel, Maine, Mr Henry Prescott, aged 77, a Revolutionary pensioner.
In Hingham, Mass, Mar 9, Mr Azariah Fuller, aged 82, a Revolutionary soldier.
In Fallsburg, N Y, on Mar 3, Mr John Tappen, in his 93rd year: a commissioned ofcr in the Revolution.
In Hyde Park, N Y, on Mar 5, Mr Peter Lansing, a Revolutionary patriot, in his 78th year.
In Charlestown, Mass, on Feb 27, Mr Danl Adams, aged 95 years & 6 months, a Revolutionary soldier, & the oldest man in the town.
In Ispwich, Mar 13, Mr Saml Lancaster, a Revolutionary pensioner.
In Piney Neck, Md, on Mar 19, Mr Nathan Allen, a soldier of the Revolution, aged 90 years.
In Danby, Vt, Feb 28, Capt Miner Hilliard, aged 82 years & 11 months, a Revolutionary patriot.
In Rome, N Y, on Mar 17, Mr Israel Denio, aged 83 years.
In Sunderland Mass, Feb 28, Mr Sylvanus Clark, a Revolutionary pensioner, aged 86.
In Sullivan, N H, Capt Eliakim Nims, a Revolutionary pensioner & a Bunker Hill man, at the advanced age of 94 years & 6 months. –Albany Citizen

Died: on Mar 22, at his residence near the Long Bridge, in Wash City, Wm Evans, in his 47th year. Born in humble life, proverty was the portion he inherited at his birth, honesty the lesson that was instilled in his tender mind. He was an industrious cheerful companion, a prompt & sympathizing friend. Death has taken from an affectionate wife & children their stay & support. –P

Trustees sale of valuable property in Wash: decree of the Circuit Court of this District, pronounced in a cause wherein Richd Cruickshank, adm de bonis non of John Ott, is cmplnt, & Catherine Ott, Chas B Ott, & others, heirs & devisees of David Ott, are dfndnts, I will expose to sale at public auction, on Apr 24 next, the following real property, to wit: part of lot 2 in square 379, Wash City, fronting upon Pa ave, with the dwlg house & store thereon, as now occupied by Dr Hall & Mr Sexsmith. –John Marbury, trustee -B Homans, auctioneer

In Chancery: Circuit Court of Wash Co, D C, Mar Term, 1846. Frances Clark, vs John F Clark & others, heirs at law of Francis C Meigs. Ratify sale of real estate in the above cause: sale of lot 27 in square 252, was sold to Letitia Clark, for the sum of $957.96; & the 3 story brick dwlg-house fronting on F st, in square 224, to Eliz & Letitia Clark for the sum of $3,000. –Wm Brent, clk

SAT MAR 28, 1846
The subscriber offers for rent the desirable dwlg over Mr Brashier's store, opposite Brown's Hotel: vacated with the exception of an ofc Dr Gould occupies in the back bldg. The Doctor would continue in the House for a liberal rent, should it suit the person that would rent it. Apply to Dr Gould, at the house, or to the subscriber. Also, for rent, his 2 story brick house, on the lot north of the Pres' House.
–G C Grammer, at the Patriotic Bank

The nomination of Peter G Washington, to be Auditor of the Treasury for the Post Ofc Dept, vice Matthew St Clair Clarke, removed, has been confirmed by the Senate.

The packet-ship **Henry Clay**, Capt Nye, from Liverpool for N Y, went ashore on Tue on Squam Beach. Mr Cooley, the 2nd mate, & another seaman, were drowned.

On Mar 15th 2 dry goods stores & one hardware store belonging to E C Noble, C F Haskell & Co, & Henry Degraff, were destroyed by fire at Marshall, Michigan. Entire loss is at $24,000.

Orphans Court of Wash Co, D C. Letters of administration on the person estate of Jas Turton, late of said county, dec'd. –Susannah Turton, adm

Teacher wanted: The Visiters & Govn'rs of Washington College, Kent Co, wish to engage the services of a competent person to take charge of the grammar school attached to said institution. Salary will be $300 per annum, in addition to the tuition money. Apply to B F Green, Sec, Chestertown.

House of Reps: 1-Cmte of Claims: adverse report on the case of J W Crane: laid on the table. 2-Cmte of Claims: adverse reports on the cases of Gideon Walker & Alex'r King: laid on the table. Same cmte: bill for the relief of John Carr, John Batty, & S Stephenson: committed. 3-Cmte of Claims: bill supplementary to the joint resolution authorizing the accounting ofcrs of the Treas to audit & settle the accounts of Wm P Zantzinger, late a purser in the U S Navy: committed. Same cmte: was discharged from the consideration of the case of Capt G Mackall: laid on the table. Same cmte: the case of Caleb Bell, adm of Matthew Bell, was recommitted to the same cmte, with additional testimony. 4-Cmte on Commerce: adverse report on the case of Jas Frazier: laid on the table. 5-Cmte on Commerce: adverse report on the case of Thos Sanford: laid on the table. 6-Cmte on the Post Ofc & Post Roads: adverse report in the case of Wm Fuller: laid on the table. 7-Cmte on Revolutionary Claims: asked to be discharged from the case of the heirs of David Hopkins, of the heirs of Jacob Cohen, the heirs of Dr Lawrence Brooke, & the heirs of Alex'r White: laid on the table. 8-Cmte on Private Land Claims: adverse reports on the cases of Ira Baldwin, A Goodenough, & Jacob Kerr: laid on the table. Also reported a bill for the relief of Jas Journey: committed. Same cmte: adverse report on the case of Mary Nations. Also reported a bill for the relief of Jos Cazillo:

committed. 9-Cmte on Indian Affairs: bill for the relief of the legal reps of Thos Murray, jr: confirmed. Same cmte: adverse reports in the cases of Jas E Rawlings & the heirs of Dr John Motlow, dec'd: laid on the table. 10-Cmte on Indian Affairs: made an adverse report on the memorial of Shapendoshia & other Miami Indians; & on the memorial of David Foster & 99 other white men, asking that said Indians may receive their annuities in Indiana: laid on the table. 11-Cmte on Military Affairs: asked to be discharged from the case of John A Webber: laid on the table. Same cmte: adverse report on the ptn of Richd Fitzpatrick: laid on the table. Same cmte: asked to be discharged from the bill to construct a military road from *Fort Adams* to Newport, R I. Also, the ptn of Wm W Hubbell: all laid on the table. Same cmte: bill for the relief of Bennett M Dill: committed. 12-Cmte on Militia: asked to be discharged from the ptn of Thos Abbott & others: laid on the table. 13-Recommended they pass: bill for the relief of Langtree & Jacobs; bill for the relief of John R Williams, with an amendment to strike out $2,000 & insert $1,250. Bill for the relief of Chas M McKenzie; relief of David S Williamson. Relief of the heirs & legal reps of Cyrus Turner, dec'd, with a recommendation that it be recommitted to the Cmte on Indian Affairs, to report in writing the facts of the case.

Episcopal High School of Va: near Alexandria, D C: Rev E A Dalrymple, Rector: located in Fairfax Co, about 3 miles west of Alexandria. The year is divided into 2 terms of 5 months each: $200 per annum for board & tuition. The post ofc of the school is Theological Seminary, Fairfax Co, Va.

$5 reward for runaway Paul Talbert, jr, aged 16 years, an apprentice to the boot & shoe-making business. The reward will be given for his apprehension, as I will never give up while life remains. –John Goldin

Died: on Mar 27, of consumption, John Joseph, only s/o the late Jas C White, aged 24 years. His funeral will take place this Sunday at 3 o'clock, from his mother's residence on 9th st, between D & E sts.

MON MAR 30, 1846
John Weisfott, who lived in Alice Ann st, Old Town, Balt, cut his throat in a fit, whilst he was in a schnr going down the Potomac. He was conveyed to the city hospital, where it is feared he will die in a short time. He has a wife & several children. He is humanely attended by Dr May.

The St Louis Republican announces the death near that city, of John Miller, formerly a Rep in Congress from Missouri, & at one time Govn'r of that State. He was also a brave ofcr in the last war. [No date-recent news.]

Wash City Ordinance: Act for the relief of Geo Stewart: that the fine imposed for a violation of the law in relation to meetings or assemblies of colored persons being held after 10 o'clock at night, be & the same is remitted: provided Stewart pay the costs of prosecution.

Investigation into the causes which led to the death of Martha Hamilton, the wife of Edw L Hamilton, of Wash City, carpenter. The mother of Martha Hamilton, who died on Fri, said that the dec'd complained that she had been beaten by her husband, Edw L Hamilton, who also stamped upon her breast on or about Mar 19. Edw L Hamilton was fully committed for trial at the next Criminal Court. Both Edw & Martha Hamilton were addicted to intemperance. Edw L Hamilton had been at one time the Pres of the Temperance Society. [Jul 4th newspaper: trial of Edw Hamilton: verdict of not guilty.]

Yesterday, Jas Tucker, a merchant from Madison Co, Va, in a fit of insanity, or mania potu, attacked Capt Ramsay & 3 of his sons, Messrs Wadsworth, David, & Douglass Ramsay, with a sharp claspknife, cutting & maiming all of them, the eldest son severely. The maniac is now in jail. [Apr 1st newspaper: although in great jeopardy by the attack of this unfortunate maniac, they were not seriously injured & are doing well.] [Jun 29th newspaper: The Jury found John T Tucker to be under the influence of insanity.]

House of Reps: 1-Bill for the relief of the sureties of Elijah J Weed, late Quartermaster of the U S Marine Corps, dec'd: recommended that it do not pass. 2-Earnest but ineffectual attempt was made to get up the bill to amend the act heretofore passed for the relief of Geo Mayfield. 3-Bill for the relief of Mary Ann Bruner: in 1837 she went to a land ofc in Indiana to purchase a small tract of land. The Register told her she could not enter the land until he went to Washington & returned. She left her money with him, which he embezzled, & she never obtained either land or money. She asks that she may now receive a grant of the land. The bill proposes to give it to her. Mr Grover moved that the bill be reported to the House, with a recommendation that it do not pass. The motion prevailed. 4-Bill for the relief of Wm Saunders & Wm R Porter, sureties of Wm Estes, a paymaster of Va militia in the war of 1812 with Great Britain, reported by the Cmte on the Judiciary. Laid aside to be reported to the House. 5-Bill to purchase the right of using the patent manger stopper, invented by & patented to her husband, Lt Mervine P Mix, U S Navy, dec'd: to strike out $4,000, the amount proposed to be paid & insert $3,000: negatives. Recommended that the bill pass. 6-Bill to authorize the payment of 7 years' half-pay of Lt Jona Dye, of the Revolutionary army, who was killed in battle, to his personal reps or descendants: recommendation that it be rejected. Motion was agreed to. 7-Cmte of the Whole was discharged from the consideration of the bill for the relief of John Stockton, late a Lt in the U S Army: & it was recommitted to the Cmte on Military Affairs. 8-Cmte of the Whole: be discharged from the consideration of the joint resolution from the Senate providing for the settlement of the claim of Peter Gorman, for work done on the U S road from the Capitol to the Navy Yard gate, & to the Congress burial ground, with a view to take it up, & act upon it in the House. Stated that it do pass. 9-Bill for the payment of the 5 years' full pay as the commutation pay of the half-pay for life to which Col Wm Grayson, of the Revolutionary army, was entitled: rejected. 10-Cmte on Invalid

Pensions: bill to repeal an act granting a pension to Peter L Allen, & a bill for the relief of Surranus Coff: read & committed. Same cmte: adverse reports on the cases of John Downs, Geo Newton, Danl Morse, Benj Rowe, Simeon Caswell, Beriah Wright, Oliver Herrick, Moses Davis, Isaac Plummer & Jared Gossage: laid on the table. Sam cmte: bill for the relief of Justin Jacobs, & a bill for the relief of Danl Pratt: committed. Adverse reports on the cases of Jonas D Platt, John Ingraham, Wm H Wilson, Chas Walsworth, & March Farrington: laid on the table. Same cmte: asked to be discharged from the ptns of Moses Holden, Stephen Benton, David Sage, John Mitchell, Asa Sprague, Danl Duggan, Levi H Parish, E C Brown, Orinda Cooper, Otis F Ladd, Wm Slocum, Jehiel Tuttle, & Giles London: laid on the table. Bill for the relief of John Campbell: committed. Bill for the relief of Jos Dusseau: committed. 11-Cmte on Invalid Pensions: bill granting a pension to Abraham Ansmen: committed. Same cmte: adverse reports on the cases of Palmer Branch, John Kline, & David Towle: laid on the table. Same cmte: bill for the relief of Griffin Kelly; relief of Benj Allen, & relief of Aquila Goodwin: all committed. 12-Cmte on the Judiciary: bill for the relief of John McAlister: committed. 13-Cmte on Revolutionary Claims: bill for the relief of the heirs of Gen Thos Sumter, late of S C: committed. Same cmte: bill for the relief of the excs of Col Abraham Bowman, dec'd: committed. Also, an adverse report in the case of Sally Ketchum: laid on the table. 14-Cmte on Naval Affairs: bill for the relief of John L Worden: committed. 15-Cmte on Naval Affairs: bill for the relief of Wilmer Shields: committed. Same cmte: reported a joint resolution to purchase the right to use Jas Hamilton's & Philip Schuyler's invention for saeing ship-timber: committed. 16-Cmte on Revolutionary Pensions: bill for the relief of Jonathan Brown: committed. Same cmte: adverse reports on the cases of Jacob Patrick, Susan Belknap, wid/o Isaac Belknap, Eliz Grennell, wid/o John Redmington; & of Nicholas Otman, Abraham Bouck, Peter Otman, & Wm Otman: laid on the table. Same cmte: bill for the relief of Martha Gray, wid/o Capt Gray, the discoverer of the mouth of the Columbia river; also, a bill for the relief of Patrick Masterton: both bills were committed. Same cmte: adverse reports on the cases of Lucy Davis, wid/o Wm Davis; of Ann Royal; Sarah Hammond; Eliz McClain; Susan Aldrich; Joanna French; Abigail Church; Abilgail Lindley; Roxanna Moore, Sally Tyler, Charity Chatfield; Esther Humphreys; Anna Bissel; Eunice Buckman; Polly Mahl; Eliz Randolph; Polly Owen; Huldah Saxon; Sarah Scovel; Catharine Adair; Mgt Corwin; Catharine Jackson; Amy Pearsey; Rebecca Boyd; Hannah Stevenson; Huldah Norris; Nancy G Van Rensselaer; John Vice; John Reid; Peter Dunbar; Mott Wilkinson; Keziah Hobart; Fred'k Gibbs; Levi Nicholls; & Noah Clark: all laid on the table. The same cmte reported sundry bills for, viz: relief of Eliz Betts; relief of Mary Phelps; relief of Mary Segar; relief of Catharine Fulton; relief of Eliz Kreider Brunot; relief of Polly Damson; relief of Francis Hutinach: severally committed. 16-Bill for the relief of Jas Jones: referred to the Cmte on Naval Affairs.

At Hancock, Delaware Co, N Y, on Mar 18, 3 children of Mr Calvin Thomas, the eldest of 14, another of 12, & a boy of 6 years, with a dght of Josiah Martin, aged about 14, were playing on a small pond coverd with ice, when suddenly the ice gave way & all the children except the d/o the Mr Martin were drowned.

Balt Conference: appointments for this District & neighboring stations, recently made by the Balt Conference of the Methodist Episcopal Church:
Washington-Foundry & Asbury: N J B Morgan, T A Morgan. Wesley Chapel: H Slicer. MeKendree Chapel: Wm G Eggleston. Ebenezer: O Ege, J M Hanson, sup.
Ryland Chapel: Geo D Chenowith
Alexandria: J Guest, S V Blake
Gtwn: H Tarring, W Taylor
Leesburg: J S Martin
Fairfax: R T Nixon, T Cornelius
Loudon: J Merriken, T C Hays
Warrenton: J Bradds, J R Durborow
Stafford: Wm Wickes, Wm F Pentz
Fredericksburg: J Lanahan
Winchester Station: Norval Wilson
Annapolis: Wm Hirst
West River: Robt Cadden, T M Reese
Calvert: Amos Smith, Jas Bunting, J W Richardson, sup
Bladensburg: F Macartney, J M Grandin, J P Simpson, W Edmunds, sup
St Mary's: T B Lemmon, Saml Ellis
Chas: Matthew A Turner, Wm H Pitcher

Died: on Mar 22, near the Navy Yard, Mrs Julia Pic, aged about 47. This estimable woman died of the small-pox. Eleven or 12 years since she was left destitute with several small children. Her greatest care was to bring up her children upright. She endeared herself to all who knew her.

Trustee's sale of valuable lots: by virtue of an act of Congress, passed Jul 20, 1840, & of the decree of the Circuit Court of Wash Co, D C, & of the Orphans Court of Wash Co, D C, made in the cause of Lewis G Davidson's heirs, I shall offer at auction on Apr 20 next, the following lots, in Wash City:
Lot 1 thru 8, in square 161
Lots 2, 4 thru 8, 11, 16, 20, 21, in square 163
Lots 3 thru 6, 13 thru 19, in square 126
Lots 6 & 7, in square 127
Lots 10 thru 12, 14 thru 16, 19, in square 165
Lots 4, 6 thru 8, 11, 13, 15 thru 17, in square 168
Lots 2, 3, 4, 19, in square 169
Lots 1 thru 5, in square 170
Lots 1 thru 25, in square 183
Lots 1 thru 6, 8 thru 16, & 18, in square 184. These lots are numbered according to Davidson's subdivision, & are in the neighborhood of the Pres' square.
–Saml G Davidson, trustee -R W Dyer, auct

Died: on Mar 25, at her residence, Pleasant Hill, Chas Co, Md, after an illness of 2 weeks, Mrs Mary T Spalding, in her 29th year. She has left a disconsolate husband & 3 infant children, together with a large circle of relatives & friends, to mourn her loss. -S

Mrd: on Mar 28, by Rev Horace Stringfellow, Mr Alex M Mahon, of Pa, to Miss Mary G, y/d/o Richd S Coxe, of Wash, D C.

By virtue of a deed of trust from Andrew Jenkins & Fanny Jenkins [late Fanny Hampton,] his wife, to the subscriber, dated Jul 5, 1841, & recorded in Liber W B 89 folios 189 thru 192, one of the land records for Wash Co, D C, I shall sell on May 2, 1846, the south half part of lot 24 in square 5, with the improvements thereon, of a small frame house. –Thos Jewell, trustee -Benj Homans, auctioneer

TUE MAR 31, 1846
Sale of household furniture: on E, near 10th st, opposite the old Medical College, the entire household furniture of a gentleman declining housekeeping.
–Chas Wallach, trustee -Boteler, Donn & Co, aucts.

Senate: 1-Cmte of Claims: asking to be discharged from the further consideration of the memorial of Nathl Wright, on the ground that a general bill was before the Senate. 2-Cmte on Private Land Claims: bill to confirm the title of the heirs & legal reps of Julius Dubuque, dec'd. Same cmte: bill to authorize the Sec of the Treas, with the approbation of the Atty Genr'l, to purchase the interest of Balie Peyton in an island at Grand Pass. 3-Cmte on Pensions: bill for the relief of Thompson H, s/o Thos Hutchinson. Same cmte: bill for the relief of Eliz Jones & others, with a written report, which was ordered to be printed. Same cmte: asking to be discharged from the further consideration of the ptn of G B Duvall, & that it be referred to the Cmte on Naval Affairs. 4-Cmte of Claims: adverse reports on the ptns of Eli Hobbs & Orlando L Rees. Same cmte: without amendment, House bill for the relief of Geo D Spencer. 5-Cmte on Indian Affairs: adverse report on the ptn of Mary B Hook. 6-Cmte on Pensions: adverse report on the ptn of Wm W Hall. Same cmte: asking to be discharged from the further consideration of the ptn of Hannah Atwood.

Mrd: on Mar 27, at N Y, by Rev Abraham Polhemus, Dr John W Scott, formerly of Lexington, Ky, to Jane Heyer, d/o the late Cornelius R Suydam, of N Y.

Died: on Sunday last, at the residence of her brother-in-law, Francis Y Naylor, on Capitol Hill, Miss Martha Maria Brightwell, d/o Mr John L Brightwell, aged 27, after a short & painful illness, which she bore with Christian resignation. Her funeral is Thu at 3 o'clock, from the residence of her father, near the Upper Bridge of Anacostia river.

The subscriber has just returned from the North with a well assorted stock of Spring & Summer goods. -Wm R Riley, corner of 8th st & opposite Centre Market.

Redemption of Virginia 6% Stock: by act of the Genr'l Assembly of Va, passed Feb 27, 1846.
1822, Dec 27: Catharine Hays: $4,000.
1822, Dec 27: Slowey Hays [transferred Nov 3, 1836, to C Hays, & now in her possession]: $4,000.
1823, Feb 22: Wm Robinson, adm of Needler Robinson, dec'd: $3,300.
1827, May 3: Geo McIntosh, of Norfolk, [transferred to Ro L McIntosh, of Norfolk, Jan 19, 1843: $10,000.
1827, May 3: same: $5,000.
Act passed Feb 24, 1823, entitled An act making more effectual provision to carry into effect the aforementioned act:
1824, Jan 30: Anne Boggs, of Fredericks Hall, Louisa Co: $400.
1835, Oct 6: Dr Thos Massie: $1,250.
1838, Oct 24: Archibald Thomas, of Richmond City: $1,000.
1839, Sep 19: Bazil Gordon, of Falmouth, Va: $3,000.
1843, Apr 8: Geo Fisher, of Richmond: $666.66+
An act passed Jan 25, 1839, entitled An act to amend the act entitled An act to provide for the construction of the Northwestern Turnpike Road:
1839, Jul 12: Lawson Burfoot, Treas of the Commonwealth, in trust for the benefit of the Cincinnati Society: $260.
1841, Jun 21: Richd Jeffers, of Richmond: $400.
1843, May 13: Hill Carter, trustee under the will of Beverly Randolph, for the benefit of Nancy Kennon & others: $180.
1843, May 13: same, for the benefit of Livinia H Deas & others: $120.
1843, Jun 8: John E Friend, infant son of E O Friend, dec'd: $1,003.
1844, Jan 22: Richd H Cunningham, adm de bonis non with the will annexed of Beverly Randolph, dec'd: $1,000.
1844, Mar 4: Mendes I Cohen: $100.
1846, Jan 14: Geo Fisher, exc of E J Carrington: $2,000.

Andrew J Joyce, Horse Shoeing & Smithing Establishment, successor to John Daley, corner of 14th & E sts, near Fuller's Hotel. Thankful for the patronage he has received from a liberal public, he solicits a continuance of the same.

Manure: will be sold on Apr 4 at the Centre Market. The manure to be scraped up & placed in convenient heaps by the Clerk of the Market, & to be taken away by the purchaser every day or market days. By order of the Mayor, John Waters, Clerk of the Market.

WED APR 1, 1846
Senate: 1-Ptn of N Y, remonstrating against the renewal of Jethro Wood's patent for a plough. 2-Ptn from Ruth Fye, for a pension. 3-Ptn from the legal reps of Ethan Allen, asking remuneration for military services performed by their ancestor.

Wash Corp: Cmte of Claims: bill for the relief of H G Corcoran: passed. 2-Ptn from Jas Casparis: referred to the Cmte of Claims. 3-Memorial from John F Tucker, Pres of the Anacostia Fire Co: referred to Messrs Magruder, Thornly, & Beck. 4-Cmte of Claims: bill for the relief of Wm Easby & K H Lambell: ordered to lie on the table. 5-Ptn of Geo Gray & others, praying the opening & grading of M st, from 16th to the upper bridge: referred to the Cmte on Improvements. 6-Ptn of Saml Kirby & others, praying the widening & extending the gutter on the west side of 8th st west: referred to the Cmte on Improvements. 7-Ptn of C Columbus, praying the remission of a fine: referred to the Cmte of Claims. 8-Ptn of Henry Barnes, praying remission of a fine: referred to the Cmte of Claims. 9-Cmte of Claims: bill for the relief of the heirs of Geo Adams: reported the same without amendment, & recommended that it be not passed.

House of Reps: 1-Ptn & documents of Geo West: referred. 2-Ptn of Henry Bruce, Cmder in the U S Navy, in relation to the prize money for the capture of the slaver ship **Spitfire**. 3-Ptn of Anna McLean, praying compensation for the services of her husband who died in the service in 1813. 4-Ptn of Peter Rambo, of Sevier Co, Tenn, praying Congress for compensation for money taken from him by the British whilst at the surrender of *Fort Niagara* in the late war. 5-Ptn of Josiah Kindred, of Morgan Co, Tenn, praying Congress to grant him a pension on account of services rendered to his country as a soldier for a period of 17 years, including the late war with Great Britain. 6-Ptn of Jos Hoget, of Mississippi, for indemnification for the loss sustained by the receipt of a U S Treas note, which had been cancelled but fraudulently reissued. 7-Ptn of David Petts, a soldier of the last war, for a pension for disabilities incurred during his services in the same.

Letters remaining in the Post Ofc, Wash, Apr 1, 1846:

Atkinson, Wm	Adams, Thorton W	Brown, F J
Adaser, C	Anderson, Benj	Brown, Richd
Abby, Wm E	Alexander, Chas A	Balch, Benj
Ashton, B	Armistead, Lt L A	Brown, E S
Armstrong, John	Brown, Arthur	Belt, Alfred C
Allen, Thos	Brown, Mrs Susan	Binks, Miss Mary
Anderson, Alex	Blake, Rev John	Blair, Wm H
Applegate, Mrs E	Bagg, John S-2	Byrne, Teresa
Alston, Jas T	Burt, Wm A	Brooks, Miss A E
Adams, West	Burt, A E	Boyd, Stephen
Ashard, Wm R	Burch, Jos A	Blount, Thos M
Allen, Maj J M-2	Bibb, T P Atticus	Belt, Capt Wm J
Archer, Wm B	Black, Mrs Ellen	Brick, Theodore

Baker, John	Clark, John	De Hass, W
Bennet, Miss M H	Crump, Mr	Darcy, Mrs Frances
Busher, Miss C E	Cameron, Col J	Dunlap, Col Jas
Banghart, J	Collins, Mrs N J	Doran, Edw
Berry, Miss Celby	Clgerle, David	Donly, Peter
Bagby, R B	Cheever, John	Dana, Jas D
Bowlin, John N	Crosby, Capt	Dennington, F C
Beecher, Wm A	Carter, Miss A M	Dawson, Geo
Billings, Moses	Coffin, John	Davis, G
Browning, Rev W	Campbell, John	Donelly & Co, P
Burnett, Ward B-2	Collins, Miss A	Downing, Miss H A
Barry, Edmund	Capretz, Jeremiah	Dyer, Miss Mary
Berry, Elisha T	Curtis, Mary	Donelson, A J-4
Bettinger, Henry	Caruthers, Madison	Dade, Mrs Gwynetta
Butler, Mrs Ann	Cochrane, John T	Downes, Gen S W-2
Bouthron, Widow	Comings, Ed S	Dickson, J,
Brooers, Miss M A	Cramer, John	brickmaker
Braiden, Miss	Canfield, Capt A	Eimon, John
Beecher, Miss A E	Closky, C B	Emmons, Calvin
Baldwin, Seymour	Campbell, John C	Everardus, Miss G
Barlett, John R	Cunningham, G S	Ewell, Rev D F
Baker, J F-4	Connell, Wm	Evans, H C
Banning, Dr E P	Curtis, Thos A	Eppes, Wyatt-2
Barker, Wm	Clarkson, Henry	Ewing, P U
Butler, Miss P	Cormick, F	Frink, John
Bridwell, Armfield	Conway, W P	Frame, David
Butler, Richd	Carusi, Lewis-2	Floyd, Jas H
Bledsoe, A T-3	Clayton, Jas F-3	Floyd, Robt J-2
Barron, Com Jas	Coston, John-2	Fisher, D
Bishop, Col A	Cotter, Abraham	Fowler, Dr W J
Barbour, J S-2	Cowan, John F-2	Fuller, Thos
Bennett, Jas H-3	Cullum, W J-3	Ferguson, Enos D
Bennett, Miss J D	Cabbell, Mr-2	Fitzgerald, Gerald
Blanchard, L	Carter, Hart-2	Fowler, Wm Q
Bulger, Miss M	Cassin, R A, U S N	Ferry, Wm
Burgevin, Miss M A	Clinton, Miss M A	Farlee, Isaac G
Bernard, J, of Lake Superior	Cuyler, Dr J M, U S A	Grant, Gen R H
	Diggs, Geo	Gray, Mrs Rena
Brownell, Lt Thos-4	Dunham, F S	Gibbs, Gov W C
Brittolph, Edw A	Dickinson, T	Gunn, W J
Clark, Mary A	Daily, Oliver A	Gregg, Josiah
Cooke, Eleuthers	Dubourjal, Mons	Green, Miss E
Cox, Jas H	Davis, John	Griggs, Geo
Chase, Oliver B	Deneale, N J	Gaines, A
Clark, Miss M A	Devaughn, Miss E	Gould, Gen J-4

Green, Geo B	Herert, Mrs	Jacoway, B J
Gough, John B-2	Hemminck, jr, J	Johnson, Col R M
Gaither, J W	Henderson, C A	Joachim, John
Gollady, Maj G S	Howard, Chas	King, Chas
Gilbert, Miss C C	Harding, H	Knox, Jas
Groran, Miss C	Hayden, Ira	Kilmiste, Mr
Godwin, Park	Higgins, Miss S	Kinzie, John H-2
Geisinger, Capt D	Henson, Miss Cely	Kehler, Jas
Graham, T M	Hopkins, Ed A	Kelly, C D
Gonder, Jos	Headman, Andrew	Klapper, Miss M S
Goette, Catharine	Hilton, Geo	Kanally, J
Hall, Jas S	Henry, G M	Kelley, Davl
Hall, Hiland	Hooper, Chas	Kurtzels, Mr
Hick, Lawrence	Hubbard, David	Kingley, John L
Hall, Jas H	Horid, Miss S A	Kingsbury, W O
Hase, John	Halsey, Col T L	Lee, Saml
Hill, Chas	Hazewell, G R-2	Lynch, John
Hill, Moses J	Hillyer, Rev S J	Lees, John
Hale, Erastus	Hamilton, R C	Long, Edw
Hart, E B	Hinton, Gen O-2	Lewis, jr, Isaiah
Hart, B S	Humphrey, Henry B	Latruite, J P
Hunt, Gen J E	Humphreys, Miss A M	Lindsley, D C B
Haig, Jas M	Hammond, M C M	Lowry, Geo W
Hall, Geo	Howard, Miss Mary	Lewis, Saml
Height, Silas-2	Hutchins, Miss S G	Lesure, Francis
Hill, E B	Iardella, John A	Leslie, Mrs M O
Hughes, A W	Iardella, N M	Lenman, J A
Hook, Maria A	Jones, J C	Lavelle, Edw
Hord, Robt	James, J Dawson	Lewis, M N
Hord, Thos-2	Jones, Com Jacob	Loveless, Jas A
Heiss, Wm	Jones, Thos F	Lamar, John B
Hickox, Virgil	Jones, Jas	Lincoln, Levi-2
Hoover, Wm	James, Chas R	Lynch, Raymond-2
Haskins, Timothy	James, Miss E V	Lancaster, Ignatius
Holman, Maj J S	Jones, Chas S	Muth, Johan
Herrick, Joshua	Junkin, Rev Geo	Morse, Cyrus E
Hutchings, John S	Jacobs, Wm M-2	More, John E
Hinston, Jas G	Janny, Shepherd	Mills, John
Henrie, Lt Dan D	Jennings, J C	Munn, Lt Sam E
Henning, Henry N	Jaeger, Professor	Mitchell, Jos
Hamilton, Josiah	Jeffers, Capt J W	Mulloy, John J
Hobby, A K	Jenkins, Lt T A	Morgan, E B
Haskin, C J-2	Jaquis, Henry	Mulloy, Thos
Herrick, Edgar H	Johnson, G W	Matlock, Mr
Harris, O C	Jessup, Wm	Moulton, Dr P

Moran, D	O'Riley, V	Reeside, jr, Jas
Mitchell, Wm-2	Owen, M J	Robertson, Jas
Murray, Nicholas	O'Neill, Geo P	Rogers, Robt
Milstead, Rob A	Pierce, Saml	Robinson, C H
Middleton, Alex	Poole, Rev W C	Rabbitt, Wm
Myers, Benj S	Pike, Jas S	Reddy, Miss M A
Milner, Jas A	Pughe, Wm	Raymond, N H
Moutel, Miss L	Pitts, Cyrus	Ryan, Wm P-2
Mulligan, Mrs C	Payne, John H	Robertson, Miss E
Mergoun, Rob	Pitts, Hiram A	Rogers, Catharine
Mendenhall, Cyrus	Price, John H	Russell, Frank S
Morton, Col J	Pease, L T	Rowan, Mrs S C
Miller, Mrs Ann	Pollock, Jas	Ready, Wm
Morris, Thos A	Parsons, Maj J-6	Ranson, J L
Mathew, Mathew	Parsons, Jas	Russell, Thos
Masters, Capt S J	Paris, Virgil D	Russell, F S
Milson, Jeremiah	Pickett, Thos B-2	Robinson, W G
Murray, Miss A	Parker, S S	Reynolds, Maj L
Mattern, Zach	Peters, jr, R	Rayner, Kenneth
Montgomery, Jas	Potter, Jas A	Rosevelt, Wm C
Mertin, Wm T	Pickering, Chas	Ridgley, Lt S C
Matthews, Henry	Peddicord, A B	Ratcliff, Miss M
Mason, Jas	Penrose, Chas B	Rubey, Addison
Mason, Col R B-2	Philips, Ellis	Reid, Joh, of Ken
Martin, Col A B	Philips, Miss E	Rockwell, Mrs J A
McKee, Rev W P	Potter, Emery	Ramsay, Miss M A
Mackur, Mrs M	Pumphrey, Mrs S	Robertson, Miss A S
Mackay, Maj A	Perry, Prof T H	Ringgold, Lt F L-2
McGregor, Miss S	Pister, J W	Riley, Col B, U S A-2
McDuffie, John T	Philips, Jas B	Robertson, Mrs E M
Magruder, Miss S	Philips, Sam	Simons, John A C
McFarland, Danl	Peters, Wm	Sykes, John M
McCullough, Sol	Pickett, Thos	Schwartz, Thos
McCauley, F G, U S N	Palmer, Lt J S, U S N	Sands, Geo
	Queen, Wm	Shaw, Mrs Mary
McConnell, M-2	Quinter, Mrs r	Smith, Mrs G H
McCauley, Capt W C	Queen, Miss Eliza	Shields, Gen Wm
Noble, Henry	Queen, Miss C	Sipe, Hezekiah
Nichols, Abr	Reed, C M	Spriggs, Rev Jos
Norris, John	Read, Andrew C	Schwartz, Dr T J
Nixon, Chas	Redd, Wm	Scott, Robt
Newton, Miss M	Right, G A	Smith, John P
O'Riley, Mary E	Reid, Jas	Starke, Reuben
Owen, Elijah	Read, Thos H	Spring, Rev G
Ogden, M	Rice, R D-3	Smith, Mrs B P

Smith, Col B P	Smith, Mr, brickmaker	Wissinger, Geo
Smith, Jas	Schemerhorn, Rev J F	Ward, Miss M A
Stoddard, J H	Todd, Wm H	Wats, Wm
Sinclair, Mgt	Turner, Danl-2	Willett, John
Slover, A	Tylor, Miss J A	Wells, Sylvanue
Stewart, Mrs L	Thomas, J C	Welch, Mr
Stevenson, Jas H	Thompson, John	Williams, H S
Sumner, Gen Wm	Thompson, Mrs J	Wiley, Miss V-2
Stevens, Wm	Thomas, C	Wheatley, Geo
Saunders, Wm J	Tansill, Lt R	Williams, J J
Staples, Thos A-5	Thompson, Chas	Webster, Ira
Sheckles, Miss C	Thomas, Jos	Williamson, Jas
Saxton, Chas-2	Tolson, Mrs B B	Williamson, S D
Sullivan, J T I	Taylor, Jas B-2	Wickham, Dr R C
Shelden, Gen W B	Tascar, Ann	Warren, Henry
Sumbey, Mrs M	Thomas, Jos	Wheeler, Jos P-4
Spencer, Thos A	Teirney, John	Walker, Richd
Spencer, Col J-2	Tozer, Mrs J A	Walker, Miss E F
Shepard, C B	Turner, H E	Wilkins, Wm
Seymour, Capt C	Taylor, Col E D-3	Wheatly, Walter
Sanford, Lt J P-2	Thompson, G	Waters, Miss H J
Sherlock, Mrs S A	Trimble, J R	Wellman, Wm A
Stewart, W W	Thornton, Miss J W A	Williams, Jas-3
Shepherd, Forrest	Thruston, Miss F C	Wilburn, Miss A M
Sommers, Miss E	Taylor, Miss M J-2	Williams, Mrs M A
Sinclair, John-2	Thomas, John D-2	Whittle, Lt W C-2
Sangster, Capt T-4	Throckmorton, C S	Whitesides, Rev H M
Selby, Wm R	Vail, Mrs E	Yates, Giles F-6
Sanderson, W	Van Meter, J J	Young, Jas C
Starkweather, Col S-3	Voltz, Geo J	Yerby, Wm-2
Stacker, Marinus	Wells, Gideon	Zachman, Chr F-2
	Ward, John L	

The inland postage on all letters intended to go by ship must be paid, otherwise they remain in this office. -C K Gardner, P M

The trial of Albert J Tirrell, charged with the murder of Mrs Bickford, has been in progress at Boston for some days. Main ground of defence was that the prisoner was subject to fits of somnambulism from his youth, which showed itself in harmless acts, but also in violent ones, such as attacks upon his wife & oter individuals while in this state: was thought this disease was connected with insanity. The mother & brother of the prisoner were called to prove this fact. Since the above was put in type we have heard of Tirrell's acquittal by the jury. The jury said the crime was not adequately proved upon him. The theory of somnambulism they did not consider at all.

A colored man, Wm Smallwood, died near Emmittsburg, Md, recently, at the advanced age of 117 years.

Died: on Tue, in Wash City, Mrs Anne Milligan. Her funeral is from her late residence, N Y ave & 15th st, this afternoon at 4½ o'clock.

Mrs Rice, at the corner of E & 5th sts, has accommodations for 10 or 12 genteel boarders, if application is made without delay.

Boots & Shoes: Pa ave, between 9th & 10th sts. –R L Smallwood & Co

Teacher wanted, a gentleman, who is qualified to teach the languages & the higher branches of an English education. Salary of $300 & liberal perquisites will be given. Apply near Millersville, Anne Arundel, Md to the undersigned. A middle-aged man would be preferred. –Rev Henry Aisquith, Dr John H Brown, Benj E Gantt, Trustees School District #48.

Valuable brick houses & lot at auction: on Apr 6: lot 7 in square 456, with 2 handsome 2 story brick houses, with back bldgs, fronting on E st, a few doors east of Mr J F Callan's drug store. –A Green, auct

Goodrich's Nat'l Geography for Schools, with a globe map on a new plan: by S G Goodrich, author of Peter Parley's Tales. –G Brooke & Co, Pa ave & 15th sts.

THU APR 2, 1846
Senate: 1-Cmte on Pensions: asking to be discharged from the further consideration of the ptn of Mary Ripley, wid/o Jeremiah Ripley, & from the ptn of the reps of Cornelius Oakley. 2-Cmte on Pensions: adverse report on the ptn of Joanna Puicey: which was ordered to be printed.

Wash: Notice is given that all licenses issued for using Carts, Wagons, & Drays, in Wash City expired on Mar 31, & must be renewed at this ofc within the next 10 days. –C H Wiltberger-Reg: Register's Ofc

All persons indebted to the late Edw Dyer are requested to make immediate payment, as it is absolutely necessary to close the estate as speedily as possible. R W Dyer is authorized to receive & receipt for any debts due the estate. –Henrietta H Dyer, excx

Valuable improved property at public sale: on Apr 22, the Farm on which he formerly resided, near Colesville, Montg Co, Md. Property to be sold for the benefit, first of Mr Smith, agent for the Bank of the U S, to settle a debt due from the purchase money; the balance for the benefit of the creditors of the subscriber, according to a deed of trust made to John Brewer, in 1845. Farm contains about 192 acres; bldgs good, with a large Tannery establishment. Property lies with 12 miles of Wash. –John Poole

Mrd: on Mar 31, at *Aspen Hill*, Anne Arundel Co, Md, by Rev Mr Richardson, Marshall P Howard, M D, of North Carolina, to Anna Norman, d/o Jacob McCeney.

$5 reward for strayed or stolen from the commons south of the Canal, a brown horse. Reward & expenses will be given for return of the horse to the Steamboat Hotel, 7th st. –John West

Attention: Meeting of the United Rifle Corps, at the house of Capt T J Williams, a few doors east of Coleman's Hotel, Apr 3 at 7½ o'clock. –Chas Calvert, jr, sec

FRI APR 3, 1846
City Ordnances-Wash. Act making appropriations for white-washing & the usual repairs of the several market-houses: for the Centre Market-house: $50. For the West Market-house: $15. For the Eastern Branch Market-house, $15. For the Capitol Hill Market-house: $10. Sums shall be payable out of the general fund. Approved: Apr, 1846.

House of Reps: 1-Ptn of Foster Demarters, of Missouri, a soldier in the late war, praying to be permitted to select 160 acres of public land in lieu of his bounty land, which is worthless. 2-Ptn of Jas Little, praying for compensation for services as keeper of the *Congressional Burial Ground*. 3-Ptn of Thos Sinclair, a soldier of the last war, for a pension for disabilities incurred in the same. 4-Ptn & accompanying papers of Anna Tarrington, wid/o Jonathan Park, a soldier of the Revolution, asking for a pension, taken from the files of the House at a former session.

Senate: 1-Documents in favor of Jacob Houseman's claim: presented. 2-Documents relating to the claim of Hannah Severance: presented. 3-Ptn from Bethiah Healey, wid/o a Revolutionary soldier, asking a pension. 4-Ptn from the legal reps of Thos Hughes, asking to be allowed commutation pay. 5-Ptn from Silvanus Smith, exc of Judah Allen, dec'd, to be allowed commutation pay. 6-Ptn from the delegation of the Tonawanda band of Seneca Indians, asking to be exempted from the operation of the treaty of 1842. 7-Cmte of Commerce: House bill for the relief of Chas G Bingley, of S C, with an amendment. 8-Cmte of Claims: bill for the relief of Jno Bronson. 9-Unfavorable report made in the case of Simeon Summers was taken up & concurred in. 10-Resolved, that the resolution in favor of the wid/o Edw Dyer, late Sgt-at-Arms, be so construed as to make the same allowance as that made to the widow of Saml Haight, late Sgt-at-Arms.

1-During the freshet in the Susquehanna last week, Fred'k Hotchkiss, an old & respected citizen of Windsor, was drowned on Wed while attempting to cross a little creek, which empties into the Susquehanna at that place. 2-It is also said that 3 children of Mr Elsira Thomas, of Chehocton, on the Delaware, in N Y, were floated off on a cake of ice & drowned.

For rent: two 2 story frame houses, at 6th & Pa ave. For terms, apply to the subscriber, or to Bernard Parsons, who lives near the premises, where the keys may be had. –Jas Rhodes

Murder in Court: during the trial of an uimportant cause in a Justice's Court at Van Buren Co, Missouri, Mr Anderson called Mr Estes, a witness on the stand, a liar, whereupon Estes attacked him, but Anderson being the strongest man, got his opponent down & dealt him furious blows, when suddenly he rolled over a corpse. On examination it was found that Estes had stabbed him 5 or 6 times with a penknife, which caused his death. He was admitted to bail, but immediately fled, & has not since been heard of.

Meeting of Ofcrs of the Army, in Detroit City, on Mar 21, 1846, Brig Gen H Brady presiding, in justice to the memory of the late Lts Edwin R Long & J R D Burnett, 2nd Infty, who died, the former on the Mar 11, & the latter on Mar 15. The arduous services of each during the late southern campaigns having, beyond a doubt, so broken their good constitutions as to have predisposed them each to an early death, & which has thus overtaken the one at age 36 & the other at age 35. H Brady, Col 2nd Infty & Brevet Brig Genr'l U S A

J P Taylor, Lt Col & Asst Com Genr'l of Subsistence
E Bakus, Capt 1st Infty
A Canfield, Capt U S Top Engineers
C S Tripler, Surgeon U S Army
H Day, Capt 2nd Infty

S P Heintzelman, Capt & Assist Quartermaster
J N Macomb, 1st Lt, U S Top Engineers
F Woodbridge, 1st Lt 2nd Artl & A D C
S P Brady, Sutler

For rent: 2 story dwlg-house on 6th st, south of Pa ave. Inquire of Jourdan W Maury, next door east of Coleman's Hotel. Possession to be had Apr 10.

SAT APR 4, 1846
New Market-House: Mayor's Ofc, Apr 1, 1846. Proposals will be received until Apr 24, for the erection of a Market-house between 7th & 8th sts north, on the open space formed by the junction of N Y & Mass ave with K st, according to a plan which may be seen at the Mayor's ofc on Mon next & every day thereafter.
-W W Seaton, Mayor   -J C Harkness, Jos Bryan, Com'rs

Appointments by the Pres, by & with the advice & consent of the Senate:
Thos P Moore, of Ky, to be Indian agent for the Indian tribes on the Upper Missouri, vice Andrew Dripps, removed.
Richd J McCulloh, to be melter & refiner of the Mint of the U S at Phil, vice Jonas McClintock, resigned.
John M McCalla, of Ky, 2nd Auditor of the Treasury, vice Wm B Lewis, removed.

John R Macmurdo, of Louisiana, Treasurer of the Branch Mint of the U S, at New Orleans, vice Horace C Cammack, removed.
Felix Grundy Mayson, to be 2nd Lt in the Marine Corps, from Nov 14 last, vice Lt Robt D Taylor, dec'd.
Reuben Burdine, of Wash, & Henry Reaver, of Gtwn, to be justices of the peace.

Lexington [Miss] Adv gives an account of a dreadful affray at Richland, Holmes Co, on Mar 7, between Richd Gage, of that county, & Jacob Varnell & Lewis Alexander, of Rankin. Squabble was over a horse race. Alexander died in half an hour of a gunshot wound, Gage died Mar 9, of a pistol shot. Varnell, the only survivor, has been arrested & committed for trial.

Mrd: on Thu last, by Rev Septimus Tuston, Mr John Wagner to Miss Anne Eliz, eldest d/o Mr Henry L Cross, all of Wash City.

Died: on Mar 22, Miss Jane Colston, d/o Col Edw Colston, of Honeywood, in her 17th year.

Senate: 1-Cmte on Naval Affairs: adverse report on the bill for the relief of G B Duvall. 2-Cmte of Claims: House bill for the relief of Smith Thurger, without amendment. 3-Cmte of Claims: House bill for the relief of John G Pierie, without amendment. Also, House bill for the relief of Adam McCulloch. 4-Cmte on Revolutionary Claims-adverse reports on the following: ptns of the legal reps of John Campbell, dec'd; of Sally Bass, heir of Chas Pasteur; of the excs of Henry Tatum, of John Fulford, of Wm Wilson, & Wm W Wilson; of Simeon Hubbard, of Wm S Jett, of Bebe Wadhams, exc of Abigail Wadhams. 5-Cmte on Naval Affairs-adverse reports on the following ptns: of Carey H Seely, of Mary D Wade, of Saml H Thompson, of Eliz Sevier, of the laborers & mechanics of the Wash Navy Yard, & of Jas Melville Gillis. 6-Cmte on the Judiciary: adverse report on the ptn of Chas Stearns. 7-Cmte on Pensions: adverse reports on the ptns of Eli Hinds & of Jemima Flood. 8-Cmte on Private Land Claims: adverse report on the ptn of Erastus Brooks.

Washington College: summer session will commence the 1st Monday of May. –R R Reed, sec, Wash, Pa.

Delaware College: will commence on Apr 22. –E W Gilbert, Pres Del College, Newark, Dela.

Mrs Clitz has several vacant rooms: between 3rd & 4½ st, Pa ave.

Runaway was committed to the jail of Wash Co, Md, on Mar 30, a negro man, who says he belongs to Col John Strothers, of Berkoley Co, Va, & was hired to Mr Jos Crane, near Charlestown, Va, from whom he absconded. Owner is to prove his property, or else he will be discharged agreeably to law. -Thos Martin, Sheriff

By virtue of a writ of distrain by Chas Calvert, sen, against the goods & chattels of Wm Brown, I have taken sundry articles of furniture, glasses, wash-stand, & castors: for sale at the Centre Market-house, on Apr 7, for cash. –Jas H Boss, Bailiff

MON APR 6, 1846
Circuit Court of Wash Co, D C-in Chancery. Wm W Corcoran, vs Alex'r M Burch & Eliz M, his wife, et al. Cmplnt's bill charges that, on or about Jul 14, 1843, he purchased, on time, from John Breckinridge, of Va, lots 20 & 21 in square 186, of Wash City, & by the terms of the sale was to receive a valid deed, with a good & sufficient title, on full payment of the purchase money; that he has duly paid the greater part of the purchase money, & is prepared to pay the residue when such title shall be made; that, after said purchase, said John died, leaving a will sufficient to pay the title to the residue of the purchase money, [& the administrator with the will annexed is made a party dfndnt,] but not sufficient to pass the legal estate remaining in him, & his title in the same has descended to his hiers at law, of whom the dfndnt Eliz M is one, & of whom all save she have executed a valid deed to the cmplnt of all their title, which deed is now held as an escrow by a 3rd party, to be delivered to cmplnt when the residue or purchase money shall be paid to said administer. The objects of the bill are to obtain from said Alexander M Burch & wife a conveyance of all their title in right of the wife to the cmplnt, on full payment of the purchase money, & general relief. And forasmuch as it is averred, & appears, that said Alex'r M Burch & wife reside & are out of D C, it is ordered that they appear on or before Aug 7 next, & show cause why the cmplnt should not have relief as prayed, otherwise the said bill may be taken against them as confessed, & a decree passed in conformity with the prayer. –W Brent, clk

Senate: Ptn from Geo W Whitton, asking to be allowed a pension. 2-Ptn from Benj Harris, of Illinois, asking to be allowed a pre-emption right. 3-Papers in the case of John Cocke: presented. 4-Ptn from Peter Von Schmidt, asking the adoption of his plan for carrying ships over bars & shoals by the U S Navy. 5-Ptn from Peter Frost, for a pension. 6-Ptn from Michl Hanson, late a seaman of the U S Navy, for a pension. 7-Ptn from the heirs of John Morrison, dec'd, asking to be indemnified against loss by the depreciation of continental currency. 8-Cmte on Private Land Claims: bill for the relief of Nathl Hogatt. 9-Cmte of Claims: bill for the relief of Geo W Walton, & a bill for the relief of Calvin Reed. Same cmte: unfavorable report on the claim of Robt Butler; which was ordered to be printed. Unfavorable report made in the case of John Brooks was taken up & concurred in.

House of Reps: 1-Memorial of Josiah Moore & 85 others, citizens of Chester Co, Pa, praying for the abolition of slavery in D C. 2-Memorial of Isaiah Jackson & 62 others, citizens of Chester Co, Pa, praying Congress to take measure for so amending the Constitution as to prohibit the Gen Gov't from requiring any portion of the people of the U S to interfere for the support of slavery in any of the States.

Wm Lee Davidson Ewing, lately a Senator in Congress from Illinois, died at Springfield, in that State, on Mar 25. He was at the time of his death Auditor of the public accounts of Illinois.

Ladies Ordinary, for the better accommodation of ladies visiting Wash on business or for pleasure. Every attention will be rendered to visiters in order to make them comfortable. –L Galabrun, European Hotel, Pa ave, near the Treasury Bldg.

An Englishman, named Fletcher, was killed on the Reading railroad, 9 miles below Pottsville, Pa, on Tue. He was standing upon the platform, contrary to orders, &, after being cautioned by the agent, was caught by one of the bridges. He was about 25 years of age, & had been in the country but a few days. His father resides in Pottsville.

Died: on Apr 3, at Balt, Mrs Hester Ann Hucorn, in her 77th year, formerly of Alexandria, but for the last 28 years a resident of Balt.

Samaritan Association meeting this evening at half past 7 o'clock. –Wm Flinn, sec

Wash Light Infty meeting this evening at half past 7 o'clock. –Wm H Clark, sec

Nat'l Blues regular meeting this evening at 7 o'clock. –M P Mohun, sec

To rent: house & store on 7th st, between F & G sts. Apply to Bates & Brother, at the Soap & Candle Factory, on G st, or to Thos Bates.

Orphans Court of Wash Co, D C. Letters of administrationon the personal estate of Hanson Davies, late of Wash Co, dec'd. –A H Lawrence, adm, ofc western wing City Hall. [Apr 7th newspaper: Orphans Court of Wash Co, D C. Letters of administration on the personal estate of Hanson Dines, late of said county, dec'd. –A H Lawrence, adm, ofc western wing City Hall.]

TUE APR 7, 1846
Public sale on Apr 9, that beautiful piece of property on C st, between 3rd & 4½ sts, lately occupied by Robt N Johnson. I believe the title to be perfectly good.
–Jos H Bradley -B Homans, auctioneer

The Oakland School, Burlington, N J: E C Wines, Principal. Nest session commences on May 4.

The Western Continent: Park Benjamin & Wm T Thompson, editors. It is a family newspaper, published every Sat in Balt, Md, & devoted to the preservation of the Union & the best interests of the South. Address the Editors or Publishers. Wm Taylor & Co, Jarvis Bldgs, North st, Balt, Md.

Orphans Court of Wash Co, D C. Letters of administration on the personal estate of Hanson Dines, late of said county, dec'd. –A H Lawrence, adm, ofc western wing City Hall.

Senate: 1-Memorial from Thos T Barclay, proposing an improvement in coinage. 2-Cmte on Naval Affairs: bill for the relief of Harriet Ward.

Proposals will be received for filling up the lots in squares 259, 260, & 324, to secure & effect their perfect surface drainage. –John Sessford, Com'r of Second Ward

Died: on Apr 5, in Wash City, after an illness of several weeks, Gen Danl Parker. His funeral will be from his residence on F st, this day at 3 o'clock. Gen Parker was a native of Massachusetts. He came to this city before the commencement of the last war, to fill the responsible post of Chief Clerk of the War Dept. From this arduous ofc, in the times in which he filled it, & his signal services & extensive capacity for business were appreciated by the administration of the excellent Madison, Gen Parker was transferred to the ofc of Adj & Inspector Genr'l of the Army, with rank of Brig Gen, which he held til 1821. In late years he was again in the chief clerkship of the Dept of War. In his last painful illness he possessed all his faculties to the end, & met death with a fortitude & resignation to which human nature is rarely equal.

The Hon Jos Vance, Rep from Ohio, while on a recent visit to his family at home, has been stricken with a serious if not alarming illness.

WED APR 7, 1846
A colored servant girl, about 16 years of age, of Jas M Torbert, went into the kitchen to kindle the fire, & her dress took fire. She lingered in excruciating pain until 5 o'clock, when she expired.

The Capitol Grounds, through the capital management of Mr Jas Maher, the public gardener, are beginning to assume a very springlike appearance.

House of Reps: 1-Memorial of Benj Crawford, in relation to his invention of a scale by which the amount of pressure & the quantity of water in steam boilers will be accurately shown. 2-Memorial of Benj Loomis, of Michigan, for a pension. 3-Ptn of Mrs Eliz Ferguson, praying for a pension.

City Ordnance-Wash. Act authorizing the Mayor to settle with Wm H Gunnell & Wm Bird, the assignees of Andrew B McLean, for the Corp Fish Dock, & other purposes. Award was rendered on Feb 23, 1846, which gives Gunnell & Bird the sum of $5,925.61in compensation. Jos Harbaugh for his services as arbitrator, the sum of $20.

Senate: 1-Cmte on Revolutionary Claims: bill for the relief of Maj Gen Alex'r Lord Sterling. 2-Cmte on Indian Affairs: bill for the relief of W H Thomas.

Mr Hughes, who has conducted the Fred'k Herald for several years, retires, & Messrs Turner & Young take charge of it-editor & printer respectively.

House of Reps: 1-Cmte of Claims: bill for the benefit of the legal reps of Gen Jas C Walson, of Ga: committed. 2-Cmte of Claims: adverse reports on the cases of Maria B Stall & Chas M Hudspeth: laid on the table. Bill for the relief of Jos C Doxey; also, a bill for the relief of John Speakman, & a bill for the relief of Phineas Capen, of Mass, administrator of John Cox, dec'd, late of Boston: all committed. Same cmte: adverse report on the case of Zenas King: laid on the table. 3-Cmte on Commerce: bill for the relief of Moses Noble, owner of the fishing schnr **Ruth**. Bill for the relief of Wm Ellery, owner of fishing schnrs **Sevo & Ida**. Bills for the relief of the owners & crews of the schnr **Good Exchange**; of the schnr **Garland**; of the schnr **Blooming Youth**; of the schnr **Fortune**. 4-Cmte on Public Lands: bill for the relief of the heirs & legal reps of Richd C Allen, dec'd, late of Florida. Bill for the relief of John Milstead, of Florida. Adverse report on the case of Allen G Johnson, of Hamilton Co, Fla: laid on the table. 5-Cmte on Revolutionary Claims: asked to be discharged from the ptn of Alanson Grant: laid on the table. 6-Cmte on Private Land Claims: bill for the relief of the legal reps of John Rundle. Bill to amend the act for the relief of the legal reps of Therese Molette, wid/o Gaspard Phiole. 7-Cmte on Indian Affairs: bill for the relief of the heirs & legal reps of Cyrus Turner, jr, reported the same back, with a report in detail of the facts: committed. Same cmte: asked to be discharged from the consideration of the ptn of Peter Crouse & others, for a grant of Indian reservation lands, & that it be laid on the table: agreed to. 8-Cmte on Military Affairs: bill for the relief of John Stockton: read twice & committed. Same cmte: bill for the relief of Jas Edwards, adm of Edw M Watson, dec'd: committed. 9-Cmte on Naval Affairs: asked to be discharged from the consideration of the ptn of N C Whitehead & others: laid on the table. 10-Cmte on Foreign Affairs: bill for settling the claims of the legal reps of Richd W Meade, dec'd: committed. 11-Cmte on Revolutionary Pensions: bill from the Senate for the relief of Goe Wentling, without amendment: committed. Same cmte: adverse report on the case of Medad Shelly: laid on the table. 12-Cmte on Invalid Pensions: adverse reports on the cases of Sarah Hildreth, wid/o John, of John I Smith, of Nathan Ashby, of Jeremiah Carter, & of Mgt C Hanson: laid on the table. Same cmte: asked to be discharged from the cases of Richd Palmer & John S Jennings: laid on the table. Same cmte: adverse report on the case of Saml T Winslow: laid on the table.

A rencontre took place on Fri last at Charlotte Hall, St Mary's Co, Md, between Mr John H Thomas, a student of law of Dalt, & Mr Geo G Ashcom, in which the latter was killed. The survivor is said to have acted only in self-defence.

Wanted, a young man thoroughly acquainted with the dry-goods business, who can bring undoubted testimonials as to his qualifications. None other need apply.
–John E Carter, Gtwn

The slave Pauline, who was condemned to be hanged at New Orleans a year ago, for cruelly beating her mistress, but respited in consequence of her then situation, suffered the full penalty of the law on Mar 28.

Died: on Apr 6, in Wash City, of erysipelas, in his 45th year, Ezekiel Starr, of the Cherokee Nation. He was a man of extraordinary firmness, moral & physical courage; always enjoyed a deep place in the affections of his family & numerous relatives. In 1834 he foresaw that the Eastern Cherokees cound not be relieved from the thralldom which surrounded them in the States, removed with his family, & joined the Western Cherokees in their new homes. In the winter of 1843-44 he came to Wash as one of the delegates to plead the cause of the Treaty party before the U S Gov't. He returned in the winter of 1844-45. Returning home last summer, he found his large family circle driven from their homes in the Nation to the State of Arizona, & his valuable brother, Jas Starr, a signer of the treaty of 1835, & an infant son, ruthlessly murdered, & their murderers stalking abroad unpunished. He arrived here 4 weeks since, at the invitation of the Pres, as one of the Delegation to adjust with the U S the many difficulties of his comrades. He was immediately attacked with the worst form of erysipelas. His funeral is this day at 4 o'clock, from Mrs Hamilton's.

The sale of lots belonging to the estate of Geo Murdock, dec'd, to take place at my auction store this evening. -R W Dyer, auct

For rent: 3 story house on 6th st, between E & F sts, east side, at present occupied by DeWitt Kent. For terms inquire of the occupant.

For sale: good brick dwlg-house, on north side of D st, commonly called Mechanics' Row, between 2nd & 3rd sts, now in the occupancy of Mr D Ridgely. Inquire of Wm Thompson, Genr'l Agent, #4, south side of Louisiana ave, beween 6th & 7th sts.

For rent: store & dwlg at Md ave & 12th st, square 299. Inquire of Mr T M Edward, the present occupier of said house, or of Edw Mattingly, near the Navy Yard.

Tavern stand for rent: the undersigned, intending to change his present business, offers for rent his establishment, at 8th & D sts, between the Genr'l Post & Patent Ofcs, fronting 60 feet on 8th st & 36 feet on D st. Possession on May 1.
–Owen Connolly, Farmers' Hotel, 8th & D sts.

$100 reward for my servant woman Sophia. She left my residence at Annapolis, Md, Apr 5, & traveled in the cars to Wash City, & went to the house of her mother, who is a free woman, named Mgt Lee, residing next door to a blacksmith's shop at L st south & 3rd st east, near the Navy Yard. She has not been heard of since Apr 6th, when her mother alleges she intended to return to Annapolis. She is a remarkable neat well-looking mulatto woman, about 28 years of age. –Thos G Pratt, Annapolis, Md

THU APR 9, 1846
Senate: 1-Adverse reports taken up & concurred in: from the Cmte on Revolutionary Claims: ptn of Eli Hobbs. From the Cmte on Claims: ptns of Orlando S Rees & of Robt Butler. From the Cmte on Indian Affairs: ptn of Mary B Hook. From the Cmte on Pensions: the ptns of Wm W Hall, Saml Knight, jr, & Joanna Quincey. From the Cmte on Naval Affairs: ptn of G D Duvall.

Died: on Apr 7, after a lingering illness of consumption, Mary Catharine, only d/o Jas Williams, in her 17th year. Her funeral is this day at 4 o'clock, from the residence of her father, 5th & H sts.

St Mary's School, Raleigh, N C: Right Rev L S Ives, D D, Visiter. Rev Aldert Smedes, Rector. Summer term will commence on Jun 4th & continue till Nov 10. Winter term is from Nov 11 till Apr 15, 1847.

By writ of fieri facias, at the suit of the Mayor, Board of Aldermen & Board of Common Council of Wash City: I have seized & taken into execution all the right, title, & interest of Edw F Valentine in & to sundry furniture and articles: sale on Apr 16, in front of the Centre Market-house, Wash City, for cash.
–H R Maryman, Constable

Marshal's sale: I shall offer to resell, at the risk & expenses of Wm Ball, on Apr 13, on the premises, for cash, all the right, title, & interest of Mary Eliz Ball, Wm W Ball, Thos Wilson, John W Wilson, Geo W Wilson, & Walter Wilson, in the following property, to wit: a 2 story brick tenement & lot of ground on the south side of Prince st, in the town of Alexandria, D C; subject to a ground-rent of $66.67; to satisfy a writ of venditioni exponas, in favor of Wm Brockett & others, against said Mary Eliz Ball, Wm W Ball, Thos Wilson, & others. –D Minor, Marshal

Orphans Court of Wash Co, D C. Ordered, on application, that letters of administration on the personal estate of Henry Culver, dec'd, be granted to Geo G Coe & Richd Dement, unless cause to the contrary be shown on or before Apr 28.
–Ed N Roach, Reg/o wills

Circuit Court of Wash Co, D C-in Chancery. Jas Dundas et al, vs Jos Forrest's reps, et al. The Trustees have reported the sale of lot 5 in square 120, Wash City, to Bladen Forrest, for $387, & a part of lot 14 in square 490, to Wm A Bradley, for $1,200: ordered that the sales be ratified. –Wm Brent, clerk

FRI APR 10, 1846
House of Reps: 1-Ptn of the heiress of Dr Fred'k Seigle, for commutation pay due for the Revolutionary services of her said ancestor. 2-Ptn of Valentine Spencer. [No other information.]

New volunteer company, The United Rifle Corps, has lately been formed in Wash City. Elected ofcrs of the corps:

Thos J Williams, Capt	Josiah Dixon, 3rd Lt
John A Hunnicutt, 1st Lt	Peter Callan, Quartermaster
Green H Barton, 2nd Lt	

Circuit Court of Wash Co, D C. Trial yesterday of a cause of ejectment, the contending parties being Gen John Mason vs Jos N Fearson, both of Gtwn. The action was brought by the plntf to recover from the dfndnt sundry lots sold by the Corp of Wash, & bought by the dfndnt at a tax sale. The Court adjourned, today being Good Friday, until next Monday.

Senate: 1-Ptn of Alex'r Wilson, of Illinois, praying for arrearages of pension. 2-Ptn from the administrator of Wm Tarry, asking commutation. 3-Cmte on pensions: adverse reports on the ptns of Reuben Mills, Abigail Rives, & Deliverance Slasson. 4-Cmte of Claims: bill authorizing the payment of a sum of money to Robt Purkis. 5-Cmte on Territories: bill to provide for the settlement of the accounts of Wm B Slaughter, late Sec of the Territory of Wisconsin.

The ship **Columbia**, W J Boothe, of & for Alexandria, from Liverpool, Feb 9, was totally lost on Apr 2 on the coast of N C: no lives were lost. The **Columbia** was owned by Messrs Wm Fowle & Son & the estate of the late Capt Wm Morrell.

Capt Saml Whitney & wife were drowned on Mar 31, while attempting to cross Penobscot Bay from Lincolnville to Castine in an open boat.

A gentleman from Harrisburg informs us that Mr David Hummel, jr, committed suicide by hanging himself in the attic of his residence. -Phil American

Mrd: on Mar 8, in Gtwn, D C, at Christ Church, by Rev Mr Gassaway, Jas Selden, of Wash, to Margaret, d/o Maj Geo W Walker, U S Marine Corps.

Died: on Apr 8, in Balt, Wm Geo Read, an eminent member of the Balt Bar, & a gentleman of high & accomplished character.

SAT APR 11, 1846
Mr S B Howes, proprietor of the N Y Mammoth Circus is now erecting a large pavilion over the 7th st bridge, on the Mall, & will open on Apr 13, with the greatest array of equestrian talent now traveling the country, in which Madame Marie McCarte, from Ducrow's Royal Amphitheatre of Paris, will appear.

The Rev B F Barrett, Pastor of the Society of the New Jerusalem in N Y C, will preach in the Capitol on Sabbath morning next, at 11 o'clock.

R A Meredith, Atty at Law, Gainesville, Ala: will attend to the security & collection of claims in Alabama & Mississippi.

Caution: The undersigned, having been infomed that Seth L Cole has offered for sale the fractional southeast quarter of section #9, in township #8, in Illinois, would inform that a bill in equity is now pending, & an injunction against said Cole & others in the Circuit Court within & for Peoria Co, Ill, in relation to said land. Since the commencement of the above named suit the Supreme Court for the State of Ill has decided that the undersigned has a perfect title to said land, & against the title of said Cole. –Isaac Underhill, Peoria, Ill: Mar 27, 1846.
[See 'Caution" in Apr 13th-below.]

MON APR 13, 1846
Reply to "Caution" of Isaac Underhill: I believe that my title to the tract mentioned is good & valid, while that under which Mr Underhill pretends to claim was not suspected or set up until after the death of the alleged grantor, Mr Bogardus; & his widow has testified that she never joined in any such conveyance, & believes that no such deed was ever given. I have no knowledge of any such decision as that referred to in the caution. –Seth L Cole [See "Caution" in Apr 11, 1846-above.]

Wanted to hire, by the year, a good steady hand, on a farm near Gtwn. –L M Morton, Gtwn

L H Berryman has opened a Feed Store on the northeast corner of C st north & 12th st west, [between Pa ave & the bridge on 12th st.]

Mrs Lanphier will open Spring Millinery on Apr 15.

Orphans Court of Wash Co, D C. Letters of administration on the personal estate of John P Van Ness, of said county. –C P Van Ness, adm

Mrs Wheeler, the young & amiable wife of Paul J Wheeler, Postmaster at Croydon, N H, was burnt to death a few days since, by her clothes taking fire while she was sitting alone in her house.

Extraordinary Longevity. Died, in Bladen Co, N C, on Oct 14 last, Mr Wm Pridgen, aged 123 years. He entered his 124th year in Jun last. He volunteered to serve his country in the Continental Army of the Revolution, &, though then exempt by reason of his being over age, he served a full term in that war, & received a pension for many years past. He has lived to follow all his children to the grave, except one, an aged dght. His grandchildren are aged people, & he has left great grandchildren upwards of 40 years of age, & great-great grandchildren about 12 years of age. He retained his faculties till his death, except his sight, which he lost a few years ago. He was able to walk until a few days before his death, when he was attacked by fever, of which he died. –Fayetteville Observer

House of Reps: 1-Recommended they pass: bill for the relief of Wiley B Parnell; relief of Isabella Baldridge, wid/o Capt John Baldridge; bill for the relief of Sampson Brown. 2-Passed: bill for the relief of Langtree & Jenkins. 3-Ptn of Jerusha Smith & others for a pension. 4-Ptn of Elias Hall, for compensation for Revolutionary losses & sufferings. 5-Ptn of Abijah J Bolton, of Trumbull Co, Ohio, praying for a pension for wounds received in the last war.

Colonization Rooms, Wash, Apr 10, 1846. From the colony of Liberia: the brig **Kent** has just brought intelligence to Feb 13. The Rev Mr Williams, missionary [white] of the Methodist Episcopal Church, had died with the fever. Of the re-captives of the Pons, about 60 had died altogether after their reaching Monrovia.

The Nat'l Magazine & Industrial Record, edited by Redwood Fisher, Apr, 1846. Another number will complete the 2nd volume of this valuable journal.

The Farmers' Library & Monthly Journal of Agriculture, edited by John S Skinner. This is the 10th number of this journal.

Very valuable bldg lots at auction: on Apr 29, on the premises, as exc of the estate of the late Danl Grinnan, lot 13 in square 378, in Wash City. It is within one square of Pa ave. –John S Welford, exc of Danl Grinnan, & com'r of F C. -R W Dyer, auct

$30 reward for runaway negro George, about 21 years of age. My son, a youth about 14 years old, has also left me, & they may be in company. –Jesse C Burroughs, Chaptico. [$20 if taken in St Mary's Co, Md.]

The subscriber has been appointed by his Honor Judge Cranch a Constable for Wash Co, D C: J F Wollard.

Meeting of the Philodemic Society of Gtwn College, on Apr 9: testimonial of our regard for the public worth & private virtues of the dec'd, Wm Geo Read. –Edmond R Smith, Oliveira T Andrews, Jas H Donegan: Gtwn College, Apr 9, 1846.

Mrd: on Apr 7, by Rev Mr Jordan, Wm Robertson, jr, of Petersburg, Va, to Caroline Agnes, d/o the late John W Lard, of Sussex Co.

Mrd: on Apr 9, in Fredericksburg, Va, at St George's Church, by Rev Dr Edw C McGuire, Wm Kerney, of N Y, to Miss Ann F L Carmichael, of Richmond, Va.

Died: on Apr 11, in Wash City, Anne, the w/o Peter Brady, aged 58. She has an enduring existence in the memory & affections of her bereaved husband & sorrowing children. Her funeral will take place from her late residence on Capitol Hill, this afternoon, at 4 o'clock.

Died: on Apr 11, Miss Stella Adeline Makepeace. Her funeral will take place from the residence of Henry Stone, on Capitol Hill, this afternoon, at half past 4 o'clock.

Died: on Mar 24, at the residence of her mother, near Piscataway, PG Co, Md, after a severe illness, Mrs Henrietta E Clements, w/o Mr Francis H Clements, leaving an affectionate husband & children to mourn their irreparable loss. She was an amiable & excellent lady.

The subscriber has taken a room on 9th st, over Mr Uttermuhle's Tailor Shop, on the 2nd square above Messrs D Clagett & Co, for the purpose of closing his business, & requests all those indebted to him to call & settle without delay. –Thos T Barnes

Senate: 1-Memorial of the heirs of Jas Beall, asking payment for money advanced by said Beall for provisions during the Revolutionary war. 2-From citizens of N Y, several memorials remonstrating against the renewal of Jethro Wood's patent for a plough. 3-Ptn from Ziba Baker, for a pension. 4-Ptn from Brian Mullanphy & Saml Hawken, of Missouri, asking that the laws of the U S may be extended over the Oregon territory. 5-Ptn from Willis J Spann & others, citizens of Florida, asking that the bill now before the Senate for the relief of Benj Chaires & others may not be passed. 6-Cmte on Revolutionary Claims: adverse reports on the following ptns: heirs of Francis Vigo; heirs of Lt Saml Beach; reps of Christopher Delazerne; reps of Benj Durkee; excs of Lt Bartholomew Van Valken. 7-Cmte of Claims: adverse report on the bill from the House for the relief of Chas Bemis. 8-Bill for the relief of Gabriel B Fanning: presented. 9-Bill for the relief of Benj Chaires & others was recommitted to the Cmte on the Judiciary.

For rent: desirable residence formerly occupied by the Hon W D Merrick, fronting the City Hall, near the Rev Mr Stringfellow's church. Apply to W H Gunnell, at his Lumber Yard, 6th st & opposite Coleman's.

For rent: 3 story brick store & back bldg, at present occupied by Randolph & Keller, on Pa ave, near 6th st. Possession given immediately. Inquire of Mr J W Baden, next door, or to Wm M Randolph.

To let, a 2 story brick house, on N Y ave, between 7th & 8th sts. Inquire of Jos Harbaugh, on 7th st, between D & E sts.

TUE APR 14, 1846
Senate: 1-Ptn from Jas Livingston, asking interest on commutation. 2-Adverse reports on the ptns of Reuben Mills; on the ptn of Deliverance Slasson; on the ptn of

Abigail Reese: in the Cmte on Pensions. 3-Acts referred: for the relief of Isabella Baldridge, wid/o Capt John Baldridge; relief of Sampson Brown; relief of Langhey & Jenkins; relief of Wiley B Pannall, of Blount Co, Alabama. 4-Cmte on the Library be instructed to inquire into the expediency of purchasing a portrait of Baron Steuben.

Breach of promise case: Miss Sarah Greer, a young lady residing in N Y, has recovered damages to the amount of $3,000 in an action for breach of promise instituted by her against Mr Eli Butler, of that city. The dfndnt had been paying attention to the plntf since 1842, & lately married another woman.

The Newark Advertiser announced the death of a Revolutionary veteran, David Tichenor, in his 88th year. He was brother to the late Isaac Tichenor, formerly Govn'r of Vermont & a Senator in Congress.

Died: on Mar 10, at *Oak Grove*, St Mary's Co, Md, Eliz Emily Matthews, consort of Wm Matthews, of that county, & oldest child of the late Geo W Neale, after a protracted illness, borne with the fortitude natural to one who discharged in life all her incumbent duties as best became her, & awaited resignedly that summons to a hereafter which, soon or late, comes to all of humanity.

$10 reward for strayed large gray horse. Reward will be paid on delivery of said horse to Owen Connolly, corner of D & 8th sts.

St Mary's Female Seminary, St Mary's Co, Md: will be opened on May 12 next, under the care & instruction of Mr E J Meany as Principal of the Seminary assisted by Mrs Meany. –C Combs, Pres of the Board of Trustees.

For sale: St Charles Hotel, Wash D C: the lease, the furniture, & fixtures of this fashionable & highly popular hotel. It fronts on B st, Pa ave, & 3rd st.
–Burlin Brown, St Charles Hotel

The undersigned, being the sole owner of *Sharp's Island*, in the Chesapeake Bay, except that part upon which the U S Gov't has had a Lighthouse erected, & having been much incommoded by persons having business to transact in connexion with said lighthouse, hereby gives notice that in future no person will be permitted to land or trespass upon the premises, or any business appertaining to said lighthouse. The undersigned regrets having to use this course in consequence of his remonstrances sent to the U S Gov't being entirely disregarded. –Jeremiah Valliant

WED APR 15, 1846
Wash Corp: 1-The Board resumed the consideration of the nomination of John Magar as Police Constable & Com'r of the fish wharf: ordered to lie on the table. 2-Bill for the relief of Wm Easby & K H Lambell: passed. 3-Cmte of Claims: bill for the relief of Michl Downey: passed. 4-Ptn of Silas H Hill & others, for the

improvement of I st, from 5th & 6th sts west: referred to the Cmte on Improvements.
4-Cmte of Claims: act for the relief of Jos C Harris: read twice.

Died: on Apr 14, Henry Clay, infant s/o Jas & Sarah B Williams, aged 5 months. His funeral is today at 3 o'clock, from the residence of his parents, 5th & H sts.

Circuit Court: Wash: Thos W Morris & wife, vs Chas Calvert et al: Exceptions to the Auditor's report. The cmplnt, Mrs Morris, is one of the 5 children of Geo Calvert & Rosalie E Stier; Mrs Calvert was one of the 3 children of Henry J Stier & Maria Louisa Peetres. The dfndnts are 2 of the 5 children of Mr & Mrs Calvert, & the excs & residuary devisees of Geo Calvert. The controversy between the parties relates to the property of Mr & Mrs Stier, which came to the hands & possession of Geo Calvert. After being in court for a considerable time, the matter was referred to an auditor, W Redin, who made a lengthy report of over 100 pages, the result of which is: that the auditor reports to the court that the balance due from the dfndnts to the cmplnts is the sum of $11,260.87, with interest from Jan 28, 1838. To this report the cmplnts find 12 & the dfndnts 5 exceptions, which have been fully argued. Today the Court delivered its opinion, over-ruling all the exceptions & confirming the report of the auditor.

T B Warder was arrested yesterday by ofcrs Fowler & Howison, of the Auxiliary Guard. The prisoner is charged, on the oath of Richd T Smallwood, with having murdered Geo Smallwood, brother of the informant, in Fauquier Co, Va, in the course of last year. Warder is also charged with being a fugitive from justice. He is in the county jail awaiting the requisition of the Executive of Virginia.

On a fine day may occasionally be seen at the Capitol, Altamont, with a basket of a few apples & cakes, which he sells & ekes out a very scanty subsistence. He is in his 92nd year, & was raised in the Washington family. He was a servant of Capt Geo Washington, & was with him at the battles of the Cowpens & Guilford Court-house, & was present at the siege of York & the surrender of Cornwallis. After the death of his master, he became the property of Dr Barry, of Tenn, in whose family he remained until his freedon was given him as a boon for his good conduct. In 1844, having survived his wife & all his children, he express a desire to come back to Va, to find some of his relations or friends. The family purchased a horse for him, gave him ample means; but when he reached the home of his childhood, there was no one living being that he knew. He wandered to this city, where he has ever since remained. The object of this is to call the attention of the benevolent to his situation, in order that it may be relieved.

Senate: 1-Ptn of Eliz Byars, asking a pension. 2-A ptn, asking that Peter Carnes have leave to withdraw his papers. 3-Ptn from John D Wyatt, asking permission to locate land in lieu of that to which he had a patent. 4-Ptn from Levi P Evans, of Arkansas, asking payment for a horse that died while in the service of the U S.

Mrd: Apr 2, in Vicksburg, Miss, at the residence of T A Marshall, by Rev Mr Davidson, Edw Roberts, of Balt, to Miss Anne M Hoblitzell, niece of Col H Stidger, of Vicksburg.

House of Reps: 1-Ptn of Mrs Candace Porter, wid/o Amos Porter, for arrears of pension due to her late husband as a wounded soldier of the Revolution. 2-Ptn & papers of the heirs of Gordon White, of Tenn, praying Congress to grant to their mother the benefit of joint resolution of Congress passed Aug 16, 1842. 3-Ptn of Elias Coon, late master & owner of the schnr **Congress**, of Stonington, R I, for fishing bounty.

Musical instruction: a gentleman accustomed to teaching wishes to locate himself in some healthy situation, where his services as a Teacher of Music will secure to him a moderate support. His wife would probably receive a few day scholars. For references address: –O Woodbarton, Gtwn, D C.

For rent: dwlg on 7th st, with a stable in the rear. –Simon Fraser, south F st.

For rent: 2 story brick dwlg: on G st, within a few yards of the War Dept. Inquire of Mr Aquila Ricketts, where the key will be left, or to the subscriber, in Gtwn.
–Judson Mitchell

THU APR 16, 1846
Senate: 1-Cmte on Pensions: asking to be discharged from the further consideration of the ptns of Priscilla Green & Martha Moore. Same cmte: bill for the relief of John Keith, of N Y. Same cmte: House bills for the relief of Sampson Brown & of Isabella Baldridge: without amendment.

Tribune of Tuesday published a letter from Waterville, Oneida Co, N Y, which states that the dwlg house of Timothy Leonard was burnt to the ground with all its contents, & Mr Leonard, his wife, & a d/o Mr Woodward, about 12 years old, perished in the flames. They were the only persons in the house.

Students of the Univ of Charlottesville, Va, got into a quarrel on Sat last, with the keepers of Raymond & Co's menagerie, exhibiting at that place. A young man named Glover, from Alabama, was killed by a blow struck by one of the keepers, J J Bailey, who was arrested & committed to prison.

Died: on Apr 1, in the vicinity of Greensboro, Ala, Jesse Hair Croom, sr, in his 56th year. He was a native of N C, & emigrated to Alabama in 1818, having, before his removal, at the age of 24 represented Lenoir Co, in N C, with credit to himself & the approbation of his constituents. [See Apr 21st newspaper.]

Died: on Mar 31, at Toronto, Canada, Mary, the beloved w/o Edw H Rugherford, & d/o Dr Robt Henderson, of Cumberland Co, Va, in her 22nd year.

Appointments by the Pres, by & with the advice & consent of the Senate.
Fred'k B Welles, of N H, to be Consul for the Island of Bermuda, in place of Alex'r J Bergen, resigned, who was appointed during the recess of the Senate, vice Wm T Tucker, recalled.
Henry B Humphrey, of Mass, to be Consul for the port of Alexandria, in Egypt, vice Alex'r Todd, recalled.
Saml Haight, of N Y, to be Consul for the Azores or Western Islands, vice C W Dabney, recalled.
John T Pickett, of Ky, to be Consul for Turks Island, vice Abraham Morrell, recalled, who was appointed in the last recess of the Senate, vice John Arthur, recalled.
Wm Nelson, to be Consul for the port of Panama, in New Grenada, vice Jeremiah A Townsend, recalled.
M Hollander, to be Consul for the port of Sedan, in France, vice Thos Hulme, jr, dec'd.
Alex'r Newman, to be postmaster at Wheeling, Va, vice J B B Hale, appointed during the last recess of the Senate, who has resigned.
Wm Nelson, to be Collector of the Customs for the district, & Inspector of the Revenue for the port of Yorktown, Va, his former commission having expired.
Wm Patterson, to be Collector for the port of Sandusky, Ohio, vice Elias H Haines, whose commission has expired.
Jas E Gibble, to be Collector of Customs for the district & Inspector of Revenue for the port of Beaufort, N C.
Wm Gray, to be Surveyor for the port of Port Royal, Va.
Jos Sibley, to be Collector for the district of Genesee, & Inspector for the port of Rochester, N Y, vice Lyman B Langworthy, removed.
John D Howard, to be Naval Ofcr for the district of Salem & Beverly, Mass, vice Abraham True, whose commission expires on Apr 12, 1846.
John Dougherty, to be Chief Engineer in the U S Revenue Service, vice Thos W Farron, resigned.
Jas McGuire, Surveyor for Alexandria D C, vice Benj T Fendall, whose commission has expired.
John S Shepperd, to be Surveyor for the port of Windsor, N C, vice Marcus C Ryan, dec'd.
Thos Addison, to be Surveyor for the port of Madisonville, Louisiana, vice Mathew Dicks, whose commission has expired.
Nathl Hawthorne, to be Surveyor for the district of Salem & Beverly, Mass, vice Nehemiah Brown, removed.
Jas N Nicholas, to be Collector for the port of Perth Amboy, N J, vice Solomon Andrews, removed.
Patrick Collins, to be Surveyor for the port of Cincinnati, Ohio, vice Isaiah Wing, removed.
Philip Poultney, to be Appraiser of Merchandise for the port of Balt, from & after May 1, 1846, vice Wm Dickinson, resigned.

Household furniture, crockery, carriage, & sleigh, at auction: on Apr 21, by virtue of a deed of trust from Patrick Gowins, for certain purposes therein expressed, at his residence, at the corner of F & 22nd sts. –R W Dyer, auct

Four or 5 members of Congress can be accommodated with board at Jas Young's Boarding-house, on Capitol Hill, for the balance of the session. 250,000 bricks for sale at reduced prices for cash. Inquire of Jas Young, N J ave, Capitol Hill.

Lafayette College, Easton, Pa: 55 miles north of Phil. Inquire of Rev N Bannatyne, of F st Church, Washington, a graduate of Lafayette; or, by letter, to the subscriber. –Geo Junkin, Pres, Easton, Pa

Palm-leaf hats just received. –W Noyes & Son, La ave, opposite Bank of Washington

For sale: 6 houses & lots, in the Northern Liberties. Inquire at the store of Moorhead & Brown. –J W Moorhead

FRI APR 17, 1846
House of Reps: 1-Cmte on Commerce, reported the following bills, viz: relief of Jos Curwen, surviving partner of Willing & Curwen. Relief of Wm B Lang. Relief of the owners of the Spanish brig **Restaurador**; owners of the ship **Herald**, of Balt; owners & crew of the schnr **Madison**. Same cmte: made an adverse report on the case of Thos Harris Hodges, administrator of John H Hodges: laid on the table. 2-Ptn of Abigail Doughty, d/o Ichabod Doughty, a soldier of the Revolution. 3-Ptn of Mathias Barne for a pension. 4-Ptn & papers of Chas McClane, of Missouri, asking Congress to confirm to him a certain tract of land in the State of Missouri, containing 640 acres, on which he had established himself & cultivated prior to the purchase of Louisiana in 1803.

The late respected founder of this paper, Saml Harrison Smith, bequeathed to the Washington Library a complete set of the Nat'l Intelligencer paper, from its commencement in 1801 to the period of his decease. This is the only perfect copy which we know of, our own set extending back only to the time of the invasion of Wash City in 1814, when all of our files & other books & property were burnt by the enemy.

Geo Douch, whilst engaged on Monday in blowing rocks about 7 miles from Balt, was killed by an accidental explosion.

Thu last in Northumberland, Saratoga Co, N Y, 2 sons of Dr Jesse Billings were out gunning, when the gun in the younger brother's hands went off accidentally, the ball hitting his brother, who survived but 30 minutes.

Orphans Court of Wash Co, D C. Letters of administration on the personal estate of Anne Milligan, late of said county, dec'd. –E Milligan, admx [Persons having claims against the estate, will present them, authenticated & passed by the Orphans' Court to Alex McIntire.]

The 4 year old s/o Mr Stephen Clark, of South Boston, fell from Alger's wharf into the dock on Wed Last. Henry Jas Poole, aged 13 years, leaped into the water & rescued the drowning child.

Mrd: on Apr 14, at St Matthew's Church, by Rev John P Donelan, Mr Wm Chambers, of Alexandria, D C, to Miss Catherine M Sherlock, of Wash City.

Mrd: on Apr 14, in Wash City, by Rev W T Sprole, Benj Barton, of Alexandria, D C, to Miss Eliza Douglas, only d/o John Kennedy, bookseller, of Wash City.

Died: on Apr 14, at the residence of John Tolson, near the Navy Yard, in Wash City, Mr Geo Semmes, about 64 years of age. The dec'd was a native of Md, having represented PG Co in the Legislature of that State for many years, & filled the ofc of Sheriff of the said county for several years.

Died: on Apr 13, in Wash City, at the residence of her grand-dght, Mrs Eliz Trucks, in her 77th year. She was an excellent mother & an exemplary Christian. May she rest in peace.

Died: on Apr 15, in Wash City, after a short illness, Mr Dominic Carre. He was a native of France.

Died: on Sunday last, in Wash City, John, infant s/o John & Louisa E Potts.

For rent: 2 story brick dwlg-house at 9th st & H sts, on a double lot, with parlors & hall handsomely papered. Apply to the present occupant. –W L Bailey

SAT APR 18, 1846
Assignees' sale of Groceries, Store Fixtures, Horse & Dray: at auction on Apr 24, at the store recently occupied by Messrs Lewis & Holland on Pa ave, near 9th st, by order of the Assignees, for the benefit of the creditors. –David Stewart & Son, Assignees -A Green, auctioneer

First rate house for rent: on the corner of G & 19th sts: there are 13 rooms, including 2 kitchens. Rent-$350. -S Burche

Journeyman watchmaker wanted. Inquire of Robt Keyworth, Wash.

Ice-cream Saloon, corner of Pa ave & 11th st. C Gautier will open on Apr 13.

By virtue of a deed of trust from Geo Heberd, dated Oct 27, 1845, recorded in Liber W B #118, one of the land records of Wash Co, D C, I shall sell at public auction, on May 5, in front of the premises, lot 4 in square 438, Wash City, with improvements-a frame house lately built. This lot fronts 50 feet on south H st, & runs back 66 feet 4 inches in a line parallel with 8th st west, the same being the corner lot.
–Walter Lenox, Trustee -R W Dyer, auct

Major Ripley, Superintendent of the U S Armory at Springfield, Mass, has been honorably acquitted, by the Court of Inquiry called to investigate his case, of all the charges exhibited against him.

Trustees sale: by virtue of a deed of trust for certain purposes therein expressed: public auction on May 1, on the premises: of the east half of lot 2 in square 455, being 26 feet on F st, by 101 lest 10¼ inches deep. It is between 6th & 7th sts. Title indisputable. –Michl Larner, trustee -R W Dyer, auct

Rev Henry W Bellows, of N Y, will preach in the Unitarian Church tomorrow: 11 o'clock & 7½ o'clock.

Mrd: on Apr 7, at Wickland, near Bardstown, Nelson Co, Ky, by Rev J Farris Smith, Hon David L Yulee, U S Senator from the State of Florida, to Miss Nannie C, d/o Hon Chas A Wickliffe, late Postmaster General of the U S.

Mrd: on Mar 24, at *Mulberry Hill*, Pickaway Co, Ohio, by Rev D Whitcomb, Jas Whitcomb, Govn'r of the State of Indiana, to Martha Ann Hurst, d/o the late Wm Renick, of the former place. –Indiana Sentinel

Mrd: on Apr 1, in Prince Wm Co, by Rev T D Herndon, Mr John H Yeatman, of Wash, D C, to Miss Sarah Jane, d/o Wm M Nalls, of Prince Wm Co, Va.

Died: on Sun last, in Wash City, of consumption, which had arrested him while on a journey homeward from the South, A Kingman Parker, s/o Ebenezer Parker, of Boston, in his 20th year. His remains were conveyed home by his afflicted friends.

Died: on Mar 29, at Orange Court-house, Va, Mrs Frances E Hume, w/o David Hume, in her 34th year, d/o the late Dr Francis Dade, of the same county.

New Grocery, Flour, & Seed Store: F C Crowley, corner of 7th & E sts.

MON APR 20, 1846
We are informed by letter of the death, by yellow fever, on the coast of Africa, of John C Spencer, jr, s/o the late Sec of War, who was attached as Purser to the U S sloop-of-war **Marion**. This bereavement falls with a crushing weight upon the hearts of his parents. –Albany Evening Journal

Capt Gustavus S Drane, of the U S Army, in command of *Fort Mifflin*, below Phil, died on Wed last, after a protracted illness, in his 57th year.

City Ordnances-Wash: 1-Act for the relief of Henry S Wood: fine imposed for violating the law in relation to dead animals, be & the same is remitted: provided he pay the costs that may have accrued thereon. 2-Act for the relief of Michl Downey: to pay to him $3.37, being the amount of a judgment paid by Downey. 3-Act for the relief of Wm Easby & K H Lambell: Payment of a claim of Wm Easby, on account of repairs to the dredging machine owned by the Corp, according to his bill dated May, 1845, the sum of $394.32; & for the payment of the claim of K H Lambell, for sundry repairs to 3 scows owned by the Corp, according to his bill dated in May, 1845: $111.10.

United Rifle Corps meeting at their Armory, corner of 12th & Pa ave, Apr 22, at 7½ o'clock. [Armory is in the bldg occupied by J E Dow, as a printing ofc.] –Chas Calvert, jr, secretary

The Providence papers come to us with their columns in mourning for the death of Ex-Govn'r Jas Fenner, which event took place on Fri. He was in his 77th year.

House of Reps: 1-Bill for the relief of Jas Hillman, & bill for the relief of Saml Jordan, from the Cmte of the Whole with a recommendation that they pass. 2-Bill asking compensation to John R Williams, of Michigan, for damage done to his property by the military in the war of 1812 with Great Britain, also reported from the Cmte of the Whole, with a recommendation that it do pass. 3-Senate bill for the relief of David F Williamson, of Arkansas; bill for the relief of Chas M McKenzie; bill to amend the act for the relief of Geo Mayfield, were passed & sent to the Senate for concurrence.

Mrd: on Apr 15, at Alexandria, by Rev J T Johnston, Cassius F Lee to Ann Eliza, d/o the late Wm C Gardner, all of that place.

Soda Fountain for sale: apply at Geo A Lane & Co, Market Space, Gtwn.

For sale or rent: 2 story frame house, nearly new, on 10th st, south of Pa ave, & adjoining Green's Row, within one square of Marsh Market. –Warren Little, on the premises.

For rent: the house just vacated by Chas Bradley, on Md ave, south side, between 4½ & 6th sts. Inquire of Chas Bradley, at the ofc of the Franklin Fire Co, or S P Franklin, Pa ave, between 9th & 10th sts.

TUE APR 21, 1846

U S & Foreign Agency, at Wash, D C: for the purpose of transacting business in Wash City, under the firm & style of Richd S Coxe & Co. Ofc-12th st, between E & F sts. Richd S Coxe, Roger C Weightman, Jas Prentiss, Wm A Bradley.

To let: 2 story brick house, with back bldg, 3 doors from 5th & G sts. Apply for the key next door. For terms to John Alexander, between 12th & 13th, Pa ave.

To let: 2 story frame dwlg-house, on 14th st, between H & I sts, & near the State & Treasury ofcs. Inquire of John McDuell, near the premises.

By virtue of a deed of trust from Henry Walker to the subscriber, dated Feb 23, 1843, & recorded in Liber W B #99, folios 299 thru 301, in the land records of Wash Co, D C: sale on Apr 20, lots 1 & 2 in square 107, with the improvements.
–Nich Callan, trustee -R W Dyer, auct

Wash City Canal: proposals will be received for renting to the highest bidder the following wharves or sections on the Canal, for 1 or 3 years, commencing May 1, 1846. The whole or any part of 17th st wharf, not less than a section. All that part from 17th st to 6th st west, lying north & south on the Canal.
–Jas A Tait, Canal Com'r, Western Division

Wanted, in a small family, a good cook & washerwoman. A slave would be preferred. Apply at Dr Blake's, n w corner of C & 3rd sts.

Cmder Richd A Jones, of the U S Navy, died at Balt in the latter part of last week.

Died: on Apr 17, at the residence of her dght, Mrs Mary L Eliason, Mrs Mary B Carter, relict of the late Landon Carter, of **Sabine Hall**, in her 67th year.

Died: on Apr 20, after a short illness, Jos Smoot, in his 49th year. His funeral is this day, at 2 p m. from his late residence on K st, in Wash City.

The following annunciation is repeated [from our paper of Apr 16, in consequence of an error in the name of the dec'd. Died: on Apr 1, in the vicinity of Greensboro, Ala, Jesse How Croom, sr, in his 56th year. The dec'd was a native of N C, & emigrated to Alabama in 1818, having, before his removal, at the age of 24, represented Lenoir Co in the Senate of N C, with credit to himself & the approbation of his constitutents.

WED APR 22, 1846

Lawrence J Brengle has been chosen Treasurer of the Chesapeake & Ohio Canal Co, in place of Philemon Chew, resigned.

Foreign newspaper: the celebrated navigator Otto de Kotzebue, s/o the dramatic writer, died at Revel, on Mar 15, aged 58. He had been 3 times round the world, making several important discoveries; but in 1839 retired from service, & lived in his family circle in Kan, in Esthonia.

Naval: Crew on board the ship **Columbus** were perfect health. The ship had lost one ofcr, Lt Todd, & 1 seaman. The ship **Vincennes** had lost 6 men by dysentery since leaving Batavia.

The dwlg of Capt Laughton, & the Observatory, on Fortress Calhoun, were destroyed on Sat by fire. He was unable to save any portion of his furniture. His loss, we feat, has been a severe one. –Norfolk Beacon

Capt Gustavus S Drane, late of the U S Army, was a gallant ofcr: he was at the storming of *Fort George* & at the battles of Wmsburg & Lundy's Lane: he served throught the Florida war, & signalized himself at the Withlacoochie. His exposure in this service contributed mainly to the prostration of his health & final dissolution. He was emphatically a duty soldier, ever ready for the most arduous service. He was a man of gentle disposition & humane heart, & was highly esteemed by all who knew him. –Phil Enquirer

Geo Tompkins, late one of the Judges of the Supreme Court of Missouri, died on Apr 5, from an attack of apoplexy, at his residence near Jefferson City.

Sixty shares of stock of the Farmers & Mechanics Bank of Fred'k Co, were sold on Tue last, by Geo Koontz, auctioneer, for $21.12½ a share, being an advance of $6.12½ on $15 paid in. -Fred'k Herald

Polly Bodine has at last been acquitted, by a jury, of the charge of having murdered Mrs Houseman, her sister-in-law, some 2 or 3 years ago. The last trial of this case took place at Newburg, Orange Co, it being found impossible to get a jury in N Y C.

The elegant mansion recently occupied by Madame Amory, in Franklin Place, Boston, was on Fri, sold at public auction for $30,000. –Atlas

The Charlestown [Va] Free Press: the fine farm of Mr Jos Shewalter, on the line of the Winchester railroad, has been purchased by Mr John R Flagg, at $50 per acre. The tract contains 354 acres, amounting to $17,700. The improvements are good, & the location a handsome one. This is a substantial evidence of the value of land in old Jefferson Co.

Rev Jos Badger, a venerable & widely known clergyman, died at Perrysburgh, N Y, on Apr 5, aged 87 years. He was a soldier of the Revolution, & was Chaplain under Gen Harrison at *Fort Meigs*.

Senate: 1-Ptn from Saml Hatwell, for a pension. 2-Ptn from the atty of the estate of Jacob Houseman, asking remuneration for advances on account of military services. 3-Ptn from Mrs Susan McCulloh, for a pension. 4-Ptn from Thos Blanchard, for the renewal of a patent. 4-Additional testimony in the case of J B Blake. 5-Ptn from Maria Maxwell, asking to be allowed commutation pay. 6-Ptn from the heirs of Col Wm Grayson, asking for commutation pay. 7-Cmte on the Library: bill for the relief of Eliz Hamilton, wid/o Alex'r Hamilton. 8-Cmte on Private Land Claims to inquire into the propriety of authorizing the legal reps of John Rice Jones, dec'd, to locate certain lands confirmed to him by the Govn'r of the Northwestern & Indiana Territories. 9-Bills referred: relief of Jas Hillman; relief of Saml Jordan; relief of the heirs of Wm Evans; relief of Chas McKenzie; making compensation to John R Williams. 10-Ptn from Saml W Ball, asking compensation for his services in negotiating a treaty with the Seminole Indians. 11-Ptn from Isaac Davenport, rep of Jos Davenport, asking a pension. 12-Cmte on the Judiciary: without amendment, & recommending its passage: bill for the relief of Abraham B Fanning. 13-Cmte of Claims: bill for the relief of Edw Bolen. 14-Bill introduced to confirm to the heirs & legal reps of Pierre Dufresne a certain tract of land: referred to the Cmte on Private Land Claims. 15-Sec of War to transmit to the Senate the proceedings of the Court of Inquiry of which Brig Gen Wool was president, lately held at Springfield, Mass, to inquire into certain charges against Maj J W Ripley, Superintendent of the Armory at that place, together with the testimony & proof taken by said court.

House of Reps: 1-Memorial of John R St John, proposing to relinquish for public use, for a consideration to be paid by the U S Gov't, his alleged invention of the means of discovering at all time & places the declination or variations of the magnetic needle. 2-Ptn of Jas Crutchett, praying Congress to employ him to furnish gas lights to the public bldgs & grounds in Wash City.

Heirs Found. It will be recollected that heirs of Miles Standish, the pilgrim of old Plymouth, were not long since advertised for, as a very large estate in England had recently been ascertained to belong to them. A Sandwich, [Mass,] paper says that at least of couple of claimants have been found. A lady in Connecticut has set up her claim to the whole inheritance; but a Massachusetts man, Mr Ethan Standish, who drives a stage from Sandwich, is believed to be entitled to at least a share of the estate, if not to the whole of it. He has, at any rate, been offered $1,000 for his chance, & has refused the offer; & he was wise enough in doing so, as the annual income of the estate is said to be $40,000 per annum.

Mrs R J Waugh, I st, opposite the north side of the West Market, has some spacious & airy rooms for rent.

Lyford's Commercial Journal: a hogshead of Md ground leaf tobacco sold at $40.25 per 100 lbs, in Balt last week. This is the highest price, says the Journal, in this or any market of the U S. It was grown on the plantation of Mr Jas Kent, in Anne Arundel Co, & sold for him by Messrs Pike & Penn, on Light st wharf.

Mrd: on Apr 14, at Fred'k, Md, by Rev J Peterkin, Jas M Ramsey, of Gtwn, D C, to Mary Eleanor Addison, eldest d/o Dr Wm Tyler.

Mrd: on Apr 19, by Rev Mr Van Horseigh, Mr F L Fortune, of Liberty, Missouri, to Miss Mary A Bruce, of Wash City.

Died: yesterday, Wm Francis, s/o Ignatius & Sarah J Mudd, aged 4 years & 6 months. His funeral is this afternoon, at 4 o'clock.

Private sale of a splendid horse, buggy, & harness, the owner having no further use for them. For particulars inquire of E H Fuller, at Fuller's Hotel.

The undersigned respectfully but most earnestly requests all persons indebted to him prior to 1846 to call at his store & settle the same on or before May 1. –Wm Fischer

New arrival: French Fancy Goods: gloves, combs, perfumery, fans, purses, & beautiful parasolets. - J H Gibbs, opposite Centre Market

All persons indebted to the subscriber are notified that their accounts must be settled on or before May 1, either by cash or short notes. –C H James, Pa ave, between 12th & 13th sts.

Orphans Court of Wash Co, D C. Saml G Davidson, trustee for the sale of the unimproved & unproductive real estate of Lewis G Davidson, dec'd, reported a further sale of said estate, made on Apr 20th, the following lots were sold: to Jos G Totten, lot 19 in square 165, for $221.42. To Jos Fraser, lot 6 in square 127, for $288.91. To Lemuel Williams, lt 7 in square 127, for $286.23. Ordered by the Court that the sales be ratified & confirmed. –Nath Pope Causin
-Ed N Roach, Reg/o wills

Orphans Court of Wash Co, D C. Letters of administration on the personal estate of Geo Semmes, late of said county, dec'd. –Wm W Hoxton, adm, Alexandria, D C

Orphans Court of Wash Co, D C. Letters of administration on the personal estate of Julia Pic, late of said county, dec'd. –John F Pic, adm

THU APR 23, 1846
Tavern establishment for sale: having determined to change my business, on May 1, I will sell at public auction my house & lot, furniture, bar fixtures, & stock & liquors. –Jas English -Geo White, auct

The extensive foundry of Mr Miles Greenwood, at Cincinnati, was almost entirely consumed by fire on Thu last. Loss is estimated at $85,000, insured for $25,000.

In the matter of Paul Rogers, dec'd. Notice is given, that if Paul Webster Rogers & Edmund Rogers, [the sons of Paul Rogers, late of Croydon, in the county of Surrey, in England, gentleman, who died on Feb 10, 1845,] or either of them, were living on that day, information of the fact is required to be given Jacob Read Rogers, of Lewisham, Kent, in England, auctioneer, & Jacob Read Rogers, the younger, of Pomeroy st, Old Kent Road, London, gentleman, the trustees of the will of the said Paul Rogers; or to Messrs Wilde, Rees, Humphrey & Wilde, of College Hill, London, their solicitors, on or before Feb 10, 1847; otherwise they will be excluded of all benefit to which they would be entitled under the will of the said Paul Rogers.

A widow lady named Good, from Pa, with 7 children, who was a deck passenger on the steamer **Sea-Bird**, on her way to Illinois, was accidentally killed on Apr 15, by a boy falling on her out of his berth while asleep. The children were taken care of by some of her relatives.

Senate: 1-Cmte of Claims: bill for the relief of Ray Tompkins & others, the children & heirs at law of Danl D Tompkins. 2-Cmte on Pensions: adverse report on the ptn of Chas Larrabee: to be printed. 3-Cmte on Commerce: bill for the relief of Chas Bingley, of Charleston, S C, with a report, which was read, setting forth a full view of the case: ordered to be engrossed for a 3rd reading.

The <u>Presbyterian Church</u> at Charleston, Va, was entirely destroyed by fire last week.

Mrd: on Apr 21, in Wash City, by Rev Mr Slicer, Mr Wm T Flick, of Phil, to Miss Mary Jane Thompson, of Wash.

Mrd: on Apr 21, at Alexandria, by Rev Mr Blake, Mr John W Lugenbeel, of Wash, to Miss Mary Frances Simpson, of the former place.

Died: on Apr 22, after a short but painful illness, Emma O'Bryon, the y/d/o Jas & Adaline O'Bryon, aged 14 months & 2 days.

Valuable land & lots of land in Wash Co & City at auction: on May 1: about 62 acres bordering on the new county road leading to Bladensburg, & adjoining the Brentwood tract & the lands of Messrs Gales, Derringer, & Burr. Also, at the same time, lots in squares 544, 501, 414, 593, 594, 653, 555, & 616, in Wash City, mostly situated near the river. The title is indisputable, & derived immediately from one of the original proprietors of the city. –A Green, auctioneer

For rent, that spacious & handsome dwlg on Pres' square, at present in the occupancy of Mrs Latimer. Possession given on Jul 10 next.

Furniture at auction: a variety of second-hand furniture: on Apr 24, at the house lately occupied by Dr Wadsworth, one door east of the Union Hotel.
–E S Wright, auctioneer

300 reams printing paper for sale. Cash paid for rags in lots of 100 lbs & over, at 3 cents per lb, delivered at my store, in Gtwn. –O M Linthicum

Orphans Court of Wash Co, D C. Letters of testamentary on the personal estate of Cmdor Wm M Crane, late of Wash Co, dec'd. –L Warrington, exc

FRI APR 24, 1846
Wash Corp: 1-Ptn from Jas McClery & others, & from J H Eberbach & others: referred to the Cmte on Improvements. 2-Cmte of Claims: asked to be discharged from the further consideration of the ptn of Robt Beale: agreed to. 3-Ptn of Chas Dyson: referred to the Cmte of Claims. 4-Ptn of Caleb Dulany, praying for the remission of a fine: referred to the Cmte of Claims. 5-Ptn of Jos Straub, praying for the remission of a fine: referred to the Cmte of Claims. 6-Communication received from Wm P Elliott, City Surveyor, in relation to a report recently made to the Board concerning the graduation of 11th st west: laid on the table. 7-Cmte of Claims: ptn of John Lee, asked to be discharged from its further consideration: agreed to. 8-Cmte on Improvements: examine the accounts of F C Crowley for grading & gravelling 11th st west, & that they report by bill for any balance due. 9-Bill for the relief of Jos C Harris: passed. 10-Cmte of Claims: made on Nov 3 last, asking to be discharged from the further consideration of the ptn of Wm J Bronough: taken up & concurred in. 11-Bill authorizing Patsy R Walker to erect a wharf: motion was negatived.

House of Reps: 1-Ptn of Ruth Pope, for a pension. 2-Remonstrance of P D Wright & 81 other citizens of Monroe Co, N Y, against renewing or in any way extending to Benj H Wood, or any other person, the patent-right heretofore granted to Jethro Wood in relation to case iron ploughs.

Army Genr'l Order: #7, War Dept, Adj Gen Ofc, Wash, Apr 9, 1846. The Court of Inquiry, whereof Brig Gen John E Wool is Pres, instituted by Gen Orders #3, of Feb 4, 1846, by direction of the Pres, to examine into certain transactions, accusations, & cmplnts made against Maj Jas W Ripley, of the Ord Dept, by Jos Lombard, Calvin Shattuck, & other citizens of Springfield, Mass, have submitted a full report of the facts & their opinions on the case. Concluded: Maj Jas W Ripley, Superintendent of this Armory, is acquitted fully & honorably of all the charges exhibited against him. [I have examined the proceedings of the Court of Inquiry in the case of Maj Jas W Ripley, & approve the findings & opinion of the Court. –Jas K Polk]

Mrs Col Cook, of Rockville, has several rooms vacant, & will be pleased to receive ladies & their families as boarders during the summer. She will also take boys & girls for the academies.

Col C S Todd, late U S Minister to Russia, returned to the U S in the last European steamer.

Appointments by the Pres, by & with the advice & consent of the Senate.
Geo Welles, Chief of the Bureau of Provisions & Clothing.
Robt Coltman, of Wash, D C, to be Warden of the D C Penitentiary, vice John H Dade, resigned.
Land Ofcrs:
Archer G Herndon, to be Receiver of Public Moneys for the district of lands subject to sale at Springfield, Illinois, from & after May 14, 1846, when his present commission will expire.
Andrew J Isaacks, to be Receiver of Public Moneys for the district of lands subject to sale at Natchitoches, Louisiana, in place of John Tucker, resigned.
Consuls:
Jas H Tate, of Mississippi, Consul at Cueno Ayres.
Gorham Parks, of Maine, Consul for the port of Rio de Janeiro, vice Geo W Gordon, recalled.
Geo H Goundie, of Pa, Consul for the City of Basle, in Switzerland, vice Seth T Otis, recalled.
Thos W Gilpin, of Pa, Consul for the port of Belfast, Ireland, vice Jas Shaw, recalled.
Thos B Abrams, of Pa, Consul for the port of Mayaguez, in the island of Puerto Rico, vice Gordon Bradley, recalled.
Chas Ward, of Maine, Consul for the island of Zanzibar, in the dominions of the Sultan of Muscat, vice Richd P Waters, recalled.
Stewart Steel, of Pa, Consul for the port of Dundee, in Scotland, vice Edw Baxter, recalled.
Robt L Longhead, of Pa, Consul for the port of Londonderry, in Ireland, vice Jas McDowell, declined, who was appointed during the last recess of the Senate, vice Jas McHenry, dec'd.
Saml D Heap, of Pa, Consul for the port of Picton, in Nova Scotia, vice John J Peavy, dec'd.
Custom-house Ofcrs:
Jas Taylor, to be Collector for the district & inspector, for the port of Wiscasset, Maine, vice Moses Shaw, removed.
Silas Weaver, to be Surveyor, for the port of East Greenwich, R I, vice Jos I Tillinghast, removed.
Edwin Wilber, to be Collector for the district of Newport, R I, vice Wm Ennis, removed.
Murray Whallow, to be Collector for the district & port of Presque Isle, Pa, vice Chas W Kelso, whose commission expired.
John B Guthrie, to be Surveyor, for the port of Pittsburg, Pa, vice Wm B Murray, removed.
Jas Fisher, to be Surveyor, for the port of Pawtuxet, R I, vice Peleg Aborn, whose commission expired.
Postmasters:
Wm N Friend, at Petersburg, Va, vice John Minge, removed.
Timothy P Spencer, at Cleveland, Ohio, vice B Andrews, removed.
Jas K Gibson, at Abbington, Va.

Promotions in the Army:
Capt John B Clark, 3rd Regt of Infty, to be Maj, Nov 26, 1845, vice Dearborn, promoted.
3rd Regt of Infty:
1st Lt Philip N Barbour, to be Capt, Nov 26, 1845, vice Clark, promoted.
2nd Lt Wm B Johns, to be 1st Lt, Nov 26, 1845, vice Barbour, promoted.
Brevet 2nd Lt Wm K Van Bokkelin, of 7th Regt of Infty, to be 2nd Lt, Nov 26, 1845, vice Johns, promoted.
Promotion in the Navy:
Albert G Clary, to be a Lt in the Navy, from Apr 11, 1845, at which time he was promoted to fill a vacancy, occasioned by the death of Lt Jas H Lockert.

A handsome service of plate has been presented to Mr J Hoffman Collamore, of Boston, by his creditors. He failed last year, & was released by the Master in Chancery on the payment of 30% on his obligations. Having since received a large legacy, he summed his creditors & paid the balance, amounting to $29,000, for which honorable conduct his creditors have paid him the above compliment.

Mr Beauvallan was tried at Paris on Mar 27 & 28 for the murder, 12 months since, of Mr Dujanier, the manager of the Presse newspaper. He was acquitted of the capital charge, & was sentenced to pay 20,000 francs [nearly $5,000,] damages to the mother & nephew of the dec'd.

Balt Co Court: on Wed, the jury in the case of Thos D Cockey vs Chas E Goodwin, to recover damages for an assault with a pistol in Sep last, when the plntf was much injured about the head from the effects of the shot, rendered a verdict awarding the plntf the full amount of damages claimed, being $10,000, with costs.

Mrd: on Apr 22, by Rev Mr Stringfellow, Jos W Arnold, of Norwich, Conn, to Eliza W, only d/o the late Jos S Berret, of Md.

Died: on Apr 12, at Balt, aged 23 years, Eliz H, the beloved wife of Jas M Sewell, & d/o the late Jos Janney, of the same place, for many years a resident of Alexandria.

Died: on Apr 22, Laura Virginia, only d/o Jas & Jane Lynch, aged 2 years & 2 months. Her funeral is this evening, at 4 o'clock, from East Capitol st.

A man by the name of Waite is about to be tried in Mississippi for the murder of Thos Shannon, who was invited to Waite's house, where he went, unarmed; the door was closed upon him, & he was assailed by 3 men with bowie knives, & finally fell, when each plunged his knife in him & fled. Their object was plunder, & the wife & dght of Waite, one of the murderers, were present. A shocking detail. –Mobile Herald

The subscriber has this day received from Boston a supply of <u>Shower Baths</u>: 7 feet high & only 2 feet square upon the floor. It is designed for chamber use, & makes a very pretty piece of furniture. It may be placed near the bed, so a person can bathe in the morning before dressing-a great desideratum, as many people neglect bathing because it requires too much time to shift their clothing. –Chas W Boteler, jr: Union & Col Fountain

For rent: large 3 story brick house, corner of 10th st & Pa ave: well calculated for a tavern or boarding-house: contains 12 rooms. For terms apply to Mich Sardo, 10th & H sts.

Orphans Court of Wash Co, D C. Letters testamentary on the personal estate of Geo O'Driscoll, late of the State of Pennsylvania, dec'd. –Walter Gwynn, exc [Persons having business with me, connected with the above estate, are to address Clement Cox, Atty at Law, Gtwn, D C. –Walter Gwynn, exc]

Notice: by virtue of 2 writs of fieri facias, against the goods & chattels of John E Dement, I have taken under said writs: 1 coach-carriage, subject to bill for repairs in favor of Thos Young, I will expose said carriage at public sale, for cash, on Apr 30, on Pa ave, opposite Gadsby's Hotel, except payment is made before that time, to satisfy judgments in favor of Richd H Harrington, use of Jas Riordan & M C Byrne, use of Caleb Buckingham. –Thos Plumsill, Bailiff

Senate: 1-Ptn from the heirs of Wm Grayson, dec'd, asking to be allowed commutation pay. 2-Cmte of Claims: bill for the relief of Jos Watson, with a report: ordered to be printed. 3-Bill for the relief of John P Skinner & the legal reps of Isaac Green were taken up: passed over for the present. 4-Bill for the relief of Chas W Bingley, of Charleston, S C, was passed.

SAT APR 25, 1846
The large hall in King's Gallery, 12th st, will be let for exhibitions or other public purposes. Also, a suite of furnished rooms for ofcs, in the basement. Inquire of E Kingman & Co, at their ofc, King's Gallery.

For rent: three 2 story brick dwlg houses on 14th st, near Capt Howell's. Two of the houses are just completed. Apply to Christopher Cammack, F st, near 15th st.

Orphans Court of Wash Co, D C. Ordered, that letters of administration be granted to Susan Eaton on the personal estate of Wm H Wynn, late of the U S Navy, dec'd, unless cause to the contrary be shown on or before May 15 next.
–Ed N Roach, Reg/o wills

Orphans Court of Wash Co, D C. Letters of administration on the personal estate of Milly Jackson, late of said county, dec'd. –Jos H Hickman, adm

Household furniture at auction on Apr 28, by order of Orphans Court of Wash Co, D C, at the residence of Mr John Tolson, at the Navy Yard, 11th & K sts, being part of the personal estate of the late Geo Semmes. -R W Dyer, auct [Jan 22nd, 1847 newspaper: Com'rs' sale of the portion of Geo Semmes' real estate remaining unsold will be offered: **Head of Frazier**, containing 5 acs. -Zach Walker, David Barry, Jas C Barry, Benj T Smith, & Thos Jenkins, Com'rs]

Trustee's sale of a lot: on May 12 next, by virtue of a deed of trust from Jos Marteni to the subscriber, dated Feb 19, 1846, & for certain purposes therein expressed: sale of lot 12 in square 813, fronting 51 feet on 5th st east, between A & B sts south. –Nicholas Callan, trustee -R W Dyer, auct

Died: yesterday, Mrs Anne Herben Jesup, d/o the late Maj Wm Crogham, of Ky, & wife of Gen Thos S Jesup, of the U S Army. She leaves an affectionate husband & a group of almost idolizing children. Mrs Jesup was born in 1798, married May 17, 1823, died Apr 24, 1846. The friends of the dec'd are invited to attend the funeral from the house of Gen Jesup, this afternoon, at 5 o'clock.

MON APR 27, 1846
Circuit Court of Wash Co, D C: jury empanelled to try the Alexandria Will case: Smoot et al vs White & Jewell. The cause originates on an issue from the Orphan's Court, & the suit is brought by the heir at law, to set aside a paper purporting to be the last will & testament of Mrs Catharine *Calder, dec'd, of Gtwn, on the ground of the incapacity of the testatrix. The will manumits a number of slaves who had been raised by the old lady, which is the principal property involved. Counsel for the plntf: Messrs J H Bradley, John Marbury, & Wm Redin. Counsel for the defence: Messrs Clement Cox & John E Addison. [May 1st newspaper: Case terminated yesterday. Verdict of the jury: "That the paper purporting to have been drawn on the 18th Jan, 1841, was the last will & testament of Catharine *Colder, dec'd." This verdict establishes the right of 12 colored person to manumission.] *Two spellings.

House of Reps: 1-Ptn of Eve Boggs for a pension. 2-Ptn of the heirs of Saml Jackson, dec'd, praying Congress to grant them the arrearges of pension due their said father at the time of his death. 3-Ptn of Jas M Lewis, praying for a pension for wounds received while in the service of the U S, during the late war with Great Britain. 4-Ptn of Jas Kegg, the principal chief, & divers other Catawba Indians, who represent that they have recently removed from S C to N C, Haywood Co; that they now own no land; that the remnant of the once powerful Catawba tribe is now reduced to about 82 souls. They humbly ask Congress to make arrangements, & adequate appropriations to remove them to the west of Arkansas, & give them a home in the woods.

All persons indebted to the late firm of Forrest & Scott are to call & pay their accounts, on or before Jun 1st next. –B Forrest

New bldgs in various parts of this metropolis. 1-Lofty edifice on 7th st, called the Odd Fellows Hall. 2- Jackson Hall, a splendid edifice on Pa ave, now on the eve of completion-the iron balustrade work in front of the bldg just completed. 3-At 1st st & Pa ave, a neat 3 story brick bldg just erected & occupied as a store & dwlg by Mr John T Killmon. This bldg was erected by Mr Stephen Coster, bricklayer, & Messrs Thos Milburn & M M White, carpenters. 4-On north side of C st, between 3rd & 4½ sts, two 4 story brick dwlg houses are now being erected for Thos Blagden & Edw Simms. 5-Mr A Baldwin, a skillful architect, residing on Louisiana ave, commenced digging the foundation of 2 brick dwlgs, which he intends to erect on the south side of D st, [Pollard's Row,] between 2nd & 3rd sts. 6-A handsome 3 story brick dwlg is now bldg on 8th st for Mr Thos Berry. 7-On H st a large brick dwlg, 2 stories high, is now erecting for Mr Sweeny. 8-On 11th st a handsome 3 story brick bldg is now being erected by Mr A Baldwin for Mr Boyd, upholsterer. 9-On 13th st 4 handsome 4 story dwlg-houses are being erected for Geo R Gaither, of Balt. 10-Mr Jos Frazer is now raising two 3 story brick houses, with back bldgs, in the 1st Ward of Wash City.

Refrigerators & Water Coolers: Jos H Nevitt, opposite Fuller's Hotel, Pa ave. The undersigned have the refrigerators, with cooler for water attached:

Mrs Thos H Benton	Wm Gadsby	Alex McIntire
Mrs Dr Laurie	Dr J M Thomas	McClintock Young
Mrs Wm Cox	Dr Thos Miller	
Mrs Kreiber	Thos Munroe	

Sale of desirable property: by deed of trust from Thornton A Doniphan, dated May 27, 1842, & recorded among the land records of Wash Co, I will offer for sale, on May 25, on the premises: lots 6, 7, & 8 in square 436, with a very good 2 story frame house, with brick basement: on F st south, near the corner of 7th st & the steamboat landing. –Richd Wallach, trustee -C W Boteler, jr, auctioneer

Wanted to hire by the year, a colored man or stout lad, who has some knowledge of working the ground, & can attend a horse. A slave who has been brought up in the country, would be preferred. –I Vivans, between 20th & 21st sts, & east of Kalorama.

Notice: the subscriber, having withdrawn for the present from the house-furnishing business, is desirous that the old business should be speedily settled up. Those persons indebted to the subscriber, or to the late firm of Boteler & Donn, will make payment to Thos C Donn, Justice of the Peace, La ave, near 7th st, where the books & accounts are left for settlement. –John M Donn

Mrd: on Apr 23, by Rev John P Donelan, Mrs Jas Daly to Miss Mary Ann Clements, all of Wash City.

Mrd: on Thu, by Rev Horace Stringfellow, Mr Smith Thompson, of PG Co, Md, to Miss Mary Ann, eldest d/o D Clagett, of Wash City.

Mrd: on Apr 23, by Rev J T Johnston, John Brookes, of Mount Calvert, PG Co, Md, to Esther J, eldest d/o Wm Fowle, of Alexandria.

Died: on Apr 22, at the residence of his mother, in Wash City, Mr Wm McLaughlin, aged about 24 years.

Died: on Mar 26, in Kirkland, Oneida Co, N Y, Deborah Raymond, aged 102 years & 5 months.

House of Reps: 1-Bill for the relief of Wm Saunders & Wm R Porter, sureties of Wm Estes, a paymaster of Virginia militia in the war of 1812 with England, was first in order: bill was rejected. 2-Bill to enable the Sec of the Navy to purchase of Mrs Mix the right of using the patent manger stopper, invented by her late husband, Capt Mervin P Mix, U S Navy, now dec'd: Cmte of the Whole struck out $5,000, the sum proposed to be paid Mrs Mix, & substituted $3,000: confirmed by the House. 3-Cmte of the Whole: bill for the relief of the sureties of Elijah J Weed, late captain & quartermaster of the marine corps; bill for the relief of Asa Armington; bill to direct the payment of 7 years' half pay due on account of the death of Lt Jonathan Dye, an ofcr of the Revolutionary army, to his widow & childrenor their reps; which bills were rejected by the House.

Very valuable property at auction: on May 27, on the premises, belonging to the estate of the late Dr Marens C Buck: part of lot 1 in square 354, with an excellent 2 story brick bldg, with basement & garret: fronts the Mall, between 10th & 11th sts, & adjoins the residence of Nicholas Tastet. Also, lots 20 & 21 in square 534, fronting on south B st, between 3rd & 4½ sts: lots belong to the same estate. -R W Dyer, auct

TUE APR 28, 1846
Senate: 1-Ptn from W A Howard, of the Revenue service, asking to be allowed the pay of navy ofcrs of his rank during the time he was engaged in co-operating with the navy & army in Florida. 2-Ptn from Alexis Argot, asking to be allowed a pension in consequence of injuries sustained while in the exploring expedition of Capt Fremont. 3-Ptn from Mary G Clitz, wid/o a dec'd ofcr, for a pension. 4-Ptn from John J Sanchez, asking compensation for property destroyed by the U S troops in Florida. 5-Documents in favor of the claim of Louis Chapperton. 6-Ptn from Saml Knapp, a Revolutionary soldier, asking arrears of pension. 7-Ptn from Mgt Heyland, asking a pension. 7-Cmte on Public Lands: without amendment, the House bill for the relief of Chas M McKenzie. 8-Cmte on the Library: joint resolution authorizing the employment of Hiram Powers to execute certain statues for the U S: ordered to be printed. 9-Cmte on Pensions: bill for the relief of Asenath Canney; bill for the relief of the heirs of Crocker Sampson: both ordered to be printed. 10-Cmte on Revolutionary Claims: ptn of Saml Beach; ptn of heirs of Christopher Delazerne; ptn of the heirs of Benj Durkee; ptn of the reps of Benj Valkenburg: concurred in. 11-Cmte on Pensions: adverse report on the ptn of Chas Larabee: also concurred in.

Important sale of real estate in Smith Co, Tenn: by virtue of a decree of the Circuit Court of Smith Co: sale of about 7,500 acres of land in quantities to suit purchasers; land belong to the estate of the late Judge Gaston, of N C, about 50 miles from Nashville, on the Cumberland river. –Will Hart, clerk

Among the strangers at present visiting our city is the Hon R M Johnson, Ex-Vice Pres of the U S, who, we are glad to learn from the "Union," is in excellent health. –Washington

Died: on Apr 27, Edw Maynard, eldest s/o Dr Edw Maynard, aged 6 years & 5 months. His funeral is this day at 4 o'clock, at his father's residence, corner of 14th & H sts.

Died: on Apr 16, at his residence near Leetown, Jefferson Co, Va, Chas Lowndes, at an advanced age. He was formerly of Gtwn, D C, but had been for many years a resident of Virginia.

WED APR 29, 1846
Senate: 1-Ptn from Jos de la Francia, asking the liquidation of a certain judgment against the agent of the Convention of West Florida, for a supply of arms for the use of that Territory. 2-Ptn from Philip Slaughter, for arrears of pension. 3-Additional documents in the case of Thos E Wilson. 4-Ptn from Creed Taylor, asking to be released as the security of H L Edington. 5-Bill for the relief of Nathl Goddard & others was taken up for its 3rd reading. 6-Cmte on Commerce be instructed to inquire into remitting to J H McLellan, owner of the American ship **Byron**, the additional tonnage duty charged on said ship on her arrival from Odessa, in consequence of having a crew of foreign seamen. 7-Cmte on the Judiciary: asking to be discharged from the further consideration of the ptn of Maria J Nourse. 8-Cmte on the Public Lands: bill for the relief of Henry H Marsh.

House of Reps: 1-Ptn of Sarah Waddle, wid/o Robt Waddle, dec'd, praying compensation for services rendered by said dec'd upon the western frontier during the difficulties with the Indians after the Revolutionary war. 2-Ptn of Messrs Chas D Abell, Joshua Allen, & 1,150 others, citizens of Hamden Co, Mass, praying that the law of Congress, passed in Aug, 1842, placing the nat'l armories under military gov't, may be repealed, & the same placed under civil gov't as heretofore.

Wash Corp: 1-Ptn from Owne Magee: referred to the Cmte of Claims. 2-Ptn of Anne R Dermott, in relation to the condition of the open space opposite the Centre Market: referred to the Cmte on Police. 3-Letter from Mr C F Lowrey, Pres of the Columbia Typographical Society, tendering a fine portrait of Franklin, to be placed in the Chamber of this Board during the time the Society may be permitted to meet therein. 4-Bill for the relief of Jos C Harris: referred to the Cmte of Claims.

Valuable town property at auction, in Alexandria: on May 5, one lot, or quarter square of ground, containing over 21,000 feet, with improvements, on north side of Duke, & west side of Henry st; subject to a rent charge of $20 per annum. Also, one lot, containing 21,000 feet, with improvements, on south side of Prince st & east of Fayette st; subject to a rent charge of $20 per annum. The above property was once called the *Garden of Eden*, & the improvements consist of a frame house & well on each lot. Also, a Tenement & Lot of Ground beginning on the east side of a 20-feet alley, running from Queen to Princess sts, between Union & Water sts, at the line or Richd Conway & Robt Adams' heirs. Also, one Tenement & Lot of Ground on the east side of Wash st. The title to the above property is indisputable. –W S & T

A little girl, aged 2 or 3 years, d/o Mr Saml Newcom, residing in the upper part of Queen Anne's Co, Md, was burnt to death a few days ago by her clothes taking fire. There was no one near when her clothes took fire, & when the father returned he found his child, an only companion, a lifeless corpse.

Rev J B McFerren will preach in the McKendree Chapel, Northern Liberties, this evening, at 8:15 p m.

Journey Barber wanted: First rate Journeyman Barber & Hair-dresser will meet with steady employment & fair wages-apply to M Dubant, Pa ave, between 12th & 13th.

The Cape of Good Hope Gazette of Jan 9th gives the details of the shipwreck of the barque **Francis Spaight**, of Liverpool, in Table Bay, with the loss of her commander, Capt Patterson, & most of her crew.

Mr Clark Mills, a native of S C, has presented to the Council of Charleston a handsome & correct bust of John C Calhoun, made out of pure white stone, found near Columbia. This first essay of Mr Mills is said to be highly successful.

Died: on Apr 28, in Gtwn, Jas Thomas, for many years a bookseller in that place. His funeral is this afternoon, at 4 o'clock, from his late residence, on West st.

Died: on Apr 14, at her residence, near Warrenton, Fauquier Co, Va, after a protracted illness, Mrs Eliz Stewart, in her 69th year. She was an indulgent parent, a kind mistress, & beloved by all who knew her.

The copartnership between the subscribers is this day dissolved by mutual consent. Business will hereafter be conducted by the senior partner, who is alone authorized to settle the business of the late firm. -Wm Noyes, sr; W Noyes, jr; & Albert Noyes

Lost, a gold & black enameled Breastpin, containing dark brown hair, & of an oblong shape; also, a bunch of keys. The finder will be rewarded.
–W Thompson, #4 Louisiana ave

For rent: a commodious 3 story brick house, on Pa ave, next to the corner of 3rd st. Inquire of Jas Owner, sr, Va ave, near the Navy Yard.

$300 reward for the apprehension & delivery to me, or to my reps, at Wash, of my servants Wm Grimshaw, called Billy, about 45 years old, a house carpenter, & of his dght, Eliz G, about 25 year old, with her infant son, 2 years old: mulattoes.
–Wm K Taylor, of Warsaw, Va

Orphans Court of Wash Co, D C. Letters of administration on the personal estate of Henry Culver, late of PG Co, Md, dec'd. –C C Hyatt, adm

THU APR 30, 1846
Senate: 1-Ptn from John Develin, asking compensation for services rendered in the ofc of the 5th Auditor. 2-Cmte on Finance: adverse report on the ptn of Jacob Clarke. 3-Cmte on Pensions: bill granting a pension to John Clarke. Also, adverse reports on the ptn of the widow of John Little & Ruth Fry. Same cmte: adverse reports on the ptns of Zebulon Mead & Eliz Myers.

Mr Jas H Piper has been appointed Chief Clerk in the ofc of Com'r of the Genr'l Land Ofc, in place of Mr John M Moore, who had for many years discharged the duties of that trust with very general respect.

Gen Wm Monroe, U S Receiver for the Clinton Land District, in Missouri, died a few days since. He had filled many important official stations in that State.

The Nashville Orthopolitan says that E Z C Judson, who lately killed Robt Porterfield, in a personal affray, had been discharged from prison, & immediately left the city for Pittsburg. Porterfield's friends made no attempt to have him arrested.

No less than 5 barns belonging to John Gibson, of Francestown, N H, all standing near each other, were struck by lightning on Sat of the week before last, & entirely consumed, together with hay & hogs.

Died: in Woodfield Co, Ky, at the residence of her sister, Mrs M W Railey, Miss Paulina Pleasants, in her 74th year. She was the eldest surviving sister of the late Gov Jas Pleasants of Va. [No date-recent notice]

Died: on Apr 24, in Ritchie Co, Va, in her 23rd year, Laura Virginia, youngest sister of R H Williamson, of Wash City. In the death of this beloved girl, many hearts will grieve & be sorrowful.

New Line to Norfolk, Portsmouth & Gosport, Old Point Comfort: whole fare from Wash to Norfolk, $5.50. For ticket or information, apply to Capt J Rogers, on board the Potomac steamboat **Powhatan** or to Geo Mattingly, agent at Wash.

Lands in Hardy Co, Va, for sale at public auction: by deed of trust, executed on Jan 22, 1839, by Chas J Nourse & Rebecca M Nourse his wife, & Geo Templeman & Mary Templeman his wife, duly recorded in book 15, page 136, in the Clerk's Ofc of said county: sale at the Exchange, in Balt, on May 16, the following lands in Hardy Co: All those tracts or parcels of land lying in said county, containing 9,365¼ acres, more or less, know & described as follows, viz: all that land, containing 4,480 acres in said county, between the North Branch of Potomac river & Stony river, being a part of Francis & Wm Deakins' tract of 25,500 acres, being the same land which was conveyed to Walter Smith, in trust, by John Templeman & wife, by deed dated Mar 31, 1809, recorded in book 6, page 396, in said county. Also, the lands in said county executed in like manner by said Templeman & wife to said Walter Smith, in trust, & dated Mar 31, 1809, & recorded in said county, in book 6, page 403, containing 5,609 acres; which said 2 tracts, containing together 10,089 acres, 345 acres sold to John Irons, Jan 29, 1846; 110¾ acres sold to M Hainline, Oct 8, 1830; 150 acres sold to R Davis, Dec 28, 1836; 118 acres sold to Elisha Hays, Aug 21, 1837; leaving 9,365¼ acres, now hereby conveyed as above mentioned.
–Rd Smith, trustee -Hoffman & Co, auctioneers

Chancery sale: by virtue of a decree of the Hon Chancellor of Md, in his Court of Chancery, made in the cause of Dundas et al, vs McCulloh et al, depending in said Court, I shall offer at auction, on May 16 next, at the Exchange, in Balt, the following real estate, in Alleghany Co, Md, & said to be advantageously located within the coal basin of that county, to wit: all that tract called *Bank Property*, being a resurvey of a part of *Western Connexion*, containing 1,622½ acres of land, according to the certificate of resurvey dated Oct, 1836, returned into the land ofc of the Western Shore of Md, & there remaining. Also, tract called *Bank Territory*, being a resurvey of another part of *Western Connexion*, containing 6,322 3/8 acres of land, according to the certificate dated Sep 27, 1836, in same land ofc. Also, *Bank Lot*, being a resurvey of another part of *Western Connexion*, containing 1,036½ acres, according to the certificate dated Sep 22, 1836, in same land ofc. All the said lands being the same which were conveyed to the Pres, Dirs, & Company of the Bank of the U S, by 3 deed from Jas M Mason, dated May 19, 1830, recorded in the land records of Alleghany Co, & also by 3 patents from the State of Md, dated May 29, 1837. Also, all that Revolutionary soldier's lot, being #2487, containing 50 acs. Also, an undivided moiety of *Mount Pisgah*, said to contain for said moiety 235 acres of land. Also, a tract called *Pleasant Ridge*, said to containg 281½ acres of land. -Rd Smith, trustee -Hoffman & Co, auctioneers

Lawrenceville Classical & Commercial High School, between Princeton & Trenton, N J: institution is long known to the public: term-$200 per annum.
-H & S M Hamill, Principal

Appointments by the Pres, by & with the advice & consent of the Senate.
Thos Hartley Crawford, of D C, to be Judge of the Criminal Court for D C, vice Jas Dunlop, resigned.
Wm Adams, to be Receiver of Public Moneys, at Johnson Court-house, Arkansas, vice Aldred Henderson, removed.
Benj Patterson, to be U S Marshal for the northen district of Alabama from & after May 8, 1846, when his present commission expires.
Wilson, Knott, to be Postmaster at Newark, N J, vice John J Plume, removed.
John T Mason, jr, to be a Purser in the Navy, vice Purser Robt J Moore, dec'd.
John F Steele, to be a Purser in the Navy, vice Purser Thos E Norris, resigned.
Edw C Doran, to be a Purser in the Navy, vice Purser Philo White, resigned.
Wm B Hartwell, to be a Purser in the Navy, vice Purser John N Todd, dismissed.
Quintin Bushee, of N C, to be a Purser in the Navy, vice C C Rice, dec'd.

Important to Brickmakers. The subscriber has just obtained letters patent for a maching for making brick of <u>dry clay</u>, which he now offers for sale. Mr Z C Robbins, Patent Agent in Wash, will assist as his agent, for Md, Dela, Pa, R I, & N Y. For other States address John Simpson, Decatur, DeKalb Co, Georgia.

New mowed grass at auction: on May 2, by request of Mr Maher, the public gardener, in the Capitol yard, 5 lots of new mowed Hay or Grass, to be positively removed by 4 o'clock same day. -R W Dyer, auct

FRI MAY 1, 1846
<u>List of letters remaining in the Post Ofc, Wash, May 1, 1846.</u>

Anderson, Miss L	Brown, J F	Burgess, Henson
Adams, Miss E	Brick, Theo	Brady, Miss S
Allen, Miss I	Burch, Jos A	Brady, Miss A
Adams, T W	Brooks, Miss Betsy	Bartin, Miss C
Andrews, J D	Butt, Richd	Barbour, John N
Anderson, J A	Brown, Jas	Brewer, Jas W
Anderson, Wm	Brown, Wm D	Baldwin, Wm
Adams, Mrs E	Bean, Miss Sarah	Burgess, Chas H
Adams, Richd	Blunt, Thos M	Besancon, Gen
Adams, Saml	Beck, Miss E S	Burroughs, Wm
Adrean, Geo W	Brown, Mrs M	Bosser, Thos
Alexander, Mrs C F	Brisco, Henry	Bradbury, Theo M
Aitkin, Wm	Burman, Miss M E	Branagan, John
Adams, John G	Bailey, Mrs	Butler, Mrs Henry
Andrews, Dr	Berry, C C	Butler, Pierce
Burke, Jas M-2	Bennett, Jas H	Bartley, Thos W
Brown, Wm, Tenn	Bowen, Chas W	Barclay, Dr Jas T
Brown, M C-2	Broadrup, Geo	Buel, Jas T
Brown, Wm G	Boswell, Mrs B	Browning, Fra S
Bridge, E T	Baltimore, Mrs A	Barrit, Thos

Barnum, Noble S
Blanchard, L
Burritt, Saml L-4
Cross, John
Camp, F M-4
Case, Thos
Choate, Mrs A
Crump, Lewis
Cook, Mrs M E
Case, A, Dep G Sire
Case, P
Chew, Jas
Crown, J Edgar
Cooke, Miss H
Cocke, Capt H H
Clarke, Alex
Clark, Aaron
Chase, Chas
Cox, Dr Saml S
Cabell, E C-2
Chapman, Mrs J S
Collins, P McD
Clinton, Miss V-2
Cady, N W
Columbus, Jerome
Carter, Danl F-4
Cornish, Rev J
Carroll, Rev Dr D L
Corser, Sol T
Crosby, Roberjot
Clinton, Geo
Crosby, Henry R
Conly, Miss Cath
Chandler, Lt
Cayhow, Miss M B
Calaghan, Chas-2
Couman, Eliz
Calahir, Jas
Carroll, J [colored]
Chandler, A G
Cramphin, Mrs C-2
Claxton, R W
Cassidy, Jas
Coffin, Isaac N
Coffin, Jas B

Campbell, Mrs E
Canedo, Juan de Dios
Degges, Geo A
Duff, John
Dant, Thos
Dove, Wm
Dorr, John W
Doyle, Lt Jas A
Dix, Maj R S-8
Drummond, Mrs C S
Dutton, Mrs A E
Dunlop, J D, of Pa
Delanu, Miss B J
Durell, Miss Ann
Daragh, Robt
Dement, John E
Donovon, Dr Jas
Duval, P S
DeKrafft, F W
Dickinson, Horace
Dorsey, Felix
Donoho, Jas
Dewey, Rev L D
Davenport, D-2
Drury, John H
Davidson, Wm S-4
Davis, Mrs H-3
Evans, Miss Fanny
Edwards, Gov J C
Edmonds, Mrs M B-2
Ely, Miss Mary D
Fry Miss Eliza
Ford, Mrs Ann
Fay, Jerub A
Foote, Henry S
Fenner, Dr E D
Feller, Thos
Foster, jr, W B-2
Ferguson, John W
Farrow, Miss M
Frazier, Robt H
Favor, Wm
Furtney, Geo H
Forncy, Col J W-3
Gist, Robt C

Grooms, Miss V
Gould, David H
Goothe, Cath
Glenn, Jos B
Graham, Col Jas
Gowdy, Geo W
Goddard, Henry
Goodman, Chas S
Gibson, John S
Graham, F
Gibson, Miss M A
Hill, John H
Hogg, Moses
Hill, Frances-2
Hord, Robt
Hull, D C
Hall, Henry
Hills, Wm
Hall, Wm S
Hurt, John
Harrises, the Miss
Hamill, Saml M
Hening, Jas
Herbert, Leonard F
Hamersley, Miss M E
Hussy, Jos G
Hussell, John
Haskins, John
Hinlin, Wm D
Hackelton, J H
Howard, Jas
Hooper, Chas
Hawkins, John D
Hayden, Dr C
Herrick, Joshua
Hofman, S-3
Herbert, Geo
Jack, Mrs Mary
Jones, John
Jones, Jas D
Jones, Thos R
James, Miss Jos
Jones, Miss A
Jenkins, Thos
Jackson, Alex

Jackson, W W	Murray, J M-2	Powell, Wm
Johnson, Miss R	Marshall, John F	Peyton, Jos H
Jenkins, John	McLean, Geo W	Pendergrast, Com G J
Keek, Mrs Jane	McKay, Mrs E A	Queen, Miss Charlotte
Key, J M	McKay, Wm	Queen, Miss Mary
King, Mrs	McJilton, Cath	Reeves, J C o/Upgate
King, Elisha	McKeever, Capt J	Rhodes, Miss E
Kortztes, Mr	Niles, Dr Stephen	Reed, Jas
Karston, Miss Jane	Neville, John S	Rhett, J B
Lawrason, Dr S C, U S N	Newton, Miss Ann	Reid, David
	Nouman, Dr A M	Rall, Mr
Loveless, Jas A	Nailor, Col W	Roche, R J
Laberdi, Francis	Nevet, Luciana-2	Russell, F
Lucas, Miss Maria	Oames, Mrs Eliza	Reed & Cheshire- Misses
Lockery, Hugh-2	Oliver, Francis E	
Lawson, Jane	O'Neale, Jas	Rice, R D-2
Lohead, Ann	O'Bryan, John	Rush, Miss Cath
Lacey, Wm	O'Neale, Geo P-2	Rose, Sam;
Linkenwater, Thos	Pharm, W	Reed, John Z-4
Marks, Mr	Peugh, Wm	Rodburn, Eph B
Mans, Isaac R	Price, Salby	Reynolds, N L
Mills, Chas H	Page, Mrs Susan	Roberts, R B
Moore, Saml S	Page, Dr Fred B	Robison, Hiram H
Mills, Lewis	Price, John W	Rogers, Aug F
May, John J	Price, Col M A	Ronkendorf, Lt
Morse, Mrs E K	Paine, Henry M	Roberts, Edm
Mann, Col H D-4	Poole, Mrs M M	Robinson, W
Marlett, Wm J	Prather, Alfred	Readils, Saml
Mackur, Mr	Parker, Chas C	Rawlins, Isaac B
Magruder, Kitty	Parker, Ely	Rogers, John A-2
Martin, John P	Parmlee, Aaron S	Smith, Mrs Fanny
Middleton, Theo	Perry, J Z	Smith, Jas F
Marcy, Laban-2	Penny, Jas-2	Shawk, Abel-3
Morris, Eliza A	Palmer, Lt Wm R	Smoot, Capt, U S N
Mather, W W	Porter, Wm	St John, John R
Morgan, Rud S	Preston, Thos L	Smith, A Austin
Milburn, Zenas	Preston, John	Simms, Jos
Moran, Jas D	Parker, Dr J W	Sage, Danl
Murray, Chas	Polly, Jas H	Steele, Jas
Marshall, David E	Ploughman, Wm	Smith, Wm
Martin, John	Pinney, Rev J B	Smith, John
Martin, H C	Pickett, Thos B	Simmes, Miss F
Murdock, Mrs	Pinkney, Lt Henry	Sprague, Dr L M
Mattingly, Jos	Pilling, Jos	Smith, Sarah H
Martin, Henry C	Peckham, Dr W H	Sweet, Isaac

Shead, Olive	Townley, J D	Walcott, Wm D-2
Shaw, Sergt John	Taylor, R	Watson, Edw A
Semmes, D R	Taylor, Jas B	Williams, Mrs F A-2
Simms, Miss M J	Teakle, Lit Dennis	Woodward, Mrs
Scott, Robt T	Talmadge, D	Watson, Miss M
Shanks, M-2	Tolson, Mrs E B	Williams, Mrs S B
Scribner, Jas	Thomas, Jas C	Waters, Rev Edw
Sinclair, John	Turner, M A	Wilson, Dr Jas
Sackett, Chas R	Tilson, Jona	Wanser, Lewis
Sedden, Alex	Towers, Jas M	Willard, Saml A
Stewart, Chas	Thomas, David	Wilson, John J
Silver, Dr Silas B	Tonge, Easton	Washington, M A
Summers, Mrs M E	Vishner, Miss C	Walker, Wm J
Smithcomb, Andw	Varlin, Miss Mary	Washington, Miss B
Stephens, Walter	Van Schoonhorn, J	Washington, C
Stephens, Jas	West, Lt Ed L	Whistler, jr, G W
Simpson, Wm L	Ward, T W	Watkins, Miss M A
Scrivener, Mr	Ware, Betsy-2	Wallace, Geo
Schermerhorn, Rev J F	West, Master B	Wallace, Geo W-2
	Wade, Jas T	Walker, Miss Bella
Smallwood, T	Work, Jos-2	Wheatley, Geo
Sheldon, Alex-2	White, Miss M C	Woodyer, Rev C
Shephard, Miss M A	White, Purser G H	Warren, Henry
Spediss, Chas	Waugh, Jacob H	Wherry, Jos
Sangston, Capt T-2	West, B R	Watson, Miss M R
Spycer, Robt	Wood, Miss Sarah	Washburn, Alex C
Tate, Wm	White, Mrs M	Weller, John
Tod, David	Wayne, Mrs	Young, Jas C
Thompson, Miss C Ann	Wayne, Jas M	Yates, Giles F
	White, Dr E C	Zachman, Christian
Tasker, Thos	Williams, Mrs J A	
Thompson, E H	Willan, Jos	

The inland postage on all letters intended to go by ship must be paid, otherwise they remain in this ofc. -C K Gardner, P M

Anacostia Fire Co: Annual May Ball on May 5. Managers:

John F Tucker, Pres	Jos McCuen	Wm Sanderson
Jonas B Ellis	Thos Kelly, V P	Jas H Meade
Thos Thornley	Thos Goss	Thos H Murphy
Thos N Adams	Danl Quigley	
Thos Tench	John Hutchison	

Tickets $1, admitting a gentleman & 2 ladies, to be obtained of the Managers, or at the door on the evening of the Ball.

The Empress of Russia is to present his dght [the Princess Olga,] on her wedding day with a diadem of precious stones, valued at 18,000,000 francs, about L750,000 sterling. The central diamond is valued at 1,000,000 francs. –English paper

Geo Hatton was, on Tue last, sentenced by Judge Scott, in the Superior Court of Loudoun Co, Va, to 3 years' imprisonment in the State Penitentiary, for shooting at & wounding Mr Jas Smith, in Feb last.

Fine beef yesterday in the stall of Mr John Walker, in our Centre Market. This beef was raised by Mr David Parsons, an emiment grazier on the South Branch.

New & Cheap Spring & Summer goods: Geo F Allen, Pa ave, between 11th & 12th sts.

The site of the late Howard Athenaeum, in Boston, has been sold to Mr Edw A Raymond for a little less than $40,000, or $4 per foot for the land. Arrangements have been made to erect an Opera House & Music Saloon. A plan has been drawn by Mr Rogers, the architect.

Luther Britton has recently been tried in Geauga Co, Ohio, for killing a man who was ordered to arrest him at a militia muster, & sentenced to the penitentiary for life.

Public Baths on C, between 4½ & 6th sts: summer season will commence May 1 & end Sep 30th. Each subscriber to pay $10, & be entitled to one bath per day for himself, or the lady of the house, or son, or dght. The house will be open from 5 a m until 10 p m. Single bath: 25 cents. –P Aiken

House of Reps: 1-Ptn of Saml Lewis, praying indemnity for losses sustained by reason of a delay occasioned by Gov't ofcrs in the execution of a contract. 2-Memorial & evidence of John P Gamble, praying compensation for the hire of mules employed in the service of the U S.

The subscriber informs the public that he has associated with him in business his brother-in-law, Mr Wm Ebert, late of Fred'k City, Md, & for the future the business will be under the firm of Ramsburg & Ebert, at the old stand, on High st, between 1st & 2nd sts, Gtwn, D C. –Jacob Ramsburg, Gtwn

For rent: the house & grounds on the corner of 14th & F sts, owned & lately occupied by Col J Kearney. Inquire of J B H Smith, at his ofc, on F st.

The party of blind children embraced in the recent exhibition of the Blind at the Capitol & Carusi's, numbered 19, 6 of whom are from Boston, [among whom is the celebrated Laura Bridgman, who from her birth has been deaf, dumb, & blind,] 7 from N Y, & 6 from Pa. Their educational exercises are nearly all of a mental character.

C Eckloff & Sons, Merchant Tailors: south side of Pa ave, between 12th & 13th sts.

Notice: Letters testamentary to the estate of Gen Danl Parker, late of Wash City, dec'd, having been granted to the subscribers, & all persons indebted to said estate are requested to make payment, & those having claims to present them to W J Duane, B W Richards, C C Parker, excs: Phil, Apr 28, 1846.

$500 Reward. Whereas one ___ Reed, s/o John Reed, of Wendron, in the county of Cornwall, England, & for many years resident in the U S, departed this life on or about 1840, & his family in Cornwall are informed that he has bequeathed to them, or some of them, property to a large amount: this is to certify that any one giving information concerning the same so that the said family may be enabled to recover their just due, shall receive the above reward, besides all reasonable expense for his trouble. All letters & communications for the family to be left at the British Consulate, Phil. –Jos Reed, Nicholas Reed, of the county of Cornwall, England.

Household & kitchen furniture at auction: by deed of trust from Wm Clare to the subscriber, dated Jan 1, 1846, recorded among the land records of Wash Co, D C: at the residence of said Wm Clare, on East Capitol st, near the east Capitol gate, Capitol Hill. –W Lenox, trustee -A Green, auctioneer

SAT MAY 2, 1846
The Retreat. P A Desaules will open this morning, on 7th st, this establishment, where his old customers & the public generally will find the choicest Liquors & all the various delicacies of the season.

Geo Earle, Merchant Tailor, #175 Chestnut st, Phil, Pa: opposite the State-house.

Trustee's sale: by virtue of a deed of trust executed for certain purposes therein expressed, the subscriber, as Trustee, will sell at public auction: on May 4, the east half of lot 2 in square 455, on F st, with a 2 story frame house, with a back bldg, when rents readily for $150 per annum. This property is adjoined on the east by Mr Lyons' row of brick houses, & on the west by a new brick house of Mrs Ann Benning. Title indisputable. –Michl Larner, trustee -R W Dyer, auct

Eutaw House, corner of Eutaw & Balt sts, Balt. H F Jackson [late of the Astor House, N Y,] & H Cranston [of the Pavilion at Rockaway, L I,] proprietors. They have leased the above Hotel which during the last 2 months has undergone a thorough renovation & refurnishing. N B-Coaches will be in readiness at the depots & landings to convey passengers & baggage free of charge to the House.

Patent Agency at Wash: Zenas C Robbins, Mechanical Engineer & Agent for Procuring patents: ofc on F st, opposite the Patent Ofc.

Notice: was committed to the jail of PG Co, Md, as a runaway, on Apr 29, 1846, a negro man, who calls himself Chas Nichols. He was a hand on board the schnr **Mary Virginia**, of Balt, Levin Wheatly, master. He is about 46 years old; says he is free, & was born near Cambridge, Dorchester Co, Md, & once belonged to Chas Goldsborough, of that county, & was purchased from Mr Goldsborough's estate by Dr Edw White, of Cambridge, by whom he was set free. Owner, if any, is to come forward, prove property, pay charges, & take him away; otherwise he will be discharged according to law. –John R Baden, Sheriff

Notice: was committed to the jail of PG Co, Md, as a runaway, on Aug 12, 1845, a negro man, who calls himself Wm Spencer, about 24 years old. He says he is free, & is from Phil, & last sailed with Capt Hand, in the packet **Argo**, from that place to Alexandria; says he can be identified by Mr Dagerty, [or Dugherty,] merchant, of Camberton & 8th sts, Phil. Owner, if any, is to come forward, prove property, pay charges, & take him away; otherwise he will be discharged according to law. –John R Baden, Sheriff

Notice: was committed to the jail of PG Co, Md, as a runaway, on Apr 29, 1846, a negro man, who calls himself Wm Hiram Boggs. He was a hand on board the schnr **Mary Virginia**, of Balt, Levin Wheatly, master. He is about 21 years old; says he was born free in Princess Anne, Somerset Co, Md; that he is recorded in the county court of that county, & that his mother lives in Balt. Owner, if any, is to come forward, prove property, pay charges, & take him away; otherwise he will be discharged according to law. –John R Baden, Sheriff

New Orleans, Apr 23. U S District Court: before Judge McCaleb: Rice Garland & Thos Curry vs, the U S. Case decided in favor of the plntfs: they claim about 40,000 acres on Black river, under a grant to Louis Bringier about 1796. A portion of the land having been sold to the U S, it is decided that the plntfs are entitled to scrip for such portion. -Bee

MON MAY 4, 1846
The May Ball at Gtwn will be given at Mr Holtzman's Pompeian Hall, an elegant & well furnished ball room.

To let: that spacious brick house & premises, the residence of the late Robt Sewall, on the highest part of Capitol Hill, within 250 yards of the n e corner of the Capitol gardens. Inquire of S Scott, on the adjoining premises.

The inauguration of Hon Edw Everett, as Pres of Harvard College, took place on Thu last. Govn'r Briggs delivered to Mr Everett the symbolical keys. A company of about 600 sat down to a public dinner. Hon Josiah Quincy, the retiring Pres, Mr Webster, Mr Everett, & Mr Winthrop, took part in the festivities.

John W Watson, a wood-engraver, was arrested in N Y on Fri, charged with forging a check for $80 in the name of Col Totten, U S Engineer. He was committed for trial.

Danl Stillwell, & his grand-dght, Miss Caroline Smith, were drowned on Apr 25 in attempting to ford the Muskingum, at Robinson's ford, 7 miles below Coshocton, Ohio.

Capt Barnum, of the U S Army, commanding the fort at Oswego, by a fall from his horse, sustained a bad fracture of the leg. Though now in tolerable comfortable condition, serious apprehensions of the result are entertained. –Utica Gaz

The first sale of house lots in the new city of Essex, Mass, took place on Tue. The amount of the sums bid for 22 lots on Essex st, [the main street of the projected city,] 41 lots on a parallel st called Common st, & 62 lots at about $3/4^{th}$ of a mile from this site, in a part intended for residence, was about $70,000.

Mrd: on Thu last, by Rev Mr Tarring, Mr Jesse F Mann to Miss Ann Anderson, all of Wash City.

Mrd: on Apr 30, by Rev John P Donelan, Lt Wm Handy, U S R M, to Ann Paine, d/o the late Wm Reddall, of Wash City.

Died: on Apr 28, at his residence, Spring Garden, Chas Co, Md, in his 59th year, Jas Brawner, who had held the commission of Surveyor of lands for the county in which he resided more than 30 years.

Died: on Apr 24, at Detroit, Mich, after a most painful illness of 3 weeks, Czarina Macomb, in her 36th year, d/o the late Gen Alex'r Macomb, & w/o Lt John N Macomb, of the U S Army.

Died: on Arp 26, at Richmond, Va, Mrs Lucy Nelson Call, relict of the late Danl Call, of that city, in her 69th year.

Masonic-ofcrs & members of New Jerusalem Lodge #9 to meet today, at the hall of St John's Lodge #11, 4½ st & Pa ave, at 2 p m, to attend the funeral of our late Brother C F Erb, at 4 o'clock. –O J Preston, sec

Notice: by virtue of a writ of fieri facias, issued by Jos W Beck, a justice of the peace for Wash Co, D C, at the suit of Hall & Brother, against the goods & chattels, lands & tenements of Jas B Phillips, to me directed: I have seized & taken in execution all his rights to one horse, cart, & harness, & same will be offered for sale on May 6, in front of the Centre Market, for cash. –E G Handy, Constable

TUE MAY 5, 1846

May Festival: Miss Mary Fulmer has been for the last year or two engaged in teaching a female school in the eastern part of this city. A few years ago she received the gold medal for excellence of conduct, at the annual exhibition of the pupils belonging to the Seminary of the Ladies of the Visitation, at the Monastery in Gtwn, an institution which is of the highest rank. The May Queen was Miss Mgt R Speisser, who also performed in musice, as did Miss Eliz S Fulmer, & Miss Georgiana Thompson. A Silver medal premium was awarded to Miss Virginia A Cutt, for proficiency in French. Other premiums were awarded to Misses

M R Speisser	E S Fulmer	E M Clark	J Herold
M C Herold	F Vanhorn	M A Herold	
J V Padgett	J A Gaddis	M A Howe	
M Cresselle	L M Speisseer	A Cull	

Senate: 1-Ptn from Isaac Foy, late a postmaster, asking reimbursement of a certain sum of money. 2-Ptn from John J Adams, of Camden, N J, asking an extension of a patent right. 3-Ptn in relation to the claims of Nat Stafford, for arrears of pension. 4-Ptn from John Ross & others, reps of the Cherokee nation of Indians, on the subject of the existing difficulties in that nation & their relations with the U S. 5-Cmte on Private Lands Claims: bill confirming the claim of the heirs & legal reps of Pierre Dufresnet to a tract of land: without amendment. Same cmte: bill for the relief of Geo Mayfield: without amendment. Same cmte: bill for the relief of Jaques Moulon. Same cmte: asking to be discharged from the futher consideration of the ptn of Wm Le Blanc. 6-Cmte on Patents: bill for the relief of the heirs of the late Uri Emmons, with a report: ordered to be printed. 7-Bill for the relief of John P Skinner & the legal reps of Isaac Green & others, was considered in the Cmte of the Whole: to be engrossed. 8-Cmte on Pensions: to inquire into the allowance of arrearages of pension to Nathl Stafford, of Vt, from the time of his disability up to Mar 30, 1846, when his name was entered upon the pension roll as a pensioner.

House of Reps: 1-Cmte of Claims: bills for the relief of Archibald Bull & Lemuel S Finch, of N Y, of Martin Thomas, & of Jacob Gideon: committed. Same cmte: adverse reports on the cases of S C Ford, of John N Ford, & John Scrivner, of Thos C Miller, of Edw Morris, of John Mason, of Edw Fitzgerald, of Marshal A Matthias, & of Jos Davis: laid on the table. Same cmte: reported bills for the relief of Michl Nourse, for the relief of David Thomas, of Phil, & for the relief of Elisha F Richards: committed. Same cmte: adverse reports on the cases of A A Crowley, of John S Tyson, adm of Jonathan W Sherburne, of the heirs of Bernard Todd, & of A C Crandell: laid on the table. Same cmte: adverse reports on the ptns of O S Rees & Jacob Stonifert: laid on the table. 2-Cmte on Commerce: bill for the relief of John Chaseaud, Consul of the U S to Syria & Palestine, reported the bill back to the House with sundry amendments. 3-Cmte on the Public Lands: bill authorizing the issuing of patents to Geo Ramey & Thos F January, for certain lands entered in the county of St Louis, Missouri: committed. Same cmte: bill for the relief of Julius Eldred & Sons: committed. Same cmte: adverse report on the ptn of Gustave de Neven: laid on the table. Same cmte: bill for the relief of Thos Scott: committed. 4-Cmte on Revolutionary Claims: bill for the relief of Eliz Converse: committed. Unfavorable reports on the cases of Nathan Beard & Lewis Whiting: laid on the table. 5-Cmte on Private Land Claims: bill for the relief of Chas Cappell. Same cmte: bill for the relief of the heirs & legal reps of Wm Dixon, dec'd. 6-Cmte on Private Land Claims: asked to be discharged from the case of Wm Moore, of Ill: laid on the table. 7-Cmte on Indian Affairs: bill for the relief of the late Jos E Primeaux & Thos J Chapman: committed. Same cmte: bill for the relief of Geo P Russell & others: committed. Same cmte: adverse report on the case of Geo M Lavender, dec'd: laid on the table. 8-Cmte on Naval Affairs: bill for the relief of the legal reps of Jas H Clarke. Same cmte: bill for the relief of the widow & heirs of Capt Silas Duncan, dec'd. Same cmte: bill for the relief of Susan Brum: committed. 9-Cmte on Revolutionary Pensions: reported a resolution to discharge the Cmte of the Whole from the bill for the relief of Geo Wentling. Bill remains on the Speaker's table. 10-Cmte on Revolutionary Pensions: bill for the relief of Anna Griffin: committed.

Mrd: on May 4, by Rev C R Hendrickson, Absalom A Anderson, of Phil, to Miss Harriet Goodall, of Wash City.

Died: on May 2, in Wash City, after a short but painful illness, Helen Choate, aged 16 years, second d/o Anthony Holmead, of Wash City, & grand-dght of the late John O Webster, of Kennebec, Maine.

Died: on May 4, Catharine Lee Clumpitt, w/o Wm H Clumpitt, in her 29th year. Her funeral is from her late residence on Mass ave, near 12th st, this day, at 4 o'clock.

1,030 acres of land at Public Auction: in Fairfax Co, Va, before the door of Newton's Hotel, Alexandria, D C, on May 25, 1846, *Woodlawn*. This tract, once a part of the **Mount Vernon** estate, contains upwards of 2,000 acres of land: a large brick barn, farm house, corn-houses, & sheds. Also, a large stone mill upon the creek, with one pair of wheat burrs, & one pair of country runners. The dwlg-house is not surpassed by any in Va in construction, style of finish, & situation, being on a high hill, in a grove of fine oaks, commanding a beautiful view of the river in front. House is built of brick, with freestone sills & lintels to windows & doors, coping of the basement also of stone, slate roof, 2 stories high, 4 rooms on a floor, spacious cellars under the house, portico in front, paved with marble, & confined by freestone; all out-houses of brick, connected with the main bldg by spacious corridors, namely, kitchen, wash-house, library, & servants' hall, which, again, by a brick wall, connect with the dairy & meat-house-well built of the best materials. *Woodlawn* is 16 miles from Wash, 9 miles from Alexandria, & 2 from *Mount Vernon*. Close to the dwlg-house is a never failing well of the purest water. –L Lewis N B-any person wishing to view the place will be shown it by John A Washington, of *Mount Vernon*, & any information given by Henry Daingerfield, of Alexandria.

For rent: small convenient 3 story brick dwlg-house on I st, between 20th & 21st st, very convenient to the West Market. Key is next door, at Wright's barber shop. For particulars inquire of Maj Geo Bender, a few doors east of the bldg.

Jos K Boyd, Upholsterer: Pa ave, between 10th & 11th sts, north side. [Ad]

Orphans Court of Wash Co, D C. Letters testamentary on the personal estate of Thos Boothe, late of said county, dec'd. –Ann Boothe, excx

Circuit Court of Wash Co, D C-in Chancery. Mrs Eliz Holtzman, Eliza Ann Holtzman, Geo H Holtzman, Wm G W White, Jas L White, vs Wm Hayman, Mary Hayman, et al, heirs of Wm Hayman, dec'd. Cmplnts' bill charges that on Dec 20, 1834, Geo Holtzman, of Wash Co, D C, was possessed of certain real & personal property within the limits of Wash Co; that the said Geo Holtzman, on the day aforesaid, devised to Wm Hayman & John Holtzman & the survivor of them, in fee & in trust, the aforesaid property; that the said property was to be held in trust by the said trustees & the survivor of them, for the benefit of the wife & children of the said Geo Holtzman, since dec'd; that the said Wm Hayman & John Holtzman have both departed this life, the said Wm Hayman surviving the said John Holtzman; that the legal title had descended to the heirs at law of the said Wm Hayman, to wit: Wm Hayman, Mary Hayman, Anne Hayman, Adelaide Hayman, Julia Hayman, Saml Hayman, & Catherine Hayman. The objects of the bill are, to obtain the substitution & appointment of a trustee for the property mentioned in the last will of said Geo Holtzman, & to vest the same in such trustee in fee upon the like trusts as are specified in said last will, & for general relief. And, forasmuch as it is averred & appears that the said Wm Hayman, Mary Hayman, Julia Hayman, Saml Hayman, & Catherine Hayman are, with the exception of the said Wm Hayman, infants, & reside & are out of D C, it is order that on or before the 3rd Mon in Oct next, they appear in Court & show cause why the cmplnts should not have relief as prayed.
–W Brent, clerk

WED MAY 6, 1846
Wash Corp: 1-Ptn of Andrew Stepper: referred to the Cmte of Claims. 2-Cmte of Claims: asked to be discharged from the further consideration of the ptn of Jas Casparis: agreed to. Same cmte: act for the relief of Jos C Harris: relief of Jacob Wechter: bills were rejected. 3-Cmte of Claims: asking to be discharged from the futher consideration of the ptn of Wm Feeney: agreed to. 4-Ptn of J S Fowler, praying remission of a fine, was taken up. 5-Ptn of Jos Frazer & others, for a paved footway; ptn of Geo M Davis & others, for curbstone: both referred to the Cmte on Improvements.

Eben H Clark, the postmaster at Cherry Hill, Wayne Co, Pa, has lately been arrested & fully committed for robbing the packages of letters which passed through his ofc.

The Nat'l Blues, under the command of Capt Tucker, had a handsome parade & target firing last Mon. They marched to the grove near Eckington, where they practised for some time by firing at a mark. The target was about 2 feet in diameter; placed at the distance of 60 years; best shot was that of Private Wm Tucker; the 2nd best was that of Private Geo Emmerich.

Mr John Paddon, professor of music, died on Mon at his residence in Cambridge, Mass, of apoplexy. He sat down to take his breakfast, leaned his head back upon his chair, & died without a struggle. He was 70 years of age.

Ky papers notice an event which occurred in Granger Co, on Clinch river, on Apr 9. An old gentleman, Albertus Arwine, a peaceable inoffensive man, suspecting some outrage was planned upon his person, loaded a musket with slugs: hearing the dogs barking he went outside; his call to the person advancing towards him were not answered; he felt a bullet pass close to his head & fired back. He struck & killed the man, who had disguised himself as a negro. The body proved to be that of his nephew, Wm Bowers, who had forged a will, & was doubtless intending to take the place of the will Mr Arwine had written: had the scheme which was laid for his murder been successfully accomplished.

Senate: 1-Memorial from John G Smith, a soldier in the late war, asking for a pension. 2-Cmte on Finance: asking to be discharged from the futher consideration of the ptns of Wm B Bend. 3-Cmte of the Whole: adverse reports on the following: ptn of Sarah Little; ptn of Ruth Frye; ptn of John G Clark. 4-Bill for the relief of John P Skinner & the legal reps of Isaac P Green: passed.

House of Reps: 1-Affidavits of O Lee & C Robinson in support of O Lee's claim: presented. 2-Ptn of Alex'r Coleman, praying to be allowed to locate a land claim heretofore confirmed & surveyed in the Old Mine concession on other public lands. 3-Ptn of Henry D Spears, of Missouri, praying compensation for a horse lost during the last war with Great Britain while in the service of the U S as a mounted ranger. 4-Ptn of John H Monroe, of Missouri, praying to be placed on the invalid pension list. 5-Memorial of Walter Sessions, praying the U S to aid him in enforcing his claim against the Provincial Gov't of Canada. 6-Ptn of Geo R Smith, of Missouri, praying compensation for additional services rendered as mail contractor. 7-Ptn & other papers of Martha Grey, of Clark Co, Ky, praying compensation for services in the last war.

Trustee's sale: by virtue of an act of Congress passed Jul 20, 1840, & of the decree of the Circuit Court of Wash Co, D C, made in the cause of Lewis G Davidson's heirs, I shall auction on May 27, the following lots, in Wash City: lots 15 & 16 in square 168; lot 1 in square 169; lots 13 thru 16 in square 126. Title indisputable. –Saml G Davidson, trustee -B Homans, auctioneer

Mrd: on Tue, by Rev John C Smith, Saml Duvall to Miss Christina, d/o Patrick Crowley, all of Wash City.

Died: on May 5, Mrs Catherine Knott, consort of Mr Geo Knott, after a brief & suffering illness, aged 24 years. Her funeral is on Wed, at 4 o'clock, from her late residence on Pa ave, between 4½ & 6th sts.

Died: on Fri, at Balt, aged 39 years, Lt Lewis G Keith, of the U S Navy.

As a party of young ladies were walking to view the Falls, near Watertown, N Y, one of their number, Frances Reed, an adopted d/o Mr Peter Howk, of that town, ventured to near th edge, became dizzy, & fell over the steep embankment, & was instantly hurried away by the current & drowned.

House of Reps: 1-Cmte on Revolutionary Pensions: adverse reports on the sundry cases, viz:

Susan Howard
Saml Fulton
John Chaney
Mary, wid/o Abel Blakeney
Ruth, wid/o Saml Pope
John W Ward
heirs of Ann Blackwell
heirs of David Avery
Wm Stubblefield
Asbel Moore
Nathl Lyford
Jos Green
Benj Guthrie
Mary B, wid/o Peter Francisco

heirs of Joshua Jones
John Hudson
Benj Johnson
John C Vansice
Abigail, wid/o Seth Watkins
Eunice, wid/o Wm Starr
Eliz, wid/o John Myers
Sarah Triplett
Sally, wid/o Benj Beekes
heirs of Jos Davenport
Ann O Wright
Eliza Briscoe
Wm Pratt

2-Cmte on Revolutionary Pensions: discharged from the consideration of the ptn of Jerusha Smith: laid on the table. Same cmte: adverse report on the case of Peter Ambler: laid on the table. 3-Cmte on Claims: adverse reports on the cases of Peter Rambo; Elijah Rose, John Rudolph; & that about the fine imposed on Capt Jona Walker, that it may be refunded: laid on the table. 4-Cmte on Military Affairs: adverse report on the case of Capt David S Rogers: laid on the table. 5-Cmte on Invalid Pensions: asked to be discharged from the ptns of Sherman Pierce, Josephine Nourse, Frances, wi/do Capt Gardiner, & Fanny, wid/o Abraham Fowler: laid on the table. 6-Cmte on Revolutionary Claims: adverse report on the ptn of the heirs of Moses Cook: laid on the table. 7-Cmte of Claims: bill for the relief of Thos Crown: committed. Same cmte: bill for the relief of the heirs of Gassaway Watkins: committed. Same cmte: adverse reports on the cases of Chas G Layton & Gideon Walker: laid on the table.

THU MAY 7, 1846
Senate: 1-Ptn from Chas M Gibson, asking remuneration for a wagon & team captured by the Seminole Indians in Florida. 2-Ptn from the heirs of Saml V Keene, for commutation with interest. 3-Supplemental memorial of the heirs & legal reps of Capt Benj Harrison, for commutation pay & bounty land. 4-Cmte on Pensions: adverse reports on the ptns of Hezekiah Wingate, Thos Hall, & Jas Updike: to be printed. Same cmte: asked to be discharged from the further consideration of the ptn of Michl Hanson, & that it be referred to the Cmte on Naval Affairs.

Early on Tue the large & splendid establishment called the N J Hotel, erected by Wm Gibbons, at Morristown, N J, was wholly consumed, involving a loss of more than $50,000, without insurance. [May 11th newspaper: Mr Baily, a druggist, & boarder in the hotel, perished in the flames. He was a native of and connected in N Y. He was a highly educated gentleman, universally esteemed.]

Line of packets between Phil & Liverpool:
packet **Thomas P Cope**: Capt H F Miercken
packet **Saranak**-new: Capt E Turley
packet **Susquehanna**: Capt A Turley
packet **Wyoming**-new: Capt J W Miercken
Passage to Liverpool, $80; to Phil, L20, without wines. -H & A Cope & Co, Phil
-Brown, Shipley & Co, Liverpool

Danl McCook has been tried at Harrisburg for an attempt to bribe Mr Piollet, a member of the Pa Legislature, was convicted & sentenced to pay a fine of $600 & the costs of prosecution.

Mr McCabe, of Balt, was robbed of $8,221 last week, while on his way to Phil in one of the steamboats. The money was taken from under his pillow, while he was sleep in one of the berths.

Session of the Supreme Court of Mass, begun at Lowell Apr 13: 2 cases of promise of marriage have been tried. 1-Caroline Frost & Wheelock Newton for breach of promise of marriage & seduction, claiming $2,000 damages. Jury gave the plntf a verdict of $2,500-$500 more than she claimed. Both of the parties belonged to West Cambridge, Mass, & are very young, & their connexions highly respectable. 2-In the other case, Lucelia Pearl sued Philander Cheswell for breach of promise of marriage & seduction, & the jury gave a verdict in favor of the plntf for $2,000.

Subscribers will to employ a Young Gentleman to instruct 6 or 8 students in the usual branches of an English Education, & the Latin & Greek Languages. Address the undersigned, to Good Luck post ofc, PG Co, Md. -Robt Bowie, Geo W Duvall

Mrd: on Mon last, at the residence of Geo W Cass, in Muskingum Co, Ohio, by Rev Mr Harrison, John Kinsman, of Kinsman, Trumbull Co, to Mrs Jane W Cass.

Mrd: on Apr 29, by Rev Wm H Pendleton, at Leeds, the residence of J K Marshall, in Fauquier Co, Va, Mr Ezra Abbott, of the same county, to Miss Sarah Hooker, late of N Y C.

FRI MAY 8, 1846
Sealed proposals for wood will be received at the ofc of the Clerk of the House of Reps, until Wed: 200 cords of the best hickory wood. –B B French, Clerk of the House of Reps. P S No coal will be wanted this season.

House of Reps: 1-Ptn of Abigail Bodfish, of Sandwich, Mass, for a pension in consideration of the services of her husband in the Revolutionary army.

Trustee's sale of stoves, grates, tools, shop fixtures, & tinware: on May 13, at the store formerly occupied by J Kell & Brother, Pa ave, near 4½ st. –A Green, auctioneer

Groceries at auction, by order of the Orphans Court of Wash Co, D C: at the warehouse of the late Jos Smoot, dec'd. –Julia A Smoot, Clement Cox, admx -Ed S Wright, auctioneer

Senate: 1-Ptn from Capt B L Lucas, for a pension. 2-Bill granting a pension to Richd Elliot: to be engrossed for a 3rd reading. 3-Cmte of the Whole: joint resolution in favor of David Shaw & Solomon T Corser: ordered to be engrossed for a 3rd reading. 4-Bill for the relief of the legal reps of John J Bulow, jr, dec'd: laid on the table.

Mrd: on May 4, by Rev Mr Eggleston, Wm H Falconer, of Balt, to Miss Mary Eliz, d/o Jos Bryan, of Wash City.

Died: on Wed, at **Haddock's Hills**, the residence of Mrs Edw Dyer, Margaret Ann, w/o H C Spalding, of Wash City, & eldest d/o Cmdor Stephen Cassin, of Gtwn, in her 34th year, leaving a husband, 2 infant children, & a large circle of relatives & friends to mourn their loss. Her funeral will move from the residence of Mrs Dyer, at half past 3 o'clock, this Fri, & proceed to St Patrick's Church, on F st, where the funeral services will be performed.

SAT MAY 9, 1846
Brick house at auction: on May 12, the well-built 2 story brick dwlg-house on D st, between 2nd & 3rd sts, in the row called Pollard's Row, lately occupied by Mr D Ridgely, & now untenanted. –B Homans, auct

Four stray cows: strayed away on May 3. Liberal reward will be paid for their return, or either of them. -Wm T Duvall, 4½ st, Wash.

The Boston Traveller announces the death of John Pickering, who died on Tue at his residence in Boston, after a protracted illness, at the age of 69. He was the s/o the late Timothy Pickering, & was, till a late period of his useful life, a resident of Salem, as Rep of which town he filled some of the highest public stations. He has resided for the last 12 or 15 months in Boston.

The 7 year old s/o Mr Solomon Brown, was killed a few days since. A little companion was whirling round with great rapidity a piece of wood notched like a saw, attached to a string, called a whirligig, when the string broke, & the notched piece struck little Brown on the throat, puncturing the windpipe, making an aperture not larger than the head of a good sized pin. It was thought a slight hurt, but soon the body began to swell, from the diffusion of air under the cellular tissue of the skin. His parents witnessed his death.
-Raleigh Register

Mrd: on May 5, by Rev Mr Donelan, Mr Wm Van Reswick to Miss Ann Olivia Bean, all of Wash City.

Mrd: on Apr 7, at the Chapel of the Prussian Embassy, at Turin, by Rev Mr Bert, Robt Wickliffe, Charge d'Affaires of the U S at Turin, to Miss Josephine Van Houton, of Rotterdam.

Mrd: on May 5, in Wash City, by Rev Smith Pyne, Wm Weir, of Phil, to Phebe Mary, d/o the late Rev Wm Hawley, of Wash City.

Died: on May 7, Mr Walter Clarke, in his 69th year. He was one of the oldest inhabitants of Wash City, having resided here upwards of 46 years. Fortified by all the rites of the Catholic Church, of which he was from childhood a zealous & practical member, he resigned his soul into the hands of his Creator. His funeral will take place this Sat morning at 9½ o'clock, from the residence of his brother, Mr Jos Clarke, on Missouri ave, between 3rd & 4½ sts.

Notice to teachers: the Trustees of the Ridgeway Academy, in Warren Co, N C, desire to employ a competent gentleman to take charge of this institution.
–Thos Carroll, sec pro tem, Ridgeway

Orphans Court of Wash Co, D C. Letters of administration on the personal estate of Ann Sheckels, of said county, dec'd, be granted to Jas Burdine, unless cause to the contrary be shown. –Ed N Roach, Reg/o wills

MON MAY 11, 1846
House of Reps: 1-Ptn of Geo Darracott & others, of Boston & vicinity, in relation to the patent laws of the U S. 2-Ptn of Saml Latimer, setting forth that he has the legal title by prior deeds to a portion of the lands attached to Old Point Comfort, & praying Congress to purchase his claim thereto.

St Louis Republican of the 30th ult: companies & ofcrs of the 6th Regt U S Infty, stationed at Jefferson Barracks, under marching orders for Texas, to leave as soon as possible.

Lt Col Wilson, Commanding	1st Lt G W F Wood
Co K: Bt Maj Abercrombie	2nd Lt S D Carpenter
Co E: Capt A S Miller	Co C: Capt J H Lamotte
2nd Lt Plummer	1st Lt G Barry
Bt 2nd Lt Dilworth	2nd Lt J Terrett
Co G: Capt E Backus	

Subscriber is desirous to sell the house in which he resides, together with the furniture. The house is larger than he requires. –Peter Brady

J & H Douglas, Florists & Seedsmen, opposite the State Dept, have this day entered into partnership.

Luther Pool, aged 22, was accidentally shot in the neck at Walnut Grove, Morris Co, N J, on Apr 25, by one of Cochran's 6-barrel pistols, in the hand of a friend who was adjusting a cap. He lived but 10 minutes.

Painful news from the Rio Grande: news of the deaths of Col Cross & Lt Porter. [Ill-advised & ill-fated movement of Gen Taylor's force from the post it at first occupied to the banks of the Rio Grande?]

TUE MAY 12, 1846
Annual election of the director for the Mineral Bank of Md was made on Mon. Col Chas M Thruston has been elected Pres, to fill the vacancy caused by the resignation of Thos J McKaig. –Cumberland Civilian

The large paper mill of Messrs Howard & Lathrop, at South Hadley Canal, Mass, was destroyed by fire on Wed: fears were entertained for the paper mill of Mr Danl Ames.

WED MAY 13, 1846
Orphans Court of Wash Co, D C. Letters of administration on the personal estate of Roderick Hampton, late of said county, dec'd. –Emily Hampton, admx

Lt Porter, who met his death on the Rio Grande, had been but a short time married. His wife is a d/o Maj Benj Lloyd Beall, formerly of this city, who is now in command of the 2nd Regt of Dragoons in Texas. Mrs Beall & dght are at **Fort Washits**, the late station of Maj Beall, where they had been left by their husbands but a short time ago.

First Ward Hardware & Variety Store: on Pa ave, between 17th & 18th sts. –Jos L Savage & Co

Gen Joel Leftwich, of Bedford: we learn of the death of this venerable soldier of the Revolution, & of the war of 1812: he died in Bedford, the country of his nativity, on Apr 20, after a lingering disease. At the time of his death he was 86 years of age: he first shouldered his musket & joined the northern army in his 16th year: was at the battle of Germantown: was with Gates in the disastrous engagement at Camden; with Greene in the battle of Guilford, in which he was severely wounded. He was at *Fort Meigs*, under Gen Harrison: & after the burning of Wash, by the British forces under Gen Ross, again at the head of a brigade, he rushed to the standard of his country, & served a 2nd tour. Gen Leftwich has represented the people of Bedford in the Legislature, & held the position of justice of the peace in that county. –Rich Whig

A Mormon settlement, under the influence of Sidney Rigdon, has been commenced in the vicinity of Greencastle, Franklin Co, Pa. They have purchased a large tract of land from Mr McLanahan, for $15,000. –Hagerstown News

Harrison Waite, Clerk of the County Court of Berkely, Va, died a few days since, very suddenly, of paralysis. He was well, & ate a hearty supper in the evening, & at midnight was a corpse.

House of Reps: 1-Cmte of Claims: adverse reports in the case of Danl Turnipseed & Jos Kager: laid on the table. 2-Cmte on Public Lands: bill for the relief of the widow & heirs of John B Chandler: committed. 3-Cmte on Private Land Claims: bill for the relief of Anthony Bessey & a bill for the relief of Isaac Guess: committed. Same cmte: adverse report on the case of Saml Reed, of Pike Co, Ohio: laid on the table. Same cmte: favorable report on the claim of Pierre Chouteau, jr, & others, for the confirmation of the "Dubuque claim," in the territory of Iowa: laid on the table. 4-Cmte on Revolutionary Pensions: adverse report on the case of Eliz Taylor, wid/o the late Maj Wm Taylor: laid on the table. 5-Cmte on Invalid Pensions: adverse report on the cases of Jesse Campbell, the wid/o David Lyman, Asa Hall, Obediah Bass, Jacob Shade, Stephen Brian, & Fielding G Brown: laid on the table. Same cmte: bill for the relief of Wm Causey, & a bill for the relief of Wilfred Knott: committed. Same cmte: asked to be discharged from the case of John Eldridge, & that the petitioner have leave to withdraw his papers. 6-Cmte of Claims: adverse report on the case of Wm Shapely: laid on the table.

For sale: on Jun 1, on the premises, the 3 story well-built brick dwlg house & lot on Water st, between Queen & Oronoco sts. Also, the 3 story brick dwlg on Union st, adjoining the steam mill on Conway's wharf. House can be converted into a warehouse if wished. –H V Ladd, or A J Fleming, Alexandria, who will show the property.

Circuit Superior Court of Law & Chancery, held for Halifax Co, Va, on Apr 8, 1846, the Pres & Dirs of the Literary Fund, plntfs, against Stephen Kent, adm of Nicholas Cole, dec'd, dfndnt. In Chancery: plntfs seeking by their suit to recover of the dfndnt & the residuum, after the payment of funeral charges, debts, & just expenses of the estate of said Nicholas Cole, dec'd, who was born in that part of the dominion of Great Britain called Ireland, & who died in the county of Halifax, Va, some time in the year 1833 or 1834 intestate: the Court, on motion of the plntf, by counsel, order & require that every person who claims an interest in the said residuum, as distributes of the said Nicholas Cole, dec'd, do appear & make themselves parties dfndnt to this suit, on or before the first day of the next term of this Court.
–Wm Holt, clerk

Circuit Court of Wash Co, D C In the cause of the ptn of Thos Jones & Sarah his wife, for the division of a part of 3 several tracts of land, called *Claim Course, Harard,* & *Girl's Portion,* in Wash Co, with bldgs, & improvements, comprising the real estate of Basil Loveless, dec'd, among the heirs at law of the dec'd, consisting of Sarah Jones, the wife of Thos Jones, Benoni Loveless, Tendall Loveless, Eliz Martin, w/o Henry Martin, Cecelia Johnson, w/o Jas Johnson, Jane Ray, w/o Wm Ray, & Charlotte Loveless, wid/o Basil Loveless, dec'd, the undersigned com'rs notifly all persons concerned that thay will proceed on May 16 next, on the above premises, to execute the commission directed to them by the Court in the above cause.
–F P Blair, Tho Carbery, T H Bowen

Mrd: on May 6, at Bloomfield, Eastern Shore, Md, by Rev Mr Brown, Richd M Harrison, of Wash City, to Miss Anne E, only d/o the late Wm Y Burke, of said county.

Mrd: on May 7, in Winchester, Va, by Rev Mr Jones, Jos F Brown, of Wash, to Miss Maria Virginia Singleton, d/o W G Singleton, of the former place.

Died: on May 6, of consumption, at her residence in Culpeper Co, Va, Mrs Sarah Ann W, w/o Benj Rosson, in her 42nd year. May she rest in peace!

Died: on May 12, after a lingering illness, Mrs Maria Bland, consort of Jno D Bland, in her 28th year.

House of Reps: 1-Ptn of Alex'r Wilson, of Fulton Co, Ill, who lost his right arm, at the shoulder joint, in the service of the U S, during the late war with Great Britain, praying an increase of his pension: referred to the Cmte on Invalid Pensions.

Notice: stolenor strayed, from the stable of John L Layton, of Cracklintown, Montg Co, Md, on May 5, a fine black horse. It will give $10 if he is taken out of the county; if taken in the county, $5, & $10 for the thief. –John L Layton

THU MAY 14, 1846
House of Reps: 1-Ptn of John J Adams, of Camden Co, N J, asking Congress to extend for his relief his patent for his new & useful plan of glattening cylinder window glass.

Died: on May 12, Mary Susannah Poor, in her 87th year, a native of Phil, but for the last 46 years a resident of Wash. Her funeral is this afternoon, at 5 o'clock, from her late residence on 14th st, above F st.

Died: on May 9, at Hampstead, L I, N Y, Eliza Matilda, the consort of P R Jones, formerly of Balt, the 3rd d/o Mr Mathias Jeffers, of Wash.

For sale or rent: 2 story frame house, nearly new, on 10th st, south of Pa ave, & adjoining Green's row, within one square of Marsh Market. Call on Warren Little, on the premises.

Stock of groceries at auction: on May 15, at the store of Wm D Windship, on Bridge st. –Ed S Wright, auct

Senate: 1-Ptn from John P Converse, asking compensation as a special agent of the Post Ofc. 2-Ptn from John M Moore, late clerk of the Land Ofc, asking compensation for extra services. 3-Cmte on Pensions: adverse report on the ptn of Michl Bowden. Same cmte: asking to be discharged from the further consideration of the memorial of Ann Kelly, & that it be referred to the Cmte on Naval Affairs. 4-Cmte on Pensions: adverse report on the ptn of Ziba Baker. 5-Cmte on Private Land Claims: bill for the relief of the heirs & legal reps of Louis de la Housange.

Small boat found: picked up between Buzzard & Poplar Points, a small skiff, painted drab, with a red stripe. Owner can have it by proving property, on application to Mr Rollings, on 7th st, south of Md ave.

Summer boarding in the country: subscriber, living about 4 miles from the Centre-market-house, on the Wash & Rockville turnpike, contiguous to the farms of N P Causin & Thos Carbery, has a few rooms unoccupied by his family. Inquire of the Messrs Thos Havenner & Son, or on the premises. –Henry Ould

FRI MAY 15, 1846
Order #20, Headquarters Army of Occupation, Camp near Matamoras, Apr 25, 1846. The remains of the late Col Truman Cross will be interred, with military honors, at 4 p m tomorrow. The funeral escort will be a squadron of dragoons & 8 companies of infty; the latter to be taken from the 2nd brig, the whole organized & commanded by Col Twiggs. Arrangements for the funeral ceremony will be made by Lt Col Payne, Inspec Gen. By order of: Brig Gen Taylor -W W S Bliss, Assist Adj Gen

A Mormon Hero. Orrin P Rickwell has been arrested at Nauvoo on several charges, among which is one of having some time since murdered Frank Worrell. He was armed with shooting-irons enough to have fired 71 shots, but surrendered himself without resistance.

Large steam boiler in the iron foundry of Mr John Watchman, of Balt, exploded yesterday: the engineer, about 21 years of age, John Easton, was killed.

Dreadful railroad accident on Tue on the Columbia railroad, at Phil: a burden car ran off the track, throwing 3 little boys who were standing on the platform. The youngest was killed instantly; the 2nd brother died a few minutes afterwards. They were the sons of Mr Anthony Elton, 24 Unin st, between Spruce & Pine. The two killed were about 8 & 10 years old. The one saved was about 13 years old.
-Chronicle

On May 4, while the brig **Maria L Hill** was lying at Johnson's plantatin, Lou, Capt Rogers, master of the brig, got up, & went on deck. He was discovered by the mate in the hold, his skull fractured & life extinct. Capt Rogers was a native of Dennis, Maine, where he had a wife & 7 children.

Alfred Jones, alias Montgomery, has been arrested at Boston on suspicion that he stole a trunk from a mail stage last winter, containing $3,700 owned by the Waltham Bank. He was detected by his passing two $100 bills of the stolen money at the bank.

Official: by the Pres of the U S of America. A Proclamation: The Congress of the U S, have declared by their act, bearing date this day, that by the act of the Republic of Mexico, a state of war exists between that Gov't & the U S.
–Jas K Polk, May 13, 1846

Mrd: on Tue last, by Rev Mr Vanhorseigh, Mr Edeson Marcellus, of Balt, to Miss Mary Eliz Austin, of Wash City.

For sale: 2 story frame house on south C st, between 3rd & 4½ st: two years old. Call on Mr Wm Wise or J Sinon for further information.

For rent: house just vacated by Chas Bradley, on Md ave, between 4½ & 6th sts. Inquire of Chas Bradley, at the ofc of the Franklin Fire Ins Co.
–S P Franklin, Pa ave, between 9th & 10th sts

Tract of land for sale: about 105 acres, between the road leading to Bladensburg & Bennings Bridge, on the Eastern Branch, & within the District line. Inquire of the subscriber, living on the premises. –T Gibson

Valuable lots at auction: by order of the Excs, the lots belonging to the estate of the late John Gadsby: lots 1 thru 12, 19 thru 22, & 28 thru 30, in square 76, on K st north, between 20th & 21st sts. -R W Dyer, auct

Sale of valuable leasehold premises on Pa ave: by virtue of a deed of trust from Isaac Kell, recorded in Liber W B, #119, folio 295: auction on Jun 17 next, the leasehold premises of lot 34 in square or reservation B, in Wash City, with a 3 story brick house on it, lately erected & occupied by said Kell for the manufacture of tin ware.
–Jos H Bradley, trustee -A Green, auctioneer

Farmers' Hotel, 8th & D sts, formerly kept by Mr Owen Connolly. The undersigned has taken the above Hotel: bar supplied with choice wines & liquors.
–Patrick Moran

SAT MAY 16, 1846
On Wed night week, in consequence of heavy rains, Mud creek, a small stream in Ohio Co, Indiana, rose to an extent never before known. The freshet carried off a log house, occupied by Mr Elias Greathouse, his wife, & 3 children, all of whom perished in the flood.

Senate: 1-Ptn from Stephen R Rowan, asked to be released from liability for money of which he was robbed. 2-Ptn from Robt Jones & Jas Bowen, asking repayment of certain duties illegally exacted. 3-Cmte of Claims: adverse report on the ptn of John Hallet. 4-Cmte on Pensions: adverse reports considered & concurred on: ptn of Thos Hale, ptn of Hezekiah Wingate; ptn of Jas Updike; & ptn of Mgt Hayland.

Richmond Times announce the death of Judge Robt Stanard, of the Court of Appeals. He was struck down by paralysis while engaged in the preparation of an opinion, in his ofc, on Mon night, & lingered until Wed night. He was in his 67th year.

On Fri last Jas McCafferty, convicted of murder, was executed at Huntingdon, Pa. He was a robust & large man, 40 years of age.

House of Reps: 1-Bill for the allowance of 5 years' full pay as the commutation of half pay for life claimed by the heirs of Capt Larkin Smith, on account of his services in the Revolutionary army, which bill had been reported from the Cmte of the Whole: passed in the affirmative. 2-Bill for the relief of Alborne Allen directs the payment to him of $857, balance due on account of a boat built by him for the Gov't: laid aside to be reported. 3-Relief of J W Nye, assignee of Peter Bargy came up: provides for the allowance of an additional sum of $5,967, balance of losses sustained by Bargy & Stuart, under contract to macadamize Pa ave, in Wash, in 1832, by reason of the visitation of the cholera & the refusal of the Gov't ofcr to suffer the work to be suspended during the sickness: laid aside to be reported.

4-Bill for the relief of Cmdor Thos Ap Catesby Jones, of the U S Navy: bill directs the accounts of Cmdor Jones, for extra expenses, incurred while rendering valuable services of a diplomatic character at the Sandwich & Otaheite Islands, during a cruise in the Pacific, some years ago, to be adjusted on principles of equity & justice. Mr Pettit said he was an ofcr of the Navy, with a regular fixed salary, & could not conceive any claim that ofcr could have on the Gov't, if his salary had been paid. Debate continued. 5-Sec of State to settle the claims of Benj E Green, for compensation as Charge d'Affaires at Mexico; &, also, of Wm M Blackford, for compensation as Charge d'Affaire at Venezuela. 6-Ptn of John Day, master of the ship **Elizabeth Bruce**. 7-Ptn of the heirs & legal reps of Lt Robt Allison asking relief.

Mrd: on May 14, by Rev Mr Stringfellow, Mr Thos W Riley to Miss Mary Young, all of Wash City.

Liberal reward for cow that strayed from the subscriber, on C st, between 2nd & 3rd sts. –J R Thompson

Jas P Tustin offers his services in the District or elsewhere as a Collector, Copyist, & Agent. Residence on 8th st, immediately in the rear of the Post Ofc.

MON MAY 18, 1846
Wash Corp: 1-Bill for the relief of Wm Buist: referred to the Cmte of Claims. 2-Cmte of Claims: bill for the relief of Andrew Steper: passed. 3-Cmte of Claims: asked to be discharged from the further consideration of the ptn of Owen Magee: agreed to. 3-Cmte on Police: asked to be discharged from its further consideration of the ptn of Wm R Golding & others. 4-Cmte of Claims: bill for the relief of Henry Gray: reported the same without amendment. 5-Cmte of Claims: asking to be discharged from the further consideration of the ptn of P L Leman: agreed to.

Obit-died: on Fri, at Fuller's Hotel, Capt John Looney, a member of the delegation representing the Cherokee Nation now in Wash City on business with the U S Gov't. He was the nephew of the celebrated chieftain Enolee, or Black Fox. He was about 70 years of age, & distinguished as a brave, honest, & good man. During the war with the Creek Indians, he joined the Cherokee regt which co-operated with the American army under the command of Gen Andrew Jackson, & at the battle of Tallodega he received a severe gun-shot wound from the enemy, & for which disability he had been allowed a pension for life by this Gov't; after the treaties of 1817 & 1819 he removed, with his family & many others of his people, to the new country acquired by the Nation from the U S, west. His signature will be found on the treaty of 1828. After the death of John Holly, he was the only surviving legitimate chief in power under the "Old Settlers," or "Western Cherokees," when the Cherokee Nation from east of the Mississippi removed & arrived in their new country west, in the spring of 1839. He has left a very worthy family & numerous friends to mourn his loss –C D

Thos C Reynolds appointed by the Pres, to be Sec of Legation of the U S at Madrid, vice Jasper H Livingston, resigned.

Mrd: on May 13, at the U S Hotel, by Rev Wm T Sprole, Leonard Bowman to Miss Caroline V B Frye, all of Va.

Stray pigs were taken up by the subscriber, a few days ago, 2 pits that were depredating on his fields. The owner can have them by proving property & paying charges. –Edw Fenwick, near Washington.

House of Reps: 1-Bill for the payment to Philip B Holmes & Wm Pedrick of $500 for the right to use a machine invented & patented by them for cutting raw hides into strips to be made up into cordage: recommendation that it do not pass. 2-Bill for the relief of the heirs of Dr John Gray, dec'd: bill direct that the sum of $5,000 be paid to the reps of Dr Gray for property destroyed by the British forces in the war of 1812, in consequence of its having been in the occupation of the U S for military purposes: laid aside to be reported. 3-Bill for the allowance of the usual bounty granted by law on fishing vessels to Nathan Smith, Chas K Smith, & others, owners of the schnr ____, lost at sea, came up: laid aside. 4-Bill for the relief of the reps of Capt Wm Smallwood Tillard, dec'd: for payment of property destroyed by the British in the war of 1812: favorable decided on by the cmte. 5-Ptn of Joel H Stubbs, of De Kalb Co, Ga, in behalf of the wid/o Benj Stubbs, a soldier in the war of the Revolution. 6-Ptn of Hannah Jackson & 73 other females of Pa for the abolition of slavery. 7-Ptn of Henry Earle & 47 others, citizens of Pa, for the abolition of slavery.

TUE MAY 19, 1846
Orphans Court of Wash Co, D C. Letters of administration on the personal estate of Wm H Wynn, late of the U S ship **Cyane**, dec'd. –Susan Eaton, admx

House of Reps: 1-Ptn of John Stevens, of Athens, Maine, for a pension. 2-Ptn of Bernard Hemken, for the confirmation of the sale of a tract of land. 3-Ptn of L Millandon & others, for the confirmation of certain entries in the New Orleans land district. 4-Ptn of Jas H Myers & 500 other citizens of Iowa, praying that there may be a new territory formed out of a part of the present Territory of Iowa, to be called Dacota Territory.

Furniture at auction on May 22, at the residence of Miss Mary White, over the store of Myers & Brother, on Bridge st: all her stock of furniture. –Edw S Wright, auct

Died: on May 18, in Wash City, Fountain Alex'r Merritt, in his 34th year. His funeral is this evening at 4 o'clock, from his late residence on Pa ave, north side, near 4½ st.

Died: on Feb 27 last, at Stirling, his residence in Saline Co, Missouri, Wm B Alexander, until within a few years a resident of Alexandria Co, D C.

In Montg Co Court, sitting as a Court of Equity, Mar Term, 1846. Mgt Dick & Robt Dick, vs Jas B Beverly & others. Object of this suit is to procure a revival of the decree for a sale of the real estate of which David Peter died seized, in Montg Co, or so much as may be necessary, for the payment of the cmplnts' debts. Bill states that on or about Jul 24, 1828, the cmplnts filed in the Court aforesaid their bill of cmplnt against Jas B Beverly & Jane his wife, Wm H Peter, Wm Ramsey & Eliz his wife, Geo H Peter, Jas C Peter, heirs & devisees of David Peter, dec'd, & Geo Peter, exc of said David, praying that the real estate of which David died seised, in Montg Co, or so much as might be necessary, might be sold for the payment of debts due the cmplnts; that a decree passed & Robt P Dunlop was appointed trustee; that the said Dunlop made sale at different times of parts of the real estate of said David, dec'd, & that the proceeds were insufficient for the payment of the debts due the cmplnts; that after the passing the decree aforesaid Wm H Peter departed this life without leaving heirs of his body, but leaving Jane Beverly, Eliz Ramsey, Geo H Peter, & Jas C Peter, his heirs at law; that the said Wm & Eliz Ramsey, Jas Beverly & Jane his wife, Geo H Peter, Jas Peter & Susan his wife, afterwards conveyed all the lands descended or devised to them by the said David Peter, lying in Montg Co, to John Marbury, of Gtwn, D C, in trust to sell the same, & after defraying the expenses of said trust, to divide the proceeds of said sale among the grantors; that the said Marbury, by virtue of said deed of trust, disposed of a part of said lands conveyed to him as aforesaid; that a part still remains unsold subject to the decree passed as aforesaid, which is still unsatisfied; that since the making of the decree aforesaid & the execution of the said deed to said Marbury, the said Eliz Ramsey has departed this life, leaving Wadsworth, David, Douglass, Marion, & Allen Ramsey, her children & heirs at law of D C; that the said Jas Peter has departed this life, leaving a widow Susan, who has since intermarried with John B Leonard, & 2 children, Sarah Peter & Calhoun Peter, his heirs at law, who are minors, & reside in Montg Co, it is May 5, 1846, ordered that notice be given & the dfndnts are to appear in this Court, in person or by solicitor, on or before Nov 1 next. –Nicholas Brewer
-Saml T Stonestreet, Clerk Montg Co Court, Md.

Senate: 1-Ptn from Josephine Nourse, asking a ptn. 2-Ptn from Thos H Duvall, asking compensation for his services as clerk of the Superior Court of ___ Co, Florida. 3-Ptn from C Alexander & T Barnard, asking indemnity for loss sustained by violation of contract in executing the printing of the Navy Dept. 4-Cmte on Customs: resolution for the relief of Lewis G De Russy: passed. 5-Bill for the relief of John Keith, of N Y, & the bill for the relief of Amos Kendall: read a 3rd time & passed.

Important from the Rio Grande-Gen Taylor at Point Isabel-Attack on his Camp-Repulse of the Mexicans-Destruction of Matamoras.

WED MAY 20, 1846
Volunteers: on motion of Lewis F Beeler, that this company be styled "Washington City Riflemen" was agreed to. Ofcrs elected-

Robt Bronaugh, Capt	Wm A Woodward, 4th Sgt
Phineas B Bell, 1st Lt	Andrew Kemp, 1st Cpl
Wm O'Brien, 2nd Lt	John Kelly, 2nd Cpl
John W Mount, 1st Sgt	Jacob C Hemmrick, 3rd Cpl
Josephus Dawes, 2nd Sgt	John P White, 4th Cpl
Lewis F Beeler, 3rd Sgt	Dr W L Frasier, Surgeon

The Sandusky [Ohio] Clarion records that on May 7th, some citizens were firing a salute to welcome the arrival of the first boat under the arrangement of the Buffalo & Sandusky line. The gun went off while 2 men were ramming down the cartridge: B W Brundage was blown into the bay, & Chas Gueyer near to the edge of the dock. The arms of both were torn off above the elbows. Brundage died immediately; Gueyer survived about 6 hours. C Simmons, who had charge of the vent, had the thumb of his left hand broken at both joints, & the bones displaced.

Wash Corp: 1-Ptn from Josiah Goodrich: referred to the Cmte of Claims. 2-Ptn of Wm Waters & others, for a crubstone & footway: referred to the Cmte on Improvements. 3-Ptn of Wm Wall, presenting a claim against the Corp: referred to the Cmte on Police.

Meeting of the United Rifle Corps at the house of Jas K Plant, O S, on C st, near 10th, this evening, at 7½.

Constable's sale: by virtue of a writ of fieri facias, for Wash Co, D C, at the suit of Thos Kelley & Peter Kelley, trading under the firm of Kelley & Son, against the goods & chattels, lands & tenements, rights & credits of S C Stambaugh: I have seized & taken in execution one bay Mare, the property of said S C Stambaugh: I will offer said property for sale on May 21, on the square opposite the Centre Market, for cash. –J W Dexter, Constable

For hire: a negro boy, between 16 & 17 years of age, of excellent character. Inquire of Dr McWilliams, near the Navy Yard, or of J F Callan.

For rent: 2 story brick dwlg-house on South A st, Capitol Hill, a few doors east of Mr Hill's Boarding House, & near the residence of John H Houston. For terms apply to John H Houston.

Headquarters Army of Occupation: Corpus Christi, Texas, Aug 30, 1845. I report the arrival at this point of 7 companies of the 7th Infty under Maj Brown, & 2 companies of volunteer Artl under Maj Gally. Maj Sewall's company, I am informed, was ordered back to Baton Rouge by Gen Gaines. –Z Taylor

Senate: 1-Ptn from A H Yarnall, for a pension. 2-Cmte on Pensions: adverse report on the ptn of Saml Hartwell. 3-Cmte on Foreign Relations: adverse report, asking to be discharged from the further consideration of the memorial of the owners of the privateer brig **General Armstrong**. 4-Bill for the relief of Mrs Pike, wid/o Gen Pike: engrossed for a 3rd reading. 5-Bill for the relief of Geo Maybee: passed.

Military movements at New Orleans: New Orleans papers of May 12.
Company of Adopted Citizens: Capt C C Whitney has nearly formed a company.
Capt Ricardo's Company: will probably muster them into the service today.
Orleans Riflemen: company of about 60 men marched down to the barracks yesterday.
Montgomery Guards: company of about 70 strong, raised within the last 2 days by Capt Geo W White, ready to be mustered into service last night.
The Fulton Guards: company enlisted in the Regt of Louisiana Volunteers, under the command of Capt Warren A Grice, & is composed of steamboat men.
Armstrong Guards: raised by Mr Saml C Reid, jr. He is the s/o the Saml C Reid who made so brilliant a battle with the Brig Gen Armstrong, during the last war.
The Black Hussars: citizens of German origin raised this fine company, the same name as that of the celebrated corps commanded by the gallant Duke of Brunswick, who was killed in the famous Belgian campaign, Jun, 1815. The company already mustered 90 men, many of whom have served in the armies of Europe.
Carrol Awake: a noble company of men from Carrol, about 70, under the command of Capt Willis Kean, who arrived in this city yesterday.
The Legion Volunteers: volunteered its services for service in the war on the Rio Grande. Gen Taylor will now have under his command as finely disciplined a brigade of citizen soldiery as any in the world. Requisition for more troops:
Maj Gen Gaines, commanding the Western division of the U S Army, has made a requisition upon the Govn'r of the following States for additional troops, to proceed as soon as ready to the Rio Grande:

Tenn to furnish 4 regts of 600 men each: 2,400
Ky the same: 2,400
Missouri 2 regts: 1,200
Mississippi 2 regts: 1,200
Alabama 2 regts: 1,200

Beautiful country seat & mill at public auction: on May 27, the Farm on which I reside, with 170 acres of land: mansion is very handsome & commodious. At the same time I will offer 2 other Farms convenient to the above-one containing 110 acres, & the other 186 acs. If not sold, these last would be exchanged for property in the District, either in the city of out of it. Distance from Balt 11 miles, on the Reisterstown rd. –E B Addison

THU MAY 21, 1846

J Rother, Gtwn Vinegar Depot, corner of Green & Olive sts: will receive during the season a superior article of spiced pickled Oysters, which he will dispose of at reasonable prices.

Senate: 1-Cmte on the Post Ofc & Post Roads: bill for the relief of Isaiah Foy, of N J. Same cmte: bill for the relief of Creed Taylor. 2-Cmte on Pensions: bill for the relief of Nathl Stafford, of Vt, with a report in writing. Same cmte: asking to be discharged from the further consideration of the ptn of John Yarnall, & that it be referred to the Cmte on Naval Affairs. 3-Ptn from Ann Dod, asking for a pension. 4-Ptn from Wm Sloan, asking passage of a law recognizing him as a citizen of the U S.

For rent: the house on 10th st now occupied by Mayor Smith, opposite St Patrick's Church.

Sale of household furniture at auction on May 22, at the boarding house of Mrs Holdsworth, on Pa ave, between 3rd & 4½ sts. –C W Boteler, jr, auctioneer

Fine Watches, Jewelry, & Silver Ware: Saml W Benedict, #5 Wall st, N Y. Mr Cottier has been head of the repairing dept for the last 5 years, & will give his personal attention to the repairing of all fine watches.

Ice Cream, Confectionary, & Refreshments: manufactured at home by the subscriber, may be had at all times during the Nat'l Fair, at his rooms & tent at the corner of 6th st & La ave, in front of the Unitarian Church. –Geo Krafft

Montgomery Volunteers: a fine looking company, about 100, under Capt Elmore, arrived yesterday on the steamboat **Dallas** from Montgomery. They are volunteers for Gen Taylor's camp in Texas. –Mobile Adv

A fine company, at least 107 men, reached here yesterday from Plaquemine & the parish of Iberville, under the command of Gen G S Rosseau as captain. They are almost all young men, & are all from the parish of Iberville. A company of about 90 men also arrived yesterday from the parishes of East Baton Rouge & Iberville, under the comman of the Rev Richd A Stewart as captain. Capt Stewart is a worthy clergyman of the Methodist persuasion, who allows nothing to prevent his discharge of that duty every citizen owes to his country in the hour of peril.
–New Orleans Picayune

Yesterday Judge Canonge gave an order to the Sheriff to release those persons in the parish prison who are confined for want of bail to keep the peace, who are willing to volunteer for Texas. A few availed themselves of this conditional discharge. –Delta

Sale this day: in front of Centre Market: sundry articles of furniture, bedding, pottery, guns & pistols, turnbuckles, carpets, boots, shoes, & hats.
–J Robinson & Co, auctioneers, opposite the Bank of Wash.

Mrd: on May 14, by Rev Dr Marbury, Mr John F Chesley, of Upper Marlboro, to Miss Henrietta E, d/o the late Dr Joseas A Beall, of PG Co, Md.

Capt Walker, [Saml H, as we suppose him to be,] lately one of the Rangers operating on the Texan frontier under Col Hays, is a native of Md, & was formerly a resident of Wash City, where he has many family connexions. He is a carpenter by trade, & is yet a young man. His first entry upon military life was as a volunteer in the company which left here for Florida in 1834; &, after returning, he resumed his occupation in this city for some time, until the spirit of adventure led him first to emigrate to Florida, & then to Texas.
-Nat'l Intell

Mrd: on May 14, by Rev Dr Marbury, Mr John F Chesley, of Upper Marlboro, to Miss Henrietta E, d/o the late Dr Joseas A Beall, of PG Co, Md.

FRI MAY 22, 1846
Appointments by the Pres, by & with the advice & consent of the Senate. 1-Seth Barton, of La, to be Solicitor of the Treas, vice Chas B Penrose, removed. 2-Geo W Sneed, to be postmaster at Florence, Ala, vice Joshua D Coffee, removed.

War movements at New Orleans: from the New Orleans papers of May 14. Appointments by Maj Gen Gaines. Gen Wm DeBuys, who volunteered as a private a few days since, to be Inspector of Volunteers in the U S service on the Rio Grande. Lewis Texada, of Rapides, to act as a Volunteer Aid-de-Camp to the Maj Gen commaning the Western Division.

Taylor Guards, young men of New Orleans are reallying with great spirit under Capt Balie Peyton, at Bravo's Exchange, where that gentleman has established his headquarters.

Still they come: a full company of volunteers, commanded by Capt Galbraith, arrived yesterday on board the ship **North Alabama** from the parish of Concordia. Also, there arrived about 250 fine fellows, from the parishes of Assumption & Lafourche Interior, commanded by Capts E F Nichols & Williams.

German Battalion: the German Volunteers have united together to form a battalion of 325 men, or 5 companies, under the command of Maj Chas Fieska.

The Newark Daily Adv records the death of another of the gallant men who served their country in the war of the Revolution, the venerable Peter B Dumont, of Somerset Co, N J. He was 87 years of age, & was among the most gallant of the "Jersey Blues" who served under Washington.

An elderly gentleman, Mr Manu, was instantly killed 2 miles from Lockport, [N Y,] on board the packet boat **Rescue**, on Thu last, by coming in contact with a bridge. He was from Macomb Co, Mich, & was a highly respectable citizen.

On Sat last 3 citizens, Mr A J Helphenstine, Mr J M Bennett, & Mr Thos P Morehead, in attempting to cross the South Branch of the Potomac, above the dam at Mr David Gibson's mill, for the purpose of fishing, discovered it would be impossible to prevent the boat from going over the dam. Mr Helphenstine leaped out of the boat & made the other side; Mr Morehead could not swim & was drowned; Mr Bennett remained in the boat & was precipitated over the fall without any injury. –Romney [Va] Intelligencer

Mr Martin S Downs was killed at Bennington, Vt, last Tue, by the bursting of a grindstone. He was polishing spindles on a dry stone, when it burst, & a large piece struck him in the forehead. He lived but 20 minutes.

Senate: 1-Several ptns from Thos T January, Geo Runey, & Wm Ramsey, asking to be allowed pre-emption rights. 2-Ptn from Wm De Courcy, asking that the benefits of the pension laws may be extended equally. 3-Ptn from the wid/o Wm Carroll, asking a pension. 4-Ptn from Jos Loranger, for compensation for a fishing seine seized by the collector of Detroit. 5-Cmte on Pensions: adverse report on the ptn of Hannah Severance. 6-Cmte on Military Affairs: be instructed into authorizing the purchase of 200 of Colt's patent rifles for the use of the troops on the southwestern frontier. 7-Cmte on Naval Affairs: be directed to report upon the merits of R F Loper's plan for constructing war steamers & other vessels; also, on the merits of said Loper's plan for constructing wrought iron cannons & mortars on the screw principle. 8-Putnam's ploughing & dredging machine to be referred to the Cmte on Commerce.

Wm Hudson, living in Pendleton Co, Va, on May 11, murdered his wife & 2 children, & maimed 4 others, 2 of whose lives are despaired of. He made his escape but 2 days later surrendered to a gentleman in Hardy Co. He says he was prompted to the deed in a state of phrensy, occasioned by improper conduct on the part of his wife, & he intended to kill himself after the horrid act, but his heart failed him.

Mr Geo G Smith, of Boston, has engraved a plate, in beautiful style, containing the whole of the Declaration, with fac similies of the signatures, on a reduced scale, surmounted with accurate likenesses of all the Presidents, from Geo Washington to Jas K Polk, & surrounded by the emblems or coats of arms adopted by all the States. Copies are being offered for the trifling price of .25. –Salem Gaz

Died: on May 21, in Wash City, Mr Lewis Sanders, in his 55th year, after a short but distressing illness, which he bore with Christian fortitude. Mr Sanders was a native of Chas Co, Md, but for the last 30 years a resident of this District. His funeral is tomorrow, from the residence of his nephew, R B Nalley, corner of 9th & G sts, at 10 o'clock.

City lots for sale: lot 18 in square 252; lot 3 in square 264; lot 12 in square 762; which will be sold upon liberal terms. Reference, Stanislaus Murray.

Notice: the undersigned has taken a house on 8th st, between D st & Pa ave, [over Tabler & Clarke, merchant tailors,] to accommodate persons with comfortable boarding. –Eliza Larcombe

For sale: a good draught Horse & a new Cart, together with the Gear. Apply to F & A Schneider, corner of 18th st & Pa ave.

For rent: the new brick house, lately finished, with an elevated basement, on 16th st, near M St Clair Clarke's, & opposite the residence of Cmdor Morris. Rent moderate to a good tenant. –Jas Carrico

Trustee's sale of valuable lot: by virtue of a deed of trust from John Young to the subscriber, dated Dec 30, 1840, recorded in liber W B, #85, folios 273 & 274, Wash Co: sale of part of lot 9 in square 290, fronting on 13th st. –Henry Naylor, trustee -R W Dyer, auct

Boarding house to let: large 3 story house formerly occupied by A R Dowson, on Capitol Hill, next door to Mrs Carter's. Apply at Mrs Carter's, next door, or to A Green, auctioneer, Concert Hall Todd's Bldgs.

Orphans Court of Wash Co, D C. Letters testamentary on the personal estate of Fountain A Meritt, late of said county, dec'd. Persons with claims are to exhibit the same with vouchers, on or before May 19 next. -Chas S Wallach, exc

Mrs Rhea, on Missouri ave, between 4½ & 6th sts, can accommodate 10 or 12 gentlemen with board, or with rooms without board. Her house is very pleasantly situated & well furnished.

SAT MAY 23, 1846
For sale: 2 light one-horse Carriages & 4 Carryalls, at very low prices. Also, a large frame bldg, built for a coach factory, on 18th st, between G st & Pa ave. –Wm Keefe

Household & kitchen furniture at auction on May 26, at the residence of Wm M Smith, on Pa ave, between 21st & 22nd sts-a lot of good furniture. –A Green, auctioneer [The house is for rent: apply to Mr Smith, at Mr L Smith's, near the Brewery, or to A Green.]

Oregon Beaver hats: Pearl Gossamer hats; Black Moleskin hats, for sale. M H Stevens & Emmons, [late Fish & Co,] occupying 2 stores, #s 1 & 2, Brown's Hotel.

Houses for rent: 2 brick dwlg-houses on N Y ave, between 8th & 9th sts, & one on 11th st, between H & I sts. Inquire of H Cruttenden

Land for sale: on the premises, to the highest bidder, on Jun 23 next, a small & beautiful Farm of about 300 acres: it is healthy, out of upwards of 50 persons in family, whites & blacks, there was not one single case of bilious fever the last year. –Chas A Pye, near Port Tobacco, Md

The subscriber will dispose of a tract of about 1,100 acres of land within 20 miles of Wash, on the Va side of the Potomac, a short distance below & in view of the Mount Vernon estate. It may be divided into 3 farms. Apply to S McKenney, Gtwn, D C.

Valuable property for sale; the Columbian Cotton Factory, on Four Mile Creek, one mile from the Potomac, half a mile from the Alexandria lateral Canal: with a 3 story brick bldg, with several other spacious 2 story brick houses; also, a large Grist Mill. Apply on the premises, or to Gen Alex'r Hunter, Marshal of the District, or to Messrs Swann & Swann, Councillors at Law, Wash.

Most awful tornado passed over Grenada, a beautiful village in Yallabusha Co, Miss, on May 7: 30 or 40 lives lost: the teacher of the male school, Mr Sample, was killed, & many of his pupils perished. Mrs F E Plummer, the teacher of the female school, with many of the children under her charge, were killed. Mr Robinson lost his father, wife, sister & child. –New Orleans Pic, 15th

Died: yesterday, after a protracted & painful illness, Mrs Ann Speiden, in her 72nd year, one of the oldest residents of Wash City. For nearly half a century she was a pious member of the Methodist Episcopal Church, & died in the full & certain hope of a blissful immortality. Her funeral is from the residence of her dght, Mrs Jno H Smoot, near the Navy Yard, on Sun afternoon, at 3 o'clock.

Died: on May 21, of convulsions, *Geoge Bender Fisk, only child of Chas B & Mary Eliz Fisk, aged 2 years & 6 months. His funeral is from his grandfather's, Maj Bender's residence, this afternoon, at 5 o'clock. *Geoge-as copied.

Died: on May 15, at Martinsburg, Va, Edmund Pendleton, s/o Col E P & Martha C Hunter, in his 5th year.

$10 reward for lost or stolen, on May 21, a small cream-colored Mare. –John Carroll Brent, Capitol Hill

Very valuable property at auction: on Jun 4, in front of the premises, the property long known as the Globe Hotel, at the corner of Pa ave & 13th st, formerly occupied by A Fuller & Mr Jas Maher. This property runs 52 feet on Pa ave: the House contains 21 rooms. Also, I shall sell lots 8 & 9 in square 355: these lots front on 14th st & P ave. -R W Dyer, auct

Tho Hon Wm Simonton, late Rep in Congress from the Harrisburg district of Pa, died at his residence in South Hanover on Mon last.

MON MAY 25, 1846
House of Reps: 1-Cmte of the Whole: bills considered-bill granting a pension to Oris Crosby; bill granting a pension to Elijah C Babbitt; bill for the relief of John Stockton, late a lt in the army; bill granting a pension to John Porter; bill granting a pension to Isaiah Parker; bill for the payment of arrears of pension due to Dorothy Terrell to John Wing; bill to pay Saml D Enochs $40 for a mare which ran off while in the public service, & has never since been heard of. 2-The bill for the relief of Philip & Eliphalet Greely, ordered to be reported to the House. 3-Bill for the relief of N & L Dana & Co, was called, & objection was interposed. 4-Next came up the bill for the relief of Emanuel Berri & John M Reese; bill for the relief of Jas G McCloud, of Iowa; & bill to confirm an entry of land made by the administrator of Jas Anderson, dec'd, of Iowa. 5-Joint resolution for the relief of Sheldon B Hays: ordered to be reported to the House. 6-Ptn of Elijah Connor, praying to be confirmed in the possession of a certain tract of land. 7-Ptn of Solomon Hartford, of Hiram, Maine, a soldier of the war of 1812 with Great Britian, praying for a pension for disability incurred while a soldier in the army of the U S. 8-Ptn of Horatio G Wood & others, praying that steel may be imported free of duty. 9-Bill for paying to Alborne Allen $500, balance claimed by him for building a revenue boat, was read the 3rd time: bill stands passed. 10-Bill to pay J W Nye, assignee of Peter Bargy & Hugh Stewart, $5,967 damage sustained by said Bargy & Stewart-under a contract for Macadamizing Pa ave, in Wash, in 1832, next came up for a 3rd reading. Bill was rejected.

On May 14, a s/o Mr Chas Curdois, aged 7 years, was drowned in the dam above the saw-mill, in this village. He was fishing from the steep bank, & fell in accidentally-so it is supposed. His body was recovered about 4 hours afterwards.
–Plattsburg Republican

Galveston Civilian of the 15th. 1-The brave & gallant Maj Brown died on the ___ from a wound received in his thigh by the explosion of one of the enemy's shells. His wound was not considered dangerous, but as he was placed in one of the bomb-proof burrows, mortification ensued from the want of fresh air. [The ___ for the date, is as written.] 2-Gen Vega is the Col Vega that was captured by the Texan forces at the slaughter of San Jacinto. He was also at the fall of the Alamo, & is a brave & accomplished ofcr.

Brasas Santiago, May 10, 1846. We had 11 killed & about 10 mortally wounded. Capt Page, of the Third, had all the lower part of his face shot off with a cannon ball. It is thought he will recover, though horribly mutilated. Maj Ringgold had the fleshy part of both his legs shot through, & horse killed. Lt Sutter slightly wounded. The Mexicans were commaned by Gen Majia.

Henry Boyland, passing directly in front of one of the guns fired after the meeting held in N Y on Tue, at the moment of firing, was so badly burnt in the face by the powder that he will lose the sight of one of his eyes, if not both.

Columbian Horticultural Society: Cmte of Arrangements:
Alex'r Suter	Wm Buist	Chas Stott
Wm Breckenridge	Mr Slater	Mr McNamee
John Douglas	Mr Shoemaker	Geo W Riggs
Wm Cammack	Geo Watterston	
Joshua Pearce	Mr Kedglie	

City Ordinances-Wash. 1-Act for the relief of G C Grammer: fine imposed for a violation of the law in relation to foot-pavements, is hereby remitted.

Mrd: on Apr 21, in Wash City, by Rev Mr Morgan, Dr Francis Lambert to Miss Mary Louisa Saffer, all of Loudoun Co, Va.

Died: yesterday, in his 26th year, after a severe illness of a week, Benj Speight, s/o the Hon Jesse Speight, Senator from Mississippi. His funeral is this afternoon, at 5 o'clock, from his late residence, [Mrs Taylor's boarding house, 9th & Pa ave.]

Orphans Court of Wash Co, D C. Letters of administration on the personal estate of Fred'l A H Lefort, late of Geneva, dec'd. –Jos E Nourse, adm

Three days later from Brasas Santiago: another battle: Gen Taylor victorious: Gen Vega taken prisoner. Battle on May 9th between the Mexican & American forces, within 3 miles of Camp Taylor. Among the killed were Col McIntosh, Lt Cochran, Col Brown, Lt Eng, & 1or 2 others whose names are not given. Col Payne, Lts Gates, Brubank, Hooe, Luther, & others were wounded. Maj Ringgold died on May 10th & was buried on May 11 with the honors of war. Exchange of prisoners: Capt Thornton & Capt Hardee & Lt Kane have been returned to the army. Lt Deas was not demanded & still remains a prisoner.

The Pope has created Dr John McLaughlin, Commandant of the Hudson Bay Co beyond the Rocky Mountains, Chevalier of the Order of St Gregory. His Holiness has conferred the honor in acknowledgment of the services rendered by the Doctor in the cause of religion since the arrival of the missionaries in Oregon.

TUE MAY 26, 1846
Senate: 1-Cmte on Indian Affairs: bill for the relief of Saml W Bell, a native of the Cherokee country, with a report in writing: referred.

$10 reward for runaway servant woman Agnes: about 50 years old, rather dark. My residence is on E st, next the Medical College. –C Buckingham

Mrd: on May 23, at St Paul's Church, N Y, by Rev Dr Wainwright, Horatio Bridge, Purser U S Navy, to Charlotte, d/o the late Josiah Marshall, of Boston.

News from the Rio Grande. On May 9, Lt Inge, of the 2nd Dragoons, Lt Cochrane, of the 4th Infty, & Lt Chadborune, of the 8th Infty, were killed. Ofcrs wounded: Lt Cols McIntosh & Payne, Capts Montgomery & Hooe; Lts Gates, Maclay, Selden, Burbank, Jordon, & Fowler, of the Infty. [May 27th newspaper: Lt Dobbins, 3rd Infty, was among the ofcrs wounded. Lt Blake, topographical engineers, after rendering distinguished service in my staff during the affair of the May 8, accidentally shot himself with a pistol the following day, & expired before night. Capt Page's wound is dangerous.]

The Hon E J Shields, for the past several years a resident of Memphis, Tenn, died in the vicinity of La Grange, Texas, on Apr 21, after being arrested for 2 days, by a sudden attack of disease, from pursuing his route to San Antonio, whither he was journeying in pursuit of health.

The death of the gallant Maj Ringgold has cast a gloom over the city of Balt. This distinguished ofcr had resided in Balt for a number of years past, & had many warm friends. –American [May 29th newspaper: Gen Saml Ringgold, was the eldest s/o the late Gen Saml Ringgold, of Wash Co, Md. His mother was a d/o Gen John Cadwalader, of Phil, a distinguished citizen in the days of the Revolution. Maj Ringgold entered the army, as Lt of Artl, in Jul, 1818, having graduated at West Point with much honor. He was selected by Gen Scott as one of his aids; he was on duty in S C in 1832; in Florida, when the Indian war occurred, then a Capt of Artl; he never recovered from the effects of his exposure during the Florida campaign. He fell in the fierce battle of May 8, the same ball killing his horse under him, & wounding him mortally. –Balt American]

Strayed or stolen from Mr John Woods, Northern Liberties, one bright bay Horse; & one sorrel Mare. Information to Mr P Moran, Farmers' Hotel, Wash: will be handsomely rewarded.

Died: on Apr 23, at Winchester, Va, Miss Sarah Nickolls G Buchanan, after a most painful illness. Her widowed mother & sister are left inconsolable. This young lady was interesting, intelligent, & accomplished. She was endeared to a large circle of relatives, friends, & a devoted mother.

Trustee's sale: by virtue of a deed of trust from John T Devaugh to me, I will offer at auction, on Jun 2, in front of the premises, all the south half of lot 14 in square 54, in Wash City, with 2 frame tenements of 2 stories. –John Pickrell, trustee
-A Green, auctioneer

Orphans Court of Wash Co, D C. Letters of administration on the personal estate of F Chas Erb, late of said county, dec'd. –Wilhelmine Erb, admx

WED MAY 27, 1846
Senate: 1-Ptn from A B Durand & others, asking that Saml F B Morse, of the Magnetic Telegraph, may be employed by the Gov't to execute a painting for one of the vacant panels of the rotundo. 2-Ptn from Oscar F Pitman, asking compensation for his services in transporting the mail.

Brvt Brig Gen Henderson, of the Marine Corps has been charged on the floor of the House of Reps, & by several of the presses opposed to the Navy, & the Marine Corps in particular, with having misapplied the public funds; in other words, with having wrongfully appropriated them to his own use. It has been asserted that his annual pay amounts to $12,698.33, as charged to him in the Navy Register for 1846. The charge of misappropriation of the public funds, as applied to Gen Harrison, is all moon-shine, or worse, mere malice. The Board adjourned sine die-Feb 28, 1845. Approved Mar 31, 1845-Upon this approval of Pres Tyler of the proceedings of the Board was Gen Henderson allowed the pay of a Brevet Brig Gen. Gen Henderson is not a disbursing ofcr, & cannot receive one cent more pay than the law allows him.
–Boston Journal

Terrible tornado, which visited the town of Grenada, Miss, on May 7, swept away a great number of bldgs, & killed a large number of people. Killed: Mrs Robinson, w/o D Robinson, & his father

Jas Whitsett, s/o Dr S Whitsett
2 children of D Rosser
1 d/o J Snider
1 s/o R Coffman
Mrs Plummer
A s/o Mr Kirwan
1 s/o J A Williamson
Wounded:
A d/o D Rosser
A s/o R Coffman
A s/o J A Williamson
2 children of Mr Gill
A s/o J Melton
Mrs Baughn
2 sons of Wm Lake
Jos, a s/o B Williams, sr
A s/o Dr Edmonds

Mrs Baughn & child
Wm Eubanks
1 s/o Rev Mr Boswell
Henry Allen, s/o Mrs Allen
2 negroes belonging to Dr Purnell
4 negroes belonging to S Caldwell
2 or 3 belonging to J Balfour

A child of the late Dr Payne
A child of Mr E Eubanks
Mrs Land, lady of T S Land
J M Sample
Marion, a s/o A S Brown
Richd Armstrong
Mrs Nelson
John Mitchell
Jas Holden

Headquarters Army of Occupation, Camp at Resaca de la Palma, 3 miles from Matamoras, May 9, 1846. Our own loss has been very heavy: Lt Inge, 2nd Dragoons, Lt Cochrane, 4th Infty, & Lt Chadbourne, 8th Infty, were killed on the field. Lt Col Payne, 4th Artl, Lt Col McIntosh, Lt Dobbins, 3rd Infty, Capt Hooe & Lt Fowler, 5th Infty, & Capt Montgomery, Lts Gates, Selden, McClay, Burbank, & Jordan, 8th Infty, were wounded. It affords me peculiar pleasure to report that the field work opposite

Matamoras has sustained itself handsomely during a cannonade & bombardment of 160 hours. But the pleasure is alloyed with profound regret at the loss of its heroic & indomitable commander, Maj Brown, who died today from the effect of a shell. –Z Taylor, Brevt Brig Gen U S A, commanding. Adj Gen of the Army, Wash.

The copartnership under the firm of Russell & Miffleton was dissolved on May 23 by mutual consent. –F A Russell, G W Miffleton. F A Russell will continue the Carriage Business at the corner of 8th & D sts.

Mrd: on May 26, in Wash City, by Rev G W Samson, Mr Munroe Harris to Miss Jane W Henderson, both of Alexandria, D C.

Died: on May 25, in Wash City, after a long & painful illness, Jamima Little, w/o Peter Little, in her 69th year. Her funeral is from her late residence, on L st, near the Navy Yard, this afternoon, at 3 o'clock.

A Boston letter states that Peter C Brooks, father-in-law of the Hon Edw Everett, has sent a draft to the gov't of Harvard Univ for the sum of $10,000 to be appropriated for bldg a new house for the residence of the President of that institution. The present house is very unsuitable for the purpose.

Wm S Ward, of the Harrisonburg Republican, was drowned on Sat last, in attempting to cross the river near Col Givens' on horseback. –Staunton Spectator

House of Reps: 1-Ptn of Mrs Ann Timmons, wid/o Saml Timmons, who was a soldier in the late war with Great Britain, & who died in the service of the U S: referred.

The Phil papers announce the death on Sun last, of the Hon Wm Drayton, formerly a distinguished Rep in Congress from State of S C, but for the last 12 or 14 years a resident of the city of Phil.

Wash News. Exhibits at the National Fair: specimens of <u>Printed Goods</u> from: manufactory of S McCredy, Phil; S McBride, of Fairmount; & T H Fulton, Balt. Saddlery, Harness, & Trunks: displays by Mr D Campbell, of this city; Wm H Horstmann & Sons, of Phil; Jenkins & Lilly & Hughson & Vail, Balt; also Messrs S & T H Hunt, of that city; R W Lewis, of Unionville, Chester Co, Pa; Trunks from A L Hickey, Summers, & John Ulrich, of Phil; Chas F Sangster, of Gtwn; John Ebert & Son, of Fred'k City, Md; Ramsburg & Ebert, of Gtwn, D C; Mr John Kunkle, of Fred'k, Md; G S Adler, of Phil; Hon Z Pratt, of Prattsville, N Y; Wm Brown, of Manchester, Carroll Co, Md; Mr D Howell, of Pine st, N Y. Piano Fortes exhibited by: T Gilbert & Co, Boston.

A reported duel at Carlisle between Gen Armour & Col Noble is pronounced, on the authority of a letter from that place, to be a hoax. –Alex Gaz

Bakehouse for sale: by virtue of a deed of trust, executed by D Sands, in order to secure the payment of a debt due to Chas Harris, & duly recorded in the Hustings Court of this city: the trustees will expose to public auction, on Jun 1, on the premises, the Leasehold Tenement between the property of the late John N Walke & the late Thos Glenn, on Commerce st, between Main & Little Water sts, being an unexpired term of years in the lot & the 3 story brick bldg thereon, used as a bakehouse. The house is insured for $2,560. The title is believed to be unquestionable. –The Trustees. H & W Pannell, auctioneers, Norfolk, Va.

THU MAY 28, 1846
Senate: 1-Ptn from Thos Bryant, asking to be allowed remuneration for the naval service of his ancestor. 2-Cmte on Pensions: adverse report on the ptn of Philip Slaughter: concurred in. 3-Cmte of Ways & Means: to pay F Gardner, late Naval Storekeeper to the African squadron, for his services as such, $437.50. To pay the reps of Thos H Storm balance due him as agent for prisoners at Barbadoes, $2,274.26.

National Fair-Wash: beautiful woolens from John Heeren, Waterville, Vt; A & A Lawrence, Boston; A J Sawyer, Dover, N H; Thos H Dickinson, Phil. Samples of Georgia plains sent by Geo Schley, of Augusta, Ga. Samples of woollen manufacture from W P Eliason, of Orange Courthouse, Va; & Messrs Wethereds, of Balt Co, Md. Mixed cotton & woollen cloths sent from Jos Ripka, Phil, & J & R Wethered, A Newman, & W & D Watt, of Pa. Woollen knitting yarn sent from Moses Hay, Phil. Hats of various descriptions: Mr Todd, Stephens & Emmons, & J Maguire, of Wash; W F Seymour, of Gtwn; Chas Oakford, G Brooks & Co, & Bacon & Hallowell, Phil; L Hunt, J L McPhail, & Elmes & Seaver, Balt. Madame Dyvernois, of Wash City, has a small case containing some elegant fancy caps. Machine Cards are exhibited by Messrs T K Earle & Co, of Worcester, Mass. We saw the sewing machine invented by Mr Elias Howe, jr, of Cambridgeport, Mass, at work. We think that if this machine can continue to work as rapidly as we saw it work, it ought to be called the "Devil among the Tailors," for it will certainly bring about a revolution in the trade. Several new articles of Furniture have been introduced: from R B Willis, Boston; D & A Crout, Phil; extension dining-table, from Mr Briggs, Roxbury, Mass, & an article of very handsome workmanship, called an "American Beehive," to be placed close to an outside wall of a room. It forms a bureau & sideboard, & also a parlor beehive, in which all the operations of that insect may be viewed whilst sitting in the parlor. The bees enter through the tubes passing through the outer wall & depart the same way; they cannot come into the room. This ingenious invention is by Mr Jas A Cutting, of Boston.

Three lives lost by spirit gas: at St Louis, on May 16, in the house of Mr Augustine Farnham. Amanda A Smith, a nurse, in filling a lamp with spirit gas, the candle came in touch with the fluid & the room filled with flame. Mr Farnham's boy of 5 years, & girl of 3 years, & the nurse, a girl of 14 years, were so badly burnt that they died during the night.

Sale on Aug 13, 1846, at the ofc of the Clerk of the Corp, at auction, the following lots & parts of lots in Gtwn; the same being seized by me for taxes due to the Corp of Gtwn. –Wm Jewell, Collector
Part of lot 49, old Gtwn: assessed to the Chesapeake & Ohio Canal Co
Part of lot 209, Beatty & Hawkins' addition: assessed to the U S Bank
Part of lot 65, in Beatty & Hawkins' addition: except 25 feet front which is owned by A H Paul: assessed to the U S Bank
Lot not numbered, being the northern lot in that part of Threlkeld's square west of Fayette st: assessed to Gabriel Duvall's heirs.
The third dividion into which lots 21 thru 24, of Holmead's addition, are divided & held by the heirs of Wm Crawford, the elder, & their assigns: assessed to Richd R Crawford.
West half of lot 270, Beall's addition: assessed to Richd B Crawford.
East half of lot 271, Beall's addition: assessed to Thos Lorman.
Lot 23, Beatty & Hawkins' addition: assessed to Mary Sands' heirs.
West half of lot 209, Deakins & Baily's addition: assessed to Thos Corcoran's heirs.
Part of lot 65, old Gtwn, from the south wall of the 2 story brick house standing on said lot 65, formerly owned by Chas King, but now owned & occupied by Thos Hunter: assessed to John Connelly's heirs.
Lot 23, Peter, Beatty, Threlkeld, & Darkin's addition: assessed to the heirs of Dr Chas A Warfield, dec'd.
Part of lot 188, Beatty & Hawkins' addition, on Market st, running back to the west boundary line of said lot 188, on which part stands the 3 story tenements originally erected & owned by Fleury Lewis, & which middlemost tenement is now claimed by Mrs Mary Ogle: assessed to Mary Ogle, but supposed to belong to the heirs of said Fleury Lewis, dec'd, & a native of France.
Lots 28 & 29, Peter, Beatty, Threlkeld, & Deakin's addition: assessed to Jas Clagett's heirs.

War Movements: 1-Ky-The Louisville Legion, under command of Col Stephen Ormsby, about 800 of the most ardent, athletic, & respectable young men of Louisville, were to embark for New Orleans on May 23.
2-Col Wm O Butler, Gen Leslie Combs, & Maj Humphrey Marshall are applicants for the command of the whole force of Kentucky volunteers, when they shall have been raised. The requisition calls for 3,000-2,000 foot & 1,000 horse. 3-Missouri-on may 16th 3 companies, numbering 240 volunteers, attached to the 64th regt, under the command of Maj Schoenethaler, left St Louis for Jefferson Barracks, where they will remain until ordered to the frontier.

Mrd: on May 25, at St John's Church, by Rev Mr Pyne, Joel S Kennard, U S Navy, to Harriet Macomb, d/o Isaac K Hanson, of Wash City.

Died: on May 10, in his 94th year, David Diffenderffer, the last ofcr of the War of Independence residing in Lancaster Co, Pa.

Died: on May 12, at Lexington, Va, in Christian peace, Anna Marsden, eldest child of Francis H & Sarah Smith, aged 10 years.

Fresh lobsters & salmon: at the Centre market, & at O B Sheckel's, opposite the market. –Chas W Arnold

Chinese Chess men, fans, ivory, seals, & gifts. For sale by Wm F Bayly, Pa ave, between 11th & 12th sts.

John McLeod declines being considered a candidate for the Mayoralty. His friends unadvisedly have brought forward his name in connexion with this ofc.

FRI MAY 29, 1846
Senate: 1-Ptn from Peter Von Schmidt, praying the purchase by Gov't of his improvement on the rotary steam-engine. 2-Cmte on Finance: adverse reports on the ptn of Henry Simpson; & on the claim of E A Ware. 3-Bill for the relief of Asenath Canney was taken up & passed.

The Pres, with the advice & consent of the Senate, has made the following appointments in the U S Army, in the Regt of Mounted Riflemen, or 3rd Regt of Dragoons, authorized by the act appoved May 19, 1846.

Col-Persifor F Smith, of Louisiana   Major-Geo S Burbridge, of Ky
Lt Col-John C Fremont, of the Army
Captains:
Wm H Loring, of Florida   Stevens T Mason, of Va
Winslow F Sanderson, of Ohio   John S Simonton, of Indiana
Saml H Walker, of Texas   John B Backenstoss, of Ill
Henry C Pope, of Ky   Bela M Hughes, of Missouri
Geo B Crittenden, of Ky   Stephen S Tucker, of Arkansas
1st Lts:
Benj S Roberts, of Iowa   Thos Duncan, of Ill
Thos Ewell, of Tenn   Wm W Taylor, of Indiana
Andrew Porter, of Pa   Andrew J Lindsay, of Mississippi
Michl E Van Buren, of Michigan   John G Walker, of Missouri
Llewellen Jones, of N Y   Spear S Tipton, of Indiana
Noah Newton, of Ohio
2nd Lts:
Thos Claiborne, jr, of Tenn   Geo McLane, of Md
Thos G Rhett, of S C   Murray Morris, of D C
Chas L Denman, of N Y   Llewellen Rague, of Ohio
Washington L Elliott, of Pa   Francis S K Russell, of Michigan
Thos Davis, of Illinois   Julian May, of D C

Nat'l Fair-Wash: Lamps, chandeliers, girandoles: W H Starr, of N Y; Cornelius & Co, Phil; & Hooper & Co, Boston. Boston & Sandwich Glass Co has a stand of beautiful articles; Mr Thos Purcell, of Wash City, is their agent; as is also Mr C S Fowler, our neighbor. Display by Henry Bayly, of Balt. Large assortment of suspenders made by Solomon Doebely, of East Kensington, Phil. Mr Goodyear exhibits an article called a gumelastic paper-holder, which appears well adapted for the purpose. D W Canfield, of N Y, has a case of finely worked gentlemen's shirts. The Franklin Clothing Store, Phil, forwarded a variety of Gentlemen's Bathing Dresses, & Dressing Gowns.

Mr Harvey, who has attained his 111th year, & is the parent stock of 5 generations, addressed an audience at the Tabernacle in N Y on Monday night for upwards of an hour.

The Telegraph line between Phil & Balt will be completed & tested this week. –Wilmington [Del] Journal

Wash Corp: 1-Cmte of Claims: ask to be discharged from the further consideration of the ptn of Wm R Golding: agreed to. 2-Bill for the relief of H G Corcoran: passed. 3-Relief of Wm Wallis: passed. 4-Bill for the relief of A G Seaman: taken into consideration & agreed to. 5-Cmte of Claims: ask to be discharged from the further consideration of the ptn of Patrick Crowley: discharged accordingly. 6-Cmte of Claims: act for the relief of Andrew Steper, & act for the relief of J Martin: both passed. 7-Relief of Renslaugh Deneale: passed.

Mrd: on May 27, by Rev Mr Eggleston, Mr Alex'r Jackson, of Warrenton, Va, to Miss Mary Eliz, d/o Robt Ricketts, of Wash City.

Mrd: on May 18, at the residence of the Hon Jacob S Yost, in Pottstown, Pa, by Rev N S S Beaman, D D, Geo M Coffin, Merchant, to Miss Sarah A Harrington, all of Troy, N Y.

The new Presbyterian Church on 8th st, to be known as the Central Presbyterian Church of Wash City, under the pastoral care of Rev Septimus Tustin, will be dedicated on Sabbath morning next. Sermon will be preached by Rev Thos B Balch, of Va. [Jun 3rd newspaper: Dedication took place last Sat: the edifice is on 8th st, on the site generously given about a year since by the late Gen Van Ness: Architect-Mr C L Coltman; Mr Jas B Philips, plasterer; venetian blinds were made by Mr Noel, of Wash City; Mr Reese, upholsterer, added much to the beauty of the pulpit & to the comfort of the minister who occupies it; pulpit was planned by Mr J C Harkness, & executed by Messrs Donovan & Gerbess. Sermon was preached by Rev Thos B Balch, of Va. Rev Septimus Tustin, chaplain of the U S Senate, was chosen pastor.]

To let: 2 story brick house on 12th st, between C & D sts. Inquire of John Alexander, Pa ave, between 12th & 13th sts.

For sale: a valuable lot of ground, on 7th st, near the corner of K st; also several lots to lease, in the vicinity of the depot. Call on Wm H Ward, on 8th st, between I & K sts. Also, a servant Girl to put out for a term of years. Call on John Wise, on 4½ st, south of the canal.

City Ordinances-Wash: 1-Act for the relief of Henry Gray: fine imposed for an alleged violation of the law in relation to keeping a dog without paying a license: same is remitted, provided he pay the expenses of prosecution. Register to pay him $5. 2-Act for the relief of Kinlaugh Deneale: fine imposed for a violation of the law relative to watering horses on Pa ave, is remitted, provided Deneale pays cost of prosecution. 3-Act for the relief of Andrew Steper: fine imposed for an alleged violation of the law relative to carts & drays: same is hereby remitted. 4-Act for the relief of H G Corcoran: fine imposed upon Mrs H G Corcoran, for an alleged violation of the law, regulating retail licences, is remitted, proved Corcoran pay the expense of prosecution. 5-Act for the relief of A E Lemerle: refund to Lemerie the sum of $14.17, which was deposited by him in the Bank of Wash to the credit of this Corp for taking out a grocery license, which intention has since been abandoned. 6-Act for the relief of Jacob Martin: fine imposed upon him for a violation of the law in relation to dogs, is remitted: provided Martin pay the costs of prosecution.

House of Reps: 1-Ptn of Chas R Allen, praying for the allowance of an account for services of guard while the U S Com'r was concluding a treaty with the N Y Indians. 2-Ptn of the trustees of the Faulkner School, in Chesterfield City, Va, praying the allowance of a year's pay, alleged to be due to the reps of Ralph Faulkner, an ofcr of the army of the Revolution.

Nat'l Fair-Wash. Mr Walbourn, of Phil, has a case of rich Stocks for gentlemen; J Hodges, of Phil, the same. L Benkert, of Phil, French bootmaker, has fine specimens of his skill shoes & boots exhibited by Henry Hearth, of Phil; some ladies shoes by Wm Ryan & Co, of that city; Francis Dane, of South Danvers, Mass, has some stout Coarse Shoes; Mr Thorne, of Phil, displays a variety of shoes; also India rubber shoes from N Haywood & Co, Lisbon, Conn. Mr Geo Rapp, of Economy, sent beautiful Silk Goods. There is a very handsome table cover embroidered by Miss Harriet E Thompson, of Wash. Silk tassels from Henry Deehring, Phil. Mr John W Gill, of Wheeling, Va, has a table of Silk Goods. Mr Henry Huber, of Phil, sent fine specimens of Saddlers' & Shoemakers' Tools: Mr Hemerick, of Newark, N J, Tailors' Shears & Scissors. Chas C Reinhardt, of Balt, collection of Surgical & Dental Instruments. In Silver & Plated Ware, the exhibition is not large: our neighbor, Mr R Keyworth, has a case of rich goods; fine goods from H W Dubosy, Phil; & A E Warner & Saml Kirk, of Balt. Mr W A Richardson, of Phil, has a fine collection of umbrellas & parasols.

Prof B Frank Palmer, of Merdith, N H, exhibits, at the Fair, an <u>Artificial Leg</u>, which is attracting great attention. He himself employs one of these legs & walks well with it.

Valuable improved property for sale: on Jun 8, on the premises, fronting on the road leading from the toll-gate, on the Balt Turnpike, to the Anacostia Bridge, containing 65 acres, with a small frame house & out-bldgs. Terms liberal.
–John A Bartruff -R W Dyer, auct

SAT MAY 30, 1846
The undersigned have appointed Mr Jos Ingle their agent & atty to settle the estate of the late Griffith Coombe, dec'd, with full power & authority to rent property & to collect rents & claims now due or which may hereafter become due to said estate.
–Mary Coombe, Jas G Coombe, excs of the last will of G Coombe, dec'd. [For rent: the large 3 sotry brick house at present occupied by the family of the dec'd, & wharf & warehouse adjoining. –Jos Ingle, Agent, Capitol Hill]

Executors sale of household furniture, watches, diamonds, & other breastpins, at auction, on Jun 5, by order of the Orphans Court of Wash Co, D C: the personal estate of Fountain A Merrett, dec'd, at his late residence on Pa ave, between 4½ & 6th sts. –Chas S Wallach, exc -C W Boteler, jr, auctioneer

For sale: 2 story brick house occupied by Mr John Underwood, on the east side of N J ave, Capitol Hill. Apply to the subscriber, next door to the premises. –Jos Ingle

Election Notices-for Mayor, one member of the Board of Alderman, & 3 members of the Board of the Common Council, of Wash, to be held on Jun 1:
1st Ward: election in the room over the West Market: Saml Drury, Saml Duvall, W H Perkins, Com'rs of Elections.
2nd Ward: election at the ofc of Nicholas Callan, on F st: Wm Drake, Nicholas Callan, Jos Abbott, Com'rs of Elections.
3rd Ward: election at the house of Jos Miller, F & 9th st: Geo Crandell, Valentine Harbaugh, John Boyle, Com'rs of Elections.
4th Ward: election at City Hall: A Coyle, Fra B Lord, sr, G C Grammer, Com'rs of Elections.
5th Ward: election at the Engine House, on Capitol Hill: Wm J McCormick, John M Broadhead, T Van Reswick, Com'rs of Elections.
6th Ward: election at the police ofc of Jas Crandall: Noble Young, Wm M Ellis, Jas Crandall, Com'rs of Elections.
7th Ward: election at the house of John T Cassel, Md ave & 7th st: Wm Lloyd, Wm Wise, M M Fisher, Com'rs of Elections.

Isaac Corbitt has purchased all the right & interest of Abraham Corbitt in & to his Umbrella Establishment, on south side of Pa ave, near 4½ st. He will keep it well supplied.

Nat'l Fair-Wash: Mr C R Barry, of Balt, has sent some very good specimens of American Mosaic in marble. Mr W Dougherty, of Wash, executed a miniature Marble Cupid. Cotton window curtains, made by a 74 year old lady, & depostited by Mr J J Greenough, of Wash City. Mr Edw K Tryon, of Phil, has a fine display of good, consisting of Rifles, from $6 to $150; Mr John Krider, of Phil, has an extensive assortment of Rifle & Shot Guns, the former from $8 to $100, the latter from $4 to $200; Pistols of every description. Mr Thos Tyrer, of Richmond, has some very elegant Shot Guns & Rifles. Mr F W Widman, of Phil, had a variety of Swords. There is a splendid collection of Military Accoutrements from J T Ames, of Cabottsville, Mass.

Mrs Anne E Bronaugh, on 10th st, has several vacant rooms.

Senate: 1-Ptn from Rezin Tevis, asking an increase of pension. 2-Ptn from Thos P Winston, asking to be reimbursed the amount of a judgment obtained against him & paid into the Treasury. 3-Ptn from Geo Ramey, asking to be confirmed in his title to a tract of land. 4-Ptn from Elias Burnell & others, asking that certain duites paid by them on undressed hides may be refunded.

Shocco Springs, Warren Co, N C: the subscriber has purchased this desirable Watering Place, & will open his house for visiters on Jun 1. –Saml Calvert, proprietor

Md Volunteers: The Govn'r tendered the command of the 2 regts [Md's requisition] to Col C M Thruston, of Alleghany, & Maj Geo W Hughes, of Anne Arundel Co, as the colonels. The Annapolis Herald states that Maj Wm H Watson, of Balt, & Capt Wm H Emory, of Queen Anne's Co, have been offered commissions as lt cols, & Capt John Pickett, of Balt, & Capt Wm B Clarke, of Hagerstown, commissions as majors. It is understood that Capt Pickell declines the appointment.
–Balt American [See Oct 16th newspaper.]

Died: yesterday, in Wash City, Cmdor Jas Renshaw, U S Navy, aged 62 years. His funeral will take place from his late residence, 19th & F sts, this afternoon at half past 4 o'clock. P S-The ofcrs of the Navy are requested to appear in undress uniform, with epaulets & caps.

Died: on May 27, at Alexandria, in his 76th year, Rev Isaac Robbins, of that town.

Died: on May 27, at his residence, in Alexandria, after a long & painful illness, Kinsey Griffith, sr, aged 60 years.

Miss R F Colton informs the ladies & gentlemen of Wash, that her Cotillon party takes place at Odd Fellows' Hall, 7th st, on Jun 2. Tickets may be had at the Nat'l Hotel, Brown's Indian Queen Hotel, & at the door.

The subscribers have on hand & manufacture to order Geo C Kellogg's Patent Ratchet Feeder & Shell Wood Pickers, hundreds of which are in operation & give perfect satisfaction. –E Kellogg & Co, New Hartford, Conn.
–E Kellogg, G C Kellogg

MON JUN 1, 1846
Nat'l Fair-Wash. Painting of a Newfoundland dog, belonging to Mr Hudson Taylor, of Wash City, was painted by the talented neighbor Mr W McLeod. There were beautiful landscapes by Mr J D Lee, & one by Mr Osgood Muzzy, both residents of Wash City. Mr Edw Stabler, of Harewood, Montg Co, Md, exhibits an improved cast-steel Screw Seal press: the impressions made on dry paper are minutely beautiful Dr Page, of Wash, has a beautiful model of his Magnetic Electric Machine. A fine Achromatic Telescope constructed by H Fritz, of N Y, is on display. Messrs J D Edwards & Co, of Elizabethtown, N J, exhibit very great varieties of Oilcloth for floors & for furniture. Fine specimens of room paper from W S Birch, of Balt. From the manufactory of Jacob Tree, of Balt, were Transparent Window Shades, deposited by L C Ducheane, of Phil. Watches & clocks from the manufactory of C Prenot, of Phil. Bookbinding, stationery, by U Hunt & Son, of Phil. Wrapping paper from cornstalks by G W Matthews, Carroll Co, Md. Marble Papers from T C Konigmacher, Phil. Mr F Lucas, jr, of Balt: illustrated Books very finely bound, from his Balt foundry. Also Types from the foundry of Alex Robb, Phil. Steel Pens from Jas French, Boston; Silver Pens & Pencil Cases from E Deacon, N Y. W Fischer, our neighbor, deposited superior American Stationery. Messrs J B Lippincott & Co, of Phil, have some splendid specimens of Bookbinding. Mr Jas Ackerman, of N Y, deposited many specimens of Lithography & Coloring. We omitted to notice a case of very superior hats from Robt Bacon & Sons, Boston.

City Ordinances-Wash: Act for the relief of Wm Wallis: that the sum of $106.69 be appropriated to be paid to Wallis, late police ofcr of the 3rd Ward, being the balance found to be due to him on settlement of his accounts in the Register's ofc.

Genteel furniture at auction on Jun 2, at the residence of Mr Jos Mountz, on Montgomer st, near Gay. –E S Wright, auctioneer

Orphans Court of Wash Co, D C. Letters of administration de bonis non on the personal estate of Fred'k Reitz, late of said county, dec'd.
–A H Lawrence, Adm de bonis non

An extensive saw-mill in the Western County, the property of Danl D Page, situated at Monk's Mound, about 8 miles from St Louis, in St Clair Co, Ill, was totally destroyed by fire on the 18th ult. How it originated no one knows. –St Louis Era

Mrd: on May 25, by Rev F S Evans, Mr Thos S Dorrell to Miss Mary Ann Daley.

Mrd: on May 28, by Rev Mr Van Horseigh, Mr John Sessford, jr, to Miss Mary A Lagree.

Mrd: on May 27, in Norfolk, Va, by Rev Upton Beall, John Randall Hagner, of Wash City, to Louisa, d/o Maj Chas H Smith, of the U S Army.

Mrd: on May 31, by Rev J P Donelan, Danl Convers Goddard, of Zanesville, Ohio, to Madeline S, only d/o the Hon Saml F Vinton, of Ohio.

Mrd: on May 26, by Rev Mr Hendrickson, Mr Geo W Goodall to Miss Roseanna Rigdon, all of Wash City.

Died: on Sun, in Wash City, Mary Ann, d/o Peter & Catherine McGuiness, in her 9th year. Her funeral is from 4½ st, near the Arsenal, this afternoon, at 5 o'clock.

Letters remaining in the Post Ofc, Wash, Jun 1, 1846.

Arth, Philip	Bragg, J C	Barton, D W
Ashard, W K-3	Beall, Miss H R	Bidault, L H
Anderson, J A-2	Boyd, Rev Geo	Bledsoe, A T
Arnot, A	Black, Col Wm-2	Billings, Geo W
Anderson, Jos R	Brooke, Edmund	Browning, Theo
Anbanal, Mr R	Brooks, Homer	Butler, H H
Allen, Chas T	Blair, J	Baldwin, Wm A
Allison, Saml P	Beers, Peter	Bentley, Chas W
Anderson, Alex	Bell, Miss Amanda	Butler, Dr John S
Allston, Jas T	Brent, Wm L	Biss, Letha
Albro, jr, Jas	Birch, Douglas	Battle, Miss Sally
Anderson, Miss L	Burt, J C	Brenner, D
Andrews, R R	Ball, Henry	Baley, John
Anderson, John P	Brown, D	Ballard, Com
Arnold, John W	Brown, Wm	Bolton, Com W C-2
Andre, Nicolaus	Brown, Miss Mary	Butler, Geo
Adams, Julius W	Brown, John-2	Bowen, Geo
Arnold, J W	Bell, J F	Bernard, C H
Allen, S S	Burgess, Wash'n	Berry, jr, John E
Armstrong, Capt W-5	Badger, L V	Baltimore, Mrs A
Anderson, Mrs M	Bowen, Theo L	Bronson, Simeon D
Allemong, Miss M E	Baker, Clinton	Benjamin, Jas
Bates, John	Bowling, Geo L	Baldwin, Moses H
Biggs, Mrs M E	Bowling, Henry	Butler, Chas
Buck, Wm M	Burgevin, Mrs Julia	Blanchard, John
Barnes, Henry	Brenneman, Aug	Bennett, Jas H-2
Beall, Geo T	Bagby, R R	Brown, Miss Sarah-2
Brown, A H	Butler, Mrs Martha	Cram, Jonathan
Beall, Miss Ann E	Brinley, Horace	Clark, John C

Clow, Danl-2
Chubb, Jonathan L
Claude, Wm Tell
Camp, Lt John D
Crane, A Judson
Cooke, Miss Eliza
Chase, Oliver R
Cole, Christopher
Clack, Franklin H
Coones, Duncan
Clark, Henry M
Choate, Mrs A C
Carr, Lt A L, U S N
Carter, F
Cassidy, Mrs Henry
Chambers, Rev J
Campbell, Rev L
Creamer, Mrs Ann
Cary, T F
Chapman, Basil-2
Collins, Mrs A
Campbell, C M
Chancey, W
Churchill, Col
Capron, Horace
Clinton, Geo W-3
Cooper, Mark A
Campbell, Wm W
Cooper, Loyd N
Colder, John
Cooper, Mrs Mary
Carroll, Jane
Carter, Mrs Mary J
Chatfield, Andrew G
Colvocoresses, Lt G M
Connell, Mary A
Caton, John
Carmichael, Danl
Cunningham, H D-2
Cushman, C C-2
Coburn, Capt J L
Cushing, Caleb-3
Croghan, Col Geo-7
Chappell, Miss Amy

Cunningham, Gen W-2
Carter, Mrs M [col]
Durr, M
Deerz, H
Digges, Danl C
Delaney, Miss B J
Dorsey, Alfred
Denham, Mrs C
Davis, W M
Dewitt, Thos H
Dippel, Mr
Delany, Caleb
Duncan, Alex
Davidson, Wm S-3
Dudley, P
Daniel, Mrs Eliza
Derring, Wm S-2
Duvall, John P-2
Davis, Harriet
Dixon, Mrs Mary
Dailey, Mary Ann
Dawson, Aaron
Deshla, David
Douglass, Jas C, U S N
Devereux, Miss
Davis, S
Downing, Mrs Jos
Davis, Miss Emma
Duffield, Nathan K
Dozier, Mrs C
Derby, Dr Geo
Donaldson, Miss C
Eyre, Miss Sarah
Edmonston, E D
Edwards, Gov J C-7
Evans, Mrs A M-2
Ellsworth, Mrs M
Eckert, Mrs R H
Ellsworth, E L
English, H
Eddy, David R-2
Ellery, Wm
Easton, Mrs S A
France, Mrs M
Fitz, Albert-2

Forbes, R B
Fobes, Alpheus-2
Floyd, John G-3
Farnham, Dr J W
Finteneau, B G
Ferris, Jonathan
Fisher, Ebenezer-2
Fortune, Thos L
Fischer, Geo I
Fenwick, Mrs Sarah
Fruturmuth, N
Franklin, Wm B
Ferguson, Robt
Farrar, Edmund W
Flowers, R K
Fitzgerald, Jas H
Fitzgerald, Wm F
Fetter, Edwin T
Fulton, Geo W
Falconer, J G
Green, Maj Nat T
Grant, Gen R H-3
Galt, Dr John M-2
Graine, Robt
Griffin, Danl
Gridley, Rev W
Graeve, Madame
Gray, A J
Gray, Henrietta
Green, Miss Eliz
Gray, Julius C
Greer, Thos
Gray, Mrs Sarah
Gwynn, Maj W
Glynn, Com Jas-4
Giddings, C M-2
Gooding, Wm
Goddard, Jas
Galligan, Thos
Giddings, Saml S
Gravatt, Miss C W
Gillis, Lt John P
Gallaher, Col David
Gartrell, Lucius J
Grantun, F F

Garner, Caroline	Hodgkinson, Miss M	Lamb, Mr
Gastin, Nelson	Hamilton, Gen J-7	Lynch, Lt Wm F
Gahan, Wm	Harrison, Maria L or	Long, Col S H
Gahan, Mrs M	Beech, Silas	Little, Warren
Gardiner, Capt W H-3	Howard, Capt	Lockrey, Edw
Hough, A J	Howard, Col Geo T	Lugenbeel, Dr J W
Hatch, Wm S	Harrington, I	Louis, Wm
Haas, David	Hinton, Robt W	Leddon, Mrs C
Hall, Edw-2	Humphries, Mrs J S	Lindsey, A J
How, jr, S G	Irvin, Gen Jas-2	Loyall, Geo
Haines, B T-2	Jones, Gen G W-4	Lively, Robt A
Hatch, Julius	Jones, Mrs Com	Lowney, N M
Hall, Horace B	James, Wm	Leighton, Miss J
Ham, Albert	Jenks, M H-2	Lockhart, John
Haight, Silas-2	Jones, Caleb	Locker, Miss R
Hay, Alex'r	Jones, S L	Lohmeyer, Henry
Helm, Thos-3	Jefferson, P-2	Leavitt, Mr
Hass, Mr De	Johnson, Miss E	Livingston, Chas
Harilson, Miss C	Jackson, Mary A	Lewis, Theodore-2
Hammack, W	Jarvis & Brown	Moore, Mrs Cerusia
Harlan, S	Johnson, Wm-2	Marks, Michl
Harrington, C B	Jasper, Wm	Mars, Wm
Holtzman, A J	Johnson, Col W R-2	Moran, Jas D
Houston, Dr D H	Judlin, A F	Mause, Isaac R-2
Harris, J G	Jackson, Miss M J	Meyer, C
Hassard, Thos	Johnson, E P	Murst, Mrs C D-3
Howard, Luther	Johson, Mr	Mitchell, Wm S
Herbert, Chas O	Jenkins, N P	Matthews, Miss R
Humphries, H B-2	King, Wm	Murphy, Wm
Hastings, John	Kirk, J W	Marquis, Wm H-2
Hoover, W P	Knox, Dr John R	Morehead, Wm G
Hollingsworth, J McH	King, Wm M	Miller, Dr F H
Hipkins, John	Kendall, Geo A	Myers, W H
Hillips, Geo	Kirkbridge, T S	Mason, Miss L R
Heywood, Nathan	Kelly, A B	Murray, Col Jas B
Hedrick, Mrs B	Kimball, John H	Munday, Geo H
Hutchins, Mrs M	Keabel, Jacob	Mitchell, H T
Hayden, Mrs M I	Kingston, Capt S B	Murdock, Mrs J H
Hoogland, Edw	Lee, Miss Emily J	Murdock, Jas H
Handy, Thos R	Lee, Kitty	Martin, John P
Harris, Mrs Kitty	Long, Mrs Aurelia	Morton, A B
Harvey, Gen T W	Lang, Benj-3	Myers, Capt Danl
Hardey, Rich B	Lyne, Mrs H A	Miller, Wm
Hunter, Milburn	Lee, Col Robt M	Marshall, Wm L
Harlse, Mrs W	Lann, L C	

Morgan, H	Newby, J W P	Redfield, Heman J
Maloy, Thos	Nelson, Miss M	Richardson, T A
Matthewson, Geo	Neville, John-2	Simms, Wm
Murphy, F G	Noland, Philip	Shiver, Lt A E
Miller, Mrs Mary	Nichols, Capt C D	Scott, Mrs Eliz
Mitchell, Jos	Niven, T M	Smith, Maj Chas H
Mason, Col R B	O'Brine, Mrs M E	Smith, Thos H-2
Morgan, Chris'r	Orphean, Chas-6	Smith, Jos L
Mason, Lewis E	Olcott, Danl	Shaw, Richd
Montgomery, Sarah	Poor, John M	Sprague, Capt J T
Maxwell, David	Price, Geo W	Smith, F O J
Morsel, Richd T	Phelps, Oliver	Schenck, Peter H
Mitchell, Gen John	Price, Miss C	Shanks, Miss V
Matchett, Rev Wm	Prindle, P A	Simms, Jos
Mixter, Geo	Perry, Hugh	Smith, S Wads'f
Montgomery, Miss C	Parker, Francis A	Smeed, A-2
Murphy, Mrs M A E	Pickett, Jas C	Springs, Alex'r
Murray, Miss Anna	Parsons, Maj J-2	Smith, Jas F
McGee, Jas	Perkins, Nicholas	Smith, Mrs Sarah
McNeill, Mrs S W	Parker, Thos	Smith, B E
McNeill, Col B P-3	Parsons, S E	Shaw, Sidney
McGroger, jr, Jas	Parrish, Col	Starr, Wm H
McKelden, D W	Parker, Leonard M	Smith, John T-3
McPherson, J W	Peekham, Mrs S W-3	Smock, John
Magarry, P	Reed, Miss Emma	Schouler, John
McCarty, Eugene	Ruse, Wm M	Sinit, Jas
McCrery, Dr	Rowe, jr, Spencer	Stinger, Mrs
MacIntyre, Rev T	Russ, Mrs Rebecca	Spencer, Chas A
McAlister, Benj	Ross, Chas	Stevens, Miss C
McFarlan, Jacob	Richards, Thos S	Swigert, Jos
McCann, Miss M	Ratcliffe, J A	Schuyler, P J
McElvin, Abraham	Rowand, Dr	Sinclair, John
McChritie, Capt J	Ringgold, Mrs H	Stewart, W W
McCutcheon, Jos	Richardson, Miss S	Swelvant, Michl
McChesney, Chas G	Robinson, Mrs E M	Shelby, A B
McCormick, Miss M	Rogers, p'd mid H	Stuart, Smith
McHenry, John H	Raymond & Co	St Clair, Gen
McDonnell, Mrs M C	Riddle, Crawford	Stedman, Dr C H-2
McAfee, Gen R B-2	Rightstine, Mrs C	Sibrey, Wm
Magruder, Capt G A	Riley, Patrick	Saltmarsh, D A-2
McCleary, Dr J F J	Robinson, Miss S	Shirving, Chas E
McConaughy, Rev D	Remington, John R-2	St John, J R
Noyes, Crosby S	Russell, J G T	Schroeder, Friede
Neutze, Johann	Rowand, Stepen R	Shuster, John
Niven, Catp J-2	Robinson, Mr	Smallwood, R T

Stanford, D R	Thompson, Wm	Woolford, Capt J
Seely, Mrs Sarah A	Topliff, Benj	Warner, Edw M
Siegmund, Fred'k	Taylor, Arthur-2	Whiting, Lt Col H
Sever, Rev E F	Thompson, Jas A	Williamson, John
Standish, Aug M	Thomas, Mrs Eliza	Weatherbee, E D
Sawyer, Warren	Thompson, Miss A E	Walker, Geo
Sewell, John	Terrill, Mrs Eliza	Warren, Henry
Smallwood, Danl	Tattnall, Capt Josiah	Williams, Geo W
Sweeny, Mrs A	Tallmadge, Gen N P	Walton, Robt N
Sexton, Miss J E-2	Vandusen, Chas H	Walker, Jas
Suggett, Wm-2	Viaton, Miss M	Wilson, J of Dayton
Saunders, R M-2	Van Reswick, J	Willard, Wm H
Schemerhorn, Rev J	Webb, Philip D	Williams, Saml M
Thorpe, C J R	White, Miss Martha	Williams, Chas K
Towne, E C	Ward, Wm	Washington, Geo
Thorn, John-3	Wells, Miss Mary	Webster, Capt J A
Tremayne, Edw	Wright,	Wilson, W C & others
Thomas, Capt J A	miss Julia	Wilburn, Mrs J
Thomas & Dyer	Wood, Mrs A	Woodward, Dr C
Tappan, Benj	Wood, Geo	Wilson, Rev J W
Toler, Danl J	Wells, John	Watson, Miss M R
Talcott, Henry A	Wood, Mrs C B	Webster, Ira
Tillman, John	Webb, Jas	Wheeler, Stephen H
Thompson, W F	Webb, Maj	Williams, Wm
Thomas, Jas	Weart, John A	Williams, Mrs M W
Thompson, Jas A	Ware, Miss A B	White, Mrs Sarah M
Thomas, David	White, C W	Young, John
Tiffany, O C	White, Geo W	Young, Mrs A J-2
Thomas, Benj B	Wright, John S	
Taylor, Miss C A	Wright, Geo	

The inland postage on all letters intended to go by ship must be paid, otherwise they remain in this ofc. -C K Gardiner, P M

Urbeling de Alvear, a student of Gtwn College, & s/o the Buenos Ayroan Minister near Washington, was drowned in the Potomac, near the Foundry, on Thu. In company with fellow-students, he was bathing in the river, under the supervision of a Professor, when he swam some distance, & it is supposed, was seized with a cramp. The body was recovered in the evening. –Advocate
+

Students of Gtwn College: meeting on the death of Urbeling de Alvear, who died on May 28, in his 18th year. Mr P Landry in the chair; Messrs Doyle, Clark, Longstreth, Andrews, Smith, & Allemong cmte. Crape to be worn for 30 days.
–Proper R Landry, Chrmn -L T Brien, Sec

Appointments by the Pres, by & with the advice & consent of the Senate:
Marcus Morton, Collector of the Customs for the district of Boston & Charlestown, in Mass, vice Lemuel Williams, removed.
Lewis Washington, Capt of the U S Navy, to be Chief of Bureau of Ordnance & Hydrography, vice Capt Crane, dec'd.
Jos Smith, Capt of the U S Navy, to be Chief of Bureau of Navy Yards & Docks, vice Lewis Warrington, transferred.
John C Watrous, to be Judge of the District Court of the U S for the district of Texas.
Geo W Brown, to be Atty for the district of Texas.
John M Allen, to be Marshal of the U S for the district of Texas.
Gershom J Van Brunt, now a Lt, to be Cmder in the Navy, to fill a vacancy occasioned by the death of Cmder Richd A Jones.
Peter W Murphy & John B Randolph, now Passed Midshipmen, to be Lts in the Navy, to fill vacancies occasioned by the death of Lt John C Henry & the promotion of Lt Gershom J Van Brunt.

L W Bickley & J W Tyson, under the firm of Hickley & Tyson, opened their ofc on F st, for the transaction of a Genr'l Exchange business. L W Bickley will transact business at his ofc, 110 Walnut st, Phil.

Orphans Court of Wash Co, D C. In the matter of the real estate of Lewis G Davidson. Saml G Davidson, Trustee, reported he sold lot 15 in square 126, in Wash City, to Lindsey Muse for $390.24. –Nathl Pope Causin -Ed N Roach, Reg/o wills

TUE JUN 2, 1846
House of Reps: David S Kauffman appeared as one of the Reps of the newly admitted State of Texas: the oath was administered by the Speaker, & he took his seat as a member of the House of Reps of the U S.

Senate: 1-Ptn from Abigail Edgerly, wid/o a Revolutionary soldier, praying that a pension may be granted her. 2-Ptn from Meigs D Benjamin, asking the payment of duties alleged to have been illegally exacted by the Collector of N Y. 3-Ptn from Dudley Walker, purser in the navy, asking to be allowed commission on certain disbursements, & for clerk-hire & other expense incurred in the public service. 4-Cmte on Public Lands: bill granting the right of pre-emption to Philip F Deering & Robt H Champion, of Iowa Co, Wisconsin Territory, with a report. 5-Cmte on Pensions: adverse report on the ptn of Smith Cram. Same cmte: asking to be discharged from further consideration of the ptn of David Curry.

Sale of excellent household furniture at auction on Jun 4, at the late residence of Wm P Zantzinger, on La ave, opposite City Hall, the entire household furniture.
–C W Boteler, jr, auctioneer

Died: on May 31, Miss Laura Cheshire. Her funeral will take place from the residence of her mother, on 6th st, Tue, at 10 o'clock.

WED JUN 3, 1846
Nat'l Fair-Wash. Mr Saml Lichtenthoeler, of Litiz, Pa, invented an apparatus for boltin & unbolting outside window shutters, without raising the sash. Mr Winslow, of Ohio, invented a machine for Cutting Laths. Mr P Coad, of Phil, exhibited a model of his Patent Graduated Galvanic Battery, adapted for medical purposes. Mr F H Opiphant, of Uniontown, Pa, sent a cabinet of Iron & its Manufactures, made at his establishment, the Fair Chance Iron Works," near Uniontown. Beautiful assortment of Locks & Knobs, exhibited by E Robinson, of Boston. Chemical products were sent from the chemical works of Saml & Philip T Ellicott, of Balt.

Returns for the Wash City Councils:
1st Ward: for Alderman: Wm B Magruder, 126; T P Morgan, 22.
For Common Council: Chas A Davis, 104; Wm Wilson, 95; Wm Easby, 86; Saml Stott, 66; G W Harkness, 61; scattering, 12.
2nd Ward: for Alderman: Wm Orme, 108; Robt Farnham, 89.
For Common Council: Lewis Johnson, 158; Saml D King, 163; Jas F Haliday, 133; Nicholas Callan, 89; J E Dow, 38; scattering, 6.
3rd Ward: for Alderman: John T Towers, 176; Stephen P Franklin, 138; Jos Bryan, 82; John Boyle, 10.
For Common Council: Jos Borrows, 139; Jas W Moorhead, 134; Silas H Hill, 132; C P Wannall, 108; J T Walker, 97; scattering, 4.
4th Ward: for Alderman: Walter Lenox, 305; scattering, 8.
For Common Council: Richd Wallach, 214; Saml Bacon, 203; Saml Burche, 179; Francis Mohun, 112; S S Coleman, 89; Aug E Perry, 54; Michl Larner, 28; scattering, 9.
5th Ward: for Alderman: Jos W Beck, 116; Jas Adams, 79; for the 2 years' term. John C Fitzpatrick, 115; Nathl Brady, 86; for the unexpired term of 1 year.
For Common Council: Peter Brady, 122; Richd Dement, 119; Aaron W Miller, 93; John Johnson, 90; John Kedglie, 46; John L Maddox, 45; John P White, 17; Z Hazel, 10; scattering, 8.
6th Ward: for Alderman: Thos Thornley, 191; scattering, 4.
For Common Council: Jas Cull, 137; Geo W Fulmer, 114; John R Queen, 95; Robt Clarke, 78; Jas Gordon, 66; scattering, 17.
7th Ward: for Aldermen: Saml Byington, 137; Ignatius Mudd, 126.
For Common Council: Wm Lloyd, 81; J W Jones, 77; John T Cassell, 56; John L Smith, 34; John Van Reswick, 31; Wm Wise, 27; Wm Bird, 27; John M Young, 18; scattering, 2.

Missouri-The St Louis Legion embarked for the seat of war on May 23. Its ofcrs are:
Alton R Easton, Col   Henry Almstedt, Adj
Ferdinand Kennett, Lt Col   Geo Johnson, Surgeon
Godfried Schoenthaler, Maj   Richd H Stevens, Assist Surgeon

I certify that John Bohlayer, of Wash Co, D C, brought before me as an estray, a black Cow. –Jas Crandell, J P [Owner to prove property, pay charges, & take her away. –John Bohlayer, Garrison, Navy Yard, Wash

The U S ship **Yorktown** has been absent from the U S 20 months, during which time she has not lost one of her crew by sickness or accident. List of the ofcrs of the **Yorktown**:
Chas H Bell, Cmder
Henry A Steele, Lt
Isaac N Morris, Acting Lt
John N Hambleton, Purser
Wm L Van Horn, Surgeon
Lewis J Williams, Assist Surgeon
Francis A Roe, Midshipman
Jos Lewis, Boatswain
Thos M Crocker, Gunner
Hugh Lindsay, Carpenter
The following ofcrs were passengers in the **Yorktown**; Thos C Eaton, Midshipman, & John Adams, Capt's Clerk, both from the ship **Marion**.

New Orleans Bulletin: wounded during the battles of May 8 & May 9:
Col McIntosh, 5th Infty, was pierced through the mouth with a bayonet, & shot in 3 places.
Col Pyne, Inspector Gen, shot in the hip.
Capt Page, 4th Infty, lower jaw, part of the tongue & upper teeth entirely shot away. He is suffering dreadfully.
Capt Hooe, 5th Infty, right arm shot off above the elbow.
Lt Gates, 8th Infty, right arm broken, & shot in the left hand.
Lt Jordan, 8th Infty, shot & bayoneted in several places.
Lt Luther, 2nd Artl, lower lip shot off.
It is expected that all the above will recover, but most of them will require great care.

In the U S Circuit Court for Pa on Sat a judgement for $14,250 & costs was entered in favor of Jas Stimpson, of Balt, against the city of Phil. Mr Stimpson is the inventor of a railroad curve which the corporation of Phil had laid down in its streets.

Mrd: on May 28, at the U S Hotel, by Rev W T Sprole, Philip H L Montague to Miss Mary Susan Coleman, all of Va.

Mrd: on May 21, in Wash City, by Rev Chas A Davis, Mr Washington Brunner, late of Circleville, Ohio, to Miss Frances C Cammack, of Wash City.

Mrd: at the residence of Hon Jonathan Robert, in Montg Co, Pa, John R Flagg, of Jefferson Co, Va, to Mrs Mary E Merritt, of the same county.
[No date–appears recent.]

Mrd: on May 18, at the residence of the Hon Jacob S Yost, in Pottstown, Pa, by Rev N S S Beaman, D D, Geo M Coffin, Merchant, to Miss Sarah A Harrington, all of Troy, N Y.

Died: on Mon last, at Winchester, Va, after a lingering illness of several years' duration, Mrs Caroline J Brent, w/o Henry M Brent, Cashier of the Bank of the Valley in Va, in her 39th years. Mrs Brent was for a number of years a member of the Old School Presbyterian Church. She has left a most affectionate & devoted husband, 3 children, & a large circle of friends to mourn their loss.

Senate: 1-Ptn from C M Hitchcock, exc of R S Hunter, asking remuneration for corn furnished the Cherokee Indians. 2-Ptn from Colby Bigs, wid/o a Revolutionary soldier, asking to be allowed a pension.

Adj Genrl's Ofc, Frankfort, Ky, May 26, 1846. Announcement to the citizens of Ky that the whole number of Volunteer assigned to be raised in this State by the Sec of War, as its quota of a requistion made on the several States, for raising a corps of 50,000 volunteers to serve for 12 months or during the war, is now full & complete, including the Louisvill Legion, which has embarked; the following Commandants of companies, with their subaltern ofcrs, having been commissioned, to wit:

1st Regt of Cavalry or Mounted Men:
1st Company, Capt Wm J Heady, of Jefferson
2nd Company, Capt A Pennington, of Jefferson
3rd Company, Capt Wm R McKee, of Fayette
4th Company, Capt Thos F Marshall, of Woodford
5th Company, Capt J C Stone, of Madison
6th Company, Capt J Price, of Garrard
7th Company, Capt G L Postlethwaite, of Fayette
8th Company, Capt J S Lillard, of Gallatin
9th Company, Capt John Shawhan, of Harrison
10th Company, Capt Ben C Milam, of Franklin

2nd Regt of Infty:
1st Company, Capt Wm H Maxey, of Green
2nd Company, Capt Franklin Chambers, of Franklin
3rd Company, Capt Phillip B Thompson, of Mercer
4th Company, Capt Speed S Fry, of Boyle
5th Company, Capt G W Cutter, of Kenton
6th Company, Capt Wm T Willis, of Jessamine
7th Company, Capt Wm Dougherty, of Lincoln
8th Company, Capt Wm M Joyner, of Kenton
9th Company, Capt Wilkerson Turpin, of Montgomery
10th Company, Capt Geo W Kavanaugh, of Anderson

For rent: that large brick bldg over the stores of Messrs Pittman & Phillips & Mr Perry, at the corner of 7th st west & market space, occupied now by Mrs Turpin as a boarding house. Inquire of the subscriber, residing in the house. –Anne R Dermott

THU JUN 4, 1846
Trustee's sale of a valuable stock of Staple & Fancy Dry Goods: by virtue of a deed of trust to me, executed & delivered by Richd C Washington, bearing date of Mar 31, 1846: sale on Jun 22, at the store lately occupied by Richd C Washington, in Wash City. –J M Carlisle, Trustee

Liberal reward for a red cow & calf that left on Sun last, from F st, near 6th st. I presume the cow is trying to make her way to Va, across the chain bridge, as she was driven a few days since from Fauquier Co, Va.
–Saml T Ashby, of the firm of Perry & Ashby.

Signor de Noronha, a self-taught violinist from South America, but originally from Portugal, gives a concert in Wash City tonight.

Teacher wanted: an elderly lady to teach 2 scholars Music, French, & the ordinary branches of an English education. Address the subscriber, living in PG Co, Md, near Bladensburg post ofc. –Marsham Waring

FRI JUN 5, 1846
Sale of desirable property: by virtue of a deed of trust from Thornton A Doniphan, dated May 27, 1842, recorded among the land records of Wash Co: sale on May 25, on the premises: lots 6, 7, & 8, in square 436, with a very good 2 story frame house: on F st south, near 7th st & the steamboat landing. –Richd Wallach, trustee
-C W Boteler, jr, auctioneer

Orphans Court of Wash Co, D C. Letters of administration on the personal estate of Com Jas Renshaw, late of the U S Navy, dec'd. –R T Renshaw, adm

House of Reps: 1-Ptn of H L Horner & 120 others, citizens of Wood Co, Ohio, asking a pension for the wid/o the Rev Jos Badger, dec'd, a chaplain of the Revolutionary army.

The copartnership existing between Farquhar & Knoblock has this day been dissolved by mutual consent. -Thos C Farquhar, Fred'k L Knoblock. Settle accounts with Thos C Farquhar.

$100 reward for runaway negro Otho Hammon, 25 years of age. He has relations living in Wash & Gtwn. -Wm J Berry, living near Upper Marlboro, PG Co, Md.

Senate: 1-Ptn from Edw H Mills, asking to be allowed to change the registry of a vessel purchased at a marshal's sale in Phil. 2-Ptn from Wade Allen, asking to be allowed compensation for extra service on a certain mail route.

Information received at the Dept of State, from the Consul of the U S at London, of the death at that place, on May 9 last, of John White, a native of Wash, D C, who died at the boarding house provided for him.

For rent: a 3 story brick house, on 4½ st, between N & O sts, **Greenleaf's Point**, & commonly known as one of Wheat's Block. Inquire next door to: Mary Wheat.

For rent, that desirable residence, together with the furniture therein, on I st north, immediately west of Com Morris'-formerly the residence of Mrs Cmdor Stewart, & more recently of the Chevalier Hulseman, Charge d'Affaires from Austria. Apply to Richd Smith. The colored woman in the house will show the premises to any applicant.

Suicide. Dr Geo W Spalding, aged 22, committed suicide at Richmond, Va, on Sat, by taking prussic acid. No cause assigned.

The Volunteers: Wash, Jun 3, 1846. Companies from Balt & Wash City, now waiting orders at the U S Barracks, under command of the following named ofcrs:
1st Co Balt Volunteers: Jas E Stewart, Capt; B T Owen, 1st Lt; Saml Wilt, 2nd Lt.
2nd Co Balt Volunteers: Jas S Piper, Capt; M K Taylor, 1st Lt, L Dolan, 2nd Lt.
Chesapeake Riflemen: Jas Boyd, 1st Lt Commanding; Jas H Ruddock, 2nd Lt.
Wash Volunteers #1: John H Waters, Capt; Wm J Parham, 1st Lt; Eugene Boyle, 2nd Lt.
Wash City Riflemen: Robt Bronaugh, Capt; Phineas B Bell, 1st Lt; Wm O'Brien, 2nd Lt.

Mrd: on Thu, in Wash City, by Rev J P Donelan, Fred'k B Page, M D, to Miss Anne Fraziette Davis, d/o Gen John Davis.

Mrd: on Jun 2, in Wash, by Rev Dr J T Brooke, of Cincinnati, Geo H Pendleton, of that city, to Alice, y/d/o the late F S Key.

Mrd: on Jun 2, by Rev John C Smith, Mr Jas G Ellis, of Wash City, to Miss Susan Falkner, formerly of New Market, Fred'k Co, Md.

Mrd: on May 28, in St Paul's Church, Berlin, Worcester Co, Md, by Rev Wm Henry Rees, Allen Bowie Howard, of Balt, to Anna M, d/o the late Hon John S Spence, of the U S Senate.

Died: on Jun 4, of consumption, in her 58th year, Alice, w/o Jos Harris, Clerk in the Gen Post Ofc Dept. Her funeral is this morning, at 10 o'clock, from the dwlg of Mrs Galvin, on C, near 3rd st.

Died: on Jun 3, after a long & painful illness, Nelson, 4th s/o Julia Ann & Adam Gaddis, aged 10 years & 3 days. His funeral will take place this day at 3 o'clock, from the residence of his father, near the Navy Yard.

Teacher wanted to take charge of a few scholars in a private family: a single gentleman is desired: liberal salary & board. Address either or both of the subscribers, at *Oak Grove*, Westmoreland Co, Va.
–G W Lewis, Lawrence Washington

SAT JUN 6, 1846
Senate: 1-Ptn from Geo Catlin, asking Congress to purchase his collection of Indian portraits & curiosities. 2-Cmte of Claims: bill for the relief of John R Williams, recommending its passage. 3-Cmte on Naval Affairs: asking to be discharged from the further consideration of the ptn of Saml R Read, & that it be referred to the Cmte on Pensions. 4-Cmte on Post Ofc & Post Roads: joint resolution from the House of Reps for the relief of Seth M Leavenworth, without amendment.

In Chancery: Jas Dundass et al, vs French Forrest et al. By order of the Circuit Court of Wash Co, D C, I am to state an account of the Trustees in the above cause, & of the creditors & reps of the late Jos Forrest, with the trust fund, & also of his personal estate. The accounts will be stated on Jun 18th, in my ofc in Gtwn, at 10 o'clock.
–W Redin, Special Auditor

Lost or strayed from me, a short haired black dog. Liberal reward for his return to Dr Washington, 6th st. -Z Collins Lee

Norfolk Beacon: A person calling himself Edw B Sullivan killed himself in that city on Tue, while in a fit of delirium. It is stated that he belonged to Washington, & that his real name is believed to be Edw B Lewis.

House of Reps: 1-Following bills were ordered to be reported with a recommendation that they pass:
relief of -

Sellers & Pennock	Lewis Hastings
Abraham Hoorback	Richd Hargrave Lee
Danl H Warren	Wm B Lang
Peter Rife	John F Richards
Geo Roush	Lewis Laing-pension
Patrick Kelly, sen	Wm Gump-pension
Wm B Ligon	Wm Pooler-pension
Ebenezer Conant	Gideon A Perry-pension
Capt John Patten	Mgt Gwynnup-pension
Solomon Russell	Leah Gray-pension
Jas Gee	Abraham Ausmen-pension
John McAlister	Griffin Kelly-pension

Benj Allen-pension
Jonathan Brown-pension
Patrick Masterson-pension
Eliz Betts, of N Y-pension
Mary Segar, of N Y-pension
Catharine Fulton, of Pa-pension
Polly Damron, of Ga-pension
John Campbell, of Maine-pension
Jos Dusseau-pension
Suranus Cobb-pension
Justin Jacobs-pension
Danl Pratt-pension
Mary Phelps, of Genesee, N Y-pension
Mary Campbell, wid/of John-pension
Wm Moss-grant of land
Jas Journey-land claim
Jose Carxillo-land claim
Reps of Geo Duvall, Cherokee Indian
Legal reps of Thos Murray, jr
Heirs & reps of Thos Kelly
Heirs & reps of Cyrus Turner
Gad Humphreys & Geo Centre
Eli Merrill [land claim]
Owners of the ship **Herald**, of Balt
Refund duties to David Thomas, of Phil
Adm of John Cox, dec'd, late of the Navy
Grant of land to the heirs & reps of John Ruddle
Jos Curwen, surviving partner of Willing & Curwen

Pay to John Carr, John Batty, & S Stevenson, seamen on board the whale ship **Margaret**, for their attendance at court as witnesses on behalf of the U S 2-Cmte of the Whole: recommendation they do not pass: pension to Wm Beard; relief of John B Donton & Curtis Humphreys, mail contractors. 3-Bill granting a pension to Maj Jas P H Porter came up in the regular order, it was stated that Maj Porter had died since the bill had been reported by the Cmte of the Invalid Pensions. It was then ordered to be reported to the House of Reps: to be there disposed of. 4-Bill for the relief of Capt John B Crozier's company of mounted Tennessee volunteers came up, with a view of recommitting it to the Cmte on Military Affairs.

Eben H Clark, late postmaster at Cherry Ridge, Wayne Co, Pa, has been sentenced to 10 years imprisonment for embezzling some $100 from a letter. It was done under an unhappy influence, & the crime confessed immediately.

Three of the volunteer companies from Osage, Cole, & Cooper Counties left St Louis on May 26 for their homes. They were sadly disappointed in not being received & marched into the service of the U S. Four other companies, which were not wanted, had made arrangements to return home the following day. In many Western States, we observe, that the difficulty is not in obtaining the number of volunteers required, but in choosing from the abundances offered.

MON JUN 8, 1846
Mrd: on Jun 2, by Rev D P McLean, Amzi C McLean, late of Ross Co, Ohio, to Margaretta, d/o John Hull, of Freehold, N J.

Died: on Jun 6, suddenly, at her residence in Wash City, Mrs Maria E Morgan, formerly of St Mary's Co, Md, in her 53rd year. Her funeral is today at 4 o'clock, at her late residence, Missouri ave & 4½ st.

Lt Chadbourne, who was among the ofcrs slain in our late encounter with the Mexicans, was a descendant of the gallant Genr'l Lincoln, of the army of the Revolution.

A father murdered by is son: in Windham, Greene Co, N Y, on Wed last, being no less than the shooting of the father, John Hitchcock, by his son. The family are given to drink a good deal. The son, who is a married man lives in the same house. The son made no effort to escape.

House of Reps: 1-Bill granting a pension due to Dorothy Terrill, dec'd: passed over informally for the present. 2-Bill granting a pension to John Porter, who had been injured in the revenue marine service-a service which Mr Hungerford believed was not recognized by the pension laws, & if this bill passed it would be creating a new class of pensioners. Bill was rejected. 3-Bill granting arrears of pension to Isaiah Parker was passed in the affirmative. 4-Bill to pay Sanl D Enochs for a mare, which ran off while in the public service many years ago, & has never been heard of, was read the third time. [Much merriment on the reading of the bill.] Passed in the affirmative. 5-Ptn of Frederic Durrive, praying to be confirmed in the purchase of a tract of land. 6-Bill to pay the heirs of Dr John Gray, late of the State of Md, dec'd, for property destroyed by the British forces in the war of 1812, came up, & passed in the affirmative. 7-Bill for the relief of the legal reps of Capt Wm Smallwood Tillard: passed in the affirmative. 8-Bill to release John Stockton, late a lt in the U S army, from a judgment, with the costs thereon, recovered against him by the U S: bill passed.

Orphans Court of Wash Co, D C. Letters of administration with the will annexed on the personal estate of Lewis Saunders, late of said county, dec'd.
–R B Nalley, adm with the will annexed.

N Y Courier & Enquirer: John C Thomas, a graduate of the Military academy, who resigned his commission of captain in the army last winter, & who for 3 years past has been the very efficient Commandant of the Corps of Cadets at West Point; Geo R P Bowman, a graduate of the Military Academy, late of the army; & Geo Webb Morrell, also a graduate of the Military Academy, & who graduated at the head of his class, late of the Corps of Engineers, have, by the advice of the authorities at Washington, & under their sanction, determined to raise forthwith a regt of volunteers in N Y C, of which they will constitute the Field ofcrs.

Rooms for rent: I am authorized to offer the spacious rooms in Mr Geo C Grammer's house, nearly opposite the hotel of the Messrs Brown, & immediately over the boot & shoe store of Mr T M Brashears. Occupying one of the rooms as an ofc, I will wait upon applicants. –P Gould

For rent: 2 story brick dwlg-house on the west side of 9th st, south of I st north. Apply for key at Haslup & Weeden's Coach Factory, near the premises.

Senate: 1-Ptn from Jesse Haven, asking to be allowed arrears of pension. 2-Cmte of Claims: unfavorable report on the claim of Wm B Foster, accompanied by a report.

House of Reps: 1-Bill to pay the heirs of Dr John Gray, late of the State of Md, dec'd, for property destroyed by the British forces in the war of 1812, came up, & passed in the affirmative.

Corpse preserver: I have purchased the right, for Wash City & County, of using Frederick & Trump's Patent Corpse Preserver, by the use of which corpses can be preserved for any length of time, & be transported to any part of the country. He is prepared for orders in his line of business, at his shop on D st, between 9th & 10th sts. —Jas K Plant N B-shrouds furnished at the shortest notice.

TUE JUN 9, 1946
Lands in Hardy Co, Va, for sale: at Public sale, under a decree of the Circuit Superior Court of Law & Chancery for the county of Hardy, Va, pronounced on Sep 22, 1844, in the case of Norman Bruce, cmplnt, against the Potomac & Alleghany Coal & Iron Manufacturing Co, dfndnts: sale in Moorefield, Hardy Co, on Aug 3: the following tracts of land on the Alleghany Mountain, in Hardy Co, Va:
400 acres on the east side of Stony river
413 acres on Elk run
400 acres southwest side of Elk run
400 acres near ***Welton Glade***
409 acres on Difficult creek
408 acres on Difficult creek
394 acres known as ***Slate Cabin Tract***
290 acres known as Slate Cabin Tract
2005+ acres near ***Big Elk Lick***, of F & W Deakin's lands
1001+ acres known as the ***Buffalo Tract***, whereon Spencer Hendrickson now resides
140 acres known as ***Benj Ray Tract***
400 acres, 340 acres, & 1000 acs: out of these 3 tracts 200 acres is excepted, being sold to Wm Shillingburg. Said 3 tracts are on Jonny Cake creek, & near the turnpike road.
1000 acs-103 acres excepted, sold to Alex'r Smith, by deed, Feb 3, 1817.
240 acres, 660 acres, 740 acres, 360 acres, 695 acs: the said last 6 tracts were land conveyed by F & W Deakins to John Templeman, by said Templeman to Bruce, & by Bruce to the dfndnts in this decree.
Inquire of Wm Seymour, atty for the plntf, or to Jos McNemar, my deputy, Moorefield, who are authorized to give information in relation to the above lands. —Job Welton, Sheriff of Hardy Co, Va

For rent: large brick warehouse on Water st, Gtwn, recently & for many years occupied by the late Jos Smoot, dec'd. Apply to Mrs Julia Anna Smoot, opposite Harman & Gordon's Brewery, Wash, or to Henry B Blagrove, Water st, Gtwn.

Geo Niles, a Revolutionary soldier, recently died at Shaftsbury, Vt, at the age of 105 years.

Carriage & horse for sale. Inquire of R B Nalley, at D Clagett & Co.

House of Reps: 1-Memorial of Geo Catlin, now in Paris, setting forth that his extensive & unique collection of Indian portraits, customs, costumes, & weapons, which cost him the exertions of 8 years of his life, & an expenditure of more than $20,000, is now in Paris, & has for more than 2 months occupied a large gallery in the Louvre for the private views of the Royal family & guests. The collection contains nearly 600 paintings, of 48 different tribes. The memorial proposes the sale of the entire collection to the U S Gov't for the sum of $65,000, the same sum proposed to the Cmte on Indian Affairs in 1837-38, when a favorable report was made.

Senate: 1-Additional documents relating to the ptn of the administrator of Jacob Houseman, dec'd: referred. 2-Ptn from Jas F Southron, asking remuneration for property destroyed during the late war. 3-Resolved: that the Pres be requested to communicate to the Senate the report of the expedition led by Lt Abert on the Upper Arkansas, & through the country of the Comanche Indians, in the fall of 1845.

WED JUN 10, 1846
Orphans Court of Wash Co, D C. Letters of administration on the personal estate of Jos A Sawyer, late of said county, dec'd. –Ann Lowry, Jas H Lowry, adms

Phil papers of Mon announce the death, on the day preceeding, by apoplexy, of the Hon Archibald Randall, of the District Court of the U S for the Pa District. He was in his 47th year.

The trial of Nutter, one of the menagerie men, for the alleged murder of Glove, one of the late students of the Univ of Va, has resulted in his acquittal.

Mrd: on Jun 2, by Rev Thos C Hayes, Mr Chas Bayne to Miss Mary Ellen, d/o Capt Thompson Ashby, all of Paris, Fauquier Co, Va.

Mrd: on Mon, by Rev John C Smith, Lt Wm J Parham [of Wash City Volunteers, Capt Waters,] to Miss Martha Rowen, all of Wash City.

Mrd: on Thu, Mr Robt Bowie, jr, of Nottingham district, PG Co, Md, to Miss Hettie D C, d/o the Hon John T Stoddert, of Chas Co, Md.

From Texas: The only news from the army was brought by the steamship **New York**, found in the Galveston papers, communicated by a vessel which arrived on Thu from Corpus Christi. She left Aransas Pass on the May 25, at which place the steamship **Sea** arrived from Point Isabel. On board the **Sea** were Mr McCleister, [supposed to have been killed in Capt Walker's scouting party,] Lt Humphreys, & Mr Rogers. McCleister was severely wounded & supposed by the Mexicans to be dead. He was found in the chaparral & taken to Matamoras, where he was well treated & recovered from his wounds. Rogers saw his father & brother butchered before him in a terrible manner before his turn came, & his own escape was owing to the fact that, while the wound upon his throat was not fatal, he had the presence of mind to feign himself dead, & was accordingly, with all the balance, thrown into the Colorado, where he managed to escape unseen & swam to the other side of the river. He made his way to Rio Grande, was taken prisoner, sent to the hospital in Matamoras, & after the battle exchanged.

Died: on May 20, at his residence near Charlotte Hall, St Mary's Co, Md, Chas Perrie, in his 34th year. He died after a painful & protracted sickness.

Died: on May 30, at Barancas, Florida, Mrs Sally Harwood, w/o Capt Francis Taylor, U S Army.

Died: on Jun 5, aged 2 weeks, Jas Robt, s/o Mary Alice & Robt Cranston.

An excursion up & down the most beautiful part of the Potomac can be made daily on board the mail steamboat **Powhatan**, Capt J W Rogers, an ofcr who is admirably fitted for the command of a fine steamboat. It passes by *Fort Washington* & Mount Vernon. –Alexandria Gaz

New Books! 1-The Argentine Republic, embracing its civil & military history, & its political condition before & during the administration of Govn'r Rosas, by Col J Anthony King, 24 years a resident of the country. The Life of Martin Luther, gathered from his own writings, by M Michelet. –Wm M Morrison, 2nd door west of 4½ st & Pa ave.

Mounted Riflemen, U S Army. Gen Orders, #18. Headquarters of the Army, Adj Gen Ofc, Wash, Jun 4, 1846. The Captains & Subalterns of the "Regt of Mounted Riflemen" have been assigned to companies, as follows:

Company A	Company C
Capt Wm J Loring	Capt Saml H Walker
1st Lt And J Lindsay	1st Lt Benj S Roberts
2nd Lt R Murray Morris	2nd Lt Geo McLane
Company B	Company D
Capt Winslow F Sanderson	Capt Henry C Pope
1st Lt Noah Newton	1st Lt Thos Ewell
2nd Lt Llewellen Raguet	2nd Lt Th Claiborne, jr

Company E
Capt Geo B Crittenden
1st Lt Llewellen Jones
1st Lt Spear S Tipton
2nd Lt Chas L Denman
Company F
Capt Stevens T Mason
1st Lt Andrew Porter
2nd Lt Thos G Rhett
Company G
Capt John S Simonson
1st Lt Wm W Taylor
2nd Lt F S K Russell

Company H
Capt Jacob B Backenstoss
1st Lt Thos Duncan
2nd Lt Thos Davis
Company I
Capt Bela M Hughes
1st Lt John G Walker
2nd Lt Julian May
Company K
Capt Stephen S Tucker
1st Lt M E Van Buren
2nd Lt Wash L Elliott

II-Major Geo S Burbridge will superintend the recruiting of the regt, to whom the Captains & Subalterns will report for instructions without delay, at Newport, Ky, where he will establish his headquarters for the present. Companies C & F will be raised in Pa, Md, Va, & Texas. The other companies will be recruited by their ofcrs in Tenn, Ky, Ohio, Indiana, Ill, & Mo, at such places as may best ensure success.

III-None but health, active, respectable men of the country, not under 19 nor over 35 years of age, will be enlisted; of good sixe & figure, & whose early pursuits in life may best qualify them for the duties & active service of mounted soldier.

IV-The established Recruiting Regulations will be strictly observed, & all the required returns, muster & descriptive rolls, monthly & semi-monthly reports, will be regularly made, & promptly transmitted through the superintendent to the Adj Gen, who will furnish the requisite funds, & blanks.

V-The Colonel & Lt Colonel will repair to ***Jefferson Barracks*** as soon as the special service in which they are now engaged will permit, where the regt will be organized, instructed, & equipped for service in the field by the earliest day practicable. The Capts & Subalterns will repair to their recruiting stations without delay, & devote their undivided attention to the service upon which they are about to enter.

Uniform:

VI-The Undress of the U S Regt of Mounted Riflemen shall, for the present, be the same as that for the Dragoons, except: The button & waist belt place shall bear the letter R instead of D.

The trousers of dark blue cloth, with a strip of black cloth down the outer seam, edged with yellow cord.

The forage cap to be ornamented with a gold embroidered spread eagle, with the letter R in silver on the shield.

The sash to be crimson silk.

Wings for coat, [according to pattern,] to be provided.

The Undress will be the only uniform required to be worn by the regt until further orders.

Strayed from my stable on May 31, a bay Mare. Reasonable reward. Communicate to me at the Third Auditor's ofc, or my residence, at Gtwn. –John Harry

Notice of copartnership: Raphael Semmes & B I Semmes, jr, having purchased the stock of goods of Semmes, Murray, & Semmes, will, from after this date, conduct the business on their own account, & under the name & style of Raphael Semmes & Co. –Raphael Semmes, B I Semmes, jr: Jun 1, 1846, Wash. The firm of Semmes, Murray, & Semmes will be continued for the purpose of liquidation.
–Raphael Semmes, Stanislaus Murray, B I Semmes, jr.

THU JUN 11, 1846
The *Potomac Mills* & other valuable real estate for sale: by decree of the Circuit Superior Court of Law & Chancery for Jefferson Co, Va, rendered in the cases of Peter Sourwein & others, plntfs, against Geo Reynolds & others, dfndnts, & in the case of Jos McMurran & others, against the same dfndnts, & Jacob Wolford, plnts, against Geo Reynolds & others, the undersigned, as Trustee & Com'r, will on Jul 11, 1846, before the tavern of Danl Entler, in Shepherdstown, Jefferson Co, Va, offer at public auction: *Potomac Mills*, with 10 or 12 acres of land adjacent thereto. Property is on the Potomac river; with large & well-built smoke-house, blacksmith's shop, workshops, with a convenient dwlg house. Also, another tract, adjoining the last tract, containing about 85 acres, which was purchased by Boteler & Reynolds from the devisees of Jacob Bedinger, dec'd. –E I Lee, Trustee & Com'r

Senate: 1-Cmte on the Post Ofc & Post Roads: bill for the relief of Wade Allen. 2-Cmte on Pensions: bill granting a pension to Wm Pittman, with a report in writing: to be printed. Same cmte: reported House bill for the relief of Isaiah Parker, & that granting a pension to Orris Crosby, without amendment. 3-Cmte on Pensions: House bill for the relief of Jas Hilman, recommending its indefinite postponement.

House of Reps: 1-Timothy Pillsbury presented himself as a member for newly admitted State of Texas; being sworn in, he took his seat as a member of the U S Congress. 2-Mr Jefferson Davis present a Memorial received from a number of ladies of N Y, subject-remonstrating a clause in the report of the Cmte on the Militia, made Jan 9, 1846, on the efficiency of the older ofcrs, the subalterns are younger men, & are scientific; they are ill calculated for active duties of the field, or for anything more than drill sgts, or men of mere routine. The ladies say a gross injustice has been done to the ofcrs of the army, & holds them up to the world as without valor, patriotism or energy. Memorial is signed:

Ann Thompson	Anna Higgins	Cornelia Smith
Mgt Walker	Lucy Floyd	Judith Nicholson
Rachael Saunders	Gertrude Lawrence	Jane Smets
Emelio Desfourneaux	Augusta Willing	Louisa Thorndike
Sarah Ann Lewis	Mary Hope	Maria McMasters
R J Ripley	Amy Thornhill	Letitia Whitehead
Susan Thornhill	Jane Hendricks	Mary Oakley
Hester Bressington	Eliz Thompson	
Jane Platt	Mary O'Neil	

The several companies of Balt Volunteers, under Lt Col Watson, were removed from their quarters in Wash City yesterday to *Fort Washington*, preparatory to their embarkation for the Southern Army. The steamship **Massachusetts**, now lying at Alexandria, has been chartered by the Gov't to take the whole battalion to the Rio Grande.

Handsome household & kitchen furniture at auction on Jun 18, at the residence of the late Jos Smoot, opposite the Brewery, Gtwn. –B Homans, auctioneer

Orphans Court of Wash Co, D C. Letters of administration on the personal estate of Ann Shekels, late of said county, dec'd. –Jas Burdine, adm

FRI JUN 12, 1846
Collector & Genr'l Agent: collection of accounts, bills, & notes. Any business left with Messrs J F Callan, E & 7th sts; or John L Smith-8th st, will be promptly attended to. –Saml C Espey

Circuit Court of Wash Co, D C-in Chancery. Augusta R Theriot, vs the heirs at law & adm of Peter Passet, dec'd, et al. The creditors of Peter Passet, above named, & all others, interested in his real estate, are to exhibit their claims, at my ofc in Gtwn, on or before Jun 22. –Clement Cox, adm

Tennessee Volunteers: 12 companies mustered into service: field ofcrs: Gen Wm B Campbell, chosen colonel; S R Anderson, lt col; Richd Alexander, major; & R Farquarson, 2nd major.

Illinois-Thos Ford, commander-in-chief of the Illinois forces, issued a proclamation that no provision has yet been made for paying the expenses of transportation to the place of rendezvous. He confidently expects the expenses will be reimbursed by the U S or by that State.

Louisville paper: Judge John J Marshall, of the Circuit Court of that city, died very suddenly on Jun 3, of apoplexy.

Michl Walsh, who was sentenced to *Blackwell's Island* for 6 months for a libel upon Mr John Horspool, was released from confinement on Sat-having received a pardon from Govn'r Wright.

Dr Edson, brother to Calvin Edson, now dec'd, the great living skeleton, is now traveling through the country, a skeleton counterpart of his dec'd brother. He is 42 years old, 5 feet 6 inches in height, & weighs only 50 pounds-a mere mass of human bones.

House of Reps: 1-Ptn of Mrs Martha Hough for arrears of pension. 2-Ptn of Wm Sporks, an invalid soldier of the war of 1812, asking a pension.

Gold watch found: inquire at the house of Wm Beach, on Va ave, near 3rd st west.

Near Schenectady yesterday, Mr Giles I Yates, superintendent of some work on the railroad, was struck by the train. Little hope of his recovery. —Albany Argus, Tue.

Died: on Jun 10, in Gtwn, D C, Mrs Isabella Thomson, in her 86th year. She was a native of Morayshire, Scotland, & upwards of 50 years a resident of Gtwn, D C. Her funeral will take place from her late residence on Market st this day, at 4 o'clock.

Died: on Mar 25 last, at Owensborough, Ky, Dr Wm Morton, eldest s/o Capt Wm Morton, of Gtwn, D C.

Died: Jun 8, at his residence, Montg Co, Md, Col Washington Owen, in his 68th year.

Died: on Jun 5, at Shepherdstown, Jefferson Co, Va, in her 18th year, Miss Ellen Eliza Hamtramck, d/o J F Hamtramck. Scarcely 3 years have flown since the dec'd graduated at the Academy of the Visitation, Gtwn, D C, with the most distinguished honors, receiving the first premiums & rewards in almost every branch taught at the institution. She was a most affectionate dght, sister, & friend.

Dan Drake Henrie, of Texas, is raising a company of Volunteers for the war in Mexico. A meeting will be held for this purpose at the City Hall on Fri at 5 o'clock.

SAT JUN 13, 1846
For sale: a very superior clinker-built copper fastened Sail Boat: made to order, in a very superior manner. Apply to Edw H Fuller, City Hotel.

Orphans Court of Chas Co, Md. Letters testamentary on the personal estate of Jas Brawner, late of said county, dec'd. —H H Dent, exc of Jas Brawner

Died: last evening, at Mrs Townly's, in Wash City, Capt John Rogers, Principal Chief of the Western Cherokees, aged about 70 years. His funeral is this evening at 4 o'clock, from this late boarding house, opposite Galabrun's, on Pa ave.

The Postmaster at St Louisville, Licking Co, Ohio, named A P Goff, was arrested on Thu last, & committed to jail, on a charge of having committed numerous depredations upon the mail. —Wheeling Times

Frankfort [Ky] Commonwealth: Judge Kinkead lately performed a very handsome act, by the appointment of Mrs Trimble, the accomplished lady of the late John Trimble, as Clerk of the Carter Circuit, in place of her dec'd husband.

Report from Gen Taylor: Camp near *Fort Brown*, Texas: May 17, 1846. "Resaca de la Palma"-May, 9. Genr'l La Vega was taken prisoner. A small company, under Capt Buchanan & Lts Wood & Hays, 4th Infty, composed chiefly of men of that regt, drove the enemy from a breastwork which he occupied, & captured a piece of artillery. An attempt to recover this piece was repulsed by Capt Barbour's 3rd Infty. Our loss-killed: Lt Inge, 2nd Dragoons, who fell at the head of his platoon while gallantly charging the enemy's battery; Lt Cochrane, 4th, & Lt Chadbourne, 8th Infty, who likewise met their death in the thickest of the fight. The ofcrs wounded were Lt Col Payne, inspector genr'l, Lt Dobbins, 3rd Infty, seving with the light infty advance slightly; Lt Col McIntosh, 5th Infty, severely, [right arm since amputated;] Lt Fowler, 5th Infty, slightly; Capt Montgomery, 8th Infty, slightly; Lts Gates & Jordan, 8th Infty, severely, [each twice ;] Lts Selden, Maclay, Burbank, & Morris, 8th Infty, slightly. Report of Capt Hawkins: Headquarters, *Fort Taylor*, Texas, May 10, 1846. May 9-2 p m, Maj Brown died, a gallant & faithful ofcr. Letter from Geo W Allen, Brvt Maj commanding 4th Infty, to Lt Col J Garland, commanding 3rd Brig: I regret to announce the death of 1st Lt E R Cochrane, of my regt, who fell at the very edge of camp, whilst gallantly leading his men into it. On the 8th Capt Page was severely, if not mortally wounded. On the 9th, 1st Lt E R Cochrane & 3 men were killed; Lts Wallen & Hays & 6 men wounded.

Callaghan's Tavern & Farm for sale: situated in Alleghany Co, Va, on the State road from Covington: farm consists of more than 50 acs. Refer to John Callaghan, the present occupant. –Uriel Terrill, Orange Court House, Va -John Yates, Halltown, Jefferson Co, Va

By virtue of a writ of fieri facias, at the suit of Benj F Middleton & Benj Beall, under the firm of Middleton & Beall, against the goods & chattels of Walter Evans, to me directed, I have seized property of said Walter Evans: 100 pieces of crockery, 1 demijohn, boxes, keg, 3 pocket handkerchiefs, barrel, & glassware, to be offered on Jun 20, in front of the Centre Market-house, for sale for cash.
--H Y Maryman, constable

MON JUN 15, 1846
The subscriber has opened a new Drug Store at the corner of 7th & I sts. Dr E M Chapin will have the management of this establishment. –Thos Haynes

Ky Volunteers, the remainder of them, consisting of 1 regt of infty & 1 of cavalry, were to rendezvous at Louisville & be mustered into the U S service on Jun 8. Field ofcrs of these 2 regts:

1st Regt of Cavalry:
Humphrey Marshall, of Louisville, Colonel
Ezekiel H Field, of Woodford Co, Lt Colonel
John P Gaines, of Boone Co, Major

2nd Regt of Infty:
Wm R McKee, of Lexington, Colonel
Henry Clay, jr, of Louisbille, Lt Colonel
Carey H Fry, of Boyle Co, Major

Senate: 1-Ptn from E P Calkin & Co, merchants at Galveston, praying indemnity for goods alleged to have been illegally seized by the collector of that port. 2-Memorial of L Taliaferro, praying an appropriation to satisfy a judgment against him, for whiskey seized by him as U S Indian agent. 3-Memorial from citizens of Pa, praying an appropriation for the widow & children of the late Judge Randall, in consideration of his faithful services. 4-Ptn of John Rederson & Chas Black, praying indemnity for the illegal seizure & detention by an ofcr of the U S of their schnrs **Creole** & **Ann M Briggs**. 5-Ptn of John McCloud, for an increase of pension. 6-Cmte on Finance: adverse report on the claim of E A Ware. 7-Cmte on Pensions: adverse report on the ptn of Smith Cram. 8-Cmte on Claims: adverse report on the claim of Wm B Foster. 9-Relief of W H Thomas, read twice & referred. 10-Bill for the relief of Nathl P Phillips: passed. 11-Bill for the relief of J Throckmorton; relief of Benj Adams & others; & relief of Orlando Saltmarsh & Wm Fuller: engrossed

Maj Gen John C Pasteur, of Newbern, N C, died very suddenly on Jun 4, of disease of the heart. He was engaged a few minutes previous to his death in drilling the Newbern volunteers for Texas.

Mrd: on Jun 11, by Rev F S Evans, Mr Saml Cooper to Miss Mary A Thompson, all of Wash City.

Death of a *Bunker Hill* Drummer. The Revolutionary veteran, Rufus Kingsley, a drummer at the *Bunker Hill* battle, died at his residence in Harford, Susquehanna Co, Pa, on May 26 last, in his 84th year. He was born in Windham, Conn, Feb 1, 1763, & entered the service as a drummer boy at age 13 years, & continued till the close of the war. His amiable companion, with whom he had lived happily for 60 years, survived her husband but 3 days, & died on May 29, nearly realizing the often expressed desire of both, that, as they had lived so long pleasantly together, they might be permitted to depart together. –Ithaca Chron

At *Camp Oakland* on Jun 6, while Mr McDonough, of the Kenton Rangers, was uncocking a pistol, it went off, killing Mr Jos Castor, of the same company, instantly. Mr McDonough was so affected that he went into a paroxysm, deep gloom was cast over the whole company. Mr Castor was from Campbell Co, & Mr McDonough from Cincinnati. No blame is attached to Mr McDonough. –Louisville Journal

N Y papers announce the death of Theodore Dwight, of that city, aged 82 years; formerly a rep in Congress from the State of Conn, & subsequently the senior proprietor & editor of the Daily Advertiser, of N Y C, afterward published by Messrs Dwight, Townsend & Walker.

Died: on Jun 13, in Wash City, of consumption, Maj Nahum Stone, Clerk in the Auditor's Ofc of the Post Ofc Dept, aged 38 years.

Died: on Fri last, suddenly, at his residence, Archibald Thompson, in his 45th year.

TUE JUN 16, 1846
Circuit Court of Wash Co, D C in Equity. Richd Cruikshank, adm de bonis non of John Ott, dec'd, cmplnt, vs Catharine Ott & others, dfndnts. John Marbury, trustee in the above cause, reports to the Court that he has sold the part of lot 2 in square 379 in Wash City, D C, to Jas C Hall, the highest bidder & purchaser thereof, at the price or sum of $8.050. –Wm Brent, clk

Senate: 1-Ptn of the heirs of Sourjohn, an Indian, asking that an award made in his favor after his death may be paid to them. 2-Ptn from John T Adams, assignee of Taylor, Little & Co, of N Y, asking that certain duties illegally exacted may be refunded to them. 3-Ptn from Chas W Churchman, of Phil, asking relief in relation to certain duties illegally exacted. 4-Cmte on Revolutionary Claims: asked to be discharged from the further consideration of the memorial of the heirs of Saml Y Keene. Same cmte: asking to be discharged from the further consideration of the memorial of the heirs of Wm Grayson, as in both cases adverse reports had been heretofore made.

Notice: Whereas, Mary Hitt, late of Rappahannock Co, Va, died, leaving 4 children, to wit: 2 sons, one named Morgan Hitt & the other Armistead Hitt, & 2 dghts, whose names are not known, but who, it is believed, resided in the Western country. And whereas, by the will of Francis James, the brother of the said Mary Hitt, it is provided that said 4 children of Mary Hitt shall take, as devisees, his real estate in Fauquier Co, provided they come forward & comply with the provisions of said will. –Stephen S Fletcher, exc of Francis James, dec'd.

Mrd: on Jun 10, at Holly Hill, Caroline Co, Va, by Elder Jas M Bagby, John P Dickinson, of King & Queen Co, to Sally Taylor, d/o P Woolfolk, of Caroline Co.

Circuit Court of Wash Co, D C: gentlemen summoned to serve on the Grand Jury during the present term:

John Kurtz, Foreman	Geo W Riggs	Isaac Clarke
John Mason, jr	Geo Parker	Benj K Morsell
Andrew Coyle	G C Grammer	Geo Thomas
Wm Gunton	John Cox	Jesse E Dow
John F Cox	Henry C Matthews	Judson Mitchell
Thos Fenwick	Thos Blagden	John Austin
Otho M Linthicum	John C Harkness	Edw Simms
Joshua Peirce	Henry Haw	

To let, the residence at present occupied by S E Cole, on 7th st, opposite the Odd Fellows' Hall. Inquire of T F Harkness, merchant tailor, on the premises.

Appointments by the Pres, by & with the advice & consent of the Senate:
1-Jas Fiora, of N Y, to be U S Consul for the city of Manchester, England.
2-Peter T Crutchfield, to be Receiver of Public Moneys for the district of lands subject to sale at Little Rock, in Arkansas, to take effect Jun 16, 1846, when the term of the present incumbent will expire.

Corporation wharf for rent: wharf is on the west side of the Wash Canal, between N st south & the south side of Ga ave, commonly called the Fish Wharf.
–Jos Cross, Com'r East Canal

WED JUN 17, 1846
Sale of excellent household furniture, at auction: on Jun 19, at the late residence of Ann Sheckells, dec'd, on Md ave, between 1st & 2nd sts. –C W Boteler, jr, auctioneer

Senate: 1-Cmte on Naval Affairs: to inquire into allowing Jas Wilson the regular compensation of sailmaker, for services performed by him on board the U S ship **Yorktown**, on her late cruise. 2-Bill for the relief of J Throckmorton: passed. 3-Bill for the relief of Benj Adams & Co & others: passed. 4-Joint resolution for the relief of Orlando Saltmarsh & Wm Fuller: passed.

Note: Chas W Boteler, sen, is fully authorized to use the name of the late firm of Boteler, Donn & Co, for signing notes & winding up the business of the said firm.
–C W Boteler, John M Donn, C W Boteler, jr

Cmdor Jones, late commander of the British squadron on the west coast of Africa, died soon after his arrival in England, whither he had returned in consequence of his failing health. –Foreign news

I wish to dispose of the valuable property known as *Seneca Mills*, on the Seneca Creek, about 20 miles from Gtwn. Apply to Clement Smith, Gtwn.

For sale: a first rate Horse, perfectly broken & safe for the carriage & saddle. Or I will rent for the month to a careful person very low. Apply to D A Gardner, on 12th st, between H & N Y ave.

$200 reward for runaway Henry Lockwood: 27 years of age, bright copper color; has a wife at R L Jenkins' near Piscataway. –John Palmer, PG Co, Md

Orphans Court of Wash Co, D C. Letters of administration on the personal estate of Maria E Morgan, late of said county, dec'd. –G C Morgan, adm

Alexandria Volunteers: now number 50: ofcrs elected on Fri:
M D Corse unanimously elected Capt   T W Ashby, 2nd Lt
Chas S Price, 1st Lt   Benj Waters, jr, 1st Sgt
-Gazette

Mrd: on Thu, at *Longwood*, Anne Arundel Co, Md, by Rev John C Smith, of Wash City, the Rev Thos Jas Shepherd, Pastor of Harmony Presbyterian Church, Lisbon, to Miss Emma, d/o Dr Gustavus Warfield, all of said county.

St Louis Republican of Jun 8: challenge of a duel between H C Broadus, of Hannibal, & John L Taylor, of Palmyra, resulted in the dreadful result of the death of the seconds. Geo W Buckner met Jos W Glover, near Palmyra: Glover shot Buckner; Buckner, wounded, seized the pistol from Glover, fired it, the ball passing through his heart. He expired immediately. Buckner died yesterday. Mr Buckner was the circuit atty for the district, residing at Bowling Green, & Mr Glover a student of law in Palmyra. [Aug 18th newspaper: the rencontre occurred on Jun 6, 1846. On May 22 last Henry C Broaddus, of Bowling-Green, challenged John L Taylor, of Palmyra, to fight a duel. A detailed description of the events can be found in the Nat'l Intelligencer of Aug 18, 1846:signed by S T Glover.

THU JUN 18, 1846
Senate: 1-Ptn from the excecutor of Z Kingsley, asking the payment of interest awarded by a judgment of the Supreme Court of East Florida under the treaty of 1819 with Spain.

Henry Kepler is now prepared to supply his friends & the public with his Celebrated Root Beer.

Meeting of Dan Drake Henrie's company of volunteers for Mexico, held at City Hall on Tue, the following were elected ofcrs:
Dan Drake Henrie, of Texas, Capt
Rich P Henry, 1st Lt
F A Klopfer, 2nd Lt
B R West, 1st Sgt
Wm M McCarty, 2nd Sgt
John W Ross, 3rd Sgt
Richd M Hanson, 4th Sgt
John Carr, 1st Cpl
R J H Handy, 2nd Cpl
Wm A Stewart, 3rd Cpl
Chas F Force, 4th Cpl

Information wanted. The subscriber has just learned, by a letter from the old country, that his brother & sister, Michl & Mary Sullivan, left Ireland for America some time during last summer. They have not been heard of since. It is supposed that they landed at N Y or Quebec. They are from the parish of Squall, county of Cork, Ireland. Any information concerning them will be thankfully received, & the person giving it rewarded for his trouble. Easter papers & papers generally are requested to give the above notice, & receive the sincere thanks of distressed brother. –Patrick Sullivan, Springfield, Clarke Co, Ohio

Stephen D Hall, s/o Carter A Hall, a promising youth aged about 16 years, was accidentally drowned on Sunday last in Spring Gardens, Balt, whither he had gone with some others for fishing.

Two men were shot in one of the southern counties of Ky on Jun 1. W D Dun, deputy sheriff, left town to arrest B H O'Neil for assault with intent to kill. In the attempt to arrest O'Neil, Benj H O'Neil & Thos Risley were shot & killed. The grand jury refused to find an indictment against the sheriff & posse.

Trustee's sale of groceries: by deed of trust from Saml Kelly to me: auction at the store house now occupied by said Kelly, at the corner of High & Gay sts, Gtwn, on Jun 24: all the stock, stand casks, & store fixtures. -John Sessford, trustee -E S Wright, auctioneer

Died: on Jun 17, Miss Catharine O'Neale, aged 30 years, a native of the county of Waterford, Ireland, but for the last 3 years a resident of Wash. Her funeral will take place today, at 11 o'clock, from the residence of Mr Jas Fitzgerald, on Pa ave, between 3rd & 4th sts.

Vegetable stalls for sale at public auction: on Jul 1, all the vegetable stalls in the Eastern Branch Market-house, for one year, commencing on Jul 1, 1846. On Jul 2, all the vegetable stalls in the Centre Market-house, for one year, commencing on Jul 1, 1846. On Jul 3, all the vegetable stalls in the West Market-house, for one year, commencing on Jul 1, 1846. -W W Seaton, Mayor

FRI JUN 19, 1846
Senate: 1-Cmte on Pensions: adverse reports on the ptns of Abigail Edgerly & Polly Biggs: to be printed. 2-Cmte on Revolutionary Claims: adverse report in the case of Wm Bryant.

House of Reps: 1-Clk of the House to pay to John Taliaferro, of Va, the compension, per diem & mileage that is allowed to members of Congress, computing the per diem from the commencement of the first session of the 12th Congress until Nov 30, 1811. Also, that he pay said Taliaferro a like compensation, per diem & mileage, computing the per diem from the commencement of the first session of the 13th Congress to & including Aug 2, 1813, & the like compensation, per diem & mileage, computing the per diem from the commence of the 2nd session of the 13th Congress until Feb 17, 1814. 2-Cmte of Claims: adverse report on the ptn of Orange H Dibble: laid on the table. Same cmte: adverse reports on the cases of Martha Cannon & Andrew H Patterson: laid on the table. Same cmte: adverse reports on the cases of Isaac Cook & Vantyne Gray & others, clerks in the N Y custom-house: laid on the table. Same cmte: adverse reports on the cases of Mrs Frances Moore, wid/o John E Moore; of Armand Martin, Geo McGahen, Hugh K Meade, Jas B McCutchen, & Catharine E Moreland: laid on the table. Same cmte: bill from the Senate for the relief of Mrs Pike, wid/o Gen Pike: committed without amendment. Same Cmte: joint resolution from the Senate for the relief of Putney & Riddle, reported the same without amendment: committed. Same cmte: bill for the relief of the heirs of Joshua Kennedy, dec'd: read & committed. Same cmte: adverse reports on the cases of

Nancy E Richards & Zachariah Walker. Same cmte: adverse report on the case of Geo W Jackson: laid on the table. 3-Cmte on Public Lands: joint resolution for the relief of the children of Stephen Johnson, dec'd: read & committed. Same cmte: bill from the Senate for the relief of Asenath Canny, reported the same without amendment. Same cmte: discharged from the further consideration of the ptn of Erastus Harvey, & from the ptn of the citizens of Paulding Co, Ohio, for a reduction of the price of public lands. 4-Cmte on the Judiciary: bill for the relief of the administrator of Francis Cazeau, dec'd: committed. Same cmte: bill for the relief of Jos Edson, late marshal of Vt: committed. 5-Cmte on Revolutionary Claims: adverse report on the ptn of the heirs of Michl Cryder: laid on the table. Same cmte: bill for the erection of a monument to the memory of Gen Herkimer, who fell in the Revolutionary war: read & committed. 6-Cmte on Private Land Claims: bill for the relief of Jas B Davenport: committed. Also, a bill for the relief of Thos B Scott, of Louisiana: committed. 7-Cmte on the Post Ofc & Post Roads: joint resolution for the relief of Geo R Smith: committed. Also, an adverse report on the case of Wm Eaves: laid on the table. Same cmte: discharged from the cases of Thos Withrow, B F Seaman, Elijah Coombes, & Jonah Blackman: laid on the table. 8-Cmte on Private Land Claims: bill for the relief of the heris of John Wall, dec'd: committed. Same cmte: bill for the relief of Eliz Burriss, her heirs or assigns: committed. 9-Cmte on Indian Affairs: adverse report on the case of Geo Jackson & others: laid on the table. Also, a bill for the relief of the heirs of Hyacinthe Lassell: committed. Same cmte: bill for the relief of John A Bryan: committed. Same cmte: adverse report on the case of L P Cheatham: laid on the table. 10-Cmte on Naval Affairs: bill for the relief of Jos Gideon. Also, a bill for the relief of David Myrlie: committed. Same cmte: bill for the relief of Cmder Jas McIntosh: committed. Also, a joint resolution to authorize the settlement of the accounts of Purser Garret Barry: committed. Same cmte: bill for the relief of Jas Pennoyer: committed. 11-Cmte on Naval Affairs: bill for the relief of Eliz M Adams; relief of Capt Thos M Newell; relief of Henry La Reintrie: bills were committed. Also, adverse reports on the cases of Susan Langreen, Chas Smith, Joshua Parker; Mary Jackson, wid/o Thos Jackson; Mary D Wade, wid/o Lt Wade; Geo A De Russy, & Gaetano Carusi: laid on the table. 12-Cmte on Revolutionary Pensions: bill from the Senate granting a pension to John Keith, of N Y, reported the same with an amendment: bill was committed. Same cmte: adverse report on the cases of Mary Crysalt & Matthew Tarker or Parker: laid on the table. [Tarker or Parker copied as written.] 13-Cmte on Invalid Pensions: bill for the relief of Harvey Reynolds: committed. 14-Cmte of Claims: adverse report on the case of Hugh K Meade: laid on the table. 15-Cmte on Revolutionary Pensions: bill for the relief of Edith Ramey; relief of Ann Clayton; relief of Jas Green; relief of Catharine Stevenson: all committed. Same cmte asked to be discharged from the cases of Squire Ferris, Eliz Ellis, & Ann Lindsley: laid on the table. 16-Cmte on Revolutionary Pensions: bill granting a pension to Silas Chatfield: committed. 17-Cmte of Claims: adverse reports on the cases of John B Wingerd & Jas Sloan: laid on the table. 18-Cmte on Patents: bill for the relief of Thos Blanchard: committed.

Gen Gaines, accompanied by his Aid-de Camp, Lt Calhoun, arrived in Wash City last evening.

Charleston News of Mon: we regret the death of the Hon Henry Middleton, on Sat last, in his 76th year. He was the descendant of a family of conspicuous in the annals of Caroline; has filled various prominent situations, both under the Genr'l Gov't & that of his own State. He was elected a rep in the Legislature of this State in 1801; chosen State Senator, which post he occupied until elected Govn'r in 1810; in 1814 was elected to rep this district in Congress & served 2 terms. In 1820, Mr Monroe conferred on him the appointment of Minister to Russia, at which Court he remained several years.

Quebec Mercury of Sat evening: last night, at 10 o'clock, a fire broke out in the Theatre Royal, St Louis st, [formerly the riding school,] at the close of Mr Harrison's exhibition of his chemical dioramas. A camphene lamp was overset, & the stage at once became enveloped in flames. Up to this house 46 bodies have been recovered from the ruins. List of the unhappy suffers:
Horatio Carwell, dry-goods merchant-Horatio, aged 6, & Ann, aged 4, his children.
Jos Tardif & Olivia Fiset, his wife.
Sarah Darah, w/o John Calvin, carter.
Jas O'Leary, aged 22, apprentice to his brother John, plasterer, St Rochs; Mary O'Leary, aged 16, his sister.
J J Sims, druggist; Rebecca, aged 23, & Kennith, aged 13, his children.
Mary O'Brien, aged 26, w/o John Lilly, tailor.
Jean Bte Vezina, aged 30.
Maria Louise Lavailee, w/o Ronald McDonald, editor of the Canadien.
Eugenie McDonald, w/o Rigobert Anger, mcechant.
Edw R Hoogs, bookkeeper, Montreal Bank; John, aged 8, & Edw, aged 6, his children.
Thos C Harrison, aged 21, from Hamilton, C W; brother to the owner of the diorama.
Harriet Glackemeyer, w/o T F Molt, aged 45; Fred'k, aged 19, & Adolphus, aged 12, her children.
Helen Murphy, an orphan, aged 20.
Emeline Worth, aged 9, d/o Edw Worth, Montreal, sister-in-law of Mr A Lentesty, grocer, of this city.
Flavien Sauvageau, aged 14, s/o Mr Chas Sauvageau, musician.
Eliz Lindsay, aged 53, w/o Mr T Atkins, clerk of Upper Town Market; Richd Atkins, aged 27, her son.
Stewart Scott, Clerk of the Court of Appeals, & Jane, his dght.
Thos Hamilton, Lt 14th Regt.
Mrs John Gibb, widow, & Jane, her dghts.
Arthur Lane, s/o Mr Elisha Lane, of the firm of Gibb, Lane & Co.
Marianne Brown, aged 25, schoolmistress, at Wood & Gray's Cove.
Jos Marcoux, bailiff.

Colin Ross, aged 26 years, plasterer, a native of Inverness, Scotland, & Agnes Black, his wife, aged 18, d/o widow Black, of Montreal.
Isaac Devlin, watchmaker, Lower Town.
John Berry, from Aberdeen, late in the employ of Messrs W Price & Co, arrived in Quebec, from Chicoutimie, on the 8th. A letter was found on his person from his brother, Jas Berry, instructing him to address him, Jas Berry, gardener & riddlemaker, North Bradford, Aberdeen.
Anne Taffe, late servant with ___ Denholm, Cape.
John Smith Kane, s/o Mr John Kane, tinsmith, of this city.
Mr John Wheatley, stationer, Lower Town.
Julia Ray, d/o Assist Commissariat Genr'l Ray.
Two bodies were not recognized.
Dile Emilie Poncy, aunt of Miss Poncy, of the Lower Town, is missing. The remains of a body, said to be a female, are supposed to be hers. The second is a Mr McKeogh, of Malbaie, a schoolmaster, who was in the theatre in company with Miss Poncy. The theatre & adjoining stables were all burnt to the ground. The most remarkable fire in America was on Dec 26, 1811, in Richmond, Va, when 600 persons were present, of whom 72 perished, among them the Govn'r of the State & the Mayor of the city. [Page 97 of the Nat'l Intell of 1811-1813: amongst those killed in the theatre fire in Richmond, Va, was Govn'r Geo W Smith.]

Criminal Court-Wash: Chas Bridgett was found guilty under 3 indictments, charging with an assault & battery upon Albert Paris, Favila Boswell, & Marianne Frazer.

Gayoso House: this spacious & elegant Hotel will be finished by Aug 1, 1846: to let for a term of years upon reasonable terms. Insolvent persons or those greatly embarrassed need not apply. Address, post paid, Robertson Topp, Jno T Trezevant, Memphis, Tenn.

Alexandria, Jun 17. Yesterday the Battalion of the District of Columbia & Baltimore Volunteers sailed from this place in the steamship **Massachusetts**, for the Rio Grande. Ofcrs composing the battalion: Wm H Watson, Lt Col; F B Shaffer, Adj; G M Dove, Surgeon

Co A: Capt J E Stewart
1st Lt B F Owen
2nd Lt Saml Wilt
Co B: Capt Jas Piper
1st Lt M K Taylor
2nd Lt L Dolan
Co C: Capt Robt Bronaugh
1st Lt Phineas B Bell
2nd Lt Wm O'Brien
Passenger: Capt R B Lawton

Co D: Capt John Waters
1st Lt Wm J Parham
2nd Lt Eugene Boyle
Co E: Capt J R Kenly
1st Lt F B Shaffer
2nd Lt Oden Bowie
Light Co: Capt Jas Boyd
1st Lt Jos H Ruddach
2nd Lt R E Hastell

I certify that Zebulon Brundidg brought before me, as an estray, trespassing upon his enclosure on 4½ st, ***Greenleaf's Point***, a black brindle milk cow. –John L Smith, J P, 8th st, near Pa ave. The owner is to come forward, prove property, pay charges, & take her away. –Zebulon Brundidg

Trustee's sale of Printing establishment: by deed of trust from J G Kleuch to the subscriber, dated Jun 1, 1846: to secure a debt due to Alfred Shucking, & also to Emil Preusier: sale, for cash, at the ofc of the Nat'l Zeitung, corner of 7th & La ave, on Jun 30, all the materials, implements, & utensils comprising the establishment, amongst which are one iron Smith Printing Press, [double medium,] with Chase & Rolling Apparatus, Type of different kinds, Cases, Composing Sticks, & Galleys, together with the dues & credits at the time of sale, & the good will & subscription list of the ofc. –Nicholas Callan, Trustee -R W Dyer, auct [All debts now due the Establishment & remaining unpaid, must be paid to the subscriber, who is alone authorized to collect the same. –Nicholas Callan, trustee]

Mrd: on Jun 16, at Claremont, near Balt, by Rev Mr Atkinson, Oliver P MacGill to Mary Clare Carroll, d/o the late Com Robt T Spence, of the U S Navy.
+
Mrd: on Tue, at Claremont, by Rev Mr Atkinson, Chas Brooke, jr, of Lancaster, Pa, to Roberta Trail, y/d/o the late Com Robt T Spence, of the U S Navy.

Died: on Jun 15, at Richmond, Va, in her 74th year, after a protracted illness, Mrs Catharine Ambler, wid/o the late Col John Ambler.

Died: on Jun 13, at Raleigh, N C, of paralysis, Louis D Henry, an eminent citizen & distinguished lawyer.

Died: on Jun 17, Mrs Margaret Donohoo, aged 103 years, a native of the county of Galway, Ireland, but for the last 60 years a resident in this country. Her funeral is today, at 3 o'clock.

SAT JUN 20, 1846
Senate: 1-Cmte on Military Affairs: House bill for the relief of John Stockton, late a lt in the U S Army, without amendment. 2-Cmte on the Public Lands: bill for the relief of Shadrach Gillet & others. Same cmte: bill for the relief of John Russell, with a report: to be printed.

Appointments by the Pres: 1-John K Kane, of Pa, to be Judge of the district court of the U S for the eastern district of Pa, vice Archibald Randall, dec'd. 2-Henry Wilson, of Ohio, to be Purser in the Navy, to fill a vacancy occasioned by the death of John C Spencer, jr.

Lewis Clephane, intending to close his present business, offers for sale on the most accommodating terms his entire stock of Perfumery & Fancy goods, together with the fixtures. –Pa ave, 3rd door east of 10th st.

To let, a genteel 3 story brick house on H st, near the Patent Ofc. Or the subscriber will rent the house in which he now lives, on Capitol Hill, near the residence of B B French. –H King

Orphans Court of Wash Co, D C. In the case of Lewis G Davidson: ratify sale by the trustees, namely, to Louis Vivans, of lots 16 & 17 in square 168, for $1,230.24, & to Jas Carico, of lot 19 in square 169, for $506.25, all in Wash City.
–Nathl Pope Causin -Ed N Roach, Reg/o wills

Mrd: on Mar 17 last, at Buenos Ayres, at the residence of the Hon Wm Brent, jr, Charge d'Affaires of the U S, by the Rev A Faber, Thos P McBlair, of the U S Navy, to Mary C Walsh, d/o Robt Walsh, Consul of the U S at Paris.

For 3 weeks past, at my residence, between 9th & 10th sts east, on Md ave, there has been 2 stray cows & calves & 1 yearling. The owners can have the same by paying costs. –Dennis Vermillion

Boarding: Mrs M Crim, 108 Walnut st, between 4th & 5th sts, Phil, having connected with her old establishment the large & commodious house adjoining. Warm & cold baths are attached to the house.

From the Dundee [N Y] Record, Jun 16. Information wanted, of a lady who, on Apr 15, 1845, married a gentleman in Detroit, Mich, by the name of Ezra Gregory, & with him left that city on the same day for a residence in or near Phil, Pa. Since her departure, nothing has been heard of them, nor their particular place of residence made known to their friends, & as it had become important to have correspondence with them, by reason of the decease of Mr Alex'r Grant, in Inverness, Scotland, who has left a large estate to be divided between his heirs in this country, [a handsome portion of which is going to Mrs Gregory,] any information concerning them, or that shall apprize Mr Gregory & wife of the necessity of their appearing at Mrs Hayse's, Washington st, Geneva, Ontario Co, N Y, on or before the 1st day of Sept next, to attend to the business, will be gratefully acknowledged by a fond mother & endearing friends, who have entertained many fears as to their safety.

MON JUN 22, 1846
Mr Wm Cammack, a worthy citizen, who is well known for his successful cultivation of strawberries, peaches, & other delicious fruits, had the misfortune to be thrown from his horse last Thu, & thereby break his leg. He is doing well, under the professional assistance & care of Dr Reiley, of Gtwn.

Criminal Court-Wash. 1-Henry Smith found guilty for assaulting with intent to kill Andrew Suter. 2-Wm Pettigrew not guilty for a riot. 3-Eliz Creamer, was indicted for keeping a disorderly house, known as *Alhambra*, at Pa ave, near the Treasury Bldg. Jacob Creamer, the husband of Eliz, was found guilty, & saying nothing of Eliz Creamer, the wife, who alone was upon trial. The Court having apprized the jury of their error, returned with a verdict of not guilty. 4-Geo Gaines, a free colored boy-aged 10 years, was found guilty with grand larceny, in stealing sundry articles, the property of Dr Gould. 5-John Hall was convicted for an assault & battery on Antonie Manuyette. 5-In the trial of the U S vs Wm M Stewart, it was reported to have been an indictment charging him with an assault with intent to kill his wife. Now, as Mr Stewart is known to be a bachelor, the statement caused no little surprise. Mr Stewart, the dfndnt in the case, was tried for an assault upon Owen Clark, a laborer employed by Dr Ritchie in putting up a fence on disputed land.

Appointments by the Pres, by & with the advice & consent of the Senate.
Jos Hall, of Boston, to be Navy Agent for the port of Boston, Mass.
Thos J Durant, to be U S Atty for the district of Louisiana, from & after Jun 30, 1846, vice Solomon W Downs, resigned.
Jas MacHenry Boyd, of Md, to be Sec of the U S Legation near her Britannic Majesty, vice Gansevoort Melville, dec'd.
Joel W Jones, of D C, to be Military Storekeeper, vice Stephens T Mason, appointed captain in the regt of mounted riflemen.
Richd W Cummins, of Missouri, to be Indian Agent for the *Fort Leavenworth* agency, from Jul 3, 1846, when his present commission expires.

Rev Mr Tustin was installed pastor of the Central Presbyterian Church, in Wash City, on Jun 14, 1846.

Hagerstown News: on Mon last, at Heyer's sawmill, near that place, a young man named John Kurfman met his death in a sudden & awful manner. He was taking a log from a wagon, when the log escaped the hold of those lowering it, & it rolled over Kurfman, crushing his head in a frightful manner, & causing his death in a few moments. He was a highly respectable young man, & has left an aged mother & several sisters who were dependent upon his exertions.

Miss Eliza Floyd, of Gorham, Me, drowned herself at Saccarappa on Thu last. She was an operative in a factory, & had committed an error, for which she was repentant, & had been forgiven; but some of her companions frightened her by saying the constable was after her, & she waded into the water & drowned.

Miss Whitman, with a party of ladies & gentlemen on the Wissahickon on a picnic, fell from a ledge of rocks over the stream & was drowned on Wed, near Phil.

Mrd: on Jun 18, at New Market, Md, by Rev P L Wilson, Jos A Gilliss, of Louisville, Ky, to Emeline Louisa, y/d/o Mr Saml Geyer, of the former place.

House of Reps: 1-Ptn of W G Kartright, for himself & others, claim for French spoliations. 2-Ptn of Wm Nicholl, of Knox Co, Tenn.

On Jun 9, as the steamer **Convoy** was coming up from New Orleans, there fell overboard & was drowned, a respectable English woman, the w/o of Robt Addison, just arrived from England, on her way to settle in Wisconsin. She had on board the boat her husband & 7 children-& they are people of intelligence & seemingly of much worth. All the money [70 sovereigns] possessed by this family she had on her person, & the whole family are now penniless-except that contributed by passengers on the boat & Capt Garrison, who refunded their passage money.

Died: yesterday, in Wash City, Ann Josephine, y/d/o Jas & Margaret Fitzgerald, aged 3 months & 21 days. Her funeral is this day at 4 o'clock, from the residence of her parents on Pa ave, between 3rd & 4½ sts.

Beautiful residence for sale: on the Heights of Gtwn, at the north termination of Congress st. There are attached to the part now offered for sale about 10 acres of land, but if desired 30 to 50 acres more might be bought with the property. The bldg contains 11 rooms altogether. This property was the residence of the Hon John C Calhoun while he was Sec of War. As it is without the limits of Gtwn, it is free from any other than a county tax, which is very inconsiderable. –B Mackall

The Hon Richd P Herrick, one of the Reps in Congress from the State of N Y, died at his lodgings in Wash City on Sat evening, after a brief illness of only 3 days.

Sale of household furniture & bar fixtures: by deed of trust from A R Jenkins to the subscriber, dated Mar 16, 1843, recorded in Wash Co land records, Liber W B #100: sale at the Metropolis House, on Pa ave, next to Jackson Hall. –A W Kirkwood, trustee -A Green, auctioneer

For rent: comfortable residence on Missouri ave, near 4½ st. Also, for sale or exchange, 2 unimproved lots in an improving part of the Wash City, & a desirable lot on Bridge st, in Gtwn, will be sold low or exchanged for property in the country. –Wm Ward, Pa ave

TUE JUN 23, 1846
Senate: 1-Hon Richd P Herrick was born in Rensselaer Co, N Y, & always resided there. In the relation of a husband & a father his example was deserving of all commendation. It is but a few weeks since his wife had to leave on a mission of maternal duty to one of their children in the North, unconscious of what was to occur. Crape will be worn on the left arm for 30 days.

Died: on Jun 22, after a lingering illness, Mrs Phillippe Carusi, in her 75th year. Her funeral is this evening, at 4 o'clock, from the residence of her son, on Pa ave, between 10th & 11th sts.

Died: on Jun 21, aged 67 years, Mrs Margaret Cassedy, a native of Ireland, but for the last 54 years a resident of the U S. Her funeral is this day, at 2 o'clock, from her late residence, near the Navy Yard. Her friends & acquaintances & those of her dght, Mrs Eleanor O'Donnell, are requested to attend.

Dissolution of the copartnership under the firm of Cotter & Thompson, by mutual consent. All claims to be presented to John Cotter.
–John Cotter, Richd R Thompson

Maramec Iron Works for sale: by authority of a power of atty from Messrs Massey & James, I will sell, at public auction, at the court-house in the city of St Louis, Missouri, Nov 2, the above Iron Works, together with 8,000 acres of land, more or less. Also, the detached tracts: 183¼ acres in township 40, near Wherry's Mill, in Osage Co. 80 acres on Benton's creek; 320 acres in township 38. 160 acres in township 37. 80 acres in township 37. One lot, nearly 1 acre, on the south bank of the Missouri river, 4 miles above Hermann. –John F Armstrong, agent, St Louis, Jun 6, 1846.

Pickled Oysters: put up at Piney Point, immediately after being taken from the water. Families supplied by the gallon or less quantities.
–J Beardsley, Pa ave, between 12th & 13th sts

$100 reward for runaway dark mulatto woman Henny, about 21 years of age. Mr John B Magruder, near Bladensburg, owns her father.
–Geo W Hilleary, near Upper Marlborough, Md.

Valuable real estate at auction: on Jun 25, in front of the premises, the following real estate in Gtwn, viz: Lots 121 & 122 in Beall's addition to Gtwn, fronting 100 feet each on Beall st by 120 feet depth. Lot 133, same addition, 40 feet front on Dunbarton st by 120 feet depth. Part of lot 144, same addition, fronting 45 feet on Montgomery st, with a brick dwlg-house, stable, pump, spring house & other conveniences. Part of lot 143, same addition, fronting 73 feet on Dunbarton st, vacant, most valuable bldg lot. Lot 151, same addition, fronting 40 feet on Montgomery st, with a well-finished frame house. All the deeds given & received, will be at the expense of the parties purchasing. –E S Wright, auctioneer

$100 reward for runaway, my house servant Geo Hamilton, about 30 years of age, of dark complexion. He has a wife at Dr Grafton Tyler's, in Gtwn, D C.
–John B Mullikin, living near Queen Anne, PG Co, Md

House & lot at private sale: the subscriber, desirous of moving into the country, offers the frame House in which he lives, on L st, between 6th & 7th sts. This house is 2 years old, built in the best manner & of the best materials, containing 6 rooms. Also, a valuable bldg lot on the corner of L 7 8th sts. –A B Gladmon

WED JUN 24, 1846
Fires: the Pilgrim House, at Plymouth, Mass, kept by Mr Jos White, was destroyed by fire on Sat. Loss $3,400: insured. The dwlg-house of Mr Isaac Hudson, in Bridgewater, Mass, was consumed on Fri.

French's Hotel, Norfolk, has been taken by our late fellow townsman, Capt F Black, so well known to the public as the obliging commander of the mail steamers on the Potomac.

Valuable real estate at private sale: a 2 story frame house & premises, on Montgomery st, fronting 31 feet, now occupied by Mr Benj F Miller. Several lots adjoining the above on Montgomery & Stoddard sts, are also offered. The whole property fronts 194 feet on Montgomery & 120 feet on Stoddard. Inquire of Mr B F Miller, on the premises, or at the ofc of Messrs Ould & Peachy.

For sale: a fine large bay Horse, Buggy, & Harness. The horse is 7 years old & well broken to harness. The buggy has been used one year, & is not injured. Apply to John Foy, at the Capitol.

For rent: large commodious house on First st, Gtwn, [one of Cox's row,] formerly occupied by the Hon Mr Payne. It is undergoing repairs & improvements under the supervision of Mr M Duffey, & will be ready for a tenant by Jun 1. Apply to John H King, High st, Gtwn.

St Louis, Mo, Jun 14. Capt Weightman's fine company of horse artillery departed last evening for *Fort Leavenworth*, whence they will take up their march for Santa Fe. Numerous friends were present to bid them farewell. They are a choice body of young men. The following are the ofcrs:

Richd Hanson Weightman, Capt — Alfred V Wilson, 3rd Sgt
Andrew J Dorn, sr, 1st Lt — [Vacancy, 4th Sgt
Edmund F Chouteau, jr, 1st Lt — W C Kennerly, 1st Cpl
John O Simpson, 2nd Lt — Clay Taylor, 2nd Cpl
John R Gratiot, 1st Sgt — John R White, 3rd Cpl
Davis Moore, 2nd Sgt — Geo W Winston, 4th Cpl

The number of privates is 105. -Daily Reveille

THU JUN 25, 1846
Orphans Court of Wash Co, D C. Letters of administration on the personal estate of Benj Leddon, late of said county, dec'd. –C E Leddon, J S Harvey, adms

I certify that Geo Gedding of Wash Co, D C, brought before me as an estray, trespassing on his enclosure, a bay Mare. –Jas Marshall, J P Owner to come forward, prove property, pay charges, & take her away. –Geo Geddings, living on the Rockville road, near the *Sligo Mills*.

House & lot at private sale: the subscriber, desirous of moving into the country, offers the frame House in which he lives, on L st, between 6th & 7th sts. This house is 2 years old, built in the best manner & of the best materials, containing 6 rooms. Also, a valuable bldg lot on the corner of L 7 8th sts. –A B Gladmon

Selby Parker informs those indebted to him that their bills are now ready on his desk & will be delivered on Jul 1. It is his intention to close his present business.

Senate: 1-Ptn from Lydia Lord, wid/o John Lord, a soldier in the war of 1812, asking for a pension.

In Balt County Court, in the case of Harriet G C Sprigg vs Thos Irwin, sen, an action to recover damages for injuries received by the plntf from falling on the pavement before the property of the dfndnt, the jury, on Sat, brought in a verdict in favor of the plntf for the sum of $900.

A yoke of oxen came to the subscriber, near Wash, on Jun 15. Owner is to come forward, prove property, pay charges, & take them away. –Thos Fenwick

Sale of furniture, tavern fixtures: the subscriber, having determined to relinquish his present business, offers for sale the entire furniture & effects in the house known as Hepburn's Hotel, on the south side of Pa ave, nearly opposite Coleman's Hotel. For many years it was used as a tavern & restaurant, formerly by Mrs Latourno. -P J Hepburn

With orders from Wash for the increase of the rank & file of the army, & reoganization of the regts now in Texas, 4 companies from each regt of U S infty & dragoons have been broken up, & their non-commissioned ofcrs & privates, except sgts, joined with the 6 remaining companies of each regt. The vacancies in the list of ofcrs have been filled from ofcrs of the disbanded companies, & the residue ordered off on recruiting service to complete the organization of the regts to 1,000 strong. The following named ofcrs arrived on the Galveston yesterday: Lts Smith, Gordon, Johns, & Van Bokkeler, of the 3rd Infty, destined for Newport, Ky; Capts Morrison & Morris, of the 4th Infty, & Capt Montgomery, & Lts Burbank, Jordan, Beardsley & Reeves, of the 4th Infty, for N Y; Lts Marcy, Ruggles & Crittenden, of the 5th Infty, for Phil; Majors Rains & Seawell, & Capts Hawkins & Lee, & Lts Hayman, Henry & Wood, of the 7th Infty, for Boston; Capt Hunter, & Lts Lowrey & Sanders, of the 2nd Dragoons, for Balt. -Picayune

Rencontre on Jun 13, in Lebanon, Ky, between 2 young men, citizens of that place, Thos Chandler & Thos Elder. Elder fired at Chandler without effect; Chandler stabbed Elder causing his death. The parties are said to be respectable. –Elizabethtown [Ky] Register

Died: on Jun 23, of congestion of the brain, Ann Virginia Cover, in her 16th year.

Died: on Jun 22, at the residence of his dght, on 3rd st, Gtwn, D C, Horatio Jones, in his 62nd year. The dec'd, for many years a resident of Gtwn, had justly endeared himself, by his truly Christian walk & conversation, to a large circle of friends.

Died: on Jun 14, in Stokes Co, N C, Walter Gwynn, infant s/o the Hon A H Shepperd & Martha P T Shepperd.

FRI JUN 26, 1846
Maj C P Montgomery, brother of the distinguished Maj L P Montgomery, of the U S Army, who fell at the battle of Horse Shoe, is now in Wash City. We have a prospectus of the Life & Speeches of Maj Lemuel P Montgomery, of the U S Army, left with us by his surviving brother. It fills up a vacuum in the history of the late war, & will be edited by Chas Cassedy. The book will contain the lives of Col Lauderdale, Col Henderson, Gen Coffee, & an accurate history of the Southern war under Gen Jackson.

Senate: 1-Cmte on Pensions: bill for the relief of Peter Engles, sr, with a report: to be printed. 2-Cmte on Pensions: adverse report on the ptn of Cecilia Carroll, which was ordered to be printed.

Wash Corp: 1-Ptn from Jas A Breast & others: referred to the Cmte on Improvements. 2-Ptn from Nathl Plants & others: referred to the Cmte on Improvements. 3-Ptn from Richd Wroe, sen: referred to the Cmte of Claims. 4-Bill for the relief of Robt Beale & John Lee: referred.

Household & kitchen furniture at auction[very good & well kept]: on Jun 30, by order of the Orphans Court of Wash Co, D C: at the residence of the late Mrs Maria E Morgan, on Missouri ave, between 3rd & 4½ sts. -R W Dyer, auct

Thos M Milburn still keeps on hand at his old stand south side of Pa ave, between 9th & 10th sts, household furniture of various kinds, as also at his residence on Mass ave, between the aforesaid sts, in the Northern Liberties, where he has a branch of his business.

Died: on Jun 25, in Wash City, Wm A Williams, in his 58th year. The dec'd was a member of the Masonic Fraternity, & Past Master of Wash Lodge 22 in Alexandria. His funeral is from his late residence on Missouri ave, this day, at 10 o'clock, the Masonic procession is in Alexandria.

Died: on Jun 24, Ann Permelia, y/d/o Elijah & Ann Eliz Dyer, aged 1 year & 10 days.

SAT JUN 27, 1846
Senate: 1-Bill for the relief of Elijah White, to be engrossed for a 3rd reading. 2-Bill in addition to the act for the relief of Walter Loomis & Abel Gay, approved Jul 2, 1836. 3-Bill to authorize the settlement of the accounts of John Crowell.

The Trustees of Wash Academy, Princess Anne, Somerset Co, Md, wish to employ a teacher to take charge of said institution from & after the 1st Mon of Oct next: salary of $600. –Wm W Handy, J W Crisfield, S W Jones, Com'rs

Died: on May 24, at his residence, near Courtland, Alabama, after a protracted illness, Col Wm McMahon, in his 66th year. Col McMahon was born in Augusta Co, Va, on Aug 12, 1780, & removed thence to the adjoining county of Rockingham in 1809, & from thence to Alabama in 1838.

Annual Commencement of the College of N J at Princeton took place on Mon. Among the speakers in the Jr Class we notice 2 from D C: Mr Chas H Key, whose theme was Modern Heroism, & Mr Frank K Dunlop, who delivered an address on the Progress of the Arts. The honorary degree of LL D was conferred on the Hon Jas McDowell, of Va.

MON JUN 29, 1846
The laying of the Corner-stone of the Methodist Episcopal Church in the 1st Ward of Wash City is to take place on Jul 1, at 5 o'clock.

Two farms for sale: about 46 acres each, on the old Bladensburg road, about 3 miles from Wash. Apply at the house-furnishing store of Boteler, Donn & McGregor, Pa ave.

Portsmouth [Va] New Era states that Miss Virginia Hope, a niece of Mrs Peed, residing in Glasgow st, in that town, was so severely burned on Mon last, in consequence of her clothes taking fire, that she died on Tue, after suffering excruciating agony.

On Jun 22, the new dwlg in the course of erection near Snow Hill, Md, by the Hon Thos A Spence, was consumed by fire. Loss $3,000.

Batavia Times: on Wed last a lad named Martin Cone, aged about 15 years, residing some 3 miles north of that village, accidentally hung himself while playing with a swing. He was alone at the time.

House of Reps: 1-Ptn of Deborah Marot & 1,014 other women of Phil, praying for the abolition of slavery in D C & the slave trade between the States.

Wm Huffington, who resided about 2 miles from Indianapolis, was accidentally killed on Jun 10. Two of his brothers were preparing a gun for shooting birds when one gun accidentally discharged shooting the brother in the heart.

Take notice: by virtue of a writ of distrain from Mathias Bouvet, & to me directed, I have seized & taken sundry goods & chattels, the property of Momus Gilbert, to satisfy rent due & in arrears to Mathias Bouvet. -Danl McPherson, Bailiff
-J Robinson & Co, auctioneers

The subscriber, being duly authorized by powers of atty from Cornelius P Van Ness & Madalina Van Ness his wife; N M Hoffman & Gertrude Hoffman his wife; Chas W Van Ness, Miss Matilda E Van Ness, Eugene Van Ness, & Edw Van Ness, heirs at law of the late Gen John P Van Ness, to manage & dispose of the real estate in D C belonging to the estate of the said John P Van Ness, & to collect all arrearages of purchase money or rents now due, or which may hereafter fall due, & to give full receipts & acquittances therfor, hereby gives notice to all persons indebted as aforesaid for rents or purchase money which have become due & payable since the death of said John P Van Ness, or which may become due, that he will receive payment thereof; & he requests all persons so indebted to call on him for this purpose. –Rd Smith

A little boy, s/o Mr Jas Wivill, living near Piney creek, Carroll Co, Md, came to his death on Jun 16, by being drowned in a spring of water near the house of his parents.

Appointments by the Pres, by & with the advice & consent of the Senate.
1-Thos Gray, Surveyor & Inspector of the Revenue for the port of St Louis.
2-Chas Obermeyer, U S Consul for the city of Augsburg, in the Kingdom of Bavaria.
3-J Geo Harris, to be Purser in the Navy, to fill the vacancy occasioned by the death of Purser Cox.
4-John D Clark, Justice of the Peace for Wash Co.
5-Edgar Snowden & Geo W P Custis, Justices of the Peace for Alexandria Co.

Mrd: on Jun 25, by Rev Mr Eggleston, Henry E Stanley to Miss Louisa E Berry, both of Wash City.

Mrd: on Jun 25, in Burkittsville, Fred'k Co, Md, by Rev Mr Houer, Jas S Carper, of Leesburg, Va, to Miss Eliz Ohr Cost, only d/o the late Geo Cost, of the former place.

Died: on May 10, after a short illness, at his residence in Montg Co, Md, Mr Basil Duvall, in his 46th year, s/o Frederic & Emesy Duvall.

Died: on Jun 28, Mary Ellen, infant d/o John & Bridget McMahon, aged 13 months & 22 days. Her funeral is this evening at 4 o'clock, from the residence of her father, corner of E & 10th sts.

Senate: 1-Ptn from Madison Allen, asking the renewal of certain land scrip which was destroyed while in his possession. 2-Cmte on Pensions: bill for the relief of Welcome Parmenter. Same cmte: bill for the relief of John England. 3-Bill for the relief of John Jones, surviving partner of John Jones & Chas Souder, & the bill for the relief of Nathl Stafford, were severally considered in the Cmte of the Whole & ordered to be engrossed for a 3rd reading. 4-Bill for the relief of Abraham B Fannin. 5-Bill for the relief of Nathl Perry & J M Reese: referred to the Cmte on Commerce. 6-Act for the relief of Philip & Eliphalet Greene: referred to the Cmte on Commerce. 7-Act for the relief of John S McLeod, of Lynn Co, Mo: referred to the Cmte on Public Lands.

Orphans Court of Wash Co, D C. Letters of administration on the personal estate of Jas Radcliffe, late of the U S Navy, dec'd. –Demares Radcliffe, adm

TUE JUN 30, 1846
Foreign Items: The Prince Royal of Denmark, who was divorced from his first wife, d/o the late King Fred'k XI, has applied to be divorced from his second, the Princess Caroline, of Mecklenburg Strelitz, on the ground of insurmountable aversion.

Copartnership under the name of John & Philip Ennis is this day dissolved by mutual consent. All debts due the firm will be collected by John Ennis, who will continue the business. –John Ennis, Philip Ennis

By virtue of an order for distress & to me directed, I shall expose to public sale on Jul 7, on Pa ave, between 4½ & 6th sts, at the 3 story brick house adjoining the store of Semmes & Murray, sundry goods seized & taken for house rent due in arrears by Mrs Whitehill to Raphael Semmes, & will be sold to satisfy same.
–R R Burr, Bailiff -R W Dyer, auct

Senate: 1-Ptn from John Mortimer, jr, asking to be reimbursed certain duties alleged to have been illegally exacted by the collector of the port of N Y. 2-Cmte on Military Affairs: bill for the relief of Josephine Nourse. 3-Following adverse reports were taken up & concurred in: ptn of Mary Biggs; of Jonthan Tyner, of Abigail Edgerby; of the reps of Jas Livingston; of the reps of Jonathan Smith; of the excecutor of Judah Allen, administrator of Wm Terry; ptn of the excx of Jas Maxwell; bill for the relief of Nathl Stafford, of Vt; bill for the relief of John Crowell, Indian Agent.

Orphans Court of Wash Co, D C. Letters of administration on the personal estate of Benj Leddon, late of said county, dec'd. –C E Leddon, J S Harvey, adms

Assignee's sale: at public auction, on Jul 6 next, all the right, title, & interest [being a life-estate in one-half thereof] of Leon R Garonski in & to lot 44 in square 503, in Wash City, together with the 3 story brick house thereon. –David A Hall, Assignees of Bankrupts -Wm Marshall, auct

Circuit Court of Wash Co, D C-in Chancery. Aug R Theriot vs Peter Porsetts, adm, et al. Ratify sale by the Trustee of lot 31 in square A, in Wash City, to Michl McDermott being the highest bidder, who became the purchaser thereof for the sum of $1,747.83, & complied with the terms of the sale. –W Brent, clk

Tract of land for sale in Montg Co, Md: 248 acres near the farm of Dr Washington Duvall, & adjoins the land of Mr Elias Berry, & is only 4 miles from Colesville. Apply to Nicholas Callan, F st.

Died: a few days ago, at Greencastle, Pa, Doct John McClellan, in his 84th year. He was a student of the late Dr Benj Rush, M D. Surgery was essentially his forte, steady hand, & vigorous nerve, were all united in him. Never disconcerted, he was a dexterous operator.

Lt Morris, of the revenue cutter **Van Buren**, died at sea on board the cutter on Jun 10.

On Wed last the body of Mr Archibald S Clarke, of this parish, was found in the pasture adjoining the plantation of Jesse Stanbrough, with life extinct. It was found that he came to his death by the accidental discharge of a yager in his own hands. Mr Clarke has left a wife & children. He was an honest man, a most industrious & useful citizen. He was a printer by profession, & for several years was the editor of the Port-Gibson Correspondent. –Madison [Louisiana] Journal

WED JUL 1, 1846
List of letters remaining in the Post Ofc, Wash, Jul 1, 1846.

Avery, Wm W	Brent, Dr A L	Butler, J W
Allen, Thos	Brown, J M	Bardin, Capt Wm
Allen, Thos D	Beams, Miss S	Bowen, Mrs F
Asbury, Coleman	Bloom, Miss A M	Beyer, Miss H
Ashard, Wm K	Brown, Ludwel H	Butler, Thos
Alston, Thos	Bokes, Rev D	Buckley, Miss A M
Archbold, Saml-2	Benham, Mrs M S	Bradley, Alexr
Arnold, Wm H	Buckner, Dr C S	Barret, Dr L
Alston, Thos	Bolton, Com	Burnet, Miss B
Armstrong, S T	Barton, Dr E H	Bryant, Mrs S J
Brown, Wilson	Boston, Robt	Browers, Mrs M A
Burke, Mrs A M	Baltzell, Miss E	Bartlin, A S H
Brown, Miss M	Barboza, J M-2	Bernard, John
Boyd, Cooper S	Bensancon, E R	Barock, Maria

Berry, Washington
Bottomer, Francis
Bent, Passed Mid, Silas-2
Blair, John, of Tenn
Cole, Mrs A H
Carr, Edw
Clitz, Mrs M G
Cook, Col Wm
Clair, Mrs M-2
Clarke, Gustavus
Crarps, Miss M
Clarke, John J
Clarke, Miss J N
Chase, Mickey
Choate, Rufus
Carr, Geo M
Crough, John
Collins, Mrs M
Connahan, Hugh
Campbell, Mrs C M
Crosby, Mrs A
Chapman, Mrs S R
Chapman, Basil
Conway, Jos
Carroll, Mrs E
Callagher, Jas
Collier, Jos
Cover, Danl
Carusi, Saml
Clements, Ignatius
Clements, Miss L
Carusi, Gaetano
Clements, Miss S
Chapman, Capt Wm W
Colquhoun, Maj W S
Cummings, Lt Col, D C
Clarkson, Maj C S-3
Deane, jr, F B
Duncan, Dr A-2
Dixon, G W
Downey, Jonas
Downey, Thos

Devond, Benj
Dana, Amasa
Doherty, Wm
Duncan, Jas L
Davis, Wm L
Downey, John
Dunohoo, Mrs H
Donohoo, Mgt
Duvall, Gen J P
Dorsey, Alfred
Douglass, Jas C, U S N
Downing, Miss H A
Edwards, Miss E J
Elliott, Mrs E
Ennis, John
Emerson, Geo
Edmond, Mrs S H
Evans, Mrs Ann
Ericsson, John
Fource, Germain
France, Mrs M
France, Mrs M A
Flagg, John G
Ferrer, Morgan
Fryers, Miss S B
Flenrickin, R P
Fisher, Edmund
Forest, Alex'r
Fowler, Mrs Julia
Frazer, Mrs L A
Forshey, Moses
Feinour, Dr Thos
Frelinghuysen, T
Fletcher, Mrs L D
Farrington, Maj R M
Grooves, Miss L J
Grey, Benj E
Grimes, Miss S M
Gwinn, Dr W M-6
Gooding, Wm
Gifford, Geo
Gibbons, Saml
Gillespie, Lt A H
Gordon, David

Gardner, Capt J L
Graham, Mrs
Hart, Saml J
Hall, Francis X
Heap, Harris
Hall, Harman
Hyde, Anthony
Hall, John
Hull, Asbury
Hook, Miss A M
Hess, Jacob
Hough, Wm J
Hevener, Peter
Howell, Gen J B
Haier, Fred'k
Hedrick, David
Hitchcock, Josiah
Hepburn, David
Handley, Miss I
Henry, Ann
Hammack, Wm
Herndon, Lewis
Harry, Jos M
Hooper, Chas-3
Howard, Gen B C
Haxall, Mrs B
Hopkins, Miss M E
Hillseman, Miss S
Hallett, Wm
Harris, Col C C
Hunter, Lt T T
Indemaur, Mr
Jones, Miss P
Jones, Arthur
Jones, Isaac
Jones, Miss C
Jones, Col J L
James, J Sexton
Jasper, Wm
Jackson, Mrs A
Jeffers, Mrs M
Johnson, Mrs H
Jackson, Capt W A
Johnston, Mrs S
Jockum, Peter

Knapp, Garey
King, Dr H-2
Krum, John M-2
Kugan, Mary
Kilian, Geo
Kearney, Comr L
Keabel, Jacob
Kenan, John
Kehoe, Miss E
Kendrick, Miss M
Lunt, Mrs Sarah
Leeds, John
Lovett, Geo S
Latham, Geo N
Lively, Wm
Lucas, Willis-2
Lohmier, Henry
Lohear, Ann
Leger, Hertz
Louis, Mrs M
Lindsley, Rev Dr P
Lyon, Miss Olivia
Lawton, Capt R B
Leslie, Maj T J
Le Brun, Capt J
Moore, Miss S
Marks, Jacob
May, Alex'r
Moore, Mrs C
Morris, Miss E
Murphy, Wm
Mastin, John P
Minor, Lt C J
Morton, Col A B
Morgan, Geo C
Moran, Mike
Mason, Mrs, Lt Col R B
Macres, Thos
Marquis, Wm H
Murray, Jas C
Miller, Wm B
Maffitt, Lt J N
Mazeen, Mrs M
Maddox, Dr

Miller, Jacob
Menairy, Frank
Meteer, Andrew
Marshall, Charlotte
Murray, Passed Mid Alex'r-3
Matchett, Miss M F
Mavin, Lt M C
Mackay, Robt
McRae, Col J J
McKeage, John
McGalway, Jos
MacGregor, Jas
MacIntire, Rev T
McMillion, John
Niles, Mrs J M
Niles, Saml
Naylor, Col W
Nelson, Geo E
Naser, Fred'k
Ord, Lt E O C
O'Brien, Wm
Owen, Robt
Piles, Lewis
Pope, Capt H
Pope, Lt John-2
Pew, Thos J
Preston, Wm C
Parker, Thos-2
Pierpont, Miss E
Philips, Mrs Ann
Patterson, Mrs E
Parrott, John
Preusser, Dr E
Pickett, Col J C-3
Reed, John
Ross, John W
Reed, Jos J
Ray, Winthrop G
Riley, Philip
Reynolds, Lt W
Roberts, John
Robinson, Fay
Rollins, Mrs L
Rawdon, Freeman

Stout, Edw C
Simms, Miss J E
Sims, Miss M
Schwartz, Mrs B
Swett, John B
Simms, Mrs S
Schad, Mrs
Schmid, Casper
Smith, Nathan
Smith, Mrs B P
Steele, Gen G K
Spring, Christian
Smith, Mrs Jane
Shields, Comr W F
Slaughter, Col W B
Stewart, Thos T
Starkey, Isaac G
Sperry, J Austin
Sherwell, Robt
Stetson, Miss M A
Strother, Mrs M
Stratten, Edw
Schermerhorn, Rev J F-3
Spillman, John
Smallwood, Danl
Suggett, Wm
Spalding, Maj D-3
Stevens, Com adm of estate
Storm, Gen H
Sheppard, Susan
Tate, Dr Jas H
Taylor, Col L G
Turner, Com D
Taylor, Jas B
Tappin, Benj
Terrett, Geo H
Thompson, Chas
Turner, Mrs C
Tansill, R, U S N
Tyock, Wm
Turpin, Eliz A H
Thomas, Miss E
Thibodeaux, Mrs J

Tillman, John	White, Mathias M	Williams, Miss M E
Taylor, Lt W W	Wright, Mrs J	Wilson, Eliz
Taliaferro, John	White, Mrs M A	Webster, Saml
Tailor, Mrs M	Weeks, Wm H	Wynn, Col W L-3
Townely, Eugene	Wills, John	Williams, Jas-2
Thomas, Geo	Wiley, Miss A V	Williams, Capt W
Tracey, Albert	Williams, Saml	Wilkinson, Comm
Tattnall, Com J	Wilson, Jas C	Jessee D
Upperman, Chas E	Wilson, Jas G	Williams, Miss M A
Voglin, Catharina	Wilson, Chas H	Williams, Jos L
Vinson, John E	Webster, Hanson	Yale, Lewis
Vinton, Thos J	Waters, Wm P	Young, jr, Benj
Wayne, Judge	Washington, Mrs M	Yonge, Chandler C
Ward, Miss M	Whiting, Lt Col Henry-2	

The inland postage on all letters intended to go by ship must be paid, otherwise they remain in this ofc. -C K Gardner, P M

On Mon last, while Mr Dove & his 2 sons were crossing the Alleghany at Dickson's Falls, their skiff sunk when near the shore. Mr Dove & his sons were drowned. Another boy with them swam to shore. –Pittsburg Journal

The Lewisburg [Va] Chronicle states that on Jun 22, 391 manumitted slaves of the late John Randolph passed through that place, on their way to their new home in the West-a large tract of land having been purchased in Mercer Co, Ohio, for their benefit. The army is headed by an old patriarch of 110 years, who rode on a horse beside the young & healthy, leading them to the land of their adoption. [Aug 10th newspaper: the last Piqua [Ohio] Register says: these unfortunate creatures have again been driven from lands selected for them. They tried to settle in Shelby Co, but, like the attempt in Mercer, it has failed. They were driven away by threats of violence. About a third of them remained at Sidney, intending to scatter & find homes wherever they can. The rest are now at the wharf in boats.] [Aug 15th newspaper: Judge Leigh, despairing of being able to colonize them in a free State, has concluded to send them to Liberia. –Richmond Republican]

Affray occurred at a circus at Nashville, on Jun 20th, between 2 young men, Coriolanus Branch, 19, the other Moore, in which Branch was killed by a stab in the breast with a knife, & a brother of his at the same time severely wounded. The dec'd was an industrious mechanic, the main reliance of a widowed mother & several children.

The subscribers offer for sale the Gazette Establishment of the Lexington [Va] Gazette. Possession to be given at the end of the present volume, in Sep next. The ofc is supplied with a first-rate hand press & a good stock of printing materials. Address O P Baldwin, Richmond, or W F Drinkard, Lexington.

The oil factory of Mr A W Quimby at Charlestown, Mass, was destroyed by fire last Sat. Loss from $30,000 to $35,000.

Criminal Court-Wash: 1-Edw Hamilton, charged with the murder of his wife, Martha Hamilton, commences today.

Mrd: on Jun 30, at the Church of the Epiphany, by Rev Mr French, Jos H Berret, of Boston, to Nannie Baynton, d/o the late Jas Abercrombie, of Balt.

Alexandria-Retrocession. Proposed dismemberment of the Permanent seat of Gov't selected by Geo Washington, under the authority of the Constitution, & the Laws of Congress passed in pursuance thereof, & with the cession, in good faith, & in perpetuity, of the ancient & honorable Commonwealth of Virginia. It was determined that the seat of the Genr'l Gov't should be under the exclusive control of the Gov't; the Legislature of Md, on May 24, 1783, resolved that there should be a fixed & permanent place of residence for the reception of Congress & their ofcrs. On Jun 28, 1783, the Legislature of Virginia: Resolved, unanimously, that, if the Legislature of Md are willing to join in a cession of territory for the above purpose with the State, [the said territory to lie on the river Potomac,] this Assembly will cede to the honorable Congress to fix their residence on either side of the said river; offering 100,000 pounds should the south side be adopted, or 40,000 pounds should the north side be determined upon, towards the erection of bldgs for Congress. Should Congress remove from such district, those land should revert to the Commonwealth. There was no intimation, much less a stipulation, for retrocession. On Dec 23, 1788, the Legislature of Md ceded any district of this State, not exceeding 10 miles square, which Congress may fix upon & accept the seat of Gov't of the U S. On Dec 3, 1789, the Legislature of Va enacted that a tract of country, not exceeding 10 miles square, or any less quantity, to be ceded & relinquished to the Congress & Gov't of the U S. Acceptance by Congress was done by the Acts of Jul 16, 1790, & Mar 3, 1791. On Jan 24, 1791, the Pres declared that all that part within said 4 lines of experiment which shall be within the State of Md & above the Eastern Branch, & all that part within the 4 lines of experiment which shall be within the Commonwealth of Va, & above a line to be run from the point of land forming the upper cape of the mouth of the Eastern Branch due s w, & no more, is now fixed upon, & directed to be surveyed, defined, limited, & located for a part of said district. The Pres issued his proclamation of Mar 30, 1791, for the purpose of amending & completing the location of the whole of the said territory of 10 miles square. We believe that the dismemberment of a part of this District, however small, will be the removal of a corner-stone from the political fabric; that it will be the first fatal act in sapping its foundation, the remote, if not proximate, consequences of which would not fail to cause poignant regret to those who might aid in its accomplishment. –Pro Patria Wash Co, Jun 30, 1846.

Furnished rooms to let: having taken the house formerly occupied by Mrs Balmain, on G, between 17 & 18th sts. Apply to Mrs A Ricketts, near the premises.

The Fourth of July will be celebrated at the Piney Point Pavilion in the usual manner, by reading the Declaration of Independence & delivering an Oration. The day will conclude with an elegant Dinner & Ball. Many distinguished members of Congress will be present, among them Gens Houston & Rusk, of Texas. The steamboat **Oceola** will leave Wash on Fri, at 3 o'clock, & will return on Sun evening. The boat **Columbia** will leave *Piney Point* on Sun, at 10 o'clock, for Wash. –Jas H Birch

For rent: convenient Boarding House on C st, near 4½ st, now occupied by Miss Gurley. Possession given on Sep 15 or earlier if desired. Apply to Dr Lindsly.

Senate: 1-Memorial of Capt Saml Walker, of Texas Rangers, praying Congress to remunerate him & his brave companions in arms for losses sustained by them in horses & rifles in the defeat they sustained in an engagement with an overwhelming force of the enemy. 2-Cmte on Indian Affairs: bill for relief of John Crowell, with instructions to settle the accounts of said Crowell, notwithstanding the act of 1845, reported the bill back in conformity with the same. 3-Cmte on Printing: to whom was referred the journal of Lt Abert, reported that the cost of printing the usual number, with lithograph plates & maps, would be $1,012.82; & the cost of extra numbers would be .45 a copy. 4-Cmte on Revolutionary Claims: the case of Thos Bryant was taken up & concurred in. 5-Cmte on Pensions: the case of Cecelia Carroll was taken up & concurred in.

Newport Herald of Sat: loss of the brig **Sutledge**, of Pictou, N S: Capt Graham, of & from the same, for Fall River, was received here by the arrival of the schnr **Dusky Sally**, Capt Wilder, of & from Hingham. On the deck lay the dead bodies of those who had been picked up from the wreck, surrounded by their kindred & friends who had been rescued from the watery grave. The **Sutledge** sailed on Jun 12, with 56 passengers; on Jun 26, being thick & foggy, came to anchor; on the following morning got under way; struck on a ledge of rocks [in the Vineyard] called the Sow & Pigs; the tide caused her to slew round, she backed off the ledge, filled, & went down, bow first, in 10 fathoms water. The boat was got out & the passengers rushed into it, when the Capt gave orders to shove her from the brig. He jumped overboard & swam to the boat, & kept her close to the brig, picking up such as jumped into the water: picking up 31 alive. The schnr **Dusky Sally** being near, sent her boat to assist, & saved 6 more alive, who were in the water, & 3 more alive from the rigging of the sunken brig. The bodies of 4 women & 12 childrenwere picked up by the 2 boats. The passengers were all foreingners, mostly Scotch, & were on their way to Pennsylvania, where they expected to find employment in the mining establishments.

THU JUL 2, 1846
Valuable Farm for sale: the subscriber, desirous of returning to his native county, Calvert, would sell at private sale, his Farm, in the forest of PG Co, about 11 miles from Upper Marlborough, containing about 600 acs: known as *Rosemount Estate*, the residence of the late Govn'r Kent. –Jos K Roberts, *Rosemount*

Senate: 1-Ptn from John Martin, an ofcr in the last war with Great Britain, asking to be allowed arrears of penson. 2-Cmte on Foreign Relations: asking to be discharged from the further consideration of the memorials of Wm R B Gales & Thos Wilson. 3-Cmte on Pensions: House bill granting a pension to Elijah C Babbit, without amendment. Same cmte: adverse report on the ptn of Resin Tevis for an increase of pension. Same cmte: asking to be discharged from the further consideration of the ptn of Saml Knapp, & that it be referred to the Cmte on Revolutionary Claims. 4-Cmte on Foreign Relations: adverse report on the ptn of John Strohecker. 5-Bill introduced for the relief of the heirs of Robt Fulton. 6-Bill introduced for the relief of Fernando Fellanny. 7-Bill for the relief of John Crowell was read a 3rd time & passed.

Wanted, a woman to do the cooking, washing, & ironing, for a small family. Apply at Mrs Hitz's dry good store, B st south, Capitol Hill.

Colonels Stephen W Kearney & David E Twiggs have been appointed by the Pres of the U S, to be Brig Genr'ls in the U S Army, in accordance with the provisions of the act of Jun 18, 1846. The nominations of Zachary Taylor, to be Maj Gen in the Army, & Wm O Butler, to be Maj Gen of Volunteers, have also been confirmed by the Senate.

Congress Hall, Cape Island, N J, is now open for the reception of visiters.
–J Miller & Sons

From the Rio Grande: 1-The boat **James L Day** arrived at New Orleans on the 23rd ult from Brasos Santiago, having sailed thence on the 20th. Among the passengers she brought over were Lt Col Payne, on his way to Washington with Mexican trophies, Majors Erwin & Fowler, Capts Smith, Stockton, & Page, & Lt Sturges-all of the army. 2-The capture of Reynosa by Col Wilson is confirmed; so is the report that Genr'ls Arista & Ampudia had both been ordered to Mexico. 3-Gen Henderson, of Texas, has been mustered into the service as a Maj Gen.

Mrd: on Jun 30, in the Church of the Ascension, by Rev Mr Gilliss, John T Gray, of Louisville, Ky, to Miss Virginia S Hook, d/o the late Capt Jos Hook, of Balt.

Mrd: on Jun 25, in Dinwiddie Co, Va, by Rev Isham E Hargrave, Mr John J Alston, of N C, to Miss Mary M Clark, of Va.

Died: on Jul 1, Mr Wm Ford, in his 48th year. His funeral is this afternoon, at 4 o'clock, from his late residence, corner of 19th & F sts.

Appointments by the Pres, by & with the advice & consent of the Senate.
Abraham Van Buren, Paymaster in the Army of the U S
Appointments in the Quartermaster's & Commissary's Depts, under the act approved Jun 18, 1846.

In the Quartermaster's Dept:
To be Quartermasters, with the rank of Major, the following:
John S Love, of Ohio   Geo A Caldwell, of Ky
Saml P Mooney, of Indiana   Levin H Cox, of Tenn
Alex'r Dunlap, of Illinois   Thos B Eastland, of Louisiana

To be Assistant Quartermasters, with the rank of Captain, the following:
T S Gilbert, of Ohio   Benj F Graham, of Ky
S H Webb, of Ohio   Robt B Reynolds, of Tenn
Thos H Wilkins, of Ohio   Jonas E Thomas, of Tenn
Robt Mitchell, of Indiana   Philip B Glenn, of Tenn
John Neff, of Indiana   Saml M Rutherford, of Arkansas
Elanson W Enos, of Indiana   Franklin E Smith, of Miss
Jas H Ralston, of Illinois   Harry Toulmin, of Ala
Henry Scott, of Illinois   Robt R Howard, of Ga
Jos Naper, of Illinois   Geo W Miller, of Missouri
Henry M Vanbeven, of Illinois   Geo Kennerly, of Missouri
Theodore O Hara, of Ky   Jos Daniels, of Texas
Geo P Smith, of Ky

In the Commissary's Dept:
To be Commissaries, with the rank of Major, the following:
Wm F Johnson, of Ohio   Julius W Blackwell, of Tenn
Jas C Sloo, of Ill   Wm Bobbitt, of Miss
Alfred Boyd, of Ky

To be Assist Commissaries, with the rank of Captain, the following:
Wm C McCauslin, of Ohio   Thos J Turpin, of Ky
Jesse B Stephens, of Ohio   Wm Garrard, of Ky
John Caldwell, of Ohio   Jas R Copeland, of Tenn
Delany R Eckles, of Indiana   Wm B Cherry, of Tenn
Christopher C Graham, of Indiana   Wm Fields, of Ark
Newton Hill, of Indiana   Robt Fenner, of Ala
J S Post, of Ill   Kemp S Holland, of Missousi
Jas M Campbell, of Ill   Thos P Randle, of Ga
Wm Walters, of Ill   Wm Shields, of Missouri
Saml Hackleton, of Ill   Amos F Garrison, of Missouri
Richd Gholston, of Ky   Stephen Z Hoyle, of Texas

FRI JUL 3, 1846

Alexandria-Retrocession Act to retrocede the county of Alexandria, in D C, to the State of Va. On Feb 3, 1846, the State of Va signified her willingness to take back the said territory ceded as aforesaid. This act shall not be in force until after the assent of the people of the county & town of Alexandria shall be given by a vote.

Wash Corp: 1-Ptn from Richd G Briscoe & others, referred to the Cmte on Improvements. 2-Ptn of Henry M Morfit & others, praying for the filling up of the gulley across K st, near 5th st: referred to the Cmte on Improvements. 3-Ptn of John Roby, praying the payment of a balance due him for repairing canal bridges: referred to the Cmte on Canals. 4-To the Cmte of Claims: act for the relief of Eliz G D Dulany, & the ptn of A G Seaman. 5-Ptn of Jas Cadem: referred to the Cmte on Improvements. The following nominations by the Mayor, were considered by the Board & confirmed:

Chas H Wiltberger, Register
Jos Radcliffe, 1st Clerk
Wm E Howard, 2nd Clerk
Jos H Bradley, Atty
Jacob Kleiber, Messenger
Isaac Milstead, Inspec of Tobacco
Jas A Tait, Com'r Western Section of the Canal
Jos Cross, Com'r Eastern Section of the Canal
Caleb Buckingham, Inspector of Fire Apparatus

J H Goddard, Wm Orme, & Ignatius Mudd, Com'rs of the Centre Market
Wm Serrin, Clerk of the West Market
John Waters, Clerk of Centre Market
H B Robinson, Assist Clerk of Centre Market
Peter Little, Clerk of Eastern Branch Market

<u>Inspectors & Measurers of Lumber:</u>
Henry S Davis
Wm G Deale
John W Ferguson
Benj Bean
Wm Douglass
John G Robinson

<u>Wood Corders & Coal Measurers</u>
Jas Gaither
John P Hilton
Saml Kilman
Nathl Plant
Richd Wimsatt
John B Ferguson

<u>Gaugers & Inspectors:</u>
Nicholas Callan for the 1st & 2nd Wards
Florian Hitz for the 3rd & 4th Wards

<u>Measurers of Bran, Shorts, & Ship-stuffs:</u>
Jas Gaither, for the 1st district
John B Ferguson, for the 2nd distrit

<u>Com'rs of the West Burial Ground:</u>
Saml Drury
John Wilson
J C Harkness
Guy Graham, Sexton

<u>Com'rs of the East Burial Ground:</u>
Jas Marshall
John P Ingle
Thos J Barrett, Sexton

That of Wm McCauley, for Sealer of Weights & Measures, was, on motion, referred to Messrs Magruder, Fitzpatrick, & Mudd.

Francis D Newcomb, late U S Surveyor Gen for Louisiana, has been acquitted on 2 indictments for defrauding the Gov't.

Western newspapers have apprized us of the death of Hon John Jas Marshall, one of the ornaments of the Bench of the State of Ky. He was the eldest s/o the late Hon Humphrey Marshall, & was born in Woodford Co, Ky, near Versailles, on Aug 4, 1785; graduated at Princeton College, N J, with the highest honors, in 1807; studied law with his maternal uncle Hon Alex'r K Marshall. In Sep, 1809, he married the only d/o Mr Jas Birney, of Danville, Ky, who, with 4 sons arrived at manhood, & one dght, survives him. He held various posts during his most active public life. He was at one time possessed of a magnificent estate; but his purse was at the service of his friends, & his name freely attached to whatever paper they presented him. He had not wholly discharged his debts when his life was terminated. For one firm alone he paid the large amount of $230,000. He has left as a legacy his example of untiring energy, unshrinking resolution, & stern integrity.

Official, from "The Union" of yesterday. A Court of Inquiry, to consist of Brvt Brig Gen H Brady, Brvt Brig Gen G M Brooke, & Col J Crane members, & Brvt Capt J F Lee recorder, has been ordered by the Pres to convene at *Fort Monroe* on Jul 18, to investigate the conduct of Brvt Maj Gen Gaines. 1-In calling upon the Govn'rs of several of the States for volunteers or militia to be mustered into the service of the U S, between May 1 & 16, 1846; & to examine the autority & circumstances under which the calls were made. 2-Similar charge with dates of between May 16 & Jun 1, 1846. 3-Mustering into the service of the U S a body of volunteers or militia of the State of Alabama, about Jun 12, 1846. 4-Giving orders, since May 1, 1846, to ofcrs of the ordnance, commissary, quartermaster, & pay depts. to issue & distribute ordnance & ordnance stores, subsistence stores, & for the disbursement & payment of public funds to certain individuals or bodies of men; & to inquire whether the persons to whom such issues or payments were ordered or made with legally in the service of the U S, or properly authorized to receive or have the custody of public property or money.

As the stage was passing between Bethlehem & Reading, Pa, on Wed night week, it was upset, & the Rev Peter Wolle, Bishop of the Moravian Church, & his lady, were severely injured-the reverend gentleman so badly that he could not survive. The stage is said to have been racing with one of an opposition line.

The case of Mr Barker Burnell, charged with embezzling the funds of the Manufacturers' Bank of Nantucket, have been quashed ab initio by the Supreme Judicial Court at Boston. It appears that measures were taken to force Mr Burnell into bankruptcy. The court left the matter standing precisely as if no proceedings had been instituted.

Mrd: on Jun 11, at Montrose, near St Louis, Mo, by Rt Rev Bishop Hawks, Dr Wm Marcellus McPheeters, late of Raleigh, N C, to Miss Pink, y/d/o the late Cary Selden, of Wash.

Died: on Jul 2, J W, infants s/o J C & M McKelden. His funeral will take place this afternoon at 2 o'clock.

Revolutionary Veteran Gone: died on Jun 25, at his residence, Cape May, near Cape Island, Jas Schellinger, pilot, in his 94th year. He was actively engaged on shipboard in our Revolutionary struggles, & was with Cmdor Barney in the hard fought battle off the capes of the Delaware, between the ship **Hyder Ali** & the ship **Monk**, resulting in the capture of the **Monk**, although of much heavier metal than the ship of the gallant Cmdor & his noble crew.

An explosion at Tue last at the powder mill of Mr Alfred Dupont, on the Brandywine, near Wilmington, Del, by which a man named Archibald Watson was so badly injured as to cause his death on Wed. He has left a wife & 4 children to mourn his death.

Senate: 1-Ptn from Andrew Parke, a soldier of the last war with Great Britian, asking to be allowed a pension. 2-Ptn from John M McIntosh, asking the payment of his claim against the U S. 3-Cmte on the Public Lands: bill for the relief of Madison Allen, of the State of Missouri. Same cmte: House bill for the relief of John G McLeod, without amendment. Same cmte: without amendment, House bill to confirm an entry of land made by the administrator of Jas Anderson, dec'd, of Iowa Territory. 4-Cmte on Revolutionary Claims: adverse report on the House bill for the relief of Nathl Bird.

Information wanted of Jos Holloran, who left this city some years since for the Western country. Any information of his place of residence will be thankfully received by his aged mother, if addressed to the care of Dr Philip Smith, of Wash, D C. –Ann Holloran

Household & kitchen furniture at auction on Jul 8, by order of the executor, at the late residence of Griffith Coomes, dec'd, near Coombe's wharf, a little west of the Navy Yard. –A Green, auctioneer

SAT JUL 4, 1846
For sale: that elegant furniture manufactured by Quantin & Lutz, of Phil, exhibited at the Nat'l Fair, is at the subscribers auction rooms: 1 fancy secretary, 1 arm-chair, 1 set of bookshelves, 1 music stand, 1 high-back chair covered with garnet plush. All of rosewood, & handsomely carved & ornamented. –B Homans, Pa ave, between 10th & 11th sts.

Thos B Griffith informs that he has removed to his former place of business in the new store next door to Mr Walter Harper & Co's fancy dry good store. He has a large assortment of all kinds of boots & shoes.

For sale: a very superior saddle & harness Horse, which the subscriber has owned for the last 4 years, warranted sound & gentle. Apply to G W Phillips, of the firm of Pittman & Phillips.

For sale of rent: the new 3 story brick house occupied by the subscriber, on L st north, between 9th & 10th sts west. The lot is 68½ feet on L st, running north 209¾ feet; yard in front of the house, with a variety of choice roses. L st, in front of this property, from 7th to 10th sts, is now being paved. The new market-house on K st north, between 7th & 8th sts, is in progress to completion. –Geo Gilliss, Agent

The Saturday Evening News, a weekly newspaper & professional directory: the first number intended to be published on Jul 4, 1846, will not be issued until Jul 18, the type & materials purchased by the subscriber not having arrived from Balt until yesterday. –Wm Thompson

House of Reps: Mr Ligon, of Md, was compelled to leave Wash in the midday train, owing to the sudden & severe illness of his wife.

Official: appointments by the Pres, by & with the advice & consent of the Senate. To be Brig Generals in the military service of the U S, in accordance with the provisions of the act [for the organization of the volunteer forces:] approved Jun 26, 1846.

Thos L Hamer, of Ohio	Thos Marshall, of Ky
Jos Lane, of Indiana	Gideon J Pillow, of Tenn
Jas Shields, of Illinois	John A Quitman, of Miss

The venerable Ashbel Green has been re-elected Pres of the Pennsylvania Bible Society. This venerable Jerseyman, who was Chaplain to Congress during Gen Washington's administration, & enjoyed a familiar intercourse with the great men of that day, is engaged in writing out the minutes of his diary-a faithful daily record of public events & the course of opinion, embracing the whole period of our history from the commencement of the Revolution.

Died: on Fri, in Wash City, Marmaduke Dove, a Master in the U S Navy, aged 70 years, long attached to the Navy Yard in this city. His funeral will take place from his residence, opposite the Marine barracks, on Jul 5, at 2 o'clock.

St Peter's Church, Capitol Hill. The patron feast of this church will be solemnly celebrated tomorrow, at 11 o'clock, the Very Rev P Verhaegen, Provincial of the Society of Jesus, will deliver an appropriate discourse, after which a collection will be taken up for the benefit of said church.

The fire-works manufactory of Mr John Bartlett, in Phil, was blown up on Fri. Mr Bartlett & his brother were in the bldg at the time, but escaped with but trifling injury.

Phil, Jul 3. Arrival of Recruiting ofcrs from the Rio Grande. Arrived on Tue night, by the Western cars: Capt Montgomery, 8th Infty; Lts Reeve, Burbank, Beardsley, Morris, & Jordan, 8th Infty; Lts Marcy & Ruggles, 5th Infty. Phil is the rendezvous for the 5th Infty, & Lts Marcy & Ruggles will remain here. The other ofcrs proceed to N Y to recruit for the 8th Infty. –U S Gazette

The brig **Francis Amy** arrived at Balt on Thu from her 2nd voyage of exploration & search after the treasure of the ship of war **San Pedro**, which was sunk off the Spanish main in 1815. She has recovered this voyage about the sum of $35,000 in Spanish money. This money was found at the bottom of the sea, about 3 feet under the sand, & beneath a coral formation, in 60 feet of water. The whole amount recovered from the wreck thus far is something more than $60,000. –American

TUE JUL 7, 1846
From our European Correspondent: Paris, Jun 16, 1846. The Criminal Court was in session last week: it was stifling in the Court; the thermomenter has risen to 87 degrees; extraordinary dispatch was practiced in the trial of Lecomte, the regicide, by the Chamber of Peers. Lecomte was dressed in a black frock-coat, with black stock, d la militaire. He wore a thick black moustache, & appeared about 45 years of age, & a powerfully-made man. Lecomte was suffered to survive only long enough for his spiritual preparation.

Among the recent deaths in N Y C, was the relict of the late Gen Ebenezer Stevens, of the Revolution, in his 91st year.

From our European Correspondent: Paris, Jun 16, 1846. Pope Gregory XVI had a swelling in the legs, but his general health was wonderful for his age. With all his political mistakes [& what could a poor monk have learnt in his cell of this wicked world's ways?] the Roman bishop is a genuine honest character. When he dies, you may fairly reproduce the words of Lord Bacon concerning his names sake & predecessor: Gregory XIII, who fulfilled the age of 83 years, an absolute good man.
+
Late from Europe. 1-Pope Gregory XVI died at the Vatican in Rome, on Jun 1, after a short illness. He was in his 81st year, & is represented to have been a good man. Cardinal Franzoni, Prefect of the Congregation of the Propaganda, aged 70, is expected to be his successor. 2-Lecomte, who attempted to assassinate the King of the French, has been tried & executed.

Alabama paper: Col John Crowell, of **Fort Mitchell**, Russell Co, Ala, died at his residence on Jun 20. He was a Delegate to Congress from Alabama whilst yet a Territorial Gov't, & the first Representative from the same district after it became of State. Since which he had for many years discharged the duties of Indian Agent for the country in which he lived.

Senate: 1-Ptn from Thos O'Neil, Deputy Marshal of the U S of the Eastern district of Pa, asking remuneration for services in arresting a fugitive from justice, charged with counterfeiting the coin of the U S. 2-Bill for the relief of the legal reps of Jno J Bulow, dec'd: postponed. 3-Bill to allow Elijah White additional compensation for services & reimbursement of expenses incurred as acting sub-agent west of the Rocky Mountains: to be engrossed & read a 3rd time. 4-Cmte of the Whole: bill granting a pension to Jos Morrison, dating back from 1835. Mr Evans explained the bill. Mr Morrison was an ofcr of the army during the late war with Great Britian, & had been wounded on board one of our ships of war on the lakes, where he had fought gallantly & acquitted himself nobly. He had volunteered on board, & found himself in the capacity, he [Mr Evans] believed of captain of marines, in which he received the dangerous & disabling wound that had unfitted him for the pursuits of civil life. The reason why the pension was antedated was, that in 1835 Mr Morrison had made application to the War Dept to be allowed a pension, but was told that he could not be pensioned by the War Dept, as he had been wounded in the naval service. Mr Morrison then made application to the Navy Dept, & was told that he could receive no pension from that ofc, because he belonged to the military branch. The case had been brought before Congress, & had passed one or the other branch every time it had been introduced, but had never had the good fortune to pass both Houses. The case was one that, from his own knowledge, he knew to be deserving of the consideration of the Senate, & he hoped it might receive it: ordered to be engrossed & read a 3rd time. 5-Bill for the relief of Henry Etting: to be engrossed. 6-Cmte of the Whole: bill for the relief of Benj Harris, of La Salle Co, Ill: to be engrossed for a 3rd reading. 7-Bill for the relief of Bent, St Vrain & Co: passed.

Died: on Jul 4, after a few hours' illness, Mrs Julia M Tayloe, w/o B O Tayloe, of Wash City, & d/o the late Hon J D Dickinson, of Troy, N Y.

Died: on Sunday last, in Wash City, of apoplexy, Mr Jas Cuthbert, aged 63 years, a native of England, but for the last 20 years a resident of Wash. His death has caused a family to mourn the loss of a kind husband & an affectionate father. His funeral is this afternoon, at 5 o'clock, from his late residence on Pa ave, 3 doors east of 4½ st.

Died: on Jul 2, at the residence of Mr Chapman, of Chas Co, Md, after an illness of 2 weeks, Wm F Herbert, late of PG Co, Md.

Died: on Jul 4, at the residence of her son-in-law, Horatio M Ward, in PG Co, Md, Mrs Hannah McCormick, relict of Alex'r McCormick, dec'd, in her 71st year, formerly a resident of Wash City for upwards of 50 years.

Balt, Jul 6, 1846. 1-I record a deliberate murder which was perpetrated on Sat at the corner of Park & Clay. A young man named Laplat Carter was killed by a person named Lewis Cummings. The assassin has not been arrested. 2-The jury, in the case of Lucy Crawford, petitioning for her freedom from H H Slatter, returned a verdict on Sat for the petitioner.

Valuable farm for sale: pursuant to a decree pronounced by the Circuit Superior Court of Law & Chancery of Fairfax Co, at the June term thereof, 1846, in the case of Albert Wren & others, vs Robt Darne & wife & others, the com'rs will on Aug 17, next, at Fairfax Court-house, offer for sale, at public auction, that valuable farm lying near to Falls Church, in said county, known as *Winter Hill*. This farm was formerly owned by John Wren, dec'd, & is now in the possession of Mr Walter Sewall. It contains, by a recent survey, 150 acres of land. –H W Thomas, W L Edwards, Com'rs: Fairfax Co, Va, Jul 1

Laws of the U S passed at the 1st session of the 29th Congress. To the <u>Winebagoes</u>: 1-For expenses of John W Quiney, a Stockbridge Indian, to the seat of gov't, while here, & returning: the sum of $200. 2-Payment to Baptiste Powlis, & the chiefs of the first Christian party of the Oneidas, stipulated in the 13th article of the treaty with the Six Nations of N Y, Jan 15, 1838: $4,000. 3-Payment to Wm Day, & the chief of the Orchard party of the Oneidas, stipulated in the 13th article of the treaty with the Six Nations of N Y, Jan 15, 1838: $3,000. 4-For the ransom of 2 white boys, Gillis Doyle & Thos Pearce, held by the Comanches in bondage, & delivered to the agents of the Gov't: $500. 4-To pay J A S Acklin, U S District Atty for the northern district of Alabama, for the professional services in defending Capt Jas H Rogers & Lt Roberts, in suits brought to recover damages for an act done by them, under the order of a superior ofcr, while in the service of the U S; also, to pay to Jos Bryan, agent of Wm Whitfield, for purchasing & distributing stock animals to the Creek Indians, pursuant to an article of a treaty made with said Indians: $489.

MON JUL 8, 1846
St Louis Republican of Jun 27 says: companies B & K, 1st Regt U S dragoons, from *Fort Atchison* & *Fort Crawford*, numbering 115 non-commissioned ofcrs & privates-with 119 horses & 15 mules-under the command of Capts E V Sumner & P St G Cook, arrived here last evening on the steamer **Gen Brooks**. Attached to the companies are Lts Hammond & Davidson, & Surgeon R A Simpson. They are destined for *Fort Leavensworth*, there to join the expedition against New Mexico.

Mr Solomon Snyder & Mr W B Rodney, members of a volunteer corps of Harrisburg, were very seriously injured on Jul 4, by the premature discharge of a cannon. The former lost one of his arms; the latter both of his eyes. He is not expected to survive.

The N Y Express says that the Califormia Expedition is going on famously, & adds: the regt of which Jonathan D Stevens is to be the Colonel is filling up with considerable rapidity. Several West Point Cadets, & even one Professor at the same institution, have eagerly joined the expedition. The regt is to be reviewed on Jul 20, & immediately afterward put into motion.

Mr Edwin Thayer, of Columbia Co, N Y, has invented a Self-Adjusting Railroad Brake. –Alb Eve Journal

Died: on Jul 7, after an illness of 12 days, Mr Salathiel Hicks, in his 25th year. His funeral is this day, at 5 o'clock, from the residence of Mrs D Galvin, C st.

Died: yesterday, after a painful & protracted illness, in her 58th year, Mrs Catharine Borrowe Ball, w/o Henry W Ball, & d/o John T Frost, of Wash City. Her funeral will take place this afternoon, at half past 4 o'clock, from her late residence on Capitol Hill.

Died: on Jul 3, George, s/o Henry & Sarah Hay, aged 7 years & 3 months.

Maysville, Jun 3. Died: on 27th inst, very suddenly, at the residence of the late Gen Henry Lee, in this county, Lt John Graham, of the U S Navy, in his 42nd year. The dec'd was born in this county, & for 28 years has been in the naval service of the country, entering first as a midshipman, & rising by regular promotion to lieutenancy. On the 22nd inst he left his residence near St Louis, & was on his way to the seat of Gov't, unsolicited by the Dept, to tender his aid in the prosecution of the war against Mexico. His absent wife, a son, & an interesting dght, just entering upon the sphere of womanhood-are smitten by a calamity which to them will be irreparable. He died of an affection of the heart. He reached this place on Fri, remained over night with his uncle, & on Sat at the home of his grandmother, with but slight & almost entirely unheeded symptoms of illness, but he was seized with a convulsion, which was radiply succeed by another, & was hurried in a few moments to his death.

A man named Isaiah Bacon has recovered damages from the city of Boston to the amount of $10,000, as compensation for injuries received by falling into a hole in the sidewalk of one of the streets. The writ directs the ofcrs to seize upon the goods of the inhabitants of the city of Boston; the said inhabitants to appear at the Supreme Judicial Court on Nov 2.

On Sat last a lad aged about 11 years, s/o a widow lady, Mrs McDaniel, residing at Selma, a place owned by Gen Geo Rust, near Leesburg, Va, was killed by being thrown from his horse. He had been sent to Gen Rust's residence, about a mile distant, on an errand. He was found with his neck & some of his limbs broken. -Chronicle

The Gtwn [Ky] Herald states that the bagging & rope factory of Mr B W Finnell, at that place, was destroyed by fire on Thu. Loss is supposed to be about $5,000

Criminal Court-Wash. U S vs Jos Lafontaine, charged with rape: verdict of not guilty. The accused has yet to be tried on another indictment, charging him with an assault & battery on the same female.

Accidents at N Y from the imprudent use of fire arms. 1-A lad, Wm Henry Willis, was severely wounded in the right arm, by the bursting of a pistol fired by another boy alongside of him, while in the Park. 2-A boy named Zilkin had 2 fingers blown off by the busting of a pistol. 3-Jas Gold, about 13 years, was severely lacerated in his left hand, in the act of firing a pistol near the American Museum. 4-Patrick Doulin, aged about 13 years, residing in Orange st, while firing off a pistol, on the Battery, was severely injured. 5-Mr Voorhies, a respectable citizen of Brooklyn, a ship carpenter by occupation, was in the act of firing a small ships' cannon, the piece burst, one of the fragments striking his leg & breaking it to pieces. The limb will probably have to undergo amputation. –N Y Sun

To the public. Having been called on by Mr Saml Hevener to inspect the steamboat **Arlington Belle**, I did, on Jul 3, & found her totally unfit & unsafe to be used for the transportation of passengers. The duty I owe the community compels me to give this notice, & to warn those who may go on her. –Wm Easby, Inspector

House of Reps: 1-Memorial of D Kleaner, agent of the German Association, praying remission of duties. 2-Ptn from Dorothy Perry, of Maine, wid/o a Revolutionary soldier, praying for a pension. 3-Ptn from Kick-o-neaks, a Cherokee Indian, in N C, asking compensation for a pre-emption right. 4-Memorial of Jefferson S Hurtsfield relating to several applications of his for patents.

Senate: 1-Ptn from Philip R J Friese, asking the payment of certain debenture bonds. 2-Four ptns from Geo Howe & Co: John Williams & Co; Jos Sill, Jas Read, & Chace & Grew: all asking repayment of duties alleged to have been illegally exacted on certain importations. 3-Three ptns of Cobb & Co; Thos P Cushing; Thos P Cushing & Co; Lambert & Slade, & Lambert, Slade & Co. 4-Cmte on the Judiciary: bill for the relief of Milledge Galphin, legal representative of Geo Galphin, dec'd, accompanied by an elaborate report: ordered to be printed. 5-Cmte of Claims: House bill for the relief of Sanl D Ennocks, with a recommendation that it do not pass. Same cmte: House bill for the relief of the heirs of Dr John Gray, without amendment. Same cmte: bill for the relief of the heris of Robt Fulton. Same cmte: House bill for the relief of William Culver, without amendment. 6-Cmte on Foreign Relations: House bill for the relief of Thos Ap Catesby Jones, without amendment. 6-Passed: bill for the relief of Henry Etting; bill for the relief of Benj Harris, of La Salle Co, Ill.

Gtwn Advocate: The floods of the rain have made 6 breaches in the Chesapeake & Ohio Canal from Gtwn up to Harper's Ferry. The boat **Charles**, from Wmsport, belonging to Mr John Emery, which was washed out with the embankment this side of Noland's Ferry, was the only one that was lost. She had on board 570 barrels of flour & 14 barrels of whiskey.

Col M G Lewis, one of the U S Com'rs who recently made a treaty on Brasas river with the Camanches & several other Indian tribes-was accompanied by his wife, of whom the New Orleans Tropic gives this account: Mrs Lewis has accompanied the expedition throughout. She started in feeble health, but returned much improved. She made presents of jewelry & clothing to the wives of the chief & captains.

Mrs Clavadetscher, former Mrs Bihler, has received a large assortment of Hair, consisting of Wigs, Half-wigs, Braids, long & short, & Curls of different kinds. Also, a variety of Fancy Goods.

THU JUL 9, 1846
Senate: 1-Cmte on Foreign Relations: bill for the relief of Joshua Dodge. Same cmte: bill for the relief of Sarah A King.

Foreign: in consequence of the death of the Pope Gregory XVI, the oldest Sovereign in Europe is now Ernest Augustus, King of Hanover, born Jun 5, 1771. The next in age is the King of the French, born Oct 5, 1773. A letter from Rone, in the Constitutionnel, states that the fortune left by the late Pope to his heirs is estimated at about eleven millions of francs.

Mr Wm M Meredith, s/o Jonathan Meredith, of Balt, was recently murdered at Independence, Mo, by Dr Harper, of that place. The Chicago Journal publishes a history of the affair, & states that Harper, without cause, became jealous of Merdith on account of an imagine intimacy with his wife, disguising his feelings, decoyed Meredith into his ofc & shot him dead. –Loudoun Chronicle

The remains of a man by the name of Duncan McKilb were brought to Cumberland, Md, for interment on Sunday last, who came to his death by plunging into the Potomac river near Green Valley Depot. –Civilian

Jas Sutherland, who resides in Bank st, in N Y, was seriously injured at Farmingdale, Long Island, by the discharge of a cannon, on Jul 4. He was dreadfully lacerated.

Frame house & lot at auction: on Jul 13, in front of the premises, belongs to the estate of the late John Glascoe, dec'd, at the corner of M & 26th sts, being the corner lot near the bridge over Rock Creek. –John Marbury, Hugh Caperton, Agents -B Homans, auctioneer

Mrd: on Jul 2, by Rev John P Donelan, Jas A McLaughlin to Anne E, d/o Jas Caden, all of Wash City.

Died: on Jul 8, in Wash City, John O'Neale, in his 32nd year. His funeral will take place from the residence of Mrs Inch, on 7th st east, near the Navy Yard, on this afternoon, at 2 o'clock.

The marriage of Count Alex'r Colonno Walewski with Mile de Ricci, grand dght of Machiavel, & the great niece of the last King of Poland, was solemnized on Jul 7 in the chapel of the Poniatowski palace at Florence, in the presence of nearly all the personages of distinction at Florence, including the Count of Larochefoucauld & Lord Holland, the French & English resident Ministers. The Grand Duke sent as his representative his Grand Equerry & Grand Chamberlain.

Geo W Buckner, age 23 years, is the same youth who, a short time since, was killed in a street fight in Palmyra with a young gentleman with whom he had become embroilded in the course of an affair of honor, to which they were neither of them original parties, but in which they mortally wounded each other. He was the s/o the late Baily Buckner, a gentleman well known in Virginia & in this District, & was a native of Rappahannock Co, Va. [From the Missouri Democratic Banner, Jun 17. A brother drops bitter tears over the bier, & a widowed mother weeps in the agony of her soul over the loss of her favorite son.]

FRI JUL 10, 1846
In the Market-handsome bldg lots in square south of square 572. This property is bounded by Indiana ave, C st north, & 2nd & 3rd sts west; 5 substantial dwlg-houses now in the course of erection by Messrs Sims, Blagden, Gunnell, & others.
–Wm W Birth, for the heirs of the late Jas Birth.

St Louis, Mo, Jul 3. Departure of the Volunteers at *Fort Leavenworth*, attached to Col Kearney's expedition, left the fort in the order stated below: Capt Waldo's company & Capt Read's company took up their line of march on the 22nd.
Capt Walton's company, Capt Parson's company, Capt Moss' company, & Capt Jackson's company left on the 26th & 27th under the command of Lt Col Ruff.
Capt Hudson's company, Capt Rodgers' company, & Capt Harrison's company left on the 29th under the command of Col A W Doniphan & Major Gilpin.
Capt Angney's company of Infty & Capt Murphy's company of Infty also left on the 29th. Capt Weightman's & Capt Fischer's companies of flying Artl were to leave on the evening of the 29th or the morning of the 30th. Col Kearney, with his staff, was to leave on the evening of the 29th & 30th. The troops at the time of their departure were in good health & excellent spirits. -Republican

Judge McCaleb, of the U S District Court, [says the New Orleans Courier,] pronounced a decision in the case, of a habeas corpus in favor of Henry Grammont, who was arrested as a deserter from Maj Gally's btln of artl, now stationed at *Fort Jackson*. Mr Grammont's enlistment was illegal, & ordered him to be set at liberty. [Gen Gaines was not authorized by the Pres to receive the btln into the service of the U S.]

Senate: 1-Cmte of Claims: bill for the relief of John Devlin.

To let: 2 story brick house south side of F st, between 11th & 12th sts, now occupied by Dr Darne. Inquire at the drug store of Wm Elliot, nearly opposite. Also, the spacious house on 7th st, over the shop of T F Harkness, Merchant Tailor, where has the key may be found.

Appointments by the Pres, by & with the advice & consent of the Senate:
Chas Mason, to be Chief Justice of the Supreme Court of Iowa from Jul 27, when his present commission will expire.
T S Wilson, to be Assoc Judge of the Supreme Court of Iowa from Jul 27, when his present commission will expire.
Chas K Gardner, to be Postmaster at Wash, vice Wm Jones, removed.
Robt N McMillan, to be Collector of the Customs for the district of Teche, & Inspector of the Revenue for the port of Franklin, La, vice Robt Royster, dec'd.
Robt Patterson, of Pa, to be a Major Genr'l [of volunteers] in the military service of the U S, in accordance with the provisions of the act approved Jun 26, 1846.
Assist Adj Genr'ls under the act of Jun 18, 1846:
Capt Geo A McCall, of the 4th Infty, to be assist adj gen, with the brevet rank of major.
Brvt Capt Wm W S Bliss, assist adj gen, to be assist adj gen, with the brevet rank of major.
1st Lt Randolph Ridgely, of the 3rd Artl, to be assist adj gen, with the brevet rank of captain.
1st Lt Geo Lincoln, of the 8th Infty, to be assist adj gen, with the brevet rank of captain.
1st Lt Oscar F Winship, of the 2nd Dragoons, to be assist adj gen, with the brevet rank of captain, in place of W W S Bliss, promoted.
In the Regt of Mounted Riflemen, or 3rd Dragoons:
Chas Ruff, of Missouri, to be captain, in place of Bela M Hughes, who declines to accept.

Vespasian Ellis, formerly U S Charge at Caraccas, has obtained from the Gov't of Venezuela the exclusive right of navigating the mighty Oronoco with steam vessels for 22 years, on term highly advantageous. –N Y Tribune

Criminal Court-Wash: 1-Jos Lafontaine was found guilty of simple assault upon Sarah Greene: sentenced to pay a fine of $1, & be imprisoned for 2 months in the county jail. 2-Negro Jas Taylor was found not guilty of larceny. 3-Andrew Hoover, jr, convicted of keeping a disorderly house, was sentenced to pay a fine of $1, & suffer one month's imprisonment. He was also found guilty of an assault & battery on Charlotte Payne: fined $5. 4-Jas Goshing, having submitted to an indictment for an assault on W M Stewart, was fined $8. 5-Julia Simms was tried yesterday for keeping a disorderly house & a house of ill-fame. The defence was made by Messrs Carlisle & Woodward. [Jul 13th newspaper: Julia Simms was acquitted.]

Louisville Journal: accident near New Albany: a hack, in which G W Powers, a 1st lt of one of the Indiana volunteer companies, & another person were riding, upset, & falling down a precipice, Powers was killed & the other person was injured.

SAT JUL 11, 1846
Senate: 1-Ptn from the reps of Lemuel P Montgomery, an ofcr in the last war with Great Britian, asking to be allowed a pension. 2-Ptn from the reps of Wm D Degges, asking permission to institute a suit against the U S for the recovery of certain lands erroneously conveyed by his excx to the Gov't. 3-Ptn from Royal E House, asking the aid of the Govn't in the construction of a magnetic telegraph between the cities of Washington & New Orleans upon a plan invented by him. 4-Ptn from J D Wychoff, asking compensation for materials furnished for the construction of the custom-house at N Y. 5-Cmte of Claims: a bill for the relief of Messrs Erskine & Eichelberger. 6-Consideration of the bill for the relief of the legal reps of John J Bulow: the Sec be authorized to withhold payment until it was proved to his satisfaction that the place of Bulow was occupied without his consent, & that such destruction was in consequence of the occupation of the U S troops. Bill was laid on the table.

The *Loveless Farm*, adjoining F P Blair's, will be sold today at 3 o'clock, on the premises, immediately on the Turnpike Road leading to Rockville, Md, about 5 miles from Wash. The farm, of 206 acres, was owned & occupied by Basil Loveless at his death. The homestead on the road was used as a tavern, & proved profitable. The sale will certainly be made at the time appointed, without bidding in by any of the heirs, none of whom are able to become the purchaser. The title is believed to be indisputable. –F P Blair, Agent, appointed to make sale & distribution among the heirs.

For rent: 3 story brick house on G st, between 14th & 15th sts. Apply to C Cammack, on F st, near 15th, in the absence of the proprietor. –D A Gardner

The Pavilion Hotel, Berkeley Springs, Va: this establishment has been recently transferred to the Blue House property of the undersigned. I have purchased, in connexion with J W Breathed, the stock & interest of "Dandy Jack" in the stage line to this place. –John Strother

Valuable farm at auction: on Aug 3, on the premises, the farm belonging to Dr Jas G Coombe, lying half a mile from the Eastern Branch Bridge, being part of a tract called *St Elizabeth*, containing 181 acres, more or less. –A Green, auctioneer

Mrd: on Jul 9, by Rev Henry B Tarring, John A Curtin, of Balt, to Mary Eliz Edwards, of Wash City, formerly of Gtwn, D C.

Mrd: on Jul 9, at Oakland, Fairfax Co, Va, by Rev Geo Woodbridge, Mr Alex'r H Terrett, of Wash, to Miss Eliz C Paine, of Richmond, Va.

Notice: Chas P Van Ness, having advertised through the public press, for the will of the late Gen John P Van Ness, of Wash City, & the undersigned, widow of the said John P Van Ness, having also good reason for the belief that such a will does, or at least did exist, a reward of $500 is offered for the discovery of the existence or fate of any such will. And all persons indebted to the estate of said Gen John P Van Ness, or having business relations therewith, are hereby cautioned against making payments & consummating contracts, or doing any other act or thing to the validity of which the sanction of the undersigned is necessary. The undersigned will ratify & carry into effect, at the proper time, all contracts & business negotiations according to the intentions of her late husband. –Mary Ann Van Ness

MON JUL 13, 1846
Senate: 1-Bill for the relief of Ross Winans: postponed until Monday next.
2-Bill for the relief of Henry Gardner & others, directors of an association called the Mississippi Land Co, was taken up & made the special order for Saturday next.
3-Bills were passed for the relief of: of Nathl Kuykendall; of Benj Ballard; of Ebenezer Ballard; of Jas Low; of Geo Gordon, of Randolph Co, Ill; of Semington Buffenberger; of Henry Newman; of Peter Von Schmidt; of Jos Kemball; of Francis Sommeraner; of Richd Kidd & Benj Kidd; of Thos Rhodes; of Jas Erwin, of Arkansas, & others; of the personal reps of Wm A Slacum, dec'd. of Wm McCauley; of John Ficklin; of Arthur R Frogge, of Fentress Co, Tenn; of Jos M Rhea, of Sullivan Co, Tenn; of Peter Capella, adm of Adnrew Capella, dec'd; of Richd S Coxe; of Harriet L Catching; of Thos Brownell; of Jos Wilson; & of John E Holland.

$50 reward for runaway negro man Huke Diggs, about 19 years of age.
–John Palmer, living at Palmerville, PG Co, Md.

P M Butler, formerly an ofcr of the U S army, afterwards Govn'r of the State of S C, & more recently Indian agent in the Cherokee Nation, has been chosen Colonel of the Regt of Volunteers called out from S C for the Mexican war.

Rev Richd Davys died suddenly in Boston on Thu last, from disease of the heart. In company with Rev Mr Deas he had been in this country about 3 years, collecting subscriptions towards bldg a Catholic Cathedral at Ardagh, in Ireland, & arrived at Boston from a tour to the West only a few days before his death.

House of Reps: 1-Bill for the relief of Sheldon B Hays: read a 3rd time & passed.
2-Bill to pay to Abraham Hoorbach the amount of a draft drawn by Jas Reeside in 1836, then a mail contractor in the Post Ofc Dept, & accepted by the Dept & duly protested for non-payment, was read the 3rd time, & the question was on its passage. Bill postponed until next Fri. Lost. 3-Bill for the relief of the heirs & legal reps of Cyrus Turner, dec'd, was passed. 4-Bill for the relief of Gad Humphrey & Geo Centre: next read. 5-Ptn of Israel Carlton, of Mass, praying for compensation for military services rendered in the Revolutionary war.

Vicksburg Sentinel of Jun 26 says: on Wed last, B G Simms, a highly respectable & worthy citizen of Hinds Co, was shot dead in the streets of Raymond by a man named Saunders, a stranger. Mr Simms leaves a most interesting family. The wretched homicide was instantly apprehended & committed.

A s/o Judge Clopton was accidentally drowned on Tue last in James river, near the railroad bridge, Richmond, Va. He was about 9 years of age.

Mrd: on Jul 7, at Camden, N J, by Rev Mr Manwarring, Chas Stott, of Wash, to Lillias M Young, d/o the late Jas Young, of Peel Hill, Lanarkshire, Scotland.

Died: on Sunday, Lydia Ellen, 3rd d/o Franklin & Sarah Edmondston, in her 16th year. Her funeral is this evening at 5 o'clock, at the residence of her father, on Mass ave, between 6th & 7th sts.

Died: Jul 11, after a short illness, by drinking cold water, Mr Robt McLenahan, marble polisher, formerly of Phil, for several years past a resident of Balt.

Died: on Jul 5, after a protracted illness of several months, Dr Thornton A Doniphan, in his 57th year, formerly a resident of King George Co, Va.

Died: on Jul 9, Graham, infant s/o John & Frances Bronaugh.

Died: on Jul 12, Emma, infant d/o Henry & Harriet J Lyles, aged 2 weeks & 1 day.

TUE JUL 14, 1846
Senate: 1-Memorial from Seneca G Simmons, asking compensation for services as secretary to the board of com'rs for treating with the Creek & Osage Indians. 2-Additional documents presented relative to the claim of Isaac Davenport. 3-Cmte on Roads & Canals: bill for the relief of Moses Shepherd. 4-Bills passed: relief of Jas Wyman; of John G Piere; of Danl Ingalls; of Jas Davidson; of Geo D Spencer; of Adam McCullogh; of Sampson Brown; of Jos Watson; of Jas Mains. 5-Bills referred: relief of Abram Horboek; & relief of Cyrus Turner. 6-Bill for the relief of Ross Winans: laid on the table. 7-Bill for the relief of Mrs Eliz Hamilton, wid/o the late Alex'r Hamilton: passed.

House of Reps: 1-Cmte of Claims: bill for the relief of Stalker & Hill. Also, a bill for the relief of the legal reps of John Lawson, dec'd. Also, a bill for the relief of John C Stewart & others: committed. 2-Cmte of Claims: adverse reports on the cases of Jas Warman & Saml Worthington: laid on the table. 3-Cmte on Commerce: was discharged from the consideration of the application of Edw H Mills for a change of the name of the barque **Pons**. 10-Cmte on Public Lands: bill to provide for the final settlement of the accounts of John Spencer, late receiver of public money at *Fort Wayne*, in Indiana: committed. 4-Cmte on the Judiciary: bill for the relief of the estate of Benj Metoyer & Francois Gaiennie, dec'd, as sureties of Benoit

Laments, late receiver of the land ofc at Natchitoches: committed. 5-Cmte on Revolutionary Pensions: to inquire into restoring to the pension roll the names of Jas Wamsley & Saml Z Jones, of the State of Va. 6-Cmte on Public expenditures: report on the memorial of Henry Elliot, recommending the adoption of the following resolution, which was agreed to: that the Clerk procure of Henry Elliot the condensed annual statements of the receipts & expenditures of the U S from 1789 to 1829, to be paid for out of the contingent fund. 7-Cmte on Private Lands Claims: adverse report in the case of Abraham Forbes: laid on the table. 8-Bill for the relief of Benj Harris, of Lasalle Co, Indiana: passed & returned to the Senate. 9-Bill granting a pension to Jos Morrison: referred to the Cmte on Invalid Pensions. 10-Bill for the relief of Bent St Vrain & Co: referred to the Cmte on Military Affairs. 11-Bill for the relief of Henry Etting: referred to the Cmte on Naval Affairs. 12-Bill to allow to Elijah White compensation for services & reimbursement of expenses incurred by him as acting sub-agent of Indian affairs west of the Rocky Mountains: referred to the Cmte on Indian Affairs: committed. 13-Cmte on Military Affairs: asked to be discharged from the ptn of John A Webber. Same cmte: bill for the relief of the widow of Elijah Bragdon, dec'd: committed. Adverse report on the ptn of Jas Adams Gregg & 7 others, asking that alterations be made in the laws in reference to the admission of surgeons & assistant surgeons in the army: laid on the table. 14-Cmte on Naval Affairs: bill for the relief of Nathl Phillips, granting him a pension of $4 per month: committed. Same cmte: bills for the relief of Lewis C Sarton, for the relief of Jas H Conly, for the relief of Wm T Walthall: committed. 15-Cmte on Revolutionary Pensions: bill for the relief of Eliz Fitch: committed. Bill from the Senate for the relief of Richd Elliot: reported the same with amendment. Same cmte: adverse reports on sundry cases, viz:

Eliz Martin	Thos Hargas	Benj Hall
Anne Smith	Abigail Doughty	Jacob H Bunner
Hannah Norton	Jas Taylor	John Stevens
Anne Pearsee	Jacob Olinger	John Boreman
Abigail Bodfish, [or Codfish]	Wm Hilton	Ann Yarrington:
	Relief Gibson	
Mary Bentley	Nancy King	

laid on the table. 16-Cmte on Revolutionary Pensions: bill for the relief of Thankful Reynolds, & a bill for the relief of Eliz Calkins: both committeed. Same cmte: bill for the relief of Amos Hunting: sent to the Senate for concurrence. 17-Ptn of J S & N J Wise, asking compensation for mail service. 18-Ptn of Newbold Cannon & 231 inhabitants of Lewis Co, Missouri, asking the establishment of a post route from Canton, in Lewis Co, to Lancaster, in Schuyler Co, Missouri. 19-Cmte on Invalid Pensions: bill for the relief of Jonathan Hoyt, & a bill for the relief of John Van Slyck: committed. Same cmte: adverse report on the case of Jas Monaghan: laid on the table. Same cmte: reported that leave be given to withdraw the papers in the cases of Giles Landon, J N Hall, Mgt C Hanson, Jehiel Tuttle, & of Lt Wendall: leave was given. Same cmte: bill for the relief of Nathl Stafford, without amendment: passed & returned to the Senate. 20-Cmte on Accounts: to audit & allow the account of N Lane, Sgt-at-Arms of this House, for furnishing a saddle-horse for his own use for 49 days, ending with May last, amounting to $49, to be paid out of the contingent fund of this House: agreed to. 21-Cmte on Expenditures of the Navy Dept: asked to be discharged from the consideration of the letter from the Sec of the Navy relative to the accounts of John T McLaughlin, & that it be referred to the Cmte on Public Expenditures.

Medical College of Louisiana: will commence on Nov 16, 1846, & continue for 4 months:
John Harrison, M D-Physiology & Pathology
Jas Jones, M D-Theory & practice of medicine
Warren, Stone, M D-Surgery
A H Cenas, M D-Obstetrics
J L Riddell, M D-Chemistry
Wm Carpenter, M D-Materia Medica
T R Le Monnier-Demonstrator of Anatomy
A J Wedderburn, M D, Dean-Anatomy

Rev Dr Judson & lady, with several other Missionaries, embarked from Boston last Sat for Burmah. Dr Judson has been laboring as a Missionary about a third of a century.

The punishment of the Pillory was on Mon inflicted at Charleston, on 2 men, Andrew Musselman & Wm Marks. The prisoners remained in the frame about half an hour, exposed to the view of about 500 white persons & 3 times that number of negroes. It is 20 years since this punishment has been inflicted there.

Concord [N H] Patriot: Mr Fales was killed at Claremont by the bursting of an old rusty cannon. He was a married man, & 27 years of age. The Newburyport Herald: a son of Capt Snowman of that town, was badly wounded in the hand by the premature discharge of a pistol while he had the ramrod in the barrel.
-Boston Traveller

Mrd: on Jul 9, at **Cedar Park**, the seat of John Mercer, West river, Anne Arundel Co, Md, by Rev Mr Brand, P McCall, of Phil, to Jane Byrd, d/o Mr Mercer.

Mrd: on Jul 7, at the Univ of Virginia, by Rev R K Meade, Prof H Courtenay to Virginia Pleasants, d/o Prof Henry Howard, M D.

Died: on Jul 12, at the family residence, **Mount Airy**, PG Co, Md, in his 18th year, Edw Henry Calvert, the eldest s/o Benedict Calvert, & grandson of Chas Calvert, the sixth Lord Baltimore. [Jul 15th newspaper: Died: on Jul 12, at the family residence, **Mount Airy**, PG Co, Md, in his 80th year, Edw Henry Calvert, the eldest s/o Benedict Calvert, & grandson of Chas Calvert, the sixth Lord Baltimore.]

First-rate Farm for sale: about 353 acs: at public auction on Aug 24: in Loudoun Co, Va, being two-thirds of the *Greenway Farm*, late the residence of Chas J Catlett, dec'd. The original estate has recently been divided among his heirs, & the portion now advertised to be sold [2/3rds] contains about 353 acres in a compact form, part of which the subscriber sells in his own right, & the balance under a power of atty. There is on it a good barn, ample stabling, granaries, corn-house, carriage house, shed for cattle, meat-house, & other necessary bldgs. The house in which the subscriber lives is a very indifferent one, but adjoining it are the walls of the old dwlg, [burnt some time since,] which would be sufficiently strong by taking a little off the top to support the requisite timbers for converting it into a comfortable, substantial, & handsome bldg. The cellars could not be better, being large, airy, & the foundation is of rock. They would be worth the interest of the money it would take to build up the house as a place for roots & apples. There are no incumbrances whatever on the property, as the right of dower in it is relinquished.
–Erskine Catlett, near Leesburg, Loudoun Co, Va.

Fine family carriage for sale: a Landeau Carriage, lined with yellow satin, made by Wood & Canfield, N Y, of the best material, & now in perfect order.
–A Green, Auctioneer & Commission Merchant, Concert Hall

WED JUL 15, 1846
Thos Woodward, our county Coroner, held an inquest last Sat in view of the body of Robt McLenehan, whose sudden death from drinking cold water was announced yesterday. We are sorry to learn that Mr Chas Miller, of Wash City, butcher, lost a valuable servant last Sat, whose sudden death resulted from a similar imprudence.

Wash Corp: 1-Ptn from J E Moss: referred to the Cmte of Claims. 2-Ptn from O J Prather: referred to the Cmte of Improvements. Same for the ptn from Andrew Small. 3-Ptn from Hugh B Sweeney, Teller of the Bank of Wash: referred to the Cmte of Claims. 4-Cmte on Improvements: bill for the relief of John G Robinson: passed. 5-Ptn from Andrew Noerr: referred to the Cmte on Improvements.

We had the surprise visit at our ofc by Henry R Schoolcraft, whose death at Sault St Marie by the hands of a half-breed Indian by the name of Tanner has been reported & generally believed. There is reason to apprehend, however, by letters received from the West, that the brother of this gentleman, Col Jas L Schoolcraft, resident at Sault St Marie & sutler to the troops at *Fort Brady*, has met with his death by being waylaid & killed in the manner described.

Senate: 1-Ptn of Theodore T Johnson & others, manufacturers of glass & soap in Phil, praying that the existing duty on soda-ash may not be increased. 2-Cmte of Claims: bill for the relief of John Spencer, late receiver of public moneys at *Fort Wayne*, Indiana: without amendment.

Illinois Volunteers: Capt Ferris Forman, of Fayette Co, has been elected Colonel of the 3rd Regt of Illinois Volunteers; Wilson W Wiley, of Bond Co, Lt Col; & Saml D Marshall, of Gallatin, Major. The question of seniority of rank, arising between Col Hardin, of the 1st Regt, & Col Baker, of the independent regt, was decided by the board of ofcrs in favor of Col Hardin. Col Baker's regt is now at *Jefferson Barracks*, having been transported thither on Sunday in the steamers Laclede & Luella. They will remain there until ordered to march to the South.

Texas Volunteers: Col A Sidney Johnson, Lt Col Ephraim McLean, & Major Wells are the ofcrs of the Texas Regt of Riflemen.

Mr Chas W Thompson, of Richmond City, Va, was drowned in the James river, near Haxall's mills, on Fri last. He was with friends & went into the river for the purpose of bathing, & ventured over his depth, it is supposed. He was about 28 years of age, of exemplary character, & had been for several years employed in the hardware establishment of Mr Thos A Rust, but had just commenced business for himself. The dec'd has left a wife & 4 children.

Died: on Jul 12, at the family residence, *Mount Airy*, PG Co, Md, in his 80th year, Edw Henry Calvert, the eldest s/o Benedict Calvert, & grandson of Chas Calvert, the sixth Lord Baltimore. [See Jul 14th newspaper.]

Died: on Jul 14, Martin Murphey, aged 40 years, a native of the county of Cork, Ireland, but for the last 18 years a resident of Wash City. His funeral is this afternoon, at 4 o'clock, from the residence of Mr Jeremiah O'Leary, Pa ave, south side, between 4½ & 6th sts.

Died: on Sunday, Lydia Ellen, 3rd d/o Franklin & Sarah Edmondston, in her 16th year. Thus have a devoted mother & a fond father been bereft of an idol of their affections.

Died: on Jul 11, in Wash City, in her 47th year, Mrs Ellen Venable.

Died: on Jul 11, in Wash City, Mrs Eliz Johnson, consort of Geo Johnson, in her 56th year, leaving a disconsolate family & a large number of warmly-attached relatives & friends to lament their heavy bereavement. The body was on the next day, deposited in the family ground at *Hays*. The funeral services were performed by the Rev Mr Berry & Rev Mr Hines. –A Friend

House of Reps:: 1-Ptn of Mrs Mary Brown, of Cheshspaugh, Mass, for a pension. 2-Ptn of Mary Boyd, of Chester Co, Pa, the widow of an old soldier, praying for a pension. 3-Remonstrance of Mrs Charity Hemintgon, of Kane Co.

For rent: a frame house on 13½ st, between C & D sts, in good condition. –Jos Scholfield, 8th st, near the Genr'l P O.

The Cincinnati [Ohio] Chronicle of Jul 9: the emancipated slaves of John Randolph, who recently passed up the Miami Canal to their settlement in Mercer Co, Ohio, met with a warm reception at Bemen. The citizens of Mercer formed themselves into one immediately, & passed resolutions to the effect that said slaves should leave in 24 hours, which they did in other boats than the ones which conveyed them there. They came back some 23 miles, at which place they encamped, not knowing what to do.

We see it stated in our exchanges that Capt May wears <u>long hair</u> & a beard because of disappointment in love. We presume such is the case, &, by a singular coincidence, every man attached to May's command is afflicted in the same way, as they all have, more or less, long hair & long beards. Such a brave set of disappointed lovers we think never before got together. –New Orleans Topic

Official-Passed Midshipmen: From the Union: Board of Examiners, Naval School, Annapolis, Md, Jul 11, 1846. It is proper to remark that the qualification & merit of Messrs R Aulick & R Savage were, in the estimation of the board, so precisely equal, that it was though admissible to determine by lot who should stand number one, & the choice fell to Mr R Aulick. –Lawrence Kearney, Pres Board of Examiners to the Hon Sec of the Navy. List of Midshipmen, in the order of rank assigned them, Jul 10, 1846.

1. Richmond Aulick
2. Robt Savage
3. R A Marr
4. Wm N Jeffers
5. Wm D Austin
6. John J Pringle
7. Edw Brinley, jr
8. Edw Simpson
9. Wm G Temple
10. Geo P Welsh
11. S P Carter
12. Wm Nelson
13. Wm H Smith
14. R M McArann
15. C W Aby
16. Chas Dyer, jr
17. Edw C Stout
18. F B Brand
19. Reuben Harris
20. John Walcutt
21. J B McCauley
22. Thos S Phelps
23. John Madigan
24. A F Warley
25. G V Denniston
26. Leonard Paulding
27. Geo A Stevens
28. F A Conover
29. S B Elliot
30. F Gregory
31. Edw Barrett
32. John W Bennett
33. Peter Wager
34. John P Hall
35. H C Blake
36. Clark H Wells
37. S B Quackenbush
38. Earl English
39. Chas Waddell
40. D Ochiltree
41. J M Bradford
42. R B Lowry
43. F P Whellock

Correct: L Kearney, Pres Board Attest: Jas Tilton, Sec of Board Approved, Jul 11, 1846 -Geo Bancroft

Lost, on Sat last, my Free Papers & a Deed for a house & lot in lot 12 & square 286, fronting on I st. Finder will be liberally rewarded by leaving them at Fuller's Hotel, or the ofc of this paper. [They were in a cigar case when lost.] -W Moulden

House of Reps: Bills from the Senate referred: 1-Bill for the relief of Benj Ballard: referred to the Cmte on Private Land Claims. 2-Bill for the relief of Ebenezer Ballard: referred to the Cmte on Naval Affairs. 3-Bill for the relief of Jas Low: referred to the Cmte on Naval Affairs. 4-Bill for the relief of Geo Gordon, of Randolph Co, Ill: referred to the Cmte on Public Lands. 5-Bill for the relief of Peter Von Schmidt: referred to the Cmte of Claims. 6-Bill for the relief of Francis Sommeraner: referred to the Cmte on Invalid Pensions. 7-Bill for the relief of Nathl Kuykendall: referred to the Cmte on the Post Ofc & Post Roads. 8-Bill for the relief of Eliz Hamilton, wid/o Gen Alex'r Hamilton. 9-Bill for the relief of Harriette L Catching: referred to the Cmte on the Judiciary. 10-Bill for the relief of Richd S Coxe: referred to the Cmte on the Judiciary. 11-Bill for the relief of Peter Capella, administrator of Andrew Capella, dec'd: referred to the Cmte on the Judiciary. 12-Bill for the relief of Richd Kidd: referred to the Cmte of Ways & Means. 13-Bill for the relief of Thos Rhodes: referred to the Cmte on Post Ofc & Post Roads. 14-Bill for the relief of Jas Erwin, of Arkansas, & others: referred to the Cmte on Indian Affairs. 15-Bill for the relief of the personal reps of Wm A Slacum, dec'd: referred to the Cmte on Foreign Affairs. 16-Bill for the relief of Thos Brownell: referred to the Cmte on Naval Affairs. 17-Bill for the relief of Robt Barclay, of Missouri: referred to the Cmte on Private Land Claims. 18-Bill for the relief of Harriette Ward: referred to the Cmte on Naval Affairs.

THU JUL 16, 1846
Senate: 1-Cmte on Pensions: bill from the House for the relief of Saml Jordan, without amendment.

Wm & Mary College: Course for the Degree of A B:
Junior Moral Class: Thos R Dew, Pres & Prof
Mathematics: Robt Saunders, Prof
Chemistry: John Millington, Prof
Nat'l Law: Beverly Tucker, Prof
Senior Year:
Senior Political Class: Thos R Dew, Prof
Mathematics: Robt Saunders, Prof
Natural Philosophy: John Millington, Prof
Independent Subjects:
Law: Beverly Tucker, Prof
Preparatory Mathematics: Robt Saunders
Classical Dept: Ancient Languages: Chas Minnigerode, Prof

Mrd: on Jul 6, in Portsmouth, N H, by Rev Dr Borroughs, Montgomery Blair, Judge of the Circuit Court of Missouri, to Miss Mary E, eldest d/o Hon Levi Woodbury.

Mobile Register of Jul 8: on the downward passage of the vessel **William Bradstreet** with a portion of the Georgia Volunteers, 2 men, Farrar, from S C, belonging to Capt Calhoun's company, the other, Macnier, of Dooly Co, Ga, belonging to Capt Turner's company, being suddenly awoke by the noise of letting off steam, jumped overboard & were drowned. R J Hanson, of Capt Calhoun's company, died on the march from Columbus to Montgomery.

Died: on Jul 11, in West Springfield, Hon Saml Lathrop, aged 75. Besides having been a long time a member of the Senate of his own State, & for some time its Pres, he was for 8 eights, [from 1818 to 1826] a Rep of his native district in Congress, & his public course was uniformly marked by integrity, dignity, & efficiency.

Died: on Jul 10, at the Warrenton Springs, Va, upon his return from Phil, whither he had gone for medical advice, Col Edw Ambler, of Rappahannock Co, the eldest s/o the late Col John Ambler, of Richmond. The dec'd was at one time a delegate from Henrico Co in the Genr'l Assembly, & was very much beloved.

FRI JUL 17, 1846
Local News: the Annual Examination of the pupils under the charge of Miss M A Tyson & Sisters was held last Wed, in their Seminary on F st: the highest premium was awarded to Miss Maria Leigh Bell; premium in Latin to Miss Jane E Young; in writing to Miss Annetta Morrow; in music to Miss Louisa McVey. Miss Carothers particularly excelled in Music.

Fire last night in the First Ward of Wash City, entirely destroyed the cabinetmaker's shop & store of Mr Chas Calvert, jr, & much of its contents.

Senate: 1-Bill for the relief of Edw Bulow: passed. 2-Bill for the heirs of Crocker Sampson, dec'd: passed. 3-Bill for the relief of Henry H Marsh, of Michigan: passed. 4-Bills for the relief of Alexis Ayot: passed. 5-Bill granting a pension to John Clark: passed.

Additional Surgeons for the Army: appointments on Jul 7, "An Act providing for the existing war between the U S & Mexico," approved Jun 18, 1846.

Surgeons:
Wm Trevitt, of Ohio
Benj Stone, of Ohio
Edw B Price, of Ill
Jas Mahan, of Ill

Robt F Richardson, of Ill
Wm M Quinn, of Ill
Seymour Halsey, of Miss
Paul F Erie, of Ga

Assistant Surgeons:
Robt McNeal, of Ohio
P H Mulvaney, of Ohio
Wm B Herrick, of Ill
Danl Turney, of Ill

Washington J Gibbs, of Ill
Henry Bragg, of Ill
John Thompson, of Miss

Appointments on Jul 14th, under the act approved Jun 18, 1846:
Surgeons:
Alex'r Hensley, of Ky
Thos L Caldwell, of Ky
Robt P Hunt, of Ky
Caleb V Jones, of Indiana

Danl S Lane, of Indiana
Jas S Athore, of Indiana
E K Chamberlain, of Ohio

Assist Surgeons:
Alex'r Blanson, of Ky
John J Matthews, of Ky
Jas B Israel, of Ky
Wm Fisdick, of Indiana
John F Walker, of Indiana

John G Dunn, of Indiana
John G Dunn, of Indiana
A E Keighway, of Ohio
John J B Hoxey, of Ga

Mr Francis Bassett, aged 82 years, was drowned while bathing in the river at Wheeling last Fri.

DISGUSTING. Female Smokers. Three ladies, apparently of the "upper ten" class, [says a N Y paper,] accompanied by 3 gentlemen, were promenading the upper part of Broadway, each smoking a regalia!

One of the crew of the steamer **James L Day**, at Mobile, had his arm blown off by the accidental discharge of a cannon which he was loading to fire a salute on Jul 4th.

Mr Arago, the French astronomer, says it is impossible to tell with certainty what the weather will be a year, a month, a week, or even a single day in advance.

Detroit Daily Advertiser of Jul 10. Jas L Schoolcraft was killed at the Sault Ste Marie last Sun. He was fired upon from a thicket & must have instantly expired. His body was found lying on his face. Suspicion of his murder rested upon an old man named Tanner, who had frequently threatened Schoolcraft. Mr Schoolcraft was sutler to the post at *Fort Brady*, & also engaged extensively in the fur & other trade. He leaves a wife, now in this city, & young children to mourn their loss.

Died: lately at New Orleans, Etienne Sylvestre, a soldier of the War of Independence, aged 90 years. He arrived in America nearly 70 years ago under the Count D'Estaing, & participated in most of the engagements that followed. After the establishment of peace he settled in Louisiana, & at the battle of New Orleans behaved with marked intrepidity.

By virtue of a wit of distrain for rent due in arrears to the estate of Gen John P Van Ness, dec'd, by Jos Martini, & to me directed by C P Van Ness, administrator of said estate, I have this day levied on the improvements on Lot 13 in square 337, consisting of a frame house, being the property of said Martini; I will proceed to sell said improvements on Jul 23, in front of said lot, on or near the corner of E & 10th sts. -D McPherson, Bailiff

Died: on Jul 10, at Troy, Capt Ephraim Whitaker, a soldier of the Revolution, at the advanced age of 81 years. He was in the battles of Germantown, Monmouth, & Saw Pits, & several minor skirmishes.

SAT JUL 18, 1846
Orphans Court of Wash Co, D C. Letters of administration on the personal estate of Marmaduke Dove, late of said county, dec'd. –Benj M Dove, adm

Orphans Court of Wash Co, D C. Letters testamentary on the personal estate of Martin Murphy, late of said county, dec'd. –Stans Murray, exc

On Jul 3, Mr Henry K Henion, of Chester Co, Pa, died from the effects of a sting in the nostril by an insect, received while lying down in a baggage car, at Columbia, waiting for a car. He was employed on the Pennsylvania railroad.

Senate: 1-House bill for the relief of Abraham Hasbrook, without amendment.
2-Bills from the House were read a 2nd time & referred: for the relief of-

Griffin Kelly	Jas Journey	Jas Gee
Abraham Ansam	John McAlister	Solomon Russell
Jos Dusseau	Mary Segur	Capt John Patton
Wm Moss	Mary Phelps	Lois Masterson
John Campbell	Eliz Betts	Ebenezer Conaut
Danl Pratt	Partick Masterson	Eli Merrill
Justine Jacobs	Jonathan Brown	Wm B Ligon
Surranus Cobb	Wm Gump	Patrick Kelly, sen
Polly Damron	Lewis Laing	Geo Roush
Catherine Fulton	Leah Gray	Peter Rife
John P Denton	Mgt Gwinnup	Danl H Warren
Jose Carxillo	Richd Hargrave Lee	Heirs of Thos Kelly

Of John Batty & Saml Stevenson, seamen on board the whale-ship **Margaret**

The Regt of Mississippi Volunteers, at Vicksburg, has elected Jefferson Davis, at present a member of Congress, Colonel; Alex K McClung, Lt Col, & Gen A B Bradford, Major.

The brig **Columbia**, Capt Barbes, bound from New Orleans for Savannah was struck by lightning on Jul 3, 60 miles from the Balize. All the crew were aloft reefing topsails at the time, when the electric fluid, in descending the mainmast, after shattering it, precipitated the whole of the men, 6 in number, into the sea, who were lost. It set the boat on fire but the Capt with the only passenger on board arrested the flames.

Obit-died: Mrs Julia M Taylor: wife, mother & neighbor. [No details.]

Gen A Disney Johnson has been elected Colonel of the 1st Regt of Texas Infty; E McLane, Lt Col; & Mr Wells, of Nacogdoches, Major. The ofcrs of the 1st Texas Regt of mounted men are as follows: J C Hays, Col; S H Walker, Lt Col; Chevallo, Major.

Died: on Jul 11, at the Markoe Home, Phil, in her 35th year, Mrs Martha M Yellowby, w/o Dr Jas B Yellowby, & d/o the late Mr Guilford Nicholson, all of Halifax Co, N C. Born & educated under the most favorable circumstances, she married in her 19th year; because of ill health & protracted sufferings, she was brought annually to the North, which experiment was successful. An acute disease in a few days prostrated her renovated strength. Husband, brother, sisters, friends, mourn her loss. [Jul 21st newspaper: correction-in her 35th year, Mrs Martha M Yellowly, w/o Dr Jas B Yellowly. –Mistake of the compositor of a letter in the proper name.]

Military. Ofcrs attached to Co F, 3rd Regt U S Artl, who sailed from N Y for California, in the beginning of the present week, in the storeship **Lexington**.
C Q Tompkins, Capt
E O C Ord, 1st Lt
W T Sherman, 1st Lt
Lucien Loeser, 2nd Lt
C J Minor, Brevet 2nd Lt
H w Halleck, 1st Lt Corps of Engineers
Dr Jas Ord, Assist Surgeon
One ordnance sgt, & 112 men

Customers desirous of settling their accounts, by cash or note, can do so at the store un Jul 20; after that time, I can be found on D st, directly in the rear of the store. –S Parker, Fancy Store, between 9th & 10th sts

House of Reps: 1-Leave was given to withdraw the ptns & papers of Mary Phelps, Anna Giffin, & Josiah Sturges. 2-Cmte of Claims: bill for the relief of Harrison Whitson: committed. Also, adverse reports on the cases of Geo Hix, David Little, & Saml Lewis: laid on the table. 3-Cmte on Private Land Claims: bill from the Senate for the relief of Benj Ballard, reported the same without amendment. Same cmte: bill from the Senate for the relief of Robt Barclay, reported the same without amendment. 4-Cmte on Military Affairs: to which was referred the joint resolution from the Senate for the relief of Lewis De Russy, reported the same without amendment. 5-Bill for the relief of gad Humphreys & Geo Centre: rejected. 6-Relief of Sellers & Pennock: laid on the table. 7-Bill granting a pension to Danl H Warren, a soldier in the war of 1812 with Great Britain, was taken up. Mr Hamlin said that he had labored most industriously for 3 years to procure the passage of this bill. It had passed the House at 2 preceding sessions, & died a natural death in the Senate: bill was passed. 8-Bills for the relief of Peter Rife; of Geo Roush; of Patrick Kelly; of Wm B Ligon; & for the legal reps of Thos Kell: all passed. 9-Bill to pay Capt John B Crozier's companies of mounted Tennessee volunteers: passed in the affirmative. 10-Bill to authorize Eli Merrill to exchange a tract of military bounty land in Illinois for other public land in that State; & the bill granting a pension to

Ebenezer Conaut: both read & passed. 11-Bill granting a pension to Capt John Patton for injuries received in the war with Great Britain in 1812; bill for the relief of Solomon Russell; bill granting arrears of pension to Jas Gee, who received 3 desperate wounds in the early part of a battle in the war of 1812 with England, & yet continused to fight bravely on till the victory was achieved; & the bill granting a pension to Wm Moss: severally came up in order: all passed. 12-Joint resolution for the relief of John B Dexton & Curtis Humphreys, mail contractors in Georgia: passed. 13-Following were passed: Bills granting a pension to Mgt Gwinnup; pension to Leah Gray; pension to Mary Campbell, of Pa; pension to Lewis Laing; pension to Wm Gump; bill for the relief of John Carr, John Patty, & S Stephenson, seamen: all passed. 14-Bill for the relief of John McAllister, of Georgia: passed. 15-Following bills were passed: relief of Jas Journey; & relief of Jose Carxillo. Pension to Jonathan Brown; pension to Patrick Masterson; pension to Eliz Betts, of N Y; pension to Mary Phelps; pension to Mary Segar; pension to Catharine Fulton; & a pension to Polly Dawson. 16-Bill granting a pension to Surranous Cobb: laid on the table, then passed. 17-Bill granting a pension to Justin Jacobs: passed. 18-Bill for the relief of Wm Beard: rejected. 19-Bills granting a pension to Danl Pratt; pension to John Campbell, of Maine; pension to Jos Dusseau; pension to Abraham Ausmen; pension to Griffin Kelly; pension to Benj Allen; & pension to Aquilla Goodwin: passed. 20-Bill for the relief of Cornelius Capen, adm of John Cox, of Boston, dec'd: passed. 21-Following bills passed: for relief of the heirs & reps of Richd C Anderson, dec'd; relief of John Milsted, of Florida; relief of Jos Curwin; relief of the owners of the ship **Herald**, of Balt; relief of Wm B Lang; relief of David Thomas, of Phil; & relief of Elisha F Richards. 22-Bills for the relief of Maj Jas H P Porter; relief of Lewis Hastings; relief of the widow of Thos Murray, jr, dec'd; & the bill for the relief of Gideon A Perry: all laid on the table. 23-We are sorry to learn that Mr Carroll, of N Y, who left his sick room a few days ago to vote upon the land graduation bill, had a relapse of illness in consequence, which yet confines him to his room, though, we are happy to learn, he is now slowly convalescent.

An Eastern papers says, Col Smith, who married John Adams' dght, writes at Madrid, in 1787, "What is called society here, is the assembling of a number of people, who immediately fix themselves at a table, & proceed to plunder themselves politely at cards." The gentleman referred to was in the military family of Gen Washington. Col Smith was one of the polished gentlemen in the U S: in height full 6 feet, a remarkably good looking man, of florid countenance. Even when somewhat advanced in life, he was perfectly erect, & in his movements of a military port. When the British evacuated N Y C on Nov 25, 1789, & the American troops marched in, Col Smith, being a New Yorker, Gen Washington conferred on him the honor of receiving a surrender of the city from the British commanding ofcr of the day. Col Smith filled various public stations, the last of which was a Rep in Congress from the Western part of this State. He was in the habit of corresponding with his mother-in-law, the mother of the Hon John Q Adams. She was a most extraordinary woman, retaining it is believed, in full vigor to her latest hour the powers of a mighty mind. –A Calm Observer: Journal of Commerce

Died: on Tue last, in Martinsburg, Va, at the residence of her son-in-law, Col E P Hunter, in her 72nd year, Mrs Sally Abell, relict of Capt John Abell, late of Elkwood, Jefferson Co, Va, & d/o Zachariah Forrest, late of St Mary's Co, Md.

Died: on Jul 14, at Concord, N H, while on a visit to his grandparents with his mother, Riley Loomis, only child of Hon John Wentworth, member of Congress, of Illinois, aged 10½ months.

Capt Talcott, with Col Hart, of Michigan, were in Dr Keeny's quarters, at Copper Harbor, the former sitting on a lounge, & the latter examining a revolving pistol belonging to the Dr. The Col supposed all the barrels were unloaded, so he carefully cocked the pistol, without regard to the direction of the barrel, snapped it, & discharged it into the shoulder of Capt Talcott. Capt Talcott is now said to be out of danger & recovering.

For rent: a 2 story brick dwlg-house, on the west side of N Y ave, near the residence of Thos Blagden, within a few minutes walk of the Capitol. To a good tenant it will be rented for $100. Apply to Richd Barry, opposite the premises.

For rent: a 3 story brick house on Pa ave, adjoining the St Charles Hotel. Also, a 3 story brick dwlg-house on N J ave, adjoining the residence of Col Gardner. Inquire of B Homans, Pa ave, between 10th & 11th sts.

Customers desirous of settling their accounts, by cash or note, can do so at the store un Jul 20; after that time, I can be found on D st, directly in the rear of the store. –S Parker, Fancy Store, between 9th & 10th sts

MON JUL 20, 1846
Centre Market: fine veal raised by Govn'r Sprigg, of PG Co, was readily sold by Mr Chas Miller at a reasonable price.

A woman named Mary Calvert, who says she is from Loudoun Co, Va, was arrested a few days ago, & committed to prison by Justice Morsell, under the following circumstances: a newly-born male white child was found in Mr Benter's coal-house, & this woman was seen a little before the child was discovered, on Sun last, hastening from the premises. She admitted that she was the mother of the child, but said she had placed it in the coal-house, hoping it would be taken care of! She was committed under the charge of inhumanly abandoning her own offspring. Coroner's verdict: the child's death was occasioned by want of substenance. She exhibited no proofs of a deranged intellect.

A colored man, Lloyd Douglass, was arrested on Fri, for having stolen a cloak belonging to the Hon Senator Niles, at Mrs Scotts' boarding house.

Imprudent drinking of cold water caused the sudden death, in Wash City, of Henry Jasper, [colored man,] a hack driver, well know in the First Ward. The jury returned a verdict that he died of apoplexy.

Senate: 1-Cmte on Private Land Claims: House bills for the relief of the heirs of Thos Kelly; relief of Eli Merrill; relief of Solomon Russell; relief of Jas Journey; & relief of Jose Darxilla: without amendment. Same cmte: asking to be discharged from the further consideration of the ptns of Isabella Stout, Jas B Davenport, & that of the heirs of Nicholas Barra, & the ptn of Thos Mullett in behalf of Francis Le Beau & others; & the ptn of J W Taylor & others. 2-Cmte on Pensions: adverse report on the ptn of Benj L Lucas. Same cmte: House bill for the relief of Amos Hunting. 3-Cmte on Naval Affairs: bill for the relief of Michl Hanson.

House of Reps: 1-To be reported to the House for passage: bills for the relief of Francis Martin; relief of Silas Waterman; relief of Elisha H Holmes; relief of Gregory Thomas & others. 2-Bill for the relief of the heirs of Robt Fulton, the great steamboat inventor, was read, as was also the report of the Cmte on Naval Affairs, containing a full exposition of the history, merits, & misfortunes of the claim. Mr Hungerford moved to amend the bill by reducing the amount proposed to be paid from $76,300 to $16,300. He rejected the $60,000 for the invention of the steam battery. It was rejected. Mr Gordon moved to amend the bill by striking out $76,300 & inserting $20,000. Motion was not inorder. Mr Gordon modified his amendment so as to insert $40,000: rejected. Bill for the relief of the heirs of Robt Fulton, dec'd, was taken up: passed without opposition. 3-Bill granting a pension to John Clark: referred to the Cmte on Invalid Pensions. 4-Bill for the relief of Wm B Keene: referred to the Cmte on Private Land Claims. 5-Bill for the relief of Edw Bolon: referred to the Cmte of Claims. 6-Bill for the relief of the heirs of Crocker Simpson, dec'd: referred to the Cmte on Revolutionary Claims. 7-Bill for the relief of Henry H Marsh, of Michigan: referred to the Cmte on Public Lands. 8-Bill for the relief of Alexis Ayot: referred to the Cmte on Invalid Pensions. 9-Bill granting a pension to Wm Poole: passed.

War Dept, Nov 11, 1837: a volunteer company, raised & organized in N Y C, has been accepted by this Dept for service in Florida without a doubt of your willingness to commission the individuals selected by them for its ofcrs so soon as their names should be presented to you, which is required by the law of May 23, 1836, before the Dept can avail itself of the services of the company. I have thereford the honor to request that you forward to Lt Col Cutler, of the army, now in N Y C, a captain's commission for Jacobus Benj Seiler, & one of a 1st Lt for Edw Gayner Lavers, who have been selected for those ranks by the company. –Joel R Poinsett, Sec of war: To his Excellency Wm L Marcy, Govn'r of N Y, Albany, N Y.

$100 for runaway negro man Henry, about 20 years of age. –Wm Clark, near Queen Ann, PG Co, Md

By virtue of an order of distrain, to me delivered, I shall expose to public sale, for cash, at the store of Jos B Glenn, on Pa ave west, Wash City, near the corner of 15th st, on Jul 24, sundry goods, to wit: a lot of toys, lot of cigars, 4 lamps, 20 boxes of blacking, wrapping paper, small scales & weights, show glass, glass jars, counters, shelving, bedstead & bedding, 3 chairs, barrels & boxes, tinware, andirons, shovel & tongs, iron pot & skillet, coffee-mill; stone jugs, lucifer matches, writing paper, seized & taken as the property of Jos B Glenn, to satisfy rent due in arrears of John Robinson. –John Dewdney, Bailiff

The copartnership in the Boot & Shoe business, existing between Wm Moore & Malcolm Douglass, is this day dissolved by mutual consent. The business will be cont'd at the old stand, Pa ave, & 10th st, by Wm Moore.
-Wm Moore, Malcolm Douglass

Lord Francis Egerton has been raised to the peerage, & his place in the House of Commons filled by an American merchant, G D Brown.

The election of a new Pope was achieved without difficulty, the conclave being in session only 48 hours. Its choice fell upon Cardinal Mastai-Feretti, who has taken the name of Pius IX. He is only 54 years of age, & is one of the youngest Cardinals ever chosen to the Papacy. He is a native of the Papal States.

Mr Mittag, the distinguished artist & naturalist of the South, is at present in Wash City & will remain a few days. He is preparing a work which will contain an analysis of the Language of Natural Forms.

The celebrated painter, Haydon, has died by his own hand, induced to this unhappy close of his career, it is said, by poverty & the ills which follow in its train. [Jul 22nd newspaper: among those from whom he solicited pecuniary assistance was Sir Robt Peel. Peel was the only party who responded, sending him a L50 note. On hearing of his melancholy exit, Sir Robt Peel sent the family L200, to relieve their more pressing requirements.]

Efforts are making in Boston & New Bedford to raise subscriptions for the relief of the sufferers by the late fire in Nantucket: estimated total loss a million & a half of dollars, & the insurance at $350,000. Jared Coffin, formerly of Nantucket, but now a resident of Brighton, Mass, gave a $1,000 for the assistance of the sufferers. Considerable sums have been collected in N Y for the same object.

Justus Hoppe, of Balt, died on board the steamer **John J Crittenden** last Mon, about 50 miles below Louisville. His complaint was congestion of the liver. Every attention was paid to him by his friends, & a physician who was on board. He was buried at Louisville.

Died: on Jul 19, Nathl Addison, infant s/o Wm & Anna Maria Orme, aged 7 months & 16 days.

Appointments by the Pres, by & with the advice & consent of the Senate: 1-Jesse B Clements, U S Marshal for the middle district of Tennessee, to take effect from Aug 6, vice Benj H Sheppard, whose commission then expires. 2-Danl Vaughan, to be Naval Ofcr for the district of Portsmouth, N H, vice John McClintock, removed. 3-Hezekiah Willard, Collector of Customs for the district of Providence, R I, vice Thos F Carpenter, who declines the appointment.

The Cincinnati Commercial states that, on Thu last, one of the Misses McCue, living on 7th st, between Sycamore & Broadway, went to market; returned home & died, as is supposed, from the effects of the heat, soon after, On Fri, the second sister died in the same manner, after returning from the funeral. On Sat, the third sister died in the carriage while attending the funeral of the second sister. The mother of the 3 young ladies was taken sick in the carriage & returned home. This calamity has created great concern in the minds of the people living in the neighborhood.

Alpheus White & Ambrose Ferguson were tried before Judge Conklin, of the U S District Court for the Northern District of N Y, at a session of the Court held at Canton, St Lawrence Co, a few days since, & found guilty of passing countereit coin. Both sentenced to the State prison of Auburn for 3 years each.

Eliphalet M Spencer murdered his wife at Jersey City last Tue. He is about 26, & was married to the dec'd, whose maiden name was Dobbin, about 15 months since. He is said to have been unkind to her-to have treated her even with violence & cruelty, & on this account she had sought the protection of the law, & refused to see him. He has been arrested a short time before the murder, on her complaint. At his request the ofcr allowed him to have an interview with her, but she locked herself in her room, & opened the door at the intercession of her brother. As soon as the door was opened Spencer rushed in & fired a pistol at her, with fatal effect. He was arrested & committed for trial. [Sep 29th newspaper: The Jury, in the case of Spencer, who was tried at Jersey City on a charge of having murdered his wife, have returned a verdict of not guilty-on the ground, we suppose, of insanity.]

Hudson & Heustis, 2 men who recently ran away from Hempstead, L I, with 2 married women of that place, were arrested at Rochester on Sun last, while on their way to the West. The "ladies" have been sent back & are probably, ere this, again at home.

TUE JUL 21, 1846
The coronation of Oscar L & his consort Eugenia, d/o Prince Eugne de Beaubarnais, as King & Queen of Norway, is fixed to be held on Oct 15 next on which occasion the Storthing will be convoked.

For rent: new brick house on I st, between 9th & 10th sts, with carriage house & stabling for 3 horses. –Jos Thompson, N Y ave, between 12th & 13th sts.

Senate: 1-Ptn from Saml & Philip T Ellicott, manufacturers of chemicals, asking that crude brimstone & saltpeter may continue to be admitted free of duty. 2-Cmte on Indian Affairs: bill for the relief of Seneca G Simmons. Same cmte: House bill for the relief of the heirs & legal reps of Cyrus Turner, without amendment. Same cmte: asking to be discharged from the further consideration of the ptn of Thos L Judge, in behalf of certain Indians; of Benj Crawford; of the exc of A R L Hunter.

From the Far West: Independence Expositor of Jul 4. On Tue, Messrs J Bond, W Parkinson, W Delany, & 2 others, arrived in our place direct from Oregon. They left Oregon City on Mar 1, 1846, for the States; delayed when crossing the summits of the Rocky Mountains, by severe snow storms; on Jun 11 they met the company of emigrants from St Joseph at *Fort Laramie*, all in good spirits. They saw 43 wagons, said by the emigrants to be Mormons. In the route thus far Brown's company had lost 120 head of cattle [60 yoke of them oxen, the remainder loose cattle.] Go ahead, seemed to be the motto. A company has cut a road through the Cascade mountains, & even bound themselves in writing in the sum of $5,000 for the fulfillment of it. In the spring of 1845, 75 persons died crossing the plains, caused by getting lost while following Pilot Meek from *Fort Bosien* to the Falls on the Columbia river. 30 wagons in the company went into the Cascade mountains, remained until spring, & were then able to come out.

House of Reps: 1-Ptn of Shadrach O'Brian, for an increase of pension.

G W Tracy, of pilot boat **Baltimore**, writes from Cape Henry, under date of Jul 15, as follows: On Wed we fell in with the schnr **Manteo**, of Washington, N C. She was on fire, & soon entirely destroyed. We picked up her crew, 8 in number, & her stern boat. The schnr **Manteo**, Capt Abbot, was a regular trader between Washington, N C & Boston.

Concord Academy will commence Jul 1: Caroline Co, Va. –F W Coleman, Principal

Household & kitchen furniture at auction on Jul 28, at the residence of Geo M Philips, on 10th st, between D & E sts. –A Green, auctioneer

Orphans Court of Wash Co, D C. Letters of administration on the personal estate of Truman Cross, late of said county, dec'd. –Wm B B Cross, A H Cross, adms

Died: on Jul 16, at Bedford Springs, [whither he had gone for the promotion of his health,] Notley Young, of PG Co, Md, in his 54th year. His death will be lamented by a very large circle of attached relatives & friends. He was the polished gentleman, kind, amiable, & sincere. His life was that of a truly pious Christian.

Petersburg [Va] Intell, Jul 18. The mysterious disappearance of Mr F Adolphus Muir has at last been accounted for. His body has been found & identified. He was murdered by Capt Wm Dandridge Epes, of Dinwiddie Co, who has for the present made his escape. Mr Muir was one of the most respectable, amiable, & inoffensive men in our country, connected with one of the most respectable families in our State. His murderer is also connected with a family as respectable as any in the country. The accursed love of money prompted the act. Muir held a bond or bonds amounting to $3,200 against Egpes-it being the balance which Epes owed for a tract of land bought by him of Muir. Circumstances: on Feb 2 last, Muir left the house of his brother, John A Muir, in Dinwiddie Co: about Feb 11th, John A Muir rec'd the following letter: Petersburg, Feb 4, 1846: Dear John, I have arrived in this place; my horse threw me, sprained my right hand; I shall leave for the North on some business. –Your brother, F Adolphur Muir
About Feb 27, a letter dated N Y, Feb 12, 1846, & signed F Adolphus Muir, directed to John A Muir, postmarked Petersburg was received. The account of what actually occurred on Feb 2 was given by the most deeply distressed wife of Epes, before she was aware that her husband was suspected of the crime of murdering Muir. She stated that Epes & Muir left the house, Epes with a double barreled gun & Muir entirely unarmed. Muir was to watch Epes kill a deer in the woods. Epes returned to his house alone, telling his wife that Muir had to go to Brunswick & had not redeemed his promise to return to dinner. On Thu last, a large party went to Epes' house & told him that he was suspected of the murder. He asseverated his innocence. Matters stood until Sunday, when Mr Lumsden, a respectable watchmaker of this town, stated that in May last Mr Epes had sold him a gold watch, which watch he had in 1843 cleaned for Mr Muir, & taken down the number. This development, with other circumstances, justified the arrest of Epes. Epes left his house on Mon, & has not been seen since. A negro on the plantation was called up & interrogated, & proceeded to a spot about 600 yeards distant from the house, & pointed out a grave. The body was found, & although a good deal decayed, was readily identified as that of Muir. Epes had told the negro that he had accidentally killed his friend, & ordered him to dig a grave. The negro's silence from that period until Wed, was doubtless produced by threats from his master. $500 reward will be given for the apprenhension of Wm Dandridge Epes, the murderer of F Adolphus Muir, of Dinwiddie Co. Epes is about 40 years of age, about 5 feet 10 inches high, of a florid complexion, with blue eyes & dark auburn hair, with a high forehead, & of athletic form, slightly inclined to corpulency. He is reserved in his manners, proud & haughty in his general demeanor. He is without doubt guilty of one of the most atrocious murders ever committed. The Govn'r will also offer a large reward for his apprehension. –John A Muir, Peter Boisseau, Petersburg, Va, Jul 1, 1846. [Exchange papers will confer a favor upon a respectable community, & aid in promoting the ends of justice, by copying the above statement.]

Died: on Jul 19, Virginia, infant d/o Maj Nicholson, aged 11 months.

Capt John Page, of the U S Army, who distinguished himself & was terribly wounded in the battle of the Palo alto, died on Jul 12 on board the steamer **Missouri**, while on his way from New Orleans to St Louis. His remains were taken to the latter city for interment. His wife & family, as also a medical attendant, were with him at the time of his death. He was a native of the State of Maine, & entered the Army as a 2nd Lt in 1818. [Oct 7th newspaper: he entered the army on Feb 13, 1818: promoted to 1st Lt on Jan 1, 1819: received the full commission of Capt in the line on Apr 30, 1831. For many years he was actively employed in the Subsistence Dept in Florida, & for a long period also filled the post of Assist Quartermaster, being the active ofcr of that dept in the original establishment of *Fort Brooke*, Tampa Bay, in 1823. In Aug, 1832, he was appointed, by the direction of Pres Jackson, emigrating & disbursing agent in the removal of the Choctaw Indians to the country west of the Mississippi river. He left Florida in May, 1841, with Gen Armistead, but returned the next year & remained until the termination of the war by Gen Worth in 1842. His regt was then relieved from duty in Florida, & he accompanied it to Jefferson Barracks, Mo, where he was permitted to repose for a time, blessed with the society of his wife & children. In May, 1844, his regt was ordered to Natchitoches, La. Capt Page accompanied his regt. In Jul, 1845, circumstances placed him temporarily at its head, & he conducted it to the shores of St Joseph's island & Corpus Christi- there almost unknown regions. For some time, disabled for duty by illness, he devoted himself to the last moment to the calls of the service & his country. That devotion he sealed with his life. He fell nobly in the action of Palo Alto, on May 8 last, while commanding the leading division of his regt in support of the battery of 18 pounders. A shot struck Capt Page on the face, carrying away the whole of the lower jaw. He was removed from the field, &, under the hands of the surgeon, displayed unexampled patience & fortitude. The day after the battle he was sent to Point Isabel, where he endured extreme suffered for nearly 2 months, during which he was never heard to complain, but was cheerful, though he could not speak. About the last of June his wound had so far healed as to enable him to take passage on a steamship for New Orleans. A few days after his departure his wife, who, impelled by the purest affection & a devotion to her husband that overcame every obstacle, had left her home in Delaware alone, & traveled several thousand miles to minister to his comfort, arrived at Point Isabel. Her disappointment at not meeting him was borne, not without grief, but with a firmness as unprecedented as it was admirable. She returned immediately to New Orleans, & there found her wounded husband prostrated & rapidly sinking. They left New Orleans on the steamboat **Missouri** for St Louis, but the heroic sufferer was doomed to expire before reaching their destination, & on Jul 12, 1846, near Cairo, he quietly gave up his spirit. His remains were taken to Jefferson Barracks & interred with the honors of war, escorted to the grave by Col Baker's regt of Illinois volunteers. Capt Page was a native of Friburg, Maine, & was born on Feb 4, 1797. -B

Died: on Jul 17, at his residence, in Anne Arundel Co, Md, Edw Lloyd Nicholson, in his 47th year. Plain & retiring in all the habits of his life; unassuming in prosperity, & uncomplaining in tribulation; upright, benevolent, & generous in the discharge of all the social duties, he has fallen, at the meridian of his day, amidst the lamentations of relatives, the regrets of friends, & the respect of all who knew him.

WED JUL 22, 1846
Wash Corp: 1-Ptn from Wm Thompson, Editor & Publisher of the Saturday Evening News, asking for the publication of the proceedings of the 2 Boards & the laws & advertisements of the Corp: which was read. 2-Ptn from Andrew Doig: referred to the Cmte on Improvements. 3-Suitable site for a market-house south of the Canal, in that part of the city known as the "Island," & probable cost of said site; & that, as a market house is being built in that part of the city known as the Northern Liberties, the distance from the several market houses may be nearly equal, & the interests & conveniences of all the people may be served: referred to Cmte on Improvement. 4-Ptn from Lambert Tree & others: referred to the Cmte on Improvements. 5-Ptn from Catharine Adamson: referred to the Cmte of Claims. 6-Ptns of Chas Dyson & Jas Fitzgerald: referred to the Cmte of Claims. 7-Ptn from Edw D Tippett: referred to the members from the 1st Ward. 8-The nominations of Saml Drury, Ignatius Mudd, & Jas Marshall, for Assessors: confirmed. 9-Cmte of Claims: asked to be discharged from the further consideration of the ptn of Richd Wroe, sen: ordered to lie on the table. 10-Ptn of Jos Fraser & others, praying alteration in the alley in square 127: referred to the Cmte on Improvements. 11-Ptn of Solomon Hersey, praying a remission of a fine: referred to the Cmte of Claims. 12-Ptn of R R Burr & others, for the opening, grading, of F st north, from 2nd to 3rd st west: referred to the Cmte on Improvements. 13-Cmte of Claims: reported a bill for the relief of Jacob Wechter, which was read. 14-Bill for the relief of Robt Beale postponed because the Board Adjourned.

H M Gage, a printer of Quincy, Ill, was seriously injured on Jul 4, while firing the cannon on the public square. His hands, wrists, arms & face were much mangled, & one of his eyes much injured.

Letter from a Baltimorean at Brasas Island states that 3 Baltimoreans had died since their departure from Wash, viz: Robt Beacham, a private in Capt Piper's company; Richd Belt, a private in Capt Kenly's company, drowned; & Geo M Cole, a private in Capt Stewart's company.

As the steamer **John J Crittenden** was approaching Paducah, Ky, on Sat week, on her way from St Louis to Louisville, a man named Garland A Hardwick, of Newcastle, Ky, together with Nathl Price, of St Louis, head engineer of the Crittenden, were drowned. Hardwick, under delirium, rushed into the cabin with a billet of wood to confront his supposed tormentors, when he was caughy by Price, & they both fell overboard forward of the wheel. They were doubtless killed by a stoke of the buckets.

Senate: 1-Cmte on Foreign Relations: without amendment, bill for the relief of Thos Ap Catesby Jones. 2-Cmte on the Judiciary: without amendment, bill for the relief of John McAlister.

Private tutor is wanted in a neighboring county in Md: one having some experience to instruct in the rudiments of the Latin & Greek languages. A member of the Episcopal Church would be preferred. -J G Chapman, House of Reps, U S

The Board of Naval Ofcrs which assembled in this city yesterday, to confer respecting the contemplated attack on the Castle of San Juan d'Ulun, is [says the Eastern papers] composed of the following ofcrs: Capts Stewart, Jacob Jones, Morris, Ridgely, Downes, Ballard, Ap Catesby Jones, Bolton, Shubrick, Kearney, Turner, Perry, Jos Smith, Rousseau, Geisinger, McKeever, Parker, McCauley, Stringham, & Breese.

Ex-Govn'r Bennett, of S C, had his left arm amputated at the shoulder blade lately, the result of an accident in the hand 25 years ago!

Died: on Jun 17, in Wash City, Walter R Stone, s/o Dr Benj Stone, of Ohio, in his 28th year. The dec'd was a native of Ohio, but has resided for the past year in Va, & was on his way to visit some friends in Fairfax, when attacked with violence by the disease which terminated his life. He displayed the qualities of a perfect gentleman, united with those of an exemplary Christian.

Died: on Jul 19, in Wash City, of cholera infantum, Virginia Sylvania, 5th child of John J & Mary G Mulloy, aged 8 months.

Very desirable farm for sale: 3½ miles from Wash City, the residence of the late Alex'r Shepherd: contains 111 acres; house is commodious, modern style, & well finished. Apply to either of the Excs, Susan D Shepherd, S Holmes, or to J C Lewis, 7th st.

The ofcrs & men who rendered such efficient service to the citizens of Nantucket during the late disastrous fire were those of the Coast Survey schnr **Gallatin** & the schnr **Wave**, commanded by Lt Chas H Davis & Lt John R Goldsborough, of the U S Navy, at present engaged in the survey of the Vineyard Sound & of the Nantucket South Shoal.

Later from the Army & Texas. On Jul 13, Col Croghan mustered into the U S service Col Baker's Regt, now at Jefferson Barracks. Arrangements are in progress for the transportation of the Illinois volunteers to the place of destination as soon as possible.

House of Reps: 1-Ptn of John Welch, & a large number of Cherokee Indians residing in N C, asking compensation for reservations, spoliations, & losses sustained by the action of the Gov't: referred.

THU JUL 23, 1846
On Sat an inquest was held at the Cathedral Hotel, St Paul's Churchyard, before Mr Wm Payne, city coroner, on view of the body of Mr Saml Butler, aged 23, s/o Mr Thos Butler, chemist, St Paul's Churchyard, who poisoned himself with prussic acid. The dec'd stated he wanted to marry, & his father, & the father of the young girl he intended to marry, both found them to be too young, & they should wait. Witness is of the opinion that the thought of the delay may have produced a temporary insanity. -Times

Senate: 1-Cmte on Pensions: House bill for the relief of Benj Allen, without amendment. Same cmte: House bill for the relief of Griffin Kelley.

Board of Naval Ofcrs assembled in Wash City on Tue, composed, if all the members attended of the following Captains:

Chas Stewart	Wm B Shubrick	G W Storer
Jacob Jones	Chas W Morgan	Isaac McKeever
Chas Morris	Lawrence Kearney	Chas S McCauley
L Warrington	F A Parker	E A F Lavallette
John Downes	Danl Turner	S H Stringham
Jesse Wilkinson	M C Perry	Isaac Mayo
Thos Ap C Jones	Jos Smith	Saml L Breese

[Convened to deliberate the best mode of attacking & capturing, by a naval force, the Mexican fortress of San Juan de Ulua.]

Naval Court Martial at Annapolis, which has been in session there for the past week, is composed of:

Capt Isaac McKeever, Pres	Lt Cadwallader Ringgold
Capt Chas J McCauley	Lt Edw G Tilton
Capt Isaac Mayo	Lt Jas H Ward
Cmder Chas Lowndes	Lt John J Almy, judge advocate

The trial of Midshipman McLaughlin is now before the Court, & when concluded the Court will proceed to the trial of Lt Cogdell. -Sun

On Fri morning, Jul 10, 40 ladies from the village of Utica, Michigan, secretly assembled, proceeded to a bowling alley, armed with axes, hatchets, & hammers, & completely demolished it. They had viewed this insidious foe to their domestic peace for some time with an anxious & jealous eye; &, having waited in vain for some legal proceeding against it, determined for once to take the law into their own hands. The bldg was 80 feet long, & the destruction was accomplished in a little less than an hour! -Detroit Daily Adv

Rencontre at a muster on Sat last in Cumberland Co, N C, between B F Atkins, a candidate for the Legislature, & Archibald McDiarmid, which resulted in the immediate death of the latter from a pistol shot. Both gentlemen belong to the same political party. –Raleigh Register

Andrew P Potter, who had been convicted of the murder of Lucius P Osborn, in Feb, 1845, was hung on Mon in the jail yard at New Haven. The execution was witnessed by from 100 to 200 persons.

The Coronation of the Pope took place at Rome on Jul 21. On this occasion Pius IX ordered the distribution of 50 marriage dowries of 50 crowns each [about 270 fr] for Rome, & 1,000 of 10 crowns each for the provinces. The new Pope's Cabinet: Cardinal Gizzi, a moderate Liberal, being named Sec of State for Foreign Affairs, or Prime Minister, & Cardinal Amati as Minister of the Interior.

FRI JUL 24, 1846
Senate: 1-Cmte of Claims: House bill for the relief of the heirs of Robt Fulton, without amendment. 2-Cmte on Pensions: House bill for the relief of Mary Campbell, wid/o John Campbell, without amendment. Same cmte, without amendment: relief of Leah Gray; relief of Danl H Warren; & relief of Peter Rife. 3-Cmte on Public Lands: House bill for the relief of John Milsted, of Escambia Co, Florida, without amendment.

Caleb J McNulty, former Clerk of the House of Reps:, a private in one of the companies of Ohio volunteers, died on board the steamboat **Alhambra**, on Jul 10, while on his way to New Orleans.

The U S Marshal for the State of Md has received the Pres' remission of the fine, & costs in the case of Jason L Pendleton, late master of the brig **Montevideo**, convicted in the District Court of the U S of being engaged in the slave trade.

We regret to hear from Washington, the sudden death of Mrs Tayloe, the w/o B Ogle Tayloe, of that city, d/o the late Mr Dickinson, of Troy, & a very highly accomplished & elegant female, long known in the circles of fashion, & yet exceedingly beloved by friends in humble life. –N Y paper

Dreadful affray on Jul 14 in St Clair Co, Ill, in which Mr Jas Duncan, an old & wealthy citizen , lost his life. It seems that from some cause he had become obnoxious to his neighbors. A body of men visited the farm of Mr Duncan & ordered him to leave the neighborhood. In reply the dec'd fired on the lynchers, & wounded one of them. The fire was returned from some 20 guns, & Mr Duncan was blown to pieces.

Prisoners escaped: Chas W Whitehouse, John Adams alias John Allen, & John Johnson, from the State prison at Charlestown, Mass. The warden offers a reward of $50 for each convict.

Mrd: on Jul 19, by Rev Mr Eggleston, Henry D Cooper to Susan Weybourn, all of Wash City.

Died on Jul 2, in Wash City, of affection of the throat, Mrs Eliz G, w/o Wm T Griffith, & eldest d/o Simeon Matlock, aged 36.

Died: on Tue last, at his residence in Gtwn, D C, Jas Keith, aged 76 years. The dec'd was for a long time an extensive merchant in Alexandria; afterwards he moved to Fred'k City, Md, & had been for the last 3 years a resident of Gtwn.

Died: on Jul 21, at Phil, after a long & painful illness, Wm Swaim, in his 63rd year. [This is the gentleman who had acquired an extensive fame by the general diffusion & use of a medicine of his preparation.] For some considerable time past Mr Swaim has been confined to his chamber, or had only reached his carriage by the assistance of others.

For rent: 3 story brick house, on 7th st, between I & N Y ave. Apply to G W Uttermuhle, next door.

For rent: large 3 story brick house on Pa ave, next door west of Edw Simm's store. The store will be rented separate from the upper part & back bldg. Apply to Geo Mattingly.

Dr Alfred H Lee tenders his professional services to the residents of Wash & its adjoining counties. Ofc on H st, near 7th.

Woodville, Miss, Jul 11. On Tue, Chas J Foster, Assessor of the Taxes for this county, was taking down the taxable property of Wm K Richardson, a young mechanic of this county, a native we believe of Dayton, Ohio. Mr Richardson gave Foster a deadly blow & was stabbed in the left lung immediately over the heart, & lived but 6 minutes after receiving the wound. Richardson was tried & bound over in the sum of $2,000. Foster was one of our best citizens, an upright & impartial ofcr. We learn there was an old grudge between them, or at least on the part of Richardson.

House for rent: formerly occupied by Mr S Ashby, on F st, near 6th. Apply to A Green.

Valuable bldg lots at private sale: lots 1 thru 4 in square 128; lot 7 in square 792; lot G & improvements in square 903; parts of square & improvements in 928; lot 22 in square 1020; & lot 14 in square 1023. –A Green, auctioneer

By virtue of 2 writs of fiera facias, issued by S Drury, a justice of the peace for Wash Co, D C, we shall expose to public sale for cash, at the West Market-house, on Jul 29; 1 sideboard & sundry articles, the property of John T Devaughn to satisfy 2 judgments & executions in favor of Wm Hagerty & Chas E Upperman. Sale at 8 o'clock, a m. -John Dewdney, F B Poston, Constables.

Very excellent household furniture at auction on Aug 5, at the residence of Mrs Potter, on Pa ave, south side, between 3rd & 4½ sts, the furniture of that large boarding establishment. -R W Dyer, auct

SAT JUL 25, 1846
Senate: 1-Cmte on Pensions: House bills without amendment: act for the relief of Patrick Kelly, sen, of Indiana Co, Pa. Act for the relief of Ebenezer Connaut, of Jefferson Co, N Y. Acts for the relief of Lewis Laing; relief of Wm Gump; relief of Patrick Masterson; act granting a pension to Jos Dessau. Also, asked to be discharged from the further consideration of the ptn of Saml R Read, & that it be referred to the Cmte on Naval Affairs. 2-Cmte on Claims: House bill for the relief of John Carr, John Batty, & Saml Stevenson, seamen on board the whale ship **Margaret**. 3-Cmte on Pensions: House bills, without amendment: acts for the relief of Mary Phelps; relief of Mgt Gwiumaph, of Hamilton Co, Ohio; & relief of Jas Gee.

Mr J B Schoener, a native of Pa, formerly a minature painter of great talent in Boston, committed suicide by cutting his throat in his room, at the American House in that city, while in a temporary state of insanity. Mr Schoener was highly esteemed & respected by a large circle of acquaintances.

Mrd: on Jul 16, by Rev Dr Empie, Mr Chas Merrewether Fry to Miss Eliz Wickham Leigh, d/o B W Leigh, all of Richmond, Va.

Mrd: on Jul 21, by Rt Rev Saml Eccleston, Archibishop of Balt, Robt H Gallaher, junior editor of the Richmond Republican, to Miss Harriet E P Marsh, y/d/o Elias Marsh, of N Y.

Mrd: on Jul 16, at Hampstead, Va, by Rev John McDaniel, Mr John E Baker to Miss Minnie Anne, d/o the late Mr Jas Blackburn, all of King Geo Co, Va.

Obit-died: on Jul 7, at Havana, of Mrs Campbell, w/o Gen R B Campbell, Consul of the U S at that place. She was the d/o Ludwell Lee, of Va, & grand-dght of Richd Henry Lee. Beautiful & accomplished, she was married very early in life to Gen Campbell, then of S C. Mrs Campbell was an exemplary wife, a fond & devoted mother, possessing all those qualifications best calculated to endear a woman to the circle in which her lot is cast.

In 1830 the last Will of Thos Pentecost was admitted to record in Dinwiddie Co, Va. He left his estate to his wife Mary Pentecost during her life, & at her death to be equally divided between his brother Wm [who it is known to the subscriber lately died in Georgia] & the testator's 3 sisters, Nancy Jackson, Eliz St John, & Martha Dials. In May last Mary Pentecost died. At the request of Wm Pentecost in his lifetime, & of his son since his father's death, I have taken charge of the estate of Thos Pentecost. Any one knowing whether either of the sisters resides, or if dead, who is entitled to her estate, will greatly oblige by giving me the information.
—R R Collier, Petersburg, Va

$50 reward for runaway negro man Dorsey Dyer, about 30 years of age: left the plantation of Wm B Beall, near Nottingham, PG Co, Md, on Jul 13. He has a wife residing on the estate of Mr Osbourn, & relations in this neighborhood & in Montg Co. —Danl C Digges, Agent for Miss S Forest, Upper Marlboro.

Disastrous fire at Fayetteville, N C, last Wed consumed bldgs, most of them being stores, either owned or occupied by the following persons:

R W Hardie	Robt A Stuart	John Mullins
Wm G Matthews	Wm E Kirkpatrick	David Shaw
J M Beasley	Mallett & Huske	Dr Gilliam
Edw L Winslow	A M Campbell	C Caison
E S Hobbs	A Marsh	J L Parker
Jas Jenkin	M McKinnon	G W Smith
David & J R Gee	F D Breece	

Fire at Naples, Ill, on Jul 15, nearly all the business part of the town of Naples was destroyed by fire. The Naples House, kept by Col C F Keener; the stone warehouse & smokehouse of E & L Vansyckles; store & warehouse of Conn & Mandlebaum; store & warehouse of Joshua Moore; & the dwlg house of Mr Vansyckles.

Col J Van Benthuysen, long known as the efficient & highly respected postmaster at Poughkeepsie, expired of apoplexy on Sun evening.

MON JUL 27, 1846
On Thu night, at the Capitol, a splendid experiment came off with the new oxhydrogen light invented by Mr Robt Grant. A flood of light, radiating like the fiery tail of some mighty comet, swept over the city, illuminating at intervals the whole length of Pa ave, the Pres' house, & different public bldgs. The light is produced by a set of gases from the combined <u>oxhydrogen</u> blow-pipe thrown upon a piece of unslaked lime-the lime point being placed in the focus of a parabolic rainbow, which revolves upon a centre. These improvements will enable the public soon to enjoy this illuminating principle at a rate much cheaper than ordinary gas or oil can be provided.

Coleman's Hotel, last Fri, was beautifully & brilliantly lighted up with Mr Jas Crutchett's solar gas. We understand there are now 90 gas lights in that extensive bldg, the smallest of which emits a flame equal to 16 candles.

Brown's Hotel, the Old Indian Queen Hotel, has been lighted for some time with gas.

Last Fri night, a young man, David Fry, was instantly killed by lightning. He & 2 other persons were taking a temporary shelter during the thunder storm, under a wagon in a field, where they had been harvesting, not far from the Long Bridge. Fry was killed instantly, & his companions were stunned. A horse near them was struck dead upon the spot.

The California Expedtion: the ofcrs of Col Stevenson's regt have been commissioned by Govn'r Wright, the commissions to take effect from Jul 16. It is understood the regt will be mustered into service this week, & will be ordered to **Fort Hamilton** for drill, preparatory to its departure from N Y by sea, from Aug 1 to Aug 15.

Fire at Cleveland, Ohio, on Jul 20th, consumed a warehouse owned by S S Stone & occupied by A Loomis, wholesale grocer, & another by A Merwin & others.

Senate: 1-Ptn of Jos Elliott, a soldier in the Revolutionary army, praying a pension. 2-Ptn from Amos Calton, in behalf of David Whelpley, praying extra compensation for his services in the exploring expedition under Gen Pike in 1805 & 1806. 3-Cmte on Pensions: House bills without amendment: relief of Aquilla Goodwin; relief of Justin Jacobs; relief of Suranus Cobb; act granting a pension to Abraham Ausman. Same cmte, without amendment, House bill for the relief of John Campbell, of Garland, in the State of Maine.

Mrd: on Jul 21, by Rev H V D Johns, Wm Emack to Miss Mary E Griffith, d/o R H Griffith, all of Balt.

Valuable city property for sale: property belonging to the estate of John McClelland: 2 brick houses on 13th st, between G & H sts.
Also, 3 fine bldgs adjoining the same.
2 brick houses on south side of N Y ave, between 13th & 14th sts.
3 fine bldg lots on the corner of H & 10th sts.
7 lots on the north side of I st, between 12th & 13th sts.
The whole of the above property will be sold on reasonable terms. Inquire of John McClelland, corner of E & 10th sts.

Railroad accident last Fri, on the Erie Railroad, about a mile from Monroe: wheel upon one of the forward cars broke, throwing the train off the track: Mr Chas Stevens, of N Y, & a s/o Dr Crane, of Goshen, were killed instantly.

Thos J Chew, late of the U S Navy, died at Brooklyn a day or two since in his 70th year. Mr Chew was the person to whom Lawrence uttered the words, "Don't give up the ship!" Chew fought with great gallantry in several naval battles in the war of 1812. He was on the deck of the frig **Constitution** in the memorable fight with the vessel **Guerriere**, & contributed to the capture of that ship. At the time of his decease he held the ofc of purser in the navy. [Aug 13th newspaper: Mr Chew was not of the U S Navy at the time of his death. He left the Navy in 1832. He was one of those unobtrusive Christians who do good silently & constantly. As a public servant, husband, father, & friend, his life was passed with integrity. He was the s/o Capt Saml Chew, who died in defence of the liberty of his country as a captain in the U S navy in the war of Independence in 1779. At age 23 Mr Chew had attained the command of a merchant ship, which he left to enter the U S navy in 1799, in the war with France. In the war of 1812 he was a purser on the frig **Constitution**, & had a post of active duty assigned to him in the battle that captured the vessel **Guerriere**. On board the ship **Chesapeake** he fought in the conflict with the vessel **Shannon**, where he received from the mortally wounded Lawrence the memorable words, "Don't give up the ship." On his return to the U S he married the d/o John Hallam, of New London, & he named his only son after his lamented friend Cmdor Lawrence, who had died in his arms. Mr Chew retired to private life in Brooklyn, Long Island, the residence of his family. He was a member of the church & vestry of St Ann's there, & was 9 years a warden. He died, lamented by all who knew him, on Jul 21, 1846, in his 70th year. The family of Mr Chew were of Va, where his ancestor, John Chew, settled anno Domini 1843. His grandfather Thos married Martha Taylor, aunt of Pres Madison, & his aunt Alice was the grandmother of Gen Z Taylor, U S Army.]

Died: on Fri last, in N Y C, Preserved Fish, in his 81st year, a respected as well as old citizen. He was long one of the most intelligent merchants of the city, & had for several years been, as he was at the time of his death, Pres of the Tradesmen's Bank.

Died: on Jul 25, in Wash City, Martha F, w/o John F Hartley, & d/o Jonathan King, of Saco, Maine.

Died: on Jul 26, in Washington, John Hill, of PG Co, Md, in his 25th year. His funeral will take place this afternoon, at 5 o'clock, from the residence of his mother, on H st.

Died: on Jul 23, at Fredericksburg, Va, Maj Hugh M Patton, Cashier of the Farmers' Bank of that place.

Trustee's sale of valuable improved property: virtue of a decree of the Circuit Court of Wash Co, D C, sitting as a Court of Chancery: sale on Aug 24, of lots 2 & 3 in square 744, on the Eastern branch, with extensive water-privilege. Also, lot 17 in square 878. The Trustee will convey to the purchaser, all the right & title of which the late Franklin Wharton died seised. –Saml Miller, Trustee

House of Reps: 1-Leave was granted to withdraw the papers of Henry Disbrow. 2-Cmte on Indian Affairs: bill for the settlement of the accounts of John Corwell, late Creek Indian agent in Georgia & Alabama, reported the same with an amendment: bill was then committed. Same cmte: adverse report on the case of Saml Douthet: laid on the table. 3-Cmte on Naval Affairs: Senate bill for the relief of Thos Brownell, reported the same with a recommendation that it do not pass: bill was then rejected. Same cmte: bill granting a pension to Ebenezer Ballard; bill granting a pension to Jas Low; bill for the relief of Henry Etting; bill for the relief of Harriette Ward: reported the said bill back to the House; they were severally committed. Same cmte: bill for the relief of Andrew Armstrong: committed. Same cmte: bill for the relief of John W Simonton, John Whitehead, & others: committed. 4-Cmte on Foreign Affairs: Senate bill for the relief of the personal reps of Wm A Slacum, dec'd: committed. 5-Cmte on Ways & Means: bill from the Senate for the relief of Richd Kidd & Benj Kidd: committed. 6-Cmte of Claims: bill for the relief of J Throckmorton; bill for the relief of Peter Von Schmidt; bill in addition to the act for the relief of Walter Loomis & Abel Gay; bill for the relief of John Jones & Chas Souder: committed. 7-Cmte of Claims: bill for the relief of the heirs of Matthew Stewart; also, bill for the relief of Benj Ogle Tayloe: committed. Same cmte: adverse report on the cases of Ruth Freeman, & Henry Parke: laid on the table. Same cmte: bill for the relief of Mary Renner: committed. 7-Cmte on the Post Ofc & Post Roads: joint resolution from the Senate in favor of David Shaw & Solomon J Corser, reported the same without amendment: committed. Same cmte: joint resolution from the Senate for the relief of Orlando Saltmarsh & Wm Fuller: committed. 8-Cmte on the Judiciary: bill from the Senate for the relief of Abraham B Fannin: passed. Same cmte: bill from the Senate for the relief of Harriette L Catching, & bill from the Senate for the relief of Richd S Coxe: committed. Also, joint resolution from the Senate for the relief of Chas S Sibbald: committed. Same cmte: bill from the Senate for the relief of the reps of Peter Capella, dec'd: recommendation that it do not pass: bill was them rejected. 9-Joint Cmte on the Library of Congress, to which was referred the memorial of Mr Catlin, asking Congress to purchase his gallery of Indian portraits & Indian collections, made a favorable report thereon, recommending that an amendment be made to the bill which has passed the House, & is now before the Senate, to establish the Smithsonian Institution, which shall provide for the purchase of said gallery. 10-Cmte of Claims: bill for the relief of Robt Roberts: committed. 11-Bill for the relief of Francis Martin: rejected. 12-Bill granting a pension to Silas Waterman: passed. 13-Bill to extend the term of the patent herefore granted to Elisha H Holmes: Passed. 14-Bill for the relief of Gregory Thomas & others: passed. 15 thru 27: The undermentioned bills were not objected to, & were reported to the House to be there disposed of, by passing them or otherwise, viz: Following are for <u>relief of</u>:

Jos Warren Newcomb;	Jacob L Vance
Joshua Shaw	Susan Brum
Fred'k Hopkins	Isaac Guess
Josiah Haskell	Wm Causey
Job Hawkins	Wilfred Knott

Dr Clark Lillybridge
Amos Kendall
Jas Williams
Jos Gideon
David Myerle
Purser G R Barry
Capt Jas Pennoyer
Eliz Adams
Thos M Newall
Henry La Reintree
John Keith, of N Y
Harvey Reynolds
Catharine Stevenson
Edith Ramey
Ann Clayton
Thos Blanchard
John C Stewart & others
Bernard O'Neil
Putney & Riddle
Nathl Philips
Lewis C Sartori
Jas H Conley
Wm T Walthall
Eliz Fitch
Thankful Reynolds
Jonathan Hoyt
John Van Slyck
Harrison Whitson

Henty Etting
Harriette Ward
John Jones & Chas Sonder
Richd Kidd & Benj Kidd
John Pickett, & others
Heirs of Hyacinth Lassell
Zachariah Simmons, of Tenn
Heirs of Sgt Maj John Champe
Heirs of John Speakman, dec'd
Heirs of Gen Thos Sumter, late of S C, dec'd
Legal reps of Thos Shields, dec'd
W P S Sanger & Geo F De Roche
Alvin C Goell, & other puposes
Geo B Russell & others
Widow & heirs of John B Chaudonia
Heirs of Stephen Johnson, dec'd
Mrs Pike, wid/o the late Gen Pike
Eliz Caltins, widow of Silas Winans
Legal reps of Jas H Clark
Legal reps of John Lawson, dec'c
Heirs of Silas Duncan, dec'd
Widow of Elijah Bragdon, dec'd
Benj Metoyer & Francois Gaiennie, dec'd
Relief of Eliz Converse, wid/o Josiah Converse

16-Relief of the heirs of John Whitsitt, dec'd, late of Lafayette Co, Missouri. 17-Relief of the administrators of Jos Edson, dec'd, late marshal of the district of Vermont. 18-Relief of Wm B Stokes, surviving partner of John N C Stockton & Co. 19-Relief of Julius Eldred, Elisha Eldred, & Francis E Eldred, for expenses & services in removing the copper rock from Lake Superior. 20-Elijah White, acting sub-agent of Indian affairs west of the Rocky Mountains. 21-Relief of the heirs of Gassaway Watkins, an ofcr of the Md continental line in the war of the Revolution. 22-Act for the relief of the legal reps of Pierre Menard, Josiah T Betts, Jacob Feaman, & Edmund Roberts, of Illinois, sureties of Felix St Vrain, late Indian agent, dec'd. 23-Bill authorizing patents to Geo Ramey & Thos F January, for certain lands entered in St Louis Co, Missouri. 24-Bill to provide for the final settlement of the accounts of John Spencer, late receiver of public moneys at **Fort Wayne**, Indiana. 25-Settlement of the accounts of John Crowell, late Indian agent. 26-Settlement of the claims of Alex'r M Cumming. 27-Pension to: Roswell Hale, Silas Chatfield, Richd Elliott, Ebenezer Ballard, & Jas Low. 28-A bill from the Senate for the payment of a small sum of money to Mrs Pike, the aged & infirm widow of the gallant Gen Pike, killed in Canada in the war of 1812 with Great Britain, for the valuable extra services rendered by her husband soon after the purchase of Louisiana from France, in several tours of exploration through the interior of that country, then a trackless wilderness, never before trodden by a white man, was taken up: it passed- yeas 88, nays 64. Bill was recommitted to the Cmte on Indian Affairs. 29-Bill for the relief of the widow of the late Thos Murray, jr, dec'd, was taken up: passed. 30-Bill for the relief of Harriette L Katching: passed. 31-Bill granting a pension of $20 a year to Richd Elliot, of Wash City, for Revolutionary services: amendment making the pension commence in the year 1846, instead of 1831: he is now understood to be very aged & infirm, & cannot live very long to enjoy his $20 a year: passed.

From the Rio Grande. The reverend gentlemen appointed by the Pres of the U S as Chaplains for the soldiers professing the Roman Catholic Religion, McElroy & Rey, arrived on Jul 8, in the steamboat **Troy**, from Point Isabel. The appointment of these gentlemen by the Pres must go far to remove the unfounded opinion prevalent in Mexico, that the U S Gov't is hostile to the Catholic religion, & that this war is waged in part against the religion professed by the Mexicans. [Jul 28th newspaper: The Catholic Chaplains sent out by Pres Polk to officiate for the soldiers professing that faith attempted this morning to address the citizens of Matamoros, but they were refused the use of the church either to speak or preach in.]

N Y Correspondence, Jul 25, 1846: Govn'r Wright has commuted the punishment of Sam Wilcox, the murderer of Saml McKinstey in Dec last. He is to be confined during life.

For sale or rent: 2 story brick dwlg, on N J ave, near the Capitol. Inquire of the subscriber, or of John R Queens, at the Capitol. –R M Combs

For rent: commodious 2 story brick house on E st, now occupied by Mr Fendall. Apply to Mr John F Callan, nearly opposite, or to the subscriber, at his residence, a few doors east of the Seven Bldgs, in the First Ward. –A McD Davis

For Trinidad, [Port Spain] The fine fast sailing new brig **Analoston**, John G Dorry master, will sail on Jul 29. For light freight & passengers, having superior state- room accommodations, apply to the Capt on board, or to F & A H Dodge, Gtwn. Passengers can be landed at Barbadoes if required.

TUE JUL 28, 1846
Senate: 1-Cmte on Indian Affairs: asking to be discharged from the further consideration of the ptn of Jos Kennedy. Also, from the ptn of Lawrence Taliaferro. 2-Cmte on Naval Affairs: adverse report on the memorial of Wm A Howard. 3-Cmte on Commerce: House bill for the relief of John Chasseaud, U S Consul for Syria & Palestine, without amendment: passed.

Obit-died: on Jun 30, in Warren Ohio, Mrs Cutler, w/o Hon Ephraim Cutler, aged 67 years. Mrs Cutler was of a class highly estimated in life, perhaps more so in death. Her married life, of almost 40 years, has been one of great retirement-latterly, of affliction & pain. –Marietta [Ohio] Intell, Jul 9, 1846 [Mrs Cutler, as Sarah Parker, was one of the dghts of Wm Parker, who was himself one of the original members of the Ohio Co, the founders of Marietta, & indeed of the State of Ohio. Mr Parker, with his large family, came out with the first settlers, about 1788, when the woman we now mourn for was still little above childhood. The Indian war & the dangers to his charge induced Mr Parker to retrace his steps as far as Westmorland Co, Pa, where they remained until savage war terminated. After her return with her relatives to Ohio, Sarah Parker become the 2nd w/o Judge Ephraim Cutler, the s/o the well-known Manassah Cutler, a man to whom a higher compliment could not be paid than to say he was worthy to be the husband of such a woman. Judge Cutler now, near if not about 80 years of age, was himself amongst the very earliest pioneers of Ohio. –Wm Darby

Laws of the U S passed at the First Session of the 29th Congress. Official Publication. Public-No 27. An Act to retrocede the county of Alexandria, in the District of Columbia, to the State of Virginia.

J H Gibbs has taken the fancy store recently occupied by S Parker, & respectfully invites the ladies & public generally to his very handsome & varied stock of French Fancy Goods, Perfumery, Fans, & Gloves. Store: Pa ave, between 9th & 10th sts.

Furniture, & buggy, at auction by order of the Orphans Court of Wash Co, D C. Being the personal estate of the late Martin Murphy. -R W Dyer, auct

Later from the seat of war. The Times says: We learn that the court martial on Capt Thornton terminated on the 15th ult, & the general impression is that he has been acquitted. One passage of his reported defence has been commented on with admiration by all in the camp at Matamoros. He said that, in the performance of the act for which he was tried-rashness or precipitancy, we believe-he did not see the numbers of the enemy; all he saw was the Mexican flag waving over American soil, & he was willing to risk his own life in an attempt to cut it down.

A curious case is now pending in the Alabama Courts. 2 sgts of Capt Desha's company of volunteers, now in Mexico, [Jas Chandler & Elijah Keer,] deserted & returned to Mobile, their place of residence. They were there arrested & placed in charge of the cmder of the Georgia regiment to be conveyed back to the army for trial. They justify their desertion by alleging the tyrannical conduct of Capt Desha & his 1st lt, Adrian. They are being retained in custody in Mobile.

Mrd: on Jul 2, in Wash City, by Rev Mr Morgan, Mr Thos Webster to Miss Mary Smith, all of Alexandria.

<u>Bethany College</u>, located in Western Virginia, Brook Co, near the Ohio river, just closed its 5th session on Jul 4. 16 young gentlemen obtained the degree of Bachelor of Arts. During the last year there were 128 students, assembled from 15 States of the Union. It is under the superintendence of Alex'r Campbell, of Bethany, Va.

Died: on Jul 27, from water on the brain, Ella Apalonia, only child of John E & Sarah A Scheel, aged 9 months & 3 days.

While the steamboat **Jas Hewett**, having on board a portion of the 1st regt of Indiana volunteers, was at the Vicksburg landing on Jul 12, Freeman H Cross, s/o the gentleman of that name belonging to the Louisville Legion, & nephew of the late Col Cross who was killed on the Rio Grande, fell from the wharf boat & was drowned.

<u>Appointments by the Pres, by & with the advice & consent of the Senate.</u>
Edw B Marache, of Pa, Consul for the island of Trinidad.
Narino de Mattey, Consul for the island of Cyprus.
Philip Geisse, of Pa, Consul for Nuremburg, in Bavaria.
Benj H Brewster, of Pa, & Edw Harden, of Ga, to be com'rs to examine claims under the treaty with the Cherokees of 1835-36.
Wm C Bettencourt, Postmaster at Wilmington, N C.
Chas R Belt, Justice of the Peace in Wash Co, D C.
Passed Midshipman Johnson Blakely Carter, to be a Lt in the navy, to fill a vacancy occasioned by the death of Lt L G Keith.
John Miller, of Missouri, to be Indian Agent at the Council Bluffs.
<u>Medical Dept, under Act of Jun 18, 1846:</u>
Danl McPhail, of Tenn, to be Surgeon.
Geo Penn, of Missouri, to be Surgeon.
Geo Johnson, of Missouri, to be Surgeon.
A Parker, of Texas, to be Surgeon.
Wm D Dorris, of Tenn, to be Assist Surgeon.
Thos M Morton, of Missouri, to be Assist Surgeon.
Richd H Stevens, of Missouri, to be Assist Surgeon.
E Tucker, of Texas, to be Assist Surgeon.
Richd P Ashe, of Texas, to be Assist Surgeon.
<u>Custom-house Ofcrs:</u>
Edmund Wilson, to be Collector of the Customs for the district, & Inspector of the Revenue for the port of Waldoborough, in Maine, in place of Parker McCobb, jr, dec'd.
John C Humphries, to be Collector of the Customs for the district, & Inspector of the Revenue for the port of Bath, in Maine, vice Amos Nourse, rejected by the Senate.
Jos H Jordon, to be Collector of the Customs for the district, & Inspector of the Revenue for the port of Frenchman's Bay, in Maine, vice Henry S Jones, appointed in the recess of the Senate, in place of Jno M Hale, removed.
Nathan Bardin, to be Surveyor & Inspector of the Revenue for the port of Bristol, in Rhode Island, vice Elkanah French, whose commission expired.

Wm J Miller, to be Collector of the Customs for the district of Bristol & Warren, in Rhode Island, vice John Howe, removed.

Benj W Bosworth, to be Surveyor & Inspector of the Revenue for the ports of Warren & Barrington, in Rhode Island, vice Wm B Snell, removed.

Russell G Hopkinson, to be Collector of Customs for the district of Vt & Inspector of the Revenue for the port of Alburg, Vt, vice Archibald W Hyde, resigned.

Augustus Jenkins, to be Collector of the Customs for the district of Portsmouth, N H, vice Lory Odell, removed.

Jacob de la Motta, to be Naval Ofcr for the port of Savannah, Ga.

Land Ofcrs:

Benj R Cowherd, to be Register of the Land Ofc for the district of lands subject to sale at Jackson, Miss, from Jul 15, 1846, when his late commission expired.

Saml Russell, to be Register of the Land Ofc for the district of lands subject to sale at Newnansville, Florida, to take effect from & after Aug 31, 1846, when his present commission expires.

John Parsons, to be Receiver of Public Moneys for the district of lands subject to sale at Newnansville, Florida, to take effect from & after Aug 31, 1846, when his present commission will expire.

Murdoch McIntire, to be Register of the Land Ofc for the district of lands subject to sale at Opelousas, in Louisiana, vice Peter L Hebrard, whose commission expired Jul 12, 1846.

WED JUL 29, 1846

The 9 days' funeral honors rendered to the dec'd Pope were concluded on Jun 13 by a Latin eulogy, delivered by Bishop Rosani. A 15 foot high fence was put around the apts in the Quirinal Palace, to be occupied by the Electoral College of Cardinals, & built up the outside windows with bricks & mortar, as as to effectually prevent all communication. On Jun 14th a large concourse assembled at the church of St Sylvestre to see the 51 Cardinals start in procession, chanting the anthem Veni, Creator. Count Rossi declared, in the name of his master Louis Philippi, that the French Gov't would in no case use their veto. On Monday a signal was given within, signifying that an election had been completed, while a revolving drawer brought out a suit of the fortunate candidate's clothes, that his pontifical robes might be prepared. Now, as all the Cardinals wore the same dress, the only clue was the size, the shoe was very small-it was recollected that Cardinal Gizzi had a tiny foot, & in an hour all Rome knew that he was Pope. But there were other Cardinals who had small feet, & one of them, The Bishop of Imola, had received a majority, after several ballottings. The heads of the various orders went to his seat, & the oldest asked, "Acceptanane electionem de te canonice factam in sammum pontificem?" "I accept," was the reply, & instantly the canopies over the chairs of the other Cardinals fell by machinery, that of the Pope alone remaining. He selected the name of Pius IX, & was the youngest Cardinal in the college, having been born in 1792, at Sinigaglia, near Ancona, where he was christened Johan Maria Mastai Ferretti. Inheriting the title of Count with a handsome fortune, he was one of the most fashionable young men at Rome; but, when about 21, was disappointed in a love affair & took orders. He was placed over the Tata Giovanni, a charitable hospital founded by a master mason for the destitute members of his craft, & in the reign of Pius VII sent as auditor of the Papal Legation to Chili, being the only Cardinal living who has been on the American continent. He was named Cardinal in 1840. On Jun 16 the place of the Quirinal was literally packed with people, watching the centre walled-up window which looked out upon the balcony. About 9:30 it was knocked down from within, & Cardinal Riario Sporza, said in a loud voice: :Annuntio vobis gaudium magnum: Papam habemus eminentissimum ac reverendissimun dominum, Mastai, qui sibi imposuit nomen Pius Novem." The Pope appeared in his pontifical robes, resplendent with embroidery, borne in a chair on men's shoulders. The tiara was on his head, & behind him 2 attendants, carrying the flabelli, or peacock-feather fans. He rose, prayed, & blessed the people

Distressing Robbery-a very hard working honest man, G Green, residing on the Island, was robbed on Sun night of a considerable sum of money, the hard earnings of 15 years' industry, to build a small tenement to shelter the family. On Sun some villain broke into the house the carried the whole precious treasure. The worthy man, who drives a cart for a living, had the misfortune to lose his horse only a few days ago.

Senate: 1-Cmte on Pensions: bill granting a pension to Eliz Pistole, wid/o Chas Pistole. 2-Cmte of Claims: bill for the relief of Hudson Johns.

Robt Clarke was elected on Sat as Alderman to represent the 6th Ward of Wash City, in place of Marmaduke Dove, dec'd.

The Rev Jas Collard, printer, of the Methodist Episcopal Book Concern in N Y C, died at his residence on Fri. He had been indisposed for several months, but had so far recovered as to attend to business again. It is supposed he was affected suddenly with an enlargement of the heart.

A gentleman named Bunker, residing in Brooklyn, N Y, was desperately wounded & probably killed at the Railroad Depot in Newark. He had gone to Newark with his wife, who remained with friends, & while returning home he attempted to leap upon one of the cars, but failing, he fell across the track, & the train severed both his legs from his body. Little hope that he could survive.

A M G D: Gtwn College, D C. Annual commencement was held Jul 28, 1846.
Degree of A M was conferred on
Mr Jos Johnson, of Miss   Mr Francis M Gunnell, of D C.
 Degree of A B was conferred on:
Eliel S Wilson, of Md   L Tiernan Brien, of Md
Richd H Clarke, of D C   Prosper R Landry, of La
Robt E Doyle, of N Y   John C Nevins, of D C
Medals awarded to: [the above &]

Jas H Donegan, of Ala
Oliveira T Andrews, of Va
John C Longstreth, of Pa
Chas DeBlanc
Bernard G Caulfield, of D C
Alex A Allemong, of S C
John C Riley, of D C
Henry B Leaumont, of La
Edmond R Smith, of N Y
Henry J Forstall, of La
Clement Cox, of D C
Adrien J B Lepretre, of La
Geo A Loyall, of Va
Francis M Hall, of Md
Edmund L Smith, of Pa
Chas H Fulmer, of D C
John Duncan, of Ala
Richd H Edelin, of Md
John V Livingston, of N Y
Chas C Longstreth, of Pa
Bennett R Abell, of Md
Geo A Dyer, of Ky
F Matthews Lancaster, of Md
John C Hamilton, of D C
Edwin F King, of D C
Geo Furt, of Va
Jules M Brou, of La
Wm E Byrd, of Va
Edmond R Smith, of N Y
Lawrence A Williams, of D C
Alfred H Byrd, of Va
Geo W Fulmer, of D C
Alfred Tete, of La
Alfred J Higgins, of Va
Jas J Pritchard, of La
Wm H Donoho, of D C
Hermogene Dufresne, of La
Henry A Fenwick, of Md
Henry W Brent, of Md
Marshall T Polk, of N C

John Savage, of Pa
Louis F Pise, of N Y
Wm Boarman, of Md
John Gormly, of D C
D Clinton Yell, of Ark
Julius C Eslava, of Ala
Oscar P Tete, of La
Geo Ritt, of N Y
Aristide L Aubert, of Ala
Louis B France, of D C
Gerald Fitzgerald, of N Y
John Gabaroche, of La
Pierre D D Delacroix, of La
Alex'r A Allemong, of S C
Oscar Olivier, of La
Clement Cox, of D C
Chas W Swift, of Mass
Robt C Kent, of Va
Julien Cumming, of Ga
Richd G Shekell, of D C
Edmond A Deslonde, of La
Florence O'Donoghue, of D C
Gregory Ritt, of N Y
Jos T Mason, of Va
Ernest L Forstall, of La
Thos G May, of D C
Simon Seyfert, of Pa
Francis Neale, of Md
Stanislaus Coiron, of La
John Lee Carroll, of Md
Thos H Dawson, of D C
John F Ellis, of Va
Edouard P Drouet, of La
Isaac Pritchard, of La
John H King, of D C
Eugene de St Romes, of La
Louis V Landry, of La
John F Ellis, of Va
Saml Lauve, of La

THU JUL 30, 1846
For rent: large 3 story brick house on Pa ave, between 9th & 10th sts, at present occupied by S Woodward as a boarding-house & refectory. Possession on Aug 15. Inquire of Nicholas Callan, Agent

Senate: 1-Cmte on Pensions: asking to be discharged from the further consideration of the ptns of Rhoda Barton & of Susanna McCulloch. Same cmte: House bill for the relief of Louis Mattison, of Jefferson Co, N Y, without amendment. Same cmte: House bill for the relief of Eliz Betts, of N Y C, without amendment. Same cmte: House bill for the relief of Capt John Patten, without amendment. 2-Cmte on Commerce: bill for the relief of N & L Dana & Co. Same cmte: bill for the relief of Philip & Eliphalet Greeley. Same cmte: House bill for the relief of the owners of the ship **Herald**, of Balt, without amendment.

House of Reps: 1-Message from the Senate disagreeing to the amendment of this House to the bill granting a pension to old Richd Elliot, a Revolutionary soldier, now residing in Wash, was taken up. The bill, as passed by the Senate, extended to Mr Elliot the benefits of the pension law of Jul, 1832, which provides that all pensions granted under it shall commence Mar 3, 1831, [& all pensions granted under it have commenced at that time,] & fixes the amount at $24 a year. The amendment of the House deprives him of the benefit of the act of 1831, which has been enjoyed by thousands of his compatriots, & makes his pension commence on Mar 3, 1846, & reduces the amount to $20 a year. [No very great boon to an infirm man 87 years old.] Mr Brodhead moved that the House recede from its amendment; which the House refused to do, & the bill was returned to the Senate with notice of this decision. 2-Cmte on Invalid Pensions: bill for the relief of Richd Kelly Read: committed.

$100 reward for the robber that broke into my house on Jul 26, & robbed me of $505 in specie, nearly the whole in half dollars. The money was in a shot-bag, & was stolen from my bed-room, in the 2nd story. -Patrick Green, 13th st, near the Long Bridge

Baltimore Female Seminary, 119 East Balt St, opposite Aisquith st, Balt, Md. A Butler Atkins, B S, & Theron H Hawkes, B A: Principals. The Fall term will commence on Sep 1; been established for 2 years. Communication of the Rev Dr Johns: Balt, Jul 17, 1846. The Misses Chisholm, who take charge of the boarding-house arrangements, are middle aged ladies, & are women of piety & character. My acquaintance with them is personal & intimate, running back some 18 years. One of these ladies is a communicant of the Church under my care, the other is a communicant in the Presbyterian Church. I may mention that Mr Atkins is a graduate of Union College, & a communicant of the Protestant Episcopal Church. Mr Hawkes is a gaduate of Williams College, Mass, & a communicant in the Presbyterian Church. The truth is, the school is what a school ought to be, & hence must succeed. –Henry V D Johns

For rent: large 3 story brick house on Pa ave, between 9th & 10th sts, at present occupied by S Woodward as a boarding-house & refectory. Possession on Aug 15. Inquire of Nicholas Callan, Agent

American forces on the Rio Grande-from Matamoros on Jul 12: At the Brasos are the Alabama & Balt regiments, & immediately opposite, on the Point, the Texan regt of infty. At Burrita is Featherston's regt Louisiana volunteers; quarter miles above, the Louisville Legion & 4 detached companies Alabama volunteers; quarter of a mile further up you come to Peyton's La volunteers & St Louis Legion; 3 miles above Burrita the Tenn regt, being all the troops below this place. Capt McCullough's Rangers are on a scout towards Monterey; Capt Wells' [late Walker's] are in or about the city; Capt Price has disbanded. Gen Burleson is on the other side of the river, with a few men, on his own hook, as is also Gen Lamar.

FRI JUL 31, 1846
Coroner Woodward held an inquest on Wed, at Gtwn, in view of the body of a woman, lately married, named Ellis, who, as there was reason to suspect, had died by violence done to her by her husband's brother. The coroner felt it to be his duty to advise the arrest of the husband as well as brother of the dec'd.

A man named Kuhn was arrested on Wed, charged with stabbing Wm Naylor, of Wash City, in an affray. The wound is not a severe one, but Kuhn has been held to bail to answer for the assault.

Arkansas Regt of Volunteers have reached the rendezvous at Wash, & ofcrs have been elected. Archibald Yell, member of Congress, was chosen Colonel; John S Roane, Lt Col; Dr Solon Borland, Major; & ___ Meager, Adj.

Letter from Capt Randolph Ridgely, relative to the removal of the remains of the late gallant Maj Ringgold, to the city of Balt, for interment in **Greenmount Cemetery**. The grave now presents a very unique & appropriate resting place. The ofcrs of Point Isabel have done everything in their power to protect the grave. Capt Ramsey of the Ordnance, suggested that it should be surrounded by a railing composed of muskets captured from the enemy. Four posts, ornamented as well as our limited means would allow, are erected, one at each corner, connected by pieces of timber, the upper having holes bored at every 6 inches, through which the musket barrels are placed, resting on the lower one; the bayonets are all fixed, & the whole painted black. Appropriate head & foot boards are erected. I propose sending this enclosure with the remains, as it would be a most appropriate protection to the monument you are about erecting in **Greenmount Cemetery**. –Randolph Ridgely, 1st Lt 3rd Artl, commanding Horse Artillery. To Capt Geo P Kane, & Capt J P Chifelle.

Wash Corp: 1-Ptn of Washington Rawlings, praying remission of a fine: referred to the Cmte of Claims. 2-Ptn of Stephen J Ober: referred to the Cmte of Claims. 3-Ptn of D L Porter, proposing to rent certain ground: referred to a select cmte.

Rio Grande: on Jul 5, M Priest, private in the Soto company of Louisiana volunteers, was accidentally shot & died on the same evening. On Jul 8 a private belonging to Maj Featherston's regt Louisiana volunteers was drowned; name unknown.

The troop ship **Crocodile**, Cmder Gower Lowe, was to be taken out of dock at Davenport yesterday, & will embark a detachment of artillery, under command of Capt Blackwood, for service at Hudson's Bay, where a wing of the 6th regt of 300 men, under the command of Maj Crofton, is to be sent. They are destined for **Fort Guerrier**, a settlement of the Hudson Bay Co, near & around which there is a population of five to six thousand hunters & trappers, trained from childhood to use the rifle, & which the military nucleus now under orders for Oregon will soon bring into a highly efficient state of tactical organization.

House of Reps: 1-Ptn of Louis Larkin, master of the schnr **Merchant**: referred. 2-Ptn of Mr Henry Carrington, exc of Mrs P LeGrand, dec'd, for arrears of pension. 3-Ptn of Eliz Clapper, wid/o Geo Clapper, a soldier of the Revolution, praying for the benefit of the act of Congress of Jun 17, 1844. 4-Ptn of P H Folger & others, of Nantucket, asking for the erection of a bldg at that place for a custom house & post ofc, those ofcs, with all the public documents, having been destroyed by the late fire.

Capt Mulholland, whose abstinence from every kind of food, except water, created some talk last winter, was said to have died in Mar; but we find by the Red River Republican that he lived until Jul 7, 1846. He went 40 days without a particle of food. On the 49th day he made signs that he wanted something to eat, but he gradually sunk as if from comsumption. –N Y Sun

Stock of groceries at auction: on Aug 5, at the corner of High & Bridge sts, Gtwn, my entire stock & fixtures. –Wm H Tenney -Edw S Wright, auctioneer

Mrd: on Jul 27, at Alexandria, D C, by Rev E Harrison, Wm H Fanning, of Wash, to Miss Willaminer Lucas, of Alexandria, D C.

Circular to the Mormons. I have come among you instructed by Col S W Kearney, of the U S Army, now commanding the Army of the West, to visit the Mormon camp, & to accept the services, for 12 months, of 4 or 5 companies of Mormon men, who may be willing to serve their country for that period in our present war with Mexico; this force to unite with the Army of the West at Santa Fe, & be marched thence to California, where they will be discharged. They shall be mustered into the service, & will be entitled to all the comforts & benefits of regular soldiers of the army; & when discharged, will be given, gratis, the arms & accoutrements with which they will be fully equipped at **Fort Leavenworth**. –J Allen, Capt 1st Dragoons. Camp of the Mormons, at Mount Pisgah, Jun 26, 1846.

Senate: 1-Cmte on Indian Affairs: joint resolution for the relief of the legal reps of the wid/o Sour John, a Cherokee Indian. Same cmte: House bill for the relief of the legal reps of Thos Murray without amendment, & recommending it be indefinitely postponed. 2-Cmte on Private Land Claims: House bill for the relief of the legal reps of John Rice Jones, dec'd. 3-Cmte on Pensions: adverse report on the ptn of John McLoud.

Manufacturers letter regarding domestic interest of the country & duties imposed on articles of imported merchandise.
Thos Lamb, Pres of the Boston Sugar Refinery
Thos Lamb, Pres of the New England Worsted Co
H L Steans, Representing Linseed Oil Manufactures
Jos S Lovering & Co, Sugar Refining interest in Phil
John Marland, Representing Worsted, Mousselines de Laines, & Flannels
Elisha Peck, Representing Iron interest
Murdock, Leavitt & Co, for Railroad Iron
Erastus Corning, Representing Iron interest
E P Tileston, Allen C Curtis, Paper interest of Mass
Russell Hubbard, Paper interest of Conn
Danl L Miller, jr, Phil Chemical manufacturing interest
John McCanles, Coal interest, Schuylkill Co, Pa
Robt Kilton, Iron interest, Lancaster Co, Pa
Benj F Pomroy, Anthracite Iron interest, Pa
John Cooper, Delegate from Columbia Co, Pa
Warren Murdock, manufacture of Iron in Wareham, Mass
Robt G Rankin, Representing the Iron & Cotton interests of portions of Dutchess & Orange Counties, N Y
M H Simpson, Representing manufactures of Wool, Cordage, Cottons, & Carpets.
Thos Chambers, Anthracite Coal & Iron
Wm A Crocker, representing all manufacture of iron in Mass; &, all the manufacture of copper in the U S
-Garrick Mallery, J Scholfield, jr, of Boston: To the Hon Danl Webster, U S Senate

Died: on Jul 30, Wm A Scott, in his 74th year. His funeral is this morning, at his late residence on Md ave, Capitol Hill. [No time given.]

Died: on Jul 27, at *Mount Pleasant*, D C, after a lingering illness, Miss Harriet M White, 3rd d/o the late Capt Jas White.

Died: on Jul 29, at *White Cottage*, [the residence of her grandfather,] of cholera infantum, Z Douglass, infant s/o Z D Gilman.

Houses & lots at auction: on Jul 31, in front of the premises: lot 125 in Beall's addition to Gtwn, fronting 60 feet on Dunbarton st, with a comfortable 2 story frame house. Also, lot 126, on the corner of Green & Dunbarton sts, with a brick dwlg house, thereon. This lot will be divided if desired. Persons wishing to purchase at private sale will made application to the subscriber. By order of the heirs of the late Jas Dickson. Terms at sale. –E S Wright, auctioneer

SAT AUG 1, 1846

Senate: 1-Cmte on Pensions: House bill for the relief of Mary Segar, of Jefferson Co, N Y, without amendment. Same cmte: bill for the relief of Anthony Connaut, accompanied by a report. Same cmte: bill for the relief of Peter Frost, accompanied by a report: ordered to be printed.

Laws of the U S, passed at the First Session of the 29th Congress. Public No 9. Joint resolution presenting the thanks of Congress to Maj Gen Taylor, his ofcrs & men. The Pres of the U S be authorized to have a medal of gold procured, with appropriate devices & inscriptions thereon, & presented to Gen Taylor, in the name of the Republic, as a tribute due to his good conduct, valor, & generosity to the vanquished. Resolution-Public No 10. A joint resolution to refund to States & individuals expenses incurred by them under calls for militia & volunteers made by Gen Gaines & Gen Taylor. Approved, Jul 16, 1846

Massachusetts Medical College, of Boston. A new Medical College is now in process of erection: situated in Grove St, on the land liberally given by Dr Geo Parkman, near the Hospital. Lectures begin in Nov.
Anatomy & Surgery, John C Warren, M D
Chemistry, John W Webster, M D
Surgery & Clinical Surgery, Geo Hayward, M D
Theory & Practice of Med, John Ware, M D
Clinical Med & Materia Med, Jacob Bidgelow, M D; Obstetrics & Med Jurisprudence, Walter Channing, M D -W Channing, Dean

$10 reward for strayed bay horse. –Henderson Fowler, living near the Navy Yard.

The Union House: the above named new & splendid Hotel, just completed, at the centre of the beautiful village of Springfield, Mass, & opened on Jul 30. –S S Seaman, who recently kept the U S Hotel & Congress Hall, at Saratoga.

List of letters remaining in the Post Ofc, Wash, Aug 1, 1846:

Ayres, J B	Atkins, Miss Charl'te	Bean, Mrs Ann
Ashard, Wm K	Archer, Miss Amelia	Burr, Robt
Adams, Richd	Atterson, Miss Evel'e	Barnes, Mrs M
Archer, Jas T	Armstrong, Miss Susan W	Birge, Alonzo W
Alger, Chas C		Browne, Lt H
Agate, Mrs E H	Allerson, Miss Eveel'e	Blackman, Wm
Armistead, Col G G	Burch, Jos F	Boyd, Stephen
Alexander, C A	Bean, Miss Sarah E	Brent, Wm
Archer, Wm	Brichy, Theodore	Brown, Mrs Andrew
Anton, Jas	Banks, Thos G	Browne, Col Wm P, of Ala
Alston, Jas T	Brown, Miss Sarah	
Anderson, Cameron	Bohn, Valentine	Betts, Edw C, of Ala
Anderson, Mrs Esther	Brooke, Robt L-3	

Boston, Miss Mary Jane
Bearney, Geo W
Bowen, Mrs Fran's S
Bradley, Gen T
Blanchard, Miss Rebecca
Barry, Jas
Butler, John W-2
Baker, Miss Ann P
Berry, Miss Susan
Barry, Jas C
Bergman, Wm H
Bagby, Robt B
Barrett, Mrs Eliz
Briceland, J N
Bryant, Miss Mary
Brenen, Miss Louisa G
Brook, Miss Elea'r-2
Butler, Henry
Burgess, Miss Mary A
Burris, Pritchard
Bledsoe, Albert T
Benson, Egbert
Benson, John-2
Baldwin, Miss Emily
Butler, Maj John B
Butler, Andrew
Blockley, Miss Mary
Bostwick, Mrs E B
Brown, Wilson, of Eli
Bradbury, Wymand-2
Byers, Thos N-5
Clark, Jas-3
Crown, Jeremiah
Clark, Miss Sarah G
Combs, Miss Mary
Clarke, Richd W
Cheairs, John T
Clare, Wm-2
Clark, John
Clark, Jas L
Cocke, Capt Harrison H

Carr, Vincent
Cain, Wm
Carne, Richd L
Clarke, Miss Kate M
Clark, John
Clark, Rev M M
Clementson, Henry
Cooper, Geo
Cooper, John
Casidy, John L
Clements, Miss Mary Llewellen
Chambers, Wm
Caulk, Robt
Cutting, Jas A-2
Colton, Miss R F-3
Cooper, Mrs Ann
Coryell, Lewis C-2
Colton, Benj
Cruger, Mrs Lydia S
Comada, Capt John
Coffin, Rev Wm H
Clempson, T G
Coburn, Jos L
Crockett, David
Crocker, Wm A
Coody, Wm S
Creighton, Fred-2
Coleman, Mrs Ann M
Campbell, Miss Virginia
Campbell, John H
Colquhoun, Miss Alice E
Calvert, Geo
Cushman, C C
Chisholm, John H
Dove, Mrs Mary
Dale, Lt J B
Duvall, Gen Jno P-8
Dulany, Capt W W
Duvall, Geo W
Dawson, Geo-2
Dement, John E
Dalton, Jonathan
Dalton, Mrs Susan

Dorsey, Miss Virgi'a
Dickerson, Mahlon-2
Earl, Mark A
Emery, Lt
Ewing, Mrs C
Edwards, Mrs Mary
Frank, Mrs Mary
Ford, Wm
Foy, Jas
Foxwell, Capt G W
Ferguson, John
Frisby, John B-2
Fossitt, Henry J
Florance, John E
Flanagan, Dominick
Fogert, Wm
Fisher, Thos H
Ferguson, Capt J
Fowler, E, of Ky
Grant, Dr E F
Gant, Rev David
Gage, Aaron
Gray, Rev S T
Gaines, Mrs Catherine
Green, Geo B
Gray, John-5
Goble, Dr J G
Gilliss, J Alex'r
Gibson, Mid Wm
Glover, John
Goddard, John M
Grigsby, Miss Eliz
Gibson, Mrs Charity
Greenhard, Sophia
Gilbert, Saml A
Gulick, John
Gibson, Miss Mary A
Gardiner, Col D S
Hall, Mrs Mary
Hill, Chas
Hide, John
Hill, Geo H
Hunt, Gen John E
Hill, Dr John

343

Hopkins, Mrs Matilda A
Hoffman, Leonard
Heide, Geo
Hewitt, Dr Richd-2
Hogans, Miss Amelia
Harman, Geo
Harrison, Edw
Harrison, Mrs Eliz
Hooper, Chas
Hammond, Lt Richd P
Hodgkin, Mrs Ann R
Harris, Maj Thos G
Hamer, John C
Harrison, Richd
Haswell, Geo R-4
Inge, John C
Ives, Jos
Jones, Wm
Jones, Miss Mary
Jones, Col Joel L
Jackson, Henry W
Jordon, Miss Harriet
Johnston, Hamilton G
Johnson, Walter R-2
Keep, Lt John A
Kuhn, Walter
Knox, Chas
Kensett, Geo P
Keoble, Jacob
Kuchland, Claus
Kunsman, Geo R
Kennedy, Dr Howard
Kimball, Mrs Helena
Kello, Capt Wm O
Lee, Jessee
Lake, Geo L
Lee, Mr [artist]
Love, Eliz Ann
Lowe, John
Lacy, Wm
Lawless, Col L E
Lamerloniere, Eug'e
Luxen, Mrs Eliz
Latham, Geo N

Lockhart, Miss Mar't
Lawson, Miss Leaner-2
Langhorne, Mid J D-2
Little, Seth
Lawrence, T Pritchard
Lanman, Lt Jos
Leonard, Capt J A B
Lyons, Miss Lavilla-2
Mann, Mrs Mary A
Meade, John L
Mills, Jos H
Moore, Jas
Muse, Lt Wm T
Morse, Mrs E K
Morse, Saml F
Muller, Rev A A
Marleind, John
Manning, Col J L-2
Myer, Ferdinand F
Muhlenburg, Dr H H
Manchester, Major
Martin, Andrew
Mayer, Elias
Murdoch, Mrs Jas H
Mason, Calvin
Myers, Capt John A
Marshall, Wm G
Miller, John S
Mortin, Robt
Myers, Mrs Susanna
Mathews, Chas S
Meriwether, Wm H
Matthews, Passed Mid J
Marcy, Capt R B
Morris, Mrs Eliza M
Martin, John
Manning, Miss Jen'ett
Miller, Jas-2
Miller, Wm J
Miller, Robt
Miller, Chas
McNeil, John A
McRae, John j
McLanahan, Mid T
McEnnis, Philip

McWilliams, And-2
McGonigal, Alex
McDonald, Col A-2
McKiernan, Jas
McGunnegle, Mid W
McDermott, Mrs Letnea
McDonell, Patrick
McCullough, Jas
Nancrede, Jos G
Niebert, Miss Mary
Nelson, Wm
Norman, Mrs Frances
Nolen, Philip
Olivier, Madame V E
O'Brien, John
Pye, Wm H
Pratt, Henry C
Phipps, Wm
Pearce, Jos
Pearks, Miss Ann E
Parker, Miss Prisc'a
Pollock, Miss Char'e
Peckham, John S
Pringle, Passed Mid J J
Porter, Henry
Pentland, Miss Susan E
Pinckney, Dr N
Potter, Geo
Pearson, Edw A
Purcell, Mrs Eliz
Porter, Mid H O-4
Ross, Dr Robt D
Rice, Owen
Rand, Mrs Mary Josephine
Ratcliff, Mrs Sarah Ann
Ready, Wm
Riley, Jas W
Richardson, Harriet
Ringgold, Fayette
Ridgeley, Jas L

Riddock, Wash'n L	Sardban, John	Webb, Jas-2
Redin, Wm H	Sewall, Mrs Caroline N-2	White, Mrs Harriet
Ridgley, Com C G		Wise, Geo
Stoops, Walter	Simms, Capt Jos	Wise, Miss Eliz A
Springs, John	Saunders, Lt W H-3	Webb, Capt S H
Smith, Jos P	Stockton, Richd C-3	Watson, Geo M
Shaw, Saml B	Stevenson, Lt c L	Wigans, Tabitha
Storrs, Ashbel-2	Swigart, Mrs Eliz	Woodward, Wm
Simms, Wm	Snobler, Miss Sophia	Williams, Hillory
Smith, Fowler R	Tydon, Dr	Williams, Jas
Scott, Isaac	Townsend, Isaac	Walker, Wm S
Smith, Wm [engraver]	Tinney, Susan	Whitehill, Mrs D
Smith, Jas F	Thompson, Wm B	Wilson, John D
Smith, Mrs L H	Tolson, Edw	Wiebster, Saml
Smith, Addison	Torrey, David K	Warren, Jos T
Shorter, Kitty	Thompson, Jas P-2	Woodland, Mary
Stevens, Wm H	Thomas, John D	Walter, Mrs Biddy
Stettson, Miss M A	Thompson, Nathan	Wilson, Jas G
Stelsee, Eliz	Travis, Capt Geo	Wineberger, Wm
Spender, Col John	Tucker, Beverly-2	Walker, Miss M
Schreppler, K T	Taylor, Thos F-2	Watson, Mrs
Stapler, Jos B	Taylor, Mrs Eliz W	Wright, Miss Susan M
Spearing, Mrs Jane	Talbot, Paul	Williams, Miss Marian
Staunton, Sergt A-3	Tailor, Miss Sarah	
Saunders, Alex	Taylor, Henry	Williams, Capt G W
Sallade, Andrew M	Trabue, Stephen F J	Winton, Miss Lucy G
Stewart, Chas	Thornton, Mid Th F	Williamson, David-2
Stanton, John H	Truston, Wm Talbot	Williams, Mrs Fra's
Sedgwick, Chas	Thompson, Gabriel R	Williams, Miss M A
Sedgwick, Saml	Van Wick, Mid	Yell, Mrs Lucy
Seward, Henry	Vincent, Wm	Young, Mildred-2
Stotenburg, Richd T	Van Ness, Mrs E	
Saville, Jos	Vaustarman, Geo W	Yeek, Chas
Stanton, Wm	Wright, John W	Yoong, Chas J
Stewart, Wm D	Ward, Geo	Young, Benj-2
Shepherd, Jas G	Wood, David M	Yearson, Richd

The inland postage on all letters intended to go by ship must be paid, otherwise they remain in this ofc. -C K Gardner, P M

Trade with 2 Sicilies. The "Union" stated a few days ago that the Dept of State had received from the U S Consul at Messina, a copy of the Tariff of the Kingdom of the Two Sicilies, as passed by a decree May 9, 1846.

Mrd: on Jul 25, in Alexandria, by Rev Job Guest, Dr J W Lugenbeel, physician to the colony of Liberia, to Miss Martha Alice Abercrombie, of the former place.

We have received the first number of the "Lake Superior News & Miners' Journal," to be issued weekly at Copper Harbor, Lake Superior, Mich, by E D Burr; John N Ingersoll, editor.

Faculty of Columbia College, N Y, have conferred the degree of Dr of Divinity on Rev Robt Emory, Pres of Dickinson College, Carlisle, Pa.

MON AUG 3, 1846

The new Baptist Church was dedicated yesterday, & the Pres & his lady, Sec of War, several Senators & Members of Congress, the Mayor, & many other distinguished individuals were there. Mr Samson is the pastor of the church; sermon was delivered by Rev G B Ide, of Phil. Mr Mann, was the architect; Messrs Finch, Pollock & Co, did the painting & bronzing of the pillars; Mr Dreyer, of Balt, did the fresco work, & Mr Armidon, did the upholstering.

Wash City Ordnance: Act in relation to the ***Northern Market-house***: to be erected on the open space at the junction of N Y ave & Mass aves with K st north. Sale of the butchers' stalls in said market shall be at rate of $20 per annum; thereafter the vegetable stalls shall be rented or sold upon the same terms.

Col W B Shubrick, the commandant of the navy yard at this place, this day resigned the command of said yard, preparatory to taking command of the U S forces in the Pacific. Cmder Dornin is now in charge of the navy yard, Wash.
–Union of Sat night

Senate: 1-Memorial of Edw D Tippett, praying the aid of Gov't to enable him to complete a model of an improved steam-engine. 2-Communication by Saml R Knox, a lt in the U S Navy, relative to the harbor at the mouth of the Columbia river. 3-Cmte on Commerce: adverse report upon the House bill for the relief of Jos Curwen, surviving partner of Wilbur & Curwen, & recommending that its consideration be postponed indefinitely, which was agreed to. Same cmte: asked to be discharged from the further consideration of the House act for the relief of Wm B Laing, & that it be referred to the Cmte on Finance. 4-Cmte on the Post Ofc & Post Roads: House bill for the relief of Sheldon B Hayes. 5-Bill for the relief of Abraham Horback: referred to the Cmte on the Judiciary.

House of Reps: 1-Cmte of Ways & Means: bill for the relief of Benj Adams & Co & others: committed. 2-Cmte on Indian Affairs: bill for the relief of Jas Erwin & others, of Arkansas: committed. 3-Following bills were passed: joint resolution for the relief of Putney & Riddle; settlement of the accounts of John Crowell, late agent for the creek Indians in Alabama; relief of Ebenezer Ballard; relief of Jas Low. 4-Bill granting a pension to Harriette Ward, wid/o Lt Ward, late of the navy, who died in service, was taken up. Much confusion arose in the hall on the question of the passage of this bill. Two hours of the day was consumed. The bill was suffered to pass without count or further difficulty or opposition.

The California Volunteers, commanded by Col J D Stevenson, embarked from N Y C, on Sat, for Govn'rs Island, where they are to remain until the 14th, when, it is said, they are to take their final leave.

Illinois Volunteers, Gen Wool, with his aide, & a large portion of the Ill volunteers, reach New Orleans on Jul 23. These troops, it is said, are destined for San Antonio de Bexar.

The Court of Inquiry ordered on Gen Gaines, at **Fort Monroe**, was organized on Wed, & consists of Gen Brady, Gen Brooke, & Col Crane; Capt Lee, Recorder. –Norfolk Herald

The sloop of war **Marion** arrived at Porto Praya on Apr 26, from the River Benin, via Cape Palmas, Monrovia, & Sierra Leone. She had lost 2 ofcrs & 2 men since her arrival on the station. The list of her ofcrs: Cmder, Lewis E Simonds; Lts, Cicero Price, Chas C Barton, & Wm C B Porter; Midshipmen, J Higgins & S J Bliss; Master, Chas C Sims; Purser, C Doran; Surgeon, J Brinkerhoff; Passed Assist Surgeon, J B Gould.

Mrd: on Jan 6 last, by Rev J P Donelan, Mr Jas Thompson to Miss Ellen Hopkins, all of Wash City.

Died: on Jul 29, in Wash, Lilian Arnot, infant d/o Francis A Dickins, of Fairfax, Va.

Board in the country may be had at a pleasant & healthy location on the Columbia Turnpike, 5 miles from the Long Bridge. Horses & carriages can be furnished if wanted. –Lewis Bailey

Caution: I hereby forewarn all persons from purchasing any portion whatever of lands belonging to the family of Wm Johnson, in the neighborhood of the boundary line of north 7th st, Wash. –Wm Johnson

For sale: lot 19 in square 456, with a 2 story brick house, located on F st, near 6th. –J P Pepper

Academy of the Visitation, B V M, Gtwn, D C. Annual distribution of premiums took place on Jul 29. Piano premium awarded to Sophronia Pickrell, of Gtwn, D C
Premiums to:
Cornelia Matthews, Lynchburg, Va
Pauline Ligon, Petersburg, Va
Mary Jane Russell, Phil
Mary Slevin, Phil
Mary King, Gtwn
Mgt Leonard, Gtn
Dora Hernandez, St Augustine, E Fla
Mary Nevins, Gtwn
Anna Grammer, Wash
Matilda Semmes, PG Co, Md
Charlotte Waterman, Balt
Matilda Grammer, Wash

Maria Ewing, Phil
Maria Beelan, Pittsburg
Elmina De Blanc, New Orleans
Anna Templeman, Gtwn
Charlotte Pierce, Tuscaloosa, Ala
Maria Huntt, Wash
Augusta Cunningham, Poughkeepsie, N Y
Eleanora Gibson, Richmond, Va
Caroline King, Wash
Fanny Huntt, Wash
Augusta Scott, Wash
Matilda Binford, Portsmouth, Va
Louisa Carroll, Balt, Md
Eliza Duncan, Montgomery, Ala
Sally Mittag, Lancaster, S C
Emily Edelin, Wash
Susan Boarman, Martinsburg, Va
Harriet Bennet, Balt
Susan Cruit, Wash
Mary Mittag, Lancaster, S C
Mary Ellen Brady, Wash
Catharine Templeman, Gtwn
Mary Adams, Wash
Mary Donoghue, Gtwn
Emily Matthews, Lynchburg, Va
Mary Turnbull, Wash
Mary Ellen Hinton, Delaware, Ohio
Maria Louis Barton, New Orleans
Glovinia Neale, Wash
Josephine Jamison, Chas Co, Md
Sienna Gwynne, PG Co, Md
Clara Mitchell, Balt, Md
Anna Josephine Briscoe, Wash
Maria Louisa Pearce, Montg Co, Md
Julia Ewing, Phil
Emily Ward, Norfolk, Va
Virginia Love, Gtwn
Sarah Stone, Wash
Maria Mitchell, Queen Anne's Co
Louisa Mitchell, Queen Anne's Co
Eliza Gwynne, PG Co
Matilda Devereux, Wash
Rosa Ford, Carlisle, Pa
Susan O Dell, Gtwn

Mary Ellen Mitchell, Gtwn
Elen Roche, Gtwn
Catharine May, Gtwn
Anne Donoghue, Gtwn
Mary Catharine Donoghue, Gtwn
Camilla Lancaster, Chas Co, Md
Eliza Fenwick, Wash
Ann Jane Carroll, Gtwn
Fanny Masi, Wash
Hester Berry, Gtwn
Jane Neale, Wash
Amanda Lepretre, New Orleans
Celestia Neale, Chas Co, Md
Mary Eliz Spalding, Wash
Ada Semmes, Gtwn
Filomena Roach, St Mary's Co
Emma Mason, **Fort Gibson**, Ark
Anna Mason, **Fort Gibson**, Ark
Sissy Devereux, Wash
Sissy Briscoe, Wash
Sophia Lepretre, New Orleans
Irene Marshall, Portsmouth, Va
Julia Cox, N Y
Cecelia Plowden, St Mary's Co
Eliz Roach, St Mary's Co
Pamela Setze, Augusta, Ga
Eliz Hanrahan, Grenville, N C
Lavinia Whyte, Petersburg, Va
Mary Ann Ennis, Wash
Catharine Lindsey, Gtwn
Sally Bayne, Wash
Rosa Queen, Wash
Sarah Lockett, Colloden, Ga
Josephine Clarke, St Mary's Co
Adelaide Clarke, Grenville, N C
Cora Dufour, St Mary's, Ga
Adele Cutts, Wash
Caroline Leib, Wash
Cora Semmes, Gtwn
Amelia Stoops, Gtwn, D C
Josephine Boucher, Gtwn
Matilda Gorham, Grenville, N C
GeorgeAnna White, Wash
Marion Crook, Balt
Mary Ellen Fenwick, Wash

Sally Peters, Poolsville, Montg Co, Md
Angelina Snider, Phil
Virginia Gross, Gtwn
Josephine Clements, Gtwn
Virginia Gross, Gtwn
Eliza O Dell, Gtwn
Marion Ramsay, Wash
Mary Ann Matthews, Lynchburg, Va

Laura Powell, Rockford, Ala
Rosalie Hickey, Wash
Estelle Bienvenu, New Orleans
Mary Payne, Tuscaloosa, Ala
Julia Young, PG Co
Eugenia Wynne, Dinwiddie, Va
Sarah Lockett, Colladen, Ga

TUE AUG 4, 1846

$50 reward will be paid for apprenhending & securing Peter, who left me a few days ago. He is about 26 years & very black. –John Parker, Hampstead, King George Co, Va

Entire stock of summer goods at within 10% of costs. –Geo W Adams, 15 Pa ave, opposite Centre Market

Removal to the shoe store formerly occupied by J H Gibbs, between 8th & 9th sts, 2 doors east of Clagett's dry good store, where there will be Shoes & Boots of every kind & quality. –T J Magruder & Co [Those indebted to Hall & Magruder to call & settle their accounts by money or notes at a short date.]

Senate: 1-Cmte on the Judiciary: ptn of the executor of Zephaniah Kingsley, asking payment of interest awarded by a judgment of the Superior Court of East Florida, under the treaty of 1819 with Spain: resolved: to be referred to the Sec of the Treas & the Atty Genr'l of the U S, to report thereon to the Senate on the first day of the next session. Same cmte: bill for the relief of John Bearden, dec'd. Same cmte: House bill for the relief of Abraham Horback, with an amendment. Same cmte: bill for the relief of John P Baldwin, owner of the Spanish brig **Gil Blas**. 2-Cmte on Pensions: asking to be discharged from the futher consideration of the following ptns: from the citizens of Ohio, for an increase of the pension allowed to Saml Hall; from Lydia Lord, wid/o John Lord; from Ann Dodd, wid/o a Revolutionary soldier; from Sarah Overbagh, wid/o Jeremiah Overbagh; from Mariah Ostrander, wid/o a Revolutionary soldier; from Benj Watson.

A most cold-blooded murder was committed at the People's Theatre, in Cincinnati, last Tue. A man named Cook, Treasurer of the Theatre, whose wife was an actress connected with the same, upon some slight provocation, stabbed Jack Reeve, the Prompter, with a knife about 6 inches in length, inflicting a wound through the heart. His death was almost instantaneous. Cook escaped with the money in the ofc.

We understand that Robt C Grier, of Pa, was nominated yesterday by the Pres to supply the vacancy on the Bench of the Supreme Court occasioned by the death of Judge Baldwin.

Trustee's sale: by virtue of a decree of Montg Co Court-in Equity, in the case of Adam Robb & others, vs Henry Harding, adm of Thos F W Vinson & others: public sale of the following real estate in said county, of which Thos F W Vinson died seized, to wit: on Sep 9, on the premises, the Farm in said county, about 2 miles from Poolesville, containing 534 acres of land, more or less; improvements are good, such as are required for farming purposes. On Sep 11, on the premises: the Farm, with improvements thereon, in said county, on the road leading from Damascus to Unity, being part of a tract called *Addition to Ray's Adventure*, containing 134+ acres, as conveyed by deed from Wm N Austin, trustee of Wm O'Neall, jr, to said Thos F W Vinson, date of Dec 17, 1842, recorded in liber B S, 12, folios 115, & is the same land upon which Philip Duvall now resides. On Sep 12, on the premises, the House & Lot in Rockville, fronting the court-house square, in which the said Thos F W Vinson resided at the time of his death, being part of lot 2, as described upon the plat of Rockville; & also the lot known as lot 3, lying between the lots respectively occupied by Dr Crossan & Dr Anderson. –Robt W Carter, Trustee

In the case of Gen Gaines: the documents read today showed that before the Gov't had received information of the battles of May 8 & 9, the Sec of War had approved of what is now regarded as not justified by the necessity of the case-that is, some of the unauthorized requisitions for troops. [Aug 5th newspaper: One of the grounds of justification is, that the Sec of War, in a letter to Gen Gaines, under date of Nov last, speaking for the Pres, used language which would authorize the Gen commanding the western division, in a case of imminent peril, to make requistitions for volunteers. –Norfolk Beacon]

Mathematical Teacher desirous of obtaining a Professorship in some Literary Institution in one of the Southern or Western States. Can furnish the most satisfactory testimonials of moral character, scholarship, & competency to teach. –H L C Burke, Richmond, Va

Ex-Govn'r Geo Howard, formerly Govn't of Md, died Aug 2, at *Waverley*, his residence in Anne Arundel Co, of apoplexy. He had been at church in the morning, & after returning home exchanged this world for another. He had endured ill health for a long time. No man possessed warmer feelings, or a nobler heart.

Mrd: on Aug 3, by Rev Brown Morgan, Mr Armistead G *Matlock to Louisa Fayette, only d/o the late John Brannan, of Wash City. [Aug 5th newspaper: Corr: Mr Armistead G *Matlack.]

Died: on Aug 2, Lauriston C Ward, of Saco, Maine, w/o Lauriston Ward, of Wash City, aged nearly 21 years.

Died: on Jul 30, at Charleston, S C, Maj Jas H Ashby, formerly of the U S Dragoons.

Notice: Matthew A J Manning, an indented apprentice to the Beacon ofc, left Norfolk for Wash on Jul 2, by permission to visit his mother, now residing here, & has not returned. All persons are cautioned against harboring or employing the said indented apprentice, under the penalty of the law.

For sale: feeling anxious to discontinue the present business in which engaged, I offer the entire stock of Boots & Shoes for sale. I have been in business some 18 years or more, & did too much credit business; consequently I find it necessary to close, to enable me to get my outstanding matters settled.
–H S Cross, Seven Bldgs, First Ward

WED AUG 5, 1846
Senate: 1-Cmte on Pensions: House bill for the relief of Catharine Fulton, of Wash Co, Pa, without amendment, & recommending that it be indefinitely postponed. Same cmte: following House bills-recommending that they be indefinitely postponed: relief of Geo Roush; relief of Jonathan Brown; & relief of Polly Dameron. Same cmte: asking to be discharged from the further consideration of the following ptns: ptn of Hector & John Butler; ptn of Robt Armstrong; ptn of Eliza Buchanan; ptn of N Nye Hall; ptn of Wm Miller; ptn of the legal reps of Saml C Montgomery; & the ptn of Wm De Courcy.

House of Reps: 1-Ptn of Wm A Carson, praying the change of name of a steamer. 2-Ptn of Harriet Ashby, wid/o Maj Jas A Ashby, praying a pension.

Announced in the Abingdon papers, the death, on Jul 23, of Mrs Sarah B Preston, wid/o the late Gen Francis Preston, only child of the distinguished Gen Wm Campbell, of Revolutionary memory, & mother of the Hon Wm C Preston, of S C. Mrs Preston was about 70 years old at her death; & was well known as a lady of high character & valuable accomplishments. –Richmond Times

Died: on Jul 29, in Wash City, Jos Burman, s/o Henrietta & Henry Thompson, aged 18 months.

Revolutionary Relics. We saw one day this week all the original papers found in Andre's boot at the time of his capture; the plan of the fortifications at West Point; the return of the number of guns; the report of Maj Bauman, commanding the artillery, to Arnold, as to the situation of the troops in case of alarm, & the number of soldiers necessary to garrison the various batteries & redoubts, from Villefranche, the engineer. Also, Arnold's pass to Maj Andre, which he exhibited too late to the 3 scouts to stay their suspicion & save himself. Had Andre, when he was arrested, merely said, I am out on particular service of Gen Arnold; here is his pass, they would have let him proceed without search. The papers are all in an excellent state of preservation, & belong to Mrs Beekman, the widow of a grandson of the late Govn'r Clinton. This lady is now having them substantially framed, as an heirloom for her children. –N Y Messenger

House & furniture for rent: property on I st, between 16th & 17th sts west, formerly occupied by Mrs Com Stewart, & more recently by the Chevalier Hulsemann. Apply on the premises.

THU AUG 6, 1846
$50 reward for negro man Mike, belonging to the estate of my dec'd husband, Thos Thompson, who left on Jul 26, from Chapel Hill, N C, in a buggy, taking with him his wife Emmeline, & their child about 3 years of age, the property of Hon A Rencher, on leave & under pretence of visiting Pittsborough for a few days. It is apprehended that they have made off westwardly, or by railroad northwardly, with the design of reaching a free State. Mike is a carpenter by trade & has been living in Chapel Hill in that capacity for the last 3 years; he is a black man, about 27 years of age; knows how to read, & is quite intelligent. Emmeline is a black woman; can read & write; is perhaps 25 years of age; has travelled North, & resided in Wash with her master & mistress, & during their absence from the U S, has been living at Chapel Hill as a washerwoman & seamstress for the students. Address either to me at Pittsborough, Chatham Co, N C; or to Chas Manly, at Raleigh; Judge Manly, at Newbern; or to Dr Johnson D Jones, at Chapel Hill. –Louisa S Thompson, Pittsborough, Chatham Co.

Female Collegiate Institute, Gtwn, Ky: the 18th session opens Sep 7.
–T F Johnson, A M, Principal

Appointments by the Pres, by & with the advice & consent of the Senate. 1-Robt C Grier, of Pa, to be one of the Assoc Justices of the Supreme Court of the U S, in place of Henry Baldwin, dec'd. 2-Jas Page, Collector of the Customs for the district of Phil.

Fort Smith, Ark, on Jul 13th the following troops left *Fort Smith* for San Antonio de Bexar, Texas, viz:
Co A 1st U S Dragoons, 75 strong. Ofcrs: Capt, Wm Eustis; 1st Lt, J Henry Carleton; 2nd Lt, Jos H Whittlesey.
Co E 1st U S Dragoons, 70 strong. Ofcrs: Capt, Enoch Steen; 1st Lt, Danl H Rucker; 2nd Lt, Abram Buford.
Co D 6th U S Infty, 80 strong. Ofcrs: Capt, Wm H Hoffman; 1st Lt, E Howe; 2nd Lt, Wm Read.
Co H 6th U S Infty, 80 strong. Ofcrs: Capt, Albemarle Cady; 1st Lt, Edw H Fitzgerald; 2nd Lt, Henry Rhea.
The whole commanded by Maj B L E Bonneville, 6th U S Infty. Capt Washington's company of light artl, is said to be under orders to proceed from Carlisle barracks, Pa, via Little Rock, Ark, to join Maj Bonneville's command; & Capt Sumner's & Capt Cook's companies, of the 1st U S Dragoons, are ordered from *Fort Atkinson* & *Fort Beauford*, Upper Mississippi, for the same purpose.

Senate: 1-Cmte on Finance: adverse report on the ptn of Edwin Bartlett: ordered to be printed. 2-Cmte on Pensions: House bill for the relief of Silas Waterman, of Wash Co, Vt, without amendment, recommending that it be postponed indefinitely, which was concurred in. 3-Relief of Zeth M Leavenworth: read a 3rd time & passed.

Bank of the Metropolis stock wanted: the subscriber wishes to dispose of the following improved property in Wash, viz: lots 8, 12, & 16 in square 299; & a lot in square 404, on 9th st. The assessed value will be accepted, & payment can be made in Bank stock at its par value. Apply to my agent, Mr Wm Lloyd, near the Potomac bridge, or to the subscriber, at his lumber yard in Gtwn. The above property is all under rent to good tenants, & yields about $750 per annum. –John Pickrell

For sale: a farm in Montg Co, Md, near the Gtwn & Rockville Turnpike road, 3 miles back of Tenallytown by the turnpike: contains 53 acres; has on it a spacious log dwlg. Apply to the subscriber, Alfred Schucking.

FRI AUG 7, 1846
Senate: 1-Cmte on the Judiciary: resolution authorizing the Sec of War to settle with David Ames, & recommending its passage. 2-Bill for the relief of the heirs of Robt Fulton, was passed by a vote of 32 to 15. 3-Bill for the relief of Mrs McRae, wid/o Col McRae: passed.

After the death of Capt Page, his widow at once left for the East, & we are happy to say met with the greatest attention on the way. No boats, railroads, or hotel would accept any pay.

Judge Pennybacker, one of the Senators from Va, has been hurried home by the sickness of one of the members of his family. –Union

The name of 1st Lt S L Fremont, 3rd Artl, was omitted in the report of the battles of Palo Alto & Resaca de la Palma, which has since been corrected at the Adj Gen's ofc, by letter from Col Twiggs. Lt Fremont belonged to the company commanded by the late Maj Ringgold, & was with him when he fell. –Union

Capt Wm Walters, of a company of volunteers in Col Baker's regt, died yesterday at the Planters' House. He was taken with a fever the day the regt left here; it changed to a congestion of the brain & terminated his sufferings. The corpse was taken to Alton on board the steamer **Luella** last evening. We think that the above, copied from the St Louis New Era of Jul 31, records the death of a former citizen of this place, who has for some years past been the Editor & Proprietor of the Illinois State Register. We know Mr Walters left his home as a private in one of the companies of Ill volunteers, was afterwards promoted to an ofc among them. He has, no doubt, friends, if not relatives, still in this city, who deeply lament his death.

Dr Wm C Waterman, of Buffalo, has been sentenced to 3 years' imprisonment in the State prison, for disinterring bodies for anatomical purposes.

The Board of Health [Washington] consists of:
Dr Wm B Magruder	Dr John F May	Dr Noble Young
John D Barclay	G C Grammer-Sec	Jas Crandell
Dr Thos Miller-Pres	Dr Fred'k May	Dr E Morgan
John Y Bryant	John P Ingle	J W Jones

Valuable improved land for sale: being disabled by advanced years & ill health from giving the requisite personal attention to my farm, about 4 miles above Gtwn, on the turnpike leading to Rockville, I have concluded to offer it at private sale, either the whole together, or in parcels, as may be preferred. The farm includes upwards of 400 acres; the bldgs include an excellent family dwlg, overseer's house, gardener's house, barn, stabling, & other necessary out bldgs. The title is perfectly good. –Chas King, Gtwn

Trustee's sale of square 138 in the 3rd Ward, by deed of trust dated Apr 26, 1845, recorded in Liber W B 121, folios 126 thru 129, Wash Co, D C. –Jos Peck, trustee -A Green, auctioneer

For sale: that desirable brick dwlg-house & lots attached, on 3rd st, Gtwn, late the property of Horatio Jones, dec'd. For terms inquire of Dr Isaac Lauck, on Bridge st, Gtwn, nearly opposite the Mayor's ofc, or on the premises.

Wash Co, D C. I certify that John B Wiltberger, of said county, brought to my knowledge that there had been taken up, as an estray trespassing on his enclosures, a large Durham bull, about 8 years old. –H Naylor, J P [Owner is to claim his property, pay charges, & taken him away from my farm, near Rock Creek Church, or I shall be compelled to put a stop to his roving propensities. –Jno B Wiltberger]

Valuable real estate at Private sale: a 2 story frame house & premises, on Montg st, now occupied by Mr Benj F Miller. Several lots adjoining the above, on Montg & Stoddard sts, are also offered. Inquire of B F Miller, on the premises, or at the ofc of Messrs Ould & Peachy, Gtwn.

By writ of fieri facias, issued by John L Smith, one of the Justices of the Peace for Wash Co: I have seized & taken goods & chattels as the property of Cotter & Thompson, to satisfy an execution in favor of Chas W Boteler, sen, John M Donn, & Chas W Boteler, jr, lately trading under the firm of Boteler, Donn & Co: 10 cane seat arm-chairs, 3 tables, large looking-glass, lamp, refrigerator, decanters & bottles of liquor, doz tumblers: same at public sale on Aug 11, in front of the Centre Market-house. –J F Wannall, Constable

SAT AUG 8, 1846
Senate: 1-Cmte on the Judiciary: asking to be discharged from the further consideration of the bill for the relief of the excs of Benj Chaires, Gad Humphries, & others. 2-Cmte on Commerce: bill for the relief of Mary G Clitz. 3-Cmte of Claims: bill for the relief of John A Rodgers. 4-Cmte on Pensions: asking to be discharged from the further consideration of the ptn of Jos Elliot, & that he have leave to withdraw his papers. 5-Bills passed: relief of John R Williams; relief of Langtry & Jenkins; relief of Isaiah Parker, pension to Orris Crosby; pension to Elijah C Babbit; relief of John G McCloud, of Linn Co, Iowa; & confirm an entry of land made by the administrator of Jas Anderson, dec'd, of Iowa Terr.

We announce the death by drowning, at Black Rock Dam, on Sat, of Col Eason Lewis, of Black Rock, N Y, while endeavoring to rescue another-Jas Griffin. They were removing obstructions in the mill feeder, when Griffin got beyond his dept, & was sinking. Lewis was drowned-Griffin was saved. –N Y News

Mr B L'Hommedieu, who was injured a few days since by the falling of a brick wall at Nantucket, died the day after the accident. He had lost all his property by the fire, & has left his family entirely destitute.

Situation as a Teacher wanted: a graduate of one of the first New England Colleges, having had charge of a popular Academy nearly 2 years. Address Wm A Walton, Milford, N H.

Miss Heaney's Academy, near the Capitol, Wash, house adjacent the residence of Col Gardner: school will resume on the 1st Mon of Sept. References:

Hon Edw Everett	Carvill & Co	D A Hall
Hon Jas Savage	Rev H W Bellows	Wm Fischer
Hon Richd Sullivan	Rev Orville Dewey	Jonathan Goodhue
Jos R Chandler	Col J B Walbach	Col N Barrett
Rev J Pierpont	Robt G Shaw	S S Coleman
Wm C Bryant	Hon J A Dix	Jas Larned
Hon Louis McLane	Hon Lewis Cass	Wm G Eliot
Hon J Thompson	Hon Philemon	Saml Dexter
Maj T L Smith	Dickerson	Jos L Locke
Dr Wm Gunton	Hon R M Johnson	G F Berteau
Hon Wm Emmerson	Maj Edmond Kirby	Hon Ed Turner
Th Nesmith	Dr Lindsly	Hon Wlfred Hennen
Rev S Tustin, Chaplain U S Senate		

House of Reps: 1-Bill from the Senate for the relief of Mrs Mary MacRea, wid/o Lt Col Wm MacRea, late of the army of the U S: referred to the Cmte on Military Affairs. 2-Cmte of Conference: bill granting a pension to old Richd Elliot, a soldier of the Revolution: agreed to.

Govn'r Wm Slade, of Vt, is not a candidate for re-election; & on the expiration of his term of ofc in Oct next will remove to the State of Ohio. -Salem [Mass] Register

We have seen a letter from Adj Gen Jones, which states that the court martial proceedings in the case of Capt S B Thornton, 2nd Dragoons, have come to hand. They exhibit the gratifying fact that he is acquitted of all the charges on which he was tried. –Richmond Enquirer

Mrs Wilmer's School, Alexandria, D C. School will be resumed on Sep 14, 1846. References:
Rev J T Johnston, Alexandria
Dr O Fairfax, Alexandria
H Daingerfield, Alexandria
Rev Dr Sparrow, Theological Seminary, Va
E R Lippitt, Editor of the Southern Churchman
O W Andrews, Shepherdstown, Va
C K Nelson, Upper Marlborough, Md
John A Selden, Chas City Co, Va
Lorenzo Lewis, Clarke Co, Va
Rev R H Wilmer, Clarke Co, Va

Landon Female Seminary, Rev Richd H Phillips, Rector: the 9th session will open on Sep 2. The pupils form part of the Rector's family, & share with his children his solicitude & watchfulness. Address the Rector, P O, Urbana, Fred'k Co, Md.

Valuable real estate at public vendue: by decree of Montg Co Court, Court of Equity, in the case of Euphrasia M Foster vs Wilbur & Edwin Foster, the subscriber, as trustee, will offer on Aug 31, on the premises recently occupied by Dexter Foster, the real estate of which said Dexter Foster died seized, lying in said county, consisting of 2 several lots of parcels of land. The first lot being all those tracts, pieces, or parcels of land, conveyed by John Harry & wife to Dexter Foster, as described in the deed of conveyance from them, recorded in the land records of Montg Co, containing 181 acres, more or less. This farm lies on the turnpike from Gtwn to Rockville, being about 5 miles from Gtwn, & is intersected by what is called the old Gtwn road, dividing the farm into 2 parts, with a good tenement on each. This farm adjoins the lands of Robt Dick, Thos W Maccubbin, & Chas King. The second lot is all that piece of land conveyed by Guy F Austin to Dexter Foster, containing 26 acres, lying about 3 miles from the first, without any improvement. -Richd J Bowie, Trustee

Died: yesterday, at the residence of his mother, in Wash City, after a painful illness of 10 or 12 days, Mr Saml Purviance Walker, 2nd s/o the late Saml P Walker. His early death is deeply deplored by his afflicted family. His funeral will take place from the residence of Mrs Walker, on E st, this afternoon at 5 o'clock.

Mrd: on Aug 6, by Rev Mr Matthews, Saml Reeve, of Wisconsin, to Miss Constantia Preuss, of Wash, the eldest d/o the late Augustus W Preuss, of PG Co, Md.

Trustee's sale of valuable Mill property: by deed of trust to us, dated Aug 16, 1842, recorded in Liber B S 11, folios 237 thru 239, land records of Montg Co, Md: sale at the auction rooms of E S Wright, in Gtwn, D C, on Aug 19: *Seneca Mills*, on Seneca creek, about 22 miles above Gtwn. It includes 93½ acres of land, more or less, being part of *Thomas' Discovery Fortified* & of *Seneca Fork or Ford*; improvements consist of a substantial merchant mill; a new mill for grinding plaster & country work; a sawmill, with the necessary dam & race. The canal furnishes a ready access to the markets of D C. –John Kurtz, Clement Cox, trustees -Edw S Wright, auctioneer, Gtwn

$150 reward for runaway negro John Ellis, 22 years of age. He has a wife at Mrs McGregor's, near Marlborough, & a free brother either in Wash or Gtwn. His mother lives near Palmer's tavern. -Jesse Talburtt, living near Upper Marlborough, PG Co, Md.

MON AUG 10, 1846

Jo Claveau, a Clown in Howe & Mabie's Circus Company, committed suicide at Iowa city on Jul 20.

The Rev A Biewend, Pastor of the German Lutheran Church, who was educated at the College of Clausthal & the Univ of Goettingen, in Germany, continues to give instructions in the Hebrew, Greek, Latin, French, & German Languages. His residence is in Gtwn, on Green st, 3 doors north of Bridge st.

The obituary notices in the London journals of the late Lord Chief Justice of the Common Pleas, Sir Nicholas Tindal, are universally & highly encomiastic. His successor, Sir Thos Wilde, is welcomed by the while Whig press.

<u>Wm the Conqueror</u> was born at Falaise in 1027. That city is about to erect a statue to his memory. Queen Victoria is exhibited as a legitimate descendant, in the 27th degree; the Archduke Chas of Austria, as the nearest-the 22nd degree. Nearly all the sovereign houses of Europe belong to the connexion. They are traced to the Emperor Charlemagne, by Matilda of Flanders, the w/o Wm Duke of Normandy. Paragraphs of heraldry are much relished on this side of the Atlantic.

A colored man, Geo Jenkins, was so cruelly beaten & maimed in a house not far from the jail, last Mon, that Dr Morgan is of the opinion that his life is yet in danger. Two colored men, Allen & Brooks, assisted by a colored woman, named Lomax, assaulted Jenkins. They have all been committed for trial.

A person named Kneeland, a painter, was drowned on Wed near Stapleton, Staten Island. He & his wife, with others, were bathing, when Kneeland, taken with a cramp, drowned.

The descendants of the late Isaac Jennings, dec'd, had a family meeting in this town last week, which is the first enjoyed by them in 30 years. There were 55 souls present: children & children-in-law-19; grandchildren-36. Of the children there are 11, [no deaths having occurred among them,] ranging from 31 to 51; of the grandchildren 11 are dead; the whole number having been 69; & of the great grandchildren there are 7. A supper & religious service made the scene one of deep & affecting interest. –Norwalk Gaz

Mr David Brooks, of Rye, Westchester Co, a retired merchant of this city, was found suspended by the neck in one of the out-bldgs attached to his residence, by a colored woman belonging to the family, when the family were absent at church. When discovered life was extinct. He has left a family. –N Y Express

For rent: brick dwlg house on C st, between 3rd & 4½ sts, recently occupied by Pishey Thompson. Also, a brick dwlg house, on Capitol Hill, near the residence of John H Houston, & recently occupied by Mr Stuart, in the coast survey service. Apply for the latter to Mr Houston, or for either to Jas Larned, 13th st west, for the owner.

A young man, Geo Hunnewell, who was arrested at Boston a day or 2 since, on charge of having set his mother's house on fire, & thus caused the death of his brother, who was burnt to death while trying to save some of the goods, has been fully committed to answer the charge.

Killed & wounded of the 8th Regt: list of ofcrs, non-commissioned ofcrs, musicians, & privates, killed or wounded in the engagements of the 8th & 9th of May, 1846. On the 8th: ofcrs killed, none: non-commissioned ofcrs killed, none; ofcrs wounded, none; non-commissioned ofcrs wounded, none:

Privates killed, 4 :
Henry A Carpenter	Henry Francis	
Adam Anthony	John Fisher, musician	

Privates wounded, 15:
Cearn Dolan	Jas Loyd, musician	Wm Sandys
John Kenneford	Henry Lewis	Alex'r Clocker
John W Bailey	Jas Malony	Jas Dolan
John Burke	Jas Holmes	Jas Patton
Jas Wilferson	Jas R Murry	Ephraim White

On the 9th follows: Ofcrs killed-1: Lt Chadbourne
Ofcrs wounded, 7:
Capt W R Montgomery   J Selden, 1st Lt   C F Morris, 2nd Lt
                      R P Maclay, 1st Lt   C D Jordan, 2nd Lt
C R Gates, 1st Lt   J G Burbank, 1st Lt
Non-commissioned ofcrs killed:
Elijah Andrews   Jas M Mullon   L W Hunt
Non-commissioned ofcrs wounded:
Theodore Finn   J C Gallagher   Adolphus Sae
John Anderson   Alfred Humphries   John Williams
R S Crismont   Thos Wiles
Privates killed:
Geo Craiten   Edw Hamesley   Harrison Hart
R Griffin   Jas Wallace
Privates *wounded:
Avery Ree____   John Flamry   Jas Wallace
Gilbert Churchill   Augustus Sellingslak   W J Haddix
John H Beatty   Geo Anthony   Patrick Malone
Henry Farrell   Joel Havens   John Long
Jas McCafferty   John Waldnan   Jas Farmer

[5 names were not readable.] The eighth suffered severely, as the report of the killed & wounded shows. This regt was commanded by Lt Col Belknap, in the absence of Gen Worth. -New Orleans Topic

The Albany Citizen announces that Judge Granger, of Saratoga Co, died on Sat week in a apoplectic fit, on board a canal boat, on his passage from Troy to his home.

Valuable lots in Wash City for sale at public auction: by deed of trust, executed on Jan 8, 1842, by the late Gen J P Van Ness, recorded in liber W B, #91, folio 196: sale on Aug 21, of lots 1, *9, & 9, in square 382. Lot 8, in square 377, with the large bldg known as the Medical College. Lots 15, 16, & part of 17, in square 293, with valuable dwlg houses thereon. The south 5 feet in width from front to rear of lot 24 & the north 15 feet width, from front to rear, of lot 25, in square 288, with a good 2 story dwlg thereon. The lots in square 382 are opposite the Centre market.
–Rd Smith, Trustee -R W Dyer, auct [*Lot 9 listed twice.]

House & lot to be raffled for the subscriber, who having determined to dispose of the property in which he now resides, at the corner of K & 15th sts, chances $5 each. Subscription lists may be seen at his store, F & 15th sts, & at Mr Hand's lottery ofc.
–W B Laub

House of Reps: 1-Bills passed: relief of Jas Gee; relief of Wiley B Parnell; relief of Ebenezer Conant; relief of Smith, Turber & Co, N Y; payment of certain volunteers & militia called out by Gen Gaines.

Naval Intelligence. The sloop of war **Jamestown**, the flag ship of the squadron on the coast of Africa, all well, arrived at Boston on Thu. She is last from the West India Islands, having touched at St Pierre, Martinique, on Jul 9. The following is a list of her ofcrs:

Cmdor, Chas W Skinner	Prof of Mathematics, Wm Flye
1st Lt, L Stoddart	Cmdor's Sec, Wm H Allmand
2nd Lt, Geo R Gray	Acting Master, J C Beaumont
3rd Lt, Jno L Henderson	Midshipmen: Wm B –[not readable]
4th Lt, I I B Walback	Thos P Eskridge
Fleet Surgeon, Wm F Patten	Boatswain, E Cavendy
Purser, Jas A Semple	Gunner, E Whiton
1st Lt of Marines, F B McNeill	Carpenter, J Cahill
Assist Surgeon, R T Maccoun	Sailmaker, J Stevens
Chaplain, M R Talbot	Purser's Clerk, A M Tabb

The St Louis Republican of Jul 31 announces the death of Capt Wm Walters, at the Planters' House, in that city, on the day before. At the commencement of the war with Mexico he enrolled himself as a volunteer, & received the appointment of Assist Commissary of Subsistence. His wife was with him during his sickness, & friends were in attendance to minister to his wants.

About 4 weeks ago through the New Orleans papers, we learn there was an unfortunate affair at Vicksburg, in a detachment of volunteers on their way to the Rio Grande, & a sergeant, named Sneed, was killed by R C Miller. We learn from the Tennessee Democrat that Miller has been tried by court martial, convicted of murder, & shot.

Arthur Goodwin, was on Wed last, elected cashier of the Farmers' Bank of Va, at Fredericksburg, in place of Hugh M Patton, dec'd.

We regret to hear of the death of Judge Clement Dorsey, of Md, who died suddenly on Thu night last, at Port Tobacco, where he was holding a session of the County Court.

Cmder Wm Chauncey Wetmore, of the U S Navy, died on Sat last, at his residence, Bergen Hill, N J.

Died: yesterday, in his 61st year, Danl Kurtz, a native of, & nearly his whole life a resident of Gtwn, D C. His worth is too well known to the circle in which he moved to require eulogy. His funeral will take place from the residence of his brother, John Kurtz, Gay st, Gtwn, this day, at 12 o'clock.

$100 reward for runaway negro man Edward, about 22 years of age. His father & grandfather, Ellick & Jerry Pratt, live in Balt, & are employed as laborers on Light st wharf; he has also relatives in Anne Arundel Co, Md, where he came from.
–John D Bowling, PG Co, Md

TUE AUG 11, 1846
Acts which have passed at the session of Congress just closed. Bills which originated in the Senate:
Final settlement of the accounts of John Crowell, late agent of the Creek Indians.
Relief of the reps of Pierre Menard, Josiah T Betts, Jacob Feaman, & Edmund Roberts, sureties of Felix St Vrain, late Indian agent.
Relief of the legal reps of Geo Duvall, a Cherokee Indian.
Relief of Mrs Pike, wid/o the late Gen Pike.
Relief of John Jones, surviving partner of John Jones & Chas Souder.
Resolution declaratory of the act of Aur 23, 1842, entitled "An act for the relief of Chas F Sibbald."
Relief of Lewis De Russy, late a paymaster of the army of the U S.
Joint resolution to correct a clerical error in the act of Jun 6, 1846, for the relief of the legal reps of Geo Duvall, a Cherokee Indian.
Joint resolution for the relief of John B Denton & Custis Humphreys.
Act to confirm an entry of land made by the administrator of Jas Anderson, dec'd, of Iowa Territory.
Relief of Wiley B Parnell, of Blount Co, Ala, & Jas A Whiteside, of Ill.
Relief of Ebenezer Conant, of Jefferson Co, N Y.
Relief of Saml D Walker, of Balt.
Act for the relief of Patrick Kelly, sr, of the county of Indiana & State of Pa.
Relief of Nathan Smith, Chas K Smith, & others.
Relief of the heirs of Dr John Gray, dec'd.
Relief of Mgt Gwinnup, of Hamilton Co, Ohio.
Relief of the heirs & legal reps of Cyrus Turner, dec'd.
Relief of Solomon Russell, of Somerset Co, Maine
Relief of Mary Segar, of Jefferson Co, N Y.
Relief of Gregory Thomas & others
Relief of the legal reps of John Ruddle.
Relief of Mary Phelps, of Genesee Co, N Y
Relief of Eliz Betts, of N Y C
Relief of Lois Mattison, of Jefferson Co, N Y
Relief of Arthur M Frogge, of Fentress Co, Tenn
Relief of Jos M Rhea, of Sullivan Co, Tenn
Relief of the heirs of Robt Fulton.
Relief of Isabella Baldridge, wid/o Capt John Baldridge
Relief of Jas Davidson, of Fentress Co, Tenn
Relief of John Chasseand, the Consul for Syria & Palestine
Relief of the heirs & legal reps of Richd C Allen, dec'd
Relief of Chas W Bingley, of Charleston, S C

Relief of John G McCloud, of Linn Co, Iowa
*Act to allow to Elijah White reimbursement of expenses as acting sub-agent for Indian affairs west of the Rocky Mountains.
Relief of Mary Campbell, wid/o John Campbell.
*Act to authorize the agent for paying pensions at Cincinnati to pay to John Wing any arrears of pension money due to Dorothy Terrill, dec'd.
Act to establish the Smithsonian Institution for the increase & diffusion of knowledge among men.
Act to retrocede Alexandria Co in D C to the State of Virginia.
*Relief of Philip & Eliphalet Greely.
Pension to John Campbell, of Garland, Maine
Joint resolution presenting the thanks of Congress to Maj Gen Taylor, his ofcrs & men
*Relief of N & L Dana & Co
Admission of the State of Texas into the Union
Relief of John Carr, John Batty, & Saml Stevenson, seamen on board the whale ship **Margaret**.
Relief of the owner & crew of the schnr **Tancred**.
Relief of the owners of the ship **Herald** of Balt.
Relief of:

Sampson Brown	John R Williams	Jas Lowe
Sheldon B Hayes	Aquila Goodwin	Amos Kendall
Seth M Leavenworth	Eli Merrill	Harriette L Catching
Adam McCulloch	Wm B Lang	Gen Wentling
Jos Kemball	Saml Jordan	Thos Brownell
Semington	Griffin Kelly	Robt Barclay
Buffenbarger	Leah Gray	Harriet Ward
Geo D Spencer	Wm Pool	Abraham B Fannin
Jas Mains	Capt John Patton	John Keith
Jas Wyman	John McAllister	Asenath Canney
Wm McCauley	Justin Jacobs	Nathl Stafford
Abraham Hoorbach	Lewis Laing	Richd Kidd &
Danl Ingalls	Patrick Masterson	Benj Kidd
John E Holland	Thos Ap Catesby Jones	Jas Erwin
Henry Etting	Wm Gump	Alexis Ayot
Jose Carxillo	Jas Journey	Putney & Riddle
Peter Rife	Jas Bogardus	Peter Gorman
Chas M McKenzie	David F Williamson	Jas Gee
John Ficklin	Isaiah Parker	Saml D Enochs
Jos Watson	Nathl Phillips	Langtry & Jenkins
Wm Elliot, jr	Benj Harris	Surannus Cobb
Danl H Warren	Benj Ballard	Benj Allen
Richd Hargrave Lee	Ebenezer Ballard	Amos Hunting

Pension to:
Danl Pratt   Orris Crosby   Elijah C Babbit
Jos Dusseau   Abraham Ansman
[*Aug 13th newspaper: Act not passed by Congress.]

Smithsonian Bill: the Managers, or Regents, as they are called, created by the bill, consist of 15 persons-3 ex officio, 3 Senators, appointed by the Pres of the Senate, 3 members of the House of Reps:, appointed by the Speaker of the House, & 6 citizens at large, [2 of them to be residents of Washington & members of the Nat'l Institute,] to be appointed by joint resolution of the 2 Houses. These appointments having been made, according to the several modes prescribed, are as follows, [with the exception of the 3 Senators:]
The Board of Regents.
The Vice Pres of the U S
The Chief Justice of the U S
The Mayor of the City of Wash
[We could now learn what Senators were appointed by the Pres of that body.]
Rep Robt Dale Owen, of Indiana
Rep Wm J Hough, of N Y
Rep Henry W Hilliard, of Ala
Rufus Choate, of Mass
Gideon Hawley, of N Y
Richd Rush, of Pa
Wm C Preston, of S C
Alex'r Dallas Bache, of Wash
Jos G Totten, of Wash
The Regents are required by the law to meet in the city of Washington on the first Mon in Sep next, to enter on the duties of their appointment.

Died: on Aug 10, Mrs Prudence Aiken, aged 90 years. Her funeral is from her late residence on C st this afternoon at 4 o'clock.

Died: on Jul 27, at his residence in Goochland Co, Va, Archibald Bryce, for many years a member of the Legislature of Va, a distinguished lawyer, & one of the most popular men in the county. By his death the community has lost a great & good man, & his family a most affectionate husband & father.

WED AUG 12, 1846
Discovery of gold recently by John H Blake, of Boston, while examining a quartz vein which was laid open in Denham, Mass, by his directions, for the purpose of ascertaining whether it was worth working for galena. This is probably the first discovery of gold in any place in New England. Besides galena, there were found in the same vein carbonate & sulphuret of copper.

Mrd: on Aug 2, by Rev Jas Donelan, Mr Thos Byrnes, late of Plattsburg, N Y, to Miss Mary Josephine Hubbard, of St Mary's Co, Md.

Died: on Aug 10, in Wash City, Wm Francis Purcell, s/o Wm F Purucell, from a violent attack of the measles, aged 15 months. 'Suffer little children to come unto me, & forbid them not, for of such is the kingdom of heaven."

Household & kitchen furniture at auction on Aug 14, at the residence of Mr John Underwood, N J ave, Capitol Hill. –B Homans, auctioneer

THU AUG 13, 1846

House & furniture for rent: residence on Capitol Hill at present occupied by the Hon W T Colquitt. Apply at the patent agency ofc of C E Tims.

Household furniture at auction on Aug 17, at the residence of Mrs Potter, on Pa ave, between 3rd & 4½ sts, the balance of her household furniture. -R W Dyer, auct

Military appointments: made in the Army by the Pres, & confirmed by the Senate. In Executive Session, Senate of the U S, Aug 8, 1846. Resolved, that the Senate advise & consent to the following promotions in the army, by brevet, for gallant & distinguished services in the battles of Palo Alto & Resaca de la Palma, in Texas, on May 8 & 9, 1846, & in the defence of **Fort Brown**, Texas, during its bombardment from May 3 to the 9th, 1846, agreeably to their nominations respectively, viz:
Lt Col Jas S McIntosh, 5th Regt of Infty, to be colonel by brevet, to date from May 9, 1846.
Lt Col Matthew M Payne, 4th Regt of Artl, to be colonel by brevet, to date from May 9, 1846.
Brevet Lt Col Wm G Belknap, major of the 8th Infty, to be colonel by brevet, to date from May 9, 1846.
Capt Edgar S Hawkins, 7th Regt of Infty, to be major by brevet, to date from May 9, 1846.
Capt Geo A McCall, 4th Regt of Infty, to be major by brevet, to date from May 9, 1846.
Capt Jos B F Mansfield, Corps of Engineers, to be major by brevet, to date from May 9, 1846.
Capt Alex'r S Hooe, 5th Regt of Infty, to be major by brevet, to date from May 9, 1846.
Capt Robt C Buchanan, 4th Regt of Infty, to be major by brevet, to date from May 9, 1846.
Capt Chas A May, 2nd Regt of Dragoons, to be major by brevet, to date from May 8, 1846.
Capt P W Barbour, 3rd Regt of Infty, to be major by brevet, to date from May 9, 1846.
Capt Jas Duncan, 2nd Regt of Artl, to be major by brevet, to date from May 8, 1846.

1st Lt Randolph Ridgely, 3rd Regt of Artl, to be captain by brevet, to date from May 9, 1846.
1st Lt Wm H Churchill, 3rd Regt of Artl, to be captain by brevet, to date from May 9, 1846.
2nd Lt Jas S Woods, 4th Regt of Infty, to be 1st lt by brevet, to date from May 9, 1846.
2nd Lt Alex'r Hays, 4th Regt of Infty, to be 1st lt by brevet, to date from May 9, 1846.
Capt Jas Duncan, 2nd Artl, to be lt colonel by brevet for gallant & highly distinguished conduct in the battle of Resaca de la Palma, to date from May 9, 1846.
Capt Chas A May, 2nd Dragoons, to be lt colonel by brevet for gallant & highly distinguished conduct in the battle of Resaca de la Palma, to date from May 9, 1846.

Mrd: on Aug 4, in Northampton Co, Va, by Rev Mr Ufford, Lt T L Ringgold, U S Army, to Miss Susan Brown, only d/o the late Hon A P Upshur.

Orphans Court of Wash Co, D C. The proceedings before this Court on Tue, in relation to the alleged marriage of the late John P Van Ness to Mrs Mary Ann Conner, caused a number of persons to attend. Mr Dent, as counsel for Mrs Van Ness, informed that Court that he had determined to leave the issue of marriage or no marriage, sent by this Court to the Circuit Court of Wash Co, D C, to be there tried before a jury. Mr Dent asked to be allowed until Fri next to frame that issue, that he might have an opportunity to consult with the gentlemen associated with him as to the suitableness of the issue. Messrs Bradley & Carlisle, counsel for the administrator, C P Van Ness, desired that the issue might be made up at once, as they expected to be absent from the city on Fri next. The Court concluded to extend the time within which the issue might be made till Fri week, for the convenience of all parties. [Aug 14th newspaper: more comformable to have inserted the words claiming to be Mrs V N.] [Aug 24th newspaper: the Circuit Court of Wash Co, D C will decide the question whether Mary A Van Ness be the widow of John P Van Ness, or not?]

Died; on Aug 4, at Detroit, Michigan, Fisher Ames Harding, one of the Editors of the Detroit Daily Advertiser; a native of Dover, Mass, & a graduate of Harvard University.

Miss Mary Simpson informs the ladies of Gtwn & Wash that she will resume giving instructions on the Pianoforte & Guitar on Sep 1 next. For terms apply to Miss Simpson at the house of her brother-in-law, Mr Saml Hein, in Gtwn, Market st, between 3rd & 4th.

$5 reward for my old saddle horse Felix, stolen from my enclosure on Aug 6. He is a beautiful black, about 10 or 11 years old, with white feet & a blaze face.
–Wm Clarke, near Queen Anne, PG Co, Md.

Mount St Mary's College, Emmitsburg, Md, will be resumed on Aug 17: board & tuition is $182 per annum. There is a daily stage from Balt to the College, & Fred'k to the College. –John McCaffrey, Pres

Balt: the little s/o Mr Henry J Rogers, superintendent of the Telegraph station in this city, who was so dreadfully scalded last evening in a bath, died this morning.

Serious if not fatal rencontre took place in the lower part of St Mary's Co, Md, the end of last week, in which Mr Wm H Dunkinson was seriously stabbed with a bowie knife in the lower groin, passed up into the kidneys, injuring in its course the main artery. At last accounts there were no hopes of his recovery. Those engaged in the rencontre are Messrs Jas B Kirk, Nelson Kirk, Philip Chandler, & Jas Chandler, the former of whom is said to have inflicted the wound. [Aug 14th newspaper: Mr Wm H Dunkinson, of St Mary's Co, Md, has died of his wounds. He was a gentleman much esteemed, & had represented his county in the Legislature.] [Aug 19th newspaper: Mr Kirk, said to have been the principal assailant of Mr Dunkinson, is a gentleman much respected in this county, & is married to a dght of Wm Redin, of Gtwn.]

FRI AUG 14, 1846
Wash Corp: 1-Ptn from O J Preston & others, dealers in wood, coal, & lumber, on the Wash City Canal, asking for the removal of obstructions in the canal west of 14th st: referred to the Cmte on the Canal. 2-Cmte of Claims: asked to be discharged from the further consideration of the ptns of J E Moss: & the ptn of Jas Casparis. 3-Ptn of Selby Parker, proposing to construct a stone wall on the alley in square 378: referred to the select cmte to which was referred the ptn of D L Porter, proposing to rent the same. 4-Ptn of Ann Smith, praying the remission of a fine: referred to the Cmte of Claims. 5-Ptn of P Moran, for the remission of a fine: referred to the Cmte of Claims. 6-Ptn of Wm Lord & others, praying for a flag footway across 5th st west, on the north side of G st north: referred to the Cmte on Improvements.

The Pres is in communication with the Gov't of Mexico, of which Paredes is the head, with reference to a Negotiation for Peace & for an adjustment of Boundary.

The Rev Mr Fenwick, the Roman Catholic Bishop of Boston, died in that city on Tue last.

Wash High School's 4th year will commence on Sep 1. –Edwin Arnold, Principal: residence 11th & F sts.

Mrs R J Waugh has determined to resume her former profession teaching school, [which she pursued many years in Alexandria & Gtwn,] aided by her dght, solicits a share of the public patronage. The school will commence Sep 1. Inquire for terms & location at T P Morgan's Drug Store, 1st Ward, near 7 Bldgs, Pa Ave. A few boarding pupils can be accommodated.

For rent: large 3 story brick house & store, corner of 10th & Pa ave. Apply to Michl Sardo, 10th & H sts.

Household & kitchen furniture at auction: Aug 20th, at the residence of Geo M Phillips, on 10th, between D & E sts, by virtue of a deed of trust from G M Phillips, recorded in the land records of Wash Co, D C, in liber W B 120, folios 91, 92, & 93, a good lot of furniture. –Walter Lenox, Trustee -A Green, auct

To let: very eligibly situated Dwlg-house on Dunbarton st, Gtwn, now occupied by Geo Poe, jr: possession on Sep 1 next, or sooner if required. –M Adler, agent

Mrd: on Aug 11, at Bowling Green, Caroline Co, Va, by Rev F W Scott, Mr Lewis Hill, of Richmond, to Miss Mary E, d/o Wm G Maury, of the former place.

Mrd: on Aug 11, at Culpeper Court-house, by Rev John Cole, Mr John R Murray, of Wash, to Miss Mary F Thompson, of the former place.

SAT AUG 15, 1846
The Ky volunteers: the regt of volunteer cavalry & mounted gunmen, from Ky, under the command of Col Humphrey Marshall, arrived at Little Rock, Ark, on Jul 25, & on Jul 29, they took up their line of march for San Antonio, via Washington & Fulton. It was deemed necessary to leave several invalids at Little Rock.

Cmder Henry W Ogden resigned his command of the ship **North Carolina** on Mon, to proceed to the ship **Independence** at Boston, & upon leaving the ship, the men, with whom he is very popular, gave him 3 hearty cheers.

N Y papers: Mr Wm M Price, late U S Atty for the district of N Y, who killed himself in a pistol-gallery by shooting a pistol ball through the centre of his forehead, was 59 years of age: D A under Gen Jackson, for 8 years. He leaves a wife & large family to deplore his death, which in letters he left behind, attributes pecuniary difficulties & the prospect of starvation of himself & family, by having lost money by thousands who not only did not repay it, but treated his claims upon them with neglect & contempt. [Aug 24th newspaper: copy of a letter written by Wm M Price: tells of the large patrimonial estate to which he was entitled upon the death of his father & his brothers: in 1816 he became an endorser of notes to a very large amount: the agent of my father's estate prevailed upon me, prior to the death of my brother Stephen, to convey to him all the estate which might come to me upon the death of either of my brothers. Said conveyances made to him are all on record; but he gave me in exchange for them the most solemn pledges that he would do what was right. He has acquired more than $100,000, & refuses to give me another cent, & I fear has driven me to fatal despair. –Wm M Rice]

For rent: comfortable dwlg house, centrally situated, containing 7 rooms. Inquire at the Cabinet Warerooms, 11th & Pa ave, Edwin Green.

Commandants of the 7 regts of U S Volunteers raised in the State of N Y for the Mexican war are:

Col Ward B Burnett	Col John A Thomas	Col J D Stevenson
Col Chas Baxter	Col John T Cairns	
Col Alex'r Ming, jr	Col R E Temple	

Montgomery Co Court, in Equity, Jul Term, 1846. Barnet T *Norris, cmplnt, vs Thos S Reid, adm of Henry A Collier, dec'd, Jos P Collier, Thos S Reid & Rachel A Reid his wife, Ann Eliza Clarke & Jas Henry Clarke, heirs at law of said Henry A Collier, & Geo W Peter, defts. The original & amended bill in this case state that Henry A Collier, late of said county, departed this life on or about the -- day of ----- intestate, & that the administration of his personal estate was granted to the dfndnt Thos S Reid, & that his personal estate is wholly insufficient for the payment of his debts. That he was at the time of his death seized in fee of a lot of land in Poolesville, in said county, & has an equitable interest in certain other lands in said county, which have descended to the said Jos A Collier his brother, Rachel A Reid his sister, & Ann Eliza Clarke & Jas H Clarke, dght & son of Henry Clarke, dec'd, who was the brother of Henry A Collier, as his heirs at law. That the said Ann Eliza Clarke & Jas Henry Clarke are infants, & do not reside within the State of Md. That the said Barnet T *Norriss is a creditor of the said Henry A Collier, & sues as well for himself as for the other creditors of the said Henry A Collier who may come in & contribute to the expenses of the suit, & prays that the said Thos S Reid may account for the personal estate of the said Henry A Collier in his hands to be administered, & that the real estate of the said Henry A Collier may be sold for the payment of his debts & for general relief. Notice is given that Ann Eliza Clarke & Jas Henry Clarke appear in this Court in person, or by a solicitor, on or before the first Mon of Mar next. –T H Wilkinson, Saml T Stonestreet, Clerk. [*Two spellings-Norris/Norriss.]

Orphans Court of Wash Co, D C. Letters of administration on the personal estate of Wm Evans, late of said county, dec'd. –Jane E Evans, admx

Mrd: on Aug 8, at Carlisle, Pa, by Rev J McClintock, Prof Spencer F Baird, of Dickinson College, to Mary Helen, d/o Col S Churchill, Inspector General U S Army.

Died: on Sat last, of apoplexy, in N Y C, Chas O Handy, Pres of the N J Steamboat Navigation Co, & for many years a Purser in the Navy. [Sep 4th newspaper: the late Chas O Handy was insured in all for $32,000; by 4 different companies. His sudden death affords a striking example of the vast importance of life insurance.]

For rent: a 2 story brick house, with back bldg & attics, excellent cellar & stable, on Md ave, between 13th & 14th sts. Apply to Jane E Evans, 3 doors west.
–Jane E Evans

Died: on Jul 25, at his residence in the State of Indiana, in his 75th year, Gen Marstin Greene Clark. He was born in Lunenburgh Co, Va, on Dec 12, 1771, & was one of a family of 29 brothers & 2 sisters, by the same father & mother. Before he was 21 years of age he left his native State & went to the West, then a wilderness. He served in the campaigns of Gen Wayne as a private soldier; & was aid to Gen Harrison at the sanguinary battle of Tippecanoe. As Indian agent, also, Gen Clark served his country with much advantage; & was repeatedly a member of both branches of the Legislature of Indiana. In 1836 he served as Elector on the Whig Electoral ticket of Indiana, & in 1840 was chosen to carry the vote of the State of Washington, which duty he performed with as much gratification as any other of his life. [Sep 16th newspaper: for some years he resided at Clarksville, Clark Co, arriving there on Jun 1, 1790. After an absence of 12 years from Va he returned, & in 1803 he married & moved with his family in 1805 to Ky, & in 1807 came to Indiana, since which time he has been a citizen of the State.]

Died: on Tue last, in the city of Boston, the Rt Rev Benedict Fenwick, for 21 years the Catholic Bishop of that diocese. His disease wan an enlargement of the heart & liver, inducing dropsy. He was a profound theologian, a learned civilian, a powerful preacher, a thoroughly read historian, & a prudent counselor in all that related to the interests of his church, & what he deemed for the welfare of his people. When he received his appointment to the New England diocese, there were but 2 Catholic churches & 2 priests within its limits. Now there are something over 50 churches & 60 priests, exclusive of those in Conn & R I, which, under his administration, have been created into an independent bishopric, & are no longer under the jurisdiction of the Bishop of Boston. Bishop Fenwick was a native of St Mary's Co, Md, & between 64 & 65 years of age. He joined the order of Jesuits, & in a few years became Pres of Gtwn College, a station he filled with great distinction till 1825, when, & only in obedience to imperative bulls from Pope Leo XII, he accepted the ofc of Bishop of Boston. Latterly he had been assisted in the duties of his ofc by Bishop Fitzpatrick, his coadjutor, appointed for that purpose in the first instance, &, in the second, to be his successor upon his death. –Post

Prospectus of the Ladies' <u>Academy of the Visitation</u>, in Gtwn, D C. It is located on the heights of Gtwn, D C. The Ladies, under whose care & superintendence the studies are conducted, are members of the religious order founded in 1610 by St Francis de Sales, & first governed by St Jane Francis Fremiot de Chantal. All boarders should observe the general regulations of exterior worship. They are allowed to visit their parents or guardians once a month. Wed & Sat evenings of each week are allotted to recreation. Young ladies from a distance: it is desirable that a merchant in town be instructed to furnish the young ladies with the requisite articles of clothing, & that provision be made if the charge devolve on the Institution. On Sundays the uniform for winter consists of a maroon colored merino dress, a cape of the same, & a black silk apron. No particular color is required except on Sundays. Letters to be addressed to the Directress of the Ladies, Academy of the Visitation, Gtwn, D C.

On Mon a party of young men & a lad went out upon Lake Winepisseogee for a sail: the boat filled & the following drowned: Lawson B Brewer, of Dorchester, Mass, aged 20 years; Saml F Perry, a scholar at Wolfsboro Academy, aged 17 years; & Everett Huggins, of Wolfsboro, aged 8 years.

By virtue of 2 writs of fieri facias issued by Thos C Donn, a J P for Wash Co, D C: at the suits of Wm R Riley & Solomon Drew, use of E M Drew, against the goods & chattels of Robt W Hinton: sale of one piano & piano cover, the property of said Robt W Hinton, on Aug 22, in front of the Centre Market-house.
–H R Maryman, Constable

Trustees' sale of valuable real estate: by virtue of a decree passed by the PG County Court, as a Court of Equity, the undersigned will expose to public sale, on the premises, on Sep 11, 1846, all the real estate of which Brook Beall, late of said county, died seised & possessed, supposed to contain about 250 acres, more or less, & which adjoins the estate of Robt W Bowie. There are on the farm an overseer's house, negro quarters, 3 large tobacco houses, a corn house, & stable.
–C C Magruder, Danl C Digges, Trustees

MON AUG 17, 1846
Outlaw killed: John Work, a notorious outlaw, & wholesale murderer & robber, was killed in Washington Co, Ark, about 2 weeks since. He had been concerned in some outrageous murders committed in & near the Cherokee nation within a year or 2 past. Work threatened the life of Mr Funkhauser, who was set up by a negro where Work might steal a horse; he led him to the place, & 8 men, with rifles in hand were waiting his coming. When he was within 10 paces, each man fired, & Work fell dead. –St Louis Republican

Fort Gaines, Ga: Dr E A Roberts & John Jacobs were arrested, supposed to have been concerned in late robberies in that vicinity. Jacobs attempted to run away & was shot & killed. Their saddle bags were literally loaded with specie, & all the tools necessary for entering houses.

Col R Peyton, brother of Hon Bailie Peyton, committed suicide recently in Sumner Co, Tenn, by shooting himself; his mind had been unsettled for several years.
–Memphis Eagle

The succession of the Right Rev John Bernard Fitzpatrick as Roman Catholic Bishop of Boston: rapidly did he rise in the estimation of those who knew the wants of the Catholic Church in New England that, in 1843, at the council of Gtwn he was nominated as a titular bishop & coadjutor to Bishop Fenwick. The nomination was confirmed by the late Pope, Gregory XVI, & on Mar 28, 1844, at Gtwn, he was consecrated by Bishop Fenwick. –Boston Post, Thu

Appointments by the Pres, by & with the advice & consent of the Senate.
Ralph I Ingersoll, of Conn, Envoy Extra & Minister Pleni to Russia, vice Chas S Todd, recalled.
Isaac H Bronson, Judge of the U S District Court for Florida.
Jos Williams, Assoc Judge of the Supreme Court in Iowa, his former commission having expired.
Chandler C Yonge, U S Atty for Florida.
Jos B Browne, U S Marshal for Florida.
Ranson Gillet, of N Y, Register of the Treasury.
Wm C Bouck, of N Y, Assist Treasurer of the U S at N Y C.
Wm Laval, of S C, Assist Treasurer of the U S at Charleston.
Henry Hubbard, of N H, Assist Treasurer of the U S at Boston.
Geo Penn, of Missouri, Assist Treasurer of the U S at St Louis.
Consuls:
Geo W Ellis, of Mass, for Bombay, vice Q C Alexander, resigned.
John W Mulligan, of N Y, for Athens, vice G A Perdicaris, resigned.
Jorgen A Flood, of Norway, for Porsgrund, in Norway, vice Jorgen Flood, resigned.
Francis W Cragin, of N H, for Paramaribo, in Surinam, vice Levi Bixby, resigned.
Wm Carroll, for the Isle of France, vice Robt P De Silver, resigned.
Land Ofcrs: Register of the Land Ofc for the district of land subject to sale at:
Louis St Martin, at New Orleans, La, to take effect from & after Aug 23, 1846, when the commission of Peter Laidlaw expires.
Elisha Taylor, at Detroit, Mich, vice Robt A Forsyth, appointed Paymaster in the U S Army.
Chas Nealey, in the Territory of Iowa, created by the act approved Aug 8, 1846.
Enos Lowe, to be Receiver of Public Moneys for the same district.
Revenue Ofcrs: to be Surveyor & Inspector of the Revenue for:
Seth Belden, the port of Hartford, in Conn, vice Penfield B Goodsell, removed.
Wm Willard, for the port of Saybrook, in Conn.
Geo T Nichols, for the port of North Kingston, in R I, vice Wm Halloway, removed.
Robt H Webb, for the port of Suffolk, Va, to take effect from & after Aug 29, 1846, when his present commission will expire.
Jesse Thomas: for the port of Nashville, Tenn, vice Jos Litton, dec'd.
Benj B Leavitt, for the port of Eastport, Maine, vice Micajah Hawks, rejected.
Revenue Ofcrs-Appraiser of Merchandise for:
Benj E Carpenter, for the port of Phil, Pa, vice Saml Spackman, removed.
Danl Burrows, reappointed Surveyor & Inspector of the Revenue for the port of Middleton, Conn.
Revenue Ofcrs-Collector of the Customs for the district, & Inspector of the Revenue for:
Jos Ramsey, for the port of Plymouth, N C, to take effect from & after Aug 29, 1846, when his present commission expires.
Hardy Hendren, for the port of Vicksburg, Miss, to take effect from & after Aug 29, 1846, when the commission of the present incumbent expires.

Jas Hewson, for the port of Newark, N J, vice Archer Gifford, whose commission expired.
Wm B Snowhook, for the port of Chicago, Ill.
Alfred Marshal, for the port of Belfast, Maine, vice Nathl M Lowney, rejected.
Silas A Comstock, to be Naval ofcr for the district of New Providence, R I, vice Moses Richardson, removed.

A vessel at N Y from Havre has brought out a marble statue of the late Stephen Girard, executed by Gevecot, a Parisian sculptor. It is intended, we presume, for the Girard College, of Phil

Mr I C Bradfield, proprietor of the Shelbyville [Tenn] Free Press, fell dead on Aug 5, whilst standing reading in his ofc at Shelbyville.

Mrd: on Aug 15, at St Patrick's Church, by Rev Jas B Donelan, Robt Kearon to Miss Mary Brannan, all of Wash City.

Died: on Aug 6, at Montreal, Wm R Casey, Civil Engineer, of N Y. In the estimation of all scientific & practical engineers he stook in the first rank of his profession.

Died: on Aug 6, of paralytic, Saml Cooper, aged 58 years, formerly of Balt.

Died: on Aug 14, James, s/o James & Norah Lynch, in his 5th year.

TUE AUG 18, 1846
For rent: a 2 story brick house, with back bldg & attics, excellent cellar & stable, on Md ave, between 13th & 14th sts. Apply to Jane E Evans, 3 doors west.
–Jane E Evans

The Coroner of Boston held an inquest on the body of Jane Jordan, w/o Wm Jordan, who committed suicide by taking laudanum, at the residence of her husband, on Thu. She was a woman of very violent temper, & committed the deed, as she said previously, in order to be revenged on her husband. [Aug 20th newspaper: Jane Jordan, w/o Wm Jordan, in Boston, in a fit of anger, on Thu night, took a large quantity of laudanum & died within an hour. The immediate cause of her anger was the unskilfulness on the part of her husband in cooking a beefsteak.]

Old battle field found lately on the farm of Marlon S Lovett, of Fred'k Co, Va: in ploughing, the plough turned up bushels of old rusty musket & rifle bullets, which had probably been embedded there for more than three quarters of a century. The ground thus giving up the messengers of death was no doubt the scene of a bloody contest between the white & Indian races, or between opposing tribes of the latter. The bones have doubtless long since decayed. –Winchester Republican

Flour at my Flour Depot: on 12th st, 2 doors north of Pa ave. –Jos Hedrick

Winchester Academy will commence on Aug 31: under the charge of the Rev J Jones Smith, A M, with a complement of well qualified assistants. –R Y Conrad, Pres
Trustees:
R T Baldwin	P Williams
T A Tidball	Jno Bruce
D W Barton	Jos H Sherrard
J M Mason	H H McGuire
W M Atkinson	W Y Rooker
A S Tidball	

Valuable tavern stand & farm for sale: the subscriber, on behalf of the proprietor, & for the purpose of satisfying the original purchase money due from Chas Cooper to Chas B Calvert, will offer at public sale, on the premises, on Aug 26, the following property: Lot 1-that spacious & old established brick built tavern known as the cross-roads, on the Washington & Brookville road, at its intersection with the Bladensburg road, in Montg Co, Md. The tavern is rented at $150 a year. Lot 2-a wood lot of 72 acres, adjoining lot 1, on the south. –Thos Connelly, near Colesville

Peter W Crane, of Chas Co, Md, has been appointed by the Govn'r of the State of Md to be Associate Judge of the first Judicial District of Md, vice Clement Dorsey, dec'd. Mr Crane is a distinguished lawyer of Chas Co. -Patriot

Col Saml Humphreys, Chief Naval Constructor in the Naval Service of the U S, died suddenly on Sunday, of apoplexy, in Gtwn. He was in his 68th year, & had been in the service of the U S for more than 33 years. [Aug 19th newspaper: Col Humphreys was the s/o Joshua Humphreys, of Phil, the first U S Naval Constructor, who has left us the frig **Constitution** & the frig **United States**, the finest ships that grace the ocean, as monuments of his skill. These vessels were planned by him & built in 1797, &, what is remarkable, as showing the cast & character of his mind, he had never seen a frigate when he planned them, & yet he built frigates which to this day have never been surpassed. Indeed, the father of Col Humphreys, by his skill, may be said to have effected a complete revolution in the whole science of Naval Architecture, causing the old "wooden walls" of England to be replaced with vessels quite of another sort. His son, the subject of this notice, was educated by his father as a naval constructor also, of which art he was a master. Some of the most beautiful ships in the navy are of his models. He was appointed Naval Constructor for the Phil navy year in 1813, & Chief Naval Constructor in 1826, which posts he filled with advantage to his country & honor to himself; the latter till the day of his death. He has left a large family & circle of friends to mourn his loss.] [Aug 24th newspaper: the relatives of the late Col Humphreys say the cause of his death was not apoplexy, as reported, but that he had long been recognized by different medical advisers as an affection of the heart.]

Robt Melvin, who was a few days ago elected Senator from Brunswick Co, N C, died on Aug 12 of bilious fever.

U S ship **Columbus**, Canton River, Mar, 1846. List of the Ofcrs of this ship:
Cmdor, Jas Biddle   Cmder, Thos O Selfridge
Capt, Thos W Wyman
Lts:
Stephen Johnston   Jas H Strong
Percival Drayton   Madison Rush, acting
Henry French
Acting Master, J M Wainwright
Capt of Marines, H B Tyler
1st Lt, N S Waldren
2nd Lt, J C Cash
Fleet Surgeon, Benajah Ticknor
Passed Assist Surgeon, Chas F B Guillou
Assist Surgeon, D L Bryan
Purser, Edw T Dunn
Chaplain, J W Newton
Sec, E St Clair Clarke
Prof, Mordecai Yarnell
Passed Midshipman, D McNiel Fairfax
Cmdor's Clerk, Jos Lewis
Midshipmen:
H A Colburn   E A Selden
Geo M Dibble   N H Van Zandt
Wm D Whiting   Chas K Graham
Gustavus Harrison   John B Stewart
Wm W Low   Byrd W Stevenson
Stephen B Luce   Jonathan Young
David A McDermut   E W Henry
Capt's Clerk, Robt Harris   Gunner, Thos Robinson
Purser's Clerk, Wm H Needles   Carpenter, Jonas Dibble
Boatswain, V R Hall   Sailmaker, Robt C Rodman
The ofcrs & crew are all well. The **Columbus** leaves in a few days for Manila.

Caleb, s/o Mr Jacob Frederick, of Spafford, came to his death on Aug 10th. He & one or two of his brothers were mowing in the field, when another lad named Breed came & wished to try his hand at the business. He took the scythe, & Caleb stepped back a little to give him room, but the first stroke he made the point of the scythe entered the groin of the unfortunate boy, severed the main artery, & he bled to death in about three-quarters of an hour. He was 10 years old. –Skaneateles Columbian

Western Academy: 11 years of this institution: will commence on Sep 1. Information from Geo J Abbott, Principal, at his residence, corner of 17th & I sts.

For rent: residence, with furniture therein, on I st north, immediately west of Com Morris', formerly the residence of Mrs Cmdor Stewart, & more recently of the Chevalier Hulseman, Charge d'Affaires from Austria. Apply to Richd Smith. The colored woman in the house will show the premises.

For sale: a tract of land of about 780 acres, in Alexandria Co, on the Columbia turnpike, about 3 miles from the Washington long bridge. Mr Mills, who lives on the premises, will show the land. Letters of inquiry may be addressed to Dr O Fairfax, Alexandria. –Henry Fairfax, O Fairfax, exc of Thos Fairfax, dec'd.

Josiah Bailey, for many years Atty Genr'l of the State of Md, died on Fri last at his late residence in Cambridge, Dorchester Co, after a protracted illness. He was probably the oldest lawyer in the State.

Died: on Aug 16, Saml Humphreys, Chief Naval Constructor, in his 68th year. His funeral is from his late residence in Gtwn, on Tue, at half-past 3 o'clock.

Died: on Mar 31 last, in Chickasaw Co, Miss, of bronchitis, Mrs Ariana B Gates, aged about 20 years, w/o Geo E Gates, & d/o Capt Geo Bowen, of Waterloo, Laurens district, S C. She & a younger sister were married at the last mentioned place on Sep 5, 1844, & left shortly after for Mississippi, in fine health & spirits, with prospects bright before them. Little did the relatives & friends of the dec'd then think that she was so soon, by a species of consumption, to be numbered with the dead.

Died: on Jun 20, at the residence of Mr Jesse Fuller, her son-in-law, in Laurens district, S C, Mrs Eliz Conant, wid/o Maj Hardy Conant, in her 95th year. During her whole life she was universally esteemed for her kind & affiable manners & friendly disposition. As a wife, she was dutiful, loving, & obedient; as a mother, tender & affectionate; an agreeable neighbor & an exemplary Christian.

Died: on Fri last, at Aspen Hill, Fairfax Co, Va, after a painful illness of 12 days, Mrs Virginia Benton, in her 19th year, consort of Mr Jas M Benton, & d/o Owen Leddy, of this city. Her death has deprived a fond & doating father of a cherished & idolized dght, a tender & devoted husband of an amiable & affectionate wife, an interesting infant of an anxious & adoring mother.

Died: Aug 15, in Wash City, Dallas, the youngest child & only son of Jas & Susan Espey, aged 18 months.

$50 reward for runaway negro man Uriah, whom I purchased of Wm Holmes, of Montg Co. He is about 19 or 20 years of age. –John Higgins, living in PG Co, Md, near Beltsville.

WED AUG 19, 1846
Naval: we lately stated that Cmder Ogden was ordered to the U S ship **Independence**, but the state of his health prevents his going, & Capt Lavellette will go in command of that ship. –Boston Journal

A boat belonging to the U S ship **Plymouth** was upset in the harbor of Montevideo on Jun 2 last, by which these 5 of her crew drowned: Henry Lincoln, Raphael Gondolpho, Saml Beahan, John Niess, & Geo Munroe. Midshipman Hoffman was in charge of the boat at the time of the upset, & to his coolness & activity, & encouraging the men, may be attributed the safety of many of the survivors, as also a seaman, Jeremiah McCarty, for Southwark, Phil, whose conduct on this occasion is above all commendation.

Isaac Primrose, a sgt of one of the companies of California Volunteers, arraigned before a court martial on a charge of mutiny, has been sentenced to confinement in irons, on bread & water, till the day of embarkation of the troops, & then to be drummed out of the regt, & be deprived of all pay for the time he has been in the service.

Private Moreton, tried for disorderly conduct, was sentenced to be confined in irons, on bread & water, for 17 days; but, owing to his youth & inexperience, together with the recommendation of the court, the sentence was remitted.

Upwards of 70 men belonging to the <u>California Regt</u> have deserted.

On Mon, from the indiscreet handling of firearms, at a tavern lately in the occupancy of Benj Fowler, on the Falls Road, near the termination limits of Gtwn, a young man, Jos Goodyear, on entering a room of the tavern where 2 young men, John Crown & Walter Hilliary, were seated, thoughtlessly caught up a gun that rested against the wall, &, without further warning than a jocular exclamation that he was going to shoot, leveled it & pulled the trigger. The gun proved to be loaded, & the 2 young men both received ghastly wounds from a heavy charge of shot. Young Crown was in all probability mortally wounded, his face being indescribably mangled. The other young man, Hilliary, is not so badly hurt, the shot having struck his left arm & breast. Young Goodyear made no effort to escape, but evinced great concern at the suffering & distress he had brought upon his companions. -Advocate

The Florida Sentinel: Mr Edw C Pittman, of Marianna, Jackson Co, while sitting in his house, on Jul 26, was shot & killed. No clue whatever has yet been discovered to the cause or the agent of this deed.

Mrd: on Aug 16, by Rev Mr Slicer, Richd G Purdy to Miss Martha Ann E Jones, both of Wash City.

Mrd: on Aug 13, at Albany, N G Whistler, U S Army, to Eliza C Hall, grand-dght of the late Francis Bloodgood.

Died: on Aug 15, after a lingering illness, Col Jas K Mullany, aged 66 years.

On Aug 8 a sad accident happened at the house of Mr Chas Gottschalk, druggist, corner of Custom-house & Royal sts, New Orleans. The brother of the gentleman, a volunteer just from Mexico, had a pistol loaded a long time, & which he was trying to discharge. At the moment when he was going to blow into the muzzle it went off, the ball entered below the eye & came out the back of the head, fracturing the skull.

To let: the dwlg-house recently occupied by Maj Geo W Walker, [who has recently removed to the country,] on Capitol Hill, fronting on Pa ave. Inquire of the execs, Susan D Shepherd, or Sylvanus Holmes.

Valuable property at auction: on Aug 26, in front of the premises, lot 10 in square 38, with the excellent 3 story brick-house in good repair thereon. The property fronts on 24th st, between Pa ave & North L st, & in the immediate vicinity of the residence of the French & Belgian Ministers. -R W Dyer, auct

THU AUG 20, 1846
Whig Convention on Sat last, assembled at Rockville to nominate a ticket for the next House of Delegates, made the choice of the following: N Holland, Lyde Griffith, Washington Bonifant, & Jas N Allnutt.

Louis Bonaparte, Ex-King, died at Leghorn, apoplexy, on Jul 24, aged 67 years.

On Aug 8, Saml Goodwin, aged 32, Danl Ray, aged 27, & Byron Briggs, aged 18, were drowned in Hinesburg pond, Chittenden Co, Vt. They repaired to the pond to bathe, but neither could swim.

Mrs Mgt Henry, a widow lady, threw herself from the window of her dwlg in New Orleans on Aug 10, while laboring under a temporary fit of insanity. She died in about an hour.

Died: on Aug 19, after a lingering illness of consumption, Mrs Susan Taylor, w/o Mr Harrison Taylor, in her 34th year, formerly of Alexandria. She was a member of the First Baptist Church, 10th st. Her funeral is from the residence of her husband, on 7th st, 4 doors above I st, today, at 12 o'clock.

The Engraving & Copperplate Printing Ofc of the subscriber is removed to near the corner of 4½ st & Pa ave. Orders for engraving or printing left at Geo Templeman's or R Farnham's bookstores will be promptly attended to & thankfully received by their obedient servant. –J V N Throop

St Mary's Female Institute, near Bryantown, Chas Co, Md. The Miss Martins, Directresses. Annual distribution of Premiums to the pupils were distributed on Aug 6, 1846. Among the visiters were the Rev Messrs Moriarty, & Kroes, & Maguire, from St Thomas'; Rev Mr Donelan, of Wash; & the venerable pastor & founder of the school, Rev Mr Courtney. Premiums were awarded to:

Eleanor Downey, Chas Co, Md
Mary F Neale, Chas Co, Md
Eliza F Dyer, of Wash, D C
Ellen Queen, Chas Co, Md
Annie Downey, Chas Co, Md
Mary G Smith, Chas Co, Md
Marie L Hamilton, Chas Co, Md
Anna Maria Bowling, Chas Co, Md
Mary C Hughes, Chas Co, Md
Olivia Dyer, PG Co, Md
Agnes Courtney, Balt, Md
Mary J Boarman
Virginia Gardiner
Priscilla L Mudd
Eleanor Downey
Rebecca Adams, Chas Co, Md
Mary A Tennison, Chas Co, Md
Mary A Tenneson, Chas Co, Md
Mary E Dyer, Chas Co, Md
Emily Bowling, PG Co, Md
Maria R Gwynn, PG Co, Md
Rosalie Boone
Ellen Rose Boarman
Martina Dyer, Wash, D C
Mary Jane Hamersley, Chas Co, Md
Josephine Freeman, Chas Co, Md
Beatrice Gardiner
Emily Boarman
Eliz Bowling
Mary O Dyer, PG Co, Md
Anna Maria Bowling, Chas Co, Md
Ellen Queen, Chas Co, Md
Marie Gwynn, PG Co, Md

Died: Aug 15, at Phil, after a protracted illness, the Hon Geo W Crabb, of Tuscaloosa, Ala, aged 41 years.

Died: on Wed, at *Rosedale*, the residence of Mr John Green, Imogen, w/o John Taylor, of Windsor, King George's Co, Va, & d/o the late Jas Mosher, jr, of Gtwn. Her funeral is Aug 21, at 9 a m, from *Rosedale*. [Aug 21st newspaper: Died: on Wed, at *Rosedale*, the residence of Mr John Green, Imogen, w/o John Taylor, of Windsor, King George's Co, Va, & d/o the late Jas Mosher, jr, of Gtwn. Her funeral is from *Rosedale* on Aug 21, at 9 o'clock; the process will proceed to Trinity Church, Gtwn, where funeral services will be performed, & thence to the *Catholic graveyard.*]

Died: on Aug 15, after a lingering illness, Col Jas R Mullany, aged 66 years.

Trustees sale: by virtue of a deed of trust to the subscriber: will be sold at public auction on Oct 24 next: part of lot 1 in square 104, in Wash City, beginning for the said part on 20th st west; with a 2 story frame house, & a like house on E st.
–D A Hall, trustee -A Green, auctioneer

FRI AUG 21, 1846
Died: Tue last, Edson, aged 17 months, y/c/o Maj Walker, U S M Corps.

Laws of the U S passed at the 1st session of the 29th Congress: 1-Payment to Horatio Greenough for a group of states to adorn the eastern portico of the Capitol, $8,000. 2-Pay the legal reps of Thos H Storm for a balance due to him as agent for prisoners at Barbadoes, $2,274.26. 3-Payment in full to Benj E Green for services while employed in Mexico as charge d'affaire: $3,000. For enlarging the law library, constructing a new stairway, & other work & the materials thereof, according to the plan of John Skirving, dated Jul 20, 1846: $2,412.

Mrs Mary L Eliason's Boarding & Day School for Young Ladies: corner of Prince & St Asaph sts, Alexandria: instruction will be resumed on Sep 8. References:
Rt Rev Wm Meade, D D, Millwood, Va
Hon Thos H Benton, Wash
Rev Chas B Dana, Alexandria, D C
Eustace Conway, Fredericksburg, Va
Henry Daingerfield, Alexandria, D C
Hon J McLean, Judge of the U S Supreme Court

The razee **Independence**, mounting 56 guns, is now ready for sea at Boston, but she is detained to fill up her complement of seamen. She lacked nearly 50. She is bound to the Pacific, & bears the flag of Cmdor Wm Shubrick. The following is a list of her ofcrs: Capt, E A F Lavalette
Lts:

Fred'k A Neville	Geo W Chapman
Richd L Page	Henry H Lewis
Fred'k Chatard	John B Randolph
Chas Heywood	

Capt of Marines: Jas Edelin	Purser: Hugh W Greene
Lt of Marines: W W Russell	Master: 1st Henry A Wise
Surgeon: J F Sickels	Master: 2nd Saml Marcy
Passed Assist Surgeon: Saml Jackson	Chaplain: Chester Norvell
Assist Surgeon: Wm A Harris	Cmdor's Sec: Henry La Rientree

Passed Midshipmen:

Austin	Warley	English	
Harris	Deniston	Stevens	
McArrann	Conover	Ochiltree	

Midshipmen:

Smith	Chandler	McKean	Sproston

Boatswain: John Mills   Carpenter: David Marple
Gunner: Benj Bunker   Sailmaker: Nicholas Buck
Her complement, all told, will be 500.

By 2 writs of fieri facias, issued by John D Clark, one of the Justices of the Peace for Wash Co, D C, I shall expose to public sale on Aug 25, one baggage-wagon, one gray horse, one set of harness, the property of Lewis Galabrun, seized & taken, in favor of Michl Miller & one in favor of Wm B Laub, & will be sold to satisfy the same. –Donald McPherson, Constable

Dwarkanauth Tagore died in England on Aug 1, in his 52nd year. He was of the most elevated rank of nobility recognized in India, & possessed an immense fortune.

The U S [Texas] ship **Austin** was found not to be worth repairing. She may be considered as condemned. The ofcrs of the Austin were expecting orders for some other vessel in the Gulf. A letter of Aug 8, informs that the U S brig of war **Lawrence** sailed last Mon for N Y. She had been condemned as not seaworthy. –Picayune

Mrd: on Tue, by Rev John C Smith, Mr John C Reeves to Miss Mary E A Waller, all of Wash City.

Mrd: on Wed, by Rev John C Smith, Mr Lorenzo Hatch to Miss Clara E Adsit, both of Fairfax Co, Va.

Mrd: on Aug 12, in N Y, by Rev Moses Marcus, Rector of St George the Martyr, Theophilus Cary Callicot, only s/o W Bulter Callicot, of Fair Hill, Cecil Co, Md, to Fitzina Halleck Lyman, only child of Mrs Lyman, of N Y, & ward of Fitz-Greene Halleck.

Died: Aug 20, Mr Wm Niblo, jr, aged 32 years. His funeral is today at 5 P M, at the residence of his brother-in-law, H Rochat, Pa ave, between 21st & 22nd sts.

Died: on Aug 7, at Mount Independence, Fauquier Co, Va, Mrs Sarah, w/o Capt Andrew Chunn.

Harrison Gray, while at a barber's shop in Tremont st, was suddenly taken ill, & conveyed to the Marlborough Hotel, where he lodged, his family being out of town, & put to bed. In a few minutes he died, supposed of a disease of the heart. Mr Gray was an intelligent bookseller, formerly largely engaged in business as one of the firm of Hilliard, Gray & Co. He was 54 years of age. –Boston Daily Adv

Valuable farm at auction: on Sep 1, the farm belonging to B M Deringer, being a part of Brentwood, lying one mile north from the Capitol on the new Bladensburg road, near the residence of Jos Gales, containing 40 to 50 acres of land, with a new 2 story house, barn, & stable. –A Green, auctioneer

Wash Co, D C: I certify that F B Poston, of said county, brought before me, as a stray, a bay mare. –S Drury, J P [The owner of the mare is to prove property, pay charges, & take her away. –F B Poston]

Smithsonian Institution: the Vice Pres has appointed the following Senators Regents of the Smithsonian Institution: Hon Geo Evans, of Maine; Hon Sidney Breese, of Ill; & Hon Isaac S Pennybacker, of Va. These appointments having completed the list, the Board of Regents consists of:

The Vice Pres of the U S
The Chief Justice of the U S
The Mayor of the City of Wash
Senator Geo Evans, of Maine
Senator Sidney Breese, of Ill
Senator Isaac S Pennybacker, of Va
Rep Robt Dale Owen, of Indiana
Rep Wm J Hough, of N Y
Rep Henry W Hilliard, of Ala
Rufus Choate, of Mass
Gideon Hawlet, of N Y
Richd Russ, of Pa
Wm C Preston, of S C
Alex'r Dallas Bache, of Wash
Jos G Totten, of Wash

The time fixed by law for the first meeting of the Board of Regents is the first Monday in Sep next.

SAT AUG 22, 1846

Woodland, a School for Young Ladies: recently organized at the former residence of R H Snowden, within 4 miles of the Laurel Depot of the Wash Railroad, is now ready for the reception of pupils. A clergyman of the Episcopal Church will reside in the family as chaplain, & assist in some of the higher branches. Apply to Mrs R Windsor, Laurel P O, PG Co, Md. References: Rt Rev W R Whittingham, D D, Balt; Rev W E Wyatt, D D; Col Capron T Snowden; R H Snowden; Dr W W Duvall, PG Co, Md.

Murder yesterday: Jack Haynes was instantly killed by a man named McCanan, a ranger belonging to Tom Greene's company, from Lafayette, Texas.

On Jul 30, at Burita, a member of Capt McIntosh's company of Louisiana volunteers, named Wm Overton, stabbed another of the company named King, who died immediately. Overton made his escape.

New Orleans papers: 1-Capt Walker is lying dangerously ill at Matamoros. Sickness among the volunteers is increasing. 2-Col Twiggs lately remarked that the last shot in the Mexican war had been fired. This is more evidence, indirect, it is true, that a peace had already been conquered.

Departure of Gen Taylor. From the Matamoros "American Flag." Yesterday morning early "Old Rough & Ready, left Matamoros for Camargo in the steamer **Whiteville**, with about half the Texan regt of infty & a few regulars.

Army promotions & appointments: War Dept, Adj Gen Ofc, Wash, Aug 12, 1846.
Promotions:
1st Regt of Dragoons: effective Jun 30, 1846:
Lt Col Richd B Mason, to be Col, vice Kearney, appointed Brig Gen
Maj Clifton Wharton, to be Lt Col, vice Mason, promoted.
Capt Eustace Trenor, to be Maj, vice Wharton, promoted
1st Lt Abraham R Johnston, to be Capt, vice Sumner, promoted to 2nd Dragoons
1st Lt Philip R Thompson, to be Capt, vice Trenor, promoted
2nd Lt Leonidas Jenkins, to be 1st Lt, vice Johnston, promoted
2nd Lt John Love, to be 1st Lt, vice Thompson, promoted
Brevet 2nd Lt Delos B Sacket, 2nd Dragoons, to be 2nd Lt, vice Jenkins, promoted
Brevet 2nd Lt Jos McElwain, to be 2nd Lt, vice Love, promoted
2nd Regt of Dragoons: effective Jun 30, 1846:
Lt Col Wm S Harney, to be Col, vice Twiggs, appointed Brig Gen
Maj Thos T Fauntleroy, to be Lt Col, vice Harney, promoted
Capt Edwin V Sumner, 1st Dragoons, to be Maj, vice Fauntleroy, promoted
1st Regt of Artl: effective Jun 18, 1846:
1st Lt Jas H Prentiss, to be Capt, vice Sibley, Assist Quartermaster, who vacates his regimental commission
2nd Lt Wm S Smith, to 1st Lt, vice Prentiss, promoted
Brevet 2nd Lt Asher R Eddy, to 2nd Lt, vice Smith, promoted
2nd Regt of Artl: effective Jun 18, 1846:
1st Lt Thos P Ridgely, to be Capt, vice Grayson, commissary of Subsistance, who vacates his regimantal commission
1st Lt Horace Brooks, to be Capt, vice Schriver, Assist Adj Gen, who vacates his regimental commission
2nd Lt Henry J Hunt, to be 1st Lt, vice Ridgely, promoted
2nd Lt Augustus A Gibson, to be 1st Lt, vice Brooks, promoted
Brevet 2nd Lt Henry F Clarke, to be 2nd Lt, vice Hunt, promoted
Brevet 2nd Lt Francis J Thomas, of the 3rd Artl, to be 2nd Lt, vice A A Gibson, promoted
3rd Regt of Artl: effective Jun 18, 1846:
2nd Lt John F Reynolds, to be 1st Lt, vice Tompkins, promoted
Brevet 2nd Lt Saml G French, to be 2nd Lt, vice Reynolds, promoted.
4th Regt of Artl: effective Jun 18, 1846:
1st Lt Chas O Collins, to be Capt, vice Dusenbery, Assist Quartermaster, who vacates his regimental commission
2nd Lt Albion P Howe, to be 1st Lt, vice Searle, Capt & Assist Quartermaster, who vacates his regimental commission
2nd Lt Julius P Garesche, to be 1st Lt, vice Collins, promoted
Brevet 2nd Lt Saml Gill, to be 2nd Lt, vice Howe, promoted
Brevet 2nd Lt Thos J Curd, of the 1st Artl, to be 2nd Lt, vice Garesche, promoted.
1st Regt of Infty: effective Jun 18, 1846:
1st Lt John M Scott, to be Capt, vice Cross, Assist Quartermaster, who vacates his regimental commission

2nd Lt John C Terrett, to be 1st Lt, vice Scott, promoted
Brevet 2nd Lt Rankin Dilworth, to be 2nd Lt, vice Terrett, promoted
2nd Regt of Artl: effective Jun 18, 1846:
1st Lt Jas W Penrose, to be Capt, vice Eaton, Commissary of Subsistance, who vacates his regimental commission
1st Lt Geo W Patten, to be Capt, vice Hetzel, Assist Quartermaster, who vacates his regimental commission
2nd Lt Julius Hayden, to be 1st Lt, vice Penrose, promoted
2nd Lt Edw R S Canby, to be 1st Lt, vice Patten, promoted
Brevet 2nd Lt Jas S Woods, of the 4th Artl, to be 2nd Lt, vice Hayden, promoted
Brevet 2nd Lt Jas M Henry, of the 7th Infty, to be 2nd Lt, vice Canby, promoted
3rd Regt of Infty: effective Jun 18, 1846:
1st Lt Jos H Eaton, to be Capt, vice Babbitt, Assist Quartermaster, who vacates his regimental commission
1st Lt Lewis S Craig, to be Capt, vice Casey, Commissary of Subsistance, who vacates his regimental commission
2nd Lt Thos Jordan, to be 1st Lt, vice Eaton, promoted
2nd Lt Don Carlos Buell, to be 1st Lt, vice Craig, promoted
Brevet 2nd Lt Henry B Schroeder, to be 2nd Lt, vice Jordan, promoted
Brevet 2nd Lt John J C Bibb, to be 2nd Lt, vice Buell, promoted
4th Regt of Artl: effective Jul 12, 1846:
1st Lt Wm W S Bliss, to be Capt, vice Page, dec'd
2nd Lt Granville O Haller, to be 1st Lt, vice Bliss, promoted
Brevet 2nd Lt Abram B Lincoln, of the 1st Infty, to be 2nd Lt, vice Haller, promoted
1st Regt of Infty:
Capt Martin Scott, to be Maj, Jun 29, 1846, vice Staniford, promoted to the 8th Infty
1st Lt Danl Ruggles, to be Capt, Jun 18, 1846, vice Clary, Assist Quartermaster, who vacates his regimental commission
1st Lt Wm M D McKissack, to be Capt, Jun 29, 1846, vice Scott, promoted
1st Lt Jos H Whipple, to be Capt, Jul 10, 1846, vice Drane, cashiered
2nd Lt John C Robinson, to be 1st Lt, Jun 18, 1846, vice Ruggles, promoted
2nd Lt Pinkney Lugenbeel, to be 1st Lt, vice McKissack, promoted
2nd Lt Jos L Folsom, to be 1st Lt, Jul 10, 1846, vice Whipple, promoted
Brevet 2nd Lt Jos P Smith, to be 2nd Lt, Jun 18, 1846, vice Robinson, promoted
Brevet 2nd Lt John A Richey, of the 4th Infty, to be 2nd Lt, Jun 29, 1846, vice Lugenbeel, promoted
Brevet 2nd Lt Patrick A Farrelly, of the 4th Infty, to be 2nd Lt, Jul 10, 1846, vice Folsom, promoted
6th Regt of Infty:
Lt Col Newman S Clarke, of the 8th Infty, to be Col, Jun 29, 1846, vice Taylor, appointed Maj Gen
1st Lt Chas S Lovell, to be Capt, Jun 18, 1846, vice Crossman, Assist Quartermaster, who vacates his regimental commission
2nd Lt John D Bacon, to be 1st Lt, jun 18, 1846, vice Lovell, promoted
Brevet 2nd Lt Winfield S Hancock, to be 2nd Lt, Jun 18, 1846, vice Bacon, promoted

8th Regt of Infty:

Maj Thos Staniford, of the 5th Infty, to be Lt Col, Jun 29, 1846, vice Clarke, promoted to the 6th Infty

1st Lt Isaac V D Reeve, to be Capt, Jun 18, 1846, vice Ogden, Assist Quartermaster, who vacates his regimental commission

1st Lt Collison R Gates, to be Capt, Jun 18, 1846, vice Hill, Assist Quartermaster, who vacates his regimental commission

1st Lt Larkin Smith, to be Capt, Jul 21, 1846, vice Worth, promoted

2nd Lt John Beardsley, to be 1st Lt, Jun 18, 1846, vice Reeve, promoted

2nd Lt Chas F Morris, to be 1st Lt, Jun 18, 1846, vice Gates, promoted

2nd Lt John D Clark, to be 1st Lt, Jul 21, 1846, vice Smith, promoted

Brevet 2nd Lt Alex'r Hays, of the 4th Infty, to be 2nd Lt, Jun 18, 1846, vice Beardsley, promoted

Brevet 2nd Lt Geo Wainwright, to be 2nd Lt, Jun 18, 1846, vice Morris, promoted

Brevet 2nd Lt Jas G S Snelling, to be 2nd Lt, Jul 21, 1846, vice Clarke, promoted

Brevets: for gallant & distinguished services in the battles of Palo Alto & Resaca de la Palma, in Texas, on May 8 & 9, 1846, & in the defence of **Fort Brown**, Texas, during its bombardment from May 3 to May 9, 1846:

Lt Col Jas S McIntosh, of the 5th Regt of Infty, to be Col by Brevet, to date from May 9, 1846

Lt Col Matthew M Payne, of the 4th Regt of Artl, to be Col by Brevet, to date from May 9, 1846

Brevet Lt Col Wm G Belknap, Maj of the 8th Regt of Infty, to be Col by Brevet, to date from May 9, 1846

Capt Edgar S Hawkins, of the 7th Regt of Infty, to be Maj by Brevet, to date from May 9, 1946

Capt Geo A McCall, of the 4th Regt of Infty, to be Maj by Brevet, to date from May 9, 1846

Capt Jos K F Mansfield, of the Corps of Engineers, to be Maj by Brevet, to date from May 9, 1846

Capt Alex'r S Hooe, of the 5th Regt of Infty, to be Major by Brevet, to date from May 9, 1846

Capt Robt C Buchanan, of the 4th Regt of Infty, to be Maj by Brevet, to date from May 9, 1846

Capt Chas A May, of the 2nd Regt of Dragoons, to be Maj by Brevet, to date from May 8, 1846

Capt Philip N Barbour, of the 3rd Regt of Infty, to be Major by Brevet, to date from May 9, 1846

Capt Jas Duncan, of the 2nd Regt of Artl, to be Maj by Brevet, to date from May 8, 1846

1st Lt Randolph Ridgely, of the 3rd Regt of Artl, to be Capt by Brevet, to date from May 9, 1846

1st Lt Wm H Churchill, of the 3rd Regt of Artl, to be Capt by Brevet, to date from May 9, 1846

Brevet 2nd Lt Jas S Woods, of the 4th Regt of Infty, to be 1st Lt by Brevet, to date from May 9, 1846

Brevet 2nd Lt Alex'r Hays, of the 4th Regt of Infty, to be 1st Lt by Brevet, to date from May 9, 1846

Capt Chas A May, of the 2nd Regt of Dragoons, Maj by Brevet, to be Lt Col by Brevet, for gallant & highly distinguished conduct in the battles of Resaca de la Palma, to date from May 9, 1846

Capt Jas Duncan, of the 2nd Regt of Artl, Maj by Brevet, to be Lt Col by Brevet, for gallant & distinguished conduct in the battle of Resaca de la Palma, to date from May 9, 1846

Appointments: Adj Genr'l Dept:

1st Lt Edw D Townsend, Adj of the 2nd Regt of Artl, to be Assist Adj Gen with the Brevet rank of Capt, Aug 8, 1846.

Medical Dept:

John F Head, of Massachusetts, to be Assist Surgeon, Aug 6, 1846

Pay Dept:

Robt A Forsyth, of Michigan, formerly Paymaster, to be Paymaster, Aug 8, 1846

Transfer:

Brevet 2nd Lt Geo H Derby, of the Ordnance Dept, to the Corps of Topographical Engineers

Appointments in the Quartermaster's, Commissary's, & Medical Dept, under the 5th section of the "Act supplemental to an act entitled-An act providing for the proscution of the existing war between the U S & the Republic of Mexico, & for other purposes." Approved, Jun 18, 1846.

Quartermaster's Dept:

Quartermaster with the rank of Major:

Nathl Anderson, of Tenn, Aug 6, 1846

Assist Quartermasters with the rank of Capt.

Rank

1-Jas H Walker, of Arkansas, Aug 4, 1846

2-Nathan Adams, of Tenn, Aug 6, 1846

3-Wm Allen, of Tenn, Aug 6, 1846

4-Zebulon C Bishop, of Missouri, Aug 6, 1846

5-Chas W Davis, of Texas, Aug 8, 1846

Commissary's Dept

Commissaries with the rank of Major:

1-Brookyns Campbell, of Tenn, Aug 4, 1846

2-Richd Roman, of Texas, Aug 6, 1846

3-Pleasant L Ward, of Ill, Aug 8, 1846

Assist Commissaries with the rank of Capt:

1-John J Clendenin, of Ark, Aug 4, 1846

2-Wm G Marcy, of N Y, Aug 6, 1846

2-John S Bradford, of Ill, Aug 8, 1846

Medical Dept: Surgeons:
1-A Parker, of Texas, Jul 22, 1846
2-Geo Penn, of Missouri, Jul 22, 1846
3-Geo Johnson, of Missouri, Jul 22, 1846
4-Danl McPhail, of Tenn, Jul 22, 1846
5-Ewing H Roane, of Arkansas, Aug 4, 1846
6-Gideon M Alsup, of Tenn, Aug 6, 1846
7-Abram S Hill, of Georgia, Aug 8, 1846
Assist Surgeons:
1-Richd H Stevens, of Missouri, Jul 22, 1846
2-E Tucker, of Texas, Jul 22, 1846
3-Thos M Morton, of Missouri, Jul 22, 1846
4-Wm D Dorris, of Tenn, Jul 22, 1846
5-Richd P Ashe, of Texas, Jul 22, 1846
6-John W Glenn, of Arkansas, Aug 4, 1846
7-John W Stout, of Tenn, Aug 6, 1846
8-J M Dove, of the District of Columbia, Aug 6, 1846
9-John M Leech, of Ill, Aug 8, 1846
Order of rank & precedence of the ofcrs of the Quartermaster's & Commissary's Depts, appointed under the 5th section of the act, approved Jun 18, 1846.
Quartermasters & Commissaries with the rank of Major:
1-Brookyns Campbell, Commissary
2-Richd Roman, Commissary
3-Nathl Anderson, Quartermaster
4-Pleasant L Ward, Commissary
Assist Quartermasters & Assist Commissaries with the rank of Capt:
1-John J Clendenin, Assist Commissary
2-Jas H Walker, Assist Quartermaster
3-Nathan Adams, Assit Quartermaster
4-Wm Allen, Assist Quartermaster
5-Wm G Marcy, Assist Commissary
6-Zebulon C Bishop, Assist Quartermaster
7-John S Bradford, Assist Commissary
8-Chas W Davis, Assist Quartermaster
Appointments in the Pay Dept, under the 25th section of the act approved Jul 5, 1838.
Additional Paymasters.
A W Gaines, of Ky, Jul 20, 1846
Geo H Ringgold, of D C, Aug 6, 1846
Casualties:
Resignations & Commissions vacated, under the provision of the 7th section of the act of Jun 18, 1846.
Capt J R Irwin, 1st Artl, Assist Quartermaster*
Capt G H Crosman, 6th Infty, Assist Quartermaster*
Capt S B Dusenbery, 4th Artl, Assist Quartermaster*
Capt D H Vinton, 3rd Artl, Assist Quartermaster*

Capt E B Alexander, 3rd Infty, Assist Quartermaster**
Capt O Cross, 1st Infty, Assist Quartermaster*
Capt S P Heintzelman, 2nd Infty, Assist Quartermaster**
Capt E S Sibley, 1st Artl, Assist Quartermaster*
Capt E B Babbitt, 3rd Infty, Assist Quartermaster*
Capt J B Grayson, 2nd Artl, Commissary of Subsistance*
Capt A B Eaton, 2nd Infty, Commissary of Subsistance*
Capt J C Casey, 3rd Infty, Commissary of Subsistance*
Capt R E Clary, 5th Infty, Assist Quartermaster*
Capt A R Hetzel, 2nd Infty, Assist Quartermaster*
Capt E Schriver, 2nd Artl, Assist Adj Gen*
Capt E Schriver, Assist Adj Gen, Jul 31, 1846
Capt E A Ogden, 8th Infty, Assist Quartermaster*
Capt J M Hill, 8th Infty, Assist Quartermaster*
Capt W Wall, 3rd Artl, Assist Quartermaster**
1st Lt F Searle, 4th Artl, Assist Quartermaster*
Assist Surgeon, Chas E Isaacs, Jul 24, 1846
Declined:
Volunteer Service:
Maj Julius W Blackwell, Commissary
Maj Levin H Coe, Quartermaster
Maj Jas C Sloo, Commissary
Capt Jonas E Thomas, Assist Quartermaster
Capt Philip B Glenn, Assist Quartermaster
Capt Wm Fields, Assist Quartermaster
Capt Saml M Rutherford, Assist Quartermaster
Surgeon Paul F Eve
Assist Surgeon Danl Turney
*Regimental Commission [only] vacated, under 7th section, act Jun 18, 1846
**Staff Commission [only] vacated, under 7th section, act Jun 18, 1846
Deaths:
Capt John Page, 4th Infty, near St Louis, Missour, Jul 12, 1846. [Of wounds received in the battle of Palo Alto, May 8.]
Capt Jos S Worth, 8th Infty, at St Augustine, Florida, Jul 21, 1846
Capt Wm Walters, Assist Commissary, [volunteer service,] at St Louis, Missouri, Jul 30, 1846
The ofcrs promoted & appointed will join their proper regts, companies, & stations, without delay; those on detached service, or acting under special instructions, will report, by letter, to the commanding ofcrs of their respective regts & corps.
Acceptances or non-acceptances of appointments will be promptly reported to the Adj Gen of the Army; &, in case of acceptance, the birth-place of the person appointed must be stated. By order: R Jones, Adj Gen

Correction:
Horatio M Vandeveer, of Ill, to be an Assist Quartermaster with the rank of Capt, [under the act of Jun 18, 1846,] to date from Jun 26, 1846, instead of Henry M Vandeven, which was a misnomer in his first nomination.

Household & kitchen furniture at auction on Aug 25, at the residence of J P Colman, on 9th st, between D & E sts. The house is for rent. Inquire of Mr Colman, on the premises. –A Green, auctoneer

Household & kitchen furniture, & a mocking bird: on Aug 26, at the residence of J W Henderson, on I, between 6th & 7th sts. –A Green, auctioneer

Mrd: on Aug 20, in Wash City, by Rev Mr Aege, Mr Thos B Brown, of Phil, to Mrs Rhoda C H Homans, of N Y.

Died: on Aug 21, in his 37th year, Jeremiah Calnan, a native of the county of Cork, Ireland, but for several years a resident of Wash City. His funeral is from his late residence on F st, between 6th & 7th sts, at 10 o'clock. [The Wash City Benevolent Society are requested to meet at their Hall at 9 a m this day, to attend the funeral of Mr Calnan, dec'd member.]

Died: on Aug 18, in Dranesville, Fairfax Co, Va, after a short but severe illness, Miss Ann Maria Louisa Drane, eldest d/o W Drane, dec'd. She has left a fond doting mother, and affectionate & devoted sisters & brothers, with a very numerous circle of friends.

MON AUG 24, 1846
Later from Mexico: the insurgents of Guadalajara had surprised & cut to pieces the troops of Gen Arevalo, who was among the slain. Gen Bravo was to take formal possession of the Presidency on Aug 28, the 30th, Gen Paredes was to leave for the seat of war.

Col A C W Fanning, of the U S Army, died suddenly in Cincinnati on Tue last, of apoplexy, in his 59th year. He entered the army in 1812; served through the war with England; was with Gen Jackson through the Seminole war; & was in service in Florida, where he participated in 2 of the most sanguinary battles. He was Lt Col of the 2nd Regt of Artl, & Col by Brevet of date Dec 31, 1835

The Raleigh Register mentions that Gen Welborn, who has been elected to the House of Commons from Wilkes Co, was a member of the first Legislature that sat in Raleigh in 1795.

The body of Bernard Kelley was found in the Alleghany river, near Pittsburg, on Thu. He had been paying his addresses to a widow lady in that vicinity, but she refused his proposals to make her a happy wife. -N Y Courier & Enquirer

Balt Patriot of Sat: the loss of the ship **Gentoo**, on her passage from Calcutta to Boston, by which a lady passenger & 2 children were drowned. We have since learned that the lady was Mrs Watt, formerly of Cincinnati, & d/o our late fellow-citizen, E S Thomas. She was on her return from Calcutta for the purpose of educating her children, & was shipwrecked on the **Gentoo** on Apr 29, at Struy's Bay, near the Cape of Good Hope. Three of the crew of the **Gentoo** were also drowned. Mrs Watt was the beautiful & brilliant Frances Ann Thomas. –Cincinnati Gaz
+
Mr Thomas, the father of this lady, accumulated a large fortune in Charleston, S C, during our war with Great Britain, removed to Balt, & invested in real estate. In the revulsion which followed his large possessions were sacrificed; he emigrated to the West, transporting his family, in a 4 horse wagon, whilst he, on foot, plodded beside them. We said all of his family, we should have excepted his son, F W Thomas, then a student of law in this city, & who soon after embarkded on that profession with most brilliant hopes of success. He wrote the novel "Clinton Bradshaw." -W O N

An inquest was held at the city prison, in N Y, on Wed, on the body of Westerla W Woodward, a native of Albany, aged 32 years, who was brought to the Police Ofc by some unknown person. He was found on his bed dead, having killed himself by severing the brachial artery of the arm with a penknife, which was found lying on his bed. -Globe

Sale of household & kitchen furniture, bar & fixtures: on Sep 2, to satisfy a deed of trust, at the Verandah Hotel, kept by Mr John Cotter, on Pa ave, between 3rd & 4½ sts, all the furniture of said establishment, which is of good quality.
–A Green, auctioneer

Orphans Court of Wash Co, D C. Letters of administration, with will annexed, on the personal estate of Jonathan Eliot, late of said county, dec'd. –Henry Eliot, admr

By virtue of a writ of fieri facias, at the suit of John Pettibone, against the good & chattels of Wm Buist, & to me directed: I have seized & taken in execution all the right of said Wm Buist in & to one cart; same will be for sale to the highest bidder for cash, on Aug 29, in front of the Centre Market-house, Wash City.
-H Y Maryman, constable

TUE AUG 25, 1846
Died: on Aug 22, Archibald Murray, infant s/o Gen Archibald Henderson, U S Marine Corps, aged 13 months & 21 days.

Land near the district for sale: the subscriber offers his plantation, lying in PG Co, Md, near the state road leading from Washington to Port Tobacco: tract contains 400 acres; improvements consist of a large & comfortable 2 story frame dwlg & all necessary out bldgs. –C A Gantt

Valuable property for sale: the subscriber, intending to remove to the West, will dispose of his farm on which he resides, on the N W Branch, in PG Co, Md: about 300 acres are bottom land; about 100 acres of woodland; comfortable frame dwlg with all necessary out bldgs. Inquiry may be made of Mr Saml Redfern, Wash, or of Mr Saml Cropley, Gtwn. –Robt Clark

Mrs Mary E Hussey, a widow lady of N Y, while bathing with friends at Rockaway, L I, was carried into deep water by the under-tow & drowned. She leaves a little boy, her only child.

Died: on Aug 11, at his residence in Jefferson Co, Va, of paralysis, Col Geo W Humphreys, aged 68; a gentleman who had filled many public stations; commander of a volunteer corps of riflemen during the war of 1812.

Springfield [Ill] Journal: Dr Todd, of this city, has furnished us with a letter from his son, Wm L Todd, who went out with the emigration to California in the spring of 1845, dated Apr 17: we left **Fort Hall** on Aug 9, in company with 10 wagons, & on St Mary's river we were joined by 15 more. When we reached the mountains we met with tribulation in the extreme. Solomon Sublette, of St Louis, who passed us at the lake on the north side of the mountain, told us afterwards that he had no idea we could get through with our wagons. We made out way to the valley; it is about 60 miles from the bay of St Francisco, about 40 from **Fort Suter**, & 25 from the Pacific Ocean. I am not so much pleased with what I have seen of the country. I do not, however, believe there was ever a more beautiful climate than we have in this country. There will be a revolution before long, & probably this country will be annexed to the U S. If here, I will take a hand in it. –Wm L Todd

In Chancery, Aug 14, 1846. Marcellus T Jones, & Wm H Jones & Sarah L Jones his wife, vs Eugene J Jones, Alice J Jones, & Wm Hughes Jones. The object of this suit is to procure a decree for a sale of certain real estate described in the bill, & have the proceeds of the sale distributed among the parties entitled. The bill states that the cmplnts, Marcellus T Jones & Sarah L Jones, & the dfndnts, Eugene J Jones, Alice J Jones, & Wm Hughes Jones, are seized as tenants in common in fee of certain real estate in Somerset Co, & that it will be for the interest of the persons entitled to have the same sold & the proceed divided; that the dfndnts are infants, & a sale cannot be made without the assistance of this Court; that Eugene J Jones & Wm Hughes Jones reside in Somerset Co, & that Alice J Jones resides out of the State of Md, & beyong the reach of the process of this Court. Absent dfndnt to appear in this Court, on or before Jan 14th next. –Louis Gassaway, Reg Cur Can

WED AUG 26, 1846
Alexandria Boarding School: 23rd annual session will commence on Sep 7. –Caleb S Hallowell & Brother, Principals, Alexandria, D C

Fairfax Co, Va: farms sold within a short time: the farm of the late Henry Hedges was sold, under a decree of the Court, to Mr A H Ives, of Pa, at $17 per acre. About 27,000 acres in this county are now held by Northern settlers. –Fairfax News

Local News: Mrs Parker, the lady of Mr Geo Parker, of this city, met with a serious injury on Mon whilst riding in a one-horse carriage. It appears that when the vehicle was near Mr Buist's garden, on 12th st, the horse took fright, & set off at a gallop towards Pa ave, & so continued for 4 squares. The carriage came in contact with a stone-step fronting Mr Riley's. Mrs Parker & her children were thrown out against the curbstone. Mrs Parker received a severe but not dangerous wound on the side of the head. The children escaped without injury. Surgical assistance was promptly rendered by Dr Dawes, & Mrs Parker was conveyed to her residence on C st.

Mr Geo Mattingly, of Wash City, narrowly escaped being drowned last Fri, while he was watering his horse in the Tiber, in the rear of the Railroad Depot. The horse, which was attached to a buggy, got into a dangerous hole & could not be extricated in time to prevent his being drowned.

Drowned, in the Gulf of Mexico, Jul 25, by the capsizing of one of the boats of the U S steamer **Mississippi**, Midshipman Wingate Pilsbury, of Maine He was an aspiring young ofcr, brave, generous, & highminded. He was singularly skilled in his profession.

Orphans Court of Wash Co, D C. Letters of administration, with the will annexed, on the personal estate of Saml Humphreys, late of said county, dec'd.
–Clement Humphreys, A A Humphreys, adms

THU AUG 27, 1846
Lost or mislaid: a note drawn by Wm Gadsby in favor of B M Deringer & by him endorsed, dated Feb 12, 1844, at 60 days, for $200. All persons are warned not to receive or pass said note, as B M Deringer is the proper owner.

Mrs Dyson & Mrs Chalmers inform that their Seminary will be re-opened for the reception of pupils on Sep 1, in the Session-room of the Baptist Church, on 19th st, between E & F sts.

Genteel furniture at auction on Aug 28, at the residence of W J Nevius, on Beall st.
–Edw S Wright, auct

For rent: one of those 3 very desirable residences on 8th st, between G & H sts, in the rear of the Genr'l Post & Patent ofcs, occupied at present by Mr Chas Murry. Inquire on the premises. –Mgt Stewart

Mrd: on Aug 25, by Rev W T Sprole, Alex'r Speer to Maria Henrietta, d/o Andrew Coyle.

Died: on Aug 24, at his residence in Talbot Co, Md, Jas Murray Lloyd, 2nd s/o the late Govn'r Edw Lloyd, of Md.

Died: on Aug 2, at New Orleans, Mrs Mary Austin Holley, in her 62nd year, wid/o the late Rev Dr Holley.

Orphans Court of Wash Co, D C. Letters testamentary on the personal estate of Wm A Scott, late of said county, dec'd. –J W Beck, exc

FRI AUG 28, 1846
Wash Corp: 1-Ptn of W G Harrison, praying to be refunded certain costs alleged to have been illegally exacted from him: referred to the Cmte of Claims. 2-Ptn of Richd T Smallwood, praying remission of a fine: referred to the Cmte of Claims. 3-Ptn of Jas Davis, praying remission of a fine: referred to the Cmte of Claims. 4-Ptn of Jos Schwarts & others, for curb & footway on the west front of squares 127 & 166: referred to the Cmte on Improvements. 5-Relief of H B Sweeney, teller of the Bank of Washington: referred to the Cmte of Claims. 6-Ptns of Alfred Prather & W R Dempster, praying remission of fines: referred to the Cmte of Claims. 7-Ptn of O J Preston & Co & others, renters of wharves on the canal, praying the clearing out of the western portion of the canal: referred to the Cmte on Canals. 8-Cmte of Claims: discharged from the further consideration of the ptn of Jas Casparis: referred to the Cmte of Claims. 9-Ptn of Jas Fitzgerald: referred to the Cmte on Claims. 10-Ptns from M A Daley, Thos Dumphey, & Ann Stewart: referred to the Cmte on Claims.

The Gtwn Advocate has passed into the hands of Ezekiel Hughes, late editor of the Fred'k Herald, who will be assisted in the editorial conduct of the Advocate by Jos F Crow.

Longevity: Mrs Ann McCannon died at Paterson, N J, on Thu last, in her 106th year.

The schnr **Maine**, of Cohasset, was run into & sunk on Aug 16, by the steamship **Hibernia**, when on her way to Halifax, in a thick fog, & 6 of her crew were drowned: John Litchfield, master; M Litchfield & son; Martin Wheelwright; H Richardson, & E Lincoln. The last two were boys. The engine of the steamer was stopped immediately, boats lowered, & 5 of the crew saved.

Died: on Aug 27, Mr Robt G Lanphier, formerly of Alexandria, in his 81st year. His funeral is this day at the residence of the family on Pa ave, near 9th st, at 12 o'clock.

Died: on Aug 24, in Gtwn, Kate Smoot, y/d/o Geo D Abbot, aged 2 years & 8 months.

Notice: for sale, 30 slaughtered Hides of my own killing, in lots to suit purchasers. A liberal credit will be given if desired. Apply to John Little, Washington

The Cambridge College Library, by actual enumeration lately made, this library consists of 51,000 volumes, exclusive of 8,000 to 10,000 pamphlets. The oldest work on American history known to exist is a letter from Columbus, translated from Italian into Latin, & published in 1494.

For rent: a first rate business stand, The large corner store-room of the house occupied by Mr S Masi, on the corner of Pa ave & 4½ st. Apply to Raphael Semmes & Co.

SAT AUG 29, 1846
Dr John T Bartow, of the U S Navy, died at Savannah, on Sat last.

A H Ayers, about 38 years of age, was found dead in Essex st, Boston, on Aug 15, having fallen from the roof of a 4 story bldg while intoxicated.

Mr John Wesley Finch & his wife met with a melancholy death on Aug 21, near Abingdon, Va. They were traveling, & encamped for the night, & were reposing in their carryall, together with a nephew, when the horse, being tethered to the wheel, took fright, turned the wagon bottom upwards, & the two old people were suffocated. The young man with them said they were returning from a visit in N C to their residence near Dresden, Weakley Co, Tenn.

Mrd: on Aug 20, at La Grange, Georgia, by Rev Thos Samford, the Hon Orlando B Ficklin, of Illinois, to Eliz B, eldest d/o the Hon Walter T Colquitt.

Breach of Promise Case: Conrad vs Williams, which has been some years before the Courts, was disposed of last week at Ithaca, N Y, by a verdict for the dfndnt. The suit commenced in Nov, 1842, & at the trial in Feb following a verdict of $8,000 was obtained, but a new trial was ordered by the Supreme Court. The third trial was tried before Hon Amasa J Parker, of the 3rd circuit. The jury agreed on thie verdict, which was rendered for the dfndnt. –Ithaca Chronicle

Died: on Aug 17, in St Louis, Missouri, Mrs Anne E Lane, w/o Dr Hardage Lane, in her 43rd year. Mrs Lane was a d/o the late Maj Chas Carroll, of N Y, & had passed more than 20 years of her life in Missouri. During the last 12 years she was a resident of St Louis. She sustained the ravages of a cruel disease for more than 2 years, with Christian fortitude. –St Louis Republican

English Classical & Mathematical School, 4½ st, between Pa ave & C st. This school will be reopened on Sep 1. –C W Feeks

$100 reward: stop the thief & runaway dark mulatto boy Danl: aged 21 years. He eloped taking a valuable horse & about $120 in money. Address "near Upperville, Loudoun Co, Va, Geo M Grayson.

Small desirable farm for sale by Geo White: containing about 80 to 84 acs: situated a little below the junction of the old Leesburg road & the Middle Turnpike: about 25 acres cleared on the west end, on which is an old dwlg-house, & out-houses, all in a dilapidate state. Title unexceptionable. Sale positive, & terms made known on the day of sale. Sale on Sep 5. –Christopher Neale, & Thos Grimes, Attys in fact for Mary P Allison, Matilda Allison, & Jas H Allison, heirs & devisees of Jno Allison & D F Allison, dec'd.

Burnt Mills for sale: property is in Montg Co, Md, on the N W Branch, direct on the road leading from Wash to Colesville: about 80 acres of land, with a grist & saw-mill in good repair, a comfortable dwlg, with other out-houses. For information apply to Nathan Loughborough, near Tenallytown, Saml Phillips, A Green, Otho Gattrell, Washington, or to the subscriber, residing on the premises. –Richd Israel

The Arkansas Intelligencer reports that Capt Leavitt & his friends, 11 in number, who started for California last April, have been murdered by the Camanches. A party of those savages were seen in possession of their guns & other arms, & the traders of Little River, in the Seminole country, believe them to be murdered.

Strayed away from the subscriber on Aug 4, a spotted Buffalo Cow: $3 to any person who will return her to John Sioussa, sr, N Y ave, between 12th & 13th sts.

Public sale of land, crops, & stock: estate is in the upper part of Prince William Co, Va, 7 miles from Brentsville: contains 1,600 acs: includes a principal dwlg & overseer's house, occupied by himself. –Saml D Williamson

MON AUG 31, 1846
Mrd: on Aug 5, by Rev Chas A Davis, John W Haines to Irene A E Chappell.

Mrd: on Aug 27, by Rev Chas A Davis, Stokeley Finacum to Mary E Fletcher.

Mrd: on Aug 27, by Rev Chas A Davis, Wm H Mortimer to Mrs Mary Ann Barnes, all of Wash City.

Wanted: the undersigned wishes to employ immediately a first-rate blacksmith; one well acquainted with making fancy fence & hand railings, & housework in general. His establishment is on C st, between 10th & 11th sts, Wash. –C Buckingham

Orphans Court of Wash Co, D C. Letters of administration on the personal estate of Jeremiah Calnan, late of said county, dec'd. –Anne Calnan, admx
+

Anne Calnan informs the friends & customers of her late husband that she intends carrying on the Bread-Baking Business with punctuality & fidelity.

Coroner Woodward held an inquest last Sat in view of the body of a colored woman Nancy Carter, who was found drowned in the Wash Canal, not far from the 12th st bridge.

TUE SEP 1, 1846
Col Johnathn D Stevenson. A motion was yesterday made for the appointment of a receiver of the property & effects of this gentleman, upon a creditor's bill filed against him, in which N Dane Ellingwood was cmplnt. The motion was granted. Will not this stop his supplies from the Gov't? He is also under bail, which was put in upon his arrest upon a writ of ne exeat, to stay within jurisdiction of the court. –N Y Tribune

Boston Custom-house: Messrs Geo F Emery, John C Leach, Leander Warren, Benj D Baxter, Wm P Loring, & David Townsend, inspectors in the Boston custom-house, have each received a letter from the Hon Marcus Morton, Collector of the port, dated Aug 27, 1846: by authority of the Sec of the Treas, another person has been appointed to perform the duties of you ofc. Your services will not be required after Aug 31. –Marcus Morton, Collector: to Geo F Emery, Inspector of the Customs, Boston.

Rev Chas A Davis, of Wash City, has been appointed Agent of the American Colonization Society for the State of Va.

David Hewlett, a member of the Gulick Guards, a volunteer company of N Y on a visit to Phil, was drowned on Sat, as he was about departing for home. In the excitement & fun of leaving, he was pretending to throw his companions overboard, & at last fell overboard himself with another. His companion was saved.

Died: on Aug 20, at his residence in Charlton, Mass, Nathan Dexter, in his 88th year. He entered the Revolutionary army as a volunteer private, from R I, &, towards the close of the war, was promoted to the rank of Major of Infty. He has left a large circle of relatives & friends to enjoy the principles of practical freedom for which he contended.

Died: on Aug 20, at the Red Sulphur Springs, Va, of consumption, in his 34th year, Jas Breckenridge Watts, eldest s/o Gen Edw & Mrs Letitia Breckenridge Watts, of Roanoke Co, Va. Born on May 26, 1812, at *Grove Hill*, [the seat of his maternal grandfather, Gen Jas Breckenridge,] he passed with distinction through his academic studies, & won his degree at Wm & Mary with high credit, & selecting law for his profession, merited his legal diploma at Va Univ. Something more than a 12 month since, he removed to N Y C. He contracted a violent infammation of the lungs, which passed into the disease that has consigned him, after 8 months of calmly sustained suffering, to his grave. –E W J

House & lot for sale, on north side of Mass ave, between 5th & 6th sts, having 21 feet front & 90 feet deep, running back to a 10 feet alley: bld is a new 2 story frame, with back bldg, containing 7 rooms, sliding doors between the parlors, & built of the best material. For terms apply to Peter Gallant, living near the premises; or to Richd L A Culverwell, Gen Agent & Collector, 9th, near I st.

Valuable real estate in PG Co, Md, for sale: by virtue of a decree of PG Co Court, as Court of Equity: sale on Sep 22, that desirable farm **Greenwood**, the late residence of Thos T Somervell, dec'd. Estate contains 663 acres; improvements are a large & very roomy dwlg house, tobacco houses, & all other necessary bldgs & out houses. Also, at the same time, 270 acres, convenient to the former. The widow's dower in the whole estate has been assigned, the outlines of which & of the whole property will be shown upon application to Jas Somervell, or Dr M J Stone.
–Will H Tuck, Trustee

State of Md, Chas Co: in Equity, Jul 31, 1846. Jeremiah W Burch vs Mary Moran, Judson Hunt, & others. Object of this suit is to procure a decree for the sale of the real estate of Alex'r Moran, late of said county, dec'd, to satisfy debts due by him at the time of his death. The bill states that Alex'r Moran departed this life in 1842, leaving a widow, Mary Moran, & without children; that Judson Hunt & Henrietta his wife, & the said Mary Moran, are the only persons known to the cmplnt as having an interest in & title to said real estate. There were brothers & sisters of the dec'd who removed from the said county many years since, & it is not known where they are, if living, & if dead, whethere or not they left heirs. The personal assets have been exhausted in the payment of debts, & the cmplnt said other creditors of Alex'r Moran, are yet unpaid, & that they are entitled to have their claims paid out of the real estate of said dec'd. The bill prays for a sale of said real estate, & for an order of publication giving notice to the absent heirs, if any, to appear in person or by solicitor, to this court, on or before Nov 26 next. –A C Magruder -W Mitchell, Clerk Chas Co Court

Mrd: on Aug 30, by Rev Mr Samson, Mr Wm A Boss to Miss Eliza A Lewis, all of Wash City.

Mrd: on Jan 15, 1846, by Rev J Van Horseigh, at his residence, Wm Linton to Miss Julia M, y/d/o Danl E Dunscomb, of Wash City.

Mrd: on Aug 30, at St Patrick's Church, by Rev Wm Matthews, Bernard Brien, of Gtwn, to Miss Mary Ann Masi, eldest d/o Francis Masi, of Wash City.

Mrd: on Thu last, at Washington, Pa, by Rev G S Holmes, Alfred Galt to Mrs Sophia Funstan, all of that borough.

The Misses Koones have resumed their School, in Pollard's Rown, & solicit the patronage heretofore extended them by their friends & the public generally.

Good chance for business. The term of the copartnership existing between T G Townshend, M B Carroll, & John R Baden, under the firm of the undersigned, having expired, we have to say that we will dispose of our entire stock of goods on very liberal terms to anyone who may wish to succeed us. Call on T G Townshend & Co, Nottingham, PG Co, Md.

Letters remaining in the Post Ofc, Wash, Sep 1, 1846.

Ames, Miss E	Bright, Mrs Jacob	Cunningham, Mrs
Adams, Mrs Mary	Boyd, Cooper S	Chandler, Lt Wm
Allen, Jas	Brown, Mrs Rebecca	Cornelia, Mlle
Angerman, John	Bowser, Adam	Cleveland, Henry W
Anderson, Mrs E E	Bailey, John E	Carter, Miss Julia
Allison, John	Binkhold, Henry L	Chapman, Wm
Allen, Jas M	Barry, Mrs Sarah	Calley, Jas
Ashton, Miss Betsy C	Barrow, jr, Alex	Cowan, Wm
Abbott, Eliz	Baker, Julia	Chalfant, L W
Abell, Alex G	Bryant, Mrs Mary	Charleton, Miss L
Armstrong, R	Bladen, Jos	Codrick, Jos
Bohn, Casimer	Baltzel, Miss Emma	Coffin, Rev Wm H
Black, Ellen	Bogert, Miss Almire	Colquitt, Miss E
Brown, Ludwell	Bagby, jr, Arthur P	Cushing, Caleb
Buck, Juna	Barry, Miss Theresa	Carmichael, Mid E T
Burns, Benj F	Bennett, John R	Covington, Michl
Bryce, Capt J W	Bennett, Alex	Cummins, Jacob W
Brown, Mrs Mary E	Bassett, John	Denham, Mrs David
Banks, Miss Mary	Buchanan, Mrs S	Dowel, Saml V
Black, Saml	Bronough, John E	Donley, Mrs Sally
Beck, Lemuel J	Bryan, Mrs C M	Dulany, Mrs Eliza C
Bell, Miss Martin A	Barrett, Thos	Doolittle, H P
Bell, Mrs Harriet	Briscoe, Miss A H	Dutton, Capt Geo
Beach, Levi	Bealer, Capt C R	Daniel, J L
Brooke, Miss M V	Buckley, Miss C	Depkin, Chas
Buck, Miss Frances	Boston, Robt	Davis, Chas W
Brooke, R L	Berkley, John F	Davis, John
Belt, Edw W	Barry, Mrs Jas D	Dowell, John
Bean, Mrs Mgt	Brady, Gen H-2	Dorsey, Mrs M M
Bixbe, Mansel	Cearires, Miss M A	David, Dr Jas B
Bragg, Joh	Cooke, Robt	Dallas, Passed
Brooke, Brig Gen G M	Cox, Miss Mary A	Midshipman A J
	Clarke, Saml	Duvall, Philip &
Brown, jr, Alex	Crane, Col J B	Raymond

Dowden, Mrs Eleanor
Drummond, Mrs C
Doniphan, Wm T
Drummons, Mrs Ann T-2
Drummond, Miss Ann S R
Ellis, Nathl M
Elezy, Miss M H
Emmons, Wm
Ennis, Gregory J
Ellis, Vespasian
Elliott, Lewis
Engard, Saml
France, Mrs Annabella
Fox, Michl
Fleet, Mrs Julia
Fleet, Jas H
Forrest, Louisa
Fortune, Mrs M A
Fremont, Lt Z
Furguson, Mrs
Fletcher, John
Florence, John
Gray, Miss Louisa
Gay, Lowman
Gill, Miss Mgt
Gray, Mrs Henrietta-2
Galt, Jacob
Graeve, Madam
Genard, Lewis
Grandin, Rev J M
Griffin, Chas T
Griswold, Mrs E A
Gleeson, Jas
Garret, Alex
Graham, Geo
Gatton, John
Groger, Mr
Grammald, Timothy
Graham, Catestry
Hume, Geo
Heath, Miss Adeline
Hart, Dr Wm P

Hass, Jacob
Hess, Conrad
Harlsee, Wm
Herbert, Alfred
Headley, John P
Henry, Rev T H-2
Hathaway, J G
Howard, Miss Emily
Hoover, Miss S E
Hampton, Miss H
Harrison, Mrs E
Heaton, Col D F-2
Hamer, Catharine E
Hunter, M J
Henning, Robt M
Howard, Wm
Haret, Miss Mary
Henning, Thos
Hatton, Jas K
Hambleton, J M-2
Irwin, Jas R
Johnson, Dr C P
Jordan, Alex
Jacobs, Jas
Jackson, Henry A
Johnson, Jas
Jett, John W
Johns, John S
Jones, Wm W
Johnson, Susan
Jordan, Richd L
Jacobs, Mrs Dolly
Johnson, Mrs Julia A
Johnson, Mrs Teny
Jackson, Wm S G
Jameisson, Elias
Jenkins, Thos
Jackson, Miss Mary
Jordan, Miss Harriet
Jeffries, Matthews
Kean, Miss Rebecca
Key, Chas W
King, Mrs John L
Kehl, John W
Kirby, Miss Blanche

Kinnines, Wm
Kantner, Isaac
Kempton, Wm J
Kunsman, Geo R
Kaufman, Mrs Jane
Keaman, Miss Mary
Kuhland, Claus
Kearney, Col Jas
Love, Miss E
Laton, Miss Jos
La Truitte, Miss B V-2
Lonelen, Mrs Bar'a
Lowry, Passed Mid R B
Lindsay, Mrs Maria
Lushy, Jas H
Lincoln, B Austin
Lacey, Miss Frances
Lyon, Caleb
Leggett, Aaron
Lewis, Lt H H
Lusby, Saml
Lindsay, Mrs Marie
Muse, Lt Wm T
May, John B
Man, Henry
Marks, Michl
Meins, Wm S
Montgomery, Maj C P-2
Miller, Nathl
Matchett, Miss M F
Miller, Aaron W-3
Morris, Miss J K
Morton, Jeremiah
Miller, Col Saml
Martin, Luther L
Mansfield, John T
Marion, Thos
Miller, Mrs C E
Moreland, Miss R L
Manning, Dr R A
Morehouse, Wm G
Minor, Ann

Merrille, Edw	Roane, Archibald	Shelden, Isaac C
Markwood, Wm	Reeves, John C, of Upgate	Sitgreaves, Lt L
Morgan, Randolph-5		Steeples, Miss A M
Mulloy, Thos	Reeves, Randolph B	Soper, Miss Sarah E
Mattern, Zacharias	Russ, Lt John A	Sullivan, Timothy
Martin, Wm	Rochel, Miss Emily	Stryker, John
Matchett, Dr Wm	Ringgold, T L, U S A	Simmons, Mrs H B
Martin, Henry B	Roberton, Wm A	Shirman, Mrs M A
Martin, Chas	Ringgold, Mrs G H	Smallwood, Miss L
Montgomery, M J-2	Robinson, Miss M	Stewart, Mrs Emma
Mason, Mrs Araann	Rockfort, Wm	Stewart, Col Wm
Magee, Miss Mary	Robinson, Fay	Shoemaker, A C P
McGruder, Mrs-2	Robbins, Jas	Timby, T R
Magill, Benedict	Rallings, Mrs C	Thompson, Mary A
McDuffie, Wm	Russell, Mgt	Trueman, jr, Josiah
McCarthy, Miss M	Roswell, Rosson	Thompson, Gen W
Magruder, John B, U S Army	Rathburn, G A	Thompson, Wm
	Russell, Lt W W	Taylor, Fran B
McJilton, Mrs C	Reyburn, Dr W P	Thornton, Mrs R
McLaughlin, J	Russell, Mrs Jane	Thruston, Miss M
McCarthy, Eugene	Smith, Miss Frances	Thomas, Capt G E
McPherson, Mrs M	Simms, Miss M J	Thomas, Mrs Ann A
McGregor, Ridout	Smith, Mrs Jane E	Thompson, Wm O
McAlpine, Wm J	Shaw, Ellen	Tillotson, Shubael
McGregor, jr, Jas	Scott, Mrs Louisa	Taylor, Geo W-2
McCarty, Col J M	Smoot, Miss S A	Taylor, Burrill B
Nildett, Dr	Smith, Thos S	Taylor, Miss Mary J
Naples, Minister from	Smith, John W	Trustee, Saml
O'Neal, J H	Smith, Clement	Tippett, Mrs Ann
O'Bryan, Miss Rose	Stoff, John Peter	Thomas, Mrs Mary
O'Sullivan, John	Smith, Jos F	Thompson, Robt
Othiltree, Midshipman David	Smith, John G	Thistle, Capt H L
	Simms, Mrs S	Underwood, Dr J R
Pieres, Richd	Stone, Geo B	Vail, Danl
Plant, Mrs Henri'ta	Snead, Holman	Watts, Rev Danl
Peck, Mrs Eliz	Smith, Jas	West, Lt E L
Price, Hibert B	Smith, Delazon	West, John W
Plant, Jas K	Scott, Henry	Whyte, Thos
Payne, Lt Col M M-5	Shaw, Lt T D	Walsh, Mrs Mary
Philips, Jas	Skinner, Usher	Wright, John S, of Chicago
Perry, Emma	Seymour, Miss B	
Rant, Miss C	Saunders, Wm	White, Mathias M
Ross, Wm	Standley, Sarah	Wood, Richd
Rhodes, Miss E	Sheckells, Richd M	Wood, Jas A
Rhodes, Foster	Selin, Miss Enag	Weeks, Wm

Wright, Lt W H	Waters, John H	Wharrey, Jos
Watson, Miss Maria	Wilgars, Mrs P	Webster, Israel B
Walker, Zacharie	Wheeler, Chas	Young, Geo E
Whitlark, Wm W	Wagner, Sebastian	Young, Mrs Eliza
Wheeler, Tureman	Whitler, Mrs Ann	Young, Augustus
Worrell, Alex	Walker, Capt J T	Young, Miss Mary
Winton, Henry L	Weston, H	Younge, C C
Watrons, Chas	Wilson, Henry, U S Navy	Zaminiski, Mr
Waters, David S		

The inland postage on all letters intended to go by ship must be paid, otherwise they remain in this ofc. -C K Gardner, P M

WED SEP 2, 1846

A colored man named Jacob Brown, belonging to Dr King, of Annapolis, was drowned on Sun in the Eastern Branch. It appears he was intoxicated, & in that condition fell into the water.

Cow lost or strayed, from the commons of Wash City: came from the neighborhood of Brookville, Montg Co, Md, & may be making for that neighbordhood agains. She left on Aug 24. A liberal reward will be given of her delivery by the subscriber. –John Prout, corner 4th st east & Va ave.

Louisville, Aug 27. The neighborhood of Jefferson & 4th sts were thrown into great consternation by the murder of a wife by her husband. Geo W Barlow, who keeps a boarding-house there, while intoxicated, fired a pistol at his wife, who immediately fell & expired. Mrs Barlow is represented to us to have been a very estimable lady. Barlow was immediately arrested, & is now in jail. –Journal

Free Trade & our Forefathers: Examining articles of the original Association, they form not merely a Tariff, but a strictly prohibitive one. Out colonial forefathers cound not legally tax British or other foreign goods: but, to defend their independence, & to make the Gov't which has injured them retrace its steps, they could renounce the use of foreign good; & they did so. In the first roll of subscribers [that at Wmsburg] will be found nearly all the most eminent names of Revolutionary Virginia. The 2nd list contains a few more remarkable ones-as of John Marshall, Geo Mason, Richd Harrison, & Wm Grayson. The Association entered into last Fri, the 22nd instant, by the gentlemen of the House of Burgesses & the Body of Merchants assembled in this city. Signed in Williamsburg: Jun 22, 1770:

Peyton Randolph, Moderator	Henry Lee
Andrew Sprowle, Chrmn o/the trade	Chas Carter, Corotoman
Ro C Nicholas	Thos Jefferson
Richd Bland	Severn Eyre
Edmund Pendleton	Thos Whiting
Archibald Cary	Edw Hack Moseley, jr
Richd Henry Lee	Geo Washington

Urwell Bassett
Spencer M Ball
Jas Walker
Edw Osborn
Southy Simpson
Richd Lee
John Alexander
John Burton
Wm Clayton
Richd Randolph
Benj Harrison
P Carrington
Jas Pride
Wm Acrill
Peter Poythress
Jas Mercer
N Edwards, jr
Richd Adams
Thos Mewton, jr
Francis Peyton
Thos Barber
Lewis Burwell
Jas Cocke
Richd Baker
Benj Howard
R Rutherford
Archibald Campbell
Jas Balfour
W Cabell, jr
Danl Barraud
Jas Mills
David Jameson
Chas Duncan
John Wayles
John Bell
Thos Adams
Henry Taylor
Alex'r Shaw
John Banister
Thos Bailey
Wm Robinson
Jas Wood
Bolling Stark
Thos Pettus
John Woodson

Henry Field, jr
Wm Roane
Wilson Miles Cary
John Blair
Jas Wallace
Richd Mitchell
Cornelius Thomas
Jas Dennistone
Wm Snodgrass
Benj Baker
Patrick Coutts
Neill Campbell
John Donelson
Neill McCoull
Thos Jett
Saml Ker
Jas Robinson
Archibald Ritchie
Saml Eskredge
Thos Stith
Jas Edmonson
Anthony Walke
John Wilson, of Augusta
Geo Logan
John Hutchings
W Lyne
Edw Ker
Alex'r Trent
John Talbott
Jos Cabell
Gardner Fleming
Saml Harwood
Humphrey Roberts
Thos M Randolph
Robt Wormeley Carter
Jerman Baker
John Gilchrist
Jas Archdeacon
Robt Donald
Jas McDowall
Alex'r Baine
John Smith
Purdie & Dixon
Jas Buchanan
Thos Scott

Alex'r Banks
John Johnson
Archibald Govan
Hugh McMekin
Foushee Tebbs
Archibald McCall
Danl Hutchings
Henry Morse
Nathl Terry
Isaac Read
Wm Rind
Benj Harrison, jr
Josiah Granbery
Jas Robb
Neil Jamieson
Walter Peter
Robt Crooks
John Winn
John Esdale
Nathl Lyttleton Savage
Jacob Wray
John Fisher
Hartwell Cocke
Edwin Gray
Danl McCallum
Jas Donald
Thos Nelson, jr
Robt Gilmour
Geo Riddell
John Bland

Robt Miller
Francis Lightfoot Lee
Merriwether Smith
Ro Munford, Mecklenburg
Roger Atkinson
J H Norton
Lewis Burwell, of Gloucester
Abraham Hite
Jas Parker
Edw Brisbane
Jas Baird
Neill Buchanan
Andrew Mackie
Thos Everard
Geo Purdie
Patrick Ramsay
Walter Boyd
John Tabb
Richd Booker
John Page, jr
Robt Andrews
John Tayloe Corbin
John Tazewell
John Prentis
Wm Holt
John Greenhow
Haldenby Dixon
Wm Russell
Thos Hornsby

The Subscribers, inhabitants of the county of Fairfax, in the Colony of Virginia, having duly considered the above agreement & association, & being well convinced of the utility & real necessity of the measures therein recommended, do sincerely & cordially accede thereto; & do hereby, voluntarily & faithfully, each & every person for himself, upon his word & honor, agree & promise that he will strictly & firmly adhere to & abide by every article & resolution therein contained, according to the true intent & meaning thereof.

John West
Wm Ramsay
John Carlyle
John C Dalton
Robt Adam
John West, jr
Harry Piper
Jas Steuart

Thos Carson
John Hite, jr
Thos Kirkpatrick
Jonathan Hall
Henry McCabe
Geo Gilpin
Will Balmain
Richd Harrison

John Muir   G Mason
Jas Kirk

The poll was opened at the Court House in Alexandria yesterday, to vote on the retrocession of Alexandria, D C, back to the State of Va. Messrs Snowden, McKenzie, Smith, & Hall made addresses in favor of retrocession; Mr Hardy, from the upper part of Alexandria Co, delivered an address on the opposite side.
For retrocession: 589   Against Retrocession: 183
Majority for retrocession: 406

For rent: 3 story bldg lately occupied by the subscriber, near the corner of 15th st, fronting on Pa ave. The front bldg has a spacious store & counting room; private passage to 8 handsome rooms on the 2nd & 3rd floors, with iron balustrade balcony looking on the ave; a fine cellar for coal & wood; good pump in the year; fine back bldg; with first rate kitchen & store rooms, which has for several years been the family part of the domain. The entire tenement is the best calculated for any business done on Pa ave. Apply to myself, at my shop, on E st, near 13th, or Darius Clagett, on Pa ave. –Jos K Boyd

For rent: large brick dwlg-house on 3rd st east & Eastern Branch, late residence of Griffith Coombe, dec'd. Inquire of Jos Ingle, agent, Capitol Hill.

Died: on Aug 31, Harriet Walling, relict of the late Wm M Walling, aged 45 years. Her funeral is from her late residence, corner of 13th & D sts, this morning at 10 o'clock.

M A Tyson & Sisters' Seminary, on F st, north side, between 12th & 13th sts: will be resumed on Sep 15.

Dedication of St Mary's German Roman Catholic Church: ceremony to take place on Sep 6. The members of the German congregation will assemble at their chapel, on 8th st, at 9 o'clock, &, preceded by the German band, will move to St Matthew's Church, & thence down 14th st to F, along F st to 5th, & up 5th st to the new church, the doors of which will remain closed till the procession arrives. The church will be dedicated by the Most Rev Archbishop in pontificals & a sermon in English will be delivered during the High Mass. A collection will be taken for the benefit of the church. A sermon in German will be delivered at 4 p m, during vespers.

THU SEP 3, 1846
Bombardment of *Fort Brown*: on Apr 26, the day after the attack & capture of Thornton's squadron of 2nd Dragoons, we were possessed of information that the enemy had crossed the Rio Grande in considerable force, & it was evident that he had in view one of two objects, either to advance on Point Isabel to cut off our supplies, or to attack Gen Taylor in position; either of which rendered the completion of *Fort Brown* of immediate necessity. On May 1 the Commanding Gen ordered the

movement of his army, designating as the garrison of **Fort Brown** the 7th Regt of Infty, Capt Lowd's company of the 2nd Artl, & Lt Bragg's battery of light artl, composed of 2 six-pounders & 12 pounder howitzers. During the day muskets were placed in the hands of evry man capable of bearing arms, & our force numbered 560 men & 40 ofcrs; 32 ofcrs & 341 rank & file 7th Infty; 3 ofcrs & 41 rank & file of Capt Lowd's Company; 4 ofcrs & 51 rank & file of Lt Bragg's company, 6 Dragoons, & one ofcr & 91 rank & file of a detachment of inefficient men left from other regiments. Of this number, 95 were on the sick report, 77 being of the number of inefficient men left from other regts, & the remainder of the 560 were citizens & sutler, 25 in number. We were surrounded by as many thousands as we had hundreds. On the 3rd the gallant Brown at his post, &, whilst giving an order to his staff ofcr to have the 7th Infty turned out to work on the defences, his attention was attracted to the first shot fired by the enemy. With a smile of joy he turned to his staff ofcr and said: "Sir, we have other work to do today; order the batteries manned; go to the right & see that every man is at his post, I will go to the left." It was noticed that the flag had been overlooked & not yet raised, when Lt Van Dorn volunteered to raise it; which was done under the fire of the enemy. The enemy's fire was opened on us from the nearest fort, called by us the "Sand-bag Battery," by the Mexicans "La Fortine Redonda," under command of Capt Passamente, a Frenchman, who took up arms for his adopted country for the protection of his family. Bragg's battery was playing upon them well & in 30 minutes after our first fire, La Fortine Redonda was abandoned. At this time Sgt Weigart, of B Co 7th Infty, was killed by a round shot. Lt Bragg was ordered to place his guns in barbette in the several bastions for defence; one commanded by Capt Hawkins; one under Lt Thomas, in the bastion commanded by Maj Seawell; one under Lt Reynolds, in the bastion of Capt Miles; the other under the direction of Lt Johnson, in the one commanded by Capt Lee. Capt Walker, sent from Capt May's command, came into the fort at 3 a m-found his return before daylight impracticable. On the 4th we were again saluted from the enemy's batteries; Capt Walker left; fire was being thrown from a gun called by the Mexicans "escopettes," [a short gun, carrying a ball nearly as large as a grape shot.] On the 5th the enemy commenced the fire. Lt Hanson, 7th Infty, with 6 dragoons, was sent out to look at the parties of infty & cavalry around us. Lt Hanson accomplished the object for which he was sent out, returned, bringing us important information. Capt Hawkins & Lee, commanded by Lt Humber, went out to clear away brushes & obstacles. May 6th: enemy's fire opened on us from La Fortine de la Flecha. At 10 o'clock today we were deprived of the services of our gallant cmder. His leg was shattered about the knee by a falling shell. Being borne to the hospital, he turned to some of his men & said, "Go to work, men. I am but one among you." He lived until the 9th, when he died of his wound. Capt Hawkins was now in command. Bragg, Thomas, Johnson, & Lansing were ordered to fire a charge of canister or grape at the enemy, whenever an opportunity offered to do execution. At 4½ o'clock, a white flag was shown at the old bldgs in rear. Two Mexican ofcrs advanced, & by direction of Capt Hawkins were met by Maj Seawell & Lt Britton, who brought him a communication signed by Gen Arista, demanding a surrender of the forces under his command, giving him one hour to reply. A council of war was held & a very appropriate reply unanimously agreed upon, & sent off in the allotted time. On the 7th, the enemy's batteries opened on us: the bombardment continued without intermission until sunset: all the instruments of the 7th Infty band were lost today by the explosion of a bombshell; & Private Moody, of H Co, lost his arm. It was now necessary to remove the traverse thrown up by Gen Worth's command before the fort was commenced, & about 9 o'clock Capt Miles, in command, with Lts Van Dorn & Clitz, with 80 men, were sent out to level it; accomplished with rapidity. This party was covered by a detachment of light infty commanded by Lt Potter. The picket-guard duty was the most dangerous duty to be performed: Sgt Wragg, Cpl Manson, privates Ballard & Melton distinguished themselves by their daring bravery in approaching the enemy's lines. Capt Manson & privates Ballard & Melton were always volunteers when there was danger service for a picket. May 8: batteries opened on us again; Capt Mansfield suggestion that a picket burn the old house near the traverse-this was done by Cpl Manson & private Ballard, who volunteered. The nat'l flag of the 7th infty was raied inside the fort by Sgt Henry. May 9: batteries open on us: the capt commanding determined to have the flag raised on the staff on the outside of the fort, &, the hallairds being unrigged, the topmast had to be lowered to replace them. Lt Hanson, with Quartermaster Sgt Henry, & privates Collins & Howard, went out to perform this duty. They found it impossible to raise the topmast, but fastened it in position, & raised the nat'l flag to the admiration of the whole command. They had been exposed to a constant fire of canister, grape, & round shot. At the suggestion of Capt Mansfield the commanding ofcr ordered a party detailed to burn the houses & fences in rear, which had been occupied by the enemy. Sgt Jones, of C Company, 7th Infty, was sent out with 10 men-private Ballard again a volunteer. Capt Mansfield accompanied this party. Lt Gantt, with 20 men, with axes, cut away the bushes between the dragoon encampment & the fort. After 2 o'clock we could perceive the advance of our artl & musketry. Lt McLaws was sent out to cut away the chaparral bushes. About 5¾ o'clock we saw the Mexican cavalry & infty in precipitate retreat to the river, but entirely out of the range of the 6 pound guns. The distinguished services of Quartermaster Sgt Henry, Cpl Manson, & private Ballard deserve the highest praise. -P

Mr Josiah Eaton, an old man, nearly 70 years of age, has just completed Capt Barclay's celebrated feat of walking a thousand miles in a thousand hours. This performance took place at the Caledonia Springs, a watering place on the Ottawa river, Canada. Eaton is a native of Woodford, Northamptonshire.

Gtwn College, D C, will be resumed on Sep 15. –Thos F Mulledy, President

Music School: Miss Eliz B Scott can take 3 or 4 additional pupils, who would be waited on at their own dwlgs, if preferred. Inquire at the residence of Mrs Eliz B Scott, G st, corner of 11th.

For sale: a part of lot 1 in square 295: it corners on 12th st west & Ohio ave. Apply to L H Berryman, 12th st west, near bridge.

Valuable farm for sale: in Fairfax Co, Va, on the Colchester road, between that & the Hunting creek road: adjoins the lands of Dennis Johnson, ___ Ashford, Saml Collard, & Mr Lloyd, & being part of a tract called *Mount Erin*, for many years the residence of Jas Francis Tracy, who by will bequeathed the same to his widow, Frances Maria Tracy, the present owner. The tract contains about 195 acres & 67 perches. Title is indisputable. Improvements are a large 2 story frame dwgl-house, with 1 story kitchen, smoke-house, & spring-house. If not disposed of at private sale before Sep 19, it will, on that day, be offered at public sale at the tavern of Saml Catts, Alexandria, D C. Apply to T L & A Tho Smith, Genr'l Agents, Wash.

Sale of household & kitchen furniture: on Sep 3, at the residence of Mr J F Hartley, on 12th st, near N Y ave. -R W Dyer, auct

Seizure of American vessels: By the arrival at Boston, on Sat, of the ship **Augustine Heard**, from Valparaiso, information received that the whaling ship **Pantheon**, Capt Dimon, of Fall River, with 200 bbls sperm oil, & sealing schnr **Leader**, Capt Pray, of New London, with 3,000 sealskins & 50 bbls seal oil, were seized at St Carlos, island of Chiloe, about 600 miles south of Valparaiso, for passing through an inland channel, which they were obliged to do by stress of weather. Capts Dimon & Pray would remain to hear from the Chilean Gov't. The crews of both vessels were turned ashore.

FRI SEP 4, 1846
Capt Chas S McCauley, a popular & highly esteemed ofcr of the Navy, has been appointed to the command of the Navy Yard at Wash, which he assumed on Sep 1, in place of Cmdor Shubrick, appointed to the command of the Pacific squadron.

In Sep, 1845, Capt Danl P Upton, of the ship **Governor Davis**, belonging to Boston, rescued the crew & passengers of the British ship **Glenview**, numering 24 in all, after they had been lashed in the rigging during 2 days. A beautiful & massive gold medal has been prepared, by order of the Queen of Great Britain, as an acknowledgment of this act, & a day or two ago it was presented by the British Minister through the Sec of State of the U S.

Miner's Journal, of Pottsville, given an account of an explosion of fire-damp on Wed last, at the colliery worked by Mr Geo Rich, on the west branch of Mount Carbon road, known as Lewis vein; followed by choke-damp: John Toley was extricated & found dead.

Public sale: by virtue of a deed of trust from Wm Hodge & wife to the undersigned, dated Jun 21, 1843, recorded in liber J B B, one of the land records of PG Co, Md:

sale on Sep 25, on the premises, the farm now in the possession of the said Hodge, containing about 124 acs. This farm is near Addison's Chapel, PG Co. –N C Stephen, C C Hyatt, Trustees

Paul Kinchy, having declined business & rented out his Confectionary Establishment to Mr John Miller, recommends Mr Miller, his successor. Location: south side of Pa ave, between 10th & 11th sts.

Mrd: on Sep 1, by Rev O Ege, Mr Geo R Ruff to Miss Sarah Jane, eldest d/o Jas Crandall, all of Wash City.

Mrd: on Aug 31, by Rev Dr Johns, at the residence of Mrs J C Washington, John S Wright, of Chicago, Ill, to Catherine Blackburn, d/o the late Henry S Turner, of Wheatland, Jefferson Co, Va.

Died: yesterday, after a short & severe illness, Henry Stone, of Wash City, in his 50th year. His funeral is this morning at 9 o'clock, from his late residence.

Died: on Aug 30, of typhus fever, Saml Bender, in his 16th year, s/o Jacob A Bender, of Wash City.

Lost, Uriel *Glasscock's draft, accepted by S E Scott, no date, at 88 days, for $1,000. Finder will confer a favor by leaving it at the Bank of Wash, or Corcoran & Rigg's, Wash. –Uriel *Glasscock [2 splgs.]

Died: in Fauquier Co, Va, Mrs Sarah Chunn, w/o Andrew Chunn, in her 58th year. She was an excellent wife, mother, & hospitable neighbor. Within 2 weeks after the decease of Mrs Chunn, on Aug 25, died her venerable relict, Andrew Chunn, in his 79th year. Fauquier has lost one of its most respectable citizens. The painful illness of which he died was but of 30 hours' duration. He was one of the oldest magistrates of Fauquier at the time of his decease.

Estray cow taken up by the subscriber near Bladensburg: owner can have by proving property & paying charges. –Richd Sedgewick

SAT SEP 5, 1846
From *Fort Leavenworth*: we regret to announce the death of Lt Col Allen, who was in command of the btln of Mormon infty at the post, on their route to join the army under Gen Kearney. He died on Aug 23, of congestive fever. Col Allen belonged to the regular army, in which he held the rank of Capt. He was detached for this special service by Gen Kearney. The last 2 companies of Col Price's regt left *Fort Leavenworth* on Aug 23.

Servant Wanted. Female servant, white or colored, a good plain cook, washer, & ironer, will find a good place in a small family. Apply to E Stubbs, G, between 8th & 9th sts.

Atlantic & Ohio Telegraph: the Dirs have chosen John B Trevor, Tresurer of their Company. The line will be pushed forward with all speed to the Ohio river. Efforts are making to reach Cincinnati before Jan.

Trustee's sale: by deed of trust, executed to me on May 26, 1845, by Philmond E Keech, of Chas Co, Md: I will expose at public sale, on Oct 7, on the premises, all that tract of land called **Maxwell's Seat**, otherwise called **Maxwell Hall**, upon which the said Philmond E Keech now resides. This tract is near Benedict, in said county, & contains about 600 acres, more or less. It has upon it a comfortable dwlg & all necessary out-houses. The terms of sale, as prescribed by the deed of trust, are cash. –John D Bowling, trustee

Grocerier, & Liquors, at auction: on Sep 10, at the Grocery store of T C Farquhar, corner of H & 7th sts. Also, the store fixtures, oil cans, lamps, counter, & shelving. –A Green, auctioneer

Died: on Sep 1, Mr Robt Speir, of Wash City, aged about 27 years.

Sheep for sale: 150 head Saxony & Meriono Sheep for sale, the property of the late Hachaliah Baily, dec'd. The above sheep were selected from flocks in Connecticut, & brought to Md in the fall of 1845. Address Jos T Baily, Rockville, Montg Co, Md. –Mary R Baily

New Fall Goods: ginghams, silks, plaids, Lama cloth, & Silk-warp Alpacas. Walter Harper & Co, Pa ave, between 9th & 10th sts.

MON SEP 7, 1846
The will of Louis Bonaparte, ex-King of Holland, who died lately at Florence, is an interesting document. It implies that he was enormously rich. Louis Napoleon, the ex-prisoner of Ham, inherits enough to equip another expedition for the imperial crown of France.

Oregon country: letter from Rev Mr Spalding to Joel Palmer, who, hailing from Oregon, is at present at Laurel, in Indiana, & has there received this letter. Nez Peres Mission, Clearwater River, Oregon Territory, Apr 7, 1846. The Oregon Territory is divided into 3 great divisions, the Lower, Middle, & Upper Regions: a most desirable climate, has fertility of soil, & rivers & mountains. [Description of Oregon continued.]

A letter from Rome of Jul 26 says: "A picture of Michael Angelo & another of Raphael have just been discovered here-the first representing the placing of Christ in the tomb, & the other the portrait of the celebrated Cardinal del Monte, similar to the fresco in the Vatican. Both works were purchased amongst a number of old, valueless pictures, one by Mr McCall, a young Scotch painter, & the other by M Cardeni, a broker."

From latest European papers. 1-The ranson demanded for the release of M Perpigna, who was carried off by banditti when traveling near Lerida, not having been sent at the time appointed, the ruffians murdered their victim. The body of the unfortunate gentleman has been found in a deep well near the road from Juncoso to Torregrosa, into which it had been thrown having stabs from a knife. A heavy stone was attached to the body in order to sink it. 2-Count de la Forest, Peer of France, had just died, at an advanced age. 3-The Baron de Damoiseau, member of the academy of Sciences, section of Astronomy, died the day before yesterday at Issy, near Paris. 4-Prince Maximilian, heir to the Crown of Bavaria, now in France, is in his 35th year. In 1842 he married Princess Marie Hedwige, cousin of the King of Prussia.

Francis Grice, naval constructor at the Brooklyn Navy Yard, has been appointed to the ofc of Chief Naval Constructor, to fill the vacancy created by the decease of Saml Humphreys. He will removed to Washington as soon as the sloop of war **Albany** is completed, which vessel was built under his direction.
[Sep 9th newspaper: Official Correction: Mr Grice has not been appointed Chief Naval Constructor. The ofc existed without any special warrant of law; the Sec of Navy determined to leave the Naval Constructors on an equal footing, & not to continue the doubtful ofc. Mr Grice has been called to Wash, for the temporary duty in connexion with his present ofc. -Union]

This is the day appointed by law for the first meeting of the Regents of the Smithsonian Institution. By direction of the Pres of the U S, a room in the Genr'l Post Ofc has been appropriated for the temporary use of the Regents, who will assemble at 12 o'clock.

Wm G Moorhead, of Ohio, appointed by the Pres, to be Consul of the U S at Valparaiso, vice Eben R Dorr, recalled.

We learn from Wilmington that Judge Rodney, the father of the late Rep in Congress from Delaware, & who has himself been prominent in his native State, died on Fri last, aged 75 years. Of a Revolutionary stock, he has borne himself in all his relations of life with unimpeachable integrity.

Genteel furniture at auction on Sep 9, at the residence of the Rev E Jones, on Prospect st, near High st. -Edw S Wright, auctioneer

Auction of the stock of dry goods, boots, shoes, & hats at the store of B Brien, near the market, on Sep 10. -Edw S Wright, auctioneer [Also, sale of the furniture & real estate, at auction, on Sep 11: at the residence of B Brien, near the market. Sale of the excellent 2 story brick house & lot, now occupied by Mr Brien. Also, the frame house adjoining, with the brick bldgs attached, fronting on Warehouse Alley.]

Mrd: on Sep 1, by Rev Mr Eggleston, Geo Washington Markward to Miss Eliz L Clarke, all of Wash City.

Mrd: in Lowell, by Rev Dr Putnam, of Roxbury, John Kebler, Counsellor at Law, of Cincinnati, to Miss Lucy Eliot, y/d/o the late Rev Jacob Abbot, of Windham, N H. [No date-appears recent.]

Died: on Fri last, Mary Debby, d/o Henry R Randall, of Wash City, aged 15 years.

Died: yesterday, at his residence, near the Navy Yard, after a short illness, Robt Middleton, in his 42nd year. His funeral is this evening at 3 o'clock.

Died: on Aug 29, at the residence of her brother-in-law, Mr Wm Burroughs, in Wash City, after a long & painful illness, Miss Rebecca Maria Greenfield, formerly of St Mary's Co, Md. A devoted dght, an affectionate sister, a constant friend; to know her was to love her; she lived a Christian.

Nurse wanted: a female, well qualified as a sick nurse, can obtain a situation by applying at the residence of Col Saml Burche.

Piano forte, household & kitchen furniture at auction on Sep 7, at the residence of Mr Amorige, on D st, between 6th & 7th sts. –A Green, auctioneer

TUE SEP 8, 1846
The <u>Smithsonian Institution</u>. The Regents of this Institution assembled in this city yesterday, in obedience to the appointment of the law creating the Institution. There were present:

The V Pres of the U S	Hon Rufus Choate, of Mass
The Chief Justice of the U S	Hon Richd Rush, of Pa
Hon Geo Evans, of Maine	Dr Gideon Hawley, of N Y
Hon L S Pennybacker, of Va	Prof A D Bache, of Wash
Hon W J Hough, of N Y	Col J G Totten, of the Corps of Engineers
Hon R D Owen, of Indiana	
Hon H W Hilliard, of Alabama	

Absent, the Hon W C Preston, of S C, who is detained in the South by indisposition, & the Hon Sidney Breese, who had proceded home to Illinois before his appointment, & of course could not have received notice early enough to enable him to return to Washington in time for the meeting. [Sep 9th newspaper: The Board of Regents was fully organized by the unanimous election of the Hon Geo M Dallas, Vice Pres of the U S, as Chancellor of the Institution, & the appointment of the Hon Mr Hough, one of the Regents, as Secretary of the Institution, whose services are of course gratuitous, & his appointment designed to be temporary, the Board at present, now being prepared to make a permanent choice.]

Prof Dew, of Wm & Mary College, Va, died in Paris a few days previous to the sailing of the last steamer. He arrived in that city only the day before his death.

Cambridge [Md] Chronicle: Gordon M Handy, Clerk of the Worcester Co Court, died at his residence in that county on Thu last. He was on several occasions a member of the Legislature of Md, & was a gentlemen of fine attainments.

Springfield, Mass, Sep 4. 1-Mr Wm Merriam, about 19 years of age, s/o Mr Wm E Merriam, of Greenfield, died on Wed from an accident on Mon last. He was employed in the grinding room of Messrs J Russell & Co's cutlery establishment in Greenfield, when his leg was caught by the drum of the wheel & his leg was crushed. His leg was amputated by Drs Deane of Greenfield, & Williams of Deerfield, but the shock was too great to his system. 2-An 18 year old girl, by the name of Hamilton, was killed in an accident in one of the carpet factories at Thompsonville yesterday. -Republican

Caution: I hereby forewarn all persons from harboring or hiring my son, Wm T Garner, as he has absconded from my house, he being yet under my control until he arrives at the age of 21 years. The law will be put in force against any that disregard this caution. –Saml Gardner, near Brandywine, PG Co, Md

Mrd: on Sep 5, in Wash City, by Rev J M Hanson, Mr Jas T Wolfenden, of Balt Co, to Miss Eliza T Brown, of Anne Arundel Co, Md.

Mrd: on Sep 3, in Phil, by Rt Rev Alonzo Potter, Mr Jos Jackson Halsey, of Fredericksburg, Va, to Miss Mildred Jackson Morton, only d/o Jeremiah Morton, of Culpeper Co, Va.

To the next of kin of John Justice, dec'd: In the matter of Wm H Bridges & Sarah his wife, John Justice, Wm Duncan & Eliz his wife, Warren Durham & Nancy his wife, Allen Justice, David Justice, Keziah Justice, Eliz Justice, Sarah Justice, Allen Robertson, Nathl Robertson, Stephen Robertson, David Robertson, Merrit Robertson, John Robertson, Wm Thompson & Eliz his wife, Wm Justice, Clayborn Justice, Wesley Edwards & Dolly his wife, & Franklin Freeman & Sarah his wife, plntfs, & Stephen Pleasants, exc of the last will of Stephen Justice, dec'd: dfndnts. Pursuant to an order of the Supreme Court of N C, directing me to inquire & state to the Court who were the children of John Justice, dec'd, [a brother of the testator, Stephen Justice,] living at the death of the said testator, to wit, in 1835, & whether any of them are since dead, & if dead, who is or are their personal reps; I do hereby give notice to all such persons, to come in & make out their kindred before me, at the ofc of said Court, in the city of Raleigh, on the 2nd Mon in Mar next, as, in default thereof, they will be excluded from all benefit in the distribution of a fund now in said Court. –Edmund B Freeman, Clerk

Died: on Sep 6, Mr Chas Straham, aged 50 years. Mr Straham has resided amongst us for many years, & is well known as an accomplished instructor of youth. His funeral is this morning, from his late residence on H st north, at 9 o'clock. His friends & acquaintances, & former & late pupils are invited to attend.

Died: on Sep 5, at the house of her son-in-law, Mr Thos Mustin, of Wash City, Mrs Mary Yoe, in the full triumphs of Christian love, aged nearly 70 years.

Died: on Sep 5, after a long & painful illness, in her 58th year, Mrs Martha Cook, a native of Lancashire, England, but for the last 28 years a resident of Wash City.

Died: on Sep 2, at the Fauquier White Sulphur Springs, Va, of congestive fever, Mrs Susan R Zantzinger, consort of Capt J P Zantzinger, U S Navy, of Cedar Grove, Norfolk Co, Va. This estimable lady arrived at the Springs just a week previous to her death, &, having been sick on the road, retired immediately to bed. Her disease baffled all the tender assiduities of her friends & the skill of her physicians. Her afflicted husband & dght were with her.

Died: on Sep 2, at New Haven, Conn, Chas Calvert Stuart, of Fairfax Co, Va, aged 50 years. For many days his sufferings were acute, but his end was peaceful & happy. Although not permitted to die in the bosom of his family circle, his last hours were soothed by the presence of a devoted wife, sister, & dght, who lavished on him every attention in the power of affection to bestow on suffering humanity.

A colored woman, Dolly, belonging to the estate of Richd Wilder, of Camden Co, N C, died on Aug 2, at age 123 years. She survived her husband some 3 or 4 years, who was 119 at the time of his death. They lived together as man & wife nearly 90 years.

M Kilmiste announces that having taken up permanent residence in Wash, he is prepared to give instruction in the most fashionable style of Dancing: Odeon Hall, 4½ st & Pa ave.

By order of the Chancellor of the State of Delaware, sitting in Newcastle Co, will be exposed to sale, at public vendue, on Oct 8, at the house of Isaac H Register, inn-keeper, in the town & hundred of Newcastle & county aforesaid, the mansion & grounds late the residence of Geo Read, dec'd, in said town. The mansion is 40 feet front by 48 feet deep, more or less; 4 rooms on a floor; the parlors & 2 of the chambers [12 in number] are fitted with grates, & there is a pump in the cellar. The house commands a view of the Delaware. Also, the lots adjoining the above, extending from Front to Market st, in said town, having very good sites for bldg on both streets. Also, the wharf lot, east of said grounds. With the improvements &

appurtenances, being part of the real estate of Mary G Read. Terms of the sale made known, by Wm T Read, Trustee of Mary G Read.

Belmont for sale: the subscriber wishing to engage in some other business, desirous of disposing of his plantation at private sale: tract contains 290 acres, adjoining Bowieville & the plantations of Mr Chas Hill, Thos E Berry, & Dr Stewart, in the Forest of PG Co, Md. There is a convenient & comfortable new 2 story frame dwlg, of 9 rooms, with all the necessary outhouses in good repair. –Richd C Bowie

John Riggles has recommenced business as a Draper & Tailor, on the west side of 8th st, near Pa ave.

For rent: a commodious 3 story brick dwlg: the last house westerly in Cox'r row, Gtwn, at present in the occupancy of the subscriber. Possession given on Oct 1. –B Forrest, Proprietor

Household & kitchen furniture at auction on Sep 10, at the residence of Chas Fletcher, at the corner of 13th & F sts. -R W Dyer, auct

WED SEP 9, 1846
Miss H McCormick & sister have resumed the duties of their School: residence on 4½ st, in Mr Ward's row of bldgs.

Land at public sale: will be sold at my residence, on Sep 14, near Mount Pisgah meeting house, Montg Co, Md, the farm upon which I now reside, containing 100 acres, improved with a new dwlg-house & kitchen. Land adjoins Col J Jackson, Mr Jas Crawford, Rev F S Evans, & others. –John S Bogan, Mongt Co, Md

Appropriations made during the 1st session of the 29th Congress:
Compensation of Pres of the U S: $25,000.
Compension of Vice Pres of the U S: $5,000.
To pay F Gardner, late Acting U S naval storekeeper to the African squadron, from Aug 24, 1844, when Floyd Waggaman ceased to receive salary, until Dec 9, 1844, when Francis Alexander proceeded to the post, 3 months & 15 days, at $1,500 per annum: $437.50
To pay the legal reps of Thos H Storm, for a balance due to him as agent for the prisoners at Barbadoes: $2,274.26.
For refunding to Jas Buchanan, late her Britannic Majesty's Consul at N Y C, moneys disbursed by him, & for compensating him for services performed in respect to the slaver *Catherine*, condemned & sold at the suit of the U S, the sum of: $2,144.75.
Payment in full to Benj E Green for services while employed in Mexico as Charge d'Affaires: $3,000.

For the ransom of 2 white boys, Gillis Doyle & Thos Pearce, held by the Camanches in bondage, delivered to the agents of the Gov't: $500.

To pay J A S Acklin, U S District atty for the northern district of Alabama, for professional services in defending Capt Jas H Rogers & Lt Roberts, in suits brought to recover damages for an act done by them, under the order of a superior ofcr, whilest in the service of the U S; also, to pay to Jos Bryan, agent of Wm Whitfield, for purchasing & distributing stock animals to the Creek Indians, pursuant to an article of a treaty made with said Indians: $489.

Life annuity to chief Bob Cole, stipulated in the 10th article of the treaty of Jan 20, 1825: $150.

Payment to Horatio Greenough for a group of statues to adorn the eastern portico of the Capitol: $8,000.

Payment of the excess of duties paid upon wines imported from Portugal into the U S by John Osborn, of
N Y C: $1,718.42.

Excess of the excess duties paid upon wines imported from Portugal into the U S by Isaac Winslow & Son, of Boston: $1,019.54.

Payment of the excess of duties paid upon wines imported from Portugal into the U S by Alex'r Soltan, of
N Y: $885.96.

Balance due to the Wyandots on the valuation of their improvements on the lands in Ohio & Michigan, ceded by the Wyandots to the U S, according to the appraisement made by Moses H Kirby & John Walker, pursuant to the 5th article of the treaty made between the U S & the Wyandots, at Upper Sanduskey, Mar 17, 1842: $57,094.24.

For payment to Wm Day, & the chiefs of the Orchard party of the Oneidas, stipulated in the 13th article of the treaty with the Six Nations of N Y, Jan 15, 1838: $2,000.

Sudden death: Thos F Jones, of Chelsea, a constable, came to his death in that town last evening, while assisting an ofcr from East Boston in catching 2 young rascals who had been committing depredations upon a garden, he suddenly fell, in running, & expired instantly. Death was occasioned by disease of the heart. -Boston Journal

Official, by the Pres of the U S of America. A Proclamation. Act of Congress approved Jul 9, 1846, entitled "An act to retrocede the county of Alexandria, in D C, to the State of Va." Done at the city of Wash, Sep 7, 1846, & of the Independence of the U S in the 71st year. By the Pres: Jas K Polk -N P Tryst, Acting Sec of State.

Mrd: on Sep 8, in Gtwn, by Rev Mr Gassaway, Thos Marshall, of Chas Co, Md, to Miss Sarah M Wyles, of D C.

THU SEP 10, 1846
Miss Mary Sullivan: Ladies Dress Maker: establishment removed from 13th st to 7th & F sts.

For rent: house on 10th st now occupied by Mrs Bronaugh as a boarding-house, aa few door north of Pa ave, containing 14 rooms. Possession on Oct 1. -R W Dyer, auct

Very handsome & superior furniture at auction on Sep 17, at the residence of the Hon Mr Bancroft, late Sec of the Navy, on Pa ave, between 16th & 17th sts. -R W Dyer, auct

Appropriations made during the 1st session of the 29th Congress:
1-That the proper accounting ofcrs of the Treasury are hereby authorized & directed to allow to Wm H Stiles, Charge d'Affaires to Austria, his salary from May 10th to Jun 30th, 1845, & to pay the same out of any other unexpended balance of the appropriations for salaries of the charges des affaires of the U S-[Indefinite.]
2-By the act for the relief of the legal reps of Pierre Menard, Josiah T Betts, Jacob Feaman, & Edmund Roberts, of the State of Illinois, sureties of Felix St Vrain, late Indian agent, dec'd. Being the amount of salary of said St Vrain remaining unpaid at the time of his death, & the sum of $200, paid by him to Mr Farnham to hand to gunsmith & blacksmith, & for which his account was never credited, with 6% interest per annum from Dec 13, 1839, being the time when the execution against the sureties of said St Vrain was satisfied: $427.40
3-Act for the relief of Thos Ap Catesby Jones: it being the balance due him on his accounts as rendered to the U S: $1,501.78
4-Act for the relief of Isaiah Parker: for arrears of pension from Mar 4, 1823, to Oct 31, 1836: $328.
5-Act for the relief of John McAllister: being the amount still due him as encouragement for his enlistmant into the army of the U S, under the provisions of the act of Congress approved Jan 27, 1814: $50.
6-Act for the relief of John Carr, John Batty, & Saml Stevenson, seamen on board the whale ship **Margaret**: for their detention, under the authority of the U S, 538 days each, at the rate of $1.25 per day, amounting to $2,016.50, to given evidence on the trial of Harper, Rodman, Latham, & Hummstor, for mutiny & setting fire to the above named ship whilst on a whaling voyage in the Pacific Ocean: $2,016.50
7-Act for the relief of the heirs of Dr John Gray, dec'd: $5,000
8-Act for the relief of Richd Hargreave Lee: for moiety of the penalty of $400, paid by said Lee, by mistake, for a breach of the revenue laws committed by him on Dec 30, 1829, after deducting from said penalty of $400 the amount of the true penalty which ought to have been paid by said Lee, according to the provisions of the act of Mar 3, 1823: $160.
9-Act of the relief of John R Williams: for damages done to his farm, known by the name of *Springwell Farm*, situated in the then Territory, now State of Michigan, while in the occupancy of the U S troops, in 1813 & 1814, & in full payment for said damages: $2,000.
10-Act for the relief of Gregory Thomas, & others: being $300 for expenses incurred by them for repairs, & $500 for detention occasioned by injuries to their pilot-boat,

by a collision with the U S steamer **Colonel Harney**, on the ocean, on the night of Oct 1, 1840: $800.

11-Act for the relief of Saml D Walker, of Balt: Being the amount of duty levied [on 441 seroons of Spanish leaf tobacco] by the act of Mar 2, 1833: $616.27.

12-Act for the relief of the heirs & legal reps of Cyrus Turner, dec'd: for depredations & injuries committed by that band of Sioux Indians known & designated as the North Sursitons of Lake Traverse Indians; which sum of money shall be deducted from any annuity which may now be or hereafter may become due from this Gov't to said band of Indians: $1,500.

13-Act to allow Elijah White reimbursement of expenses incurred by him as acting subagent of Indian affairs west of the Rocky Mountains: $2,176.59

14-Act for the relief of Abraham Horbach: being the amount of a draft drawn by Jas Reeside on the Post Ofc Dept, dated Apr 18, 1835, payable on Jan 1, 1836, & accepted by the Treasurer of the Post Ofc Dept; which said draft was endorsed by said Abraham Horbach, at the instance of the said Jas Reeside, & the amount drawn from the Bank of Phil, & at maturity said draft was protested for non-payment, & said Horbach became liable to pay, in consequence of his endorsement, & did pay, the full amount of said draft [including interest.]: $8,197.21

15-Act for the relief of Henry Etting: being a portion of the amount expended by him in prosecuting a suit against the Commercial Bank of New Orleans, to recover public moneys deposited therein: $2,606.

16-Act for the relief of John E Holland: [Indefinite.]

17-Act for the relief of Amos Kendall: for such counsel fees paid by said Amos Kendall, or bound himself to pay, & all other necessary or unusual expenses incurred & not prepaid by plntfs in the suit instituted by Wm B Stokes & others against him for acts performed whilst Postmaster Genr'l of the U S: [Indefinite.]

18-Act for the relief of John Chasseaud, the consul of the U S for Syria in Palestine: for salary while acting as said counsul: [Indefinite.]

19-Act to provide for the final settlement of the accounts of John Crowell, late agent for the Creek Indians: [Indefinite.]

20-Act for the relief of Wm B Lang: for excess duties to this amount, paid by said Lang: $415.22

21-Act for the relief of the heirs of Robt Fulton: for claims of the said Robt Fulton against the U S, due at the time of the death of the said Fulton, for inventing floating steam-batteries, & superintending the construction of the steam frig **Fulton**, for the detention of, & damages to, his steamboat **Vesuvius**, & for the great benefits conferred on the country by his improvements in the application of steam to navigation: $76,300.

22-Act for the relief of Jas Gee: for arrearage of pension at the rate of $4 per month, from Sep 22, 1837, to Dec 3, 1842: $230.

23-Act for the relief of the owners of the ship **Herald**, of Balt: for extra tonnage duty charged upon said ship by the collector of the port of N Y, in Sep, 1844: [Indefinite.]

24-Act for the relief of Nathan Smith, Chas K Smith, & others: for fishing bounty: [Indefinite.]

25-Act for the relief of Richd Kidd & Benj Kidd: for balance remaining unpaid & interest thereon of a judgment recovered by them in the U S circuit court for the southern district of N Y against Saml Swartwout, late collector of the port of N Y, for duties illegally exacted: [Indefinite.]
26-Act for the relief of Jas Erwin, of Arkansas, & others: for losses sustained by contracts with the U S: [Indefinite.]
27-Act for the relief of John Jones, surviving partner of John Jones & Chas Souder: [Indefinite.]
28-Act for the relief of Langtry & Jenkins: for damage sustained by them in consequence of the violation of a contract on the part of the Gov't agents, in refusing to receive 3,000 pairs of shoes contracted to be received at the Cherokee agency, in the summer of 1838, for the use of poor & destitute Cherokees, to equip them for their removal west: $1,443.65
29-Act for the relief of Nathl Stafford: for amount of arrearage due to him, at the rate of $8 per month, from May 17, 1814, to Mar 30, 1846, at which time his pension, already allowed, commenced under existing laws: $3,060.
30-Act for the relief of Saml D Enochs: for a mare lost in the service of the U S: $80.
31-Act for the relief of the legal reps of Geo Duval, a Cherokee Indian: [Indefinite.]
32-Act for the relief of Abraham B Fannin: [Indefinite.]
33-Act for the relief of Putney & Riddle: [Indefinite.]
34-Act for the relief of Lewis De Russey, late a paymaster in the army of the U S: [Indefinite.]
35-Act for the relief of Peter Gorman: [Indefinite.]
36: By the resolution declaratory of the act passed Aug 23, 1842, entitled: An act for the relief of Chas F Sibbald: [Indefinite.]
37-Act for the relief of Jos Kemball: for work done on Madison barracks, at Detroit, in 1816: $198.47
38-Act for the relief of Geo D Spencer: for taking the census of 2 precincts in Montgomery Co, Md, in 1840: $76.23
39-Act for the relief of Adam McCulloch: for his legal title of *Goat island*, in Maine, [whereon a lighthouse has been built by the U S]: $300.
40-Act to establish the Smithsonian Institute, for the increase & diffusion of knowledge among men: for the erection of suitable bldgs, & for other current incidental expenses, such sum of interest as may have accrued on fund, on Jun 1 next: $242,129.00
41-Act for the relief of Semington Buffenbarger: for money wrongfully received by the Receiver of the land ofc at Waupaukonetta district, in the State of Ohio, for the n e quarter of the n e quarter of section 4, in township 6 south, of range 8 east: $50.
42-Act for the relief of John G Pierie, for the sum exacted on the entry of the brig **Aldrick** at the N Y custom-house, as foreign tonnage, because of having foreign seamen, who were shipped from Oporto from necessity: $102.25
43-Act for the relief of Mrs Pike, wid/o the late Gen Pike: for compensation for 2 years' extraordinary services in 2 exploring expeditions by the said Genr'l [then Lt] Pike to the sources of the Mississippi, in 1805 & 1806, & to the sources of the Arkansas & Great Platte, & through New Mexico, in 1806 & 1807: $3,000.

Trial of Coleman C May, for the murder of Wm J McDearmon, of Appomattox Co, last fall, was ended at Amherst courthouse, Va, on Thu last, after 11 days: jury gave in a verdict of acquittal without leaving the jury box.

Died: on Sep 5, at Kingston, Canada, Sarah, w/o Mr Francis Hall, senior editor & proprietor of the N Y Commercial Adv, in her 60th year. Mr & Mrs Hall were making their annual tour through Canada; &, having visited Quebec & Montreal, were proceeding to the Falls. On Mon, Mrs Hall was attacked with a fit of apoplexy, & on Wed with a second fit, from which time there was not expectation that she would recover.

FRI SEP 11, 1846

American Colonization Society will send an expedition to Liberia, to sail from Norfolk, Va, about Nov 15 next: excecutors & others having slaves under their care intended for this vessel, to to have them ready in time. They should be well supplied with beds, bedding, clothing, cooking & farming utensils, & such other articles as may be necessary to their comfort & happiness. The present demand in Liberia is for Teachers & Ministers of the Gospel. Free people of color competent to discharge the duties of either of these professions, is earnestly requested. –Wm McLain, Sec: Sep 9, 1846, Colonization Rooms, Wash.

Mr F G McConnell, a Rep in Congress from Alabama, yeterday, in a fit of delirum, at the St Chas Hotel, in Wash City, committed suicide by stabbing himself in the abdomen & then cutting his throat. Mr French, Clerk of the House of Reps, has taken charge of the remains to give them proper interment.

Wash Corp: 1-Ptn from Matthew Wright & Jos Rapetti: referred to Cmte on Improvements. 2-Ptns of Edw Sweeny & of C Columbus: referred to Cmte of Claims.

Appointments by the Pres: 1-Geo Bancroft, of Mass, to be Envoy Extra & Minister Pleni of the U S for the United Kingdom of Great Britain & Ireland, vice Louis McLane, recalled at his own request. 2-John Y Mason, of Va, to be Sec of the Navy of the U S, vice Hon Geo Bancroft, resigned.

Trustee's sale of valuable land: by deed of trust from Michl Downey to the subscriber, dated Mar 13, 1844, recorded in Liber W B 107, folios 172 thru 174, of the land records for Wash Co, D C: dale on Oct 1, of the following: part of the tract called **Long Meadows**, beginning at the corner of a half acre, which had been sold to the Turnpike Road Co, & running to the corner of the land of the same tract sold to Alex'r Forrest; thence to to outlines of the whole tract of **Long Meadow**, it being on a line with the road leading to Bladensburg; to the beginning, containing 2 acres of land; it being the same property which was conveyed by Patrick McGee to John Kincart on or about Jun 12, 1841, with all improvements thereon.
–Thos Collins, Trustee -R W Dyer, auct

Died: on Sep 9, at his residence in Wash City, Mr Rezin St Clare, aged 83 years.

At Exeter, Mr C H Cole met his death on Aug 17 from the effects of a sixpence, which he had accidentally swallowed 8 years before. After death a post mortem examination found the coin was lodged in the right bronchia, the lung being in a state of complete gangrene.

Maj Thos McGough & a man named Bigelow were killed on the Portage, Pa railroad on Aug 31. The cause was the breaking of the crank, which was caught by the driving wheel of the locomotive. The accident also caused injuries to several of the other passengers.

Savannah papers inform us of the death, in that place, of Dr Wm A Caruthers, formerly of Lexington, Va. He had won considerable distinction by several novels, illustrative of the ancient manners & customs of Va. The last of these, "The Knights of the Horse Shoe," was sent to us a few days ago by a friend of the author. –Richmond Whig [No date-recent news.]

Mrd: on Sep 6, at St Peter's Church, by the Rev Mr Van Horseigh, Agrigole Favier, of Wash, to Miss Albertine Marshal, of Ghent, in Belgium.

Mrd: on Sep 7, in St Luke's Church, Phil, by Rev W W Spear, Saml Frey Glenn, of New Orleans, to Mary Virginia, d/o Col John H Sheburne, all formerly of Wash.

SAT SEP 12, 1846
Mrd: on Sep 9, at Gettysburg, Pa, by the Rev J C Watson, John H Oyster, of Wash, to Miss Phebe Ann Flohr, of Gettysburg.

Died: on his return from the Springs, at Buchanan, Bottetourt Co, Va, after an illness of 2 weeks, John C Herbert, late of PG Co, Md, aged 71 years.
[No date-recent item.]

Died: Wed last, in PG Co, Md, Rebecca, y/d/o Henry J & Mary Rose Bowling, aged 5 years & 6 months.

Capt Thompson, of the U S Army, was prostrated by lightning, on the parade-ground at Jefferson Barracks, Missouri, on Sep 2, while exercising a squad. Two privates were also slightly injured. The fluid tore up the earth directly in front of the troops.

Household furniture at auction: by virtue of a writ of distrain, to me directed, against the goods & chattels of Jas Cuthbert, dec'd, to satisfy Saml Miller for rent due & in arrears: sale on Sep 18, at the house occupied by the said J Cuthbert, on Pa ave, known as the Adelphi Hotel, 3rd door east of 4½ st. –Thos Woodward, Deputy Marshal -B Homans, auctioneer

A 4 year old d/o Mr Stephen McCalla, of Harrisburg, died last week after eating the berries of a poisonous place called nightshade.

Balt, Sep 11. Very beautiful sword presented to Capt Ker, U S Dragoons, now in this city, by his friends in Balt, as a testimonial of their regard for him. The Capt soon returns to join Gen Taylor's army, with whom he fought with on May 8 & 9.

MON SEP 14, 1846
Points of Honor: Col Montgomery was shot in a duel about a dog; Col Ramsey in one about a servant; Mr Featherston in one about a recruit; Stern's father in one about a goose; Gen Barry was challenged by a Capt Smith for declining a glass of wine at a dinner on a steamboat, although the Gen had pleaded as an excuse that wine invariably made him sick; & Lt Crowther lost his life in a duel because he was refused admittance to a club of pigeon shooters. -Noah's Messenger

Loss of life by the bursting of the boiler of the steamboat **Excelsior**, in N Y, on Thu last: Danl Slauson, a native of New Lebanon, Conn, aged 78, father-in-law of Alderman Gilbert of N Y; Wm Hall, carpenter, of N Y; & Geo Van Weart, of Coxouckle, the 2nd engineer. They all died at the City Hospital a few hours after they were taken off the wreck. One of the hands, named William, is missing.

T Leger Hutchinson was on Tue last elected May of Charleston, S C.

Anton Lizardo, near Vera Cruz, Aug 29, 1846. Loss of the beautiful U S brig **Truxton**, that sailed from here in the early part of the month for Tampico. On the 15th, a Scotchman was taken out of a Mexican prize to pilot him, but who, whether from design or accident, run him aground. Ofcrs attached to the **Truxton**, who have gone to Tampico: Cmder E W Carpender; Acting Master, Isaac N Briceland; Passed Midshipmen John P Bankhead, & Geo B Bissell; Purser, Geo F Cutter; Assist Surgeon, John S Messersmith; Midshipman, Simeon S Bassett; Capt's clerk, H Wilkinson; together with about 50 petty ofcrs & seamen. Lts Hunter & Berryman are on board the ship **St Mary's**. [Sep 24 newspaper: Cmder Carpender as late as Aug 24, was then at Tuxpan. His disaster was not the result of any misplaced confidence in the Scotch captain whom he had on board, but from the peculiar character of the coast.]

Notice: committed to the jail of Kent Co, Md, on Aug 29, a negro man who calls himself Alfred Harris: appears to be about 25 years old: says he is free, that he was born on Federal Hill, Balt City, that he has been a sailor a part of his life, & also worked at the brickmaking business. The owner, if any, is to come forward, prove property, pay charges, & take him away, or he will otherwise be discharged according to law. -Geo W Spencer, Sheriff, Kent Co, Sep 9, 1846.

Died: on Sep 12, Margaret Barrett, after a long protracted illness, aged 19 years. Her funeral is from the residence of her mother, Mrs Mary Barrett, on 9th st, near N Y ave, this morning at 10 o'clock.

Died: on Sep 5, after an illness of 13 days, Julia Louisa, 2nd d/o Robt B & Emeline Clokey, aged 17 years & 13 days.

Died: on Sep 6, in Richmond, Va, Mrs Mary Eliza G Jordan, aged 25 years, consort of David Jordan, & d/o Mr Chas A Grice, of Portsmouth, Va.

Braddock's defeat: it appears from the dispatch received at White Hall, on Aug 26, 1755, that the army under Braddock left *Fort Cumberland* in the latter part of Jun, reached on Jul 8 within 10 miles of the Forks of Monongahela, Pittsburg, on the 9th was met by the enemy & untterly defeated-Braddock mortally wounded, & died on the 13th. –Wm Darby

Cincinnati Atlas of Tue: Capts Moore & Ramsey, of this city, & Capt Bradley, of Sandusky, have all returned home, having been compelled to relinquish their respective commands for the present on account of continued sickness. These ofcrs all belong to the 1st Regt of Ohio volunteers; they are on furlough for 3 months. Maj Giddings, formerly capt of the Dayton Infty, has nearly recovered from his long illness, & Lt Brescount, of the same corps, is getting well. Capt Mitchell is lying dangerously ill at the hospital in Matamoros with the brain fever. His case was conceived extremely critical. Col Morgan & Lt Col Irwin, of the 2nd Regt, were in the hospital at Camargo. Capt Worthington, of the 2nd Regt, had the intermittent fever at Matamoros.

TUE SEP 15, 1846
Army Medical Board, lately in session in N Y C, has recommended the following for appointment to the Medical Staff of the Army:

Robt Newman, Pa	Josephus M Steiner, Ohio
Horace R Wirtz, Pa	Robt C Wickam, Va
Israel Moses, N Y	Chas P Dyerle, Va
John f Hammond, S C	Elisha J Bailey, Pa

Mrd: on Aug 20, at Ann Arbor, Michigan, by Rev Mr Taylor, Dr N K Maniates, of Marshall, Michigan, [formerly of Wash City,] to Miss M Arabella Becker, of the former place.

Died: at her residence, on Captiol Hill, after a short but painful illness, Mrs Philomela C Buck, wid/o the late Dr A A Buck, in her 52nd year. Her funeral is at 3 o'clock this day. [No death date given.] [Sep 16th newspaper correction: Mrs Buck was the wid/o the Hon D Azro A Buck, formerly a Rep in Congress from Vt, & not of *Doctor* Buck.]

Died: in Jul last, at the residence of her brother, Mr C D Kelly, in Boone Co, Indiana, Mrs Isabella McAller, wid/o the late John McAller, formerly of this city.

House to let: the dwlg house lately occupied by E Lindsley, on Pa ave, opposite to Coleman's Hotel. Apply to John P Ingle.

Groceries, feed & fixtures at auction: on Sep 16, at the store of John T Crow, on the Canal, his entire stock & fixtures. –E S Wright, auctioneer

WED SEP 16, 1846
The Boonslick [Missouri] Times states that there is now living in Prairie township, Howard Co, one of Harmer's old soldiers, who is yet hearty & active, has 22 children, 70 grandchildren, & 29 great grandchildren. Six of the old man's children are yet single. 55 of the number are now living in Prairie township.

Bloody affair at Pawpaw Island, at the foot of Millikin's Bend, on Mon: Col W B Minor had rented a woodyard on the island to Col Wilkinson. Minor, getting tired of the contract, wished Wilkinson to give it up. Wilkinson refused. Two sons of Minor, on Mon, secreted themselves in a hut on the island, & when Wilkinson & his 2 sons, & a man named Boggs appeared, the Minors fired upon them until they all fell. Col Wilkinson & one of his sons was killed on the spot, the other & Boggs were severely wounded. Col Minor & his 2 sons were arrested & imprisoned at Richmond, La, & the court finding no evidence against the father discharged him, & remanded the 2 sons to prison to be tried for murder. –Louisville Journal

Gen Jos Chandler, aged 75, a resident of Augusta, Maine, visited N Y C a few days since, & lodged at Walker's Hotel. He retired on Fri, but was found next morning, with his clothes on, lying on his bed, entirely dead. He was one of the general ofcrs of the last war, & served on the Northern frontier, & was for several years a Senator in Congress from Maine. [See Sep 19th newspaper.]

Late disaster on board the steamer **Enterprise**, on the Rio Grande. Killed-Enoch Tucker, A Boswell, Tenn; Mr Seaps, Texas; Thos Gaufney, N Y, 2nd cook. Badly wounded-Lt Dearing, of the Louisville Legion; Wm A Crook, C B Crook, Tenn; Capt Woods, Wm Grey, Jacob Bowridge, Thos Eagle, Texas; J C Howard, sutler, Balt; Jos Grigsby, Mr Hickey, sutlers, Louisville Legion; Taber, pilot; Thos Henepee, Saml Martin, Patrick Kelly, Frank Tallant, deck hands; J F Clark, mate. Slightly wounded: Milton Cunningham, Jas Wilson, Tenn; J Wheeler, J Humerick, Matthew Samson, Christian Coleman, Texas; j Downing, Mr Adams, sutlers, Louisville Legion; Edmond Newell, clerk; Capt Kelsey, Conn; W Arthines, fireman; Henry A Emmons, mate; Dr H S Tudor. [Sep 15th newspaper: The Matamoros Flag of Aug 26 informed that the steamer **Enterprise**, on her upward trip, having on board Capt Wood's company of Texas volunteers, with 2 companies, we believe, from Tenn, burst her boilers a short distance above Raynosa.]

Died: on Sep 13, in Balt, Wm John, in his 13th year, s/o Thos C Dunlevy, of that city.

Died: on Aug 29, in Nashville, Tenn, Mrs Needham Washington, late of Waterloo, Va, aged 64 years, after an illness of 6 weeks, sustained with great fortitude & exemplary Christian resignation.

Died: on Sep 9, at Brattleborough, Vt, Lt Col Greenleaf Dearborn, of the U S Army. He commenced his military career at a Lt of Artl, in Mar, 1812, & served with distinction during the war with Great Britain, & in that with the Seminole Indians. As a son, husband, father, soldier, & citizen, her presented an admirable illustration of those exalted principles which give luster to the human race. Col Dearborn left *Fort Snelling* [his late command on the Upper Mississippi] early in the spring, to join his regt serving with the army in Mexico; but, finding his health impaired, was unable to proceed to the South. On the recommendation of his surgeon, he reluctantly received leave of absence, & repaired to his native State.

Died: on Sep 8, in Wash City, Wm Wallace, aged 1 year & 8 months, y/s/o Josiah & Susannah Hoffman, of Balt.

Died: on Sep 9, at Cleveland, Ohio, Chas, s/o J Edmund Millard, of Wash City, aged about 15 months. The parents left this city about 2 weeks since with their sick child, in the vain hope that a change of atmosphere would restore him to health.

N Y, Sep 14, 1846. Govn'r Wright has pardoned Silas Tompkins, Lewis Knapp, & Anson K Burrill, anti-Renters. They were sentenced for 2 years, & had served 16 months of the time. The pardon restores them to the rights of citizenship.

Jesse Garner, well know in PG Co, Md, & to the police of Wash City, was arrested last Sun by ofcr Adams, under the charge of kidnapping a slave belonging to Mr Jos Soper, who resides near Mr Judson Naylor's. Garner brought the negro to the city tied on a horse, & then offered him for sale to Mr Josias Clements. Garner was committed to jail. [Sep 30th newspaper: Garner was released from confinement a few days ago; opinion of several gentlemen from PG Co, one of whom became Jesse's security, that he had no intention of kidnapping the negro, but committed the act while under the influence of strong drink. The prisoner made a solemn promise of reformation.]

For rent: 2 story brick dwlg-house on 13th st west, 2nd door north of E st north. Apply to B Willet, next door south.

THU SEP 17, 1846
Mrd: on Sep 15, by Rev E M P Wells, Mr Richd M Scott, of Fairfax Co, Va, to Miss Virginia, eldest d/o Dr Jas S Gunnell, of Wash City.

Mrd: on Sep 15, by Rev H Stringfellow, Mr Francis Lamb to Miss Eliz Sessford, all of Wash City.

Mrd: on Sep 6, by Rev H Stringfellow, Mr Benjamin F Price to Miss Mary Umphreys.

Mrd: on Sep 7, by Rev H Stringfellow, Mr Wm L H Smith to Miss Martha Ann Holland.

Mrd: on Sep 10, by Rev H Stringfellow, Mr Solomon Bell to Miss Catharine Snauber.

Died: yesterday, of pulmonary disease, Mr Thos Martin, in his 24th year. His funeral is from his late residence on Capitol Hill, today at 3 o'clock.

Died: on Sep 15, after a short illness, Wm B Laub, in his 38th year. His funeral is from his late residence, at 9 o'clock this morning.

Died: on Sep 16, Miss Julia Randall, d/o John Voorhees. Her funeral is from the residence of her father, near the corner of 10th & E sts, tomorrow at 4 o'clock.

Died: on Sep 15, in Wash City, of typhus fever, Henry E Stanley, of Blockley, Gloucestershire, England, in his 26th year. The friends & acquaintances of the dec'd, & different societies of which he was a member, are requested to attend his funeral today, at 2 o'clock, proceeding from the house of Mr T Barnard, 18th st, to McKendree Chapel, where the ceremonies will be performed.

Valuable farm at private sale: advertised to be sold at auction on Sep 15, was not sold, & will be sold for a great bargain. This farm is on the back road leading from Wash to Bladensburg, near the farms of Mr Tucker & Mr Bates. It contains 93 acres of good land, with a good dwlg-house. –A Green, Auctioneer & Cmmission Merchant, Concert Hall.

Jacob A Bender, Bricklayer, will attend to buildings, fixing grates, boilers, & all kinds of fireworks requiring brick flues; also, to measuring bricklayer's & stonemason's work. Residence on H st, next corner to 6th st. Orders may be left at the ofc of J L Smith, magistrate, on 8th st, near Pa ave.

Household furniture at auction on Fri next, at the late residence of Mrs James, on Pa ave, between 12th & 13th sts, over King's lace store. -R W Dyer, auct

FRI SEP 18, 1846
$100 reward for runaway negro man Cornelius Shaw, age 21 years.
–Y C Magruder, Wash

The Hon Saml A Foot died at his residence in Cheshire Sep 15, after an illness of some months'. He has served the State with great fidelity for many years, having been often a Rep in the Legislature, Speaker of the House, a Rep & Senator in Congress, & Govn'r of the State. –New Haven Palladium

The celebrated Elihu Burritt, the American Blacksmith, is at present engaged in a pedestrian tour through England, & has furnished the editors of the British papers with 26 receipts using Indian cornmeal.

Mrd: on Sep 14, at Burlington, N J, by Rt Rev Bishop Doane, Jas Morse, of Newburyport, Mass, to Mrs Josephine Nourse, d/o Arthur J Stansbury, of Wash.
+
Mrd: on Sep 15, at the same place [Burlington, N J,] Henry M Nourse to Cora, y/d/o the same.

Died: on Sep 5, Albert Greenwell, aged 1 year & 26 days, s/o B O & Eliz C Greenwell.

Died: on Sep 1, at Oakland, PG Co, Md, Saml Glenn Mayo, s/o Capt I Mayo, U S Navy, aged 2 years & 7 months.

Trustee's sale of house & lots: by deed of trust, recorded in Liber W B 116, folios 451 thru 453: sale on Oct 19, of lots 3, 6, 7, 13, 14, 15, & 16, in square 917, in Wash City, together with a comfortable 2 story frame dwlg house, nearly new, on one of the said lots. –E Evans, Trustee -B Homas, auctioneer

Local Affairs: Rev J P Donelan has been removed from the pastoral care of St Matthew's Church of Wash City to the Church of St Vincent de Paul, in Balt, Md, & that his brother, Rev Jas B Donelan, has been appointed pastor of St Matthew's in his stead. Rev Mr Parsons, of Balt, has been made assistant pastor of St Patrick's Church in place of Rev J B Donelan, transferred to St Matthew's.

Yesterday the Wash Light Infty, under command of Lt Tate, attended the funeral of the late Thos Martin, a much respected member of that corps. They march with reversed arms from the residence of the dec'd to St Patrick's grave-yard, where he was interred.

Wash Corp: 1-Ptn of H B Sawyer: referred to the Cmte of Claims. 2-Ptns of R R Golden, Josiah Goodrich, & of Jane Fagan: all referred to the Cmte of Claims. 3-Ptn of Conrad Finkman: referred to the Cmte of Claims. 4-Ptn of Benj Homans, praying remission of a fine: referred to the Cmte of Claims. 5-Ptn of Josiah Essex, praying payment of a balance due him for work done on the Wash Asylum: referred to the Cmte of Claims.

SAT SEP 19, 1846
Mrd: on Sep 16, in Wash City, by Rev H Stringfellow, Wm S Burch to Mary Hurdle.

Wash City property to be sold for taxes-Dec 12 next: -A Rothwell, Collector. [Tax year Chart: 1841 thru 1845: with additional years noted prior to 1841]
Alexander, John & Adelaide, & Edw F: 43-45

Alexander, Chas: 41-45
Adams, Geo R: 42-45
Adams, Jas: 42-45
Adams, Mgt: 43-45
Atkinson, Francis: 43-45
Atkinson, Geo: 43-45
Appleton, John: 42-45
Butler, Abraham: 42-45
Berry, Brooke M: 42-45
Bean, Benj: 43-45
Bean, Benj: 43-45
Burns, Chas: 41-45
Boteler, Chas W: 42-45
Birch, Geo A: 43-45
Birch, Geo A: 44-45
Barnes, Elias: 43-45
Bender, Jacob: 43-45
Burch, Jas A: 44-45
Beck, Lambert S: 43-45
Baker, Mary A: 42-45
Bestor, O H: 43-45
Brown, O B: 41-45
Brooke, Richd: 42-45
Burch, Saml & Offa Wilson: 40-45
Buist, Wm: 43-45
Bradley, Wm A: 41-45
Barnes, Wm H: 42-45
Biddle,Clement: 1835-45
Buckey, Geo: 42-45
Bontz, Henry & Wm Kalb: 1843
Bradford, Henry: 42-45
Bosworth, Josiah: 41-45
Benning, Jas, Lucy, & others: 41-45
Breckenridge, John: 43-45
Boardley, John B: 41-45
Bryan, Maria H: 43-45
Berry, Mildred: 42-45
Bulfinch, Thos: 42-45
Bryden, Wm: 42-45

Caldwell, Elias B: 41-45
Cruttenden, Joel: 43-45
Campbell, Jas: 42-45
Clarke, Saml: 43-45
Clagett, Sarah E: 43-45
Cross, Eli: 43 & 45
Combs, R M; 44-45
Conner, Thos: 44-45
Conner, Thos: 41-45
Corcoran, Thos: 42-44
Connelly, Thos, of John: 44-45
Corcoran, W W: 42-45
Cooper, Wm: 1838-45
Cranch, Wm G: 43-45
Chambers, Benj: 40-45
Clements, Chas A: 43-45
Coddington, Camilla: 43-45
Clarke, Eliz: 43-45
Conley, John T: 43-45
Crampton, Jas: 43-45
Clarke, Letitia: 42-45
Clarke, Letitia: 42-45
Craig, Maria: 41-45
Carroll, Michl: 44-45
Craven, Nancy: 43-45
Callan, Nicholas, in trust for Jane Lynch: 43-45
Connelly, Owen, 41-45
Crowley, Patrick: 43-45
Carroll & Prout: 1839-45
Caldwell, Timothy, & John Moore: 43-45
Davis, Alex'r M D: 43-45
Digges, Geo: 41-45
Drury, John H: 43-45
Davidson, John: 42-45
Duff, John: 42-45
Dove, Jos: 43-45
Drummond, Noah, in trust: 41-45

Donoho, Patrick: 38-45
Donaphon, Thornton A: 1839-45
Doyle, John: 42-45
Ennis, John: 42-45
Edmonston, Nathan: 43-45
Eckloff & Wagler: 44-45
Evans, Wm: 44-45
Edelin, Elexius: 44-45
Eastburn, Manton, & others: 42-45
Ellicott, Philip T: 43-45
Fales, Barnabas: 1839-45
Freedy, Christian: 43-45
Friend, Eleanor: 42-45
Fowler, Hanson: 44-45
Freer, Jas B: 43-45
Foulkes, John E, & others: 43-45
Follansbee, Jos: 41-45
Fowler, Saml: 41-45
Fairfax, Ferdinand: 41-45
Forrest, Richd: 42-45
Flint, Thos, & others: 43-45
Furlong, Valentine D: 41-45
Goldsborough, C W: 44-45
Grammer, G C: 41-45
Gideon, Jacob: 42-45
Glover, Jane, & B Chambers: 41-45
Greer, Wm: 42-45
Gore, Christopher: 43-45
Gray, John: 42-45
Groff, Michl: 41-45
Harrington, Anna M: 41-45
Harrison, Benj: 43-45
Hackney, Barton: 41-45
Hines, David: 43-45
Hickey, Danl G: 44-45
Handy, Edw G: 43-45
Handy, Edw G: 41-45
Howard, Flodoardo: 42-45
Hill, Gustavus: 43-45
Holland, John E: 43-45
Hall, Jas C: 43-45
Hall, Jas C: 43-45
Hoban, Jas: 42-45
Hamilton, Matthew: 43-45
Houston, Mary T: 41-45

Hayre, Mary: 1839-45
Higden, Mary Ann & J C: 42-45
Harkness, Saml: 43-45
Handy, Saml W: 43-45
Herbert, Thos: 43-45
Herty, Thos & Jas & Mary Ann & N Callan, jr: 1839-45
Hazle, Zachariah: 42-45
Hickey, Cecilia A: 43-45
Hill, Henry: 1839-45
Hoffman, Jacob: 42-45
Hunter, John: 42-45
Hollohan, John T: 42-45
Horsey, Outerbridge: 1834-45
Hickey, Wm: 43-45
Hemmersly, Wm: 1833-45
Hollins, Wm: 1839-45
Hall, David: 41-45
Johnson, Catharine M: 43-45
Jordan, Richd L: 43-45
Ingle, M: 24-45
Jones, J H, & Eliz: 41-45
Jewell, Wm: 41-45
Kirkwood, Wallace: 41-45
Kedglie, Ann: 44-45
Kelly, Bernard: 42-45
Kierman, Chas: 44-45
Knippel, Danl: 42-45
Kane, Elias: 42-45
Kingman, Eliab: 43-45
Kendrick, Geo W: 43-45
Kedglie, John: 44-45
Kiernan, Patrick: 35-45
Key, Henry S: 42-45
Key, John T: 42-45
Kay, Jas, & John J: 43-45
Key, Philip: 42-45
Lefevre, Ann M, & others: 44-45
Corcoran, Thos: 41-45
Lynch, Ambrose: 43-45
Lindsay, Adam: 1835-45
Leckie, Robt: 1839-45
Leckie, Robt & B O Shekel: 41-45
Lewis & Coats: 42-45
Laidler, Eliza: 42-45

Lutz, John: 43-45
Lewis Lawrence: 43-45
Lloyd, Thos: 43-45
Law, Thos: 42-45
Lee, Wm: 42-45
Lambell, Wm: 43-45
Lowe, Wm W: 42-45
McCerrin, Andrew: 42-45
McCormick, Andrew T: 42-45
Minturn, Benj G: 43-45
Mullen, Dolly: 43-45
Meigs, Francis C: 42-45
Maher, Jas: 42-45
McKean, Jas P: 42-45
McCormick, Jas M: 43-45
Marlow, J W: 43-45
McCormick, Jas M: 43-45
Martin, Jas M: 43-45
Martin, Jas E: 45
Milstead, Judson: 42-45
Milburn, Mgt: 40-45
Miller, Robt: 41-45
Magruder,Wm B: 43-45
McPeak, Wm: 42-45
McLaughlin, Wm: 41-45
Moscrop, Henry: 41-45
Mason, John: 40-45
Mountz, John, in turst for Miss Chateline: 43-45
Madison, Jas: 41-45
McKim, Jas: 43-45
Naylor, Henry: 44-45
Neilson, Hall: 43-45
Nicholls, Wm S, in trust: 41-45
Nash, Michl: 42-45
Orr, Benj G: 40-45
Orme, Wm: 42-45
Phillips, Jas B: 1836-45
Patton, Dolly Ann: 43-45
Peters, Henry: 1839-45
Paulding, Jas K: 43-45
Pettibone, John: 43-45
Peetsch, John C: 42-45
Parker, Selby: 41-45
Pettibone, Mgt: 42-45

Preston, Wm: 41-45
Prout, Wm: 1829-45
Peter, America P: 43-45
Payne, Danl: 43-45
Palmer, Eliakim: 42-45
Parrot, Richd: 41-45
Pratt, Wm: 1839-45
Shyrock, Henrietta: 42-45
Shyrock, Henrietta: 41-45
Seavy, Jas D: 41-45
Simms, M A E: 43-45
Semmes & Murray: 43-45
Smith, Richd: 43-45
Stott, Saml, & J C Harkness: 41-45
Shekels, Thos: 44-45
Simpson, Tobias: 43-45
Stewart, Wm H: 43-45
Stewart, Wm H: 43-45
Rice, Mary: 41-45
Riggs, Saml: 41-45
Rench, Jacob & Lodowick Young: 43-45
Ringgold, Tench: 42-45
Shaff, Arthur: 43-45
Scholfield, Andrew: 43-45
Swann, Caleb: 43-45
Smith, Jas: 41-45
Sands, Julia M: 43-45
Swift, Jonathan: 1835-45
Stewart, Wm W: 42-45
Scott, Jas W: 1839-45
Stoddart, Rebecca: 43-45
Sewall, Thos: 42-45
Sidebotham, Wm: 43-45
Tyler, John: 1838-45
Tyler, Robt: 43-45
Taylor, Wm H: 42-45
Thomas, Amelia, & Hanson, Gassaway: 42-45
Tayloe, B O: 43-45
Taylor, John: 43-45
Taylor, John, jr: 42-45
Thaw, Jos: 43-45
Talbot, John: 42-45
Towles, Jas: 43-45

Towles, Jas: 43-45
Thomas, Jas: 44-45
Taylor, John: 41-45
Venable, Eliz: 42-45
Venable, Chas: 43-45
Van Ness, Benj: 41-45
Wagler, F A: 43-45
Wood, Ferdinand F: 43-45
Watterston, Geo [in trust for Mary Sweeney]: 42-45
Watterston, Geo & John Kedglie: 41-45
Wilson, Henry: 43-45
Wilson, John A, Offa, & others: 40-45
Wilson, John: 42-45
Wright, Richd: 42-45

Weightman, R C: 43-45
Webster, Sereno S: 43-45
Wilson, Alex'r: 43-45
White, John B: 42-45
Ward, Richd R: 44-45
Whalen, Nicholas: 42-45
Young, McClintock: 43-45
Young, Moses: 41-45
Young, Eleanor: 1824-45
Young, Geo W, Nicholas, Notley, Ignatius, & Benj, & Sarah E Clagett: 43-45
Young, Ignatius F & Geo W: 43-45
Young, Morduit: 41-45
Young, Notley, D D: 43-45

New Boot & Shoe Store: south side of Pa ave, between 9th & 10th sts.
–Malcolm Douglass

Two deaths by hydrophobia in Pittsburg this week: Mr John Pritchard, a young man 18 years of age, who was bitten by a dog 9 months ago, & Mr Gustavus Sandoll Chandler, who was bitten 4 months ago. A man named Sprat was also suffering from the dreadful malady, & was not expected to survive.

A splendid sword was presented to Lt, now Capt Randolph Ridgely, of the late Maj Ringgold's Flying Artl, by the citizens of Balt, for his gallantry & military services in the battles of Palo Alto & Resaca de la Palma.

Some of our brethren in N Y have confounded Gen Jos Chandler, who died suddenly in that city last Sat, with Gen John Chandler. Both gentlemen were residents of Augusta. The latter, however, was uncle to the former, was a Gen in the U S Army, & a Senator of the U S for Maine, & died, as we believe, some time since.
–U S Gazette [See Sep 16th newspaper.]

Died: yesterday, Ann Scott, in her 90th year, wid/o Wm A Scott. Her funeral will taken place this afternoon at 2 o'clock, from the residence of her brother, Jos L Scholfield, on 8th st.

MON SEP 21, 1846
Orphans Court of Wash Co, D C. Letters of administration, with the will annexed, on the personal estate of Wm Ford, late of said county, dec'd.
–Peter Brady, Adm, W A

Mrd: on Sep 17, by Rev Mr Gillis, Mr John T Tonge, of Wash City, to Miss Margaret Ellen, 3rd d/o Richd & Rebecca Butler, formerly of West River, Anne Arundel Co, Md.

Died: yesterday, in her 88th year, Mrs Margaret Draine, a native of county Antrim, Ireland, & for the last 25 years a resident of this city. Her funeral is from the residence of her son-in-law, Mr John Sinon, corner of 4½ st & Md ave, this afternoon at 3 o'clock.

U S schnr **Flirt**, off Vera Cruz, Aug 25, 1846: letter to Col Bankhead, U S A: subject-the Prisoners of the Truxton. Being a friend of your son's, I take the liberty to alleviate the solicitude of your family on the receipt of the news of the loss of his vessel, & the capture of her ofcrs & crew by the enemy, with the exception of Lts Hunter & Berryman. Your son was quite well when he left the vessel; the ofcrs are enjoying all the honors of war, & are residing with the Lt Govn'r at Tuspan, a person very kindly disposed towards them; & that the province itself has declared for peace. Sincerely hoping your son will shortly be restored to you.
–Geo Harrison Starr, U S N

TUE SEP 22, 1846
For rent: commodious brick house with a capacious back bldg, brick stable, carriage house: on north side of East Capitol st, about 100 yards east of the Capitol square. Apply nearly opposite to Mrs Rebecca Burche, or to John C Burche, at Col Saml Burche's.

Desirable residence for sale: the subscriber offers for sale the house & lot which he at present occupies: the house was built 5 years ago, & is good condition, contains 9 rooms, fronts 25 feet on E st, running back 180 feet to a paved alley 30 feet wide.
–R C Washington

Mount Hebron Estate for sale: under a deed of trust to the subscribers: sale on Nov 21, at the Auction Store of R W Dyer, Wash City: the above estate in Fairfax Co, Va, near the Little River Turnpike: contains 1,084 acres of land or thereabouts: the bldgs consist of a 2 story brick dwlg-house 38 by 19 feet, 2 others, a barn, a stable, spring-house, smoke-house, & the walls of a large brick factory. Apply to the subscriber at the Bank of Wash, or to Mr J T O Wilbar, residing on the farm.
–Wm Gunton, Jas Adams, Trustees

Notice: by virtue of a writ of fieri facias issued by B K Morsell, a J P for Wash Co, D C, I shall expose to public sale, for cash, on Sep 26, opposite the Centre Market-house in Wash, one wagon & gear, seized & taken as the property of Wm Buist, & will be sold to satisfy a judgment in favor of Middleton & Beall against the said Wm Buist. –R R Burr, Constable

First session of the Board of Regents of the Smithsonian Institution: Sep 7, 1846: Wm McPeak appointed doorkeeper & messenger.
Sep 8: Hon Geo M Dallas was elected Chancellor-by ballot.
Wm J Hough was elected Secretary-by ballot.
Wm W Seaton is appointed Chairman of the Executive Cmte.
Cmte appointed to carry out the provisions of the act to establish the Smithsonian Institution: appointed-Mr Owen, Mr Hilliard, & Mr Bache.
Cmte appointed to prepare a report upon the subject of the formation of a library: appointed-Mr Choate, Mr Hawley, & Mr Rush.
Sep 9: Mr Owen presented to the Board, in behalf of David D Owen, M D, of Indiana, a plan, drawing, & specifications of a bldg for said Institution. Mr Owen also presented a plan & drawings for the same by Mr Robt Mills, Architect, of Wash. It was resolved that Mr Rush be a cmte to ascertain, through the solicitors formerly employed by him on behalf of the U S in the suit to obtain the Smithsonian bequest, or otherwise, whether Madame de la Batut still survives; &, if not, what steps are necessary to be taken to obtain the fund reverting to the U S at her death, being a portion of the original property of Jas Smithson, retained by the English Court of Chancery, in order to furnish, in the shape of interest, an annuity to said Madame de la Batut. And, in case the said Madame de la Batut survives, to adopt measures by which her decease may be communicated to the Board whenever that event may occur. Wm Archer, Architect, of Wash City, presented to the Board a plan & drawings for a bldg for the Institution, together with specifications & estimates of the cost: referred to the Cmte on Building. –Wm J Hough, Sec Smithsonian Institute

Mrd: on Sep 17, in Fauquier Co, Va, by Rev John Ogilvie, Geo W Adams, of Wash, to Miss Ann M, d/o Z R English, of the former place.

Appointments by the Pres: Geo Latimer, of Pa, to be Consul of the U S for the port of St Johns, in the island of Puerto Rico, vice Henry G Hubbard, dec'd. The Gtwn Advocate states that Capt Clement Smith, cmder of the Independent Greys of Gtwn, on Fri, received an appointment of captaincy in the Regt of the U S mounted riflemen.

St Louis Daily Union of Sep 14: announces the death of Luke E Lawless, on Sat last. Judge Lawless was as much esteemed as a man, as he was admired for his thorough legal attainments.

Died: on Thu last, Mrs Margaret Mercer, of Belmont, Loudoun Co, Va. This excellent lady has left many of her kindred & friends to weep for her loss. Her character & influence has been every where appreciated; & her memory will live green & fresh upon the minds of all.

WED SEP 22, 1846
From the Pacific: several men had been lost in a gale at sea from the American whale ship **Luminary**, Warren, R I, on Mar 8. Unfortunate men who were lost: Dr Browne, a native of Balt, where his family & friends now reside. Mr E W Athearn belonged to Tisbury, Martha's Vineyard, where his family-a wife & 4 children are now living. Geo Cummins, B S Edgartown; Nelson Atherton, carpenter, Rhode Island; Michl Antonio, Corco, Western Islands; Wm E Jone, cooper, N Y C; & Bob, a Tahitian. –Honolulu Friend, a Sandwich Islands paper.

The will of Louis Bonaparte, ex-King of Holland, was opened at Florence, on the 26th ult: after recommending his soul to God, he desires that his body be taken to St Leu, near Paris, to be buried near his father Chas Bonaparte & his eldest son, dec'd in Holland in 1807. He desires the body of his 2nd son, who died in Italy in 1831, to be also transported there. He applies 60,000fr for the erection of a tomb. He says: I bore the name of that village for 40 years, & I have loved that place better than any other. He makes a present of the property which he possessed in Holland to the municipal administration of Amsterdam, in order that the annual proceeds may be applied to succouring persons injured by inundations. Property is worth about a million of francs. He leaves a large sum to the poor of Florence. He leaves to the Grand Duke of Tuscany the colossal bust of the Emperor Napoleon executed by Canova. He leaves to 4 sisters of the hospital of St Leu, an annual sum of 100 fr; each; also, 2,500fr to the poor of Civita-Nova. He leaves to his brother, Jerome Bonaparte, Prince de Montford, the property of box in a theatre at Florence, valued at 60,000fr; to his nephew Napoleon, s/o the Prince de Montfort, a fine diamond; & to his other nephew Jerome a similar souvenir; to the Princess Mathilde de Demidoff a suite of rubies & diamonds; to his nephew Louis, s/o Prince de Canino, his handsome villa de Montughi, with it dependencies & furniture, valued at 200,000fr; to his ward, Francesco Castel Vecchio, a sum of 150,000fr. After some legacies to his servants & executors, he concludes with: I leave all my other property, the palace of Florence, the estate at Civita-nova, all, in fact, that constitutes my heritage at the period of my death, without reserving any thing except the legacies mentioned above, to my universal heir, Louis Napoleon, my only remaining son, to whom also I bequeath, as a particular mark of my tenderness, my Dunkerque, placed in my library, with all the decorations & souvenirs which it conatins; I leave him all the objects sent me from St Helena, & which had belonged to my brother the Emperor Napoleon, all enclosed in a piece of furniture made expressly for the purpose. –Florence, Dec 1,1 845.

Wash Corp: 1-Cmte of Claims: asked to be discharged from consideration of the ptns of the following named persons: W B Lewis; R J Pollard; Jno Chambers; Mrs M A Daly; two ptns of Jas Fitzgerald; Mrs Ann Stewart; Mrs Jane C Adamson; & Thos Drempey. 2-Ptn of Allison Naylor & others, praying the grading & paving of an alley in square 258: referred to the Cmte on Improvements.

A soldier by the name of Ring, by birth from the old Granite State, N H, was among others of the 3rd infty, advancing to do his best in the action, when he came to the rear of the artl that Capt May was charging on. Some of the party shot the gunner, who had already touched the quick-match from the cannon before it had burnt to the powder. This gallant feat was performed in sight of a 1,000 Mexicans; &, in so doing, it is estimated he saved at least 50 lives, as Capt May's squadron was within 150 yards of the mouth of the cannon at the time. The cannon was loaded with grape-shot. [Capt May can be found on Jul 15th & Sep 3rd newspapers.]

Household & kitchen furniture at auction on Sep 29, at the residence of Mrs Stillson, on Pa ave, south side, between 14th & 15th sts, opposite A Fuller's Hotel.
–A Green, auctioneer

A young man named Geo W Little, who came from Balt, & was employed by Mr Jos Prather, met his death last Mon, when returning from market with Mr Prather's butcher wagon, on 5th & M sts north, the horse became unmanageable & set off with the wagon down a hill. In attempting to stop the animal Mr Little fell down & both wheels of the wagon passed over him, causing such injury in the small of his back as to produce death in a few minutes. He was a young man of excellent character, the only s/o a widowed mother, & a member of the Northern Liberty Division of the Sons of Temperance.

Foreign Items: 1-Lord Elgin, appointed Govn'r-Gen of Canada, is to be succeeded as Govn'r of Jamaica by Sir C E Grey, late Govn'r of Barbadoes; while Lt Govn'r Col Reid, from Bermuda, will replace Sir C E Grey, & he himself will be succeeded at Bermuda by Capt Elliott. 2-Lord Geo Bentinck is a 2nd s/o the Duke of Portland & a major in the army. His lordship was born in 1802. The late Right Hon Geo Canning had a high opinion of his abilities.

H Ernest Vass will take a few addition pupils, to whom he will give instructions in music on the Piano Forte. Apply at Mr Anderson's Music Store, Pa ave, near 12th st.

THU SEP 24, 1846
Notice: by virtue of 2 orders of distrain, for house rent due to Frances Hanna by Charity Gibson, I shall exporse at public sale, in front of the Centre-market house, on Sep 29, the following goods & chattels, to wit: a bureau, a table, a washstand, bowl & pitcher, 1 looking-glass, 12 chairs, a pair brass andirons, shovel & tongs, 10 pictures in frames, a workstand, a lot of glass-ware, 4 candlesticks.
–H R Maryman, Constable

Mrd: on Sep 22, by Rev Mr Morgan, Mr David Hines, of Wash, to Miss Christiana Rheem, formerly of Alexandria.

Wood for sale: on the premises adjoining the Great Falls directly on the canal, 1,000 cords of wood. –Danl C Digges, Agent for proprietor, Upper Marlboro, Md.

John Shelton, Atty at Law, Raymond, Hinds Co, Miss: practices in all Courts of Hind Co, & in various Courts held at Jackson, the capital of the State. References:
Jas Littlefield, Boston
W & R Kelly, N Y
Nathl Weed & Co, N Y
Hon J H Gholson, Petersburg, Va
R W Henry, Richmond, Va
R S French, Norfolk, Va
Dr Chas Cocke, Albemarle Co, Va
Dr Edq A Broddus, Monticelo, Ga
Messrs Martin, Pleasants & Co, New Orleans
Messrs Slark, Day Stauffer & Co, New Orleans
Messrs Clements, Belknap & Co, New Orleans
Messrs J Bonner & Co, New Orleans

Household & kitchen furniture at auction on Oct 1, at the residence of Mrs King, on 13th st west, near the corner of B st south. –A Green, auctioneer

Died: on Sep 22, of enlargement of the heart, Mrs Ann Fletcher. Her funeral is this afternoon, at 2 o'clock, at the late residence of the dec'd, on Camp Hill.

Died: on Sep 22, Saml Enoch, 2nd s/o Jos & Octavia Bryan, in his 17th year. His funeral is this afternoon at 2 o'clock, on N Y ave, near the corner of 10th st.

Died: on Sep 15, in Wentworth, Rockingham Co, N C, after an illness of 45 days, Miss Lucinda S, d/o the Hon Robt Martin. She was stricken down on the very eve of her marriage. Her bethrothed, hastening with pride & joy to claim his lovely bride, arrived in time to close her eyes in death & consign his all to the gloomy precincts of an untimely grave. The gorgeous trappings that were to clothe her youthful loveliness for the bridal day, shrouded her lifeless form in the cold embrace of remorseless death! She died a Christian; with the universal regrets of all who knew her. W

For sale: a valuable estate, called **Hesse**, in Matthews Co, Va, on the Piankatank river, & in sight of the bay: contains 500 acres, with a 2 story brick dwlg-house, in good condition. Apply to Robt Wallace, King George, Va.

For sale: that very desirale residence, of the late Mr Chas Strahan, on H st, opposite the new Episcopal Church of the Ascension. Apply on the premises, or to Geo Sweeny, Notary Public, 7th st.

FRI SEP 25, 1846
Mrs Ann Speir, [successor to Mrs Parker,] has located in the rear of Harper & Co's store, on D st, between 9th & 10th sts, with all kinds of Fashionable & Plain Millinery & Mantua-making.

Belmont Institute: this Seminary for Young Ladies, so long & so ably conducted under the auspices of its late lament head, Miss Margaret Mercer, are informed that it will be continued under the superintendence of Mrs Mary S Mercer, of Cedar Park, Md, assisted by the same highly accomplished teachers. Please address communications to Mrs Mary S Mercer, Belmont Post Ofc, Loudoun Co, Va. [Under title of "The Late Miss Margaret Mercer." For the last 7 or 8 years Miss Mercer has been a resident of Va; taking up her location in a remote neighborhood, she lived to witness the complete triumph of her untiring zeal, & the accomplishment of her most favorite plans. In passing the highway which conducts the stage to the Belmont Seminary, a humble spire in an adjacent wood marks the location of a neat little church, built by her own indefatigable labors. It was here that the last said offices of love & respect were paid her. It was here in this little temple that the triumph of her labors were being developed, as each succeeding Sabbath called together the objects of her untiring solicitude.

Handsome new furniture at auction on Mon next, at the warerooms of Jos K Boyd, on Pa ave, near 11th st. -R W Dyer, auct

Wreck of the brig **Helen McLeod**: the schnr **P Holt**, Capt Holt, at N Y from St Mary's Georgia, makes the following report: the brig **Helen McLeod**, which left Balt on Sep 2 for New Orleans, was dismasted in the late equinoctial gale, & when last seen was in such a condition as to leave no doubt that she soon after sunk with all on board. The following is a list of the ofcrs, crew, & passengers of the **Helen McLeod**:

Thos Marston, master
Saml Edwards, chief mate
Wm R Richardson, 2nd mate
Seamen-6:
1-Wm Borroughs
2-John Valentine
3-John Charden
4-John Wilkinson
5-Wm Moore
6-Francis Monmonier
Wm Collers, cook

Cabin passengers: Mrs Amos & 2 dghts
In the steerage: a lady & 3 gentlemen, names not known; & Wm Sewall, colored. On Sep 11th Capt Holt saw a ship with everything gone but her foremast; she had no boats; appeared to be a new vessel of about 160 tons; at half past 11 spoke her, the captain reported 3 or 4 feet water in the hold, & in a sinking condition; she lay perfectly unmanageable; stood past her perhaps a mile; put the vessel under working sail, tacked ship & went to windward of her, with the intention of boarding her, but did not think it prudent, as the sea ran irregular & rough, although my crew volunteered to a man to attempt it, when I should think proper. Kept off, & spoke the schnr **Silas H Wright** bound to St Domingo, [since put back to N Y.] We running near together. It came to blow a complete hurricane from the southward.

Excellent household & kitchen furniture at auction on Sep 30, at the residence of Mrs Spalding, on 4½ st, near Pa ave: very good & worthy the attention of persons furnishing. -R W Dyer, auct

For rent: the large 3 story brick house on Pa ave, next door west of Edw Simms' store. Apply to Geo Mattingly.

Pennsylvania against N Y. Sweet potato measuring 3 feet & 1 inch, when first dug from the ground was raised, by John McKay, of Delaware Co. –Native Eagle

Orphans Court of Wash Co, D C. Letters of administration on the personal estate of Salathet Hick, dec'd, be granted to John P Pepper, unless cause to the contrary be shown. –Ed N Roach, Reg/o wills

Mrd: on Sep 15, in West Troy, N Y, by Rev N S S Buman, D D, Dr W B H Brown, of Wash, to Miss Adelaide J Harrington, of Troy, N Y.

J Edgar will commence a Juvenile Singing School, on G st, near 11th st, on Sep 26.

The complete works of the Rev Andrew Fuller, with a memoir of his life, by Andrew Gunton Fuller, reprinted from the 3rd London edition; revised, with additions, by Jos Belcher, D D: in 3 volumes: for sale by Wm Q Force, Pa ave, corner 10th st.

Died: on Sep 14, at his residence, near Dumfries, Va, suddenly, in his 55th year, Wm A Weaver. He was a native of Dumfries, near which he breathed his last, & was prepared for his useful active life at the Gtwn College, in this District. He entered the navy when quite young, & was twice a prisoner during the late war with Great Britain, & was wounded in the action between the vessel **Shannon**, & the ship **Chesapeake**, when the latter vessel was captured. After the war he continued several years in the service, where, among other evidences of his merit, he was appointed flag Lt to the squadron in the Mediterranean, under the command of Cmdor Stewart. After he left the navy much of his life was devoted to agricultural pursuits, though he was occasionally called for other services. In 1832 he was selected by Mr Livingston to edit the Diplomatic Correspondence of the U S, from the treaty of peace, in 1783, to the commencement of the present gov't under the federal constitution, in 1789; & in 1840 he was appointed by Mr Forsyth superintendent of the 6th census; for the manner in which he executed these trusts he received from Mr Livingston & Mr Foysyth the fullest approbation.

SAT SEP 26, 1846
Elegant & extensive property for sale: the late residence of Mr Armfield, on Prince st, in Alexandria. The House is brick, built of the best materials, contains 15 rooms, & has a wide hall through the centre. Out houses of brick, covered with metal; wash house, cistern above ground, 2 bathing & 2 dressing rooms, fine green house, & a brick 2 story double house for servants. The flower gardens extend from Patrick to Henry st; the vegetable garden is large & productive. Apply to Wm D Nutt, at the Treasury Dept.

The brig **Washington** arrived in command of Lt John Hall. The names of those lost in the gale are Lt Bache, Benj Dalloff, Jas Dorsey, John Washburn, Saml Schroader, Peter Hanson, Edw Grennen, a seaman named Counsel, Wm Stanford, & 2 colored servants, Francis Butler & Lewis Maynard. [Oct 23rd newspaper: tribute by the Cliosophic Society, Princeton, N J, Oct 12, 1846: deep regret of the loss of Lt Geo M Bache, U S Navy, on Oct 8 last, while in command of the U S brig **Washington**.]

Navy Dept, Sep 24, 1846. Information received at this Dept of the death of the following persons:
On Jul 27, John Folwell, landsman, attached to one of the vessels of the Brazil squadron.
On Aug 15, John Harvey, quarter gunner, died on board the ship **Potomac**, Gulf squadron.
On Aug 17, John B Martin, ordinary seaman, jumped overboard from the ship **Falmouth**, in a fit of insanity, & was drowned.

Valuable small farm at private sale: farm contains 56 acres, & is about 1½ miles from Gtwn, on the Va side, in Alexandria Co. There is a small house & stable on it. Apply to Robt Cruit, F st, between 14th & 15th sts.

To let: a 2 story frame house, fitted up for a grocery store, fronting on 12th st & Mass ave. Inquire of the proprietor, Thos Robbins, near the premises.

Mrs H A Peters will re-open her School for little boys & girls on Oct 1. Her residence is on E st, between 8th & 9th sts.

Mrd: on Sep 17, at Rutland, Vt, by Rev A Walker, Lt Benj Alvord, U S Army, to Miss Emily Louise, d/o Mr Henry Mussey, of that town.

MON SEP 28, 1846
New Bldgs in & near Pa ave: 1-Jackson Hall is one of the largest & handsomest edifices in this metropolis: 2-Mr Robt Keyworth just put a lofty bldg at the s w corner of 6th st & Pa ave: called Washington Hall. It contains 4 stories, & seems to vie with Coleman's Hotel, on the opposite of the avenue. 3-Messrs Haslup & Weeden erected a spacious bldg near the Centre Market space, at C, 9th st & La ave: intended to be used as a coach factory. 4-Mr Thos Young has commenced the erection of a substantial bldg on the south side of Pa ave, near the corner of 4½ st, which he intends for a coach factory. 5-Mr Boyd erected 2 very handsome stores on Pa ave & 11th st. These bldgs are ornamental to our widely-extending metropolis.

Died: on Sep 25, in Balt, Thos W Pairo, in his 74th year, & for the last 40 years a resident of Wash City.

Died: on Sat last, after a short illness, Bianca Niles, in her 17th year, y/d/o W Ogden Niles, late of Balt.

Police Intelligence: late arrest. 1-On Sat last, Jos Lafontaine was committed for trial, charged with robbing a person named Elijah Duling, from Fauquier Co, Va, of his pocket-book containing $15. The cmplnt was in a stating of intoxication last Fri night when the robbery was committed. 2-Jas Butler, a colored by, was committed to jail on Sep 24 charged with setting fire to the livery stable of Mr Allison Nailor.

Marine disaster to U S troops. The brig **Excel**, Macy, arrived at N Y from Savannah, spoke on Sep 12 ship **Ocean**, of Providence, from N Y, for Balize, with U S troops on board. She experienced the late gales & received considerable damage. The Capt said that he had lost some of the crew or some of the U S troops overboard in the gale, which was not perfectly understood.

Late from the army: from the New Orleans Tropic, Sep 19. 1-The schnr **Edward Tilletston**, bound to this port from the Brasos, with 68 discharged soldiers, was blown ashore near the Sabine. Six had died previous to this disaster. 2-On Sep 16 a volunteer, Jas Hoffman, from Nashville, Tenn, jumped overboard & was drowned; & another died in a few hours afterwards, named Benj Hartwell. 3-There was near 600 sick volunteers in the hospital at Camargo, & they were dying fast.

Nashville, Tenn, Sep 17. Peer Bagwell was arrested in this county about 4 weeks since, & committed to jail on a charge of horse-stealing. In his possession, when arrested, were found $17 in coin & $32 in paper-all counterfeits. Devolopments made by him while in jail led to the arrest of R Hampton & L Barnwell, blacksmiths, residing on Mill Creek. Henry Carter, gunsmith, of this place.

$50 reward for runaway negro man Uriah, whom I purchased of Wm Holmes, of Montg Co, Md. He is about 19 or 20 years of age. –John Higgins, living in PG Co, Md, near Beltsville.

TUE SEP 29, 1846
Died: on Sep 24, in Md, David Cooly, aged 44 years, formerly of Deerfield, Mass.

Wash Co, D C: I certify that John Owens, of said county, brought before me as an estray, a gray horse. –E W Smallwood, J P. [Owner is to prove property, pay charges, & take him away. –John Owens.]

For sale: 2 story brick house & lot of ground, together with an adjoining lot: house contains 9 rooms, including the attic story, with passage, basement, kitchen, & cellar: carriage-house, stable, cow-sheds, & milk-house: premises are on 17th st west, near the public Depts. Will be sold or exchanged for an improved & productive farm of moderate size, near the city. Inquire of S Lewis, on the premises. [Oct 13th newspaper: the same property is advertised again. Inquire of S Lewis, on the premises, or Geo M Philips, Agent, 10th st.]

For rent: house at present occupied by the subscriber, with or without the furniture. The house is nearly new & built in the best manner, contains 11 rooms, with high ceilings, elegant marble mantels in parlors, & closets & wardrobes in each of the 4 principal chambers: property is on H st, between 9th & 10th sts. For particulars apply to J A M Duncanson.

For rent: a most valuable 3 story brick bldg, the residence of the late Jos Smoot, on K st, 2 squares above Mr Fox's, the late British Minister. The house is large & commodious; out-bldgs are a fine brick stable & carriage-house. Apply at the residence, or to Mr Cox, Gtwn.

Wanted to hire: a colored Woman as housemaid in a small family. She must come well recommended for honesty & good conduct. A Catholic would be preferred. Inquire of Mr Fischer, at Stationer's Hall.

From Balt & the North: 1-Edw D Martin appointed Clerk of Worcester, Co, Md, in place of the late G W Handy. 2-The young man Kelly, who murdered Miss Carle, has been arrested & imprisoned for trial.

Notice: public sale on Oct 1, one hogshead of tobacco, seized & taken under execution as the property of John Penny, & sold to satisfy a claim due J Mistard, issued by N Brady, a justice of the peace in & for Wash Co, D C.
–John Fowler, Bailiff

Trustee's sale: by decree of the Circuit Court of Wash Co, D C: in a cause wherein Alex'r Hanna & wife are cmplnts, & Eliz Bohrer & others are dfndnts: sale on Oct 30th next of the following very valuable lots, late part of the estate of Fred'k Grammer, namely: Lot 5 in square 294; Lot 13 in square 343 Lot 14 in square 378. Last 2 lots are near the Medical College, E & 10th sts. –W Redin, Trustee
-B Homans, auct

Md nominations for the State Legislature: election to be held on Oct 7.
For the Senate:
Chas M Keyser, Balt City
Wm Pierce, Cecil Co
Mathias George, Queen Anne's Co
Jas M Fooks, Worcester Co

David W Naill, Fred'k Co
Zabdiel W Potter. Caroline Co
Wm B Clarke, Wash Co
Dr S P Smith, Alleghany Co

For House of Delegates:
Balt City:
John P Kennedy

A B Patterson
Jos Simms

Wm Bayley
J M Harris

Anne Arundel Co:
John Johnson

Howard M Duvall
Saml Thomas

Edwin P Hayden
Thos Donaldson

St Mary's:　　　　　　Wm H Dunkinson　　　　Henry Fowler
John A Jones　　　　　Geo D Coad

Kent Co:　　　　　　　Saml W Spencer
Wm F Smyth　　　　　 R Chambers Wickes

Calvert:　　　　　　　 John Turner
Thos J Graham　　　　 H D Billingsley

Chas:　　　　　　　　 Danl Jenifer, jr
Henry H Hawkins　　　 John D Freeman

Talbot:　　　　　　　　Nicholas Rice
Alex'r H Seth　　　　　 H Goldsborough, jr

Somerset:　　　　　　 John H Done　　　　　 Saml B D Jones
　　　　　　　　　　　 Jas Phoebus　　　　　　Benj Lankford

Dorchester:　　　　　　Danl M Henry　　　　　Benj Travers
Jacob Wilson　　　　　 Wm Frazier

Cecil　　　　　　　　　Jas W Morgan　　　　　John Conard
Jas H Jamar　　　　　　Edw T Tarring

PG Co:　　　　　　　　Philemon Chew　　　　　Thos Duckett
John D Bowling　　　　Thos Martin　　　　　　Edmund B Stephen

Queen Anne's:　　　　 P G Hopper, jr
Wesley Clements　　　 Thos H Kemp

Worcester:　　　　　　 Wm Laws　　　　　　　Ebenezer Hearn
L L Derickson　　　　　Saml S McMasters

Fred'k:　　　　　　　　Jacob Root　　　　　　 Thos Turner
Peter Grabill　　　　　　Jeremiah S Morrison　　 Geo Doub

Harford:　　　　　　　 Abraham Cole　　　　　Geo C Davis
B F Walters　　　　　　Oliver H Thomas

Caroline:　　　　　　　Jos Pearson
Geo W Harrington　　　Robt H McKnott

Washington:　　　　　 Geo French　　　　　　Wm E Doyle
Hezekiah Boteler　　　　Isaac Motter　　　　　　John J Bowles

Montgomery:	Jas N Alnutt	Lyde Griffith
Nathan Holland	Washington Bonifant	
Alleghany:	Stephen McKinley	Danl C Bruce
Peter Ritner	John M Brewer	
Carroll:	Thos Hook	Chas Devilbiss
Andrew G Ege	Jas M Shelman	R R Booth
Abraham Wampler	Upton Scott	

The U S ship **Preble** ordered to convoy the California Expedition. Her ofcrs:
Cmder, Wm F Shields
Lts-4: Jos Lanman, Edw C Ward, jr, Thos M Mix, Albert G Clary
Sailingmaster, Silas Bent   Assist Surgeon, John L Burt
Surgeon, Danl Egbert   Purser, Henry Wilson
Passed Midshipmen-3: Edw Brinley, jr, Jas B McCauley, Homer C Blake
Midshipmen-4: Wilson McGunnegill, Wm F Shunk, Edgar Brodhead
Capt's Clerk, Eugene Lees   Sailmaker, Timothy J Griffin
Boatswain, Benj Wakefield   Surgeon's Steward, Wm Marsh
Gunner, Henry Ward   Ship's Steward, Chas B Sterling
Carpenter, Thos Coleman

WED SEP 30, 1846
The central division, or army of Chihuahua, may be detailed as follows:
Birg Gen John E Wool commanding
Col S Churchill, Inspector Genr'l & Chief of the Staff
Capt O Cross, Chief of the Quartermaster Dept
Capt W D Fraser, Corps of Engineers
Lt Irvin McDowell, Aid-de-camp, & Acting Assist Adjutant Genr'l
Lt C P Kingsbury, Ordnance Dept
5 companies U S Dragoons, under Col W S Harney: 300
1 company U S field Artl, under Capt J M Washington: 100
2 companies U S 6th Infty, under Major B L E Bonneville: 160
1 regt Arkansas cavalry, under Col A Yell: 750
2 regts Illinois Infty, under Col J J Hardin: 1,600
1 company Kentucky Infty, under Capt Williams: 90
Total: 3,000

A little girl, Cecelia Baumer, was stolen or strayed from her parents, on Jun 17 last, at a public celebration at Hoboken, near N Y C. Nothing has been heard of her since. She had scars of burns on the palms of her hands, & her age is 4 years & 5 months. Any information will be thankfully receiverd & liberally rewarded by her parents. Address F H Baumer, 121 Bowery, N Y.

To the Editors of the Nat'l Intell: Gentlemen: accounts of the recent death of Darwin E Stanton, of this city, at Steubenville, Ohio, have appeared in the public papers. They are so various that I deem it proper to send the following extract from a letter from his brother, E M Stanton, to use. After stating that Dr Stanton had been sick since Sep 12 with chills & fever, & great pain in the head, & affection of the brain, he says: "During all the time he evinced great anxiety & distress of mind, with frequent delirium, & expressed the opinion several times that his medical attendants did not understand his case & were not treating it properly. His friends, on the other hand, were assured by his physicians that he was out of danger, & I parted from him on Tue night the 22nd, in the belief that he was free from danger & would speedily recover. That night, a paroxysm of his disease returned, & although two men were staying in the room, he got possession of his razor without their noticing it & inflicted a severe wound on his throat, & suffered considerable loss of blood before it was discovered. The wound was not, in itself, any ways dangerous, but the loss of blood weakened him, & the violence of his disease increased with great rapidity. I got to him about 4 or 5 o'clock in the morning & remained with him until his death, which took place about half past 6 at night. He continued insane all the time, with one or two slight intervals." That the character of Dr Stanton may not suffer in consequence of his attempt to commit suicide, I will state that more upright, honorable, kind-hearted man did not live, & that for temperance & sobriety he was an example to his fellow-men. Yours, respectfully, B B French.

Mrd: in the U S Consular House, Monterey Calf, by Thos O Larkin, U S Consul, Jas Williams, of Cape Girardeau Co, Missouri, to Miss Mary Patterson, of Jackson Co. Mr John Harris, of Brighton, Monroe Co, N Y, to Miss Drucilla Shadden, of Jackson Co, Arkansas-all arriving in California, via the Rocky Mountains.
[No date-current item.]

Died: yesterday, of a lingering illness of several months, in her 29th year, Mary Ann, d/o the late Cmdor Thompson, & w/o Gen M Head, of the Treasury Dept. Her funeral is from the residence of her afflicted husband at Miss Wilson's, on F st, corner of 12th st west, this afternoon at 4 o'clock.

Died: on Sep 23, in Brooke Co, Va, Dr Darwin E Stanton. The dec'd was twice a member of the Virginia House of Delegates from Brooke Co, & the last 2 sessions of Congress was one of the clerks in the House of Reps. Immediately on his return from Washington with his family, he was seized with a violent disease, accompanied with inflammation of the brain, &, after a severe illness, he has been cut off in the prime of life, leaving an afflicted family & a large circle of relatives & friends to mourn his loss. –Steubenville Gaz

Dog lost, $5 reward: small dog of the European terrier species: answers to the name of Tip. –Eliz Schofield, 6th st.

THU OCT 1, 1846
Letters remaning in the Post Ofc, Wash, Oct 1, 1846.

Anderson, Jos A
Angermann, John-2
Archer, Miss Ame'a
Ashley, Wm
Allison, Henry S
Bock, Johanna
Bruce, Edw C
Buse, Geo
Brown, Miss Eliz
Brown, John
Burke, Capt M
Brooks, Jas W
Bond, Miss Mar'a E
Brown, Miss M Ann
Bell, Miss Letty
Boss, Jas H
Brooks, Howard
Brown, Abraham
Bond, Chas M
Brown, Michl C
Bulter, Henry
Bergen, Alex J
Butler, Walter
Bronson, Miss Jane
Birkhead, Midle'n
Bowman, Alex'r
Briscoe, Miss S A
Bunnell, Eliah
Broadrup, Geo
Bentley, Jos
Butler, J Wilkins-2
Baltimore, Thos
Baltimore, Mrs A
Bostock, Wm L
Bennett, Gen A G
Becker, Julia
Cole, John T
Clarke, Mrs H E
Clarke, Capt M M
Clarke, Robt
Chick, Maj Nath
Cammack, Wm
Collins, Mrs M J

Cater, Henrietta
Clover, jr, Lewis P
Campbell, Wm
Croggin, Isaac N J
Chellar, John B-2
Chapman, Alex
Curtis, Littleton
Cambloss, Geo W
Corson, Miss Pe'a P
Challess, Lenoir
Carmalt, John
Dick, John
Darne, Jas
Davis, Jas
Dixon, Mr
Davenport, Dudley
Dixon, Augustus
Dalton, Mr Susan
Dickinson, Reuben
Darby, Jas
Dunlop, Jas
Davis, Miss Fra's M
Danford, Miss Ann E
Dobbyn, Mrs Ma'da
Duvall, Gen J P
Elliott, Mrs Eliz
English, Mrs C G
Evans, Miss M Ann
English, Mrs M E
Evans, Miss Fanny
Evans, Miss Josep's
Evans, Miss Sarah A
Equal, Div S of T
Eustis, Judge-3
Ford, Mrs Ann E
Ford, Miss Mary
Ford, Miss Eliza
Frost, Danl
Forshee, Rev Mr
Ferguson, Enos D
Fenno, Geo Q
Fritzpatrick, Mrs M
Fairfield, Mrs M A

Fortune, Thos L
Fisher, Emanuel
Gould, Jas
Gray, Miss Eliz
Green, Allen B
Grimes, Wm H
Garrett, Mrs C
Gratton, Jas
Glover, John B
Gallagher, John
Garney, Capt Edw
Gibson, Mrs Car'e-2
Garner, Mrs Pris'a
Gooding, Mrs E A
Gadsby, Mrs P
Gedney, Comm J R
Garnett, Lt Rd B
Goings, Miss Anna
Goings, Patrick
Getty, Acting Master R H-3
Hull, Alex'r
Hup, Rev John
Hall, Mrs Mary
Hughes, Thos-2
Hill, Eliz
Hais, Lt
Haight, SilAs-2
Heitmuller, Albre't
Hammond, Debby
Hollidy, Jos
Higgins, Rebecca
Howard, Mrs A F
Harris, Henry C
Houser, Wm
Horan, Mrs Mary
Henderson, Francis G W
Harrison, Wm R
Heintzleman, Capt S P
Hamilton, R C-6
Ingle, Mrs Mary

Ingersoll, Lt Harry	Murphy, Mrs M A E	Ridings, Fred'k
Jones, Miss Virgi'a	Marquis, Wm-2	Robey, Leonard S
Jones, Miss Mary J	Myers, Lawrence	Reeder, Richd
Johnson, Danl C	Merchant, And's-2	Richards, Miss S E
Johnson, Wm-3	Myers, Capt A C	Robinson, Sarah
Jackson, Wm S G	Milnes, Mrs Eliz C S	Reider, Mrs Lydia
Jackson, Miss Jane	Mattchett, Rev Wm	Ramsay, Mrs Eliza
Jordon, Alex'r	McRae, J J	Ratcliff, Louis
Jordan, Thos	McCarty, Thos	Robinson, Eleanor
King, Gen W M-2	McKenney, Patrick	Roberts, John
Kirk, Miss Mary H	McGowan, Robt	Reckless, Col J W
Key, Mrs S M	McFarran, Jas	Robinson, Miss Ma'a
King, Wm R	McIlroy, Benj	Rollins, Wm Emery
King, John	McQuigin, Capt	Riddle, John
Kingsbury, John	McDonald, Mrs A B	Ringgold, Lt T L-2
Kensett, Geo P-2	McClery, Dr J F J-2	Ringgold, Maj G H
Kunsman, Geo R	McCarty, Col John	Smith, Benj R
Kelly, Nathl	Noyes, Robt	Scott, Mrs Eliz P
Kellogg, Capt John	Nicholson, Com	Shield, David
Kennedy, Miss C S	Nelson, Mrs Recec's	Smith, Thos S
Lowe, Mrs Eliza	Obane, Monsieur	Shields, Wm
Leigh, Lt Wm	O'Conner, John	Smith, Mis Harriet
Lee, Mrs Robt E	O'Brien, John	Scheel, John E
Lee, Mrs Mary R	Ogden, John F	Simms, John thos
Lefebre, Mrs E	Oliver, Thos	Smith, John [fifer]
Lonsure, John	Pen, Mrs Matilda	Sloan, W H
Lucas, Sarah	Pool, Miss Rachael	Smith, Casper
Leddy, Hugh	Price, Hiland B	Straine, Lt Isaac G
Lucas, Mrs Ann M	Prevost, Henry M	Smith, Jas H
Lattimore, Miss M	Patton, Miss L Ann	Scott, Miss Mary E
Moore, Mrs Car'e	Powell, Miss J C	Scott, Miss Ann
Mount, Mrs M A-3	Parsons, John	Starke, Thos E
Mauss, Isaac R	Pringle, Mrs Ann R	Stetson, Miss M A
Moore, Dr S P, U S A	Powell, Jas R	Somerville, Robt
Moore, David	Philips. Jas B	Stewart, Carter
Moore, John	Philips, Reuben A	Simpson, Thos P
Matlock, Mrs A G	Pendleton, Edw H	Suter, Miss Frances
Moody, Priscilla	Pendleton, Mrs J S-2	Summers, John
Murdock, Mrs Eliza	Powers, Wm	Schiffler, Martin
Moulder, Andrew J	Pupo, Miss Harriet	Shorter, Wesley
Martin, Henry Clay	Rhett, Lt Thos G	Sumby, Mary
Montgomery, Sarah	Ricks, Jas T	Shorter, Nelson
Middleton, Theo's	Rhind, Pd Mid E C	Schureman, W D W
Martin, Geo-2	Ray, John R	Shiner, Mrs Marg't
Martin, John R	Rogers, Col John	Sangster, Capt Th-2

Stambaugh, Col S C-5	Vantyne, Dr J	Wilson, John
Skinner, Usher-6	West, Mrs Rosetta	Walker, Mrs Thos
Todd, John N	White, Chas W	Watkins, Miss M
Todd, Wm H	Walsh, Jas	Williams, Henry C
Timby, T R	White, Mathias M	Waller, Jas D
Tascoe, Thos	White, Henry	Watson, J
Thomas, Mrs Ann A	White, Jas W	Wheeler, Truman
Taylor, Henry	Wood, Wm N	Watkins, Miss M A
Thomas, John C	Ward, jr, Isaac L	Walter, Mrs Biddy
Tennison, Capt W A	West, Mrs Eliz E	Whittlesy, David C
Thorburn, Fred'k	Welsh, Aikman	Wineberger, Wm
Thayer, Jos	Williams, Mrs M	Williams, Jas-2
Thomas, Dr T	Williamson, Miss	Warley, Pd Md A
Timothy Division	Martha L	Younger, Edw
S of T	Wilkins, John	Younger, Sarah
Venner, Mrs Henreitta	Williams, Wm	

The inland postage on all letters intended to go by ship must be paid, otherwise they remain in this office. -C K Gardner, P M

Died: on Tue last, after an illness of 7 weeks, of pulmonary consumption, Saml Burche, in his 60th year. He was formerly during many years the able & faithful chief clerk in the clerk's ofc of the House of Reps, in which capacity he always enjoyed, in the highest degree, the respect of the members of the House. He was at the time of his death, as he had often been previously, a member of our City Council. His funeral will take place from his late residence tomorrow at 2 o'clock. [Members & ofcrs of the Boards of Adlerman & Common Council are respectfully requested to attend. –W W Seaton, Mayor]

Highly valuable real & personal estate at public auction: by deed of trust from Thos B Offutt, the undersigned, as trustee, will offer at public sale, on Oct 17, at the residence of Thos B Offutt, the following: the farm upon which Thos B Offutt now resides, formerly owned by Saml Hambleton, lying in Montg Co, about 18 miles from Wash, & about 1 mile from the main road leading from Monocacy to Gtwn, containing about 258 acres of land. Improvements are a large & comfortable dwlg, 36 feet by 30 feet, a large barn, kitchen, meat-house, corn-crib, dairy, & all other convenient out-bldgs. If the above real property is sold on the day of the sale, there will also be offered for sale the following personal property: 2 fine horses, cattle, hogs, household & kitchen furniture, farming utensils, corn in the loft, wheat & oats in the straw.
-John Brewer, Trustee

FRI OCT 2, 1846
Isaac Franklin, who begain life as a boatman, died recently at his residence in Sumner Co, Tenn, leaving an immense estate, the most of which he bequeathed to a seminary to be built on his own plantation in that county. The property so bequeathed is estimated at $600,000.

Ceremony on Sun last in The Roman Cathedral at Montreal-the elevating to the episcopal dignity of the Rev Mr Blanchet, one of the canons, who was nominated at Rome for the ofc of Archbishop of Oregon. His title is Archbishop of Wallawalla. 7 dioceses are now formed in Oregon, & provisionally 3 prelates superintend them, the Archbishop & 2 Bishops.

Liberal reward for strayed or stolen light bay mare, from the stable of P Moran, on Sep 28. –C Emmerick, corner of 9th & D sts.

Engine for sale: of one horse power, stroke of piston 6 inches, bore of cylinder 3 inches, boiler 4 feet long & 1 foot diameter, suitable for driving a lathe, cutting machine, or fan. See it in operation at the residence of N B Vanzandt, 12th & Mass ave. The owner has no use for it, & it will be sold much under its real value.

Household & kitchen furniture at auction on Oct 8, at the late residence of Mrs Buck, dec'd, on Capitol Hill, east of the north Capitol gate-excellent lot of furniture. –A Green, auctioneer

$100 reward for runaway negro man Chas Southern, about 24 years of age; ran away from the subscriber residing near Benedict, Chas Co, Md. –Philemon E Keech

Orphans Court of Wash Co, D C. Letters of administration on the personal estate of Thos W Pairo, late of said county, dec'd. –Chas W Pairo, exc

The St Louis Republican announces the recent arrival of an express at **Fort Leavenworth** from New Mexico, bringing the gratifying news of the entrance of Gen Kearney into Santa Fe without the firing of a gun or any opposition from the Mexicans whatsoever. This occurred on Aug 15, & the entire dept was formally taken possession of in the name of the United States. Thos W Pairo, late of said county, dec'd. –Chas W Pairo, exc

Died: on Sep 29, Francis Marion, y/s/o Cornelius & Catharine Colison, in his 5th year.

The friends & acquaintances of the late Col Saml Burche are respectfully invited to attend his funeral from his late residence this day at 2 o'clock.

For sale: 2 story dwlg in the 1st Ward, occupied by the subscriber, near the corner of I & 17th sts, & nearly opposite the residence of Mrs Gen Macomb. Inquire at the premises-Jno M Moore.

SAT OCT 3, 1846

The Hon Thos Sergeant, one of the Associate Judges of the Supreme Court of Pa, has resigned that ofc. The Bench loses a brilliant luminary. –U S Gaz

Drowning of 18 men by the overturning of a boat at Kingston, Canada West: they were employed on the Gov't works at Cedar Island, & were returning home in a boat, & made for the town, round Point Frederick. Most of them lost left wives & children. On one family, 5 of them having perished-the father, the husband, 2 brothers, & a brother-in-law were laid down dead before the agonized wife & sister. They were recent emigrants, only 6 weeks in the country. 14 women were made widows, & 72 children left orphans. [No names given.]

Paris, Aug 30, 1846. I am happy to inform you that Vanderlyn's "Landing of Columbus" wants but some slight touches to complete it, & it will be embarked for the U S in a few days. [Since the above was placed in the hands of the compositors, we discover that Mr Vanderlyn has arrived in N Y, having the picture here described. –Editors]

Marlborough Gaz: John Manning has declined being an independent candidate for the House of Delegates. Dr Tolson also declines.

Revolution: Capt Tynders has been deposed, & henceforth Mr John L Austin succeeds him as Capt of the Empire Club.

Teacher wanted: the Trustees of the Upper Marlborough Academy wish to engage for the ensuing year a single gentleman competent to teach a full course of Math & the Elementary branches of a sound English education. Salary will be $350 per annum. Apply to John B Brooke, Pres Board of Trustees U M A.

Orphans Court of Wash Co, D C. Letters of administration on the personal estate of Ann Scott, late of said county, dec'd. –Jos Scolfield, adm

Proposals will be received until Oct 10 for the bldg of a Grist Mill in Gtwn. For further particulars see Mr Saml Redfern, Grocery store, Wash. –Andrew R Ray & Brother

Mrd: on Aug 5, 1846, by Rev Geo W Samson, Adolph Fred'k Ahrens, of Phil, to Maria Virginia Antoinette, d/o Jas Townley, of Wash City.

Mrd: on Sep 29, at the Church of the Epiphany, by Rev Mr French, Conrad Pileto Eliz, d/o Col R P Pile, all of the Island of Barbadoes.

Died: on Oct 2, John Wayne, aged 88 years, many years a resident of Fred'k Co, Md. His funeral will take place from the residence of John L Wirt, North Capitol st, Capitol Hill. [No date or time for the funeral.]

Died: on Sep 29, Wm Thornton, infant son, & on Sep 30, Anna Hamilton, w/o Lt Thornton A Jenkins, U S Navy.

Died: on Sep 28, at **Bellwood**, St Mary's Co, Md, after a few days illness, in his 3rd year, Geo Washington Done, s/o the Rev W P C Johnson & Ann E Johnson.

For rent: 3 story brick house south of Capitol garden, either with or without furniture. Apply on the premises, or at C E Tim's ofc, 8th st, between E & F sts.

MON OCT 5, 1846

Cmdor Chas W Skinner took command of the Gosport Navy Yard on Thu, & hoisted his pennant on board the receiving ship **Pennsylvania**.

Died: on Fri last, at the residence of John W Maury, in Wash City, Sarah Ann, w/o Robt H Maury, of Richmond, Va, & oldest d/o Richd C Wortham, of the same place, in her 29th year.

Died: on Oct 4, after a long & painful illness, of pulmonary consumption, Miss Adeline Collins, in her 38th year. Her funeral is from the residence of Mrs Goldsmith, on 2nd st, Capitol Hill, this day, at 3 o'clock.

Tavern for rent: the hotel on the corner of 14th st & Md ave, at the Long Bridge, leading to Alexandria. Inquire at my Woodyard, 10th st & canal. –Peter Casanave

Public Sale: by virtue of a mortgage from Matilda Hatton & Jos Hatton, to the undersigned, dated Nov 6, 1842, he will sell at public sale to the highest bidder for cash, on Oct 17, several likely negroes. Sale at the late residence of Jos Hatton, at 10 o'clock. –T I Marshall

Wash Light Infty regular month meeting of the corps will be held in the armory on this evening, at 7 o'clock. By order: W H Clark, Sec

Samaritan Association meeting at the City Hall, this evening, at half past 7 o'clock. –Wm Flinn, Sec

Desirable tavern stand for sale: in Wash City, between Pa ave & City Hall, known as the Farmer's Hotel, corner of 8th & D sts, fronting 100 feet on D, by 57 feet on 8th st. A portion of the above now rents for the interest of $11,000. Apply to Owen Connolly, Proprietor, or to A Green, Auctioneer.

Farm for sale: in Montg Co, Md, within 1½ miles from Wash City: lies adjoining the lands of Elisha W Williams & Geo Dawson, & contains about 400 acs. If desired, city property will be taken in lieu of the deferred payments. Apply to Jeremiah Williams, Gtwn.

Orphans Court of Wash Co, D C. Letters testamentary on the personal estate of Henry Stone, late of said county, dec'd. –John G Stone, Philip Stone, excs

For sale: a farm containing 41 acres, with a small house & stable. Owner leaving the city. Situation is beautiful, a 1½ miles north of the Capitol, adjoining Brentwood. Inquire of the subscriber, at Galabrun's Hotel, or at the wharf at the foot of 17th st, near the late Gen Van Ness' residence. –Calhoun M Derringer

Trustee's sale of valuable lot: by virtue of a deed of trust from O Connolly & T McGuire to the subscriber, dated Mar 13, 1846, recorded in Liber W B 126, Wash Co, D C land records. Sale in front of the premises on Oct 16, all that part of lot 18 in square 407 fronting 25 feet on 8th st west & running back 50 feet, with the improvements thereon. –Geo Mattingly, trustee -R W Dyer, auct

Tribute of respect was paid to the memory of Lt Geo M Bache, U S Navy, by the U S Coast Survey at Wash. Intelligence was announced of the loss of Lt Bache, while in command of the brig **Washington**, & engaged on duty connected with the survey of the coast. He received his education in Phil; about 8 years ago he entered upon the duties of the coast survey; he was first under Cmder Gedney; he looked to the exploration of the Gulf stream as the crowning labor upon his work. He had made one very successful cruise, & was returning from a second, the results of which are reported to have been not less interesting than those of the first, when overtaken by the storm of the 7th & the hurricane of the 8th of Sept. All that nautical skill & intrepidity could do were tried to save his ofcrs, crew, & vessel, & the very manoeuvre which gave them safety rendered it impossible that he should recover the deck when swept from it. His after sufferings may be imagined, but are known only to the God & father who has received his spirit. Honorable fame is the inheritance of his orphan children.

Orphans Court of Wash Co, D C. Letters testamentary on the personal estate of Alex'r C W Fanning, late of the U S Army, dec'd. –Harriet O Read, excx

Balt: 1-A little child, s/o Mr Jos Minning, of this city, fell from the 2nd story window of its father's dwlg Oct 2, & was killed. 2-On Oct 3 a young man named Merchant fell from the top of a new bldg on which he was at work & died instantly.

TUE OCT 6, 1846
Letter to the Editors from an ofcr at Pensacola, dated Sep 25: It is very sickly ashore. Most are down with the fever. The Rev C H Alden, Chaplain of the yard, died early on yesterday morning, & was buried in the afternoon with military honors. A number of men have been lost at the forts at the mouth of the harbor.

Fayetteville [Tenn] Journal: fire destroyed the house of Mr Jas Gill, some 13 miles from Fayetteville. Three of his children perished and the 4th received severe burns, & it is doubtful he will recover. Mr Gill himself was also badly burnt.

For rent: a 2 story frame house on 19th st, near Pa ave. Apply to S C Davison, on G st, near 19th, or at the Treasury Dept.

Mrd: on Oct 4, by Rev G W Samson, Mr Lewis I Burkhart to Miss Mary Ann Parsons, both of Wash City.

Died: on Sun last, at the residence of Thos Young, in Wash City, Jas J Crane, of St Mary's Co, Md, s/o Col Geo Crane, of the same county, aged about 25 years. His funeral is this afternoon at 3 o'clock, from the residence of Thos Young, on Missouri ave.

Died: on Sep 1, at Cincinnati, Ohio, Dr J Henry Wintrode, of Hanover, Pa in his 25th year. He was sincere & ardent as a friend, exemplary & moral as a citizen, & with a strong desire to be useful to the community.

For rent: desirable 3 story frame dwlg, containing 10 rooms, on 6th st, between F & G sts. Apply to Chas Lyons, 10th st.

On Sep 24 near Burlington, Vt, 3 young men, Cheney, Thompson, & Connolly, went out upon the lake in a small row-boat, & were upset. Cheney died from cold & fatigue; Thompson became deranged & perished. Connolly was taken up insensible but it is thought he will recover.

Groceries, liquors, & store fixtures at auction: on Oct 8, at the store occupied by the late Wm B Laub, 15th & F sts. –R W Dyer, auct

Orphans Court of Wash Co, D C. Letters testamentary on the personal estate of Wm B Laub, late of said county, dec'd. –E A Laub, excx

Strayed or stolen from the subscriber, a roan Horse; also, at the same time, a sorrel Horse. $5 reward for each Horse. –Catherine Pearson, Brentwood
–Jas A Shaw, Agent

Maryland House, [late Verandah Hotel.] The undersigned has taken that commodious house recently occupied by Messrs Cotter & Thompson, north side of Pa ave, between 3rd & 4½ sts: board $1 per day; meals prepared at a few minutes' notice, at any hour, & sent to any part of the city when ordered.
-Leonard P Roby

Notice is given that the partnership lately subsisting between Jas B Bragdon & Chas E Twombly, of Wash City, under the firm of Bragdon & Twombly, was dissolved on Oct 1, 1846, by mutual consent. All debts owing said partnership are to be received by Jas B Bragdon. –Jas B Bragdon, Chas E Twombly

WED OCT 7, 1846
The Defence of the *Alamo* in 1836. Letter from on ofcr of the Army: San Antonio de Bexar, Texas, Aug 24, 1846. On Feb 23, 1836, Santa Anna entered San Antonio de Bexar & took possession of the town without firing a gun. The small garrison of 130 men, under the command of Wm Barret Travis, retired, as he advanced, to the Alamo, on the opposite side of the river. On the 25th, the siege on the *Alamo* began. The Mexican Gen received large reinforcements, & his army now numbers 1,000. The siege continues for 10 days. Travis shows himself on the walls, cheering on his undaunted followers. Around him are Crockett, Evans, & Bonham, roused to a last struggle, for they know their doom is sealed. Travis receives a shot, staggers & falls. He dies not unavenged. A Mexican ofcr rushed upon him, & is about to plunge his sabre into the bosom of the fallen man, when, gathering all his energies for a last effort, he bathes his own sword in the blood of his enemy, & they die together. The conflict becomes hand to hand. The carnage has been so terrible that the slain are piled up in heaps. Crockett has been conspicuous in the melee, wherever the blows fell hottest & thickest. At one glance he sees that the fate of the *Alamo* rests upon himself alone. Travis has fallen; Evans is no more; Bowie expires upon a bed of sickness, pierced to the heart by a Mexican bayonet; Bonham fell before his eyes, & he finds himself the only living warrior of the 163 who had been his comrades. Crockett makes his way to the door of the chapel. At length a ball from a distant rifle pierces him in the forehead: he falls backward to the earth, in the streams of gore which curdle around him. No groan escapes his lips; no cry of agony gratifies the implacable rancor of his enemies: he dies, & the *Alamo* has fallen. -K

A machine for cutting wrought nails has been invented by Mr J H Holcomb, of Brandon, Vt, which with 2 men will make as many nails per day as 40 or 50 men can do, & with a great saving of iron.

The New Orleans Times mentions the death in that city of an Italian named Roscende, who had served as a city watchman for the last 26 years. He was a miser in his habits, & at his death left an estate of $25,000 to $30,000.

The U S sloop of war **Plymouth**, Henry Henry, Cmder, arrived at N Y on Sun from Rio Janeiro: she was absent 2 years & 6 months, during which time she has been in Europe, Asia, Africa, & South America. List of her ofcrs:
Cmder, Henry Henry
Lts-4: Henry Darcantel, Dominick Lynch, Lewis C Sartere, Wm May
Surgeon, Wm F McClenahan   Capt's Clerk, Geo F Geessinger
Assist Surgeon, Thos P McBlair   Passed Midshipmen: Courtlandt
Acting Master, Wm L Blanter   Benham
1st Lt of Marines, Wm L Young
Midshipmen-4: Greenleaf Celley, Jefferson Maurey, Wm G Hoffman, Chas McGarg
Acting Boatswain, John Featherson   Acting Carpenter, Chas W Babbett
Gunner, Thos Dewey   Sailmaker, Henry Bacon
Passengers: Lt Wm P Griffen, Lt W L Drayton, Acting gunner, Francis Dawson.

On Wed an intemperate, malevolent, & quarrelsome Irishman, Jas Gough, shot his wife & one of his children, a boy about 5 or 6 years of age. He was in the employ of Mr Jos Savage, as a laborer upon his coarse salt fields, & resided in a shanty a few rods from the road. After an argument at dinner, Gough took down his gun & fired hitting his wife in her left arm, hitting the backhead of the boy. The latter at the time was clinging to his mother. [Where this happened is not given; but it is under other local items.]

Mrd: on Sun last, by Rev Mr Matthews, Mr John H Reiss to Miss Eliza Loveless, all of Wash City.

German Benevolent Society Ball: Cmte of invitations & reception:
G Strobel   M Kaiser
Mr Lockmeyer   B Ostermayer
Wm Voss   Mr Grammer
T Schlegel   F Stutz
Mr Hoehn   G Willner
J H T Werner   Mr Rheinhard
Mr Hansam

For rent: a large house on Capitol Hill, now occupied by Mrs Mount as a boarding house. Apply to Benj E Green, or to Jas Adams.

THU OCT 8, 1846
Died: on Oct 7, in Wash City, Mrs Jasabella McGarvey, in her 37th year, a native of the county of Donegal, Ireland. Her funeral is from her late residence at the railroad Hotel, at 3 o'clock tomorrow.

Died: on Oct 3, at the residence of his son, V Pulizzi, Mr Felice Pulizzi, in his 76th year, a native of Cantania, in the island of Sicily, & has resided in Wash City for the last 41 years. [See Oct 14th newspaper.]

Died: on Oct 6, at the residence of her father, on 10th, between G & H sts, Harriet, w/o Mr Oliver Barron, & eldest d/o Benj & Harriet Williamson, of Wash City, in her 22nd year.

Died: on Sep 28, in Warren Co, N C, Mrs Birchett Ransom, wid/o the late Mr Seymour Ranson, in her 80th year. During her long, active, & useful life she never made an enemy for a moment, nor spoke unkindly of mortal. Retaining her mental faculties until the last sand of life had run, she died in peace.

For sale, a small farm containing about 100 acres, one mile south of Beltsville, PG Co, Md, immediately on the Railroad. Circumstances beyond the control of the owner make it necessary for him to sell, or it could not be purchased for double its value. Apply at Beltsville. –Wm Coale

St Charles Hotel: having leased the entire upper part of the hotel, consisting of 30 or 40 rooms, I am prepared to receive transient or permanent guests by day, week, month, or year. –C J MacLellan

Orphans Court of Wash Co, D C. Letters testamentary on the personal estate of Robt Tweedy, late of said county, dec'd. –Arian Tweedy, Jacob Gideon, excs

Handsome furnished residence for rent: situated on G st, near 17th st west, lately occupied by Gen Gratiot. Apply soon, near the premises, to Mrs E Ricketts.

For rent: commodious house on south side of Capitol Hill, formerly known as the Bank of Washington. It contains 5 rooms on the lower floor, & 6 on the 2nd story, besides large passages & closets, & several rooms in the basement. Apply at the ofc of Henry M Morfit, on 4½ st, near Pa ave, or at the house.

Paper hangings, painted window shades, rich curtain tassels, loops & cords, bell-pulls, oil cloths, & table covers: Stephen P Franklin, importer & dealer, at his old stand, on Pa ave.

New furniture at auction on Oct 12, at the Cabinet Ware Rooms of Mr J E W Thompson. -R W Dyer, auct

The copartnership existing between O S Paine & J H McBlair is this day dissolved by mutual consent. Mr J H McBlair is alone authorized to settle the affairs of the firm. McBlair will continue the family grocery business at the old stand, north side of Pa ave, between 17th & 18th sts.

FRI OCT 9, 1846
Commencement of the Columbian College took place last Wed in the Rev Samson's Church, on E st: the Pres of the U S & 2 members of the Cabinet, were present. Oration by J C Bagby, Stevensville, Va; by W J Brookes, Hamburg, S C; by R Burton, Petersburg, Va; by J Hammitt, Phil; by R S Haynes, Bruington, Va; by J Pickett, Fauquier, Va; by H Stringfellow, jr, Wash; by A J Huntington, College Hill, D C; & by T W Haynes, Bruington, Va. Poem by G P Nice, Phil. Music. Conferring of degrees-Benediction. Candidates for the 2nd degree:

P A Aylett, Alabama	C Graham, S C	E G Smallwood, N C
R L Butts, Georgia	J A Haynes, Va	A B McWhorter, Alabama
J R Garlick, Va	A J Huntington, D C	
A Gindrat, Alabama	T P Janes, Georgia	J W M Williams, Va

The honorary degree of LL D was conferred on Hon Isaac Davis, of Mass, & on Hon J B O'Neale, of S C.

Lime, wood, & coal: Walter Warder, corner 12th & C sts north, near the Canal.

For sale: a valuable lot of woodland, 4 miles north of Wash, near Rock Creek Church, containing 55 acres, & will cut from 25 to 30 cords of wood to the acre. Apply to Thos McCormick, Alexandria, Va, or of Mr Majors, at the Toll Gate, 7th st road.

Extensive sale of household furniture, plated ware, china & glass ware: by deed of trust from L Galabrun to the subscriber, dated Jun 27, 1846, at the European Hotel, on Pa ave, between 14th & 15th sts, on Nov 2 next. –Johnson Hellen, trustee -R W Dyer, auct

Wash Corp: 1-Ptn of John Lewis, praying remission of a fine: referred to the Cmte of Claims. 2-Ptn of John Hilliary, praying remission of a fine: referred to the Cmte of Claims. 3-Ptn of Amandies Baumback, praying remission of a fine: referred to the Cmte of Claims. 4-Act for the relief of Michl Joyce: referred to the Cmte on Improvements.

Wm Milburn has removed his Furniture Store to the east side of 7th st, opposite to Messrs Gales & Seaton's printing ofc.

Died: on Sep 29, at his residence in Montg Co, Md, after a short & severe illness, Baker Waters, aged 68 years. Maryland has lost one of her most valuable & respectable citizens. In his family he has left a place as a husband & a brother which can scarcely be supplied.

I hereby give notice that the Library of Congress will be closed on Oct 20th, & re-opened Nov 17. –John S Meehan, Librarian

Business stands for rent: the store on the eastern corner of 7th & E sts, with or without dwlg above, at present occupied by John Suter. Also, the large store on the s e corner of 4½ st & Pa ave, now fitting up. Apply to Raphael Semmes & Co, Pa ave.

J T & C King will remove their Lace Store, between 12th & 13th sts, next week to the splendid store lately fitted up by J K Boyd, between 10th & 11th sts. Ladies who will call this week may expect to receive about $2 worth of goods for $1. –J T & C King

For rent: 2 houses, 1 brick & 1 frame: on the east side of 7th st, between G & H sts. Apply on the premises to Alex'r Talburt.

SAT OCT 10, 1846
In Chancery: Circuit Court of Wash Co, D C: Amos Binney, adm, cmplnt, vs, the heirs of Jas Thomas, dec'd, Byron Wilkinson, Paul Spofford, Thos Tileton, et al, dfndnts. By decree of the Court dated Mar 15, 1846, it was ordered that the said cmplnt's bill should be taken for confessed against the said dfndnts, unless they appear & make answer to the said bill on or before the 4th Mon of Oct, 1846. The said absent dfndnts are warned to appear. –D A Hall, Solicitor for cmplnt

Mrd: on Oct 1, at New Bedford, Mass, at the residence of Hon Jos Grinnell, Nathl P Willis to Miss Cornelia Grinnell, the adopted d/o Mr Grinnell.

At the meeting of the Stockholders of the Navy Yard Bridge Co at the Bank of Wash, on Oct 6, the following were elected Directors for the ensuing year:
Wm Gunton-Pres   John Davis [of Abel]   Alex'r H Lawrence
Alex'r McWilliams   Jas Owner

Life lost on Tue to the careless habit of walking upon the railroad track. Mr John Pond, a worthy citizen of Hopkinton, was run over by the noon train of cars from Worcester, & killed instantly. –Boston Paper

The venerable Dr Waterhouse died at his residence in Cambridge, Mass, on Oct 3, at the advanced age of 92 years. He was born at Newport, R I, & resided there until 1775, when he was sent to London to be placed under the charge of Dr Fothergill, a maternal relative. After pursuing his studies in Edinburgh, he graduated at the Univ of Leyden. On his return to his native land, he was elected to a professorship in Harvard Unis, & 62 years ago was chosen Prof of Natural History in Brown Univ. He was ardently attached to the profession of medicine, as well as its kindred sciences, particularly botany, in which he acquired a high reputation. –Providence Journal

On Thu week, in Morgan Co, Va, a young man named Selvestin Michael was shot by another, Peter Fenner. They went out together in hunt of wild turkeys, when Fenner accidentally shot & killed Michael.

St Stephen's Chapel [Protestant Episcopal] was dedicated to Divine service on Mon last, in Boston. The bldg & lot cost upwards of $22,000, all of which was paid by Wm Appleton, who presented the whole to the Bishop.

MON OCT 12, 1846
Hasty Memoranda of the operations of the American Army before Monterey, Mexico, from Sep 19 to Sep 24. On the 19th Gen Taylor arrived before Monterey with a force of about 6,000 men; on the 20th, Gen Worth was ordered with his division to move by a circuitous route to the right to gain the Saltillo road & to storm the heights above the Bishop's Palace; he had to continue his route on the 21st; on the same morning the 1st division of regular troops, under Gen Twiggs, & the volunteer division, under Gen Butler, were ordered under arms to make a diversion to the left of the town; this battery was ordered to open upon the citadel & town; immediately after the 1st division, with the 3rd & 4th in advance, under Col Garland, were ordered to skirmish with the enemy on the left of the city; this attack was directed by Maj Mansfield, Engineer, Capt Williams, Topographical Engineer, & Maj Kinney, Quartermaster to the Texas division. The bldg was occupied by infty; the first division was followed & supported by the Mississippi & Tennessee & the 1st Ohio Regts, the 2 former Regts being the first to scale & occupy the fort. The 3rd, 4th, & 1st Infty & the Balt Btln remained at the garrison of the captured position, under Col Garland, assisted by Capt Ridgely's

battery. On the 22nd Gen Worth stormed & carried successively the heights above the Bishop's Palace. Both were carried by a command under Capt Vinton, 3rd Artl. The company of Louisiana troops under Capt Blanchard performed efficient & gallant service as part of Capt Vinton's command. On the evening of the 22nd, Col Garland & his command were relieved as the garrison of the captured forts, by Gen Quitman with the Miss & Tenn Regts, & 5 companies of the Ky Regt. Troops were thrown into the streets to reconnoitre, & soon became hotly engaged with the enemy; supported by Col Wood's Regt of Texas Rangers,dismounted, by Bragg's light battery, & the 3rd infty. On the 24th a communication was sent to Gen Taylor from Gen Ampudia, under a flag, making an offer of capitulation, to which Taylor refused to accede, as it asked more than the American cmder would under any circumstances grant. At the same time a demand to surrender was in reply made upon Gen Ampudia: he was granted one hours to accept or refuse. Before the expiration of the hour, an ofcr was sent on the part of Gen Ampudia to inform the American Gen that, to avoid the further effusion of blood, & the nat'l honor being satisfied by the exertions of the Mexican troops, he had, after consultation with his Genr'l Ofcrs, decided to capitulate, accepting the offer of the American Genr'l. Terms of capitulation were in effect as follows:

Ofcrs should be allowed to march out with their side arms.
Cavalry & infty should be allowed to march out with their arms & accoutrments.
Artl should be allowed to march out with one battery of 6 pieces & 20 rounds of ammunition
All other munitions of war & supplies should be turned over to a board of American Ofcrs appointed to receive them.
Mexican army should be allowed 7 days to evacuate the city, & that the American troops should not occupy it until evacuated.
The **Cathedral Fort**, or **Citadel**, should be evacuated at 10 a m on the 25th, the Mexicans then marching out & the American garrison marching in. The Mexicans allowed to salute their flag when hauled down.
There should be an armistice of 8 weeks, during which time neither army should pass a line running from the Rinconada through Linares & San Ferdnando.
This lenient offer of the American Genr'l was dictated with the concurrence of his Gen'ls, & by motives of good policy & consideration for the good defence of their city by the Mexican army.

Killed:

Capt Williams, Topographical Enginineers	Lt Hoskins, 4th Infty
Lt Terrett, 1st Infty	Lt Woods, 4th Infty
Capt L N Morris, 3rd Infty	Capt McKavett, 8th Infty
Capt Field, 3rd Infty	Col Watson, Balt Btln, Sep 21
Maj Barbour, 3rd Infty	Capt Battlem, 1st Tenn Regt
Lt Irwin, 3rd Infy	Lt Putnam, 1st Tenn Regt
Lt Hazlitt, 3rd Infty	A Lt in a Germany company

Wounded:

Maj Lear, 3rd Infty, severely	Capt Bainbridge, 3rd Infty, very slightly

Lt R H Graham, 4th Infty, severely
Capt Lamotte, 1st Infty, slightly
Lt Dilworth, 1st Infty, severely
Maj Abercrombie, 1st Infty, slightly
Lt Wainwright, 8th infty, slightly
Lt Rossell, 5th Infty, slightly
Lt Potter, 7th Infty, slightly
Maj Mansfield, Engineers, slightly
Gen Butler, Volunteer Division, slightly
Capt Gillespie, Texas Rangers, mortally, since dead

Col Mitchell, Ohio Volunteers, slightly
Col McClung, Miss Regt, severely
Maj Alexander, Tenn Volunteers
Lt Allen, Tenn Volunteers
Lt Scudder, Tenn Volunteers
Lt Nixon, Tenn Volunteers
Capt Dowler, Miss Regt
Lt Thomas, Texas Regt
Lt Armstrong, Ohio, severely

Intelligence received of the shipwreck of the brig **Rienzi**, of Boston, & the loss of 16 lives, in the gale of the 15th & 16th ult, to which the Great Western was exposed. Capt Small, his mate, & young son, about 16 years of age, together with 2 boat steerers, ship-keeper, & steward, were drowned in the cabin. Some were drowned in the forecastle, & others were washed overboard. The survivors remained on the wreck for 10 days, & all the provisions they had was about half a deck bucket of bread, which had been socked for 48 hours in salt water. They were rescued by the vessel **Minerva**, 5 in number, 2 boys having died the day before. The poor fellows were mere skeletons, & would have probably died during the night if they had not been relieved.

Nothing has been heard of the steamer **Great Britain**. Her day of sailing was fixed for Sep 22. If she sailed on that day, this is the 19th day she has been out.

Died: on Oct 5, in Boston, Mrs Juliana Jump, w/o Dr Thos L Jump, & d/o the late Gen Robt R Johnson, of N C.

Died: yesterday, after a short illness, Alice, the d/o Robt & Rose Greenhow, aged 4 years. Her funeral is from the residence of the parents, in F st, tomorrow, at 4 o'clock.

A general Court Martial was convened on board the U S ship **North Carolina**, in N Y harbor, on Fri, for the trial of such cases as may come before it. The following ofcrs compose the Court:
Capt Benj Cooper, Pres
Capt Salters
Capt Stringham
Capt McIntosh
Capt Bigelow

Capt Hudson
Capt Engle
Lt Ellison
Lt Calhoun
Garrett R Barry, Judge Advocate

Notice is hereby given that from & after this date I will not pay any bill or bills unless contracted by myself in person. –Chas Gordon

TUE OCT 13, 1846

Our esteemed countryman, the Rev Dr Robt Baird, now in Europe, on his second mission in the cause of Temperance, happened to be in Russia at the time of the marriage of the Grand Duchess Olga, d/o the Emperor of Russia, to the Crown Prince of Wurtemberg. Dr Baird was honored with an invitation to be present at the marriage. In his letter dated St Petersburg, Jul 15, 1846 he gives an account of the wedding which took place [on the 1st old style, but the 13th according to the new] at the chapel of the Palace. Next to the Empress stood her brother, the Prince of Prussia, the heir to the throne of that country. Next to him stood the Duchess of Leuchtenberg, the oldest d/o the Emperor, & her sister-in-law, the wife of his imperial highness Alex'r Nicholauvitch, the heir of the throne of Russia. Next to them stood Prince Nicholas, & Michael, who are youths from 18 to 10 or 12 years. Next to them stood the Grand Duke Michael, the brother of the Emperor. Next to him was the Duke of Leuchtenburg. The Prince was dressed in the uniform of a Wurtemberg ofcr of the highest rank: a fine looking man, of between 23 & 24 years of age. The Grand Duchess is 24 years of age, & is older than her husband by some 6 months: she is a beautiful woman: she is even called the most beautiful woman in Europe. Her dress was magnificent, as may be supposed. She is above medium height of ladies, had bright blue eyes, a fair bonde complexion, & auburn hair. During the whole service the Emperor, the Empress, all the members of the Imperial family, & many of the spectators, crossed themselves frequently, according to the custom of the Greek Church, with much apparent devotion. It was easy to see that the Emperor doted upon his beloved daughter. The marriage ceremony, according to the Protestant manner, took place immediately after in one of the large rooms of the palace. It was simple, serious, & appropriate, but contained nothing worthy of a particular notice. It was performed by Dr Pauffler, a worthy Protestant divine. Dinner followed at 4 p m.

The brig **Casket**, of Beverly, arrived at Boston on Thu, from Kabenda, west coast of Africa, in command of Lt C C Barton, of the U S sloop-of-war **Marion**. The **Casket** was seized by the **Marion** on suspicion of being concerned in the slave trade. –Journal

List of ofcrs of the U S frig **Cumberland**: French Forrest, captain; Saml F Hazard, 1st Lt, Raphael Semmes, 2nd Lt; John A Winslow, 3rd Lt; Francis B Renshaw, 4th Lt; Edwin J De Haven, 5th Lt; Mathew C Perry, 1st master; J Hogan Brown, 2nd master; Alvin Edson, capt of marines; Waters Smith, fleet surgeon; Nathl Wilson, purser; Fitch W Taylor, chaplain; Wm S Bishop, assist surgeon; E Ross Colhoun, Alex'r J Dallas, Reginald Fairfax, & Jos S Day, passed midshipmen; Nathl T West, Jas L Johnson, Walter W Queen, Alex'r Habersham, Robt B Stover, M J Smith, Jos A Seawell, & Geo B Hodge, midshipmen; Henry R Weightman, capt's clerk; Chas Johnson, boatswain; Elijah Haskell, gunner; Amos Chick, carpenter; Thos J Boyce, sailmaker; Wm S Brooks, purser's clerk; Michl Shay, ship's steward. The **Cumberland** bearing the broad pennant of Cmdor David Conner; Lt C W Morris, signal ofcr; W D McLeod, sec.

Mrd: on Oct 6, at Brooklyn, N Y, at the Church of the Emanuel, by Rev Mr Vinton, Dr Henry W Tabb, of Auburn, Va, to Miss Ellen A Foster, of Phil.

Mrd; on Oct 8, at Alexandria, Va, by Rev Jas T Johnston, Jas U Dennis, of Somerset Co, Md, to J Cecilia Hooe, y/d/o Bernard Hooe.

Died: yesterday, at his residence in Gtwn, after a long illness, Raphael Semmes, widely known & valued as one of our most extensive merchants & excellent citizens. His funeral will take place from his late residence on tomorrow forenoon at 10 o'clock.

Died: on Oct 8, in Balt, after an illness of 4 weeks, of congestion of the brain, Julia, d/o the late Hon John C Herbert, of PG Co, Md, aged 26 years.

Died: on Oct 1, Col Byrd C Willis, of this town, aged 65 years. During the war he served in the regular Army with the rank of Capt of Infty, but, as his motive for entering the service was a purely patriotic one, he did not continue in the Army after the war. The rest of his life, except a residence of 11 years, from 1825 to 1836, in Florida, was spent here. –Fredericksburg Herald

An inquest was held lately in Staffordshire, England, before G Hutchins, coroner, at the house of Mr Thos Sower, Sun Inn, Brockmoor, on the body of Jane Webb, aged 6 years, who was found drowned in the canal near Mr Firmstone's works at the Ley Colliery. Her body at first could not be found: a young woman insisted that they should get a loaf of bread & put quicksilver in it & it would float to the body if it was in the water. This was done & the loaf & quicksilver were thrown into the water & it floated to a certain spot, turned round several times, & remained. Beneath this spot the lost child was found. –Cist's Adv

Mr Hoyt, who was shot at Richmond on Sep 27, by Mr Wm R Myers, died of his wounds on Fri last.

Land for sale: 120 acres fronting on Rockville turnpike, a mile of the Gtwn corporation line, & north of the land of Mr John Green. Also, 15 acres on the same road, being the meeting-house lot. Also, 50 acres adjoining Tenallytown, & immediately north of Mrs Syles' farm. Apply to Richd Smith, or to Chas J Nourse.

Public sale: by deed of mortgage from Wm H Ward to John Van Riswick, dated Jan 8, 1846, recorded in Liber W B 121, folios 1 & 2, of the land records of Wash Co, & also in liber A 1, pages 287 to 289, of transfers of patent rights in the U S Patent Ofc, I shall offer at auction, on Oct 17, at my auction rooms, a Steam Engine, Planing Mill, Saw Mill, Circular Saw, & Patterns, & the Scow on which they are placed, now lying at or adjacent to a wharf in Gtwn, D C. Also, the exclusive right of using the Woodworth Patent Planing Machine for D C, said exclusive right to continue until Dec 27, 1849. -R W Dyer, auct

Household & kitchen furniture at auction on Oct 16, by order of the Orphans Court of Wash Co, D C, at the residence of the late Wm Ford, on F st, between 20th & 21st sts. -R W Dyer, auct

Lost or mislaid: a note drawn by Edw S Wright, dated Gtwn, Sep 30, 1846, at 4 months payable to the order of Benj Homans, & by him endorsed, for $118.18. Finder will confer a favor & receive the thanks of the subscriber by leaving it at his auction store.
–R W Dyer, auct

Desirable bldg lot at auction: on Oct 15, on the premises, lot 22 in reservation 11: fronts on 2nd st west, between B & C sts; it adjoins the property of R Dement & J Acker, opposite the Railroad outer depot.
–B Homans, auct

Toledo Land Agency: Elisha Whittlesey & Co have associated to establish an extensive land agency at Toledo, Ohio. They will take charge of & sell lands in Northern Ohio, Southern Michigan, & Northern Indiana. –Elisha Whittlesey, O H Knapp, J W Scott, & J Fitch

Balt & the North: Oct 12. Joy at the recent victory of our arms at Monterey; sorrow for the fate of our gallant townsman, Col Wm H Watson. Thus, in the meridian of manhood, has our noble-hearted fellow citizen found a soldier's & patriot's death; he was probably in his 37th & 38th year; has filled some important stations in our State gov't; held a prominent position as a member of the Balt bar. He has left a wife & 2 children, a son & a dght, of the ages of about 15 & 13 years. The sad tiding of his death was communicated to Mrs Watson last night. She is now quite indisposed.

WED OCT 14, 1846

Wash Corp: 1-Cmte of Claims: act for the relief of Thos Baker: read. 2-Expediency of changing the location of the Centre Market: twice read. 3-Nominations from the Mayor for Superintendents of Chimney Sweeps: W A Robinson, Geo Y Bowen, John E Keenan, Jas Littleton, David Westerfield, N B Wilkinson: all were confirmed, except that of John E Keenan, which was rejected. 4-Jacob Kleiber was confirmed as Inspector of Flour & Salted Provisions. 5-Wm M McCauley was confirmed as Sealer of Weights & Measurements. 6-<u>Trustees of the Public Schools duly elected</u>:

Robt Farnham	J T Van Reswick	John F Callan
Geo J Abbott	Abel G Davis	W B Randolph
J F Hartley	Thos Donoho	Ignatius Mudd
Geo Watterston	Valentine Harbaugh	Craven Ashford

7-<u>Police Magistrates duly elected</u>:

Saml Drury	T C Donn	Reuben Burdine
Saml Smoot	John L Smith	Jas Crandall
John D Clark	Thos Donoho	Benedict Milburn
B K Morsell	Jas Marshall	John W Williams

Counterfeiters arrested: The Nashville Union of Oct 1 says-Yesterday 4 men, calling themselves Wm C Spencer, Wm Brown, Jas Johnson, & Wm Boyd, were arrested for possession of counterfeit money.

Lewistown [Pa] Gaz: some days since 3 young ladies, Miss Kipperling, Miss Bare, & Miss Baker, were suddenly drowned. They had gone to the spring house to secure some articles, as a flood was threatening. While there the rain fell in torrents, & the torrent rushing in it at the door was so great as to bar egress.

Mrd: on Oct 13, at Gtwn, D C, by Rev Alex Shiras, Ferdinand W Risque, of St Louis, Mo, to Miss Caroline Salmona, d/o John Pickrell, of the former place.

Died: on Oct 12, at the residence of his brother-in-law, Capt Wm I Belt, in the Forest of PG Co, Md, Edmund Coolidge, of Wash City, in his 37th year. His funeral is at that place on Wed, at 12 o'clock.

Died: on Oct #, at the Navy Yard, after a short illness, Mr Felice Pulizzi, in his 76th year. He was a native of Catania, in the island of Sicily, at which place he was born in 1771. In 1805, during the war with Tripoli, he entered the service of the U S, & after the termination of that war he migrated with a wife & 3 children to this country, intending to make it the home of his adoption & the native home of the children with whom he might subsequently be blessed. He renounced allegiance to his own country, espoused the cause of freedom, & he came to enjoy the inestimable rights of an American citizen. He has left behind him children & grand-children whose grief would be in vain to attempt to describe. A kinder father never lived.
–J A L [Death notice in Oct 8th newspaper.]

Monterey, now in possession of Gen Taylor, is the capital of the State of New Leon. It is on the Fernando river: has well paved streets & mostly 1 story stone bldgs: population is about 12,000, & the city is on the main traveling route from the Rio Grande to the city of Mexico.

Miss Jane E Biscoe will open on Oct 15, a handsome assortment of fashionable millinery, on Pa ave, next door to D Clagett's.

Mr G Doub, one of the Whig Delegates elected to the Legislature of Md on Wed last, from Fred'k Co, died on Sunday after a short illness. A special election will be held to fill the vacancy.

Strayed away from the residence of the subscriber, on Oct 7, a Red Buffalo or Muley Cow. Liberal reward for her return to the owner on F st, between 12th & 13th sts, Wash.
–Wm H Dietz

Horses, carriages, carts, household & kitchen furniture at auction on Oct 21, at the residence of Mr Z Hazel, on Md ave. –A Green, auctioneer

Single & double-barrel guns, hunting apparatus, & powder flasks, for sale.
–John W Abden, Pa ave & 6th st

THU OCT 15, 1846
Alexandria Boarding School, founded in 1824 by the subscriber, & conducted by him till 1842, & since that time by Caleb S & Jas S Hallowell, will resume on Nov 16. It is particularly calculated for those who design engaging in the business of Teaching. –Benj Hallowell. Rockland, Md, Nov 3, 1846 [Application may be made to the subscriber, at Sandy Spring Post Ofc, Montg Co, Md, or to his nephews, Caleb S Hallowell & Brother, Alexandria, Va. It is proper to state that no smoking or use of tobacco is allowed among the students.]

Died: on Tue last, at his residence in Wash City, after a protracted illness, the Rt Rev Henry S Fox, late her Britannic Majesty's Minister Plenipotentiary to the Gov't of the U S. [Oct 16th newspaper: Hon Henry Stephen Fox was born in 1791, the s/o Gen Henry Edw Fox, 3rd s/o Henry Fox, the first Lord Holland. He was thus the nephew of the celebated Chas Jas Fox, & cousin of the late amiable & enlightened Lord Holland. We may add that through one of his female ancestors, he inherits the blood of merry King Chas II, & consequently of Henry IV. In his younger days Mr Fox was well known in the beau monde of London as one of a coterie of elegant, gay, & witty gentlemen of high birth. In 1815 he visited the continent, & in Rome he contracted the malaria fever. He entered the diplomatic career & was the first Minister Pleni of Great Britain to Buenos Ayres; same to Rio de Janeiro, then to this Gov't in 1836.] [Oct 17th newspaper: the funeral of the late Mr Fox took place yesterday. The remains of the dec'd were conveyed to the *Congressional Cemetery*, & deposited in the public vault to await the instructions of his connexions in England.]

Notice: by virtue of a writ of fieri facias, issued by Jas Marshall, a justice of the peace for Wash Co, D C, I shall expose to public sale for cash, opposite the Centre Market-house, Wash City, Oct 17th, one gray mare, seized & taken as the property of Patrick Going, & will be sold to satisfy a judgment in favor B L Jackson & Wm B Jackson, trading under the firm & style of B L Jackson & Brother. –R T Mills, Constable

New Dry Goods Store: T T Barnes & J R Mitchell, having formed a copartnership, will open on Oct 19, the store lately occupied by Boteler & McGregor, between 8th & 9th sts. –Barnes & Mitchell

Col Jacob G Davies is re-elected Mayor of Balt, Md, by a majority of only 84 votes-the vote being, for Davies 8,877, for Levering 8,793.

FRI OCT 16, 1846
The late Capt Williams, of the Topographical Engineers, now numbered among the brave who were killed at the battle of Monterey, is honored in the Gtwn Advocate: "Capt Williams was a resident for some time & married in this town. He married a d/o the estimable widow of the late Thos Peter, at whose residence the orphans of Capt Williams now remain, their mother being also dead".

Tribute to the late Col Watson: Balt Clipper of Oct 13. City Court-The battles of the 8th & 9th of May were brilliant, but those of the 21st, 22nd, & 23rd of last month will far excel in brilliancy of action, in desperate daring, & in noble deeds the others. In those we mourn the death of Col Wm H Watson, a member of this bar, of great moral worth, of undeniable courage. He leaves a wife & children.

Letter from Col Saml R Curtis, commanding the 3rd Regt of the Ohio Volunteers, dated Matamoros, Sep 7, 1846. In my regt there are 150 on the sick list. By disease & death I have seen my ranks already reduced from 780 to 620. So far as life & death are concerned, I would rather risk a battle once a week, with my regt in the north, than remain in a climate so unnatural to them.

Fayetteville Observer: at the recent session of the Presbytery of Fayetteville, N C, the long pending case of the Rev Mr McQueen, who was suspended in 1841 from functions of the ministry & from the communion of the Church, for marrying the sister of his dec'd wife, again came up, & by a majority of 4 votes the reverend gentleman was restored to his former position in the Church. A protest & cmplnt were entered by a portion of the ministry, under which the case was carried up to the Synod of N C, at its session at Greensborough last week. [Oct 19th newspaper: The Synod of N C refused, by a large majority, to entertain the appeal from the Presbytery of Fayetteville, against the decision of the the latter body. So the question may be considered as settled in favor of the Reverend gentleman. –Raleigh Register.]

$10 for a Cygnet Ring lost between the alley that leads to Walker & Kimmell's stables from Pa ave & the Circus, with the initials J R B engraved on it. Apply at the Wash telegraph Ofc, Jos R Bailey.

Mrd: on Wed, by Rev John C Smith, Mr Benj Snyder to Miss Louisa E Waples, both of Phil

Died: on Oct 15, Thomas, only s/o John Walker, victualler, born Oct 17, 1844. His funeral is today at 3 o'clock P M, from the residence of his parents, N Y ave & 3rd st.

Died: on Oct 14, in Upper Marlboro, Md, after an illness of 6 weeks, Catherine Brent, y/c/o Danl C & Zuleima Digges.

SAT OCT 17, 1846
To the Public. In self defence, I am compelled to state that I purchased from Mr Reuben Burdine all his right, being two-thirds, & one-third from the administrator of A Vancoble, dec'd, all their right for the District of Columbia to Woodworth's Patent Planing Machine. There has been great diversity of opinion as to the right of the old assignees. –John Pettibone

New Upholstery & Paper Hanging Establishment: David A Baird, for many years engaged in the business in N Y C: has commenced business on 8th st, the 2nd house from Pa ave.

Dissolution of copartnership existing under the firm of Jas W Berry & Co, by mutual consent. –Wm & Geo McLean & Co. J W Berry, Oct 1, 1846. [The business will be continued, at the old stand, 7th st, & will continue to sell every description of Groceries. –J W Berry]

Names of the Reps to the next Congress who are ascertained to be elected:

Whigs:
Jos R Ingersoll
John Freedley
John W Hornbeck
Abraham R McIlvaine
John Strohm
Jas Pollock
Geo N Eckert
Henry Nes
Jasper E Brady

Whigs:
John Blanchard
Andrew Stewart
Locofocos:
Chas Brown
Chas J Ingersoll
Wm Strong
Richd Brodhead
Native:
Lewis C Levin

MON OCT 19, 1846

City Ordinances: Wash. 1-Act for the relief of John G Robinson: sum of $23.44 be paid to him, in payment of his bill for certain repairs to the City Hall.

From Mexico: the sloop of war **John Adams** brought as passengers Cmder Carpender & a number of the crew lately belonging to the brig **Truxton**. All who became prisoners by the loss of this vessel have been set at liberty on parole; but a portion of them were on board the storeship **Relief**, which was not expectd to sail for Pensacola until she received on board some 10 or a dozen of the sick, for whom a cutter has been dispatched to Tuspan. Cmdor Perry arrived out on the 22nd ult. Jackson, who was condemned to death for striking an ofcr, was hung on the 15th. Impression prevailed in the squadron that Cmdor Conner contemplated another attack upon Alvarado, but nothing definite was known about it.

The preliminary trial, before the Mayor of Richmond, of Wm R Myers, S S Myers, & Wm S Burr, the first as principal & the others as accessories in the shooting of the late D M Hoyt, closed on Fri last. Bail was refused, & the parties were recommitted to jail. [Oct 28th newspaper: the Court met yesterday: Court stood 5 to2 for acquittal: parties were discharged. –Richmond Times of yesterday]

John Fisk was on Mon last chosen town clerk of Middleton, Conn, this being the 50th year he has been elected to that ofc. He has also entered upon his 24th year as town treasurer.

Appointments by the Pres:
John Romeys Brodhead, Sec of Legation of the U S near her Britannic Majesty, vice McHenry Boyd, recalled at his own request.
Thos J Mulhollan, Receiver of Public Moneys at Champagnole, Arkansas, vice Albert G Rust, resigned.
Wm H Brian, of Gtwn, D C, Justice of the Peace for Wash Co.
Nathan Clifford, of Maine, U S Atty Gen, vice John Y Mason, resigned.
Edw D Reynolds, Purser in the Navy, vice Purser Breese, dec'd.
John Miller, Register of the Land Ofc at Batesville, Arkansas, vice Robt C Newland, dec'd.
Peter H Kemp, Receiver of Public Moneys at Greensburg, Lousiana, vice G W Womack, resigned.

Wed at the U S Hotel in Hartford, Conn, a murdered man was found, Mr Danl F Olcott, of the firm of Olcott & Co, livery stable keeper. Another man, Lewis L Holcomb, of St Louis, formerly of Granby, Conn, in Hartford, on a visit, was also found dead. A suit was pending between them. In the room, Mr Olcott breathing his last. A revolving pistol, belonging to Holcomb, was found with 4 barrels discharged. Mr Olcott was a single man, about 40. Mr Holcomb was a widower, aged 35, with one child, & was to have been married on the same day of the dreadful occurrence. The sum in dispute was about $3,000. –N Y Courier of Fri

N Y, Oct 16. Recruits for the Army: nearly 600, now at the principal depot at *Fort Columbus*, Govn'r Island, under the superintendence of Col R B Mason, of the 1st Dragoons, to be organized into a btln of 4 companies. The btln will be officered as follows, viz:
Brevet Maj E S Hawkins, 7th Infty, & recruits of the 7th Regt of Infty, with which 1st Lt S G Simmons, of the same regt, is assigned to duty.
Brevet Maj G Wright, 8th Regt of Infty, will command the recruits of the 8th, with which 1st Lt J Beardsley, of the same regt, is assigned to duty.
Capt Geo Morris, 4th Infty, will command the recruits of the 4th Infty, with which 1st Lt H D Wallen, of the same regt, is assigned to duty.
Capt D Ruggles, 5th Infty, will command the detachment of the 5th Infty, with which 2nd Lt W H Tyler, 5th Infty, is assigned to duty. Assist Surgeon S P Moore is assigned to duty with the command.
They will embark on the steamship **Massachusetts**, as soon as she is ready for sea; will disembark at Point Isabel, Texas, for such service as the contingencies of war may require. Capt Hawkins will be remembered as the cmder of the Fort opposite Matamoros after the death of Maj Brown. –Jour Com

John Wood, Cashier of the Bank of Rothe, N Y, left there last month for N Y & England, for his health. He left N Y Sep 18, in the steamer **Massachusetts**, for Newport, R I. His trunk arrived at Newport, but nothing has been heard from him. His friends think he must have fallen overboard in crossing the Sound.

Private sale of fine young Mare, with Saddle & Bridle. My only reason for parting with her is that I have no use for her. –M Delany, Druggist, corner of 4½ st & Pa ave.

Woodland for sale: on Oct 21, on the premises, 26 acres of land, on the road leading to Rock Creek Church, adjoining the lands of N L Queen, W G Deale, & E J Middleton. Inquire of J F Callan, E & 7th sts. -R W Dyer, auct

Details of the late battle of Monterey confirm the sad rumor that Capt Lewis N Morris, of this city, fell at the head of his regt, during the progress of that sanguinary conflict. He was a native of this state; grandson of Lewis Morris, one of the signers of the Declaration of Independence, & eldest s/o Capt Staats Morris, who served as aid-de-camp to Gen Wayne, during the Indian wars, at the close of the Revolution. He graduated at West Point Military Academy in 1820, as 2nd Lt of Artl, but was soon after attached to the 3rd Infty, then, & for several years after, stationed on the Western frontier. He served in the Black Hawk war, in 1832, was promoted to a Captaincy in Oct,1833. In Nov, 1840, he was ordered to Florida, until 1843. He went to Corpus Christi with Gen Taylor, & commanded the 3rd Regt in the well-fought battles of Palo Alto & Resaca de la Palma. In the battle which has terminated his career, he accompanied the command of Maj Lear, in his gallant charge upon the masked batteries within the walls of Monterey. He was among the foremost of the column, & when Maj Lear fell wounded, he took command. He fell, pressing forward to the capture of the battery, under a murderous & sweeping fire from the enemy. Capt Morris was in his 46th year. He has left a wife & family. –Albany Journal

Died: on Oct 13, at Portsmouth, Va, Mr Jos Whipple, in his 48th year, well known as an able advocate of the Temperance cause. His funeral is on Oct 25, from his late residence, Navy Yard Hill. [No time given.]

Died: on Oct 11, at Cambridge, Mass, Thos Breese, Purser U S Navy. He was born in Newport, R I; in early life he left Newport attached to the personal staff of Cmdor Perry; was in the combat on Lake Erie with his friend & cmder; assisted in discharging the last gun, which was fired on board the vessel **Lawrence**. Shortly after he received a commission as purser, & has been since uninterruptedly employed. A protracted & distressing disease of the heart was supported with the fotitude of a man & the resignation of a Christian.

Balt, Oct 17. Mrs Mowatt, the accomplished actress & authoress, met with a severe accident whilst performing in the Holiday st Theatre last night. During the last act, required to leave the stage in great haste, she ran with violence against the feet of one of the actors, which, while lying on a sofa, protruded beyond a reasonable distance. She struck these obstacles with her breast, & suffered severe pain. She continued acting till the play ended. With her husband she proceeded to Barnum's Hotel, but began to throw up blood profusely, & fainted. Her condition was considered extremely critical. [Oct 20th newspaper: Mrs Mowatt, afflicted on Fri last by the bursting of a blood vessel, is recovering rapidly.]

TUE OCT 20, 1846
Excellent household & kitchen furniture at auction on Oct 23, at the residence of Mrs Strahan, on H st, between 9th & 10th sts, immediately opposite the Church of the Ascension. -R W Dyer, auct

The Royal Academy of Sciences of Berlin has elected as a corresponding member M J P Secchi, a Jesuit of Rome. This is said to be the first instance of a Jesuit becoming a member of the Berlin Academy.

Two children of Mr Saml Condit, of Orange, have been cut down with Hydrophobia, communicated by a small pet dog belonging to the family. –Newark Daily Advertiser

From the Rio Grande: New Orleans Bee of Oct 12. Col McClung, of Mississippi, died of the wounds received at the battle of Monterey. [Oct 22nd newspaper: Lt Col Alex'r McClung, of Jackson, Miss, who was Marshal of the Eastern district, appointed by Gen Harrison, died of his wounds. He was a nephew of the late Chief Justice Marshall, & fell heir to a large portion of the talent which has rendered that family one of the most remarkable we ever knew. He was a lawyer of full practice. –Richmond Whig]

Mrd: on Oct 18, by Rev N J B Morgan, Mr Robt A Connell to Miss Ellen M White, both of Wash City.

Died: on Oct 18, Jas Crampton, in his 53rd year. His funeral will take place this afternoon at 3 o'clock, from his late dwlg on 12th st, between E & F sts.

Died: on Oct 18, after a lingering illness, Mary Ann Cook, aged 21 months & 26 days, only d/o Jas A & Eliz S Bowen. Her funeral is today, at 10 o'clock, from her parents residence, Md ave, one door west of 4½ st.

Died: on Sep 20, at his residence in Hardeman Co, Tenn, Gen Calvin Jones, in his 73rd year. He was a native of Massachusetts, where he was educated. He removed in early life to Raleigh, N C, where he established a high reputation for honor & probity. He emigrated to Tenn 14 years since. In the region of country in which he spent his ripe old age, he was regarded by all as a pious Christian, & a most valuable citizen.

WED OCT 21, 1846
Wash Corp: 1-Ptn from Harvey Cruttenden: referred to the Cmte on Improvements. 2-Ptn from M Kilmiste, a teacher of amusing arts: referred. 3-Ptn from Andrew Noerr & others: referred to the Cmte on Improvements. 4-Ptn from C Gautier & others, confectionaery: referred. 5-Ptn & papers from Richd Davis, relating to an injury to his carriage by the breaking of Md ave bridge: referred to the Cmte of Claims. 6-Ptn from Zackariah Hazel: referred to the Cmte of Claims. 7-Bill for the relief of Thos Baker: passed.

New York, 1789. St Tammany's Society, or Independent Order of Liberty. This being a Nat'l Society, consists of Americans born, who fill all ofcs, & adopted Americans, who are eligible to the honorary posts of Warrior & Hunter. It is founded on the true principles of patriotism, & has for its motives charity & brotherly love. The ofcrs consist of one Grand Sachem, 12 Sachems, 1 Treasurer, 1 Secretary, & 1 Doorkeeper. It is divided into 13 tribes, which severally represent a State; each tribe to be governed by a Sachem, the honorary posts in which are one Warrior & one Hunter. Ofcrs for the present year. Wm Mooney, Grand Sachem

Sachems:

White Matlack	Jonathan Piersee	Gabriel Furman
Oliver Glean	Thos Greenleaf	Abel Hardenbrook
Philip Hone	Jas Tylee	Corlandt Van beuren
John Burger	John Campbell	Jos Gadwin

Thos Ash, Treas   Gardner Baker,
Anthony Ernest, Sec   Doorkeeper

May 12, [or May 1, old style,] 1789, was the Anniversary of St Tammany, the Tutelar Saint of America. On this occasion markees were erected on the banks of the Hudson, about 2 miles from the city, for the reception of the brethren of the Society, & an elegant entertainment provided, which was served up precisely at 3 o'clock.

+

New York, 1797. Tammany Society, or Columbia Order.

The Nat'l Society was instituted in 1789, & is founded on the true & genuine principles of Republicanism. Ofcrs of the present year:

Wm Mooney, Grand Sachem   John P Pearss, Sec
Richd Davis, Father of the Council   John Swartwout, Sagamore
Wm Boyd, Treas   Jos Dunkley, Wiskinkie

Council of Sachems

Nicholas Evertson	John Waldron
John Mersereaw	Tos Timpson
Richd Davis	Stanton Latham
Thos Greenleaf	Jas Teller
Josiah G Pierson	Jacob De la Montagnie
Wm Whitehead	Christian Tupper
John J Johnson	

Geo G Warner, Scribe of the Council
John Swartwout, Reader of the Declaration of Independence for Jul 4.

+

May 12, 1797: The Tammany Society, or Columbian Order, celebrated their anniversary festival, in their Wigwam, in Broadway. Mr John L Johnson delivered a political oration.

Mrs Ellen Jones has reopened her School for Young Ladies, at her residence on F st, between 19th & 20th.

In Chancery. John Ham & Mary his wife, Thos O Sheetz & Eliz his wife, Michl Runner & Sarah his wife, Wm Johnson & Ann Magill his wife, David C Newcomer & Virginia his wife, David L Ham, & Jos'h Sherrick & Sarah his wife, cmplnts, against Judith Ham, Mgt Stoner, Jacob Harmer & Eliz his wife, Benj Wagoner, Eliz Wagoner, Augustin A Biggs & Mgt his wife, Ann S Wagoner, Amanda S Wagoner, Magdalena Bougher, Peter Ham, John Pursivall & Sarah Jane his wife, Louis Lauck & Emily his wife, Jacqueline Ham, Andrew J Ham, Davis S Cox & Mary Leight his wife, & Enos Kessinger & Mgt Ann his wife, dfndnts. The bill states that Peter Ham, late of Wash Co, Md, died seised of part of lots 1 & 13 in square 118, in Wash City, as described in said bill, & whereon stands the easternmost house of the Seven Bldgs or houses built upon said square, fronting upon Pa ave, having by his will devised the same to his wife, Mgt, for her life, & after her death directed the same to be sold, & the proceeds divided between his children & grand-children; that said Peter & Mgt Ham have both departed this life; & that the cmplnts & dfndnts are the children & grand-children of said Peter, & the descendants of such as have died; & the object of the said bill is to have the said property sold & the proceeds divided between the cmplnts & dfndnts according to the will; & it having been made to appear to the Court that all the dfndnts reside beyond the jurisdiction of the Court; warning said dfndnts to be & appear in person or by solicitor in this Court, on or before the 4th Mon of Mar next. –Wm Brent, clk
-Redin, for cmplnts

Mr Fred'k Pierpont Walter, a much respected merchant of New Orleans, was suddenly killed in that city on Oct 3 by the fall of the cornice of an unfinished house.

Floyd, the portrait & historical painter, is now in Wash, engaged upon a picture entitled "The Surrender of Santa Anna." The portraits of the Mexican & Texan Generals are recognized by all who have seen the originals. –Alex Gaz

Horrible butchery occurred at Lancaster, Pa on Sat. A man named John Haggerty, after shooting a horse in the street near his own house, went to the residence of Mr Melchoir Fordney, an aged & highly esteemed citizen, who, with his wife & child, he deliberately murdered with an axe. Fordney & his wife were killed instantly; the child only lived a few hours.

Mrd: on Oct 20, by Rev Mr Holmead, Mr John H Phillips. Of Carlisle, Pa, to Miss Emeline W, d/o Anthony Holmead, of Wash City.

Died: on Oct 17, in Wash City, Wm M, y/s/o the late Thos B Dyer, in his 21st year.

Died: on Oct 19, at the residence of Mr Enoch Tucker, in Wash City, Mrs Mary Williams, aged 77 years.

For rent: the house on F, near 14th st, known as the residence of the late Richd Forrest. Inquire at the store of Mr J J Joyce, 13th & F st.

House & lot at auction: Fri next, in front of the premises, part of lot ___, in square 456, on E st, between 6th & 7th sts. The house is a 2 story brick, adjoining the residence of David Saunders. -R W Dyer, auct

THU OCT 22, 1846
The remains of Cmdor Stephen Decatur are to be removed from Washington to Phil next week, & are to be received & reinterred with appropriate ceremonies in the yard of St Peter's Church. A monument is also to be erected over them.

Amid the storm & rain on Tue last there appeared at the polls in East Bethlehem township, an aged citizen, Thos Farquhar, who case his ballot for the Whigs. On the day of the election he was over 96 years of age.

Rev Henry R Wilson, lady, 4 children, & 3 Hindoo orphans, arrived at N Y on Oct 4, in the ship **Hedrick Hudson**, from London. Mr Wilson was obliged to leave his missionary labors in India on account of the serious & protracted illness of Mrs Wilson. He was the founder of a flourishing orphan institution at Futtegurh.

Household & kitchen furniture at auction on Oct 26, at the residence of Mr Geo Gilliss, on L st, between 9th & 10th sts, a short distance N E of Franklin Row.
–B Homans, auctioneer

Valuable land, negroes, & personal estate for sale: at the request of Mrs Frances T Barbour, who wishes to be relieved from the cares & perplexities that the possession of a large estate devolves upon her, & to enable her to equalize the advancements which have been made to her children, I shall, on Dec 2 next, on the premises, offer for sale, at public auction, that beautiful south mountain farm called *Frescati*, the late residence of Judge Barbour, dec'd, containing about 1,300 acres of land, in Orange Co. The Mansion House is a large fire-proof brick bldg; all necessary out bldgs & other houses. I shall also offer for sale from 40 to 50 negroes. –Richd K Field, for Mrs Frances T Barbour, excx & devisee of Judge P Philip Barbour, dec'd.

Trustee's sale: in execution of an order passed by the worshipful Thos Duckett, Chief Justice of the Orphans' Court of PG Co, passed on the petition of Robt Ghiselin, an insolvent debtor, the subscriber, as Trustee, will offer at public sale on Nov 24 next, at the residence of said Ghiselin, in said county, distant about 2 miles from Nottingham, his entire real & personal estate, to wit: his dwlg plantation of about 1,000 acres, more or less; commodious dwlg, overseer's house, & all other bldgs. Fifty slaves, men, women, & children. An ample stock of horses, oxen, cows, sheep, & hogs. A large crop of corn & tobacco now in the houses, &, lastly, the household & kitchen furniture. To a gentleman of fortune who desires a country residence already stocked & furnished, I offer a rare opportunity for investment. –Th S Alexander, trustee

Copartnership formed this day under the style of Terrett & Clarke, & bought out the establishment of J W Clarke & Co. General variety of Staple & Fancy Dry Goods: store on Pa ave, 3 doors east of 10th st. –Alex'r H Terrett, John W Clarke

Came to the subscriber's premises, *Cross Keys*, 7th st, on Oct 20, a roan colored Horse. Owner can have him by paying charges & taking him away. –J Francis

FRI OCT 23, 1846
New Orleans Picayune: we learn that Capt J B Nones, of the revenue cutter **Forward**, has been suspended from his command by Com Webser for non-compliance with orders, & that Lt McGowan has been placed in command. Nones was dispatched to the Gulf by Com Webster, with orders to report to Com Conner, to act under his orders until Webster arrived. When Webster arrived, & ordered Nones to hoist the revenue flag; Capt Nones replied that he could not do so until he was detached from the command of Conner, when he should be pleased to recognize Capt Webster as his commanding ofcr. Great nonsense all around. -Alex Gaz

New London Morning News: letter from a correspondent at Norwich, gives the account of the death of a young woman, d/o Mr Jacob Welden, in one of the factories in Greenville, on Mon last. She was killed when her hair became caught in the revolving shaft, & her neck was broken. Her mother had asked her dght to go there to allow her friend the opportunity to leave.

Valuable property for sale: the subscriber will sell his present residence, on the corner of 3rd & D sts: a 2 story brick bldg, conveniently arranged house. He will also sell the lot on the corner opposite & east of the residence of Gen Hunter, fronting 54 feet on C & 160 feet on 3rd st. –D W Middleton

For rent: 2 small 3 story brick dwlg houses on I st, between 20th & 21st sts, in the neighborhood of the West Market. Inquire of Maj Geo Bender, on I st, or at the Ordnance Dept.

The late Lt John Chapman Terrett, of the 1st Infty: entered the army in 1839, & served in Florida until 1841; proceeded with his company to the Upper Mississippi; there, on the Missouri, he remained until his company was ordered to Mexico, & there he has nobly died a soldier's death. He was a native of Fairfax Co, Va, & a brother of Capt B A Terrett, 1st Regt of Dragoons, U S A, who accidentally shot himself on the western frontier, [at *Fort Scott*,] about 18 months since, as he was dismounting from his horse with a pistol in his hand. Another brother still remains in the service of his country as an ofcr in the Marine Corps. -C

Died: on Oct 21, in Wash City, at the residence of Thos C Magruder, Miss Eliz Morgan, of consumption, formerly of St Mary's Co, Md, in her 58th year. Her funeral is this afternoon, at 3 o'clock.

Died: on Oct 20, Theodore, infant s/o Leonard & Winifred Harbaugh, aged 7 months & 13 days.

Trustee's sale of houses & lots: deed of trust from Wm V Hickey to the subscriber, made Jul 10, 1843, recorded in liber W B 106, folios 133 thru 136, in the land records of Wash Co, D C: sale on Nov 3 next, of 5 undivided sixth parts of lots 1, 18, 27, 24, & 23, in the subdivision of square numbered north of square 743, as laid down on the plat of Wash City, with improvements thereon. On lot 27-a 2 story brick house. The property fronts on N J ave, between L & M sts south. –Jas Adams, trustee
-R W Dyer, auct

The injunction granted by the Circuit Court to restrain the subscriber from carrying on his business of burning lime having been dissolved, he is now ready to comply with any orders left at his kiln, on 20th st. –W T Dove

SAT OCT 24, 1846
To let: a house on G st, between 13th & 14th sts. Low to a good tenant. –A H Young

Died: on Oct 12, at *Avonwood*, Jefferson Co, Va, of a protracted illness, Mrs Bennett Taylor, in her 66th year, the eldest d/o the late Edmund Randolph, Sec of State & Atty Genr'l of the U S.

Pensacola, Oct 12, 1848. 1-On Oct 10 the U S steamer **General Taylor** took fire alongside the wharf of this yard, & in a short time burnt to the water's edge. Her engine may be of some value. 2-We have been visited at this yard for a month past with a fever called by a variety of names-pernicious, congestive, bilious, malignant fever-a near relation of Yellow Jack. Our chaplain, Mr Alden, Miss Lynch, & several others have died of it. There are about 120 patients now in the hospital near this place.

Mrd: on Oct 19, at Alexandria, Va, by Rev Mr Dana, Jas J Dickens, of Wash, to Miss Augusta M Thompson, of the same place.

For rent: the commodious dwlg recently occupied by Maj Walker, on the Navy Yard road. Apply to Susan D Shepherd, Sylvanus Holmes, excs. Key next door.

For sale or exchange: the heirs of the estate of John H Terrett, dec'd, of Fairfax Co, Va, being prepared to give a clear title or deed to said estate, wishing to dispose of the farm & all landed property left by said John H Terrett, offer for sale, or exchange in city property in Washington, a farm of about 450 acres, with a comfortable dwlg-house & out-bldgs: 7 miles from Washington & 6 miles from Alexandria. Apply to the subscriber, on 9th st, between H & I sts, Wash. –Julia Terrett

MON OCT 26, 1846
Mrd: on Oct 20, in Norfolk, by Rev Mr Caldwell, Dr Carter P Johnson, of Richmond, to Anne Love, d/o the late Henry Forrest, of Wash.

Died: on Oct 17, at his residence in Bladensburg, Md, Dr Benj Day, in his 49th year. Dr Day was a native of Calvert Co, studied medicine under his uncle, Dr Rollings, a celebrated physician of Tenn, & was graduated at the Univ of Md with Dr Davis, Speaker of the House of Reps, & several other distinguished men. Twenty-two years have elapsed since Dr Day commenced his profession amongst us. -K

City Ordnance-Wash. Act in relation to the Northern Market-house: upon the completion of the market house to be erected on the open space at the junction of N Y & Mass aves with K st north, the Mayor is hereby authorized to cause the stalls therein [butchers' as well as vegetable stalls] to be sold to the highest bidder. Butchers' stalls shall be at the rate of $20 per annum. The market will be ready for occupation & use on Nov 3 next. -W W Seaton, Mayor

Notice is hereby given to Mrs Henrietta Behrens, if she be living, to return to the undersigned, from whom she has been living separated for 10 years past, or to inform him of her whereabouts within 2 months from date, else he will consider himself as discharged from all obligations towards her, under the presumption of her death or unwillingness ever to return. -Fred'k Behrens, Wash, Oct 26, 1846

Circuit Court: Robt Fulton, the first inventor of the application of steam power to navigation, performed various services to the Gov't, & for these services & some losses experienced in the service of the U S, claimed a considerable amount. In 1815 Robt Fulton died, leaving 4 children, 3 dghts & 1 son, the latter named Robt Fulton, jr. These heirs presented their claim before Congress, & did so for a number of years, without abtaining anything. Robt Fulton, jr, made a contract with Mr Isaac N Coffin, in consideration of Coffin's services in urging the claim, in aurguing before cmtes, & he agreed to pay him 20% upon his [Robert's] share of what Congress would grant. Robt Fulton, jr, died in 1840 intestate. In Jan, 1845, Coffin obtained from the Orphans Court of Wash Co, D C letters of administraction on the estate of Robt Fulton, jr. Congress, in Aug, 1844, passed an act appropriating over $76,000 to the payment of these claims. In Sep, 1846, a Mr Crary, of N Y, arrived with letters of administration on the estate of Robt Fulton, jr, obtained from the Surrogate of N Y. Both administrators claimed Robert's share. The Govt concluded to pay over to Crary; whereupon Mr Coffin obtained an injunction restraining the Treas of the U S from so doing. No decision has yet been made. [Nov 11th newspaper: that both administrators claimed Robert's share-this was a mistake. Robt's share was claimed at the Treasury by the 3 surviving heirs, as belonging to them exclusively, in capacity of heirs only, to the exclusion of the administrator on his estate, & the letters of administration obtained in N Y by Crary were taken out since the injunction. It was also stated in our notice that the Gov't, after some deliberation, concluded to pay over to Crary. This also was a mistake, as the Gov't had come to no final decision when the injunction was obtained, but to the contrary; as, although the Treasury warrant was made out for the whole sum appropriated, on Crary's application for the whole, but three-fourths was paid by the dept to the 3 sruviving heirs, the other fourth being retained by the Treasury before the injunction was obtained.]

Orphans Court of Wash Co, D C. Letters of administration on the personal estate of Salathel Hicks, late of said county, dec'd. –J P Pepper, adm

TUE OCT 27, 1846
Death of a Centenarian. The venerable Baltis Stone, well known in Southward as the oldest inhabitant, & a veteran of Revolutionary times, died on Thu last. At an early age the dec'd entered the army as a rifleman, along with his father, who sealed his devotion for his adopted country with his life's blood. Baltis Stone was with Washington in every campaign of the Revolutionary struggle, & witnessed the battles of Bunker Hill, Trenton, Germantown, Red Bank, & others, & yet escaped without receiving a wound. He has received a pension from Gov't, as a reward for these services, for many years. He was 103 years & 16 days old at his death. He was able to walk, supported by his staff, until within a few months past. He gradually wasted away, from extreme old age, until his frame was scarcely the weight of an infant. –Phil Chron

The body of Alex'r T Hays, formerly of Ohio, but for the last 8 or 9 years a resident of Lexington, Ky, was found horribly mutilated in the suburbs of Lexington on Oct 17. The murderer is not known. The dec'd was a printer by trade, but had been engaged in various pursuits, the last was that of a druggist. He was about 50 years of age, & a peaceful, inoffensive man.

Ofcrs who fell at Monterey. 1-Lt Chas Hoskins, 4th Infty, was killed in the gallant charge in the streets of Monterey on Sep 21, was a native of N C; graduated at West Point in 1836, & was Adjutant of his regt at the time of his death. As Quartermaster in the old Cherokee nation in 1838, under Genr'ls Scott & Wool, his services were pre-eminent in all the operations preliminary to the removal of the Cherokees. 2-Brevet Maj Philip N Barbour, 3rd Infty, also fell on Sep 21, was a native of Ky, & graduated at West Point in 1834. He was breveted a Capt for gallant services in Florida on Apr 15, 1842. He was breveted a Major from May 9 last for gallant conduct in the battle of Resada de la Palma. He fell at Monterey in the thickest of the fight, whilst his regt was subjected to that murderous fire from masked batteries in the streets, which, after severely wounding its commander, Maj Lear, killed 3 capts & 2 subalterns, & left the regt commanded by its youngest captain. He was a relation of the Barbours of Va. 3-2nd Lt J S Woods, 2nd Infty, then on duty with the 4th Infty, who was killed in the same charge, was a native of Pa: graduated at West Point in 1844: breveted a 1st Lt for his gallantry on May 9 at Resada de la Palma, whilst serving in the 4th Infty, in capturing a field piece from the Mexicans with a very few men. He was a young & modest ofcr, s/o a clergyman in the interior of Pa. The citizens of his native town had just presented a sword to him for his gallantry on May 9. 4-1st Lt Douglass S Irwin, 3th Infty, killed at the battle of Monterey, was the s/o Maj Irwin, of Old Point Comfort. Lt Irwin was educated at West Point, & distinguished himself in the Florida war. Each one of the ofcrs of the regular army who have fallen in those brilliant battles at Monterey were graduated at West Point, except Lt Terrett, 1st Infty, from Va, a young ofcr of high promise.

Within the past week Lt Col Fauntleroy has arrived at this place emaciated, worn, & entirely prostrated by severe illness & exposure, & is now lying ill at the barracks. A few months since Lt Col Hitchcock, the pride & ornament of the service, passed up the river equally reduced in health & strength. God grant them a speedy & full recovery. –Baton Rouge Gaz

Gold bracelet found up on the avenue a few days ago, which the owner can have by calling at Mr Jos Howard's, Garrison st, near the Navy Yard, proving the same & paying all costs.

Leeches! W C Choate has received a large supply of prime European Leeches, just imported. Physicians in the country can be supplied at the shortest notice. The Sulphur Bath will be in readiness at all hours. Mrs Choate will attend to the ladies. Corner of La ave & 6th st.

Public sale of old bridge materials: public auction on Oct 30, the material of the Md ave bridge. –Jos Cross, Com'r Eastern Section Canal.

For rent: commodious 2 story brick house on E st, lately occupied by Mr Fendall. Apply to Mr John F Callan, nearly opposite, or to the subscriber, at his residence, a few doors east of the Seven Bldgs, in the First Ward. –A McD Davis

For rent: commodious & neat brick house on 12th st, containing 8 good rooms. Key is at Mr Holmead's grocery store, corner of N Y ave & 12th st, or to M Caton.

Mrd: on Oct 25, by Rev P D Chenoweth, Mr John H Taylor to Mrs Jane Usher, all of Wash City.

Mrd: on Oct 20, by Rev Mr Sprole, Mr Beverly W Butler, of Balt, to Miss Ellen A Phillips, of Wash City.

Mrd: on Oct 2, in Lafayette Co, Missouri, by Rev Mr Simpson, Dr Wm D Digges, of Lexington, to Miss Ann Kavanaugh.

Died: on Oct 26, Col Thos Corcoran, in his 52nd year. His funeral is Wed at 4 o'clock, from his late residence in Franklin Row.

Died: on Sep 26, at Urbana, Ohio, at the residence of her son, the Hon Jos Vance, Mrs Sarah W Vance, aged 85 years, a native of Fred'k Co, Va. She has left 7 sons & dghts & 24 grandchildren & great-grandchildren. Mrs Vance emigrated 64 years ago to the West, crossing the mountains on horseback, & carrying her eldest son, then an infant, in her arms. After being left almost alone of that community founded by a Boon & a Kenton, she also has passed away, & is now numbered with her contemporaries.

$1,000 reward: Richd J Turner, late a book-keeper in the Mechanic's Bank of Balt, absconded about Oct 20th: since which it has been discovered that through false entries frauds have been committed on the Bank. Richd J Turner is about 30 years of age, 5 feet 8 inches in height, reddish brown hair, a small artery in the left cheek always pulsating, which is easily observed; has a remarkably large foot, down look, with an inability to meet your eye; is courteous & bland in his manners. Above reward for his apprehension & delivery to the civil authorities of this city. By order: John B Morris, President

WED OCT 28, 1846
For sale: subscriber offers well finished brick house in which he now resides, on north side of D st, between 2nd & 3rd sts, called Pollard's Row, being the 3rd house from 3rd st. Inquire of Wm Thompson, Genr'l Agent, 6th & La ave.

Serious accident at Wheeling on Fri resulted in the instant death of Mr Robt Boyd, iron merchant, & in injury to Mr John W Bowring, Mr Washington Bowring, 2 German laborers, & another man named Myers. The wall of an unfinished bldg fell upon them.

Died: on Fri last, suddenly, aged 14 years, Geo Alex'r, s/o the late Capt Chas McIntire, of Alexandria.

Trustee's sale: deed of trust from Erasmus H Roper to the undersigned, dated Jul 21, 1840, recorded in Liber W M 83, folios 1 et sq: public auction on Dec 3 on the premises: lot 9 in square 317-lot is enclosed & has a frame stable on it.
–Geo Gilliss, trustee -B Homans, auctioneer

Balt: the remains of Cmdor Decatur arrived from Washington in the cars this afternoon, en route for Phil. Our military & the "Old Defenders" were out to do honor to the illustrious dead as an escort. [Oct 29th newspaper: the remains of Cmdor Stephen Decatur were on Tue last quietly removed from the vault at **Kalorama**, in this vicinity, where they were placed at the time of his death in 1820, to Phil, where they are to be finally deposited & a monument erected over them. We were aware of the intention to make this removal of all that remains of the illustrious dec'd, but, knowing the desire of the friends that it should take place without parade, we did not announce it. The Sec of the Navy & a few private friends were there.] [Oct 31st newspaper: the remains of Cmdor Decatur were interred on Thus, beside the grave of his father, in St Peter's Churchyard. The military were out on the occasion, under command of Gen Cadwalader: the bells were tolled & minute guns fired from the navy yard.]

Local News: An old man, Michl Lucia, a native of St Lawrence Co, N Y, came into the watch house last Sunday for lodgings. While there he cut his throat from ear to ear, but did not succeed in severing the jugular vein. Capt Goddard kept him till morning, Dr Hall attended to his wounds, & he was committed to jail for safe keeping.

Household & kitchen furniture at auction on Oct 29, at the late residence of Isabella Thompson, dec'd, on Market st, Scotch Row. –E S Wright, auctioneer

THU OCT 29, 1846
Boots & Shoes: A Hoover & Son, opposite Brown's Hotel, Pa ave.

House to let: brick house on I st near the residence of Mrs Gen Macomb. Apply to Jos Ratcliff.

Mrd: on Oct 27, by Rev Mr Martin, Mr Zachariah B Beall to Miss Mary R, d/o the late Henry D Hatton, all of PG Co, Md.

Mrd: on Oct 20, at Upperville, Fauquier Co, Va, Peter Wilson, of Wash, to Miss Margaret R Brown, d/o the late Jas Brown, of Martinsburg, Va.

Died: on Oct 27, after a severe illness, John L Brightwell, aged 68 years. His funeral is from his late residence, on the eastern side of the Anacostia river, this day, at 11 o'clock.

Headquarters Army of Occupation, Camp near Monterey, Sep 27, 1848. We are glad to hear the report of the death of Col McClung, of the Mississippi volunteers, was totally unfounded. An ofcr who left Monterey on Oct 6th says he was improving, & it was thought he would recover. His friends will regret to hear that Lt Dilworth, of 1st Infty, has died of his wounds. Lt Graham, 4th Infty, was still alive-he is so desperately wounded that his recovery would be deemed a miracle. Maj Lear, 3rd Infty, is doing well, & it is believed that he will recover. The death of Mr Hermann S Thomas, of Harford Co, Md, will be deeply felt in his native State. He had joined McCulloch's rangers to see active service, & fell in storming the second height. Capt Owen, formerly Lt, of the Balt Btln, left Monterey on Oct 6, & we are indebted to him for many interesting details. He informs that the American loss in the 3 actions is set down at 561 killed & wounded. The Mexican loss is believed to exceed 1,000. Other accounts say from 600 to 800. In the American Flag we find announced the death of Capt Robt Mitchell, Assist Quartermaster to the Indiana Volunteers-he died at Matamoros on the 7th inst. A warm eulogium is paid to him in the Flag. We regret that certain difficulties had occurred at Carnargo which it was grievously feared would lead to two private hostile meetings, in which two of our citizens were to take part. Brig Gen Marshall, of Ky, had demanded satisfaction from Col Balie Peyton, of this city, & a meeting would take place probably on the 11th inst. Another difficulty was to be arranged in a similar mode, between Capt Musson, of this city, & Capt Shivers, of Texas. We hope an adjustment may have been effected without resort to arms.

Household & kitchen furniture, & piano forte at auction: on Nov 2, at the residence of Mr Rhea, on Missouri ave, between 4½ & 6th sts, fronting the Canal, a splendid & large lot of furniture. –A Green, auct

Orphans Court of Wash Co, D C. Letters testamentary on the personal estate of Eliz Morgan, late of said county, dec'd. –Edwin C Morgan, exc

The Roman Catholic Advocate says: 1-A Colony of missionaries, of the order of St Benedict, started for Munich on Jul 29, for the U S of A, to form at St Joseph, in Pa, the first monastery of Benedictines. It is composed of the Rev Fr Boniface Wimmer, [prior;] F Maximillian Goetner, 2 theologians, 4 scholastics, & several lay brothers. On the eve of their departure, the evangelical laborers assisted together at a solemn ofc, celebrated by the Rt Rev Dr Reisack, the Bishop coadjutor of Munich, to call the blessings of Heaven on their long journey, & on their generous undertaking. 2-On Fri, the 9th, the ceremony of taking the veil took place for the first time in Chicago. At a grand Pontifical High Mass, celebrated by Rt Rev Dr Quarter, two of the devoted ladies that embarked from Pittsburg to form in Chicago a foundation of the Order of Mercy, received at the hands of the Bishop the white veil. The names of the postulants are Miss Mary Eliza Corbitt, called in religion Sister Mary Josephine, [choir sister,] & sister Mary Eve Juridth, called in religion Sister Mary Veronica, [lay sister.]

For rent: 2 story house on 4½ st, between Pa ave & C st. Inquire of Jas Williams, next door, or at his wareroom, 7th st.

Smoking chimneys cured. The undersigned is prepared to set Grates, Stoves, & Furnaces, in the neatest & most durable manner, at the shortest notice. Orders through the post ofc, or left at his residence on N Y ave, north side, between 12th & 13th sts, will meet with immediate attention. –John Plant, Bricklayer

FRI OCT 30, 1846
Wash Corp: 1-Cmte of Claims reported the ptns of Z Hazel, H B Sawyer, & Conrad Finkman, as not having been testified to in accordance with the rules of the Board. 2-Nominations from the Mayor for scavengers: John Cox, John Spurling, & Jas Hollidge. Also, Wm B Wilson as market master for the Northern Market. All confirmed except those of Hollidge & Wilson-ordered to lie on the table. 3-Bill for the relief of Thos Baker: referred to the Cmte of Claims. 4-Ptn of Ann R Dermott: referred. 5-Cmte of Claims: bill for the relief of A Baumback: passed. 6-Cmte on Improvement: bill for the relief of Michl Joyce: passed. 7-Bill for the relief of C Columbus: passed.

Letter from Monterey on the Pacific to the editor of the Alexandria Gaz contains the annexed notice of our interesting young countryman, Lt Col Fremont. The letter is dated Jul 20: "Col Fremont's party arrived here yesterday, having had some pretty hard fighting with the Mexicans & Indians. They number about 200, & are the most daring & hardy set of fellows I ever looked upon. They are splendid marksmen, & can plant a bullet in an enemy's head with their horses at a full gallop. They never think of eating bread, but live upon meat all the time. They never sleep in a house, but on the ground, with a blanket around them, their saddle for a pillow, & a rifle by their side. I should like to give you some more minute account of them, but time will not admit."

Hardware, Glass, & Crockery Ware at auction: on Oct 31, at the store-house formerly occupied by C P Wannall, at the corner of 9th & I sts. –A Green, auctioneer

A sailor named Jackson, lately hung on board the ship **St Mary's**, was an Irishman, a young man of 27, of considerable talent & some education. His offence consisted in knocking down the 1st Lt several times on the quarter-deck, & uttering mutinous & insubordinate language. He was convicted by a court of 11 ofcrs, Capt F, of the frig **Cumberland**, being the President. His case excited considerable sympathy, & the Cmdor confirmed the sentence very reluctantly. New Orleans Times [Oct 13th newspaper: Note-Capt French Forrest, of the frig **Cumberland**.]

A house in Leyden, Mass, occupied by Mr Lyman Lamb, was destroyed by fire on Thu last, while Mr Lamb & his wife were absent, & Mr Lamb's 2 children, 1 four years old & the other 2½ years, perished in the flames, together with all of their household furniture, clothing, & provisions.

Valuable house for sale: late the residence of Dr G W May, dec'd, at the corner of D & 9th sts, in the Third Ward. Inquire at this ofc.

Corp of Wash: every person who shall apply for a tavern or ordinary license shall produce to the Mayor a certificate, signed by the Com'r & 6 respectable freeholders of the ward in which such person resides.

By whom premises were examined & certified	By whom recommended
1st Ward:	
Benedict Jost, square 168 Pa ave.	
Jacob Brodbeck	Jacob Brodbeck
H Haney	H Haney
Jas Kelly	Jas Kelly
Geo Krafft	Geo Krafft
Chas A Schneider	Chas A Schneider
F A Wagler	F A Wagler
2nd Ward:	
Andrew Hancock, square 292, Pa ave.	
John France	John France
Nathl Plant	Nathl Plant
C P Sengstack	C P Sengstack
Wm Morrow	Wm Morrow
Geo A W Randall	Geo A W Randall
Jas A McColgan	Jas A McColgan
Abraham Butler, square 254, north F st.	
E Simms	E Simms
McClintock Young	McClintock Young
Jas Larned	Jas Larned
Michl Nourse	Michl Nourse

Jos S Wilson
Allison Nailor
J Galabrun, square 225, Pa ave
A Fuller
E Evans
Geo Lamb
Wm B Laub
C H James
M R Callan
Conrad Turkman, square 292, Pa ave ave
C Utermohle
L Lepreux
C Eckloff
C P Sengstack
Wm Morrow
N Traverse
Wm Thomas, square 267, 14th st, & Md ave
P G Howle
Peter Cazenave
Wm Evans
John Pettibone
J S Harvey
John Laskey
Geo McCauley, square 225, Pa ave
Jas H Caustin
M R Callan
S W Handy
Geo Lamb
Wm Morrow
C H James
Azariah Fuller, square 225, Pa ave
Jas Anderson
E Evans
C H James
John Hands, jr
Robt Cruit
Jas Laurie
Henry Kuhl, square 294 or 291, Pa ave
C Utermohle
C P Sengstack
C Eckloff
J McColgan
John France
Nicholas Traverse
Job Corson, square 255, 11th & E sts

Jos S Wilson
Allison Nailor

A Fuller
E Evans
Geo Lamb
Wm B Laub
C H James
M R Callan

C Utermohle
L Lepreux
C Eckloff
C P Sengstack
Wm Morrow
N Traverse

P G Howle
Peter Cazenave
Wm Evans
John Pettibone
J S Harvey
John Laskey

S W Handy
Geo Lamb
Wm Morrow
M R Callan
Jas H Caustin
C H James

Jas Anderson
E Evans
C H James
John Hands, jr
Robt Cruit
Jas Laurie

C P Sengstack
E Eckloff
J McColgan
John France
C Utermohle
Nicholas Traverse

Richd Wimsatt	Richd Wimsatt
K H Lambell	K H Lambell
J W Martin	J W Martin
Geo Mattingley	Geo Mattingley
Lewis Thomas	Lewis Thomas
Thos W Riley	Thos W Riley

3rd Ward

P H King, square B, Pa ave
Alex'r Lee	Alex'r Lee
J M Johnson	J M Johnson
Andrew Small	Andrew Small
J P Pepper	J P Pepper
S Hyatt	S Hyatt
E Lindsley	E Lindsley

E C Baker, square ___
M Delany	M Delany
Stanislaus Murray	Stanislaus Murray
J M Johnson	J M Johnson
Alex Lee	Alex Lee
Edw Simms	Edw Simms
Thos Young	Thos Young

H H Sweeting, square 490, C st
Levi Pumphrey	Levi Pumphrey
Alex'r Lee	Alex'r Lee
J P Pepper	J P Pepper
R Burdine	R Burdine
John W Maury	John W Maury
W G W White	W G W White

Wm Benter, Square 491
Alex'r Lee	Alex'r Lee
J M Johnson	J M Johnson
A F Kimmell	A F Kimmell
B F Middleton	B F Middleton
J P Pepper	J P Pepper
John W Maury	John W Maury

Burlin Brown, square res 12, Pa ave & 1st st.
Chas Lee Jones	Chas Lee Jones
John A Smith	John A Smith
Wm B Kibbey	Wm B Kibbey
W H Upperman	W H Upperman
Wm Gadsby	Wm Gadsby
Jas H Birch	Jas H Birch
Jas Fitzgerald	Jas Fitzgerald

P A De Saules, square 431, 7th st.
Geo W Sweeny	Leonard Harbaugh

Leonard Harbaugh	John R Hendley
John R Hendley	Jos Harbaugh
Jos Harbaugh	Thos Baker
Thos Baker	Geo W Sweeny
Francis Mattingley	Francis Mattingley
Jas Fitzgerald, res 10, Pa ave	
Patrick Moran	Patrick Moran
Martin Murphy	Martin Murphy
W H Upperman	W H Upperman
Thos Young	Thos Young
Michl McDermott	Michl McDermott
J M Johnson	J M Johnson
Jas Cuthbert, res 10, Pa ave.	
Wm H Upperman	Edw Simms
Jas Fitzgerald	Wm H Upperman
Alex'r Lee	Jas Fitzgerald
J M Johnson	Alex'r Lee
John W Maury	J M Johnson
Edw Simms	John W Maury
Patrick Moran, square 575, Pa ave	
Martin Murphy	Martin Murphy
Jas Fitzgerald	Jas Fitzgerald
Jas H Birch	Jas H Birch
Chas Lee Jones	Chas Lee Jones
Wm H Upperman	Wm H Upperman
John Purdy	John Purdy
J S Hall, square B, Pa ave	
Alex'r Lee	Alex'r Lee
J M Johnson	J M Johnson
S Hyatt	S Hyatt
Andrew Small	Andrew Small
E Lindsley	E Lindsley
B O Sheckell	B O Sheckell
John West, square 461, 7th st.	
B O Sheckell	B O Sheckell
Chas Stott	Chas Stott
Z D Gilman	Z D Gilman
S Hyatt	S Hyatt
Jos Peck	Jos Peck
E Lindsley	E Lindsley
J H Eberbach, square 407, 8th & E sts.	
Thos Baker	Thos Baker
Thos Baker	Leonard Harbaugh
John F Boone, jr	Owen Connolly
Leonard Harbaugh	C W Utermohle

Owen Connolly
G W Utermohle
Fred'k Stutz, square 408, F st
J H Eberbach
Owen Connolly
G W Utermohle
R Bihler
Thos Cookendorfer
Vincent Masi
Jas Long, square ____
Alex Lee
Frank Taylor
R C Weightman
Jos Peck
Z D Gilman
Thos Pursell
S Hyatt
John Foy, square ___.
J H Eberbach
S P Franklin
J C McGuir
C Buckingham
F Masi & Co
Robt T Patterson
Owen Connolly, square 407, 8th & D sts
G W Utermohle, sen
J H Eberbach
F Masi & Co
Jos Harbaugh
John Foy
Thos Donoho
Jas Davis, square 461, Pa ave
B O Sheckell
S Hyatt
E Lindsley
Z D Gilman
Jos Peck
Jas Long
John Donovan, reservation 12, Pa ave
Martin Murphy
Jas Fitzgerald
W H Upperman
Pat Moran
Geo Parker
Chas Lee Jones

John Foy
Wm Steiger

Owen Connolly
G W Utermohle
Vincent Masi
R Bihler
Thos Cookendorfer
J H Eberbach

Alex Lee
Frank Taylor
R C Weightman
Jos Peck
Z D Gilman
Thos Pursell
S Hyatt

S P Franklin
J H Eberbach
J H McGuir
C Buckingham
F Masi & Co
Robt T Patterson

Wm T Steiger
G W Utermohle, sen
John Foy
J H Eberbach
Jos Harbaugh
Thos Donoho

B O Sheckell
S Hyatt
E Lindsley
Z D Gilman
Jos Peck
Jas Long

Martin Murphy
Jas Fitzgerald
W H Upperman
Pat Moran
Geo Parker
Chas Lee Jones

B Shad, reservation 12, B & 2nd sts.
Pat Moran   Pat Moran
Martin Murphy   Martin Murphy
Jas Fitzgerald   Jas Fitzgerald
W H Upperman   W H Upperman
Wm Greason   Wm Greason
Chas Lee Jones   Chas Lee Jones
Jesse Brown, square 460, Pa ave
Alex Lee   Alex Lee
J M Johnson   J M Johnson
Z D Gilman   Z D Gilman
Jas Long   Jas Long
A Coyle   A Coyle
Levi Pumphrey   Levi Pumphrey
Wm Samuels, square 454, 7th st
J A Donohoo   J A Donohoo
Jos Beasly   Jos Beasly
Levi Pumphrey   Levi Pumphrey
Jonathan Forrest   Jonathan Forrest
R Jones   R Jones
Saml Bacon   Saml Bacon
Thos Baker
Leon'd Harbaugh   Leon'd Harbaugh
John R Hendley   John R Hendley
Jos Harbaugh   Jos Harbaugh
J H Eberbach   Raphael Jones
Raphael Jones   J H Eberbach
Saml Bacon   Saml Bacon
A R Jenkins, reservation 10, Pa ave.
Wm H Upperman   Wm H Upperman
Edw Simms   Edw Simms
Alex'r Lee   Alex'r Lee
J M Johnson   J M Johnson
Fred'k Cudlip   Fred'k Cudlip
J P Pepper   J P Pepper
S S Coleman, square 491, Pa ave
Alex'r Lee   Alex'r Lee
E Lacy   E Lacy
J P Pepper   J P Pepper
John W Maury   John W Maury
B F Middleton   B F Middleton
Benj Beall   Benj Beall
J R Hendley, square 431, 7th st
Geo Sweeny   Jas D Hendley
F Mattingley   Leonard Harbaugh

Jos Harbaugh
Geo Sweeny
F Mattingley
Jos Harbaugh
Fred'k O'Neal, square 407, 7th st
John Foy
J H Eberbach
Patrick Moran
Thos Baker
G W Utermohle
Thos Donohoo
Geo Topham, reservation 10, Pa ave.
Wm H Upperman
Jas H Birch
J M Johnson
F Cudlip
Edw Simms
John P Pepper
<u>4th Ward.</u>
E Rupert, square 729, East Capitol.
V Mallion
D Homans
Edmund Reilly
Chas McNamee
J B Phillips
John A Lynch
Jas H Birch, square res 10, Pa ave
Wm H Upperman
Fred'k Cudlip
M Delany
Thos Young
Michl McDermott
R E Simms
J Casparis, square 688, A st & N J ave.
C K Gardner
Wm J Wheatley
Simon Brown
Jas T Frye
N C Towle
Fred'k May
John Cotter, res 10, Pa ave
J M Johnson
Edw Simms
F Cudlip
W H Upperman

Wm Gaham
Jas D Hendley
Leonard Harbaugh
Wm Gaham

John Foy
Patick Moran
Thos Baker
G W Utermohle
J H Eberbach
Thos Donohoo

Wm H Upperman
Jas H Birch
J M Johnson
F Cudlip
Edw Simms
John P Pepper

V Mallion
Edmund Reilly
Chas McNamee
J B Phillips
Jno A Lynch
D Homans

Wm H Upperman
Fred'k Cudlip
M Delany
Thos Young
Michl McDermott
R E Simms

Robt Brown
C K Gardner
Wm J Wheatley
Simon Brown
Jas T Frye
N C Towle

J M Johnson
Edw Simms
F Cudlip
W H Upperman

Jas Fitzgerald	Jas Fitzgerald
Alex'r Lee	Alex'r Lee
6th Ward	
John A Golden, square 928, 8th st.	
John Boylayer	John Bohlayer
Thos Bayne	Thos Bayne
F S Walsh	F S Walsh
J R Queen	J R Queen
R M Combs	R M Combs
S Tench	S Tench
7th Ward	
Peter Jones, square 356, Water st.	
Henry N Young	J W Martin
Geo Hercus	Lewis Thomas
Simon Fraser	Simon Fraser
Jas Mitchell	Jas Mitchell
Lewis Thomas	Geo Hercus

Broke into my garden & premises, several times, & destroyed my celery, corn, etc, a roan colored Filly. Owner can have her by paying charges, damages, & taking her away. –John King, 7th st, near the Toll Gate.

Circuit Court of Wash Co, D C: motion to dissolve the injunction in the case of Henry Carter vs J M Carlisle, J B Gardiner & Co, Franklin Gardiner, & R C Washington. It appears that Mr Washington was engaged in the dry goods business in Wash City in 1845, & had some of his paper remaining out in Sep 1845, at which time he & Mr Carter became partners in the same business; they continued as partners till Jan, 1846. During the partnership all Mr Washington's paper was retired & the partnership paper substituted to an amount upon which the parties differ; that the terms of the dissolution were that Mr Carter should take goods to the amount he invested in the partnership, & that Washington should pay all debts.

Household & kitchen furniture at auction on Nov 4, at the residence of Mrs Timms, on Capitol Hill, nearly opposite the south gate of the Capitol. -R W Dyer, auct

Farm at private sale: wishing to leave the neighborhood in which my family at present resides, I offer for sale my Farm, near Beltsville Post Ofc, Balt & Wash Railroad, Md, 12 miles from Wash: contains about 200 acs. Title is indisputable. The house has 8 rooms, a stable, carriage-house, corn-house, servants' house, & a fine ice-house. During my absence Alfred Hunter will show the premises. –Thos T Turner

Mrd: on Oct 28, by Rev Jas B Donelan, John Thos Lenman to Miss Jennett Raldon Hunter, all of Wash City.

Mrd: on Oct 27, by Rev O Ege, Francis Keithley to Miss Jane Eliza Chancey, all of Wash City.

Died: on Oct 29, after an illness of 9 days, Mrs Mary Brooks, in her 66th year, a native of County Down, Ireland, & for the last 30 years a resident of Wash City. Her remains will be conveyed for interment to St Patrick's Church this afternoon at 4 o'clock, where the funeral services will be performed. Friends & acquaintances of the dec'd, & ofher family, are respectfully invited to attend the funeral from her late residence on the corner of F & 5th sts.

Notice: Wm Hill, of Wash, Tin, Stove, & Grate Dealer, having transferred & assigned all his book debts, accounts, & other evidences of debt to the subscribers, & constituted them his attys to collect the same, the debtors of said Wm Hill are notified to make payment to the subscribers, or one of them, & to no other persons. –Ed M Linthicum; John Marbury, jr; Chas A Buckey, Gtwn, D C.

SAT OCT 31, 1846
Store for rent, next to Brown's Hotel, recently occupied by R France & Co. Inquire of Wm B Todd.

Jobbing Gardening. Newell & Kerr, Gardeners, at Mr Buist's, H st, between 11th & 12th sts.

Mrs D Potter has permanently taken that large house adjoining Douglas' Green-house, near the State Dept, & last in the occupancy of the Prussian Minister, will be able to accommodate a few more permanent or transient boarders.

Letter to Mr Calvin Goddard, belonging to one of the District companies, dated Monterey, Sep 27, after announcing his own safety: "We had about 30 men killed & wounded in our squadron. Col Watson was as brave a man as ever lived. Sgt Truscott had his head shot off by a cannon ball. Gen Taylor sent in to bury our dead, but the Mexicans refused permission. The Lancers killed the wounded men whenever they got a chance. Lt Boyle led us like a man & gallant soldier. Capt Waters is safe. Tell L Fitzgerald that Thomas is safe. He acted like a man. Tell John Porter that the two Murphys are safe. Jas Williams is also safe; he would have written, but had no paper. Tell Jas Shreve that Jim Darkey, a negro boy, followed Lt Boyle through the battle, with his musket. Capt Bronaugh sends his best respects. Lt Bell joins with him. Tell Mr J E Norris that his brother was struck with a grape shot in the side. Another bullet hit him in the face, but he is walking about; the latter only knocked the skin off."

Changes in the Phil Custom House: following gentlemen have just been removed: Abraham Martin, Cashier; J S Cummings, J C Pechin, Thos Vallettee, Chas P Hays, Thos Latimer, & Saml Eckel, clerks; besides about 15 inspectors. –Phil Inquirer

Orphans Court of Wash Co, D C. Letters testamentary on the personal estate of Raphael Semmes, late of said county, dec'd. –B I Semmes, jr; Thos Semmes, excs

Balt: Christ Church, of Balt City, under the pastoral charge of Rev H D V Johns, which has been undergoing thorough repairs for some months, is to be re-opened on Sabbath next for divine service.

Mrd: on Oct 27, by Rev Dr J S Reese, Capt Jas Guy, of Alexandria, Va, to Miss Susan Potter, d/o Mr Saml Potter, of Fairfax Co, Va.

Died: on Jul 26 last, in Clarksville, Tenn, Mrs Lucinda Reynolds, consort of the Hon Jas B Reynolds, formerly for several years an esteemed Rep in Congress from that district. She was born on May 28, 1781, in the State of Va, from which State her family emigrated to the West at a period when the country was infested with Indians & not yet reclaimed from the wilderness. She was married to Mr Reynolds, [who was her 2nd husband] in Feb, 1829.

Died: on Oct 25, at St Julien, Spottsylvania Co, in her 68th year, Mrs Mary Champe Brooke, w/o the Hon Francis T Brooke.

Died: on Sep 22 last, at Fred'k, Md, David Steiner, aged 49 years. He was distinguished through life for strick integrity & a rigid adherence to the attributes of the high-minded, honorable, & just man.

Died: on Oct 26, at Rockville, Montg Co, Md, Iver McIver Campbell, aged 65 years.

Mrs S Hamilton, south side of Pa ave, between 9th & 10th sts, will this day open new & fashionable Millinery, including latest fashions & patterns, to which she invites the attention of the ladies.

MON NOV 2, 1846
Trustee's sale of house & lot: by deed of trust from Henry Wilson to the subscriber, dated Jun 4, 1842, recorded in liber W B 94, folios 324 thru 325, in the land records of Wash Co, D C: sale on Dec 2, in front of the premises: lot 1 in subdivision of square 374, with 2 story brick house on the front & a frame house on the rear: property fronts 100 feet on 10th st west, between H & I st north. –Jas A Kennedy, trustee
-R W Dyer, auct

City Ordnance-Wash; 1-Act for the relief of C W Stewart, that the fine imposed on him for an alleged violation of an ordinance of this Corp relative to the keeping or harboring of dogs, the same is hereby remitted: Provided, the said Stewart pay the cost of prosecution.

Mrd: on Nov 1, by Rev Mr Van Horseigh, John Edw Thompson, of Wash City, to Eliz Herbert, formerly of Balt.

Died: on Nov 1, Miss Charlotte Clubb, aged 45 years. Her funeral is this afternoon at 3 o'clock, from the residence of her brother, on I st near 6th st.

Letters remaining in the Post Ofc, Wash, Nov 1, 1846.

Ayres, Lt G W
Anderson, Capt R
Addison, Henry S
Adams, Saml
Alexander, Dr R B
Adams, Henry
Andree, Cornel
Beard, Lewis
Bross, Wm
Black, Richd
Browne, John
Botts, Alex'r L
Ball, Wm
Bates, Miss Cath'e
Black, Mrs Eliza
Brown, Jos
Boyd, Jos K
Ball, Miss Sidnor
Burges, Joshua
Butler, Wesley
Bussell, John H
Baggott, Jas
Bruning, Henry-2
Bartlett, Nelson
Brewer, John W
Bull, Martin
Berry, Jas A
Bowman, Wm W
Baltzell, Emma
Burgwin, Henry A
Botter, jr, Jas
Bagman, Wm
Burnett, Chas A
Butler, John W
Bean, Miss Mgt E
Bender, Miss Lucy A
Brown, Miss Cath G
Bennett, Gen Alfred
Baltimore, Amelia A
Butlar, Miss Eliz E
Bingham, John K

Bohrer, Benj R
Baxter, Morris
Bainbridge, Mort-2
Bryan, Wm H
Berry, Brooke M
Clark, Miss Maria
Coe, Miss Guinetta
Chase, Miss Jane C
Cox, Mrs L
Chick, Nathl
Cooke, Miss Ann
Carter, Caroline M
Cooper, Saml
Cooper, Miss Prise
Cavanaugh, Dennis
Chapman, Thos J
Caustin, Augustus
Carroll, Mrs Harriet
Collier, Jos
Creamer, John
Cannon, Minor M, or J W
Chandler, Thos A
Cearns, Miss Mary A
Chew, Miss Clarissa
Deitz, Geo
Dean, John
Dean, Miss Cath'e
Darrell, Julia Ann
Dewey, Rev Orville
Dishman, John
Dunbar, Jane
Eaton, Capt J H
Espey, Wm
Edgertown, Robt C
Emmett, Mrs C
Eland, Eliza
Elmore, Col F H-2
Everett or Joe Sweeney
Fahr, August
French, Miss Roso

Fisher, Miss Marg
Fenton, Chas W
Fagin, Jane
Frederick, Thos
Fraser, Jas
Fitzhugh, John W
Febiger, Pas'd Mid John C
Fowler, Rev Wm C
Guy, Wm B
Green, Allen B
Grey, Richardson
Green, Noah
Gray, Mrs Mary E
Greene, John L
Gray, Notley
Graves, Thos J
Gray, Geo
George, Wm M
Grinnell, Frank
Gardner, John L
Gleason, Thos M
Garltand, Mrs Eliza
Gilliss, J Alex'r
Gurhett, Miss Lucr'a
Gladden, Mrs Sarah
Howe, Wm
Hill, Wm
Howe, Dr Saml G
Hughes, Miss M A
Hough, Miss Cath'e
Hall, Matthew M
Hall, Isaac
Hull, Miss Rebecca
Hill, Mrs Nancy
Hall, Ephraim W
Hasler, John
Harvey, Wm
Hernandez, John C
Hayden, Dr Chas
Hoover, Miss S E

Hammling, Chris'n	Lovenskiold, A de	Rosier, Mrs Mary
Hawkins, Chas G	Moore, Jas	Rice, Geo W
Harper, Jas A	Minck, John	Robertson, Wm H
Hutton, John, of Dublin	Miller, Mrs R E	Rogers, Chas J
	Mahorney, Richd	Richards, Jos
Harvey, jr, John	Moran, Mrs Nancy	Ready, Wm
Howard, Col Geo T	Morris, Thos A	Ridings, Fred'k
Howard, Jas M	Murphy, Edw-2	Rodgers, Miss Cath
Hunter, Lt Chas G	Merrill, Beanham	Rogers, Mrs Sarah A
Henrich, Marion	Miller, Henry	Robertson, Nelson R
Hotchkiss, Gideon-2	Meredith, Mrs Mary	Sour, jr, Col M
Ingraham, Edw	Miller, Jas N	Steel, Jas R
Jones, Mrs Persis	Minge, Louisa & J	Simms, Wm
Jones, Dangerfield	Brown	Simmes, Miss Jane
Jamaison, Miss Jos	Marshall, Mrs Char	Simmes, Miss M J
Janney, Paul	McLain, Wm	Simms, John Thos
Johnston, Zach's	McCloud, Danl A	Smith, Edw H
Jarvis, Mrs Marg't	McFarland, Jas	Smith, Wm
Jirdinston, Mrs Lue	McLaughlin, B L	Sangster, Capt Tho
Johnson, Chas	McCauley, Geo	Savin, Harvey W
King, Wm	McGehee, Mrs C	Starkey, Isaac G
Kuhn, Walter E	McJilton, Mrs C	Stebbins, Henry
Kelly, Jos C	McDonnell, Wm	Stuard, Mrs Ann M
Klockgether, Lewis	McCormick, Wm	Siminton, John
Knuckel, John C	Macoudry, Capt F W	Sinclair, John
Laub, Miss Mary	McCleary, Dr J Z J	Smallwood, Rich T
Love, John S	McCarty, Miss Jane	Sinclair, Rev Jos
Lee, John	Neutze, John Chr	Stockdale, Thos P
Little, Capt Geo	O'Bryon, John	Samuel, Henry
Lucane, Jas T	Otto, John	Shelton, Mrs Sarah
Luxin, Mrs Eliz	O'Hara, Theodore	Stewart, Wm E
Lewis, Cmdor	O'Bryon, Fred-2	Seiden, Mrs E L
Lewis, Edw	Onego, Marano	Somers, Miss Eliza
Lively, Robt A	O'Nail, Jas	Seward, Henry
Lanier, Jas F D	O'Bryon, John F-2	Schiminger, Jerry
Lenhart, Peter	Page, Mrs Sophia	Sweeney, Mrs Mary
Leggitt, Aaron	Plant, Geo H	Sullivan, Marshall-2
Lewis, Miss Agnes	Prince, Jos H	Tuffley, John
Lakey, Mrs Martha	Patterson, Wm	Tolson, Edw
Lavege, John	Philips, Miss Aman	Thomas, Henry G-2
Looby, Terence	Philips, Mrs Cecilia	Tarbos, Lyman
Lavalette, Capt	Pettit, Alfred	Townsend, Lem R
Lincoln, B Austin	Quastoff, Theodore	Turner, Mrs Eliz
Lemon, Rev Nich	Rich, Dr Jas S	Tayloe, John-2
Lefebre, Mrs E	Rest, Levi	Thompson, John H

Talbot, Tobias F	Wall, Thos	Wooster, Chas F
Thompson, Geo	Wood, Mrs A J	Williams, Welling'n
Tilghman, Henry	Wood, Mrs Chris'a	Wiley, Ann Virg'a
Taylor, John A	Wood, Nicholas	Wilson, Mary Ellen
Tippett, Edw	Whitney, Jos	Wharton, Dr John O
Tilley, Miss Bar'a A	Waller, Mrs M H	Wiley, Wilotto
Tolson, Miss Mary E	Waters, Geo	Webster, Lt John A
Vermillion, Miss Eliza	Williams, Jas	Williams, Wm A
	Webster, Caroline	Warner, Matilda
Wright, Sarah J	Watkins, Miss J A	Yale, G
Wood, Jas A	Wilkinson, John A	Yates, Francis
Welsh, Wm	Williams, Saml	Young, Jacob

The postage due to the U S on letters & packets directed to Mexico & all other foreign Gov'ts, except the British Canadian Provinces & New Brunswick, must be prepaid, otherwise they cannot be sent. –C K Gardiner, P M

TUE NOV 3, 1846
Public sale of real & personal property: by deed of trust from Jas Davidson, late of Anne Arundel Co, Md, dated Jan 2, 1845, recorded in Liber W S G 27, folio 569, a land record of Anne Arundel Co, Md: sale on the premise of said dec'd, on Dec 1: a valuable farm, containing 232¼ acres, in the neighborhood of Davidsonville, Anne Arundel Co, & adjoins the lands of Dr R S Steuart, David McBrogden, & others. Improvements consist of a comfortable dwlg, & all other houses for farming & planting purposes. Also, 15 servants, slaves for life. –Thos Davidson, trustee [Also, on the same day & at the same place, the subscriber will sell, by order of the Orphans' Court, the residue of the personal property of Jas Davidson, dec'd, consisting of a valuable stock of horses, cattle, sheep, hogs; farming implements, household & kitchen furniture. –Thos Davidson]

Fatal accident. In Stokes Co on Oct 15, Abram & Hampton Vanhoy, 2 brothers, went out to hunt turkeys: one brother accidentally shot & killed the other brother. [The brother killed was not identified.] The dec'd was 30 years of age, & has left a young wife & 2 or 3 children. –Greensboro Patriot

A large & fine Newfoundland dog, the property of F H Gerdes, was lost or stolen on Fri last from the farm of Mr Smith Thompson, near Beltsville, Md. A very liberal reward will be paid for any such information to Mr J B Gluck, Assist U S Coast Survey, Wash, which may lead to the recovery. Dog answers to "Bush."

Notice: I hereby forewarn all persons indebted to me from paying any accounts to E M Linthicum & Co. -Wm Hill

Died: on Nov 1, in Balt, Charles, infant s/o Chas & Mary Jane Pairo.

WED NOV 4, 1846
Obit-killed: at the capture of Monterey, Mexico, on Oct 22, Capt W G Williams, U S Topographical Engineers: born in this country, the greater portion of his childhood & early youth was passed in England; returning to his nativity while yet a boy, his mother being dec'd, his father engaged in business which required his absence, & he was left to carve out his own destiny. He succeeded in procuring an appointment to West Point, through his own efforts. At the close of his course at West Point, his rank was among the first of the class. After a career of 22 years he joined the army at Matamoros, & accompanied it to Monterey. Here it was decreed that his career of honor & usefulness should cease. Here he was too severely wounded to retire, & was left to die in the hands of the enemy. The interesting children he left will ever cherish his memory as one of the kindest & most affectionate of parents. –A F

Balt Sun furnishes the following list of the persons killed & wounded at the battle of Monterey who belonged to the Balt & District Btls: Wash, Nov 2, 1846. From a letter date Sep 30, received in this city from Capt Piper, of the Balt Volunteers, by his brother, Dr John R Piper.
Col Wm H Watson's body was brought into camp by Lt Taylor, assisted by privates Hyde & Simpson, who risked their lives under a heavy cannonade to rescue it from where it fell.
Co A-Capt Stewart's: Jos Files, wounded in the left arm, since amputated. Albert Hart, color sgt, wounded in the right arm, since amputated. Robt Caples, in the abdomen. Wm Lee, in the groin. Malcolm Wilson, in the left arm. Wm Alexander, in the leg.
Co B-Capt Piper's: Patrick O'Brien, killed. Wm F Powelson, 1st sgt, wounded in the left wrist. Geo Harold, in the right arm, badly.
Co D-Capt Waters, of Wash: 1st Sgt Truscott, killed by a cannon ball. Chas Yerst, wounded in the leg. A Parris, in the side, slightly.
Co E-Capt Kenly: Alex'r Ramsay, killed. Jos Wharry, killed. Jas Henry, wounded in the left arm. Henry Elslen, in the thigh, slightly.
Co F-Capt Boyd's: Geo A Herring, s/o Henry Herring, of Balt, killed. Henry Clifford, wounded in the left arm. Wm Kelly, in the right leg, badly. Melvin Stone, in the right foot, slightly. Geo Pearson, of Co F, died on Mon, having been sick for 10 or 12 days. No reference made to Co C, commanded by Capt Bronaugh, which was on camp duty during the battle. -Sun

David W Dixon, a free mulatto, was arrested on suspicion of a recent robbery in Wash City. Property in the amount of $500 was found in the dwlg-house & premises of the prisoner. Mr W C Eckloff, Mr C S Fowler, Mr Jonathan T Walker, & Messrs Young & Steer, merchant tailors: all identified their property.

Wreck of the barque **Meteor**, of Alexandria: Capt Janney sailed from Balt for St Thomas, on Sep 3, & was wrecked in the disastrous gale of the 7th & 8th. The only survivors of the crew, John Thompson & Wm Deany, seamen, arrived at Balt on Mon, from St Thomas, they having been taken off by the barque **Chancellor**, of New Haven, & carried to Antiqua.

Notice: by virtue of a writ of fieri facias, to me directed, I shall expose to public sale for cash, on Nov 7, one double-cased Gold Watch, seized & taken as the property of Thos L Thruston, & will be sold to satisfy a judgment in favor of the Pres & Trustees of the Patriotic Bank of Wash. –R R Burr, Constable

Mrs M Lare, Fashionable Dressmaker, 10th st, west side, south of Pa ave, has just received her Fall & Winter Fashions, & is prepared to execute all orders in her line.

Mrd: on Nov 3, at Gtwn, by Rev Mr Shiras, Mr Reuben H Meriweather, of Harewood, Balt Co, Md, to Miss Hester A, d/o Dr Austin, of Gtwn.

Two or three dressmakers wanted immediately. Apply to Miss Mary Ann Sullivan, on F st, between 6th & 7th sts.

THU NOV 5, 1846

Judge Danl B Tallmadge, of N Y, formerly of the Superior Court, & brother of Hon N P Tallmadge, died in Richmond, Va, on Thu last, while on a visit to his brother-in-law. He was about 60 years of age. –Tribune

The remains of the lamented Col Cross are expected to reach this city in the train of cars which leaves Balt on Fri at 5 o'clock, p m. They will be escorted to the cars by the citizen soldiery of Balt.

By an order of distrain I shall expose to public sale for cash at the house of F O'Neal, on 9th st, between D & C st, Wash City, on Nov 7, household & kitchen furniture, & sundry articles, taken as the property of F O'Neal, to satisfy rent due in arrears to Jane Woodruff: sale on the premises. –J F Wollard, Bailiff

Miniature Painting & instruction in Drawing: Miss Eliz Milligan, at her residence, one door east of the corner house on N Y ave & 15th st west.

For rent, the commodious dwlg, now in the occupancy of John H Smith, on 17th st, between I & H sts. Inquire of S P Franklin.

Trustee's sale: by decree of the Circuit Court of Wash Co, D C, in a cause wherein Sabret E Scott is cmplnt, & John Lynch & others are dfndnts, I will sell at public auction on Nov 27, on the premises: lots 11 thru 13 in square 728, with the bldgs & improvements. –H Naylor, Trustee -R W Dyer, auct

Orphans Court of Wash Co, D C. Letters testamentary on the personal estate of Saml Burche, late of said county, dec'd. –C H Wiltberger, Silas H Hill, Thos Blagden, excs

For sale or rent: 2 story brick dwlg on the corner of north C & 1st sts east. Apply to Chas E Ball, Green's Row, Capitol Hill.

FRI NOV 6, 1846

The Hon Andrew Beaumont, of Pa, appointed by the Pres Com'r of the Public Bldgs, vice Wm Noland.

Lt J S Jackson, late of Capt C M Clay's company of Ky Volunteers, has just returned home from Port Lavacca, having resigned his ofc on account of a difficulty between Capt Thos F Marshall & himself, which resulted in a duel. Finding measures would be taken by Col Marshall for punishment of this violation of the rules of the army, Lt Jackson & Lt Patterson, who was the friend of Capt Marshall on the occasion referred to, both resigned, & started for Monterey with a view to solicit a reinstatement at the hands of Gen Taylor, &, if unsuccessful, to be at present at the anticipated battle at Monterey. They learned of the battle & the armistice, & both returned to Ky, where they will remain a few days, & then return to the army. Capt Marshall, we understand, is determined to stand trial, & remained with his regt. –Lexington Gaz

Female Union Benevolent Society: 8th annual meeting held on Nov 3, Wash. Elected for the ensuing year:

Directresses:
Mrs Laurie
Mrs O B Brown
Mrs M St C Clarke
Mrs Mills
Mrs Webb, Sec
Mrs Whitman, Treas

Managers:
Mrs Wm A Bradley
Mrs C S Fowler
Mrs Anderson
Mrs Wm Cox
Mrs L Powell
Mrs Easby
Mrs Tucker
Mrs John Davis
Mrs Stelle
Mrs Purdy
Mrs Milburn
Mrs Dr Bradley
Mrs Simon-Brown
Mrs Columbus Munroe
Mrs Macomb
Mrs Drake
Mrs Hall
Mrs N Rice
Miss L Stott
Miss R Lowry
Miss Whitman
Mrs Luce
Mrs Randolph
Miss Moore

Negro man for sale: by order of the Orphans Court of PG Co, Md: sale on Nov 9, at the jail in Wash, D C. -Chas Hill, Guardian of Eliz S Hall.

Mrd: on Nov 4, by Rev Henry Slicer, Mr Geo Burns to Miss Mary Ellen, y/d/o Mr John Brown, both of Wash City.

Mrd: on Thu last, in Lynchburg, by Rev Mr Kinckle, Richd M Toler, one of the Editors of the Richmond Whig, to Miss Frances, d/o the late Dr Wm H B Christian, of the former place.

Mrd: on Sep 24 last, in Staunton, Va, by Rev Mr Castleman, Mr Wm Boswell Johnson to Miss Margaret Sarah, 2nd d/o Mr John B Breckenridge, all of that place.

Died: on Nov 5, Mrs Eveline McCormick, w/o Wm J McCormick, in her 39th year. Her funeral is at 10 o'clock on Sat.

Died: on Oct 31, at Elizabethtown, N J, at the residence of his father-in-law, Jas Crane, Wm B Beverley, Lt U S Navy, aged 32 years.

Died: on Oct 31, at Burlington, N J, aged 34 years, Susan Harriet, w/o John Henry Gilliat, of Newport, R I, & d/o Henry Schroeder, jr, formerly of Balt.

Died: on Nov 5, Wm Henry, only s/o Jeremiah Crown, in his 17th year.

United Brothers of Temperance, Jr Assoc, #1, to meet at the Northern Liberties Engine House today at 1 o'clock, to attend the funeral of our late brother, Wm Crown. Members of sister associations are invited to attend. By order: Wm W Grant, 1st Vice Pres

For hire, 2 servant men, one an excellent house-servant, the other a first rate carriage driver. Apply to Jas Mankin, at the Patriotic Bank, or to the subscriber, on 8th st, between L & M sts. –Wm K Dent

SAT NOV 7, 1846
To let: dwlg house, containing 6 rooms, with a good yard attached. Inquire of Jos Scholfield, 8th st, near the Genr'l Post Ofc.

For rent: new 3 story brick dwlg house on 13th st. Apply to Mr Wm Morrow, grocer, Appollo Hall, near the premises, or at the residence of the subscriber, F & 5th sts, opposite the Wesley Chapel. –Francis I Brooks

The remains of the lamented Col Truman Cross reached Wash last night in the Balt cars, & were conveyed to his late residence & that of his bereaved family in Franklin Row. They were accompanied from the Rio Grande by his eldest son, & in Balt escorted to the Railroad depot by several volunteer companies. At the Wash depot the remains were received by the Mayor of Wash & several members of the City Councils, by a large number of citizens, by the Wash Light Infty, & by a detachment of the Auxilliary Guard, under Capt Goddard. The military company, with solemn music, escorted the body to the late residence of the dec'd. Public interment will take place on Mon next, at 11 o'clock.

Strayed from the subscriber on Wed last, a red & white Steer, very fat, weighs about 1,000 pounds, horns rather forward. Liberal reward for his recovery.
–Wm H Wall, *Greenleaf's Point.*

Destruction of shipping at Havana: list from the Consul at Havana of vessels lost or damaged in that port during the terrible hurricane of the 10th & 11th.
American:
vessel **Rapid**, Ward, sunk, will be got up
vessel **Iowa**, Thompson, ashore, uninjured
vessel **Mudara**, Rich, lost, passengers & crew saved
vessel **Childe Harold**, Crosby, much damaged
vessel **Madeline**, Shanklan, sunk
vessel **Cybele**, Morrill, ashore
vessel **Echo**, Smith, sunk
vessel **Lisbon**, Messer, dismaster
vessel **Mohawk**, Crocker, wrecked
vessel **Nancy Prats**, Stevenson, safe
vessel **Smyrna**, Sprague, slightly damaged
vessel **Venezuela**, Fowler, dismaster
vessel **Millinoket**, Ellen, slightly damaged
vessel **Oak**, Foxter, dismasted
vessel **Titi**, Brown, badly damaged
vessel **Cumberland**, Hadley, damaged
vessel **Planet**, Jacobs, sunk
vessel **Merchant**, Kean, dismasted
vessel **Isabella**, Robby, safe

Maj Moses V Grant, of Ky, Commissary in U S army, died at Port Lavacca on Oct 5.

Mrd: on Nov 5, by Rev O Ege, John D Evans to Miss Isabella Nesmith, both of Wash City.

Mrd: on Oct 28, at Alexandria, Va, by Rev J T Johnston, Edmund B Duval, of Marietta, PG Co, Md, to Caroline D, y/d/o the late Wm M Lansdale, of Md.

Mrd: on Nov 5, by Rev Mr Eggleston, Mr Geo Humes to Miss Priscilla W Duvall, both of Wash City.

MON NOV 9, 1846
Official report of 1st Ohio Regt: from the Cincinnati Adv-Nov 2: Col Weller's Report: First Regt of Ohio Volunteers, now under my command, was led by its commanding ofcr, Col A M Mitchell, unto the attack made on Monterey on the 21st inst. On the 22nd we remained in camp, the men worn down & exhausted. On the 23rd we took to the field again, to sustain Capt Webster's batteries, & subsequently into the fort which fell into our hands the first day; kept possession of it until the 24th, when we were relieved. In the battle of the 21st Adj A W Armstrong was severely wounded in the leg, making amputation of the limb necessary; 1st Lt Hett, of Co H, was killed; 1st Lt Niles, of Co E, was severely wounded; Capt George, of the 2nd Rifle, & Lt Motear, of Co B, slightly wounded. Co F, under Lt Beargrand, had been detailed as a guard for the camp, & was

not in the actions. –John B Weller, Lt Col 1st Regt O V: to Brevet Gen Hamer, 1st Field Brigade of Volunteers

Later from the seat of the war: 1-The steamship **McKim** arrived at Galveston on Oct 23 from Brazos St Iago: on board: most of Capt Shriver's company of Mississippi & Texas volunteers, Col Balie Peyton, Gen A S Johnson, Mr Kendall, of Picayune, & a large number of discharged volunteers, making about 300 in all. 2-Lt Col McClung was rapidly recovering from the effects of his wounds. He received his wounds whilst saving his sword aloft & cheering his men, shouting "Victory!" The musket ball struck him on his left hand whilst holding his scabbard to his hip, & cut off 2 of his fingers, glancing from the scabbard & entering his abdomen, fracturing in its course the bone above the hip joint. 3-Lt Price, whose death has been announced, is alive & now at New Orleans. 4-The duels between Col Balie Peyton & Gen Marshall, & also between Capt Musson, of La, & Capt Cheeves, of the Texas Volunteers, have all been amicably arranged. 5-Col W S Fischer, cmder of the ill-fated Mier expedition, & Capt Fank S Early, of the Wash Texas Volunteers, & a hero of Monterey, died in Galveston on the 26th inst.

<u>Official list of the killed & wounded: 1st Ohio Regt at the storming of Monterey, Sep 21, 1846.</u>
Invincible Riflemen: W H Harris, killed, shot in the breast with grape
Josiah A Kellum, severely wounded-arm amputated above the elbow
Saml Myers, severely wounded-grape shot fractured jaw & lodged in the throat
E Wade, slightly; spent ball in the head
Montgomery Guards: Rich Welch, killed. John Farrell, slightly wounded-contusion of arm & side
John Clarkin, severely wounded-contusion of arm by grape
Wm Work, severely-musket ball through the foot, amputated
Vandeventer, slightly-contusion of the shoulder by a shell
John Flannagan, contusion of hip & side from a charge of horse
J Ryan, slightly-flesh wound of leg by a musket ball
Dayton Co: W G Davis, orderly sgt, killed
D F Smith, pvt, killed
Kelley Cox, killed-shot through the head by grape
E Reese, killed-residence Cleveland
Thos McMurray, killed
Lewis Motter, 1st lt, severely wounded
Alex'r McCarter, 2nd lt, slightly-musket ball in the leg
Dayton German Co: Jas McCloskey, pvt, killed
Geo Phale, pvt, killed
Wm Weber, pvt, killed
T Went, pvt, severely wounded
Chas Logan, pvt, severely wounded
Portsmouth Co: John W Hewlett, pvt, killed
Griffin Sowards, severely wounded-grape shot through the thigh

Alfred Donahue, pvt, severely wounded-grape shot through the thigh
Silas Burril, severely wounded-musket ball through the leg
Jas Lambeck, pvt, slightly wounded-contusion by a shell
Cincinnati Cadets: N H Niles, 1st lt, severely wounded-musket ball through the hip
Wm Miller, 3rd sgt, slightly wounded-contusion of hip & sie by a shell
W J Hogan, slightly wounded-spent ball in thigh
Geo W Fitzhugh, 1st cpl, slightly wounded-spent ball in thigh
Thos D Egan, pvt, killed
Robt Doney, pvt, slightly wounded-contusion of hip by shell
Brown County Boys: A F Shaw, pvt, severely wounded-musket ball through the arm
John Fletcher, pvt, severely wounded-grape shot in the thigh
A B McKee, pvt, severely wounded-musket ball through the hand
Cincinnati German Co: Matthew Hett, 1st Lt, killed-commanded company
Geo Meyer, cpl, severely wounded-musket ball losdged in arm-extracted
E J Dehooler, pvt, severely-grape shot in thigh & musket ball in arm
Henry Weber, pvt, severely-musket ball in right side-extracted at left breast
Henry Meyer, pvt, severely-musket ball through arm-extracted
Butler Boys: Jas George, Capt, severely wounded-contusion of head by shell-not dangerous
Geo Webster, 1st sgt, slightly-contusion by spent ball-not dangerous
Geo Lowfellow, 2nd sgt, severely-musket ball through thigh-not dangerous
J Pierson, pvt, severely-musket ball through the chest-not dangerous
John H Longley, cpl, slightly-contusion from spent ball
R H Alcott, pvt, slightly-contusion from shell
Stephen Freeman, pvt, killed
Oscar Behnee, pvt, killed
These men were murdered & shocking mangled by Lancers, who came upon them whilst the latter was conducting the former, who was slightly wounded, into camp---unarmed!
Field & Staff: Col A M Mitchell, severely wounded-an esquipette [2½ oz] ball through the leg. [The Colonel's favorite horse, presented him by the Cincinnati Bar, was killed.]
Adj A W Armstrong, 2nd Lt of Cincinnati Cadets, severely wounded-grape shot through the knee-leg amputated above the knee-recovery doubtful.
-E K Chamberlin, Surgeon, U S A: Monterey, Sep 24, 1846
The Cincinnati Cadets owned the Regimental Flag, a beautiful silk banner presented to them by the ladies of Cincinnati. It was carried during the whole action by Sgt Lundy, & though riddled by musket, canister & grape, & its staff shot off a few inches above his head, the gallant & fearless Sgt kept it waving during the whole day, & now has it floating on a Mexican lance captured from the enemy!

Died: on Nov 7, at the residence of Mr Saml Cropley, Gtwn, Mr Saml John Barnard, aged 40, & for nearly 20 years past a resident of the District. His funeral is today at 2 p m, to start from Mr Corpley's.

City Ordinances: 1-Act for the relief of Eliz G Dulany: fine imposed for an alleged violation of an act in relation to the keeping of dogs, is hereby remitted: Provided: she pay the costs of prosecution. 2-Act for the relief of Michl Joyce: payment of the claim of Joyce for repairing a breach in the arch on 11th st west, furnishing all materials for the same, the sum of $67.08 to be paid to him.

Headquarters Nat'l Blues to parade this Mon at half past 8 o'clock, in full winter uniform, to attend the funeral of the late Col Cross. By order of the Captain: Geo Emmerich, O S

Ocean Scenes, from Old Seaman. Capt Geo Little, of Balt, will deliver addresses at the Foundry Methodist Chapel, G & 14th sts, this evening, & relate many of the dangers of the great deep, viz, battles, capture of cannibal Indians, conflict with pirates, & many other perils, showing the Interposition of Divine Providence in his rescue. He will dispose of his book entitled "The Cruiser," which may be had at the Chapel.

Union Brothers of Temperance to meet in their Hall this evening at 6½ o'clock. –H W Dowden, Rec Sec

TUE NOV 10, 1846
THE Home Journal, by Geo P Morris & N P Willis: will be issued on Nov 21: entertaining reading, passing events, a paper which families may keep up with the times. Address: 107 Fulton st, N Y.

French & English Boarding School: Mrs David H Burr is prepared to receive an additional number of young ladies. Located corner of E & 9th st, Wash.

The undersigned, having been appointed Scavenger of the 5th Ward, informs the citizens of that ward that he is prepared to execute the duties of his ofc with promptness. Any orders left at the store of J Kilmon, the store of Geo Bean, or the store of Phillips & Smallwood, will be promptly attended to. –John T Killmon [Note: 2 spellings of Kilmon/Killmon.]

For rent: the store & dwlg house on Md ave & 12th st west: good stable. Inquire of Edw Mattingley, near the Navy Yard, Wash.

Spain: The marriage of the Queen of Spain to her cousin Prince Don Francisco d'Assis, & of her sister the Infanta Louisa Fernanda to the Duke de Montpensier, y/s/o the King of the French, took place on the 10th ult-the treaty of Utrecht & the protest of the British Gov't to the contrary notwith standing. Queen Christiana was observed to raise her handkerchief to her eyes more than once during the ceremony. On the 11th the "veiling," as the solemn religious ceremony consequent on state marriages is termed, took place in the church of Atocha.

Circuit Superior Court of Law & Chancery of Fauquier Co, held on Oct 12, 1846. Philip S Johnson & Austin B Weedon, excs of Frances Kerton, dec'd, plntfs, against Edw Sanderson, Geo E Sanderson, Betsy Sanderson, Frances Sanderson, & Kitty, Hannah, Edmund, & Willis, negro slaves, dfndnts-in Chancery. From the bill & exhibits, the will of Anthony Kerton was admitted to probate in the County Court of Fauquier on Oct 24, 1803, whereby he devised to his widow, Frances Kerton, all his estate, real & personal, for life, & after her death to his brothers, John & Thos Kerton, & his sister Eliz Kerton, or their legal reps, who were at that time said to be subjects & residents of the kingdom of Great Britain, & have so continued, if now alive, or that if dead their legal reps; & the said Frances Kerton, having recently died, having made her last will & testament whereby she appointed Philip S Johnson & Austin B Weedon her excs, which will was admitted to probate, & the said excs qualified, in the County Court of Fauquier on Feb 23, 1846. The Court doth order that publication be made for 3 months, warning the said John, Thos, & Eliz Kerton, if they be living, or their legal reps if they be dead, to appear before this Court on the Tue after the first Mon in May, 1847, & assert any claim they may have or think fit to prefer against the estate of the said Fances Kerton, dec'd, growing out of the provisions of the will of Anthony Kerton aforesaid, & her possession of the property mentioned in said will; & that, in default of such appearance, the Court will proceed finally to dispose of the assets of the estate of said Frances Kerton, dec'd, & to declare her slaves free, in conformity with the provision of her will. –Wm F Phillips, Clerk

European Correspondent: Sir Charles Wetherell's personal estate has just been administered to by Lady Wetherell, & a stamp duty paid on L250,000.

The remains of Col Cross were yesterday conveyed to their final resting place in **Congress burying-ground**. The funeral was attended by the Pres of the U S & all of his Cabinet, by all the ofcrs of the army & navy now in Wash City, by the Mayor & a number of the clergy & citizens of Wash: service was performed by Rev Septimus Tustin. The remains were escorted from the late residence of the dec'd, in Franklin Row, by the Wash Light Infty, the Nat'l Blues, & the Union Guards, volunteer companies of Wash City. The Potomac Guards, under the command of Lt Bomford, also attended. Citizens in hacks, on horseback, & on foot, followed the dec'd to his grave.

Mrd: on Nov 8, by Rev Mr Ege, Mr Wm P Cannon to Miss Julia A Evans, all of Wash City.

Died: yesterday, at his lodgings in Wash City, Cmdor John B Nicholson, of the U S Navy, in his 63rd year. He was a native of Richmond, Va, & entered the navy as a midshipman in 1805, on board the brig **Hornet**, then under command of Cmdor Chauncey. At the capture of the Macedonian frig, the late Cmdor served as 4th Lt of the **United States**, & was the first Lt of the ship **Peacock**, &, after her brilliant fight with the Epervier, the cmder of the prize ship, which he bought safely into port.

Mrs E W Randell, Fancy Dressmaker: removed to the east side of 10th st, 5 doors south of Pa ave. [Ad]

Clothing & Fancy Store: P Brenner & Son: Pa ave, between 11th & 12th sts. [Ad]

WED NOV 11, 1846
New Orleans Picayune: we learn that Lt Graham, of the army, died of his wounds since our last advice.

Despatch of Gen Pedro De Ampudia to the Mexican Sec of War, announcing the surrender of Monterey: was dated Headquarters in Monterey, Sep 26, 1846. Proclamation of Genr'l Jose Mariano De Salas, the acting President, to the people of Mexico, announcing the loss of Monterey, followed.

Rencontre-from the Memphis Eagle: took place on Oct 21, in Somerville, Tenn, between Wm A Lacy, & J A Wilson, both young gentlemen of the bar, in which Mr Wilson was killed from a pistol shot by Mr Lacy.

Appointed Scavenger of the 5th Ward: Jas Sparlin.

The Cumberland Citizen has passed into the hands of A Cary, formerly of Va. It will continue to advocate Whig-men & measures.

Mrd: on Nov 10, by Rev Job Guest, Mr Jourdan W Maury to Miss Sally M, eldest d/o Geo McNeir, of Wash City.

Mrd: on Nov 3, in Christ Church, Gtwn, by Rev Mr Gassaway, Rev Geo Armistead Leakin, Rector of Trinity Church, Balt, to Anna Maria, only d/o Hezekiah Miller, of the former place.

The funeral of the late Cmdor Nicolson will taken place this morning, at 11 o'clock, from Mrs Ulric's boarding house. The Ofcrs of the Army & Navy, & the friends & acquaintances of the dec'd, are respectfully invited to attend.

United Brothers of Temperance, Junior Encampment, are to meet at the Northern Liberties Engine-house today at 1 o'clock, to attend the funeral of our late brother, Jas Lee. –Wm W Grant, 1st Vice Pres

For sale: 5 houses & lots, 2 of them on 18th st, between I & K sts, & 3 in I st, between 18th & 19th sts. Apply to the subscriber, Dorcas Walker, residence on 18th st, between I & K sts.

Maine Mercer Potatoes: now landing from the schnr **Joseph**, & for sale in lots to suit purchasers. Apply to Peter Berry, Water st, Gtwn.

Trustee's sale of valuable lot: by deed of trust from John Walker to the subscriber, dated May 15, 1844, recorded in Liber W B, #109, folios 299 & 300: sale on Dec 15, on the premises, lot 6 in square 555, with improvements. The lot is a corner lot, fronting about 150 feet on N J ave & 109 feet on north M st. –Henry Naylor, Trustee -R W Dyer, auct

Burch's Patent Chinmey Top: for an improved cowl for the cure of smokey chimneys: Wm S Burch, Inventor & Patentee, residence F st, between 9th & 10th sts. N B: all kinds of brick work, such as setting grates, furnaces, & cooking ranges, neatly & promptly executed. [I certify that within 18 months past Mr Burch has placed 11 of his ventilators on the flues of chimneys of the Hall of the House of Reps & the ofcs & committee-rooms attached thereto-the ventilator has effectually cured every chimney. –B B French, Clerk of the House of Reps, Feb 27, 1846. Like endorsement from Geo C Whiting, A S H White: Genr'l Land Ofc, Feb 21, 1846. Mr Burch placed his "Chimney Cap' on the top of the flue, & then the fireplace [the back of which had been entirely broken out to accommodate a Franklin stove] was restored to its former shape. Since which there has been no smoke at all.

Orphans Court of Wash Co, D C. Letters testamentary on the personal estate of John L Brightwell, late of said county, dec'd. –Thos R Brightwell, exc

Late from the Army. The latest date from Monterey, the 16th: Lt Graham's remains were followed to the grave 3 days since by Gen Taylor & nearly all the ofcrs. [Nov 30th newspaper: the remains of the lamented Lt Richd H Graham were consigned to the tomb, with appropriate funeral honors, on Oct 13, Mr Rey, our Chaplain officiating. –Camp near Monterey, Mexico, Oct 26, 1846.] [Same paper: Washington, Nov 29, 1846: may his memory be ever cherished, above all in the honored city of his birth. –B]

THU NOV 12, 1846
Gen Kearney. This gallant ofcr is a native of N Y: married the step-dght of the celebrated Clark, of St Louis, who penetrated, with Merriwether, to the Columbia river. He is between 50 & 55 years of age: the Gen entered the army in 1812: for the last 15 to 20 years he has been stationed in the Far West-at St Louis, & generally at **Fort Leavenworth**, on the Missouri, in the dragon service. He ranks very high as an energetic, & accomplished ofcr. -N Y Globe

The brig **Alvarado**, commanded by Capt Harding, lying in Georgetown Bay, S C, was entirely destroyed by fire on Wed: fire originated in the galley. At the time the captain was on shore, having been unwell for some time previous. 3 persons perished, including a young man about 18 years of age, a nephew of the captain of the brig **Judge Whitman**.

Fisheries for rent: on the Potomac known as the ***Sycamore***, ***High Point***, & ***Stony Point***, for 2 or 5 years, separately or together. –Philip Otterback, near the Navy Yard, Wash

Public sale of personal property: by deed of trust from Robt Clark, of PG Co, Md, dated Sep 23, 1844, recorded in the clerk's ofc of Fairfax Co Court, Va, the subscriber, as trustee, will proceed to sell on Dec 2, on the premises, on the *High Point* estate, the personal property contained in said conveyance, consisting of live stock & farming utensils, 2 nets from 10 to 12 hundred fathoms long, & all the rope & corks appertaining to them, & all other implements, used by the said Robt Clark in the fishing business. –H Naylor, Trustee N B: the steamboat **S S Coleman** is employed to take down & bring back all who may wish to attend the above sale.

Balt, Nov 11. Master Hernandez, attached to the Equestrian company now performing at the Roman Amphitheatre in this city, fell from his horse while riding in the ring last night, & was very dangerousely, if not fatally, injured.

Case of the U S vs Francis Thomas: indictment for libel. Circuit Court of Wash Co, D C: Nov 9, 1846. Cause postponed till the first Monday of March next due to the health of Judge Cranch.

Mrd: on Nov 5, at the residence of F Hitz, on Capitol Hill, by Rev Mr Sprole, Jerimias Capritz to Miss Anna Magdalina Hitz, all of Wash City.

Died: on Nov 2, at his residence, in Chas Co, Md, Wm Penn, in his 72nd year.

Died: on Oct 30th, at the Naval Hospital, Brooklyn, Richd Russell Waldron, Purser in the U S Navy, aged 45 years-a gentleman of high character as an ofcr, & highly esteemed for his personal qualities by those who knew him, & they were many.

Died: on Oct 19, at Maysville, Ky, after a protracted & very painful illness, Mrs Augusta Ranson, consort of Richd Henry Ranson, of Lewis Co, in her 37th year.

Died: on Oct 31, in Oglethorpe Co, Ga, after a long & painful illness, Edw Jones, aged 74 years within a few days. The dec'd was a native of Montg Co, Md, whence he emigrated at the age of 12, with his father, Wm Jones, to Columbia Co, Georgia.

Notice: application has been made at the Mayor's Ofc for a renewal of the bond given by the com'rs of low grounds, dated Jul 9, 1822, for lot 8 in reservation 12, to Benj O Tyler, in viture of a public sale made by said com'rs, on that day, of said lot to Tyler, & which said bond has been assigned to the subscriber, & become lost or mislaid, & cannot be found. Unless cause shall be shown to the contrary, at the Mayor's Ofc, on or before Nov 25, 1846, a renewal of said bond will be granted to the subscriber. –Wm Morrow

FRI NOV 13, 1846
Killed, Wounded, & Missing, on the part of the American Army, in the storming of Monterey on Sep 21, & the subsequent engagements on Sep 22 & 23, 1846.
Gen Twigg's Division:
Killed:
Wm H Watson, Lt Col, Balt Vol
L N Morris, Capt, 3rd Inf, Sep 21
G P Field, Capt, 3rd Inf, Sep 21
P N Barbour, Brev Maj, 3rd Inf, Sep 21
C Hoskins, 1st Lt & Ad, 4th Inf, Sep 21
J C Terrett, 1st Lt, 1st Inf
D S Irwin, 1st Lt & Ad, 3rd Inf, Sep 21
R Haslett, 2nd Lt, 3rd Inf, Sep 21
J S Woods, Bvt 1st Lt, 2nd Inf, Sep 21
Geo Waitman, 1st Sgt, 3rd Artl, Co E
John Eagle, Pvt, 3rd Artl, Co E
Lovell Gregory, Pvt, 3rd Artl, Co E
Henry Snower, Pvt, 3rd Artl, Co E
T J Babb, Sgt, 3rd Inf, Co D
W Patrick, Pvt, 3rd Inf, Co D
J Newman, Pvt, 3rd Inf, Co D
C Torskay, Pvt, 3rd Inf, Co D
J Young, Pvt, 3rd Inf, Co D
Wm Brown, Sgt, 3rd Inf, Co F
Wm Mich'e, Pvt, 3rd Inf, Co F
J Harper, Pvt, 3rd Inf, Co F
C K Brown, Pvt, 3rd Inf, Co H
J Stubert, Pvt, 3rd Inf, Co H
Edgar Lavalette, Pvt, 3rd Inf, Co I
Edw Reilly, Pvt, 3rd Inf, Co K
Benj Bradt, Cpl, 4th Inf, Co E
Thos Salsbury, Pvt, 4th Inf, Co A
Henry Conline, Pvt, 4th Inf, Co D
Edw Carey, Pvt, 4th Inf, Co D
Allen J Vanceal, Pvt, 4th Inf, Co D
Michl McGouth, Pvt, 4th Inf, Co E
John Weeks, Pvt, 4th Inf, Co E
Jas S Doble, Pvt, 4th Inf, Co E
Peter Andrews, Pvt, 4th Inf, Co E
Peter Judge, Pvt, 4th Inf, Co E
Jas C Pennington, Pvt, Texas V
Martin Enwul, Pvt, 1st Inf, Co E
Thos W Gibson, Pvt, 1st Inf, Co G
Thos Perkins, Pvt, 1st Inf, Co G
Lawson Stuart, Pvt, 1st Inf, Co G
Jos Wolf, Pvt, 1st Inf, Co G
Geo Beck, Pvt, 1st Inf, Co G
Richd Bunchan, Pvt, 1st Inf, Co C
H K Brown, Pvt, 1st Inf, Co C
J Carroll, Pvt, 1st Inf, Co C
Marcus French, Pvt, 1st Inf, Co K
John Savage, Pvt, 1st Inf, Co K
Mica Hatch, Pvt, 1st Inf, Co E
Wm Raymond, Pvt, 1st Inf, Co E
Francis Sheridan, Cpl, 1st Inf, Co E
John Truscott, 1st Sgt, Balt Bat, Co B
G A Herring, Sgt, Balt Bat, Co F
Alex'r Ramsay, Pvt, Balt Bat, Do E
Jos Worry, Pvt, Balt Bat, Co E
Patrick O'Brien, Pvt, Balt Bat, Co B
Wounded:
W W Lear, Major, 3rd Inf, severely
H Bainbridge, Capt, 3rd Inf, Co B, slightly
J J Abercrombie, Brev Maj, 1st Inf, Co B, slightly
J H Lemott, Capt, 1st Inf, Co B, severely
R H Graham, 1st Lt, 4th Inf, Co B, since dead
R Dilworth, 2nd Lt, 1st Inf, Co B, since dead
Philip Swartwout, Sgt, 3rd Artl, Co C, slightly
John Edwards, Pvt, 2nd Drag
Wm P Holschea, Pvt, 2nd Drag, slightly
John Lee, Pvt, 3rd Artl, Co C, slightly
Michl McCarthy, Pvt, 3rd Artl, Co C, slightly

Theodore Fricken, Pvt, 3rd Artl, Co C, slightly
Bendt Nelson, Pvt, 3rd Artl, Co C, slightly
Bartholomew Stokes, Pvt, 2nd Drag, Co B,-slightly
Geo Wolf, Cpl, 3rd Artl, Co E, slightly
S D Coal, Pvt, 3rd Artl, Co E, severely
Thos Heuson, Pvt, 3rd Artl, Co E, severely
Wm Gilmore, Pvt, 3rd Artl, Co E, severely
John McCarthy, Pvt, 3rd Artl, Co E, severely
M Reilly, Pvt, 3rd Artl, Co E, severely
W R Goed, Cpl, 3rd Artl, Co E, slightly
Austin Clark, Pvt, 3rd Artl, Co E, mortally
P E Holcomb, Pvt, 3rd Artl, Co E, slightly
Thos Wajan, Musician, 3rd Inf, severely
G Brownley, Sgt, 3rd Inf, Co A, severely
Emit Hadduck, Pvt, 3rd Inf, Co C, slightly
D Maloney, Pvt, 3rd Inf, Co C, slightly
J Hagan, Pvt, 3rd Inf, Co C, slightly
P White, Pvt, 3rd Inf, Co C, slightly
C Ichle, Pvt, 3rd Inf, Co C, severely
N Farley, Pvt, 3rd Inf, Co C, severely
C Leslie, Pvt, 3rd Inf, Co D, severely
D Preslie, Pvt, 3rd Inf, Co D, severely
J D Ritters, Pvt, 3rd Inf, Co D, severely
W H McDonnell, Pvt, 3rd Inf, Co D, slightly
Ischa B Tucker, Pvt, 3rd Inf, Co D, severely
M Tyler, Pvt, 3rd Inf, Co F, severely
Jos Morris, Pvt, 3rd Inf, Co F, severely
W Mullen, Pvt, 3rd Inf, Co H, severely
W Rooke, Pvt, 3rd Inf, Co H, severely
J Treel, Pvt, 3rd Inf, Co H, severely
D Boyle, Pvt, 3rd Inf, Co H, slightly
T Clair, Pvt, 3rd Inf, Co H, slightly
Wm H Bowden, Pvt, Co I, severely
J Mansfield, Pvt, 3rd Inf, Co I, severely
C Adams, Pvt, 3rd Inf, Co I, severely
Edw Astin, Pvt, 3rd Inf, Co I, severely
Jas Calhoun, Pvt, 3rd Inf, Co I, severely
J Kerns, Pvt, 3rd Inf, Co I, severely
M Regan, Pvt, 3rd Inf, Co I, severely
L Sours, Pvt, 3rd Inf, Co K, severely
David Pottsdaner, Pvt, 3rd Inf, Co K, severely
G E Radwell, Pvt, 3rd Inf, Co K, severely
Thos O'Brien, Pvt, 3rd Inf, Co K, severely
Geo W Anderson, Sgt, 4th Inf, Co A, slightly
Robt Sanders, Sgt, 4th Inf, Co B, dangerously

Thos Mannigan, Sgt, 4th Inf, Co E, dangerously
Jas Ryan, Sgt, 4th Inf, Co E, severely
Thos Hyam, Cpl, 4th Inf, Co A, severely
Jas Wyley, Cpl, 4th Inf, Co B, dangerously
Danl McDonnell, Cpl, 4th Inf, Co C, slightly
Wm Albison, Cpl, 4th Inf, Co D, severely
Matthew McCormick, Cpl, 4th Inf, Co E,- severely
Wm Taylor, Pvt, 4th Inf, Co A, severely
E Henderson, Pvt, 4th Inf, Co A, slightly
Wm Holborn, Pvt, 4th Inf, Co A, severely
Wm Petty, Pvt, 4th Inf, Co A, dangerously
Wm Johnson, Pvt, 4th Inf, Co A, slightly
John Hill, Pvt, 4th Inf, Co C, severely
E Barnum, Pvt, 4th Inf, Co D, severely
Robt Halden, Pvt, 4th Inf, Co D, severely
Wm A Jones, Pvt, 4th Inf, Co D, severely
Jas Myers, Pvt, 4th Inf, Co D, severely
Aaron Wriggle, Pvt, 4th Inf, Co D, severely
Andrew Smith, Pvt, 4th Inf, Co D, since dead
Wm C Jones, Pvt, 4th Inf, Co E, dangerously
John Maguire, Pvt, 4th Inf, Co E, severely
John McDuffy, Pvt, 4th Inf, Co E, dangerously
John Banks, 1st Sgt, 1st Inf, Co K, slightly
Patrick Myles, 1st Sgt, 1st Inf, Co K, severely
E Bessie, 1st Sgt, 1st Inf, Co E, slightly
T H Haller, 1st Sgt, 1st Inf, Co E, slightly
John Tigart, 1st Sgt, 1st Inf, Co E, slightly
E Garver, 1st Sgt, 1st Inf, Co C, severely
Denton Conner, Cpl, 1st Inf, Co G, severely
Robt Aikens, Cpl, 1st Inf, Co C, severely
Augustus Lapple, Cpl, 1st Inf, Co C, severely
C Smith, Musician, 1st Inf, Co K, slightly
Wm McCarty, Pvt, 1st Inf, Co K, severely
Patrick Neely, Pvt, 1st Inf, Co K, slightly
John Saunders, Pvt 1st Inf, Co K, slightly
Wm Norlin, Pvt, 1st Inf, Co E, slightly
Robt E Wooley, Pvt, 1st Inf, Co E, severely
Jas Crawley, Pvt, 1st Inf, Co G, slightly
H Duchart, Pvt, 1st Inf, Co G, slightly
Francis Faulkler, Pvt, 1st Inf, Co G, severely
A Ryan, Pvt, 1st Inf, Co G, slightly
John Wilson, Pvt, 1st Inf, Co G, slightly
Jacob Smidt, Pvt, 1st Inf, Co G, severely
Chas Ratcliff, Pvt, 1st Inf, Co G, slightly
Jas Delany, Pvt, 1st Inf, Co K, severely

H Shrieder, Pvt, 1st Inf, Co G, severely
John Gallagher, Pvt, 1st Inf, Co C, severely
Levi Smith, Pvt, 1st Inf, Co G, severely
Peter M Cabe, Pvt, 1st Inf, Co E, severely
W P Poulson, 1st Sgt, Balt Bat, Co B, slightly
Robt Caples, Pvt, Balt Bat, Co A, dangerously
Jas Piles, Pvt, Balt Bat, Co A, severely
Alvert Hart, Pvt, Balt Bat, Co A, severely
Wm Lee, Pvt, Balt Bat, Co A, severely
Jacob Hemming, Pvt, Balt Bat, Co B, slightly
Geo Aunuld, Pvt, Balt Bat, Co B, severely
Chas Peck, Pvt, Balt Bat, Co D, slightly
Andrew J Norris, Pvt, Balt Bat, Co D, slightly
Geo Allen, Pvt, Balt Bat, Co E, slightly
Jas Henry, Pvt, Balt Bat, Co E, slightly
Harry Elting, Pvt, Balt Bat, Co E, slightly
Wm Kelly, Pvt, Balt Bat, Co F, severely
H Gifford, Pvt, Balt Bat, Co F, slightly
Melvin J Stone, Pvt, Balt Bat, Co F, slightly
E W Stevenson, Pvt, Balt Bat, Co A, severely

Missing:
E Gormley, Pvt, 3rd Inf, Co I, presumed to be dead
Geo O'Brien, Pvt, 3rd Inf, Co I, presumed to be dead

Gen Butler's Division:

Ohio Regt: Killed:

Mathew Hett, 1st Lt	Jas McCockey, Pvt, Co C
W G Davis, 1st Sgt, Co B	Geo Phale, Pvt, Co C
D F Smith, Pvt, Co B	Wm Weber, Pvt, Co C
O B Coxe, Pvt, Co B	John Havolett, Pvt, Co D
Elijah Reese, Pvt, Co B	T D Egan, Pvt, Co E
Thos McMurray, Pvt, Co B	Stephen Freeman, Pvt, 1 R
W H Harris, Cpl, 1 R	Oscar Behnee, Pvt, 2 R
Richd Welch, Pvt, Co A	

Wounded:

W O Butler, Maj Gen	John Farrell, Pvt, Co A
A M Mitchell, Col, severely	John Clarken, Pvt, Co A
A W Armstrong, Lt & Adj, severely	Wm Work, Pvt, Co A
Lewis Morter, 1st Lt, slightly	Thos Vande Venter, Pvt, Co A
N H Niles, 1st Lt, severely	John Flannigan, Pvt, Co A
H McCarty, 2nd Lt, slightly	Jeremiah Ryan, Pvt, Co A
Jas George, Capt, slightly	Michl Gilligan, Pvt, Co A
Saml Myers, Pvt, 1 R	Tobias Went, Pvt, Co C
Josiah A Kellam, Pvt, 1 R	Chas Segar, Pv, Co C
Edw Wade, Pvt, 1 R	Griffin Lowerd, Pvt, Co D
Wm Maloney, 1st Sgt, Co A	Alfred Donoghue, Pvt, Co D

Jos Lombeck, Pvt, Co D
Silas Burrill, Pvt, Co D
Wm Miller, Sgt, Co E
G W Fitzhugh, Cpl, Co E
Robt Doney, Pvt, Co E
Adam F Shane, Pvt, Co G
John Fletcher, Pvt, Co G
A B McKee, Pvt, Co G
Geo Myer, Cpl, Co H

E J Spoole, Pvt, Co H
Henry Weber, Pvt, Co H
Henr Myer, Pvt, Co G
Geo Webster, Sgt, 2 R
Geo Longfellow, Sgt, 2 R
John F Longley, Cpl, 2 R
John Pearson, Pvt, 2 R, since died
R H Alcott, Pvt, 2 R
Henry Humphries, Pvt, 2 R

Tennessee Regt: Killed:
W B Allen, Capt, Sep 21
S M Putnam, 2nd Lt, Sep 21
John B Porter, Pvt, Co C
Wm H Robinson, Pvt, Co C
John A Hill, Sgt, Co D
B F Coffee, Pvt, Co D
E W Thomas, Pvt, Co E
Booker H Dolton, Pvt, Co F
Isaac Gurman Elliot, Pvt, Co G
Peter H Martin, Pvt, Co G
Edw Pryor, Pvt, Co G
Benj Soaper, Pvt, Co G
Henry Collins, Pvt, Co H

Jas H Allison, Pvt, Co I
Jas H Johnston, Pvt, Co I
Jas B Turner, Pvt, Co I
R D Willis, Pvt, Co I
Jos B Burkitt, Pvt, Co K
Jas M L Campbell, Pvt, Co K
A J Eaton, Pvt, Co K
A J Gibson, Pvt, Co K
Finlay Glover, Pvt, Co K
A J Pratt, Pvt, Co K
Wm Rhodes, Pvt, Co K
John W Sanders, Pvt, Co K
G W Wilson, Pvt, Co K

Wounded:
R B Alexander, Major, severely
J L Scudder, 1st Lt, severely
G H Nixon, 1st Lt, slightly
J C Allen, 2nd Lt, severely
F F Winston, Cpl, Co B, slightly
J L Bryant, Pvt, Co B, severely
Alex'r Bigam, Pvt, Co B, severely
D C Fleming, Pvt, Co B, severely
Mackey Roney, Pvt, Co B, severely
Jas Thompson, Pvt, Co B, severely
David Collins, Pvt, Co B, severely
A S Duval, Pvt, Co B, slightly
T B Powell, Pvt, Co B, slightly
Wm B Davis, Pvt, Co C, slightly
Jos Law, Pvt, Co C, slightly
Jas York, Pvt, Co C, mortally
Wm Young, Pvt, Co C
Richd Gifford, Pvt, Co C, slightly
A V Stanfield, Pvt, Co C, slightly
Asa Lamb, Pvt, Co C, slightly
J J Argo, Cpl, Co D, slightly

Jas Todd, Pvt, Co D, severely
Thos Vickens, Pvt, Co D, severely
W D Cabler, Pvt, Co E, since dead
Jas M Vance, 1st Sgt, Co F, severely
Geo W Gilbert, Sgt, Co F, slightly
Chas M Talley, Pvt, Co F, slightly
Michl Crantze, Pvt, Co F, severely
R C Locke, Pvt, Co F, severely
J F Raphile, Pvt, Co F, since dead
Thos Kelly, Pvt, Co F, severely
Albert Tomlinson, Pvt, Co F, severely
Julius C Elliott, Cpl, Co G, severely
R A Cole, Pvt, Co G slightly
Jas H Jenkins, Pvt, Co G, severely
A G Stewart, Pvt, Co G, severely
Gulinger Holt, Sgt, Co H, severely
Jas Patterson, Cpl, Co H, slightly
Charley Arnold, Pvt, Co H, slightly
J J Blackwell, Pvt, Co H, slightly
Jos Crutchfield, Pvt, Co H, slightly
J Freeman, Pvt, Co H, severely

J D Gilmer, Pvt, Co H, severely
P O Hale, Pvt, Co H, slightly
Danl C King, Pvt, Co H, severely
C B Maguire, Pvt, Co H, severely
S S Reaves, Pvt, Co H, severely
A W Reaves, Pvt, Co H, slightly
Augustin Stevens, Pvt, Co H, slightly
Thos N Smith, Pvt, Co H, slightly
C B Ward, Pvt, Co H, slightly
Chas Davisk, 1st Sgt, Co I, severely
Robt W Green, Cpl, Co I, severely
Eli Brown, Pvt, Co I, severely
W F Bowen, Pvt, Co I, severely
Peter Eugles, Pvt, Co I, severely
Robt Flannigan, Pvt, Co I, severely
Wm Lowery, Pvt, Co I, slightly
S N Macey, Pvt, Co I, slightly
E G Zachary, Pvt, Co I, severely

Missing:
Felix Wordzincki, Pvt, Co F

Mississippi Regt:Killed:
L M Troeur, Pvt, Co C
Silas Mitcham, Pvt, Co E
Saml Potts, Pvt, Co G
Jos H Tenelle, Pvt, Co H
Wm H Grisam, Cpl, Co I

Wounded:
Alex R McClung, Lt Col, dangerously
R N Downing, Capt, severely
Henry T Cook, 1st Lt, slightly
Rufus K Arthur, 2nd Lt, slightly
L T Howard, 2nd Lt, severely
Henry H Miller, Pvt, Co B, dangerously
J H Jackson, Pvt, Co B, dangerously
A Lainhart, Pvt, Co B, severely
J L Anderson, Pvt, Co B, severely
G H Jones, Pvt, Co B, slightly
John D Markham, Cpl, Co C, severely
H B Thompson, Pvt, Co C, slightly
E W Hollingsworth, Sgt, Co D, slightly
Dr G W Ramsay, Pvt, Co D, mortally
Alphius Cobb, Pvt, Co D, dangerously
Geo Wills, Pvt, Co D, severely
W Huffman, Pvt, Co D, severely
O W Jones, Pvt, Co D, severely

W M Alfred, Cpl, Co K, severely
John H Kay, Cpl, Co K, severely
A S Alexander, Pvt, Co K, severely
M C Abinathy, Pvt, Co K, slightly
Jesse Brashars, Pvt, Co K, severely
J M Bailey, Pvt, Co K, severely
Campbell G Boyd, Pvt, Co K, severely
B L Commons, Pvt, Co K, slightly
J W Curtis, Pvt, Co K, severely
H H Dadson, Pvt, Co K, severely
John Gavin, Pvt, Co K, slightly
Aaron Parks, Pvt, Co K, slightly
F Richardson, Pvt, Co K, severely
A G Richardson, Pvt, Co K, severely
Thos C Ramsay, Pvt, Co K, severely
John Vining, Pvt, Co K, severely
M D Watson, Pvt, Co K, severely
Thos Thompson, Pvt, Co F

R R Morehead, Pvt, Co I

Jos Heaton, Pvt, Co I
Jos Downing, Pvt, Co I
Danl D Dubois, Pvt, Co H
John M Tyree, Pvt, Co K

Wm Orr, Pvt, Co D, slightly
D Love, Pvt, Co D, slightly
Jos H Langford, Sgt, Co E, slightly
A P Barnham, Pvt, Co E, mortally
H W Pierce, Pvt, Co E, dangerously
Wm Shadt, Pvt, Co E, dangerously
W H Fleming, Pvt, Co E, severely
Jacob Frederick, Pvt, Co E, slightly
John Coleman, Pvt, Co E, slightly
Wm P Spencer, Pvt, Co E, slightly
M M Smith, Pvt, Co E, slightly
Jas Kilvey, Pvt, Co E, slightly
J Williamson, Pvt, Co G, dangerously
A W Taig, Pvt, Co G, dangerously
Warren White, Pvt, Co G, severely
Robt Bowen, Pvt, Co G, severely
Fred'k Mathews, Pvt, Co G, mortally
Benj F Roberts, Pvt, Co G, slightly
Avery Noland, Pvt, Co G, slightly
Francis A Wolf, Sgt, Co I, dangerously
C F Cotton, Pvt, Co I, severely
Geo Williams, Pvt, Co I, severely
Nat Massie, Pvt, Co I, slightly
Wm H Bell, Sgt, Co K, dangerously
E B Lewis, Pvt, Co K, dangerously
D B Lewis, Pvt, Co K, dangerously
Carles Martin, Pvt, Co K, dangerously
Jas L Thompson, Pvt, Cl K, slightly
John Stewart, Pvt, Co K, slightly
John McNorris, Pvt, Co K, slightly
R W Chance, Pvt, Co B, mortally
P W Johnson, Pvt, Co C, severely
Robt Grigg, Pvt, Co H, slightly
Platt Snedicox, Pvt, Co K, mortally
<u>Kentucky Regt: Wounded:</u>
Valentine Deutche, Pvt
Lewis Young, Pvt
Jos Bartlett, Pvt, Co I
Philip Smith, Pvt, Co I
Thos Alender, Pvt, Co K
Genr'l Worth's Division:
<u>Killed:</u>
H McKavett, Capt, Co E, 8th In, Sep 21
W Rihl, Pvt, Co A, 8th Inf
Chas Hamm, Pvt, Co G, 4th Artl

J F Watner, Pvt, Co I, 4th Artl
Irwing, Pvt, Co I, 4th Artl
Miller, Pvt, Co I, 4th Artl
P Fickicson, Pvt, Co C, 7th Infty
S G Alleng, Pvt, Ph, La volun's
John Francis, Pvt, Ph, La volun's
Wounded:
N L Rossell, 1st Lt, 5th Infty
Band, Sgt Maj, NC S, 5th Infty
McManus, Pvt, Co E, 5th Infty
Grubb, Pvt, Co G, 5th Infty
Schriveigman, Pvt, Co G, 5th Infty
Bell, Pvt, Co H, 5th Infty
Ingalls, Pvt, Co I, 5th Infty
Grelan, Pvt, Co K, 5th Infty
McGuirk, Pvt, Co K, 5th Infty
Hendricks, Pvt, Co K, 5th Infty
R C Catlin, Capt, Co F, 7th Infty
J H Potter, 2nd Lt, Co I, 7th Infty
R S Cross, Sgt, Co C, 7th Infty
S P Oakley, Cpl, Co K, 7th Infty
M Fleming, Pvt, Co D, 7th Infty
C Gersbenberger, Pvt, Co E, 7th Infty
Jas Myers, Pvt, Co E, 7th Infty
A Renebeck, Pvt, Co E, 7th Infty, died Sep 27
N White, Pvt, Co K, 7th Infty
Morron, Cpl, Co K, 1st Artl, died Oct 7
Jas Harvey, Pvt, Co H, 4th Artl, died Sep 28
Louis Kirk, Pvt, Ph, La volun's
W Burton, Pvt, Ph, La volun's
M Morton, Pvt, Ph, La volun's
Basse, Pvt, Co A, 2nd Artl, badly w'd
Michl Noonon, Pvt, Co H, 4th Artl
Jos Grey, Pvt, Co H, 4th Artl
Stephen Edwards, Pvt, Co G, 4th Artl
Theopolis Bowis, Pvt, Co G, 4th Artl
Jas Lynch, Pvt, Co A, 3rd Artl, died Sep 30
Mark Collins, Pvt, Co A, 3rd Artl
Dennis Kelly, Pvt, Co A, 3rd Artl
Amos Collins, Pvt, Co A, 3rd Artl
John Reinecke, Pvt, Co A, 3rd Artl
Isaac Dyer, Pvt, Co A, 3rd Artl
Boyd, Pvt, Co I, 4th Artl, died Oct 9
Ragan, Artificer, Co I, 4th Artl
Paul Bunzey, Pvt, Co K, 2nd Artl

Geo Wainwright, 2nd Lt, Co A, 8th Infty
Rock, Sgt, Co B, 8th Infty
Wilis, Sgt, Co D, 8th Infty
Marshall, Sgt, Co D, 8th Infty
R Riley, Pvt, Co E, 8th Infty
Lauce Tacey, Pvt, Co H, 8th Infty
Jas McKnight, Pvt, Co H, 8th Infty
<u>Colonel Hays' Regt</u>
Herman S Thomas, Pvt, Co A, killed Sep 22
Armstrong, Pvt, Co A, badly wounded
Fielding Alston, Pv, Co A, badly wounded
John P Waters, Pvt, Co A, badly wounded
C E De Witt, Pvt, Co A, badly wounded
Oliver Jenkins, Pvt, Co A, slightly wounded
J F Minter, Pvt, Co A, slightly wounded
Thos Law, Pvt, Co A, slightly wounded
John Rabb, Pvt, Co C, slightly wounded
Wm E Reese, Lt, Co D, slightly wounded
Danl McCarty, Pvt, Co D, killed
J W D Austin, Pvt, Co E, killed 21st
Jesse Perkins, Pvt, Co E, slightly wounded
N P Browning, Pvt, Co F, slightly wounded
Roundtree, Sgt, Co G, slightly wounded
J B Walker, Cpl, Co H, slightly wounded
Wm Carley, Pvt, Co H, badly wounded
R A Gillespie, Capt, Co I, killed
Gilbert Brush, Pvt, Co I, slightly wounded
John M Fullerton, Cpl, Co K, killed
J B Barry, Sgt, Co K, slightly wounded
F F Keys, Pvt, Co k, slightly wounded
Col Woods' Regt of Texas Rangers-Operating in the eastern part of the city on the 23rd.
Killed-Geo Short & Thos Gregory
<u>Wounded:</u> Baker Barton, Chas G Davenport, Ira Grisby, & Calvin Reese.
*J Buchanan, H P Lyon, & C W Tufts were left behind on special duty, & are supposed to be killed.

Desirable residence for sale: subscriber intending to remove from the city, offers his dwlg house for sale. Apply to John A Smith. –H Stringfellow

Trustee's sale of warehouse: by deed of trust from Jos Smoot to me, dated Jun 11, 1844, recorded in Liber W B 104, folios 409 through 413, in the land records of Wash Co: sale on Nov 28, in front of the premises, all that valuable lot, with a 2 story brick warehouse & other improvements thereon, in Gtwn, on the corner of Jefferson & Water sts, fronting 85 feet on the east side of Jefferson & 58+ feet on the north side of Water. –Clement Cox, Trustee -Edw S Wright, auctioneer

Groceries: J T Radcliff, 7th st, 2 doors north of Oldd Fellows' Hall.

Galena Gaz: the Hon Caleb Cushing has hastend home, in consequence of information of the death of his brother. The paper states that this gentleman has acquired by contract [for a company of which he is a principal member] the valuable mills & lumbering property of the Falls of St Croix, with the intention of carrying on a largely increased business. He will return again in the winter or spring.

Grand Lodge of the Independent Order of the Odd Fellows of D C: ofcrs elected Nov 9 for ensuing year:

Jos Borrows, Grand Master
Flodoardo Howard, deputy Grand Master
Thos Jewell, Grand Warden
Chas F Lowrey, Grand Sec

Walter Lenox, Grand Treasurer
Wm W Moore, Grand Rep
Jos Beardsley, Grand Rep

$5 reward for return of a strayed light gray Horse: if returned to me at Carusi's Saloon. –A Carusi

A full length statue of Jean Nicot has recently been erected in the court-yard of the tobacco entrepot at Gros Cailou. Jean Nicot was the first person to introduce that vile or healthful-opinions are divided on the subject-plant into France, whose Treasury now receives from it an income of one hundred & ten millions a year. He was Lord of Villemain, Sec of Henry II, & ambassador of Francis II to Portugal. He was born in 1530, & died at Paris in 1600. Although he has obtained the credit of the introduction of this plant, it really belongs to a Dutch merchant, one of those original herring fishermen who controlled the commerce of the world.

By virtue of a writ of distrain, to me directed, by Wm Jones, against the goods, chattels, & improvements found on the premises of J Martini, on 10th st, between D & E sts, now in the occupancy of the said Jos Martini, I have this day levied on all the improvements to satisfy Wm Jones for rent due & in arrears, & will sell the same, on the premises, on Nov 19, to the highest bidder for cash. –Richd I A Culverwell, blf

Died: on Nov 7, in N Y C, after a short illness of 8 days, Jas M Dever Middleton, of Balt, & formerly of Wash City.

The State of Louisiana presented a superb sword to Gen Z Taylor, lately, for the high opinion entertained of his conduct during his whole military life, & especially in the battles of May 8 & 9. The design originated with Messrs Hyde & Goodrich, of New Orleans, & the sword was manufactured by A P Ames, of Springfield, Mass.

SAT NOV 14, 1846

Desirable house, possession given on Dec 1, & garden lot containing from 4 to 5 acres, & convenient out-bldgs. –Wm T Baldwin, adjoining the premises, half miles east of the Capitol, fronting C & 10th sts.

Md Mining Co: Coal Yard, Broad st, Cumberland, Md, near Dry Run Bridge. Prices of Coal at the Yard: for lump or screened coal, $2 per ton. A box of orders will be left at the store of Mr J Mason Maguire. -Geo S Green, Agent, Cumberland

Ernest Dreyer, of Balt, Fresco Painter, is prepared to paint the walls & ceilings of dwlgs & public bldgs, in a style that cannot fail to please. He is now engaged in Wash City. Leave address at Messrs J & G S Gideon's ofc, on 9th st. –Ernest Dreyer

Trustee's sale: under authority of a deed of trust, dated Oct 30, 1845, recorded in Liber W B #118, folio 453: sale on Dec 15, on the premises, Lot 18 in square 127. –W Redin, trustee

The trial of Dr Wm Tyler, of Fred'k, on a charge of malpractice in treating Ex-Govn'r Thomas, by administering certain drugs to him some 15 years since, has resulted in a verdict of acquittal upon the first count, & upon the others a ***nolle prosequi*** was entered.

Fine sheep: Col Josiah W Ware, of Clarke Co, near Berryville, has given some attention to this subject, & has supplied himself with sheep which will bear a comparison with any in the country, & from which he has raised his now superior stock: of the Cotswold breed. He sold this fall 30 Wethers to Mr Otterback, of the Wash Marrket. A lot of 9 were purchased yesterday by Mr Jacob Pittman, of this county, who is taking them to his new residence in Augusta. –Winchester Republican +

Notice to my Customers & Lovers of Good Mutton. I shall have [during this winter] the finest & best Mutton ever exhibited in our market. I have purchased a lot of 30 of Col Josiah W Ware; I have another lot of Col Edw J Smith, 60 in number, of the Bakewell & Southdown. Also, another lot of De McCormick, of the best Southdown. I have spared no pains in selecting them myself. –Philip Otterback

The Magnetic Telegraph: lines have been built from Boston to Lowell; from Troy to Saratoga; from Syracuse to Oswego; from Auburn to Ithaca, which is progressing to Elmira; from Buffalo to Lockport, which is to be extended to Lewiston, to be connected across the Niagara, with a line to Toronto; from Phil to Harrisburg, to be extended to the West. This is covered with a beautiful iron cord. The length of the lines now constructed is about 1,300 miles. A line is in progress from Boston to Portland. A line will be immediately put up from Washington to Petersburg, Va, if there be no difficulty about the right of way; & none is apprehended. An effort will be made to raise the necessary funds to carry the Southern line through to New Orleans next season.

Galt House [Louisville, Ken,] for rent: well known establishment, now occupied by Mr Isaac Everett, offers it for rent for one or more years, from & after Jan 1, 1847. Address to W H Pope, Pres Galt House Co.

Mrd: on Nov 1, on board the steamer **Die Vernon**, by Esquire Waugh, of Scott Co, Miss, Mr Baptiste Vran to Madam Charlotte Hoffman. The happy groom is a Spaniard, who had just arrived from the Rio Grande; the fair bride, a widow, was taken from the ship which brought her from Germany, & the first time they met was on board the **Die Vernon**, where each had taken passage for this place. Neither could understand a word the other said, but with an occasional aid of an interpreter, on the 2nd day out from New Orleans, the widow surrendered, & the following day they were married by a Justice of the Peace on board. –St Louis Republican

Mrd: on Nov 12, in Wash City, by Rev Geo W Samson, Mr Ignatius M Knott to Miss Susan C Bell, both of Wash.

Mrd: on Nov 12, by Rev John P Donelan, of St Vincent de Paul's Church, Balt, Md, Wm W Beckenbaugh, of Fred'k City, Md, to Miss Margaret Ann, y/d/o the late Saml Stewart, of Wash City.

Late from Santa Fe: from the St Louis Republican of Nov 7. By the arrival at *Fort Leavenworth*, on Oct 30, of Lt Col Ruff, of the Missouri volunteers, we learn that Gen Kearney left for Calif on Sep 25, taking with him Companies B, C, G, K, & I, 1st U S Dragoons, in all about 400 men, mounted on mules. The route of this small command was considered by many of the oldest & most experienced mountaineers & traders as one of great hardships & suffering, if not absolutely impracticable-being down the Rio Grande to Socoro, [an old Spanish town,] formerly of much importance from the garrison stationed there, about 200 miles to Santa Fe; thence west to the Gila, [pronounced Heela;] then to the Gulf of Calif, into which the Gila empties; thence n w to Monterey, on the Pacific. This route is called the Copper Mine route. This command is accompanied by: Gen Kearney, commanding; Capt Johnston, 1st Dragoons, aid-de-camp; Capt Turner, 1st dragoons, Adj Gen of the "army of the West;" Maj Thos Swords, Quartermaster U S Army; Assist Surgeons John S Griffin & R Simpson, of the Medical Staff of the army; Maj Sumner, commanding Dragoons; Capts Cook, Moore, Burgwin, & Grier, 1st Dragoons; & Lts Love, Hammond, Nobel, Davidson, & McIlvaine, of the same regt. The scientific part of the expedition is under command of that meritorious ofcr, 1st Lt W H Emory, of the corps of Topographical Engineers, & consists of 1st Lt Warner, Engineer Corps; Mr Bestor, of D C, & Mr Stanley, employed at Santa Fe as the artist of the expedition. The command is also accompanied by Mr Fitzpatrick, Mr Robidoux, & a guide, Taos, who take with him for his own riding 5 mules, so difficult is the route in his estimation & experience. The troops left in Santa Fe & vicinity are Maj M Lewis Clark's btln of horse artillery & a part of Col Price's regt, with Capt Angney's & Capt Murphy's companies of infty.

Balt, Nov 13. Richd J Turner, formerly Clerk of the Mechanics Bank of Balt, charged with defrauding that institution out of large sum of money, & for whose arrest $1,000 was offered, has been taken prisoner. He was arrested on Sat last at Kingston, Canada, by Jacob Cook, of the firm of Cook, Zell, & Ridgley, Balt, assisted by Mr Germine, an ofcr of the Province.

Mrd: on Oct 4, in the streets of Vicksburg, near the Perry Landing, by N G Brydone, Mr Willis G Wheeler, of Madison Co, Miss, to Miss Catharine Smith. The parties were removing westward.

Died: on Oct 31, at Lovingston, Va, in his 53rd year, Robt Currie Cutler. He was in the actual performance of his duties during the last Superior Court, as Clerk of that Court, when extreme illness compelled him to desist, & at once confined him to his bed, which he exchanged only for the damp, damp vault. As an ofcr he had few, if any, equals. He was Clerk or Sec to every public body in the county in which he served. More than 30 years ago [before he settled at Lovingston] he discharged for 10 years the duties of Clerk in the ofc of the Nat'l Intelligencer, whose proprietors have always cherished a friendly remembrance.

MON NOV 16, 1846
Hon Wm Kent, recently appointed Royal Professor of Law in the Cambridge Law School, has taken up his residence in the house formerly occupied by Judge Story. On dit, that the distinguished commentator on American law will take up his residence at Cambridge. –Law Reporter

The New Orleans papers announce the arrival of Gen Brooke in that city, to take command of the Western Div of the Army, the headquarters of which have been established in that city.

Letters from Monterey announce the death of 2 Balt Volunteers, from wounds received in the late battle: Robt Caples & Wm P Alexander, both members of the Balt & District Btlns.

Circuit Court of Wash Co, D C: motion was made to the Court for a rule upon the Pres & Sec of War, to show cause why Lt Jas W Shaumburg should not be restored to the station in the army held by him previous to Mar, 1845. It appears from the papers of Lt Shaumburg, that in 1834, he was appointed 2nd Lt in the U S Dragoons; in 1836 he was promoted to 1st Lt; that before he received his promotion, he forwarded his resignation as 2nd Lt, which resignation was not received at the War Dept till 3 months after the promotion. Immediately he addressed the Dept stating his resignation applied only to his 1st commission. The Gov't thought propery to do otherwise, & his name was struck from the roll of the army. In Oct, 1842, Pres Tyler reversed the decision, & restored Mr Shaumburg to 1st Lt & placed his name at the head of the list. In Mar, 1845, Mr Sec Marcy informed Lt Shaumburg that the Pres had considered the matter, & concluded that his name was improperly place on the army list, & he could not be considered an ofcr of the U S Army. [Nov 18th newspaper: Corrections: Mr Schaumburg was commissioned 2nd Lt of Dragoons in 1833; on Jun 6, 1836, by letter of that date, from *Fort Demoins*, on the Upper Mississippi, he tendered his resignation as 2nd Lt, to take effect Oct 31, 1836. Letter was received at the Adj Genrl's Ofc on Jun 23, 1836, endorsed by Gen Macomb, recommended to be accepted, to take effect Jul 31, 1836, & approved L C, Mr Cass then being Sec of War. On Jun 30, 1836, it was announced, in Genr'l Order #44, that the resignation of 1st Lt Jas W Schaumburg, 1st Regt of Dragoons, had been accepted by the Pres, to take effect Jul 31, 1836. On Jul 1, 1836, signed by the Pres of the U S, countersigned by the Sec of War, Schaumburg was commissioned as 1st Lt of Dragoons, & that commission was transmitted to him. On Jul 6, 1836, in Genr'l Orders #46, the promotion of 2nd Lt Schaumburg to the rank of 1st Lt of Dragoons, to take date from May 1, 1836, vice Noland, resigned, was announced. In Jan, 1844, Pres Tyler decided that he was entitled to the rank of 1st Lt. On Mar 24, 1845, Pres Polk reversed the decision: the name of Jas W Schaumburg to be erased from the official Army Register.]

Mr Wm Lacy, keeper of the light-boat at the mouth of Port Tobacco creek, fell a few days ago, whilst trimming his lights, & broke his neck.

Fatal Rencontre: from the Van Buren [Ark] Intelligencer of Oct 17: On Oct 5, Col Holland Coffee & Mr Chas Galloway met at Coffee's Bend, in Texas, where a difficulty ensued which resulted in the death of the former. Col Holland leveled a gun at Galloway, when Galloway ran under it & stabbed his assailant in the heart with a bowie-knife.

The dwlg house of Mr Thos Cook, in Lewistown, Trumbull Co, Ohio, was burnt down during the night of Oct 31. Mr Cook was absent, & Mrs Cook, having got her children out in safety, returned for a pocket-book, & while in the bldg it fell upon & consigned her to a fiery death.

Mr Robt Nicholson, of Raleigh, N C, retired to bed on Wed last, & about 12 o'clock, his wife awoke, & found him dead by her side. –Raleigh Register

Mrd: on Sep 17 last, in Gtwn, by Rev Josiah Varden, Wm Henry Norvill, of Va, to Miss Margaret Roberta Ballard, of Wash.

Sale of valuable leasehold premises on Pa ave: by virtue of deed of trust from Isaac Kell, recorded in Liber W B #119, folio 295: sale on Nov 25, the leasehold premises of lot 34 in square or reservation B, in Wash City, with a large 3 story brick house lately erected upon it, & occupied by said Kell for the manufacture of tin-ware. The lease is for 7 years from May 20 last, at an annual rent of $219.75, payable quarterly, with the privilege of purchasing the fee simple of said premises at any time within said term for the sum of $3,662.50. –Jos H Bradley, Trustee -A Green Auctioneer

For rent: house on C st, lately occupied by Mr Beeler. Rent low to a good tenant. Inquire of the undersigned at Birch's U S Hotel, Pa ave. –W D Potter

TUE NOV 17, 1846
At the late term of the Court of Common Pleas of Huron Co, Ohio, Miss Cynthia Ann Clark obtained a verdict of $4,000 against Howard Morse for a breach of marriage promise.

Chancery Sale: by virtue of a decree of the Circuit Court of Wash Co, D C, sitting as a Court of Chancery, made in the cause of Jas Dundas et al, vs Bladen Forrest et al, reps of Jos Forrest, dec'd, the subscribers will offer at auction, in front of the premises, on Dec 1 next, all those parts of Lots 13 & 14 in square 80 in Wash City, with improvements, including a 2 story frame front bldg & brick back bldg, that may be connected or used as separate tenements. –French Forrest, Clement Cox, Trustees -R W Dyer, auct

Balt, Nov 16. I learn that Mrs Caton, relict of the late Richd Caton, died yesterday at Elkridge, the residence of her son-in-law, Mr McTavish, British Consul. She was the eldest d/o Chas Carroll of Carrollton. She survived to a ripe old age, like her distinguished father, & leaves several children, among whom is the Marchioness of Wellesley.

Being duly authorized by the Pres of the U S A, I hereby make the following appointments for the Gov't of New Mexico, a Territory of the U S. The ofcrs thus appointed will be obeyed & respected accordingly.
Chas Bent, Govn'r   Francis P Blair, U S Dist Atty
Donaciano Vigil, Sec of Territory   Chas Plummer, Treasurer
Richd Dallam, Marshal
Eugene Leitensdorfer, Auditor Pub Acc'ts
Joab Houghton, Antonio Jose Otero, & Chas Beaubien, to the Judges of the Superior Court. Given at Santa Fe, the capital of the Territory of New Mexico, Sep 22, 1846, & in the 71st year of the Independence of the U S. –S W Kearney, Brig Gen U S A

Mr Ephraim Murray, employed at the Gosport Navy Yard, on the St Lawrence, by some accident, fell last Sat from the scaffolding, & immediately expired. He has left a wife & 3 or 4 children to mourn his death.

Died: on Thu last, at Alexandria, Mrs Ann Thornton Emerson, w/o Mr John P Emerson, & d/o the late Capt Hezekiah Reeder, of Culpeper Co, Va, in her 28th year.

Died: on Thu last, at Alexandria, Mary T Baggett, aged 27 years.

On Sat, says the Cincinnati Atlas, as the mail train was on its way to Springfield, Wm G Farmer, locomotive engineer, was struck on the head by the reversing lever of his engine at the Waynesville water station, & died in a few moments.

WED NOV 18, 1846
The Hon Theodorick Bland, Chancellor of Md, was found dead in his bed in Annapolis on Mon, having died from a disease of the heart. He was in his 70th year. He was a gentleman of the old school. The dec'd represented the city of Balt in the House of Delegates on several occasions when parties were Federalists & Democrats. –Clipper

Col T F Hunt, U S Army, on Nov 7, notified officially to Gen Vega & other Mexican ofcrs, prisoners in New Orleans, that they have been exchanged for Capt Carpender & the crew of the brig **Truxton**. It was dated Wash, Oct 28, signed by Gen Winfield Scott. –New Orleans Times

Gtwn: the house of Mr Saml Wardell, of Gtwn, was robbed on Sunday of some $80 in paper & specie. Robbers unknown at this time, but it appears to be a person well acquainted with the premises.

Gtwn: Inquest was held on the body of Christopher Quinn, who drowned on Sunday night in the Canal. It is supposed that he was intoxicated at the time. He has a brother & son at Williamsburg, N Y, but no relations here.

Gtwn: On Sunday, the body of a negro man, named Jas Williams, died suddenly in the northeastern part of the town. And, on Sat, the body of a colored child, in the service of Mr Henry King, drowned in Rock Creek.

Wash Corp: 1-Ptn of Francis Huttenburg, praying remission of a fine: referred to the Cmte of Claims. 2-Ptn of John O'Leary, praying the remission of a fine: referred to the Cmte of Claims. 3-Act for the relief of John Roby: read twice.

Mrd: on Nov 10, by Rev Henry M Mason, D D, Thos H Matthews, of Balt, to Rebecca J D, d/o the Hon Nicholas Martin, of Walnut Grove, Talbot Co, Md.

Died: on Nov 17, Lucinda Clark, in her 31st year, [2nd d/o Alex'r Talburt, of Wash City,] w/o Wm D Clark, formerly of PG Co, Md, but for several years past a resident of Wash City. Her funeral will be from the residence of the family on I st north, between 6th & 7th sts, this afternoon at 2½ o'clock.

In Chancery: Alex'r Hanna & Louisa C his wife, cmplnts, & Eliz Bohrer, Eliza Grammer, Chas West & Mary his wife, Catharine, Anna, Eliza, Wm, & John A Grammer; Henry F Mayer, Henry Emmons & Henrietta E his wife, & Ernestina M Mayer, dfndnts. Wm Redin, trustee, reported the sale of the lots decreed to be be sold in the said cause: John France became the purchaser of lot 5 in square 294, for $817.02; Gotlieb C Grammer of lot 13 in square 348, for $786.18; & Wm Orme of lot 14 in square 378, for $1,171.21, all in Wash City. –W Brent, clerk

Orphans Court of Wash Co, D C. Letters of administration on personal estate of Wm G Williams, late of Topographical Corps of Engineers, dec'd. –John P C Peter, adm

Trustee's sale: by decree of the Circuit Court of Wash Co, D C, in Chancery, in a cause in which Fred'k L Keller is cmplnt & Henrietta C Keller & Chas Keller, dfndnts, I will sell, on Dec 19, at public auction on the premises the following property on the corner of 12th & Md ave, Wash City: lots 18 thru 23 in square 327. –A H Lawrence, Trustee –R W Dyer, auct

THU NOV 19, 1846
Foster Rhodes, U S Naval Constructor, died at Pensacola on Nov 7.

Hon Wm Findlay, formerly Govn'r of Pa, & Senator of the U S from that State, died on Sun at Harrisburg, in his 79th year.

Lorenzo Lewis, of Jefferson Co, has disposed of the *Wood Lawn* estate [comprising 2,000 acs] in Fairfax Co, Va, to a company of Pennsylvanians, principally Friends, who will settle on the land, & proceed to its cultivation by forming nurseries & gardens. We hail with pleasure every movement that will go to improve the adjacent country. –Alexandria Gazette

Mrd: on Nov 5, at Waterloo, the residence of Mr Luke W B Hawkins, by Rev Lemuel Wilmer, Henry H Hawkins to Miss Mary H Hawkins, d/o the late Col Francis W Hawkins, all of Chas Co, Md.

Mrd: on Oct 22, at St Mary's Chapel, near Natchez, by Rev Wm W Giles, Wm Meade Addison, of Balt, to Miss Eliza W Girault, of Natchez.

Died: on Nov 15, at his residence in Centreville, Queen Anne's Co, in his 73rd year, the Hon Lemuel Purnell, late Associate Judge of the 2nd Judicial District, after a painful & protracted illness.

Balt, Nov 18. A new company of volunteers, to be under the command of Capt Thos G Richards, is about forming in the western section of our city. They now number about 60 members. They design offering their services to the Gov't as volunteers for the army of occupation. If accepted, well; if not, they propose going to Mexico at their own expense.

FRI NOV 20, 1846
Circuit Court of Wash Co, D C-in Chancery. John Carroll, vs Danl Carroll, trustee, & Thos Mason. The bill charges that said Thos Mason is indebted to cmplnt in a certain sum of money, long since due & in arrears, & which is secured by a deed of trust, executed by said Thos Mason to said Danl Carroll, as trustee for a certain lot of parcel of ground in Gtwn, with the appurtenances, all particularly described in said deed; & that said Danl Carroll has removed beyond seas, & cannot execute the trusts of said deed. The objects of the bill are, the substitution of another trustee & general relief. As it is represented that said Danl Carroll resides & is out of D C, & in parts beyond

seas, it is ordered that said Danl Carroll, on or before the 4th Mon in Mar next, appear in Court & show why the cmplnt shall not have relief as prayed. –Wm Brent, clk

Saml Carusi, Prof of Music, having returned to Wash City, offers his professional services in all its branches. Applications are to be made before Oct 1, at Mr Nathl Carusi's, between 10th & 11th sts, Pa ave.

For sale: one plain counter & 2 mahoghany counter cases, suitable for stationers, confectioners, or dealers in fancy articles. Apply to Jas Galt, Watchmaker, between 9th & 10th sts, Pa ave.

SAT NOV 21, 1846

The War: it is now 6 months since the Nation found itself involved in a War without the consent of the Legislative authority, & to the surprise, not merely of the great body of the People, but also of the comparatively few who had reason to suppose themselves pretty thoroughtly informed of the state of public affairs. This state of war was, as every one knows, brought on by the march of our army into the territory west of the Nueces, then wholly in possession of Mexico, posting that army in front of a Mexican fortress, & erecting a battery within gunshot of it. The Executive is, therefore, undoubtedly responsible for the existence of this war, & for all the consequences which may grow out of it; a responsibility which the Administration cannot cast off, if it would, & which, in truth, it has shown a disposition to enlarge rather than to shrink from, by it avowal of designs of conquest, & by already establishing civil gov'ts within the Mexican territory-acts not less against the Constitution than was the first inception of the war.

Valuable Jefferson land for sale: the subscriber, being desirous of removing to the South, offers for sale his landed estate, 3 miles n e of Charlestown: contains 600 acres & a commodious brick dwlg house, containing 11 rooms; also, the necessary out-bldgs. The dwlg commands a beautiful view of the Blue Ridge & North Mountains. To a gentleman of fortune, who desires a country residence, an opportunity is now afforded rarely to be met with. Wm T Washington, near Charlestown, Jefferson Co, Va.

Capt Randolph Ridgely is supposed to have lost his life at Monterey about 3 weeks ago. Our information is derived from John Deshon, one of the owners of the steamship **Sea**, & who came passenger in the ship **Uncas**, which arrived here yesterday from Brasos, is to this effect: Capt Hill, the U S Quartermaster at Brasos, informed Mr Deshon that an express had just arrived from Monterey, communicating the sad intelligence that Capt Ridgely, being on an unruly horse, & riding down a steep hill, was thrown, the horse falling upon him. At the time the express left Monterey Capt Ridgeley was wholly insensible, & no hopes were entertained of his recovery. We must hope that Capt Ridgely will be spared to his country, which cannot afford to lose so brave & chivalrous & meritorious an ofcr. -New Orleans Tropic

Centreville [Queen Anne's Co, Md] Sentinel: a colored man belonging to the estate of the late John Sparks died near that place last week, at the advanced aged of 122 years.

$3 reward to anyone who will deliver to me, on the south side of Capitol Hill, a Cow which strayed away about a week ago from my stable. –Wilson M C Fairfax

Mrd: on Nov 19, by Rev Mr Tarring, Mr John B Turton to Miss Sarah A Riggles, all of Wash City.

Mrd: on Nov 19, by Rev O Ege, Mr Henry B Otterback to Miss Rosella Gaddis, all of Wash City.

Mrd: on Nov 19, at Annapolis, Md, by Rev E M Van Deusen, Frank H Stockett to Miss Mary Priscilla, eldest d/o the late Maj Wm I Hall, of Anne Arundel Co, Md.

Died: on Nov 5, in Marshall Co, Missouri, Mrs Lucy Stansbury, w/o Chas F Stansbury, formerly of Wash. She was a native of Portsmouth, N H, & had recently removed to Missouri, with a view to settling in the West, but was cut off y the bilious fever, so prevalent in all that region. -S

We learn that Capt Goddard & one of his ofcrs yesterday arrested on the farm of N Queen, near Wash City, a man named Alison McDonald, who stands charged by the Grand Jury lately sitting in Mongt Co, Md, with the willful murder of his wife in said county. He was committed to await the requisition of the Md authorites.

Timber wanted immediately: Posts for a line of Telegraph from Wash, through Gtwn & Alexandria, to Fredericksburg, Va, & thence to Richmond. They must be 35 feet long, straight, & 5 inches in diameter at the top, excluding the bark. –Amos Kendall, Agent, for Proprietors. Wash, Nov 20, 1846

MON NOV 23, 1846
On Fri Mr Gustavus Fallen, a grocer in Bridge st, Boston, was walking upon the Providence railroad track, in Rosbury, & was struck & killed by the Dedham train.

Hugh Kerman, from PG Co, Md, has 2 valuable horses stolen from his a few days ago, by some daring villain, who took them from a trough in 7th st, while they were feeding, in the day time.

The public will be pained to learn that the venerable John Quincy Adams was yesterday seized with a paralysis of his left side, which for a time rendered him nearly insensible. He had just left the residence of his son, the Hon Chas F Adams, in Mount Vernon st, in a state of health, when the gentleman with whom he was walking suddenly perceived that he was laboring under some severe affection of his limbs, & was obliged to assist him to prevent his falling. He was conveyed back to his son's house & received immediate medical aid. After a short time his consciousness

returned, & he was much relieved & able to converse, & not considered in immediate danger. Mr Adams is, we believe, about 80 years of age.
–Boston Advertiser of Fri.

Sailing of Missionaries. Rev Mr Spaulding & Dr Scudder & 2 dghts, accompanied by a number of other missionaries with their wives, sailed from Boston on Wed in the ship **Flavio** for India.

Boston Transcript: in the latter part of July last, Capt Seth Burgess, of Phipsburg, Maine, died in that town of typhus fever. Since that time 5 of his children, residing in the same house, of ages from 16 to 28 years, have fallen victims to that disease.

Mr Gaiennie, a clerk in the house of Hewitt, Heran & Co, was drowned on Nov 12 in the river a few miles below New Orleans. He was well known & universally beloved.
-Tropic

Mrd: on Nov 19, by Rev Mr Sprole, Mr J W Colley to Miss Mary J Plunkett, both of Wash City.

Mrd: on Nov 19, by Rev Mr Morgan, Wm McLane to Miss Eliza J Mattingly, all of Wash City.

Died: on Nov 22, Mrs Cecilia, w/o Hon D Higgins, late of Norwalk, Ohio, aged 53 years. Her funeral is at 12 o'clock, this day, from Mrs Manning's, on 13th st.

On Fri, a lad about 7 years of age, s/o Mr Jos Crook, fell into the river near Green's wharf, Alexandria. Mr John W Green, being on the adjoining wharf, hastened to his rescue. He had to be drawn out by the means of a grappling iron: the usual remedies were resorted to, & after awhile, vitality was restored. -Gaz

Mrs L Beeler, C st, near 4½ st, can accommodate some families, by the year or otherwise: charges according to times. The situation is in a healthy & central part of the city.

Household & kitchen furniture at auction on Nov 23, at the Housefurnishing Rooms of W S Clary, on Pa ave, between 19th & 20th sts, near the West Market.
–A Green, auctioneer

Mrs Spier [successor to Mrs S Parker] will open on Nov 19, a splendid assortment winter Millinery. Residence D st, rear of Harper's.

TUE NOV 24, 1846
Obit-died: on Sep 29 last, in San Augustine City, Texas, Mr Saml Benton, youngest & last brother of the Hon Thos H Benton, aged about 60 years. Mr Benton was a native of N C, whence he removed to the State of Tennessee, & thence to the city of St Louis,

where he resided several years. Removing to Texas about 1822, he became distinguished as a supporter of the claims of the colonists to a liberal recognition of their rights on the part of Mexico. –From the St Louis Reveille.

For rent: 2 story brick house, neatly & completely furnished, near the corner of H & 21st, west. Inquire at Jackson Hall. –Jas Blair

Gen Peter S Van Orden died on Nov 8, in his 84th year. He had been a member of the State Legislature from Rockland Co, N Y, for a number of years, & was the general who commanded the troops on Harlem heights in the last war. He was also a soldier of the Revolution.

Commissioned Ofcrs killed & wounded during the operations before Monterey, Mexico, from Sep 21 to Sep 23, inclusive.
Killed: M Hett, 1st Lt, 1st Ohio reg, Sep 21
Wounded:
W G Williams, Capt, top engin'rs, Sep 21, mortal
J H F Mansfield, Bt Maj, engineers, Sep 21, severely
J L Abercrombie, Bt Major, 1st Infty, Sep 21, slight
J H Lemott, Capt, 1st Inf, Sep 21, severely
J C Terrett, 1st Lt, 1st Inf, Sep 21, mortally
R Dilworth, 2nd Lt, 1st Inf, Sep 21, mortally
W W Lear, Maj, 3rd Inf, Sep 21, dangerously
H Bainbridge, Capt, 3rd Inf, slight
R H Graham, 1st Lt, 4th Inf, dangerously
N B Rossell, 1st Lt, 5th Inf, slight
R C Gatlin, Capt, 7th Inf, Sep 23, severely
J H Potter, 2nd Lt, 7th Inf, Sep 22, severely
Gen Wainwright, 2nd Lt, 8th Inf, Sep 22, severely
W O Butler, Maj Gen, vol service, Sep 21, severely
A M Mitchell, Col, 1st Ohio reg, Sep 21, severely
A W Armstrong, Adj, 1st Ohio reg, Sep 21, severely
Jas George, Capt, 1st Ohio reg, Sep 21, slight
Lewis Matter, 1st Lt, 1st Ohio reg, Sep 21, slight
A McCarty, 2nd Lt, 1st Ohio reg, Sep 21, slight
N H Niles, 2nd Lt, 1st Ohio reg, Sep 21, slight
R B Alexander, Major, 1st Ten reg, Sep 21, severely
J L Scudder, 1st Lt, 1st Ten reg, Sep 21, severely
G H Nixon, 1st Lt, 1st Ten reg, Sep 21, slight
J C Allen, 2nd Lt, 1st Ten reg, Sep 21, severely
A H McClung, Lt Col, Miss reg, Sep 21, severely
R N Downing, Capt, Miss reg, Sep 21, slight
H F Cook, 1st Lt, Miss reg, Sep 21, slight
R H Arthur, 2nd Lt, Miss reg, Sep 21, slight
L S Howard, 2nd Lt, Miss reg, Sep 23, severely

R A Gillespie, Capt, 1st Texas, Sep 22, mortally
W E Reese, 1st Lt, 1st Texas, Sep 22

A man named Jas Conners was accidentally shot on Nov 17, at Troy, N Y, in a store on North Second st, by his cousin, Michl Conners, & so badly wounded that no hope is entertained of his recovery. –Troy Whig

Lt John T McLaughlin, U S Navy, left Washington on Sat to take command of the iron steamer **Hunter**, at New Orleans, destined to aid in the operations of the Gulf Squadron.

Jas Jefferson, a boy between 9 & 10 years of age, left the home of his parents in Alexandria, on Nov 16, since which time they have not found or learned anything satisfactory respecting him. He is a delicate boy in appearance, with light hair, hazel eyes, a mole on the right cheek, & a scar on the left temple near the eye. He was last seen at Cazenove's wharf. Information left at the Public School, of which he was a pupil, will be conveyed to his afflicted parents. [Nov 28th newspaper: the body of Jas Jefferson, the lad who had been missing at Alexandria since Nov 16, was found last Mon, in the dock above Cazenove's wharf, & was conveyed to his afflicted parents. The lad was accidentally drowned by slipping from the wharf. –Gaz]

Deaths of the Pioneers: from the Nashville Banner, Nov 14. 1-Col Wm Martin died at his residence in Smith Co on Nov 4, after an illness of 4 weeks, in his 81st year. Wm Martin was born in Va, on Nov 26, 1765, & when yet hardly 15 years of age, towards the close of the Revolutionary war-he took part in a campaign against the Indians. About 1786 he first came to Tennessee, as the cmder of a company of men sent by the State of N C to protect the frontiers; & he may be considered, therefore, as one of the Pioneers of the West. After peace had been secured to the early settlers of the wilderness, he returned to Va, &, having married, removed to S C. Here he was soon elected to the Legislature; in 1798, he removed to this State & settled upon the spot where he breathed his last. In 1812 & 1813 he commanded the 2nd regt of old volunteers, & was with Gen Jackson in the Creek campaign, & participated in the battle of Taledega & other engagements. 2-Died on Oct 16, 1846, at his residence, in Bedford Co, Tenn, Capt Matt Martin, aged 83 years. In Feb, 1780, he became a volunteer in the service of his country, & served 4 or 5 terms of duty, to the end of the war, under Generals Pinckney, Sumter, & Green, & Col Clark. He was in 4 battles, among them the battle of Guilford, N C. He was born in Charlotte Co, Va, Dec 26, 1763; but at the time of the Revolution was a citizen of '96 in S C. Some time after the war he removed to Bourbon Co, Ky, & then to Bedford Co, Tenn, in 1808, where he continued to reside until death closed his mortal career.

For rent: desirable house just erected by the subscriber on 8th st north, between 6th & 7th sts, adjoining his own residence. Apply on the premises or at the Bank of Washington to Hugh B Sweeney.

Balt, Nov 23: an explosion this morning, at the powder mills of Jas Beatty, 7 miles from Balt, on the York road, killed 4 white men & one colored man. Their names are: Jas Bush, Francis Woodward, Wm Branden, a German named Kanoot, & a colored man named Neilson Winger. They were literally blown to atoms.

Died: in Balt City, Col Jas Morris, s/o John B Morris, of Balt City. He died last night, after a brief & painful illness, from constipation of the bowels. Few men possessed better or nobler qualitles.

Mrd: on Nov 22, by Rev W G Eggleston, Mr Adam Keizer to Miss Hannah Williamson, all of Wash City.

Died: on Nov 20, at Hayfield, Fairfax Co, Va, Wm H Foote, in his 65th year. For many years he was the magistrate of his county, & discharged with the utmost kindness his various domestic duties, & bore through life the character of an estimable & upright citizen.

WED NOV 25, 1846
Bombardment of Tabasco: sketch of the proceedings of Com Perry, with the detachment of vessels sent under him against Tabasco: object of the expedition was to cut out certain prizes anchored in the river: these were all taken. When the city was summonded to surrender, the people were all in favor of yielding at once. The Govn'r & soldiery opposed it. The Govn'r would not allow anyone to leave, so it is feared most of those killed during the bombardment were not soldiers: some of the regulars were killed. The squadron consisted of the steamer **Mississippi**, Com Perry; steamer **Vixen**, Cmder Sands; ship **Bonita**, Lt Commanding Benham; ship **Reefer**, Lt Sterret; ship **Nonita**, Lt Hazard; revenue steamer **McLane**, Capt Howard; revenue cutter **Forward**, Capt Nones; 200 seamen & marines from the ship **Raritan** & frig **Cumberland**, under the command of Capt Forrest, Lts Gist, Winslow, Walsh, & Hunt; Capt Edson & Lt Adams, of the Marines. They left Anton Lizardo on Oct 16, & arrived at Frontera on the 23rd. Captured steamer **Petrita** & steamer **Tabasyaeno**, & several small vessels. On the 24th & 25th ascended the river 72 miles to Tabasco; the current very rapid; towed by the **Petrita** & **Vixen**; passed Devil's Turn at 2 p m; landed & spiked four 24 pounders. Arrived off Tabasco at 6 p m; anchored in line ahead, 150 yards from shore. Summoned the city to surrender. Govn'r refused. Fired 3 shots from the **Vixen**-one cut down the flag-staff of the fort, &, as the colors fell, we thought they had surrendered. An ofcr came off with a request that we would spare their hospitals, which was granted. At 5 o'clock landed 200 seamen & marines, but it was too late to attack the fort, they were ordered on board. This was Sunday, & the Cmdor was reluctant to commence the attack on that day. Captured one brig, 5 schnrs, 2 steamers, 1 sloop, & many small craft & lighters. Monday, 26th, at daylight, a sharp fire of musketry from shore, which was returned by our great guns, firing at the flash. A white flag was shown by the civilians on shore, no doubt with the consent of the Govn'r. Lt W A Parker got ashore with his prize vessel near the city, & was attacked by about 80 soldiers, whom he beat off with about 18 men, losing only one & having

but 2 wounded. This affair last 30 minutes. Lt C W Morris was dispatched to him with orders, &, passing the heavy fire of the enemy, was wounded in the neck by a musket ball. Lt Morris stood up in his boat & cheered the men, most gallantly, until he fell in the arms of Midshipman Cheever, who was with him. The Cmdor commenced cannonading in earnest from the **Vixen, Bonita, Nonita,** & **Forward,** & in half or 3/4ths of an hour almost demolished the city-sparing the houses of the foreign Consuls & such as appeared to be inhabited by peaceful citizens. At about midday the fleet left Tabasco, & as it passed, fired musketry & great guns, swept them completely of every living thing. Lt Morris died on the 1st inst on board the **Cumberland** & was buried with the honors of war at Lizardo. [Nov 30th newspaper: Lt Morris was buried on a small island called Salmidina, which is a short distance from the point of Anton Lizardo. –Picayune] [Same newspaper: the remains of the lamented Lt Chas W Morris have been exhumed & placed on board the **Raritan** to be conveyed to Pensacola as soon as the affair of Tampico is over.] [Dec 3rd newspaper: Boston Journal: Mr Morris was well known in Boston & vicinity; he was a native of this State, & entered the service in 1829: his family, consisting of a wife, the d/o Richd Devens, of Charlestown, & children, reside in Charlestown.]

Mayor's Ofc, Gtwn, Nov 17, 1846. In compliance with the general desire, I hereby respectfully recommend the citizens of this town to observe Thu, Nov 26, as a day of solemn thanksgiving to Almighty God for his goodness & mercy to our land & nation- to reverently recognize Him as our wise ruler & bountiful benefactor.
–H Addison, Mayor

Latest from Monterey: The steamship **Massachusetts** arrived at New Orleans on the 16th inst, from Brasos Santiago, having left there on the 12th inst. She took our to Brasos troops from N Y. Capt Lamotte, of the 1st Infty, came over on her. He was severely wounded at Monterey, but we were happy to find him in the finest spirits, & he is doing well. The gallant Maj Lear, 3rd Infty, has died of his wounds. He was buried on the 1st inst. -Picayune

Mrd: on Nov 24, in Wash City, by Rev Mr Gilliss, W M Caldwell, U S Navy, to Caroline Eveline Archer, only child of Brig Gen Towson, Paymaster Genr'l U S Army.

Mrd: on Nov 17, by Rev Mr Coombes, Stephen Belt to Miss Celeste, d/o Capt John Gwynn, all of PG Co, Md.

Died: on Nov 23, in Wash City, Mrs Harriet S Jarboe, consort of F M Jarboe, in her 25th year. She was married near 12 months ago. The immediate cause of her death, it is believed, is not known. She suffered but little, & that only at short intervals. Her funeral is this morning at 10 o'clock, from her late residence, on M st south, between 3rd & 4th sts east.

Died: on Nov 23, Mrs Margaret McLaughlin, in her 53rd year, a native of county Derry, Ireland, but a resident of Wash City for a number of years. Her funeral is this evening, at 3 o'clock.

Lots at auction: on Nov 30, in front of the premises, lot 7 in square 580, on 2nd st west, between C & D sts south. Apply to Wm F Purcell, atty in fact for the party.
–R W Dyer, auct

Mose K Crofut, about 45 years of age, a respectable character, & a professor of religion, committed suicide yesterday in Milford, by suspending himself from the rafters of his barn. He had been in mercantile pursuits, & had become embarrassed that some of his creditors in this city attached him the evening previous. His embarrassment & the processes against him, had the effect to unsettle his mind.

For rent: the 2nd store west from the corner of 7th st, fronting on Market space, at present occupied by Mr Wm M Perry. Apply to the subscriber, at Mrs Turpin's, over the store. –Anne R McDermott

Rooms for rent: Mrs E Sexsmith has 2 rooms, Pa ave, between 9th & 10th sts.

By order of the Orphans Court of Wash Co, D C: subscriber will sell, on the premises, on Mon next, all the personal property of John L Brightwell, dec'd, consisting of corn, fodder, hay, rye, rye straw, & stock of various kinds. –Th R Brightwell, adm

By virtue of an order of distrain for house rent due Wm G W White by Julia Fleet, I will expose at sale, in front of the Centre Market-house, in Wash, on Dec 1: furniture, bedding, glassware, & sundry articles. -H R Maryman, Bailiff

THU NOV 26, 1846
Capt S H Stringham has received orders to take command of the line of battle ship **Ohio**, now being fitted out at Charlestown Navy Yard, & to proceed to sea with all possible dispatch, under sealed orders. The following ofcrs have received orders to join the **Ohio**: Cmder L M Goldsborough; Surgeon B Washington; Purser John Debue. Lt Neville, with a draught of seamen, 85 men, destined for the **Ohio**, arrived at the Navy Yard in Charlestown on Fri last. Another draught of 100 men, from Balt, arrived on Sat, & a large draught from N Y on Sunday.

The sloop of war **Falmouth**, Cmder Jarvis, arrived at Boston from Pensacola, whence she sailed Oct 25th: she brought the following passengers: Lts J M Gardiner, J H Sherburne; Midshipmen A H Otis, W Murdaugh, W L Powell, N T West, J T Barrand, A F Monroe; Boatswain Saml Drew; Carpenter Luthe Manson; Sailmaker J G Gallagher.

Mrd: on Nov 19, by Mr Pyne, Mr Albert J Webb, of Winthrop, Maine, to Miss Harriet Farrell, of Wash.

Gale on Lake Erie-wreck of vessels: many lives lost: Buffalo Commercial Advertiser accounts of the loss: schnr **Helen Strong** & the schnr **Indian Queen**; the beaching of the schnr **Cleveland**, schnr **Dayton**, schnr **J H Lyon**, ship **United States**, ship **H H Sizer**, ship **Chas Howard**, & ship **Huron**, the the n w gale of Thu. Two passengers, a man & woman, names not known, were lost off the **Helen Strong**, & 4 hands of the **Oceola**. Buffalo, Monday: On Sat morning 16 dead bodies floated ashore at Barcelona. The shore for miles along the lake is strewn with fragments of vessels. Dead bodies were being picked up along shore.

Vessels, belonging to port of Marblehead, Mass, with their crews, all lost in the great gale on Sep 19. Of the men, 43 left widows, & children amounting to 151:

schnr **Zela**:
Wm Hooper	Saml Blackler, jr	John Wallis
Thos Caswell, jr	John D Bowden	
Amos Humphreys	John White	

schnr **Pacific**:
John Cross	John Bates	Robt Devereaux
Isaac Wadden	Edw Homan	
John Hunt	Eleazer Leach	

schnr **Liberty**:
Eben Lecraw	Thos Doliber	Robt Blair
John Lancey	Geo Lemaster	
Richd Goss	Saml Graves	

schnr **Sabine**:
Saml Dogg	Henry Pitman	Edw H Dixey
Benj Garney	Jos Homan	
Nickolance Florance	David Pierce	

schnr **Salus**:
John Trefry	Wm Girdler	John Green
Benj Martin	Jos Atkins	
Fred'k Donaldson	Thos Pedrick	

schnr **Senator**:
Chas Chadwick	Mark H Giles	John Glover
John Gilbert	Elisha D Pedrick	
Jos Green	Edw Dixey, jr	

schnr **Warrior**:
Sans Standley	Benj Dodd	Saml Goodwin
Geo Bridgeo	Wm Blackler	
Moses Peachey	Edw Humphrey, jr	

schnr **Trio**:
Wm G Bridgeo	John Courtis	Jas Eeatland
Edw F Trefry	Jos Bowden	
John R Meelzard	Wm Harris	

schnr **Clinton**:
John White   Nehemiah Stone

schnr **Minerva**:
Franklin Stevens	Archibald Sinclair, jr	Spanish boy
Osmond C Stacey	Wm Wooldridge	
Michl Phillips	Philip Thrasher	

On Sat last, at Merchants' Hotel, Phil, Judge Wagonseller, of Union Co, Pa, underwent the most severe operation known to surgery. He had an enormous tumor upon his left shoulder. The operation was performed by Dr D Gilbert, Prof of Surgery in Pa Medical College, & consisted in the removal of the entire arm & shoulder, including $1/3^{rd}$ of the collar bone, & a large portion of the shoulder blade. The patient is doing well. –U S Gaz

Public sale of corn & fodder: on Nov 30th, at the farm lately occupied by me, about 3 miles from Wash, on the old Bladensburg road, near the farm of Mr E Tucker. –C W Boteler

Boarding: Mrs Mann, having fitted up those 2 elegant houses, [about 2 years since erected,] Nos 1 & 2 Phil Place, [11th & H sts,] Wash City, in the most comfortable & fashionable manner, is now prepared to receive boarders on moderate terms.

To let: a handsome residence for a gentleman: spacious brick house & premises, the residence of the late Robt Sewall, with every requisite for a large family, standing single on the highest part of Capitol Hill, within 250 yards of the n e corner of the Capitol gardens. Inquire of S Scott, on the adjoining premises.

Proclamation: to the citizens of Wash. That the Mayor is requested to set apart Nov 26th in thanksgiving & praise to Almight God, by which the blessings of life, health, & every necessary comfort have been bestowed on us; & believing it right & proper, as a community, to return thanks of these blessings. –Saml Bacon, Pres of the Board of Common Council; Jno D Barclay, Pres of the Board of Alderman. Heatily approved by W W Seaton, Mayor, on Nov 13, 1846.

Mrd: on Nov 19, by Mr Pyne, Mr Albert J Webb, of Winthrop, Maine, to Miss Harriet Farrell, of Wash.

Mrd: on Nov 24, by Rev Geo W Samson, Mr Thos Hall to Miss Eliz Grimes, both of Wash.

Mrd: on Nov 15, by Rev Mr Moran, John W Williams to Miss Mary Cammack, all of Wash City.

Mrd: Nov 12, by Rev Mr Nelson, Mr Chas Clagett to Miss Mary, d/o Baruch Mullikin, all of PG Co, Md.

SAT NOV 28, 1846
Farm for sale: subscriber will offer, on the premises, on Dec 13 next, the farm called the *Forrest*, in Montg Co, Md, on the main road leading from Gtwn to Fred'k. Farm contains about 250 acres of land. –Zach Maccubbin

Clarksville [Tenn] Jeffersonian: Mr J M Jackson, a Methodist preacher, & a tanner by trade, was murdered in cold blood last Fri in Clarksville, by a fiend in human shape, by the name of Moon, a citizen of Missouri. It seems that Jackson owed Moon money, which he expected to pay in a short time. Moon, without any passion, shot Jackson with a pistol. He died immediately. Moon was arrested.

N Y paper: the sloop **Aurora**, Capt Sturdevant, & sloop **Ann Strong**, Capt Dayton, were wrecked on the Long Island shore, near Greenport, on Sun. On boarding the wreck of the **Aurora**, the body of one of the crew was found lashed to the quarter rail. It is feared that all on board perished, viz: Capt S Sturdevant; Mr S Smith, part owner of the cargo; Mr D Norton; & Solomon, a black man, all of Port Jefferson. The body found is supposed to be that of Norton. All hands on the **Ann Strong** escaped to shore, where they were hospitably entertained at Mr Mapes' dwlg.

Rev Thornton Fleming, one of the first Methodist Ministers who preached the Gospel west of the Alleghany Mountains, died at the residence of his son-in-law, Rev David Sharp, in Elizabeth, Alleghany Co, Pa, on Sat last. There was only one older Methodist preacher in the U S, Rev Ezekiel Cooper, of the Phil Conference. –Pittsburg Gaz

To Inventors: Patent Agency at Wash, D C, by Wm P Wm P Elliot, formerly of Patent Ofc, [for 20 years, & for many years official Surveyor of Wash City,] has relinquished all business to devote his whole time to the service of inventors, patentees, & persons interested in patents. Ofc opposite the Patent Ofc, corner of F & 8th sts: residence adjoining the Washington House, Capitol Hill. –W P Elliot

Persons killed, wounded, & drowned during the expedition to Tabasco. Killed: Chas Raimond, seaman of the ship **Raritan**. Wounded: Chas W Morris, Lt, of the frig **Cumberland**, since dead. John Southerland, & Geo Pearce, seamen of the **Raritan**. Drowned: Richd W Butler, ordinary seaman, of the **Raritan** Benj McKenny, seaman, of the **Cumberland**. –M C Perry

The Van Ness Trial was continued on Wed: Mr Chas Mann, who had married in Phil, & Rev Mr Sprole, who had often performed the marriage ceremony in Pa, were called to the stand & examined as to the customs of marriage in that State. Following witnesses gave testimony on the part of the dfndnt: Mr & Mrs Hover, Mr Christian, Alderman Bulkley, & Alderman Elkinton, of Phil. [Nov 30th newspaper: case was continued by the examination of Mrs Hagan, [a female who lived in the family of Alderman Christian, late of Phil,] Miss Lenan, Thos Carbery, & C K Gardner.]

For sale: a new one-horse Carriage. –Wm Keefe, 18th st, between Pa ave & G st.

MON NOV 30, 1846
E Ridgway appointed agent for D C & Alexandria for the sale of Thos S Williamson's celebrated Susquehanna Slate, & is prepared to furnish it at the shortest notice.

The fine old mansion at the corner of Chestnut & 7th sts, Phil, the residence of the late Mr Swain, is to be torn down. The present owner intends to erect a 5 story high bldg of brown granite stone: the lower floor is for stores, the upper floors for public purposes, such as concert rooms.

Wash Corp: 1-Ptn from Mary French: referred to the Cmte of Claims. 2-Ptn from H B Sawyer: referred to the Cmte of Claims. 3-Papers from John Fletch regarding a flag footway: referred to the Cmte on Improvements. 4-Ptn of David S Waters, for remission of a fine: referred to the Cmte of Claims. 5-Cmte of Claims: relief of Jas Casparis, without amendment.

Boarding: Mrs Edw H Edelin, on Capitol Hill, rear of ***Duff Green's Row***. Mrs Edelin is provided with good servants, & will endeavor to give general satisfaction.

Orphans Court of Wash Co, D C. Letters of administration on the personal estate of Cmdor John B Nicolson, dec'd, be granted to Maj Thos L Smith, unless cause to the contrary be shown on or before Dec 13 next. –Ed N Roach, Reg/o wills

Loss of the steamship **Atlantic**, which was driven ashore in Long Island Sound, during the gale of Thu last: The passengers left Boston on Wed, reached Allyn's Point: left New London for N Y when the steam-pipe running into the steam-chimney bursted, rendering the engine entirely usless. The disabling of the steamer in a perfect hurricane, rendered her entirely unmanageable, superadded to the anguish of the scalded, intense cold, & the terror of all on board, is indescribable.

<u>Ofcrs & passengers lost:</u>
Capt Dustan, of the steamship *Atlantic* Sarah Johnson, chambermaid
Dr Hassler, of the Navy   Sarah Ruby, of Providence,
Lt Norton, of the Army   chambermaid
A clergyman named Armstrong   Eliza Wacob, servant of Mrs Lewis
Mrs Hilton, stewardess

John Walton, Mrs Jane Walton, & their children, John, Jas, & Eleanor Jane, all one family, from West Newburgh, for Pennsylvania.
Robt Vine & Jacob Walton, of the same family, saved.
The following are the names of such of the crew lost as far we have been able to astertain: John Gleason, Thos Gedney, Mich Dougherty, Chas Tyley, & John Macfarlan.

Passengers Saved:

Capt Geo W Cullum, U S Eng Corps	Thos Gooding, Boston
Seabury Brewster, N Y	Nahum Reise, Newark, N J
Capt Peter Hann, Portland	E V Booth, Boston
C C Orr, Louisville, Ky	Edw Maddox, Boston
Joel R Andrews, New London	Chas Mitchell, Norwich
Lt E Maynard, U S Navy	C Peterson, Boston
Lt C S Stewart, U S Engineers	Henry Van Wart, Birmingham, Eng
Chas Cadnedy, N Y	Varnham Marsh, Haverhill, Mass
Hiram Tarbox, Lisbon, Conn	Jas Wilson, Boston
Francis Herrick, Boston	Nathl Atwood, Mass
Geo W Rogers, New London	Richd Atwood, Mass
C C Comstock, New London	T O Gould, Adams' Express
Thos Truesdell, N Y	Jas Monroe, Adams' Express

Ofcrs of the Boat saved:

Jas Stetson, 2nd capt, very badly hurt	R W Duncan, 2nd mate
Chas Woodworth, barkeeper	John Keefer, steward
W W Boyld, clerk	Eli Birdsell, 2nd engineer
Capt N M Allen, pilot	John L Gale, 3rd engineer
Chas Crandall, 2nd pilot	Mr Baker, engineer of the gasometer
Dennis Spellans, wheelman	Chas Christian
Elias Kington, 1st mate	

Jas M Dobbs, 1st engineer, picked up out of the water entirely senseless, was restored, but remains blind. Mr Boyle, the clerk of the boat, escaped by lashing on his person a couple of life preservers, with which the boat fortunately was well supplied. He expresses the conviction that but for these not a person could have been saved. Every kindness was shown to the sufferers by Mr Winthrop, who resides upon Fisher's island. There is every reason to suppose that the gentleman referred to as the clergyman named Armstrong, was the Rev Dr Armstrong, for so many years the corresponding secretary of the American Board of Foreign Missions. He was expected at N Y, & had left Boston with the intention of going there, & nothing has been heard of him since he left home. [Dec 2nd newspaper: the bodies of 2 highly respectable citizens have been brought to their families from the wreck of the steamship **Atlantic**, whose fate was not certainly known before, viz: Mr Moses Kimball, of the firm of Kimball & Brown, who was returning from Massachusetts, his native State; & Mr Wm Burbank, of the firm of Burbank & Chambers, morocco dealers, in Ferry st. All the bodies at New London, with one exception, had been claimed by friends. Among the lost were 2 gentlemen of Boston, Mr Orlando Pitts, Sec of the Boylston Ins Co, & Mr French, of the Merchant's Ofc, both on their way to this city to spend Thanksgiving day with their friends. The body of Rev Mr Armstrong had several life preservers secured to his person. One of the survivors [the brother-in-law to the lad whose father, brothers, & sisters were lost] was married on Sat last. The family were on their way to purchase a farm & settle in the vicinity of Lancaster, Pa. Lt Norton, one of the lost, had been stopping in this city for several days, on a visit at Capt A Bassett's. He entered the Military Academy from the State of Ohio in 1838, & graduated in 1842. Surgeon C A Hassler had just arrived at Boston, after a 3 years' cruise in the U S ship **Falmouth**, & was on his way to Brunswick, N J, the place of his residence. He has left a devoted wife & 4 children to mourn his loss.]

TUE DEC 1, 1846
The Saturday Evening News: a weekly newspaper, published by the undersigned in Wash City, at $3 per annum with the subscribers' business cards, & at $1 per annum without the business card. –Wm Thompson

Household & kitchen furniture at auction on Dec 4, at the residence of Mr Wurdemann, on Capitol Hill, [1st house immediately north of the north capitol gate. Apply to A Green auctioneer, or to Mr Wurdeman, Coast Survey ofc.

Trustee's sale: in execution of an order passed by the worshipful Thos Duckett, Chief Justice of the Orphans' Court of PG Co, Md, passed on the petition of Robt Ghiselin, an insolvent debtor, the subscriber, as Trustee, will offer at public slae on Dec 29, at the residence of said Ghiselin, in said county, distant about 2 miles from Nottingham, his entire real & personsl estate, to wit: his dwlg plantation of about 1,000 acres, on which are a commodious dwlg, overseer's house, & all other bldgs needed for the convenience of the family & the cultivation of the estate. Fifty slaves, men, women, & children. An ample stock of horses, oxen, cows, sheep, & hogs. A large crop of corn & tobacco now in the houses; &, lastly, the household & kitchen furniture.
-Th S Alexander, Trustee

Orphans Court of Wash Co, D C. Letters of administration on the personal estate of Ebenezer H Stanley, late of said county, dec'd. –Louisa E Stanley, admx

Orphans Court of Wash Co, D C. Letters of administration on the personal estate of Capt Richd T Janney, of said county, dec'd. –Anna Janney, admx

The ivory comb factory of Julius Pratt & Co, at Meriden, Conn, took fire on last Fri & was wholly consumed: loss about $75,000. 30,000 pounds of ivory is said to have been stored in the cellar.

Mrd: on Nov 29, by Rev G W Samson, Mr Peyton Carley to Miss Martha Ann Butler, both of Wash.

Mrd: on Nov 19, at the residence of Hon A P Maury, in the vicinity of Franklin, Tenn, by Rev A N Cunningham, Hon M P Gentry to Miss Caledonia Brown.

Mrd: on Nov 29, by Rev H Slicer, Mr Jas S Brady to Miss Teresa Ann Venable, all of Wash City.

Mrd: on Oct 27, in Danville, Ky, by Rev F M Maury, Mr John W Venable, of Wash City, to Miss Sarah E Farnsworth, formerly of Hartford, Conn.

Died: on Nov 30, in Wash City, Mrs Mary Cooper, in her 82nd year. Her funeral is this day at 2 o'clock, from her late residence on Capitol Hill.

Died: on Nov 30, James Henry, y/s/o Saml H & Ann Marks, aged 3 years, 1 month & 18 days. His funeral is this day at 2 o'clock, from the residence of his father, near the Protestant Church, Navy Yard.

Died: on Nov 27, in Wash City, Mrs Sarah, w/o Mr Wm H Fales, aged 41 years.

Mr Denton Offutt will remain a short time in Wash City, & will reduce all kinds of vicious horses [kicking or stubborn] to a docility unknown before; or teach them to ride, work, or to follow, lay down, or to be shod; in short, he will render them fit for all the uses for which the horse is employed, or no pay will be demanded. Mr Offutt has satisfactory references from his own State, Ky, as well as other States. He may be seen at Levi Pumphrey's stables, 6th st.

Letters remaining in the Post Ofc, Wash, Dec 1, 1846:

Adams, Geo F	Brogden, Benj F-2	Cook, John K
Abbott, jr, Richd	Borland, Mrs Mary	Clair, Wm-2
Archer, Jas J	Blacklar, Chas R	Curd, Lt Thos J-2
Ashby, Jas	Butler, Mrs Ann	Crane, Col J B
Brown, John	Baker, Mrs Julia	Caldwell, Miss A
Beech, Miss Jane	Barry, Mrs Julia	Carter, Amos K
Brook, Gen C	Bagman, Wm	Cormick, Wm
Brown, Wm	Burn, Wm	Cogswell, Pearson
Brown, Thos	Barry, Griffith C	Chambers, John
Bates, Wm	Barry, Jas C	Cannon, John W-2
Bell, Miss Ellen N	Bledsoe, A T	Coston, John
Bell, Wm	Beaty, Wm R	Carrol, Miss Eliz
Beall, Chas R	Butler, John W	Calhoughn, Wm
Brooks, Miss Eliz	Bosher, Geo L	Colquhoun, Wm S
Brown, Chas P	Butler, Col P M	Conner, Wm
Brown, Arthur	Broors, Mrs Mary A	Carter, Jas
Bruce, Sandy	Burritt, Saml L-2	Campbell, Maria
Bell, Mrs Ann E	Clarke, John H	Comstock, J Gris
Brent, jr, Wm	Cole, John T	Carusi, Saml-2
Brent, Mrs Jane	Crown, J Edgar	Cabell, Edw C-4
Bastinelli, Titus-5	Coombe, Dr Jas G	Chauncey, J L USN

Dunn, Wm T	Fairfield, Mrs M A-2	Hamilton, Mrs Eliza
Dank, Thos	Foster, Moses	Hooe, Miss Eliz M
Darnes, Jas	Fowler, Hannah A	Hall, Miss Amanda C
Dudley, Allen	Fitzgerald, Mrs M	Harrman, Miss Car'e
Douglass, Wm	George, Miss Pris	Ingle, J S
Davis, Isaac R	Groff, Wm D	Jones, Miss M
David, Gen John	Gray, Mrs Sarah	Johnson, Miss E A
Davis, Oliver	Grimes, Wm	Jeffres, Mathias
Doniphan, Miss C	Gales, Rev Moses	Johnson, John
Davis, Jas	Gray, Rev S T-2	Jamaison, Rev J M
Dowdy, Jas A	Green, Jas	Jenkins, Miss Eliz
Davis, Mrs E C	Glenn, Mrs Eliz	King, Wm R
Dorsey, Alfred	Gray, John	Kean, Mrs Sarah E
Donally, Patrick	Greenville, Bened't	Kirk, Miss Mary H
Duncan, Mrs Betsy	Guyton, Mrs Ophe	Kendel, Louis
Dowden, Denis D	Goddard, Mrs Ann	Kensett, Geo
Duvall, John	Gormley, Simon	Lane, Newton
Duvall, Marcelus	Glasscock, Enoch	Lewis, John S
Duer, Pas Mid J K	Grimes, Miss S M	Loveless, Jas A
Depkine, Chas	Howe, Saml G	Leffler, Shepard
Delafield, J Jan-2	Hill, John	Latham, Robt W-2
Drummond, Mrs H A	Hall, Hiland	Lunday, Emma
Dobbins, Mrs Jas C	Howe, Rev W H	Le Moyne, Julius
Daniel, Mrs Araminta	Hobbs, Wm	Lovelace, Saml H
Englebrecht, O USD	Harrison, Mrs E O	Logan, Wm
Eaton, Mrs Cath's	Hazewell, Geo R	Lemon, Lucy A
Evans, John	Howard, John	Moore, Miss S J
Ellithrop, Wm F	Harrison, Thos B	Miles, Mrs Har't A
Ewing, Col R C	Hamilton, Miss A V	Morse, Geo E
Easton, Capt J H-3	Harper, Mary Ann	Morgan, Miss Fanny
Espy, Prof Jas P	Hilliary, John B-2	Meredith, Miss S
Ford, Geo E	Hazard, Robt R	Mulloy, Thos J
Ford, Miss Laura E	Hodson, John	Morris, Mrs E M
France, Jas	Henry, Thos W	Magruder, Capt G A
French, Thos	Hornley, Allen	Murphy, Mary A E
Foy, Mrs Sarah	Hamann, Augustus	Manning, Mrs Nancy
French, Edm F-2	Hudson, Capt	McGarr, Mrs Cath
Fry, John	Harris, Maria	McDonal, Sarah
Freeman, Mrs Mary	Henson, Adnrew	McCully, Geo
Fuller, Cornelius	Henry, Hugh F	McKenna, Mrs M
Fitzhugh, Capt A-2	Henry, Richd P	McClelland, Mrs R
Fagan, Jane	Harrison, Wm R	McClenahan, Dr W F
Fraleigh, Chas L	Hewitt, Miss Mary	Nail, Bryan
Freelon, Capt t W	Houser, Wm	Nowlan, Louisa
Fruhling, Caspar	Hansjacob, Chas	Ogden, Danl

Page, Miss M S-3	Schad, B	Vincent, Wm
Plant, Jos	Smallwood, Richd	Van Brancken, Saml
Polk, Capt Wm W	Shonnard, Miss C	Van Zandt, Jos-4
Pratt, Dr Ambrose	Seymour, Andrew	West, Lt E L
Posey, Mrs Adelane	Sawtell, Edwin	Wright, Chas J
Pickrell, Miss A M	Sabin, H W-2	Wolf, Henry
Pumphrey, Miss K L	Saunders, Mrs Ellen	Wiley, Violetta
Palmer, Miss Cath	Sheahen, Mrs Fran	Wallace, Ellen
Roach, Mrs Eme E	Slemaker, Jas-2	Wagoner, Mrs Cath
Rabbit, Mrs M A	Slemmer, L	Williams, Jane
Ridings, Fred'k	Sullivan, Marshall	Wheeler, Alex
Roberts, Miss M A	Sommers, Mrs Susa	Williams, Mrs E
Rollings, Miss L J	Somers, Lafayette	Williams, Mrs Susan
Robinson, Miss S H	Thomas, John W	& Miss
Robertson, Mrs M-2	Tolson, Mrs E B	Wanzer, Mrs Louis
Ruggles, Draper	Taylor, Miss M M	Young, Ellie
Rennolds, Miss M D	Thompson, Wm, saddler	Young, Benj F
Rowan, John	Tomlinson, Jos	Yates, John
Riley, F B	Turner, Jeremiah	Young, Rev A L
Sims, Miss M J	Tyer, Henry G	Young, Jas C
Stras, Miss E C	Turner, Com D-3	
Stanks, Sergeant	Tansitt, Grandes'n S	

The postage due to the U S on letters & packets directed to Mexico & all other foreign Gov'ts, except the British Canadian Provinces & New Brunswick, must be prepaid, otherwise they cannot be sent. –C K Gardner, P M

WED DEC 2, 1846
The late Wm H Foote, of Fairfax Co, Va, has made the Female Free School of Alexandria the residuary legatee, in fact, of his whole estate. He has also left it 10 shares of Potomac Bank Stock, as a legacy to be paid forthwith.

Capt Bacon, of the steamer **Chancellor**, informs that among his cabin passengers from New Orleans were 3 volunteers from the Rio Grande, who had been discharged because of sickness. Edw Cokely, of Green Co, Ken, 18 or 19 years of age, delirious, jumped overboard. He was drowned, although every effort was made to rescue him. His mother, we understand, is widow lady, & resides in Green Co. –Louisville Courier

The train of cars which left Balt on Mon for Cumberland ran off the track 4 miles this side of Point of Rocks, & a passenger, Hugh Haughey, who was standing on the platform of one of the cars, was thrown from the car & instantly killed.

Mr Robt McFarlan, a young lawyer in Fred'k Co, Md, committed suicide on Fri last, by hanging himself whilst in a state of temporary insanity.

The following list of the passengers & crew of the steamship **Atlantic** was made up from the books of the Company, & is believed to be correct, or nearly so:

Passengers, Boston to N Y:

Atwood, probably found
Atwood, probably found
Symes, not found
Hassler, body found
Maynard, not found
Giddings, not found
Burbank, body found
Partridge, saved
Western, body found
Orr, not found
Cullum, saved
Leverett, not found
Van West, saved
Cunningham, not found

Burbank, [probably A A Burbank,] not found
Houghton, saved
Solace, body found
Kimball, body found
Cassidy, body found
Collamore, body found
Hirsch, saved
Armstrong, body recovered
Booth, found, probably
Hanna, found, probably
French, body recovered
Pitts, body recovered
Baldwin, not found
Mary Jordan, not found

Miss Sarah Drake perished in a snow storm near the county poor-house in Orange Co, N Y, on Thu last.

Miss Nano Hayes, of Louisville, Ky, has obtained $6,000 from Mr John Hayes, a merchant of that city, for a breach of marriage promise.

Mrd: on Dec 1, by Rev H Slicer, Mr Cary W White, of Balt, to Miss Julia A Carroll, of Wash City.

It is stated that 4 or 5 acres of land, belonging to Mr Ledyard, on the east bank of the Cayuga Lake, sunk a few days ago, & have entirely disappeared.

Jas Field had been declared guilty of murder in the first degree, for killing his aged mother, in order to avoid the expense of maintaining her. The trial took place in Crawford Co, Indiana. –U S Gaz

Ball at Odd Fellows' Hall: Managers, announce that it will be held at the Grand Saloon or Odd Fellows' Hall, on Dec 9. Managers:

E G Eastman
W L Dixon
L Parmele
Andrew Tate
M H Stevens
Walter Lenox
A G Herold
T A Provost

H S M Farnham
S W Walker
Wm M Perry
Hugh Latham
F D Stewart
T M McCalla
F Eckloff
Levin Jones

Edw Drew
Wm H Topping
Saml S Coleman
John S Cunningham
Chas King
T W Johnson
Saml L Harris
John T Towers

J W Colley	Robt Ould	A H Lawrence
Jas T King	John Mead	G E Jillard
Jos B Tate	W P Zantzinger	J W Eckloff
J B Bragdon	J F J McClery	S Yorke AtLee
J R Ashby	Robt S Waters	Alex'r Settle
F J Waters	A V Fraser	John Thaw
W W Wall	J A McLaughlin	Jesse E Dow
E C Eckloff	Nathn Hammond	A W Kirkwood
Geo M Sothoron	John Sessford, jr	Jas Cathcart
Wm B Magruder	F W Fuller	E S Hough
A M Thomas	W T Wallace	Geo Cochran
Z K Offutt	Oliver Denham	J C McGuire
F B Lord, jr	R C Johnson	W F Bayly

Tickets will be $2, & may be had at: Coleman's & Brown's Hotels; King's Congress Hall, Delany's Drug Store, Thompson's Refectory, Stevens & Emmons' Hat Store, Bayly's Stationery Store, V Harbaugh's Drug Store, F W Fuller's Drug Store, McClery & Clement's Drug Store, T P Morgan's Drug Store, G M Sothoron's Drug Store, Gtwn, & Hugh Latham, Alexandria, or any of the Managers.

THU DEC 3, 1846

Mrs Mount has taken that desirable residence on the corner of 4½ st & Pa ave & is fitted up for the reception of a mess of Members & their Ladies. Terms moderate & servants attentive.

Handsome furnished parlor & chamber attached, will be rented on reasonable terms. Apply on 18th st, between I & K sts, first house south of the Brazilian Minister. –Mrs Dorcas Walker

By virtue of a writ of fieri facias, issued by Thos C Donn, one of the Justices of the Peace in & for Wash Co, D C, at the suit of Jas Riordan, against the goods & chattels of Jos Cross: I have seized & taken in execution all the right, title, & interest of the said Jos Cross in & to one carryall: sale on Dec 8 in front of the Centre Market House, in Wash City. –H R Maryman, Constable. [The above sale is to pay a debt of Walter Evans, & levied on at my instance. –Jos Cross]

Balt, Dec 2. 1-A letter received in Balt, dated Norwich, states that Mr Robt Hope, of Balt, was among those who were lost in the wreck of the steamship **Atlantic**. He had gone to the East on business. 2- Preparations are being made by our military & citizens generally for the funeral of the lamented Maj Ringgold. His body is expected here in the course of 8 days to 2 weeks.

Mrd: on Dec 1, by Rev W T Sprole, Benj Cooley to Miss Eliz Ann Grooms, both of Montg Co, Md.

Died: on Nov 27, on his way from St Louis, Missouri, to Wash, D C, John Andrew Jackson, s/o John F Jackson, of Fauquier Co, Va, aged 16 years.

FRI DEC 4, 1846
For rent: 2 story brick house near the corner of H & 21st st, west. Inquire at Jackson Hall. –Jas Blair

For rent or sale: desirable residence: the middle house of the Seven Bldgs. Apply to Chas J Nourse, or T P Morgan, Druggist, near Seven Bldgs.

There is a good bit of discrepancy in the different accounts of the saved & lost by the wreck of the steamship **Atlantic**. The following list is the most perfect of any which we have seen.

Passengers Lost:

Rev Dr W J Armstrong	Orlando Pitts	Jas Walton
Dr C A Hassler, USN	Chas French	Eleanor J Walton
Lt A H Norton, USN	A F Collamore	Ald Burbank
Moses Kimball	Dr J M Weston	Wm B Solace
Isaac Fitz	John Walton	M Cassidy
Miss Mary Jordon	Mrs J Walton	Eliza Wacob
	John Walton, jr	

Crew Lost:
Capt Dustan
John Gleason, porter
Thos Gebney, waiter
Michl Dougherty, waiter
Chas Riley, waiter
John McFarland, waiter
Warren Smith, cook
Wm Willett, cook
Mary Ann Hilton, stewardess
Sarah Johnson, chambermaid
Sarah Ruby, chambermaid

There are 5 bodies amongst those not positively indentified. One man, on whom was found a linencambric handkerchief, marked Archibald Austen. One woman & a child, supposed to be from Salem, Mass, on their way to N J. A Miss Smart, so supposed, as yet not known. One body of a man at Fisher's Island, so cut to pieces that he could not be identified. Part of a body, from the waist to the neck, so mangled that it cannot be identified. Also, several parts of bodies, lying in different parts of the island.

A Soldier's Gratitude. A late Washington letter in the True Sun: the last will of Capt McKavett, of 8th Infty, killed in Worth's division at the storming of Monterey, arrived in the city. It was found in his trunk after the battle. He wills to the Orphan Asylum in N Y C, where he was nutured in his childhood, nearly all his effects, including a farm in the State of N Y, & some money due him as pay.

Valuable land for sale: being empowered by Mr Jos R Willett, I will offer at public sale, on the premises, on Dec 10, that tract of land lying immediately on the Railroad, at the intersection of the Wash & Balt Turnpike road, near Bladensburg: contains about 80 acs. –Chas B Calvert

A very distressing accident occurred in Chas Co, Md, a few days ago, in the family of Mr Wilson Compton. Two of his children, a little boy & girl, nearly of the same age, were playing together in the yard, & just as the former was about to strike a stick of wood with an axe, his sister stooped to pick it up & received the blow upon her head. She died the next day.

SAT DEC 5, 1846
Boarding: Mrs E Y Arguelles has a number of pleasant rooms which can be had cheap with board. Residence nearly opposite Coleman's Hotel, Pa ave.

Furnished rooms: the parlor & 5 well furnished chambers lately occupied by Capt Ramsay, of the Navy, situated on Pa ave, between 1st & 2nd sts. –J F McDuffie

Mrs E O Robinson's Boarding House, corner of 1st & B sts, Capitol Hill, one street north of the Old Capitol. She has 3 comfortable chambers & a parlor, with or without board.

Sale of 3 story brick house & ground on square 742, fronts on N J ave: on Dec 23. –Thos Carbery, Agent of Ben Pollard. -R W Dyer, auct

Circuit Court of Wash Co, D C-in Chancery. Walter Smith & David English, surviving trustees of the estate of Henry Foxall, dec'd, vs Wm Parrott, Thos W Williams & Eliza Williams, [late Eliza Parrott,] his wife, heirs at law of Richd Parrott, dec'd. Object of the bill of cmplnt is to procure a decree to foreclose the equity of redemption of the dfndnts in a certain part of the tract of land called **Rock of Dunbarton**, in said county, containing about 4½ acres of land, which Thos Beall, of George, conveyed to the said Richd Parrott, by his deed dated Jan 11, 1813, & which the said Richd Parrott conveyed, by way of mortgage, to the said Henry Foxall by 2 deeds; one dated Jun 8, 1814, & the other Sep 27, 1821, to secure the payment of sundry debts in the said deed mentioned with interest thereon, unless the said dfndnts shall pay, or bring into the said Court to be paid, to the said cmplnts, as trustees & devisees of said Henry Foxall, the sum of $5,590.09, which they allege to be due for principal & interest on the said mortgage deed. The bill states that the said Richd Parrott, in his life time, to wit, on Jun 18, 1814, conveyed to said Henry Foxall, in his life time, & to his heirs, the above mentioned real estate; which is particularly described in the said bill & deed therewith exhibited, by way of mortgage, to secure the payment of the sum of $1,662.50, with interest thereon from the date last aforesaid, which was then due & owing from Parrott to Foxall; that Parrott afterwards, on Sep 27, 1821, by his deed of that date reciting the preceding mortgage, & stating that the debt thereby secured was still due, with a large arrear of interest thereon, to said Foxall; & that he, Parrott, was further indebted to Foxall in the sum of $300, did convey the same premise to the said Foxall in fee simple to secure the debt of $300, & interest from the date of said last named deed, as well as the debt first aforesaid. That the said Parrott, though requested by the said Foxall after the date of the last deed to pay the said debts, did not pay the same or any part thereof in his lifetime, & died some time in 1822, without having paid any part of said principal debts or of the interest, leaving 2 children his heirs at law, viz: Wm Parrott & Eliza Parrott; which said Eliza Parrott has since married one Thos W Williams. The bill states that Henry Foxall departed this life in 1821, leaving a will, in which he devised all his estate, real & personal, including the said mortgage, debt, & premises, to Jacob Hoffman, the cmplnts Walter Smith & David English, & one Leonard Mackall, & survivors of them, in fee simple, for certain uses & purposes in the said will mentioned; that the said Wm Parrott & Eliza Williams, & her said husband reside out of D C. Notice to the absent dfndnts to appear in this Court, on or before the 1st Mon of Apr next. –Wm Brent, clk

For rent: 2 story brick house, with attic & back bldg, on 18th st, between H & L. Inquire of E A Cabell, south side of H st, between 17th & 18th sts.

Orphans Court of Wash Co, D C. Letters of administration, with the will annexed, on the personal estate of Eliz J Kidwell, late of said county, dec'd. –A Rothwell, adm, w a

Orphans Court of Wash Co, D C. Letters testamentary on the personal estate of Thos Corcoran, late of said county, dec'd. –Emmily Corcoran, excx [Emmily as written.]

Letter from Edwin M Stanton, brother of the late Dr D E Stanton: Steubenville, Nov 23, 1846. Robt L Patterson, Pres Mutual Benefit Life Ins Co, N Y. Acknowledging receipt of yours of Nov 18, enclosing a check for $2,908,83, payable to the order of Mrs Nancy Stanton, allow me to express for myself & for my brother's widow & children our thanks for the just & honorable manner in which this business had been transacted by your company. Your obedient servant, Edwin M Stanton.

Mrd: on Dec 1, in Phil, by Rev Mr Howe, Peter V Daniel, jr, of Richmond, Va, to Mary, d/o Jas Robertson, of Phil.

Died: on Nov 30, of consumption, Mr Jacob P Norton, printer, aged 63 years, only s/o the Rev J Norton, of Billerica, Mass. [Dec 8th newspaper: Died: on Nov 30, at Lowell, Mass, of consumption, Mr Jacob F Norton, printer, aged 53 years, only s/o the Rev J Norton, of Billerica, Mass. Mr Norton was a Lt in the 4th Regt of Infty from the commencement to the close of the last war with Great Britain.]

MON DEC 7, 1846
Local Affairs: handsome improvements on Pa ave: the Fountain Bldgs, by Mr Cyrus Ward; Washington Hall, by Robt Keyworth; the lofty edifice, near the Centre Market, by Messrs Haslup & Weeden. New & elegant stores: those of Messrs W Harper & Co, Messrs Barnes & Mitchell, dry good merchants; Messrs J T & C King, lace merchants; Mr Young's Coach establishment, on the south side of Pa ave. Old stores have been greatly improved by the addition of new & handsome fronts, & splendid lamps & lights, aided by the brilliant gas-lights of Messrs Coleman, Brown, & Morrison. Turning from Pa ave into 4½ st, may be noticed, the commodious private dwlgs erected

in this city. It is at present occupied by the proprietor, Mr W G W White, who has spared neither pains or expenses to render it, inside & out. Mr P R Fendall has lately erected a capacious brick dwlg on the corner of the same street, which is ornamental to that side of Louisiana ave. Into C st, we approach 4 elegant brick dwlg lately erected on the north side by Messrs Blagden, Simms, Gunnell, & Tucker. The 2 dwlgs erected by Messrs Blagden & Simms have obtained the name of *Ashland Place*.

To let: a new 2 story frame house, situated in a respectable part of the town, on the north side of Dunbarton st, lately in the occupancy of Mr Henry King. Apply to Richd Cruit, Bridge st, Gtwn, near the bridge.

The steamship **McKim** arrived at New Orleans on Nov 27 from Brasos Santiago, & brought disabled & discharged volunteers, besides the ofcrs whose names are contained in the following list:
Majors McLane & Graham, bearers of dispatches from Gen Taylor
Capt G T M Davis, bearer of dispatches from Gen Wool

Maj Carnes	Lt Cable
Col McCook	Lt R G Mitchell
Col Cazenau	Lt W H Miles
Capt J M Scott	H G Heartt
Capt Hughes	A J Hedrick
Capt Mason	F C Humphreys
Capt Kell	W H Saunders
Capt Lillard	P A Jones
Capt Todd	Chas White
Capt Porter	Mr Hamilton
Capt Kemp	Mr Kennedy
Capt J McMann	Mr Sherman
Capt Rodgers	Mr O Riley
Capt Breath	Mr O Yerger
Capt Davis	Mr J Dale
Capt Bell	Col Cook
Capt Templeton	

Naval Ofcrs who were on board the steamship **Atlantic**: Lt Maynard happily survived, & Dr Hassler perished to save others. Lt Maynard gives an account of the heroic conduct of Dr Hassler, who thought not of himself until others were provided with floats & life-preservers, & placed in a position to be the more readily attended to when the vessel struck; for you must know we counted fully on her striking some 30 or 40 yeards from shore. But his noble heart stopped not here; for there was a child & a little boy whose parents were too feeble to take care of them. One only had been provided for, & the other he would willingly have taken himself but for my advice to the contrary, as I considered him too weak & feeble for the task, & he would have only involved them both in a common ruin. He then went, at my request, in search of some more robust person, for I thought that I had seen among the passengers one or two gentlemen who had the appearance of seafaring men, & I felt assured that no true hearted tar would hestitiate a moment to undertake the task. Dr Hassler adjusted life preservers of the ladies, procured doors, & tying ropes & cords upon them, to cling to when in the water, & encouraged them much by his composed & cheerful countenance & encouraging words. Dr Hassler was instantly killed on the striking of the vessel.

Mrd: on Dec 3, at Richmond, by Rev Dr Empie, Robt Ould, of Gtwn, D C, to Miss Sarah A Turpin, only d/o the late Thos J Turpin, of Richmond.

A Treatise on Insanity: the author, Mr G Grimes, who for a number of years was an inmate of the Lunatic Asylum in Tennessee, & who has fortunately been cured of his malady, has written the above volume.

Rooms to let, for one or more weeks, not furnished, adjoining the U S Hotel. Apply to John A Donohoo, T F Simms, Wine Merchant, on the first floor.

TUE DEC 8, 1846
House & lot at auction: on Dec 10: on the premises, lot 15 in square 480, with a small frame house upon it, nearly new. It is at present occupied by the subscriber, on 5th st, in rear of the old Poor House. Terms made known at sale. –Jos Ballinger
-R W Dyer, auct

Wm A Richardson, Merchant Tailor, Pa ave, between 19th & 20th sts, is about to close his business in the First Ward, & it is necessary that those who are indebted to him should call & settle their accounts. The store & dwlg will be for rent-possession on Jan 1. Apply to Wm P Drury, next door. –Wm A Richardson

Orphans Court of Wash Co, D C. It is this day ordered that Geo Kirby, exc of John B Kirby, dec'd, appear in this Court on Dec 15, to show cause why his letters testamentary on said estate should not be revoked.
-Nathl Pope Causin -Ed Roach, Reg/o wills

Oils, Colognes, Perfumery, Combs, Brushes, & Soaps: P Brenner & Son, Pa ave, between 11th & 12th sts.

Excellent furniture at auction on Dec 11, at the residence of Rev H Stringfellow, on Indiana ave. Also, a fine cow. –B Homans, auctioneer

Mr Orland Pitts, a young gentleman of Roxbury, one of those lost in the steamship **Atlantic**, had his life insured at the New England Mutual Life Ins Co, of Boston, for $2,000. He has by this prudent step, by the payment of only $43 in premiums, made some provision for a widowed mother & family of sisters, for whose support he was the main dependence. –Boston Transcript

From Europe. 1-Thos Moore, the bard of Erin, is dangerously ill. The Ballinasloe Star says he is in rapidly declining health: Ireland's most honored poet. 2-The marriage of Geo Chas Constantine, Earl of Elgin & Kincardine, the newly appointed Govn'r Genr'l of Canada, with the Lady Mary Louisa Lambton, eldest d/o the late & sister of the present Earl of Durham, & niece of Earl Grey, was solemnized on Sat week, by special license, at St Peter's Church, Eaton Square, in the presence of a select circle of friends of both families. His Excellency is expected to embark soon for North America to enter on the official duties of that colony, & the Earl will be accompanied by his bride.

Fisher's Island, the scene of the recent wreck of the steamship **Atlantic**, is the sole property of Wm Winthrop, of New London, & is cultivated as a farm. A son of Mr Winthrop now resides on the island, & his house offered shelter & hospitable accommodation to the survivors of the **Atlantic**. Fisher's Island once belonged to Connecticut; but the grant to the Duke of York, in 1664, carried with it not only this island, but a considerable part of Long Island previously appertaining to the same colony, together with the adjacent islands, all of which have ever since formed a part of NY. The Winthrops have owned the Fisher's Island from the first settlement of the country to the present time. –Commercial Advertiser

Balt: the old family mansion of the late Gen Saml Smith, until recently in the occupancy of his son John S Smith, was sold on Sat at auction at $30,100. It was purchased by our opulent & enterprising merchant Johns Hopkins.

Mrd: on Dec 3, in Wash City, by Rev G W Samson, Rev Geo W Dorrance to Miss Eliza Bartella McDuell, both of Wash.

Criminal Court-Wash: gentlemen on the grand inquest:
Thos Carbery, foreman	Lewis Johnson
John Carter	John Boyle
John C Rives	Henry Addison
Jacob Gideon	Thos Thornley
Wm A Bradley	Geo Sweeny
Robt White	Robt S Patterson
Saml McKenney	Wm Robinson
Joshua Peirce	G W Young
Geo Lowry	Geo Watterston
O M Linthicum	Chas R Belt
Hamilton Luffborough	Robt Keyworth

WED DEC 9, 1846
Fresh Groceries: Sylvanus Holmes, 7th st, Wash.

The Charleston papers notice the death of the Hon Henry Deas, late Pres of the State Senate, a model of a Southern gentleman.

Mrd: Dec 2, in Wash City, by Rev Mr Ege, Mr Truman Boush to Miss Jane Deneal, both of Fairfax Co, Va.

Died: yesterday, after an illness of several weeks, Mrs Elmira Fowler, w/o Mr Jas E Fowler, formerly of Phil, leaving a husband & several small children to mourn their loss. Her funeral is from her husband's residence, on 11th st, near F, today at 2 o'clock. Friends & members of the E st Baptist Church are invited to attend.

Naval: A Court of Inquiry has been ordered to assemble on board the U S ship **Pennsylvania**, at Norfolk, to inquire into the loss of the U S brig **Truxton**. The Court is compossed of the following ofcrs: Capt David Geisinger, Pres; Capt Chas S McCauley & Capt Andrew Fitzhugh, members; Lt Geo P Upshur, Judge Advocate.

From the Sandwich Islands: from the Honolulu Polynesian of Jun 27: account of the public proceedings connected with the visit of Cmdor Stockton to Honolulu, conveying Anthony Ten Eyck, the new Com'r from the U S to the Hawaiian Islands, & Joel Turrell, the new Consul. The U S frig **Congress**, bearing the broad pennant of Cmdor Stockton arrived off Honolulu on Jun 9, & on the 16th a communication was sent by the Cmdr to the Minister of foreign relations, Robt C Wylie, which resulted in an informal conference the next day at which the pending difficulties were settled, &, by direction of his Majesty Kamehameha III, Mr Geo Brown, the former U S Com'r, resumed his functions until Mr Ten Eyck & Cmdor Stockton & suite were admitted to an audience at the palace. The Cmdor presented the ofcrs of his suite, viz: Capt S F Dupont, Lt Com Howison, Lt L F Schenck, Lt L P Green, Lt A F V Gray, Surgeon Mosely, Purser Speiden, Chaplain Colton, Lt Marines L Zeilein, Cmdor's Sec L P Norris, Midshipman S Lee. [The Polynesian says of the audience: may we bury in oblivion all the unhappy differences which have arisen between your Gov't & our late Com'r, Geo Brown.]

THU DEC 10, 1846
Senate: 1-Memorial from Hayne N Solomon, asking indemnification for the services of his father in the Revolutionary war.

Musical instruction: Wm Walter, Professor of Music, late from Germany: instruction on the Piano & in vocal music. Apply at Confectionary Store of Mr John Miller, on Pa ave, where reference will be given.

Public sale: by order of the Orphans' Court of PG Co, Md, on Dec 14, at the farm of the late Benj Day, part of the personal estate of said dec'd, consisting of a number of valuable negroes; horses, cattle, sheep; crop of tobacco; & farming utensils.
Immediately after the sale the late residence [in Bladensburg] of said dec'd will be sold; also, the household & kitchen furniture, medicines, medicine stands, medical books, & a number of Law-books, & Barouche & Sulkey.
–Septimus I Cook, adm of Benj Day, dec'd.

Mrd: on Dec 8, in Wash City, by Rev Smith Pyne, Frank Grinnell, of Massaachusetts, to Miss Marion Gales Johnson, y/d/o Gen Robt R Johnson, of N C, dec'd.

Mrd: on Dec 3, at Kilmarnock, Lancaster Co, Va, by Rev J Lewis Shuck, Pastor of the First Baptist Church, Canton, China, the Rev Thos W Tobey, Missionary to China, to Miss Isabella Hall, 3rd d/o the Rev Addison Hall, & sister of the late Mrs Henrietta Shuck.

Boarding: Mrs Jos Harbaugh, on 7th st, a few doors from the Genr'l Post Ofc: can accommodate a mess of members of Congress with boarding & rooms, or with rooms.

Norfolk Herald: loss of the U S sloop-of-war **Boston**, Cmder Geo F Pearson, while on her way from N Y for Vera Cruz. On Nov 15th, during a heavy black squall, she struck on the an outer reef of the island of Eleuthera, [one of the Bahamas,] & drove up within 50 yards of shore, broadside on. All the ofcrs & crew succeeded in reaching the shore in safety, where they were living in tents. The schnr **Volante**, which brought the above information to Norfolk, also brought as passenger Midshipmen Temple & Smith, & 10 of the crew. The remainder were left on the island. The **Boston** was lying high & dry, & bilged, stripped of everything except the guns & water-tanks, which it was impossible to get out.

FRI DEC 11, 1846
Criminal Court-Wash. 1-Thos Jackson & Jas Fitzgerald were indicted for renting houses to females of bad character, to be used as houses of ill fame. Both were found guilty. 2-Wm Mattingly was found guilty of a riot in Gtwn with intent to kill several persons.

Wash Corp: 1-Ptn from Jas McColgan: referred to the Cmte of Claims. 2-Ptn of C K Sanderson, for the remission of a fine: referred to the Cmte of Claims. 3-Cmte of Claims: asking to be discharged from the ptn of Edw Sweeney, & taken up & agreed to. 4-Bill for the relief of Jas Casparis: passed.

Senate: 1-Ptn from Chas Gilham, for a pension. 2-Ptn from the administrator of Francis Pass, for indemnification for spoliations by the U S troops in Florida, in 1812 & 1813.

House of Reps: 1-Ptn of John Smith, of Henry Co, Ky, asking compensation for services rendered by himself & father during the Revolution. 2-Ptn of John Morrison, of Cuyahoga Co, Ohio, for a pension for Revolutionary services.

Geo S C Dow, et al, recovered $1,000 from the owners of the iron steamboat **Bangor**, which was burnt last year in Penobscot bay, it being for damages for goods destroyed on the boat. –Kennebec [Me] Jour

Misses T E & M Horne, Fashionable Dressmakers & Milliners, [late of Balt,] south side of Pa ave, between 12th & 13th sts. Evening dresses made in the most fashionable styles at the shortest notice.

Died: on Nov 15, at Cowansville, Rowan Co, N C, in his 77th year, P S Ney, a men of learning, whose death is severely flet in the community in which he lived.

Died: on Oct 9 last, at Winchester, Clark Co, Missouri, in her 82nd year, Mrs Eliz Chaplin, widow of Jeremiah Chaplin, & d/o Jas Nourse, formerly of Berkeley Co, Va, dec'd.

New Orleans, Dec 3. Arrival of troops: Capt G B Crittenden, Lts S S Tipton & Julian May, & 68 privates & non-commissioned ofcrs of the regt of Mounted Riflemen, Co E, arrived in this city yesterday from Jefferson Barracks, Missouri, & will leave in a few days for the seat of war. Capt W F Sanderson, of Co B, & Lts Raquet, Newton, & Gordon are expected down on the next boat. This company consists of 76 men. -Picayune

General Orders #52: War Dept, Adj Gen Ofc, Wash, Nov 30, 1846. Promotions & Appointments in the Army of the U S, made by the Pres, since the publicationof the Army Register, Sep, 1846.
Promotions:
Medical Dept: Assist Surgeon John B Porter, to be Surgeon, Oct 4,1846, vice Wharton, dec'd.
Corps of Topographical Engineers:
1st Lt Jos E Johnston, to be Capt, Sep 21, 1846, vice Williams, killed in battle.
2nd Lt Eliakim P Scammon, to be 1st Lt, Sep 21, 1846, vice Johnston, promoted.
Brevet 2nd Lt Wm B Franklin, to be 2nd Lt, Sep 21, 1846, vice Scammon, promoted.
3rd Regt of Artl:
2nd Lt Jos Stewart, to be 1st Lt, Oct 17, 1846, vice Gilham, resigned.
2nd Lt Richd W Johnston, to be 1st Lt, Oct 27, 1846, vice Ridgely, dec'd.
Brevet 2nd Lt Jos F Farry, of the 4th Artl, to be 2nd Lt, Oct 17, 1846, vice Stewart, promoted.
Brevet 2nd Lt Louis D Welch, to be 2nd Lt, Oct 27, 1846, vice Johnston, promoted.
1st Regt of Infty:
1st Lt John H King, to be Capt, Oct 31, 1846, vice Jouett, promoted Major, 3rd Infy.
2nd Lt Benj H Arthur, to be 1st Lt, Sep 21, 1846, vice Terrett, killed in battle.
2nd Lt Theophilus d'Oremieulx, to be 1st Lt, Oct 31, 1846, vice King, promoted.
Brevet 2nd Lt Wm L Crittenden, of the 5th Infty, to be 2nd Lt, Sep 21, 1846, vice Arthur, promoted.
Brevet 2nd Lt Chas C Gilbert, of the 1st Infty, to be 2nd Lt, Sep 27, 1846, vice Dilworth, dec'd.
Brevet 2nd Lt Parmenus T Turnley, of the 2nd Infty, to be 2nd Lt, Oct 31, 1846, vice d'Oremieulx, promoted.

2nd Regt of Infty:
Brevet 2nd Lt David R Jones, to be 2nd Lt, Nov 23, 1846, vice Martin, resigned.
3rd Regt of Infty:
Capt Wm R Jouett, of the 1st Infty, to be Major, Oct 31, 1846, vice Lear, dec'd.
1st Lt Jas M Smith, to be Capt, Sep 21, 1846, vice Morris, killed in battle.
1st Lt Wm H Gordon, to be Capt, Sep 21, 1846, vice Field, killed in battle.
1st Lt Danl T Chandler, to be Capt, Sep 21, 1846, vice Barbour, killed in battle.
2nd Lt Israel B Richardson, to be 1st Lt, Sep 21, 1846, vice Smith, promoted.
2nd Lt Wm T H Brooks, to be 1st Lt, Sep 21, 1846, vice Gordon, promoted.
2nd Lt Andrew W Bowman, to be 1st Lt, Sep 21, 1846, vice Chandler, promoted.
2nd Lt Geo Sykes, to be 1st Lt, Sep 21, 1846, vice Irwin, killed in battle.
Brevet 2nd Lt Jas N Ward, 6th Infty, to be 2nd Lt, Sep 21, 1846, vice Richardson, promoted.
Brevet 2nd Lt Barnard E Bee, to be 2nd Lt, Sep 21, 1846, vice Brooks, promoted.
Brevet 2nd Lt Wm Rhea, of the 6th Infty, to be 2nd Lt, Sep 21, 1846, vice Bowman, promoted.
Brevet 2nd Lt Henry B Clitz, of the 7th Infty, to be 2nd Lt, Sep 21, 1846, vice Sykes, promoted.
Breve 2nd Lt Wm H Wood, of the 7th Infty, to be 2nd Lt, Sep 21, 1846, vice Hazlitt, killed in battle.
4th Regt of Infty:
2nd Lt Henderson Ridgely, to be 1st Lt, Sep 21, 1846, vice Hoskins, killed in battle.
2nd Lt Allen H Norton, to be 1st Lt, Oct 12, 1846, vice Graham, dec'd.
2nd Lt Jenks Beaman, to be 1st Lt, Nov 27, 1746, vice Norton, dec'd.
Brevet 2nd Lt David A Russell, of the 1st Infty, to be 2nd Lt, Sep 21, 1846, vice Ridgely, promoted.
Brevet 2nd Lt Alex'r P Rodgers, to be 2nd Lt, Oct 12, 1846, vice Norton, promoted.
Brevet 2nd Lt Delancy F Jones, of the 7th Infty, to be 2nd Lt, Nov 27, 1846, vice Beaman, promoted.
5th Regt of Infty:
Capt Jos H Whipple, to be Capt, to date from Jun 29, 1846, vice McKissack, Assist Quartermaster, who vacates his regimental commission.
1st Lt Danl H McPhail, to be Capt, Jul 10, 1846, vice Drane, cashiered.
1st Lt Jos L Folsom, to be 1st Lt, to date from Jun 29, 1846, vice Whipple, promoted.
2nd Lt Mortimer Rosecrants, to be 1st Lt, Jul 10, 1846, vice McPhail, promoted.
Brevet 2nd Lt Fred'k Myers, to be 2nd Lt, Nov 23, 1846, to fill a vacancy.
8th Regt of Infty:
1st Lt John T Sprague, to be Capt, Sep 21, 1846, vice McKavett, killed in battle.
2nd Lt Chas D Jordon, to be 1st Lt, Sep 21, 1846, vice Sprague, promoted.
Brevet 2nd Lt Thos G Pitcher, of the 5th Infty, to be 2nd Lt, Sep 21, 1846, vice Jordon, promoted.
Appointments: Medical Dept:
Robt Newton, of Pa, to be Assist Surgeon, Oct 30, 1846.
2nd Regt of Infty:
Maurice Maloney, Sgt Major, to be 2nd Lt, Nov 27, 1846.

Transfers:
2nd Lt Francis J Thomas, 2nd Artl, to the 3rd Artl, to take place on the Army Register next below Lt French.
2nd Lt Josiah H Carlisle, 3rd Artl, to the 2nd Artl, to take place on the Army Register next below Lt Clarke.
Brevet 2nd Lt Thos J Wood, Topographicl Engineers, to the 2nd Dragoons, to take place on the Army Register at the head of the list of brevet 2nd Lts attached to the Dragoon Arm.
Appointments in the Quartermaster's Commissary's, & Medical Depts, under the 5th section of the :Act supplemental to an act entitled-An Act providing for the prosecution of the existing war between the U S & the Republic of Mexico, & for other purposes," approved Jun 18, 1846.
Quartermaster's Dept:
Assist Quartermasters with the rank of Capt:
Hugh O'Donnell, of Ohio, Oct 7, 1846.
Geo V Hebb, of Tenn, Oct 13, 1846.
Ralph G Norvell, of Indiana, Dec 2,1846.
Commissary's Dept:
Commissary with the rank of Major:
Fred'k A Churchill, of Ohio, Nov 24, 1846.
Assist Commissary with the rank of Capt:
Francis M Dimond, of Rhode Island, Oct 26, 1846.
Medical Dept:
Wm B Washington, of Tennessee, to be Surgeon, Oct 29, 1846.
Appointments in the Pay Dept, under the 25th section of the act approved Jul 5, 1838.
Additional Paymasters:
Hiram Leonard, of N Y, Nov 24, 1846.
Wm Rich, of D C, Nov 24, 1846.
David W Stone, of N C, Nov 30, 1846.
Casualties-Regular Army.
Resignations:
1st Lt Wm Gilham, 3rd Artl, Oct 17, 1846.
2nd Lt John W Martin, 2nd Infty, Nov 23, 1846.
2nd Lt Norman Elting, 4th Infty, Oct 29, 1846.
Commissions vacated-under the provisions of the 7th section of the Act of Jun 18, 1846:
Capt J H Prentiss, Assist Adj Gen, Jun 18, 1846, 1st Artl. [Staff commission [only] vacated.]
Capt W M D McKissack, 5th Infty, Jun 29, 1846, Assist Quartermaster. [Regimental commission [only] vacated.
Capt S H Drum, Assist Quartermaster, Aug 18, 1846, 4th Artl. [Staff commission [only] vacated.]
Deaths:
*Major W W Lear, 3rd Infty, at Monterey, Mexico, Oct 31, 1846.
**Brevet Major P N Barbour, Capt 3rd Infty, at Monterey, Mexico, Sep 21, 1846.

**Capt L N Morris, 3rd Infty, at Monterey, Mexico, Sep 21, 1846.
**Capt W G Williams, Toporaphical Engineers, at Monterey, Mexico, Sep 21, 1846
**Capt H McKavett, 8th Infty, at Monterey, Mexico, Sep 21, 1846.
**Capt G P Field, 3rd Infty, at Monterey, Mexico, Sep 21, 1846.
Brevet Capt Randolph Ridgely, 1st Lt 3rd Artl, & Assist Adj Gen, at Monterey, Mexico, Oct 27, 1746.
**1st Lt C Hoskins, Adj 4th Infty, at Monterey, Mexico, Sep 21, 1846.
*1st Lt R H Graham, 4th Infty, at Monterey, Mexico, Oct 12, 1846.
**1st Lt D S Irwin, Adj 3rd Infty, at Monterey, Mexico, Sep 21, 1846.
**Brevet 1st Lt J S Woods, 2nd Infty, at Monterey, Mexico, Sep 21, 1846.
**1st Lt J C Terrett, 1st Lt, at Monterey, Mexico, Sep 21, 1846
1st Lt Allen H Norton, 4th Infty, at sea, Nov 27, 1846.
**2nd Lt R Hazlitt, 3rd Infty, at Monterey, Mexico, Sep 21, 1846.
*2nd Lt R Dilworth, 1st Infty, at Monterey, Mexico, Sep 27, 1846.
Surgeon W L Wharton, at Port La Vaca, Texas, Oct 4, 1846.
Surgeon Lyman Foot, at Port La Vaca, Texas, Oct 4, 1846.
Casualties in the Staff authorized by the Act of Jun 18, 1846, for the "Volunteers called into the service of the U S."
Resignations:
Major Wm F Johnson, Commissary, Nov 11, 1846.
Capt Thos J Turpin, Assist Commissary, Nov 25, 1846.
Capt Thos H Wilkins, Assist Quartermaster, Sep 16, 1846.
Capt Wm Garrard, Assist Commissary, Nov 11, 1846.
Capt Jas M Campbell, Assist Commissary, Oct 26, 1846.
Surgeon Robt P Hunt, Oct 14, 1846.
Declined: Capt Wm Allen, Assist Quartermaster
Deaths:
Capt Robt Mitchell, Assist Quartermaster, at Matamoras, Mexico, Oct 7, 1846.
*Died of wounds received in the attack on Monterey, Sep 21, 1846.
**Killed in battle.
The ofcrs promoted & appointed will join their proper regts, companies, & stations without delay; those on detached service, or acting under special instructions, will report by letter to the commanding ofcrs of their respective regts & corps.
Acceptances or non-acceptances of appointments will be promptly reported to the Adj Gen of the Army; &, in case of acceptance, the birthplace of the person appointed will be stated. By order: R Jones, Adj Gen

SAT DEC 12, 1846
J R Woodruff, Piano Forte Manufacturer & Practical Tuner, has located in one of the Six Bldgs, where he is prepared to take orders. Musical instruments of every description repaired in the most perfect manner. Orders will be received at Beers' Temperance Hotel; the Furniture & Piano ware-room of Brown & Wilson, 7th st; the Conveyancing ofc of Mr Anthony Hyde, F st, next to Mr Pairo's; & at R H L Valland's, Gtwn, at his residence, or through the post ofc. Terms for tuning: $1.

Orphans Court of Wash Co, D C. Letters testamentary on personal estate of Edmund Coolidge, late of said county, dec'd. –W B Bowie, exc

Notice to Mariners: a beacon, 50 feet high, with a black ball on it, has been erected on **Sand Key**, where it will remain until a light shall be established there. It may be seen in ordinary weather 9 miles. An American ensign is hoisted at daylight every day on the flagstaff at the U S barracks, Key West, & may be seen in ordinary weather 10 miles. –S R Mallary, Col & Sup

Trustee's sale: by decree of PG Co Court, as a Court of Equity, the subscriber, as trustee, will offer at public sale, on the premises, Dec 21 next, the tract of land in PG Co, called **Retreat**, containing 550 acres, more or less, which the late John Pumphrey purchased of Wm Tolson. Improvements are a good dwlg-house, tobacco house, & all necessary out-houses. Persons wishing to purchase are referred to C C Magruder, the atty for the trustee, about the title to the land. –Wm P Pumphrey, Trustee

New Orleans Bulletin to the 28th: the steamer **Neptune** arrived at Tampico on Nov 22, with 450 regular troops, under command of Col Gates. The **Neptune** sailed from Tampico on the 24th, & encountering a heavy norther, was driven back & wrecked on the bar; all hands saved; the vessel a total loss.

The Alexandria Volunteers for the Mexican war were organized on Wed by the election of the following ofcrs of the company, viz:
Montgonery D Corse, Capt   Benj G Waters, 2nd Lt
Turner W Ashby, 1st Lt   Jas S Douglass, 3rd Lt

Mrd: on Dec 8, in St John's Church, Gtwn, by Rev A Shiras, Thos S Murray, of New Hope, Pa, to Gertrude Russel, d/o Steuben Butler, o/Wilkesbarre, Wyoming Valley, Pa.

Sale of Dec 12th, at the residence of Mr S M Jarboe, near the lumber yard of Mr Blagden, Navy Yard, the whole of his household & kitchen furniture. Also for sale, an excellent Iron Axle Cart, nearly new, a superior set of Cart Harness, & a valuable Draught & Saddle Horse. –Wm Marshall, auctioneer

Stalls in the Northern Market will be rented to the highest bidder on Dec 14: sundry Butcher's Stalls & Vegetable Stands. Terms cash. By order of the Mayor: W B Wilson, Clerk Market.

MON DEC 14, 1846
Official: Major Turnbull, of Wash City, Capt J E Johnston, Lt Scammon, Lt Derby, & Lt Hardcastle, all ofcrs of the Corps of Topographical Engineers, will leave Washington tomorrow for the army of the west. They will travel the nat'l road, descend the river, & expect to join Gen Scott at Brasos Santiago.

The Whigs of Monroe Co just elected that sterling Whig, John S Waters, to the Legislature, to fill the vacancy occasioned by the death of Capt Eller, who died on the Rio Grande.

Register's Ofc Wash, Dec 10, 1846. List of persons taking out licenses under the laws of the Wash Corp.

Adams, John G: Grocery
Aigler, Jacob: Confectioner
Allen, G F: Dry Goods
Adams, Geo W: Grocery
Adams, Wash: Retail
Allen, John: Dry Goods
Allen, W: Retail
Ailier & Thyson: Retail
Adams, Alex'r: Retail
Addison & Cockren: Retail
Barnes & Mitchell: Dry Goods
Barry, Francis: Hats, boots, shoes
Bulley, A F: Shop
Braddock, John: Slave hire
Bean, Geo: Retail
Buckley, T F: Confectioner
Beardsley, Jos: Confectioner
Bevan, Thos: Retail
Baily, B S: Retail
Barne, H: Confectioner
Brown, Jesse: Tavern
Byrne, Theresa: Retail
Brereton, Saml: Retail
Brereton, John: Retail
Brown & Hyatt: Dry goods
Brown & Hyatt: Boots & shoes
Barr, J R: Retail
Baden, J W: Hardware
Buchman, J H: Retail
Beall, R M: Retail
Bacon, S & Co: Retail
Benter, Wm: Tavern
Bury, Wm: Hats
Black, Barbara: Retail
Bayne, Thos: Boots & shoes
Berry, J W: Retail
Butler, Abraham: Tavern
Durns, G & Co: Boots & shoes
Brashears, W B: Retail

Bragdon & Bro: Dry goods
Borremans, Chas: Retail
Bayly, W F: Hardware
Baker, Thos: Tavern
Braxton, R T: Hack
Beasley, J: Hack
Burrell, John: Hack
Beasley, Jos: Hack
Bush, Jas, Hack
Butler, Jas: Hack
Bruce, Chas: Hack
Clitch, F: Hardware
Collins, Thos: Retail
Clarke, D B: Hardware
Campbell & Coyle: Hardware
Caton, John: Grocery
Contor, Peter: Shop
Coyle, Fitzhugh, Hardware
Coyle A & Son: Shoes & boots
Corcoran, H G: Retail
Clarvoe, J H: Shop
Capretz, Jer: Shop
Corson, Job: Tavern
Clarke, J B: Dry Goods
Copp, Moses: Ten pins
Copp, Moses: Shop
Coburn, W A: Dry goods
Cammack, C: Dry Goods
Cull, Jas: Boots & shoes
Casparis, Jas: Ten pins
Clavadetscher, L: Dry goods
Creutzfeldt, W: Shop
Costell, John: Retail
Combs, R M: Dry goods
Carter, Henry: Dry goods
Carter, R W & Co: Dry goods
Cannon, Danl: Retail
Comly, C A: Hardware
Clarke & Briscoe: Dry goods

Clagett, Darius: Dry goods
Casparis, Jas: Tavern
Croggan, Isaac: Retail
Callan, J F: Hardware
Clarke, R B: Boots & shoes
Combs, M R: Boots & shoes
Clements, Josiah: Tavern
Connor, John: Retail
Columbus, C: Confectionaer
Cole, Alvin: Stage
Chew, W: Hack
Clarke, Cornelius: Hack
Davy, Charlotte: Grocery
Davis, Richd: Dry goods
Daly, Jas: Retail
Dodds, Jos: Retail
Dodds, Jos: Boots & shoes
Dillow, W: Retail
Delany, Michl: Medicines
Duvall & Bro: Dry goods
Douglas, J: Shop
De Saules, P A: Tavern
Devery, Chas: Dry goods
Davis, Jas B: Retail
Dyer, R W: Auction
Donohoo, Jno A: Retail
Duvall, Saml: Retail
DeNeale, R: Retail
Dalton, Wm: Hack
Davis, Jas R: Hack
Egan, W & Son: Dry goods
Eddy, Stephen, Hardware
Erb, Wilhelm: Shop
Ellis, Henry: Retail
Eliot, Wallace: Hardware
Eberbach, J H: Tavern
Elliott, J W: Stage
Earle, Robt: Hack
Earle, Robt: Hack
Earle, Robt: Hack
Earle, Robt: Hack
Fugitt, F J: Retail
Fellar, Thos: Retail
Fearson, J C: Retail
Foy, John: Tavern

Finkman, Conrad: Tavern
Farnham, R: Hardware
Fowler, C S: Grocery
Fitman, Thos: Retail
Fletcher, Mont'y: Retail
Fisher, Geo A: Shop
Farrar, John M: Ten pins
Fitzgerald, J: Shop
Favier, A: Confectioner
Fleming, John: Hack
Fleming, John: Hack
Fisher, David: Hack
Goodin, H: Retail
Greason, Wm: Shop
Guion, H C: Dry goods
Galligan, J & Son: Dry goods
Groupe, Wm: Dry goods
Geffers, W J: Retail
Greenfield, H C: Retail
Green, Owen: Retail
Goddard, Isaac: Retail
Gilman, Z D: Medicines
Green, Amon: Retail
Gardner, J B: Medicine
Gautier, Chas: Confectioner
Golding, Sing: Hack
Givney, Bernard: Hack
Goldin, F: Hack
Henning, Stephen: Retail
Hitz, Flo: Retail
Hannon, H M: Tavern
Hall & Wilson: Dry goods
Hagerty, W: Retail
Humes, Geo: Retail
Hoffman, Henry: Shops
Hoover, A & Son: Boots & shoes
Haynes, Thos: Hardware
Hall, Edw: etail
Hall & Bro: Dry goods
Hepburn, H C: Retail
Hooe, P H & Co: Dry goods
Hertscamp, H: Shop
Hunt, Ethel: Dry goods
Hunt, Ethel: Boots & shoes
Hitz, Anna: Dry goods

Hall, John: Groceries
Hancock, Andrew: Tavern
Homans, Benj: Auctioneer
Homans, Benj: Retail
Hagerty, Danl: Retail
Harbaugh, Valent'e: Medicines
Hines, C & M: Grocery
Horning, John: Confectioner
Holmead, Anthony: Retail
Higgins, Mary: Slave
Hubbard, J: Retail
Hughes, Wm: Retail
Hines, David: Retail
Hendley, J R: Tavern
Haney, Hugh: Retail
Handy, Saml W: Retail
Harbaugh, L: Retail
Harvey, J S & Co: Retail
Hensley, Geo: Hack
Joyce, Michl: Retail
Johnson, T W & Co: Dry goods
Jackson, B L & Bro: Retail
Jarboe, Benedict: Retail
Johnson, J M: Dry goods
Joyce, J J: Retail
Jones, Chas S: Slave
James, C H: Medicines
Jones, Ann: Groceries
Iardella, J B: Medicines
Jones, Peter: Tavern
Jost, Benedict: Shop
Jasper, W T: Hack
Jamieson, E: Hack
Jeffers, w J: Hack
Johnson, Davy: Hack
Knott, Geo A: Confectioner
King, J T & Co: Dry goods
Kuhl, Henry: Tavern
Killman, J T: Retail
Kersey, Edw: Shop
Krofft, John M: Confectioner
King, P H: Tavern
Kelcher, Jas: Hack
Kingsbury, Thos: Hack
Kiger, Rachael: Hack

Kelcher, Jas: Hack
Leddy, O: Retail
Lindsley, Eleazer: Hardware
Lepreux, L & A: Retail
Lawrence, J: Hardware
Lord, Wm: Retail
Leiberman, C H: Medicines
Looby, Pat M: Shop
Lane & Tucker: Dry goods
Lucas, Benedict: Retail
Lusby & Duvall: Dry goods
Laskey, Lucy A: Shop
Long, Jas: Tavern
Lewis, John: Hack
Lewis, John: Hack
Looby, Terrence: Hack
Looby, Terrence: Hack
Moran, D: Grocery
M'Clery & Clements: Medicines
Millson, J: Retail
McGill, Thos: Retail
Moulder, J W: Retail
Miller, Jas: Grocery
Magruder, T J & Co: Hats & shoes
Magee, Eliz: Retail
Murray, Owen: Retail
McPherson, W S: Retail
Morrow, Wm: Retail
McPherson, H W: hardware
Morsell, B F: Retail
McCafferty, Wm: Confectioner
Murray, Sarah: Retail
Mattingly, F: Hats
Marshall, Wm: Retail
Marshall, Wm: Dry goods
Murray & Simms: Retail
Macoby, Jas: Retail
McQuinn, B: Shop
Morrison, W M: Hardware
Miller, John: Confectioner
Masi, F & Co: Hardware
Masi, Seraphim: Hardware
Morgan, Henry: Boots & shoes
McGarvey, P & Co: Tavern
Moran, Patrick: Tavern

Mills, R T: Retail
McKolgan, Jas: Retail
Magee, R F: Hack
Moran, Patrick: Hack
Mullin, Basil: Hack
Norris, A L: Retail
Norbeck, Geo: Confectioner
Ober & Ryan: Retail
Orme, F M: Retail
O'Leary, John: Retail
O'Donnell, John: Confectioner
O'Hare, C S: Retail
Parker, G & T: Retail
Pierce, John: Retail
Padgett, R G: Retail
Perry & Ashby: Dry Goods
Parsons, M L: Retail
Pumphrey, Saml: Retail
Peters, J A: Retail
Peetsch, E C: Shop
Patterson, R S: Medicines
Pursell, Thos: Grocery
Pancoast, W P: Grocery
Provost & Wallingsford: Billiards
Provost & Wallingsford: Shop
Pascoe, C: Boots & shoes
Queen, E F & Bro: Retail
Quigley, W: Shop
Ryan, Jno T: Retail
Ryley, W R: Dry goods
Randall, G A W: Retail
Randall, G A W: Hats, boots & shoes
Reed, B W: Retail
Ruff, Geo A: Groceries
Roemelle, J C: Retail
Rawlings, W A: Dry goods
Robey, L S: Tavern
Redfern, Saml: Retail
Rupert, Eve: Tavern
Rigden, Eliza: Retail
Ruff, J A: Boots & shoes
Ricketts, Aquilla: Grocery
Ready, John: Retail
Read, Jas: Retail
Shaw & Durr: Groceries

Sweeny, H M: Retail
Simms, Ann: Grocery
Sweeting, H W: Tavern
Simms, Elex: Retail
Stewart, Donald: Retail
Schwartz, A J: Hardware
Savage, Geo: Hardware
Savage, J L & Co: Hardware
Stock, F F: Retail
Simms, Monsieur: Slight of hand
Sutherlan, Isabel: Retail
Simpson, Presley: Grocery
Stevens & Emmons: Dry goods
Stevens & Emmons: Hats
Simms & Sons: Retail
Shadd, B H: Tavern
Sweeny, Mary: Retail
Stewart, Geo W: Retail
Stott, Saml: Retail
Sweeny, Edw: Shop
Stott, Chas: Medicines
Sterns, J: Magical delusions
Semmes, T F: Retail
Smith, Stewart: Retail
Scheckell, B O: Tavern
Skirving, Jas: Hardware
Stutz, F: Tavern
Samuels, W: Tavern
Smallwood, D: Hack
Stewart, Chas: Hack
Smith, Richd: Hack
Smallwood, Dennis: Hack
Smithson, John H: Hack
Thornley, Thos: Retail
Taylor, Franck: Hardware
Tucker & Son: Dry goods
Trimble, Matthew: Retail
Taylor, John H: Retail
Tench, S: Retail
Tench, S & Son: Retail
Terrett & Clarke: Dry goods
Todd, Wm B: Hats
Thompson, Jas: Retail
Talty, Michl: Shop
Thompson, R R: Tavern

Thompson, R R: Ten pins
Thomas, Wm: Tavern
Traverse, Elias: Retail
Turner, Thos: Hack
Turner, Henry: Hack
Visser, J: Dry goods
Venable, G A: Groceries
Voss, W: Hardware
Von Essen, Peter: Hack
Upperman, W H: Retail
Walsh, F S: Medicines
Wecatt, Susan: Dry goods
White, Fred'k: Retail
Wright, Henry: Retail
Weichman, J C: Boots & shoes
Wroe, Saml: Retail
Wilkins, John L: Retail
Ward, Michl: Shop
White & Bro: Dry goods
Wheeler, E: Hardware
White, N W: Retail
Williams, Z: Retail
Williams, Z: Boots & shoes
Woodward, Clem: Hardware
West, John: Tavern
Wall, S T: Dry goods
Wheatly, Geo: Retail
Wormley, Jas: Hack
Wannell, Chas: Grocery
Young, Wm: Retail
Young, A H: Retail
Yates, Wm H: Hack

Licenses:
Auctioneer: $100
Billiards: $100
Boots & shoes: $20
Confectionery: $10
Dry goods: $20
Grocery-$20
Hack: $10
Hardware: $20
Medicines: $20
Retail: $20
Slave: $2
Slight of hand: $2
Shop: $60
Stage: $10/$20
Tavern: $60
Ten pins: $40

City Ordinances-Wash: 1-Act for the relief of Jas Casparis: fine imposed for an alleged breach of an ordinance in relation to taverns, is remitted: Provided-Casparis pay the costs of prosecution.

For rent: new furnished & house in the western part of the city. Apply to Thos P Morgan, 7 Bldgs.

In the breast pocket of Mr Chas French, who perished in the wreck of the steamship **Atlantic**, was found the minature of his only brother, Benjamin. It was a beautiful painting executed in London. It was carefully wrapped in a linen handkerchief, marked with his whole name, & placed it in the breast pocket of his coat, thus showing that some of his last thoughts were upon his brother. This picture, with a penknife & a small key, were forwarded to Mr French's friends. Nothing yet has been heard of his watch, purse, or valise.

The appointment of Professor Henry to the Secretaryship of the Smithsonian Institution is hailed with the liveliest satisfaction.   U S Gaz

The Massachusetts Volunteers. Edw Webster's company of volunteers was to have been mustered into the U S service on Wed, but we learn that, in consequence of orders from Washington, nothing short of a regiment will be received into pay & service of Gov't from Massachusetts. Capt Webster's company is full, & now awaits the formation of the regiment. –Boston Journal

St Mary's County Court-Court of Equity, Dec Term, 1846. Saml B Anderson & others, vs Edw Spalding, adm of Andrew Greenwell, dec'd, & others, heirs of said dec'd. Bill in Equity filed for the sale of the real estate of Andrew Greenwell, dec'd. The bill states that said Andrew Greenwell died largely indebted to the cmplnts in this cause & to divers other persons; that his personal estate is insufficient to pay the same; that Andrew Greenwell, died intestate, leaving Eleanor Greenwell, a sister, Anastia, wife of Henry Greenwell, Eliz Greenwell, Eliz Joy, nieces, & Matilda Yates, wid/o John G Yates, dec'd, who was a nephew of dec'd, his heirs at law; that the said Andrew left real & person property of great value; that Edw Spalding became administrator of said personal estate, by whom it has been duly administered, & that said personal estate was insufficient to pay the debts of the Andrew, & prays for the sale of the real estate of said Andrew for the payment of his debts. The bill also states that Eliz Greenwell is a resident of D C: it therefore ordered that she appear in this Court on the first Mon of May next, either by atty or in proper person. –Peter W Crain -Wm T Maddox, Clerk St Mary's County Court

Balt: Dec 13. Mr Hiram Cranston, one of the proprietors of the Eutaw House in Balt City, was very dangerously if not fatally stabbed on Fri by a man named Patrick Dawson, a hack driver. Dawson, intoxicated, was refused liquor in the bar-room. Dawson became enraged, & when Mr Cranston assisted him to the door, Dawson drew a dirk-knife & plunged it into Mr Cranston's right breast.

Norfolk Herald: The loss of the steamship **Atlantic** in Long Island Sound has deprived us of Chas A Hassler, Surgeon U S Navy, who had just returned in impaired health from long & arduous service in the sloop-of-war **Falmouth**. His devoted attachment to his family can never be forgotten by any who knew him. May God of his great mercy protect the fatherless & the widow. –W

Mrd: on Nov 24, at *Belle View*, near Bryantown, Md, by Rev Mr Courtney, Mr John D Freeman, jr, to Miss Maria P Hotton, all of Chas Co.

For sale or rent: the Grocery Store on the corner of 12th st & N Y ave. –Michl Talty, 7th st

Woodland for sale: covered with oak, hickory, chestnut, pine & cedar wood, on the eastern side of the Eastern Branch of the Potomac, from twenty to three hundred acres. Inquire of D A Hall, at his ofc, adjoining Concert Hall, near Brown's Hotel.

TUE DEC 15, 1846
The Hon Francis Brengle died at Fred'k on Thu night last, in his 40th year.

Senate: 1-Ptn of Sarah E Graham, wid/o Lt John Graham, U S Navy, for a pension. 2-Ptn from Geo Taylor, for indemnification for French spoliations prior to 1800. 3-Ptn from Clara Williams, asking to be permitted to locate a military land warrant. 4-Ptn from S Calvert Ford, asking the payment of certain moneys received by a paymaster of the U S Army as trustee for him. 5-Ptn from Arnold Naudain, asking payment for suspended contract of certain floating lights. 6-Ptn from Seth Banister, asking commutation pay for the services of his father in the Revolution. 7-Ptn from Leslie Combs, asking the payment of a debt due him by the late Republic of Texas. 8-Ptn from Wm G Davis & his wife, asking compensation for property destroyed the the U S troops in the Seminole war. 9-Ptn from John Capo, asking indemnity for destruction of property by the U S troops in the war od 1812. 10-Ptn from A H Cole, a sutler in the army, asking payment of advances made to U S soldiers in Florida. 11-Ptn from Titian R Peele, asking indemnity for losses sustained by wreck of the U S ship **Peacock**, while engaged in the exploring expedition. 12-Ptn from J Knox Boyd, asking remuneration for his services in the recapture of the frig **Philadelphia** in 1804.

House of Reps: 1-Announcement of the death of Gen Felix Grundy McConnell, late a Rep from the State of Alabama. He died on Sep 10 last, in Wash City, in a moment of insanity, when he fell an unconscious victim to blows inflicted by his own hand. He was born in Nashville, Tenn, on Apr 5, 1809; removed with his father to Fayetteville, Tenn, in 1811, & there continued to reside until 1834, when he located in Talladega, Ala. The House tenders to the surviving widow & relatives the expression of sympathy on this afflicting bereavement. 2-Ptn of Patrick Smith, of Buffalo, N Y, for compensation for services to the U S. 3-Ptn from Stacey Lamphin, of Black Rock, N Y, for back pay as pensioner. 4-Ptn of Ira Baldwin, of Buffalo, for pay & bounty lands. 5-Ptn of Stephen York, of Clarence, N Y, for compensation for services to the U S. 6-Ptn of Abraham Forbes, of N Y, for bounty lands.

Valuable lands for sale in Loudoun Co & Fairfax Co: by authority of a decree, pronounced by the Circuit Superior Court of Law & Chancery for Fairfax Co, at its Nov term, 1846, in the suit of R H Cockerille et al against R H Cockerille's heirs et al: sale of 1,200 acres in Fairfax Co, the residence of the late R H Cockerille, about 4 miles s w from Dranesville. Said tract is now divided into 9 fields. One tract in Loudoun Co contains about 300 acres, near Gum Springs: is a good grass farm. Another tract, containing about 320 acres, now in the occupancy of W W Presgraves: has usual improvements. One other tract of about 140 acres, in the occupancy of Mr Ellmore. Another tract adjoining the lands of John J Coleman & others, contain about 146 acres. One other tract of 60 acres, adjoining the lands of R M Newman, all in timber. -H W Thomas, R H Cockerille, Com'rs

Teacher wanted : the Principal of the New Balt Academy, from an anxious wish for repose, after a service of some 20 years, having retired from the institution, the Trustees are desirous of supplying his place with a competent Teacher.
–Chas Hunton, Pres of Trustees of New Balt Academy.

$100 reward for runaway negro man John Campbell, about 26 or 27 years of age: absconded from the farm of Mr Jas F Neale, to whom he had been hired. He has a wife at Mr John Crismond's, near Allen's Fresh. –Francis Posey

WED DEC 16, 1846
Criminal Court-Wash: Trial of Jos Lafontaine-found guilty for robbing Mr Wm Wells of $100 while coming home from the races last Oct.

Wash Corp: 1-Cmte of Claims: asked to be discharged from the further consideration of the ptn of Ann Gadsby: agreed. 2-Cmte of Claims: bills for the relief of A Baumback; & the relief of C Columbus; & the relief of Richd Davis: passed. 3-Ptn of Eliz Moran, for remission of a fine: referred to the Cmte of Claims. 4-Ptn of Wm Cross, for remission of a fine: referred to the Cmte of Claims. 5-Cmte of Claims: ptn of John B Hilleary: passed. 6-Bill for the relief of Josias Goodrich: passed. 7-Ptn of Ann Luckett, for remission of a fine: referred to the Cmte of Claims.

Senate: 1-Additional documents presented in the claim of Jacob Houseman, for remuneration for spoliation by the Indians in Florida. 2-Ptn from Peter Grover, asking compensation for injuries received while in the service of the U S. 3-Ptn from A S Dearborn, wid/o Lt Col G Dearborn, of the U S Army, asking for a pension. 4-Ptn from Geo Hervey, asking the payment of a balance claimed to be due him. 5-Ptn from Anne B Cox, asking payment of an admitted balance due to the late Nathl Cox, former navy agent at New Orleans. 6-Ptn from Elisha L Keen, asking to be repaid a sum of money advanced by him on account of Gov't. 7-Ptn of Wm H Basset, asking the payment of money claimed to be due him as U S Marshal for the western district of Louisiana. 8-Ptn from Jose de la Francia, asking the payment of a judgment obtained in his favor from the U S. 9-Three several memorials from Maria S Johnson, excx of Chas Johnson; from Eliz & John Lestor, & from Marianne Champagne, of Florida, asking indemnification for spoliations prior to 1800. 10-Memorial from Cmder Jas McIntosh, asking payment for extra services. 11-Ptn from the legal reps of Thos Manning, asking indemnity for French spoliations prior to 1800. 12-Ptn from Jonas Bokes & others, asking payment for lost Treasury notes. 13-Ptn from Robt Diederick, asking to be paid the value of a package of dry goods lost by the ofcrs of the customs at N Y.

Miner K Kellogg, of Cincinnati, Ohio, a distinguished American artist is now a resident at Florence, for the purpose of studying the ancient masters & improving his skills. He has acquired the reputation of being one of the first painters of the age.

Wash Co, D C: I certify that Geo Steward, of said county, brought before me as a stray a gray gelding. -Nathl Brady, J P [The owner of the above horse is requested to call on me, near the Navy Yard market, prove property, pay charges, & take him away. --Geo Steward]

Balt, Dec 15: 1-The physicians now consider Mr Cranston, of the Eutaw house, out of immediate danger. 2-The remains of the late Major Ringgold, on arriving in this city, are to be placed in an appropriate cenotaph, to be erected in the rotundo of the Exchange, where they will remain, guarded by military, until the day of the final funeral procession, which will be probably in a week after the body reaches Balt.

House of Reps: 1-Ptn of A Baudouin & A D Robert, of New Orleans city, praying for remuneration for loss of a flat boat loaded with ice, caused by a collision with the steamer **Colonel Harvey**, a vessel belonging to the U S. 2-Ptn of Lawrence Garvey, of N Y C, for remuneration for injuries done to the light-house at Pass Manchae by a severe storm, during its erection & previous to its completion. 3-Ptns of Danl Wilson & Rosewell Bates, invalid soldiers of the last war, for a pension. 4-Ptn & other papers of John McIntosh, of Estell Co, Ky, praying for a pension as an invalid soldier in the service of the U S in 1813. 5-Ptn & other papers of John Fugatt, of Bath Co, Ky, praying for a pension as an invalid soldier in the service of the U S in 1813. 6-Ptn & other papers of Jesse W Jackson, of Lewis Co, Ky, praying for a pension as an invalid soldier in the service of the U S in 1813. 7-Ptn of Nathan M Lounsbury for arrears of pension. 8-Ptn & documents of Nicholas James, of York Co, Pa, a soldier of the Revolutionary war, asking a pension. 9-Ptn & documents of Michl Weidner, of York Co, Pa, a soldier of the Revolutionary war, asking a pension. 10-Ptn & documents of Mgt & Agnes Bigham, heirs at law of Thos Anman, praying the reimbursement of advancements made & payment for services rendered by him during the Revolutionary war. 11-Ptn & documents of Capt Jacob Lehman, of York, Pa, a soldier of the war of 1812, asking for arrears of pension. 12-Ptn & documents of Jacob Stone Ciphen, of Adams Co, Pa, asking for compensation for a mare lost by him whilst engaged in the service of his country in the last war. 13-Ptn of Ruth Freeman, wid/o Capt Thos Freeman, late of Butler Co, Ohio, praying for compensation for services rendered in the war of 1812, & for moneys advanced to the soldiers under his command. 14-Memorial of Mrs Susanna Prentiss, of Casenovia, N Y, wid/o Lt Manasseph Prentiss, who died in the service of the U S in the war of 1812, praying for a pension or such other relief as may be just. 15-Ptn of Wm Rotch, jr, of New Bedford, for himself & Wm Handy, the only surviving owners, 12 in number, of the whaling ship **Fox**, captured & condemned prior to 1800, asking remuneration for the unlawful capture & condemnation of said ship. 16-Ptn of Alex'r Wallace, of Pa, a Revolutionary soldier, praying for a pension. 17-Ptn of Capt Alex'r McEwen, of Pa, praying for a pension. 18-Ptn of the heirs of Jerusha Farrington, for a pension. 19-Ptn of Lt Wm E Starke, of the U S marine corps, praying for the allowance made to assistant quartermasters of the army for the performance of duties similar to those in the marine corps. 20-Ptn of Danl Buck, of Hartford, Conn, exc of Josiah Hempstead, dec'd, praying for indemnity for French spoliations.

Mrd: on Dec 13, by Rev Oliver Ege, Mr John A Wilson to Miss Adelaide Bury, all of Wash City.

Mrd: on Dec 13, in Wash City, by Rev G W Samson, Mr Evan Hughes to Mrs Lucinda Henning, both of Wash City.

Mrd: on Dec 15, at St Patrick's Church, by Rev Mr Parsons, Mr Wm Mark O'Brien to Miss Eliza Theresa McQuillian, all of Wash City.

Mrd: on Dec 8, at *Foust Hill*, near Fredericksburg, Va, by Rev Edw C McGuire, D D, Dr Geo Warren Thornton, of Kanawha Co, to Miss Margaret, d/o Geo Hamilton.

Died: on Oct 25, at Buffalo, N Y, Frances Charlotte Martin, w/o Lt J W Martin, 2nd Infty, U S Army, & d/o Capt G Truscott, R N, aged 22 years.

Died: on Oct 30, in the Island of Barbadoes, Mrs Ann Eliza O'Neal, w/o Col Thos Whitfoot O'Neal, & only d/o Col John Carter, of Gtwn, D C.

Died: on Dec 7, at his residence, Long Old Fields, PG Co, Md, Jos Dunlap, aged 82 years, formerly of King Geo Co, Va, but for the last 42 years a resident of PG Co, Md. He was a man of color, very favorably known as the keeper, for many years, of a public house known by the name of Dunlap's Tavern.

THU DEC 17, 1846
Senate: 1-Ptn from Susan E Gordon, asking compensation for property destroyed by the U S troops during the Creek war. 2-Ptn from Judith Whelton, asking a pension, for the services of her late husband, Jas Hilbard, in the U S naval service. 3-Ptn from Nathl Philips, for arrears of pension. 4-Ptn from Richd M Livingston, asking the commutation pay due his grandfather, Col Jas Livingston. 5-Additional documents relating to the claim of Sarah E Graham. 6-Ptn from Columbus Alexander & Theodore Barnard, asking indemnity for a violation of a contract by the U S for printing for the Navy Dept. 7-Ptn from Thos H Noble, asking compensation for charcoal furnished to the U S. 8-Ptn from Thos Talbot & others, asking to be indemnified for certain depredations committed by the Pawnee Indians. 9-Ptn from Wm Barcaly, asking to have his title to a tract of land confirmed by the Gov't. 10-Ptn from Lloyd Slemmer, asking to be allowed the pay of an acting master's mate during the time for which he perfomed that service. 11-Ptn from Richd G Dove, asking compensation for services as assistant messenger in the ofc of the 3rd Auditor. 12-Ptn from S D Dakin, for himself & others, asking that the Sec of Navy may be authorized to contract with them for dry docks at the several naval stations. 13-Ptn from the heirs of the late David Henshaw, asking indemnification for spoliations by the French prior to 1800. 14-Additional documents in favor of the claim of Andrew Moore. 15-Ptn from Henry Wright, in relation to injuries done the property of Wm Bunce by U S troops. 16-<u>Bills on leave</u>: bill granting a pension to John Clarke. Bill for the relief of Mary McRae,

wid/o Lt Col McRae, of the U S Army. Bill for the relief of Jos Wilson. Bill for the relief of Shadrach Gillet & others. Bill granting a pension to Jos Morrison. Joint resolution in favor of David Shaw & Solomon T Corser. 17-Reolution submitted: that the Sec of the Senate procure for the use of the Senate 10,000 copies of the topographical map of the road from Missouri to Oregon, compiled by Chas Preuss; the cost not to exceed $2,600.

House of Reps: 1-Ptn of Eben S Coffin for indemnification for French spoliations prior to 1800.

Latest from the Gulf Squadron: on the night of Nov 26, about midnight, the U S brig **Somers**, then lying at Green Island, about 4 miles from Vera Cruz, sent a boat with Lt Parker, Passed Midshipman Robt Clay Rogers-Passed Midshipmen J R Hynson, with 5 men, & burnt the Mexican brig **Creole**, lying moored to the Castle of St Juan. The following is a list of ofcrs of the U S brig Somers: Raphael Semmes, Lt Cmder; M G L Claiborne, 1st Lt; Jas L Parker, 2nd Lt; Jno H Wright, Passed Assist Surgeon; John F Steele, Purser; Henry A Clemson, Acting Master; Robt Clay Rogers, John R Hynson, Passed Midshipmen; Francis G Clarke, Midshipman. They also succeeded in capturing 7 prisoners-no one injured except Passed Midshipman Hynson, who was burnt by firing his pistol into some powder to set the brig on fire; he is doing well.

FRI DEC 18, 1846
J F Caldwell, Dental Surgeon, is now in Wash, at Mrs B W Bates', on Pa ave, between 17th & 18th sts, where he is ready to perform any operation in Dental Surgery.

Senate: 1-Ptn from the heirs of A L Duncan, asking indemnity for losses caused by the seizure of the ship **Iris** by the U S brig **Lawrence**. 2-Ordered that the memorial of the heirs & legal reps of Louis de la Housaye, on the files of the Senate, be referred to the Cmte on Private Land Claims. 3-The ptn of Caleb Greene, on the files of the Senate: be referred to the Cmte of Claims. 4-That the ptn of Clara H Pike, on the files of the Senate: be referred to the Cmte on Pensions. 5-That the ptn of Wm B Keene, on the files of the Senate: be referred to the Cmte on Private Land Claims. 6-Ptn from David Melville, administrator of Benj Fry, asking payment of claims for French spoliations prior to 1800, & expressing the hope that the honor of the U S may be preserved, & justice to the claimants no longer delayed. 7-Ptn from C S McKim, excx of Alex McKin, asking indemnity for French spoliations prior to 1800. Also, ptn from the heirs of Thos Rutter, to the same effect. 8-Bill for the relief of John R Williams: introduced.

The following troops sailed from N Y on Sat last for Point Isabel: 1st Lt J H Gore, 4th Infty, commanding; Dr J Simmons, U S A, Assist Surgeon; 1st Lt J G Burbank, 8th Infty, commanding 100 recruits 4th Infty; 1st Lt C D Jordon, 8th Infty, commanding 68 recruits 8th Infty; 2nd Lt E Hayes, 3rd Artl, commanding 68 recruits 5th Infty; 2nd Lt T F Castor, 2nd Dragoons, commanding 80 recruits 2nd Dragoons; 2nd Lt J N G Whistler, 7th Infty, commanding 100 recruits 7th Infty.

New Drug Store: corner of F & 9th sts: Wm C Greenleaf.

Orphans Court of Wash Co, D C. Letters of administration on the personal estate of Wm Digges, late of said county, dec'd. –Margaret O Digges, admx

House of Reps: 1-Bill for the settlement of the claim of John K Williams. 2-Election of a Chaplain: nominated: Rev Mr Sprole; Rev Mr Dewey; Rev Mr Taylor; Rev Mr Gurley; Rev Mr Tinsley; Rev Mr Morris; Rev Mr McIvor; Rev Mr Storrs. On the third time to vote the names of the following were remainingt:
Sprole-103 votes-elected   Storrs-3 votes
Dewey-48 votes   McIvor-1 vote
Tinsley-18 votes   Gurley-1 vote
3-Ptn of Richd A Clements, adm of J N Mullican, with additional evidence.
4-Memorial of Jas Bancker, a Revolutionary pensioner, for arrears of pension.
5-Ptn of John W Pore, of Franklin, Ala, asking relief for losses sustained by the removal of the Indians by the Gov't of the U S. 6-Memorial of John McClintock & 20 others, merchants of Portsmouth, N H, praying indemnity for French spoliations prior to 1800. 7-Ptn of Jos Cogswell, of Tamworth, N H, praying for a pension. 8-Memorial of Thos Allen, praying payment for printing the compendium of the 6th census of the U S for the use of Congress, under the act of Sep 1, 1841. 9-Memorial of Catharine Williamson, wid/o the late Capt John Williamson, of Phil, praying indemnity for injuries committed by France prior to 1800. 10-Ptn of Wm Hilton, of the State of Maine, for arrearages & increase of pension. 11-Ptn of the heirs of Col A Laughrey, for military bounty land. 12-Ptn & papers of Saml Reed, were taken from the files & referred to the Cmte on Private Land Claims. 13-Ptn & papers of Martha Hough, for arrears of pension with withdrawn from the files of the House.

Criminal Court-Wash. 1-Eliza Jackson, [colored,] acquitted of stealing $200 worth of clothes from Coleman's Hotel. 2-Jas Butler, [colored,] not guilty for setting fire to the stable of Allison Naylor. 3-Thos McLaughlin was acquitted of a charge of riot.
4-Lacy, the negro convicted of stealing Mr A Naylor's horse: sentenced to hard labor in the penitentiary for 3 years.

A tombstone, intended to be placed on the contiguous graves of Sir Walter Scott & Lady Scott, at Dryburg, has been cut at Aberdeen. It is a block of beautiful red granite, 7 feet long by 6½ feet broad, & weighs nearly 5 tons. The upper surface is cut in the form of the top of a double sarcophagus. The following is the simple inscription:
Sir Walter Scott, Baronet,
Died Sept., A D 1832
Dame Charlotte Margaret Carpenter,
wife of
Sir Walter Scott, of Abbottsford, Baronet,
Died at Abbottsford, May 15, A D 1826.

The Sisters of Charity, in charge of St Vincent's Orphan Asylum, desire to return their grateful thanks to Mrs Julia Keep, for her charitable donation of $25, at all times acceptable, but at this inclement season truly valuable to the institution.

Mrd: on Wed, in Wash City, by Rev Mr Robb, Levy D Slamm, of N Y, to Miss Jane Morsell, of Wash.

Mrd: on Dec 15, by Rev Henry Slicer, Mr Thos H Trent to Miss Jane F Sale, all of Va.

Died: on Dec 16, at *Montanverd*, Mrs Sally N Peter, aged 42 years, w/o Maj Geo Peter, of Montg Co, Md. Mrs Peter was amiable in all the relations of social life, fond & affectionate in the family circle, & most kind & hospitable to numerous relatives & friends, who all grieve at her premature death.

SAT DEC 19, 1846
House of Reps: 1-Bills from the Cmte of the Whole in Jul last, viz: Relief of
Roswell Hale
Joshua Shaw
Fred'k Hopkins
Josiah Haskell
Job Hawkins
Wm J Price
Chas G Ridgely
Dr Clark Lillybridge
Zachariah Simmons, of Tenn
Sgt Maj John Champe
John Speakman
Jacob L Vance
Legal reps of Thos Shields, dec'd.
Jos & Lindsay Ward, of Wisc Territory
Relief of W P S Sanger & Geo F De la Roche
Heirs of Gen Thos Sumter, late of S C, dec'd.
Heirs of John Whitsill, dec'd, late of Lafayette Co, Missouri
Relief of Wm B Stokes, surviving partner of John N C Stockton & Co
Bill for the relief of Jos Warren Newcomb, which at his request had been informally laid aside, owing to the absence of the member [Hon Danl P King] who had reported it, as he [Mr Ashmun] believed there would be not opposition to the bill. 2-Bill for the relief of Julius Eldred, Elisha Eldred, & Frencis E Eldred, for expenses & services in removing the copper rock from Lake Superior: passed.

Wm P McConnell, Resident Dentist, has practiced upwards of 20 years, 7 of which in Europe & 8 in Wash & in other cities. This information is given for the benefit of strangers. Ofc opposite Jackson Hall, Pa ave.

Notice: by an order of distrain & to me directed, I shal expose to public sale, on Dec 22, on the open space opposite the Centre Market, in Wash City, Sunday furniture & goods, seized & taken as the property of Wm Riccar, to satisfy rent due in arrears of B W Bell. –J F Wollard, Bailiff

A young man, Jas Still, of Buffalo, who attempted to jump on a car on the Buffalo & Niagara Falls railroad on Tue last, fell & received such serious injury as to cause his death the following Friday.

Mrd: on Dec 9, at Ashton Hall, by Rev Mr Dole, Chas T Butler to Virginia, y/d/o the late Thos Van Swearingen, all of Jefferson Co, Va.

Mrd: on Nov 26, at Millbrook, Buckingham, by Rev Wm C Meredith, Hon Edmund W Hubard to Miss Sarah A Eppes, d/o Mrs Martha B Eppes & the late John W Eppes, former Senator in Congress from Va.

Died: on Dec 13, in Wash City, in his 19th year, Allen Harwood Crabb, eldest s/o Capt H N Crabb. His funeral is at the residence of his parents on M st, between 4th & 5th, tomorrow, at 2 o'clock.

The subscriber has been appointed by the Orphans' Court of York Co, Auditor to make & report to said Court a distribution of the estate of Geo Willet, late of Manheim township, York Co, Pa, dec'd, in the hands of John Nunemacher, exc of said decedent, among the heirs & legal reps of said dec'd, & will attend for that purpose at his ofc, in the borough of York, in York Co, on Jan 9 next, when & where all persons interested may attend, if they think proper, & they will be heard. –Jacob Glessner, Auditor

MON DEC 21, 1846
Criminal Court-Wash: 1-David W Dixon, a free mulatto, was found guilty in 7 cases of larceny & one of petit larceny: identified as the property of John T Sullivan, Jonathan T Walker, W C Eckloff, W H Prentiss, & others.

City Ordinances-Wash: 1-Act for the relief of Josiah Goodrich: he is hereby released from a judgment rendered against him as security for Geo McCauley, provided Goodrich pay the costs of prosecution. 2-Act for the relief of C Columbus: fine imposed is remitted: provided he pay the costs of prosecution. 3-Act for the relief of A Baumback: fine imposed for an alleged violation of an ordnance in relation to the licensing of carts, is remitted, together with the costs of prosecution.

Judge Martin [so long] the Chief Judge of the Supreme Court of Louisiana died in New Orleans on Dec 10, aged 84 years.

Norwich [Conn] Courier: Elijah Hubbard, for 20 years Pres of the Middleton Bank, died suddenly, from apoplexy. [No date-current item.]

Boston Advertiser: U S Circuit Court: Chas Goodyear vs Ebenezer Seaver et al. In this action, involving the validity of certain India Rubber Patents, of great value, verdict was taken yesterday for the plntf.

$50 reward for pocket-book lost, containing $330: lost in the streets of Wash City, on Dec 18. The money was all in Virginia, chiefly Richmond $20 bank notes. Reward if returned to Harry Sweeting's Virginia House, or to this ofc, or to R R Wilson, Paris, Fauquier Co, Va.

Mrd: on Nov 14, at St John's Church, in Wash City, by Rev Smith Pyne, Mr Wm F Pettet to Mrs Frances A Robinson, both of Louisville, Ky.

Died: on Sep 7 last, at Goshen, Orange Co, N Y, the Hon Jeromus Johnson, formerly a Rep in Congress from N Y C.

Senate: 1-Bill for the relief of Alvin C Goell: laid on the table. 2-Ptn of John Moore White, of N J, heir of Maj John White, asking compensation for the Revolutionary services of his father. 3-Ptn of Thos Macy & others, of Nantucket, asking remuneration for French spoliations prior to the year 1800. 4-Ptn of Mrs Sarah Davis, asking pay for services of her dec'd husband, Wm Davis, as assist topographical engineer in 1814. 5-Ptn of Jas H Overstreet & Geo B Didlake, asking relief from their suretyship for B J Harrison. 6-Memorial of Wm A Ridgely, for the estate of John Dumeste, dec'd, for indemnity for French spoliations prior to 1800. 7-Ptn of Mrs Flora Boyd, of Monroe Co, Va, [who is the widow of Jas Boyd, dec'd, a Revolutionary soldier,] praying for a pension. 8-Ptn of Mrs Ann Royall, [the widow of Wm Royall, dec'd.] 9-Ptn Thos Atwater, of New Haven, Conn, exc & heir of Elnathan Atwater, dec'd, praying for indemnity for spoliations committed by France previous to 1801. Also, the ptn of Jacob Seber, of Middletown, Conn, for the same purpose. 10-Ptn of Eliza Stevens, wid/o Cmdor Holdup Stevens, praying an extension to her of the navy pension laws. 11-Ptn of Saml Gray, for a pension. 12-Mr Harper asked to withdraw the ptn & papers of Eliz Clopper from the file of the House of Reps:, & that they be referred to the Cmte on Revolutionary Claims. 13-Ptn of Charlotte Dorr, wid/o Andrew C Dorr, of Boston, praying for the passage of a bill of indemnity for French spoliations prior to 1800. 14-Ptn of Harriet Carter, wid/o the late Nathl Carter, of West Newton, Mass, praying a continuance of her pension. 15-Ptn of Stephen Tilton, of Boston, for a bill of indemnity for French spoliations prior to 1800. 16-Motion of Mr Hungerfood, the papers of the heirs of Adino Goodenough, on the file of the House, were referred to the Cmte on Private Land Claims. 17-Ptn of Ruliff Van Brunt, heretofore presented Dec 23, 1844. 18-Ptn of Geo Newton, heretofore presented Feb 5, 1840. 19-Ptn of the Vestry of Washington Parish for an extension of the <u>Congressional Burying Ground</u>.

Jas T Buckingham, [of the Boston "Courier,"] we regret to see it stated in the Boston papers, has met with a sad loss in the decease of his wife, who died at Cambridge, the place of his residence, on Tue. She was a highly estimable lady, much beloved & respected by all who knew her.

Rockville Academy is located in Rockville, Montg Co, Md, 15 miles from Wash, in one of the most healthy protions of the State. –O C Wright, Principal

Appointments by the Pres, by & with the advice & consent of the Senate. 1-Thos J Mulhollan, Receiver of Public Moneys at Champagnole, Ark, vice Albert G Rust, resigned. 2-Peter G Kemp, Receiver of public moneys at Greensburg, La, vice G W Womack, resigned. 3-Henry Niel, Register of the land ofc at Batesville, Ark, vice John Miller, appointed in the recess of the Senate in the place of Robt C Newland, dec'd. 4-Wm G Flood, Register of the land ofc at Quincy, Ill, from Jan 8 next, when his present commission will expire.

TUE DEC 22, 1846

Wm B George, formerly of Greene Co, Alabama, if yet alive, will confer a favor upon his brother, Jas G George, & will also learn matters of importance to himself, by making known his present residence, & if any other person has any information concerning him, they will confer a favor upon me by addressing a letter, to Hopewell, Greene Co, Ala. When last hear from he was in Pittsburg, Ark. –Jas G George

Teacher wanted in the 2nd election district of Kent Co, Md. Apply to the Trustees of primary school #3: Thos C Kennard, Danl Jones, & Benj Howard.

Senate: 1-Ptn from Margaret Casmick, wid/o Maj Caxmick, late of the marine corps, asking a pension. 2-Papers relating to the claim of Maria J Nourse: referred to the Cmte of Claims. 3-Ptn from Jas Riley, asking the pay due his father for services in the Revolutionary war. 4-Ptn from the heirs of Wm Frost, dec'd, asking commutation pay. 5-Ptn from Monmouth B Hart & others, securities of Purser Benj F Hart, asking for relief. 6-Ptn from the heirs of Jos Wilson, asking some equitable adjustment of his claims for services in the Revolutionary war. 7-Ptn from Peter Von Schmidt, asking to be paid for his model of a dry dock. 8-Ptn from the heirs of Jas Stagg, of Pa, asking payment for his services in the Revolutionary war. 9-Ptn from Wm Sanders & W R Porter, asking to be released from a judgment obtained against them by the U S as sureties of Wm Eustis. 10-Bill for the relief of the heirs of John Paul Jones: introduced on leave. 11-Cmte on the Library: bill for the relief of Eliz Hamilton, wid/o Alexander Hamilton.

Chewar Gaz: Col Jas Gadsden, Pres of the S C Railroad Co, has been appointed Brig Gen by the Pres of the U S, to take command of the Regts of Volunteers from the States of Va, N C, & S C.

WED DEC 23, 1846

Criminal Court-Wash: 1-J N Fearson, of Gtwn, found guilty in 2 cases of assault & battery: one for assaulting with intent to kill Geo H Holtzman, proprietor of the Union Hotel; one for an assault upon a negro, Rob Fletcher. 2-Jos Goodyear, one of the Auxiliary Guard, was found guilty of aggravated assault & battery upon John L Crown & Thos Hillery.

The ofcrs of the 2nd Regt of U S volunteers of N Y have elected Maj Patrick Calhoun, of the Army, Colonel of the Regt, in place of Chas Baxter, resigned.

The Van Ness Case: the testimony in this trial has occupied that Court for nearly 5 weeks, & was closed on Mon, after the examination of the following witnesses: Josiah Dixon, Richd Smith, Wm Easby, of Wash City, also of Alderman Brazier & Dr Jos Leon, of Phil. Mr Bradley moved the Court to instruct the jury that, "Even if the jury shall believe all the evidence on the part of the petitioner to be true, still there is no evidence from which they can lawfully infer that a marriage every took place between the said petitioner & John P Van Ness."

The Field Ofcrs of the 1st Pennsylvania Regt of volunteers were elected on Fri last, & are as follows: F M Wyncoop, Col; S W Black, Lt Col; F S Bowman, Major.

Senate: 1-Ptn from the heirs of Henry Stouffer, asking indemnity for French spoliations prior to 1800. 2-Ptn from Mary Dashiell, wid/o Henry Dashiell, late of Balt, to the same effect. 3-Ptn from Jas W Simmons, in behalf of his wife, heir of the late Wm Broadfoot, merchant, of Charleston, S C, for indemnity for French spoliations prior to 1800. 4-Ptn from Geo Roush, asking for a pension for Revolutionary services. 5-Ptn from Thos J Randolph, asking Congress to purchase the papers of Thos Jefferson. 6-Ptn from Thos Douglass, late district atty in East Florida, asking compensation for certain extra legal services in defending suits instituted against the U S. 7-Ptn from Gen John McNeil, an ofcr in the last war with Great Britain, asking a pension. 8-Letter from Capt Mordecai, at the U S arsenal, to Col Benton, in favor of soldiers enlisted in the ordnance dept. 9-<u>Bills introduced on leave</u>: relief of Thos Brownell; relief of John Stockton, late a lt in the U S Army; & relief of the heirs of Jas Ramsey. 10-Cmte on Military Affairs: bill for the relief of Mary McRae, wid/o Lt Col McRae, without amendment. 11-Cmte on Foreign Relations: bill for the relief of Joshua Dodge.

House of Reps: 1-Ptn of John Spear Smith, rep of the late Gen Saml Smith, of the city of Balt, asking indemnity for French spoliations prior to 1800. 2-Memorial of Benj Loomis, for an invalid pension. 3-Memorial of John Sample for claims for services in the last war. 3-Ptn of A A Lincoln & many other founders of metal, for a provision to protect their patterns. 4-Ptn of Elisha Denison, adm of Felix Carpenter Ellis, for a law to authorize the payment of the pension of said Ellis due in his lifetime. 5-Refer from the files of the Clerk the ptn & papers of Ira Bladwin. 6-Memorial of Jas W Simmons, of Houston, Texas, in behalf of B Louisa Simmons, his wife, heir of the late Wm Broadfoot, merchant of Charleston, S C, asking indemnity for French spoliations prior to 1800. 7-Ptn of Chas Shepard & others, in favor of granting interest or commutation pay to Maj Moses Van Cowper. 8-Ptn of John R Townsend & C Bolton & others, asking indemnity for French spoliations prior to 1800. 9-Ptn of Alex D Peck, for confirmation of a tract of land in the parish of Morehouse, La. 10-Ptn of Fielding Pratt, praying a pension on account of injuries received in the service of the U S during the late war with Great Britain. 11-Ptn of Mott Wilkinson, for an increase of pension. 12-Ptn of Sally Gregory, for a pension. 13-Ptn of Eliz H Thatcher, of Saco, Maine, asking indemnity for French spoliations prior to 1800. 14-Ptn of Nathl Gilbert, exc of the estate of Geo Gilbert, praying compensation for losses sustained by French spoliations prior to 1800. 15-Ptn of John Dunham, an heir of the estate of Danl Dunham, & Patrick Fanning, an heir to the estate of John Thornton, praying compensation for losses sustained by the French spoliations prior to 1800. 16-Ptn of R T J Wilson, asking indemnity for French spoliations prior to 1800. 17-Ptn of N Whittles, asking indemnity for French spoliations prior to 1800. 18-Ptn of the heirs of Lt Apollos Cooper, an ofcr of the Revolution. 19-Ptn of the heirs of Lt John Wallace, dec'd, asking commutation pay for Revolutionary services. 20-Memorial of Mrs Nancy Denow, for military bounty land, on account of the services of Francis Popham, in the war of the Revolution. 21-Ptn of the administrator of the estate of Geo Brent, dec'd, praying for commutation pay & pension due said estate. 22-Ptn of Chester Parrish, for arrears of pension. 23-Memorial & documents of John R Edie & sister, sole reps of Lt John Edie, an ofcr of the war of the Revolution, for the one year's pay & interest under the resolution of Congress of Nov 24, 1778. Also, the memorial & documents of the heirs of Capt Barnet Eichelberger, of Col Hartley's Regt, for arrearages of pay & interest due under resolution of Congress of Nov 24, 1778, & also for bounty land. 24-Papers of Uriah Brown, relating to his invention of a fire-ship. 25-Ptn & papers of Lucy O'Bryon.

Balt, Dec 21. The mortal remains of the late gallant Maj Ringgold repose, under a military guard of honor in the rotundo of the Exchange. The large hall has been thronged with visiters. There sleeps the dead warrior, shrouded in sable, beneath the hallowed folds of his country's flag. Around the cenotaph are various military trappings worn by the dec'd in the conflict where his bright career ended: his uniform, sword, & the saddle on which he sat when the fatal cannon-ball struck down both horse & rider. It is terribly shattered, & in many places exhibits stains of blood. There, too, may be seen the faithful teamster, Kelley, who was wounded while fighting in the same battle with his cmder. He has but one arm. This brave soldier, though humble, proves a vigilant sentinel. He watches by the coffin like one who has lost a friend, & entertains visitors by rehearsing incidents of the war. Balt, Dec 22: the great & imposing funeral of the late Maj Ringgold is now over. The procession was formed on Broadway, Fell's Point, & took up the line of march about 12 o'clock, presenting the finest military display seen in our city for years. A Horse fully equipped with the equipments of the dec'd, was led by Kelly. Relatives of dec'd, in carriages. The military followed: religious ceremonies at the grave performed by Rev Drs Wyatt, Johns, & Roberts.

The following companies were in attendance:
Laurel Troop, Col Capron, PG Co
Fred'k Hussars, Capt Edw Schley
Howard Light Horse, Col Carroll
Ringgold Dragoons, from Rocky Springs, near Fred'k
Hagerstown Horse Guards, Capt Clarke
Potomac Dragoons, Maj Harris, Sharpsburg
Co A Delaware Dragoons, Maj Andrews
Light Guards, Wilmington, Delaware, Lt Derrie
Harford Light Dragoons, Harford Co

The Laurel Riflemen, from PG Co
The Cecil Grays, & deputations from the Nat'l Grays & 2nd company of State Fencibles, of Phil

Mrd: on Dec 19, in Christ Church, by Rev Mr Bean, John P Ingle to Mildred H Baker, d/o the late Philip Baker, all of Wash City.

Mrd: on Nov 26, near Jackson, Mississippi, by Rev Mr Montgomery, David Fisher to Margaret, eldest d/o Wm Gahan, formerly of Wash City.

Mrd: on Aug 2 last, at the British Embassy, Paris, by the late Bishop Luscombe, Dr Lardner to Mary, only d/o Col Spicer, late of the 12th Lancers, the marriage having been previously solemnized in the U S.

Wash Corp: 1-Bill for the relief of John Roby: passed. 2-Special license to M Kilmiste: passed. 3-Relief of John C Rogers: passed. 4-Ptn from P A DeSaules, for remission of a fine: referred to the Cmte of Claims. 5-Act for the relief of Thos Dumphrey: passed. 6-Ptn of W H Parker, for remission of a fine: referred to the Cmte of Claims. 7-Bill for the relief of Jacob Wachter: passed. 8-Bill for the relief of Eliz Moran: passed. 9-Cmte of Claims: asked to be discharged from the further consideration of the ptn of P Moran.

Appointments by the Pres:
Quartermaster's Dept:
Hugh O'Donnell, of Ohio, to be assist quartermaster, with the rank of Capt, Oct 7, 1846, to fill a vacancy
Geo V Hebb, of Tenn, to be assist quartermaster, with the rank of Capt, Oct 13, 1846, to fill a vacancy
Ralph G Norvell, of Indiana, to be assist quartermaster, with the rank of Capt, Dec 2, 1846, to fill a vacancy
Geo M Lanman, of Pa, to be assist quartermaster, with the rank of Capt
Commissary's Dept:
Fred'k A Churchill, of Ohio, to be commissary, with the rank of Major, Nov 24, 1846, to fill a vacancy
McDonough J Bunch, of Tenn, to be assist commissary, with the rank of Capt, Aug 18, 1846, to fill a vacancy
Geo T Howard, of Texas, to be assist commissary, with the rank of Capt, Aug 27, 1846, to fill a vacancy
Francis M Dimond, of R I, to be assist commissary, with the rank of Capt, Oct 26, 1846, to fill a vacancy
Isaac R Diller, of Pa, to be assist commissary, with the rank of Capt.
Medical Dept:
Alex'r Perry, of N Y, to be surgeon, Aug 21, 1846
David McKnight, of Tenn, to be surgeon, Sep 10, 1846
Wm B Washington, of Tenn, to be surgeon, Oct 29, 1846, to fill a vacancy

John C Reynolds, of Pa, to be surgeon
Geo B Sanderson, of Missouri, to be assist surgeon, Aug 20, 1846
Wm C Parker, of N Y, to be assist surgeon, Sep 2, 1846, to fill a vacancy
Enoch P Hale, of Tenn, to be assist surgeon, Sep 10, 1846
Thos C Bunting, of Pa, to be assist surgeon

THU DEC 24, 1846
Senate: 1-Bill for the relief of Fernando Fellanny: introduced on leave. 2-Cmte on Private Land Claims: bill for the relief of the legal reps of John Rice Jones. Also, bill for the relief of Wm B Keene. 3-Cmte on Revolutionary Claims: bill for the relief of the heirs of Crocker Sampson, dec'd. 4-Cmte on the Judiciary: bill for the relief of Richd C Coxe. Also, bill for the relief of Thos Douglass, late U S atty for East Florida. 5-Cmte on Public Lands: House bill for the relief of Julius Eldred & other, without amendment.

We are glad to announce the return to Wash City, from a visit to Europe, to his family & his mission in this city, of Baron Gerolt, Minister Resident of Prussia to the U S.

Mr McClean, of Pa, has been called away from Wash City for a few days by the unwelcome intelligence of the death of his father, Judge McClean, of Harrisburg.

Boarding: handsome suit of rooms, adjoining, all fronting the street, can now be had at the St Charles Hotel. –C H MacLellan

The subscriber has resumed the practice of the law in Boston, Mass. Ofc #4, State st. –Francis Brinley

Classical instruction: the subscriber, an Italian, of liberal education, proposes to open a School in Wash City on Jan 1st next. He is competent to give instruction in the Latin, French, Italian, & Greek languages, as well as in mathematics, philosophy, & rhetoric. Address "Classical Teacher," care of Rev Mr Alig, at St Mary's Church, 5th st. –Americus Zapponi

Our paper on Sat contained a notice of the death of Robt Thom, the British Consul at Ningpo, in China. A gentleman of this city, who has recently returned from China, & one who knew him well, informs us that he was considered one of the best Chinese scholars in the country. He had been for a long time a resident of China. During the Chinese war he was the principal interpreter to Sir Henry Pottinger.
–N Y Courier & Enquirer

FRI DEC 25, 1846
Mammoth Christmas Plum Cake: weighing 600 pounds, may be seen at the confectionary store of subscriber Dec 24. After the exhibition, it will be cut up in quantities to suit purchasers. –Geo Krafft, 18th st & Pa ave, First Ward, Wash.

Public sale of land: by virtue of a decree of the Circuit Superior Court of Loudoun Co, Va, pronounced at the Oct term, 1846, in the case of Dawson vs Dawson: sale at public auction, on Feb 8, 1847, in Leesburg, the following tracts & lots of land: *The Iron Ore Lot*, containing 60 acres, in Loudoun Co, near the Point of Rocks. The *Mountain Lot of Woodland*: originally a part of the land of Saml Clapham, dec'd, described as *Wood Lot, #6*: about 15¼ acs. The parcel called *Peach Island*, containing about 10 acres, in the Potomac river, nearly opposite the Point of Rocks. The undivided interest of the late Saml Dawson in the *Razor Tract*, being seven-elevenths thereof: the whole tract contains about 186 acres, adjoins the lands of B Shreve & Gunnell Saunders. The bldgs are inferior. –Chas Gassaway, Com'r

The continental papers announce the death of the celebrated Swedish poet Dr Esaias Tegner, Bishop of Wexio. [Late Foreign correspondence. –No date.]

Appointments by the Pres:
Geo Bancroft, of Mass, to be envoy extraordinary & minister plenipotentiary of the U S at the court of the United Kingdom of Great Britain & Ireland, vice Louis McLane, at his own request recalled.
John R Brodhead, of N Y, to be sec of the legation of the U S near his Britannic Majesty, vice Jas McHenry Boyd, resigned.
Nathan Clifford, of Maine, to be Atty Gen of the U S, vice John Y Mason, resigned.
Lambert Reardon, to be deputy postmaster at Little Rock, Arkansas, vice Wm E Woodruff, resigned.

Field ofcrs of the Virginia Regt: Beverley Randolph, of Warren, Lt Col
John F Hamtramck, of Jeff Co, Col   Jubal A Earley, of Franklin, Major
These gentlemen, we believe, are graduates of West Point. –Richmond Whig

Com'rs sale: by virtue & in pursuance of a decree of the Circuit Court of Wash Co, D C, as a Court of Chancery, in the matter of the heirs of Geo Semmes, late of said county, dec'd, the undersigned Com'rs will offer at public sale, on Jan 19, 1847, on the premises where the dec'd resided, nearly opposite the Wash Navy Yard, part of a tract of land called *St Elizabeth*, containing about 127 acres, with improvements; & immediately thereafter 5 acres of land called *Blue Plains*, with the improvements thereon, [know as the former residence of the late Capt John B Kirby.] –Zachariah Walker, Benj P Smith, David Barry, Jas C Barry, & Thos Jenkins, Com'rs

Senate: 1-Ptn from Cornelius P Van Ness, asking for his share of the goods seized by him while collector of customs for the district of Vermont, & forfeited for illegal importation. 2-Ptn from Josiah Colston, asking that his accounts as late purser may be opened & certain allowances made him. 3-Ptn from Naomi Davis, wid/o Gen Danl Davis, asking for a pension. 4-Joint resolution explanatory of the act for the relief of Mary Ann Linton: bill introduced on leave. 5-Cmte on Pensions: bills granting a pension to Jos Morrison; & granting a pension to John Clark. Bill for the relief of

Hugh W Dobbin, an ofcr in the last war. 6-Cmte on Post Ofcs & Post Roads: joint resolution for the relief of David Shaw & Solomon Corson.

Notice is given that the partnership between Jas B Bragdon & Wm H Bragdon, under the name of Bragdon & Brother, has been this day dissolved by mutual consent.
–J B Bragdon, W H Bragdon

House of Reps: 1-Ptn from Saml M Asbury. 2-Memorial of Geo Eckert, adm of John Eckert, jr, dec'd, of Pa, asking indemnity for French spoliations prior to 1800. 3-Ptn & papers of Matthew Guy, of Clark Co, Ky, were withdrawn from the files, & referred to the Cmte of Claims. 4-Ptn of J L Hedge, adm on the estate of B Hedge, asking indemnity for French spoliations prior to 1800. 5-Ptn & documents of Jos Taylor, of Pa, asking invalid pension as a soldier in the late war. Ptn & documents of Peter Myers, for the like purpose. 7-Ptn of Jos Parrot, of Ohio, praying for a re-issue of land scrip. 8-Ptn of the exc of Col Philip Van Courtlandt, for commutation. 9-Ptn & papers of Elzakin Ruckin, of Carter Co, Ky, were withdrawn from the files, & referred to the Cmte on Invalid Pensions. 10-Ptn & other documents of Jas Fugatt, of Bath Co, Ky, were withdrawn from the files, & referred to the Cmte on Invalid Pensions. 11-Ptn of Benj Allen, sr, of Clark Co, Ky, praying for a pension. 12-Ptn in favor of increasing the pension of Sutherland Mayfield. 13-Memorial & ptn of Wm L Clarke & others, praying indemnity for French spoliations. 14-Ptn & papers of Thos Copeland, praying payment for services rendered to the Gov't. 15-Ptn of Hannah Stevenson, wid/o Fred'k P Stevenson, an ofcr of the Revolution, for a pension.

Criminal Court-Wash: 1-The U S vs Huddleston: 3 indictments, in which the dfndnt was charged with shooting 3 boys who had entered his wagon for the purpose of stealing peaches & other fruits waiting for the market in the First Ward. It appears that the dfndnt, a respectable farmer of Montg, Md, having repeatedly warned the boys, shot at them for the purpose of making tham an example, as he had been frequently robbed. The boys were not dangerously wounded. The Jury returned a verdict of not guilty in each case. 2-The Court sentenced David W Dixon, free mulatto, who was found guilty of grand larceny in 7 cases, & of petit larceny in one case: to be imprisoned 3 years for stealing valuable stationery from Mr J T Sullivan, & one year for each of the other cases. Dixon was also sentenced in the petit larceny case for a short term of imprisonment in the county jail. 3-J De Lafontaine, convicted of robbing Mr Wells, of PG Co, Md, was sentenced to 3 years imprisonment in the Penitentiary.

Died: on Dec 20, at Annapolis, Md, after a protracted illness of 7 months, Miss Eliz Maria, 4th d/o Mr Saml Peaco, of that city.

MON DEC 28, 1846
Private sale, 2 lots, 13 & 16, in square 163, adjoining Messrs Webster & Corcoran's residences. For terms apply to B Forrest, through the Gtwn Post Ofc.

Silvester Ball, at German Hall: The German Benevolent Society will give their 2nd Ball, on Dec 31, 1846, for the benefit of the Society. Tickets at $1.59, admitting a gentleman & 2 ladies, may be obtained of the following Managers, of G Lohs, Gtwn, Wm Voss, & at the door. Cmte of Arrangements:

Geo Willner	Peter Emmerich	J G Hempler
Peter Freeman	Peter Krafft	Ferdinand Schlegel
F Hausam	H Kaiser	J Keese

The only French Corsets in Wash: store on 10th st, one door from Pa ave. Subscriber has a supply of slate-colored linen drilling & satin jean, double, long, & short, at the low price of from $1 to $2 per pair. Skirt bodies & hair tourneurs: .57; gentlemen's money belts: $1.25; Spanish riding belts: $2, a fine article for health. –Madame A D Clermon

City Ordnances-Wash: 1-Act to grant a special license to Matthew Kilmiste for theatrical & other performances at the Odeon Hall, for the sum of $9 a week, payable in advance, to commence from Nov 30, 1846. 2-Act for the relief of John Roby: sum of $10.25 be paid to him for sundry repairs alleged to have been done by him to several of the bridges across the canal during 1845. 3-Act for the relief of John C Rogers: to pay the balance due to him for grading 22nd st, & for making a wooden trunk across 22nd st west: the sum of $273.67.

Spanish language taught: J F Mullowny will give private lessons. Inquire at Mrs Turpin's boarding house, corner of 7th st & Pa ave.

For rent: comfortable house, with back bldg: on 6th st, in sight of Coleman's Hotel. Apply to Dr B Washington, nearly opposite.

Gen Erastus Root, the veteran politician, died on Thu last, in N Y, having reached that city from his residence at Delhi, N Y, on his way to visit his dght, Mrs Hobbie, & his grandchildren at Wash City. He was 74 years old. He first came to Congress as a Member of the House of Reps in 1803, served 2 years, & again in 1809; elected to 3 subsequent Congresses. He was born in Hebron, Conn, in 1772: graduated at Dartmouth College, N H. He was a remarkable man, tall & stout, with great physical power & energy, a ready & effective debater, well-informed, & confident in his own opinions.

Wash Co, D C: I hereby certify that Zebulon Brundige, of said county, brought before me as strays, trespassing upon his enclosure, one brindle cow & a yearling. –John L Smith, J P [N B: Owner to come forward, prove property, pay charges, & take them away. –Zebulon Brundige, near the Penitentiary]

Mrd: on Dec 24, in Wash City, by Rev Geo W Samson, Mr Chas A Anderson to Miss Eliza Sandiford, both of Wash City.

Died: on Dec 22, at Phil, Mrs Catharine Ustick, w/o Stephen Ustick, & d/o Geo Beck, in her 41st year.

Died: on Dec 26, after a brief illness, Ada, d/o Ferdinand & Margaret Jefferson, in her 7th year.

New Grocery Store: in the spacious west room in the Jackson Hall Bldg, Pa ave. –Michl Caton

Explosion of 60 kegs of powder on Wed last: the city of Providence was alarmed by the explosion in the powder house belonging to Messrs Storey, Wood & Veder. The bldg was about 2 ½ miles from the bridge near the residence of L C Eaton. The mansion house of Mr Eaton was much injured, & some of the furniture destroyed. The farm house on the estate was much injured, & the trees & fences blown down.

Died: on Dec 26, in Wash City, John McLeod, aged about 80 years. He was a native of Ireland, but for more than 40 years past was a citizen of Wash, during all of which time he was successfully engaged in the education of youth & the embellishment of the city, having built 4 handsome seminaries & done more by his system of education than any other man who ever resided among us. His popularity as a teacher may be estimated from the fact that he was at the time of this death engaged in teaching the 3rd generation, having taught the fathers & grandparents of his pupils. His funeral will take place at 3½ o'clock this afternoon from his academy, 9th st, near H st.

Thirty second anniversary of the Columbia Typographical Society: Anniversay Supper on the first Sat in Jan, at P H King's Congress Hall, on Pa ave. Cmte of Arrangements:
C F Lowrey	Thos Caton	John H Thorn
Thos W Howard	Patrick H Brooks	
Geo W Cochran	Wm E Kennaugh	

TUE DEC 29. 1846
House of Reps: 1-Memorial & accompanying documents of Louis W Trimelli, Consul of the U S at Oporto, Portugal: laid before the House. 2-Memorial of W Z G Morton, of Boston, proposing that Congress should purchase, for the use of the army & navy, a right to use the process for preventing pain during surgical operations: referred to a select cmte of 5 members.

Senate: 1-Ptn from Alfred G White, asking to be remunerated for moneys unjustly taken from him by the Post Ofc Dept. 2-Ptn in behalf of the Rev Peter Parker, secretary & interpreter of the Chinese Mission, asking compensation for his services as acting com'r in China. 3-Ptn from Wm M Blackford, late Charge d'Affaires at New Grenada, asking the usual allowance made on the return of ministers from abroad. 4-Ptn from W T G Morton, offering to the Gov't, for the use of the army & navy, the purchase of his process for preventing pain in surgical operations. 5-Ptn from Uriah Brown, of Ill, relative to a system of coast & harbor defence. 6-Bill for the relief of the legal reps of Jacques Moreclan: introduced on leave. Same for the joint resolution for the relief of Wm H Thomas. 7-Cmte on Public Lands: bill for the relief of Cadwallader Wallace. 8-Bill for the relief of Eliz Hamilton, wid/o the late Alex'r Hamilton: changed the title to "A bill to purchase the papers of the late Alex'r Hamilton." [Note-in the House of Reps below, Morton, of Boston, is W Z G.]

It is with deepest sorrow that we have to announce that the Hon Alex'r Barrow lies at the point of death in the city of Balt, whither he went last week on a short visit, & where he was seized with a sudden & violent malady on Fri night. By the latest account, his physicians despaired of his life. [Dec 30th newspaper: notice of the death, on Dec 29, of Senator Barrow. The remains of the dec'd were brought from Balt last evening to in the railroad train, & was received by the whole body of the Senate, its Pres, & ofcrs, & numerous private friends. His body was followed in solemn procession to the Capitol. The funeral ceremonies will take place Dec 31, at 12 o'clock.]

Morris Co, Mendham, N J, Oct 29, 1846. Dr Seth W Fowle: Dear sir, this may certify that I am about 75 years of age, was forn & always resided in this town. In Oct, 1845, I took cold, & for 6 months I was afflicted with the influenza, & the worst cough I have ever experienced in my whole life. I got a bottle of Schenck's Sirup; it did me good; did not cure me. At last my physician advised me to take Dr Wistar's celebrated Balsam of Wild Cherry, which I did so, & I believe that it saved my life.
-Ephraim Sanders

W S Berrell & J S Burr, auctioneers, 297 Market st, near 8th, north side, Phil, Pa. Executor's sale of the estate of the late Isaiah Lukens, dec'd: comprising his most valuable inventions, clocks, quadrants, sextants, cabinet of minerals, chemicals, philosophical apparatus, air cung, chronometer, steam engines, turning lathes, & his superior rifle, with graduating & tlelscopic sights, together with case. Also, will be sold at the same time, 1 very superior THEODOLITE, with arch & tripod, in complete order.

Pew #55 in St John's Church, on the ground floor, near the altar, will be offered at public sale, at the Church, on Dec 30, at 12 o'clock. Also, at private sale, several eligible Pews on the ground floor. –B Homans, auct

New Hardware Store: s e corner of Bridge & High sts, entrance 1st door from the corner in either st. –Muncaster & Dodge, Gtwn.

Balt, Dec 28. The mortal remains of Lt Cochran, who fell in the conflict with Mexico, arrived here this morning from New Orleans in the ship **Montgomery**. They will be escorted from the vessel, probably tomorrow, by the Eagle Artillery to the Philadelphia cars, & taken on their way home for final interment. The same vessel brought a number of the effects of the late Maj Ringgold.

Mrd: on Dec 15, in Trinity Church, Chas Co, Md, by Rev Jas Abercrombie, Wm H Hebb, of St Mary's Co, to Miss A Caroline Penn, d/o the late Maj Wm Penn.

Mrd: on Dec 17, at Mattaponi, by Rev Mr Sweet, Mr Richd L Ogle to Priscilla M, d/o Robt W Bowie, all of PG Co, Md.

Mrd: on Dec 22, at *Omshaw Hill*, PG Co, Md, by Rev Mr Nelson, Saml H Berry to Miss Ann Rebecca, d/o the late Alex'r Mundell, all of the above county.

Died: on Dec 27, suddenly, Butler Maury, in his 25th year. His funeral is today at 2 p m, from his lodgings at Mrs M Hill's, corner of F & 19th sts.

Died: on Dec 28, at the house of her son, Mr W T Compton, in Gtwn, D C, aged 84 years wanting one day, Mrs Chloe Compton, d/o the late Leonard Briscoe, of St Mary's Co, & relict of the last W S Compton, of Wash Co, Md, confiding in the atonement, & trusting in the love of Him who is able to keep the soul unto salvation. Her funeral is this afternoon, at 2 o'clock, from the residence of Mrs C on Gay st, Gtwn.

Died: on Dec 1, at *Oak Ridge*, of a protracted illness, Miss Mary C Allen, y/d/o the late Wm Allen, of Caroline Co, Va.

Died: on Dec 18, Miss Mary Columbia Burnett, aged 16 years & 1 month.

Notice: I hereby caution dry goods dealers & otherss from crediting any one on my account from this date, without my written order, as I shall pay no accounts without. –Nicholas Travers

WED DEC 30, 1846

The Fourth Presbyterian Church, on 9th st, Rev Mr Smith's, was undergoing some improvements: the walls & ceiling have been painted in fresco, by Mr Ernest Dreyer, of Balt, in a style superior to any thing of the kind we have ever yet witnessed in this city. The wood work has been very neatly repainted by Mr Thos Stanely, of Wash City. Repairs have been made by Mr Wm Dougherty, of Wash City.

New Drug Store: on the south side of Pa ave, between 4½ & 6th sts. –L E Massoletti

The New Orleans papers: accounts from the Squadron off Vera Cruz to Dec 13: loss on Dec 8, off Green Island, the brig **Somers**, under the command of Lt Semmes, while engaged in blockading that port. She was struck by a heavy squall, capsized, & sunk in 20 or 30 minutes. There were about 80 persons on board, of whom 24 perished, & 15 drifted ashore on spars & hen-coops, & were taken prisoners by the Mexicans. Among the lost are acting Master Clemson & Passed Midshipman Hynson. Others were saved by the ofcrs of the English & French vessels, lying under Sacrificios, who risked their own lives in open boats. List of the men supposed to have been lost in the wrecking of the **Somers**, from which must be deducted the 15 who, it has since been ascertained, drifted ashore & were taken prisoners of the Mexicans:

Ofcrs & men lost: Henry A Clemson, Acting Master; John R Hynson, Passed Midshipman

Wm G Brazier	Wm Elmsley
Ebenezer Terrell	Wm Quest
Chas H Haven	John Hargrave
Jas Ryder	Wm McCardy
Jas Thompson	John Christopher Myers
Chas Loew	Clement C Willen
Thos Young	Thos McGowan
Wm Gillan	Jos Antonio
Matthias Gavel	Adolph Belmente
Major Cain	Manuel Howard
Dennis Kelly	Wm W Powers
Alex'r Anker	Henry W Spear
Chas McFarland	Jas Chapman
Jas Fennel	Lewis Johnson
Chas True	Jonatius Leopold
John Day	Thos Jefferson
Wm Purdy	Wm H Rose
Edw McCormick	Peter Hernandez

Ofcrs & men saved:
R Semmes, Lt Commanding;
Lt M G L Claiborne
Lt John L Parker
Purser, J F Steele
Passed Assist Surgeon, John H Wright
Midshipman, Francis G Clark
Purser's Steward, Edmund T Stevens
Yeoman, Jacob Hazard

Amos Colson	Wm F Thompson
Wm Johnson	Christopehr Lawrence
Mathew Buck	Jos Todd
John McCargo	Stephen Maynard
John G Van Norden	Sal Bennett
Chas Seymour	Thos D Burns
John Williamson	Wm Power
John Pollen	Jos Skipsey
John Smith	Jos Jones
Henry Strommell	Chas Nutlee
Thos Mulhollen	Washington Cooper
Geo Wakefield	Wm Dix
Wm Keys	Francis A Waldeon
Wm Toland	Jas Chambers

Jos Files, one of the brave Balt volunteers, who was severely wounded at Monterey, [having lost an arm & been wounded in the leg,] is at present in this city. Being disabled from earning a living by manual labor, he is thrown on the generosity of the public, & will gladly receive any assistance which the humane & patriotic may choose to contribute. He is at the Monterey House, Pa ave, opposite Coleman's.

House of Reps: 1-Bill for the relief of Jas Glynn: committed to the Cmte of the Whole House. 2-Cmte of Claims: bill for the relief of Geo Parsons: committed to the Cmte of the Whole. Same cmte: bill for the relief of Elisha F Richards: committed to the Cmte of the Whole. 3-The ptn of Cmder Henry Bruce, of the U S Navy, in reference to prize money for the capture of the slaver **Spitfire**, be allowed to be taken from the files, for the purpose of being returned to the memorialist, at his own request. 4-Ptn of Caleb Bell, administrator of Matthew Bell, asking for money due said Matthew at the time of his death as a Dragoon in 1834. 5-Ptn of Peter Huston, a Lt in the northwestern army during the last war with Great Britain, asking a pension. 6-Bill for the relief of Thos Scott, register of the land ofc at Chillicothe, for services connected with the duties of his ofc. 7-Ptns of Thos C Wales, of Boston, & of S H Babcock, of Boston, severally praying indemnification for French spoliations prior to 1800. 8-Ptn of John N Breckhouse & John Simpkins, administrators of Covington Simpkins, dec'd, praying indemnity for French spoliations prior to 1800. 9-Ptn of Geo Wilkes & 1,300 citizens of N Y C, in favor of a Nat'l Railroad to the Pacific ocean. 10-Ptn of Saml Allen, for allowance of commissions. 11-Ptn of Saml Gladding, praying for remission of duties. 12-Ptn of Philip Allen & others, praying indemnity for spoliations committed by the French Gov't previous to 1800. 13-Ptn of Josiah Colston, praying that the accounting ofcrs of the Treas may be directed to open his accounts as purser in the navy, & make him sundry allowances. 14-Ptn of Joice Billups, asking indemnity for French spoliations prior to 1800. 15-Ptns of David Anthony, of Fall river, Reuben Cook, of Provincetown, & T B White, of New Beford, asking remuneration for French spoliations prior to 1800. 16-Ptn of Chas Foreman, of Carroll Co, Ohio. 17-Memorial of Wm W Yerby, of Hinds Co, Miss, asking to be permitted to complete & perfect his entry [as assignee of Thos Jordan] to a certain quarter section of land therein described. 18-Ptn of the legal reps of Lemuel P Montgomery, dec'd, prayin a pension & bounty lands. 19-Memorial of Willis Wilson & Wm W Wilson, heirs of Willis Wilson, dec'd, petitioning Congress for 5 years' full pay due the latter for Revolutionary services. 20-Resolved that leave be given to withdraw from the files of the House the ptn & papers of Jeremiah Murphy, asking for a pension. 21-Resolved that John Mitchel have leave to withdraw his ptn & papers, which have been referred to the Cmte on Invalid Pensions, from the files of the House.

Toys at Auction: at the store of Wm B Lewis, on Pa ave, between 12th & 13th sts. -R W Dyer, auct

Military & Civic Ball: by the Washington Light Infty: on Jan 9, at the spacious Saloon in Odd Fellows' Hall. Managers:

Lt J B Tate	Wm H Clarke	P H King
Lt J B Philips	Wm Morgan	M E Bright
Serg Jas Kelly	Andrew J Joyce	F J Waters
Serg E Varden	Jas Powers	Jas G Ellis
John S Marl	Geo Becker	Jas H Mead
John P Stallings	Lt J F Tucker	Edw Rice
Judson Warner	Ensign J Mead	Wm Garner
Richd I Brown	H W Sweeting	Franklin Beers
Jas Bouseau	Wm E Morcoe	S H Warner
Jas Booth	Jas Y Davis	Henry Kuhl

THU DEC 31, 1846
The undersigned wish to engage a teacher for the ensuing year. One who is competent to teach the necessary branches of a sound English education. Applicants will please address Edw D Boone, Beantown, Md. Good board can be obtained very near the school on moderate terms. –E D Boone, W A Mudd, J Dyer, Trustees

U S steamer **Vixen**, Tampico, Dec 2, 1846
List of the ofcrs of the steamer **Vixen**:
Joshua R Sands, Cmder   Alex'r Maury, acting master
*John Contee, 1st Lt   A F Sawyer, Assist Surgeon
Passed Midshipmen-3: John Mathews; Wm M Jeffers; Edw Simpson
Wm B Floyd, Capt's clerk
Engineers-3: Jas Atkinson; Saml Archibold; Chas Coleman
 [She goes by the name of the "fighting **Vixen**."]
*Antonio Lizardo, Dec 8: Lt Contee has been transferred to the ship **Mississippi** on account of his bad health, having been seriously ill with fever, but is now doing well.

Young Ladies Seminary: the Sisters of Charity, of St Joseph's House, having removed from East Broadway, N Y, will on or about Jan 15 next open an Academy for Young Ladies in Wash City, on the south side of E st, between 6th & 7th sts, one door west of the residence of Richd S Coxe. In this seminary will be taught all the higher branches of an English education, with music, French, & Spanish.

A

Abbot, 318, 392, 410
Abbott, 33, 116, 128, 145, 208, 236, 374, 397, 460, 535
Abby, 151
Abden, 461
Abel, 114
Abell, 112, 190, 314, 337, 397
Abercrombie, 210, 284, 345, 457, 504, 524, 578
Abert, 102, 254, 285
Abinathy, 509
Aborn, 184
Abrams, 184
Aby, 307
Academy of the Visitation, 369
Acken, 16
Acker, 460
Ackerman, 238
Acklin, 294, 414
Acott, 23
Acrill, 401
act to retrocede, 414
Act to retrocede, 333
Adair, 30, 147
Adam, 56, 402
Adams, 2, 12, 22, 25, 39, 52, 53, 56, 99, 102, 143, 151, 191, 194, 197, 202, 213, 239, 245, 246, 261, 262, 263, 266, 313, 325, 331, 342, 346, 348, 349, 378, 385, 386, 397, 401, 422, 423, 426, 430, 431, 452, 472, 489, 505, 522, 526, 535, 553
Adamson, 321, 432
Adaser, 151
Addison, 25, 116, 124, 173, 181, 187, 220, 272, 317, 489, 520, 527, 545, 547, 553
Addition to Ray's Adventure, 350
Adkinson, 132
Adler, 135, 230, 367
Adrean, 194

Adrian, 333
Adsit, 380
Aege, 388
Agate, 11, 29, 342
Ahrens, 447
Aigler, 553
Aiken, 198, 363
Aikens, 506
Ailier, 553
Aisquith, 156
Aitkin, 194
Alamo, 451
Albison, 506
Albrecht, 8
Albro, 239
Alcott, 498, 508
Alden, 449, 472
Aldrich, 147
Aldrick, 2, 56
Alender, 510
Alexander, 25, 31, 41, 56, 81, 85, 88, 89, 91, 151, 159, 178, 194, 218, 234, 258, 342, 371, 387, 401, 413, 426, 457, 470, 489, 492, 508, 509, 516, 524, 534, 562
Alexandria-Retrocession, 284
Alford, 65, 104
Alfred, 509
Alger, 175, 342
Alhambra, 271
Ali, 120
Alig, 43, 572
Allemong, 239, 243, 337
Allen, 25, 34, 41, 47, 51, 56, 69, 73, 87, 127, 135, 143, 147, 151, 157, 163, 190, 194, 198, 215, 226, 229, 235, 239, 244, 248, 251, 257, 260, 279, 280, 290, 313, 323, 325, 340, 357, 361, 362, 385, 386, 397, 407, 457, 507, 508, 524, 533, 551, 553, 564, 574, 578, 580
Alleng, 511
Allerson, 102, 342
Allison, 216, 239, 394, 397, 443, 508

Allmand, 360
Allnutt, 377
Allston, 239
Almond, 2
Almstedt, 245
Almy, 323
Alnutt, 102, 441
Alston, 56, 151, 280, 286, 342, 512
Alsup, 386
Altamont, 171
Alvear, 243
Alvord, 437
Amati, 324
Ambler, 206, 269, 309
Ambrozine, 6
Ames, 134, 210, 237, 353, 397, 513
Amidon, 48
Amorige, 410
Amory, 179
Amos, 435
Ampudia, 286, 456, 501
Amridge, 55
Anbanal, 239
Anderson, 2, 7, 25, 31, 47, 55, 56, 68, 70, 79, 85, 89, 93, 102, 121, 122, 151, 158, 194, 201, 203, 226, 239, 258, 290, 313, 342, 350, 355, 359, 361, 385, 386, 397, 433, 443, 480, 489, 494, 505, 509, 558, 575
Andre, 239, 351
Andree, 489
Andrew, 88
Andrews, 25, 43, 70, 74, 86, 110, 122, 168, 173, 184, 194, 239, 243, 337, 356, 359, 402, 504, 533, 570
Angel, 15
Angell, 10
Anger, 267
Angerman, 397
Angermann, 443
Angier, 16
Anglea, 89
Angney, 298, 515
Anker, 579
Anman, 561

Ansam, 311
Ansman, 363
Ansmen, 147
Anthony, 69, 358, 359, 580
Antomarchi, 25
Anton, 342
Antonio, 432, 579
Appleby, 64
Applegate, 56, 151
Appleton, 426, 455
Arago, 310
Archbishop of Wallawalla, 446
Archbold, 280
Archdeacon, 401
Archer, 25, 151, 342, 431, 443, 527, 535
Ardis, 125
Aredondo, 141
Arevalo, 388
Argo, 508
Argot, 189
Arguelles, 541
Arista, 286, 404
Arlig, 136, 140
Armand, 136
Armfield, 436
Armidon, 346
Armington, 17, 189
Armistead, 42, 62, 71, 117, 151, 320, 342
Armor, 6, 78
Armour, 230
Armstrong, 21, 30, 64, 73, 97, 107, 112, 120, 134, 151, 220, 229, 239, 273, 280, 330, 342, 351, 397, 457, 496, 498, 507, 512, 524, 532, 533, 538, 540
Armstrong Guards, 220
Arnold, 9, 79, 185, 233, 239, 280, 351, 366, 508
Arnot, 239, 347
Arth, 239
Arthines, 422
Arthur, 173, 509, 524, 548
<u>Artificial Leg</u>, 236

Artman, 2
Arundell, 56
Arwine, 205
Asbury, 102, 280, 574
Ash, 468
Ashard, 151, 239, 280, 342
Ashby, 2, 25, 163, 248, 254, 263, 325, 350, 351, 535, 539, 552, 556
Ashcom, 163
Ashe, 334, 386
Ashford, 406, 460
Ashland Place, 543
Ashley, 443
Ashmun, 565
Ashton, 36, 86, 89, 137, 151, 397
Aspen Hill, 157
Aspin Grove, 124
Aspinwall, 102
Astin, 505
Atchison, 89
Athearn, 432
Atherton, 432
Athore, 310
Atkins, 267, 324, 338, 342, 529
Atkinson, 10, 151, 269, 373, 402, 426, 581
AtLee, 539
Atocho, 25
Atterson, 342
Atwater, 567
Atwell, 7
Atwood, 149, 533, 538
Aubert, 337
Augur, 72
Augustus, 297
Aulick, 76, 97, 307
Aunuld, 507
Ausman, 328
Ausmen, 250, 313
Ausment, 34
Austen, 540
Austin, 214, 262, 307, 350, 356, 379, 447, 493, 512
Avery, 206, 280
Avonwood, 472

Ayers, 141, 393
Aylett, 453
Ayot, 309, 315, 362
Ayres, 2, 184, 342, 489

B

Babb, 30, 504
Babbatt, 55
Babbett, 451
Babbit, 286, 355, 363
Babbitt, 226, 383, 387
Babcock, 89, 580
Baber, 129
Bache, 363, 381, 410, 431, 437, 449
Backenstoss, 233, 256
Backus, 210
Bacon, 17, 52, 56, 109, 114, 231, 238, 245, 292, 295, 383, 451, 484, 530, 537, 553
Baden, 96, 169, 200, 397, 553
Badger, 179, 239, 248
Bagby, 152, 239, 262, 343, 397, 453
Bagg, 71, 151
Baggett, 518
Baggott, 489
Bagman, 489, 535
Bagwell, 438
Bailey, 39, 113, 117, 134, 172, 175, 194, 347, 358, 375, 397, 401, 421, 463, 509
Baily, 207, 408, 553
Bainbridge, 2, 456, 489, 504, 524
Baine, 130, 401
Baird, 2, 368, 402, 458, 464
Baker, 2, 26, 56, 67, 97, 103, 109, 115, 122, 152, 169, 213, 239, 306, 320, 322, 326, 343, 353, 397, 401, 426, 460, 461, 467, 468, 478, 481, 482, 484, 485, 533, 535, 553, 571
Bakus, 158
Balch, 89, 151, 234
Baldridge, 55, 118, 168, 170, 172, 361

Baldwin, 2, 26, 43, 90, 92, 98, 111, 144, 152, 188, 194, 239, 283, 343, 349, 352, 373, 514, 538, 559
Baley, 239
Balfour, 229, 401
Ball, 2, 55, 56, 64, 97, 119, 165, 180, 239, 295, 401, 489, 493
Ballard, 33, 82, 90, 239, 301, 308, 312, 322, 330, 331, 346, 362, 405, 517
Ballinger, 544
Ballman, 26
Ballou, 50
Balmain, 284, 402
Balster, 80
Baltimore, 194, 239, 443, 489
Baltzel, 397
Baltzell, 56, 115, 280, 489
Baly, 39
Bancker, 123, 564
Bancroft, 98, 126, 307, 415, 418, 573
Band, 511
Banghart, 26, 152
Bangs, 109
Banister, 401, 559
Bank Lot, 193
Bank Property, 193
Bank Territory, 193
Bankhead, 420, 430
Banks, 25, 102, 342, 397, 402, 506
Bannatine, 29
Bannatyne, 174
Banning, 152
Bannon, 53
Barber, 16, 401
Barbes, 311
Barbour, 152, 185, 194, 260, 364, 384, 456, 470, 474, 504, 549, 550
Barboza, 280
Barcaly, 562
Barclay, 137, 162, 194, 308, 312, 354, 362, 405, 530
Bardin, 280, 334
Bare, 461
Bargy, 34, 215, 226

Barker, 17, 56, 103, 125, 152
Barlett, 152
Barlow, 103, 400
Barnard, 2, 95, 102, 142, 218, 424, 498, 562
Barne, 174, 553
Barnes, 2, 51, 89, 151, 169, 239, 342, 394, 426, 462, 542, 553
Barnet, 65
Barney, 290
Barnham, 510
Barnum, 26, 115, 195, 201, 466, 506
Barnwell, 438
Barock, 280
barque **Chancellor**, 492
barque **Francis Spaight**, 191
barque **Meteor**, 492
barque **Pons**, 302
barque **Quebec**, 11
Barr, 553
Barra, 315
Barrand, 528
Barraud, 401
Barret, 80, 280
Barrett, 116, 167, 288, 307, 343, 355, 397, 421
Barrit, 194
Barron, 152, 452
Barrot, 6
Barrow, 397, 577
Barry, 3, 56, 103, 123, 152, 171, 187, 210, 237, 266, 314, 331, 343, 397, 420, 457, 512, 535, 553, 573
Barstown, 120
Bartell, 103
Bartin, 194
Bartle, 101
Bartlett, 138, 291, 353, 489, 510
Bartley, 69, 194
Bartlin, 56, 280
Barton, 50, 56, 103, 107, 117, 166, 175, 222, 239, 280, 338, 347, 348, 373, 458, 512
Barton Hall, 87
Bartow, 393

Bartruff, 80, 236
Basil, 3
Bass, 15, 112, 159, 211
Basse, 511
Basset, 560
Bassett, 310, 397, 401, 420, 534
Bastinelli, 535
Bates, 42, 46, 102, 116, 132, 161, 239, 424, 489, 529, 535, 561, 563
Battee, 91
Battle, 239
Battlem, 456
Batty, 144, 251, 311, 326, 362, 415
Batut, 431
Baudouin, 561
Baughn, 229
Bauman, 351
Baumback, 454, 478, 560, 566
Baumer, 441
Baxter, 142, 184, 368, 395, 568
Bayard, 3, 38, 41, 56, 99, 103
Bayes, 136
Bayley, 103, 439
Bayly, 56, 103, 233, 234, 539, 553
Bayma, 103
Bayne, 56, 77, 254, 348, 486, 553
Baynton, 284
Beach, 99, 102, 169, 189, 259, 397
Beacham, 321
Beacon, 48
Beahan, 376
Beal, 36
Beale, 88, 183, 276, 321
Bealer, 397
Beall, 2, 3, 25, 47, 102, 119, 142, 169, 210, 221, 222, 239, 260, 327, 370, 430, 477, 484, 535, 541, 553
Beam, 56
Beaman, 56, 234, 246, 549
Beams, 2, 280
Bean, 16, 37, 47, 56, 67, 89, 102, 194, 209, 288, 342, 397, 426, 489, 499, 553, 571
Beard, 2, 41, 56, 139, 203, 251, 313, 489

Bearden, 349
Beardsley, 70, 273, 275, 292, 384, 465, 513, 553
Beargrand, 496
Bearney, 343
Beaseley, 2
Beasley, 327, 553
Beasly, 484
Beatty, 359, 526
Beaty, 535
Beaubarnais, 317
Beaubien, 518
Beaudont, 65
Beaumont, 2, 360, 494
Beauvallan, 185
Beck, 2, 48, 56, 80, 151, 194, 201, 245, 392, 397, 426, 504, 576
Beckenbaugh, 515
Becker, 421, 443, 581
Bedell, 70
Bedinger, 257
Bee, 74, 549
Beech, 113, 241, 535
Beecher, 152
beehive, 231
Beekes, 206
Beekman, 351
Beelan, 348
Beeler, 109, 219, 518, 523
Beers, 239, 581
Beetley, 25
Beggs, 21
Behnee, 498, 507
Behrens, 473
Beilstein, 32
Beirne, 26, 56
Belcher, 436
Belden, 371
Beldon, 103
Belgian Minister, 377
Belknap, 147, 359, 364, 384, 434
Bell, 55, 86, 108, 112, 115, 117, 125, 144, 219, 227, 239, 246, 249, 268, 309, 397, 401, 424, 443, 487, 510, 511, 515, 535, 543, 565, 580

Belle Haven, 113
Belle View, 558
Bellows, 56, 176, 355
Bellville, 56
Bellwood, 448
Belmente, 579
Belmont, 413
Belsher, 26
Belt, 47, 151, 321, 334, 397, 461, 527
Belton, 71
Bemis, 169
Bend, 205
Bender, 109, 140, 204, 225, 407, 424, 426, 471, 489
Benedict, 56, 221
Benedictines, 478
Benham, 280, 451, 526
Benj Ray Tract, 253
Benjamin, 161, 239, 244
Benkert, 235
Bennet, 152, 348
Bennett, 21, 80, 152, 194, 223, 239, 307, 322, 397, 443, 489, 579
Benning, 199, 426
Benns, 2, 94
Benris, 100
Bensancon, 280
Benson, 66, 343
Bent, 281, 441, 518
Benter, 314, 553
Bentinck, 433
Bentley, 2, 128, 239, 303, 443
Benton, 36, 147, 188, 375, 379, 523, 569
Bequette, 41
Berchil, 2
Bergen, 173, 443
Bergman, 103, 343
Berkeley, 77
Berkley, 397
Bernard, 79, 137, 152, 239, 280
Beron, 22
Berrell, 577
Berret, 185, 284
Berri, 39, 55, 226

Berry, 20, 21, 26, 47, 74, 103, 109, 152, 188, 194, 239, 248, 268, 278, 280, 281, 306, 343, 348, 413, 426, 464, 489, 501, 553, 578
Berryman, 167, 406, 430
Bershandt, 81
Bert, 209
Berteau, 355
Besancon, 194
Besaneon, 103
Besch, 56
Bess, 102
Bessey, 211
Bessie, 506
Best, 47
Bestor, 426, 515
Bethany College, 334
Bethune, 88
Bettencourt, 334
Bettinger, 2, 152
Betts, 82, 90, 147, 251, 311, 313, 331, 338, 342, 361, 415
Bevan, 553
Beverley, 495
Beverly, 218
Bevin, 138
Bexley, 88
Beyer, 78, 280
Bibb, 2, 151, 383
Bickford, 155
Bickley, 3, 244
Bidault, 239
Biddle, 3, 25, 46, 103, 120, 374, 426
Bidgelow, 342
Bidlack, 19
Bidleman, 54
Bidwell, 103
Bienvenu, 349
Biewand, 16
Biewend, 357
Big Elk Lick, 253
Bigam, 508
Bigelow, 43, 419, 457
Biggs, 239, 265, 279, 469
Bigham, 78, 561

Bigs, 247
Bihler, 75, 297, 483
Bill, 25
Billing, 28, 113
Billings, 99, 152, 174, 239
Billingsley, 440
Billups, 580
Binford, 348
Bingham, 31, 489
Bingley, 8, 55, 102, 157, 182, 186, 361
Binkhold, 397
Binks, 151
Binney, 454
Birch, 2, 96, 103, 238, 239, 285, 426, 481, 482, 485, 518
Birchmore, 17
Bird, 6, 31, 56, 79, 162, 245, 290
Birdsell, 533
Birge, 342
Birney, 289
Birth, 298
Biscoe, 461
Bisham, 36
Bishop, 2, 36, 56, 152, 385, 386, 458
Biss, 239
Bissel, 30, 147
Bissell, 123, 420
Bitts, 56
Bixbe, 397
Bixby, 371
Black, 151, 239, 261, 268, 274, 397, 489, 553, 569
Black Fox, 216
Black Hussars, 220
Blackburn, 326, 407
Blackford, 19, 216, 576
Blacklar, 535
Blackler, 529
Blackman, 266, 342
Blackwell, 206, 287, 387, 508
Blackwell's Island, 258
Blackwood, 340
Bladen, 397
Bladwin, 569

Blagden, 47, 123, 139, 188, 262, 298, 314, 493, 543, 552
Blagrove, 254
Blair, 14, 34, 70, 151, 212, 239, 281, 300, 308, 401, 518, 524, 529, 540
Blake, 9, 84, 90, 148, 151, 178, 180, 182, 228, 307, 363, 441
Blakeney, 206
Blanchard, 3, 56, 103, 117, 152, 180, 195, 239, 266, 331, 343, 456, 464
Blanchet, 446
Bland, 212, 400, 402, 519
Blanson, 310
Blanter, 451
Blatchford, 56
Blatchley, 103
Bledsoe, 152, 239, 343, 535
Bleight, 2, 91
Bliss, 213, 299, 347, 383
Blockley, 343
Blodget, 2, 17
Bloodgood, 377
Bloom, 280
Blount, 9, 94, 151
Blue, 14
Blue Plains, 573
Blunt, 52, 194
Boardley, 426
Boardman, 60
Boarman, 103, 112, 337, 348, 378
boat **Charles**, 296
boat **Columbia**, 285
boat **Elizabeth**, 17
boat **James L Day**, 286
Bobbitt, 287
Bock, 443
Boden, 137
Bodfish, 208, 303
Bodine, 179
Bogan, 413
Bogardus, 7, 9, 14, 17, 167, 362
Bogart, 56
Bogert, 397
Boggs, 150, 187, 200, 422
Bohee, 72

Bohlayer, 246, 486
Bohn, 342, 397
Bohrer, 103, 109, 439, 489, 519
Boisseau, 319
Boker, 125
Bokes, 280, 560
Bolan, 62
Bolen, 180
Bolivar, 126
Bolon, 29, 315
Bolton, 115, 168, 239, 280, 322, 569
Bomford, 119, 500
Bonaparte, 32, 377, 408, 432
Bond, 48, 56, 88, 109, 318, 443
Bondurant, 44
Bonham, 451
Bonifant, 377, 441
Bonner, 434
Bonneville, 72, 352, 441
Bontz, 56, 426
Booker, 402
Boon, 475
Boone, 378, 482, 581
Boorman, 88
Boose, 81
Booth, 65, 441, 533, 538, 581
Boothe, 166, 204
Boreman, 303
Borland, 339, 535
Borremans, 88, 129, 553
Borroughs, 308, 435
Borrows, 245, 513
Bosher, 535
Boss, 65, 160, 396, 443
Bosser, 194
Bostock, 443
Boston, 102, 280, 343, 397
Bostwick, 134, 343
Boswell, 26, 194, 229, 268, 422
Bosworth, 335, 426
Boteler, 26, 93, 149, 186, 188, 221, 236, 257, 263, 277, 354, 426, 440, 462, 530
Botner, 56
Botter, 489

Bottomer, 281
Botts, 489
Boucher, 109, 348
Bouck, 147, 371
Bougher, 469
Boughton, 115, 118
Boulanger, 42
Boun, 56
Bourdon, 45
Bouseau, 581
Boush, 546
Boussac, 85
Bouthron, 152
Bouvet, 278
Bowden, 213, 505, 529, 530
Bowen, 2, 7, 34, 56, 61, 79, 98, 194, 212, 215, 239, 280, 343, 375, 460, 467, 509, 510
Bowers, 205
Bowie, 207, 254, 268, 356, 370, 451, 552, 578
Bowis, 511
Bowles, 440
Bowlin, 152
Bowling, 239, 361, 378, 408, 419, 440
Bowman, 2, 3, 147, 217, 252, 443, 489, 549, 569
Bowridge, 422
Bowring, 476
Bowrum, 103
Bowser, 397
Boyce, 36, 458
Boyd, 2, 51, 52, 102, 117, 147, 151, 188, 204, 239, 249, 268, 271, 280, 287, 306, 342, 397, 402, 403, 435, 437, 454, 460, 465, 468, 476, 489, 492, 509, 511, 559, 567, 573
Boyden, 3
Boyland, 226
Boyld, 533
Boyle, 56, 109, 114, 236, 245, 249, 268, 487, 505, 533, 545
Boylston, 533
Brackenridge, 103
Bradbury, 194, 343

Braddock, 25, 421, 553
Bradds, 148
Braden, 56
Bradfield, 372
Bradford, 15, 31, 41, 56, 307, 311, 385, 386, 426
Bradley, 14, 109, 110, 122, 125, 140, 161, 165, 177, 178, 184, 187, 214, 215, 280, 288, 343, 365, 421, 426, 494, 517, 545, 569
Bradley tract, 137
Bradt, 504
Brady, 3, 19, 26, 31, 39, 76, 86, 98, 127, 158, 169, 194, 210, 245, 289, 347, 348, 397, 429, 439, 464, 535, 561
Bragdon, 303, 331, 450, 539, 553, 574
Bragg, 239, 309, 397, 404, 456
Braiden, 3, 152
Brainard, 2
Branagan, 194
Branch, 82, 90, 147, 283
Brand, 304, 307
Branden, 526
Brannan, 3, 56, 103, 350, 372
Branson, 26
Brashars, 509
Brashears, 252, 553
Brasher, 36
Brashier, 144
Brass, 102
Bravo, 388
Brawner, 201, 259
Braxton, 41, 56, 553
Brayton, 3
Brazer, 127
Brazier, 7, 569, 579
Breadford, 26
Breasha, 134
Breast, 276
Breath, 543
Breathed, 300
Breck, 7
Breckenridge, 227, 395, 426, 495
Breckhouse, 580

Breckinridge, 160
Breece, 327
Breed, 374
Breese, 56, 322, 323, 381, 410, 465, 466
Brenen, 343
Brengle, 178, 559
Brennan, 76
Brenneman, 239
Brenner, 239, 501, 544
Brent, 2, 25, 37, 38, 61, 75, 95, 100, 116, 160, 204, 239, 247, 270, 280, 337, 463, 519, 535, 570
Brereton, 6, 117, 553
Brescount, 421
Bressington, 257
Brewer, 156, 194, 218, 370, 441, 445, 489
Brewster, 70, 334, 533
Brian, 211, 465
Briceland, 343, 420
Brichy, 342
Brick, 56, 151, 194
Bridge, 194, 227
Bridgeo, 529, 530
Bridges, 411
Bridgett, 268
Bridgham, 116
Bridgman, 41, 92, 198
Bridwell, 152
Brien, 336, 396, 409
brig **Aldrick**, 417
brig **Alvarado**, 502
brig **Analoston**, 332
brig **Boxer**, 36
brig **Casket**, 458
brig **Columbia**, 311
brig **Creole**, 563
brig **Excel**, 438
brig **Francis Amy**, 292
brig **General Armstrong**, 220
brig **Gil Blas**, 349
brig **Helen McLeod**, 435
brig **Hornet**, 500
brig **Judge Whitman**, 502

590

brig **Kent**, 168
brig **Lawrence**, 563
brig **Maria L Hill**, 214
brig **Montevideo**, 324
brig of war **Lawrence**, 380
brig **Plato**, 30
brig **Restaurador**, 174
brig **Rienzi**, 457
brig **Somers**, 563, 578
brig **Sutledge**, 285
brig **Truxton**, 420, 464, 519, 546
brig **Vixen**, 111
brig **Washington**, 437, 449
Briggs, 2, 200, 231, 261, 377
Brigham, 6, 30
Bright, 22, 62, 102, 397, 581
Brightwell, 109, 149, 477, 502, 528
Bringier, 200
Brinkerhoff, 347
Brinley, 239, 307, 441, 572
Brisbane, 402
Brisco, 194
Briscoe, 3, 30, 33, 206, 288, 348, 397, 443, 553, 578
British ship **Glenview**, 406
Brittolph, 152
Britton, 198, 404
Broadfoot, 569
Broadhead, 2, 26, 56, 236
Broadrup, 194, 443
Broadus, 264
Brockenbrough, 40
Brockett, 113, 165
Brodbeck, 479
Broddus, 434
Brodhead, 338, 441, 464, 465, 573
Brogden, 535
Brokenboro, 56
Brokenborough, 26
Bronaugh, 219, 237, 249, 268, 302, 415, 487, 492
Bronough, 26, 183, 397
Bronson, 66, 157, 239, 371, 443
Brooers, 152
Brook, 2, 68, 136, 343, 535

Brooke, 2, 56, 102, 137, 144, 156, 239, 249, 269, 289, 342, 347, 397, 426, 447, 488, 489, 516
Brookes, 189, 453
Brooks, 2, 11, 25, 47, 56, 66, 112, 116, 120, 132, 151, 159, 160, 194, 230, 231, 239, 357, 358, 382, 443, 458, 487, 495, 535, 549, 576
Bross, 489
Brou, 337
Brower, 56
Browers, 280
Brown, 2, 14, 16, 17, 19, 20, 25, 31, 47, 55, 56, 65, 69, 75, 84, 88, 89, 102, 103, 113, 116, 118, 121, 122, 127, 137, 139, 144, 147, 151, 156, 160, 168, 170, 172, 173, 174, 194, 207, 209, 211, 212, 219, 226, 227, 229, 230, 239, 241, 244, 251, 252, 260, 267, 280, 302, 306, 311, 313, 316, 318, 328, 342, 343, 351, 362, 365, 388, 397, 400, 404, 411, 426, 436, 443, 458, 460, 464, 465, 477, 481, 484, 485, 489, 490, 494, 496, 504, 509, 533, 534, 535, 539, 542, 546, 551, 553, 570, 576, 581
Browne, 2, 3, 84, 114, 133, 135, 141, 342, 371, 432, 489
Brownell, 122, 128, 152, 301, 308, 330, 362, 569
Brownett, 110
Browning, 152, 194, 239, 512
Brownley, 505
Brubank, 227
Bruce, 25, 151, 181, 253, 373, 441, 443, 535, 553, 580
Bruen, 30
Brum, 44, 203, 330
Brundage, 219
Brundidg, 269
Brundige, 575
Bruner, 2, 17, 146
Bruning, 3, 489
Brunner, 246
Brunot, 147

Brush, 512
Bruton, 42
Bryan, 2, 46, 56, 92, 103, 132, 158, 208, 245, 266, 294, 374, 397, 414, 426, 434, 489
Bryant, 44, 86, 92, 231, 265, 280, 285, 343, 354, 355, 397, 508
Bryarly, 112
Bryce, 363, 397
Bryden, 426
Brydone, 516
Buchanan, 6, 19, 25, 55, 77, 141, 228, 260, 351, 364, 384, 397, 401, 402, 413, 512
Buck, 79, 189, 239, 379, 397, 421, 446, 561, 579
Buckey, 26, 426, 487
Buckham, 103
Buckingham, 83, 186, 227, 288, 394, 483, 567
Buckler, 103
Buckley, 280, 397, 553
Buckman, 147
Buckner, 68, 137, 264, 280, 298
Buel, 194
Buell, 383
Buffalo Tract, 253
Buffenbarger, 2, 84, 86, 97, 362, 417
Buffenberger, 301
Buford, 9, 352
Buist, 141, 216, 227, 389, 391, 426, 430, 487
Bulfinch, 426
Bulger, 56, 152
Bulkley, 532
Bull, 2, 7, 56, 130, 134, 202, 489
Bullen, 134
Buller, 43
Bulley, 26, 553
Bullock, 116
Bulow, 43, 208, 293, 300, 309
Bulter, 443
Buman, 436
Bumbaugh, 2, 20
Bumbough, 98

Bump, 13, 55
Bunce, 78, 562
Bunch, 571
Bunchan, 504
Bunker, 20, 336, 379
Bunker Hill, 261
Bunnell, 443
Bunner, 303
Bunting, 148, 572
Bunzey, 511
Burbank, 56, 103, 141, 228, 229, 260, 275, 292, 359, 533, 538, 540, 563
Burbridge, 233, 256
Burch, 102, 151, 160, 194, 342, 396, 426, 502
Burche, 175, 245, 410, 430, 445, 446, 493
Burdell, 26
Burdine, 159, 209, 258, 460, 463, 481
Burfoot, 150
Burger, 468
Burges, 116, 489
Burgess, 2, 88, 194, 239, 343, 523
Burgevin, 152, 239
Burgwin, 2, 489, 515
Burke, 19, 26, 102, 107, 194, 212, 280, 350, 358, 443
Burkhart, 450
Burkitt, 508
Burleson, 339
Burman, 194, 351
Burn, 535
Burnell, 103, 237, 289
Burner, 103
Burnet, 88, 280
Burnett, 3, 152, 158, 368, 489, 578
Burns, 109, 121, 397, 426, 494, 553, 579
Burnt Mills, 394
Burr, 14, 68, 182, 279, 321, 342, 346, 430, 464, 493, 499, 577
Burrell, 553
Burril, 498
Burrill, 423, 508
Burriss, 266

Burritt, 195, 425, 535
Burroughs, 168, 194, 410
Burrows, 371
Burt, 56, 151, 239, 441
Burton, 20, 401, 453, 511
Burwell, 401, 402
Bury, 553, 562
Buse, 443
Bush, 20, 25, 491, 526, 553
Bushee, 194
Busher, 152
Bussell, 489
Butlar, 489
Butler, 3, 15, 56, 77, 103, 125, 152, 160, 165, 170, 194, 232, 239, 280, 286, 301, 323, 343, 351, 426, 430, 437, 438, 443, 455, 457, 475, 479, 489, 507, 524, 531, 534, 535, 552, 553, 564, 566
Butt, 194
Butterfield, 8
Butts, 453
Byars, 171
Byers, 343
Byington, 39, 47, 245
Byrd, 304, 337
Byrne, 2, 103, 151, 186, 553
Byrnes, 364

C

Cabbell, 152
Cabe, 507
Cabell, 26, 195, 401, 535, 542
Cable, 543
Cabler, 508
Cadden, 57, 148
Cadem, 288
Caden, 47, 297
Cadnedy, 533
Cadwalader, 228, 476
Cadwell, 57
Cady, 42, 195, 352
Cahill, 360
Cahoone, 134

Cain, 343
Cairns, 368
Caison, 327
Cake, 253
Calaghan, 195
Calahir, 195
Calder, 187
Caldwell, 11, 57, 229, 287, 310, 426, 472, 527, 535, 563
Calhoughn, 535
Calhoun, 36, 103, 191, 218, 267, 272, 309, 457, 505, 568
California Regt, 376
Calkin, 261
Calkins, 303
Call, 201
Callaghan, 3, 19, 129, 260
Callagher, 281
Callan, 18, 28, 33, 44, 56, 62, 67, 76, 101, 103, 109, 156, 166, 178, 187, 219, 236, 245, 258, 269, 280, 288, 332, 337, 338, 426, 427, 460, 466, 475, 480, 554
Callayham, 99
Calley, 397
Callicot, 380
Calloway, 26
Calnan, 119, 127, 388, 394, 395
Caltins, 331
Calton, 328
Calvert, 3, 157, 160, 171, 177, 237, 304, 306, 309, 314, 343, 373, 540
Calvin, 267
Camara, 57
Cambloss, 443
Cambridge College Library, 393
Cameron, 112, 124, 152
Cammack, 77, 159, 186, 227, 246, 270, 300, 443, 531, 553
Camp, 195, 240
Camp Oakland, 261
Campbell, 3, 45, 57, 70, 88, 89, 90, 103, 109, 128, 141, 147, 152, 159, 195, 211, 230, 240, 251, 258, 281, 287, 311, 313, 324, 326, 327, 328,

334, 343, 351, 362, 385, 386, 401, 426, 443, 468, 488, 508, 509, 535, 551, 553, 560
Canby, 383
Canedo, 195
Canfield, 3, 26, 57, 152, 158, 234, 305
Canino, 432
Canney, 189, 233, 362
Canning, 69, 433
Cannon, 42, 265, 303, 489, 500, 535, 553
Canny, 266
Canonge, 221
Canova, 432
Capella, 43, 76, 112, 301, 308, 330
Capen, 163, 313
Caperton, 25, 41, 103, 297
Caples, 492, 507, 516
Capo, 559
Cappell, 68, 203
Capretz, 152, 553
Capritz, 503
Capron, 240, 570
Capt, 443
Carbery, 38, 109, 212, 213, 532, 541, 545
Cardeni, 409
Carey, 26, 504
Carico, 270
Carle, 439
Carleton, 71, 352
Carley, 512, 534
Carlisle, 74, 248, 299, 365, 486, 550
Carlton, 8, 301
Carlyle, 57, 402
Carmalt, 443
Carmichael, 168, 240, 397
Carnac, 138
Carnan, 57
Carne, 343
Carnell, 57
Carnes, 171, 543
Carothers, 75, 309
Carpender, 420, 464, 519

Carpenter, 25, 47, 117, 210, 304, 317, 358, 371, 564
Carper, 278
Carr, 2, 3, 84, 90, 114, 144, 240, 251, 264, 281, 313, 326, 343, 362, 415
Carre, 175
Carrico, 135, 224
Carrington, 150, 340, 401
Carrique, 19
Carrol, 535
Carrol Awake, 220
Carroll, 12, 15, 57, 95, 100, 103, 195, 209, 223, 225, 240, 276, 281, 285, 313, 348, 371, 393, 397, 426, 489, 504, 518, 520, 538, 570
Carryl, 57
Carscillo, 11
Carson, 70, 127, 134, 351, 402
Carter, 57, 68, 82, 103, 150, 152, 163, 164, 178, 195, 224, 240, 293, 307, 334, 350, 395, 397, 400, 401, 438, 486, 489, 535, 545, 553, 562, 567
Carusi, 26, 31, 43, 57, 96, 107, 127, 129, 152, 198, 266, 273, 281, 513, 521, 535
Caruthers, 152, 419
Carver, 3, 57
Carvill, 355
Carwell, 267
Carxillo, 251, 311, 313, 362
Cary, 42, 400, 401, 501
Casanave, 448
Case, 195
Casey, 93, 372, 383, 387
Cash, 374
Casidy, 343
Casmick, 568
Casparis, 151, 204, 366, 392, 485, 532, 547, 553, 554, 557
Casper, 103
Cass, 207, 355, 517
Cassedy, 273, 276
Cassel, 236
Cassell, 245
Cassidy, 20, 103, 195, 240, 538, 540

Cassin, 152, 208
Castleman, 495
Castor, 261, 563
Caswell, 85, 147, 529
Catalano, 12
Catching, 121, 301, 308, 330, 362
Cater, 443
Cathcart, 539
Cathedral Fort, 456
Catholic graveyard., 378
Catlett, 305
Catlin, 117, 250, 254, 330, 511
Caton, 11, 240, 475, 518, 553, 576
Cattin, 103
Catts, 406
Caulfield, 337
Caulison, 103
Caulk, 343
Causey, 85, 211, 330
Causin, 181, 213, 244, 270, 544
Causten, 36, 48, 99
Caustin, 480, 489
Cavanaugh, 489
Cavendy, 360
Cavillion, 3
Cayhow, 195
Cazeau, 43, 266
Cazenau, 543
Cazenave, 480
Cazenove, 525
Cazillo, 144
Cearires, 397
Cearnes, 103
Cearns, 489
Cedar Park, 304
Cenas, 304
Center, 79, 116
Centre, 301, 312
Centre Market-house, 157
Chace, 296
Chadborune, 228
Chadbourne, 73, 229, 252, 260, 359
Chadwick, 529
Chaffee, 117
Chaires, 77, 90, 141, 169, 355

Chalfant, 397
Challess, 443
Chalmers, 103, 391
Chamberlain, 18, 57, 133, 310
Chamberlin, 498
Chambers, 3, 68, 175, 240, 247, 341, 343, 426, 432, 533, 535, 579
Champagne, 560
Champe, 99, 331, 488, 565
Champion, 244
Chance, 510
Chancey, 240, 487
Chandler, 195, 211, 276, 333, 355, 366, 379, 397, 422, 429, 489, 549
Chaney, 57, 206
Channing, 342
Chapin, 79, 134, 260
Chaplain, 179
Chapman, 51, 57, 72, 91, 125, 195, 203, 240, 281, 293, 322, 379, 397, 443, 489, 579
Chappell, 240, 394
Chapperton, 189
Charden, 435
Charlemagne, 357
Charles, 141
Charleton, 9, 397
Chase, 40, 56, 120, 152, 195, 240, 269, 281, 489
Chaseaud, 202
Chasseand, 87, 361
Chasseaud, 332, 416
Chatard, 379
Chatfield, 61, 147, 240, 266, 331
Chatman, 103
Chaudonia, 331
Chauncey, 500, 535
Cheairs, 343
Cheatham, 113, 266
Chedal, 11
Cheever, 23, 83, 86, 102, 152, 527
Cheeves, 497
Chellar, 443
Cheney, 450
Chenoweth, 475

595

Chenowith, 26, 148
Cherry, 115, 117, 287
Chesebro, 115
Cheshire, 244
Chesley, 221, 222
Cheswell, 207
Chetwood, 50
Chevallo, 312
Chew, 21, 95, 178, 195, 329, 440, 489, 554
Chezum, 46
Chichester, 56
Chick, 36, 443, 458, 489
Chifelle, 339
Child, 79
Childs, 66
Chilton, 57, 103
Chipman, 57, 115
Chisholm, 338, 343
Chislom, 47
Choate, 103, 195, 203, 240, 281, 363, 381, 410, 431, 475
Choteau, 128
Chouteau, 211, 274
Christian, 494, 532, 533
Christmas Plum Cake, 572
Chubb, 240
Chunn, 380, 407
Church, 55, 147
Churchill, 43, 57, 70, 240, 359, 365, 368, 384, 441, 550, 571
Churchman, 262
Ciphen, 561
Cisson, 57
Citadel, 456
Clack, 240
Clagett, 3, 9, 169, 188, 232, 254, 349, 403, 426, 429, 461, 531, 554
Claiborne, 233, 255, 563, 579
Claim Course, 212
Clair, 281, 505, 535
Clapham, 573
Clapp, 142
Clapper, 340
Clare, 199, 343

Clark, 18, 23, 26, 42, 56, 67, 92, 103, 114, 116, 138, 143, 147, 152, 161, 175, 185, 195, 202, 204, 205, 239, 240, 243, 251, 271, 278, 286, 309, 315, 331, 343, 369, 380, 384, 390, 422, 448, 460, 489, 502, 503, 505, 515, 518, 519, 525, 573, 579
Clarke, 3, 18, 33, 45, 47, 57, 68, 71, 79, 120, 122, 127, 138, 140, 144, 192, 195, 203, 209, 224, 237, 245, 262, 280, 281, 336, 343, 348, 365, 368, 374, 382, 383, 384, 397, 410, 426, 439, 443, 471, 494, 535, 550, 553, 554, 556, 562, 563, 570, 574, 581
Clarken, 507
Clarkin, 497
Clarkson, 152, 281
Clarvoe, 553
Clary, 185, 383, 387, 441, 523
Claude, 240
Clavadetscher, 75, 297, 553
Claveau, 357
Claxton, 25, 26, 103, 195
Clay, 87, 108, 260, 494
Clayton, 103, 152, 266, 331, 401
Clement, 539
Clements, 19, 26, 89, 98, 103, 130, 169, 188, 281, 317, 343, 349, 423, 426, 434, 440, 554, 555, 564
Clementson, 343
Clempson, 343
Clemson, 563, 578, 579
Clendenin, 385, 386
Clephane, 270
Clermon, 135, 575
Cleveland, 397
Clewell, 74
Clgerle, 152
Clifford, 465, 492, 573
Clinch, 91
Clinton, 103, 152, 195, 240, 351
Clitch, 553
Clitz, 74, 118, 159, 189, 281, 355, 405, 549

Clocker, 358
Clokey, 421
Clopper, 45, 567
Clopton, 302
Closky, 152
Clough, 98
Clover, 443
Clow, 240
Clubb, 489
Coad, 245, 440
Coal, 505
Coale, 103, 452
Coaly, 79
Cobb, 134, 251, 296, 311, 313, 328, 362, 509
Coble, 45
Coburn, 20, 72, 134, 240, 343, 553
Cochran, 25, 51, 70, 115, 210, 227, 539, 576, 577
Cochrane, 26, 152, 228, 229, 260
Cocke, 87, 160, 195, 343, 401, 402, 434
Cockerill, 57
Cockerille, 559
Cockey, 185
Cockrell, 10
Cockrill, 3
Coddington, 426
Codfish, 303
Codman, 103
Codrick, 397
Coe, 94, 165, 387, 489
Coff, 147
Coffee, 26, 222, 276, 508, 517
Coffin, 3, 26, 152, 195, 234, 246, 316, 343, 397, 473, 563
Coffman, 229
Cogdell, 323
Coggswell, 122
Cogswell, 535, 564
Cohen, 144, 150
Coiron, 337
Cokely, 537
Colburn, 48, 374
Colby, 119

Colclasier, 138
Colder, 240
Cole, 26, 30, 54, 71, 86, 133, 167, 212, 240, 262, 281, 321, 367, 414, 419, 440, 443, 508, 535, 554, 559
Coleman, 26, 29, 35, 57, 95, 118, 128, 157, 158, 169, 205, 245, 246, 275, 318, 328, 343, 355, 422, 437, 441, 484, 510, 538, 539, 542, 559, 564, 575, 580, 581
Colemus, 29
Coles, 56
Colgate, 103
Colhoun, 458
Colison, 446
Collamore, 123, 185, 538, 540
Collard, 33, 336, 406
Collers, 435
Collett, 8
Colley, 57, 523, 539
Collier, 103, 132, 281, 327, 368, 489
Collings, 26
Collins, 57, 70, 74, 152, 173, 195, 240, 281, 382, 405, 418, 443, 448, 508, 511, 553
Colman, 103, 388
Colonization Society, 418
Colquhoun, 281, 343, 535
Colquitt, 135, 364, 393, 397
Colson, 579
Colston, 159, 573, 580
Colt, 57, 103, 223
Coltman, 20, 39, 184, 234
Colton, 26, 57, 103, 237, 343, 546
Columbus, 151, 195, 374, 478, 554, 560, 566
Colvocoresses, 240
Comada, 343
Comb, 56
Combs, 3, 170, 232, 332, 343, 426, 486, 553, 554, 559
Comelly, 57
Comier, 57
Comings, 152
Comly, 553

Commons, 509
Compton, 541, 578
Comstock, 26, 372, 533, 535
Conant, 250, 359, 361, 375
Conard, 440
Conaut, 311, 313
Condit, 467
Cone, 277
Congress burying-ground, 500
Congressional Burial Ground, 36, 95, 157
Congressional Burying Ground, 567
Congressional Cemetery, 462
Coninx, 21
Conklin, 19, 97, 317
Conley, 331, 426
Conlin, 57
Conline, 504
Conly, 195, 303
Conn, 327
Connahan, 281
Connaut, 326, 342
Connell, 152, 240, 467
Connelly, 232, 373, 426
Conner, 365, 426, 458, 464, 471, 506, 535
Conners, 525
Connolly, 109, 164, 170, 215, 448, 449, 450, 482, 483
Connor, 226, 554
Conover, 307, 379
Conrad, 373, 393
Conroy, 103
Constantine, 545
Contant, 89
Contee, 581
Contor, 553
Converse, 102, 203, 213, 331
Conway, 15, 31, 152, 191, 211, 281, 379
Coody, 343
Cook, 1, 3, 33, 56, 86, 103, 130, 183, 195, 206, 281, 294, 349, 352, 412, 467, 509, 516, 517, 524, 535, 543, 546, 580

Cooke, 26, 34, 103, 152, 195, 240, 397, 489
Cookendorfer, 483
Cooley, 539
Coolidge, 461, 552
Cooly, 438
Coombe, 126, 236, 290, 300, 403, 535
Coombes, 266, 527
Coombs, 128, 143
Coomes, 290
Coon, 172
Coones, 240
Cooper, 3, 51, 57, 62, 103, 130, 147, 240, 261, 325, 341, 343, 372, 373, 426, 457, 489, 531, 535, 570, 579
Cope, 207
Copeland, 25, 39, 287, 574
Copp, 93, 553
Coppee, 74
Corbin, 3, 26, 402
Corbitt, 3, 236, 478
Corcoran, 14, 109, 151, 160, 232, 234, 235, 407, 426, 427, 475, 542, 553, 574
Cormick, 3, 152, 535
Cornel, 57
Cornelia, 397
Cornelius, 148
Corning, 341
Cornish, 195
Cornog, 16
Cornwall, 85
Cornwallis, 171
Corpley, 498
Corse, 263, 552
Corser, 195, 208, 330, 563
Corson, 443, 480, 553
Cortwite, 79
Corwell, 330
Corwin, 57, 147
Coryell, 20, 343
Cost, 278
Costell, 553
Coster, 188
Costin, 3

Coston, 26, 84, 152, 535
Cotter, 95, 152, 273, 354, 389, 450, 485
Cottier, 221
Cottman, 88
Cotton, 72, 510
Couman, 195
Coumbe, 3
Counsel, 437
Couper, 91
Courter, 3
Courtis, 530
Courtney, 26, 378, 558
Coury, 3
Coutant, 82
Couts, 71
Coutts, 56, 401
Covell, 66
Cover, 276, 281
Covert, 103
Covington, 397
Cowan, 117, 152, 397
Cowdin, 114
Cowherd, 335
Cox, 3, 57, 91, 93, 96, 103, 109, 122, 132, 152, 163, 186, 187, 188, 195, 208, 251, 258, 262, 274, 278, 287, 313, 337, 348, 357, 397, 413, 439, 469, 478, 489, 494, 497, 512, 518, 560
Coxe, 31, 56, 121, 149, 178, 301, 308, 330, 507, 572, 581
Coy, 68
Coyle, 44, 110, 236, 262, 391, 484, 553
Crabb, 378, 566
Crabtree, 89
Cragin, 371
Craig, 383, 426
Craigmiles, 55
Crain, 125, 558
Craiten, 359
Cram, 239, 244, 261
Cramer, 152
Cramphin, 195
Crampton, 426, 467
Cranch, 100, 168, 426, 503
Crandal, 3
Crandall, 92, 236, 407, 460, 533
Crandell, 95, 109, 202, 236, 246, 354
Crane, 95, 103, 111, 131, 144, 159, 183, 240, 244, 289, 328, 347, 373, 397, 450, 495, 535
Cranston, 199, 255, 558, 561
Crantze, 508
Crarps, 281
Crary, 473
Craven, 426
Crawford, 1, 3, 9, 38, 70, 89, 92, 98, 122, 162, 194, 232, 293, 318, 413
Crawley, 506
Craypo, 57
Creamer, 240, 271, 489
Creighton, 343
Crenshaw, 134
Crepon, 57
Crerar, 67
Crescraft, 103
Cresselle, 202
Cresson, 88
Creutzfeldt, 553
Crim, 270
Crisfield, 277
Crismond, 560
Crismont, 359
Crittenden, 74, 103, 233, 256, 275, 548
Crocker, 246, 341, 343, 496
Crockett, 343, 451
Crofton, 340
Crofut, 528
Croggan, 554
Croggin, 443
Crogham, 187
Croghan, 57, 240, 322
Crook, 348, 422, 523
Crooks, 2, 402
Croom, 172, 178
Cropley, 390, 498

Crosby, 8, 55, 103, 114, 152, 195, 226, 257, 281, 355, 363, 496
Crosman, 386
Cross, 26, 29, 125, 159, 195, 210, 213, 263, 288, 318, 334, 351, 387, 426, 441, 475, 493, 495, 499, 500, 529, 539, 560
Cross Keys, 471
Crossan, 350
Crossfield, 77
Crossman, 383
Crough, 281
Crouse, 163
Crout, 231
Crow, 392, 422
Crowell, 62, 277, 279, 285, 286, 292, 331, 346, 361, 416
Crowley, 20, 65, 176, 183, 202, 206, 234, 426
Crown, 3, 103, 195, 206, 343, 376, 495, 535, 568
Crowther, 420
Crozet, 141
Crozier, 85, 117, 251, 312
Cruger, 343
Cruickshank, 143
Cruikshank, 262
Cruit, 122, 348, 437, 480, 543
Crump, 3, 26, 57, 82, 103, 152, 195
Cruse, 98
Crutchett, 26, 180, 328
Crutchfield, 263, 508
Cruttenden, 92, 139, 142, 224, 426, 467
Cryder, 110, 266
Crysalt, 266
Cudlip, 484, 485
Cull, 202, 553
Cullum, 103, 152, 533, 538
Cully, 115
Culver, 17, 94, 165, 192, 296
Culverwell, 46, 82, 142, 396, 513
Cumming, 55, 331, 337
Cummings, 103, 281, 293, 487
Cummins, 103, 271, 397, 432

Cunningham, 122, 150, 152, 240, 348, 397, 422, 534, 538
Curd, 382, 535
Curdois, 226
Curry, 11, 200, 244
Curse, 42
Curtin, 300
Curtis, 3, 52, 57, 152, 341, 443, 463, 509
Curwen, 174, 251, 346
Curwin, 313
Cushing, 26, 240, 296, 397, 513
Cushman, 35, 69, 99, 240, 343
Custis, 3, 278
Cuthbert, 293, 419, 482
Cutler, 3, 26, 315, 333, 516
Cutt, 202
Cutter, 247, 420
Cutting, 231, 343
Cutts, 49, 83, 136, 348
Cuyler, 26, 57, 88, 152

D

D'Anville, 103
d'Assis, 499
D'Estaing, 310
d'Oremieulx, 548
Dabadie, 69
Dabney, 173
Dacota Territory, 217
Dade, 103, 152, 176, 184
Dadson, 509
Dagerty, 200
Dailey, 26, 57, 83, 240
Daily, 152
Daingerfield, 203, 356, 379
Dakin, 562
Dale, 132, 343, 543
Daley, 150, 238, 392
Dallam, 518
Dallas, 36, 126, 397, 410, 431, 458
Dalloff, 437
Dalrymple, 145
Dalton, 343, 402, 443, 554

Daly, 20, 188, 432, 554
Dameron, 351
Damoiseau, 409
Damron, 251, 311
Damson, 147
Dana, 3, 45, 55, 136, 152, 226, 281, 338, 362, 379, 472
Dandridge, 57
Dane, 235
Danford, 443
Danforth, 3, 57
Daniel, 57, 109, 240, 397, 536, 542
Daniell, 53
Daniels, 287
Dank, 536
Dann, 103
Dant, 195
Daragh, 195
Darah, 267
Darby, 421, 443
Darcantel, 451
Darcy, 152
Darkey, 487
Darling, 88, 114
Darne, 73, 294, 299, 443
Darnell, 3, 26, 57
Darnes, 536
Darracott, 209
Darrah, 26
Darrell, 489
Darxilla, 315
Dashiell, 569
Davenport, 29, 50, 68, 180, 195, 206, 266, 302, 315, 443, 512
Davezac, 68
David, 3, 103, 146, 397, 536
Davidson, 2, 47, 57, 73, 85, 86, 103, 112, 125, 148, 172, 181, 195, 205, 240, 244, 270, 294, 302, 361, 426, 491, 515
Davies, 42, 57, 73, 132, 161, 462
Davis, 3, 26, 29, 31, 38, 42, 51, 69, 72, 75, 86, 92, 93, 97, 103, 122, 126, 139, 141, 147, 152, 193, 195, 202, 204, 233, 240, 245, 246, 249, 256, 257, 281, 288, 311, 322, 332, 385, 386, 392, 394, 395, 397, 426, 440, 443, 453, 455, 460, 467, 468, 473, 475, 483, 494, 497, 507, 508, 536, 543, 554, 559, 560, 567, 573, 581
Davisk, 509
Davison, 449
Davy, 554
Davys, 301
Dawes, 219, 391
Dawson, 69, 152, 153, 240, 313, 337, 343, 448, 451, 558, 573
Day, 36, 57, 65, 87, 132, 158, 216, 294, 414, 458, 473, 546, 579
Dayly, 20
Dayton, 50, 111, 421, 531
de Alvear, 243
De Blanc, 348
De Bree, 80
De Courcy, 223, 351
de Grass, 51
De Hass, 152
De Haven, 458
de Kalb, 102
De Krafft, 93
De la Montagnie, 468
De la Roche, 102, 565
de Mattey, 334
De Meyer, 107
De Neale, 57
De Roche, 331
De Russey, 417
De Russy, 218, 266, 312, 361
De Saule, 11
De Saules, 481, 554
De Silver, 371
De Witt, 3, 103, 512
Deacon, 103
Deakin, 253
Deakins, 193, 253
Deale, 288, 466
Dean, 3, 489
Deane, 281, 411
Deany, 492
Dearborn, 67, 141, 185, 423, 560

Deardorff, 22
Dearing, 422
Deas, 72, 150, 227, 301, 545
DeBellevue, 89
DeBemo, 3
DeBlanc, 337
Debow, 51
Debue, 528
DeBuys, 222
Decatur, 12, 470, 476
Decker, 103
Dedman, 3
Deehring, 235
Deering, 244
DeGeisse, 103
Degges, 195, 300
Degraff, 26, 144
Degrand, 118
Dehooler, 498
Deitz, 47, 489
DeKoven, 26
DeKrafft, 195
Delacroix, 337
Delafield, 118, 536
DeLand, 26
Delaney, 3, 240
Delano, 114
Delanu, 195
Delany, 240, 318, 466, 481, 485, 506, 539, 554
Delazerne, 169, 189
Deleny, 57
Delezenne, 99
Dell, 348, 349
Demarters, 157
Dement, 3, 41, 165, 186, 195, 245, 343, 460
Demidoff, 432
Deming, 6, 79, 139
Dempster, 123, 392
Deneal, 546
Deneale, 84, 152, 234, 235
DeNeale, 109, 123, 554
Denel, 14
Denevue, 85

Denham, 3, 240, 397, 539
Denholm, 268
Denio, 143
Denison, 91, 569
Deniston, 379
Denman, 233, 256
Dennett, 57
Dennington, 152
Dennis, 459
Denniston, 307
Dennistone, 401
Denny, 73
Denow, 570
Dent, 37, 259, 365, 495
Denton, 102, 311, 361
Depkin, 397
Depkine, Chas, 536
Derby, 103, 240, 385, 552
Derickson, 440
Deringer, 380, 391
Dermott, 190, 247, 478
Derrie, 570
Derring, 240
Derringer, 37, 182, 449
Desaules, 199
DeSaules, 571
Desberry, 132
Desfourneaux, 257
Desha, 333
Deshla, 240
Deshler, 116
Deshon, 521
Deslonde, 337
Dessau, 138, 326
Deutche, 510
Devaugh, 228
Devaughn, 152, 326
Develin, 192
Devenish, 103
Devens, 527
Devereaux, 529
Devereux, 240, 348
Devery, 554
Devilbiss, 441
Devlin, 39, 47, 268, 298

Devond, 281
Dew, 308, 411
Dewdney, 316, 326
Dewee, 8
Dewees, 93
Dewey, 57, 195, 355, 451, 489, 564
Dewitt, 240
Dexter, 69, 219, 355, 395
Dexton, 313
Dials, 327
Diamond Mine, 119
Dibble, 64, 265, 374
Dick, 25, 218, 356, 443
Dickens, 8, 472
Dickerson, 88, 343, 355
Dickey, 39, 133
Dickins, 347
Dickinson, 3, 26, 75, 103, 152, 173, 195, 231, 262, 293, 324, 443
Dickover, 57
Dicks, 173
Dickson, 3, 57, 141, 152, 341
Didlake, 567
Diederick, 560
Dietz, 39, 461
Diffenbach, 20
Diffenderffer, 233
Digges, 3, 240, 327, 370, 426, 433, 463, 475, 564
Diggs, 3, 103, 152, 301
Dill, 145
Diller, 571
Dillow, 554
Dilworth, 210, 383, 457, 477, 504, 524, 548, 551
Dimon, 406
Dimond, 550, 571
Dimsdale, 98
Dines, 161, 162
Dinnies, 3, 57, 103
Dippel, 109, 110, 240
Disbrow, 78, 330
Dishman, 489
Ditty, 50
Dix, 72, 73, 195, 355, 579

Dixey, 116, 529
Dixon, 3, 26, 57, 74, 87, 89, 102, 103, 166, 203, 240, 281, 401, 402, 443, 492, 538, 566, 569, 574
Doane, 425
Dobbin, 112, 317, 574
Dobbins, 228, 229, 260, 536
Dobbs, 533
Dobbyn, 443
Dobbyns, 55
Doble, 504
Dockerty, 57
Dockray, 57
Dod, 221
Dodd, 30, 349, 529
Dodds, 554
Dodge, 3, 22, 61, 68, 297, 332, 569, 577
Dodson, 3
Doebely, 234
Dogg, 529
Doherty, 281
Doig, 321
Dolan, 249, 268, 358
Dole, 566
Doliber, 529
Dolton, 508
Donahue, 498
Donald, 17, 401, 402
Donaldson, 57, 240, 439, 529
Donally, 536
Donalson, 95
Donaphon, 427
Done, 440, 448
Donegan, 168, 337
Donelan, 16, 21, 29, 37, 44, 84, 95, 136, 140, 175, 188, 201, 209, 239, 249, 297, 347, 364, 372, 378, 425, 486, 515
Donelly, 152
Donelson, 26, 133, 152, 401
Donely, 57
Doney, 498, 508
Doniphan, 33, 188, 248, 298, 302, 398, 536

Donley, 26, 397
Donly, 152
Donn, 17, 149, 188, 263, 277, 354, 370, 460, 539
Donnelly, 3, 57
Donoghue, 127, 337, 348, 507
Donoho, 40, 195, 337, 427, 460, 483
Donohon, 61
Donohoo, 269, 281, 484, 485, 544, 554
Donovan, 234, 483
Donovon, 195
Donton, 251
Doods, 3
Dooley, 20
Doolittle, 397
Doran, 152, 194, 347
Dorn, 26, 274
Dornay, 103
Dornin, 346
Dorr, 195, 409, 567
Dorrance, 545
Dorrell, 238
Dorris, 334, 386
Dorry, 332
Dorsey, 57, 117, 195, 240, 281, 343, 360, 373, 397, 437, 536
Dort, 67
Doty, 69, 70
Doub, 440, 461
Douch, 174
Dougherty, 3, 173, 237, 247, 533, 540, 578
Doughty, 92, 109, 174, 303
Douglas, 100, 101, 124, 175, 210, 227, 554
Douglass, 3, 93, 107, 218, 240, 281, 288, 314, 316, 429, 536, 552, 569, 572
Doulin, 296
Douthet, 330
Dove, 20, 195, 268, 283, 291, 311, 336, 343, 386, 426, 472, 562
Dover, 140
Doverwater, 123

Dow, 37, 103, 177, 245, 262, 539, 547
Dowden, 398, 499, 536
Dowdy, 536
Dowel, 397
Dowell, 397
Dowler, 457
Dowling, 113, 119, 127
Downes, 69, 152, 322, 323
Downey, 12, 103, 170, 177, 281, 378, 418
Downing, 15, 26, 57, 92, 152, 240, 281, 422, 509, 524
Downs, 147, 223, 271
Dowson, 57, 224
Doxey, 163
Doyle, 21, 77, 113, 195, 243, 294, 336, 414, 427, 440
Dozier, 240
Draine, 430
Drake, 122, 236, 494, 538
Drane, 177, 179, 383, 388, 549
Draper, 3
Draugn, 134
Drayton, 230, 374, 451
Drempey, 432
Dresser, 79
Drew, 92, 96, 370, 528, 538
Dreyer, 346, 514, 578
Drinkard, 283
Dripps, 158
Drouet, 337
<u>Drowning</u>, 447
Drudge, 131
Drummond, 26, 195, 398, 426, 536
Drummons, 398
Drury, 51, 125, 195, 236, 288, 321, 326, 381, 426, 460, 544
Duane, 199
Dubant, 191
Dubois, 509
Dubosy, 235
Dubourjal, 152
Dubuque, 149, 211
Duchart, 506
Ducheane, 238

Duckett, 440, 470, 534
Duckworth, 13
Dudley, 240, 536
Duer, 51, 536
Duff, 195, 426
Duff Green's Row, 532
Duffey, 274
Duffield, 240
Duffy, 7
Dufour, 348
Dufresne, 180, 337
Dufresnet, 202
Dugdale, 51
Duggan, 147
Dugherty, 200
Dujanier, 185
Duke of Brunswick, 220
Dulany, 3, 36, 39, 57, 183, 288, 343, 397, 499
Dulay, 26
Duley, 3
Duling, 438
Dumas, 26
Dumeste, 567
Dumont, 222
Dumphey, 392
Dumphrey, 571
Dun, 265
Dunbar, 3, 26, 147, 489
Duncan, 26, 45, 57, 88, 91, 116, 203, 233, 240, 256, 281, 324, 331, 337, 348, 364, 365, 384, 385, 401, 411, 533, 536, 563
Duncanson, 92, 439
Duncanston, 128
Dundas, 93, 165, 193, 518
Dundass, 250
Dunham, 3, 152, 570
Dunin, 86
Dunkinson, 366, 440
Dunkley, 468
Dunlap, 57, 115, 152, 287, 562
Dunlevy, 423
Dunlop, 68, 194, 195, 218, 277, 443
Dunn, 3, 57, 103, 132, 310, 374, 536

Dunning, 94, 103
Dunohoo, 281
Dunscomb, 396
Dupont, 290, 546
Dupre, 117
Duralde, 10
Durand, 229
Durant, 271
Durbin, 88
Durborow, 148
Durborrow, 70
Durell, 195
Durham, 411
Durkee, 99, 169, 189
Durr, 77, 240, 556
Durrive, 252
Dusean, 79
Dusenbery, 382, 386
Dusseau, 147, 251, 311, 313, 363
Dustan, 532, 540
Dutton, 99, 195, 397
Duval, 117, 195, 417, 496, 508
Duvall, 3, 22, 26, 45, 83, 86, 103, 109, 137, 149, 159, 165, 206, 207, 208, 218, 232, 236, 240, 251, 278, 280, 281, 343, 350, 361, 381, 397, 439, 443, 496, 536, 554, 555
Dwey, 26
Dwight, 26, 103, 261
Dwinell, 3
Dyckman, 112
Dye, 31, 146, 189
Dyer, 7, 14, 18, 29, 33, 39, 41, 47, 75, 77, 93, 100, 103, 125, 126, 135, 148, 152, 156, 157, 208, 243, 269, 277, 307, 327, 337, 377, 378, 430, 469, 511, 544, 554, 581
Dyerle, 421
Dygert, 25, 117
Dyson, 47, 183, 321, 391
Dyvernois, 231

E

Eagle, 422, 504

Earl, 343
Earle, 51, 92, 199, 217, 231, 554
Earley, 573
Early, 497
Easby, 39, 47, 109, 122, 151, 170, 177, 245, 296, 494, 569
Eastburn, 427
Eastland, 287
Eastman, 69, 538
Easton, 69, 214, 240, 245, 536
Eaton, 57, 186, 217, 246, 383, 387, 405, 489, 508, 536, 576
Eaves, 266
Eberbach, 183, 482, 483, 484, 485, 554
Eberle, 29
Ebert, 198, 230
Eccleston, 136, 140, 326
Echardt, 103
Eckel, 487
Eckert, 240, 464, 574
Eckhart, 57
Eckles, 287
Eckloff, 83, 199, 427, 480, 492, 538, 539, 566
Edds, 3
Eddy, 240, 382, 554
Edelin, 3, 57, 337, 348, 379, 427, 532
Edes, 40
Edgar, 88, 133, 436
Edgartown, 432
Edgerby, 279
Edgerly, 244, 265
Edgerton, 57
Edgertown, 489
Edie, 570
Edington, 190
Edmond, 281
Edmonds, 3, 10, 195, 229
Edmondston, 302, 306
Edmonson, 401
Edmonston, 77, 240, 427
Edmunds, 148
Edson, 258, 266, 331, 458, 526
Edward, 164

Edwards, 10, 74, 103, 114, 163, 195, 238, 240, 281, 294, 300, 343, 401, 411, 435, 504, 511
Edwing, 57
Eeatland, 530
Eells, 16
Egan, 498, 507, 554
Egbert, 441
Ege, 16, 22, 148, 407, 441, 487, 496, 500, 522, 546, 562
Egerton, 316
Eggleston, 16, 47, 99, 148, 208, 234, 278, 325, 410, 496, 526
Ehringhaus, 103
Eichelberger, 300, 570
Eichner, 103
Eimon, 152
Eland, 489
Eldendice, 132
Elder, 131, 276
Elderdice, 132
Eldred, 76, 202, 331, 565, 572
Eldridge, 211
Elezy, 398
Elgin, 433
Eliason, 178, 231, 379
Eliot, 100, 355, 389, 410, 554
Elis, 129
Elkinton, 532
Eller, 553
Ellery, 163, 240
Ellicott, 245, 318, 427
Ellingwood, 395
Elliot, 9, 126, 208, 299, 303, 307, 332, 338, 355, 362, 508, 531
Elliott, 1, 3, 13, 26, 44, 57, 103, 135, 183, 233, 256, 281, 328, 331, 398, 433, 443, 508, 554
Ellis, 3, 17, 20, 23, 26, 39, 76, 87, 97, 148, 154, 197, 236, 249, 266, 299, 337, 339, 357, 371, 398, 554, 569, 581
Ellison, 64, 457
Ellithrop, 536
Ellmore, 559

Ellsworth, 19, 26, 68, 240
Elmer, 88
Elmes, 231
Elmondorf, 57
Elmore, 221, 489
Elmsley, 579
Elslen, 492
Elting, 26, 507, 550
Elton, 214
Elwell, 57
Ely, 82, 195, 196
Elzey, 57
Elzy, 103
Emack, 328
Emerson, 57, 281, 518
Emery, 296, 343, 395
Emmerich, 205, 499, 575
Emmerick, 111, 446
Emmerson, 355
Emmett, 489
Emmons, 3, 57, 77, 99, 152, 202, 224, 231, 398, 422, 519, 539, 556
Emory, 3, 20, 57, 237, 346, 515
Emperor Francis, 32
Empie, 326, 544
Eng, 227
Engard, 398
Engelbrecht, 57
England, 98, 279
Engle, 41, 457
Englebrecht, 536
Engles, 276
Englis, 118
English, 57, 181, 240, 307, 379, 431, 443, 541, 542
English Hill, 113
Ennis, 20, 38, 39, 64, 76, 119, 127, 184, 279, 281, 348, 398, 427
Ennocks, 296
Enochs, 55, 226, 252, 362, 417
Enolee, 216
Enos, 287
Entler, 257
Entwistle, 3
Enwisle, 103

Enwul, 504
Epervier, 500
Epes, 319
Eppes, 152, 566
Equal, 57, 443
Erb, 201, 228, 554
Ergood, 3
Ericson, 51
Ericsson, 281
Erie, 309
Ernest, 468
Erskine, 300
Erwin, 57, 286, 301, 308, 346, 362, 417
Esdale, 402
Esher, 57
Eskredge, 401
Eskridge, 360
Eslava, 337
Espey, 258, 375, 489
Espy, 107, 536
Essex, 98, 425
Essex, Mass, 201
Estes, 146, 158, 189
Etting, 64, 293, 296, 303, 330, 331, 362, 416
Eubanks, 229
Eugles, 509
Eustis, 71, 352, 443, 568
Eva, 132
Evans, 3, 16, 25, 50, 57, 78, 90, 100, 103, 127, 140, 143, 152, 171, 180, 195, 238, 240, 260, 261, 281, 293, 368, 372, 381, 410, 413, 425, 427, 443, 451, 480, 496, 500, 536, 539
Eve, 387
Everard, 402
Everardus, 152
Everett, 3, 10, 82, 200, 230, 355, 489, 515
Eversole, 132
Everts, 70
Evertson, 468
Ewell, 71, 132, 152, 233, 255

Ewing, 26, 57, 152, 161, 343, 348, 536
Exeter, 55, 64
Eyre, 240, 400

F

Faber, 3, 270
Fagan, 425, 536
Fagin, 489
Faherty, 39
Fahr, 489
Fahy, 3
Fail, 129
Failes, 26
Fairchild, 70
Fairfax, 36, 356, 374, 375, 427, 458, 522
Fairfield, 443, 536
Faithful, 34
Falconer, 208, 240
Fales, 57, 304, 427, 535
Falkner, 249
Falknew, 26
Fallen, 522
Fannin, 279, 330, 362, 417
Fanning, 169, 180, 340, 388, 449, 570
Fannon, 57
Fardy, 3
Farelly, 74
Farlee, 152
Farley, 505
Farmer, 11, 359, 518
Farnham, 31, 39, 61, 231, 240, 245, 377, 415, 460, 538, 554
Farnsworth, 11, 535
Farquarson, 258
Farquhar, 248, 408, 470
Farr, 20, 103
Farrar, 240, 309, 554
Farrell, 359, 497, 507, 528, 530
Farrelly, 383
Farrer, 31
Farrington, 61, 147, 281, 561
Farrish, 57

Farron, 173
Farrow, 78, 195
Farry, 74, 548
Faulkler, 506
Faulkner, 235
Fauntleroy, 382, 475
Favier, 419, 554
Favor, 57, 104, 195
Fay, 195
Fayette, 350
Fays, 6
Feady, 26
Feagans, 26
Feaman, 82, 331, 361, 415
Fearson, 134, 166, 554, 568
Featherson, 451
Featherston, 339, 420
Febiger, 489
Feeks, 393
Feeney, 204
Feinour, 3, 281
Fellanny, 286, 572
Fellar, 554
Feller, 195
Felt, 99
Felton, 81
Female Smokers, 310
Fendall, 173, 332, 475, 543
Fennel, 579
Fenner, 177, 195, 287, 455
Fenno, 443
Fenton, 57, 104, 489
Fenwick, 26, 57, 104, 217, 240, 262, 275, 337, 348, 366, 369, 370
Feretti, 316
Ferguson, 17, 26, 47, 96, 110, 112, 129, 152, 162, 195, 240, 288, 317, 343, 443
Feriton, 20
Ferraris, 32
Ferrell, 55
Ferrer, 281
Ferretti, 335
Ferris, 240, 266
Ferry, 152

Fetchtig, 115
Fetter, 240
Fewell, 137
Fickicson, 511
Ficklin, 17, 85, 94, 97, 112, 301, 362, 393
Field, 260, 401, 456, 470, 504, 538, 549, 551
Fields, 287, 387
Fieska, 222
Files, 492, 580
Filler, 7
Fillies, 104
Finacum, 394
Finch, 130, 134, 202, 346, 393
Findlay, 520
Fink, 131
Finkman, 425, 478, 554
Finlay, 54
Finley, 19
Finn, 359
Finnegan, 81
Finnell, 295
Finteneau, 240
Fiora, 263
Firmstone, 459
Fischer, 181, 238, 240, 298, 355, 439, 497
Fisdick, 310
Fiset, 267
Fish, 329
Fisher, 57, 77, 95, 104, 132, 136, 150, 152, 168, 184, 236, 240, 281, 343, 358, 402, 443, 489, 545, 554, 571
Fisk, 37, 225, 464
Fitch, 26, 39, 303, 331, 460
Fitman, 554
Fitz, 540
Fitzgerald, 3, 41, 72, 121, 152, 202, 240, 265, 272, 321, 337, 352, 392, 432, 481, 482, 483, 484, 486, 487, 536, 547, 554
Fitzhugh, 104, 489, 498, 508, 536, 546, 553

Fitzpatrick, 39, 47, 145, 245, 288, 369, 370, 515
Flagg, 3, 179, 246, 281
Flamry, 359
Flanagan, 123, 343
Flannagan, 497
Flannegan, 140
Flannigan, 507, 509
Fleet, 3, 398, 528
Fleming, 3, 43, 211, 401, 508, 510, 511, 531, 554
Flemming, 104
Flenrickin, 281
Fletch, 532
Fletcher, 20, 39, 84, 109, 112, 117, 120, 161, 262, 281, 394, 398, 413, 434, 498, 508, 554, 568
Flewellen, 57
Flick, 117, 182
Flinn, 39, 161, 448
Flint, 427
Flocke, 104
Flohr, 419
Flood, 159, 371, 568
Florance, 343, 529
Florence, 398
Flowers, 240
Floyd, 22, 23, 117, 152, 240, 257, 271, 469, 581
Flyblock, 57
Flye, 360
Fobes, 240
Fogert, 343
Folger, 340
Follansbee, 427
Folsom, 383, 549
Folwell, 437
Fontane, 71
Fooks, 439
Foot, 425, 551
Foote, 195, 526, 537
Forbes, 26, 57, 89, 103, 104, 138, 240, 303, 559
Force, 44, 62, 264, 436

Ford, 57, 103, 104, 121, 139, 142, 195, 202, 258, 286, 343, 348, 429, 443, 459, 536, 559
Fording, 104
Fordney, 469
Foreman, 17, 580
Forest, 281, 327
Forman, 306
Forney, 26, 104, 195
Forrest, 93, 94, 95, 138, 165, 187, 250, 314, 398, 413, 418, 427, 458, 469, 472, 484, 518, 526, 531, 574
Forshee, 443
Forshey, 281
Forstall, 337
Forsyth, 70, 371, 385, 436
Fort Adams, 24, 145
Fort Atchison, 294
Fort Atkinson, 352
Fort Beauford, 352
Fort Bosien, 318
Fort Brady, 305, 310
Fort Brooke, 320
Fort Brown, 260, 364, 384, 403
Fort Columbus, 465
Fort Crawford, 294
Fort Cumberland, 421
Fort Gaines, 370
Fort George, 91
Fort Gibson, 348
Fort Guerrier, 340
Fort Hall, 390
Fort Hamilton, 328
Fort Jackson, 298
Fort Laramie, 318
Fort Leavensworth, 294
Fort Leavenworth, 271, 274, 298, 340, 407, 446, 502, 515
Fort Meigs, 179, 211
Fort Mifflin, 24, 177
Fort Mitchell, 292
Fort Monroe, 289, 347
Fort Niagara, 151
Fort Scott, 471
Fort Smith, 23, 142, 352

Fort Snelling, 423
Fort St Philip, 18
Fort Suter, 390
Fort Taylor, 260
Fort Washington, 255, 258
Fort Washits, 210
Fort Wayne, 302, 305, 331
Fortress Calhoun, 179
Fortune, 181, 240, 398, 443
Fossitt, 343
Foster, 7, 17, 44, 88, 89, 104, 110, 130, 145, 195, 253, 261, 325, 356, 458, 536
Fothergill, 455
Foulkes, 427
Fountain, 186
Fource, 281
Foust Hill, 562
Fowl, 6
Fowle, 17, 57, 166, 189, 577
Fowler, 3, 68, 102, 104, 116, 122, 139, 152, 171, 204, 206, 228, 229, 234, 260, 281, 286, 342, 343, 376, 427, 439, 440, 489, 492, 494, 496, 536, 546, 554
Fox, 2, 57, 65, 398, 439, 462
Foxall, 541
Foxter, 496
Foxwell, 343
Foy, 76, 103, 118, 202, 221, 274, 343, 483, 485, 536, 554
Fraleigh, 536
Frame, 152
France, 26, 57, 240, 281, 337, 398, 479, 480, 487, 519, 536
Francia, 190, 560
Francis, 89, 358, 471, 511
Francisco, 206
Frank, 343
Franklin, 79, 177, 190, 214, 234, 240, 245, 445, 453, 483, 493, 548
Franzoni, 127, 292
Franzonia, 47
Fraser, 117, 172, 181, 321, 441, 486, 489, 539

Frasier, 219
Frazer, 119, 188, 204, 268, 281
Frazier, 144, 195, 440
Fred'k XI, 279
Frederick, 253, 374, 489, 510
Free Trade, 400
Freedley, 464
Freedy, 427
Freelon, 536
Freeman, 17, 63, 90, 117, 131, 137, 330, 378, 411, 412, 440, 498, 507, 508, 536, 558, 561, 575
Freer, 427
Freidenberger, 57
Frelinghuysen, 87, 107, 118, 281
Fremiot, 369
Fremont, 189, 233, 353, 398, 478
French, 3, 16, 19, 30, 31, 39, 48, 53, 91, 119, 134, 147, 208, 238, 270, 284, 334, 374, 382, 418, 434, 440, 442, 447, 489, 502, 504, 532, 533, 536, 538, 540, 550, 557
Frescati, 470
Fricken, 505
Friend, 142, 150, 184, 427
Friends, 520
Friese, 296
frig **Columbia**, 131
frig **Congress**, 546
frig **Constitution**, 329, 373
frig **Cumberland**, 36, 86, 458, 479, 526
frig **Fulton**, 416
frig **Philadelphia**, 12, 559
frig **Potomac**, 76
frig **Savannah**, 80
frig **United States**, 111, 373
Frink, 152
Frisby, 343
Fritz, 238
Fritzpatrick, 443
Frogge, 17, 100, 112, 301, 361
Frost, 31, 35, 90, 160, 207, 295, 342, 443, 568
Frothingham, 39

Fruhling, 536
Fruturmuth, 240
Fry, 26, 103, 192, 195, 247, 260, 326, 328, 536, 563
Frye, 205, 217, 485
Fryers, 281
Fugatt, 561, 574
Fugett, 3
Fugitt, 110, 554
Fulenwider, 49
Fulford, 112, 159
Fuller, 3, 26, 43, 57, 92, 104, 142, 143, 144, 152, 181, 216, 225, 259, 261, 263, 308, 330, 375, 433, 436, 480, 536, 539
Fullerton, 512
Fulmer, 3, 202, 245, 337
Fulmore, 47
Fulton, 3, 29, 51, 147, 206, 240, 251, 286, 296, 311, 313, 315, 324, 351, 353, 361, 416, 473
Fulton Guards, 220
Fundler, 7
Funk, 22
Funkhauser, 370
Funstan, 396
Furguson, 398
Furlong, 427
Furman, 468
Furt, 337
Furtney, 195
Fye, 151

G

Gabaroche, 337
Gaddis, 202, 250, 522
Gadsby, 188, 215, 391, 443, 481, 560
Gadsden, 568
Gadwin, 468
Gage, 159, 321, 343
Gaham, 485
Gahan, 241, 571
Gaiennie, 302, 331, 523

Gaines, 45, 131, 137, 152, 219, 220, 222, 260, 267, 271, 289, 298, 342, 343, 347, 350, 359, 386
Gaither, 24, 153, 188, 288
Galabrun, 161, 259, 380, 449, 454, 480
Galbraith, 222
Gale, 23, 51, 71, 533
Galer, 3
Gales, 37, 87, 182, 286, 380, 454, 536
Gallagher, 3, 45, 124, 359, 443, 507, 528
Gallaher, 44, 240, 326
Gallant, 39, 396
Galley, 26
Galligan, 240, 554
Galloway, 52, 517
Gally, 219, 298
Galphin, 62, 296
Galt, 104, 240, 396, 398, 515, 521
Galvin, 14, 249, 295
Gamble, 198
Gammon, 3
Gant, 343
Gantt, 69, 156, 389, 405
Garden of Eden, 191
Gardiner, 12, 50, 71, 91, 104, 109, 206, 241, 243, 343, 378, 486, 491, 528
Gardner, 9, 28, 35, 60, 72, 74, 107, 155, 177, 197, 231, 263, 281, 283, 299, 300, 301, 314, 345, 355, 400, 411, 413, 445, 485, 489, 532, 537, 554
Garesche, 382
Garland, 3, 84, 88, 200, 260, 455
Garlick, 453
Garltand, 489
Garner, 26, 241, 411, 423, 443, 581
Garnett, 104, 443
Garney, 443, 529
Garonski, 57, 280
Garrard, 287, 551
Garret, 398
Garrett, 443

Garrison, 104, 272, 287
Gartrell, 240
Garver, 506
Garvey, 561
Gassaway, 29, 97, 166, 390, 414, 501, 573
Gastin, 241
Gaston, 190
Gates, 3, 71, 211, 227, 228, 229, 246, 260, 359, 375, 384, 552
Gathir, 72
Gatlin, 524
Gatsell, 57
Gatton, 57, 398
Gattrell, 67, 394
Gaufney, 422
Gault, 20
Gautier, 175, 467, 554
Gavel, 579
Gavin, 509
Gay, 62, 277, 330, 398
Gebney, 540
Gedding, 275
Gedney, 104, 443, 449, 533
Gee, 98, 250, 311, 313, 326, 327, 359, 362, 416
Geessinger, 451
Geffers, 554
Geisinger, 153, 322, 546
Geisse, 334
Genard, 398
Gentry, 78, 534
George, 104, 439, 489, 496, 498, 507, 524, 536, 568
Gerbess, 234
Gerdes, 491
German Battalion, 222
Germine, 516
Gerolt, 572
Gersbenberger, 511
Getter, 99
Getty, 71, 443
Gevecot, 372
Geyer, 271
Ghiselin, 470, 534

612

Gholson, 434
Gholston, 287
Gibb, 267
Gibble, 173
Gibboner, 23
Gibbons, 57, 207, 281
Gibbs, 91, 147, 152, 181, 309, 333, 349
Gibert, 26
Gibons, 3, 104
Gibson, 3, 7, 26, 56, 57, 81, 82, 85, 94, 104, 125, 184, 192, 195, 207, 214, 223, 303, 343, 348, 382, 433, 443, 504, 508
Giddings, 57, 240, 421, 538
Gideon, 2, 30, 79, 83, 104, 202, 266, 331, 427, 453, 514, 545
Giffin, 312
Gifford, 281, 372, 507, 508
Gilbert, 14, 86, 93, 113, 153, 159, 278, 287, 343, 420, 508, 529, 530, 548, 569
Gilchrist, 401
Giles, 520, 529
Gilham, 547, 548, 550
Gill, 229, 235, 382, 398, 449
Gillan, 579
Gillespie, 4, 58, 281, 457, 512, 525
Gillet, 269, 371, 563
Gilleylieu, 79
Gilliam, 327
Gilliat, 495
Gilligan, 507
Gillis, 16, 159, 240, 430
Gilliss, 31, 271, 286, 291, 343, 470, 476, 489, 527
Gillott, 57
Gilman, 128, 341, 482, 483, 484, 554
Gilmer, 141, 509
Gilmore, 505
Gilmour, 402
Gilpin, 184, 298, 402
Gindrat, 453
Gipson, 58
Girard, 372

Girault, 520
Girdler, 529
Girl's Portion, 212
Gist, 104, 195, 526
Givens, 73, 230
Givney, 554
Gizzi, 324, 335
Glackemeyer, 267
Gladden, 70, 489
Gladding, 580
Gladmon, 274, 275
Glascock, 407
Glascoe, 297
Glasscock, 536
Glazier, 121
Glean, 468
Gleason, 26, 489, 533, 540
Gleeson, 398
Glendy, 57
Glenn, 21, 26, 42, 195, 231, 287, 316, 386, 387, 419, 536
Glessner, 566
Glove, 254
Glover, 104, 140, 172, 264, 343, 427, 443, 508, 529
Gluck, 491
Glynn, 240, 580
Goat island, 417
Goble, 104, 343
Goddard, 10, 13, 29, 66, 91, 138, 139, 190, 195, 239, 240, 288, 343, 476, 487, 495, 522, 536, 554
Goddart, 23, 78
Goden, 56
Godey, 20
Godwin, 3, 153
Goed, 505
Goel, 89
Goell, 331, 567
Goetner, 478
Goette, 153
Goff, 259
Going, 462
Goings, 443
Gold, 296

Golden, 32, 129, 425, 486
Goldin, 554
Golding, 216, 234, 554
Goldsborough, 200, 322, 427, 440, 528
Goldsmith, 448
Gollady, 153
Gonder, 153
Gondolpho, 376
Good, 40, 182
Goodall, 203, 239
Goodenough, 144, 567
Goodhue, 355
Goodin, 554
Gooding, 240, 281, 443, 533
Goodman, 95, 195
Goodrich, 57, 135, 156, 219, 425, 513, 560, 566
Goodsell, 371
Goodwin, 58, 147, 185, 313, 328, 360, 362, 377, 529
Goodyear, 234, 376, 566, 568
Goodyer, 104
Gookin, 115
Goothe, 195
Gordon, 45, 58, 90, 95, 104, 119, 133, 150, 184, 245, 254, 275, 281, 301, 308, 315, 457, 548, 549, 562
Gore, 427, 563
Gorham, 348
Gorman, 20, 26, 65, 104, 146, 362, 417
Gormley, 536
Gormly, 20, 337
Gorsuch, 100, 101, 107
Goshing, 299
Goss, 89, 197, 529
Gossage, 147
Gottschalk, 377
Gouche, 53
Gough, 80, 104, 153, 452
Gould, 3, 24, 49, 119, 144, 152, 195, 252, 271, 347, 443, 533
Goundie, 184
Gouverneur, 39

Gov, 152
Govan, 402
Gowdy, 195
Gowins, 174
Grabill, 440
Graeve, 104, 240, 398
Grafton, 116
Graham, 4, 11, 19, 57, 58, 77, 101, 104, 153, 195, 281, 285, 287, 288, 295, 374, 398, 440, 453, 457, 477, 501, 502, 504, 524, 543, 549, 551, 559, 562
Graine, 240
Grammald, 398
Grammer, 26, 57, 144, 227, 236, 252, 262, 347, 354, 427, 439, 452, 519
Grammont, 298
Granbery, 402
Grand Duchess Olga, 458
Grandin, 148, 398
Granger, 74, 359
Grant, 26, 61, 72, 74, 83, 104, 152, 163, 240, 270, 327, 495, 496, 501
Grant,, 343
Grantun, 240
Gratiot, 26, 58, 274, 453
Gratton, 443
Gravatt, 240
Graves, 44, 52, 57, 89, 489, 529
Grawford, 3
Gray, 12, 35, 51, 63, 88, 104, 109, 128, 140, 147, 151, 152, 173, 216, 217, 235, 240, 250, 252, 253, 265, 278, 286, 296, 311, 313, 324, 343, 360, 361, 362, 380, 398, 402, 415, 427, 443, 489, 536, 546, 567
Grayson, 2, 9, 84, 85, 95, 102, 142, 146, 180, 186, 262, 382, 387, 394, 400
Greason, 484, 554
Greathouse, 215
Greaves, 52
Greeley, 338
Greely, 55, 226, 362

Green, 3, 11, 50, 57, 87, 94, 97, 98, 104, 107, 110, 116, 134, 136, 141, 144, 152, 153, 172, 182, 186, 202, 205, 206, 213, 216, 224, 240, 266, 291, 325, 336, 338, 343, 367, 378, 379, 394, 413, 443, 452, 459, 487, 489, 509, 514, 523, 525, 529, 536, 546, 554, 578
Greene, 3, 26, 62, 104, 114, 211, 279, 299, 379, 381, 489, 563
Greenfield, 410, 554
Greenhard, 343
Greenhow, 115, 402, 457
Greenleaf, 100, 126, 468, 564
Greenleaf's Point, 249, 495
Greenmount Cemetery, 339
Greenough, 237, 379, 414
Greenville, 536
Greenway Farm, 305
Greenwell, 67, 104, 425, 558
Greenwood, 181, 396
Greer, 170, 240, 427
Gregg, 30, 122, 152, 303
Gregory, 39, 41, 104, 116, 119, 270, 307, 504, 512, 569
Gregory XVI, 370
Grelan, 511
Grennell, 147
Grennen, 437
Grew, 296
Grey, 57, 104, 205, 281, 422, 433, 489, 511, 545
Grice, 57, 81, 97, 104, 220, 409, 421
Gridley, 240
Grier, 80, 349, 352, 515
Griffen, 47, 451
Griffin, 51, 57, 126, 203, 240, 355, 359, 398, 441, 515
Griffith, 4, 26, 237, 290, 325, 328, 377, 441
Grigg, 510
Griggs, 3, 57, 152
Griggsby, 3
Grignon, 104
Grigsby, 343, 422

Grimes, 21, 57, 281, 394, 443, 531, 536, 544
Grimshaw, 192
Griner, 26
Grinnan, 168
Grinnell, 455, 489, 547
Grisam, 509
Grisby, 512
Grisse, 107
Griswold, 398
Groff, 427, 536
Groger, 398
Grooms, 195, 539
Grooves, 281
Groran, 153
Grose, 26
Grosman, 139
Gross, 11, 104, 113, 119, 349
Groupe, 554
Grover, 115, 146, 560
Grubb, 511
Guerber, 26
Guess, 123, 211, 330
Guest, 148, 345, 501
Gueyer, 219
Guier, 125
Guild, 42
Guillou, 374
Guion, 554
Gulick, 26, 343
Gump, 128, 250, 311, 313, 326, 362
Gunn, 118, 152
Gunnell, 1, 119, 162, 169, 298, 336, 423, 543, 573
Gunton, 262, 355, 430, 455
Gurhett, 489
Gurley, 78, 122, 285, 564
Guthrie, 57, 184, 206
Guy, 488, 489, 574
Guytan, 104
Guyton, 536
Gwinn, 3, 281
Gwinnup, 117, 311, 313, 361
Gwiumaph, 326
Gwynn, 186, 240, 378, 527

Gwynne, 348
Gwynnup, 250

H

Haas, 241
Habersham, 56, 87, 458
Hache, 74
Hackelton, 195
Hackerman, 119
Hackleton, 287
Hackney, 427
Haddix, 359
Haddock's Hills, 208
Hadduck, 505
Hadley, 496
Hagan, 505, 532
Hager, 58, 104
Hagerty, 20, 104, 326, 554, 555
Haggerty, 469
Hagner, 239
Hahn, 70
Haier, 281
Haig, 153
Haight, 157, 173, 241, 443
Haines, 69, 173, 241, 394
Hainline, 193
Haistor, 4
Halbach, 61
Halden, 506
Hale, 6, 19, 79, 104, 153, 173, 215, 331, 334, 509, 565, 572
Haley, 98
Haliday, 245
Hall, 4, 19, 26, 30, 41, 58, 66, 88, 99, 104, 107, 110, 118, 122, 143, 149, 153, 165, 168, 195, 201, 207, 211, 241, 262, 264, 271, 280, 281, 303, 307, 337, 343, 349, 351, 355, 374, 377, 378, 402, 403, 418, 420, 427, 428, 437, 443, 454, 476, 482, 489, 494, 522, 531, 536, 539, 547, 554, 555, 558, 576
Hallam, 115, 329
Halleck, 312, 380

Haller, 58, 383, 506
Hallet, 215
Hallett, 26, 281
Halloway, 371
Hallowell, 231, 390, 462
Halsey, 153, 309, 411
Halsted, 52
Halt, 104
Ham, 241, 469
Hamann, 536
Hambaugh, 89
Hambleton, 246, 398, 445
Hamer, 291, 344, 398, 497
Hamersley, 195, 378
Hamesley, 359
Hamill, 193, 195
Hamilton, 4, 22, 26, 27, 29, 62, 70, 87, 98, 104, 108, 132, 140, 146, 147, 153, 164, 180, 241, 267, 273, 284, 302, 308, 337, 378, 411, 427, 443, 447, 488, 536, 543, 545, 562, 568, 577
Hamlin, 27, 58, 312
Hamm, 510
Hammack, 241, 281
Hammersly, 134
Hammitt, 453
Hammling, 490
Hammock, 4
Hammon, 248
Hammond, 4, 6, 58, 71, 104, 116, 147, 153, 294, 344, 421, 443, 515, 539
Hampson, 78
Hampton, 8, 19, 87, 149, 210, 398, 438
Hamtramck, 259, 573
Hancock, 4, 383, 479, 555
Hand, 200
Handley, 130, 281
Hands, 480
Handy, 26, 58, 73, 107, 136, 201, 241, 264, 277, 368, 411, 427, 439, 480, 555, 561
Haney, 479, 555
Hanison, 137

Hanks, 104
Hann, 533
Hanna, 117, 433, 439, 519, 538
Hannon, 554
Hanover, 27
Hanrahan, 348
Hansam, 452
Hansell, 76, 104
Hansford, 61
Hansjacob, 536
Hanson, 4, 16, 72, 148, 163, 207, 232, 264, 303, 309, 315, 404, 411, 428, 437
Hara, 287
Harard, 212
Harbaugh, 83, 162, 169, 236, 460, 472, 481, 482, 483, 484, 485, 539, 547, 555
Hardcastle, 552
Hardee, 227
Harden, 334
Hardenbrook, 468
Hardey, 241
Hardie, 327
Hardin, 4, 27, 58, 70, 116, 306, 441
Harding, 58, 153, 350, 365, 502
Hardwick, 321
Hardy, 118, 133, 403
Haret, 398
Hargas, 303
Hargrave, 250, 286, 579
Harilson, 241
Harise, 58
Harkness, 39, 47, 92, 109, 158, 234, 245, 262, 288, 299, 427, 428
Harlan, 69, 115, 241
Harlse, 241
Harlsee, 398
Harman, 254, 344
Harmer, 422, 469
Harney, 104, 382, 441
Harnfeldt, 54
Harold, 492
Harper, 14, 88, 290, 297, 408, 415, 434, 490, 504, 523, 536, 542, 567

Harrett, 27
Harrington, 109, 186, 234, 241, 246, 427, 436, 440
Harris, 26, 27, 39, 50, 51, 58, 68, 78, 87, 94, 100, 104, 133, 153, 160, 171, 183, 190, 204, 230, 231, 241, 249, 278, 281, 293, 296, 303, 307, 344, 362, 374, 379, 420, 439, 442, 443, 497, 507, 530, 536, 538, 570
Harrises, 195
Harrison, 2, 48, 55, 58, 110, 129, 179, 207, 212, 229, 241, 267, 298, 304, 340, 344, 369, 374, 392, 398, 400, 401, 402, 427, 443, 467, 536, 567
Harrman, 536
Harry, 123, 256, 281, 356
Harshman, 14
Hart, 9, 26, 85, 103, 104, 136, 153, 190, 281, 314, 359, 398, 492, 507, 568
Hartford, 226
Hartley, 329, 406, 460, 570
Hartly, 143
Hartman, 22
Hartnett, 20
Hartwell, 23, 36, 194, 220, 438
Harvey, 4, 27, 39, 58, 82, 234, 241, 266, 274, 279, 437, 480, 489, 490, 511, 555
Harvie, 58, 104
Harwood, 255, 401
Hasbrook, 311
Hase, 153
Haskell, 36, 58, 82, 110, 129, 144, 330, 458, 565
Haskin, 153
Haskins, 153, 195
Hasler, 489
Haslett, 69, 504
Haslinger, 140
Haslup, 109, 253, 437, 542
Hass, 241, 398
Hassard, 58, 241
Hassler, 532, 534, 538, 540, 543, 558
Hastell, 268

Hastings, 99, 241, 250, 313
Haswell, 344
Hatch, 241, 380, 504
Hathaway, 398
Hathway, 31
Hatton, 9, 198, 398, 448, 477
Hatwell, 180
Haughey, 537
Hausam, 575
Haven, 100, 104, 253, 579
Havenner, 82, 213
Havens, 359
Havolett, 507
Haw, 10, 262
Hawes, 73
Hawken, 169
Hawkes, 338
Hawkins, 4, 89, 92, 104, 195, 260, 275, 330, 364, 384, 404, 440, 465, 490, 520, 565
Hawks, 289, 371
Hawlet, 381
Hawley, 31, 79, 209, 363, 410, 431
Hawthorne, 173
Haxall, 281, 306
Hay, 55, 231, 241, 295
Hayden, 1, 42, 153, 195, 241, 383, 439, 489
Haydon, 316
Hayes, 78, 254, 346, 362, 538, 563
Hayland, 215
Haylate, 8
Haymaker, 61
Hayman, 204, 275
Haynes, 260, 381, 453, 554
Hayre, 427
Hays, 26, 44, 58, 104, 148, 150, 193, 222, 226, 260, 301, 306, 312, 365, 384, 385, 474, 487, 512
Hayse, 270
Hayward, 27, 88, 342
Haywood, 80, 235
Hazard, 36, 88, 458, 526, 536, 579
Hazel, 135, 245, 461, 467, 478
Hazell, 120

Hazeltine, 4
Hazewell, 153, 536
Hazle, 427
Hazlitt, 72, 456, 549, 551
Hazzard, 61, 88
Heacock, 138, 139
Head, 385, 442
Headley, 398
Headman, 153
Heady, 247
Heaight, 104
Healey, 157
Healy, 6
Heaney, 355
Heap, 184, 281
Hearn, 440
Hearth, 235
Heartt, 543
Heath, 35, 398
Heatley, 46
Heaton, 26, 398, 509
Hebard, 26
Hebb, 550, 571, 578
Heben, 58
Heberd, 176
Hebert, 73
Hebrard, 335
Hebron, 120
Heckerman, 104
Heckrote, 58
Heckrott, 4
Hedge, 574
Hedges, 391
Hedrick, 241, 281, 373, 543
Hedwige, 409
Heeren, 231
Hefferman, 67
Heide, 344
Height, 153
Hein, 365
Heintzelman, 158, 387
Heintzleman, 443
Heiss, 110, 139, 153
Heitmuller, 443
Helfrichoder, 27

Hellen, 66, 454
Helm, 104, 241
Helphenstine, 223
Hemerick, 235
Hemintgon, 306
Hemken, 217
Hemmersly, 427
Hemminck, 153
Hemming, 507
Hemmrick, 219
Hempler, 575
Hempstead, 561
Henckle, 132
Henderson, 4, 22, 31, 47, 104, 115, 153, 172, 194, 229, 230, 276, 286, 360, 388, 389, 443, 506
Hendley, 11, 482, 484, 485, 555
Hendren, 371
Hendricks, 257, 511
Hendrickson, 16, 203, 239, 253
Henepee, 422
Hening, 195
Henion, 311
Henley, 26
Hennen, 355
Henning, 113, 153, 398, 554, 562
Henrich, 490
Henrie, 26, 153, 259, 264
Henry, 75, 77, 81, 95, 153, 244, 264, 269, 275, 281, 304, 374, 377, 383, 398, 405, 434, 440, 451, 492, 507, 536, 557
Henry IV, 462
Henshaw, 26, 64, 88, 109, 120, 136, 562
Hensley, 310, 555
Henson, 153, 536
Hepburn, 58, 275, 281, 554
Herbert, 58, 87, 195, 241, 293, 398, 419, 427, 459, 488
Hercus, 486
Herdelbrinck, 4
Herert, 153
Herin, 41
Heritage, 132

Herkimer, 266
Hernandez, 4, 347, 489, 503, 579
Herndon, 91, 102, 176, 184, 281
Herold, 202, 538
Herrick, 4, 27, 147, 153, 195, 272, 309, 533
Herring, 8, 29, 492, 504
Herrity, 21
Hersey, 321
Hertscamp, 554
Herty, 427
Hervand, 100
Hervey, 134, 560
Heser, 4
Hesler, 136
Hess, 26, 281, 398
Hesse, 434
Hett, 496, 498, 507, 524
Hetzel, 58, 72, 141, 383, 387
Heuson, 505
Heustis, 317
Hevener, 281, 296
Hewett, 104
Hewitt, 344, 536
Hewlett, 395, 497
Hews, 11
Hewson, 372
Heydon, 49
Heyer, 271
Heyl, 13, 82
Heyland, 189
Heywood, 241, 379
Hick, 436
Hickey, 139, 230, 349, 422, 427, 472
Hickman, 4, 26, 104, 108, 186
Hickox, 27, 153
Hicks, 295, 474
Hicster, 36
Higden, 427
Higgins, 4, 41, 72, 85, 153, 257, 337, 347, 375, 438, 443, 523, 555
High Point, 503
Higinbotham, 104
Hiland, 153, 536
Hilbard, 562

Hilcox, 104
Hildreth, 58, 163
Hill, 4, 10, 26, 58, 62, 66, 71, 83, 93, 104, 115, 118, 153, 170, 195, 245, 287, 302, 329, 343, 367, 384, 386, 387, 413, 427, 443, 487, 489, 491, 493, 494, 506, 508, 521, 536, 578
Hilleary, 273, 560
Hilliard, 143, 363, 380, 381, 410, 431
Hilliary, 31, 376, 454, 536
Hillips, 241
Hillman, 25, 177, 180
Hillseman, 281
Hillstock, 104
Hillyer, 153
Hilman, 257
Hilton, 30, 99, 139, 153, 288, 303, 532, 540, 564
Hinds, 86, 159
Hines, 4, 35, 96, 110, 125, 306, 427, 433, 555
Hinkle, 132
Hinlin, 195
Hinston, 153
Hinton, 33, 58, 153, 241, 348, 370
Hipkins, 26, 104, 137, 241
Hirsch, 538
Hirst, 104, 148
Hitchcock, 247, 281, 475
Hite, 22, 63, 402
Hitt, 262
Hitz, 286, 288, 503, 554
Hix, 102, 312
Hoban, 38, 44, 62, 69, 76, 427
Hobart, 147
Hobb, 53
Hobbie, 575
Hobbs, 141, 149, 165, 327, 536
Hobby, 153
Hoblitzell, 172
Hocke, 104
Hodge, 36, 406, 458
Hodges, 99, 174, 235
Hodgkin, 88, 344
Hodgkinson, 241
Hodskin, 26
Hodson, 536
Hoehn, 452
Hoff, 4
Hoffman, 4, 58, 61, 72, 97, 133, 141, 193, 278, 344, 352, 376, 423, 427, 438, 451, 515, 542, 554
Hofman, 195
Hogan, 99, 498
Hogans, 4, 344
Hogatt, 160
Hoge, 58, 89
Hoget, 151
Hogg, 195
Hoit, 26
Hoke, 49
Holborn, 506
Holbourn, 104
Holcomb, 451, 465, 505
Holden, 104, 135, 147, 229
Holding, 114
Holdridge, 4
Holdsworth, 221
Holgate, 125
Hollaga, 26
Holland, 17, 27, 98, 100, 124, 175, 287, 298, 301, 362, 377, 416, 424, 427, 441
Hollander, 173
Holley, 58, 392
Hollidge, 478
Hollidy, 443
Hollingsworth, 15, 241, 509
Hollins, 58, 427
Hollohan, 427
Holloran, 290
Holloway, 73
Holly, 216
Holman, 153
Holmead, 46, 81, 203, 469, 475, 555
Holmes, 34, 55, 70, 84, 92, 115, 217, 315, 322, 330, 358, 375, 377, 396, 438, 472, 545
Holoham, 20
Holohan, 20

Holschea, 504
Holt, 212, 402, 435, 508
Holton, 43
Holtzman, 200, 204, 241, 568
Holyoke, 83
Homan, 529
Homans, 18, 109, 142, 143, 149, 161, 205, 208, 258, 290, 297, 314, 364, 388, 419, 425, 439, 460, 470, 476, 485, 544, 555, 577
Homas, 425
Homer, 104
Homiller, 142
Hompkins, 58
Hone, 468
Hooe, 4, 58, 137, 227, 228, 229, 246, 364, 384, 459, 536, 554
Hoogland, 241
Hoogs, 267
Hook, 58, 64, 90, 149, 153, 165, 281, 286, 441
Hooker, 208
Hoomer, 27
Hooper, 27, 58, 104, 124, 153, 195, 234, 281, 344, 529
Hoorbach, 301, 362
Hoorback, 250
Hoover, 4, 47, 63, 153, 241, 299, 398, 477, 489, 554
Hope, 68, 257, 277, 539
Hopkins, 4, 20, 27, 39, 58, 79, 104, 144, 153, 281, 330, 344, 347, 545, 565
Hopkinson, 335
Hoppe, 316
Hopper, 440
Horan, 443
Horbach, 416
Horback, 78, 346, 349
Horboek, 302
Hord, 104, 153, 195
Horid, 153
Hornbeck, 464
Hornblower, 27
Horncastle, 58

Horne, 548
Horner, 51, 61, 112, 129, 248
Horning, 555
Hornley, 536
Hornsby, 402
Horrel, 58
Horsey, 427
Horspool, 258
Horstmann, 230
Horton, 70
Horwell, 104
Hosie, 37
Hoskins, 456, 474, 504, 549, 551
Hoskum, 7
Hotchkiss, 157, 490
Hotton, 558
Houer, 278
Hough, 40, 53, 54, 104, 241, 259, 281, 363, 381, 410, 431, 489, 539, 564
Houghton, 518, 538
Housage, 77
Housange, 213
Housaye, 563
House, 35, 94, 300
Houseman, 157, 179, 180, 254, 560
Houser, 443, 536
Housman, 133
Houston, 39, 104, 219, 241, 285, 358, 427
Hover, 532
How, 241
Howard, 7, 36, 47, 58, 104, 139, 153, 157, 173, 189, 195, 206, 210, 241, 249, 281, 287, 288, 332, 350, 398, 401, 405, 422, 427, 443, 475, 490, 509, 513, 524, 526, 536, 568, 571, 576, 579
Howe, 58, 72, 202, 231, 296, 335, 352, 357, 382, 489, 536, 542
Howell, 36, 110, 186, 230, 281
Howes, 166
Howison, 171, 546
Howk, 206
Howle, 480
Hoxey, 310

Hoxton, 181
Hoy, 19
Hoyle, 287
Hoyt, 5, 104, 303, 331, 459, 464
Hubard, 566
Hubbard, 4, 8, 23, 29, 39, 114, 137, 153, 159, 341, 364, 371, 431, 555, 566
Hubbell, 145
Huber, 40, 235
Hubley, 26, 58
Hucorn, 161
Huddleston, 574
Hudson, 206, 223, 274, 298, 317, 457, 536
Hudspeth, 163
Huffington, 278
Huffman, 509
Huger, 58, 127
Huggins, 370
Hughes, 4, 8, 58, 68, 78, 99, 153, 157, 163, 233, 237, 256, 299, 378, 390, 392, 443, 489, 543, 555, 562
Hughson, 230
Hujill, 13
Hull, 10, 64, 80, 101, 195, 251, 281, 443, 489
Hulme, 173
Hulseman, 249, 375
Hulsemann, 352
Hum, 58
Humber, 72, 74, 404
Hume, 104, 176, 398
Humerick, 422
Humes, 58, 496, 554
Hummel, 166
Hummstor, 415
Humphrey, 25, 26, 58, 116, 153, 173, 182, 301, 529
Humphreys, 4, 6, 77, 79, 99, 102, 147, 153, 251, 255, 312, 313, 361, 373, 375, 390, 391, 409, 529, 543
Humphries, 241, 334, 355, 359, 508
Hungerfood, 567
Hungerford, 17, 252, 315

Hunnewell, 358
Hunnicutt, 166
Hunt, 4, 26, 27, 31, 52, 58, 73, 104, 125, 141, 153, 230, 231, 238, 310, 343, 359, 382, 396, 519, 526, 529, 551, 554
Hunter, 4, 20, 25, 36, 38, 58, 64, 78, 104, 111, 125, 225, 232, 241, 247, 275, 281, 314, 318, 398, 420, 427, 430, 471, 486, 490
Hunting, 303, 315, 362
Huntington, 88, 115, 453
Hunton, 560
Huntt, 348
Hup, 443
Hurdle, 4, 20, 426
Hurlbert, 58
Hurlburt, 122
Hurseley, 26
Hurst, 104, 115, 176
Hurt, 195
Hurtsfield, 296
Huske, 327
Hussell, 195
Hussey, 58, 390
Hussy, 195
Huston, 580
Hutchings, 153, 401, 402
Hutchins, 33, 104, 153, 241, 459
Hutchinson, 2, 40, 85, 90, 149, 420
Hutchison, 4, 197
Hutinach, 147
Huttenburg, 519
Hutton, 4, 490
Hyam, 506
Hyatt, 11, 192, 407, 481, 482, 483
Hyde, 47, 88, 90, 281, 335, 492, 513, 551
Hyman, 54
Hynson, 563, 578, 579

I

Iardella, 4, 153, 555
Ichle, 505

Iddins, 22
Ide, 346
Imaum of Museat, 93
Inch, 297
Indeman, 104
Indemaur, 281
Indiantown, 63
Ingalls, 71, 100, 124, 302, 362, 511
Inge, 228, 229, 260, 344
Ingersoll, 346, 371, 464
Ingham, 90
Ingle, 58, 128, 236, 288, 354, 403, 422, 427, 443, 536, 571
Inglehart, 115
Ingles, 33
Ingraham, 35, 55, 147, 490
Ingram, 58
Inman, 37
Ireland, 58
Iron Ore Lot, 573
Irons, 4, 193
Ironside, 140
Irvin, 70, 241
Irvine, 27
Irving, 100, 107
Irwin, 4, 27, 275, 386, 398, 421, 474, 504, 549, 551
Irwing, 511
Isaacks, 184
Isaacs, 387
Isherwood, 20, 27, 104
Ishy, 58
Isley, 19
Israel, 310, 394
Ives, 165, 344, 391

J

Jack, 195
Jackson, 4, 17, 21, 24, 27, 38, 58, 80, 89, 94, 104, 129, 147, 160, 186, 187, 195, 196, 199, 216, 217, 234, 241, 266, 276, 281, 298, 320, 327, 344, 367, 379, 388, 398, 413, 444, 462, 464, 479, 494, 509, 525, 531, 540, 547, 555, 561, 564
Jacobs, 104, 145, 147, 153, 251, 311, 313, 328, 362, 370, 398, 496
Jacoway, 153
Jaeger, 153
Jamaison, 4, 58, 104, 490, 536
Jamar, 440
Jameisson, 398
James, 4, 139, 153, 181, 195, 241, 262, 273, 281, 424, 480, 555, 561
Jameson, 401
Jamieson, 402, 555
Jamison, 348
Janes, 453
Janis, 31
Janney, 104, 185, 490, 492, 534
Janny, 153
January, 202, 223, 331
Jaquis, 153
Jarboe, 527, 552, 555
Jarrett, 89
Jarvis, 490, 528
Jasper, 241, 281, 315, 555
Jeffers, 118, 150, 153, 213, 281, 307, 555, 581
Jefferson, 27, 121, 241, 400, 525, 569, 576, 579
Jefferson Barracks, 256, 306
Jeffres, 536
Jeffries, 398
Jenifer, 19, 61, 83, 440
Jenkin, 327
Jenkins, 27, 78, 125, 131, 149, 153, 168, 170, 187, 195, 196, 230, 241, 263, 272, 335, 355, 357, 362, 382, 398, 417, 447, 484, 508, 512, 536, 573
Jenks, 134, 241
Jennings, 58, 153, 163, 358
Jerrey, 10
Jervis, 58
Jessup, 153
Jesuit, 467
Jesuits, 369

Jesup, 34, 47, 187
Jett, 42, 48, 99, 137, 159, 398, 401
Jewell, 149, 187, 427, 513
Jewett, 27
Jillard, 539
Jirdinston, 490
Joachim, 153
Jockum, 281
John, 340
Johns, 185, 275, 328, 336, 338, 398, 407, 488, 570
Johnson, 4, 7, 9, 15, 35, 39, 42, 48, 55, 58, 63, 69, 70, 72, 79, 80, 88, 94, 104, 119, 121, 125, 137, 140, 153, 161, 163, 190, 196, 206, 212, 214, 241, 245, 266, 281, 287, 305, 306, 312, 325, 331, 334, 336, 344, 347, 352, 355, 386, 398, 402, 404, 406, 427, 439, 444, 448, 457, 458, 460, 468, 469, 472, 481, 482, 484, 485, 490, 495, 497, 500, 506, 510, 532, 536, 538, 539, 540, 545, 547, 551, 555, 560, 567, 579
Johnston, 15, 27, 36, 72, 94, 104, 116, 177, 189, 281, 344, 356, 374, 382, 459, 490, 496, 508, 515, 548, 552
Johson, 241
Joines, 80
Jone, 432
Jones, 4, 9, 15, 27, 34, 46, 47, 52, 58, 62, 63, 69, 72, 78, 79, 80, 84, 87, 104, 109, 121, 125, 142, 147, 149, 153, 178, 180, 195, 206, 212, 213, 214, 215, 216, 233, 241, 244, 245, 256, 263, 271, 276, 277, 279, 281, 296, 299, 303, 304, 310, 322, 323, 330, 331, 334, 340, 344, 352, 354, 356, 361, 362, 376, 387, 390, 398, 405, 409, 414, 415, 417, 427, 440, 444, 467, 468, 481, 482, 483, 484, 486, 490, 503, 506, 509, 513, 536, 538, 543, 549, 551, 555, 568, 572, 579
Jonston, 104

Jordan, 58, 69, 118, 132, 168, 177, 180, 229, 246, 260, 275, 292, 308, 359, 362, 372, 383, 398, 421, 427, 444, 538, 580
Jorden, 58
Jordon, 27, 228, 334, 344, 444, 540, 549, 563
Jost, 479, 555
Jouett, 548, 549
Jourdan, 34
Journey, 30, 144, 251, 311, 313, 362
Joy, 558
Joyce, 20, 34, 43, 150, 454, 469, 478, 499, 555, 581
Joyner, 247
Judd, 70
Judge, 318, 504
Judik, 4
Judlin, 241
Judson, 139, 141, 192, 304
Juicey, 29
Jump, 457
Junkin, 153, 174
Junkins, 116
Juridth, 478
Justice, 411

K

Kager, 211
Kaiser, 452, 575
Kalorama, 476
Kamehameha III, 546
Kanally, 27, 153
Kane, 4, 54, 125, 227, 268, 269, 339, 427
Kanoot, 526
Kantner, 398
Karston, 196
Kartright, 272
Katching, 332
Kauffman, 244
Kaufman, 398
Kavanaugh, 247, 475
Kay, 427, 509

Keabel, 241, 282
Kealey, 48
Keaman, 398
Kean, 220, 398, 496, 536
Kearney, 104, 198, 282, 286, 298, 307, 322, 323, 340, 382, 398, 407, 446, 502, 515, 518
Kearon, 372
Kearsley, 41
Kebler, 410
Kedglie, 52, 91, 227, 245, 427, 429
Keech, 408, 446
Keefe, 224, 532
Keefer, 533
Keek, 108, 196
Keen, 560
Keenan, 460
Keene, 207, 262, 315, 563, 572
Keener, 327
Keeny, 314
Keep, 565
Keer, 333
Keese, 575
Kegg, 187
Kehl, 398
Kehler, 153
Kehoe, 282
Keighway, 310
Keith, 27, 34, 68, 172, 206, 266, 325, 331, 334, 362
Keithley, 487
Keitt, 4
Keizer, 526
Kelcher, 555
Kell, 123, 208, 215, 312, 517, 543
Kellam, 507
Keller, 8, 34, 169, 520
Kelley, 82, 96, 100, 117, 153, 219, 323, 388, 570
Kello, 344
Kellogg, 4, 58, 80, 104, 238, 444, 560
Kellum, 20, 497
Kelly, 4, 37, 79, 83, 84, 104, 114, 147, 153, 197, 213, 219, 241, 250, 251, 265, 311, 312, 313, 315, 326, 361,

362, 422, 427, 434, 439, 444, 479, 490, 492, 507, 508, 511, 570, 579, 581
Kelsey, 58, 422
Kelso, 184
Kemball, 86, 97, 301, 362, 417
Kemble, 27
Kemff, 14
Kemp, 219, 440, 465, 543, 568
Kempton, 398
Kenan, 282
Kendall, 92, 119, 218, 241, 331, 362, 416, 497, 522
Kendel, 536
Kendrick, 104, 119, 282, 427
Kenly, 268, 321, 492
Kennard, 232, 568
Kennaugh, 576
Kenneday, 11
Kennedy, 4, 55, 175, 265, 332, 344, 439, 444, 488, 543
Kenneford, 358
Kennerly, 274, 287
Kennett, 245
Kenniston, 130
Kennon, 150
Kensett, 64, 344, 444, 536
Kent, 164, 180, 212, 285, 337, 516
Kenton, 475
Keoble, 344
Kepler, 60, 264
Ker, 88, 401, 420
Kerchum, 99
Kerlin, 31, 90
Kerman, 522
Kern, 4
Kerney, 58, 104, 168
Kerns, 505
Kerr, 4, 104, 144, 487
Kersey, 555
Kerton, 500
Kervand, 101, 136
Kessinger, 469
Ketchum, 58, 128, 147
Kew, 22

Key, 45, 50, 52, 58, 69, 87, 107, 126, 196, 249, 277, 398, 427, 444
Keys, 512, 579
Keyser, 439
Keyworth, 175, 235, 437, 542
Kezer, 104
Kibbey, 481
Kick-o-neaks, 296
Kidd, 98, 301, 308, 330, 331, 362, 417
Kidwell, 4, 20, 39, 61, 109, 120, 542
Kierman, 427
Kiernan, 427
Kiger, 4, 555
Kilian, 282
Killin, 52
Killman, 555
Killmon, 46, 188, 499
Killum, 4
Kilman, 288
Kilmiste, 96, 129, 153, 412, 467, 571, 575
Kilmon, 499
Kilton, 341
Kilvey, 510
Kimball, 2, 19, 66, 84, 241, 344, 533, 538, 540
Kimmell, 463, 481
Kincart, 418
Kinchey, 126
Kinchy, 407
Kinckle, 494
Kindred, 151
King, 2, 13, 20, 47, 53, 58, 65, 98, 101, 104, 109, 122, 129, 130, 144, 153, 163, 196, 232, 241, 245, 255, 270, 274, 282, 297, 303, 329, 337, 347, 348, 354, 356, 381, 398, 400, 424, 434, 444, 454, 481, 486, 490, 509, 519, 536, 538, 539, 542, 543, 548, 555, 565, 576, 581
King Chas II, 462
King of Bavaria, 75
Kingley, 153
Kingman, 186, 427
Kingsbury, 153, 441, 444, 555
Kingsley, 261, 264, 349
Kingston, 241
Kington, 533
Kinkead, 259
Kinney, 455
Kinnines, 398
Kinsman, 116, 207
Kinzie, 153
Kipperling, 461
Kirby, 40, 151, 355, 398, 414, 544, 573
Kirk, 235, 241, 366, 403, 444, 511, 536
Kirkbridge, 241
Kirkland, 66
Kirkpatrick, 327, 402
Kirkwood, 272, 427, 539
Kirwan, 229
Klapper, 153
Kleaner, 296
Kleiber, 288, 460
Kleine, 35
Kleuch, 269
Kline, 147
Klockgether, 490
Klopfer, 264
Knapp, 189, 282, 286, 423, 460
Kneass, 114
Kneeland, 358
Knight, 58, 78, 80, 138, 165
Knippel, 427
Knoblock, 248
Knott, 4, 13, 58, 194, 206, 211, 330, 515, 555
Knowles, 4, 84
Knowlton, 102
Knox, 16, 53, 153, 241, 344, 346
Knuckel, 490
Kolb, 27
Konigmacher, 238
Kooms, 104
Koones, 50, 109, 130, 397
Koontz, 179
Kortztes, 196
Kotzebue, 179

Krafft, 130, 221, 479, 572, 575
Krebs, 27, 58
Kreiber, 188
Krider, 237
Kroes, 378
Krofft, 555
Krum, 282
Kuchland, 344
Kugan, 282
Kugur, 4
Kuhl, 480, 555, 581
Kuhland, 398
Kuhn, 339, 490
Kunkle, 230
Kunsman, 344, 398, 444
Kurfman, 271
Kurtz, 58, 262, 357, 360
Kurtzels, 153
Kuykendall, 81, 301, 308

L

L'Hommedieu, 355
La Barron, 70
La Caze, 64
La Reintree, 331
La Reintrie, 266
La Rientree, 379
La Truitte, 398
Laberdi, 196
Labranche, 10
Lacey, 196, 398
Lackey, 110
Lacy, 4, 128, 344, 484, 501, 517, 564
Ladd, 79, 90, 147, 211
Lafayette, 2, 85, 88, 537
<u>Lafayette College</u>, 174
Lafontaine, 295, 299, 438, 560, 574
Lagrand, 105
Lagree, 239
Laidlaw, 371
Laidler, 427
Laing, 250, 311, 313, 326, 346, 362
Lainhart, 509
Laird, 23, 53, 105

Lake, 229, 344
Lakey, 490
Lally, 105
Lamar, 153, 339
Lamaris, 65
Lamb, 4, 42, 109, 241, 341, 424, 479, 480, 508
Lambeck, 498
Lambell, 12, 109, 151, 170, 177, 428, 481
Lambert, 58, 227, 296
Lamborne, 21
Lambton, 545
Laments, 303
Lamerloniere, 344
Lamme, 27, 98
Lamnie, 58
Lamotte, 210, 457, 527
Lamphere, 55
Lamphier, 51
Lamphin, 559
Lanahan, 148
Lancaster, 143, 153, 348
Lancey, 529
Land, 229
Landon, 303
Landry, 243, 336, 337
Lane, 177, 267, 291, 303, 310, 393, 536, 555
Lang, 39, 128, 134, 174, 241, 250, 313, 362, 416
Langdon, 23, 124
Langford, 510
Langhey, 170
Langhorne, 344
Langlois, 41
Langreen, 90, 266
Langtree, 145, 168
Langtry, 78, 115, 355, 362, 417
Langworthy, 41, 173
Lanham, 14
Lanier, 58, 490
Lankford, 440
Lanman, 344, 441, 571
Lann, 241

Lannum, 58
Lanphier, 134, 167, 392
Lansdale, 105, 496
Lansing, 6, 41, 143, 404
Lanton, 58
Lapple, 506
Larabee, 189
Larcombe, 224
Lard, 168
Lardner, 571
Lare, 13, 130, 493
Larkin, 340, 442
Larkins, 138
Larned, 73, 355, 358, 479
Larner, 27, 58, 176, 199, 245
Larochefoucauld, 298
Larrabee, 50, 182
Laskey, 480, 555
Lassell, 266, 331
Latham, 282, 344, 415, 468, 536, 538, 539
Lathrop, 51, 133, 210, 309
Latimer, 4, 91, 122, 182, 209, 431, 487
Laton, 398
Latourno, 275
Latreal, 27
Latruit, 105
Latruite, 153
Latson, 4, 27
Lattimore, 444
Laub, 359, 380, 424, 450, 480, 490
Lauck, 354, 469
Lauderdale, 276
Laughlin, 39
Laughrey, 564
Laughton, 179
Laurie, 16, 29, 31, 88, 107, 122, 188, 480, 494
Lauve, 337
Lavailee, 267
Laval, 371
Lavalette, 379, 490, 504
Lavallette, 323
Lavege, 490

Lavelle, 153
Lavellette, 376
Lavender, 35, 203
Lavers, 315
Law, 428, 508, 512
Lawler, 41
Lawless, 344, 431
Lawrason, 196
Lawrence, 4, 18, 27, 39, 44, 47, 58, 81, 94, 115, 153, 161, 162, 238, 257, 329, 344, 455, 520, 539, 555, 579
Laws, 55, 440
Lawson, 10, 17, 196, 302, 331, 344, 504
Lawton, 268, 282
Lay, 68, 77
Layton, 206, 212
Le Beau, 138, 315
Le Blanc, 202
Le Brun, 282
Le Cage, 1
Le Moyne, 536
Le Seigneur, 22
Leach, 395, 529
Leachman, 16
Leake, 104
Leakin, 501
Lear, 31, 456, 466, 474, 477, 504, 524, 527, 549, 550
Learcock, 27
Leaumont, 337
Leavens, 105
Leavenworth, 39, 250, 353, 362
Leavitt, 116, 142, 241, 341, 371, 394
Lebrun, 4
Leckie, 427
Lecomte, 292
Lecraw, 529
Leddon, 241, 274, 279
Leddy, 375, 444, 555
Ledyard, 538
Lee, 2, 4, 30, 40, 61, 69, 104, 105, 109, 153, 164, 177, 183, 203, 205, 238, 241, 250, 257, 275, 276, 289,

295, 311, 325, 326, 337, 344, 347,
362, 400, 401, 402, 404, 415, 428,
444, 481, 482, 483, 484, 486, 490,
492, 501, 504, 507, 546
Leech, 386
Leeds, 136, 282
Leekie, 105
Lees, 153, 441
Lefebre, 444, 490
Lefevre, 427
Leffler, 117, 536
Lefort, 227
Leftwich, 211
Leger, 282
Legg, 137
Leggett, 398
Leggitt, 490
Legion Volunteers, 220
LeGrand, 340
Lehman, 19, 139, 561
Leib, 348
Leiberman, 555
Leigh, 21, 283, 326, 444
Leight, 469
Leighton, 4, 27, 241
Leiper, 105
Leitensdorfer, 518
Leland, 115
Leman, 4, 216
Lemaster, 529
Lemerle, 235
Lemmon, 148
Lemon, 490, 536
Lemott, 504, 524
Lenan, 532
Lendrum, 58
Lenhart, 490
Lenman, 84, 153, 486
Lenox, 11, 176, 199, 245, 367, 513, 538
Lentesty, 267
Leon, 569
Leonard, 27, 172, 218, 344, 347, 550
Leopold, 579
Lepretre, 337, 348

Lepreux, 77, 480, 555
Leseur, 105
Leslie, 73, 282, 505
Lester, 19, 141
Lestor, 560
Lesure, 153
LeTruit, 4
Leverett, 538
Levin, 464
Lewis, 4, 41, 58, 67, 105, 153, 158,
175, 187, 198, 203, 230, 232, 241,
246, 250, 257, 297, 312, 322, 355,
356, 358, 374, 379, 396, 398, 427,
428, 432, 438, 454, 490, 510, 520,
532, 555, 580
Ley, 141
Lichtenthoeler, 245
Lightall, 58
Lightfoot, 8, 35, 96
Lighthall, 4
Ligon, 250, 291, 311, 312, 347
Lillard, 247, 543
Lilley, 81
Lilly, 90, 230, 267
Lillybridge, 102, 331, 565
Lincecum, 84
Lincoln, 74, 153, 252, 299, 376, 383, 392, 490, 569
Lindenberger, 58
Lindley, 147
Lindsay, 115, 233, 246, 255, 267, 398, 427
Lindsey, 35, 241, 348
Lindsley, 58, 88, 109, 153, 266, 282, 422, 481, 482, 483, 555
Lindsly, 285, 355
Linkenwater, 196
Linsley, 69
Linthicum, 25, 183, 262, 487, 491, 545
Linton, 18, 140, 396, 573
Lippincott, 105, 238
Lippitt, 356
Litchfield, 392

Little, 9, 20, 72, 92, 98, 122, 157, 177, 192, 205, 213, 230, 241, 262, 288, 312, 344, 393, 433, 490, 499
Littlefield, 37, 434
Littleton, 27, 460
Litton, 371
Lively, 241, 282, 490
Livingston, 27, 58, 79, 117, 169, 217, 241, 279, 337, 436, 562
Lizardo, 420
Lloyd, 4, 236, 245, 353, 392, 406, 428
Locke, 33, 113, 355, 508
Locker, 241
Lockert, 185
Lockery, 196
Lockett, 348, 349
Lockhart, 241, 344
Lockmeyer, 452
Lockrey, 241
Lockwood, 263
Loder, 138
Loeser, 71, 312
Loew, 579
Lofftus, 4
Logan, 401, 497, 536
Lohead, 196
Lohear, 282
Lohmeyer, 241
Lohmier, 282
Lohs, 575
Lomagne, 130
Lomax, 27, 105, 357
Lombard, 183
Lombardi, 124
Lombeck, 508
London, 51, 147
Lonelen, 398
Long, 27, 40, 58, 75, 153, 158, 241, 359, 483, 484, 555
long hair, 307
Long Meadows, 418
Longfellow, 508
Longhead, 184
Longley, 498, 508
Longstreth, 243, 337

Longwood, 264
Lonsure, 444
Looby, 490, 555
Loomis, 62, 105, 162, 277, 314, 328, 330, 569
Loomiss, 27
Looney, 216
Loper, 223
Loranger, 223
Lord, 105, 236, 275, 349, 366, 539, 555
Lord Holland, 462
Lord of Villemain, 513
Loring, 233, 255, 395
Lorman, 232
Lothar, 32
Loughborough, 394
Louis, 241, 282
Lounsbury, 561
Love, 137, 287, 344, 348, 382, 398, 490, 510, 515
Lovelace, 27, 536
Loveless, 153, 196, 212, 452, 536
Loveless Farm, 300
Lovell, 383
Lovenskiold, 490
Lovering, 341
Lovett, 282, 372
Low, 64, 301, 308, 330, 331, 346, 374
Lowd, 404
Lowe, 90, 100, 340, 344, 362, 371, 428, 444
Lowerd, 507
Lowery, 509
Lowfellow, 498
Lowndes, 190, 323
Lowney, 241, 372
Lowrey, 11, 190, 275, 513, 576
Lowrie, 88
Lowry, 27, 47, 58, 153, 254, 307, 398, 494, 545
Loyall, 241, 337
Loyd, 98, 99, 358
Lucane, 490

Lucas, 92, 196, 208, 238, 282, 315, 340, 444, 555
Luce, 31, 374, 494
Lucia, 476
Luckett, 560
Ludlow, 23, 58
Lufborough, 109
Luffobrough, 105
Lugenbeel, 182, 241, 345, 383
Lukens, 577
Lukins, 27
Lumsden, 319
Lunday, 536
Lundy, 498
Lunen, 105
Lunt, 58, 104, 282
Lupton, 105
Lusby, 109, 398, 555
Luscombe, 571
Lushy, 398
Luther, 227, 246, 255
Lutz, 290, 428
Luxen, 344
Luxin, 490
Lyford, 180, 206
Lyles, 302
Lyman, 134, 211, 380
Lynch, 153, 185, 241, 372, 427, 451, 472, 485, 493, 511
Lyne, 105, 241, 401
Lynn, 115
Lyon, 7, 15, 105, 117, 282, 398, 512
Lyons, 122, 199, 344, 450
Lytle, 54

M

M'Clery, 555
Mabie, 357
Macartney, 148
Macauly, 112
Maccoun, 360
Maccubbin, 356, 531
Macdaniel, 136
Mace, 81, 105
Macey, 509
Macfarlan, 533
MacGill, 269
MacGregor, 282
Machiavel, 298
MacIntire, 282
Mackabee, 105
Mackall, 144, 272, 542
Mackay, 154, 282
Mackey, 53, 88
Mackie, 402
Mackur, 154, 196
Maclane, 105
Maclay, 7, 141, 228, 260, 359
MacLellan, 453, 572
Macmurdo, 159
Macnier, 309
Macoby, 555
Macomb, 122, 158, 201, 232, 446, 477, 494, 517
Macoudry, 490
MacRae, 24
MacRea, 23, 355
Macres, 282
Macy, 438, 567
Maddox, 245, 282, 533, 558
Madigan, 307
Madison, 64, 162, 428
Maffitt, 282
Magar, 17, 170
Magarry, 242
Magee, 4, 190, 216, 399, 555, 556
Magill, 399, 469
Magnetic Telegraph, 514
Magnier, 56
Magruder, 137, 151, 154, 196, 242, 245, 273, 288, 349, 354, 370, 396, 399, 424, 428, 471, 536, 539, 552, 555
Maguire, 59, 109, 231, 378, 506, 509, 514
Magum, 105
Mahan, 309
Maher, 162, 194, 225, 428
Mahl, 147

Mahon, 27, 105, 149
Mahorney, 490
Maine, 124
Mains, 17, 85, 100, 302, 362
Majia, 226
Major, 58
Majors, 454
Makepeace, 169
Makintosh, 59
Malcolm, 75
Mallary, 552
Mallery, 341
Mallet, 1
Mallett, 327
Mallion, 485
Mallison, 132
Mallory, 133
Mallowny, 114
Malone, 359
Maloney, 505, 507, 549
Malony, 358
Maloy, 242
Man, 398
Manchester, 344
Mandlebaum, 327
Maniates, 421
Mankin, 17, 495
Manly, 105, 352
Mann, 27, 40, 69, 76, 196, 201, 344, 346, 530, 532
Mannigan, 506
Manning, 27, 47, 105, 128, 344, 351, 398, 447, 523, 536, 560
Manouvrier, 114
Mans, 196
Mansfield, 364, 384, 398, 405, 455, 457, 505, 524
Manson, 405, 528
Manu, 222
Manuyette, 271
Manwarring, 302
Mapes, 531
Marache, 334
Marble, 11, 61

Marbury, 38, 143, 187, 218, 221, 222, 262, 297, 487
Marcellus, 214
Marchioness of Wellesley, 518
Marcoux, 267
Marcus, 380
Marcy, 59, 196, 275, 292, 315, 344, 379, 385, 386, 516
Marion, 59, 398
Markham, 509
Markoe, 39
Marks, 4, 196, 241, 282, 304, 398, 535
Markward, 410
Markwood, 4, 399
Marl, 581
Marland, 341
Marleind,, 344
Marlett, 196
Marlow, 428
Maron, 27
Marot, 278
Marple, 379
Marquis, 241, 282, 444
Marr, 307
Marrin, 137
Marron, 44
Mars, 241
Marsden, 233
Marsh, 190, 309, 315, 327, 441, 533
Marshal, 372, 419
Marshall, 18, 19, 27, 59, 67, 69, 105, 107, 123, 172, 196, 208, 227, 232, 241, 247, 258, 260, 275, 280, 282, 288, 289, 291, 306, 321, 344, 348, 367, 400, 414, 448, 460, 462, 467, 477, 490, 494, 497, 512, 552, 555
Marston, 435
Marteni, 82, 187
Martin, 10, 12, 17, 27, 38, 43, 51, 58, 59, 74, 102, 105, 125, 147, 148, 154, 159, 196, 212, 234, 235, 241, 265, 286, 303, 315, 330, 344, 398, 399, 422, 424, 425, 428, 434, 437, 439, 440, 444, 477, 481, 508, 510, 519, 525, 529, 549, 550, 562, 566

Martine, 46
Martini, 310, 513
Martins, 378
Maruder, 59
Marvin, 4
Maryman, 33, 34, 114, 121, 165, 260, 370, 389, 433, 528, 539
Masi, 47, 348, 393, 396, 483, 555
Mason, 25, 58, 59, 62, 69, 73, 81, 105, 113, 118, 154, 166, 193, 194, 202, 233, 241, 242, 256, 262, 271, 282, 299, 337, 344, 348, 373, 382, 399, 400, 403, 418, 428, 465, 519, 520, 543, 573
Massey, 45, 273
Massie, 88, 150, 510
Massoletti, 58, 578
Masters, 154
Masterson, 251, 311, 313, 326, 362
Masterton, 147
Mastin, 282
Matchett, 16, 242, 282, 398, 399
Mather, 196
Mathew, 154
Mathews, 16, 58, 344, 510, 581
Mathias, 89
Matlack, 350, 468
Matlock, 92, 109, 153, 325, 350, 444
Mattchett, 444
Matter, 524
Mattern, 154, 399
Matthews, 27, 44, 105, 154, 170, 238, 241, 262, 310, 327, 337, 344, 347, 348, 349, 357, 396, 452, 519
Matthewson, 242
Matthias, 202
Mattingley, 12, 105, 481, 482, 484, 485, 499
Mattingly, 27, 47, 164, 192, 196, 325, 391, 436, 449, 523, 547, 555
Mattison, 90, 338, 361
Mattock, 105
Maull, 118

Maury, 76, 80, 109, 158, 367, 448, 481, 482, 484, 501, 534, 535, 578, 581
Maus, 58
Mause, 241
Mauss, 444
Mauzy, 61, 96
Mavin, 282
Maxey, 247
Maximilian, 409
Maxwell, 36, 88, 242, 279
Maxwell Hall, 408
Maxwell's Seat, 408
May, 4, 76, 96, 105, 110, 115, 145, 196, 233, 256, 282, 307, 337, 348, 354, 364, 365, 384, 385, 398, 404, 418, 433, 451, 479, 485, 548
Maybee, 220
Mayer, 121, 344, 519
Mayfield, 55, 146, 177, 202, 574
Maynard, 105, 190, 437, 533, 538, 543, 579
Mayo, 36, 115, 126, 323, 425
Mayson, 159
Mazeen, 282
McAfee, 242
McAlister, 147, 242, 250, 311, 322
McAller, 422
McAllister, 37, 313, 362, 415
McAlpine, 399
McArann, 307
McArrann, 379
McArthur, 27
McBane, 1
McBee, 87, 94
McBlair, 19, 270, 451, 453
McBride, 42, 230
McBridge, 105
McBrogden, 491
McCabe, 4, 207, 402
McCafferty, 215, 359, 555
McCaffrey, 366
McCaleb, 200, 298
McCall, 299, 304, 364, 384, 402, 409
McCalla, 158, 420, 538

McCallen, 21
McCallion, 105
McCallum, 402
McCanan, 381
McCanles, 341
McCann, 21, 242
McCannon, 392
McCardy, 579
McCargo, 579
McCarran, 21
McCarte, 166
McCarter, 497
McCarthy, 399, 504, 505
McCarty, 45, 242, 264, 376, 399, 444, 490, 506, 507, 512, 524
McCaskill, 138
McCathran, 97
McCauley, 85, 94, 97, 154, 288, 301, 307, 322, 323, 362, 406, 441, 460, 480, 490, 546, 566
McCausleind, 105
McCauslin, 287
McCaw, 32
McCeney, 157
McCerrin, 428
McChesney, 242
McChritie, 242
McClain, 147
McClane, 174
McClaughey, 105
McClay, 229
McClean, 12, 572
McCleary, 242, 490
McCleister, 255
McClellan, 69, 280
McClelland, 59, 105, 132, 328, 536
McClenahan, 451, 536
McClery, 183, 444, 539
McClintock, 70, 158, 317, 368, 479, 564
McCloskey, 497
McCloud, 55, 226, 261, 355, 362, 490
McClung, 117, 311, 457, 467, 477, 497, 509, 524
McClure, 27, 32

McCobb, 334
McCockey, 507
McColgan, 479, 480, 547
McCollins, 105
McConaughy, 242
McConnell, 43, 154, 418, 559, 565
McCook, 105, 207, 543
McCorgle, 13
McCorkle, 70
McCormick, 236, 242, 293, 413, 428, 454, 490, 495, 506, 514, 579
McCoull, 401
McCoy, 21
McCrate, 71
McCreary, 22
McCrery, 27, 242
McCuchen, 99
McCue, 317
McCuen, 197
McCulloch, 39, 100, 159, 338, 362, 417, 477
McCullogh, 302
McCulloh, 14, 121, 158, 180, 193
McCullough, 59, 154, 339, 344
McCullum, 36
McCully, 536
McCutchen, 265
McCutcheon, 39, 242
McDaniel, 295, 326
McDearmon, 418
McDermott, 127, 280, 344, 482, 485, 528
McDermut, 374
McDiarmid, 324
McDonal, 536
McDonald, 27, 37, 64, 267, 344, 444, 522
McDonell, 344
McDonnell, 59, 242, 490, 505, 506
McDonogh, 88
McDonough, 261
McDougal, 105
McDowall, 401
McDowell, 37, 45, 105, 184, 277, 441
McDuell, 8, 178, 545

McDuffee, 27
McDuffie, 59, 154, 399, 541
McDuffy, 506
McElroy, 332
McElvain, 117
McElvin, 242
McElwain, 382
McEndree, 59
McEnery, 70
McEnnis, 344
McEwen, 561
McFaran, 42
McFarlan, 27, 242, 537
McFarland, 59, 154, 490, 540, 579
McFarlane, 105
McFarran, 444
McFee, 42
McFerren, 191
McGahen, 265
McGalway, 282
McGarr, 536
McGarvey, 452, 555
McGaughey, 2
McGee, 4, 242, 418
McGehee, 490
McGill, 555
McGonigal, 344
McGough, 419
McGouth, 504
McGowan, 444, 471, 579
McGrath, 59, 65
McGraw, 27, 105
McGray, 59
McGregor, 53, 154, 277, 357, 399, 462
McGroger, 242
McGruder, 399
McGuiness, 239
McGuir, 483
McGuire, 39, 114, 168, 173, 373, 449, 539, 562
McGuirk, 511
McGunnegill, 441
McGunnegle, 344
McHatton, 102

McHenry, 59, 60, 184, 242
McIlroy, 444
McIlvain, 73, 88
McIlvaine, 464, 515
McIntire, 175, 188, 335, 476
McIntosh, 27, 150, 227, 228, 229, 246, 260, 266, 290, 364, 381, 384, 457, 560, 561
McIntyre, 59
McIvor, 564
McJilton, 196, 399, 490
McKaig, 210
McKavett, 456, 510, 540, 549, 551
McKay, 196, 436
McKeage, 282
McKean, 379, 428
McKee, 154, 247, 260, 498, 508
McKeever, 27, 196, 322, 323
McKeim, 27
McKelden, 242, 290
McKelly, 40
McKenna, 536
McKenney, 225, 444, 545
McKenny, 27, 59, 531
McKenzie, 29, 78, 145, 177, 180, 189, 362, 403
McKeogh, 268
McKibbin, 40
McKiernan, 344
McKilb, 297
McKim, 125, 428, 563
McKinley, 441
McKinnon, 327
McKinstey, 332
McKinstry, 19
McKissack, 383, 549, 550
McKissick, 125
McKnight, 41, 512, 571
McKnott, 440
McKocky, 76
McKolgan, 556
McLain, 418, 490
McLanahan, 211, 344
McLane, 87, 233, 255, 312, 355, 418, 523, 543, 573

McLaughlin, 31, 41, 79, 92, 126, 189, 227, 297, 304, 323, 399, 428, 490, 525, 528, 539, 564
McLaws, 405
McLean, 4, 15, 41, 52, 59, 132, 139, 151, 162, 196, 251, 306, 379, 464
McLellan, 190
McLemore, 27, 59, 105
McLenahan, 302
McLenehan, 305
McLeod, 92, 128, 233, 238, 279, 290, 458, 576
McLoud, 340
McMahon, 277, 279
McMakim, 27
McMann, 543
McManus, 511
McMasters, 257, 440
McMekin, 402
McMillan, 299
McMillion, 282
McMoreland, 20
McMurran, 257
McMurray, 497, 507
McNair, 42, 94
McNamara, 59, 105
McNamee, 227, 485
McNeal, 309
McNeil, 27, 116, 344, 569
McNeill, 105, 242, 360
McNeir, 501
McNemar, 253
McNorris, 510
McNulty, 324
McPeak, 428, 431
McPhail, 231, 334, 386, 549
McPheeters, 289
McPherson, 69, 91, 109, 242, 278, 310, 380, 399, 555
McQueen, 463
McQuigin, 444
McQuillian, 562
McQuinn, 555
McRae, 78, 282, 344, 353, 444, 562, 569
McRea, 14, 78
McReam, 105
McReynolds, 27
McRoberts, 80
McTavish, 518
McVey, 309
McWhorter, 453
McWilliams, 119, 219, 344, 455
Mead, 4, 58, 117, 192, 539, 581
Meade, 39, 88, 163, 197, 265, 266, 304, 344, 379
Meager, 339
Means, 27
Meany, 170
Mebane, 52
Medary, 70
Medill, 9
Meehan, 454
Meek, 4, 141, 318
Meelzard, 530
Meigs, 143, 428
Meins, 398
Meinung, 74
Melson, 118
Melton, 229, 405
Melville, 19, 271, 563
Melvin, 118, 374
Menairy, 282
Menard, 23, 81, 82, 90, 102, 331, 361, 415
Mendenhall, 154
Mercer, 21, 76, 87, 304, 401, 431, 435
Merchant, 444, 449
Merchants, 10
Meredith, 167, 297, 490, 536, 566
Mergoun, 154
Meritt, 224
Meriweather, 493
Meriwether, 344
Merrett, 236
Merriam, 411
Merrick, 169
Merriken, 148
Merrill, 6, 89, 251, 311, 312, 315, 362, 490

Merrille, 399
Merrit, 110
Merritt, 217, 246
Merriwether, 502
Mersereaw, 468
Mertin, 154
Mertons, 137
Merwin, 328
Messer, 496
Messersmith, 420
Messinger, 13
Meteer, 282
Methodist Episcopal Church, 277
Metoyer, 302, 331
Metternich, 32
Mewton, 401
Meyer, 27, 131, 241, 498
Mich'e, 504
Michael, 455
Michael Angelo, 408
Michelet, 255
Mick, 7
Middleton, 33, 36, 154, 196, 260, 267, 410, 430, 444, 466, 471, 481, 484, 513
Miercken, 207
Miffleton, 230
Milam, 247
Milburn, 122, 188, 196, 276, 428, 454, 460, 494
Miler, 58
Miles, 4, 93, 117, 404, 536, 543
Milford, 115
Millandon, 217
Millard, 423
Miller, 6, 29, 30, 37, 39, 43, 51, 70, 73, 91, 105, 116, 117, 119, 122, 125, 145, 154, 188, 202, 210, 236, 241, 242, 245, 274, 282, 286, 287, 305, 314, 329, 334, 335, 341, 344, 351, 354, 360, 380, 398, 402, 407, 419, 428, 465, 490, 498, 501, 508, 509, 511, 546, 555, 568
Millers, 30
Milligan, 156, 175, 493

Millington, 308
Mills, 58, 122, 129, 153, 166, 169, 191, 196, 248, 302, 344, 375, 379, 401, 431, 462, 494, 556
Millson, 555
Milner, 154
Milnes, 444
Milson, 154
Milstead, 27, 154, 163, 288, 428
Milsteads, 105
Milsted, 313, 324
Minck, 490
Mines, 105
Ming, 368
Minge, 116, 184, 490
Minnigerode, 308
Minning, 449
Minnix, 77
Minor, 124, 134, 165, 282, 312, 398, 422
Minter, 512
Minturn, 428
Miranda, 78, 126
Mistard, 439
Mitcham, 509
Mitchel, 580
Mitchell, 6, 27, 42, 58, 59, 69, 77, 82, 83, 105, 117, 147, 153, 154, 172, 229, 241, 242, 262, 287, 348, 396, 401, 421, 457, 462, 477, 486, 496, 498, 507, 524, 533, 542, 543, 551, 553
Mittag, 316, 348
Mix, 146, 189, 441
Mixner, 27
Mixter, 242
Moddrell, 25
Mohun, 64, 84, 120, 161, 245
Molette, 163
Molt, 125, 267
Monaghan, 303
Monmonier, 435
Monnier, 304
Monroe, 42, 105, 192, 205, 267, 528, 533

Montague, 246
Montanverd, 565
Montgomery, 51, 74, 80, 154, 214, 228, 229, 242, 260, 275, 276, 292, 300, 351, 359, 398, 399, 420, 444, 571
Montgomery Guards, 220
Moody, 405, 444
Moon, 117, 531
Mooney, 287, 468
Moore, 4, 17, 20, 22, 27, 58, 82, 94, 105, 113, 116, 122, 123, 132, 135, 138, 147, 158, 160, 172, 192, 194, 196, 203, 206, 213, 241, 265, 274, 282, 283, 316, 327, 344, 421, 426, 435, 444, 446, 465, 490, 494, 513, 515, 536, 545, 562
Moorefield, 253
Moorehead, 105
Moorhead, 174, 245, 409
Moors, 39
Moran, 27, 96, 100, 154, 196, 215, 228, 241, 282, 366, 396, 446, 482, 483, 484, 485, 490, 531, 555, 556, 560, 571
Morcoe, 581
Mordecai, 75, 569
More, 137, 153
Moreclan, 577
Morehead, 223, 241, 509
Morehouse, 398
Moreland, 142, 265, 398
Mores, 98
Moreton, 376
Morfit, 119, 288, 453
Morgan, 16, 27, 33, 58, 59, 105, 148, 153, 196, 227, 242, 245, 251, 263, 276, 282, 333, 350, 354, 357, 366, 399, 421, 433, 440, 467, 471, 478, 523, 536, 539, 540, 555, 557, 581
Moriarty, 378
Mormon, 211, 214
Mormons, 318, 340
Morrell, 166, 173, 252
Morrill, 496

Morris, 15, 19, 88, 105, 135, 154, 171, 196, 202, 224, 233, 246, 249, 255, 260, 275, 280, 282, 292, 322, 323, 344, 359, 375, 384, 398, 456, 458, 465, 466, 476, 489, 490, 499, 504, 505, 526, 527, 531, 536, 549, 551, 564
Morrison, 27, 42, 52, 64, 105, 125, 160, 255, 275, 293, 303, 440, 542, 547, 555, 563, 573
Morron, 511
Morrow, 4, 62, 78, 97, 309, 479, 480, 495, 503, 555
Morse, 27, 45, 47, 51, 58, 105, 114, 142, 147, 153, 196, 229, 344, 402, 425, 518, 536
Morsel, 242
Morsell, 19, 58, 105, 138, 262, 314, 430, 460, 555, 565
Morter, 507
Mortimer, 279, 394
Mortin, 344
Morton, 25, 42, 46, 70, 122, 154, 167, 241, 244, 259, 282, 334, 386, 395, 398, 411, 511, 576, 577
Mosby, 70
Moscrop, 428
Moseley, 400
Mosely, 546
Moses, 58, 115, 421
Mosher, 378
Moss, 102, 251, 298, 305, 311, 313, 366
Motear, 496
Motlow, 44, 145
Motta, 335
Motter, 440, 497
Moulden, 105, 308
Moulder, 444, 555
Moulon, 202
Moulton, 59, 153
Mount, 4, 219, 444, 452, 539
Mount Airy, 304, 306
Mount Erin, 406
Mount Hebron Estate, 430

Mount Ida, 112
Mount Pisgah, 193
Mount Pleasant, 341
Mount Vernon, 203
Mountain Lot of Woodland, 573
Mountford, 114
Mountjoy, 51
Mountz, 4, 85, 238, 428
Moutel, 154
Mouton, 66
Mowatt, 466
Mudd, 98, 131, 181, 245, 288, 321, 378, 460, 581
Muhl, 31
Muhlenburg, 344
Muir, 319, 403
Mulberry Hill, 176
Mules, 27
Mulhollan, 465, 568
Mulholland, 340
Mulhollen, 579
Mullanphy, 169
Mullany, 377, 378
Mulledy, 405
Mullen, 428, 505
Muller, 16, 80, 135, 139, 344
Mullett, 315
Mullican, 564
Mulligan, 154, 371
Mullikin, 60, 273, 531
Mullin, 556
Mullins, 327
Mullon, 359
Mullowny, 575
Mulloy, 59, 153, 322, 399, 536
Mulvaney, 309
Muncaster, 577
Munday, 241
Mundell, 578
Mundy, 40
Munford, 402
Munn, 4, 153
Munro, 91
Munroe, 122, 188, 376, 494
Murdaugh, 528

Murdoch, 109, 344
Murdock, 164, 196, 241, 341, 444
Murgatroyd, 82
Murphey, 306
Murphy, 4, 8, 27, 47, 58, 59, 82, 128, 197, 241, 242, 244, 267, 282, 298, 311, 333, 444, 482, 483, 484, 490, 515, 536, 580
Murray, 16, 29, 59, 87, 94, 98, 105, 110, 121, 132, 145, 154, 184, 196, 223, 241, 242, 251, 257, 279, 282, 311, 313, 332, 340, 367, 389, 428, 481, 518, 552, 555
Murry, 358, 391
Murst, 241
Muse, 244, 344, 398
Musselman, 304
Mussey, 141, 437
Musson, 477, 497
Mustin, 412
Muth, 153
Muzzy, 238
Myer, 23, 59, 344, 508
Myerle, 331
Myers, 36, 118, 154, 192, 206, 217, 241, 344, 444, 459, 464, 476, 497, 506, 507, 511, 549, 574, 579
Myles, 506
Myrlie, 266

N

Nail, 536
Naill, 439
Nailor, 196, 438, 480
Nairy, 119
Nalle, 4
Nalley, 223, 252, 254
Nalls, 176
Nally, 59
Nancrede, 344
Naper, 287
Naples, 399
Napoleon, 4, 32, 408, 432
Naser, 282

Nash, 428
Nat'l Intelligencer, 174
Nations, 144
Naudain, 559
Naylor, 1, 149, 224, 282, 339, 354, 423, 428, 432, 493, 502, 503, 564
ne exeat, 395
Neale, 56, 101, 170, 337, 348, 378, 394, 560
Nealey, 371
Needles, 374
Neely, 506
Neff, 27, 287
Neilson, 38, 428
Neiser, 4
Nelson, 4, 19, 68, 108, 173, 242, 282, 307, 344, 356, 402, 444, 505, 531, 578
Nes, 4, 464
Nesle, 7
Nesmith, 355, 496
Neutze, 242, 490
Nevet, 196
Neville, 196, 242, 379, 528
Nevins, 336, 347
Nevit, 27
Nevitt, 188
Nevius, 391
New bldgs, 188
New Bldgs, 437
New Market-House, 158
new Pope, 316
Newall, 331
Newbury, 105
Newby, 242
Newcom, 191
Newcomb, 55, 80, 288, 330, 565
Newcomer, 469
Newell, 266, 422, 487
Newland, 4, 465, 568
Newman, 97, 173, 231, 301, 421, 504, 559
Newton, 59, 79, 80, 105, 147, 154, 196, 203, 207, 233, 255, 374, 548, 549, 567

Ney, 548
Niblo, 380
Nice, 59, 453
Nicholas, 4, 116, 173, 400
Nicholauvitch, 458
Nicholl, 272
Nicholls, 25, 53, 140, 147, 428
Nichols, 9, 30, 116, 132, 154, 200, 222, 242, 371
Nicholson, 4, 27, 257, 312, 319, 320, 444, 500, 517
Nickerson, 65
Nicolson, 501, 532
Nicot, 513
Niebert, 344
Niel, 568
Niess, 376
Nildett, 399
Niles, 105, 196, 254, 282, 314, 437, 496, 498, 507, 524
Nims, 143
Niven, 242
Nixon, 9, 82, 148, 154, 457, 508, 524
Nobel, 515
Noble, 4, 65, 105, 144, 154, 163, 230, 562
Nock, 90, 102
Noel, 59, 85, 234
Noerr, 305, 467
Nolan, 113
Noland, 242, 296, 510, 517
Nolen, 344
Nones, 471, 526
Norbeck, 556
Norlin, 506
Norman, 344
Noronha, 248
Norris, 39, 47, 78, 105, 132, 147, 154, 194, 368, 487, 507, 546, 556
Norriss, 98, 368
North, 27
Northe, 105
Northern Market, 473
Northern Market-house, 346
Northup, 48, 90

Norton, 105, 303, 402, 531, 532, 540, 542, 549, 551
Norvell, 116, 379, 550, 571
Norvill, 517
not wanted, 251
Nouman, 196
Nourse, 102, 115, 190, 193, 202, 206, 218, 227, 279, 334, 425, 459, 479, 540, 548, 568
Nowlan, 536
Noyes, 24, 119, 174, 191, 242, 444
Nunemacher, 566
Nutlee, 579
Nutt, 436
Nutter, 254
Nye, 33, 34, 144, 215, 226

O

O'Brian, 318
O'Brien, 27, 59, 112, 219, 249, 267, 268, 282, 344, 444, 492, 504, 505, 507, 562
O'Brine, 242
O'Bryan, 196, 399
O'Bryon, 17, 182, 490, 570
O'Conner, 444
O'Donnell, 273, 550, 556, 571
O'Driscoll, 186
O'Hara, 69, 490
O'Hare, 556
O'Leary, 267, 306, 519, 556
O'Nail, 490
O'Neal, 70, 92, 399, 485, 493, 562
O'Neale, 196, 265, 297, 453
O'Neall, 350
O'Neil, 127, 257, 265, 293, 331
O'Neill, 27, 59, 105, 154
O'Riley, 20, 154
O'Sullivan, 399
Oak Grove, 170, 250
Oak Ridge, 578
Oakford, 231
Oakley, 133, 156, 257, 511
Oakwood, 80

Oames, 196
Obane, 444
Ober, 339, 556
Obermeyer, 278
Ochiltree, 307, 379
Ochis, 105
Odell, 335
Offley, 14, 27
Offutt, 85, 445, 535, 539
Ogden, 55, 111, 154, 367, 376, 384, 387, 444, 536
Ogilvie, 431
Ogle, 232, 578
Ohr, 278
Olcott, 242, 465
Old Dominion, 113
Oldham, 31, 79
Olinger, 303
Oliver, 59, 196, 444
Olivier, 337, 344
Oliy, 7
Omshaw Hill, 578
Onego, 490
Opie, 49
Opiphant, 245
Ord, 89, 282, 312
Order of Mercy, 478
Orleans Riflemen, 220
Orme, 27, 111, 245, 288, 317, 428, 519, 556
Ormsby, 232
Orndorff, 51
Orne, 60
Orphean, 242
Orr, 45, 46, 428, 510, 533, 538
Osborn, 59, 401, 414
Osborne, 97
Osbourn, 327
Osgood, 97, 98
Osmond, 10
Ostermayer, 452
Ostrander, 90, 349
Otero, 518
Otey, 88
Othiltree, 399

Otis, 51, 139, 184, 528
Otman, 147
Ott, 143, 262
Otterback, 38, 502, 514, 522
Otto, 490
Ould, 25, 213, 274, 354, 539, 544
Overbagh, 349
Overstreet, 567
Overton, 18, 29, 79, 103, 381
Owen, 4, 21, 29, 55, 116, 147, 154, 249, 259, 268, 282, 363, 381, 410, 431, 477
Owens, 80, 438
Owner, 192, 455
oxhydrogen, 327
Oyster, 419

P

Pack, 81
packet **Argo**, 200
packet boat **Rescue**, 222
packet-ship **Henry Clay**, 144
Paddon, 205
Padgett, 97, 202, 556
Page, 27, 50, 80, 94, 105, 196, 226, 228, 238, 246, 249, 260, 286, 320, 352, 353, 379, 383, 387, 402, 490, 537
Paige, 4
Paine, 196, 201, 300, 453
Pairo, 127, 437, 446, 491, 551
Palmer, 1, 70, 115, 154, 163, 196, 236, 263, 301, 357, 408, 428, 537
Pancoast, 556
Pannall, 170
Pannell, 231
Paredes, 366, 388
Parham, 249, 254, 268
Paris, 154, 268
Parish, 41, 147
Park, 157
Parke, 290, 330
Parker, 8, 25, 47, 55, 98, 107, 109, 115, 154, 162, 176, 196, 199, 226, 242, 252, 257, 262, 266, 275, 282, 312, 314, 322, 323, 327, 333, 334, 344, 349, 355, 362, 366, 386, 391, 393, 402, 415, 428, 434, 483, 523, 526, 556, 563, 571, 572, 576, 579
Parkinson, 318
Parkman, 342
Parks, 69, 184, 509
Parmele, 39, 143, 538
Parmenter, 27, 105, 279
Parmeter, 43
Parmlee, 196
Parnell, 118, 168, 359, 361
Parris, 47, 492
Parrish, 242, 570
Parrot, 428, 574
Parrott, 4, 40, 282, 541
Parson, 298
Parsons, 99, 154, 158, 198, 242, 335, 425, 444, 450, 556, 562, 580
Partee, 27
Partridge, 538
Paschal, 41, 105
Pascoe, 556
Pass, 547
Passamente, 404
Passet, 258
Pasteur, 159, 261
Paton, 92
Patrick, 59, 504
Patten, 90, 118, 250, 338, 360, 383
Patter, 41
Patterson, 5, 19, 53, 173, 191, 194, 265, 282, 299, 439, 442, 483, 490, 494, 508, 542, 545, 556
Pattison, 45
Patton, 27, 102, 311, 313, 329, 358, 360, 362, 428, 444
Patty, 313
Pauffler, 458
Paul, 124, 232
Paulding, 126, 307, 428
Payne, 16, 105, 154, 213, 227, 228, 229, 260, 274, 286, 299, 323, 349, 364, 384, 399, 428

Payson, 114
Peach Island, 573
Peachey, 529
Peachy, 274, 354
Peaco, 574
Peak, 27
Peake, 97
Peale, 98
Pearce, 29, 97, 227, 294, 344, 348, 414, 531
Pearks, 344
Pearl, 207
Pearsee, 303
Pearsey, 147
Pearson, 344, 440, 450, 492, 508, 547
Pearss, 468
Pease, 27, 105, 116, 154
Peavy, 184
Pechin, 487
Peck, 39, 121, 341, 354, 399, 482, 483, 507, 569
Peckham, 344
Peddicord, 59, 154
Pedrick, 34, 114, 217, 529
Peed, 277
Peek, 123
Peekham, 242
Peel, 316
Peele, 559
Peer of France, 409
Peetres, 171
Peetsch, 428, 556
Peirce, 38, 262, 545
Pelham, 15
Peltier, 102
Pember, 61
Pen, 444
Pendergrast, 105, 196
Pendleton, 59, 208, 225, 249, 324, 400, 444
Penland, 89
Penn, 180, 334, 371, 386, 503, 578
Penney, 5
Pennington, 105, 247, 504
Pennock, 250, 312

Pennoyer, 45, 98, 110, 266, 331
Penny, 196, 439
Pennybacker, 40, 353, 381, 410
Penrose, 4, 154, 222, 383
Pentecost, 327
Pentland, 344
Pentz, 148
Pepper, 18, 32, 117, 135, 347, 436, 474, 481, 484, 485
Perche, 138
Perdicaris, 371
Perham, 118
Perison, 59
Perkins, 11, 22, 35, 82, 95, 97, 98, 236, 242, 504, 512
Perpigna, 409
Perrie, 4, 255
Perry, 36, 89, 99, 105, 126, 154, 196, 242, 245, 247, 248, 250, 296, 313, 322, 323, 370, 399, 458, 464, 466, 526, 528, 538, 571
Peter, 218, 368, 402, 428, 462, 519, 565
Peterkin, 181
Peters, 59, 142, 154, 349, 428, 437, 556
Peterson, 533
Pettet, 567
Pettibone, 128, 389, 428, 463, 480
Petticord, 27
Pettigrew, 271
Pettit, 69, 105, 135, 216, 490
Petts, 151
Pettus, 401
Petty, 506
Peugh, 196
Pew, 282
Pew #55, 577
Peyroux, 31
Peyton, 43, 69, 149, 196, 222, 339, 370, 401, 477, 497
Phale, 497, 507
Pharm, 196
Phelan, 105

Phelps, 27, 49, 59, 88, 105, 124, 147, 242, 251, 307, 311, 312, 313, 326, 361
Philippi, 335
Philips, 27, 43, 59, 105, 154, 234, 282, 318, 331, 399, 438, 444, 490, 562, 581
Phillips, 18, 50, 59, 109, 201, 247, 261, 291, 303, 356, 362, 367, 394, 428, 469, 475, 485, 499, 500, 530
Phiole, 163
Phipps, 344
Phoebus, 440
Phoenix, 18
Pic, 148, 181
Pickell, 237
Pickering, 154, 209
Pickett, 81, 105, 154, 173, 196, 237, 242, 282, 331, 453
Pickins, 105
Pickrell, 25, 228, 347, 353, 461, 537
Pierce, 4, 33, 55, 59, 67, 69, 105, 109, 154, 206, 348, 439, 510, 529, 556
Piere, 302
Pieres, 399
Pierie, 159, 417
Pierpont, 282, 355
Pierre, 17, 100
Piersee, 468
Pierson, 468, 498
Pike, 33, 154, 180, 220, 265, 328, 331, 361, 417, 563
Pile, 81, 447
Piles, 282, 507
Pilling, 49, 59, 196
Pillow, 291
Pillsbury, 257
pilot boat **Baltimore**, 318
Pilsbury, 391
Pinckney, 344, 525
Piney Point, 273, 285
Pinkney, 18, 71, 196
Pinn, 137
Pinney, 196
Piollet, 207

Piper, 192, 249, 268, 321, 402, 492
Pise, 337
Pister, 154
Pistole, 336
Pitcher, 74, 148, 549
Pitman, 229, 529
Pittman, 24, 89, 247, 257, 291, 376, 514
Pitts, 95, 154, 533, 538, 540, 544
Pius IX, 316, 324, 335
Pius VII, 336
Placy, 102
Plain, 137
Plant, 219, 253, 288, 399, 478, 479, 490, 537
Plants, 276
Plater, 25
Platt, 30, 147, 257
Platte, 7
Pleasant Ridge, 193
Pleasanton, 71
Pleasants, 1, 27, 101, 192, 304, 411, 434
Ploughman, 196
Plowden, 348
Plumbe, 44
Plume, 194
Plummer, 10, 15, 110, 147, 210, 225, 229, 518
Plumsill, 186
Plunkett, 523
Poe, 367
Poensel, 59
Poindexter, 5
Poinsett, 315
Points, 4
Polhemus, 149
Polk, 183, 214, 223, 332, 337, 414, 517, 537
Polkenhorn, 105
Pollard, 34, 45, 130, 188, 208, 397, 432, 541
Pollen, 579
Pollock, 78, 154, 344, 346, 464
Polly, 196

Pollygreen, 23
Pomeroy, 133
Poncy, 268
Pond, 455
Pool, 27, 59, 105, 210, 362, 444
Poole, 4, 154, 157, 175, 196, 315
Pooler, 99, 250
Poor, 213, 242
Pope, 183, 206, 227, 233, 255, 282, 335, 515
Pope Gregory XVI, 292, 297
Pope Leo XII, 369
Popham, 570
Poplar Fields, 137
Pore, 564
Porsetts, 280
Porter, 4, 6, 7, 17, 19, 23, 27, 41, 44, 45, 55, 59, 74, 89, 98, 105, 117, 146, 172, 189, 196, 210, 226, 233, 251, 252, 256, 313, 339, 344, 347, 366, 487, 508, 543, 548, 568
Porterfield, 139, 192
Posey, 537, 560
Postlethwaite, 247
Poston, 326, 381
Potomac Mills, 257
Potter, 27, 72, 154, 324, 326, 344, 364, 405, 411, 439, 457, 487, 488, 511, 518, 524
Pottinger, 572
Potts, 105, 175, 509
Pottsdaner, 505
Pouiston, 59
Poulson, 507
Poultney, 173
Powders, 5
Powel, 59
Powell, 5, 27, 45, 80, 122, 196, 349, 444, 494, 508, 528
Powelson, 492
Power, 105, 579
Powers, 189, 300, 444, 579, 581
Powlis, 294
Poythress, 401
Prall, 105

Prather, 20, 196, 305, 392, 433
Pratt, 2, 4, 59, 147, 165, 206, 230, 251, 311, 313, 344, 361, 363, 428, 508, 534, 537, 569
Pray, 9, 406
Preble, 12
Prenot, 238
Prentis, 402
Prentiss, 27, 59, 178, 382, 550, 561, 566
Presbyterian Church, 182, 234
Prescott, 79, 143
Presgraves, 559
Preslie, 505
Prestman, 105
Preston, 4, 19, 196, 201, 282, 351, 363, 366, 381, 392, 410, 428
Preusier, 269
Preuss, 29, 140, 357, 563
Preusser, 282
Prevost, 141, 444
Price, 4, 59, 65, 76, 94, 133, 154, 196, 242, 247, 263, 268, 309, 321, 339, 347, 367, 399, 407, 424, 444, 497, 515, 565
Pride, 401
Pridgen, 167
Priest, 339
Prieur, 116
Prime, 27
Primrose, 376
Prince, 490
Princess Caroline, 279
Princess Olga, 198
Prindle, 242
Pringle, 12, 21, 27, 105, 307, 344, 444
Printed Goods, 230
Pritchard, 141, 337, 343, 344, 429
Prout, 124, 400, 426, 428
Provest, 138
Provost, 538, 556
Pryor, 508
Pugh, 65
Pughe, 154
Puicey, 156

Pulizzi, 452, 461
Pulsifer, 55
Pumphrey, 22, 154, 481, 484, 535, 537, 552, 556
Pupo, 444
Purcell, 134, 234, 344, 364, 528
Purdie, 401, 402
Purdy, 5, 20, 122, 376, 482, 494, 579
Purkis, 166
Purkitt, 120
Purnell, 229, 520
Pursell, 64, 79, 483, 556
Pursivall, 469
Putnam, 223, 410, 456, 508
Putney, 86, 88, 265, 331, 346, 362, 417
Pye, 107, 225, 344
Pyne, 16, 31, 34, 140, 209, 232, 246, 528, 530, 547, 567

Q

Quackenboss, 14, 83, 94
Quackenbush, 307
Quantin, 290
Quantrill, 5, 10
Quarls, 5
Quarter, 478
Quastoff, 490
Queen, 36, 49, 113, 154, 196, 245, 348, 378, 466, 486, 522, 556
Queen Christiana, 499
Queen of Norway, 317
Queen of Spain, 499
Queen,, 378
Queens, 332
Quest, 579
Quigley, 197, 556
Quimby, 27, 59, 72, 284
Quinby, 141
Quincey, 165
Quincy, 200
Quiney, 294
Quinlein, 59
Quinn, 309, 519

Quinter, 27, 154
Quitman, 291, 456

R

Rabb, 512
Rabbit, 537
Rabbitt, 154
Race, 99
Radcliff, 126, 513
Radcliffe, 1, 5, 40, 279, 288
Radford, 73, 80
Radwell, 505
Ragan, 5, 78, 511
Raggio, 5
Ragon, 48
Rague, 233
Raguet, 255
Railey, 88, 192
Raimond, 531
Rains, 275
Rall, 196
Rallings, 399
Ralston, 88, 287
Rambo, 151, 206
Ramey, 142, 202, 237, 266, 331
Ramsay, 5, 59, 105, 146, 154, 349, 402, 444, 492, 504, 509, 541
Ramsburg, 198, 230
Ramsey, 25, 181, 218, 223, 339, 371, 420, 421, 569
Ramsford, 105
Rand, 69, 344
Randall, 2, 109, 254, 261, 269, 410, 424, 479, 556
Randell, 501
Randle, 287
Randolph, 10, 15, 21, 28, 36, 76, 147, 150, 169, 244, 283, 307, 379, 399, 400, 401, 460, 494, 569, 573
Rankin, 44, 141, 341
Ransom, 125, 141, 452
Ranson, 71, 154, 503
Rant, 399
Rantoul, 27, 69

Rapetti, 418
Raphael, 408
Raphile, 508
Rapp, 235
Raquet, 548
Rardaf, 105
Rareshide, 65
Ratcliff, 105, 154, 344, 444, 477, 506
Ratcliffe, 43, 78, 81, 242
Rathbun, 70
Rathburn, 399
Raub, 5, 85, 86
Rawdon, 282
Rawlett, 28
Rawlings, 145, 339, 556
Rawlins, 196
Rawls, 9, 70
Ray, 105, 140, 212, 268, 282, 377, 444, 447
Rayan, 59
Raymers, 142
Raymond, 154, 172, 189, 198, 242, 504
Rayner, 154
Raynor, 70
razee **Independence**, 379
Razor Tract, 573
RCC Church, 7
Rea, 105
Read, 36, 45, 59, 66, 70, 75, 121, 154, 166, 168, 250, 296, 298, 326, 338, 352, 402, 412, 413, 449, 556
Readils, 196
Ready, 20, 124, 154, 344, 490, 556
Real, 40
Reaney, 59
Reardon, 573
Reaver, 159
Reaves, 509
Reckless, 444
Rector, 71
Redd, 154
Reddall, 39, 47, 201
Reddy, 54, 154
Rederson, 261

Redfern, 47, 52, 390, 447, 556
Redfield, 118, 242
Redin, 18, 171, 187, 250, 345, 366, 439, 514, 519
Redmington, 147
Redonda, 404
Ree___, 359
Reed, 15, 27, 44, 59, 82, 98, 109, 154, 159, 160, 196, 199, 206, 211, 242, 282, 556, 564
Reeder, 5, 47, 444, 518
Rees, 70, 149, 165, 182, 202, 249
Reese, 39, 53, 132, 148, 170, 226, 234, 279, 488, 497, 507, 512, 525
Reeside, 154, 301, 416
Reeve, 292, 349, 357, 384
Reeves, 27, 105, 196, 275, 380, 399
Regan, 505
Register, 412
Reid, 59, 72, 147, 154, 196, 220, 368, 433
Reider, 5, 444
Reiley, 5, 59, 105, 106, 270
Reilly, 485, 504, 505
Reily, 28
Reinecke, 511
Reinhardt, 235
Reintzel, 66
Reisack, 478
Reise, 533
Reiss, 452
Reitz, 238
Relfe, 35
Remington, 242
Rench, 428
Rencher, 352
Renebeck, 511
Renick, 176
Renner, 330
Rennolds, 537
Renolds, 59
Renshaw, 80, 237, 248, 458
Rest, 490
Retreat, 81, 552
retrocede Alexandria, 362

retrocession of Alexandria, 403
Retter, 28
revenue cutter **Forward**, 471, 526
revenue cutter **Van Buren**, 280
Rey, 332, 502
Reybold, 32
Reyburn, 399
Reynolds, 19, 59, 140, 154, 196, 217, 257, 266, 282, 287, 303, 331, 382, 404, 465, 488, 572
Rhea, 17, 74, 100, 224, 301, 352, 361, 477, 549
Rheem, 433
Rheinhard, 452
Rhett, 73, 196, 233, 256, 444
Rhind, 444
Rhodes, 5, 39, 59, 107, 124, 158, 196, 301, 308, 399, 508, 520
Ricardo, 220
Riccar, 565
Ricci, 298
Rice, 5, 11, 122, 154, 156, 194, 196, 344, 367, 428, 440, 490, 494, 581
Rich, 75, 114, 406, 490, 496, 550
Richard, 105
Richards, 59, 199, 202, 242, 250, 266, 313, 444, 490, 520, 580
Richardson, 5, 51, 70, 79, 105, 113, 148, 157, 235, 242, 309, 325, 344, 372, 392, 435, 489, 509, 544, 549
Richey, 74, 96, 130, 383
Richmond, 117, 139
Rickards, 59
Ricketts, 87, 125, 172, 234, 284, 453, 556
Ricks, 5, 444
Rickwell, 214
Riddell, 304, 402
Riddle, 21, 40, 49, 85, 86, 242, 265, 331, 346, 362, 417, 444
Riddock, 345
Ridgeley, 344
Ridgely, 79, 164, 208, 299, 322, 339, 365, 382, 384, 429, 455, 521, 548, 549, 551, 565, 567

Ridgley, 154, 345, 516
Ridgly, 39
Ridgway, 32, 532
Ridings, 444, 490, 537
Rife, 79, 250, 311, 312, 324, 362
Rigden, 556
Rigdon, 28, 211, 239
Rigg, 407
Riggles, 413, 522
Riggs, 14, 109, 227, 262, 428
Right, 154
Rightstine, 242
Rihl, 510
Riley, 52, 54, 71, 100, 150, 154, 216, 242, 282, 337, 344, 370, 391, 481, 512, 537, 540, 543, 568
Rind, 402
Ring, 433
Ringgold, 92, 134, 154, 226, 227, 228, 242, 323, 339, 344, 353, 365, 386, 399, 428, 429, 444, 539, 561, 570, 577
Riordan, 186, 539
Ripka, 231
Ripley, 86, 105, 156, 176, 180, 183, 257
Risley, 265
Risque, 461
Ritchie, 59, 101, 105, 271, 401
Ritner, 441
Ritt, 337
Ritter, 28, 59
Ritters, 505
Rives, 14, 19, 88, 109, 166, 545
Roach, 20, 56, 111, 127, 135, 136, 165, 348, 436, 532, 537, 544
Roane, 113, 339, 386, 399, 401
Robb, 238, 350, 402, 565
Robbins, 59, 194, 199, 237, 399, 437
Robby, 496
Roberson, 59
Robert, 59, 246, 561
Roberton, 399
Roberts, 5, 23, 27, 53, 54, 59, 82, 89, 90, 132, 141, 172, 196, 233, 255,

282, 285, 294, 330, 331, 361, 370, 401, 414, 415, 444, 510, 537, 570
Robertson, 5, 59, 62, 69, 105, 106, 117, 154, 168, 411, 490, 537, 542
Robey, 444, 556
Robidoux, 515
Robins, 89
Robinson, 5, 35, 54, 59, 69, 84, 96, 105, 106, 109, 110, 137, 150, 154, 196, 201, 205, 221, 225, 229, 242, 245, 278, 282, 288, 305, 316, 374, 383, 399, 401, 444, 460, 464, 508, 537, 541, 545, 567
Robison, 196
Roby, 5, 6, 31, 46, 132, 288, 450, 519, 571, 575
Rochambeau, 78
Rochat, 380
Roche, 196, 348
Rochel, 399
Rock, 512
Rock of Dunbarton, 541
Rockfort, 399
Rockwell, 5, 76, 78, 154
Rodburn, 196
Rodebaugh, 85
Rodgers, 5, 59, 105, 298, 355, 490, 543, 549
Rodman, 374, 415
Rodney, 69, 294, 409
Roe, 246
Roemelle, 556
Roers, 59
Roff, 65
Rogers, 20, 56, 59, 90, 92, 99, 106, 133, 142, 154, 182, 192, 196, 198, 206, 214, 242, 255, 259, 294, 366, 414, 444, 490, 533, 563, 571, 575
Rolando, 106
Rolling, 269
Rollings, 213, 473, 537
Rollins, 17, 282, 444
Roman, 385, 386
Romley, 138
Roney, 508

Ronkendorf, 196
Rooke, 505
Rooker, 373
Root, 40, 440, 575
Roper, 476
Rosani, 335
Rosas, 255
Roscende, 451
Rose, 59, 118, 196, 206, 579
Rosecrants, 72, 549
Rosedale, 378
Rosemount Estate, 285
Rosenthal, 17
Rosevelt, 154
Rosier, 490
Ross, 5, 8, 13, 98, 130, 202, 211, 242, 264, 268, 282, 344, 399
Rosseau, 221
Rossell, 457, 511, 524
Rosser, 19, 229
Rosson, 59, 212, 399
Roste, 105
Roswell, 6, 59, 399
Rotch, 561
Roth, 7
Rother, 220
Rothwell, 125, 426, 542
Rouge, 45
Roundtree, 512
Roush, 79, 250, 311, 312, 351, 569
Rousseau, 66, 322
Rowan, 41, 132, 154, 215, 537
Rowand, 27, 242
Rowe, 147, 242
Rowen, 254
Rowland, 71, 98
Royal, 147
Royall, 567
Royster, 299
Rozzell, 10
Rubey, 154
Ruby, 532, 540
Rucker, 5, 352
Ruddach, 268
Ruddle, 251, 361

Ruddock, 249
Rudenstein, 115
Rudolph, 206
Ruegger, 50
Ruff, 59, 128, 298, 299, 407, 515, 556
Ruggles, 106, 275, 292, 383, 465, 537
Rugherford, 172
Rumsey, 117
Rundle, 163
Runey, 223
Runnells, 40
Runner, 469
Rupell, 5
Rupert, 485, 556
Ruse, 242
Rush, 196, 280, 363, 374, 410, 431
Rusk, 142, 285
Russ, 242, 381, 399
Russel, 59
Russell, 28, 29, 41, 49, 59, 74, 94, 105, 106, 142, 154, 196, 203, 230, 233, 242, 250, 256, 269, 311, 313, 315, 331, 335, 347, 361, 379, 399, 402, 411, 549
Rust, 71, 97, 105, 295, 306, 465, 568
Ruth, 53
Rutherford, 20, 22, 287, 387, 401
Rutledge, 80
Rutter, 563
Ryan, 28, 154, 173, 235, 497, 506, 507, 556
Ryder, 579
Ryland, 16, 38, 79
Ryley, 556
Rynders, 106
Ryon, 27

S

Sabin, 537
Sabine, 5
Sabine Hall, 178
Sacket, 73, 382
Sackett, 197
Sadtler, 48
Sae, 359
Saffer, 227
Sage, 147, 196
Sailor, 78, 97, 98
<u>Saint Mary Mater Dei</u>, 136
Salas, 501
Sale, 138, 565
Salisbury, 5
Sallade, 345
Salmon, 15
Salonron, 141
Salsbury, 504
Salter, 59
Salters, 457
Saltmarsh, 5, 43, 92, 242, 261, 263, 330
Samford, 393
Sample, 225, 229, 569
Sampson, 55, 99, 113, 189, 309, 572
Samson, 1, 16, 38, 46, 76, 230, 346, 396, 422, 447, 450, 453, 515, 531, 534, 545, 562, 575
Samuel, 490
Samuels, 130, 484, 556
Sanchez, 114, 189
Sand Key, 552
Sanders, 1, 17, 28, 223, 275, 505, 508, 568, 577
Sanderson, 19, 59, 155, 197, 233, 255, 500, 547, 548, 572
Sandford, 113
Sandiford, 575
Sands, 154, 231, 232, 428, 526, 581
Sandwich Islands, 130
Sandys, 358
Sanford, 28, 59, 113, 144, 155
Sanger, 102, 331, 565
Sangster, 155, 230, 444, 490
Sangston, 197
Sansbury, 60
Santa Anna, 451
Santangelo, 44
Saranak, 207
Sardban, 345
Sardo, 186, 367

Sartere, 451
Sarton, 303
Sartori, 331
Satterwhite, 106
Saturday Evening News, 291, 534
Saunders, 19, 28, 82, 90, 92, 100, 116, 146, 155, 189, 243, 252, 257, 302, 308, 345, 399, 470, 506, 537, 543, 573
Sauter, 7, 138
Sauvageau, 267
Savage, 28, 55, 211, 307, 337, 355, 402, 452, 504, 556
Saville, 345
Savin, 490
Sawtell, 537
Sawyer, 23, 48, 88, 89, 97, 107, 231, 243, 254, 425, 478, 532, 581
Saxon, 147
Saxton, 155
Sayers, 59
Sayre, 89
Scammon, 548, 552
Scarpa, 142
Schad, 282, 537
Schaeffer, 97
Schaumburg, 71, 517
Scheckell, 556
Scheel, 334, 444
Scheffer, 5
Schellinger, 290
Schemerhorn, 155, 243
Schenck, 242, 546, 577
Schermerhorn, 197, 282
Schiffler, 444
Schiminger, 490
Schlamp, 138
Schlegel, 452, 575
Schley, 231, 570
Schmid, 282
Schneider, 224, 479
Schnell, 138
schnr **Blooming Youth**, 163
schnr **Brewster**, 65
schnr **Cleveland**, 529

schnr **Clinton:**, 530
schnr **Comet**, 40
schnr **Congress**, 172
schnr **Cyrus Chamberlain**, 133
schnr **Dayton**, 529
schnr **Dusky Sally**, 285
schnr **Edward Tilletston**, 438
schnr **Enterprise**, 30
schnr **Flirt**, 430
schnr **Fortune**, 30, 163
schnr **Gallatin**, 322
schnr **Garland**, 163
schnr **Garnet**, 84
schnr **Good Exchange**, 163
schnr **Helen Strong**, 529
schnr **Indian Queen**, 529
schnr **Industry**, 84
schnr **J H Lyon**, 529
schnr **Joseph**, 501
schnr **Leader**, 406
schnr **Liberty**, 529
schnr **Lurana**, 99
schnr **Madison**, 174
schnr **Maine**, 392
schnr **Manteo**, 318
schnr **Martha**, 65
schnr **Mary Virginia**, 200
schnr **Merchant**, 138, 340
schnr **Minerva**, 530
schnr **P Holt**, 435
schnr **Pacific**, 529
schnr **Rainbow**, 65
schnr **Ruth**, 65, 163
schnr **Sabine**, 529
schnr **Salus**, 529
schnr **Senator**, 529
schnr **Silas H Wright**, 435
schnr **Tancred**, 362
schnr **Trio**, 530
schnr **Two Brothers**, 84
schnr **Union**, 84
schnr **Van Buren**, 89
schnr **Victory**, 92
schnr **Volante**, 547
schnr **Warrior**, 529

schnr **Wave**, 126, 322
schnr **Zela**, 529
schnrs **Creole & Ann M Briggs**, 261
schnrs **Sevo & Ida**, 163
Schoener, 326
Schoenethaler, 232
Schoenthaler, 245
Schofield, 442
Scholfield, 306, 341, 428, 429, 495
Scholtz, 127
Schoolcraft, 130, 305, 310
Schouler, 242
Schreppler, 345
Schriveigman, 511
Schriver, 382, 387
Schroader, 437
Schroeder, 242, 383, 495
Schucking, 353
Schureman, 444
Schuyler, 28, 62, 147, 242
Schwarts, 392
Schwartz, 154, 282, 556
Scoby, 117
Scofield, 28
Scolfield, 447
Scott, 5, 13, 20, 21, 23, 39, 40, 41, 47, 48, 59, 68, 72, 80, 88, 99, 106, 115, 149, 154, 187, 197, 198, 200, 203, 228, 242, 266, 267, 287, 341, 345, 348, 367, 382, 383, 392, 399, 401, 405, 407, 423, 428, 429, 441, 444, 447, 460, 474, 493, 519, 530, 543, 552, 564, 580
Scotts, 314
Scovel, 147
Scovell, 59
Scribner, 59, 106, 197
Scrivener, 142, 197
Scrivner, 202
Scudder, 457, 508, 523, 524
Seaman, 234, 266, 288, 342
Seaps, 422
Searight, 5, 72, 106
Searle, 106, 382, 387

Seaton, 39, 52, 97, 158, 265, 431, 445, 454, 473, 530
Seaver, 231, 566
Seavy, 428
Seawell, 36, 275, 404, 458
Seber, 567
Secchi, 467
Sedden, 197
Sedgewick, 407
Sedgwick, 345
Seeley, 122
Seely, 20, 90, 159, 243
Segar, 147, 251, 313, 342, 361, 507
Segur, 311
Sehwier, 5
Seiden, 490
Seigle, 166
Seiler, 315
Seitz, 12
Selby, 5, 155, 428
Selden, 55, 109, 112, 166, 228, 229, 260, 289, 356, 359, 374
Selfridge, 374
Selin, 399
Sellers, 250, 312
Sellick, 143
Sellingslak, 359
Semmes, 77, 96, 175, 181, 187, 197, 257, 279, 347, 348, 393, 428, 454, 458, 459, 488, 556, 563, 573, 578, 579
Semple, 68, 360
Seneca Fork or Ford, 357
Seneca Mills, 263, 357
Sengstack, 479, 480
Seoncia, 106
Sequire, 6
Sergeant, 5, 446
Sergt, 197
Serrin, 288
Serruys, 87
Servant, 41
Sessford, 37, 77, 162, 239, 265, 424, 539
Sessions, 205

Seth, 440
Settle, 539
Setze, 348
Sever, 243
Severance, 157, 223
Sevier, 22, 112, 130, 159
Sewall, 31, 60, 200, 219, 294, 345, 428, 435, 530
Seward, 345, 490
Sewel, 65
Sewell, 185, 243
Sexsmith, 143, 528
Sexton, 243
Seyfert, 337
Seymour, 28, 59, 60, 106, 155, 231, 253, 399, 537, 579
Shackelford, 77, 96
Shackleford, 48
Shad, 484
Shadden, 442
Shade, 5, 211
Shadt, 510
Shaff, 428
Shaffer, 106, 128, 268
Shaiffer, 51
Shaler, 5, 82
Shane, 508
Shanklan, 496
Shankland, 5
Shanks, 197, 242
Shannon, 35, 185
Shapely, 211
Shapley, 65
Sharp, 92, 531
Sharp's Island, 170
Sharples, 16
Shattuck, 183
Shaumburg, 516
Shaw, 9, 35, 79, 106, 134, 154, 184, 197, 208, 242, 327, 330, 345, 355, 399, 401, 424, 450, 498, 556, 563, 565, 574
Shawhan, 247
Shawk, 196
Shay, 458

Shead, 197
Sheahen, 537
Sheburne, 419
Sheckel, 233
Sheckell, 482, 483
Sheckells, 263, 399
Sheckels, 209
Sheckles, 155
Sheetz, 469
Shekell, 337
Shekels, 258, 428
Shelby, 242
Shelden, 155, 399
Sheldon, 197
Shellenberger, 28
Shelly, 163
Shelman, 441
Shelton, 434, 490
Shepard, 155
Shephard, 197
Shepherd, 26, 72, 88, 106, 112, 134, 155, 264, 302, 322, 345, 377, 472
Sheppard, 282, 317
Shepperd, 22, 173, 276
Sherburn, 36
Sherburne, 2, 10, 47, 202, 528
Sheridan, 7, 504
Sherlock, 106, 155, 175
Sherman, 41, 69, 87, 90, 115, 312, 543
Shermer, 132
Sherrard, 373
Sherrick, 469
Sherwell, 282
Sherwood, 114
Shewalter, 179
Shield, 444
Shields, 5, 9, 28, 147, 154, 228, 282, 287, 291, 331, 441, 444, 565
Shiflett, 55
Shillingburg, 253
Shiner, 444
ship **Augustine Heard**, 406
ship **Austin**, 380
ship **Bonita**, 526
ship **Byron**, 190

ship **Cataraqui**, 54
ship **Chesapeake**, 111, 329, 436
ship **Columbia**, 166
ship **Columbus**, 179, 374
ship **Crocodile**, 340
ship **Cyane**, 217
ship **Elizabeth Bruce**, 216
ship **Enterprise**, 12
ship **Falmouth**, 437, 534
ship **Flavio**, 523
ship **Frolic**, 134
ship **Genr'l Greene**, 111
ship **Gentoo**, 389
ship **Governor Davis**, 406
ship **H H Sizer**, 529
ship **Hedrick Hudson**, 470
ship **Herald**, 174, 251, 313, 338, 362, 416
ship **Huron**, 529
ship **Hyder Ali**, 290
ship **Independence**, 367, 376
ship **Iris**, 563
ship **John Milton**, 89
ship **John Minturn**, 89
ship **Luminary**, 432
ship **Margaret**, 251
ship **Marion**, 246
ship **Minerva Smyth**, 11
ship **Mississippi**, 581
ship **Monk**, 290
ship **Montgomery**, 577
ship **Nonita**, 526
ship **North Alabama**, 222
ship **North Carolina**, 367, 457
ship **Ocean**, 438
ship of war **San Pedro**, 292
ship **Ohio**, 528
ship **Peacock**, 500, 559
ship **Pennsylvania**, 448, 546
ship **Plymouth**, 376
ship **Portsmouth**, 80
ship **Potomac**, 437
ship **Preble**, 441
ship **Raritan**, 526, 531
ship **Reefer**, 526

ship **Relief**, 30
ship **Saratoga**, 44
ship **Spitfire**, 151
ship **St Mary's**, 420, 479
ship **Uncas**, 521
ship **United States**, 529
ship **Vincennes**, 179
ship **Warren**, 80
ship **Wasp**, 134
ship **Yorktown**, 246, 263
Shipley, 207
Shippen, 81, 99, 110
Shiras, 461, 493, 552
Shirman, 399
Shirving, 242
Shiver, 242
Shivers, 477
Shoemaker, 106, 227, 399
Shonenburg, 106
Shonnard, 537
Shore, 59
Short, 88, 512
Shorter, 345, 444
Shower Baths, 186
Shreve, 34, 102, 487, 573
Shrieder, 507
Shriver, 497
Shropshere, 8
Shubart, 99
Shubrick, 76, 131, 322, 323, 346, 379, 406
Shuck, 547
Shucking, 269
Shunk, 59, 441
Shurbrick, 131
Shurtcliff, 106
Shuster, 242
Shyrock, 428
Sibbald, 62, 330, 361, 417
Sibley, 173, 382, 387
Sibrey, 242
Sickels, 379
Sidebotham, 428
Sidney, 28
Siegmund, 243

Silcox, 95
Sill, 129, 296
Sillcox, 59
Silver, 197
Siminton, 490
Simm, 325
Simmes, 28, 196, 490
Simmons, 5, 59, 98, 137, 219, 302, 318, 331, 399, 465, 563, 565, 569
Simms, 5, 28, 59, 94, 109, 138, 188, 196, 197, 242, 262, 282, 299, 302, 345, 399, 428, 436, 439, 444, 479, 481, 482, 484, 485, 490, 543, 544, 555, 556
Simonds, 347
Simons, 154
Simonson, 256
Simonton, 225, 233, 330
Simpkins, 580
Simpson, 5, 59, 62, 78, 98, 110, 148, 182, 194, 197, 233, 274, 294, 307, 315, 341, 365, 401, 428, 444, 475, 492, 515, 556, 581
Sims, 267, 282, 298, 347, 537
Sinclair, 5, 28, 60, 155, 157, 197, 242, 490, 530
Singleton, 212
Sinit, 242
Sinon, 214, 430
Sioussa, 394
Sipe, 154
Siscoe, 81
Sisters of Charity, 565, 581
Siter, 133
Sitgreaves, 399
Sizer, 125
Skaggs, 28
Skidmore, 59
Skillman, 28
Skinner, 28, 95, 106, 141, 168, 186, 202, 205, 360, 399, 445, 448
Skipsey, 579
Skirving, 6, 379, 556
Slack, 106
Slacum, 15, 301, 308, 330

Slade, 76, 296, 356
Slamm, 565
Slark, 434
Slasson, 166, 169
Slaston, 23
Slate Cabin Tract, 253
Slater, 227
Slatter, 293
Slaughter, 77, 128, 166, 190, 231, 282
Slauson, 420
slave Pauline, 164
slaver **Catherine**, 413
slaver **Spitfire**, 580
Slaymaker, 70
Sleight, 21
Slemaker, 119, 537
Slemmer, 537, 562
Slevin, 347
Slicer, 148, 182, 376, 494, 535, 538, 565
Slidell, 5, 43
Slight, 12
Sligo Mills, 275
Sliver, 98
Sloan, 221, 266, 444
Sloat, 80
Slocum, 28, 147
Slocumb, 68
Sloman, 59
Sloo, 134, 287, 387
sloop **Ann Strong**, 531
sloop **Aurora**, 531
sloop **Levant**, 80
sloop of war **Albany**, 409
sloop of war **Falmouth**, 528
sloop of war **Jamestown**, 360
sloop of war **John Adams**, 464
sloop of war **Marion**, 347
sloop of war **Plymouth**, 451
sloop-of-war **Boston**, 56, 547
sloop-of-war **Falmouth**, 558
sloop-of-war **Marion**, 176, 458
Slover, 155
Small, 305, 457, 481, 482
small-pox, 52

Small-Pox, 23
Smallwood, 5, 52, 60, 64, 106, 109, 124, 156, 171, 197, 242, 243, 282, 392, 399, 438, 453, 490, 499, 537, 556
Smart, 540
Smead, 71
Smedes, 165
Smeed, 242
Smeltzer, 93
Smets, 257
Smidt, 506
Smith, 5, 6, 7, 8, 14, 16, 17, 18, 19, 20, 25, 28, 31, 36, 38, 39, 41, 42, 47, 53, 59, 60, 68, 70, 71, 73, 74, 77, 78, 88, 100, 106, 107, 113, 116, 118, 128, 135, 137, 148, 154, 155, 156, 157, 163, 168, 174, 176, 187, 190, 193, 196, 198, 201, 205, 206, 215, 217, 221, 223, 224, 231, 233, 239, 242, 243, 244, 245, 249, 253, 254, 257, 258, 263, 264, 266, 268, 269, 271, 275, 278, 279, 282, 286, 287, 290, 303, 307, 313, 322, 323, 327, 333, 337, 345, 354, 355, 359, 361, 366, 373, 375, 378, 379, 380, 382, 383, 384, 399, 401, 402, 403, 406, 416, 420, 424, 428, 431, 439, 444, 458, 459, 460, 463, 481, 490, 493, 496, 497, 506, 507, 509, 510, 512, 514, 516, 531, 532, 540, 541, 542, 545, 547, 549, 556, 559, 569, 573, 575, 578, 579
Smithcomb, 197
Smithson, 431, 556
Smithsonian Bill, 363
Smithsonian Institute, 417
Smithsonian Institution, 362, 409, 410, 431
Smock, 242
Smoot, 1, 59, 97, 178, 187, 196, 208, 225, 254, 258, 392, 399, 439, 460, 512
Smull, 18
Smyth, 440

Snauber, 424
Snead, 399
Snedicox, 510
Sneed, 222, 360
Snell, 335
Snelling, 74, 384
Snider, 229, 349
Snobler, 345
Snodgrass, 5, 401
Snow, 114
Snowden, 5, 278, 381, 403
Snower, 504
Snowhook, 11, 372
Snowman, 304
Snyder, 42, 294, 463
Soaper, 508
Solace, 538, 540
Soley, 71
Sollers, 5
Solomon, 531, 546
Soltan, 414
Somerly, 17
Somers, 490
Somervell, 396
Somerville, 444
Sommeraner, 98, 301, 308
Sommers, 106, 155, 537
Sonder, 331
Soper, 5, 399, 423
Sothoron, 25, 59, 539
Souder, 121, 279, 330, 361, 417
Soule, 5, 8
Soult, 45
Sour, 490
Sourjohn, 262
Sours, 505
Sourwein, 257
Southerland, 132, 531
Southern, 446
Southron, 254
Sowards, 497
Sower, 459
Spackman, 371
Spalding, 2, 55, 79, 149, 208, 249, 282, 348, 408, 435, 558

Spanish fort, 133
Sparks, 69, 522
Sparlin, 501
Sparrow, 356
Spaulding, 523
Speakman, 76, 163, 331, 565
Spear, 10, 419, 579
Spearing, 345
Spears, 205
Spediss, 197
Speer, 39, 391
Speicer, 28
Speiden, 225, 546
Speight, 227
Speir, 408, 434
Speisser, 202
Spellans, 533
Spelman, 106
Spence, 249, 269, 277
Spencer, 2, 15, 30, 59, 69, 85, 86, 99, 106, 115, 149, 155, 166, 176, 184, 200, 242, 269, 302, 305, 317, 331, 362, 417, 420, 440, 460, 510
Spender, 345
Sperry, 282
Spice, 106
Spicer, 571
Spier, 523
Spillman, 282
Spires, 59
Spofford, 454
Spoole, 508
Sporks, 259
Sporza, 336
Sprague, 106, 147, 196, 242, 496, 549
Sprat, 429
Sprigg, 59, 67, 106, 131, 275, 314
Spriggs, 154
Spring, 154, 282
Spring Hill, 91
Springs, 242, 345
Springwell Farm, 415
Sprole, 16, 138, 175, 217, 246, 391, 475, 503, 523, 532, 539, 564
Sproston, 379

Sprowle, 400
Spurling, 478
Spycer, 197
St Clair, 24, 30, 242
St Clare, 419
St Elizabeth, 300, 573
St John, 180, 196, 242, 327
St Martin, 371
St Mary Mater Dei, 140
St Mary's German, 403
St Romes, 337
St Tammany's Society, 468
St Vrain, 82, 90, 293, 303, 331, 361, 415
Stabler, 238
Stacey, 530
Stacker, 139, 155
Stafford, 202, 221, 279, 303, 362, 417
Stagg, 568
Staines, 5, 106
Stalker, 302
Stall, 163
Stallings, 581
Stambaugh, 219, 445
Stanard, 215
Stanbrough, 280
Standish, 180, 243
Standley, 399, 529
Stanely, 578
Stanert, 61
Stanfield, 508
Stanford, 243, 437
Staniford, 383, 384
Stanitt, 13
Stanks, 537
Stanley, 278, 424, 515, 534
Stanly, 20
Stansberry, 44
Stansbury, 98, 425, 522
Stantan, 106
Stanton, 47, 76, 134, 345, 442, 542
Stapler, 345
Staples, 60, 155
Staring, 85
Stark, 401

Starke, 106, 154, 444, 561
Starkey, 89, 282, 490
Starkweather, 155
Starr, 108, 164, 206, 234, 242, 430
State of Texas, 362
Stauffer, 434
Staunton, 345
steamboat **Alhambra**, 324
steamboat **Arlington Belle**, 296
steamboat **Bangor**, 547
steamboat **Belle Zane**, 7
steamboat **Dallas**, 221
steamboat **Excelsior**, 420
steamboat **Jas Hewett**, 334
steamboat **Missouri**, 320
steamboat **Oceola**, 83, 285
steamboat **Powhatan**, 192, 255
steamboat **S S Coleman**, 503
steamboat **Troy**, 332
steamboat **Vesuvius**, 416
steamer **Chancellor**, 537
steamer **Colonel Harney**, 416
steamer **Colonel Harvey**, 561
steamer **Convoy**, 272
steamer **Die Vernon**, 515
steamer **Engineer**, 56
steamer **Enterprise**, 422
steamer **Gen Brooks**, 294
steamer **General Taylor**, 472
steamer **Great Britain**, 457
steamer **Hunter**, 525
steamer **James L Day**, 310
steamer **John J Crittenden**, 316, 321
steamer **Luella**, 353
steamer **McLane**, 526
steamer **Mississippi**, 391, 526
steamer **Missouri**, 320
steamer **Neptune**, 552
steamer **Petrita**, 526
steamer **Sea-Bird**, 182
steamer **Tabasyaeno**, 526
steamer **Vixen**, 526, 581
steamer **Whiteville**, 381
steamship **Atlantic**, 532, 533, 538, 539, 540, 543, 544, 545, 557, 558

steamship **Hibernia**, 392
steamship **Massachusetts**, 258, 268, 465, 527
steamship **McKim**, 497, 543
steamship **New York**, 255
steamship **Sea**, 255, 521
Steans, 341
Stearners, 106
Stearns, 53, 141, 159
Stebbins, 490
Stedman, 242
Steel, 184, 490
Steele, 194, 196, 246, 282, 563, 579
Steen, 9, 352
Steenbergen, 91
Steenrod, 82
Steeples, 399
Steer, 492
Steiger, 483
Steiner, 421, 488
Stelle, 47, 122, 494
Stelsee, 345
Steper, 216, 234, 235
Stephen, 407, 440
Stephens, 5, 31, 197, 231, 287
Stephenson, 144, 313
Stepper, 5, 204
Sterling, 84, 129, 163, 441
Stern, 420
Sterns, 556
Sterret, 526
Sterritt, 129
Stetson, 80, 282, 444, 533
Stettson, 345
Steuart, 67, 402, 491
Steuben, 170
Stevens, 77, 98, 106, 118, 134, 155, 217, 224, 242, 245, 282, 292, 294, 303, 307, 328, 334, 345, 360, 379, 386, 509, 530, 538, 539, 556, 567, 579
Stevenson, 147, 155, 251, 266, 311, 326, 328, 331, 345, 347, 362, 368, 374, 395, 415, 496, 507, 574
Steward, 561

658

Stewart, 5, 8, 14, 21, 23, 28, 34, 49, 50, 53, 70, 71, 84, 98, 106, 113, 119, 123, 145, 155, 175, 191, 197, 221, 226, 242, 249, 264, 268, 271, 282, 299, 302, 321, 323, 330, 331, 345, 352, 374, 375, 391, 392, 399, 413, 428, 432, 436, 444, 464, 488, 490, 492, 508, 510, 515, 533, 538, 548, 556
Stickney, 125
Stidger, 172
Stier, 132, 171
Stiles, 19, 415
Still, 566
Stillson, 433
Stillwell, 116, 201
Stimpson, 246
Stinger, 242
Stirman, 141
Stith, 90, 401
Stock, 556
Stockdale, 490
Stockett, 522
Stockton, 51, 94, 112, 118, 146, 163, 226, 252, 269, 286, 331, 345, 546, 565, 569
Stoddard, 70, 106, 155
Stoddart, 360, 428
Stoddert, 254
Stoff, 399
Stokely, 68
Stokes, 74, 94, 331, 416, 505, 565
Stone, 5, 17, 28, 31, 36, 59, 73, 106, 109, 116, 117, 169, 247, 261, 304, 309, 322, 328, 348, 396, 399, 407, 448, 474, 492, 507, 530, 550
Stone Bridge, 63
Stonecipher, 30
Stoner, 469
Stonestreet, 218, 368
Stonifert, 202
Stony Point, 502
Stoops, 345, 348
Storer, 323
storeship **Lexington**, 312
storeship **Relief**, 464
Storey, 576
Storm, 81, 231, 282, 379, 413
Storrs, 345, 564
Story, 9, 516
Stotenburg, 345
Stott, 91, 122, 227, 245, 302, 428, 482, 494, 556
Stouffer, 569
Stout, 113, 115, 282, 307, 315, 386
Stover, 92, 458
Straham, 412
Strahan, 434, 467
Straine, 444
Stras, 537
Stratten, 282
Straub, 183
Street, 106
Streets, 5
Stringfellow, 8, 16, 149, 169, 185, 188, 216, 424, 426, 453, 512, 544
Stringham, 322, 323, 457, 528
Strobecher, 30
Strobecker, 43
Strobel, 452
Strohecker, 286
Strohm, 464
Strommell, 579
Strong, 40, 82, 374, 464
Strother, 282, 300
Strothers, 159
Stryker, 399
Stuard, 490
Stuart, 6, 36, 70, 113, 117, 122, 215, 242, 327, 358, 412
Stubblefield, 92, 206
Stubbs, 5, 39, 127, 217, 408
Stubert, 504
Sturdevant, 531
Sturgeon, 47
Sturges, 286, 312
Sturgis, 117
Stutz, 452, 483, 556
Sublette, 390
Suggett, 243, 282

Sullivan, 33, 47, 76, 109, 119, 127, 155, 250, 264, 355, 399, 414, 490, 493, 537, 566, 574
Sumbey, 155
Sumby, 444
Summeraner, 13
Summers, 5, 99, 106, 157, 197, 230, 444
Sumner, 155, 294, 352, 382, 515
Sumter, 147, 331, 525, 565
Susquehanna, 207
Suter, 227, 271, 444, 454
Sutherlan, 556
Sutherland, 86, 116, 297
Sutter, 226
Sutton, 106
Suydam, 149
Swaim, 325
Swain, 532
Swan, 41, 103
Swann, 225, 428
Swart, 61, 99
Swartwout, 417, 468, 504
Swartz, 59
Sweeney, 59, 60, 92, 305, 392, 429, 489, 490, 525, 547
Sweeny, 188, 243, 418, 434, 481, 482, 484, 485, 545, 556
Sweet, 196, 578
Sweeting, 481, 556, 567, 581
Swelvant, 242
Swentzell, 132
Swett, 59, 282
Swift, 140, 337, 428
Swigart, 345
Swigert, 242
Swords, 515
Sycamore, 502
Sykes, 154, 549
Syles, 459
Sylvestre, 310
Symes, 538
Symington, 84, 86, 106

T

Tabb, 360, 402, 458
Taber, 422
Tabler, 67, 224
Tacey, 512
Taffe, 268
Taft, 80
Tagore, 380
Taig, 510
Tailor, 283, 345
Tait, 20, 109, 178, 288
Talbert, 145
Talbot, 5, 345, 360, 428, 491, 562
Talbott, 401
Talburt, 21, 454, 519
Talburtt, 357
Talcott, 243, 314
Taliaferro, 60, 261, 265, 283, 332
Tallant, 422
Talley, 508
Tallmadge, 68, 243, 493
Tallman, 28
Talmadge, 197
Talty, 556, 558
Tandy, 2
Tanner, 305, 310
Tansill, 119, 155, 282
Tansitt, 537
Taos, 515
Tappan, 28, 60, 106, 243
Tappen, 143
Tappin, 282
Tarbos, 490
Tarbox, 533
Tardif, 267
Tarker, 266
Tarring, 16, 148, 201, 300, 440, 522
Tarrington, 13, 157
Tarry, 166
Tascar, 155
Tascho, 5
Tascoe, 445
Tasker, 197
Tastet, 47, 189

Tate, 106, 184, 197, 282, 425, 538, 539, 581
Tatham, 60
Tattnall, 243, 283
Tatum, 28, 99, 159
Tayloe, 293, 324, 330, 428, 490
Taylor, 28, 30, 36, 38, 42, 60, 61, 69, 70, 84, 92, 99, 106, 117, 119, 128, 142, 148, 155, 158, 159, 161, 184, 190, 192, 197, 210, 211, 213, 218, 219, 220, 221, 227, 230, 233, 238, 243, 249, 256, 260, 262, 264, 268, 274, 282, 283, 286, 299, 303, 311, 315, 329, 342, 345, 362, 371, 377, 381, 383, 399, 401, 420, 421, 428, 445, 455, 458, 461, 466, 472, 475, 483, 487, 491, 492, 494, 502, 506, 513, 537, 543, 556, 559, 564, 574
Taylor Guards, 222
Tays, 78
Tazewell, 402
Teachum, 119
Teakle, 55, 197
Teal, 70
Tebbs, 402
Tegner, 573
Teirney, 155
Telegraph line, 234
Teller, 468
Temple, 307, 368
Templeman, 91, 193, 253, 348, 377
Templeton, 60, 543
Ten Eyck, 19, 546
Tench, 134, 197, 486, 556
Tenelle, 509
Tennant, 106
Tenneson, 378
Tenney, 340
Tennison, 378, 445
Tenny, 60
Terrell, 226, 579
Terret, 25
Terrett, 71, 210, 282, 300, 383, 456, 471, 472, 474, 504, 524, 548, 551, 556

Terrill, 243, 252, 260, 362
Territt, 5
Terry, 279, 402
Tete, 337
Tevis, 18, 237, 286
Texada, 222
thanksgiving, 527
Thatcher, 569
Thaw, 47, 428, 539
Thaxter, 116
Thayer, 134, 295, 445
thefrig **Cumberland**, 531
Theriot, 258, 280
Thibodeaux, 282
Thillon, 28
Thistle, 399
Thody, 87, 94
Thom, 572
Thomas, 1, 5, 30, 37, 49, 55, 60, 79, 106, 107, 147, 150, 155, 158, 163, 188, 191, 197, 202, 243, 251, 252, 261, 262, 282, 283, 287, 294, 313, 315, 330, 345, 361, 368, 371, 382, 387, 389, 399, 401, 404, 415, 428, 429, 439, 440, 445, 454, 457, 477, 480, 481, 486, 487, 490, 503, 508, 512, 514, 537, 539, 550, 557, 559, 577
Thomas P Cope, 207
Thomas' Discovery Fortified, 357
Thompkins, 78
Thompson, 2, 5, 10, 15, 22, 28, 30, 60, 61, 64, 79, 90, 95, 106, 110, 116, 117, 119, 120, 123, 155, 159, 161, 164, 182, 188, 191, 197, 202, 216, 235, 243, 247, 257, 261, 262, 273, 282, 291, 306, 309, 318, 321, 345, 347, 351, 352, 354, 355, 358, 367, 382, 399, 411, 419, 442, 450, 453, 472, 476, 477, 488, 490, 491, 492, 496, 508, 509, 510, 534, 537, 539, 556, 557, 579
Thomson, 259
Thomure, 31
Thorburn, 445

Thorckmorton, 43
Thorn, 15, 55, 243, 576
Thorndike, 257
Thorne, 28, 235
Thornhill, 257
Thornley, 197, 245, 545, 556
Thornly, 39, 151
Thornton, 2, 5, 28, 84, 90, 106, 155, 227, 333, 345, 356, 399, 403, 447, 562, 570
Thorp, 26
Thorpe, 243
Thrasher, 530
Thrift, 5, 28, 106
Throckmorton, 155, 261, 263, 330
Throop, 377
Thruston, 5, 68, 155, 210, 237, 399, 493
Thurber, 28, 60
Thurgar, 100
Thurger, 159
Tichenor, 170
Ticknor, 374
Tidball, 373
Tiffany, 5, 243
Tigart, 506
Tileston, 341
Tileton, 454
Tilghman, 5, 106, 491
Tillard, 217, 252
Tilley, 491
Tillinghast, 184
Tillman, 243, 283
Tillotson, 399
Tilson, 197
Tilton, 11, 307, 323, 567
Tim, 448
Timberlake, 28, 106
Timby, 399, 445
Timmons, 230
Timms, 135, 138, 486
Timothy, 60, 445
Timpson, 468
Tims, 364
Tindal, 357

Tinney, 345
Tinsley, 564
Tippett, 1, 62, 64, 321, 346, 399, 491
Tipton, 233, 256, 548
Tirrell, 155
Titcomb, 28
Titian, 44
Titus, 5, 28, 51, 60, 102, 106
Tobey, 547
Tod, 197
Todd, 5, 64, 92, 100, 106, 155, 173, 179, 183, 194, 202, 224, 231, 371, 390, 445, 487, 508, 543, 556, 579
Todsen, 46
Toland, 579
Toler, 44, 106, 243, 494
Toley, 406
Tolson, 5, 155, 175, 187, 197, 345, 447, 490, 491, 537, 552
Tomlinson, 508, 537
Tompkins, 28, 106, 110, 121, 179, 182, 312, 382, 423
Tonge, 197, 430
Toomy, 95
Topham, 485
Topliff, 243
Topp, 268
Topping, 102, 538
Torbert, 162
Torplen, 5
Torrey, 345
Torskay, 504
Totten, 60, 181, 201, 363, 381, 410
Toulmin, 287
Towers, 197, 245, 538
Towle, 133, 147, 485
Towles, 428
Towne, 243
Townely, 283
Townley, 5, 106, 197, 447
Townly, 259
Towns, 60
Townsend, 60, 173, 261, 345, 385, 395, 490, 569
Townshend, 397

Towson, 527
Tozer, 155
Trabue, 5, 345
Tracey, 128, 283
Tracy, 5, 318, 406
Trail, 269
Traver, 8
Travers, 106, 109, 440, 578
Traverse, 480, 557
Travis, 345, 451
Tree, 238, 321
Treel, 505
Trefry, 529, 530
Tremayne, 243
Trenholm, 47
Trenor, 382
Trent, 401, 565
Trescott, 5
Trevitt, 309
Trevor, 408
Trezevant, 268
Trieste, 28
Trimble, 79, 106, 155, 259, 556
Trimelli, 576
Tripler, 158
Triplett, 206
Trippe, 85
Trochart, 60
Troeur, 509
Trontfeller, 106
Trott, 115
Troxell, 70
Trucks, 175
True, 579
Trueman, 399
Truesdell, 533
Trull, 133
Trump, 253
Trunnell, 60
Truscott, 487, 492, 504, 562
Trustee, 399
Truston, 28, 345
Tryon, 115, 237
Tryst, 414
Tschiffely, 106

Tuck, 396
Tucker, 25, 31, 35, 79, 82, 97, 106, 109, 122, 146, 151, 173, 184, 197, 205, 233, 256, 308, 334, 345, 386, 422, 424, 469, 494, 505, 530, 543, 555, 556, 581
Tudor, 422
Tuffley, 490
Tufts, 512
Tuner, 28
Tupper, 106, 468
Turber, 359
Turkman, 480
Turley, 207
Turnbull, 348, 552
Turner, 5, 10, 51, 56, 60, 74, 79, 106, 115, 145, 148, 155, 163, 197, 251, 282, 301, 302, 309, 318, 322, 323, 355, 361, 407, 416, 440, 476, 486, 490, 508, 515, 516, 537, 557
Turney, 98, 309, 387
Turnipseed, 211
Turnley, 548
Turpin, 247, 282, 287, 528, 544, 551, 575
Turrell, 546
Turrill, 114
Turton, 144, 522
Turvey, 113
Tustin, 216, 234, 271, 355, 500
Tuston, 16, 68, 125, 159
Tuttle, 147, 303
Tweedy, 453
<u>Twigg</u>, 504
Twiggs, 213, 286, 353, 381, 382, 455
<u>Two Sicilies</u>, 345
Twombly, 450
Tydon, 345
Tyer, 537
Tylee, 468
Tyler, 96, 106, 147, 181, 229, 273, 374, 428, 503, 505, 514, 516, 517
Tyley, 533
Tylor, 155
Tynders, 447

Tyner, 70, 279
Tyock, 282
Tyree, 509
Tyrer, 237
Tyson, 28, 47, 202, 244, 309, 403

U

Ufford, 365
Ulric, 501
Ulrich, 230
Umphreys, 424
Underhill, 39, 167
Underwood, 76, 88, 236, 364, 399
Ungher, 18
Updike, 23, 207, 215
Upham, 69
Upperman, 283, 326, 481, 482, 483, 484, 485, 557
Upshur, 365, 546
Upton, 406
Usher, 28, 475
Ustick, 576
Utermohle, 480, 482, 483, 485
Uttermuhle, 169, 325

V

Vaden, 60
Vail, 155, 230, 399
Valentine, 84, 165, 435
Valiant, 132
Valkenburg, 99, 189
Valkenburgh, 62
Valland, 551
Vallettee, 487
Valliant, 170
Van Antwerp, 41
Van Benthuysen, 327
Van beuren, 468
Van Bokkeler, 275
Van Bokkelin, 185
Van Brancken, 537
Van Brunt, 244, 567
Van Buren, 23, 106, 141, 233, 256, 287

Van Campen, 125
Van Cortlandt, 123
Van Courtlandt, 574
Van Cowper, 569
Van Deusen, 522
Van Dieman's Land, 54
Van Dorn, 404
Van Dusen, 60
Van Dyck, 79
Van Horn, 246
Van Horseigh, 16, 67, 100, 181, 239, 396, 419, 488
Van Houton, 209
Van Meter, 155
Van Ness, 31, 68, 92, 106, 115, 121, 131, 167, 234, 278, 301, 310, 345, 359, 365, 429, 449, 532, 569, 573
Van Norden, 579
Van Orden, 524
Van Renssealer, 30
Van Rensselaer, 88, 147
Van Reswick, 209, 236, 243, 245, 460
Van Riswick, 459
Van Schoonhorn, 197
Van Sissen, 28
Van Slyck, 303, 331
Van Swearingen, 566
Van Tyne, 5
Van Valken, 169
Van Valkenburg, 99
Van Valkenburgh, 49
Van Wart, 533
Van Weart, 420
Van West, 538
Van Zandt, 60, 374, 537
Van Zant, 92
Vanalstine, 69
Vanalston, 36
Vanbeven, 287
Vance, 41, 78, 94, 162, 330, 475, 508, 565
Vanceal, 504
Vancoble, 463
Vanderlyn, 447
Vanderpoel, 49, 60

Vanderpool, 28
Vandervoort, 6
Vandeveer, 388
Vandeven, 388
Vandeventer, 497
Vandon, 13
Vandusen, 243
Vandyke, 61
Vanforsen, 5
Vanhorn, 202
Vanhorseigh, 214
Vanhoy, 491
Vannoy, 94
Vanroy, 100
Vansice, 206
Vansyckles, 327
Vantyne, 265, 445
Vanzandt, 19, 106, 446
Varden, 132, 517, 581
Vardin, 108
Varlin, 197
Varnell, 159
Varney, 28
Vass, 87, 433
Vaughan, 317
Vaustarman, 345
Vaye, 68
Veasie, 107
Vecchio, 432
Veder, 576
Vega, 226, 227, 260, 519
Venable, 306, 429, 535, 557
Venner, 445
Venter, 507
Verdon, 60
Verhaegen, 291
Vermillion, 28, 270, 491
Vernooye, 5
Vesey, 106
vessel **Childe Harold**, 496
vessel **Cumberland**, 496
vessel **Cybele**, 496
vessel **Echo**, 496
vessel **Guerriere**, 329
vessel **Iowa**, 496

vessel **Isabella**, 496
vessel **Lawrence**, 466
vessel **Lisbon**, 496
vessel **Madeline**, 496
vessel **Merchant**, 496
vessel **Millinoket**, 496
vessel **Minerva**, 457
vessel **Mohawk**, 496
vessel **Mudara**, 496
vessel **Nancy Prats**, 496
vessel **Oak**, 496
vessel **Planet**, 496
vessel **Rapid**, 496
vessel **Shannon**, 329, 436
vessel **Smyrna**, 496
vessel **Titi**, 496
vessel **Venezuela**, 496
vessel **William Bradstreet**, 309
Vezina, 267
Viaton, 243
Vice, 147
Vickens, 508
Vigil, 518
Vigo, 169
Villefranche, 351
Vincent, 1, 64, 345, 537
Vincins, 5
Vine, 533
Vining, 509
Vinson, 283, 350
Vinton, 5, 28, 239, 283, 386, 456, 458
Vishner, 197
Visser, 138, 557
Vivans, 188, 270
Voglin, 283
Voltz, 12, 155
Von Essen, 557
von Kaunitz, 32
Von Ritter, 106
Von Schmidt, 62, 97, 160, 233, 301,
  308, 330, 568
Voorhees, 127, 424
Voorhies, 296
Vose, 72
Voss, 452, 557, 575

Vowell, 14
Vrain, 23, 81
Vran, 515
Vroom, 88

W

Wachter, 571
Wacob, 532, 540
Waddell, 5, 307
Wadden, 529
Waddle, 190
Wade, 8, 89, 106, 110, 113, 122, 159, 197, 266, 497, 507
Wadhams, 137, 159
Wadsworth, 28, 146, 182, 218
Wager, 307
Waggaman, 47, 413
Wagler, 34, 46, 52, 75, 427, 429, 479
Wagner, 117, 125, 159, 400
Wagoner, 60, 469, 537
Wagonseller, 530
Waid, 87
Wailes, 106
Wainwright, 227, 374, 384, 457, 512, 524
Waite, 185, 211
Waitman, 504
Wajan, 505
Wakefield, 441, 579
Walbach, 14, 355
Walback, 107, 360
Walbourn, 235
Walch, 60
Walcott, 197
Walcutt, 307
Waldeon, 579
Waldnan, 359
Waldo, 298
Waldren, 374
Waldron, 6, 468, 503
Wales, 580
Walewski, 298
Walke, 231, 401

Walker, 2, 5, 6, 9, 17, 28, 41, 60, 72, 76, 81, 92, 93, 96, 100, 109, 116, 129, 141, 144, 155, 166, 178, 183, 187, 197, 198, 206, 222, 233, 243, 244, 245, 255, 256, 257, 261, 266, 285, 310, 312, 339, 345, 356, 361, 377, 378, 381, 385, 386, 400, 401, 404, 414, 416, 422, 437, 445, 463, 472, 492, 501, 502, 512, 538, 539, 566, 573
Wall, 60, 106, 115, 219, 266, 387, 491, 495, 539, 557
Wallace, 23, 28, 106, 197, 359, 401, 537, 539, 561, 570, 577
Wallach, 149, 188, 224, 236, 245, 248
Wallen, 260, 465
Waller, 6, 46, 380, 445, 491
Walley, 60
Walling, 403
Wallingsford, 138, 556
Wallis, 234, 238, 529
Wallston, 116
Walsh, 106, 258, 270, 399, 445, 486, 526, 557
Walson, 163
Walsworth, 147
Walter, 345, 445, 469, 546
Walters, 287, 353, 360, 440
Walthall, 303, 331
Walton, 45, 160, 243, 298, 355, 533, 540
Wampler, 441
Wamsley, 303
Wannall, 245, 354, 479
Wannell, 47, 557
Wanser, 197
Wanzer, 537
Waples, 463
War, 521
Ward, 5, 11, 38, 41, 60, 61, 74, 77, 94, 97, 106, 112, 155, 162, 197, 206, 230, 235, 243, 272, 283, 293, 308, 323, 330, 331, 345, 346, 348, 350, 362, 385, 386, 413, 429, 441, 445, 459, 496, 509, 542, 549, 557, 565

Wardell, 519
Warden, 30
Warder, 6, 171, 453
Wardwell, 98
Ware, 9, 45, 80, 90, 117, 197, 233, 243, 261, 342, 514
Warfield, 232, 264
Wargatt, 106
Waring, 91, 127, 136, 248
Warley, 307, 379, 445
Warman, 302
Warner, 40, 235, 243, 468, 491, 515, 581
Warren, 28, 38, 55, 60, 155, 197, 243, 250, 311, 312, 324, 342, 345, 362, 395, 432
Warrens, 40
Warrington, 131, 183, 244, 323
Washburn, 28, 197, 437
Washington, 31, 33, 39, 55, 60, 64, 96, 106, 107, 144, 171, 197, 203, 243, 244, 248, 250, 283, 284, 291, 313, 352, 400, 407, 423, 430, 441, 486, 521, 528, 550, 571, 575
<u>Washington Parish</u>, 6
Watchman, 214
Waterhouse, 455
Waterman, 55, 315, 330, 347, 353, 354
Waters, 5, 6, 8, 28, 60, 96, 132, 142, 150, 155, 184, 197, 219, 249, 254, 263, 268, 283, 288, 400, 454, 487, 491, 492, 512, 532, 539, 552, 553, 581
Watkins, 36, 65, 137, 197, 206, 331, 445, 491
Watmough, 60
Watner, 511
Watrons, 400
Watrous, 244
Wats, 155
Watson, 6, 17, 28, 41, 45, 53, 54, 80, 89, 90, 100, 106, 107, 124, 128, 163, 186, 197, 201, 237, 243, 258, 268, 290, 302, 345, 349, 362, 400,

419, 445, 456, 460, 463, 487, 492, 504, 509
Watt, 231, 389
Watterston, 47, 70, 109, 124, 227, 429, 460, 545
Watts, 28, 69, 395, 399
Waugh, 88, 180, 197, 366, 515
Waverley, 350
Wayles, 401
Wayne, 24, 64, 197, 283, 369, 447, 466
Weakly, 134
Weart, 243
Weatherbee, 243
Weaver, 5, 60, 184, 436
Webb, 5, 28, 48, 106, 243, 287, 345, 371, 459, 494, 528, 530
Webber, 145, 303
Weber, 497, 498, 507, 508
Webser, 471
Webster, 2, 28, 87, 106, 113, 155, 200, 203, 243, 283, 333, 341, 342, 400, 429, 491, 496, 498, 508, 558, 574
Wecatt, 557
Wechter, 204, 321
Wedderburn, 304
Weed, 7, 85, 146, 189, 434
Weeden, 253, 437, 542
Weedon, 500
Weeks, 283, 399, 504
Weems, 119
Weichman, 557
Weidnen, 44
Weidner, 561
Weigart, 404
Weightman, 76, 109, 178, 274, 298, 429, 458, 483
Weil, 60
Weir, 209
Weisfott, 145
Welborn, 388
Welch, 60, 74, 84, 116, 155, 323, 497, 507, 548
Weld, 74, 112
Welden, 471

Welford, 168
Weller, 197, 496, 497
Welles, 28, 173, 184
Wellman, 116, 155
Wells, 5, 28, 106, 155, 243, 306, 307, 312, 339, 423, 560, 574
Welsh, 64, 106, 307, 445, 491
Welton, 253
Welton Glade, 253
Wendall, 112, 303
Went, 497, 507
Wentling, 68, 122, 163, 203, 362
Wentworth, 314
Werle, 28
Werner, 452
Wescott, 28
West, 8, 17, 25, 28, 36, 60, 83, 98, 151, 157, 197, 264, 399, 402, 445, 458, 482, 519, 528, 537, 557
Westbrook, 5
Westerfield, 460
Western, 538
Western Connexion, 193
Weston, 400, 540
Wethered, 231
Wethereds, 231
Wetherell, 500
Wetmore, 29, 39, 60, 360
Weybourn, 325
whale ship **Margaret**, 326, 362, 415
Whalen, 429
Whales, 28
whale-ship **Margaret**, 311
Whaley, 61
whaling ship **Fox**, 561
whaling ship **Pantheon**, 406
Whallow, 184
Wharrey, 400
Wharry, 492
Wharton, 329, 382, 491, 548, 551
Wheat, 42, 79, 126, 249
Wheatley, 155, 197, 268, 485
Wheatly, 155, 200, 557
Wheaton, 133

Wheeler, 5, 60, 70, 115, 155, 167, 243, 400, 422, 445, 516, 537, 557
Wheelwright, 392
Whellock, 307
Whelpley, 328
Whelton, 562
Wherry, 197
Whetmore, 8
Whigeron, 5
Whipple, 383, 466, 549
Whistler, 60, 72, 197, 377, 563
Whitaker, 80, 311
Whitcomb, 94, 176
White, 5, 9, 19, 22, 28, 56, 60, 62, 68, 69, 78, 82, 84, 86, 98, 106, 107, 115, 116, 117, 144, 172, 181, 187, 188, 194, 197, 200, 204, 217, 219, 220, 243, 245, 249, 274, 277, 283, 293, 303, 317, 331, 341, 345, 348, 358, 362, 394, 399, 416, 429, 445, 467, 481, 502, 505, 510, 511, 528, 529, 530, 538, 543, 545, 557, 567, 576, 580
White Cottage, 128, 341
Whiteall, 72
Whitehead, 163, 257, 330, 468
Whitehill, 279, 345
Whitehouse, 325
Whiten, 28
Whitesides, 155
Whitfield, 294, 414
Whiting, 6, 46, 72, 73, 203, 243, 283, 374, 400, 502
Whitlark, 400
Whitler, 400
Whitman, 271, 494
Whitmore, 5
Whitney, 28, 60, 87, 97, 106, 122, 166, 220, 491
Whiton, 360
Whitsett, 94, 110, 229
Whitsill, 565
Whitsitt, 331
Whitson, 312, 331
Whittell, 97

Whitten, 86
Whitter, 60
Whittingham, 381
Whittle, 155
Whittles, 570
Whittlesey, 6, 28, 71, 88, 352, 460
Whittlesy, 445
Whittley, 106
Whitton, 160
Whon, 22
Whyte, 348, 399
Wick, 134, 345
Wickam, 421
Wickes, 148, 440
Wickham, 155, 326
Wickliffe, 28, 176, 209
Widbeck, 6
Widdicombe, 127
Widman, 237
Wiebster, 345
Wigans, 345
Wiggins, 6
Wilbar, 430
Wilber, 184
Wilbur, 346
Wilburn, 243
Wilcox, 78, 332
Wilde, 182, 357
Wilder, 285, 412
Wiles, 359
Wiley, 155, 283, 306, 491, 537
Wilferson, 358
Wilgars, 400
Wilheim, 60
Wilis, 512
Wilkes, 580
Wilkeson, 88
Wilkins, 20, 28, 155, 287, 445, 551, 557
Wilkinson, 30, 35, 60, 80, 94, 147, 283, 323, 368, 420, 422, 435, 454, 460, 491, 569
Willan, 197
Willard, 3, 107, 197, 243, 317, 371
Willen, 579

Willet, 423, 566
Willett, 5, 155, 540
William, 420
Williams, 5, 6, 15, 20, 25, 28, 30, 31, 35, 47, 52, 60, 68, 77, 78, 106, 107, 109, 119, 129, 134, 145, 155, 157, 165, 166, 168, 171, 177, 180, 181, 197, 222, 229, 243, 244, 246, 250, 276, 283, 296, 331, 337, 345, 355, 359, 362, 371, 373, 393, 411, 415, 441, 442, 445, 448, 453, 455, 456, 460, 462, 469, 478, 487, 491, 492, 510, 519, 524, 531, 537, 541, 542, 548, 551, 557, 559, 563, 564
Williamson, 13, 22, 31, 60, 78, 95, 145, 155, 177, 192, 229, 243, 345, 362, 394, 445, 452, 510, 526, 532, 564, 579
Willing, 174, 251, 257
Willis, 31, 107, 115, 169, 231, 247, 296, 455, 459, 499, 500, 508
Willner, 452, 575
Wills, 283, 509
Wilmer, 49, 356, 520
Wilson, 5, 14, 15, 16, 20, 22, 25, 28, 30, 36, 38, 43, 60, 66, 78, 82, 100, 106, 122, 129, 132, 141, 147, 148, 159, 165, 166, 190, 210, 212, 243, 245, 263, 269, 271, 274, 283, 286, 288, 299, 301, 334, 336, 345, 400, 401, 422, 429, 440, 441, 442, 445, 458, 470, 477, 478, 480, 488, 491, 492, 501, 506, 508, 533, 551, 552, 561, 562, 563, 567, 568, 580
Wilt, 249, 268
Wiltberger, 156, 288, 354, 493
Wimer, 70
Wimmer, 478
Wimsatt, 288, 481
Winans, 62, 88, 301, 302, 331
Windship, 213
Windsor, 381
<u>Winebagoes</u>, 294
Wineberger, 345, 445
Wines, 161

Wing, 55, 116, 173, 226, 362
Wingard, 62
Wingate, 83, 207, 215
Winger, 526
Wingerd, 137, 266
Winlow, 94
Winn, 402
Winne, 5, 60
Winship, 40, 299
Winslow, 5, 36, 163, 245, 255, 327, 414, 458, 526
Winston, 41, 237, 274, 508
Winter, 137
Winter Hill, 294
Winthrop, 200, 533, 545
Winton, 345, 400
Wintrode, 450
Wirt, 447
Wirtz, 421
Wise, 98, 214, 235, 236, 245, 303, 345, 379
Wishart, 51
Wissinger, 155
Wistar, 577
Witherell, 139
Withrow, 125, 266
Witt, 44
Wivill, 278
<u>Wm the Conqueror</u>, 357
Wofford, 106
Wolf, 504, 505, 510, 537
Wolf Marsh, 63
Wolfe, 5
Wolfenden, 411
Wolfinger, 28
Wolford, 257
Wollard, 168, 493, 565
Wolle, 289
Womack, 465, 568
Wood, 5, 22, 28, 29, 60, 62, 72, 73, 74, 99, 106, 133, 151, 169, 177, 183, 197, 210, 226, 243, 260, 275, 305, 345, 399, 401, 422, 429, 445, 456, 465, 491, 549, 550, 576
Wood Lawn, 137, 520

Wood Lot, #6, 573
Woodbarton, 172
Woodbridge, 158, 300
Woodbury, 9, 134, 308
Woodcock, 98
Woodford, 106
Woodland, 345, 466, 558
Woodlawn, 203
Woodruff, 493, 551, 573
Woods, 5, 88, 106, 117, 228, 365, 383, 385, 422, 456, 474, 504, 512, 551
Woodson, 42, 94, 401
Woodward, 65, 97, 106, 108, 130, 172, 197, 219, 243, 299, 305, 337, 338, 339, 345, 389, 395, 419, 526, 557
Woodworth, 28, 459, 463, 533
Woodyard, 137
Woodyer, 197
Wool, 180, 183, 347, 441, 474, 543
Wooldridge, 530
Wooley, 506
Woolfolk, 262
Woolford, 243
Woolman, 5, 28
Wootton, 60
Worden, 13, 147
Wordzincki, 509
Work, 197, 370, 497, 507
Wormley, 137, 557
Worrell, 127, 214, 400
Worry, 504
Worth, 134, 267, 320, 359, 384, 387, 405, 455, 510, 540
Wortham, 448
Worthen, 98
Worthington, 119, 302, 421
Wragg, 405
Wray, 42, 402
Wren, 294
Wriggle, 506
Wright, 5, 6, 10, 15, 25, 28, 49, 60, 61, 69, 70, 114, 132, 133, 140, 141, 147, 149, 182, 183, 204, 206, 208, 243, 258, 273, 283, 328, 332, 340,

345, 357, 399, 400, 407, 418, 423,
429, 460, 465, 491, 537, 557, 562,
563, 567, 579
Wroe, 96, 276, 321, 557
Wurdemann, 534
Wyatt, 15, 171, 381, 570
Wychoff, 300
Wyles, 414
Wyley, 506
Wylie, 95, 546
Wyman, 17, 85, 100, 124, 302, 362, 374
Wyncoop, 569
Wynn, 186, 217, 283
Wynne, 349
Wyoming, 207

Y

Yager, 28
Yale, 283, 491
Yarnall, 220, 221
Yarnell, 374
Yarrington, 303
Yates, 6, 28, 60, 107, 155, 197, 259, 260, 491, 537, 557, 558
Yearson, 345
Yeatman, 107, 176
Yeek, 345
Yell, 60, 337, 339, 345, 441
Yellowby, 312
Yellowly, 312
Yerby, 155, 580
Yerger, 543
Yerst, 492
Yoe, 412
Yonge, 283, 371
Yoong, 345
York, 508, 559
Yost, 99, 234, 246
Young, 6, 28, 33, 47, 54, 60, 65, 91, 92, 96, 98, 107, 110, 135, 155, 163, 174, 186, 188, 197, 216, 224, 236, 243, 245, 283, 302, 309, 318, 345, 349, 354, 374, 400, 428, 429, 437, 450, 451, 472, 479, 481, 482, 485, 486, 491, 492, 504, 508, 510, 537, 542, 545, 557, 579
Younge, 400
Younger, 107, 445
Yulee, 176

Z

Zabriskie, 60, 127
Zachary, 509
Zachman, 107, 155, 197
Zaminiski, 400
Zantzinger, 8, 35, 144, 244, 412, 539
Zeilein, 546
Zeitung, 269
Zell, 516
Zilkin, 296
Zock, 99

www.ingramcontent.com/pod-product-compliance
Lightning Source LLC
Chambersburg PA
CBHW070904300426
44113CB00008B/928